Presented to

ישראל

RICHARD ELLIOTT ALPERT

on your

HEBREW SCHOOL GRADUATION

by the

Sisterhood of Temple Beth El

FALL RIVER, MASS.

Mrs. Harvey Trieff Pres.

Dr. Moshe Babin Rabbi

June 5, 1976 Sivan 7, 5736

THE BOOK OF

JEWISH KNOWLEDGE

BOOKS BY NATHAN AUSUBEL

THE BOOK OF JEWISH KNOWLEDGE
PICTORIAL HISTORY OF THE JEWISH PEOPLE
A TREASURY OF JEWISH FOLKLORE
A TREASURY OF JEWISH POETRY
A TREASURY OF JEWISH HUMOR
SUPERMAN: LIFE OF FREDERICK THE GREAT

THE BOOK OF JEWISH KNOWLEDGE

An Encyclopedia of Judaism and the Jewish People,
Covering All Elements of Jewish Life from
Biblical Times to the Present

by NATHAN AUSUBEL

CROWN PUBLISHERS, INC. NEW YORK

To the memory of my father and mother,
Yisroel ben Shloima and Frimet bas Elimelech—gentle people
who in a world of dross and tumult walked beside the still waters.

The example of their own devout lives taught me the urgency of finding a motivation for my own. The ethical and spiritual truths I learned from them I have entered in this, *their book*. May these truths drawn from the accumulated wisdom and humanity of the Jewish people find their continuity in the lives of others! Selah.

Library of Congress Catalog Card Number: 62-20063

Printed in the United States of America

Sixth Printing, May, 1974

ACKNOWLEDGMENTS

Acknowledgments by an author of the assistance he has received from others in the preparation of his work can sometimes be only perfunctorily polite and often little more than a symbolic gesture. This, I want to stress, is not how I wish to acknowledge my indebtedness to those who worked with me unstintingly through the long years I wrestled with this project. The sum of all their help collectively has been more substantial than their suggestions in the planning of the book, more creative than the criticisms they offered, and far more fastidious than the editorial corrections they made. In the true sense of the word they were my collaborators, although I alone must bear the responsibility for opinions, interpretations, inadequacies and errors.

In this spirit I wish to express my gratitude to Nat Wartels, President of Crown Publishers; to Crown's Editor-in-Chief, Herbert Michelman; to Naomi Rosenbach, the editor of the manuscript; and to my wife, Marynn Older Ausubel.

Possibly the explanation for their special interest in this book was their intellectual commitment to the idea that the diffusion of knowledge about the life, religion, and culture of the Jewish people, when observed through the prism of the modern historical approach and against the background of general culture, could well serve a very useful purpose for inquiring readers in the twentieth century.

CONTENTS

A FOREWORD

THE DISTINCTIVE CHARACTER OF JEWISH KNOWLEDGE

The learned Jews of ancient times showed no less dedication in their pursuit of knowledge than the scholar-priests of Egypt, the Magi of Persia, the pundits of India, and the philosophers of Greece. Nonetheless, they gave it a markedly different emphasis. In that emphasis, no doubt, lay the individuality of traditional Jewish culture.

Each people in the family of mankind plays, as it were, a different instrument in the orchestra of civilization, contributing with its system of cultural values its own characteristic tone, timbre, and color to the total ensemble. The ancient Greeks, for example, prized knowledge more highly than any other value in their culture—even more than beauty. Their philosophers, scientists, and poets revered it because it enlarged the understanding, made possible the search for philosophic certainty by means of rational demonstration, and helped lay bare the secrets of physical reality. But the Jews followed a divergent intellectual course because the religious determinants and the circumstances of their group-life were so different.

On examining Jewish writings of former times one cannot help being struck by the singular fact that the chief criterion applied in testing the validity of any branch of knowledge—even of such non-religious studies as the natural sciences and medicine—was whether the acquisition of such knowledge would be likely to improve the moral understanding of the Jew: would be able to instill in him a purer love for God—activate a deeper piety—and make him live more righteously. Even such a "God-intoxicated" freethinker as Baruch Spinoza, when he was investigating the possibilities of achieving "human blessedness," concluded triumphantly that the highest bliss attainable for man was to cherish an "intellectual love of God." Intellect wedded to religion and ethics had, indeed, endured as a very venerable tradition in Jewish culture.

One needs go no further than the second chapter of the Book of Genesis to note in the Gan Eden myth the moralistic orientation of knowledge among the ancient Jews. After God had breathed into man's nostrils "the breath of life," runs the Biblical account, he planted a garden eastward in Eden, "and there He put the man whom He had formed. And out of the ground made the Lord God to grow every tree that is pleasant to the sight, and good for food; the tree of life also in the midst of the garden, and *the tree of knowledge of good and evil*. . . ."

This moralistic view, although expressed so naïvely in folkloric terms, could well serve as the matrix in which preponderant traditional Jewish thinking was cast, the end-goal being the increase of the good and the eradication of the evil.

Notwithstanding the fact that in various periods in their long history—especially during the cultural hegemony of Hellenism in Greco-Roman times and during the modified continuation of Hellenism in the Arabic-Jewish Golden Age—knowledge among the Jews was broadly humanistic both in its range and intensities of intellectual interests, the overwhelming characteristic of their culture was always religious. And although some of the outer forms of the Jewish religion (contrary to popular belief) were variable at different times and under changing conditions, its inner content and goals remained constant. The same passionate concern for truth, for the welfare and ennoblement of the human being, for ethical conduct, for moral climate of justice, peace, and benevolence in which a more equitable society would be able to develop, marks every historic stage of development in the Jewish religion, whether it be Mosaic, Prophetic, or Rabbinic.

To be sure, there were other cultures besides the Jewish which cherished ethical ideals and goals and created sizeable literatures about them. But as Philo, the Platonist rabbi of first-century Alexandria, and other Hellenist Jews pointed out, such values were cultivated among non-Jews only by an elite which included the most advanced of the moral philosophers, poets, and teachers. The great masses of the people, even in republican Athens, during the memorable days of Socrates, Plato, Aristotle, and Euripides, were kept suppressed and illiterate, in line with the antisocial philosophy of slavocracies, in which the common people were looked down upon as mere chattels or beasts of burden.

It was different with the Jews. The pursuit of learning—especially Torah learning—was highly revered among the Jews during the Second Temple period; it had been elevated to an exalted form of religious worship by Ezra the Scribe about the year 444 B.C.E. The obligation to study perpetually the precepts, laws, and teachings contained in the Scriptures had evolved in time into a religious-national dedication. The internal conditions and social organization of Jewish community life made it possible for even the poorest and the humblest to acquire at least some learning; many of the most illustrious of Rabbinic sages, like Hillel and Akiba, sprang from the common people. It is, therefore, not to be wondered at that, in the democratic and ethical climate of Jewish community life (in which all men, at least theoretically, stood equal), illiteracy and ignorance were scorned because they prevented the individual from acquiring an adequate knowledge of the religious-cultural heritage of Israel.

This is how the foundations of Jewish intellectuality, which was preponderantly religious and ethical in its preoccupations, were laid down by its teachers to serve for almost twenty-five centuries as a way of life and as a fortress for the spirit throughout Israel's never-ending trials and calamities.

Many thoughtful persons have been considerably puzzled, perhaps because they possess an inadequate knowledge of Jewish life, history, and culture, about why and how the Jewish pattern of civilization acquired such an all-embracing religious coloration while other cultures, in large part, continued secularist.

What the historical factors may have been that gave rise to such a single-minded and continuous preoccupation among the Jews is open to speculation. Yet one significant circumstance is plain: This religious-moralistic emphasis stemmed from the fact that in great part traditional Jewish knowledge found its matrix in the theocratic society of ancient Israel.

The term "theocracy" was actually invented and defined for the benefit of Greek-reading Gentiles in Rome by the first-century Judean historian, Josephus, in his defense of the Jewish religion, "Against Apion": "Some people [he wrote] have entrusted the supreme political power to monarchies, others to oligarchies, still others to democracies. Our lawgiver [i.e., Moses] was not attracted by any of these political forms, but gave to his constitution the form of what, to use a strained expression, may be termed *a theocracy,* placing all rule and authority in the hands of God."

The "constitution" of this God-ruled society was embodied in the laws contained in the Jewish Scriptures—the Torah or Pentateuch. All of Jewish life, in every one of its multitudinous departments and activities—even in those which might appear to the modern person to be incontestably secular in character—fell under the sovereign rule and supervision of religion in the theocracy. Supervised at first by the Temple priesthood and in later times (under Greco-Roman rule) by the Sanhedrin and the Rabbinic Sages, were not only the doctrines, beliefs, and dogmas of religion, the various rites and customs, ceremonies, observances, institutions, and practices, but also the civil and criminal laws, ethics and morals, and commercial, agricultural, familial, and social relations.

This religion-oriented pattern of Jewish knowledge, for all its variations and secularistic inclusions, remained fixed in Jewish life for most of the time. It was only in periods of intense assimilation that acculturated forms began to emerge. Such was the case when the Jews first fell under Greek cultural influence. Then, except for their Jewish identity and religious observances, they were not distinguishable from ethnic Greeks. The Greek historian Megasthenes (third century B.C.E.) was quoted by Clement of Alexandria as having noted that "all matters of natural science spoken of among the ancients are also taught by the philosophers outside of Greece . . . In Syria [which included Palestine] by those called Jews." Whatever happened to the teachings or investigations of those early Jewish scientists? No written record is extant of them.

No better authority on the erudition and acumen of contemporary Jews could be found than the philosopher Clearchus of Soli. He quoted his master, Aristotle, as having said that, while he was traveling in Syria, he had ample opportunity to engage in philosophical discussion in Greek with a Jew whom he described as having "the soul of a Greek." This Jew, went on Aristotle, "conversed with us and with other philosophical persons, and made a trial of our skill in philosophy; and as he had lived with many learned men, he communicated to us more information than he received from us."

Who could that Jewish philosopher of the fourth century B.C.E. have been to have earned such high praise from Aristotle? No knowledge of his identity or of any writing of his is extant, nor is, for that matter, the writing of many another Jewish savant; their works seem to have vanished into thin air.

THE PAST AND THE PRESENT

The history of a people, to paraphrase the analogy of the Psalmist ("A thousand years in Thy sight are but as yesterday"), takes place in but one instant in the eternity of the world. Notwithstanding that the recorded life of the Jewish past has been crowded into such a cosmic moment, its religious-cultural continuity for between three and four thousand years has probably been the longest ever achieved by any religious-ethnic group.

To the history-conscious devout Jew, the past seems as real as the present, for he conceives of both as being woven inextricably together by the same moral purposefulness. In its covenant with God at Mount Sinai, legendarized with such epic drama by the Biblical chronicler of the Book of Exodus, collective Israel declared itself to belong to YHVH forevermore, to constitute for him "a kingdom of priests and a holy nation" so that it might fulfill his will on earth for mankind. This became the leitmotif of its historic existence and reason for being, century after century. Therefore, it explains the pervasive role of tradition and custom in the unitary design of Jewish religious life. It could also explain the passionate dedication of most Jewish parents to preserve, to teach, and to transmit the spiritual certitudes and precepts of the ancestral heritage, built in and around the Torah, to their children who, in turn, were expected to indoctrinate their own children with the same beliefs, truths, and ethical values. These verities they considered immutable—they were convinced that they were extending and perpetuating this knowledge in a golden chain of continuity until "the end of time."

In the spiritual sense, time remained timeless! After the doctrines about the Messiah and the establishment by him of the Righteous Kingdom of God *on earth,* about Immortality, the Resurrection, and the Last Judgment, had all sunk firm roots into the partly mystical soil of Jewish belief during the post-Biblical period, the future, too, became joined with the past and the present, being synthesized into one indivisible, historic certainty. Life for Israel had now assumed a well-charted grand design, like the blueprint of an architectural plan.

One could, consequently, jump to the facile conclusion that, in seizing hold of what it assumed to be "absolutes," the Jewish religion was condemned to a state of permanent immobility and stagnation. But the actual fact is that, while the major traditional doctrines, principles, attitudes, and practices were clung to tenaciously, their historical development was continuous, adjusting to each new set of circumstances and to the cultural influences of the general environment and the spirit of the times; at no time in Jewish history did its religion remain static. To substantiate this, one need only point out that nowhere in the Torah of Moses is there any mention made of a belief in Immortality, the Resurrection, the Last Judgment, or the Messiah. These doctrines, startlingly new, first unfolded in a much later historic age, clearly showing their borrowings and adaptations from other religions. Like all expressions of culture, religion, too, is organic in character and follows laws of growth and change all its own.

It is extraordinary, indeed, that even in the earliest recorded time the Jews considered themselves an ancient people. The memory of their ancestral past kept obtruding constantly and nostalgically; tradition had already become venerated in Jewish life as far back in time as the Wandering in the Wilderness. The thirty-second chapter in the Book of Deuteronomy narrates, in a mood both elevated and instructive, how Moses, the great lawgiver and poet, as his life drew to a close, taught all the assembly of Israel the words of this song:

> Give ear, ye heavens, and I will speak;
> And let the earth hear the words of my mouth.
> My doctrine shall drop as the rain,
> My speech shall distil as the dew . . .
>
> *Remember the days of old,*
> *Consider the years of many generations;*
> *Ask thy father, and he will declare unto thee,*
> *Thine elders, and they will tell thee.*

The philologist Max Müller, defined in an aphorism the relation of the past to the present: "There is but one key to the present and that is the past." And the past of the Jewish people—as many Jews and also enlightened Gentiles have perceived it—was its imperishable glory. At the very center of its religious culture, radiating outward and penetrating deeply into every nook and cranny of its group-life, was its belief in One God. Now other faiths, too, like the Akhenaton sun-religion in ancient Egypt during the Eighteenth Dynasty (*c.* 1370 B.C.E.), and Zoroastrianism in Persia (*c.* eighth century B.C.E.), were essentially monotheistic, abounding with ethical implications. But it remained for the genius of Moses the Liberator and of those inspired "tormentors" of Israel's conscience, the defenders of the poor and weak against their oppressors—the Prophets Amos, Isaiah, Hosea, Micah, and Jeremiah—to evolve a new conception of the One God: one that was moral and just and girt with holiness. From this hitherto unprecedented idea developed a new ethos in which ideas and sentiments of humanity, brotherly love, mutual aid, and social responsibility predominated. It was a new light intended to lead mankind out of the pathless jungle of animism, cruelty, greed, and war.

Indeed, it was an awesome design of man's untapped potential for good and for self-perfection; this optimism remained, despite the fact that during several cultural periods in Jewish life the pure vision of Moses, the Prophets, and the Rabbinic Sages suddenly darkened and was distorted by a general sliding back into superstition and fanaticism. The fundamentalists wished the people to exchange the rational for the irrational, the spiritual and ethical content of religion for the merely trivial and the formalistic. The gentle philosopher of Amsterdam, Spinoza, himself driven out of the Jewish community by the self-righteous fanatics for the unforgivable crime of thinking honestly and for not conforming, mused bitterly in his essay "On Superstition" over the ironic condition of man: "The multitude, ever prone to superstition, and caring more for the shreds of antiquity than for eternal truths, pays homage to the Books of the Bible, rather than to the Word of God." The generality of men, the philosopher seemed to suggest, do the very opposite of that which would serve their best interests: They throw away the kernel and keep the chaff.

In assessing the intellectual tonality or moral characteristic of each of the religions of antiquity, the German philosopher Hegel, himself a believing Christian, commented that the Jews had "created the religion of sublimity." Whatever meaning the word "sublimity" may have held for him—and it is doubtful whether in its frame of reference was included anything outside of the Bible since he was not knowledgeable about Rabbinic and later Jewish thought, belief, and practice—he, nevertheless, recognized that this "sublimity" was a quality of idealistic aspiration for the moral betterment of man and the ennoblement of life. Viewed through the refined lenses of Talmudic interpretation, it would appear that the quest for sublimity was the motivating force behind all authentic Jewish religious experience.

One could plausibly hold that the central doctrine in the Jewish religion—one from which streamed forth all other principles of faith and works—was that of "the sanctification of life." The traditional Jewish view has been that when God created man He made him in His own image, from which flowed the corollary that man was to consider himself as the co-creator of God—that is, the co-creator of his own life as well as of a more just society. Bearing upon his human personality this divine imprimatur, man was thus faced with the unavoidable necessity of living up to his distinction by imitating God in His ethical attributes. It obliged him to regard all life as sacred and inviolable, to work tirelessly to improve himself intellectually and morally, to seek truth and understanding through Torah-study, meditation, and perpetual self-examination, and (not least) to love his fellow man "as himself" and, in his behalf, perform *maasim tobim* (good deeds). In this way, he would not only bring "blessedness" upon himself and others but he would help hasten the redemption of Israel and all humankind from evil, oppression, social inequity, and war.

The Cabalists and their adherents, although their esoteric questing for God and for control of "the invisible powers" had strong religious and ethical motivation, nonetheless remained morbidly life-denying. Theirs was a philosophy of renunciation and of self-subjugation, one that was shared by the monks and nuns of the Roman Catholic Church; by the practice of austerities and mortifications they strained mightily to escape from the "impure" prisons of the flesh in which their "pure" souls were confined. But aside from these mystics—and the Cabalists could justifiably be called sectaries—the vast majority of Jews, at all times and in every part of the world, were always able to say "yes" to life.

There lurks a paradox—even a colossal irony—in the fact that the Jews, at the very time that they were trapped in the midst of never-ending martyrdom and persecution by their enemies, were nevertheless able to give their full-throated affirmation to life. What are the mysterious reservoirs of strength within the mind and spirit of man that enable him to triumph spiritually even when he is engulfed by disaster? Inasmuch as the Jew of tradition valued—nay, revered—life so highly because it was the creation of God, therefore he exalted it as being both good and perfectable without limit.

This optimistic outlook—a paean to the potential good in life and in man himself—stood, for the greater part, in opposition to most of the cynical or pessimistic thinking and to antisocial practices that were current in the ancient world. An unnamed Hebrew psalmist in the Dead Sea Scrolls, living in fellowship with other Essenic sectaries, in the hush of the Judean wilderness some eighteen or nineteen centuries ago, lifted up his voice in this inspired doxology:

> I give thanks to Thee, O my God!
> For having bound my soul in the bundle of life.

And so it would appear that, in the main, life—and not death—was the final goal that Jews elected to strive for, although in some periods of great calamity and despair there were powerful undertones of escapism into the morbid, and a drifting away from reality into superstition and a fascinated contemplation of the World-to-Come.

TRADITION AND CUSTOM

It is doubtful whether there has ever been in history a people on whom custom has held such an enduring grip as the Jews. Throughout the entire ancient East, civilizations remained locked for centuries in undeviating custom. The Jews, too, were rapt in this reverence for permanence, for the preservation of the sanctified cultural forms of the past. The Book of Proverbs expressed this attachment to antiquity in the admonition: "Remove not the ancient landmark which thy fathers have set." (22:28.)

In a sense, all ethnic and religious groups in the human family, whether they are advanced or merely primitive in their stages of cultural development, are governed by fixed attitudes, beliefs, and traditions that eventually become translated into generally accepted practices and folkways. The American Zuñi Indians have a profound saying: "Custom is the cup of life." Custom, too, has been the cup of Jewish life from which Jews have been steadily drinking.

In a very significant way, their traditions, customs, and religious observances have been the binders holding Jews together for three millenniums, frequently supplementing, and sometimes even superseding, the written laws of the Torah. The Sages of the Talmud (most of them down-to-earth rationalists) not only recognized the incisive bearing of custom on the configurations of the daily life, they also treated them as popular practices that laid the foundations for their jurisprudence. The Mishnah, the repository of the Oral Traditions in the Jewish religion regarded by the devout as the body of extra-Scriptural laws, and which was handed down by word of mouth from generation to generation until its codification, *c.* 200 C.E., tried to establish the legal principle that "custom always precedes law." By this the Rabbinic teachers of antiquity did not wish to imply that custom took priority *in authority* over the laws of the Torah, but only that, before a law can acquire its legal definition, it first must exist for a long, long time as a living custom among the masses of the people.

Considering the holy urgency felt by the Jewish masses for perpetuating their group life, both biologically and religiously—in a kind of priestly guardianship that they themselves placed over their identity during certain disruptive historical periods—their rigid and excessive observance of custom and the minutiae of ritualism often resulted in what has sometimes been stigmatized as the stagnation of true Jewish religious values. The additional fact that the Jewish people was so fantastically fragmentized and dispersed into all the far corners of the earth, naturally led to the emergence of a multiplicity of regional customs and observances (such, for instance, as marked off the Central and East European Ashkenazim from the Spanish-Portuguese Sefaradim, and both of these groups in turn from the "Oriental" Jews of Arab and Middle-Eastern countries). This situation was greatly deplored by the philosopher-rabbi of the twelfth century, Maimonides; he was fully aware of the religious confusion it caused and of its divisive consequences for the Jewish people.

It is possible that some of the blame for these divergencies—if blame it should be called at all—could be laid at the door of the Rabbinic Sages themselves. Rationalists and, in the main, individuals of strong beliefs and moral principles, they strove to lay down firm guidelines for piloting the faithful through the unknown, and sometimes dangerous, shoals of religious consistency; they considered that the strict observance of tradition, custom, and symbolic rite and ceremony was the most effective pedagogic medium available for maintaining that consistency. "Man should never deviate from established custom," taught the Rabbinic jurists who, being socially and ethically conditioned in their thinking, became impatient sometimes with the empty legalism that often enough frustrated the true intention of law *as justice.*

A classic illustration of the antipodal divisions frequently to be met with in Jewish religious, legal, and social thinking is that which occurred in early Rabbinic times, while the Second Temple still stood. It concerned the formula of *lex talionis*—that primitive and brutal law which not only was universally followed by all peoples in ancient society but was also formally expressed in the Biblical law for the tribalistic Israelites as "an eye for an eye and a tooth for a tooth."

At one extreme in their attitude to this law stood the fundamentalist and ruling-class Sadducees, who were more interested in following the letter of the Scriptural law and in maintaining their power than in fulfilling its obvious intention of dispensing justice. Opposed to them, fortunately for the hard-pressed Jewish masses, were the Pharisees—those Rabbinic creators of the humane and ethical philosophy of life, belief, and pratice that was immortalized in the "Sea of the Talmud." (This was the source from which Jesus and the early Jewish Christians drew virtually all of their ethical convictions and teachings.) The Rabbinic Sages recoiled from the barbarous "eye for an eye" Scriptural law. The dictates of conscience and the feelings of compassion for the imperfections, errors, and follies of mankind prompted them to work for the abolition of that law and of many another implacable law that, paradoxically, as a throwback to the primitive past of Israel, had managed to survive through the centuries. In substitution of the *lex talionis* they provided, by a reinterpretation of the law, that the offender pay a money fine or property damages to the person whom he had, whether intentionally or accidentally, injured.

It is a melancholy reflection to dwell upon, but the progress of mankind never seems to advance irresistibly in a straight line toward certain goals. Neither does it always move in a logical sequence—from a lower to a higher stage of moral and social development. In fact, it has been noticed to move quite erratically, uncertainly, and unpredictably—sometimes forward, but too often receding—like the surf that rolls in and out of the sea driven by wind and tide. There have been several long periods in history when the Jewish people, held in the vise of petrified laws, customs, and rites, defensively driven into that position by the savagery of its persecutors, remained backward at the very time when the Christian world around them was moving forward. Such a time, to cite one instance, was the so-called Jewish Dark Ages which had descended upon the Ashkenazic ghetto-communities following the violent Catholic reaction during the Counter Reformation in the sixteenth century and continuing well into the nineteenth century in the countries of Central and Eastern Europe.

There were always courageous voices being raised in reasoned opposition to the stultification of the Jewish religion by an excessive preoccupation with the minutiae of ritualism, a situation which came into being when custom either miscarried or had been perverted by the imposition of fanatical authority.

One celebrated example of such critical resistance to custom was that furnished by Rabbenu Tam, the grandson of the celebrated Rashi ("The Prince of Commentators") and himself the foremost religious authority for the Ashkenazim of his twelfth-century generation. Tam consistently led the attack against the tyranny of some well-rooted customs and, simultaneously, against the slavishness of many of the pious who unthinkingly venerated them.

In his rabbinical decisions (Responsa), Rabbenu Tam made caustic references to the inanity of certain time-revered customs. He ventured the opinion that those customs had conceivably been instituted by fools but, having become sanctified by the passage of time and religious observance, were ultimately accorded the authority of general acceptance—a distinction which could hardly make them any less foolish or more meaningful. In one passage, he could not resist the temptation of quipping: He observed slyly that the Hebrew word for custom—*minhag*—when inverted, could in an approximate way read *Gehinnom* (i.e., "Gehenna" or "Hell").

What informed student of civilization is not aware that in many significant areas of religion and culture among all peoples are to be found certain incongruities in dogma, principle, symbolism, and practice—values that seem diametrically oppossed to one another; the most ethical and spiritual ideas jostling with the crassly materialistic and barbarous? This oddity of irreconcilables and of petrification also applies to the Jewish religion. Intellectually honest Jews—and their number is manifestly legion—being forearmed with an enlightened and rationalistic approach to the problems of religious faith and practice, are soberly conscious that in Judaism, too, there is present a wide assortment of primitive survivals, magical notions, and superstitions—observances that have been steadily and indiscriminately accumulating ever since the predawn of Jewish history. But these contradictions or cultural throwbacks can hardly be justification for any attempt to denigrate Judaism. The fact is that Christianity, Islam, Buddhism, and other religions, too, are encrusted with similar embarrassments.

Nevertheless, what distinguishes Jewish culture in the over-all vista of Jewish life is its spiritual afflatus, its down-to-earth wisdom, its ethical practices, and, perhaps quite uniquely, its steadfast commitment to the creation of a more righteous and humane society. Possibly no non-Jew ever succeeded as well as the great Russian writer Maxim Gorky in summarizing the quintessence of Judaism—not just Judaism *as religion* but Judaism as comprising *the total civilization* of the Jewish people—a comprehensive unity which, in cultural terms, it really is.

> In my early youth [wrote Gorky] I read—I have forgotten where—the words of an ancient Jewish sage, Hillel: "If you are not for yourself, who will be for you? And if you are for yourself alone, what are you?" The inner meaning of these words impressed me with their profound wisdom, and I interpreted them for myself that my life should be better, and I must not impose the care of myself on other people's shoulders; but if I am going to take care of myself alone—of nothing but my own personal life—it will be useless, ugly, meaningless. This thought ate its way deep into my soul; and I say now with conviction: Hillel's wisdom served as a strong staff on my road, which was neither easy nor even. I believe that Jewish wisdom is more all-human and universal than any other; and this not only because it is the first born, not only because of its immemorial age, but also because of the powerful humaneness that saturates it, because of its high estimate of man.

It is not unnatural that Jews who are closely identified with their Jewishness, whether religiously or Zionistically, or merely emotionally, ethnically, or culturally, should feel a certain glow of pride when they contemplate the progressive achievements of their people. Perhaps somewhat paradoxically this elation also seems to be shared, although to a far less extent, by many Jews who, ostensibly, have either little or no binding ties with their ancestral heritage. It is a moot question, indeed, to ask the actual psychological reasons behind this kind of fleeting identification with the Jewish group. Complex they certainly must be. The late Edward Sapir, the American anthropologist who himself seems not to have had any formal affiliations with the Jewish religion and who demonstrated only the scientific humanist's impartial interest in Jewish culture, and who appears not to have participated in any organized aspect of Jewish community life, still became intrigued by the irony of this psychological phenomenon:

> Even the most sophisticated Jew is proud of at least two things. While he may have no personal use for a Savior, it pleases him to think that his ancestors gave one to Christendom; and though comfort and enlightenment may long have disabused him of the necessity of a God, he takes satisfaction in the thought that his remoter ancestors invented the purest kind of a God that we have record of: the God of monotheism. Such a Jew has one of the keenest of known pleasures, which may be defined as the art of endowing others with a priceless boon that one finds is more convenient to dispense with for one's own part.

While it is patently true that, in the past, the principles and practices of the Jewish religion were primarily keyed to the traditional theocratic philosophy of Jewish life, in more modern times an ever increasing number of Jews, both knowledgeable and cultured, no matter what the extent of their affiliation with Judaism might be, have been actively pursuing non-Jewish interests—interests based on scientific and purely secularistic premises and goals. Such, after all, do represent the major cultural characteristic of twentieth-century civilization in which Jews are playing an undeniably important role.

The knowledgeable student of Jewish history and culture knows that, throughout the centuries, ever since the Hellenistic age, there have been many thousands of Jews, questioning and groping "seekers of truth," who, in a variety of ways, have striven to achieve a comfortable reconciliation between religious belief and rational certitude. Most of these Jews have considered themselves successful in effecting a harmonious synthesis between the two supposedly diverse elements, but there have also been a number of Jews who have confessed their frustration in this attempt.

To cite merely one example of diametrically opposite approaches to religion in Jewish cultural history: Toward the end of the twelfth century, the philosopher-rabbi Maimonides perfected the principles and the methodology that had been pioneered by earlier Jewish savants for explaining and validating the doctrines and precepts of the Jewish religion by means of demonstrable proof; namely, by applying to them the tools of philosophy, especially of Aristotelian logic. The illustrious Schoolmen of the Church—Albertus Magnus, Alexander of Hales, and most especially Thomas Aquinas, the foremost philosopher of medieval Catholicism—later seized upon Maimonides' method when his *Guide to the Perplexed* was translated into Latin, and applied it triumphantly to Christian theology.

But in Jewish religious-intellectual circles, besides many enthusiastic adherents, there also arose intense opposition to Mimonides' efforts at reconciliation. Two generations before him, the great poet-rabbi Judah Halevi, although himself well-schooled in Greek-Arab philosophy, nevertheless expressed his scorn for what he seems to have considered was a forced and mixed marriage being arranged by the philosophical rabbis. He held staunchly that faith and reason had absolutely nothing in common with each other, and that the Jewish religion stood in no need of bolstering by secularist thought and scientific proofs. Religion, he averred, was to be regarded as strictly a matter of spiritual faith; one either "believed" or did not!

Ever since the Golden Age of Jewish culture during medieval times in Moorish Spain and in Arab lands of North Africa, there have been many thousands of questioning Jews who have struggled to achieve some sort of harmonious—or, at least, comfortable—reconciliation between the dictates of traditional religious beliefs and the criteria of scientific thought. Certainly, during the second half of the twentieth century, a majority of Jews, somewhat set apart from one another by different sectarian philosophies and observances of the Jewish religion, whether of Modern Orthodox, Chasidic, Conservative, or Reform movements, have been successful in bridging the seeming impasse and in effecting an *acculturated* (as differentiated from the opportunistic, chameleon term *assimilated*) synthesis of Judaism with general secularistic culture.

At the same time, however, and standing at the opposite pole, there do remain a great number of Jews who, at varying distances and for different reasons, have kept themselves aloof from any Jewish religious affiliation. For that matter, many of them have not even sought any appreciable degree of ethnic, national, or cultural identification with the Jewish people. Their aim, usually stated with complete candor, is to blend completely into the Gentile cultural environment and so shed the impedimenta of their Jewishness.

The Jewish religion in our time presents far less of a monolithic unity in the values of faith, piety, and observance than it did in former centuries, when, in the religious separatism that existed within the semiautonomous ghetto, life was much less complicated; it was then relatively easy and feasible for the rabbinic and lay authorities to impose absolute comformity in religious observance and conduct on the entire Jewish community. At the same time, it should also be added, the difficult circumstances of Jewish life in those centuries perhaps made religious authoritarianism unavoidable and, at times, even necessary.

It stands to reason that, in recoiling over and over again from the unceasing whiplash of persecution and too-real threats of death and forced conversion, the Jews should have felt the need to close ranks in greater group unity and for the purpose of mutual aid. The more ferocious and implacable the blows that were dealt them by their enemies, the more adamant became their resistance—not resistance with arms, for they had no arms, nor, probably, would they have chosen to use them even in self-defense had they possessed them, since, during the Middle Ages and also later, the Jews by conviction were pacifists, but resistance *by the might of the spirit.*

They little know, who despise me so,
That shaming me does cause my pride to glow.

Thus sang Judah Halevi, the twelfth-century "Singer of Zion."

Who can have any doubt but that one of the chief catalysts responsible for drawing Jews together in an indestructible identity and fellowship while at the same time helping to preserve the Jewish religion through all of its vicissitudes was the brutal excesses of the enemies of the Jews? For the student of history it should suffice merely to take note of the ironic fact that besides the sustaining power of its religion and its ethnic way of life, what best preserved the Jewish people from extinction were the hatred and savagery of the anti-Semites of history. By segregating the Jews in ghettos, their persecutors merely preserved them; by massacring the Jews, their persecutors only made them draw closer in their resistance.

It is also plain that the Jews, struggling for physical and moral survival in an implacably vengeful world, should have sought reassurance, strength, and healing for their bruised spirits in their religion. This historic truth is admitted even by liberal Christian theologians and knowledgeable Jewish unbelievers. The will of the Jewish people to endure—to the everlasting bafflement of many non-Jews—was derived from the continuum of its religion, from its ethical and moral way of life, from its traditional culture, and from the closely knit character of its semiautonomous community organization. The miracle of it all—and it almost seems like a miracle—is that, under the disheartening circumstances of Jewish life it nevertheless was possible for the average Jew to achieve reasonable personality integration, a realistic view of himself and of his environment, to maintain high standards of personal conduct in settings of community usefulness, and, remarkably enough, to faithfully practice his religion and pursue learning—not only "for the sake of Heaven" but for the betterment of life itself.

Even in the most backward and superstition-ridden periods of the Jewish religion (psychologically considered) the harassed Jew, the rejected "orphan" of the world, found in it anodyne for his macerated human pride. From his more than three-thousand-year-old cultural-ethical heritage he was able to draw the moral fortitude with which to listen to the mocking voices of his persecutors and yet remain steadfast within and unafraid. The will to survive and to wait for a better day so that truth and righteousness might be vindicated was at the bottom of traditional Jewish hopefulness. "Make you a new heart and a new spirit," were the words with which the Prophet Ezekiel tried to rouse grieving Israel during its captivity in Babylonia: "For why will ye die, O house of Israel?" (18:31.)

THE AUTHOR'S NOTE TO THE READER

This work, it should be kept in mind, is *not* a Jewish encyclopedia in the conventional sense, but a book of Jewish knowledge arranged in encyclopedia form. This format I have considered necessary for practical reasons in order to give the articles presented maximum interest and usefulness. I hope that the format will facilitate the reader in finding readily and in using efficiently whatever information he may be looking for on any one of the several hundred subjects that have been treated here. Cross references to related articles, aided by a comprehensive index, should provide him with adequate leads for enlarging his knowledge and—hopefully—also his understanding of and insights into Jewish life and thought.

A merely cursory examination of the contents of this volume should satisfy the reader that I have set for myself one principal task: to examine and analyze the many traditional facets of Jewish knowledge which, collectively, make up the cultural heritage of the Jewish people. For the benefit of the reader who is both enlightened and inquiring, I have attempted to approach each subject from the historical point of view, critically when necessary, but objectively at all times. Inasmuch as no body of knowledge is ever created in a vacuum or in cultural isolation but is part of the grand design of the total life and civilization of mankind, I have tried to examine, as far as possible, all aspects of Jewish knowledge in that general frame of reference. Moreover, I have applied some of the principles, findings, and tools of judgment that have been provided the modern investigator of culture by the social disciplines. On the conscious level, I have avoided engaging in any special pleading or in interpreting any aspect of the Jewish religion, whether doctrine, institution, practice, or moral value, from a sectarian position of bias. Applicable to my approach is the classic aphorism: "I love Plato, but I love truth more."

My intention, regardless of whether or not I have wholly succeeded in fulfilling it, has been to discuss all matters with fair-mindedness and detachment. A work such as *The Book of Jewish Knowledge* is bound by necessity to treat of controversial—some readers might even consider them inflammatory—matters in the areas of religious belief and observance. Therefore, the conscientious author can least afford to be dogmatic, sectarian, or magisterial in expressing his own opinions. This problem has always proven both vexing and challenging to every intellectually honest writer who has been obliged to grapple with it, and many a work has foundered on it, usually because of the author's timidity, compromise, and fear of giving offense.

The noted rabbinical scholar Solomon Schechter once made this ironic observation concerning the multiplicity of interpretations it is possible to give any single Biblical writing: "Twenty-two German universities and half a dozen English universities have issued their Commentary on Isaiah, each different from the other. What a delight it would be to have Isaiah rise from the dead and tell us what he actually meant by the passages."

Wherever possible, I have sought to present different points of view and evaluations so that the open-minded reader would be able the better to draw from them his own conclusions. Nevertheless, I must emphasize that I do not consider that the mere factual presentation of information such as is usually found in the conventional encyclopedia—no matter how detailed, precise, and correct it may be—is sufficient for a thoughtful understanding of the nature of the Jewish heritage or of any of its aspects. In all conscience, as a serious popularizer of Jewish knowledge, I could not bypass the necessity of probing for *insights,* both for the reader's enlightenment and for my own, into the dynamics of Judaism, Jewish life, and culture.

The demands of unity and balance in my design and the requirements of reasonable consistency have led me to exclude, important as they may be otherwise, such materials as I consider only peripheral and which, if included, would but clutter up the text and blur the outlines of the synthesis I am aiming at. To mention only a few of the categories found in every well-constructed Jewish encyclopedia, I have deliberately omitted data about the hundreds of Jewish communities in the world and information about religious, educational, philanthropic, social, and fraternal Jewish organizations.

With the sole exception of a biographic article about Moses, I have not included *as separate entries* biographic sketches of any other eminent contributors to Jewish religious and secular culture. Notwithstanding such omission, the reader must not suppose that I have neglected to treat of any really significant Jewish personality. Numerous passages in the texts of the several hundred articles that comprise this work cite from, discuss, and refer to the Jewish great and near great among the rabbis, legists, moralists, scholars, poets, mystics, and thinkers. In addition, in order to assist the reader, thumbnail biographies of more than one hundred Jewish notables (including cross references to articles in which they appear prominently) are to be found in the book under the heading SOME ARCHITECTS OF JEWISH CIVILIZATION. Still other luminaries, though not included in this roster, are nevertheless also cited from or referred to throughout the text. Their names appear in the Index of Persons.

Finally, the reader should keep in mind that no single article on any given subject contains all the relevant data; discussion of it may also occur within other articles, possibly in a different context or with other implications. For this very reason, for a proper and fuller understanding of any particular subject, it is advisable to make use of the cross references with which the various entries are concluded, and, in addition, to consult the comprehensive General Index.

Technical Symbols and Devices

I have tried to follow with reasonable consistency the practice which is employed in modern historiography of writing the first letter of all pronouns that refer to God in lower case, namely, *he, him, who, whom,* and *whose.* The only exceptions to this rule were made to prevent confusion of meaning. However, where these pronouns appear in quoted passages from the Bible, Apocrypha, Pseudepigrapha, Talmud, and other Jewish religious writings, I have preserved intact the mode of orthography traditionally used in English, i.e., He, Him, Me, Mine, etc.

Another distinction the reader must make is between my deliberate use of *Rabbinic* (with a capital *R*) when I am referring to the religious teachers in the Talmud—the Rabbinic Sages—and of *rabbinic* (with a lower-case *r*) when I merely wish to indicate rabbis of post-Talmudic times.

An explanation may be expected about my use of the chronological symbols: B.C.E. ("Before the Common Era") instead of B.C. ("Before Christ"—which means the Messiah), and C.E. ("Common Era") instead of A.D. (*Anno Domini,* in Latin, for "the Year of Our Lord"). Such usage has become customary for Jewish writings in very recent decades. For one thing, Jews are not Christians, and their religious loyalties do not include a recognition of Jesus as either the Messiah or "Lord" (God), or even as the focus of all history. A similar sectarian calculation in chronology, evidently introduced in imitation of the Christian one, has been followed by the Mohammedans, who reckon time from the year of the Hegira—the flight of the Prophet of Allah from Mecca to Medina. The traditional chronological system of the Jews, incidentally, commences with the Biblical year of Creation (*see* CHRONOLOGY, JEWISH).

Faced with the peculiar dilemma posed for them in such unacceptable religious symbolism, yet recognizing that they were living in a predominantly Christian society and that some practical accommodation to their environment was necessary, religious Jews in English-speaking countries devised the symbols B.C.E. and C.E. These symbols, without making any alteration in the chronology of general usage, eliminated the religious references and implications.

Of very minor significance, no doubt, is the single letter difference appearing in my spelling of the Hebrew *yeshibah* and *yeshivah;* both refer to the rabbinical academy or seminary. Wherever *yeshibah* appears in the text, it is intended to indicate some Rabbinic academy which existed during the Talmudic age or in subsequent centuries among the Sefaradim, who pronounced the word as *yeshibah.* The Ashkenazim of Central and Eastern Europe, differing somewhat in their Hebrew phonetic system, transformed the hard *b* into the softer *v,* and pronounced the word as *yeshivah.* To refer to a Polish or Lithuanian *yeshivah* as a *yeshibah* would consequently appear unnatural and incongruous.

In conclusion, I would like to warn the reader not to expect to find complete consistency in my transliterations from the Hebrew and the Yiddish into English. No scientific system has yet been devised that can be considered more than partially successful or even acceptable to a concensus of scholars. Keeping in mind that my work is chiefly directed to the general reader, I have transliterated Hebrew and Yiddish words phonetically.

N. A.

THE BOOK OF

JEWISH KNOWLEDGE

A

ABODAH. *See* PRAYER AND WORSHIP; PRAYER SERVICE.

ACADEMIES, RABBINIC. *See* YESHIBAH.

ACCENTS, MUSICAL. *See* MUSICAL ACCENTS.

AFIKOMON

At the outset of the Seder, the home religious evening service for Passover, the head of the household breaks off half of the middle of the three matzot placed on the festive table before him, and conceals it with a great flourish for all the children to see, under the pillow or cushion on which ancient custom requires him to lean "royally," in a grand-banqueting posture. In the course of the evening, one of the children present is expected to "steal" the piece of matzah and, at the end of the Seder service, exact a "ransom" for its return.

This piece of matzah goes by the name of *afikomon*. The etymology of this word is somewhat uncertain. Some scholars believe it to be a corruption of the Greek word *epikomion* (dessert) or *epikomon* (a gay pastime or revel with instrumental music, song, and dance, which usually wound up a Greek banquet). Others still see it as derived from the Chaldaic *afi-kuman* (literally: "dish-remover") because the afikomon was traditionally the last thing eaten at the paschal meal, after which the table was cleared of the dishes and Birkat ha-Mazon (Grace After Meals) was recited. Everyone at the Seder was required to eat a piece of the afikomon, probably so that the last taste on the mouth should be that of matzah, the historical symbol of the Egyptian Bondage and the Liberation.

This custom of first "concealing" and then "stealing" and "ransoming" the afikomon has a delightful folk-origin. It all came about by a deliberate misinterpretation of the Scriptural prescription for eating matzah on Passover: ". . . and ye shall eat it in haste." The Talmudic Rabbis, with playful facetiousness, interpreted this to mean: "We should make haste to finish eating the matzah so that the children do not fall asleep." The passage, within the context of the whole sentence, also lends itself to still another rendering: ". . . that the matzot are 'snatched' [gobbled] during the night of Passover." Only one step separates the word "snatch" from "steal," and "steal" it has remained to this day.

Besides the shrewd introduction of ancient "nursery rhymes" and children's songs into the narration of the Haggadah (*see* PASSOVER), the afikomon treasure-hunt was another pedagogic device of the Rabbis for keeping the small fry awake and sustaining their interest in the proceedings of the Seder.

One medieval notion was that the afikomon possessed magic properties. The ignorant among the Jews of Poland and Russia used to tie a piece of afikomon in a corner of their fringed four-cornered undergarments (tzitzit) as an amulet against the Evil Eye. (North African Jews still wear it on a string around their necks, also in the belief that it wards off evil.) Another folk-belief held that "if you eat a lot of afikomon you live long." That is why, in commenting on the hardihood and longevity of a very old person, the Yiddish-speaking Jew is wont to quip. "My, what a lot of afikomon he must have eaten!"

AGADA. *See* TALMUD, THE.

AKEDAH. *See* SACRIFICE OF ISAAC.

ALEPH-BET. *See* HEBREW ALPHABET.

ALI'AH. *See* TORAH-READING.

ALIYAH. *See* ZIONISM.

ALMEMAR. *See* BEMA.

ALPHABET, HEBREW. *See* HEBREW ALPHABET.

AMIDAH. *See* SHEMONEH ESREH.

AMORA, AMORAIM. *See* GEMARA (*under* TALMUD, THE).

AMUD. *See* PULPIT.

AMULETS (in Hebrew: pl. KEMIOT, s. KEMIAH; meaning "something hung on"; namely, worn around the neck, like a pendant, medallion, or necklace)

The wearing of amulets as magic charms to ward off harm, illness, or misfortune from hostile demons, evil spirits, the Evil Eye, sorcery, and the plottings of enemies, has been a common device in many cultures, from the most backward to the most developed. The ancient Egyptians and Babylonians were greatly addicted to amulet-wearing; the Israelites who were their contemporaries shared in that practice. The point need hardly be labored that the tefillin and the mezuzah, at the point of their most primitive origins, had the character of magic amulets, affording protection by virtue of their sacred texts and the name of God. The fact that they became spiritualized with time and were endowed by the Sages of the Talmud with a memorable symbolism, only demonstrates what vast conceptual distances the Jewish religion traversed in its development. Nor should one neglect to note that, beginning with the fourth century, Christians began to wear the cross as an amulet. The religious medals of modern times are merely extensions of the same protective principle; they are, in the language of ethnology, but "magic charms."

There were some Rabbinic Sages who looked askance at the wearing of amulets; they denigrated them as "an idolatrous practice." Hai Gaon (*d.* 1038), rector of the Babylonian Talmudic Academy of Pumbeditha, in his feuding against the rival Academy of Sura, wrote with scorn: "Sorcery and amulets sprang from the Academy of Sura because it is situated close to Babylon and the House of Nebuchadnezzar." Nevertheless, he did not doubt that an amulet upon which the mystic names of God and of succoring angels were invoked against a specific demon who was believed to have caused a person to fall sick, was entirely efficacious. A Cabalistic formula, incomprehensible to moderns but once highly prized for curing and warding off disease, began in this ritualistic wise: "In the name of Shaddai [one of the mystic names of God], who created heaven and earth, and in the name of the Angel Raphael, the memuneh in charge of this month, and by you, Smmel, Hngel, Vngsursh, Kndors, Ndmh, Kmiel, S'ariel, Abrid, Gurid, memunim of the summer equinox, and by your prince, Or'anir, by the angel of the hour and the star, in the name of the Lord, God of Israel, who rests upon the Cherubs, the great, mighty, and awesome God, YHVH Zebaot is His name, and in Thy name, God of mercy, and by Thy name, Adiriron, trustworthy healing—God . . . save me by this writing and by this amulet. . . ."

It is of special interest that the philosopher-rabbi Maimonides, himself perhaps the foremost doctor and medical scientist of the twelfth century who was equally famed as a rationalist, saw "medical" merit in the wearing of amulets: "It is not inconsistent that a nail from the gallows to heal wounds and the tooth of a fox (as cure for insomnia) have been permitted to be used as cures," he wrote in his *Guide to the Perplexed*. How had he arrived at that conclusion?

"These things were considered in former days as facts that had been established by experiment. They served as cures in the same manner as the hanging of a peony over a person subject to epileptic fits . . . and the vapors of vinegar and marcasite to the swelling of hard tumors. For the Rabbinic Law permits as medicine everything that has been verified by experiment, although it cannot be explained by analogy."

A fourteenth-century Hebrew Cabalistic work of the Rhineland listed the special curative and "preventative"

Silver container for an amulet designed to be worn, containing the Tables of the Commandments and the mystical Hebrew name of God—Shaddai—*in the center. Italy, 18th century. (Courtesy of Joseph B. Horwitz Judaica Collection, Cleveland.)*

powers of semiprecious stones when worn as amulets: The ruby, called "the stone of preservation," when worn by a pregnant woman, prevented miscarriage; the topaz cooled off the over-ardent lover; the emerald rejuvenated the aged; the carbuncle endowed the wearer with great strength; the sapphire worked extraordinary cures; the amethyst lent the courage of a lion; the onyx made friends for its holder and won for him public respect and success.

Of course, just as the Egyptians in Hellenistic times wore amulets containing magic papyri, so did the Jews wear brass or silver amulets in the shape of medallions, necklaces, bracelets, and rings—many holding bits of parchment with Hebrew Scriptural passages or the mystic names of God inscribed upon them. Inasmuch as pregnant women and small children required most protection against the invisible powers —the former against the machinations of Lilith the Temptress, and the latter against the Evil Eye, invoked by envious or wicked persons—most of the amulets that Jews wore were guards against the latter two. Some merely were in the shape of tiny golden hands with the Hebrew word *Shaddai* (one of the names for God), engraved upon them against the Evil

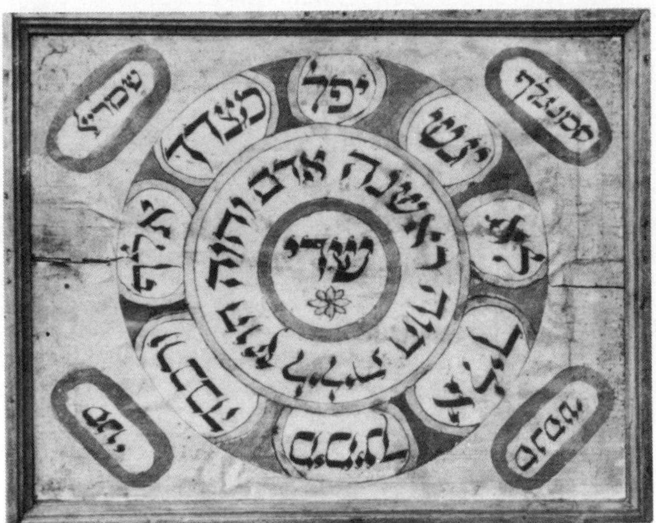

Cabalistic amulet hung on the wall of a lying-in room. Early 19th century.

Eye. Others bore the engraving of the so-called Seal of Solomon. Still others were decorated with the hexagram (the Magen David or "Star of David") or with the menorah. Common too were the inverted pyramidal acrostics on parchment of incomprehensible words arranged in the well-known abracadabra design:

Akrabokus
krabokus
rabokus
abokus
bokus
okus
kus
us
s

The fame of Jewish amulets, spread through the works of mystification by the Jewish Cabalists among susceptible Christian savants and clergy of the late Renaissance, had some startling results. Martin Luther related how once he introduced to Albert of Saxony a Jew who had given that ruler an amulet with a Hebrew inscription to protect him, so he claimed, against any attempt on his life. Angered by the notion that he required special protection against assassins, Albert hung the medallion around the Jew's neck and, to demonstrate to him how ineffective its protection was, started hacking murderously at him with his sword.

The amulet custom among Jews, however much the great majority regards it as a superstitious practice, has greatly declined since the turn of the twentieth century. Yet it is still potent as a folkway among the more backward Jews of North Africa and Arab lands. The fact is that amulets are still being worn by many tradition-bound Chasidim in New York, London, Jerusalem, and other Jewish centers. Apparently, they are able to concur with Hai Gaon: "Amulets are written . . . in order that angels may help."

See also ANGELS; CABALA; DEMONS; EVIL EYE; GOD, NAMES OF; MEZUZAH; SATAN; SHEM HA-MEFORASH; TEFILLIN; TZITZIT.

ANANITES. *See* KARAITES.

ANGELS (from the Greek, meaning "messengers"; in Hebrew: pl. MALACHIM, S. MALACH)

In spite of the fact that the religion of Israel is presumed to be thoroughly monotheistic, the Jews in Biblical and also in later historic ages, held many "idolatrous" notions in common with the animists (nature-worshipers) among the surrounding peoples. One was a belief in the existence of mediating angels and demons (or devils): a dualistic opposition of good and evil spirits struggling for the control of man's conscience and the direction of his conduct.

Angels were thought by the Jews to be incorporeal and eternal beings, dazzling with light, luminous with purity. They never fell ill, they never died; they did not eat or sleep, nor did they suffer any of the misfortunes that were the lot of humans. If God ruled the universe in *absolute* power, the angels, doing God's bidding, could be considered *secondary* powers. For the devout of every century, and for quite a number of people even in our own time, reality did not possess sharply defined lineaments; ideas about the natural and the supernatural became indistinguishably fused. The effort to penetrate the mystery of existence strained to the utmost the imaginative, let alone the rational, faculties. In the blurred thinking of the monotheistic Jew and of the polytheistic pagan (and, at a later period, of Christian and Mohammedan believers as well), the universe was populated by a vast conglomeration of angels—celestial creatures that had been created by God to serve him as his special "messengers" to accomplish his will in the world. They remained invisible, in keeping with their divine character, until it was time for them to make their presence manifest and their mission known; then they could assume a variety of physical shapes and disguises, including, occasionally, human form.

The Jews of ancient days, together with the Egyptians, Babylonians, Persians, and Greeks, believed that angels resided in all the forces of nature. The Psalmist, in a hymn of pantheistic praise (Psalm 104:4), describes God the Creator as one

> Who makest winds Thy messengers,
> The flaming fire Thy ministers.

He, like all other Jews, believed that invisible spirits (demons as well as angels) animated all of physical creation, and that they could be seen in sun, star and planet, heaven and earth, fire and water, light and darkness, wind and rain, thunder and lightning etc. In Rabbinic writings, the angels were designated collectively as *Pamaliah shel Ma'alah*, ("the Family of Heaven"). They were referred to also as "the Hosts of Heaven" and "the Sons of God."

In military formations of "hosts" and "cohorts," each of the angelic categories (the twelfth-century philosopher-rabbi, Maimonides, claimed there were ten) was said to be ruled over by an archangel: Samael, or Satan, chief of the evil spirits, was the Prince of Death; Gabriel was the Prince of Fire; Rahab, the Prince of the Sea; Dumah, the Prince of Gehinnom (Purgatory); Ridiah, the Prince of Rain, Lailah, the Prince of Night and Conception; Michael, the Prince of Israel (i.e., its guardian and steadfast advocate before God); Raphael, the Prince of Healing (bearing aloft to the Throne of Mercy the contrite prayers of man); and Uriel, the Prince of the Light of God (i.e., the disseminator of Torah truth). The Talmud states categorically: "The names of the angels came into the possession of Israel from Babylonia."

During the tumultuous final centuries before the Destruction of the Temple, when religious thinking became delirious with Messianic expectation and apocalyptic visioning, the numbers and the varieties of angels multiplied fantastically. From that time on, they were carefully regimented in categories to distinguish rank and function. In the first place were the illustrious Angels of the Presence who surrounded God like so many royal courtiers. Then came the Angles of Sanctification, for holiness was perhaps the principal ethical attribute of God. There were also Angels of Destruction to carry

Ancient Israelite conception of an angel. Ivory, 9th century B.C.E. Discovered during the excavation of King Ahab's palace in Samaria. (The Jewish Museum.)

out God's stern judgments against the wicked. But it is difficult to mark off one kind of angel from the other: cherubim, seraphim, *chayyot* ("living creatures"), offanim ("wheels"—an innovation by the Prophet Ezekiel), and *arelim* (an obscure term). God was said to be surrounded by the worshipful "hosts" of cherubim as he sat on the Throne of Glory in the Seventh Heaven. This image immediately recalls the "divine attendants," those minor deities in Greek mythology, who were described as "courtiers" surrounding each major god or goddess and doing their bidding.

The seer Enoch of the first century B.C.E. wrote down with the breathless excitement of an eye-witness:

> Behold! I saw a very great light, and all the fiery hosts of archangels, and of the incorporeal powers, and of the lordships, and of the principalities, and of the dominions: cherubim and seraphim, thrones, and the watchfulness of the many eyes (offanim). Ten hosts of angels according to their rank. Night and day, without ceasing, they sing:
> "Holy, holy, holy is the Lord God of [angel] Hosts!
> Heaven and earth are full of Thy glory!"

The Prophet Ezekiel, who preached in Babylonia to the Jewish captives in the sixth century B.C.E., was exposed to, and inevitably impressed by, the prevailing religious, mythic, and artistic values of his environment. When he described angels, it was as though they were actual and stylized figures he had just seen on some Babylonian sculptured relief. "As for the likeness of their faces, they had the face of a man; and they had the face [i.e., the appearance] of a lion on the right side; and the face of an ox on the left side . . . and their wings were stretched upward; two wings of every one were joined one to another and two covered their bodies." (Ezekiel 1:10-11.)

Archaeologists digging on the site of the palace of the Jewish king Ahab in Samaria (ninth century B.C.E.) unearthed an ivory carving of a cherub that could reasonably serve as a realization in sculpture of Ezekiel's description. The angel has a human face topped with long hair dressed in contemporary fashion. The head is set on the body of a Babylonian-style lion that has wings stretching upward from the back. It was only during the Middle Ages in Europe that Jewish figure-representations of angels in illuminated Hebrew Haggadot (S. Haggadah) and other illustrated sacred texts dispensed with the traditional animal body. No doubt this was done in order to spiritualize that primitive visualization.

So staggering in number had this celestial population grown as a result of the embroidering fancy of the early mystics, that the Rabbinic Sage of the third century C.E., Simeon ben Lakish, set himself the monumental task of taking a census of the angels in all seven heavens. His survey revealed the following: Under each of the 12 signs of the zodiac there were assembled 30 "hosts" of angels. Each host was composed of 30 "camps." Each camp boasted 30 "legions." Each legion was made up of 30 "cohorts." There were 30 "corps" in each cohort. Finally, each corps consisted of 365,000 "myriads." And, inasmuch that there were 10,000 angels in a myriad, perhaps it would be better to leave to a modern computing machine the task of arriving at the exact total of all the "messengers" of God.

Of particular significance in Jewish religious thinking was the active role played in the Bible by angels in the protection of Israel. "Behold!" God reassured the Israelites when they broke out of their Bondage in Egypt and journeyed toward the Promised Land, "I send an angel before thee, to keep thee by the way, and to bring thee into the place which I have prepared. Take ye heed of him and hearken unto his voice."

Jewish medieval conception of angels. Angels destroying Sodom and Gomorrah. (From an illumination of a Hebrew Bible, c. 1288. The British Museum.)

There was hardly a time of national crisis when the myth-weaving folk did not conjure up the appearance of redeeming angels in order to explain the miracle of Jewish survival. An angel of protection went, as a matter of course, into battle with the armies of Israel and, in the specific instance of the Assyrian general Sennacherib, dealt him a crushing blow. Who was this guardian angel and invincible ally of Israel? It was said to be the Archangel Michael, who outranked even Gabriel in the degree of his holiness and might. Moreover, he was the one who stepped forward before the Tribunal of Heaven to advocate the cause of Israel whenever it was charged with wrongdoing before God. He introduces himself in the Apocalypse, the Testament of Levi, in these words: "I am the angel who intercedes for the people of Israel that it may not be smitten utterly, for every evil spirit attacks it."

Eleazar ben Judah of Worms, the thirteenth-century Cabalist who composed the remarkable Book of the Angels, declared that angels were created by God in order to ensure righteousness among men, and that each individual soul, when it is sent into the world, is accompanied by an angel whose duty it is to guide and protect it through the mazes of an existence that is steeped in sin and error.

The simple-minded and the faithful always had a childlike trust in the ever-present helpfulness of angels. Didn't the Angel Gabriel rescue the boy Abraham from the fiery pit into which Nimrod had cast him? Hadn't he also, in the nick of time, stayed Abraham's sacrificial knife during the binding of his son, Isaac?

For generations, since Rabbinic times, Jewish children, before they shut their eyes in sleep, have recited the ancient Hebrew plea for angel protection:

> In the name of the Lord, God of Israel! May Michael be at my right hand and Gabriel at my left, before me Uriel and behind me Raphael, and above my head—the Divine Presence of God [the Shelchinah].

See also DYBBUK; SATAN.

ANIMALS, "CLEAN" AND "UNCLEAN"

Fundamental to the Jewish dietary laws is the distinction made in the Bible between those animals it specifies as being ritually "clean" or "permitted" for human consumption and those that it marks as being "unclean," and therefore not "fit" —in fact, "an abomination."

The listing of "clean" and "unclean" animals is principally found in Chapter 11 of Leviticus and in Chapter 14 of Deuteronomy. Categorically it is stated in the Bible: "There are the living things which ye may eat among all the beasts that are on the earth." (Leviticus 11:2.) Under the dietary laws, only those four-footed animals that have a cloven hoof and chew their cud can be eaten, and these include the ox, the cow, the sheep, the goat, the hart, the gazelle, the roebuck, the pygarg, and the antelope. Animals that possess only one of the required characteristics (like the camel, the rock badger, and the hare, which chew their cud but do not have a cloven hoof, or the pig, which has a cloven hoof but does not chew its cud) are terefah—"unclean" or "forbidden." "Unclean" animals also include the mouse and weasel, as well as the lizard and every other creature that crawls.

Of those creatures that live in the waters, only fish that have both fins and scales may be eaten; all others that have "not fins and scales . . . and . . . that swarm in the waters . . . they are a detestable thing unto you."

The list of forbidden fowl is large and includes all birds of prey (the eagle, the vulture, the falcon, the kite, the raven, the hawk, the sea-mew, the owl, and the cormorant), as well as most wild fowl.

Also counted as "unclean" is the carcass of any clean animal—whether or not it died of natural causes, or by accident—that was not ritually slaughtered. It is a curious fact that for any person merely to touch a carcass makes him "unclean" until the evening.

It is understandable why those Jews who unbendingly followed every ritualistic prescription should have refused, as a matter of religious principle, to search for the objective reasons that determined what animals should be regarded as "clean" or "unclean." This held equally true with every other aspect of the dietary laws. For the observing Jew it was all very uninvolved; he readily accepted the laws and commandments of the Torah as having been divinely revealed to Moses, who taught them to Israel as the Jewish way of life. They were not to be questioned or argued about; their hidden meanings were not to be probed. But it was otherwise with the intellectual and philosophically trained Jews, in particular those of the Greco-Roman era, the Middle Ages, and modern times. They found a need to reconcile their faith with the dictates of reason. In the celebrated "Letter of Aristeas," written in Greek by that expositor of Judaism during the third century B.C.E., we find the Jew Aristeas critically examining the dietary laws, which, he stated, had been given to the Jews to inculcate in them the spirit of justice, to awaken pious reflections, and, by their means, to help form the character of the individual. To prove his contention, he pointed to the fact that in kashrut, birds of prey are forbidden as food so the Jew might recall the first principle of social justice: *not to prey on others.* About two centuries later, Philo of Alexandria, who was a Platonist philosopher as well as a rabbi, attempted to interpret Scriptural law by means of the Greek method of allegory, assigning a human vice to every creature branded in the Bible as "unclean," and reading into every prohibition a devout exhortation to man to take himself in hand and master his "unclean" passions and habits.

The Talmudic Sages, being also intellectually conditioned to the challenges of reason, presented their explanation in this wise: "All these things [i.e., the eating of the flesh of 'unclean' animals] are forbidden because they deprave the blood and make it susceptible to many diseases. They pollute the body and the soul."

Among all the animals forbidden to Jews, none was fenced off with more severe and uncompromising strictures than the pig. Until recent times, the eating of pork (*chazzir* in Hebrew; *chazzer* in Yiddish) was considered by the believing Jew to be equal to apostasy; even today, many Orthodox Jews consign a Jew who eats pork to the lost and the damned. The folk-Jew, outraged in his sensibilities, expected that the rascal would have to expiate for this cardinal sin in the fiery furnace of Gehinnom (Gehenna), the original Jewish model for the Christian Hell. So notorious was this revulsion of the Jew against the flesh of the pig that, when the Seleucidan king, Antiochus (Epiphanes) IV, after he had overrun Judea, ordered the Jews to sacrifice pigs on their altars, including the one in the Temple in Jerusalem, the decree stirred up such horror and outrage among the conquered Jewish people that it sparked the popular revolt led by the Maccabees in 168 B.C.E.

In Germany, the Jewish religious prohibition against eating swine's flesh was treated with ridicule. Sculptured in relief in the Regensburg Cathedral is the so-called Jewish Sow (Judensau), *13th century.*

The baffling fact is that no Jewish religious observance aroused so much ridicule and resentment among the anti-Semites through history as the taboo against eating pork. Both Philo of Alexandria and Josephus of Rome, outstanding chroniclers of their time, mention the jeering mobs who harassed Jews on the streets, forcing them publicly to eat the flesh of swine; German anti-Semites of the Middle Ages, not unlike their later Nazi counterparts, obscenely caricatured the Jew in association with the pig (one or two old churches even illustrated this subject permanetly in sculpture).

Maimonides, the medieval authority in both religion and medicine, commented: "The principal reason why the laws forbids swine's flesh . . . is that the pig's habits and its food are very dirty and loathsome. . . ." And because trichinosis is known to be caused by eating pork, many doctors today are not unsympathetic to this opinion.

The student of comparative religions will see that the Jew was not alone among ancient peoples in having animals designated "clean" and "unclean." The Babylonian code, the Laws of Manu, also carried a prohibition against the eating of birds of prey, and the Babylonians permitted all animals (with the exception of the camel) that chewed the cud to be eaten because they were ritually "clean." Likewise, in Egypt, the priests were enjoined against "defiling" themselves by eating fish-devouring birds.

Many anthropoligists, both Jewish and Gentile, feel that there must have been a primitive origin for the concepts of "clean" (kasher or kosher) and "unclean" (terefah or trefah) that antedated the dietary laws in the Bible, and they consider these taboos too a carryover from a primitive system of totemism that must have flourished among the Hebrews, who they say belonged to totem-clans and who, like all nature-worshipers, placed a taboo on all animals they held sacred. (The ancient Egyptians had imposed such a taboo on the cat, the cow, and the bull because they worshiped them as deities.)

Evidence does exist (drawn from the Bible) that remote ancestors of the Jews were organized into totem-clans. For instance, Chapter 49 in Genesis describes the insignias of the Twelve Tribes, depicted on the standards or banners which they carried on the long march out of Egypt: "Judah is a lion's whelp . . . Issachar is a large-boned ass . . . Naphtali is a hind . . . Benjamin is a wolf . . ." etc. Anthropological investigations have shown that in animism or nature-worship, the aboriginal clan has for its totem either an animal, a bird, or a plant (Joseph's insignia was a grapevine) from whom the clan members trace their supposed descent. Each member of the clan carries a representation of the clan-god on his body, often in the form of a tattoo. ("Ye shall not imprint any marks [i.e., tattoos] on you," sternly admonished the monotheistic reformer in Leviticus 19:28.) The individuals belonging to a totem-clan are forbidden to eat the flesh of their totem, which is considered sacred.

In the case of the Twelve Tribes of Israel, which were, as the Bible reveals, constituted of a considerable number of clans, the totem of each clan must have been accepted into the common pantheon of totems when the tribal federation was formed.

It is interesting to note that those animals mentioned in the Bible as "unclean"—taboo—were exactly forty-two in number.

See also DIETARY LAWS; MEAT, SALTING OF; MEAT AND MILK; SHECHITAH; SHOCHET; TEREFAH.

ANIMALS, COMPASSION FOR (in Hebrew: TZAAR BAALE CHAYYIM)

The traditional Jewish attitude toward animals and man's treatment of them is stated in the medieval Hebrew work Sefer Chasidim (The Book of the Pious): "Be kind and compassionate to all creatures that the Holy One, blessed be He, created in this world. Never beat nor inflict pain on any animal, beast, bird, or insect. Do not throw stones at a dog or a cat, nor kill flies or wasps." The reason for this was a simple one: Animals, having been created by God, are endowed by him with a certain spirituality; they even possess wisdom and goodness to a degree.

The humane regard among Jews for people extended also to encompass animals. But behind it was the all-pervasive feeling of compassion urged upon the righteous: "As the Holy One, blessed be He, has compassion upon man, so has He compassion upon the beasts of the field. . . . And as the Holy One, blessed be He, has compassion upon the beasts of the field, so is He filled with compassion for the birds in the air." (Midrash.)

The kind treatment of animals was made part of the moral climate of Jewish living, and had nothing whatsoever in common with animal worship, so prominent in the ancient world. Its primary literary source was, of course, the Torah. In the Fourth Commandment, ordaining the Sabbath as the day of rest from all toil, the beast of burden was included as a beneficiary of its blessings together with the man-servant, the maid-servant, and the stranger. The Torah also carries a prohibition against muzzling the ox "when he treadeth out the corn" in order that he may be free to nibble when he gets hungry. The Babylonian Sage, Rab, even established the rule that, before a man could sit down to eat, he first was obligated by the dictates of conscience to feed his animals because they could not help themselves. The Talmud, supporting its view on various Scriptural passages, held that, in order to save an animal's life, or merely to relieve it when it was in pain, it was permitted the pious to break any ordinance of Sabbath observance. In fact, the extensive regulations that ordered ritual slaughtering (shechitah) were motivated entirely by humane considerations: to cause the animal as little pain as possible.

Concerning the Biblical injunction "And whether it be cow or ewe, ye shall not kill it and her young both in a day," the philosopher-rabbi Maimonides (twelfth century) pointed out, in his *Guide to the Perplexed,* "that the principle of 'sympathy with brute creation' is here involved in no small degree, in that the love and compassion of the mother for her young is implanted in the feelings of dumb creatures as it is in the human heart."

See also SHECHITAH.

ANTI-SEMITISM: THE "RACIAL PURITY" MYTH

The "Scientific" Myth: Semites and Aryans. In reality, the term "anti-Semitism," with its biologic and racial connotations, was first used in 1879 by Wilhelm Marr, the founder of the notorious Anti-Semitic League, who, ironically, was said to be the baptized son of a Jewish actor. Having everywhere a grass-roots anti-Jewish movement of sizable proportions to cater to, the word "anti-Semitism" was soon in general currency, and since the cult of science had become very popular during the last quarter of the nineteenth century, all of the "scientific" postulates of the term were eagerly accepted by the hordes of the half-baked, the partly informed, the uninformed, the gullible, the neurotic, and the malicious.

Marr based his term "anti-Semitism" on *racial identity,* averring that the "inborn" character of Jews or Semites—the presumed descendants of Shem, one of the three sons of Noah mentioned in the Bible—was antithetical to the noble character of Aryans (Marr had in mind, when he said "Aryans," Teutons and Nordics such as Germans, Austrians, Scandinavians, Dutch, English, French, etc.). Broad-mindedly, he conceded that Jews could not help being what they were; namely, morally and physically inferior humans, because Nature had so pre-determined.

This mixed fodder of pseudo-scientific nonsense that was being fed by the rabid racists to the ignorant and the unthinking either amused or outraged the eminent men of science of that time. It drew from Friedrich Max Müller, the great Orientalist and philologist, this censure:

> It is but too easily forgotten that if we speak of Aryan and Semitic families, the ground of classification is language and language only. There are Aryan and Semitic languages, but it is against all rules of logic to speak . . . of an Aryan race, of Aryan blood, of Aryan skulls, and to attempt ethnological classification on purely linguistic grounds.

It all began this way: In the year 1808, and quite innocently, in the course of his philological researches, Friedrich von Schlegel, the noted Sanskritist (a Catholic who was married to Dorothea, Moses Mendelssohn's daughter), noticed a kinship between Persian and Sanskrit on the one hand and the Teutonic languages (German, Swedish, Dutch, etc.) on the other. From these observations and from others made by a number of philologists, he finally wove an elaborate hypothesis which held that these "related" tongues were derived from a common ancestor-language called "Aryan," one that had supposedly been spoken by a people named "Aryans" who inhabited the land of "Aryana." Needless to say, "Aryan" was a lost and forgotten language, the "Aryans" themselves had disappeared into historic limbo, and as for the land "Aryana"—there were only bare references to it in the Zend Avesta, the half-mythic scriptures of Persian Zoroastrianism (written *c.* 1000 B.C.E.), but where Aryana lay there was not the slightest intimation.

It was from these hypothetical Aryans, the inhabitants of the hypothetical country Aryana, who spoke a hypothetical tongue called Aryan, that the nineteenth-century anti-Semites among the German professors, journalists, and demagogic pamphleteers derived both their noble ancestry and their pride in constituting the "master-race" of mankind. There is no doubt but that the national chauvinism which followed the stupendous triumph of the Germans over the French during the Franco-Prussian War in 1870 greatly stimulated the development of the anti-Semites' "scientific" principle of Aryanism; it made it appear persuasive. At the same time, drawing from the same ancient literary source of inspiration —the Zend Avesta—the nineteenth-century anti-Semites applied the Zoroastrian principle of the duality and the deadly opposition declared to be existing between the deity of light (Ormuzd) and the deity of darkness (Ahriman) to the equally deadly opposition supposedly existing between the Aryan race (the German "master-race") and the Semitic race (the Jewish "slave-race"). The conclusion some of the academic German anti-Semites came to was that just as the Persian god of light was locked in unyielding battle with the god of darkness until the latter was defeated—so must "the Aryan race" engage in mortal combat with Jewry until the latter was destroyed.

The legal aspect of the term "Aryan" was disposed of with finality decades later when in its decision in United States *vs.* Bhagat Sing Thind (1923), the United States Supreme Court paid its respects to it in this fashion:

> The Aryan theory as a racial basis seems to be discredited by most, if not all, modern writers on the subject of ethnology. A review of their contentions would serve no useful purpose. It is enough to refer to the works of Deniker (*Races of Man,* p. 317), Keane (*Man: Past and Present,* 445-6), Huxley (*Man's Place in Nature,* p. 278), and to the *Dictionary of Races* (Senate Document 662, 61st Congress, 3d Session, 1910–11, p. 317).
>
> The term "Aryan" has to do with linguistic, and not at all with physical characteristics, and it would seem reasonably clear that mere resemblance in language, indicating a common linguistic root buried in remotely ancient soil, is altogether inadequate to prove common racial origin. There is, and can be, no assurance that the so-called Aryan language was not spoken by a variety of races living in proximity to one another. Our own history has witnessed the adoption of the English tongue by millions of Negroes, whose descendants can never be classified racially with the descendants of white persons, notwithstanding both may speak a common root language.

On the question of the "racial purity" (*limpieza*) of the Aryans or of the Jews, quite the concensus among reputable anthropoligists was, and still is, that it too was a myth wholly unrelated to reality. A typical expression of the view about the Jews as a "race" is given by the noted English scientists Julian S. Huxley and A. C. Haddon in *We Europeans: A Survey of Racial Problems* (1936):

> The Jews can rank neither as a nation nor even as ethnic unit, but rather as a socio-religious group carrying large Mediterranean, Armenoid and many other elements, and varying greatly in physical characteristics. Like many other groups, its members are held together by external pressure of various kinds, partly by a long historic memory, partly by a sense of common suffering, partly by religion. These factors, acting through long ages, have produced a common consciousness which is relaxed when the pressures are relaxed and intensified with the reverse process.

As for the "racial purity" claims made on behalf of the German people by the "Aryan" apologists, the eminent French anthropoligist, Pittard, made this observation at the turn of this century: "There is as much difference between a Pomeranian from the Baltic Coast and a Bavarian from the Ammer Massif, as there is between a horse and a zebra."

In the years intervening between the Franco-Prussian War and the unification of all German states in 1871, and Hitler's seizure of power in Germany in 1932, there was a relatively large number of Jews in Germany whose worldly fortune began to look up. Under Prince Bismarck's opportunistic policy of reaction and liberalism at one and the same time, the country's Jews acquired full civil emancipation and, therefore, equal opportunities under the law in every field of endeavor. It is certain that during the three decades that wound up the nineteenth century, the great industrial and commercial expansion of Germany gave many Jews a ready outlet for their talents. Many became rich—and pillars of society—as manufacturers, merchants, bankers, doctors, engineers, musicians, lawyers, and writers.

That the element of envy (or resentment) entered into the thinking of many anti-Semites toward their fellow Germans of Jewish extraction needs no further comment. Ever since the Knights of the Cross late in the eleventh century raised the cry of *"Hab hab!"* ("Give give"), the enemies of the Jews during the ensuing centuries in every country of Europe became adept at mingling their love of Jewish money and possessions with the unction of pious sentiment. This combination of feeling was undoubtedly the spark behind the mass-petition signed by 300,000 Prussian citizens in 1880—and followed by two days of near-riotous debate in Parliament—asking the Iron Chancellor (Bismarck) to exclude the Jews from all schools and universities and not allow them to hold public office. The petition declared: "The blending of the Semitic with the German element of our population has proved a failure. We are now faced with the loss of our superiority through the ascendancy of Judaism, whose steadily increasing influence springs from racial characteristics which the German nation cannot and must not tolerate unless it wishes to destroy itself."

How different was the approach to the well-advertised "Jewish" failings (as if other peoples did not share the same shortcomings!) by Robespierre during the French Revolution. Pleading with the delegates of the National Assembly that they include the Jews in the humane provisions of the Rights of Man, he said: "The vices of the Jews are born of the abasement in which you [Christians] have plunged them. Raise their condition, and they will speedily rise to it." One hundred and fifty-four years later (in 1945) the American psychologist W. M. Krogman courageously touched on the same subject and virtually in the same manner as Robespierre: ". . . centuries of injustice and of rigorous competition [have forced the Jew to] compensate . . . by a tremendous drive . . . this fact has given him a set of behavioral attitudes and responses that are often characteristic to the point of recognition and group definition . . .but that is *cultural, not biological.*"

As the old saying goes, the Jews were damned if they did and damned if they didn't. The Rev. Dr. Stöcker, the Kaiser's fashionable preacher at Potsdam, declared: "The Jews are at one and the same time the pace-setters of capitalism and of revolutionary socialism, thus working from two sides to destroy the present political and social order."

The Beginnings of the Myth. The German anti-Semites, always strong in their national penchant for metaphysics, for reaching "scientific" conclusions, and for drawing up precise formulations of them, developed their hatred of the Jew into an irrefutable scientific system—so they thought. It has often been observed that, when societies or groups of men want certain of their actions to appear to others less objectionable and more "righteous" than they actually are, they adorn them with high-sounding intellectual, moral, and legal rationalizations—perfuming the stench, as it were, by such sanctions. However as Max Nordau, the noted Jewish journalist and wit (1849–1923) once dourly observed about the "intellectual" antics of the anti-Semites: "The pretexts change, but the hatred remains."

The hatred of the anti-Semites in Germany and Austria remained, but beginning with the middle of the nineteenth century, a brand new pretext was furnished—this time by the intellectuals and the professors: ethnologists, biologists, psychologists, and historians—and aimed at the complete suppression (*see* Luther's program) and even physical extermination of the Jews. This new approach had been pioneered by two men: Count Joseph Arthur de Gobineau (1816–82) and Houston Stewart Chamberlain (1885–1927).

Gobineau, a French diplomat and Orientalist, who issued his *Essay on the Inequality of the Human Races* in four volumes (Paris, 1853–55), took for his thesis the proposition that the Jews (Semites) were "a mongrel race" and that "everything great, noble, and fruitful in the works of man . . . belongs to one family (Aryan), the different branches of which have reigned in all civilized countries of the globe."

The other intellectual mentor of the German anti-Semites, Chamberlain, was the son-in-law of the composer Richard Wagner, who, on his own, had mercilessly flayed the Jews in his not-so-musical essay, "Judaism in Music." Chamberlain was the author of perhaps the most libelous work ever produced on the subject of the Jews and published under the completely misleading but academic title *The Foundations of the Nineteenth Century* (1899). It won the enthusiastic patronage of Kaiser Wilhelm II and sold almost one million copies in the German language alone. A choice reflection in the book is this: ". . . the Jewish race is altogether bastardized, and its existence is a crime against the holy laws of life . . ."

Speaking of "the holy laws of life," another equally influential and pious enemy of the Jewish people, the Rev. Dr. Adolf Stöcker, Wilhelm I's Court preacher and the leader of the anti-Semitic bloc in the Reichstag, also entered the lists as a champion of "holiness." But the sanctity he fought for was the so-called purity of German blood. He stated: ". . . modern Judaism is an alien drop of blood in the German body—one with destructive power." It was Stöcker, the founder in 1878 of the Christian Socialist Party, who at that time coined the slogan which became a battle cry of the Nazis against the Jews a half century later: *"Deutschland—erwache!"* ("Germany—awake!") The Christian Socialists also adopted a central plank in their political program calling for a Germany which would be *Judenrein* (purified of Jews).

Curiously, in this preoccupation with the racial purity of the German people, Chamberlain and Stöcker, as also the other intellectual leaders of the ever proliferating German anti-Semitic movement—Wilhelm Marr, Hermann Ahlwardt, Heinrich van Treitschke, Count Walter Puckler-Muskau, and the philosopher Eugen Dühring—had "scientific" views with the *limpieza*, purity of blood (obsession of the Spanish racists during the fourteenth century.

The Jewish problem no longer was to be a concern for the Christian religion. The intellectual anti-Semites, like the beer-hall rabble-rousers, were violently opposed to the conversion of the Jews to Christianity on account of the "taint" of "Jewish blood" that could enter the pure German bloodstream through intermarriage. This stand was entirely consistent with their "racial purity" notions, and was clearly expressed by the popular rhyming jingle:

Was der Jude glaubt ist einerlei
In der Rasse liegt die Schweinerei

("What the Jew believes is meaningless;
In the race lies the swinishness.")

Dühring, from his lofty eminence as a philosopher, gave the following genocidal counsel to the German people on how to deal with the Jews: They were not be hampered by any "scruple, to use the most modern methods of disinfection." From his "philosophy of disinfection" to the gas chambers of the Nazis, where six million Jews were asphyxiated in the 1940's, was just one step removed and only six decades away.

See also CHRISTIANITY, JEWISH ORIGINS OF; CHURCH AND PERSECUTION; COMMUNITY, SELF-GOVERNING; CONVERSION OF JEWS; DISPUTATIONS, RELIGIOUS; FEUDAL SOCIETY, POSITION OF THE JEWS IN; "HOST DESECRATION" CALUMNIES; KIDDUSH HA-SHEM; KOL NIDRE; MARRANOS AND THE INQUISITION; MASSACRES: THE CRUSADES, THE BLACK DEATH; MONEYLENDERS; NAZIS, THE; PERSECUTION IN "MODERN" DRESS; POGROMS IN SLAVIC LANDS; "RITUAL MURDER" SLANDERS; SEPARATISM, JEWISH; SHYLOCK MYTH, THE; WANDERING JEW; YELLOW BADGE.

ANUSIM. *See* CONVERSION OF JEWS; MARRANOS AND THE INQUISITION.

APIKOROS. *See* EPIKOROS.

APOCRYPHA, THE

When the second and third divisions of the Bible—Prophets and Holy Writings (Hagiographa)—were being compiled by the "Men of the Great Assembly" in the closing centuries of the Second Temple era, it was inevitable that some of the writings under consideration should be rejected. Undoubtedly, those successors to Ezra the Scribe and his editorial continuators in the compilation of the Bible must have set for themselves certain criteria of judgment when they made their selections. But what those standards may have been is not known exactly. Yet there are found several interesting hints in the Talmud concerning them.

One of these oblique references touches on the rejection from the Scriptural canon of the Wisdom Book, Ecclesiasticus (often referred to in Hebrew as "The Wisdom of Ben Sirach"). That work was composed in Hebrew by Jesus ben Sirach (*c.* 200 B.C.E.), a poet-intellectual of Jerusalem. The latter-day Rabbinic Sages observed in the Talmud that on the occasion when the Men of the Great Assembly rejected Ecclesiasticus from the canon, they established the editorial policy not to allow into the Scriptures any book of such "recent" composition as Ben Sirach's. What may have been implied in that decision was that the "Age of Inspiration" had already passed. It also could have meant that time to prove the extent of the "inspiration" and the validity in terms of sanctity of any religious writing was necessary.

But it is on this very point (of proper "aging" of a work) that the bedevilment enters for the student of the literary history of the Bible, for it has been fairly well established by modern scholarship that the books of Daniel and Esther, which were found acceptable to the Biblical editors, had been written several decades *after* Ecclesiasticus!

Some Biblical students have asked the question—which is perhaps rhetorical only—why it was that, despite their original doubts and the ensuing controversy over them, the Men of the Great Assembly found Proverbs, Ecclesiastes, and Job sufficiently "inspired" to merit inclusion in the Scriptures, yet turned down Ecclesiasticus. A quite objective evaluation shows the latter work to be no more sophisticated and skeptical than the former are. In fact, purely as a literary composition of individuality, it compares favorably with them. There is no sure answer to why it was refused.

One possible explanation for its exclusion could very well have been because, in his religious-political outlook, Ben Sirach seems to have been a patrician Sadducee. And it should be recalled that the latter-day editors of the Biblical canon, which was fixed with finality by a Rabbinical Synod in Galilee as taking place twenty-five years after the destruction of Jerusalem by Titus in 70 C.E., were principally plebian Pharisees who had been waging a bitter and continuing war against the aristocratic Hellenized Sadducees. It should also be noted that some of the Sadducean views that Jesus ben Sirach expressed in Ecclesiasticus—for example, his explicit denial of the Pharisaic doctrines of physical resurrection after death and of the immortality of the soul—ran violently counter to Rabbinic teachings.

Apparently, Ecclesiasticus and similar religious works were being widely read by Jews everywhere—even in Judea, the fountainhead of Jewish traditionalism. This may be inferred from the fact that early in the second century C.E., the illustrious Tanna (Sage) of the Mishnah, Akiba ben Joseph, who was one of the chief architects of the Oral Tradition (*see* MISHNAH, *under* TALMUD), had declared with unconcealed scorn that the Jew who read any other than the twenty-four canonical writings included in the Bible would have no share in the bliss of the righteous in the World-to-Come. It was also strictly forbidden to read from the extra-Biblical writings in the synagogue or House of Study to avoid endowing them through such readings with the same sanctity and prestige that were reserved for the canonical writings. Nonetheless, despite all the strictures, exhortations, and prohibitions, they were being widely read at the time outside of the synagogue.

During the Rabbinic period, which coincided with that of the Hellenistic intellectual and religious assimilation, when Greek-speaking Jews felt impelled by the pressures of their environment to try to harmonize the tenets of their Hebraic faith with the intellectual values of Greek culture, there were many Hellenized Jews in Judea, especially in Egypt and elsewhere throughout the Roman empire, who did not see eye to eye with Akiba. In fact, at a much earlier period (possibly during the second century B.C.E.), a number of those extra-Biblical rejected writings had been translated from the Hebrew and Aramaic and were included in the Septuagint, the Bible of the Alexandrian Jews, written in Greek, which ultimately became, in part, the Scriptures of Christianity.

Quite obviously, Jewish religious ideas flowed in two divergent currents. At the very time that Hellenism was extending the intellectual horizons of Jews with Greek philosophy, science, and literature, it was also acting as a solvent on some of the most cherished traditional religious forms and beliefs in Jewish life of the past.

There are fourteen writings not found in the Hebrew Bible which made their way first into the Greek Septuagint and, five hundred years later, from there into the Latin version, the Vulgate. Collectively those writings (some of those extant are only fragments) are called the Apocrypha. This word, which seems to have been used first by Jerome, the Hellenist Church Father of the fourth century who edited the Vulgate, is the plural form of the Greek word *apokryphon*, which means a writing of "hidden" lore. Employed in that sense, "Apocrypha" connotes a group of esoteric writings which were intended only for initiates or illuminati in mystic knowledge. It was from the inept use of this word by Jerome that the mistaken notion arose that the writings in the Apocrypha had been kept out of the Bible because it had been decided that they should not be in general circulation (as were the canonized Scriptural books) on account of the "secret" wisdom that they contained.

That Jerome was in error can be inferred from the fact that the prophecies of Isaiah ben Amoz, and even more so those of Ezekiel, contain mystic revelations that have engaged the puzzlement of readers to this day. Nevertheless, those writings were included in the Bible canon, although the Talmud makes note of the doubts that the inclusion of Ezekiel first stirred up. No less esoteric was the book of Daniel, dealing as it does with the marvelous, the supernatural, and the hinted-at mysteries of "the appointed time of the End [i.e., the End of Days]."

Most of the fourteen writings in the Apocrypha can hardly be characterized as containing "hidden" wisdom. Ecclesiasticus and The Wisdom of Solomon, which are the major literary works in the collection, are sophisticated but moralizing Wisdom books; Judith, like The Book of Esther in the Bible, is a patriotic chronicle-romance; Susanna is a gay *divertissement* with a moral; Tobit personalizes the ideal of true piety in fictionalized form; and First and Second Maccabees are merely devout chronicles of the events that took place in the Hasmonean uprising of 168 B.C.E. The only work to which the meaning of *apokryphon* (in the Jewish sense) may be applied is the Second Book of Esdras. This is in the nature of an apocalypse, a "revelation" of the hidden mysteries concerning the establishment of the Messianic kingdom, the Resurrection of the dead, and the Last Judgment.

See also BIBLE, THE; CHACHMAH; DEAD SEA SCROLLS; ESSENES; HELLENISTS, JEWISH; MESSIAH, THE; MESSIAHS, WOULD-BE; PHARISEES; POST-BIBLICAL WRITINGS; PSEUDEPIGRAPHA; SADDUCEES; THERAPEUTAE.

ARABIC-JEWISH "GOLDEN AGE"

There has hardly been a people that stepped across the stage of history which did not, at one time or another, look back with nostalgia upon a certain period of its group-existence and appraise it as being its "golden age"—the high-water mark of its power and glory. But among the Jews (no doubt because they are an older people than most) the chief preoccupation was with culture—religious culture, specifically—not with power and glory, and this had been nurtured by them continuously for some twenty-five centuries. From the time of Ezra and the Scribes (q.v.) and the Men of the Great Assembly (*see* TALMUD, THE), the Jews had gone through at least three such "golden ages," namely, the Biblical, the Talmudic, and the Arabic-Jewish, first in Babylonia and North Africa, and then in Spain, during the Middle Ages.

The Golden Age of the Jews in Islamic North Africa, Babylonia, and Southern Spain may be said to have taken place from the ninth to the thirteenth centuries. Much of it was a result of the outgrowth of the cultural influences and fusion with the remarkable Arab culture which was the successor to the then moribund Greek civilization. When, in 529 C.E., impelled by his Christian zeal to root out the last vestiges of pagan intellectuality, the Emperor Justinian had ordered closed all the schools of philosophy in Athens, he probably had not realized that the Arabs would become the preservers of Greek philosophy and science. Not that Mohammed and his successors in Islam during the seventh and eighth centuries did not try to suppress these interests among the faithful, but it was without avail; the love for philosophy, science, and literature which the Greeks had fostered throughout the Mediterranean world during the Age of Hellenism was already too deeply ingrained to be eradicated.

Living in the heart of the Arab world, the Jews first served their apprenticeship in the sciences of Mohammedan intellectual masters; but, in time, they became their collaborators in developing the general culture of the region. Yet, remarkably, while doing so, both Arabs and Jews succeeded in retaining their own religious identities and integrity of conviction. So long as secular ideas and knowledge did not conflict with Jewish doctrines, they were pursued by Jews with enthusiasm.

A striking example of this breadth of interest was the savant Maimonides (Rabbi Moses ben Maimon, 1135–1204). He was a fervent adherent of the philosophy of Aristotle, who had summed up all of Greek thought in his original encyclopedic system and had perfected for thinking men that precise intellectual instrument for testing the validity of ideas: logic. Nevertheless, whenever Aristotelian postulates ran counter to the tenets of the Jewish religion, of which Maimonides was a devout believer and champion, he did not hesitate to reject them and to give forthright reasons for doing so; he was no slavish emulator.

What chiefly characterized Jewish thought in this epochal period was its search for unity—the attempt to reconcile faith with reason, theology with philosophy, the acceptance of authority with freedom of inquiry.

In Arab countries in the Near East and in the North of Africa, where there existed this free intermingling of cultures, there blossomed a rich and unique Jewish intellectuality in *Arabic*. After Mohammed had vanquished Babylonia in 632 C.E. in his jihad or holy war of conquest, the great and ancient Jewish community in that country, which for many centuries had been the world center of Rabbinic learning under the Talmudic Sages and the Geonim (*see* GEONIM; TALMUD, THE) went into a decline. At the same time, it exchanged Aramaic for Arabic as the vernacular, but also used it, in addition to Hebrew, as the language of literary expression.

Beginning with the tenth century, especially in the kingdom of Cordova under the enlightened Omayyad caliphs Abd-al-Rahman and his son, Al-Hakim, there appeared a

Thomas Aquinas (1224–74), the most illustrious of all Christian Scholastics, revered as "Doctor Angelicus" by the Church, took Maimonides' Guide to the Perplexed *as his own "guide" in reconciling religious dogma with reason and in developing his theological-philosophical system in* Summa Theologica *and other writings. The great debt Christian thought owes, through Thomas and other Schoolmen, to "Rabbi Moyses" has received but scant recognition.*
In the above altarpiece by Francesco Traini at Sta. Caterina in Pisa, Thomas Aquinas is depicted as victorious over Averroës (Ibn Roshd), the foremost Moorish philosopher who was generally mistaken for a Jew (note the yellow badge on arms). Aristotle (right) and Plato (left) illuminate the Angelic Doctor with their philosophy while he in turn casts his rays of wisdom on the Dominican Order, which he headed.

Traditional portrait of Maimonedes (Moses ben Maimon), called "The Rambam" by the Jewish folk.

Opening lines in the "Ode to Zion" by Judah Halevi. (From a 15th-century illustrated Hebrew manuscript. Hamburg University Library.)

galaxy of encyclopedic Jewish scholars, historians, philologists, lexicographers, grammarians, religious philosophers, mathematicians, astronomers, doctors, and poets. Besides conveying their own religious-cultural values, their writings also showed clearly the enormous impact of the Greco-Arab civilization of the period. From that time on, there was little differentiation in cultural forms, language, and taste among the Jewish communities in Babylonia, Egypt, Tunisia, Arabia, Algeria, Morocco, and Southern Spain. Together they constituted a monolithic Arab-oriented Eastern Jewry. But unlike the assimilationist Jewish Hellenists of an earlier period in the same geographic area, these Jews were, in religious belief and practice, firm traditionalists.

How deeply rooted the love of secular learning was among the religious Jews of the age may be learned from the testament that was written for his son by Hai Gaon (998–1038), the last of the illustrious line of the Geonim in Babylonia:

> I have provided you, too, with books on all the sciences . . . I have also made exhausting journeys to distant lands and brought for you a teacher of the secular sciences, counting neither the expense nor the dangers of the journey . . . you have also seen how distinguished scholars have taken the trouble to come from distant lands for the sake of my intercourse and instruction, and to consult my library . . .

In the Jewish microcosm of the Islamic world during the Middle Ages, peopled by so many individuals who were fired by a sincere love of learning—secular as well as religious, as Hai's own intellectual interests reveal—it is no overstatement to say that the ranks of the Jewish scholars, scientists, and poets swelled until they reached the proportions of a small army. During the eleventh century, Ibn Usaibia, a Mohammedan scholar, listed fifty Jewish authors writing in Arabic alone on medical subjects (and this at a time when printing did not exist and the cost of hiring copyists was prohibitive!). Taking this massive intellectual achievement into account, it is hardly possible in a brief summary such as this to do more than single out the major luminaries (principally for illustrative purposes) of the principal trends they represented.

Philosophers and Scholars. The most gifted, and perhaps also the most versatile of all the Jewish intellectuals in the Arab Diaspora, was Saadia ben Joseph, better known as Saadia Gaon (882–942). He served as the rector or Gaon of the foremost yeshibah (Talmudic Academy) of Babylonia—that in Sura—and by virtue of that eminence was recognized by the Jews of the world as its chief religious authority. A brilliant writer on a great variety of philosophic and scientific subjects, Saadia attempted to create a synthesis between traditional Jewish religious beliefs and scientific principles as they had taken shape in the Arab milieu of his day. In his famous work, Sefer Emunat ve'Deot (The Book of Beliefs and Opinions), he tried, for the first time, to establish an orderly system of Judaism—an aim, however, in which Maimonides was more successful two centuries later with his monumental Mishneh Torah.

Saadia might be said to have pioneered the scientific method (according to medieval terms) in Judaic studies. He was not only the first Hebrew grammarian and lexicographer of distinction, but he translated the entire Bible into classical Arabic, an achievement of incalculable religious and cultural consequences for those Jews—and they apparently must have been numerous—who had no knowledge of Hebrew. At the same time, his translation also made available to the Arabs one of the primary sources of the religion of Islam.

Saadia also laid the groundwork for a vigorous cultivation by numerous scholars and rabbis of Hebrew grammar and Biblical exegesis on a philological basis, thus effecting a virtual revolution in Jewish religious studies. Some of the foremost Hebrew philologists, lexicographers and grammarians in the tenth and eleventh centuries in North Africa, Babylonia, and Spain who followed in Saadia's pioneering steps were Menachem ben Saruk, Dunash ben Labrat, Judah Cheyuj, Samuel ibn Nagrela, Moses ibn Gikatilia, Levi ibn Al-Taban, Abulwalid ibn Janah, Aaron ben Asher, Judah ibn Koreish, Dunash ben Tamin, and Isaac ben Moses Halevi.

Chief Rabbi Isaac Halevy Herzog of Israel praying before the traditional tomb of Maimonides in Tiberias during the international observance of the 750th anniversary of the great thinker's death. (American Friends of the Hebrew University.)

 Arabic-Jewish "Golden Age"

Page from an illuminated parchment manuscript of Maimonide's Guide to the Perplexed. *(American Friends of the Hebrew University.)*

But most important of all in this group of scholars was the great exegete and liturgical poet of Spain, Abraham ibn Ezra (1093–1167). The possessor of a vast erudition and restless creative urge, he found both the time and the originality to initiate a new method of Biblical interpretation. This was his own extension and development of Saadia Gaon's pioneer efforts in Scriptural exegesis by means of philology. He rejected Maimonides' allegorical method of interpretation as being artificial, and justified his own method of free research. Some Jewish scholars refer to Ibn Ezra as the real founder of the modern "Higher Criticism" methodology in Biblical studies. In applying this method, he was the first to point out, from internal evidence, that the Book of Isaiah was really *two* books—the conjoined works of two different prophets: Isaiah ben Amoz, who preached in Jerusalem during the eighth century B.C.E., and the "Deutero-" or "Second" Isaiah, who lived about two hundred years later in Babylonian Captivity.

Ibn Ezra's commentary on the Pentateuch is rivaled in authority only by Rashi's among Orthodox Jews. (*See* COMMENTARIES, RABBINICAL.)

Bachya ibn Pakudah (*c.* 1050– *c.* 1100) was primarily a philosopher of ethics. His principal work, The Duties of the Heart, remained one of the basic interpretive works of Jewish ethics for many centuries. Warmly devout, Bachya was less concerned with reason than with faith, maintaining that the conscience in man was even superior in authority to moral doctrine. He, too, like so many of his Jewish and Arab contemporaries, was philosophically an eclectic. His treatise on ethics was permeated by strains of Persian Sufi mysticism and Platonic idealism, but principally by the traditional Jewish ethics that were profoundly concerned with righteousness and the happiness of human beings.

Aside from Maimonides, who was the most original of all Jewish thinkers of the Middle Ages, another who exerted a powerful continuing influence on Western Christian thought was the philosophical poet, Solomon ibn Gabirol (1021–1058). He was a Neo-Platonist philosopher—in fact, the first philosopher Spain produced—and an opponent of the Jewish Aristotelians in the eleventh century. It is, indeed, ironic that he, a rabbinical luminary, was able to influence Christian Scholasticism more than Jewish thought. Actually, until his rediscovery in 1848 as a Jewish philosopher, he had, so to speak, dropped out of sight, almost at the very beginning of his career, nine hundred years previously. It has been conjectured that upon the publication of *Mekor Chayyim* ("The Fountain of Life"), he had fallen into disfavor on account of the manner of his application to the Bible of the mystical Neo-Platonic doctrines of emanations in vogue in Christian theological and philosophical thinking since the writing of the Gospel of John (second century). Ibn Gabirol's interpretation was considered to run contrary to the traditional Jewish beliefs about God and Creation that are presented in the Hebrew Scriptures; therefore, it was condemned.

In essence, Gabirol's central premise was that, by itself, matter had no reality; it required form to take on existence, something that only the Divine Will was able to accomplish. Furthermore, argued the philosopher, not only material but also spiritual substances, exclusive of God himself, who existed *outside* of the universe He created, had a material substratum. This belief, and its implications, were considered dangerously heretical by rabbinical fundamentalists—so much so that in 1656 (a far less enlightened Jewish period than the eleventh century!), a religious court in Amsterdam ordered the excommunication, for his expression of a similar view and other heresies, of the youthful philosopher Baruch Spinoza.

About 1150, under the garbled and unrecognizable name of Avicebrol, Solomon ibn Gabirol's *Fountain of Life*, which had been originally composed in Arabic, was translated into Latin as *Fons Vitae* by a Christian scholar. No one suspected that the author was a Jew—and a rabbi at that; it was assumed that he was a great but obscure Christian (or even Arab) philosopher of an earlier period. "Avicebrol" (or "Avicebron," as he was also known) found fervent champions among the great Scholastics of the Church, primarily John Duns Scotus, Alexander of Hales, and William of Auvergne, the last-mentioned describing him as the "unique and the most noble of all philosophers." A lively controversy then ensued between the Neo-Platonist Franciscan philosophers (with Duns Scotus and Alexander of Hales on the side of the Neo-Platonic *Fountain of Life*) and their Aristotelian Dominican opponents (Albertus Magnus and Thomas Aquinas, who condemned the book as heretical and unsupported by the proofs of reason).

Another poet-philosopher who was even more revered by the people than Gabirol was Judah (Yehudah) Halevi (1085–1140). Among Jews he was honored not only for his eloquent Hebrew verses but also as a stalwart defender of the Jewish religion against its critics. This popular adulation was built on his work *Kuzari,* an apologetic treatise written in lively dialogue form. Because of its succinct manner of exposition, argumentation, and analysis of the ethical thought of the Jewish religion, it became a classic in Jewish literature.

Despite the fact that Halevi was himself a philosopher, combining Neo-Platonism and Sufi mysticism with his fervent piety, he nevertheless vigorously opposed the attempt by so many Jewish thinkers of his age to substantiate the truths of faith by proofs of speculative philosophy. He attacked the Aristotelian doctrine of the eternity of matter and reaffirmed his faith in the Scriptural declaration that God had created the world out of nothing (*creatio ex nihilo*). In *Kuzari,* in the course of his repudiation of philosophy—he attacked it not per se as philosophy but as the presumed key to religious certainty—he declared: "I consider him to have attained the highest degree of perfection who is convinced of religious truths without having scrutinized and reasoned over them."

Shortly after the publication of the *Kuzari,* an eminent historian and Aristotelian—probably the first such among Jews—Abraham ibn Daud (1110–80) issued a work, *Emunah Ramah* ("Sublime Faith"), in which he sought to prove that the physical and metaphysical teachings of Aristotle did not in any way conflict with the tenets of the Jewish religion. Ibn Daud wrote: "It is an error, generally current, that the study of speculative philosophy is dangerous to religion. True philosophy not only does not harm religion; it confirms and strengthens it."

Here, in the main, in the opposing views of Judah Halevi and Abraham ibn Daud—both near contemporaries, both rabbis, and both philosophers—was dramatically presented the dilemma faced by all thinking, religious Jews not only of the Middle Ages but every other age. During the Protestant Reformation, the crisis of choice for intellectual Christians was posed in the theological challenge: *Faith or Works?* During the Middle Ages—in many ways a more intellectual time than that of the Reformation—the disturbing problem, not only for Jews, but for Christians and Mohammedans as well, was whether it was possible for a devout person to reconcile his faith with reason, or theological dogma with the scientific method.

For eight hundred years, Maimonides, known intimately to the Jewish folk as "the Rambam" (a name which is the Hebrew mnemonic of "Rabbi Moses ben Maimon") has been worshipfully regarded as the Jewish religious thinker, scholar, and physician par excellence. The popular encomium of him, phrased in the involuted style of some Hebraic folk-sayings, has been: "From Moses to Moses there has not arisen anyone like Moses." In full agreement with this Jewish evaluation of Maimonides, a Catholic analyst of medieval philosophy, Richard McKeon, has commented: "The second Moses, like the first, set forth a Law for his race which has become part of the later history of the Jews . . . his organization of the Law in view of its scientific foundation and rational significance involved profound changes in Jewish thought and the thought of the world. Each succeeding age has found philosophers who have borrowed from him, and in each age his doctrine has seemed novel and even dangerous."

On noting some of his opinions, one can readily see why Maimonides was considered by some Jewish fundamentalist thinkers to be dangerous. As a thoroughgoing rationalist, he recognized the limitations of the intellect. In his reply to a query from a correspondent, he wrote: "I declare that there is a limit to the knowledge of man, and so long as the soul is in the body it cannot know what is beyond Nature." In the introduction to his great religious-philosophical work, *A Guide to the Perplexed* written (*c.* 1190), he announced his intellectual independence, correctly anticipating the storm of abuse his work would arouse in fundamentalist circles. (The book was burned in Montpelier, [so charged the adherents of Maimonides], by order of the Dominicans at the instigation of the local fanatical rabbis.)

Maimonides wrote: ". . . When I have a difficult subject before me—when I find the road narrow, and can see no other way of teaching a well-established truth except by pleasing one intelligent man and displeasing ten thousand fools—I prefer to address myself to the one man, and to take no notice whatever of the condemnation of the multitude."

Born and raised in Mohammedan Cordova in Spain, the early life of Maimonides was filled with insecurity and trouble. When the Almohádes (the Islamic zealot sectarians of North Africa) overran Cordova in 1148, the family of Maimonides fled, since conversion to Islam or flight were the only choices left to the Jews. After years of wandering, during which the young philosopher-rabbi-doctor pursued his encyclopedic studies with remarkable concentration, he settled

Joseph Solomon del Medigo (1592–1655). Encyclopedic scholar, scientist (a pupil of Galileo's), physician, and rabbi who was one of the last distinguished inheritors of the humanism of the Arabic-Jewish Golden Age. Scientifically oriented by philosophy, mathematics, optics, mechanics, and astronomy, his nonconformist course was marked by harassments from the religious fundamentalists, obliging him to wander abroad in search of a livelihood. At one time he was court physician to Prince Radziwill, ruler of Lithuania.

in hospitable Egypt where, ultimately, he became court-doctor to Saladin the Great in Cairo. At that time Maimonides started what was to be one of the busiest and most creative careers in Jewish intellectual history.

Like Abraham ibn Daud, Maimonides was a disciple of the Greek philosopher Aristotle, but he viewed his master's thought through the interpretive prism of Avicenna (Ibn Sina, 980–1037), the great Arab savant and encyclopedic genius. (It should be noted here that, in secular and scientific studies, the Jews of that age deferred to the more knowledgeable leadership of the Arab scholars.) In all his writings Maimonides attempted to reconcile faith with reason, and the Scriptures with the philosophy of Aristotle. He averred in his Ethical Testament that reason was the great gift of God: "It is through the intellect that the human being has the capacity of honoring God." Because of this, he concluded, philosophy and Judaism were reconcilable and not oppositional.

The first important religious-philosophical work of Maimonides, which took him ten years to produce, was his Commentary on the Mishnah (1168); he wrote it in Arabic under the title Siraj (Light; in Hebrew: Meor). Its most significant part, dealing with philosophy, psychology, and ethics, was called Shemoneh Perakim (Eight Chapters). Twelve years later, Maimonides completed the monumental Mishneh Torah (Repetition of the Law), sometimes also called Yad ha-Chazakah (The Strong Hand). This work, written in Hebrew and arranged into fourteen divisions, brings together in a remarkable achievement of logical codification *all* the laws in the Bible and the Talmud. (*See* COMMENTARIES, RABBINICAL.)

But the work for which Maimonides has been most celebrated throughout the centuries is *A Guide to the Perplexed* (in Hebrew: *Moreh Nebuchim;* in Arabic—the language in which it was originally composed, in 1190—*Dalalat al Hairin*). Always forthright in the views he held, the philosopher stated thus his aim in writing the book:

> The object of this treatise is to enlighten a religious man who has been trained to believe in the truth of our holy Torah, who conscientiously fulfills his moral and religious duties and at the same time has been successful in his philosophical studies. Human reason has attracted him to abide within its sphere; and he finds it difficult to accept as correct the teaching based on the literal interpretation of the Torah . . .

Hebrew astrolabe. (From Tobias Cohen's scientific work, Ma'aseh Tobiah, *1707.)*

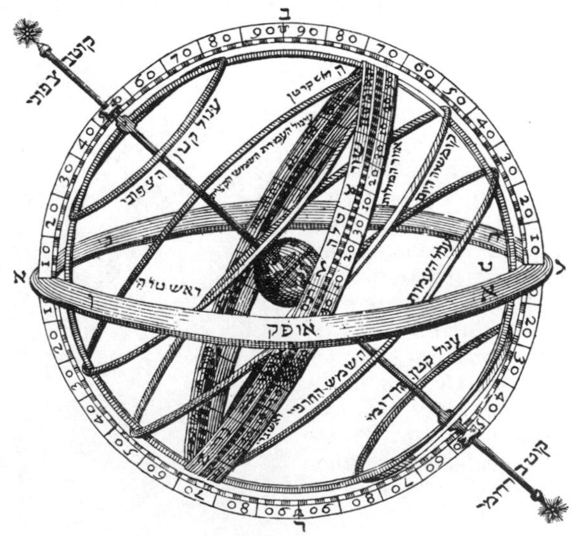

Maimonides sought many ends in his critical re-examination of Jewish religious doctrines and beliefs. He tried to strip the popular conception of God, his attributes, and his nature, derived from a literal reading of the Scriptural text, of all their materiality and anthropomorphisms (the imposition of the human form, with its corporeal characteristics and its qualities, upon the Deity.) He also advanced his famous twenty-five propositions to prove the existence of God by philosophical and scientific certitudes, a method which was eagerly adopted and elaborated upon by the great Scholastic philosopher of the thirteenth century, Thomas Aquinas. Although Thomas was better acquainted than Maimonides with the works of Aristotle, nevertheless, he lacked a persuasive method for *reconciling* the Greek's philosophy with Christianity.

A progressive thinker, Maimonides believed that man was endowed with free will; he had faith in ability of the human being to perfect himself by developing his intellectual and moral faculties. His view that prophecy did not have a supernatural character but was "the most perfect development of the imaginative faculty," stirred up much hostile criticism. In Amsterdam in the seventeenth century, adherence to this view of Maimonides was one of the heresies charged against the twenty-four-year old philosopher Spinoza, and it contributed not a little to his excommunication from the Jewish community.

Aside from his impact on the most enlightened thinkers among Jews in his own day and in subsequent centuries, the influence of Maimonides on Christian thought and on European civilization in general (for reasons that hardly need going into here) has not yet fully been gauged. The Dominican theologians, Albertus Magnus and Thomas Aquinas, both convinced Aristotelians, found him a heartening ally. They also found a ready dialectical method in *A Guide to the Perplexed* when it was translated into Latin. It has been noted by Christian scholars that during the thirteenth century, the foremost theologians at the University of Paris quoted "Rabbi Moyses" with approval on almost every point of his doctrine. This approval, in part, was also given by a host of other thinkers of varying periods—Duns Scotus, Leibnitz, and, of course, Spinoza.

On March 30, 1935, the eight hundredth anniversary of the birth of Maimonides was celebrated through the world by Jews, Christians, and Mohammedans. Universities and learned societies, newspapers and periodicals in many languages, rabbis, clergymen, and mullahs, Biblical and Talmudic specialists, scientists, doctors, and just ordinary people took part in the commemoration of the life of a man of great intellect and character—one whose real distinction probably was that he followed a life of reason and sought truth wherever he could find it, perceiving it according to his own lights and loyalties, and remaining steadfast in its defense, whatever the opposition.

One of the most original and individualistic thinkers of the Middle Ages was Gersonides (Levi ben Gerson, 1288–1344), a rabbi-scholar of Bagnols (in the south of France), known to the Christian Schoolmen as "Leo Hebraeus" and also as "Maestro Leon de Bagnols." Like Maimonides, he was a bold and independent thinker who also excelled in many branches of learning, religious as well as secular. A Biblical exegete and Talmudist, he was also a brilliant astronomer and mathematician, and a philosopher committed to Aristotelianism. He was so well known and admired by the Schoolmen and later Christian theologians, that in the sixteenth-century editions of the Latin translations of Aristotle, his commentaries, esteemed as authoritative, were incorporated with the works of the Greek philosopher.

Levi ben Gerson won wide fame—although in some places only "notoriety"—with his principal philosophic work, The Wars of the Lord (in the Hebrew original, Milchamot Adonai); his fundamentalist critics cleverly twisted this title to read "The Wars Against the Lord." In religious matters—especially as concerned the Scriptures—he remained consistently a champion of reason versus revelation. His challenges caused a great furor in his day. Typical was his defiant declaration: "The Torah cannot prevent us from considering to be true that which our reason urges us to believe." Also, like Maimonides, he looked upon the intellect of a person as the essence of his soul. From this he drew the proposition that the immortality of a human being depended on how true his intellectual ideas were.

Detail of a map of the world by Yehudah Cresques, great Mallorcan cartographer. (Bibliothèque Nationale, Paris.)

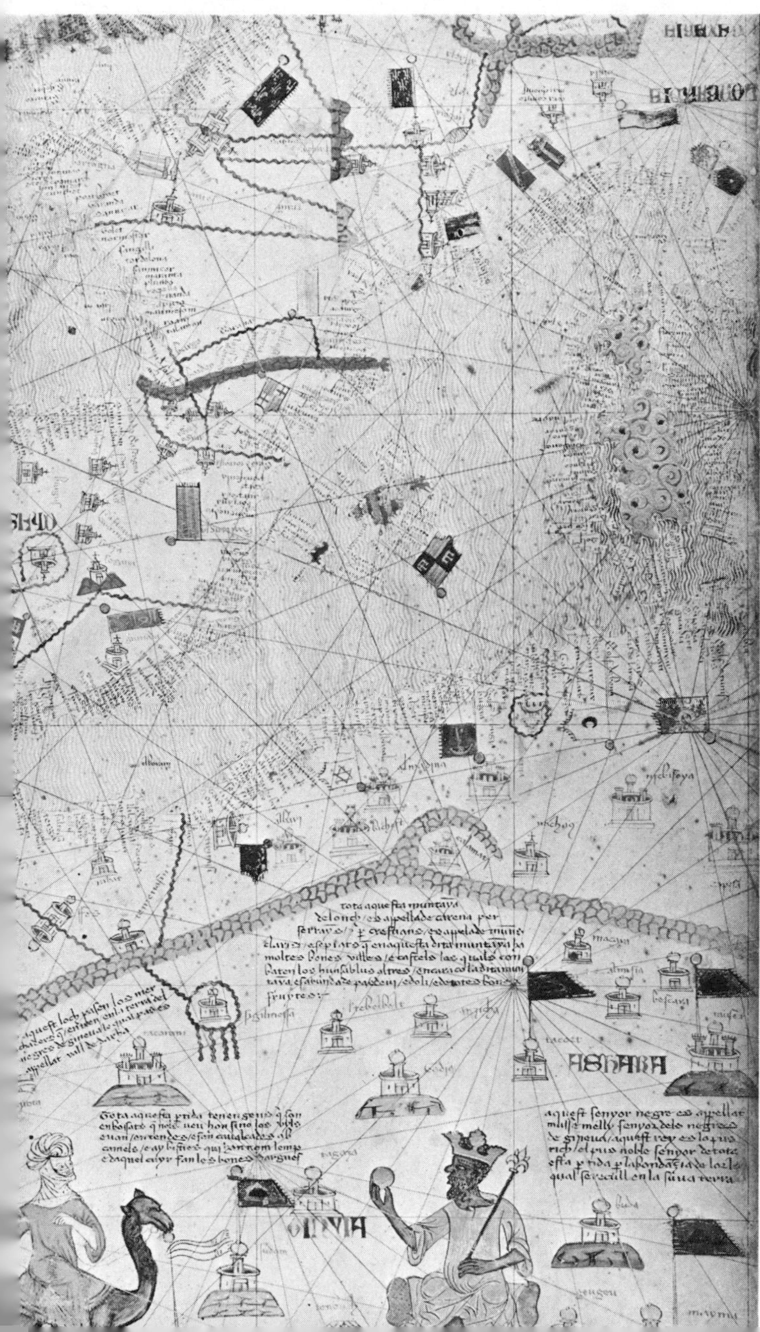

Perhaps the last original religious philosopher among the Jews of the Middle Ages was Chasdai Crescas (b. Barcelona, 1340–*c.* 1410). He arose as the Golden Age began to decline on account of the loss of prestige in Jewish life of philosophy and science. He was a vigorous anti-Aristotelian, forced into opposition against Maimonides and Levi ben Gerson because of his conviction that the philosophical accomodations made by them on behalf of Judaism were bound, sooner than later, to lead to its ruination. His criticism of the two Aristotelian masters in his principal work *Light of God* (*or Adonai*), was frequently sharp. There is a certain irony in the fact that he employed the dialectics and nomenclature of philosophy in his attempt to controvert their alleged philosophical encroachments into the Jewish religion, arguing, as Judah Halevi had several centuries before, that the reconciliation between the revelation on Mount Sinai with the alien logic of a Greek philosopher was highly artificial and spurious.

The Great Poets. In his history, *The Book of Tradition*, Abraham ibn Daud, the Aristotelian philosopher, gibed gaily: "In the days of Chasdai [ibn Shaprut, 915–990], the poets began to twitter." The Jewish Golden Age in Spain had already arrived and it needed the poets "to twitter" for its soul. The requirements of the liturgy in the synagogue gave impetus to it. The hymns, prayers, and meditations, composed in Hebrew, were called *piyyutim* (s. piyyut, from the Greek word *poetes*, meaning poet). Jewish psalmody in the Middle Ages was attuned to the themes of hope, despair, and exhortation. Many poems were elegies on Jewish massacres and laments for the desolation of Zion—Israel's ancient love and departed glory. Thus these poems were far more than liturgical verses; they constituted an intimate record of Jewish history and the Jewish way of life.

It was the fate of Jewish literature until modern times to be canalized mainly into religion. This was because the persecuted Jews, in all the lands of their fragmentation, found a sustaining strength in the consolations of their faith. One striking characteristic of the liturgical poetry by the Spanish masters was the almost negligible degree of religious parochialism to be found in it. Perhaps this was because they strove to universalize their religious sentiments, in so doing, they succeeded in keeping out the distortions that usually are caused by sectarian dogma and ritualism. For whatever other purposes they may have been written, the piyyut (liturgical poem), the selichah (penitential prayer), and the kinnah (martyr elegy) were composed by poets who were

Abraham Zacuto's Almanach *(1496).*

Tab eclipsis luminariu et primo de sole								
nnmer9 annornz	nomina mensiuz	dies	digiti	feria	hore	minut	finis eclipsis hore	minu
1493	octob	10	9	5	0	0	1	20
1502	septeb	30	8	6	17	28	19	12
1506	Julii	20	3	2	1	49	3	3
1513	martii	7	4	1	23	49	1	9
1518	Junii	7	10	2	18	22	19	17
1524	ianuar	23	9	2	3	12	4	6
Tabla de eclipsib9 lnne								
1494	septeb	14	17	1	17	5	2	33
1497	ianuar	18	17	4	3	50	7	18
1500	noueb	5	13	5	10	17	13	30
1501	maii	2	19	1	15	33	19	6
1502	octob	15	14	7	10	15	12	9
1504	februa	29	16	5	10	47	14	13
1505	aug9	14	15	5	5	42	9	6
1508	Junii	12	23	2	15	21	19	0
1509	Junii	2	7	7	9	29	2	3
1511	octob	6	13	2	9	11	2	25
1514	ianuar	29	16	2	14	20	16	3
1515	ianuar	19	15	7	5	0	6	42
1516	Julii	13	14	1	10	0	12	30
1519	noueb	6	20	1	5	50	6	48
1522	septeb	5	15	6	11	22	12	4
1523	martii	1	17	1	7	30	9	14

Jewish doctor attending St. Basil. The wearing of the "Jew's Hat" (Judenhut) *was enforced by decree of the Lateran Council under Pope Innocent III, in 1215. (From an illustrated German manuscript, 13th century.)*

Isaac Israeli, one of the great doctors of the Middle Ages. (From the frontispiece of the Latin translation of Isaac's medical works.)

devout in their love of God and of their fellow men. Therefore, they sought with their verse to solace, to guide, and to divert the troubled gaze of the Jewish people from its many sorrows to a serene contemplation of the verities which are eternal.

The non-religious themes of many of the poems had a wide range. Some extolled the sentiments of family attachment, friendship, the brotherhood of man, and the loyalty of the individual Jew to his people. There were verses in praise of righteous men, that in lofty measures, sent winging panegyrics to learning and wisdom. But conversely, they also touched on the grief of separation, the brevity of life, old age, death, and the "vanity of vanities" tenuousness of the wordly hope. From all evidence, there was in the "Jewish nightingales" of Moorish Spain, a strong element of the Persian Sufi mysticism and world-weariness, just as there was in Omar Khayyám and Hafiz.

Living in the midst of the highly developed Islamic civilization with which Spanish-Jewish culture was so closely interwoven, the Hebrew poets continued with the poetic patterns begun centuries before by the pre-Mohammedan poets of Arabia. They freely adapted into Hebrew versification Arabic poetic forms such as the *makama* (rhyming prose) and the *ghazel* (short lyric), and despite the horrified admonitions of the pietists, they also composed a great many love songs. In a later century, in the year 1415, the Portuguese rabbi, Solomon Alami, had warned the devout: "Avoid listening to love songs which excite the passions. If God has graciously bestowed on you the gift of a sweet voice, use it in praising Him." Nevertheless, in all of medieval literature, the Arabic and Persian included, there are found no more exquisite love songs than those penned in Hebrew by Judah Halevi and Moses ibn Ezra. They are suffused by a delicate sentiment and refinement of thought, and without moral preachment or argument, reveal obliquely the traditional Jewish respect and high regard for woman in what was, probably, the most advanced attitude toward her among all peoples in medieval Europe.

It was by a remarkable combination of historic circumstances at this particular juncture in the development of the art of Hebrew poetry, that a galaxy of the most exquisite Jewish poets, writing in Hebrew, arose in the Mohammedan kingdom of Cordova in southern Spain. The foremost of these unquestionably were the rabbis-philosophers-scholars Solomon ibn Gabirol (1021–58), Judah Halevi (1085–1140), Moses ibn Ezra (1070–1138), and the latter's kinsman, Abraham ibn Ezra (1093–1167). All were men of genius and of arresting intellectual versatility, in their own way equaling the universality of interest and expression found in the most gifted men of the Italian Renaissance: Leonardo da Vinci, Petrarch, and Michelangelo. Their poetic palette was rich, their expressive range broad: they composed verses in every form known to their age. The world, it must be added, has still to discover their inspired singing. To any one of these four poets could be applied the famous lines that Heinrich Heine, the Jewish lyrist of Germany, once penned about Judah Halevi:

> Yes, he was a master-singer,
> Brilliant pole-star of his Age,
> Light and beacon to his people!
> Wondrous, mighty was his singing.

The Scientists. It was entirely predictable that the intellectual life of the Jews, being so soberly keyed to reality, to rationalism, and to naturalism, should stimulate many of them to take an active interest in the sciences. The scientific attitude was acquired quite early by Jews, when they came in cultural contact with Egyptian, Babylonian, Greek, Roman, and Arab practitioners in the sciences. It eventually became a tradition that was fully matured during the closing years of the Jewish Commonwealth. At that time, Yochanan ben Zakkai, the most authoritative Rabbinic Sage of his generation, thus eulogized scientific inquiry: "He who understands astronomy and does not pursue the study of it, of that man it is written: 'But they regard not the work of the Lord, neither do they consider the operation of His hands.'"

However, the scientific enthusiasts among the Talmudic Sages were sharply opposed by a school of Rabbinic thought whose spokesmen declared wrathfully: "He who ponders over the following four things might as well not have been born: What is above, what is below, what is in front and what is behind." This fundamentalist view was motivated principally by the protective desire "to build a fence around the Torah," that is, to keep out secularist and "alien" thought. The conflict between these two opposing points of view became exceedingly bitter during the Middle Ages, which, however "dark" they may be judged to have been by some,

 Arabic-Jewish "Golden Age"

were actually a time of searching and testing, of rationalistic groping and dawning. Science and philosophy were considered by their rabbinic votaries such as Saadia Gaon, Maimonides, and Levi ben Gerson as being entirely compatible with, and even complementary to, Rabbinic studies and the profession of traditional religious beliefs. This liberal attitude was especially prominent among the cultured and enlightened rabbis of Spain, the Provence, and southern Italy.

This outlook was diametrically the opposite among the German Jews and other Ashkenazim. Rabbi Asher ben Yechiel, the celebrated thirteenth-century Talmudist, once boasted–and with feeling, too: "It is well that I know nothing of profane science. I thank God for this, that He has saved me from it, because philosophic proof leads the people away from the fear of God and His teachings."

Jewish scientists and scholars during the Middle Ages stood, at it were, with one foot in each of two civilizations—one in the Greek-Arabic-Jewish and one in Christian Europe. Beginning with the thirteenth century, Jewish intellectuals constituted, in large measure, the active leaven which made European culture rise. This was because of their philosophic-scientific eruditon, in general, and their knowledge of language, in particular. These Jews were the most indefatigable translators into Latin and other European languages of the

Page from an illuminated parchment manuscript of Maimonides' Mishneh Torah (1296).

scientific writings of the Greeks, Arabs, and themselves, and were critical interpreters as well. But they were much more than fluent transmitters and intermediaries of this variegated knowledge; they also made significant and original contributions of their own to virtually all branches of science and thought. Only in recent decades have the academic historians of science begun to reappraise their achievements in a more objective manner, without the philistine prejudice that so often in the past had shut the Jewish contributions out of all scholarly consideration.

One of the earliest, and also one of the most gifted, mathematicians and astronomers in Spain, was Abraham bar Chiyya (*d. c.* 1136) who became known to the learned Christian world as Abraham Savasorda. In the judgment of the late George Sarton, the eminent historian of scientific thought, he was the foremost mathematician of the twelfth century in Europe. Among his more imporant scientific works—the first to have been written in Hebrew—were *The Foundations of Understanding*, an encyclopedia embracing arithmetic, geometry, astronomy, optics, and music; a book on astronomy, *Form of the Earth;* and two astronomical tables used for navigation: *Calculation of the Course of the Stars* and *Tables of the Prince*. One of the most important scientific works produced in the Middle Ages was Abraham's *Chibbur ha-Meshihah,* which dealt, in an original way, with geometry and algebra; this was translated into Latin in 1145 by the apostate Jewish mathematician, Plato of Tivoli, under the title of *Liber Embodorum*, and won Abraham great renown among Arab and Christian scholars. But above and beyond all these considerations, according to some authorities, Abraham's principal distinction lies in the fact that he was the first writer to introduce the scientific method of the Greeks and the Arabs *into Europe*.

Another outstanding rabbinic mathematician and astronomer was Immanuel Bonfils, of fourteenth-century France; his astronomical tables were extensively used by mariners and explorers. Recent researchers have brought to light the fact that he had invented a decimal system about 140 years before the first one became known in Europe.

Because the Jewish scholars of the Middle Ages in Spain and in Arab lands pursued their well-known pattern of multiple cultural interests, they became, in a literal sense, encyclopedists who tried to excel in several fields. Quite often, as in the case of Maimonides and Abraham ibn Ezra, they combined dazzlingly the varied callings of rabbi, astronomer, doctor, mathematician, grammarian, philosopher, poet, Biblical exegete, Talmudic commentator, etc.

One such "universal thinker" was the philosopher, Levi ben Gerson (*see above*). Besides his command of the other learned disciplines, he was an eminent astronomer (he influenced Copernicus), a mathematician, and, in a casual way, also an inventor of some note. He has been credited with the invention of the camera obscura, the first ancestor of the camera, by describing precisely its optical principle. He also, reputedly, was the inventor of the "Jacob's Staff," a quadrant used for four centuries by navigators including Columbus, Magellan, Martin Behaim, and Vasco da Gama. Another quadrant in general use during the Renaissance was the *quadrans Judaicus,* invented by the noted physician and astronomer, Jacob ben Makkir (*d.* 1308).

The knowledge of astronomy that was possessed by an unusual number of intellectual Jews during the Middle Ages found a practical outlet in the service of navigation. The famous Alfonsine Tables, widely used by navigators and also by the great astronomers Kepler and Galileo, were arranged in 1272 for King Alfonso by two astronomers of Toledo, Judah ben Moses and Isaac ibn Sid (the latter also happened to be a chazzan [cantor]). Astronomical tables in a later period were also drawn up by Abraham Zacuto (1450–1510) and Joseph Vecinho, the chief astronomers and cartographers to Manuel the Great of Portugal, and were consulted by Columbus on his voyage. The foremost cartographers in Europe for many centuries were Jews, most famous being Yehuda Cresques of Mallorca who was employed by Henry ("the Navigator") of Portugal.

Doctors. As far back as the Alexandria of the Greek Ptolemies, Jews had been prominent as healers. In a later age, living among the cultured Arabs (the continuators of Greek medical science), Jews in time achieved a fame equal with them as the foremost medical practitioners and writers during the Middle Ages. To be a doctor was generally considered by Jews the most exalted moral and worldly calling a Jew could aspire to. Doctoring was lucrative, yet it was also a highly respected profession. It had always been that way in Jewish life, as the eulogy of the doctor by Jesus ben Sirach (*c.* 200 B.C.E.) testifies: "Honor the physician! His knowledge allows him to walk with raised head, and gains for him the admiration of princes. If you fall ill, cry to the Lord, but also call for the physician. . . ."

The medical profession has always had an enormous appeal for Jews. Centuries of social idealization fixed for them its revered tradition. The doctor's calling, in the opinion of most Jews, was much to be preferred to the despised and compulsory occupations of moneylending (*see* MONEYLENDERS), trading, and dealing in junk and old clothes. The doctor could claim great humanitarian and social usefulness—all the more important to Jews because of their religious belief that the alleviation of pain and suffering is one of the most meritorious pursuits of benevolence. To this day, the number of Jewish doctors exceeds, in proportion to their number, those of other ethnic groups.

One of the greatest doctors of the Middle Ages—court physician to two Fatimid caliphs and a noted philosopher as well—was Isaac Israeli (*b.* Egypt, *c.* 855–*d.* Tunis, *c.* 955). His medical and philosophical works, written in Arabic, were subsequently translated into Latin as *Opera Omnia Isaci* and were carefully studied and much admired by Albertus Magnus, Thomas Aquinas, and Vincent of Beauvais. His treatises "On Fever" and "On Diet" remained authoritative in medical practice in Europe for five centuries.

With the possible exception of the redoubtable Isaac Israeli, the most famed Jewish physician of the Middle Ages was Maimonides (*see above*). Besides being Saladin's court doctor he also wrote in Arabic on a wide variety of medical subjects, including diet, poisons and their antidotes, opthalmology, and hemorrhoids. His treatises were widely circulated and studied everywhere.

For at least one thousand years Jews were among the most honored healers in Europe. Some of the early medieval writers on medical subjects who brought luster to their names in Christian Europe were Meshulam ben Kalonymos, Joseph ben Gorion, Todros of Narbonne, and Zedikiah (the court physician to the Carolingian kings, Louis the Meek and Charles the Bold). Three great medical figures during the tenth century were Haroun of Cordova, Yehudah Chaioug of Fez, and Amram of Toledo, the last named being widely regarded as one of the most eminent medical scientists of the age.

The study of medicine was introduced as part of the regular curriculum in rabbinic yeshibot about the year 1000.

Parochet in the synagogue at Dubno, Lithuania. Presented in 1727.

Parochet (Ark curtain) in the Altneuschul (the "Old-New Synagogue"), Prague. Presented in 1697.

Of the long line of rabbi-physicians who were graduated from them, many served caliphs and emperors, popes and kings, bishops and princes, as well as the common people.

See also COMMENTARIES, RABBINICAL; FREE WILL; GOLDEN MEAN, THE RABBINIC; RABBINICAL DECISIONS; RABBI; TALMUD, THE; TORAH STUDY; YESHIBAH.

ARBAH KANFOT. *See* TALLIT KATAN.

ARBAH KOSOT. *See* PASSOVER.

ARBAH KUSHYOT. *See* PASSOVER.

ARBAH MINIM. *See* "FOUR SPECIES, THE."

ARBAH TURIM. *See* LAW, JEWISH.

ARK CURTAIN (in Hebrew: PAROCHET).

Before the Ark of the Law in every synagogue hangs a curtain. Its symbolic import is nostalgic with the never forgotten memories of the Jewish people of the Golden Age of their history. It commemorates the curtain that the Israelites hung before the Ark in the portable Tabernacle during their wanderings in the wilderness. Even more poignant for the pious is its association with the curtain which, in later centuries, hung before the Holy of Holies in the sanctuary in Jerusalem and which only the high priest could draw aside once a year, on Yom Kippur, during his performance of the solemn rites of atonement.

The materials out of which the Ark curtain and its valance (kaporet) were made in former times is unknown. But those still in existence–the oldest extant were made during the Renaissance in Italy–are of red velvet, plush, silk, satin, or sometimes, flower-patterned brocades, and show clearly the artistic impact of that period in the fine fabrics, simple designs, well-modulated colors, good taste, and exquisite needlework of their Jewish embroiderers. Except for the Hebrew inscriptions that are delicately stitched or appliquéd with gold or silver thread, there are virtually no other motifs or figures on the old Italian parochet to distract the attention.

It was different when the decadent Baroque period began. The parochet then blossomed out magnificently and showily with pseudoclassic Greek urns, vases with flowers, Torah Crowns, tablets of the Ten Commandments, and the Temple pillars of Jachin and Boaz. To add to the confusion in the design, there were depictions of well-known Biblical incidents and representations of the sacred vessels that had been employed in the Temple service in Jerusalem: the Sea of Brass (laver), the menorah, the altar of incense, and the table of shewbread. Hebrew inscriptions also were worked into the design. A favorite one was the verse of the Psalmist: "I have set the Lord always before me."

See also ART, CEREMONIAL.

ARK OF THE COVENANT (in Hebrew: ARON HA-KODESH, meaning "Holy Ark")

The Ark of the Covenant was the portable chest in which, according to Biblical tradition, Moses deposited the stone tablets of the covenant entered into by God and the Children of Israel at Mount Sinai. Therefore, the Ark was worshiped as Israel's holiest shrine from the time of the construction of the Tabernacle in the Sinai wilderness and for several centuries thereafter, through the time when it reposed in the Holy of Holies in the Temple at Jerusalem.

The Psalmist, describing the Ark from the point of view of the average Israelite of his day, declared it to be "the strength and glory of the Lord." As such it had been regarded by the Twelve Tribes as they trudged through the Wilderness toward the Promised Land. They carried it before them as a palladium (or protection) against misfortune–particularly against the numerous enemies they met on their way who tried to plunder and destroy them.

The growth of the idea of a universal, ethical God, as may be judged from the Bible record itself, was a very gradual one. The primitive worship of the Ark as being literally the "house" in which God "lived" is an excellent illustration of the slow evolutionary process in the religious thinking of the Jews. Like the Egyptians, the Babylonians, the Canaanites, and all the others of their ancient contemporaries, they too were animists – nature-worshipers. They were organized into totem-clans, each of which gave formal acceptance to the concept of the God of Israel but also worshiped its own animal or plant deity. It was perhaps too much to expect that the Israelites of the Exodus, who had lived as slaves in a land whose people worshiped the cat, the cow, the snake, and the River Nile, would be able to disengage themselves from such primitive beliefs overnight.

To be sure, Moses, their enlightened leader and teacher, held to religious and ethical values that were far in advance of the age, but he was also a realist. After the Israelites–and the "mixed multitude" that had joined them in the Exodus and spurred them on in this–had fashioned for themselves a Golden Calf before which they danced and adored, Moses (and this is merely a large conjecture) may have reluctantly reached the conclusion that what his simple-minded and confused followers were badly in need of was a *physical* symbol of God if they were to remain faithful to him. This symbol was not to be abstract nor spiritual but tangible and concrete–one which they could plainly see with their own eyes so they could readily grasp its meaning.

Perhaps that was the reasoning which led Moses to commission the artist-craftsman Bezalel, "at the Lord's bidding," to construct the Aron ha-Kodesh to serve as a repository for the stone tablets on which, "with the finger of God," were inscribed the Ten Commandments–the object of the most awesome veneration for the Israelites.

The Bible gives a most detailed account (in Chapter 25 of Exodus) of the design and construction of the Ark of the Covenant: a large rectangular chest of acacia wood with its surfaces, inside and outside, overlaid with pure gold. Two cherubim–God's angelic messengers–surmounted the chest. They were sculpted in gold, their wings outstretched protectingly in an arc over the chest. Because the Israelites were constantly on the move, the Ark was made portable. Bezalel, its designer, fixed into its sides four massive gold rings through which were passed two staves, also of acacia wood overlaid with gold, so the Ark could be carried by the Israelites in their wanderings.

The awe-inspiring reverence in which the Ark was held by the folk may be inferred from what the Bible had God say to Moses: "I will meet with thee and I will speak with thee from above the Ark lid." Literally and definitely, God "lived" in the Ark, the people was convinced.

Even after the Israelite tribes had settled in Canaan, the Aron ha-Kodesh continued to serve as the supreme talisman against their numerous and unrelenting enemies. It was carried into battle on numerous occasions. It is narrated in I Samuel (4:3-5) that during the fighting at Aphek (presumably in 1080 B.C.E.), when the Elders of Israel saw that the tide of battle was turning against them, they started to lament: "Wherefore hath the Lord smitten us today before the Philistines? Let us fetch the Ark of the Covenant of the Lord out of Shiloh unto us, that He may come among us, and save us out of the hand of our enemies." Finally, when the principal priests who had gone to fetch it returned bearing it, "All Israel shouted with a great shout, so that the earth rang." When the Philistines heard the shouting they were thrown into a panic: "God has come into the camp!" they cried. And they fled. They too shared the view of the Israelites that the Ark was "the house" of God.

When Solomon completed the building of the Temple on Mount Zion, he had the Ark placed in the Holy of Holies. Precisely what made this inner sanctuary so ineffably sacred to the Jews was the presence of the Ark of the Covenant in it. This chest was surrounded with an aura of incomparable holiness and unapproachability. Only the high priest was allowed to enter the Holy of Holies, and then only once a year on Yom Kippur (the Day of Atonement). Rabbinic legend of a later age, standing breathless before the unutterable magic powers it assumed were vested in the Ark, insisted that any Jew other than the High Priest entering the Holy of Holies would be instantly struck dead by God, so very ultimate in profanation would such an act be.

What finally happened to the Ark–it completely vanished–remained one of those tragic mysteries and romantic speculations that preoccupied latter-day pious Jews. One hypothesis appealing to some Biblical scholars is that, at some unspecified period in turbulent Jewish history, the Ark was carried off as a war-trophy, possibly together with Rehoboam, the king of Judah, by Shishak, the king of Egypt, in the tenth century B.C.E. Another possibility suggested is that it may have disappeared during one or another of the several invasions of Israel by the Assyrians several centuries later. Whatever the historic explanation for it may be, the memory of the Ark of the Covenant is preserved by the Ark of the Law which is found in every snyagogue in the world today.

See also ARK OF THE LAW; TEN COMMANDMENTS.

ARK OF THE LAW (in Hebrew: ARON HA-KODESH; in Yiddish: UREN KOIDESH, meaning "Holy Ark")

The Ark is simply a closet, lined inside with silk or velvet, in which is deposited in an upright position the parchment Scroll of the Law (Sefer Torah). It is made of wood, marble, or stone, and stands against the synagogue wall which faces in the direction of Jerusalem. It is either a part of the fixed edifice or an independent moveable unit. An embroidered curtain made of silk or velvet (the parochet) hangs before it in imitation of the "veil" which once separated the worshipers from the Ark of the Covenant, first in the desert Tabernacle (or Tent of Meeting) and later in the Temple in Jerusalem.

Today the Ark of the Law is virtually a physical descendant of the ancient Ark of the Covenant in which Moses deposited the Tablets of the Commandments, according to the Biblical account. But instead of the original stone tablets with their rudimentary Decalogue, the Ark of the synagogue is the repository for the Sefer Torah, the parchment scroll containing the Five Books of Moses (the Pentateuch). For that reason, it became the most arresting single feature in the interior of the Jewish house of worship. Like the altar of the Christian church—which, incidentally, was both conceptually and architecturally derived from the Aron ha-Kodesh of the ancient Judean synagogue—the Ark of the Law is elevated and is separated from the rest of the floor-level by several ascending steps.

As has been the case with other Jewish religious objects and architectural features of the synagogue, the design of the Ark has varied markedly with each time and country, yet in every instance it has harmonized with or reflected the artistic tastes and architectural forms that were in fashion in the Gentile culture in which the Jewish community happened to be planted.

On the basis of fragmentary archeological evidence and of bare references and mere hints found in early Jewish writings, it can be inferred that during the Greco-Roman and medieval periods the Ark was made relatively simple and not marred by too much ornamentation. One illustration of the Ark discovered on a fragment of gold glass made sometime during the Roman period in Judea and preserved in a museum in Rome, shows that in design it was much unlike those made in later periods and today. It was not a closet with doors that could be opened or closed. Instead, it had round horizontal apertures in which the Torah Scrolls were deposited. But with the beginning of the Baroque art period, during the late sixteenth and seventeenth centuries, when the chaste neoclassical tradition of the Rennaissance had begun

Representation on funerary gold-glass found in the Jewish catacombs of Monteverde in Rome (1st to 4th centuries C.E.*) of an Ark of the Law (Aron ha-Kodesh). The tubular horizontal niches held the Torah Scrolls.*

An Ark of the Law sculpted in relief on the rock wall of a corridor in the catacombs at Bet Shearim, Israel, 3rd century C.E.

to wane, making way for the ornate and the ostentatious, the design of the Ark, whether in wood or in marble, also began to reflect this undiscriminating taste. The human form being prohibited in the ornamentation of the Ark, as in the rest of the synagogue structure, the stonecutters, sculptors, and woodcarvers who built the Ark drew their decorative motifs instead from the inexhaustible wealth of composition, design, and form which is found in trees and flowers and in the entire animal kingdom. Ever since the Renaissance, as far as can be ascertained, the Ark has been decorated on top with the twin tablets of the Ten Commandments, often flanked on either side with a lion rampant, the whole being surmounted by the Crown of the Torah. Sometimes the representation of a deer is introduced into this composition as an addition in order to fulfill symbolically the images and values evoked in the saying of the Fathers: "Be as fleet as a hart and strong as a lion to do the will of your Father who is in Heaven." (Pirke Abot 5:23.)

An extravagant feature of baroque taste was the introduction of two columns of marble or granite to frame the Ark structure. These were, supposedly, symbols of Israel's ancient glory—the two sacrificial pillars of Jachin and Boaz which had stood in the Temple court of Jerusalem. In latter-day synagogue structures, these pillars were cut either in fluted Renaissance style or in the serpentine or screw-shape commonly appearing in Central European baroque church architecture.

See also ARK OF THE COVENANT; ARK CURTAIN.

The Ark of the Law in the Sefaradic (Portuguese) synagogue in Amsterdam.

Ark of the Law in the synagogue of Mikulov (Nikolsburg), Moravia. BELOW

ARON HA-KODESH. *See* ARK OF THE COVENANT; ARK OF THE LAW.

ART AMONG THE JEWS

The Roman historian Tacitus, examining the condition of contemporary Jewish culture, noted with scorn, although quite objectively: "Jews look upon every attempt to represent their God under the appearance of human form as a profanation of Heavenly nature." What we have here is merely a non-Jew's paraphrase of the Second Commandment: "Thou shalt not make unto thee a graven image, nor any manner of likeness, of any thing that is in heaven above, or that is in the earth beneath, or that is in the water under the earth." (Deuteronomy 5:8.)

What inspired this prohibition? Many cultured people throughout the centuries have been perplexed by its harsh and all-inclusive hostility to representational art. Few laws in the ritual codes of world religions have proven as effective and thoroughgoing. Quite demonstrably, it was the image-worship (practiced in contemporary religions) which the ancient Israelites so abhorred that inspired this prohibition. It paralyzed, although not to the exent popularly believed, the creation of painting and sculpture among Jews during much of their long history. This fear of animistic image-worship–of representations of the cow, the cat, the bull, and the snake, or of the moon, the sun, and the stars–was very real and threatening to the worship of the One God, in the judgment of Moses, the Prophets, and later Jewish religious teachers.

They were haunted by the possibility that the Israelites–who, to begin with, had also been animists or nature-worshipers–might, by the apparently innocent means of images, be led imperceptibly to revert to their old idolatry.

The historical fact is that the ancient Jews were never quite free of the inclination to idol-worship. This is proven not only by the tireless admonitions, exhortations, lamentations, and alarms sounded by the Prophets in the Bible, but by significant discoveries of archaeologists. In recent decades, they have unearthed in Palestine and in the State of Israel a number of clay figurines, crudely modeled, of the Babylonian goddess of love and procreation, Ishtar (Astarte). These sculptured objects are attributed to the early period of the Second Temple, and so can hardly be reckoned as being of little significance not only in the development of the God-idea among the Jews but also in reference to the effectiveness of the Scriptural ban on graven images.

Jewish theological belief in the Oneness and Unity of God existed as a small island of dissent that was fixed precariously in the middle of a raging sea of idolatry which constantly threatened to engulf it. The Prophets and other advanced religious elements in ancient Israel, in order to keep the ethical stream of their religion unmuddied, were forced to wage a perpetual, although not always successful, struggle against idolatry in all its backward, immoral forms, including the allure of its images. That the early Christians, being Jews, also showed this traditional fear of graven images as constituting a sure road to idolatry, is proven by the complete absence of any graphic or sculptural representations of God or Jesus in the art work by Christians discovered in the catacombs of Rome. The reverencing of images in Christianity came much later, when the religion had sufficiently accommodated itself not only to the image-worship of the Romans but also to the esthetic values of Roman culture, in which art, and specifically sculpture, figured so highly.

But who can say that there always prevailed among Jews just one single interpretation of the Second Commandment? True, while the prohibition against art was most precisely stated and even made clearer by elaborating statements elsewhere in the Bible (as in Leviticus 26:1), there was found a compelling need at various times by cultured Jews for artistic creation, especially during such epochs as the Hellenistic and the Italian Renaissance, when architecture, painting, and sculpture achieved such an astonishingly high valuation in society. In response to this clamor for visual beauty among Jews, the more worldly among their rabbis saw fit to revise, in certain limited ways, the Scriptural ban against art; they presumably squared it with their religious conscience first and then reinterpreted the Second Commandment in accordance with "the spirit of the times."

It cannot be denied that there were long stretches of time, in particular Jewish communities when the Biblical prohibition against graven images, especially those made of "figured stone," was scrupulously observed. In such periods, it was practically impossible for Jews to make representations of any kind–whether in wall-paintings, easel-paintings, engravings, drawings, ivory and wood carvings, sculpture in clay, metal, or stone; or whether of human beings, of animals, of birds, or of fish. Yet, in different historical settings, all sorts of permissive exceptions were sanctioned by broad-minded rabbis.

During the Middle Ages in Western Europe, when sculptured likenesses of people or of animals were forbidden by some religious authorities, the execution of paintings on synagogue walls were somehow tolerated so long as they did not depict the human face and figure. However, with rare exceptions this was not the case in the culturally less advanced Rhineland. On the contrary, some rabbis there specifically banned the painting of frescoes or murals in the synagogues, claiming that they were too distracting to allow proper worship. Nonetheless, revealing a reasonable tolerance, they permitted artist-craftsmen–among whom were both Jews and Christians–to carve out on the massive wooden street-doors of the synagogues representations of lions, stags, eagles, birds, and snakes, and also flowers, the imaginary Tree of Life, designs of vine tendrils, wreaths, leaves, etc.

Despite all these liberalizations from time to time, the strict traditionalists among the rabbis in every generation refused to deviate whatsoever from the law. They condemned the watering-down of the Second Commandment by others as being an invitation to the unwary to slide into apostasy and idolatry. An interesting illustration of the bitter opposition to these innovations is furnished by the stand of the German

A symbolic rendering of the Ten Commandments topped by Cherubim. (From a 13th-century Hebrew Pentateuch of Perpignan, France.)

Almost faceless and armless representation in the catacombs of Bet Shearim, Judea, of a man holding up a menorah. In the opinion of many rabbis, any substantial disfigurement of the face in a piece of sculpture took the work out of the category of idol and did not, therefore, violate the prohibition of the Second Commandment: "Thou shalt have no other gods before me. Thou shalt not make unto thee a graven image, nor any manner of likeness. . . ." While this commandment was rigorously observed by the Jewish people for the greater part of three thousand years, yet there were instances when it was either ignored entirely or modified in various ways.

Roman jug found by Yigael Yadin, the Hebrew University archaeologist, in a Judean desert cave together with Bar Kochba's letters. Like the faceless man in the Bet Shearim catacomb decoration (above), the face of the pagan god on the jug was also found disfigured. (American Friends of the Hebrew University.)

Sculptured relief on the marble sarcophagus of a Jewish notable found in Bet Shearim, Judea, and dating from the 3rd century C.E. *Being in itself a violation of the Second Commandment (prohibiting idolatry), it shows also the extent of the assimilation of the Hellenistic culture by Jews, for the sculptor has portrayed the Greek mythological story of Leda and the Swan.*

"Spring." Mosaic representation in Bet Gubrin, Judea, 3rd century C.E.

rabbi Moses Sofer (1762–1839). When his congregation proposed to install in the synagogue above the Ark of the Law a stained-glass window including a sun radiant and bearing the appropriate Hebrew inscription: "From the rising of the sun, even to its going down, let the name of the Lord be exalted," he protested that worshipers who bowed before the Ark as they came into the synagogue would, in effect, really be worshiping the sun, although unwittingly.

But a view diametrically opposite to this was apparently held by some Palestinian rabbis of the fifth century C.E. In the exquisite mosaic floor of the Bet-Alpha Synagogue, which was uncovered by archaeologists in 1939, there is a remarkable symbolic representation of the sun executed in the Hellenistic manner. It shows the figure of a human rider in the chariot of the rising sun drawn by fiery horses. This discovery both astonished and puzzled some students of Biblical culture, who could explain it only as being a phenomenon, unique and exceptional.

This theory had to be sharply revised a few years later when the third-century synagogue of Dura-Europos, in lower Syria, was uncovered and found to be in a remarkable state of preservation. From the Greek inscriptions on the wall-paintings in the synagogue, one learned that the structure had been rebuilt in 245 C.E. by a certain Samuel, the *archisynagogos* who was also a Cohen (priest), and that he accomplished his goal with the assistance of other pious Jews of Dura. Now this synagogue is situated practically next door to a Christian church, erected in 232, which was dug up at the same time. And, amazing to relate, the murals in both the synagogue and the church are of the same general artistic character, and painted in the Hellenistic manner!

The historian Michael I. Rostovtzeff, who took part in the discovery, noted that the style of the murals in the Dura synagogue were also strikingly similar to those decorating the temple of Zeus Theos in Greece. From the individual Greek inscriptions on several of the wall-paintings, it appears that each was a gift to the synagogue from a donor who chose his own theme and commissioned his own Jewish artist to paint it. The subjects were mostly of well-known Biblical episodes and of illustrious individuals such as Ezra

The baking of matzot. The representation of humans with bird faces was deliberately made by fundamentalists in order to comply with the prohibition of the Second Commandment. (Illustration from the Vogelkopfhaggada*—the "Bird-Head Haggadah"—Germany, early 14th century.)*

David anointed King of Israel. (From the frescoes in the Dura-Europos synagogue, Syria, c. 250 C.E. *Courtesy of Yale University Art Gallery.)*

Ezra reading the Torah before the people. (From a fresco in the Dura-Europos synagogue, Syria, c. 250 C.E. Courtesy of Yale University Art Gallery.)

Floor mosaic of the Zodiac in the Hellenistic synagogue at Bet-Alpha, with representation of the human face and figure. Palestine, 6th century C.E. (The Jewish Museum.)

and David, and all panels, without exception, depicted the human face and figure!

From the above facts one can deduce that, in the first centuries of the Common Era, and probably even earlier, there must have flourished in the Greco-Roman milieu a professional and artistically sophisticated class of Jewish painters, architects, sculptural stonecutters, and skilled workers in mosaic. Obviously, they, as well as their rich Jewish patrons, in esthetic ideas and tastes, were thoroughly Greek. And, finally, the most interesting conclusion drawn was that neither the figured floor-mosaic in the Bet-Alpha Synagogue nor the murals depicting Biblical incidents in the Dura-Europos Synagogue (nor even, for that matter, the emergence of a professional class of Jewish artists), could have been possible without the official sanction of the Rabbinic authorities!

The art of Hebrew book- and scroll-illumination, actively practiced by Jews during the Middle Ages before the advent of printing, employed, without any hesitation, the human face and figure as well as animals and birds, in illustrations of the Bible, the Psalter, the Passover Haggadah, and the Book of Esther (the Megillah)–proving that religious sanction was available for them, also. Several centuries later, there were Jews in Italy who even had their portraits painted or sketched, or worked in bas-relief on metal medallions. There were, of course, varying degrees of tolerance toward "graven images." Some rabbis allowed only portraits in profile, forbidding depiction of the full face. Nonetheless, there are extant a number of portraits of Jews in full face, dating from late-Renaissance times, and strikingly enough, one of them is of the famous humanist and chief rabbi of Venice, Leone da Modena (1571–1648)!

Whatever religious laws and regulations there were to inhibit the practice of the graphic and plastic arts among Jews, a great deterrent during the art-worshiping Middle Ages and the Renaissance was the exclusion of Jews from the strictly Christian artist-guilds. Christian students, in those days, customarily received their art education as apprentices to master painters, sculptors, and goldsmiths, and developed their talents in the course of the years while working in the *botegas* (workshops) of the individual master-artists. However, young Jewish artist-craftsmen had to acquire their knowledge and skills by themselves, the younger from the older, and although there was some opportunity for apprenticeship to Jewish "masters," the professional calling customarily was kept "in the family," a proud heritage of talent handed down from father to son. In this connection, it is interesting to note that the artist Marc Chagall is directly descended from Isaac Segal, an eighteenth-century synagogue decorator and painter of Mohilev, Russia!

Curiously enough, because the Christian artist-guilds did not include illuminators, seal-engravers, bookbinders, minters, and embroiderers, the frustrated Jewish artist-craftsmen, in search of new outlets, took advantage of this neglect and became excellent workers in those fields.

Perhaps one view, more widely shared among rabbis of former times than is generally believed, was that expressed by the rabbinical scholar and philosopher Profiat Duran (known to Christian Schoolmen as "Maestre Duran the Aristotelian"), who wrote that "looking on beautiful shapes and pleasing sculpture in a synagogue enlarges the soul, quickens the heart and increases the power of the mind." A great majority of Jews today would be ready to agree with this view.

See also SYNAGOGUES; TOMBSTONES.

ART, CEREMONIAL

Since the instinct for beauty in the graphic and plastic arts could not be suppressed in the Jewish people despite the absolute prohibition against graven images contained in the Second Commandment, it expressed itself in tangential fashion and in a number of ways. In particular, it was turned into intellectual and religious channels. It found one outlet in exalted religious poetry, a form of art in which the Hebrew liturgists excelled. The Jewish concept of beauty, sprung from the puritan soil of its religion, did not have as its main emphasis the esthetic or the sensual, as did the Egyptian, the Greek, and the Roman, but rather the spiritual and the moral. ". . . Worship the Lord in the beauty of holiness," exhorted the ancient Singer of Zion (Psalm 29).

Yet artistic expression did enter into Jewish life, but in a rather roundabout way. It was the Jews' love for the Torah which gave this expression religious sanction by, so to speak, an "escape clause" of exceptionalism which is implicit in a Rabbinical precept called in Hebrew *chiddur mitzvah.* This "extra precept" imposed upon the pious the duty of exceeding in performance the written demands of each of the 613 commandments (mitzvot) found in the Torah: They were *to add* something to them–just a little more than what could be considered just sufficient. This minute excess was meant to serve as a symbolic love-offering–a testament of boundless devotion from the individual Jew to his faith.

The ancient Rabbis had constructed this unique precept upon the Scriptural affirmation: "This is my God and I will glorify Him." (Exodus 15:2.) But the word "glorify" they interpreted to mean "beautify." This was the way Rabbi Ishmael, the celebrated Judean teacher of ethics in the first century C.E., interpreted the matter. He asked (as it were, rhetorically): Can a mere human being "glorify" his Creator? Not at all! Therefore, he concluded, the real and inner meaning of the word "glorify" was "beautify." And since it certainly was not God who stood in any need of being beautified but man himself, for that reason man was called upon to "beautify" his life with the commandments of the Torah. One of the ways he could accomplish this was by adorning all objects used in the performance of the rites and ceremonies of the Jewish religion.

Thus, when a Jew built himself a succah, he made it as beautiful as he could. When he made a lulab, he had to fashion it in beauty. Also beautiful had to be the shofar, tefillin, tzitzit, etc. If a man wished to donate a Sefer Torah to the synagogue, he had to make sure it was "written in his honor with the finest ink, with the best quills, by the most skillful scribe, and that it was wrapped in the purest of silks." In this way grew the tradition of religious art among Jews–i.e., in the making of ritualistic and ceremonial vessels, ornaments and furnishings as *objets d'art.* As such, they constituted a unique form of religious worship in the estimation of the Rabbis. So great, in fact, was this reverence for beauty in religious articles, that the Rabbis urged that, if a man is about to purchase a ceremonial object but suddenly sees another one that impresses him as being still more beautiful, he be urged to buy the more beautiful, provided it would not involve more than one-third additional expense and it would not result in his impoverishment.

Concretely, what do we know of Jewish religious and ceremonial art? Unfortunately, very little. The troubled history of the Jewish people has been such that the art and artifacts of entire Jewish historic periods have vanished from the earth as if they had never existed. This holds true even of an epoch so rich in cultural development and creativity as that of Hellenistic Alexandria during the Talmudic age, where for more than five centuries Jews were able to express themselves more fully and freely than in most periods of their long, dismal history. Yet hardly a trace remains of that culturally brilliant period; we have merely some random fragments of its literature and philosophy in Greek, and almost nothing at all of architecture, art, and artifacts.

Especially pertinent, to the modern student of Jewish culture is the ceremonial art of the Jews of Europe. But where can one find examples of it produced *before* the sixteenth century? Hardly any ceremonial art objects made before that time have survived the thorough destruction and looting of Jewish communities by mobs. No one can tell for certain what the Torah ornaments of the early Renaissance—not to mention the Middle Ages–were or looked like. The earliest objects extant today are of late Renaissance and Baroque times. Sad to relate, most of the oldest examples we have stem from the rococo, that degenerate period in baroque art. These are characterized by excessive ornamentation and by an unrestrained flamboyance, making use of bright red velvets, vivid gold and silver embroidery and appliqué, and a profusion of glittering semiprecious stones. Significantly, the farther back most of these art objects go toward the Renaissance, the simpler and more refined in taste and the lovelier they are.

Besides the impact of Christian cultural influences during the Baroque period on objects of Jewish ceremonial art, there is also possible another explanation, in terms of economics, for the increase in the opulence and love of display which are revealed in them. With the rapid rise of the Christian middle-class in Europe (from the sixteenth century on), an ever growing number of Jews was also able to acquire middle-class status and a corresponding increase in affluence. There emerged a sizeable number of Jewish merchants, exporters-importers, "court Jews" (shtadlonim) who acted as fiscal agents for the numerous princelings of Europe, shipowners, brokers, and factors, and finally, in the eighteenth century, factory owners. They were able to acquire for home use or to donate to their synagogues elaborately decorated Ark curtains and Sifrei Torah (Torah Scrolls) with their silver and gilded ornaments. These they commissioned Christian as well as Jewish silversmiths, artist-weavers, and embroiderers to make for them. The Christian silversmiths were employed simply as a matter of expediency. Because they belonged to guilds, they naturally had received better training in their art-crafts and, unlike their Jewish colleagues, had more extensive experience in them since they had an unlimited field of operation. Jews, not allowed to belong to these guilds, found fewer opportunities to develop their talents or to obtain commissions. Yet there were Jewish silversmiths, woodcarvers, weavers, and embroiderers, including Wolf of Augsburg (seventeenth century) and Jeremiah Zobel of Frankfort (early eighteenth century), who displayed real skill and refinement of style.

A unique development in connection with Jewish ceremonial art during the Baroque period was the emergence of a highly skilled class of artist-embroiderers and weavers *who were women.* They designed, wove, and embroidered Ark curtains and Torah mantles with great skill and creative imagination.

In more than one instance, the pride of artistic creation was registered by the Jewish artist-craftsman on his handiwork. On a red and green velvet Ark curtain, dated 1772, which is found now in the Jewish Museum in New York, the following Hebrew inscriptions is executed in appliqué: "The work of my hands in which I take pride, with the help of God. Jacob Koppel Gans, son of Judah Leb Goldsticker [i.e. . . . Judah Leb the Gold Embroiderer]."

The art objects produced for ceremonial use in both synagogue and home were surprisingly numerous. They included, first of all, the interior furnishings of the synagogue itself, together with the Ark curtain, the Torah Scrolls and their silver ornaments, the laver, shofar, Channukah lamp, and Perpetual Lamp. Then came, for home use as well as for congregational use, Kiddush goblets, Sabbath lamps and candlesticks. Channukah lamps, modified menorot, communal wedding rings and engraved ketubot (marriage contracts; s. ketubah), silver-appliquéd prayer-shawl collars, silver spice-boxes for the Habdalah service, mortars and pestles (merzhers) for pounding spices, special Sabbath, Passover, and other festival platters, fine bookbindings for sacred works, illuminated Pentateuchs, Megillot for Purim, Haggadot for Passover, etc.

The widespread use of these and other ceremonial art objects–made of the finest materials, from brass to gold, from linen to silk–and the religious eagerness to have them made as beautiful as possible, resulted in a lively activity in the art crafts among Jews. Seemingly, denied fuller expression in the media of representational art, the Jews' preoccupation with ceremonial objects amounted to a compensatory creativity.

See also ARK CURTAIN; BEMA; LAMP, PERPETUAL; MENORAH; SABBATH CEREMONIAL ART *(under* SABBATH); TORAH ORNAMENTS.

"ARYAN" MYTH, THE. *See* ANTI-SEMITISM; PERSECUTION IN MODERN DRESS.

ASARAH B'TEBET. *See* FASTING AND FAST DAYS.

ASCETICISM. *See* ASCETICS, JEWISH.

ASCETICS, JEWISH

While the main current of Jewish religious thought was a rationalistic one and represented an affirmation of the physical life with all its sensory pleasures, limited only by the requirements of moderation and encouraging joy and laughter, there were, nevertheless, also cultists who followed the life-negating ascetic way. They set themselves apart from the general Jewish community and devoted themselves with a burning fanaticism to penance through the practice of austerities, prayer vigils, and such mortifications of the flesh as fasting and flagellation, hoping to escape thereby the carnal snares set for them by the adversary of man, Satan.

The historian of the first century C.E., Josephus, observed at first hand: "The Essenes reject pleasure as an evil, but esteem continence and the conquest over our passions as a virtue." There were others in Judea besides the members of this pre-Christian Jewish sect of guilt-plagued idealists who struggled desperately to escape the tyranny of the senses. This renunciation-approach to life is found in a statement in an early Midrash: "The souls of the righteous always strain to leave this world for the bliss of the World-to-Come." This constituted, perhaps in the disguised form of an excessive pietism, a drive to self-destruction. Such was the outlook, for instance, of the first-century Mishnah Sage, Tzaddok. It is noted in the Talmud that for forty years he fasted every single day (until evening) in order that, with his penance, the Temple in Jerusalem might not suffer destruction. In fact, he became so emaciated that every bit of food he swallowed could be seen moving down his gullet. However, such austerities, declared the Rabbis reprovingly, constituted not only a sinful rejection of life but also a blasphemous rebuke to God for having created man at all. On the Day of Judgment, they warned, the ascetic will have to give account before the Tribunal of Heaven for every (permitted) pleasure he, out of perverseness, had denied himself in life!

Ascetic and mystical notions among Jews were encouraged by the political and religious calamities that befell the nation during the last period of the Second Commonwealth. (The Cabala had probably its origins at that time.) The Talmud notes: "From the day on which the Temple was destroyed, God had banished laughter." The Jewish people collectively went into a perpetual mourning. Such pervasive grief became uncomfortably depressing and drove many Jews to take a completely irrational outlook on life.

The Rabbinic teachers were alarmed and sought to stem the contagion of pietistic morbidity. A Talmudic chronicler relates: "When the Second Temple was destroyed, many in Israel took it upon themselves to abstain from meat and wine." Thereupon Rabbi Joshua ben Levi tried to reason with them. "My sons, why do you not eat meat nor drink wine?" he asked. To this, the dedicated mourners answered: "Shall we eat meat of which offerings used to be brought upon the [Temple] altar but have now ceased? Shall we drink wine of which libations used to be poured upon the altar but have now ceased?" Astounded by this line of reasoning, Rabbi Joshua wished to pursue it to its illogical conclusion, so he continued: "In that case, let us stop eating bread since the meal-offerings too have ceased." This argument threw the mourners into confusion. "Quite right," they agreed, "so we will live on fruit instead." But how could they think of such a thing? remonstrated Joshua. "How can we eat fruit if the offering of the first fruits also have ceased?" The mourners once more were baffled. "Quite right," they agreed. Then at least they could drink water, they answered hopefully. "What!" exclaimed the Sage ironically! "Shall we drink water since the water-libation [in the Temple] has also ceased?" The mourners, finding no other argument to fall back on, were silent.

The upsurge of asceticism in the Middle Ages among the Jews of Europe–no doubt precipitated by the life-rejecting monastic trend in contemporary Christianity–with a vigor it had not experienced for almost a thousand years, prompted Judah (Yehudah) Halevi, the great twelfth-century Hebrew poet, to make a plea to the ascetic escapists for their return to reality: "The servant of God does not withdraw himself from secular contact lest he become a burden to the world and [likewise] the world to him. He does not hate life, which is one of God's bounties granted to him. . . . On the contrary, he loves this world and a long life, because they afford him opportunities of deserving the World-to-Come."

Until the advent of Chasidism in the eighteenth century, ascetic practices were very much in vogue among the Cabalists of Europe, and, in particular, among those settled in the Palestinian communities of Hebron, Tiberias, Jerusalem, and Safed during the sixteenth and seventeenth centuries. But these austerities they performed not merely as acts of penance for their own personal sins, but in order that they might hasten the long-delayed coming of the Messiah and the Redemption. Although the East European Chasidim were the continuators of the Cabalists, they rejected all forms of asceticism. Israel Baal Shem, their founder, declared in his Testament: "Weeping is an exceeding great evil, for man must serve in joy."

See also CABALA; CHASIDIM; DEAD SEA SCROLLS; ESSENES; GOLDEN MEAN, THE RABBINIC; MARRIAGE AND SEX; MESSIAH, THE; MONASTICISM, JEWISH; SIN AND SINNER; THERAPEUTAE.

ASERET HA-DIBROT. *See* TEN COMMANDMENTS.

ASHKENAZIM (Hebrew pl.; s. ASHKENAZI)

For the sake of convenience, during the Middle Ages Jews were quite arbitrarily divided into two main categories. Those Jews who lived in Spain, Portugal, and the Provence were designated as Sefaradim; those who lived in Germany and in East European countries where the Judeo-German venacular, Yiddish, was spoken, were called Ashkenazim. While each only incidentally represented a separate cultural stream that was based on geographic location and the language of daily use, each principally came to have a somewhat different nusach (text and order of prayer) and minhag (religious customs and ceremonies). The Minhag Ashkenaz and the Minhag Sefarad reveal differences in the liturgy, ritual, religious customs and ceremonies, and also in the manner of pronouncing Hebrew and in the character of the music of the synagogue.

The *name* Ashkenaz figures in the post-Creation myth related in Genesis 10:3, in the list of Noah's grandsons. How the word became associated with German Jews is not altogether clear. But somehow, in their fanciful distribution of races and peoples throughout the known world, the rabbinical demographers of the Middle Ages fixed on Germany as the land where the Biblical Ashkenaz and his progeny were settled after the Sin-Flood.

The *word* Ashkenaz, denoting Germany, appears quite often beginning with the eleventh century. Rashi of Troyes (1040–1105), "the Prince" of Biblical commentators, made several references to German as being "the language of Ashkenaz." That footloose rabbi of the twelfth century, Benjamin of Tudela, makes reference to Germany in his Hebrew travelogue as "Alamania, otherwise called Ashkenaz."

The Ashkenaz order of prayer (Nusach Ashkenaz) differs in some striking respects from the Nusach Sefarad. Whereas, it was averred, the Nusach Sefarad was a lineal descendant of the Babylonian Jewish tradition, note was also made in the first Ashkenaz prayer-book for the Holy Days–the Machzor Vitry, compiled by a pupil of Rashi's, in France–that the order of prayer of the German Jews followed the tradition that had been established in Tiberias, in Galilee, during Rabbinic times. Possibly it may have begun that way, but the prayer service, the manner of pronouncing Hebrew, and also the divergent character of the cantillations (musical modes) for reading from the Torah must have undergone some remarkable changes. In one matter alone–that of the liturgical music that has become traditional in the synagogues of Germany, Austria, and Eastern Europe–the musical impact of the Central and East European Christian environment is plainly to be seen.

As a historic demonstration of how a cultural form placed in different geographic settings undergoes considerable modifications, let us consider the origin of the Polish minhag. Following the Black Death in Europe (in 1348–49), when the Jews were accused of poisoning the wells, lakes, and rivers (*see* MASSACRES: THE CRUSADES, THE BLACK DEATH), they were butchered by the tens of thousands. Thereupon a massive flight of German Jews took place into the Polish provinces. It was not long before the Minhag Ashkenaz of Germany, in its new Slavic environment, underwent certain modifications and became known as the Minhag Polen (Polish) to distinguish it from the older minhag of Germany.

See also CHASIDIM; PRAYER AND WORSHIP; SEFARADIM; SIDDUR.

ASSIDEANS. *See* ZEALOTS.

ASSIMILATION. *See* ANTI-SEMITISM: THE "RACIAL PURITY" MYTH; APOCRYPHA; ARABIC-JEWISH "GOLDEN AGE"; ASHKENAZIM; BIBLE, THE; CHANNUKAH; CHEDER; CONVERSION OF JEWS; DIETARY LAWS; ENLIGHTENMENT, THE JEWISH; FOLK MUSIC AND DANCE; GHETTO; HEBREW LANGUAGE, HISTORY OF THE; HEBREW LITERATURE, MODERN; HELLENISTS, JEWISH; HYMNS OF THE SYNAGOGUE; INTERMARRIAGE; INTOXICATION; JEWISH LANGUAGES; KARAITES; MARRANOS AND THE INQUISITION; MASORAH; PHARISEES; POST-BIBLICAL WRITINGS; PRAYER AND WORSHIP; SAMARITANS; SANHEDRIN; SEFARADIM; SHADCHAN; THEATRE, OPPOSITION TO THE; WEDDING CUSTOMS.

ATONEMENT, DAY OF. *See* YOM KIPPUR.

AUTO-DA-FÉ. *See* CONVERSION OF JEWS; MARRANOS AND THE INQUISITION.

AYIN HA-RAH. *See* EVIL EYE.

Constantine's order to the Roman decurions of Cologne concerning the Jews, indicating the existence of a Jewish community in that city early in the 4th century. (Biblioteca Apostolica Vaticana.)

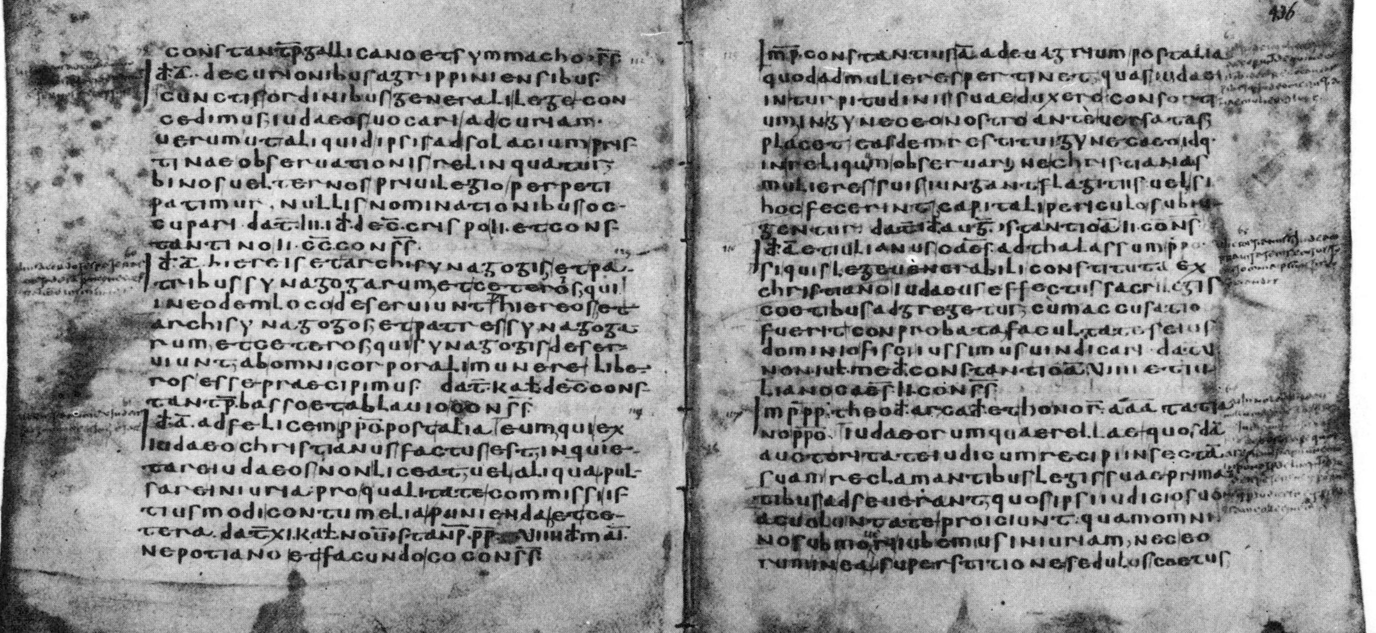

B

BAAL BRIT. *See* CIRCUMCISION.

BAAL KOREH. *See* TORAH-READING.

BAAL TEFILLAH (Hebrew, meaning "master of prayer" or "precentor")

The ancient Rabbinic teachers in the Talmud urged: "If you have a sweet voice, glorify God with the gift he has given you. Chant the Shema and lead the people in prayer."

It was considered a great honor for a man to be chosen by the elders of a congregation to lead it in prayer. The old Talmudic description for a leader of prayer was shaliach tzibbur (the messenger of a congregation). Formerly, in the Temple service in Jerusalem, it had been the officiant priest who had acted as the leader of prayer in intercession with God for the worshipers. But with the development of the synagogue as a communal institution and the growth of the prayer service, it was the precentor, himself one of the worshipers assembled, who acted as their advocate, symbolically.

The Rabbis agreed that the title "messenger of the congregation," if it were at all to conform with the objective of collective worship—i.e., communion with God—had to be vested in a man of unblemished character. Otherwise, his pleading would not be found acceptable by God, who was all knowing. Judah ben Illai, the Rabbinic teacher of the second century, listed a few of the baal tefillah's qualifications. He had to be knowledgeable in the Torah and sincerely pious. In his own family life, and in his dealings with others, he was to be of proven righteousness and be well liked. His appearance had to be attractive, his attire spotless, his manner modest and pleasant. He had to "know all the prayers and benedictions by heart," and he was to chant them with "a sweet voice" and musical sensibility, and pronounce every Hebrew word with a clear diction so that the worshipers would be able to follow him throughout. But it was most necessary that he possess true illumination in the spiritual art of prayer so that he might communicate properly to the listening congregation all the interior meanings of the prayer texts. Lastly, it was desirable that he be poor, for only he who had suffered himself would be able to plead with conviction for the needs of the straitened and the sorrows of the afflicted.

The durability of tradition and folk-custom among religious Jews has been impressive. In the fullness of time there were changes in Jewish historic circumstances. The liturgy of the synagogue grew, and its ceremonialism became more elaborate and also less informal. Musical tastes too underwent remarkable changes. For more sophisticated worshipers, the unpaid humble leader of prayer, intoning the traditional modal melodies, even though he was the "messenger of the congregation," no longer was satisfying. The professional chazzan or cantor, vocally well-endowed and competently trained in his special art, began to supplant him, at least at the Sabbath and High Holy Day services in the larger and more affluent congregations. Yet the baal tefillah never disappeared entirely, nor did his chanting of the prayers cease. It is not infrequent even today, in some Orthodox synagogues, to find the chazzan, with the aid of a choir, leading the service in tones magnificently grand-operatic, while below, in the basement of the building, a minyan (the quorum necessary for worship) of the old-fashioned pious, impervious to change, wrapped in their prayer shawls, follow the chanting of the baal tefillah.

Baal tefillah. (From an illuminated machzor [prayer book for the festival] of the 14th century. Leipzig University Library.)

Baal tefillah. (Sketch by Sheva Ausubel.)

See also CHAZZAN; PRAYER AND WORSHIP.

BABYLONIAN TALMUD. *See* TALMUD, THE.

BADCHAN, BADCHANIM. *See* MERRYMAKERS, TRADITIONAL JEWISH.

BADGE, YELLOW. *See* YELLOW BADGE.

BAHIR, THE. *See* CABALA.

BALFOUR DECLARATION. *See* ZIONISM.

BAR MITZVAH (Hebrew, meaning "Son of the Commandment"; in common usage, refers merely to the status or ceremony of BAR MITZVAH)

In the thinking of modern times, a boy of thirteen is still considered, more or less, a child. But in former centuries, and under conditions of life other than those that prevail today, the maturation process of children took place at a much more rapid tempo. A boy of thirteen, in the sober hard scheme of the European ghetto, was considered to be standing on the very threshold of manhood. The religious ceremony of Bar Mitzvah was calculated to celebrate the notable occasion when he left his childhood behind him.

There is little question but that the origin of the idea concerning maturity at thirteen years goes far back into the shadowy past of Jewish historic beginnings. It can be inferred from general practices in the religions of the ancient Semitic East as well as of primitive peoples of today that the status derived from male maturity was at first determined solely by the biologic yardstick. At the age of puberty, a boy was automatically considered a bona fide man. However, before he was allowed to take his rightful place among his male adult peers, he had to undergo successfully the ordeals, often severe and painful, imposed by the rites of tribal initiation. It is quite probable that, before the dawn of Hebrew-Israelite history, the rite of circumcision was one of these ordeals, but that, in the humanizing development of Jewish ideas, attitudes, and practices, was transferred to the eight-day-old infant. Among Jews, starting with the final Second Temple period, what had formerly been a tribal rite of initiation took on a moral, spiritual concept, marking an important religious-social milestone in the life of every male Jew.

A Mishnah elaboration written during the first century C.E., makes reference to thirteen years as being the appropriate age for beginning the fulfillment of all the 613 Biblical mitzvot or commandments. "Until the thirteenth year," observed the Tanna (Sage) Eleazar, "it is the father's duty to raise his son. But after that, he must say: 'Blessed be He Who has taken from me the responsibility for this boy.'" This, in brief, is the whole significance of Bar Mitzvah.

In antiquity, the Bar Mitzvah boy in Jerusalem was led by his father to the Temple priest or to the Elder to receive his blessing, his moral counsel, and his prayer "that he may be granted a portion in the Torah and in the performance of good deeds." In our day, the rabbi performs the same function.

The Bar Mitzvah ceremony usually takes place in the synagogue at the morning prayer-service on the first Sabbath after a boy has passed thirteen. He is honored by being "called up" for the first time to read from the Scroll of the Torah before the entire congregation. Upon the conclusion of his reading, when he has recited the second benediction, his father steps forward to the reading desk and recites aloud the ancient formula for moral severance: "Blessed be He who releases me from the responsibility of this child."

In past centuries, this ceremony constituted a dramatic point of departure: The child was considered no longer dependent upon his father, his moral conduct and piety thenceforth became his own responsibility. Now he was eligible for many of the religious privileges enjoyed by his father and by all male adults. He was allowed to become part of the minyan, the quorum of ten which is mandatory for holding public worship. Also, he could serve as one of the three male adults whose presence was required by Rabbinic law for the recitation of Grace After Meals, and, like his elders, he now had to wear tefillin (phylacteries) at morning prayer.

In days gone by, under the special religious-cultural conditions of Jewish community life in the ghetto, the thirteen-year-old lad had already absorbed an astonishing amount of religious culture; he was usually by that time somewhat of a Torah scholar, and in many instances had already been trained in the intricate dialectics of Talmudic argumentation. Consequently, time-honored custom required that, on the afternoon of the Sabbath of his Bar Mitzvah, he deliver a discourse (drosho or derashah) before his guests, including kinfolk and neighbors assembled for the celebration in his home, either on the theme suggested by the Torah portion of the week or on some point of Talmudic law. It was essentially an expository lecture in which he was able, to the delight or disappointment of his knowledgeable audience, to reveal the extent–or lack–of

Grandfather of Bokharan origin instructing Bar Mitzvah boy in Jerusalem in putting on tefillin (phylacteries). (Israel Government Information Services.)

Bar Mitzvah feast in Algiers.

his Torah learning and logical acumen. At a later period, with the breakup of close Jewish community life in the ghetto and the loosening simultaneously of religious authority and observance, this custom declined in popularity and deteriorated in intellectual content.

While, in our time, in the English-speaking world, the Bar Mitzvah boy sometimes still delivers a discourse, it no longer mirrors his intellectual accomplishments, but is, more often than not, a memorized singsong declamation full of pious sentiments about God, Torah, and father and mother. Actually, the Bar Mitzvah himself has little part (if any) in its preparation; his rabbi and Hebrew teacher supplies him with the Hebrew text and the inevitable version of the "Bar Mitzvah speech." The Hebrew portion of the speech is merely a gesture of reverence to tradition, for today, in our culturally assimilated environment, not too many adult Jews outside of Israel understand very much Hebrew. All that the Bar Mitzvah boy has to do is memorize the two addresses, or, in increasing instances, his English "speech" only. In tradition, he is given from three months to a year of extra-curricular drilling by his rabbi or Hebrew teacher in the admittedly difficult reading and cantillation of the weekly portion from the Hebrew Pentateuch and the Haftarah (the accompanying selection from the Prophets).

In the life of the European ghetto, a Bar Mitzvah was an occasion for much rejoicing, after the synagogue service, in the home of the boy's parents, and here not only relatives but almost the entire Jewish community took part. At such times overtones of religious meaning and of group interdependence were struck. In modern Jewish society, the folk-character of the Bar Mitzvah party (perhaps in keeping with the general trend in Jewish cultural and social life today) has become, in many cases, uncomfortably formal and practically devoid of religious or social significance. It is customary in the United States, for example to hold an elaborate party in a hotel or restaurant banquet room on the evening of the Bar Mitzvah Sabbath or on the Sunday afternoon or evening following. The kind of food, drink, music, and entertainment provided offer a sharp contrast to the simple and heartfelt traditional Jewish ways and tastes which, not so long ago, prevailed. The one who feels best rewarded by the celebration is the Bar Mitzvah boy himself; he is literally almost smothered with gifts.

See also HAFTARAH; MITZVOT; MUSICAL ACCENTS; TEFILLIN; TORAH-READING.

BAT KOL (Hebrew, meaning "Daughter of the Voice," i.e., the voice of God)

The Bat Kol was the proclamatory instrument of God's will and intention, his judgments and his promises, his warnings and his commands, made to chosen individuals, even to communities, and sometimes to all of Israel. It became a standard fixture of Jewish legend and the Cabalistic and Chasidic tales of the tzaddikim (the wonder-working rabbis).

A well-known feature of many primitive religions is the belief that demons and spirits which are invisible to man nonetheless speak with clear voices to him. The concept of the Bat Kol may have had that kind of origin. Concerning the divine revelation of the Torah and the covenant with God entered into by the Children of Israel at Sinai, the Bible says Moses told them: ". . . Ye heard the voice of the words, but saw no similitude; only ye heard a voice." (Deuteronomy 4:12.)

The Bat Kol sounded at extraordinary times, according to the Bible and the Talmud. For example, at the very instant when God took away the soul of Moses with a kiss, the Bat Kol rang out over the Israelite camp with the lament: "Moses is dead! Moses is dead!" It also gave dire warning or passed judgment upon the doers of evil, as when, in the prophecy of Daniel (4:28): ". . . There fell a voice from heaven, saying, O king Nebuchadnezzar, to thee it is spoken; the kingdom is departed from thee."

The Bat Kol was said to have been heard by the Rabbinic Sages when they had very important decisions to make. It is stated in the Talmud: "A Bat Kol announced two times at the assemblies of the Scribes [i.e., the Men of the Great Assembly]: 'There is a man here who is worthy to have the Holy Spirit rest upon him.' On one of these occasions, all eyes turned to Hillel; on another, to Samuel the Lesser."

References to the Bat Kol abound also in the New Testament. St. John obviously had such a visitation: "I was in the [Holy] Spirit on the Lord's day, and heard behind me a great voice, as of a trumpet." (Revelation 1:10.)

Like the Holy Spirit, the Bat Kol too is represented in Jewish tradition by the symbolism of a dove.

See also HOLY SPIRIT; SHECHINAH.

BATHING. *See* BURIAL RITES AND CUSTOMS; MIKVAH.

BAT MITZVAH (Hebrew, meaning "Daughter of the Commandment")

The granting to the woman in contemporary Judaism of a religious status closer to that of the privileged male is particularly reflected in matters pertaining to public worship and the symbolism of the faith. Today, in American Conservative and Reform congregations, girls are expected to enter into their initiation as religious "adults" at thirteen in a ceremony paralleling that of boys when they are Bar Mitzvah. In Conservative parlance, the ceremony is called Bat Mitzvah; in Reform synagogues, the rite of Confirmation usually takes the place of the Bat Mitzvah.

In Conservative practice, the Bat Mitzvah ceremony is hardly different from that of Bar Mitzvah, except that it generally takes place on Friday night. Then the girl-initiate is called up to the pulpit, she recites the appropriate blessings in Hebrew, and chants the portion of the week from the Haftarah (the excerpts from the Prophets). Furthermore, in those congregations adhering to tradition, she cantillates the lines according to the ancient musical modes in which she, like the Bar Mitzvah boy, has been instructed especially for the occasion.

See also BAR-MITZVAH; CONFIRMATION; MUSICAL ACCENTS; TORAH-READING.

BATLAN (Hebrew s., meaning "idler"; pl. BATLANIM)

Like the luftmensch (the "man of air"), the batlan was a product of the stagnant and economically depressed conditions in East European ghetto life. He spent much of his waking time within the synagogue or the House of Study (Bet ha-Midrash). There he hopefully waited for any opportunity that might turn up for earning a few desperately needed coins, grateful for the welcome distraction from his enforced idleness that the constant group exercises of piety and Torah-study afforded him. Not least among his compensations were the human warmth and fellowship he found among his fellow Jews there, many of them also batlanim like himself. Strictly speaking, the batlan was a man without a trade or calling. Consequently, he had no social status.

Perpetually unemployed, he deteriorated by degrees, and thereby lost both his human dignity and his self-confidence. He found relief, however, in much futile talking and learned discussions. Were it not for certain essential but marginal services that he was occasionally asked to render the congregation, he would have been, in a literal sense, a superfluous man—a fifth wheel to the wagon. He considered himself lucky indeed if he was asked to join nine other worthy but maladjusted individuals like himself to constitute the Ten Batlanim of the synagogue, a customary institution since Rabbinic times. (With their regular attendance at services, the batlanim assured the presence of a minyan, the quorum of ten worshipers required for holding public prayer.) For this service, the batlan was paid a trifling but steady remuneration from the congregational treasury. Sometimes, if he was truly fortunate, he would also be "hired" to recite the mourner's Kaddish thrice daily for families left without a male survivor over Bar Mitzvah age. Or sometimes he would be paid to engage in daily group-study of the Mishnah in the Bet ha-Midrash in memory of someone who had died.

Immigrant peddler of suspenders and collar buttons on a Lower East Side street in New York, 1904.

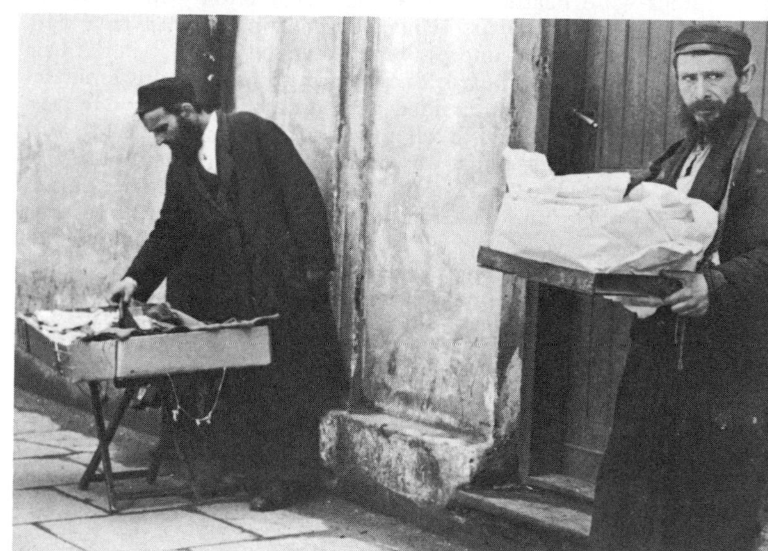

Street "merchants." Poland, pre-World War II. (R. Vishniak. Joint Distribution Committee.)

Jewish peddler. Hamburg, 18th century.

In more modern times, the "batlan" designation was also given to the misfit Torah scholar and yeshivah bachur (Talmudic student). Max Nordau, the famous European journalist and Zionist leader of pre-World War I days, also wished to include in this category of Talmudic misfits their secular equivalents among the many Jewish students found at European universities and in the peripheries of other intellectual areas. He noted ironically: "Among the Jews alone the delusion exists that a man can study without any money . . . working with the head without filling the stomach and without having to cover one's nakedness." True enough, commented Nordau, the batlan-intellectual undertook to do occasional jobs to preserve the spark of life in himself, but they were ill-paying jobs, like private tutoring. Because they consumed so much of his time, they left him little leisure and less tranquillity to apply himself systematically to his studies. So he usually ended as a half-baked intellectual, frustrated, and an embittered failure in the world.

BEARD

There is no question but that the average male Jew, in the course of several thousand years, steadfastly observed the Biblical injunction: "Ye shall not round the corners of your heads, neither shalt thou mar the corners of thy beard." (Leviticus 19:27.) Accordingly, he wore his beard full blown, without interfering in any way with its natural contours. Said the Talmudic Sages: "The adornment of a man's face is his beard." That was how God had intended it to be–one of the external signs for differentiating between a man and a woman.

It has been observed that adult male Semites in ancient times wore beards. Whoever has seen statuary in the round or in relief of the Assyrians and Babylonians must have carried away a vivid impression of "rounded corners" in the hair of both head and beard. These were modishly and effeminately set in "dips," or braided with ordered regularity. It was, therefore, to be able to tell apart Jews from non-Jews in physical appearance and to discourage any imitation by the former of the latter in their way of life, lest they progress gradually from cultural assimilation to outright religious apostasy, that the above-mentioned commandment was formulated.

While the folk-Jews, at all times, clung loyally to their revered and untrimmed patriarchal beards, there were upper-class assimilationists who broke readily with religious law and tradition in this respect, as in many others, in their eagerness to conform, chameleon-like, to the fashions of the Gentile world. On the frieze, (now in the British Museum) celebrating in sculptured relief Sennacherib's crushing victories over the Israelites, a number of aristocratic Jewish captives are depicted with fashionable Assyrian-style "rounded" heads and "rounded" abbreviated beards, both being exquisitely waved, trimmed, curled, and braided.

Certainly, not all peoples of antiquity wore beards. The Egyptians and the Hittites, for example, were clean shaven. Yet, although the Israelites were slaves in Egypt for centuries, they nevertheless did not follow the beardless example of their masters. The clean-shaven Greeks and Romans also had a positive distaste for beards in general and for untrimmed ones in particular. During the Hellenistic period, when they exerted the dominant political and cultural influence in the Mediterranean world, the Jewish beau monde, always opportunistic, hit upon certain devices by which to sidetrack the sacrosanct Biblical commandment and Rabbinic regulations concerning hair and beard, and Rabbinic law swayed by the force of Greek and Roman fashions among Jews, sought a graceful compromise. The Sages revised and formulated the commandment in this way: They forbade the removal of the hair from the face with a razor. Further, they ruled that it must not be plucked out with tweezers but must be cut off close to the roots.

Interpreting this ingeniously phrased law, the Jewish fashionables of Jerusalem and Alexandria averred that they were not violating the law if they clipped their beards close to their skin with some other cutting instrument than the razor. This set a precedent for the sophisticated Jews of medieval Germany, Italy, Spain, and France, they proceeded to clip their beards with scissors. To add irony to the situation, beginning with the thirteenth century, many Church and State authorities in Christian Europe ordered Jews living under their jurisdiction not to shave off their beards nor even to trim them but instead grow them full length so that they might be more easily recognized as Jews!

A Polish Jew. (Etching by Hermann Struck.)

During the seventeenth century, pumice stone and other depilatories were introduced. These, while legalistically avoiding the razor, nonetheless gave the persons using them a clean-shaven appearance. But these depilatories (which, curiously, are still being used today by some Orthodox men anxious to conform to the current clean-shaven fashion yet even more anxious to comply with the religious law) left the skin in a perpetually irritated state.

To the average enlightened Jew of our time, this matter would hardly seem to be one worthy of serious discussion, yet for centuries, in practically every generation, it served as a subject for heated controversy and even division in Jewish community life, especially in Eastern Europe. It has to be stressed, however, that the traditionalist point of view always prevailed. In Slavic lands, until the turn of the twentieth century, practically all Jews wore beards. They wore them full and untrimmed, as their forefathers had done in ancient Israel. It was quite unthinkable for any male adult to be without one. But ever since the Nazi slaughter of six million Jews, thousands of Jewish youths, shaken and bruised in their consciousness of being Jews, have been driven by their emotional insecurity to embrace an Ultra-Orthodoxy in which wearing beards, natural and untrimmed, is again a matter of no trifling consideration.

BEDIKAT CHAMETZ. *See* PASSOVER.

BEMA (BIMAH) (Greek, meaning "stage" or "speaker's tribunal")

Being considerably Hellenized, the Jews during the Roman period adopted both the word *bema* and the architectural feature it stood for from the Greeks. No doubt it must have had an even earlier historic origin among the Jews, but under another name. For instance, we read in the Book of Nehemiah (8:4-8) that when Ezra the Scribe stood before the returned exiles in the Temple court in Jerusalem and read to them from the Pentateuch, the raised platform on which he stood above the assembly in order that he might be seen and heard by all, was called a migdal (tower). This kind of rostrum was, it is indicated, also an architectural feature of the Second

Bema in wooden synagogue of Gwozdziec, Poland, 1640.

Bema in a wooden synagogue at Gombin, Poland. Erected 18th century. ABOVE

Bema in foreground, Ark of the Law in background. German synagogue, 17th century. CENTER

Temple court. But, when the Temple was no more, the bema in the interior of the synagogue became a commemorative symbol of the holy altar that had formerly stood there. And in place of the Temple altar to which sacrifices had formerly been brought, the bema served as the synagogical stage or platform, and here the Scroll of the Torah was unrolled for public cantillation of the weekly portion and of associated passages from the Haftarah (excerpts from the Prophets).

During the Middle Ages, the bema also served as a lectern from which the chazzan (cantor) could lead the prayer service, and the pulpit from which the preacher could deliver his sermon and the gabbai (the synagogogical treasurer) or shammes (the sexton) could make announcements of the contributions pledged for the support of the synagogue or other acts of benevolence by those "called up" for reading aloud from the Sefer Torah.

The bema may be described as a square or rectangular platform. Frequently, it has an ornamental curved front or back. Three steps or more elevate it above the floor-level of the synagogue. It is open on the sides in order to be visible to all, and sometimes has a cupola, supported by four or more posts or pillars, overhead. The whole is encircled by ornamental balustrades or railings made of wood, marble, or metal, with lamps fixed on each pillar to furnish bright illumination. Only two objects stand on the bema—the reading desk that is covered with a richly embroidered or appliquéd velvet cloth upon which is laid the Sefer Torah for public reading and a bench. At the upper end of the bema, three descending steps lead to the three ascending steps before the Ark. However, in many modern synagogues, both the bema and Ark are joined together to form one architectural unit, and the same platform serves both without the inconvenience of having to use steps between them.

Traditionally, the bema was erected in the center of the synagogue interior. The earliest mention of this location is found in the contemporary description of the Great Synagogue in Alexandria during the second century B.C.E. But, in time, other traditions also prevailed. During the sixteenth century, for example, the Cabalists decreed that the bema be built near the eastern (mizrach) wall of the synagogue, facing in the direction of Jerusalem. The Sefaradim of Spain, Portugal, and Italy preferred to put the bema at the western wall. In medieval Germany, the synagogue architecture, taking for its model the Gothic church, physically found no reason for placing the bema in a central position because that space was already utilized by the usual Gothic double-aisled arrangement of seats for the worshipers. Hence the bema became merely a raised platform or a cupola supported by columns, and it was erected on the side.

The earliest synagogues of Europe having been destroyed by the enemies of the Jews, the modern student of synagogue architectural styles can study a miniature in the British Museum in the so-called Sarajevo Haggadah, an exquisitely illuminated Hebrew manuscript produced in Northern Spain during the thirteenth century. In this miniature, the bema and not the Ark, as one might expect, constitutes the most distinguishing, and by implication perhaps also the most important, feature in the unknown artist's conception of the synagogue interior. Quite likely, this represented the prevailing view of medieval Spanish Jewry. Several centuries later (in the synagogues of Bohemia and Poland especially), the bema was treated by the architects as an independent unit. It consisted of a simple raised platform enclosed by iron grills or an iron cupola-like canopy with iron railings or a raised stone rostrum framed among four huge central piers which also served as supports for the ceiling vaults.

Most curiously, as all students of church architecture will recognize, the bema shows a close identity with the presbyterium in the Christian house of worship. The logic of this resemblance lies in the natural assumption that the primitive Christian Church, by virtue of its original Jewish character, adopted and later also adapted the bema together with other religious and architectural features of the synagogue such as the Perpetual Lamp, the institution of prayer, the reading from Scriptures, psalmody, and the sermon.

Not only in the presbyterium of the Christian church was the post-Biblical bema perpetuated, but also in the Mohammedan mosque, for Islam was, almost equally with Christianity, a "daughter" religion of Judaism and adopted not a few Jewish religious ideas, practices, and institutions, beginning with the seventh century. The bema in the mosque became the *al-mimbar* or *al-membra,* the Arabic equivalent for "pulpit." Subsequently, the Jews in Mohammedan lands used the derivative almemar (the East European Jews sometimes say almemar) to designate the bema.

See also SYNAGOGUE, THE; TORAH READING.

BENEDICTIONS. *See* CHILDREN, BLESSING OF; GRACE AFTER MEALS; HABDALAH; KADDISH; KIDDUSH; LIFE, JEWISH VIEW OF; MARRIAGE; PASSOVER; PRIESTLY BLESSING; RESURRECTION; SABBATH; SABBATH LIGHTS; SHIVA; SUCCOT; WEDDING CUSTOMS.

BENEVOLENCE, ACTS OF. *See* BURIAL RITES AND CUSTOMS; CHARITY; HOSPITALITY; HOSPITALS; LOANS, FREE; SICK, VISITING THE.

BENSCHEN. *See* GRACE AFTER MEALS.

BERIT MILAH. *See* CIRCUMCISION.

BET CHAYYIM. *See* CEMETERIES; TOMBSTONES.

BET CHOLIM. *See* HOSPITALS.

BET DIN (Hebrew, meaning "House of the Law"; thus, law court)

When the Jewish state was abolished by the Romans in 70 C.E. the Rabbinic Sage Yochanan ben Zakkai instituted the Bet Din in Yabneh. This was a religious supreme court which was intended to take the place of the defunct Jerusalem Sanhedrin (q. v.) that, in its final period, had been largely confined to issuing sterile decisions on purely religious matters.

The area of jurisdiction allowed the Bet Din by the Roman authorities was narrow, covering the areas of ritual and ceremony and certain secondary civil matters which were not considered to infringe upon the interests or the prestige of the imperial government. But under the courageous leadership of such Rabbinic eminences as Gamaliel II and Judah ha-Nasi (the compiler of the Mishnah), the Bet Din achieved a different and morally superior luster than had the more glittering Sanhedrin. Whereas the Sanhedrin had very often served as a pliant tool of Judea's foreign oppressors and of its own corrupt Hasmonean and Herodian kinglets, the integrity of the Bet Din soon enough was found by the Roman authorities to be too much of a stumbling block to their efficient suppression of the Jewish people. This was because, in effect, it had become one of the few existing instruments for the forging of Jewish national unity–the last thing Rome wanted. So the Roman authorities began to whittle down its judicial powers and create for it all kinds of restrictions and difficulties. No longer able to function properly, the Bet Din became moribund in the fourth century.

The functions of the Bet Din already had existed in the period of the Sanhedrin in three forms. It is noted in the Talmud: "At first, disputes in Israel were judged only by the court of seventy-one [Sanhedrin] in the Chamber of Hewn Stone [in the Temple area in Jerusalem], and other courts of twenty-three [for criminal cases] which were in the cities of the Land of Israel, and still other courts of three [for civil cases]." In subsequent times, the Bet Din consisted of a tribunal of three judges, sitting only in the larger Jewish centers. Why panels of three? "Judge not alone, for none may judge alone save One [i.e., God]," was one of the sayings of the Mishnah Fathers. During the Middle Ages, most Jewish communities in Europe, being relatively poor and small, were forced to ignore this tradition (of having three judges) from purely practical considerations. They had only one rabbi to constitute the court.

It was in the late Talmudic period that a judicial functionary (called in Hebrew *dayyan*) first appeared on the Jewish scene. He was a trained legal-religious specialist who served as a communal judge. To qualify for his post, he had to be proven a thorough Torah scholar and well versed in all the intricacies of Jewish law. He also had to enjoy a high reputation in his community for intellectual objectivity and fairness. The calling of dayyan was followed in Jewish life until fairly recent times, probably because–to cite one explanation–the exercise of limited self-rule by the Jewish ghetto-communities in Christian and Mohammedan lands made the religious authority by the Bet Din possible. This was particularly true of that semi-autonomous Jewish communal organization called the *kahal* which flourished in Poland beginning with the sixteenth century.

In the more or less lay society of today, where there exists in some countries, as in the United States, a separation of church and state, the Bet Din no longer finds much practical reason for functioning. Nevertheless, many Orthodox Jews still make use of the Bet Din, but mostly for those civil matters which in Jewish law have also a religious character, such, for example, as marriage and divorce (it must be remembered that all Jews who wish to follow the religious tradition and practice are obliged to contract a religious marriage). The Bet Din that was established in 1958 by the (Orthodox) Rabbinical Council of America was planned to serve as "a clearing house within the Orthodox Jewish community for rendering decisions in the areas of marriage, divorce, family status and mixed marriages."

Anachronistically, there still survives today the old Jewish practice of submitting personal grievances to a Din Torah (Law of the Torah) for a trial according to Jewish law. It sometimes happens that if a dispute arises between two strictly observing Jews who are opposed to airing their differences in a civil court, one summons the other to a Din Torah before an Orthodox rabbi who is asked to judge between them, but only according to Jewish law and tradition.

In a broader area and in the large cities there function today quite a number of Jewish Boards of Arbitration. These operate informally as tribunals in civil disputes. Unlike parties in a suit before the Din Torah, Jews who apply to these "courts" for judgment or mediation are not necessarily Orthodox. It is merely because of a historic conditioning over many centuries that some Jews prefer to settle their disputes privately–so to speak, "within the family" rather than to air them before what, in former times, only too often proved to be hostile tribunals of non-Jews.

See also SANHEDRIN.

BET HA-KNESSET. *See* SYNAGOGUE, THE.

BET HA-MIKDASH. *See* TEMPLE, THE.

BET HA-TALMUD. *See* BET HA-MIDRASH.

BET HA-MIDRASH (Hebrew, meaning "House of Study"; sometimes also called BET HA-TALMUD)

The obligatory and universal requirement for all male Jews to study the Torah began with the religious revival initiated by Ezra and the Scribes (Soferim) in the fifth century B.C.E. This objective was rigorously pursued with, of course, an ever accelerated tempo and knowledgeability by the Jews in Judea, as well as in Babylonia and other Jewish foreign settlements. It was logical that religious-educational institutions should spring up for the systematic study, analysis, and discussion of the precepts of the Torah and of their practical application to the problems of daily living. In addition to the elementary school (or Talmud Torah) and the yeshibah (or academy for higher Torah-learning), the establishment of the Bet ha-Midrash, probably during the second century B.C.E., followed in response to the general need for adult studies which, for pious Jews, soon began to constitute a perpetual and ardent preoccupation that usually came to an end only the day they died.

The Bet ha-Midrash was a public House of Study. No Jewish community of any size, if it was concerned with religious, cultural, and group interests, could afford to be without one–or sometimes several. Medieval Jewish custom required that the Bet ha-Midrash be kept open night and day. And every Jew, regardless of whether he was a native of the community in which it was established or merely a homeless stranger, or what his station in life was or what the extent of his intellectual equipment might be, was welcome to enter and to pursue in it the study of the Torah.

But this extraordinary development in the democracy of Jewish learning did not spring up all at once. In early Rabbinic times, many an acrimonious verbal duel took place between the democratic and the aristocratic proponents of education. Most epochal, from a historic point of view, was the debate that raged for generations between the opposing Rabbinic schools of Hillel and Shammai. Shammai and his adherents were fiercely opposed to popular education; they demanded that only an elite of the well-to-do and the intellectually endowed should be admitted to the House of Study. The School of Hillel just as militantly upheld the opposite view–that the Bet ha-Midrash should be open to all, regardless of station in life, material possessions, or intellectual qualifications. Hillel and his supporters were merely following a revered tradition that had been affirmed by the earlier religious teachers, the "Men of the Great Assembly" (*see* SCRIBES; TALMUD, THE). They claimed that this tradition had been

Expounding Torah in the Bet ha-Midrash (House of Study) in pre-Hitler times in Poland. (Painting by M. Minkowski. The Jewish Museum.)

transmitted from one generation to the next by the wise men of Israel, starting with Moses and the Prophets, and, finally, had become a rallying point for the pious in early Rabbinic Judaism. "Raise up many disciples," exhorted the Mishnah Fathers.

The disciples of the School of Shammai, stemming largely from the upper class, argued, like so many advocates of restricted higher education today in Western countries, that "only those who are wise, humble, and of reputable, well-to-do parents should be taught the Law." For, they insisted, only such superior individuals would be able to profit from Torah study. The equalitarian Hillelites countered to this: "All, without exception, should share in this privilege, inasmuch as many transgressors in Israel, when brought close to the Torah, became righteous, pious, and even perfect men."

In the end, the democratic view of Hillel and his disciples prevailed, and it became a fixed and incontrovertible tradition in Jewish collective life through all the centuries.

In the Bet ha-Midrash, the pious gathered to listen to the exposition of Torah by learned scholars. This consisted of lectures of an academic character (more popular informative discourses and inspirational sermons for the less knowledgeable were delivered in the synagogue itself on Sabbath afternoons). There were also study groups presided over by learned men, and these groups applied themselves ardently to the exploration of the deeper meanings of the Biblical text and of the Oral Tradition of the Mishnah. Without a doubt, it was the influence during Hellenistic times of Greek philosophy, with its strong emphasis on logic, that led to the development of an analytical and critical method of reasoning in Talmudic intellectual discussion. But Rabbinic logic, following fanciful rules of its own, was far less precise and persuasive than the balanced logic of the Greeks. The vagaries of Talmudic logic often surprise and baffle the sophisticated modern reader. However, most of the time the Rabbinic teachers are really impressive with a wisdom that springs from deep reflection and a practicality that can be derived only from a commonsense and down-to-earth approach to life, people, and all their problems and ways.

The esteem in which the House of Study was held by Jews in every age may be inferred from that Rabbinic law which states that, while it is permissible to transform a synagogue into a House of Study, *to do the reverse is forbidden.* In the ascending scale of religious values, the study of the Torah was placed even higher than the recitation of prayer. This was because it was recognized as constituting the cement that held together the national-religious life of the Jews, and it was always regarded as such. Therefore, these words of encouragement from the Talmud: "He who proceeds from the synagogue to the House of Study–that is, from the prayer service to the study of the Torah–he will be privileged to behold God's majesty! Thus says the Psalmist: 'They go from strength to strength.'"

The man who was the first to arrive at the House of Study and who was also the last to leave it, was deemed the most pious and, therefore, most worthy of grace. Furthermore, those devoted wives who with rejoicing sent their husbands off to the House of Study and who upon their return hastened out to welcome them home with warmth and appreciation–of these women the Rabbis said: They should be honored as the most meritorious in Israel.

Beginning with the thirteenth century, when Jewish existence in Europe had turned harsh and somber and Jews were forcibly confined within dank ghetto walls, the combination of poverty and the restrictions of living space led many

Jewish communities to fuse the functions of the House of Study with those of the synagogue and the Talmud Torah, sometimes even housing all three in one building. This may explain why, in medieval Germany, the combined synagogue, House of Study, and Talmud Torah was given the noncommittal name of *Judenschule* by Christians. Soon the Jews themselves began using that term: going to the synagogue for prayers was called "going to *Schule*," and in latter-day Yiddish, the word became *shul*.

The unstable Jewish group existence, brought to a sorry pass by persecution, legal and economic restrictions, expulsions, and massacre, made the House of Study also a House of Refuge for the numerous uprooted and bewildered Jews moving about unceasingly in flight from their enemies or in search of new roots. It gave asylum to thousands of footloose wanderers and involuntary beggars who had neither home nor money, nor any means of livelihood in view. But at least here, among their own, they no longer felt like strangers and outcasts. Sometimes they found material assistance, however small, in addition to the warmth of "kinfolk." And in the familiar bookish setting of the House of Study and the synagogue, institutions attuned to those verities all believing Jews have revered as eternal and redemptive, they succeeded in reviving the moral strength and the hope with which to pick up again and again the thread of continuity for their lives.

See also TALMID CHACHAM; TALMUD, THE; TORAH STUDY; YESHIBAH; YESHIVAH BACHUR.

BET OLAM. *See* CEMETERIES; TOMBSTONES.

BIBLE, THE

The People of the Book. The nineteenth-century historian of the Jewish religion, Leopold Zunz, once gave a felicitous characterization of the Bible. He said it had served as "the portable fatherland of the Jews." This was no exaggeration. Approximately the same idea had already been expressed nine centuries before by the rabbinical savant Saadia, the Gaon (Rector) of the Yeshibah of Sura: "Israel is a people only by virtue of the Torah." That view still is held by devout traditionalists.

This phenomenon of a Scripture that combines in itself a philosophy of religious belief, worship, law, and guide for moral conduct, and which, in the not-too-remote past, embraced and governed the totality of Jewish life, was observed with awe by Heinrich Heine, the great poet of Germany. Himself a forthright freethinker, he nevertheless could not restrain his wonderment:

> The Jews may console themselves for having lost Jerusalem, and the Temple, and the Ark of the Covenant, and the golden vessels, and the precious things of Solomon. Such a loss is merely insignificant in comparison with the Bible–the imperishable treasure which they have rescued. If I do not err, it was Mohammed who named the Jews "The People of The Book"–a name which has remained theirs to the present day and which is deeply characteristic. A book is their fatherland, their treasure, their ruler, their bliss, and their bane. They live within the peaceful boundaries of this book. Here they exercise their inalienable rights. Here they can neither be driven along nor despised. . . . Absorbed within the confines of this book, they observed little of the changes which went on about them in the actual world: nations arose and perished; states bloomed and disappeared; revolutions stormed forth out of the soil; but they sat bowed down over their book and noticed nothing of the wild tumult of the times which passed over their heads.

Without the Bible–in its unique Jewish sense of "Torah," it has been considered by the devout as redemptive when realized as a *total way of life*–it is impossible to imagine that the Jews could have survived as a distinctive people or as a religious fellowship for so many centuries and through so many vicissitudes. Inexhaustible have been the speculations of the

King David playing on his harp. Miniature in Northern French style. From a 13th-century Hebrew manuscript. (The British Museum.)

Moses silences the Red Sea during the Exodus from Egypt. (From a German machzor, 13th or 14th century.)

historians concerning the circumstances that made the Bible and, most particularly, the Torah (the Five Books of Moses) the total preoccupation of the Jews.

How the folk itself conceived of its Torah-dedication is illustrated by a remarkable legend that is related in the Talmud. As the Israelites stood assembled at the foot of Mount Sinai to enter into their solemn Convenant with God, there suddenly descended from heaven and remained suspended miraculously over their heads, an apparition of *The Book* and, beside it, one of *The Sword*. "Choose!" commanded the Bat Kol (the "Daughter of the Voice" [of God]) from Heaven. "You can have one or the other, but not both–either The Book or The Sword! If you choose The Book, you must renounce The Sword. Should your choice be The Sword, then The Book will perish."

The Rabbinic weaver of this morality then concluded exultantly that the Israelites made the most memorable decision in the history of mankind: They chose *The Book!* "Thereupon, the Holy One–blessed be He!–said to Israel: 'If you keep what is written in The Book you will be delivered from The Sword, but should you fail to keep it, in the end The Sword will destroy you!'"

Grim commentary to this ultimatum by God is the fact that in the history of the Jews, so largely written in blood and suffering, it was their very devotion to The Book which so frequently led to their destruction by The Sword, a weapon which not they but their enemies wielded.

What Is the Bible? Actually and contrary to the popular misconception of it–the Bible is not just *one* book. It is a "library" or collection of sacred Jewish writings. In Hebrew it is called *Tanach*. That is because the three Hebrew consonants standing for *T N CH*, which make up the word in abbreviation, represent the three divisions of the Scriptures: *T* for *Torah* (the Pentateuch or Five Books of Moses), *N* for *Nebiim* (Prophets), and *CH* for *Chetubim* (Writings). Thus: TNCH. The word is pronounced, when the appropriate vowel sounds are added, as *Tanach*.

The Tanach derived its name in English, "Bible," from the Greek word *biblia*, which means "books." In the calculation of the Jewish Scriptural tradition, differing from that of the Christian–in both instances following a curious sort of editorial arithmetic–there are twenty-four separate *biblia* in the Bible, although by actual count there are thirty-nine. And it is most important that they should be thought of as such: in the *plural sense*. That is because they were not all written at one time nor even in one particular culture-period of Jewish history. For that matter, they were not collated by a single compiler nor even revised by one editor. In fact, the reverse is true. Modern Biblical scholarship, at its most objective level and employing reasonably scientific methods of investigation, using the tools provided by comparative studies in religion, archaeology, folklore, ethnology, philology, and paleography, has proven quite persuasively, even if not always conclusively, that the component books of the Bible were produced over a vast time-span going back to mist-shrouded antiquity, and that they took on definite literary shape from the period beginning either in the tenth or ninth century B.C.E. Furthermore, the stamp of different ideological and stylistic hands is strongly in evidence in the Hebrew texts.

Much of the material pertaining to religious beliefs, moral values, laws, and social outlook found in the Pentateuch, which constitutes the core of the Bible, represents a superimposed projection into the remote and hallowed past of their own more advanced views by the Scriptural editors, chroniclers, moralists, and legists–Ezra the Scribe and the "Men of the Great Assembly" (*see* SCRIBES, TALMUD, THE)–who lived from the fifth to second centuries B.C.E. The seventeenth-century philosopher Spinoza even held that the Pentateuch had been written (or rewritten) by Ezra the Scribe and then attributed by him to the incomparable lawgiver, Moses–ostensibly because he hoped thereby to achieve a greater authority for the work among the people.

For this reason, the unpracticed reader of the Bible should guard against becoming unduly baffled or disconcerted when he discovers–as in Job, Ecclesiastes, and Proverbs–conceptual and qualitative differences and some striking contradictions in thought, symbolism, feeling, style, and idiom. The most knowledgeable opinion among scholars today is that

Palimpsest page of Bible from the Cairo Genizah. Upper writing is Hebrew, 11th century. Lower writing is Greek translation by Aquila, 6th century.

Vatican manuscript of the Greek Septuagint version of the Book of Exodus.

בראשית

ברא אלהים את השמים ואת הארץ: והארץ היתה תהו ובהו
וחשך על פני תהום ורוח אלהים מרחפת על פני המים: ויאמר
אלהים יהי אור ויהי אור: וירא אלהים את האור כי טוב ויבדל
אלהים בין האור ובין החשך: ויקרא אלהים לאור יום ולחשך קרא
לילה ויהי ערב ויהי בקר יום אחד: פ
ויאמר אלהים יהי רקיע בתוך המים ויהי מבדיל בין מים למים:
ויעש אלהים את הרקיע ויבדל בין המים אשר מתחת לרקיע ובין
המים אשר מעל לרקיע ויהי כן: ויקרא אלהים לרקיע שמים ויהי
ערב ויהי בקר יום שני: פ
ויאמר אלהים יקוו המים מתחת השמים אל מקום אחד ותראה
היבשה ויהי כן: ויקרא אלהים ליבשה ארץ ולמקוה המים קרא
ימים וירא אלהים כי טוב: ויאמר אלהים תדשא הארץ דשא עשב

First page of the Bible printed in Naples in 1492 by Joshua Solomon ben Israel Nathan Soncino.

Hyksos fortress, c. 1700 B.C.E., excavated near Tel Aviv in 1951. (Israel Government Information Service.)

Title-decoration of a 16th-century Bible, reading "Chumash" ("Pentateuch").

Parchment Pentateuch in Hebrew, bearing a note that the copyist was Yehoshua ben Eliyahu, the Sofer of Ochsenfurt, Germany, and that it was prepared for Rabbi Chaim, the son of "Rabbi Chaim the Martyr." Brussels, 1310.

Lot's wife turned into a pillar of salt. (From the Sarajevo Haggadah, 14th century.)

some of the books in the Bible, and most particularly the Five Books of Moses, underwent extensive and continuous recasting, reformulation, interpolation, and revision until early in the second century B.C.E., when the last of the "writings" –Ecclesiastes, Esther, and Daniel–were selected.

To further illustrate this point: the Book of Psalms, for example, constitutes not the single creation of the poet-king David, as Jewish tradition has stubbornly claimed in the face of internal evidence (found within the text itself), but an anthology of hymns composed by a considerable number of Hebrew liturgical poets who varied in the degree of their literary skill and inspiration. This explains too why the Psalms as a whole do not represent a unified religious-ethical philosophy and why they are not on one level of literary culture and sophistication. They, in fact, represent in poetic form all the stages of religious and cultural development of the Jewish people over a time-span of perhaps eight centuries, most probably beginning with David the Psalmist.

As regards the Book of Isaiah, modern Biblical criticism has conclusively proven by internal evidence, both philological and historical, that it was composed not by Isaiah ben Amoz (eithth century B.C.E.) alone, but, beginning with Chapter 40, by another prophet, also called Isaiah, who for convenience is called the "Second Isaiah" or "Deutero-Isaiah." Nothing is known of him except that he probably lived in Babylonian Captivity during the sixth century B.C.E. But the loftiness of his sentiments and the beauty of his poetic eloquence make him worthy of being coupled with Isaiah ben Amoz.

The priestly compilers of the Tanach–Jewish tradition refers to them as having been Ezra the Scribe and his continuators: the 120 luminaries who, over a period of about two centuries, until *c.* 200 B.C.E., comprised the "Men of the Great Assembly" or–"Men of the Great Synagogue" arranged it into three main divisions. This ordering has remained unaltered for at least two thousand years:

I. THE PENTATEUCH (in Hebrew CHUMASH)

This division consists of the Five Books of Moses which Jews call "the Torah": (1) Genesis (in Hebrew: Bereshit); (2) Exodus (Shemot); (3) Leviticus (Vayikra); (4) Numbers (Ba-Midbar); (5) Deuteronomy (Debarim).

II. THE PROPHETS (NEBIIM)

The Prophets are arranged in two distinct categories:

1) The "Earlier Prophets" consist of the following writings: Joshua, Judges, I and II Samuel, and I and II Kings. To the modern reader, the inclusion in this prophetic classification of those works which are preponderantly chronicles, seems hardly tenable.

2) The "Later Prophets" actually comprise the authentic writings of the Prophets as such, but they, too, are confusingly arranged in two categories: the "Major" Prophets (of whom there are three) and the "Minor" Prophets (who number 12). However, this editorial separation by the Men of the Great Assembly when they closed the Biblical canon by no means implies the degree of importance accorded the Prophets; "major" merely describes the longer texts and "minor," the shorter ones. The Major Prophets are (1) Isaiah, (2) Jeremiah, and (3) Ezekiel; the Minor Prophets are (1) Hosea, (2) Joel, (3) Amos, (4) Obadiah, (5) Jonah, (6) Micah, (7) Nahum, (8) Habakkuk, (9) Zephaniah, (10) Haggai, (11) Zechariah, and (12) Malachi.

III. THE [HOLY] WRITINGS (CHETUBIM OR KETUBIM)

Sometimes these works are called by their Greek name, Hagiographa (Holy Writings), or "the remainder of the Sacred Writings." They comprise a miscellany of literary compositions–two "Wisdom Books," a psalter, an anthology of love songs, a religious-national elegy in verse, a bucolic romance, an apocalypse, a philosophical-moralistic epic, and four chronicles–(1) Psalms (in Hebrew: Tehillim); (2) Proverbs (Mishleh); (3) Job; (4) Song of Songs (Shir ha-Shirim); (5) Ruth; (6) Lamentations (Echah); (7) Ecclesiastes (Kohelet); (8) Esther (also called the Megillah or Scroll of Esther); (9) Daniel (who is actually a prophet but for some reason was placed in this division); (10) Ezra; (11) Nehemiah; and (12) I and II Chronicles.

THE PENTATEUCH

Torah: More Than "Law." A widespread misconception exists among many Jews–and among a great number of Christians as well–that the proper translation for "Torah" is "Law." This error was most likely an inadvertent one originally, no doubt the fault of the Jewish translators in Alexandria in the third century B.C.E. who prepared the Greek version of the Bible, called the *Septuagint*. Probably because of the predilection for the law fostered in them by their Hellenistic cultural environment, they rendered the Hebrew word-concept incompletely, so that it emerged as "Law." And inasmuch as the Septuagint version of the Scriptures was used almost universally by the Jews outside of Judea and the Aramaic-speaking regions in the Greco-Roman world –for few Jews there knew any Hebrew or even Aramaic (Targum)–it was natural that the translation of Torah as "Law" should have been entered in Jewish post-Biblical writings composed in Greek or translated from Hebrew into the Greek language. These included, besides the books of the rabbinical philosopher Philo of Alexandria (*c.* 20 B.C.E.–40 C.E.) and the philo-Roman historian Josephus (37–105 C.E.), the Jewish writings that traditionally have been classified as Apocrypha (q.v.) and Pseudepigrapha (q.v.). And since the Christian Gospels and related works in the New Testament were originally written in Greek but followed the textual authority of the Greek Septuagint Bible instead of the Hebrew original, it stands to reason that their writers, too, equated the Hebrew "Torah" with the Greek "Law." Thus, in the most natural way, this concept entered into the preachments and writings of the Apostolic Fathers, and from them, as was inevitable, into the nomenclature of all languages of Christendom, where it has remained unchanged to this day.

Had the Torah merely comprised a legal code (it is often referred to, erroneously, as "the Mosaic Code"), paralleling in its content such other codes as the Code of Hammurabi, Justinian's Corpus Juris Civilis, and the Code of Napoleon, it would be hard to understand how it could have won the enduring and passionate devotion of the Jewish people when such devotion so often culminated in martyrdom. Obviously, then, the Torah had to be something *far more* than a dry inventory of laws, statutes, ordinances, and regulations to have aroused such a powerful moral and emotional response in the Jews.

It is undeniably true that the "Law" is the dominant and most influential elements among the several components of the Torah. The 613 laws, commandments, and ordinances that were found listed in it by the Rabbinic Sages obviously were intended by Moses and other anoymous lawgivers to meet all the requirements and exigencies possible–whether doctrinal, ceremonial, institutional, moral, economic, or social –in the total experience of man living in that uniquely Jewish, God-governed society of ancient times, the theocracy. Nevertheless, the concept of Torah among Jews is much wider and runs deeper than just "Law"; in its complete etymological meaning, "Torah" also connotes "doctrine," "instruction," and "guidance." Even the most cursory paging through the Pentateuch will show that the Torah attempts to be an all-embracing inspirational guide to belief and worship, and to cover all the ramifications of individual and social conduct. It is, therefore, an oversimplification to think of Torah as being merely "Law." The Torah is also a genealogical chronicle of Israel's beginnings and includes the biographies of its illustrious ancestors and early leaders. It is, in addition, a fervent preachment: It perpetually teaches and moralizes. Tirelessly, it exhorts the individual Israelite, as well as the entire collective of Israel, to eschew wrongdoing and to turn to the ways of truth, righteousness, mercy, and justice, in imitation of God's own attributes; to abandon the worship of idols and to find the living God in the practice of the precept "Love thy neighbor as thyself," which, as Rabbi Akiba said in the second century, is the central principle of the Jewish religion.

Modern Biblical Criticism. For devout Jews, the Torah has always towered over all of life and all creation as an immutable and eternal testimony to the will of God. For them, every word in the Biblical text shimmers with the incandescence of truth as it had been revealed by God himself to Moses on Mount Sinai; they read it in its literal and precise sense. If the text said something was so—that was the way it was! Was it an incident that involved the supernatural? Was it the breathless recounting of a miracle? Was it an unaccountable inconsistency and contradiction, an irreconcilable confusion in sequence, an unconvincing calculation in chronology? What did it matter? Nothing was too wondrous for the Creator of Heaven and Earth to accomplish. Therefore, the believing Jew *knew* that every individual mentioned in the Five Books of Moses had actually lived, and what was said about him or her was indisputably true. In fact, it was unthinkable that even a single word in the Torah should be exposed to challenge or doubt by the frivolous, the curious, or the skeptical.

For countless centuries it was a fixed and hallowed tradition that Moses was the sole author of the Torah—the Five Books of Moses. But for a long time now, informed Jewish scholarship has rejected this notion as being utterly untenable. The Biblical scholar Dr. Solomon Schechter once illustrated the dilemma in logic that had to be faced by the unyielding Scriptural traditionalists. He ironically observed that Moses could hardly have written the Five Books unless he also recounted the details of his own death and burial! The Bible did not lend itself to such an unrealistic premise, for it had stated in forthright terms (suggesting the passage of centuries since Moses) and as a complete refutation of any such impossible claim: "So Moses the servant of the Lord died there in the land of Moab. . . . And he was buried in the valley in the land of Moab . . . and no man knoweth his sepulchre unto this day. . . . And there hath not arisen a prophet since in Israel like unto Moses, whom the Lord knew face to face." (Deuteronomy 35:5-10.)

It should not pass without notice, however, that to correct this oversight, another far less venerable tradition arose which blandly credited the authorship of Moses' obituary to his disciple and successor, Joshua!

Whereas the other nineteen "books" in the Bible were revered in varying degree as having been divinely inspired, it was the Torah-Pentatuech that was first elevated to the supreme height of holiness. It constituted the primary and immutable source of the Jewish religion and way of life. For twenty-four centuries—ever since 444 B.C.E., when Ezra the Scribe had promulgated it as the Scriptures and, together with the priests and Levites, had taught and explained it to the people assembled before the Water-Gate of the Temple on Mount Zion—the Jews had faithfully followed the lonely but certain road that their ancestors had charted for them: "to walk in God's Torah which was given by Moses, the servant of God, and to fulfill all the commandments . . ."

Pool of Hezekiah (Pool of Siloam). (Sketch by Otto H. Bacher, 1887.)

Colossal figures of Ramses II, "the Pharaoh of the Exodus," at the entrance to the rock temple of Abusimbel, 13th century B.C.E.

Mount Sinai—"the Mount of the Lord"—where, according to the Bible, Israel accepted the Torah as its way of life and inheritance.

Believing Jews always regarded the Torah with awe as well as with love and rapture. They revered it, above all, as the repository of all truth; they declared it to be perfect, unalterable, and everlasting, for had it not been revealed by God directly to Moses for the guidance of Israel, in righteousness and for its ultimate redemption?

It stands to reason that the conclusions of objective Biblical scholarship today are receiving scant recognition or sympathy from those devout Jews who still hold tenaciously to the traditional view of the immutability of the Torah and the certainty that Moses himself wrote it at the dictation of God.

One fundamental consideration should enter into any objective appraisal of the Torah-Pentateuch, whether it be of its literary materials, its doctrines, ceremonial institutions and rites, or of its ethical and social value-systems. It is this: that ever since history was first recorded, it constituted a body of *continuously growing and developing* Scripture; it did not receive its final revision and authoritative imprimatur from Ezra the Scribe until 444 B.C.E.

At first—whatever unverifiable materials the early Scriptures may have consisted of, or whether they had first appeared in written form merely as notations of cherished and long-remembered Oral Traditions of bygone ages—they most definitely responded to the special conditions and problems of life in the tribalistic Israelite society. This was a way of life that, from all existing evidence, had an uninvolved nomadic-pastoral character. Certainly, many of the advanced laws included in the Pentateuch could have had no factual kinship to this primitive social organization in which marriage by capture, the blood-feud, and the *lex talionis* (the eye-for-an-eye law of retaliation) prevailed. But undoubtedly, during the subsequent historic period in the settled agricultural economy that followed the conquest of Canaan, life grew more complex. The Bible offers evidence that the new conditions became troubling to the religious leaders of Israel, as they did, indeed, to the Prophets during the First Commonwealth. Presumably, they had found the existing and much older Scriptural texts, laws, and moral teachings entirely inadequate and outmoded.

This hypothesis may be deduced from the fact that the Five Books of Moses are what one may describe as a literary palimpsest—one layer superimposed on the other. In these, enlightened ideas, attitudes, laws, and preachments—some of which clearly could have arisen only in advanced post-Exilic times, during the existence of the Second Temple—are found jostling earlier and more backward ones. On the surface, these differing laws and values, being indiscriminately thrown together, are hardly distinguishable one from the other, since

Illumination from a parchment Pentateuch manuscript, copied in 951 by a sofer (scribe) for a Rabbi Nathan and an Elder, Isaac ben Joshua. (Leningrad Library.)

The ziggurat, or Babylonian tower-in-stages, which recalls the Tower of Babel mentioned in the Bible.

A group of Israelites (or Canaanites or some other Semitic-language-speaking migrants) entering Egypt. Detail from a wall-painting in an Egyptian tomb at Beni-Hasan, XII Dynasty, c. 1900 B.C.E.

there is no indication in the Biblical text of their chronological emergence in Jewish history. Yet modern critical scholarship has found other means for determining such matters.

Nonetheless, the history of the composition of the Bible, and especially of the Pentateuch, whatever the ingenious theories that have been spun about it, still remains nebulous and inconclusive, the Higher Biblical Criticism to the contrary. The amazing diversity possible in "scientific" conclusions and interpretations was once satirized by Solomon Schechter (himself no mean hand at Biblical criticism), thus: "Twenty-two German universities and half a dozen English universities have issued their Commentary on Isaiah, each different from the other. What a delight it would be to have Isaiah rise from the dead, and tell us what he actually meant by the passages."

Modern Jews differ considerably in their historic conceptions of as well as in their interpretations of the Bible. The variations depend on denominational bias and philosophy, and these, in turn, depend on whether one is Ultra-Orthodox, Chasidic, Neo-Chasidic, Modern Orthodox, Conservative, Liberal, agnostic, or outright secularist.

That there must be a certain measure of truth in the tradition that Moses composed the Five Books of Moses, goes without saying; the folk-memory—even if it often exaggerates romantically—at times can be more precise and reliable than a written text, which, often enough, has been tampered with. This is strongly indicated by a categorical declaration in Pirke Abot (The Chapters of the Fathers), that treatise of the Mishnah which is a record of the Oral Traditions of the Jewish religion, wherein the transmission of the Torah is charted in this "genealogical" descent: "Moses received the Torah on Sinai, and handed it down to Joshua; Joshua to the Elders; the Elders to the Prophets; and the Prophets handed it down to the Men of the Great Assembly . . ." etc. Yet, notwithstanding this authoritative Oral Tradition, no claim whatsoever is found anywhere in the Pentateuch that God revealed *all* of the 613 precepts and commandments directly to Moses. Probably because of this singular omission as well as for other cogent reasons, the celebrated commentator of the Bible and poet-scholar of Toledo, Abraham ibn Ezra (1093–1167), cast a shadow upon the reliability of this tradition, and he was the first to do so.

A plainspoken Protestant Biblical scholar, Millar Burrows, has put the matter quite bluntly: ""What we really need, after all, is not to defend the Bible but to understand it." This is a difficult prescription of intellectual self-discipline for those to take who habitually have regarded the Torah with worshipful awe as being the repository of immutable truth and prophecy, and who have relied upon it to guide their fragile bark of faith safely through the shoals and reefs of personal, familial, and societal relations.

There is no question but that the Pentateuch (and the same would also hold true of a number of other writings in the Bible) was *rewritten* probably as much, if not more, than it was *written*. The experts, whether rightly or wrongly, assume that the *written* text (as we know it) dates from the ninth to the second centuries B.C.E., and to the knowledgeable reader, it is a curiously composite and many layered record of ancient Jewish civilization.

Open-minded scholars and teachers of religion of all faiths have tried to see the Pentateuch "in the round," observing it from every conceivable perspective. At the same time that it remains, for many of them, a document of spiritual and moral grandeur, having great historical and cultural interest, they cannot help but recognize that, in a manner of speaking, it is also an omnium-gatherum of literary materials. In many places there are contradictory views and values, making for inconsistency and irreconcilability. This embarrassment logically stems from the haphazard juxtaposition of laws and teachings that were pieced together, pastiche-like, sometimes arbitrarily, in folkloristic fashion. They were the products which had been transmitted culturally for many centuries, had been written by different hands, and represented the thinking and value-systems of many diverse minds and historic culture periods. In short, the whole is a fabulous overlay, one upon the other, of different Scriptural writings.

The Bible itself does not attempt to conceal this fact. It specifically refers to its borrowings from even more ancient Scriptural sources, such as the Book of Yashar, mentioned in II Samuel 1:18, and the Book of the Wars of the Lord, mentioned in Numbers 21:14. While the contents of the Book of the Wars of the Lord remain unknown, there exists a persuasive explanation in Rabbinic tradition about the Book of Yashar. Chiyya bar Abba, the third-century Rabbinical scholar, asks in the Talmud: "What is meant by the Book of Yashar?" He answers in catechizing fashion: "It is the book of Abraham, Isaac, and Jacob, they being called 'righteous [in Hebrew: *yesharim,* of which the singular is *yashar*].' "

Of course, neither of these works nor any of the other "lost" and discarded books that are mentioned in other parts of the Bible, in Josephus' writings, and in the Talmud are any longer in existence. But it is certain that much of their materials, although without attribution, were utilized by the latter-day Biblical compilers, especially Ezra, for the final fashioning of the Pentateuch.

It can safely be regarded as axiomatic by the student of cultural history that laws and religious value-systems do not spring all of a sudden full-blown from the minds of single individuals—even of geniuses. In the ancient world, it took countless generations of accrued creative effort on the part of a people to crystallize its ideas before they could even be written down. The normal process of cultural diffusion of influences from other ethnic groups went on at the same time.

That there are many strands from which the textual fabric of the Pentateuch was woven may be seen in the treatment given in it to the Ten Commandments. The obvious fact is that *there are two* and not a single version of the Decalogue. One is given in Exodus 20:1-14; the other is presented in Deuteronomy 5:6-18. It is assumed that Ezra himself incorporated both of these texts for reasons unknown today. He had apparently extracted them from two different versions of the Book of the Covenant. The two vary only slightly in content but considerably in language. The curious discrepancies in the two texts always created an impasse in logic for those rigid but erudite traditionalists who insisted that every word, even every letter, in the Ten Commandments had been revealed by God to Moses "face to face," and then had been written down "with the finger of God." (*See* TEN COMMANDMENTS.)

There is more than a tinge of irony for Jews in the thought that the first Biblical scholar to make the discovery that the Pentateuch was the composite product of *at least two* different documents was a French Roman Catholic, Jean Astruc (1684–1766), who thereby became the founder of modern Biblical criticism. He had arrived at his hypothesis in an interesting way. Nonplused by the obviously unnecessary repetitions and confused chronology in the narrative portions of the Book of Genesis, he was even more puzzled by the fact that two entirely different names were being used to designate God. One was the ineffable Name, *YHVH,* which is pronounced "Yahveh" (in 1518 it was written for the first time as "Jehovah" by Peter Gallatin, the confessor of Pope Leo X). The other was the odd plural rendering *Elohim* (*s. El*)—for God. (*See* GOD, NAMES OF.)

From the appearance in the text of these two different names, Astruc deduced that there had been effected a fusion of two separate Scriptural documents in Genesis, most probably by Ezra the Scribe. Wherever the name Elohim appeared, Astruc ascribed the passage in which it was set to the documents that he named "Elohist," and the passages in which YHVH occured he attributed to the "Yahvist" or "Jahvist" version.

Later Biblical researchers—principally the German pioneers of the "Higher Criticism" in the nineteenth century—thought that they had found evidence of still other "borrowed" literary ingredients in the composition of the Pentateuch: three, four, and even five different sets of codes and narrative myths. Their followers of more recent times have come up with theories isolating a virtually inexhaustible series of subdivisions within the already classic five divisions. Because of their very intricate (and sometimes bewildering) character, and regardless of whether one is prepared to accept their validity or not, these hypotheses are appropriate for study by erudite specialists only. For the general reader—who would only find himself at sea in the turbulent waters of learned controversy—it is sufficient to be cognizant of the fact that many modern Biblical scholars (both Jews and Christians, and religionists and secularists alike) are of the firm opinion that the Pentateuch is a blending of at least several Scriptural documents.

The document presumed to be the oldest and believed to have originated in the southern kingdom of Judah either in the tenth or the ninth century B.C.E., is the so-called Yahvist, or Jahvist (indicated by the key-letter *J*). The document called Elohist (indicated by *E*), some scholars feel, originated in the northern kingdom of Israel, possibly during the eighth century B.C.E.

The other documents are those labeled the Covenant Code (incorporated in Chapters 21-23 of Exodus), which is the oldest collection of Jewish laws, the Deuteronomic Code, the Priestly Narrative, and the Priestly Code.

The Deuteronomic Code—with the possible exception of certain laws and practices that had specific reference to conditions that existed in a later historic period—is identical in part with the Book of the Covenant of Josiah. It is recorded in Chapters 23 and 24 in II Kings that, while the priests under the High Priest Hilkiah were engaged in making repairs in the Temple of Jerusalem in 621 B.C.E., they unearthed a long-forgotten covenant. It was the dramatic discovery of this document which prompted the then reigning King Josiah to institute his monotheistic reforms and to reintroduce the old ceremonial and ritual practices to displace the blatant idolatry and animism into which the Jewish religion had relapsed by that time.

The Priestly Code comprises the ecclesiastical and ritual laws found in Exodus, Numbers, and Leviticus. Some scholars conjecture that those laws originated in Babylonia during the seventy years' span of the Captivity, and were, presumably in the middle of the fifth century 2.3.5. revised, rearranged, and put into "appropriate" places in the Scriptural texts by Ezra the Scribe.

Yet, in all objectivity, a word of caution should be sounded. These classifications, divisions, and subdivisions of the Scriptural materials, their dating included, are largely inferential and conjectural. Some of them, comments Millar Burrows in *What Mean These Stones?*, "rest on false assumptions and unreal, artificial schemes of historical development. And what shall the patient (the layman) do when the physicians (the Biblical specialists) disagree? He must do what he has to do in other matters: choose the best authorities he can find and trust them though not too far, having more confidence in a general concensus than in one writer."

THE PROPHETS

The Prophetic Writings. **If the Torah—the Five Books of Moses—can be said to symbolize the *intellect* of the Jewish religion, then the Prophetic Writings must be considered its *heart*.** For in their utterance of the loftiest sentiments and in their aspiration towards a more humane society free from war, hunger, and oppression, their like is not found in all of the sacred literatures of mankind. Rabbinical Judaism was built upon their religious-ethical foundation. The authors of the Prophetic Writings, in a stirring way were backwoodsmen of the spirit; they hewed paths of light through the darkness of the social jungle of antiquity. The French archeologist-historian, Salomon Reinach, aptly assessed them thus: "The Prophet was the interpretor of the highest conscience of the people."

It is hard to determine the full cultural significance of the Prophetic Writings to the Jewish people, but its tremendous impact can be judged from the mere fact that for more than two thousand years, Jews in their synagogues universally have observed perhaps their most revered custom: that of reading aloud, in conjunction with the weekly portion from the Torah, appropriate selections from the Prophetic Books—the Haftarah. This most solemn practice was instituted for the purpose of keeping the teachings which they proclaimed ever fresh and green in the consciousness of the Jewish people.

"Professional" Seers. The earliest Hebrew prophets were hardly distinguishable from the prophets in other ecclesiastical systems of the ancient Near East. All religions—the Jewish included—had developed in an institutional manner "schools" of prophets and prophetism. These produced prognosticators who combined in themselves the professional functions of seers, diviners, astrologers, and necromancers, trained in the secret and superstitiously feared arts of their calling. In the Temple cult of the Jews, the prophets were organized as one of the twenty-four orders of the priesthood. In the sanctuary on Mount Zion (this was also true of the earlier sanctuaries in Bethel, Dan, Beersheba), and the royal court, they presumably read the future and issued predictions in concert, like a glorified Greek chorus. There were also "local" Prophets in various towns performing individually their professional services "for a fee" to the ordinary folk. This fact is clearly indicated in I Samuel (9:7-8), where it is noted that before Saul went to consult "the seer," Samuel, he made sure that his servant had with him "a present to bring to the man of God." This "present" consisted of a fourth shekel of silver. The mental association one has of the seer with the modern fortuneteller is inescapable. It becomes even more convincing in the description of Samuel as "a man of God . . . all that he saith cometh surely to pass."

The role of the "professional" prophet in Jewish life as a prognosticator seems to have been a durable one. Even as late as the middle of the fifth century B.C.E. the governor of Judah, Nehemiah, had sought the prophets' predictions in connection with his project for the rebuilding of Jerusalem's walls. In the end, thoroughly disillusioned, he denounced them in this wrathful prayer: "Remember, O my God, Tobiah and Sanballat, according to these their works, and also the prophetess Noadiah, and the rest of the prophets that would have me put in fear [i.e., with their dire predictions]." (Nehemiah 6:14.)

The performance of miracles by means of magic or legerdemain was expected of every prophet; it was an essential element in the popular image of him. The folk readily endowed even the "master of all the Prophets," Moses, with such capabilities. To frighten Pharaoh, he turned rivers into blood: "And the magicians of Egypt did in like manner with their secret arts; and Pharaoh's heart was hardened." (Exodus 7:22.) Apparently, in his formal training as a "prophet," Moses had acquired a complete repertory of magic tricks, secret formulae, and incantations with which to achieve alleged supernatural ends. He read divine signs in a remarkable assortment of things—for instance, in the entrails or liver of an animal; he detected hidden mysteries by observing the manner in which birds flew; he "cast lots"; he interpreted dreams; and he also made astrological calculations. He employed all these methods to predict the future, to ensure good fortune, and to divert disaster.

The Prophet of every ancient religion, whether of YHVH (God) or of the Canaanite deity Baal, bore a strong resemblance to the shaman—the practitioner of magic in primitive religions. By a psychic kind of auto-intoxication, he would bring himself into a trancelike ecstasy until he reached a state of divine seizure. Then he experienced extra-sensory visions and heard "revelations," and he prophesied!

Music was also endowed by the early Jews with the attributes of magic and was employed as a stimulant for prophecy. By its means, the seer or prophet was helped to transport himself into a state of inspired frenzy. The Greek soothsayer also relied on music to waft himself into a prophetic trance.

It is related in the Bible that when Elisha wished to prophesy, he demanded: "But now bring me a minstrel."

Israelite prisoners impaled and shot by Assyrian archers during siege. War-relief of Tiglath-Pileser III, 745 B.C.E.–727 B.C.E. (The British Museum.)

Jewish prisoners with their burdens in Assyria before the Babylonian Captivity (6th century B.C.E.).

Israelite tribute-bearers sent by King Jehu to the Assyrian king Shalmaneser III (859 B.C.E.–824 B.C.E.). Relief on the Black Obelisk of Shalmaneser. (The British Museum.)

Assyrian soldier driving captives (possibly Israelites) before him. Fragment of an alabaster frieze from the palace of Sennacherib (705 B.C.E.–680 B.C.E.) at Nineveh. (The Metropolitan Museum of Art.)

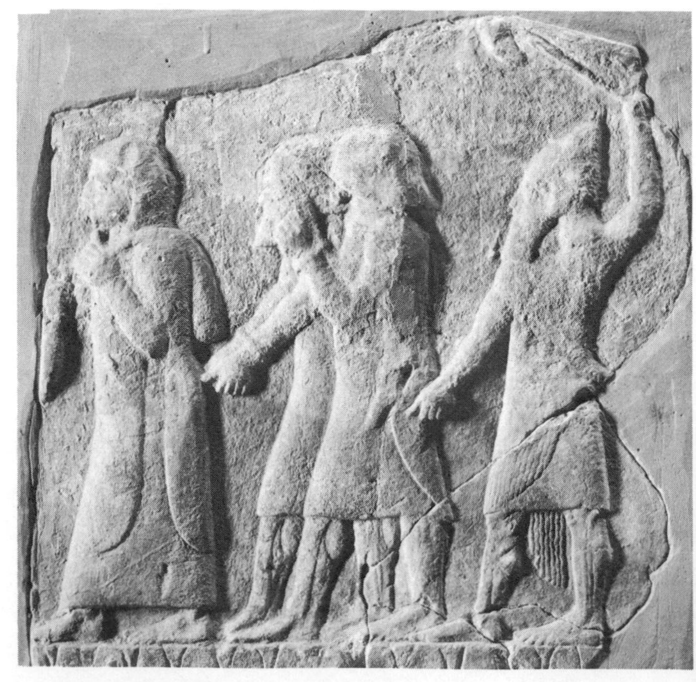

That was done. "And it came to pass, when the minstrel played, that the hand of the Lord came upon him." In a far less elevated mood was King Saul when he met a prophet-band "coming down from the high place with a psaltery, and a timbrel, and a pipe, and a harp, before them." He apparently experienced a divine seizure as he listened to their playing. ". . . and the spirit of God came mightily upon him and he prophesied among them." (I Samuel 10:10.)

"The Still Small Voice." But suddenly a fresh wind began to blow across the Biblical landscape. An entirely different strain of prophecy, based on a new system of religious harmonics, was heard. It no longer included the wild antics and hysteria of the shaman, or of the disreputable seer and diviner.

> They are confused because of wine,
> They stagger because of strong drink.
>
> ISAIAH 28:7

Now was heard the voice of the socially motivated prophet, inflamed by a passion for humanity, righteousness, and truth. Even the unknown chronicler of I Samuel clearly recognized the qualitative difference between the seer and the prophet. He noted (9:9): ". . . he that is now called a prophet was beforetime called a seer." Samuel himself went under the name of "seer."

Among the first of the authentic Prophets, although he left no written record of his teachings, was Elijah of Tishbi, "the Thunderer of the Lord." While—out of cultural inertia, no doubt—still holding on to some of the old seer's magic tricks, he nevertheless did appear—a spectral figure, gaunt of face, with blazing eyes and with long, matted hair, and dressed in the skin of a wild ass—before the royal reprobates of Israel, Ahab and Jezebel. He came to denounce them to their faces—something the old-fashioned seer would never have done—for their fashionable worship of the baalim, the idols of the Canaanites, and to upbraid them both for their persecution of the prophets of YHVH and the social crimes they perpetrated.

"Is it you, you troubler of Israel?" cried the outraged despot.

"Not I, but you and your father's house are the troublers of Israel!" retorted Elijah.

What were the inner motivations of such a prophet? How did he come by his propetic mission?

When Elijah was being hunted by the king's men, he hid in a cave and cried aloud to God:

> ". . . the children of Israel have forsaken Thy covenant, thrown down Thine altars, and slain Thy prophets with the sword; and I, even I only, am left; and they seek my life to take it away."

Thereupon the inner revelation of the authentic prophet, in all its awesome drama, is unfolded, as narrated in I Kings 19:11-12.

> And, behold, the Lord passed by,
> And a great and strong wind rent the mountains,
> And broke in pieces the rocks before the Lord;
> But the Lord was not in the wind;
> And after the wind an earthquake;
> But the Lord was not in the earthquake;
> And after the earthquake a fire;
> But the Lord was not in the fire.

Where then was the Lord?

The answer came simply: "And after the fire a still small voice."

That is where the Lord was—*in the still small voice* of Elijah's conscience.

What was true of Elijah was equally true of the later (and also greater) canonical Prophets—Amos, Isaiah, Micah, Hosea, Jeremiah, Ezekiel, and the rest. They too listened attentively to the "still small voice"; they "heard" God speak to them. They followed this voice wherever it bade them, at whatever personal cost to themselves. There was no other way, inasmuch as they spurned all compromise with the truth as they conceived it to be and with their principles as they avowed them.

The Social Background. There can be no genuine understanding of the Prophets without a prior insight, however limited, into the social, political, economic, and religious problems that beset the Israelite society of their period.

During the rule of Israel by the Judges—a historic period which ended with the establishment of the absolute monarchy under Saul (*c.* 1030 B.C.E.)—there occurred a gradual transition that changed the Jews from a nomadic-pastoral to an agricultural people. The most far-reaching changes in Jewish life resulted from this upheaval.

In the old days, under the simple and democratic social organization of the patriarchal clan and the tribe, there were no basic distinctions such as "rich" and "poor." The Mosaic program for equal distribution of the land was epitomized by the simple declarative sentence: "The earth is the Lord's." Each farmer had the privilege of keeping the land allotted to him *in trust,* but he could no longer hold legal title to it after the trumpet of Jubilee (q.v) announced the end of the fiftieth year, when the land automatically reverted back again "to the Lord"—its rightful owner. Under such conditions, mutual needs and common dangers tended to make all men feel their interdependence within the social unit of clan and tribe.

But, ultimately, the footloose nomadic shepherds were obliged by the changed circumstances of life after the conquest of Canaan to turn for subsistence to a fixed existence on the land, and the overwhelming number of Israelites became, almost overnight, agricultural smallholders. In a collateral movement with the new agricultural economy and monarchial political system, towns and even cities emerged to complicate the already difficult situation. In time, however, there moved up a class of big landowners who, by means of physical coercion and corrupt practices in collusion with the princely judges, began to absorb great areas of the land—the holdings belonging to the small farmers.

Once they were landless and dispossessed, the poor countrymen were driven by hunger into the towns, where they were once more victimized, but this time by the nobles, the dishonest merchants, the corrupt judges, and the king's tax-collectors.

The social upheaval that occurred was responsible for the emergence of the remarkable puritan sectaries called Rechabites. These dissidents stubbornly separated themselves from the rest of Israel as if it had become pest ridden. Just before the Destruction of the First Temple by Nebuchadnezzar (586 B.C.E.), their leader had instructed them: "Ye shall drink no wine, neither ye, nor your sons, forever. Neither shall ye build house, nor sow seed, nor plant vineyard, nor have any; but all your days ye shall dwell in tents [i.e., like their tribal ancestors in the Golden Age of Moses]." (Jeremiah 35:6-7.)

As the agricultural economy and the towns grew, an active and flourishing merchant class sprang up. It traded principally in produce and grains, exporting them in large quantities. From this commerce the members of this group amassed much wealth. Eventually, they even succeeded in seizing control of the grain market, and thus were able to create a virtual monopoly on all the necessities of life, raising prices at will. The people, already impoverished, were forced to pay if they wished to eat.

To compound this evil—and there were many such occasions—the crops would fail in times of drought or they would be destroyed by invasions of locusts. Then the poor farmer would be forced to turn to the rapacious moneylender. The dread of having his little house and land-strip taken away from him by his creditor haunted him. To stave off that disastrous event, when the pinch began he would make a still wilder plunge into debt, pledging first his clothes, then his household goods, and finally, the all-important tools with which he worked. Then, when he had exhausted all of his material belongings, he was left with no choice but to sell himself, his wife, and his children as bond servants.

Half-crazed with grief, a mother cried out to the Prophet Elisha: ". . . the creditor has come to take unto him my two children to be bondmen!" And the Prophet Isaiah, seeing this outrage and inhumanity, lashed out indignantly in the name of God and pointed an accusing finger at the perpetrators.

> ". . . for ye have eaten up the vineyard;
> The spoil of the poor is in your houses.
> What mean ye that ye beat my people to pieces,
> And grind the faces of the poor?"
>
> ISAIAH 2:14-15

But what of justice? From whom could the afflicted seek redress? The tribal elders who had always been in deep sympathy with the people, like fathers to their children, had been ousted unceremoniously by the kings from their traditional judicial and administrative offices and had been replaced with degenerate princelings who tried to emulate their rulers in avarice and cruelty. They accepted bribes and issued judgments against the poor, had them flogged, threw them into prison, and sold them into bondage.

"The Troublers of Israel." Starting with the prophets Amos and Isaiah, during the eighth century B.C.E., the shaman-seer school of prophecy came to an end. The fact is that unlike the Earlier Prophets—Samuel, Nathan, Elijah, and Elisha—who not only performed magic tricks or miracles but also belonged to the professional guild of oracular predictors, the Later Prophets were neither wonder-workers nor professional prognosticators. Quite the contrary. The canonical Prophets generally stood in defiant opposition to the rulers and corrupt government officials, and to their pliant tools, the priests and the official prophets. They considered themselves to have received their prophetic mandate directly from God. They pitted the ethical monotheism of Moses against the idolatry-ridden and formalistic Temple cult.

It was a spontaneous response to conditions—a compulsion from within—that quickened the spring of prophecy in them. For example, the Prophet Amos, who was of humble origin and social condition, disclaimed any special qualification or preparation for his exalted mission as Prophet. When the High Priest of the old sanctuary at Bethel taunted him for being nothing but a mercenary diviner, thus: "O, thou seer, go, flee thee away into the land of Judah, and there eat bread, and prophesy there: But prophesy not again any more at Bethel, for it is the king's chapel, and it is the king's court. Then answered Amos . . . I was no prophet, neither was I a prophet's son; but I was an herdsman and a gatherer of sycamore fruit; and the Lord took me as I followed the flock, and the Lord said unto me: Go, prophesy unto my people Israel. Now therefore hear thou the word of the Lord." (Amos 7:12–16.)

And the word of the Lord that the herdsman of Tekoa

Map of Pithom and environs, discovered in 1883 by E. Naville.

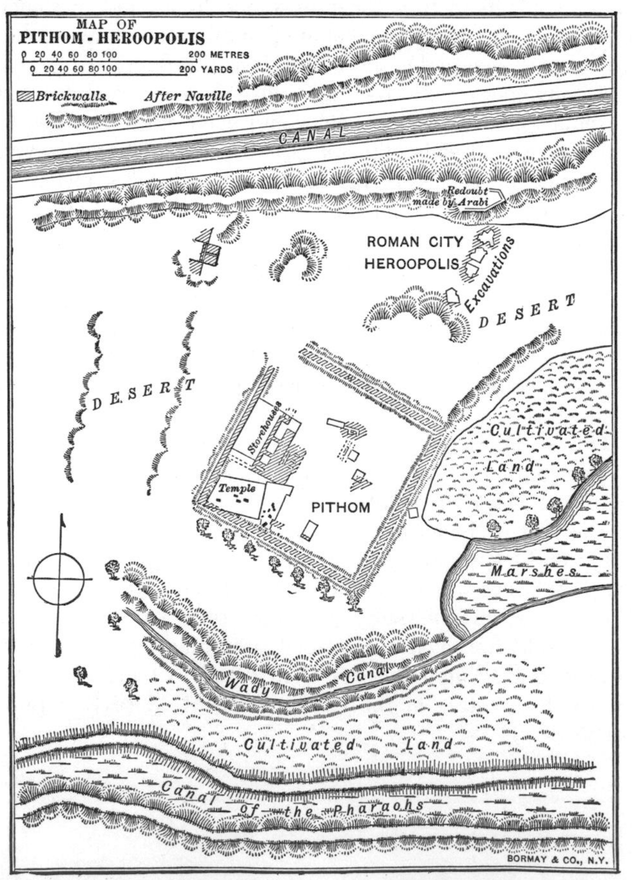

The Mesha Stele (Stone) on which Mesha, king of Moab, recorded his victories over Ahab, king of Israel, c. 850 B.C.E. This is the oldest historical inscription extant in any Hebrew dialect. (The Louvre Museum.)

uttered against the perpetrators of evil in the Land of Israel blistered and withered; even after twenty-seven centuries it still seems to boil like molten lava.

For the causes to which they were dedicated, the Prophets were reconciled to the inevitability of suffering, social rejection, and calumny, of being persecuted by the rulers—even of undergoing martyrdom. Because he opposed the bandit-like preparations by King Ahab for aggressive war against an unsuspecting neighbor, the Prophet Micaiah, the son of Imlah, raised his lone voice against the crime. But the king of Israel had him silenced with blows and a peremptory order to his officials: "Put this fellow in the prison, and feed him with bread of affliction and with water of affliction . . ." (I Kings 22:27).

The class origin of the Prophet had nothing to do with his fate in the world. The greatest of all the Prophets, Isaiah ben Amoz (eighth century B.C.E.) was a scion of one of the princely houses of Jerusalem. But he too was persecuted for his teachings. In time there even arose a tradition that he had suffered martyrdom, though it is unverified by any other documentary source than the apocryphal work in Greek, The Ascension of Isaiah, in which his martydom is related.

Two centuries after Isaiah ben Amoz, when the Prophet Jeremiah publicly began opposing King Zedekiah's conspiracy with Egypt for war against King Nebuchadnezzar of Babylonia, the Jewish princes belonging to the war party petitioned Zedekiah: "Let this man, we pray thee, be put to death: for as much as he weakeneth the hands of the man of war . . ."

Each of the social Prophets felt impelled by a religious-moral imperative to transmit his message which, he sincerely was convinced, had been conveyed to him by God. During the sixth century B.C.E., while in captivity in Babylon, the Prophet Ezekiel described how he had been instructed by God: "And thou, son of man, be not afraid of them. . . . And thou shalt speak My words unto them, whether they will hear, or whether they will forbear." (Ezekiel 2:6-7.)

The Prophets of Israel, in particular Isaiah ben Amoz and Jeremiah, vividly recorded their opinions and sentiments on the burning political issues and social problems of the day. They claimed that they saw a significant connection between the crushing blows inflicted on the Jewish people by its external enemies—the Egyptians, Assyrians, and Babylonians—and the no less crushing blows dealt it by its own despotic and corrupt ruling class. It was their conclusion that the wounds received from both kinds of "enemies" would in the end prove fatal to Israel: They would seal the doom of the state and the dismemberment of the nation.

The Prophets played a memorable role in the drama of the Jewish national life in their time. For the modern reader there can be only one assessment of them: They were inspired preachers and teachers whose evangel of reform pursued idealistic objectives—religious, political, social, and ethical. They were patriots whose lonely voices could not be stilled even by death. They articulated the grievances and woes of the people in a society similar to those which prevailed elsewhere in the ancient world, where the commonalty had no voice in public affairs and in which a small ruling class, corrupted by luxury and power, preyed upon the poor and the weak and strove to negate the democratic traditions and ethical practices first instituted by Moses.

As religious reformers, the Prophets were scornful of the empty formalism in religious worship that prevailed in their day. They inveighed against the priestly class and against the yes-saying "official" guild of sycophantic prophets. Both of these groups, they charged, had a vested interest in the preservation of the monarchial despotism and, therefore, chose to remain oblivious or indifferent to the spiritual hunger of the people and to the desperate circumstances of their lives.

> For every one from the least even unto the greatest
> Is given to covetousness,
> From the prophet even unto the priest
> Every one dealeth falsely.
>
> JEREMIAH 8:10

But none of the Prophets, not even the dourest of them, ended their exhortations on a dissonant note. In imitation of their own God's love and compassion, they themselves remained eternally hopeful, their faith in the good in mankind and in the redemptive power of truth, undiminished. Pleaded Isaiah ben Amoz:

> Come now, and let us reason together,
> Saith the Lord:
> Though your sins be as scarlet,
> They shall be as white as snow.
>
> ISAIAH 1:18

Unearthing an ancient building from the days of King Ahab (9th century B.C.E.*) at Hazor. (American Friends of the Hebrew University.)*

Tower of David (Migdal David), Jerusalem. (Israel Office of Information.)

Ruth among the gleaners. From a Hebrew manuscript of France, c. 1750. (With permission of the Library of the Jewish Theological Seminary of America.)

THE HOLY WRITINGS

The illuminations, the attractions, and delights to be found in the Bible are inexhaustible. It does seem as if each literate reader without exception must find in it some value or intangible sentiment that responds to his culture or to his special interest and outlook on life. For the devout believer, it naturally plumbs the depths of spirituality; for him it is a "well of living waters." It also serves him as a religious-ethical guide for his chosen way of life. To the humanist and the student of civilization, regardless of whether he is a religionist or freethinker, it is a fascinating collection of documents for tracing the development of the history, the religion, and the culture of the Jewish people. Much of its materials is also of inestimable interest to the student of literature. Many of the individual compositions, especially several of the Prophets, the Psalter, Ecclesiastes, Proverbs, Job, Lamentations, and The Song of Songs (Song of Solomon) are distinguished by an intellectual force and a poetic orginality of great beauty and expressiveness.

Few among the writings that are included in the last division of the Hebrew Scriptures–the so-called Holy Writings or Hagiographa–seem to have any special connection one with the other. They really constitute a miscellany of liturgical and devotional hymns (Psalms), an anthology of love-poems (Song of Songs), aphorisms and wise sayings (Proverbs and Ecclesiastes), perhaps the most stupendous morality play in verse ever written (Job), a narrative about a supposedly historical happening (Esther), a bucolic romance (Ruth), elegiac verses on the national Jewish grief (Lamentations), an apocalyptic visioning of the End of Days (Daniel), and straight chronicles of great authenticity (Ezra, Nehemiah, and the two books of Chronicles).

However, in a bird's-eye view of the Bible such as this, it is not practicable to deal separately with all the thirteen individual books found in the Holy Writings, nothwithstanding the fact that each of those documents is intrinsically of great interest to the student of Jewish religion, history, folklore, ethics, anthropology, and–not least–literature.

But it is impossible to pass over without comment works of such magnitude and significance as Psalms, Proverbs, Ecclesiastes, and the tragedy of Job. Those works have left an indelible imprint on the content of Western thought and literature.

The Psalms. The 150 hymns that comprise the Book of Psalms contain some of the most unforgettable poetry ever written. They discourse with an ingenuous openness upon all the passions that have ever wracked and fevered the human heart. They give spontaneous utterance to every variety of joy and grief, hope and despair, humility and arrogance, love and hate, pity and revenge, serenity and disquietude, as well as to many other throbbings and compulsions felt by the restless spirit of man.

The composition of the Book of Psalms was attributed by ancient Jewish tradition to David, the almost legendary poet-king of Israel. Him, next to Moses, the plain folk had adopted as the greatest of its national heroes. In the same way that the Greeks considered that Apollo had invented the art of music, so, too, did the Jews believe that King David was the founder of the art of poetry.

While it is true that 73 of the 150 psalms in the Psalter carry the name of David as their author, modern Biblical scholarship is able to agree on one poem only as being convincingly of Davidic composition. And that one, oddly enough, is not included in the Book of Psalms but in the Second Book of Samuel, where it found its way from the now lost but more ancient Book of Yashar (Book of the Righteous). This poem is David's "Lament upon the Death of Saul and Jonathan."

Many of the Psalms carry unmistakable attributions of authorship to Moses, Solomon, Asaph, "the Sons of Korach," Heman, and Ethan. All these facts offer indisputable evidence that the Book of Psalms is an anthology of hymns that must have been written by a number of poetic hands during many centuries and collated at a later date from several collections. It may be noted as of some significance that the Psalms are ordered into five separate books or anthologies, which are linked by doxologies or "praisings" of God.

Why was David named as the poet of the Book of Psalms? Serious Biblical scholars hold the view that when

The Judgment of Solomon. Hebrew manuscript, France, c. 1750. (With the permission of the Library of the Jewish Theological Seminary of America.)

Remnants of a public building (center) from the time of King Ahab (9th century B.C.E.*) and (left) a casemate town-wall from the days of King Solomon (10th century* B.C.E.*). (American Friends of the Hebrew University.)*

"Abraham's Well" in Beersheba, in Israel's Negev. Believed by some archaeologists and hydrologists to be authentic. (Israel Government Tourist Office.)

Lamp filler for oil lamp of ancient Palestine. (The Jewish Museum.)

Weight in the form of a lion bearing the inscription maneh melech *(royal weight). Ancient Palestine.*

Ezra and the Scribes were working on their selection of the sacred works to be included in the Scriptural canon, they thought to add greater prestige and acceptability to a specific writing by attributing its composition to some august and universally revered personage. This is why the writing of Job was attributed to Moses, the two Wisdom Books (Proverbs and Ecclesiastes) to King Solomon, and the Psalms entirely to King David.

Of considerable historic significance is the presence in some of the Psalms of certain elements that were not exclusively of Hebraic creation. The fact of the interchange of myths, legends, beliefs, practices, rites, and ceremonies among the neighboring peoples of the Near Eastern Fertile Crescent, including the ancient Israelites, has been well established by painstaking modern scholarship. This cultural diffusion extended as well to literary forms and styles.

It is incontrovertible that the peoples contemporary with and adjacent to Israel–the Canaanites, Babylonians, and Egyptians–also composed psalm-hymns for their temple liturgies. There is a surprising degree of correspondence among them all, notwithstanding the fact that the Hebrew Psalms, probably composed at a later time, strike spiritual and ethical sonorities rarely heard in the others. For instance, Psalm 104 shows a remarkable affinity in style and content to Pharaoh Akhenaten's celebrated Hymn to the Sun, which is found in the Egyptian Chapters of Coming Forth by Day (popularly referred to as The Book of the Dead). An arresting resemblance has also been noted between Psalm 139 and another of Akhenaten's ecstatic invocations to the sun-god Ra. Not so long ago, many similarities were noted between the Ugaritic text of a Phoenician psalm written on a cuneiform tablet discovered at Ras Shamra and the Hebrew Psalm 29. Both poems quite plainly are parallel in simile, ideas, and style.

The Psalms fall into three main categories: (1) Praise and Thanksgiving, (2) Supplication and Repentance, (3) Condemnation and Censure. The religious uses for the 150 psalms were of several kinds. There were those clearly intended for the Temple service. They were to be sung in plain chant by the Levites to the accompaniment of their stringed and woodwind instruments. Many of the Psalms, especially among the last fifty, were made to serve purely liturgical purposes in the ancient synagogue. The prayer-leader (baal tefillah) presumably chanted each verse, with the worshipers responding antiphonally.

Not a few of the Psalms are of the moralistic or wisdom-teaching kind. These were expected to be memorized by the individual and recited publicly by him for his moral improvement and the deepening of his understanding. There are other Psalms which, on their face, must have been intended for private devotions only. They are characterized by a deep inwardness, a soul-searching, an "accounting" made to God by the contrite, sin-laden soul. This type of "bookkeeping of the conscience," called *cheshbon ha-nefesh* in Hebrew, is a religious-ethical concept of fundamental importance in the Jewish religion.

The Wisdom Books. A more earthy kind of poetry than the hortatory verse of the Prophets or the threnodies to God of the Psalmists is found in the Biblical writings called "Wisdom Books": Proverbs, Ecclesiastes, and Job. They are composed in pithy verse, and at least the first two works are marked by much sophistication, worldliness, and a skepticism that is in equal measure mellow and ironic. For their time, these writings were considered intellectually challenging. Read in the light of our day, they appear to be steeped in a kind of aristocratic *Weltschmerz*–a twilight mood of world-weariness and disenchantment with life.

The writers of Proverbs and Ecclesiastes–presumably upper-class Jews belonging to the Sadducean religious-political party of the Second Temple period (*see* SADDUCEES)–utter with aplomb the most astonishing heresies. Among these is the Sadducean disbelief in the immortality of the soul and in the World-to-Come–two subjects of bitter controversy that engaged in rebuttal all the passions and dialectical skill of the rival Pharisees. Ecclesiastes, for example, is colored by the hedonistic views of Greek Epicurean philosophy. It preaches a resignation to life and a quietism in all of its affairs. It also advances a *raisonné* for the full enjoyment of the life of the senses since the grave is man's cold destination. This is a point of view hardly consonant with the puritanism that is traditional in Jewish life and with the moral significance it endows human strivings.

The Jewish pursuit of wisdom (chachmah) was part of the universal quest among all intellectually advanced peoples in ancient society for greater knowledge and understanding of man and the universe. If Jewish wisdom reveals a physiognomy of its own, it is only because the Jews, like every other branch of the human family, inevitably followed their own peculiar course, charted by their own special history and cultural traditions. There is no denying that, in Biblical times, there constantly went on a "borrowing" and also a "lending" of knowledge among peoples. This is the normal process of cultural diffusion. The civilizations of mankind in their totality have always constituted a common reservoir of accumulated wisdom from which each people, to the extent of its contact with other peoples, drew selectively for its own needs.

All the advanced Near Eastern and Middle Eastern neighbors of Israel, such as the Egyptians, Assyrians, Babylonians, and Persians, created "wisdom" literatures of their own. For them, as for the Jews, wisdom's validity was as a practical guide to daily living, leading to a happier and more righteous existence. Among each one of these peoples, proverbs and "teaching" epigrams were in general currency, and wisdom books which have survived the ravages of time and change were produced. In fact, it may be surmised that these writings, products of cultures having greater antiquity than that of the Jews, served as literary models for the latter.

Already, at the end of the Third Millennium B.C.E., the Babylonians boasted a book of proverbs–"a wise book"–to teach right and profitable conduct. There is also extant a Babylonian literary work (believed to have originated during the fifteenth–fourteenth centuries B.C.E.), which, on account of its sophistication and intellectual skepticism, has been called the "Babylonian Book of Ecclesiastes." Other Babylonian compositions of this type, perhaps also more ancient in origin than the Jewish, were: The Pessimistic Dialogue Between a Master and a Slave, and The Complaint of a Wise Man on the Injustice of the World.

The Egyptian priest-scribes, too, were wholeheartedly dedicated to the pursuit of wisdom. They produced books of proverbs and epigrams almost four thousand years ago. The best-known, believed to have been written sometime during the tenth to seventh centuries B.C.E., was The Teaching of Amenemope. This celebrated work shows striking similarities to the Hebrew Book of Proverbs.

Whereas the Greeks developed their special kind of wisdom–secular philosophy–in a formal intellectual way, the Jews produced wisdom writings that were merely didactic and random *sententiae*: wise reflections and moralistic sayings presented in popular aphoristic style. Wisdom to Jews was not the be-all and end-all intellectual pursuit that philosophy was to the Greeks. It was concerned neither with metaphysics nor with logic. Wisdom to Jews had a direct practical purpose and was trained on many aspects of reality. More precisely, it served as an auxiliary aid to the understanding of "right conduct." It helped clarify the precepts of the Torah, and, above all, it aimed to strengthen the individual's faith in God. Appropriately, the author of Ecclesiastes (whether it was Solomon or, as the Bible critics aver, someone else) makes the categorical statement that "the beginning of wisdom is the fear of the Lord."

No reference was ever made by Jews, as by the Greek and Roman philosophers, to the achievement of intellectual truth by means of understanding. The emphasis was invariably on *religious and moral truth,* acquired by means of observing the precepts of the Torah—a matter that was largely determined by unquestioning faith and indoctrination.

Whatever its borrowings from the Babylonians, the Egyptians, and the other great peoples of ancient times, the Wisdom Literature of the Jews boasts its own individuality. Its moralistic fervor, its passionate concern for better human relations, its impregnation with world-sorrow, its ceaseless intellectual probing into the whys and the wherefores of a tumultuous existence that invariably ends on a note of irony or disenchantment, lend to it a literary originality and also a moral gravity that the wisdom literatures of other peoples do not possess in the same measure.

Ecclesiastes may have been written during the third century B.C.E., as some scholars claim. Certain students see stamped upon it a worldliness and disenchantment characteristic of the Persian and Greek cultures in decline at the time. A number of Aramaic expressions found in the text also suggest to philologists its post-Exilic composition. It was the poet Heine, himself a prince among doubters, who dubbed Ecclesiastes "The Song of Songs of Skepticism."

The poetic gnomic writings of the ancient Jews are not narrow or sectarian. They possess the *élan* of the universal. They pose human problems that are peculiar to no people or period. In essence, they are timeless. What daring challenges they raise! What is the purpose of human existence? And what is either the profit or justification for all the fevered, tormented, and seemingly senseless activities of mankind? Why do the righteous suffer and the wicked prosper? bitterly ponders Job, "God's Afflicted Man." Is the world whirling in moral chaos, or is there a Providence guiding it along its course? And, demands Job, if there is a God in Heaven, where in a troubled life are the evidences of His divine justice?

Not a few thoughtful students of the literature of the Bible have marveled over the strange inclusion in it of these skeptical writings. Apparently, the Biblical compilers and editors must have set for themselves certain guidelines and ground rules to follow in order to justify their inclusions or exclusions. But what those criteria for selection may have been is not known today, since no record pertaining to them was left behind. However, during the first and second centuries of the Common Era (to merely repeat a well-remembered oral tradition) the Talmud took note thus of a controversy that was being debated between the liberal Rabbinic school of Hillel and the opposing fundamentalist school of Shammai (*see* TALMUD, THE): "The Sages sought to suppress the Book of Ecclesiastes (Kohelet) because its words contradict one another. Why then did they not suppress it?"

And the answer given was at best a legalistic evasion: "Because it begins with words of Torah and ends with words of Torah."

But even giving a venerated place to these works in the Bible could not silence all the criticism. At a later time, the Mishnah Sages continued to debate their sanctity, although they approached the question from a different angle—obliquely—asking whether, because of its heretical views, Ecclesiastes was to be considered *on an equal level of sanctity* with the other books of the Bible.

Modern scholars have attempted to reconstruct the editorial technique by which such essentially skeptical writings as Ecclesiastes, Proverbs, and Job were made part of the sacred Scriptures. They think it was the result of a diplomatic compromise. Each of these works—by convenient editorial interpolation, as the above-cited passage from the Talmud indicates—opened and closed with devout affirmations of God's omnipotence, justice, and providence. They certainly must have enjoyed a tremendous popular vogue to have been accorded such tolerant treatment in order that they might be made acceptable for inclusion in the Bible.

See also ART AMONG THE JEWS; BIBLICAL MYTHS, SIGNIFICANCE OF; BIBLICAL RESEARCH, TOOLS OF; CHACHMAH; COMMENTARIES, RABBINICAL; DOCTRINES IN JUDAISM; "EYE FOR AN EYE"; GOD, NAMES OF; HAFTARAH; HEBREW LANGUAGE, HISTORY OF; "HEBREWS," "ISRAELITES," "JEWS"; JUBILEE; LAW, JEWISH; LIFE, SANCTIFICATION OF; MASORAH; MITZVOT; MUSIC, ANCIENT JEWISH; MUSIC IN THE TEMPLE; MUSICAL INSTRUMENTS OF THE BIBLE; SABBATICAL YEAR; SACRIFICE OF ISAAC; SANHEDRIN; SCRIBES; SHEMA, THE; SLAVERY AND THE SLAVE; TEITSCH-CHUMASH; TEMPLE, THE; THEOCRACY; TORAH-READING; TORAH SCROLL; TORAH STUDY.

BIBLE, MASORETIC TEXT OF. *See* BIBLE, THE; MASORAH.

BIBLE, MUSICAL INSTRUMENTS OF THE. *See* MUSICAL INSTRUMENTS OF THE BIBLE.

BIBLICAL CRITICISM. *See* BIBLE, THE.

BIBLICAL MYTHS, SIGNIFICANCE OF

The Torah's framework is the narrative; it comprises the larger part of the Scriptural text. Unmistakably, it is in the nature of a primitive chronicle in which historic fact becomes entangled in the thickets of myth and magic, miracle, and legend. While no enlightened reader of our day can read the Torah as authentic history, neither can he afford to dismiss it as childish myths. For that matter, neither can he justifiably denigrate the historic nucleus around which the myths are conceivably wrapped. The modern scientific attitude toward myths has been cogently defined by Sigmund Freud: He perceived in them "the dust of former beliefs"; therefore, they have a historic-cultural reality of their own.

Like several other tribal sagas among the more advanced peoples of ancient times, the Torah narrative, in rude but powerfully expressive prose, achieves a cosmic sweep. It begins with the very beginning—with the Creation of the world by God and with the dawn of the human race. The primeval history of Israel is traced, seemingly guided along its predestined course by the selfsame First Cause. The history tells of Adam's fall and of Paradise Lost, and of Adam's first descendants, straying and groping to achieve even a rudimentary sense of morality amidst the savagery of the jungle. The hypocritical evasion of the fratricide Cain to the questioning of God after he has murdered his brother Abel—"Am I my brother's keeper?"—is a stirring declaration for the sanctity of life. And the moral question it raises rings ever louder today in the troubled conscience of mankind.

In a similar vein runs the morality-epic of the Sin-Flood, with the blood-drenched earth crying out at its intolerable burden of human evil that had to be swept away by the cleansing Deluge before man could again resume his advance in civilization. These myths hold a special significance for the modern reader. They mark the birth of conscience, at least in the didactic allegorizing with which they are slanted in the Book of Genesis.

It is well to keep the fact in mind that, however small, relatively speaking, the literary compass of the Pentateuch may be, the myths and legends included in it find an unusual number of analogues in the mythologies and religious literature of other ancient peoples, especially those that are set forth in the cuneiform writings of the Sumerian, Babylonian, and Ugaritic tongues. Only in the moralistic "teaching" emphasis with which some of these stories are angled in the Bible do they differ from their non-Israelite parallels. Yet–a word of caution–the fact that these myths and legends are found in the Bible by no means establishes their priority of appearance in cultural history.

Most religions have their creation-myths, and the story of Creation that is told in the Bible merely follows the general pattern of myths of the same genre. In these, man, feeling himself overwhelmed by the mystery of life and by the inexplicable whys and wherefores of the orderly vastness of the Universe, attempts to explain their origin and to trace it back to a First Cause. It is, perhaps, not co-incidental that there appears a surprising similarity between the account of the Creation in the Jewish Scriptures and certain of the cosmological myths that have been discovered in the sacred writings of other Semitic peoples and even also of non-Semitic neighbors of Israel.

There is an early Egyptian myth which describes how Ra, the Egyptian sun-god, created the world and man by means of his divine powers. There is still another Egyptian myth which ascribes the production of the world to the scribe-god Toth. Interestingly, like YHVH in the Bible, Toth, who was invested with supreme magical powers and mastery over words, "spoke" all creation into existence until the universe was completed.

Similarly, the folk-memory of many ancient neighbors of the Israelites seems to have been haunted by the recollection of some cataclysmic flood that occurred far back in primeval history; the mythic accounts of it were probably inspired by its echoing terrors. The Biblical story of the Deluge, too, finds many close analogues. A Babylonian tablet with the cuneiform text of a sin-flood saga similar in moralistic tone to that in the Bible was unearthed in Mesopotamia in 1872. It is narrated in the eleventh canto of the Gilgamesh epic which, it is believed, was composed *c.* 2000 B.C.E. This version is, therefore, to be considered even of greater antiquity than the one found in Genesis. Like the Biblical myth, it too comments sadly on the corrupt spirit that overshadowed the first created humans, who like the descendants of Adam and Eve, had been disobedient and ungrateful to their gods for all the good they had done for them; therefore, the gods resolved to be done with them: to drown them and wipe them off the face of the earth.

In all important details, the exploits of the righteous man, Utnapishtim (the Babylonian prototype of Noah, who was chosen by God to continue life on earth) and Noah are the same: Utnapishtim constructs a seaworthy "ark," and he takes along with him on his divinely directed voyage a pair of animals and birds from each of the species. When those preparations are completed, the great god Marduk (like YHVH in the Bible) unleashes the retributive floodwaters, and after seven days of buffeting by the storm and with the aid of a dove and a raven, the ark of Utnapishtim finally comes to rest on Mount Nisir (in the Genesis version Noah's Ark lands on Mount Ararat). Also, like Noah, Utnapishtim, the members of his family, and all the animals and birds on board his ark step out onto dry land, offering a sacrifice of thanksgiving to their divinities for having reached journey's end in safety.

A most significant resemblance has also been noted between the life stories of Moses (thirteenth century B.C.E.) as recounted in the Bible and that of Sargon the Elder (*c.* 2600 B.C.E.), the first great king of Babylonia, as it is rendered in a supposedly "autobiographic" inscription that was unearthed at the site of Nineveh in Mesopotamia. Both great rulers–for the obvious purpose of magnifying their native genius–are separately depicted by the weavers of their national myths as having been handicapped by almost insuperable difficulties from the start. Of the humblest origins both had been born unwanted by their heartless societies: Moses, the son of an Israelite slave in Egypt, facing the death that was decreed by Pharoah for all first-born male offspring of his Jewish slaves; Sargon, condemned to a similar cruel fate because of his illegimate birth. (Because of the facts of his birth, the Babylonian king ordered inscribed on the stele of his statue: "My mother was lowly, my father I knew not.")

The developments in the life of each are identical. Like Moses' mother, Jochebed, Sargon's was also desperate to save the life of her beloved child. So, like Jochebed, she placed him "secretly" in a "basket of bulrushes," which she made watertight with bitumen, and sent it floating down the river, on a course fraught with unknown dangers but charted by the guiding hand of Providence, to greatness and a glorious destiny.

Mention should also be made of the fact that there is a real mythological resemblance between the missions of Moses and Hammurabi, the lawgiver of the Babylonians who came before Moses. Not only are their resemblances in certain elements of their legislation (*see* TEN COMMANDMENTS) but also in the manner in which each acquired his divinely composed code. Moses received his "Tables" directly from YHVH on Mount Sinai; Hammurabi's were handed to him personally by Shamash, the Babylonian sun-god, who had written them.

Nor should it pass without mention that the romantic saga about Joseph and his brothers, who formed the family clan of the Patriarch Jacob that settled in Egypt, found a surprising parallel in the Egyptian legend "The Story of the Two Brothers" and in the Syrian legend "The Story of Idrimi." Again, both of these tales are believed to be of more venerable vintage than the Biblical narrative about Joseph.

All those myths and legends eloquently attest to the fact that, in a large measure, the diffusion of culture is an unceasing process. The stories found in the Five Books of Moses were not the sole invention of the Israelites; they represent the collaboration with other peoples in working out the shape and content of ancient civilization, in a cultural interchange that has been a *sina qua non* of progress.

With regard to the great similarities that are found in the beliefs and customs of many peoples, the eminent English anthropologist, James G. Frazer, presents the scientific view. He states that "Many of these resemblances are to be explained by simple transmission, with more or less modification, from people to people." The explanation for the arresting parallel lines present in ancient tales and beliefs can in some instances be explained "as having originated independently through the similar action of the human mind in response to similar environment."

By a direct progression, the Biblical narrative abruptly abandons the mythic tales about prehistoric man. It next introduces the reader to the subject of his greatest interest: the early history of Israel. As in a spectacle-drama, the progenitors of the Jews–their Founding Fathers and Mothers: the Patriarchs Abraham, Isaac, and Jacob, and the Matriarchs Sarah, Rebeccah, Rachel, and Leah–parade across the stage of the undimming memory of the folk.

These tribal annals treat of Joseph and his brothers and of the Israelite settlement in Goshen, of the subsequent enslavement of the Israelites by the Pharaohs, climaxed by their revolt and flight from Egypt under the hero-lawgiver Moses. Then follows the narrative of the long wandering in the Wilderness and the fierce struggles for survival against hunger and hostile tribes, with the people buoyed up only by the power of Moses' will and the vision of the beckoning homeland in Canaan. The climax is reached in the most epochal event in the recollection of the Jewish people: the Revelation at Mount Sinai and Israel's acceptance of the Torah from God through the instrumentality of Mosheh Rabbenu–"Moses our Teacher"–as its everlasting inheritance and mission in the world and in history.

All these narrative sequences, unquestionably possessing the core of historic truth, are cast in the diaphanous dream-mood of the soaring supernatural and of the miraculous. Possibly only highly imaginative children or primitive peoples, uncorrupted by the sophistications of civilization, could be capable of such transports of feeling and poetic evocations.

Nevertheless, all personalities, events, and images are projected with an astonishing detachment and intellectual honesty. The unknown Biblical chroniclers, revealing an almost austere attachment to truth, make no effort to romanticize, prettify, or glorify their national heroes, whether it be "the first Jew" Abraham, the Patriarch Jacob, or "the most righteous of men," Moses. They do not gloss over any of their misdeeds and do not try to reconcile the glaring contradictions and faults in their characters. Moreover, they are made to emerge on the stage of life in an altogether convincing manner *as human beings*, and whatever their inconsistencies and moral divagations may be, they are portrayed as groping for understanding and rectitude. This delineating realism demonstrates a devotion to truth and balance which only a highly developed moral conscience and intellectual objectivity could have been capable of.

Certainly, the modern Jew's preconceptions about his ancient forebears–in which, self-flatteringly, he disposes of them as his intellectual inferiors in knowledge, logic, and "enlightened" thinking–deserve factual re-examination.

It is true that a medieval traditionalist like Rashi (Rabbi Solomon ben Isaac of Troyes, 1040–1105) interpreted the Pentateuch (its myths and legends included) almost uncritically, in a literal but highly ingenious word-by-word manner. He told bluntly the way he read the Scriptures: "I do not pretend to give any but the natural meaning." Because of this unswerving loyalty to tradition, he frequently involved himself in monumentally intricate, and even implausible, explanations in order to vindicate the sacred text.

Yet there was still another ancient tradition in the interpretation of Scriptures which took a contrary position to that of Rashi. Nearly a thousand years before, a Rabbinic Sage in the Talmud commented significantly: "As a hammer strikes many sparks, so does a single verse of Scripture have many meanings." This tradition certainly was not one on which the literalists depended.

This keen assessment of the symbolic content of the Bible was even more forcefully expressed and defended by Philo, the rabbinic and Platonist philosopher of Hellenistic Alexandria (*c.* 20 B.C.E.–*c.* 40 C.E.). Having been trained in the precision and refinements of the Greek logical method, he remonstrated with the Biblical literalists of his day: "It is folly to suppose that the universe was made in six days, or in time at all. . . ." How was it possible, asked he, for the world to have been created "in the beginning," as it is stated in Genesis, since "time did not exist before there was a world?" As a devout Jew and a rabbi but at the same time a thoroughgoing Hellenist, Philo sought and found for himself an intellectually more satisfactory solution for his dilemma on how to interpret the Biblical myths and anthropomorphisms (the physical and human attributes with which God was provided plentifully in Holy Writ): He interpreted them not according to their literal sense but as allegories and as symbols of inner meanings. This method, said Philo, was not at all original with him, since for many generations it had been followed by the Therapeutae (q.v.), the Jewish monastic sectaries near Alexandria who had preserved "the writings of men of old, the founders of their way of thinking, who had left many memorials of the form used in allegorical interpretation." But of these writings none are extant today.

A medieval Biblical commentator, the poet-scholar Abraham ibn Ezra, like Philo and the Therapeutae, also employed the allegoric interpretation of Scripture. To illustrate his method: Apropos of the Biblical commandment, "And thou shalt write them on the tablets of thy heart," he inquired slyly of the literalists how such a thing could be possible. Obviously, he concluded, this commandment was not meant to be understood except in its metaphoric and allegoric sense.

For the reason why Scriptural ideas were presented to the believer in allegoric form and adorned by literary metaphors, the great Jewish philosopher Baruch Spinoza (1632–77), himself a pioneer among modern Biblical critics, gave this explanation (in *Tractatus Theologico-Politicus;* 1670): "All Scripture was written primarily for an entire people . . . consequently, its contents must necessarily be adapted, as far as possible, to the understanding of the masses . . . Its object is not to convince the reason but to attract and lay hold of the imagination." For example, said Spinoza, had Moses stated that it was only an east wind that had divided the Red Sea for the Israelites and not a miracle, it would have made no impression on the simple-minded, who usually are literalists but at the same time are also highly imaginative. Therefore, the Biblical account of the miracles and the wonders, of the weaving in of ravishing myths and tales of the marvelous, was given in order to entrance, to suggest, to teach, and, finally, to lead to faith and right conduct.

See also BIBLE, THE; BIBLICAL RESEARCH, TOOLS OF; DEAD SEA SCROLLS.

BIBLICAL RESEARCH, TOOLS OF

What are the more reliable tools and yardsticks of Biblical research today?

There are quite a few, and they are drawn from a variety of disciplines: from archaeology, from comparative studies of folklore, ancient religions, and cultures in the Near and Middle East, from investigations in ancient Semitic languages, requiring a greater and more correct knowledge of Hebrew vocabulary and grammar, and from literary and inscriptional archaeology. For example, Semiticists have identified in the Pentateuch texts words and terminology that are not Hebrew at all but, in fact, a more ancient Semitic language–Akkadian–the classic tongue of the Assyrians and Babylonians.

Another important source of illumination for the true meaning of certain Biblical words has been the cuneiform writings discovered about 1930 at Ras Shamra, in northern Syria. These were composed in Ugaritic, a language cognate with Hebrew, Akkadian, Canaanite (Phoenician), Aramaic, Moabite, etc. Being older, it is believed, than the Hebrew that was used in the Bible, Ugaritic has greatly aided philologists in clearing up some verbal obscurities in the Hebrew text.

Professor Solomon Schechter at Cambridge University among old Hebrew manuscripts reclaimed from the Cairo Genizah (Storehouse).

Hebrew University students of archaeology and an Israeli soldier search for ancient metal objects with a mine detector. (American Friends of the Hebrew University.)

Hebrew University archaeology students digging at entrance to a cave in the Judean desert. (American Friends of the Hebrew University.)

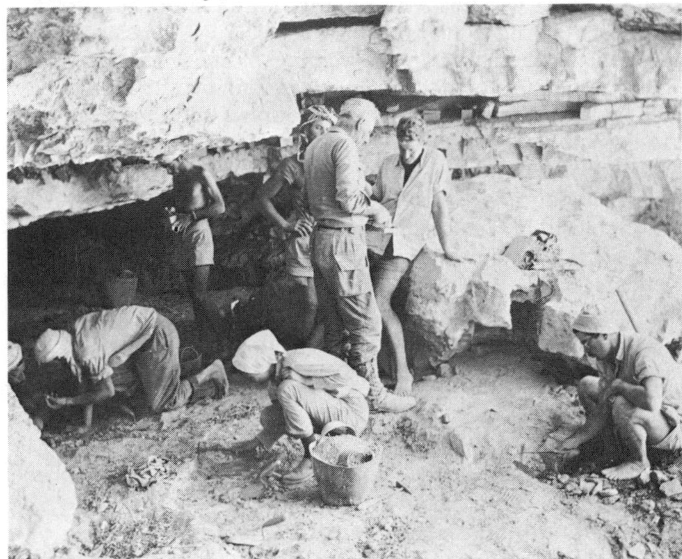

Processing a Dead Sea Scroll with the aid of the IBM 705 electronic computer are Jesuit Father Roberto Busa, a Biblical scholar, and Paul Tasman, IBM engineer. (IBM World Trade Corp.)

Hebrew University archaeologist at work in a Judean desert cave. (American Friends of the Hebrew University.)

Artifacts and tools, believed to be from Chalcolithic times (Bronze Age), dug up by Israeli archaeologists. (American Friends of the Hebrew University.)

A case in point in which paleography (the science of deciphering ancient manuscripts and inscriptions) supplied the solution, was the correct identification of the underground Pool of Siloam by archeologists in 1880. On a stone wall in the tunnel of an ancient conduit-pool in Jerusalem was discovered a carved inscription in archaic Phoenician-Hebrew lettering that bore neither date nor any other clue to what it might have been. The identification was possible only after a painstaking examination of *the shape of the letters* and a comparison of them with those that had been used in the Mesha inscription on the Moabite Stone (*c.* 850 B.C.E.), showed that there were striking similarities in both. With the approximate date thus ascertained, a quick thumbing of the Bible revealed that the pool in question corresponded perfectly with the description in II Kings 20:20 of the conduit pool that had been built in Jerusalem to supply the inhabitants with water at the time of Sennacherib's siege of the Holy City during the reign of Hezekiah (720–692 B.C.E.).

Literary archaeology is, curiously, a kind of scholarly sleuthing. By means of a minute and systematic examination of the language employed in the Bible, by making note of the slightest variations in vocabulary, syntax, and literary style, Semitic philologists have been enabled to trace in a chronological manner and with a surprising degree of exactitude the alterations that have taken place in Biblical Hebrew. They have been able to follow the course in the steady development of the language used in the Pentateuch–to cite the most significant examples from the ninth or eighth century B.C.E. to the time of Ezra the Scribe, who edited (or rewrote) the Five Books of Moses in 444 B.C.E. From this fact alone it can be seen that, even more than studies of ruins and monuments, and of ancient art and artifacts, literary archaeology (the examination of inscriptions and manuscripts) has proven of the greatest importance in a critical study of the Bible. Two well-known illustrations of this have been furnished by the discovery in 1897 of the discarded old Hebrew fragments in the Genizah (storeroom) of the great Cairo synagogue and, in 1947, of the Dead Sea Scrolls in a cave in Jordan.

But still enough, such methods should not be considered entirely accurate, nor infallible as scientific tools. Time and again, Biblical experts have pointed out that some documentary evidence or part of a text was mistranslated or misinterpreted. It was enough for a researcher to misread a single key word in the text, or even one unvoweled Hebrew consonant, to start a false scent down the wrong trail. Not infrequently, sectarian zeal or discoverer's enthusiasm led a scholar to leap to a hypothesis which later philological investigation or newly discovered archaeological data knocked into a cocked hat.

In recent years, in addition to the application of chemical analysis and X-ray photography, there has emerged a new technique for dating ancient objects and manuscripts. This is W. F. Libby's radioactivity test–the Carbon-14 method–which utilizes nuclear physics, chemistry, and electronics. Even electronic computers have been enlisted in seeking solutions to questions that are far too complex and laborious for the Biblical research scholar to undertake by himself.

See also BIBLE, THE; DEAD SEA SCROLLS.

BIKKUR CHOLIM. *See* SICK, VISITING THE.

BILU. *See* ZIONISM.

BIMAH. *See* BEMA.

BIRKAT COHANIM. *See* PRIESTLY BLESSING.

BIRKAT HA-MAZON. *See* GRACE AFTER MEALS.

BLACK DEATH. *See* MASSACRES: THE CRUSADES, THE BLACK DEATH.

BLESSING, PRIESTLY. *See* PRIESTLY BLESSING.

BLESSING OF CHILDREN. *See* CHILDREN, BLESSING OF.

BLOOD ACCUSATION. *See* RITUAL-MURDER SLANDERS; THE SEDER (*under* PASSOVER).

BONDAGE, THE. *See* PASSOVER; PIDYON HA-BEN; SLAVERY AND THE SLAVE.

BREAD OF AFFLICTION. *See* PASSOVER.

BRIT ABRAHAM. *See* CIRCUMCISION.

BRIT MILAH. *See* CIRCUMCISION.

BROTHERHOOD

One day in the second century C.E., a group of Rabbinic teachers of ethics in Judea became absorbed by the following challenge: What Scriptural saying could sum up by itself the quintessence of the Torah? Each one volunteered his favorite saying. Ben Azzai recited the verse: "In the day that God created man, in the likeness of God created He him." (Genesis 5:1.) Ben Azzai thus implied that, because man bore

Christian (left) and Jew (wearing the prescribed Judenhut *or "Jew's hat") extending a hand of amity to each other. The letter* P *stands for* pax*—"peace." (From Sachsenspiegel, Germany, 1220.)*

the moral imprimatur of divinity, he was endowed with the potential of all the virtues which, if he but willed to develop them, could add greater dignity and nobility to his stature as a human being. For that reason, it logically followed that all the teachings concerning humanity and moral goodness stemmed from the belief that man was made in the image of God.

Ben Azzai's colleague, Rabbi Akiba, made a different choice; he recited the commandment: "Love thy neighbor as thyself." (Leviticus 19:18.)

From the context of subsequent discussion concerning this matter, it could be seen that both of these verses were considered fully complementary to each other; both represented the same fundamental truth but were arrived at from different approaches. The rationale for this was simple. By loving his neighbor, man was merely vindicating the divine image in which he was cast.

The Pharisee teachers of ethics during the Second Temple period expressed this doctrine, even more simply than the Bible. "Love all men," they urged. They did not say: "Love certain men," or "Love good Men," or "Love the Jews." They said plainly: ". . . *all* men!"

The concept of brotherhood emerged from the fundamental Jewish view that universal man stood above all considerations of country, race, and religious creed. Like the anthropologists of today, the ancient moralists of Israel seemed to have been well aware that there existed no such thing as racial purity, that the Jews were biologically "mixed." Witness the pointed reminder by the Prophet Ezekiel to the Jew that "the Amorite was your father, and your mother was a Hittite."

All men came from the same source, declared the Talmud. Having been fashioned by the same Creator out of the same materials, all were equal and, therefore, brothers. "The dust that entered into the making of the first man was gathered from every land in the world," runs the old Jewish folk-belief. Why did the Creator do that? asked the Rabbinic Sages. They answered: "It was done in order that, in times to come, no nation should be able to boast: 'From my earth was Adam made! Therefore, I am greater, more worthy than all other nations.' "

While it is patently true that not a few Jews in modern times have succumbed to the disease of group pride that stems from a misinterpretation of the Jewish historic-religious concept of "the Chosen People," love for *all* peoples has been a dominant tradition in Jewish thought and practice. One has only to read a few of the ethical teachings and sayings lovingly perpetuated by the Jewish folk in every generation to recognize that brotherly love in the framework of human equality has been one of the continuing national ideals of "the Chosen People." Some of these teachings are: "He is worthy of honor who honors mankind." "Despise no

creature; the most insignificant person is the work of your Maker." "He who hates another human being hates God." "I call heaven and earth to witness that, whether a person is Gentile or Jew, man or woman, manservant or maidservant, upon each, according to his conduct, will the Divine Presence [Shechinah] rest."

See also CHOSEN PEOPLE, THE; GENTILES, JEWISH ATTITUDE TOWARD.

BROTHERS AND SISTERS. *See* FAMILY RELATIONS, TRADITIONAL PATTERNS OF.

BURIAL CLOTHES (in Hebrew: TACHRICHIM)

In different degrees, all peoples observe what might be best described as the cult of death. Having had their ethnic and

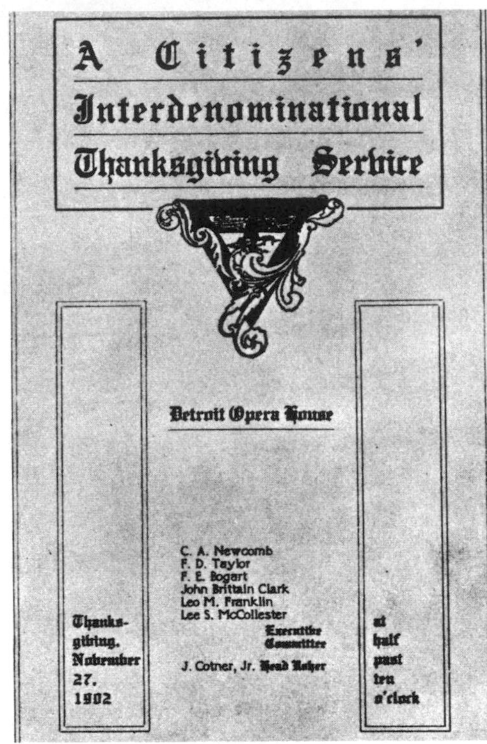

A Citizens'
Interdenominational
Thanksgiving Service

Detroit Opera House

C. A. Newcomb
F. D. Taylor
F. E. Bogart
John Brittain Clark
Leo M. Franklin
Lee S. McCollester
Executive Committee

J. Cotner, Jr. Head Usher

Thanksgiving. November 27. 1902

at half past ten o'clock

Program cover of the first Citizens' Interdenominational Thanksgiving Service, organized in 1902 by Rabbi Leo M. Franklin of the Reform Temple Beth-El in Detroit, Michigan. This was possibly the earliest forerunner of the Conference of Christians and Jews in the U.S.A.

"Music brings good fortune to all people," says Archbishop Hakim at the first Jewish-Arab Music Conference at Acre, in December, 1960.

religious origins in the Fertile Crescent, and being geographically situated within the cultural-diffusion orbit of the death-cult of Osiris in Egypt, the Jews were always preoccupied with questions concerning death, the soul, immortality, and physical resurrection. In consequence, mortuary matters received their due attention

The Jews' concern with death was also reflected in the tombs they built and in the choice of shrouds in which their dead were attired for burial. Until the destruction of Jerusalem, in 70 C.E., the burial clothes of the well-to-do were elegant; they were made of costly stuffs, especially of finely woven byssus, in parvenu imitation of patrician Greek and Roman fashion. So tyrannical did this custom of ostentatious burial become, that many families impoverished themselves because of the expense entailed. This lavishness in funeral matters of course did not occur to the same degree among the masses, who were very poor. Nevertheless, to the extent that their means allowed, social convention required that they too deck out their dead in showy fashion—an extravagance these same dead were never indulged in while they were alive. The situation finally reached a scandalous point, with some poor families even abandoning their dead, leaving the cost and the bother of interment to communal charity.

What had begun as a social vanity on the part of the rich had grown into a social evil for the entire people. The Patriarach Rabban Gamaliel II became sorely troubled, for it seemed to him as if it almost had become a forbidden luxury for the poor to die. Accordingly, some time during the first quarter of the second century C.E., he issued a Rabbinical decree forbidding ostentatious obsequies. Thenceforth, it was required that every Jew, regardless of whether he was rich or poor, a learned scholar or an illiterate, illustrious or of humble station, be buried *in exactly the same way*—in cheap, unadorned linen burial clothes (tachrichim).

Before Gamaliel himself died, he left instructions that he was to be buried in a coarse linen shroud which was not to cost more than one zuz (a small coin). In grateful memory of his sensitivity to the needs and the pride of the poor, it became ever after traditional to drink in his honor one of the ten cups of wine that are taken during the Meal of Condolence in the house of mourning upon the return of the bereaved family from the funeral.

During the Middle Ages, the custom arose whereby a Jew, as he started to grow old, prepared his own *tachrichim*. He sewed them *with his own hands*—as an act of humility because the shadow of the grave was already falling on him. He figured that it was always good to be ready in such matters; who could tell when the Angel of Death might appear to take his soul away? The great Rashi of Troyes (Rabbi Solomon ben Isaac) noted that in his day (in the eleventh century), in the Franco-German Rhineland, this was already the prevailing custom. And so it has continued to this day, but only among the Ultra-Orthodox, who resist change in religious practice at all costs. The pious man cuts out his burial clothes and sews them by hand with large, loose stitches, leaving the thread-ends unknotted, possibly as a symbol of the incompleteness that is in the life of man. (A less lofty speculation suggests that this type of sewing may be inspired by a childlike, primitive notion that when the Messiah comes and the dead rise in their graves, it will be easier for them to get out of their shrouds.)

The male shroud or tachrichim has consisted since the Middle Ages of three separate garments: a shirt, pantaloons, and a coat that covers both and is tied at the waist with a sash, and there are accessory white stockings and cap. Since the white garment is traditionally looked upon as a symbol of purity, having been worn by the ancient priests in the Temple rites at Jerusalem, the coat of the shroud, called a *kittel* by Yiddish-speaking Jews, is put on by the male worshiper in the synagogue on the Day of Atonement; he also wears it at the Seder, the Passover home prayer-service over which he officiates in a quasi-priestly role.

Although not considered an essential part of the shroud, the prayer shawl (tallit) that the deceased man wore during his lifetime, is wrapped around him over the shroud, but with one or more of its fringes (tzitzit) removed. Also, whenever available, the worn-out, discarded wrappers from a Sefer Torah (the Sacred Scroll) are sometimes used for their supposed sanctifying effect.

The Jewish woman, traditionally occupying a secondary position in religious life, was in former times not the object of as much ritualistic attention as the man. The burial clothes required for her were even simpler: a white linen apron-like dress, tied at the waist by strings, and a flat cap.

See also BURIAL RITES AND CUSTOMS; KITTEL.

BURIAL RITES AND CUSTOMS

The burial rites of the Jews—at least, of those who still adhere to the ancient customs of their people—are elaborate. They are also precise and thoroughgoing. To quite a few of them clings the suspicion that at one time they may have been little more than primitive practices, so that the religious beliefs they now purport to dramatize may once have been only tribal taboos. Yet, although they have hardly changed ritualistically, in the civilizational process, some of them have acquired, with time and with the development of religious values, new allegoric and spiritualized meanings. Also, because of the natural diffusion of folk myths and folkways, there are observable, in Jewish burial customs since prehistoric times, a wide range of accretions tapped from various sources that were not originally Jewish. Only in such a realistic context can the burial and mourning rites of the Jews be understood. This would also no doubt be true of the death rites in any other religion: They have to be *re-examined* in historical and anthropological terms of reference.

The extraordinary attention given by the Jewish religion in ancient times to mortuary matters was in keeping with similar preoccupations among all other peoples. There is more than a hint in the Jewish burial rites during the Biblical and Hellenistic periods of the influences that flowed from the overpowering, as well as appalling, death-cult of Osiris in Egypt. One telling proof of this is furnished by the funerary artifacts and domestic utensils that have been found in Jewish burial places of Greco-Roman times. In the catacombs of Torlonia, which served as the cemetery for the wealthy Jews of Rome, and in sepulchers unearthed by archaeologists in ancient Samaria and Judea, the funerary objects turned up consisted of clay jars, bowls, and oil-lamps, and also gold-glass bowls and bottles with the representation of Jewish religious symbols upon them. The reasonable assumption is that some of these vessels, like those found in Egyptian tombs, contained symbolic food and drink for the dead.

There is ample evidence also that other Jewish mortuary notions and customs were adopted from the Phoenicians, the Babylonians, the Syrians, the Persians, the Greeks and Romans, the Buddhists, the Mohammedans—even from the medieval Christians.

To a surprising extent, traditionalist Jews today still follow the ritual pattern for interment that was fixed by the Rabbinic Sages after the destruction of the Second Jewish Commonwealth. And this pattern has been preserved not merely because religious custom among the Jews has been valued as sacrosanct, but also because of the logical implications that the Jews have drawn, since the Messiah-expect-

Mourners at Jewish cemetery in Tunis. The tentlike figures in white are bereaved Jewish women; the men in the foreground are reciting Hebrew prayers for the souls of the departed.

Funeral procession. Galician town, 19th century.

Funeral procession. Utrecht, Holland, 1657.

ing post-Biblical age, from their doctrinal certainty that the dead will rise again for the Last Judgment and Eternal Life in the End of Days. It is mainly because of this belief that the most scrupulous and lavish care is taken by Jews in the preparation of their dead for burial. This is to prevent any *physical* injury from happening to any part of the body so that, when the shofar blast of the Resurrection is sounded by the Messiah, the dead can rise *intact,* and with their souls restored to them.

Also unmistakable is the fact that the principal emphasis in the traditional obsequies is laid not on the perishable body but on the indestructible soul–"the lamp of the Lord," the Mishnah teachers (Tannaim) called it. Fervently, therefore, during the rites for the dead sounds the throb of prayer, and timeless is the symbolism of the rites which are performed. The soul, "separated" only temporarily from the body (the believers are confident), must be ceremoniously "escorted" out of its terrestial home with supplications that are winged to God in compassionate intercession on its behalf.

Whenever death does not occur suddenly, the traditional rites among the Orthodox begin at the very bedside of the dying person. They constitute, as it were, the prologue to the awesome drama of death. But they are performed by the living in fraternal consolation to fellow creatures upon whom the great shadow has begun to fall. This task, considered an enormous act of merit, falls to the lot of the Chebrah Kaddishah, the Holy Society, which also prepares the dead for burial and makes the necessary arrangements for the funeral. The members of this "Holy Brotherhood," men of great fortitude and piety, perform their tasks in fulfillment of the teaching of Chamah ben Chaninah, the second-century Rabbinic Sage of Judea: "The Holy One–blessed be he–buried the dead, as it is written: 'And he [Moses] was buried [by God] in the valley in the land of Moab.' Therefore, do ye likewise: bury the dead."

As the dying person's end nears, the members of the "brotherhood" assemble at his bedside to recite supplications appropriate for the occasion from the Hebrew Psalter. This they do from the most generous of motives and from consideration of piety. Yet they are probably unaware of the fact that the ritualistic intent of the psalm-reading stemmed originally from a folk myth about the actual mechanics of dying. This is first noted in the literature of the post-Biblical era–a time of active cultural diffusion and religious syncretism among the peoples in the Mediterranean world. The Jewish Hellenistic writers evoked a frightening image of the dying person, picturing him as engaged in a desperate battle for life with that implacable technician of death, the Angel Sammael, sometimes also called Satan. With naked sword poised for the fatal thrust, this spectral messenger of God's will bides his time; well does he know what the outcome will be. For that very reason, the members of the Chebrah Kaddishah, usually men getting well on in years, cannot allow the dying person to struggle alone in the unequal combat with the terrible swordsman of heaven. So they huddle gallantly at his bedside and ring him around with the protective wall of their prayers, that they might thereby encourage the soul in its ordeal.

The Rabbinic rule, always strictly observed among the pious, has been not to leave a dying person alone, even for one moment, but to revive his ebbing soul by the recitation without pause of Psalms. Ostensibly, this permits the soul to depart taking with it the spiritual solace of its fellow Jews. Yet there is still another explanation possible for this curious custom. It is advanced by anthropologists, who point to the

Washing of hands before leaving the Jewish cemetery in Prague. (Painting by a local artist, 1773.)

Sewing shrouds for the dead as an act of piety.

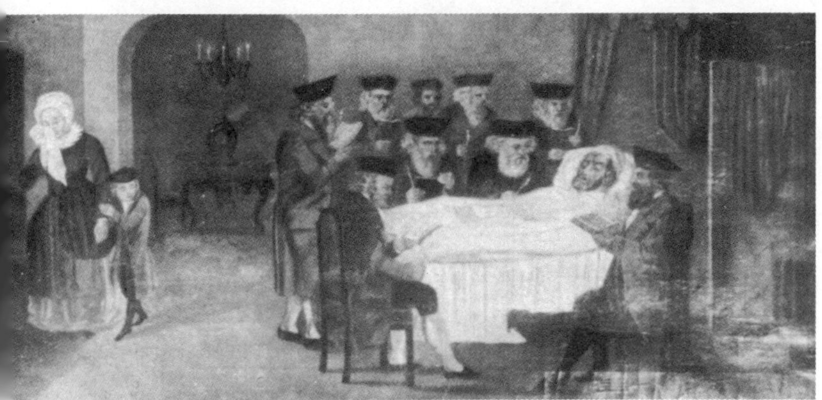

Members of the Chebrah Kaddishah reciting psalms at the bedside of a dying man. Prague, 18th century. (Paintings by a local artist.)

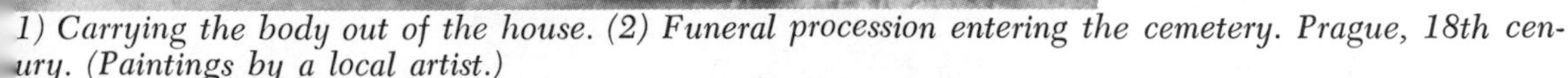

1) Carrying the body out of the house. (2) Funeral procession entering the cemetery. Prague, 18th century. (Paintings by a local artist.)

After the funeral, friends serve "the mourner's bread of affliction" to the bereaved family. (From Kirchner's Jüdisches Ceremoniell, *1726.)*

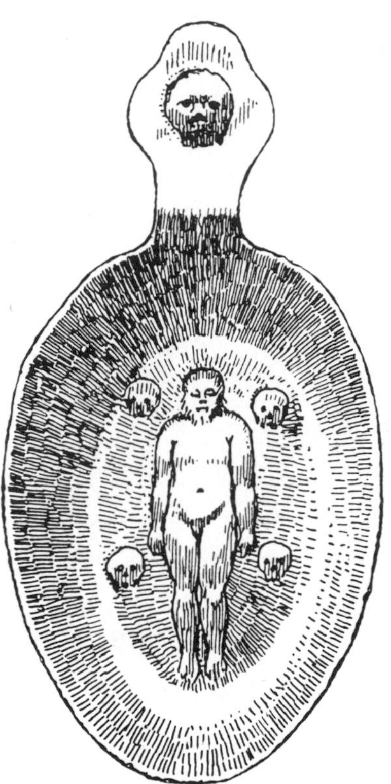

Silver water-dipper (dated 1707) used for washing the dead. Lublin, Poland.

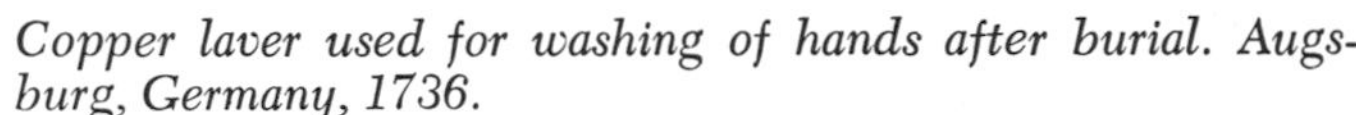

Copper laver used for washing of hands after burial. Augsburg, Germany, 1736.

Water pitchers used by Che brah Kaddishah (Holy Broth erhood) in the washing of th dead for burial. Moravic Austria, 18th century.

Silver wine goblet belonging to the Chebrah Kaddishah of Worms, Germany, 1608–09. Following a burial, the members of the society would eat and drink to cheer themselves up.

"Rabbi Samuel prepared the bodies and Judah buried them." Jewish inscription in Greek found in one of the 3rd-century rock catacombs of Bet Shearim, the seat of the Bet Din following the Destruction of Jerusalem in 70 C.E. *One of the chief acts of piety possible for a Jew was to take part in the interment of a fellow Jew. Note the menorah, the ancient symbol of Jewish identity. It is quite possible that the Judah mentioned in the inscription was Judah ha-Nasi, the President of the Bet Din and the final codifier of the Oral Law—the Mishnah—c. 200* C.E.

Sefaradic rite for the dead. Portuguese Jews of Amsterdam making circuits around the coffin, intoning psalms. (Engraving by Bernard Picart, 1723.)

widespread belief among primitive peoples which holds that, at the time just before death and until interment is completed, evil spirits of demons mill about invisibly in the air, seeking to penetrate the body in order to cause it grave injury. This offers one quite plausible explanation of why potsherds are placed over the eyes and mouth of the Jewish dead before burial; that is, to keep those eerie and dangerous intruders from entering the helpless body.

Some close students of the mortuary rites and beliefs of various ethnic groups, including the anthropologist Sir James Frazer, have put forward still another intriguing hypothesis. It concerns a widely diffused primitive notion which holds that somehow–and for reasons that are not entirely clear–the soul or "ghost" of a dead person is potentially dangerous to his surviving kin. This belief, apparently, could supply the rationale for the Jewish custom of burying the dead as soon as possible, and of the haste with which the grave is filled and closed–all so that the demonic "ghost" of the deceased has no chance to do harm to the members of his family. The Biblical injunction practiced in former times made burial on the same day as death mandatory; today it is less precipitate, although it waits, usually, only until the following morning.

Many are the strange customs still observed by Jews on behalf of the dying for which there do not seem to be any explanations of a rational or genuinely religious order. These are, obviously, what once were primitive taboos and magical rites that somehow managed to survive unchanged into the scientific age. To give one example: a Rabbinical regulation requires that no part of a dying person's body may be allowed to protrude from his bed, but the whole must be completely covered. To prevent the occurrence of such a dire accident, some of the Ultra-Orthodox barricade the sickbed all around with a wall of furniture. Should the dying person, nevertheless, succeed in pushing out a limb, no one is permitted to touch it with the intention of putting it back in place. The same taboo applies when, after death has occurred, the body is lowered to the floor or ground. Then great care is to be taken that no part of the covered body be exposed.

It would be natural to expect that the fervent recitation of selected Psalms by the Chebrah Kaddishah at the bedside of the dying has a logical motivation. It most certainly has. It is primarily intended to give spiritual solace to the one about to depart, provided he can still hear and is lucid enough to understand the sacred words, but if he has already lost consciousness, then it is done for the benefit of his soul that is to be "separated" from its envelope of flesh.

Yet there is still another purpose to this hymning, and it is, frankly, a magical one. It is called "psalmomancy" by Biblical anthropologists. It attempts to change, even at the last minute, by the magical intervention of a specific psalm–the 119th–the celestial "decree" that has been issued for the death of an individual. The ancient Jewish mystics apparently had found a technique for its effective recitation. There are twenty two separate verses in the Psalm, and each begins in seriatim with a different letter of the Hebrew alphabet, thereby forming an acrosticon. By freely reshuffling the verses so that the proper name of the dying person can be formed out of the verses of the acrosticon, the believers hope to effect his miraculous cure.

Still another magical manipulation employed in the attempt to save the dying person is the changing of his name–a magical device well known among many primitive tribes. Among the Jews, this practice is, without doubt, of prehistoric origin. The first mention of it is found in the Bible, and it concerns the Patriarch Jacob, who, when he became frightened by the approach of his pursuing brother Esau, promptly changed his name to Israel in order to escape the vengeance that he anticipated. This masquerade with intent to deceive is similar to the practice of very small children who, by closing their eyes, pretend that no one sees them. The changing of the name is designed to "fool" the Angel of Death, whose "warrant" is made out only in the name of a particular individual.

The Talmud highly commends this practice, stating: "Four things cause an evil decree that is passed on man to be canceled. There are: charity, prayer, changing a name, and a change in conduct." From this Rabbinic prescription arises the following practice, which is a kind of Scriptural lottery device. The Hebrew Chumash (the Pentateuch) is opened at random; the first name that the searchers come across mentioning one of the three Patriarchs–Abraham, Isaac, or Jacob–is promptly given to the dying man. Similarly, if it is a woman who is dying, the first name of a Matriarch stumbled upon–Sarah, Rebecca, Rachel, or Leah–is bestowed on her. The medieval rabbinic formula–one that is still in use among the undeviating Orthodox–expresses the judgment that the decree of death from that moment on (i.e., the changing of the name) is invalid because "he [or she] is now another person, who no longer is called by his [or her] former name. As his [or her] name has been changed, may the evil decree be changed from law to mercy, from death to life. . . ."

There are a number of other customs connected with dying, but not all of these, it should be added, consist of taboos or rites of spirit-placation. Some are of genuine religious or ethical character. At a proper moment, for example, the Confession (Viddui) is recited with the dying person, and if he is no longer able to speak, it is read to him. When the members of the Holy Society see that the end is approaching, they recite the following formula, repeating it three times: "Go! since the Lord sends you! Go! and the Lord will be with you! The Lord God is with him and he will ascend [namely, the departing soul will ascend to Heaven]."

Following this, all who are present rise and, gazing compassionately into the face of the dying person, repeat three times this doxology: "The Lord reigns; the Lord has reigned; the Lord will reign for ever and ever! Praised be His name Whose glorious Kingdom is for ever and ever!" And as the moment arrives when, seemingly, the soul is about to "separate" itself from the body, the members of the Holy Society, in the most fervent manner, raise their voices in the hortatory Shema, the most sacred, and also the briefest, of all Hebrew prayers. It is the ages-old credal affirmation that Moses taught Israel more than three thousand years ago at Mount Sinai: "Hear, O Israel, the Lord our God, the Lord is One!" This they intone without pause seven times, putting up, as it were, a constant prayer-shield of protection for the ebbing spirit, striving mightily to end the Shema on the all-important climactic word *Echad* ("One") at the very instant when the dying person heaves his last sigh and is still.

When death finally occurs, all echo with one voice the cosmic resignation of the Ancient Man of Sorrows:

> Naked came I out of my mother's womb,
> And naked shall I return thither:
> The Lord gave, and the Lord hath taken away;
> Blessed be the name of the Lord.
>
> JOB 1:21

First the eldest son or another close relation bends over the beloved dead and gently closes the eyes–"the windows of the soul." Then the members of the "brotherhood" remove the body from the bed and place it on the floor on its back, with the feet toward the door (a primitive symbolism that still defies explanation). Special care is taken to see that the fingers are not closed–why, is not known. A black pall (or any other covering garment) is spread over the corpse. At its head are placed two lighted wax candles, and sometimes a towel and a glass of water as well (because of a curious folk notion that the soul of the deceased, in the guise of a little bird, likes to drink water and to bathe near its former human tenement, the corpse). The position of the bed is reversed–another baffling custom–and every mirror in the house is covered and turned to the wall. This last practice, however, is less puzzling than the others, for in the view of primitive man, the reflection of a human being, whether seen in the water or in any polished surface, is his soul. Thus, if the soul or "ghost" of the dead should see the reflected image of any mourner, it might try–out of love, surely–to "snatch" the live relative away to the other world. A frightening prospect, indeed! Therefore, the urgency (without understanding the reason for it) for covering the mirrors in a house where a person has died.

Before being placed in its coffin, the corpse must be put through the rite of thorough washing and purification called *taharah*. This is the last service performed for the deceased before burial, and, depending on the sex of the dead person, it is carried out by either the male or female members of the Holy Society. They raise the corpse from the floor where it has been lying and place it on a special "purification" or taharah board. They remove the shroud and place a white sheet underneath the body, and then, with the humility prescribed by the Rabbinic Sages of old, they turn to the corpse and gravely beg its forgiveness for the indelicate attentions of washing and cleansing that they are about to pay it. This, in itself, attests to the traditional Jewish conception of the great dignity that is vested in the human being, even in death.

In post-Biblical times, the corpse, after its "purification," was anointed with essence of myrrh and aloes; at a later period, it was also made fragrant with rosewater and oil of roses. The Gospel of John narrates how, after the crucifixion of Jesus by the Romans, Nicodemus the Pharisee surreptitiously "brought a mixture of myrrh and aloes . . . Then they took the body of Jesus, and wound it in linen clothes with the spices, as the manner of the Jews is to bury."

After the body is washed and dried, it is wrapped in a white linen shroud sewn with large loose stitches with flaxen thread. If the deceased was a pious man–and who is not?–he is wrapped in his prayer shawl, the well-worn tallit that was his daily companion when he communed with God. For the religious Jew, this serves to the very end as a symbol of his love-marriage to the Torah from which he chooses never to be divorced–not even in death.

Until the time of Rabban Gamaliel II, the Patriarch of Judea during the second century C.E., coffins were made of expensive materials, and in the case of patrician and wealthy Jews, were highly ornamented and decked with garlands of flowers. In Rome, the remains of some wealthy Jews were even deposited in Roman-style marble sarcophagi with sculptured lids. In Hellenistic Alexandria, sarcophagi of the Jews, like those of the Egyptians, were of fine wood, often bearing the portrait of the deceased, painted in colors dipped in hot wax, on their lids. When the lavishness of interment reached a scandalous peak in Judea, Rabban Gamaliel put a ban on it and also on the erection of tombs. He declared testily: "It is not necessary to erect mausolea! For the righteous, their good deeds alone are the memorial!" During the Middle Ages, among the Jews in Spain, the use of coffins was dispensed with entirely, being regarded as a meaningless custom. The body, dressed only in its shroud, was laid directly in the grave.

Today–and this holds true only of Orthodox traditionalists –the coffin is made of plain pine boards, it is unpainted, and it shows all the knots and imperfections of the grain. Instead of being nailed, the boards are glued together. The coffin is purposely made plain, for in death all men are equal. The way the ancient Sages put it: The single destiny of all living creatures is "worms and maggots." This is possibly intended as a grim reminder that even man's best handiwork–including expensive and presumably "indestructible" coffins of bronze and silver–is beneath the contempt of worms, which, it is expected, will find their way inside anyway.

The obsequies performed for the dead among all peoples, whatever their stage of cultural development, are regarded generally with awe and with respect. But religious Jews, for a number of historic and cultural reasons, are literally reverential toward funerals. And should the fact be pointed out that the interment of Jewish corpses takes place with such unusual speed that it might be taken as a sign of disrespect–as a desire to get rid of the dead as quickly as possible–let it also be noted that in Jewish religious belief, a corpse constitutes a "defilement." The most general view is that this "defilement" clearly was a taboo–a customary tribal prohibition–which was no doubt entered into the code of Mosaic Laws to root out the persistent death-cult practices that had been followed by the ancient idolatrous Hebrews like other contemporary peoples. The Biblical commandment is stern: "He that toucheth the dead . . . shall be unclean seven days." (Numbers 19:11.)

While this taboo involving the dead affected every single Jew, it was exceptionally demanding of the cohen or priest, who, strictly required to maintain his Levitical purity, was not permitted to go near a corpse nor to enter into a house where one lay. To avoid becoming "defiled," he was also forbidden to enter a burial ground. If this taboo was applied with greater severity to the priests than to ordinary people, it was because it was the priests who used to officiate at the death-cult rites in early times.

The funeral cortege has always been treated with enormous reverence by the Jews. In former centuries, every passer-by was bound by religious protocol to follow it, if not to the cemetery, at least for a certain polite distance. Even the study of the Torah or the recitation of prayer could be interrupted for the performance of this meritorious act (mitzvah). The Talmudic Sages cautioned: "Whoever sees a body being conveyed for burial and does not accompany it, commits a sin because of the injunction: 'Whoso mocketh the poor blasphemeth his Maker.'" (Proverbs 17:5.) This simile equating the dead with the poor is as logically true as it is quaint, for who could be poorer than the dead who possess nothing, and who more humble than they who lie supine and still? And so by not paying proper honor to the human personality–which the deceased possess even in death–the living are showing their contempt for the dead and, by extension, for God as well.

When the funeral pocession reaches the cemetery, the mourners crowd around the freshly dug grave. The coffin is lowered slowly while either the rabbi or chazzan (cantor) intones: "May he come to his resting place in peace." This hope for the departed soul is based on the Scriptural verse in Exodus: "And also the whole of this people will come to its [resting] place in peace.

One of the Holy Brotherhood then pries open the coffin lid. In preparation against the Day of the Resurrection, he places a little sack of earth from the Holy Land under the head of the dead person to pillow him. He also sprinkles some of the sacred earth over the body. Sometimes the custom is observed of loudly calling out the Hebrew name of the dead man (or woman), exhorting him not to forget it through the long night of sleeping in the ground, so that, when the Messiah calls out his name, like a father summoning his beloved son, the resurrected dead will get up instantly and turn his face full to the golden sun rising over Mount Zion.

After this, the immediate kin perform the rite of keriah. The traditional four-inch rent is made in the upper corner of the mourner's garment. For a parent, it is made on the left side, over the heart; for other close kin, on the right side. The mourners cast a little earth on the coffin of their beloved, then leave the rest to the gravediggers. The rabbi or chazzan now begins the recitation of the prayer Justice of the Judgment, and the male mourners repeat after him the ancient words of reconciliation with death:

> "The Lord gave and the Lord has taken away;
> Blessed be the name of the Lord."

When interment has been completed, the officiant recites the supplication: El Moleh Rachamin (O God, full of compassion!), following it on certain days with Psalm 49, beginning, "Hear this, all ye peoples!" and on other days with Psalm 16, beginning, "Keep me, O God." The closest male kin of the deceased recite the Kaddish standing beside the freshly filled grave.

As the mourners start to leave the cemetery, all those present form two rows between which they pass. Comfort is extended to them through the traditional heartfelt prayer: "May God console you together with all those who mourn for Zion and Jerusalem!" With these words, all those present at the burial become identified with the grief of the mourners, praying for the early coming of the Messiah, when, the pious ardently believe, death and grief and evil will all be abolished forevermore.

Once more, like a recurring theme in a symphony, the consolation of the Resurrection is sounded. Before those present leave the cemetery, they are required by custom to pluck some grass, and as they throw it over their shoulders, they recite: "He remembers that we are dust." This is a poetic metaphor extracted from the Psalmist's hope: "And may they blossom out of the city like grass of the earth." Because of "defilement"—they having been in the presence of a corpse—everyone has to wash his hands before leaving the cemetery.

As if to recall to the living the difference between the eternal verities and the dross of the world, the charity-collectors, rattling their coin boxes at the gates of the cemetery, exhort those departing in the words of the Wise King: "*Tzedakah tatzil mi-mavet!*" "Righteousness delivers from death!" (Proverbs 11:4.)

Burial rites today no longer are what they used to be. The changes in the outer circumstances of the life of the Jews have also caused corresponding changes in their religious ideas and practices. Traditionally minded Jews more or less still follow the old ways, but the only really thoroughgoing observers today are found among the Ultra-Orthodox, in particular among the members of the Chasidic sect, but these represent only a small minority among religious Jews.

Changes in burial customs began to be apparent as early as the last decades of the eighteenth century, when the Jewish Enlightenment movement, the Haskalah in Hebrew, first made its appearance in Germany under the aegis of Moses Mendelssohn, "the German Plato." By the middle of the nineteenth century, Reform Judaism had succeeded in throwing overboard as impediments to rational faith many of the burial rites which it considered to be no longer tenable nor, indeed, to have any relationship to modern living and the religious needs of enlightened Jews. In 1846, the Breslau Conference of Liberal Jews adopted a resolution disavowing most of the burial and mourning rites that had been practiced for so many centuries without ever being exposed to critical analysis or revision. Except in the extreme wing of Orthodoxy, even the Chebrah Kaddishah has virtually ceased to exist. Nowadays, the commercial funeral chapel and the professional mortician have taken its place.

It is both difficult and imprudent to indulge in any sweeping generalization about which religious groups among the Jews are committed—and to what extent—to the traditional burial customs. Yet it is easy to see that some of them have made remarkable accommodations to the Gentile environment. More and more, the Jewish funeral parlor that serves the wealthy and the comfortable middle class is beginning to resemble the Protestant funeral parlor. It has the same identifying marks: the hushed decorum, the soft, insinuating organ music, the banks of flowers, the churchly-looking benches, and candelabra on the walls. Even more, the inexpensive pine coffin of former days has practically disappeared, its place having been taken by the expensive bronze casket with sleek, polished surface.

Perhaps the single most un-Jewish burial practice—and one entirely unknown in all previous Jewish religious experience—is the present-day custom—in a certain sense it is a modern expression of primitive magic—that requires the display in the coffin of the body of the dead person. If a man, he is usually decked out in a black tuxedo jacket, white dress shirt, and black tie; if a woman, she is often garbed in evening dress or in a chic afternoon frock. Before the "viewing," the mortuary cosmetician and the hairdresser, like make-up artists in the theatre, try to effect a glamorous and flattering transformation in the appearance of the dead. Sometimes they succeed in making the corpse look more than lifelike!

Just the same, there are still a great many Jews who remain faithful to the ancient burial and mourning rites—some out of reverence for religious tradition, some out of inertia, and not a few because of a sentimental nostalgia for the old "Jewish" ways that their grandfathers and grandmothers followed in a Jewish life that to them seems quite remote and vanishing.

See also BURIAL CLOTHES; CEMETERIES; DEATH; IMMORTALITY; KITTEL; RESURRECTION; SHIVAH; SOUL, THE; TOMBSTONES; WORLD-TO-COME.

C

CABALA (Hebrew, meaning "traditional lore")

In its long history, Jewish religious thought has been characterized by two major trends complementary of each other. No doubt the more preponderant of these two has been *rationalism*. This is represented by the larger part of the Talmud and the vast commentary literature written around it since the sixth century. The other has been *mysticism*, and this has been systematized in the numerous writings which, collectively, are called the "Cabala." Of these, the Sefer Yetzirah (Book of Creation), the Bahir (Brilliance), and the Zohar (Splendor) proved the most influential and enduring.

Nevertheless, it would be erroneous to assume that the rationalism of the Talmud is not also intertwined with the mystical and the abstruse, or that the Cabala is entirely divorced from reason or, for that matter, even opposed to knowledge. The difference between the two supporting camps has been principally one of emphasis. The rationalists chose logic (such as that developed by the Talmudic Sages) as their principal tool for apprehending God, for achieving wisdom (chachmah) and righteousness. The Cabalists tried to reach the same objectives, but in addition, strained after magical and supernatural goals, utilizing "the hidden wisdom."

For centuries, mystical beliefs, fantasies, and rites wrack-

Cabalistic "signs" adorning the Hebrew word melech—"king" (i.e., King of the Universe). (From an illuminated parchment manuscript of a 13th-century machzor [festival prayer-book]. Hamburg State Library.)

The Ten Sefirot—the "Mystic Spheres of God." (From the Cabalistic work Sefer Yetzirah, first printing, Mantua, Italy, 1562.)

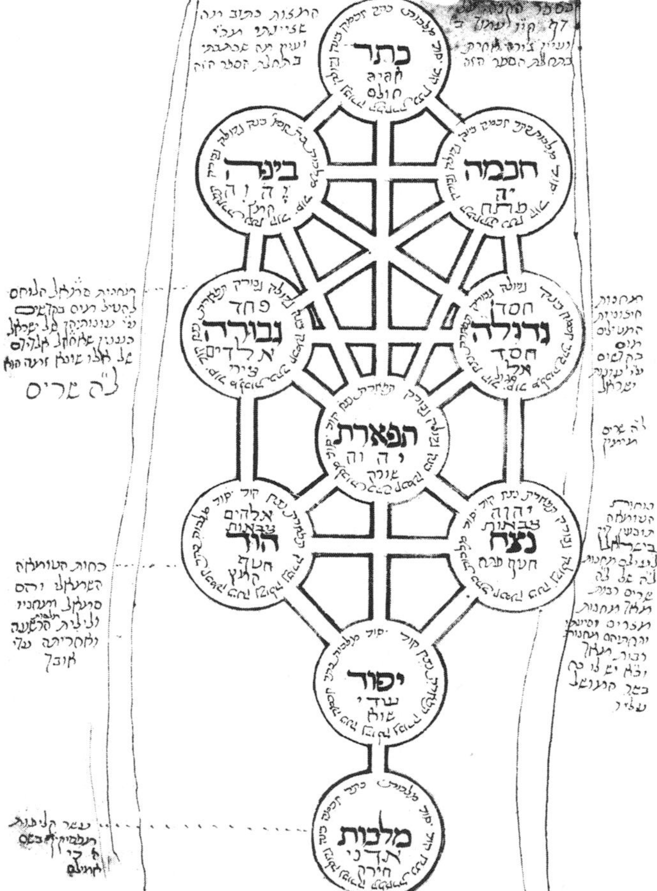

The hand-carved Aron ha-kodesh (Ark of the Law) in the synagogue of The Ari—"The Lion" (the celebrated 16th-century Cabalist Isaac Luria)—in Safed, Palestine. Legend tells of The Ari's initiation into the deepest mysteries of the Cabala by Elijah the Prophet behind this Ark.

Rabbi Naphtali Cohen, of Frankfurt, Germany, making the sun shine at night by means of his Cabalistic powers. Rabbi Cohen (d. 1719) was accused of starting with his esoteric experiments the Great Fire of January 14, 1711, which subsequently destroyed the Frankfurt ghetto.

ed Jewry in Western Asia, North Africa, and Europe like a fever. It is not too difficult to understand the allure that the supernatural and the miraculous held for a people as persecuted and as helpless in the grip of their enemies as the Jews. Denied the natural and concrete means for coping with reality—even at the barest minimum of physical survival—they grasped at the magical and at the wondrous the way a drowning person clutches at a piece of driftwood. If mysticism served them at all, it served mainly as an imaginary crutch upon which to lean while they wrestled with the terror of their lives. Many a time, an excessive preoccupation with the "invisible powers" made the credulous Jewish masses easy prey for visionaries. These were mostly of two varieties: idealists with overwrought imaginations or charlatans intent on performing their magical mumbo-jumbo from either purely mercenary motives or from egotistical power-drives. These adventurers—would-be messiahs mostly, whether nobly or evilly intentioned— flung countless thousands of the deluded and the simple-minded into a state bordering on hysteria or involved them repeatedly in activities that led them only into disaster.

Contrary to popular belief, the Cabala was not created by the Jews of Europe during the Middle Ages. Jewish mysticism goes much farther back into remote times. The history of the Cabala wound a labyrinthine and uncharted course. Emotionally, the Cabala proved to be an intoxicating brew. It combined in itself many contradictory elements: the gentleness of traditional Jewish ethics and practices, a mystically poetic conception of nature and of the soul of man, a morbid occultism, and a dazzling miscellany of superstitions. It also loaded itself down with borrowings of theosophical lore from many religions. For instance, it adopted the Hindu doctrine of metempsychosis—the transmigration of the soul; it took over much of the Chaldean system of astrology and Babylonian-Persian angelology and demonology; it derived its trinitarian notions from the syncretized Serapis-Isis cult of Hellenistic Egypt. Also, it abandoned itself with a desperate passion to numerological reckonings. It constructed its theologic system in part on the Neo-Platonic doctrine of emanations, partly on the gentle quietism of the Mohammedan Sufi sect, and partly on the asceticism of the medieval Church in Europe.

In Hellenistic Egypt, at the time of the Second Temple, the Jewish "wisdom-seekers"—the Gnostics—had already begun to develop a system of hidden lore about the supramundane world. Since for them it was a scrupulous concern of religious principle *not* to write down the secret "wisdom" they had acquired, they transmitted it in the most guarded manner by word of mouth to the few chosen individuals who, because of their supposed purity of character and nobility of intellect, were deemed worthy of receiving it. In consequence, only a small elite was at any one time engaged in the development of the esoteric doctrines and practices that, centuries later, were called Cabala.

The Jews were not alone among the ancient peoples who sought to acquire such esoteric knowledge. In Hellenistic Egypt—a prime locale in antiquity for the fusion of Persian, Egyptian, Hindu, Greek, Jewish, and other brands of religious mysticism—the numerological theories and formulas that had been worked out in the sixth century B.C.E. by the ingenious Greek philosopher-mystagogue Pythagoras were enthusiastically accepted in sophisticated intellectual circles. Among the devout numerologists of pre-Christian Alexandria was Philo, the earnest Platonist-rabbi (*c.* 20 B.C.E.–40 C.E.).

The organized sects of Jewish mystics—the Judean Essenes, the Damascus New Covenanters, and their Egyptian counterparts, the Therapeutae—living apart in their own withdrawn or monastic communities, also were consumed by a thirst for "the hidden wisdom." According to Philo, who was a contemporary, the seal of silence was imposed upon those sectaries by their rabbis: "I bid ye, initiated brethren, who listen with chastened ears, receive these truly sacred mysteries in your inmost souls, and reveal them not to one of the uninitiated, but laying them up in your hearts, guard them as . . . the noblest of possessions . . . the knowledge, namely, of the First Cause, and of virtue, and moreover of what they generate."

What were their intellectual preoccupations? They were directed at the value of all values—the unraveling of the mysteries of heaven and earth, of soul and matter—and at the untying of "the master-knot of human fate." They strained to tear away the obscuring veil from the face of reality; they sought to apprehend—more by intuition and less by reason—the presence of the invisible and hidden reality in that which was merely manifest to the senses. They had to penetrate the phenomena of nature in order to find what significant kernels of the spiritual might be concealed within their outer husks. For the mystics, there seemingly was neither opposition nor contradiction between matter and spirit. Because their quest for God was obsessive, it made them frantic to find out all about His nature and His attributes. They believed that it was by the mediating means of the divine essence of God—the soul—that man was able to rise above the dross and impurities of corporeal life and effect a union with Him.

Babylonia, having become the chief intellectual and religious center of world Jewry after the destruction of the Jewish state in Judea, served during the period of the Geonim (589–1038) as an inexhaustible source for Cabalistic beliefs. In the course of fraternal cultural-religious interchanges, the Babylonian rabbinic mystics initiated many of the Jews in Germany, France, Italy, and Spain into the Cabala. Only to a chosen few did they transmit their theosophical ideas and speculations about God, the secrets of Creation, the spirit world, and the World-to-Come.

At first the Cabala was largely theoretical. But with the onset of the Middle Ages and the intensification of the persecution of the Jews in Europe, a powerful new trend made its appearance in the ranks of the mystics. This was the "Practical Cabala." From poetic fantasy and imaginative abstraction, the pursuit of "the hidden wisdom" had led its votaries into the shadowy and wondrous areas of the magical realization and the miraculous wishful-thinking.

The early medieval Cabalists—at least, the more cultivated speculative ones of Spain and the Provence—held to a unified conception of the universe. They were pantheists (in the Hebraic, not in the Greek sense) who perceived the immanence or indwelling of God in all creation, in all matter. Therefore, they visualized Him as standing outside, above, and beyond the created universe. He had made it, He was of it, yet He himself was not in it. And He had neither beginning nor end. Accordingly, they named Him *En Sof*—"Without End."

This symbolic name for God was coined by the philosophically trained Cabalist, Rabbi Azriel ben Menachem of Catalonia. Attempting to reconcile the mythic Biblical account of the Creation with Aristotle's concept of the eternity of the world, he wrote in his Cabalistic work the Bahir in 1240: "He [i.e., God] was alone, without form and without resemblance to anything else. . . . Hence it is forbidden to lend Him any form or similitude, or even to call Him by his sacred name [i.e., YHVH]." And so, recognizing him to be formless, boundless, and infinite, he was to be referred to as *En Sof*—"the One Without End."

The Cabalists assumed that God himself had not been

directly involved in the stupendous work of the Creation. What then? He had accomplished His task by the mediating instrumentality of His divine attributes or emanations. These the Jewish mystics called *Sefirot* (Spheres). The Gnostics, during the last period of the Second Temple, had taught this very doctrine, as had also Philo of Alexandria. There were the Ten Sefirot, each one, in turn, flowing outward from the preceding one; so all of the first nine streamed from the tenth one—their supreme source: *En Sof*.

As devotees of "the hidden wisdom," the mystics frantically searched the Biblical texts for hints and signs, for symbolic allusions and "secret" meanings. They even took a magical view of the aleph-bet (the Hebrew alphabet), considering it potent with a divine fire. The Cabalists claimed that by means of the twenty-two Hebrew letters had God created the world—had his sacred commandments been formed and revealed to Moses for Israel's salvation. The Cabalists were convinced that if the letters of the Hebrew alphabet could be combined in the right manner and then added up according to the numerical values the Cabalists gave them, the awesome creative powers with which the Hebrew letters were endowed could be released by the "elect," and the most stupendous of miracles accomplished. The Talmud gravely observed that "Bezalel [the artist-craftsman who had made the Ark of the Lord for the Tabernacle in the Wilderness] knew how to arrange the letters by which heaven and earth had been created."

The certainty of the Cabalists that there was concealed a supernatural dynamism-potential in the aleph-bet led them to search for the secret, ineffable, and unutterable name of God, as well as for the "right way" of pronouncing it. In the Hebrew Bible, the Deity is represented by the Tetragrammaton or four letters standing for *Y H V H (Yod Hay Vav Hay)*, yet the name is pronounced by the devout, not directly but allusively, as *Adonai* (My Lord). The Cabalists were confident that, once in possession of that secret knowledge which in former times had been revealed only to a small number of the "elect," they would be able to perform the most dazzling of wonders, even to bringing the Messiah and the Redemption!

In the eerie myths and legends of Jewish folklore that arose during the Middle Ages—a natural outcropping from the overheated Cabalistic climate of life in the ghetto—there was found the popular notion that if Jesus of Nazareth had been able to perform the miracles ascribed to him by Christians, including his accomplishment of walking dryshod on the waters of the Sea of Galilee, it was only because he had made himself master of the "secret" name of God. This name—the *Shem ha-Meforash*—symbolically represented in the Hebrew Scriptures by the Tetragrammaton YHVH, was, for the Cabalists, equivalent to the philosopher's stone with which the alchemists sought to turn base metals into gold. A tenth-century "wonder-working" book advised anyone who wished "to walk upon the water without wetting his feet" to write upon a plate of lead the following formula in which the letters of the Tetragrammaton were variously arranged:

HBKSHFHYAL	YHVHH	ASRGHYAL	YHVHH
HZASNHYAL	YHVHH	MUDDGHYAL	YHVHH

The great medieval rationalist Maimonides (Moses ben Maimon [1135–1204]) tactfully tried to discourage all those who dabbled dangerously in the alchemical pots of "hidden wisdom." In the Mishneh Torah he wrote: "Now these things are exceedingly profound, and not every intellect is capable of sustaining them. Wherefore, Solomon in his wisdom says, respecting them, by way of parable: 'The lambs are for your clothing.' [Proverbs 27:26.] So the Sages say in explanation of this parable: 'The things which conceal the mystery of the Universe, let them be as a garment to you; meaning—keep them to yourself.' "

The book called the Zohar, a name which some people erroneously use interchangeably with the generic term Cabala, contains the most systematic exposition of Jewish mysticism. It presumably was composed by the Spanish rabbinical Cabalist Moses Shem-Tob de Leon (1230–1305). In order to lend it greater authority, its authorship was spuriously attributed to the second-century Rabbinic Sage of Judea, Simeon bar Yochai. Besides being an encyclopedia of Jewish lore, the Zohar also serves as a mystical commentary on the Torah. In its own abstruse and allegoric fashion, it deals with astrology, astronomy, the Ten Sefirot, the Creation, the transmigration of souls, angelology, demonology, and the mystic "science of numbers." Applied in a practical way to the Torah text, the Zohar purports to give the numerical value of each of the Hebrew letters contained in various Scriptural words and verses, all of which can supposedly be added up for the achievement of magical ends.

The Cabalists were tireless and inexhaustibly inventive in their arrangement and scrambling of Hebrew passages of the Bible into squares, triangles, and other geometric forms. Sometimes they constructed word-patterns horizontally, sometimes vertically, at other times backwards or even upside down. To illustrate: the name Elijah in Hebrew can be written in tabular form 130 different ways simply by juggling its letters. In English the name Elijah can be partly patterned as follows (reading from left to right):

Elijah	Ehlija	Ejahli	Eijahl	Elhija
Elahij	Eljahi	Elhaji	Eljiah	Ealijh
Eahlij	Eajhli	Eaijhl	Ealhij	Ehalij
Ehlaij	Ehijla	Ehjial	Ehialj	Ehjail

And so on.

Next to the Bible itself, Cabalistic writings were revered, by their knowledgeable devotees and superstitious folk alike, above all other sacred Jewish writings. For that reason—because they smacked of heresy—they fell into greater disrepute among rabbinical rationalists than they actually deserved. Inadequate acquaintance with its literature and history made the Cabala appear to many as merely a silly hodge-podge of numerological hocus-pocus, alphabetical abracadabra, childish beliefs, extravagant dream-symbolisms, and primitive superstitions. This unpleasant impression was fortified by observing what use the Cabalists made of magical amulets, talismans, incantations, exorcisms, and the recitations of what sounded like pure gibberish.

An example of Cabalistic use made of the various names of God and angels, arranged according to a scrambled "secret" code, is that for conjuring up the Prince of Demons. In the tenth-century Cabalistic book, *The Sword of Moses*, the following magical formula was directed to be written down on a laurel-leaf: "I conjure you, Prince whose name is Abraksas, in the name of SLGYY HVH YH GUTYUS HVH AFRNUHH HVH ASGNUHH HVH BTNUSYY HVH, that you come and reveal to me all that I will ask of you, and do not delay!"

These magical uses became dominant with the emergence of the so-called Practical Cabala in Germany during the Middle Ages and reached the ultimate in development with the establishment in Safed, Galilee, of the Cabalist wonder-working center of "The Lion." (This was the Cabalist name for ARI, Rabbi Isaac Luria, 1533–71.)

The Cabala had a number of goals, but two of them were fundamental. Both were motivated by social-ethical considerations that had been traditional with the Jews. The more obsessive of these was concerned with the redemption of the Jewish people by a divine instrumentality. This the Cabalists hoped to achieve by apprehending God through the lambent flame of love. By undergoing a spiritual purification and rebirth, they expected to hasten the coming of the Messiah. The second objective, which was closely linked to the first, was to find the means for surmounting the difficulties that Jews were made to suffer in their daily lives and to frustrate the evil designs of their enemies. This they felt sure they could accomplish by the exercise of magic: by invoking the aid of invisible powers. Indeed, the Cabalists floundered in a marshland of superstition and pietism.

The search for new mystic formulae and anodynes provided many a broken human reed with an excellent mode of escape from unhappy reality. Paradoxically enough, in trying to lighten the burden of the Jews' plight, the Cabalists only succeeded in adding to it. Besides massacre, hunger, epidemics, expulsions, and ceaseless persecution—their regular portion in life—many Jews now had to cope with the additional terrors of a nightmarish world which was haunted by Satan and the Evil Eye, and populated by transmigrating souls, moaning specters, cackling demons, and agonized dybbukim (the evil spirits or souls of the dead that inhabit the living bodies of the possessed).

Falling during the Middle Ages under Christian monastic influence, with its rejection of the life of the senses, the medieval Jewish Cabalists, too, mortified the flesh in order to subjugate it. This was their paradoxical way of purifying and uplifting the soul. They strove to break Satan's deadly grip upon themselves by the power of penitential prayer and atonement through self-inflicted suffering.

Yet, to sum it all up, behind the obscurantist, the magical, the superstitious, and the unintelligible, there nevertheless glowed a moral incandescence and a humanity. The Zohar, in a revelation of truth, stated the ever old but always new affirmation of the potential of good that resides in man: "In love is found the secret of Divine Unity. It is love that unites the higher and the lower stages of existence, that raises the lower to the level of the higher—where all become fused into one."

See also CHASIDIM; DYBBUK; ESSENES; GOLEM, THE; LAMED-VAV TZADDIKIM; MESSIAH, THE; MESSIAHS, WOULD-BE; MONASTICISM, JEWISH; SHEM HA-MEFORASH; THERAPEUTAE.

CABALISTS. *See* CABALA; CHASIDIM.

CALENDAR, JEWISH (in Hebrew: LUACH)

For more than sixteen hundred years, believing Jews have remained loyal to the Jewish calendar, most often reckoning chronological time from it instead of from the Christian calendar adopted by the Western world. The difference between the two calendars lies in the principle of their computation: the Gregorian calendar is solar, the Jewish one is lunar. The latter evolved over a period of many centuries, going through a number of formulations, much experimentation, and a great deal of controversy.

Because the economy of the early Jewish society was in the main agricultural, the first calendars clearly reflected the special interests and occupations of the soil. One of the earliest of Hebrew calendars, rudimentary in form, was discovered by archaeologists several decades ago in a mound near the site of the ancient town of Gezer in Palestine. While part of the rock-inscription was undecipherable, that which could be read made plain reference to eight months in farmer-almanac fashion:

A month of fruit harvest.
A month of sowing.
A month of after-grass.
A month of flax harvest.
A month of barley harvest.
A month of everything else;
A month of vine pruning.
A month of fig harvest.

Before the Jewish calendar was finally fixed in 358 C.E. by the Patriarch Hillel II in the name of the Bet Din (*which see*) in Jerusalem, it was very unprecise. Time was reckoned by arbitrary means. The science of astronomy was still in swaddling clothes, certainly as far as Jews were concerned. If the learned among them turned to a study of the heavenly bodies, it was only to find a solution to a utilitarian religious need: to determine the exact dates of festivals and fast days so that Jews everywhere could observe them at one and the same time. Unlike the ancient Greeks, Babylonians, and Egyptians, Jews prior to this time had not displayed any particular enthusiasm for the study of astronomy. This feeling undoubtedly had something to do with the religious antipathy that Jews felt for idolatry and for sun-, moon-, and star-worship which were so general among the peoples of the ancient world.

The main interest of the Rabbinic astronomers was to establish, with reasonable certainty, the beginning of each month (Rosh Chodesh). Thus they watched intently for the new moon to appear in the sky. For centuries, during the time of the Second Temple, the Sanhedrin in Jerusalem had held the sole religious authority to proclaim the beginning of the month when two astronomers, called "witnesses," testified that, with their own eyes, they had observed the crescent moon in the sky. Only then did the Sanhedrin dispatch swift messengers in all directions—to Judea, Syria, Babylonia, and elsewhere—to proclaim the New Moon. Torches were lit and fire signals were relayed from peak to peak in the hills of Judea to distant communities.

But it stands to reason that such primitive means of communication must have proven ineffective and confusing for communities located at great distances from Jerusalem, especially after the final Dispersion, which began in 70 C.E. A fixed calendar, formed on precise calculations, had to be created if Jewish religious life was to be synchronized in all the far-flung places—in Greece, Babylonia, Egypt, Cyrenaica, Persia, and Rome.

The study of astronomy for calendrical purposes became a necessary part of the rabbinic curriculum. Many were the "model" calendars presented to the Sanhedrin by the scientific-minded among the Sages. Rabbi Akiba attempted to draw up a uniform lunar calendar during the early portion of the second century C.E. by intercarlating, or adding, an extra month, thus making for a "leap year" of thirteen months. This idea of a leap year almost caused a disastrous schism between the Jews of Judea and those of Babylonia. The quarrel was extremely passionate and lasted for a whole generation.

There were still other notable attempts at calendar-making. The Babylonian savant, Mar Samuel (*c.* 165–250), of the Academy of Nehardea, wrote several astronomical treatises on the calendar. He reckoned the length of the solar year at 365 days and 6 hours; his Rabbinic colleague, Adda ben

Hebrew calendar in an illuminated 13th-century Pentateuch manuscript.

Ahava (*b.* 183) who followed Ptolemaic notions, placed it at 365 days, 5 hours, 55 minutes, and 25/57 seconds.

Despite the fact that the Jewish calendar finally became fixed in 358 C.E., there was no end to the criticisms and disputes leveled at its inaccuracies for centuries thereafter. Among its critics were the illustrious scientist-doctor Isaac Israeli (North Africa, ninth century) and the foremost religious authority of the age, Saadia Gaon (Babylonia, tenth century). Many corrections were offered subsequently, but there was no unanimity among them. It is evident that there must have been a basic error somewhere in the computation.

The Jewish calendar year consists of twelve lunar months: Nissan, Iyar, Sivan, Tammuz, Ab, Ellul, Tishri, Cheshvan, Kislev, Tebet, Shebat, and Adar. Says the Talmud: "The names of the months and the names of the angels were brought from Babylon." According to the Jewish calendar, the moon makes a complete circuit around the earth in 29 days, 12 hours, 44 minutes, and 3 seconds. And so the Rabbinic astronomers gave 29 days each to the months of Tebet, Adar, Iyar, Tammuz, and Ellul, and 30 days each to Tishri, Shebat, Nissan, Sivan, and Ab. Cheshvan and Kislev were purposely left flexible; sometimes they were allotted 30 days, at other times 29. This was done in order to allow for the rearrangement of certain holy days, lest they fall on "prohibited days." For example, there was a Rabbinic ruling that Yom Kippur could not take place on a Friday or on a Sunday. By manipulating the number of days—30 or 29—in Cheshvan and Kislev, this difficulty could be surmounted.

But it was infinitely more difficult to overcome the discrepancy in the time between the lunar and solar years, as the Rabbis had computed them. The solar year was calculated by them to be 365 days, 6 hours, 48 seconds; the lunar year was fixed at 354 days, 8 hours, 48 minutes, and 36 seconds. Accordingly, the lunar year was less than the solar year by 10 days, 21 hours, and 12 seconds. To allow this time differential to go unreconciled would only result in throwing the dates of the Jewish festivals into confusion. And so the Rabbinical astronomers came up with a solution. They would add (or intercarlate) one additional month every third year in each cycle of 19 years. In this way, there would be a thirteenth month—Ve Adar (the Second Adar)—in seven leap years of the nineteen-year cycle; namely, in the third, sixth, eighth, eleventh, fourteenth, seventeenth, and nineteenth years.

Jews, like some other ancient peoples, reckoned each day from evening to evening, in accordance with the description of it given in the Book of Genesis: "And there was evening and there was morning, one day." The day, which consists of twenty-four hours, concludes at nightfall—the borderline between the day that is past and the day about to begin. It is signalized by the appearance of three stars of the second magnitude, clearly visible to the naked eye. (Some modern astronomers assume that, under average conditions of the atmosphere, these stars can be seen early in the evening, when the sun is seven degrees below the horizon.) The week, of course, has seven days. But with the exception of the seventh day, Shabbat (the Sabbath), they have no names but are referred to as "the first day," "the second day," etc. It is also well to note, that, although the religious New Year (Rosh Hashanah) begins with the first day of Tishri, the Jewish calendar designates the month of Nissan, in the springtime, as the beginning of the civil year.

See also NEW MOON; ROSH CHODESH.

CANDLE-LIGHTING. *See* CHANNUKAH LAMP; SABBATH; SABBATH LIGHTS.

CANTILLATION. *See* MUSICAL ACCENTS.

CANTOR. *See* CHAZZAN.

CANTORIAL MUSIC. *See* CHAZZAN.

CEMETERIES

For the religious Jew, the cemetery had far greater significance than that of a mere burial place. From the time of the Greco-Roman period in Jewish history, it was inseparably tied in with the Jew's belief in the immortality of the soul and the physical resurrection of the body. The various names given to Jewish burial grounds present eloquent testimony to this. Commonly, and also interchangeably, used have been *Bet Olam* (House of Eternity) and *Bet Chayyim* (House of the Living), a conception derived from Isaiah 26:19:

> Thy dead shall live, my dead shall arise—
> Awake and sing, ye that dwell in the dust—

Not to be overlooked is the colloquial Jewish term *Dos Guteh Ort* (The Good Place). One need only contrast these Jewish names with the English word "cemetery," which is derived from the Greek *koimeterion* (meaning "the place where the dead sleep") to gauge the profound difference between these concepts of interment.

The Jewish burial ground had its mortuary sights fixed on eternity and on the spiritual certainty that, at the final accounting which would take place at the Last Judgment, to every human being reward would be meted out for a righteous life and punishment for an evil one.

Confidence that the dead will rise bodily at the End of Days is expressed in the words of the benediction that each visitor, upon entering a cemetery, is expected to address comfortingly to all the dead lying in their graves: "Blessed be the Lord our God, King of the Universe, Who created you in justice, Who maintained and supported you in justice, Who caused you to die in justice . . . and Who is certain to bring you to life again in justice."

But this divine justice, the pious believed, could not be achieved for the dead unless their remains were interred in *consecrated* ground. Thus, Jews, wherever their forced wanderings took them, were always passionately concerned with acquiring cemeteries where they could "slumber" among their own until the shofar-blast of the Resurrection would sound for them. "It is sweet for a man to repose among his fathers," was always a favorite Jewish saying. The dying Patriarch Jacob had pleaded with his sons in Egypt: "I am to be gathered among my people; bury me with my fathers!" And this they did. They carried his body back to the Israelite homeland in Caṇaan, and there they laid it to rest beside the bones of his father, Isaac, and of his grandfather, Abraham, in the family sepulcher within the Cave of Machpelah at Hebron.

During the Middle Ages, the custom became general for Jews, individually and congregationally, to visit their cemeteries in times of severe persecution, calamity, epidemic, or illness. They would pray before the graves of beloved ancestors or of sainted rabbis, and implore them to intercede with God in their behalf. On Tishah b'Ab—the Ninth of Ab, the fast day that commemorates the Destruction of the First and Second Temples in Jerusalem—the entire Jewish community of a city or town would march in procession around its cemetery, intoning penitential prayers. Similarly, during Ellul—the Hebrew month of penitence—it was the custom to visit, pray, and indulge in self-examination before the graves of ancestors and of learned rabbis.

It is by no means an overstatement to say that, in the institutional scheme of the Jewish religion, next to the establishment of the synagogue, which was to serve as the center for divine worship and for Jewish community life, the acquisition of a plot of ground consecrated for burial was considered of the greatest urgency. For more than two thousand years, in all the uncounted migrations, expulsions, and flights of Jews from place to place, their first concern was to find security for their lives; but, paradoxically, their very next thought was to find security for their bodies when death would come. Strangers in a hostile world while alive (it should be kept in mind that the civil emancipation of the Jews did not begin until the end of the eighteenth century, following the social revolutions in the American Colonies and in France), they did not wish to be buried as pariah-strangers, as was so often the case, along the fenced-off fringes of Christian cemeteries where lay criminals, heretics, and suicides. What would they do on the Day of Resurrection, when all the Jewish devout would rise from their graves? Were they interred in unconsecrated ground, they would be doomed, like all soulless matter, to lie inert in their graves, slumbering through eternity.

A phenomenon of unusual socio-religious interest was the appearance, toward the end of the nineteenth century, in the United States, Canada, and Great Britain, of the so-called landsmanshaften, the fraternal societies composed exclusively of Yiddish-speaking immigrants from the same town in "the old country." Strange is the fact that these clubs and lodges, made up of fellow-townspeople (landsleit) from all the regions of Eastern Europe, sprang up quite spontaneously in the big cities to meet the urgent needs of the new arrivals not only for the practice of mutual aid and for the reassurance which the familiar brings but also for cemetery plots! It is a matter of statistical record that, before the out-

Israelite infant of Patriarchal period (18th–17th centuries B.C.E.*) buried in a jar. (American Friends of the Hebrew University.)* LEFT

Ossuaries or stone caskets in which the bones of the dead were deposited in a second "burial" after the flesh had fallen away. Second Temple period. (American Friends of the Hebrew University.)

break of World War II, in New York City alone there were active in cemetery arrangements more than three thousand such organizations, in addition to the thousands of religious congregations that shared the same preoccupation. During the lifetime of a member, his landsmanshaft devoted itself to providing him with "benevolent aid," if he needed it. Then, when he, his wife, or any of his sons and daughters died, it marshaled all of its forces and assets to give them decent and proper burial in consecrated ground. Of all practical matters touched upon in the constitutions and by-laws of these numerous societies, the provisions for the burial of members and their families were most important.

Indicative of the prime importance given by Jews to owning their own cemeteries is the third of seven requests made in the celebrated petition of Rabbi Menasseh ben Israel of Amsterdam. This was addressed to the Privy Council of Oliver Cromwell on November 13, 1655, asking for the admission of Jews to England, from which they had been expelled four centuries before, in 1290, and seeking to "be allowed to have a plot or cemetery outside the city for burying our dead without being molested by anyone."

It had become commonplace for Jews living in Christian countries to suffer molestation from jeering mobs as they bore their dead in procession to the cemetery. The desecration, or even outright destruction, of their burial grounds usually accompanied every massacre or riot against the Jews. Their tombstones were, not infrequently, "appropriated" by the Christian clergy for the construction of new churches. Even in our day there hardly remains a Jewish graveyard in all the countries of the world which, at one time or another, has not suffered acts of vandalism and profanation at the hands of anti-Semites. One case of such overt hostility is detailed in the complaint by Nathan Levy, of Philadelphia, published in the *Pennsylvania Gazette* in 1751. He wrote that "unthinking persons had fired several shots against the Jews' burying ground."

Interesting, culturally, are the stern prohibitions laid down by several enlightened popes and princes during the Middle Ages against this abuse of the religious and human sentiments of Jews. Pope Gregory X issued a bull on October 7, 1272, in which he raised the threat of excommunication for such ghoulish acts of vandalism: "We decree, in order to halt the wickedness and avarice of evil men, that no one shall dare to wreck or destroy a cemetery of the Jews, or to dig up human bodies for the sake of getting money [by holding the Jews up for ransom]."

When Premysl Ottakar II of Bohemia decided to extend legal status to the Jews living in his domain, he included in his decree of 1254 the warning: ". . . and if a Christian does damage, in any wicked way, to their graveyard, or enters it by force, he should be condemned to death."

It is not difficult to understand why, since their enemies persecuted them so consistently in life, they should also wish to harass them in death. The Jew who died posed a problem that was, to say the least, fantastic. It was far from easy for him to be buried! Everywhere, restrictive measures operated against it. In all of England during the eleventh century there was only one Jewish cemetery; it was situated in London and guarded against desecrators and vandals by high walls. No person of modern times can at all imagine what tremendous problems and hazards burial for those Jews who lived in remote parts of the country and whose bodies had to be borne to London, involved. Similarly, and at the same time, the only cemetery allowed to Jews in the entire kingdom of Bavaria was situated in Regensburg.

The journey of a Jewish funeral party to the cemetery was really an odyssey, and sometimes even an episode in gory tragedy. It was costly, fatiguing, time-consuming, and–worse–dangerous to life and limb. The mourners, too few in number and not permitted to carry arms, were ready prey for fanatics, robber-bands, feudal lords, and rapacious municipal authorities in all of the cities and towns that they had to

Staircase leading to individual tombs in rock catacombs of Bet Shearim, near Haifa, 1st and 2nd centuries C.E. *(American Friends of the Hebrew University.)* LEFT

More than 200 sarcophagi from the 2nd and 3rd centuries C.E., *resting in rock niches, have been discovered in the catacombs of Bet Shearim, near Haifa, by archaeologists of the Hebrew University. (Israel Government Tourist Office.)*

pass through. They were obliged to pay at every step of the way (the levies varied in different places): a tax for the right to use the public highway, a tax for passing through the town, a tax for forming a funeral procession, a tax for the coffin, a tax for having a grave dug, etc. The "taxes"—both official and unofficial—extracted from the mourners were so onerous and outrageous that they stirred the ire of Friedrich the Belligerent, king of Austria. Therefore, when in 1244 he granted a protective charter to the Jews in his provinces, he stated with brutal forthrightness in Article 13: "Likewise, if the Jews, as is their custom, should transport any of their dead either from city to city, or from province to province, or from one Austrian domain into another we do not wish anything to be demanded of them by our customs officers. However, should a customs officer extort anything, then he is to be punished for *praedatio mortui,* which means, in common language, robbery of the dead."

During the long Biblical age (from the time of the conquest of Canaan by Joshua) and through the early centuries following the end of Judea as the Jewish state, affluent and prominent Jews who died were buried in caves and grottoes.

Stone sarcophagus from the 2nd century C.E. *found in the rock catacombs of Bet Shearim, near Haifa. (American Friends of the Hebrew University.)*

This is No. 20 of the 30 rock catacombs discovered in ancient Bet Shearim, near Haifa, containing 140 tombs with Hebrew inscriptions. Hellenistic ornamentation and scenes from Greek mythology, sculptured in relief, decorate some of them. Bet Shearim after the Destruction, was the seat of the Bet Din under the Patriarch Judah ha-Nasi (c. 200 C.E.*). (American Friends of the Hebrew University.)*

They were put to rest in niches and vaults (hypogea) carved out of solid rock wall, and closed off with a large stone, circular in shape and whitened with chalk, which was rolled across the entrance as a warning to passers-by against profanation, and to the priests that they were not to approach, for proximity to the dead would automatically make them impure. Certain scholars of mortuary customs speculate that this whitened stone may have been the precursor of the tombstone as we know it. The "Tombs of the Kings" in Jerusalem still serves as the most interesting example extant of hewn-rock sepulture, which was already an ancient practice when Abraham purchased the Cave of Machpelah for a family tomb some four thousand years ago.

It was the custom—at least it was in Judea during the Second Temple period—that the body of the eminent deceased be left lying for a certain number of years in the rock chamber until the flesh had fallen away, so that all that was left was the skeleton. Afterward, the bones would be carefully gathered and wrapped in linen, anointed with fine aromatic oil and wine, and tied up securely in the manner of the Egyptian mummies. Then, in a second funeral, they would either be buried in the ground or placed in an ossuary (a stone box designed in imitation of the Roman funerary urn). But the ordinary masses, being too poor to afford the luxury of a rock chamber, found their final resting place in the most natural of sepulchers—Mother Earth: "Dust thou art and to dust shalt thou return."

Familiar to the world are the cavernous catacombs lying underneath the city of Rome which were used as burial places for the early Christians. Less well-known, certainly, is the fact that the Jewish colony of that time in the Imperial City also laid its dead to rest in the so-called Jewish catacombs. These latter contain several cubicles with nearly faded wall-paintings of plants and animals and epitaphs in Greek that are ornamented with such Jewish religious symbols derived from the Temple ceremonial in Jerusalem as the menorah, the shofar, the lulab and etrog, the laver, etc. Even a few funerary clay lamps and shards of gilded glass have been discovered there by archaeologists.

After the final Dispersion of the Jews of Judea in 70 C.E., life for them in all their foreign settlements became more difficult and constricted. Even the cemeteries became extremely crowded, since the purchase of additional land was rarely permitted Jews, especially by the Christian and Mohammedan rulers during the medieval period. In consequence, when Hai Gaon (*d.* 1038) became the supreme religious authority of Babylonian Jewry, he rendered a Rabbinic decision making it permissible to bury bodies one layer upon another, provided that at least seven handbreadths of earth separated them. All Jewish cemeteries in Europe during the Middle Ages, having no other choice, adopted this vertical method of burial.

In the old cemetery in Prague, archaeologists discovered as many as twelve banks of graves, one lying on top of the other. This resulted in an uneven surface, and presented a weird spectacle of crowding, a sinking into the earth of tombstones at every conceivable angle. That this kind of cemetery, forced upon the Jews against their will by their desperate plight, violated their sensibilities, may be deduced from the traditional expression of remorse so frequently made when graves had to be removed. In 1903, when the municipal authorities of Prague ordered sections of the old Jewish cemetery dug up and the bodies—or what remained of them—re-interred in another spot, an inscription in Hebrew was put up on the cemetery wall. It was a supplication to God to

Photograph taken about 1875 of a section of the Jewish cemetery in Prague.

Entrance into Jewish cemetery at Cracow, Galicia, before the Nazi occupation.

Rabbi David de Sola Pool, spiritual leader of Shearith Israel Synagogue in New York City, stands beside the grave of Gershom Mendes Seixas, who was rabbi of the congregation during the American Revolution. The grave is in one of the oldest cemeteries in the New World (dating back to the 17th century), the Spanish-Portuguese cemetery on the "New Bowery" in which are buried some of the most prominent Jews of old Nieuw Amsterdam. (Photo by Marynn Ausubel.)

forgive the sin that had been committed by the Jews of Prague when they violated the final rest of the dead with such extreme rudeness.

In former centuries, each cemetery had a house of ablution (taharah) in which the Chebrah Kaddishah (Holy Brotherhood) washed the dead and prepared them, according to ancient ritual practices, for burial. There, too, the devout intoned prayers and recited appropriate selections from the Book of Psalms. In our own time, while Orthodox cemeteries still maintain the traditional taharah house, its practical uses have become sharply curtailed; American Conservative and Reform Jews, for instance, have delegated those last attentions for the dead entirely to the professional morticians operating the commercial funeral parlors and "chapels."

More and more in their appearance Jewish cemeteries have come to resemble those of Christians. The least changing, understandably, are the burial grounds of the Orthodox. Here the graves lie unusually close to one another, the many tombstones giving a cluttered-up impression. The explanation for this odd unconcern with external appearances is that, from the Middle Ages on, an austere spirit began to manifest itself among Jews toward their dead; it was the immortal soul and not the tenement of clay, crumbling into dust in the ground, that was considered important. The same kind of indifference with which the body was regarded was extended to the grave. Grass that grew over and around it was allowed to run wild; no flowers or shrubs were planted around the gravestone. Whether this attitude stemmed originally from a taboo is not clear, but there did exist an unchanging rabbinic prohibition against using anything found in a cemetery for any other purpose whatsoever than what was strictly required for the interment of the dead. That is why the traditional cemetery gives such an utterly unkempt and neglected appearance, seeming scornful of any visual mark of beauty.

But the cemeteries of other Jews than the Orthodox have sharply diverged from this custom. More and more in their externals these have come to resemble the well-kept burial grounds of Christians.

See also BURIAL CLOTHES; BURIAL RITES AND CUSTOMS; IMMORTALITY; MENORAH; MERIT OF THE FATHERS; RESURRECTION; SHIVAH; TOMBSTONES; YAHRZEIT; YIZKOR.

CEREMONIAL OBJECTS, JEWISH. *See* ART, CEREMONIAL.

CHACHAMIM, TALMIDAI. *See* SAGES, RABBINIC.

CHACHMAH (Hebrew, meaning "wisdom")

What furnished the key to the "highest good"? *Wisdom,* answered the ancient Egyptians, Babylonians, Persians, Greeks, and Jews. As to what constituted the "highest good," they were not in full agreement. The Greeks, for example, endowed wisdom with an intellectual goal. The concept of Jewish chachmah differed from it in many ways; chachmah had an over-all social and moralistic coloration. The "highest good," in Jewish belief, was the disinterested practice among one's fellow men of righteousness and "loving-kindness." By means of knowledge, the application of reason, and the conclusions of the understanding, the seeker of truth was enabled to enter into a state of inner grace through the most splendid portal of all: *the wisdom of being good and of doing good.*

The Talmudic Sage, Rabba, gave it definition in succinct form: "The aim of wisdom is repentance and the performance of good deeds." The moral content of wisdom was also stressed by the poet-philosopher of Spain, Solomon ibn Gabirol (1021–58). He called chachmah "the fountain of life" that streams from God, and thus he titled his well-known philosophical work *Mekor Chayyim* (*Fons Vitae,* in Latin). But upon one thing Jewish tradition has agreed: The Torah is the principal repository of wisdom. "There is no wisdom without Torah," categorically states the Cabalists' "scriptures," the medieval Zohar.

Yet the intellectual Jewish view on this matter in former times was hardly parochial. Talmudic Judaism, it should be recalled, had its blossoming in the midst of Hellenistic civilization. Nurtured, in part, in the spirit of contemporary Greco-Roman culture, it was humanistic up to the point where it was not considered a violation of religious scruple to say with the Rabbinic teachers: "Find the hour between day and night in which you can learn the wisdom of the Greeks."

It has been a noticeable characteristic of intellectual Jews in every age that they have attempted to reconcile Jewish cultural values and those of the dominant Gentile culture and to show that a certain kinship existed between them. During the Hellenistic period, religious and secular Jewish writers alike attempted to draw comparisons (these were not infrequently a little strained) between Jewish chachmah and Greek wisdom, which was called philosophy. One Jewish philosophical writer in Alexandria, Aristobulus (180–146 B.C.E.), claimed that Plato had read the Torah and other writings of the Jews "and had manifestly studied all that is in them." He also asserted that when Alexander the Great visited Jerusalem, his teacher, Aristotle, had accompanied him there, and in the holy city of the Jews, the Greek philosopher had obtained the wisdom-writings of King Solomon. The naïve implication Aristobulus thus forwarded was that what had helped make Aristotle a great philosopher, was the chachmah he had acquired from Solomon's writings.

Seeing what corrosive assimilationist effect Greek philosophy, with its logical skepticism and challenges, had on Jewish traditional thinking, some Rabbinic authorities in late Hellenistic times declared open war against it. One wrathful defender of the faith is quoted in the Talmud as having cried: "Cursed be the man who has his son taught Greek philosophy!" This complaint was without a doubt well justified in fact, and was aptly expressed by another Sage: "There were a thousand students in my father's academy. Five hundred studied Torah and five hundred studied Greek philosophy, but of the latter were left only my nephew and I. . . ."

Some Jewish seekers after wisdom ended their quest (for chachmah) in apostasy. The classic example held up to young Jewish intellectuals in every generation of the dangers inherent in the skeptical philosophy of the Greeks, was Elisha ben Abuyah (sometimes called Acher), the brilliant teacher of Rabbi Meir (second century C.E.). His absorption with Greek philosophy led him in the end to abandon the faith of his fathers and thus become the "beneficiary" of the execrations of his Jewish contemporaries.

The intervention of Greek philosophy, especially that of Plato and Aristotle, into rabbinic theology during the Middle Ages, stirred up a storm of opposition from the traditionalists. In 1322, the philosophical Spanish-Jewish writer, Joseph ibn Caspi, wrote a bitter diatribe against the ban clapped on the philosophical method of Jewish religious inquiry by the rabbinical literalists of his day. His plaint was: "How can I know God, and that He is One, unless I first know what knowing means, and what constitutes unity? Why should these matters be left to non-Jewish philosophers? Why should Aristotle retain sole possession of the treasures of wisdom that he stole from Solomon?"

To the Jew of every generation who pursued the self-same ancient traditions and values, acquiring chachmah was no idle objective. He deemed it an exalted ethical ideal wherewith to perfect himself in virtue as well as to bring more light and moral understanding to all mankind with the end-aim of a more noble and just existence. The Sages—and it was recognized that not every Jew had the innate capacity for becoming a sage—were driven by complex social-moral motivations to seek chachmah and to open the windows of understanding to the humblest of people. They ventured to do this by means of simple pedagogic illustrations:

> "What is the best thing in the world?" asked the Rabbinic teachers.
> "A good heart.
> "What is the worst?
> "A bad heart."

In Jewish belief, most of the time, there existed no validity for wisdom without the saving grace of love for people. Even if they were wrong anatomically, the ancient teachers of the Jewish religion were correct ethically when they considered the seat of the intellect to be not in the brain but in the heart.

See also ETHICAL VALUES, JEWISH; SAGES, RABBINIC; TALMID CHACHAM; TORAH STUDY.

CHAD GADYA (Aramaic, meaning "One Kid")

This Passover song, sung at the close of the Seder service, was not known among European Jews before 1590, when it first appeared in a Haggadah printed in Prague. From all appearances, it is nothing but a nursery song that must have enjoyed a wide popularity among the German and Polish Jews of medieval times. Because the Seder, celebrated during the first two nights of Passover week, is strictly a home service, "Chad Gadya," in all likelihood, was included to provide the small children with an active part in the joyous ceremony of recalling the liberation of the Jews from their bondage in Egypt.

Some scholars interpret the song, constructed out of cumulative rhymes, as a moral allegory illustrating the Scriptural *lex talionis* principle of "an eye for an eye," which pursues all evildoers inexorably. All the animal characters and objects in the song are purported to represent the various oppressors of the Jewish people throughout their history—the Babylonians, the Egyptians, the Romans, the Greeks, the

Turks, etc.–each of which, by acts of divine retribution, is sooner or later destroyed for persecuting the "one only kid"–the Jewish people.

> Then came the Holy One, blessed be He,
> And destroyed the Angel of Death
> That slew the butcher
> That killed the ox
> That drank the water
> That quenched the fire
> That burned the stick
> That beat the dog
> That bit the cat
> That ate the kid.

Paulus Cassel, the eminent nineteenth-century German folklorist, was one of those who held to this view. To him, "Chad Gadya" appears in all its true sublimity by the side of our popular ballads which consist of ironical and satirical views concerning the condition of the world.

A number of parallels to "Chad Gadya" have been found in various bodies of European and Eastern folklore. As recently as 1872, the French scholar, Gaston Paris, unearthed an old French ballad, "Le Chanson du Chevreau," which bears a striking similarity to "Chad Gadya." It is also worthy of note that in 1835 there appeared in New York a pamphlet titled *A Kid, a Kid, or the Jewish Origin of the Celebrated Legend*: *The House That Jack Built.* Also, in 1863, a Henry George, in London, published a booklet with the descriptive title *An Attempt to Show That Our Nursery Rhyme, "The House That Jack Built," Is an Historical Allegory, to Which Is Appended a Translation and Interpretation of an Ancient Jewish Hymn.* In fact, it has generally been conceded by English folklorists that "The Pig That Wouldn't Go Over the Stile" (also called "The Old Woman and Her Pig"), "Tity-mouse and Taty-Mouse," and several other folk tales, are modeled on "Chad Gadya." There are, in addition to the above-mentioned, a Kaffir version in South Africa, another in modern Greek known as "The Tragedy of the Child," and a Siamese analogue. But upon what song "Chad Gadya" is modeled, no one has yet discovered.

From all this, it can be inferred that cultural diffusion is a process that is unceasing among all the peoples of the earth, and folklore and folksong constitute a common currency for all mankind.

CHALITZAH (Hebrew, meaning a "taking off," an "untying")

Biblical law provided that, if a man died and left his wife childless, his surviving brother, if unmarried, was required to "take her to him to wife." The resulting union was called "levirate marriage" or, in Hebrew: *yibbum*. The principle behind it was the performance of an act of brotherly devotion and piety by the survivor, whereby he would "raise up unto his brother a name in Israel." This merely meant that, in marrying his sister-in-law, he would be perpetuating his brother's memory by continuing his line.

While levirate marriage was universally recognized and revered as fulfilling a law commanded by Scripture, the surviving brother frequently found himself in an embarrassing position: For various reasons he might consider it either inconvenient or undesirable to marry his brother's widow. After all, she might very well be childless as his wife, too, and barrenness was always a supreme tragedy in Jewish family life. For such an exigency the Rabbinic jurists, who were generally compassionate and realistic men, devised the rite of chalitzah, whereby the reluctant brother–and sometimes his brother's widow, as well–could be set free from the prospects of a tie that might prove burdensome. It is a cause for wonderment

Rite of chalitzah. Holland, 1683.

that the ceremony of chalitzah is still practiced today by many Orthodox Jews who follow strictly the directions for its performance exactly as found in the Book of Deuteronomy.

Ninety-one days have to elapse after the death of the husband before chalitzah can be effected. It is performed before three rabbinic judges, either in the synagogue or in the home of a rabbi, and involves the use of a special shoe of traditional design called "the chalitzah shoe." The sole and upper of this shoe, which is the property of the congregation, are sewed together by leather thongs, and it is laced and strapped on the foot of the surviving brother by strings arranged in an intricate design. The unfortunate man who wears the shoe is required to walk in it for a distance of four cubits in the presence of the three judges, after which his sister-in-law recites the accusation: "My brother-in-law refuses to raise unto his brother a name in Israel. He will not marry me!"

In reply, the man recites laconically: "I do not wish to take her." Publicly rejected, his sister-in-law kneels down and takes off from his foot the chalitzah shoe, which she flings from her in feigned indignation. And, since time-honored custom, which is not always pretty, requires it of her, she spits contemptuously before him and recites the following words, which rasp out with the bitterness of an anathema: "Thus shall it be done to the man who will not build up the house of his brother, and his name shall thenceforth be called in Israel 'the house of him who had his shoe loosened'!" This last phrase she repeats three times, and the assembled judges and witnesses also recite it after her three times. Then the castigated brother returns the shoe to the judges, who respond with these grieving words: "May it be the will of God that Jewish women may no longer have to be subjected to [the humiliation of] chalitzah!"

Special shoe used in the rite of chalitzah. Germany, 18th–19th centuries.

It should be remembered that the practice of levirate marriage has been common among primitive and even aboriginal peoples, ancient as well as modern. The Aztecs of Mexico, for instance, had a law that required the widow either to marry a brother of her deceased husband or, if he had none, a member of his own clan. The wife, it should be noted, always represented property: She was a chattel, and as such, was expected to remain "in the family."

A resolution concerning this practice, adopted by congregations of American Reform Judaism at a convention in Philadelphia in 1869, was, in effect, a declaration of war against it: "The precept of levirate marriage and of chalitzah has lost for us all meaning, import, and binding force."

See also DIVORCE; DOWRY; MARRIAGE.

CHALLAH. *See* SABBATH.

CHAMETZ. *See* PASSOVER.

CHAMISHAH ASAR BI'SHEBAT (Hebrew, meaning "the fifteenth day of [the Jewish month of] Shebat")

No pretense was made in early Jewish religious writings that Chamishah Asar Bi'Shebat was anything but an agricultural or "nature" festival; there is not even one mention of it in the Bible. That it is a survival of a very ancient festival of prehistoric times, when the Israelites were not yet monotheists but were animists or nature-worshipers, can be readily supposed. In the Jewish calendar of the holy days, this holiday was accorded by the Rabbinic Sages a very modest position as a semifestival; the Sages overlaid many Jewish folkways and customs, however secular their character, with a quasi-religious patina.

The first mention of Chamishah Asar Bi'Shebat—the day on which the Judean farmer used to figure the mandatory tithes (taxes) of his produce for the Temple—was made in the Mishnah without attributing to it any historic or religious significance. It was clearly indicated as a festival of an agricultural character; it occurred at the time of the very first stirrings of new life in the earth that presaged the coming of spring in Eretz Yisrael (the Land of Israel). The Mishnah Fathers referred to it as *Rosh Hashanah Lallanot*—"the New Year of the Trees."

But perhaps the real significance of Chamishah Asar Bi-'Shebat is the manner in which it has been transformed from an agricultural festival of the ancient inhabitants of Israel to a national tree-planting festival by the present-day inhabitants of Israel. It is now called *Tu Bi 'Shebat,* with the phonic sound *tu* representing in Hebrew the letters *tet* and *vav,* whose combined numerical value is fifteen; in Hebrew, *chamishah asar* means "fifteen."

Tree-planting by Israeli schoolchildren on Tu Bi'Shebat. (Israel Office of Information.)

Since the final Dispersion of the Jews in 70 C.E. (after the Temple was destroyed), it became the custom among the "exiles" to taste all obtainable fruits and nuts from Palestine: figs, dates, almonds, oranges, lemons, the fruit of the carob tree (St. John's Bread, called *bokser* in Yiddish), etc. By eating of these fruits, the "exiles" associated themselves in a physical sense with the land of their forefathers.

An elaborate ritual for the celebration of Chamishah Asar Bi'Shebat was introduced by the Cabalists of Palestine in the seventeenth century. On the eve preceding the festival, during the rite of fruit- and nut-tasting (among the Cabalists, everything they did was ritualistic), they would read "between courses" excerpts from a fruit-and-tree "anthology" that was culled from the Bible, the Zohar, and writings by the celebrated Cabalist of the seventeenth century, Rabbi Nathan of Gaza. (He was the visionary who had played the role of Elijah, the herald of the Redemption, to the would-be Messiah, Sabbatai Zevi, thereby throwing all of Jewry and part of Christendom and Islam into turmoil and confusion. *See* MESSIAHS, WOULD-BE.)

In symbolic numerical equation with the fifteenth of Shebat, the Cabalists tasted exactly fifteen fruit courses. Today in Israel, the same number of fruits and nuts—dates, figs, grapes, raisins, lemons, oranges, apples, bananas, almonds, cactus pears, etc.—are eaten, although mostly without benefit of the reading from sacred texts. Nevertheless, the Ultra-Orthodox Sefaradim of Jerusalem, many of them descendants of the old Cabalists, celebrate the festival in nearly the same way that their forefathers did, four centuries ago. On the night preceding the holiday, they assemble in festive mood in their synagogues and yeshibot (Talmudical academies) to sing, dance, and also to pray and read from Nathan of Gaza's compilation of agricultural excerpts, and they do not disperse until the break of dawn.

On Tu Bi'Shebat, all the schoolchildren of Israel—in city, town, village, kibbutz, and moshav—engage in a vast tree-planting operation. Despite the many millions of trees already planted in Israel, there is still in that country which was denuded of cover and made arid by many centuries of neglect a desperate need for further reforestation. Tu Bi'Shebat in modern Israel is therefore considered a national holiday with patriotic and social implications. The Israelis, physically and emotionally involving all the children in the tree-planting operation, use it as an educative instrument to make the children conscious of their nation's needs and of their own responsibilities as future citizens, in fulfillment of the Scriptural verse from Leviticus 19:23:

> And when ye shall come into the land, and shall have planted all manner of trees for food . . .

See also CABALISTS; ERETZ YISRAEL.

CHANNUKAH (Hebrew, meaning "dedication"; hence, "the Feast of Dedication"; also known as "the Feast of Lights")

Although Channukah is numbered among the "minor" festivals in the Jewish religious calendar for reasons that, in part, are baffling, in the national consciousness of the Jews it ranks only second to Passover (Pesach) in historical significance. Like Passover, it, too, is commemorated as a historic festival of liberation. In Egypt, more than a thousand years before Channukah was instituted, the enslaved Jews, led by Moses, threw off the yoke of bondage in an uprising that marked the beginning of a new historic era for Israel as a people, and for its adoption of the laws and ethical values of the Torah as a way of life. A comparable heroic feat was accomplished in Judea in 168 B.C.E., when small insurrectionary bands of dedicated Jews, under the leadership of the

A Channukah draydl, early 19th century. Jewish children of Central and East European extraction have played the game of trendel *or* draydl *on Channukah for many generations.* ABOVE LEFT

Channukah celebration. (Copper engraving in Jüdisches Ceremoniell, *by Paul Christian Kirchner, Nüremburg, 1724.)* ABOVE RIGHT

Antiochus (Epiphanes) IV. (From a drawing by Ralph Illgan after a contemporary coin.) BELOW

Jewish children playing Channukah draydl, a game resembling the English put-and-take, c. *1900. (Pen sketch by Clara Epstein.)* BOTTOM

Hasmonean priest Mattathias and his son, Judah the Maccabee ("the Hammer"), routed the armies of the megalomaniac Seleucidan despot, Antiochus IV (called Epiphanes, "the Risen God"), after three years of savage guerrilla fighting.

The story of that unique struggle is chronicled in I and II Maccabees, writings which are included in the extra-Biblical anthology of semisacred books, the Apocrypha, and in the Scroll of Antiochus, a brief work that probably was produced in Babylonia long before the tenth century. From these writings one gathers that it was a fiercely contested war, precipitated by the ruthless suppression decreed by Antiochus for the practice of the Jewish religion.

Antiochus aimed to end the religious and cultural separatism of the Jews and to bring Judea into line so he could carry through his plan for a monolithic Hellenic empire. In a consistent program, he initiated a series of actions for the rapid and complete Hellenization of the Jews and for their conversion to the polytheistic religion of the Greeks.

The Roman historian Tacitus gave this version of Antiochus' intentions: "In dealing with the Jews, his object was to remove their superstitions, to give them Greek customs." The Jewish chroniclers of his time attributed to Antiochus a more malevolent motivation. They defined his intention to be "that all [nations] should be one people [i.e., Greek], and that each should forsake his own laws," noting that he had ordered the Jews to suspend their traditional worship in the Temple and to cease offering sacrifices to their God. To bring the matter to a decisive head, Antiochus directed that the Jews make a public demonstration of their divorce from their religion by violating its laws and practices: that they "profane the Sabbath and the feasts and . . . pollute the sanctuary [i.e., the Holy of Holies] . . . that they should build altars and temples and shrines for idols; and should sacrifice swine's flesh . . . and that they should leave their sons uncircumcised." And as for the Jew who did not obey the word of the king, he would die!

The events involving the Jews in Judea moved in a steady acceleration of horror. On the fifteenth day of the month of Kislev, in the year 168 B.C.E., the Temple sanctuary was desecrated by the enemy. A gigantic statue of Zeus Olympus was raised on a pedestal behind the Altar of Sacrifice. The Temple courts, where formerly the Levites had raised their voices in reverent Hebrew psalmody, now became the scene of lewd bacchanalian revels. In those acts of outrage and in the national humiliation of the Jews, their own High Priest, Jason, and the Sadducean upper-class sycophants and opportunists played their collaborationist parts only too well.

A cry of anguish convulsed the people. Many refused to obey the decrees of the conqueror. Thousands were slain, and thousands more fled into the wilderness or hid in caves. They wandered about, dressed in the skins of sheep and goats, famished and hunted, daring to show their faces in the villages only in the dark of night.

It was at this juncture of national tribulation that love for their religion and their people flamed among the Jews into a passion such as they had never before experienced. It led them into a course of action which marked the historic beginning not only of self-conscious peoplehood but also of the tradition of martyrdom, in which, to die *al kiddush ha-Shem* (to sanctify the Name) was valued as the highest virtue, the most glorious of all destinies. This tradition two centuries later was carried over into Christianity by the early Jewish Christians, and martyrdom subsequently became a classic feature of Gentile Christianity.

The Maccabean uprising in 168 B.C.E. was an inevitable consequence of these events. Many were the heroic deeds, the acts of self-immolating sacrifice, that the guerrilla bands, unused to warfare and fighting at first with the most primitive of weapons, performed against the well-armed and superbly trained Seleucidan troops. The latter were decisively beaten at Emmaus in 165 B.C.E., an outcome which was the cause for universal amazement.

When the victorious insurgents swept into Jerusalem, the most heartbreaking desolation met their eyes. They found the Temple profaned and half-ruined. Its great gates had been burned and the priests' chambers demolished. After smashing the idol of Zeus and clearing the Temple courts of all the debris, the Jews purified the sanctuary. (Without this historical background, it would be impossible to understand the character and significance of Channukah.)

On the twenty-fifth day of Kislev (December) in the year 165 B.C.E., Judah the Maccabee, before a solemn convocation of the people, rededicated the Temple on Mount Zion. He lit the lamps of the great menorah, offered incense on the Golden Altar, and brought burnt-offerings to the Altar of Sacrifices.

In commemoration of these stirring events, Judah decreed that, on the same day every year thereafter and until the end of time, the Jews were to celebrate Channukah for eight days. They were to kindle lights nightly during this period as soon as the first stars appeared, adding a new light to the others each night of the festival. That is the reason why Channukah is also known as the Feast of Lights. Its outstanding physical symbol is the nine-branched menorah. One branch, standing higher than the others and called the *shammes*–the "servant" or "verger"–acts as pilot, or escort light, to the others each night of the festival.

Since Channukah, like Pesach, was instituted not merely as a solemn commemoration but as a festival of rejoicing, it was considered appropriate by the ancient Rabbis–the transmitters of tradition–that the people recall the triumph of their ancestors in their struggle for freedom and for their Jewish identity with songs of praise and thanksgiving. And just as the entire family participates, on Passover, in the Seder, so the entire family participates in the lighting of the menorah on Channukah at home.

The oddity is that this festival is considered, in the main, to be a secular one, notwithstanding the fact that the Maccabees fought for and bled in defense of the Jewish religion. Although work is permitted on this holiday, Channukah, nevertheless, has a strong religious side to it. The lighting of the Channukah menorah, both in the home and in the synagogue, is accompanied by the recitation of appropriate benedictions and hymns of praise and thanksgiving.

The theme of Channukah has been open to two different interpretations. The simple-minded, always in search of the magical and the miraculous, have accepted the supernatural explanation that was given in the Talmud several centuries after the Maccabean insurrection: "When the Hasmoneans [the priestly Maccabean clan] prevailed against the Greeks, they made search in the Temple, and found only one jar of oil which stood there untouched and undefiled, with the seal of the high priest. It contained sufficient oil for one day's lighting only. But a miracle was wrought therein, and they lit the lamp(s) with it for eight days."

To the thoughtful, the moral of the epic of Channukah has been that there exists no power on earth able to crush the free, aspiring spirit in man. This triumphant view was articulated by the Prophet Zechariah, three-and-a-half centuries before the Maccabean revolt: "Not by might nor by power, but by my spirit, saith the Lord of hosts."

See also CHANNUKAH LAMP; SADDUCEES; ZEALOTS.

CHANNUKAH LAMP

Many Jewish religious customs and traditions have grown out of historic events. One of these is the kindling of the Channukah lamp. This is lighted during the eight days of the Channukah festival, which commemorates the triumph, in 165 B.C.E., of the Jewish people, led by the Maccabees, in their religious-patriotic war against the Syrian conquerors of Judea. Several different reasons have been ascribed to the origin of this custom, perhaps the most convincing being the symbolic one: It is meant to serve as an inspiration to the Jews of all succeeding generations by recalling that a devoted Israel, in defiance of the decrees of Antiochus (Epiphanes) IV, the Seleucidan tyrant, did not allow "the light of Torah" to be extinguished.

At first, the custom was to kindle an oil lamp outside of the house, so that all passers by could see the festive light with which the liberation was celebrated, and pause and reflect upon its significance. But after the Rome of the Caesars was transformed into the Holy Roman Empire, the Christian Church forbade such "ostentatious" celebration by the Jews. Thenceforth, the lamp had to be unobtrusively lit *inside* the house. In later, less oppressive times, it was allowed to stand on the window sill.

When the modified menorah was introduced during the Middle Ages to serve as a Channukah lamp, and when candles were substituted for oil in post-Reformation times, the candles used were judged to be insolently large. This was because they resembled Christian votive tapers. In consequence, Jews discreetly reduced the size of their Channukah lamps and made diminutive candles to fit them. This custom of using small candles in the Channukah lamp became traditional, and furnishes the curious explanation why Channukah candles are still so small today.

The first Channukah lamps made in Judea during the Roman period–and archaeologists have provided us with an abundance of examples dug up during the past fifty years–were of the same general character as the earliest Sabbath lamps. They were of clay, of primitive design, and had nine oil spouts, each containing a flaxen wick. These lamps were displaced during the Middle Ages by modified menorot, modeled on that in the Temple, but supplied with nine instead of seven branches: one for each of the eight days of the festival, and a ninth serving as the shammash or shammes, namely, the "servant" or pilot-light from whose flame the candles were lit. Starting with one candle on the first night of the festival, an additional one was kindled on each successive night, until there were—not counting the shammes—eight candles burning on the concluding night.

Not only the home but also the synagogue was furnished with a Channukah lamp. In the latter, it was a fixed, ceremonial art-object, and was placed to the right side of the Ark. For synagogue use, it was, naturally, large in size and elaborately designed, and most often wrought in brass.

The Channukah lamp for home use did not necessarily have to be in the shape of the modified menorah. Over the course of centuries, it took on an infinite variety of shapes, designs, and ornamentation. In more recent centuries, in keeping with their growing affluence, the rich began to show a preference for Channukah lamps of silver instead of brass. These allowed the artist-craftsman greater opportunity for elaborate design, finer workmanship, and the exercise of his inventiveness, which could result in an end product for ostentatious display. Many lamps made during the late Renaissance, as can be observed today by the sophisticated eye, were beautiful and simple in design, but the stifling rococo taste of the seventeenth century eventually displaced them. The mass-produced Channukah lamp of today shows an inevitable decline in good taste and, of course, also in quality of workmanship and skill.

See also CHANNUKAH; ART, CEREMONIAL.

Channukah lamp. Frankfurt, c. *1675.* TOP RIGHT

Channukah lamp. France, 14th century. CENTER RIGHT

Brass Channukah lamp of Eastern Europe, 19th century. (Courtesy of Joseph B. Horwitz Judaica Collection, Cleveland.) BOTTOM RIGHT

Iraqi children lighting Channukah candles in a ma'abarah (an Israeli reception center for new immigrants). BELOW

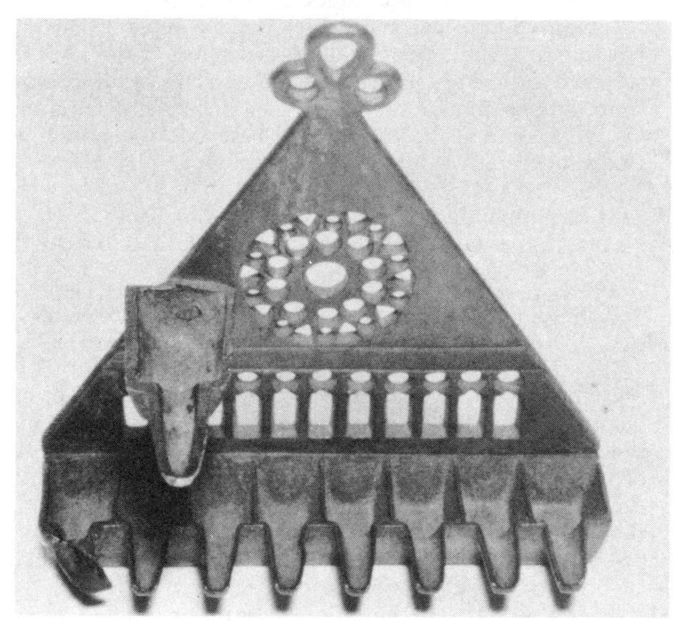

CHANNUKAH MENORAH. *See* CHANNUKAH LAMP.

CHAPTERS OF THE FATHERS. *See* TALMUD, THE.

CHARITABLE SPIRIT, THE. *See* ETHICAL VALUES, JEWISH.

CHARITY (in Hebrew: TZEDAKAH, meaning, literally, "righteousness")

Ever since the Jews began to lead their own ethnic group-life in ancient Israel, they have shown an unflagging concern for helping those less fortunate than themselves. These have included the hungry, the sick, and the old, as well as all the other needy and helpless. This activity in benevolence and mutual aid intensified and kept pace with the growing difficulties of the Jewish people. The development of an ethical consciousness in the plain folk played no small part in the rise of this universal philanthropy. In the Hellenistic age, it was noted—not always with a flattering intention—by many non-Jews as one of the identifying marks of the Jewish character. To some sophisticated Romans who had close contact with Jewish life, it appeared as a most curious, even an incredible, preoccupation.

There is a notation in the Talmud about an argument—whether real or apocryphal is not known—between Rabbi Akiba and Turnus (Tineius) Rufus, the governor of Judea. The Roman asked Rabbi Akiba: "If, as you say, your god loves the poor, why then does he not support them?" A reasonable question, certainly! Rabbi Akiba replied that if God left the care of the poor to the benevolence of the Jews themselves it was purposely "so that we may be saved by its merits from the punishment of Gehinnom [Gehenna or Purgatory]." On what authority did the Rabbi base this assumption about God's intention? Akiba cited this passage:

> Is it not to deal thy bread to the hungry,
> And that thou bring the poor that are cast out to thy house?
> When thou seest the naked, that thou cover him,
> And that thou hide not thyself from thine own flesh?
>
> ISAIAH 58:7.

It is for a very special reason that the obligation of giving charity is accorded such an arresting place in the teachings of the Rabbinic moralists. Not only did they assume that an act of charity saved the giver from the fires of Gehinnom, but they lauded it as an activity that "uplifts the soul," and one that is "equal to the merit of all the other mitzvot [the 613 precepts of the Torah]." Most important of all, they claimed, "it brings the Redemption nearer."

At every Jewish burial all over the world today, as the collectors of charity move among the mourners, they shatter the silence of grief with the urgent proclamation: "*Tzedakah tatsil mi-mavet!*" ("Charity saves from death!")

An index as to how Jews regard the giving and the taking of charity may be found in the very meaning of its Hebrew equivalent: *tzedakah.* Although the word actually means "righteousness," it also carries the connotation of "justice." In other words, what is given to the poor and is accepted by the poor belongs to them *by moral right!* By right? What right? This is the way the ancient Rabbis tried to explain it:

If poverty existed, it was society that was principally at fault, since it permitted the oppression of the poor and the weak. Such a condition was considered to be a violation of natural law, and the widespread practice of benevolence merely served as one form of atonement and amelioration. When the Psalmist sang: "The earth is the Lord's and the fulness thereof," the principle of that right was clearly noted. The same principle was given the force of law by the Scriptural text: "Mine is the silver and mine is the gold, saith the Lord of Hosts." And, since, obviously, God gave the earth and "its fulness thereof"—its silver and its gold—only to the rich and to the powerful, the Sages deduced from that fact that God owed a material debt to the poor because they were left empty-handed. Accordingly, to have this debt repaid by the rich to the poor would constitute an act of "justice" and, therefore, of "righteousness."

Furthermore, they believed that when God gave wealth to the rich, he did not give it to them *outright,* nor did he do so to reward them for their actions or for any special merit. He merely gave it to them in trust *for the poor!* Thus they—the rich—were only, so to speak, God's fiscal agents on earth *for the poor.* To extend tzedakah "with a full hand" to the poor, therefore, fulfilled its true inner meaning as an act of "righteousness." From this was developed the axiom that, if the rich were really honest and God-fearing, they would eagerly distribute the wealth they were holding in trust from God to God's innumerable *creditors*—the poor, the sick, the helpless, the needy, etc.

The Rabbinic teachers, who were men close to the people, argued that if this debt to the poor was not paid—being dishonestly withheld by "God's agents"—then the poor, whenever they were driven to desperation by the wretchedness of their condition, had every right to raise their voices to Heaven in bitter complaint. Said Judah ben Simon (Palestine, fourth century): "The poor man sits and complains to God: 'Why am I different from the rich man? He sleeps in his bed, and I? I sleep here [in the street]!' " Should the rich close their ears to this justified complaint then, warned the Rabbis, they sin in the gravest way against God and the natural law. "It is not written," they pointed out " 'the poor man,' but 'your brother,' in order to show that both mean the same thing."

While the most advanced among the Rabbinic teachers had an indestructible faith in the compassionate impulses of the heart, they were at the same time also sober-minded men with few illusions. Even if their teachings were trained on soaring objectives and were designed to awaken the slumbering conscience, nevertheless, their methods were firmly planted in reality. Consequently, they considered it wise to formalize the practice of benevolence *as a religious obligation.* Without the pressure of religious law, they realized, many ungenerous or unjust individuals might be tempted to conveniently avert their gaze from the unfortunate and the needy. Therefore, the warning of the second-century Mishnah Sage, Joshua ben Korha: "He who turns his eyes away [from a needy person] is to be considered as a worshiper of idols!"

The Sages took the realistic view that, being what they were, human beings could not be expected to behave like the proverbial angels. In any design for ethical living, their frailties and contradictory drives had to be considered, and with more objectivity than harshness. This same view had to be applied even to the measure of righteous conduct—all too pitifully small—that was expected from the pious in their fulfillment of the ethical commandments and precepts of the Torah. True, the teachers of Jewish ethics felt it their duty always to point up the purest and the noblest possibilities in conduct to the individual. Yet they were not unmindful of the need of dangling before him the expectation of some concrete reward, whether the promise of prosperity in this life or the certainty of bliss in the World-to-Come. For in doing good, as in everything else, it did seem that men required incentives —even illusory ones.

But one austere Rabbinic moralist dissented vigorously from this tolerant view. He could not resist shooting a satiric barb at the calculating "benefactor" who wishes to strike a pious bargain with God, *quid pro quo,* trading his lean acts of charity toward his fellow men for the fat rewards of Paradise. He compared him to a customer who enters a shop and

Passover benevolence. (Top) Dishing out sacramental wine to the poor. (Bottom) Distributing matzot. (From the Sarajevo Haggadah, Spanish, 13th century.) ABOVE LEFT

"The Bodleian Bowl" (bronze) used for the collection of money to support a yeshibah in Acre, Palestine. Oxford University, second half of 13th century. CENTER LEFT

Alms box (with padlock) for the support of a Talmud Torah. Central Italy, 17 century. (Courtesy of Joseph B. Horwitz Judaica Collection, Cleveland.) BOTTOM LEFT

Alms box of Halberstadt Synagogue. Germany, 1761. BOTTOM RIGHT

Jewish communal officials distributing clothing to the poor. Germany, early 18th century. BELOW

snaps at the proprietor: "Here's the sack. . . . Here's the money. . . . Here's the measure. . . . Quick, the grain!"

There was also a reverse side to the problem of tzedakah. Jews—and this also included Jesus and other early Jewish-Christians—believed that works of charity brought forgiveness of sins. Consequently, there were—and for that matter still are—people who gave charity out of the promptings of a guilty conscience. They regarded their acts of charity as placatory acts of expiation to God or as amends for the wrong they had done to their fellow men. This kind of giving was merely a new form for an older and more primitive practice: In Temple days, expiatory "sin-offerings" were brought constantly upon the altar; but when the sanctuary on Mount Zion lay in ruins, the Sages warned against the disasters which would overtake those who failed to help "God's needy."

The Jewish moralists also had to face the presence of the motive of vanity in many givers. Certain people derive a sense of power and pleasure from their ability to give to charity—publicly!—looking forward to the pathetically brief burst of applause it brings from their fellow men. Oddly enough, much of the time Jewish tradition treated such givers of charity "with charity"! The rabbis did not always condemn them, nor did they moralize too much about their motives. On the contrary, they deliberately encouraged *all* giving, whatever the reason behind it! They understood well enough that people often act out of mixed, and sometimes contradictory, motives. What if an individual did perform a benevolent act out of some unworthy calculation? They saw nothing flagrantly wrong in any act so long as it led to good results. And to help the suffering and the needy was the greatest good that could be desired! For that reason, it was not difficult for a Talmudic Sage to state: "He who says, 'I am giving this money as charity in order that my sons may live,' or, 'I am giving this money that I may inherit Eternal Life,' such a man is to be considered as perfectly righteous."

The Sages were sound educational psychologists. They believed fervently in man's ability to improve. Doing good is a *habit,* they thought, a pattern of conduct which can become spontaneous after long and sustained practice. "Let a man . . . perform good deeds, even if at first it is not for their own sake. In time, he will come to do them for their own sake."

It should not come as a surprise, therefore, that on account of such indoctrination and conditioning by daily practice, there have always been an astonishingly large number of Jews devoted to works of benevolence for *benevolence' sake alone.* This attitude, characterized as "the purity of the intention," became early a powerful tradition in Jewish life, and it has endured down to our own time. The passionate brother-feeling and respect for the human personality was eloquently expressed in the apocryphal Testament of Issachar, a Hebrew work written, significantly enough, perhaps two centuries before Jesus: "If any man was in distress, I joined my sighs with his, I shared my bread with the poor . . . I loved the Lord; likewise also every man with all my heart."

Even the poor, for the same moral reasons, were expected to dispense charity to those equally poor or even poorer than themselves. There was also a practical reason for actively involving the poor in the miseries of their brethren. Following the large-scale massacres and persecutions during the Middle Ages and as late as the seventeenth century, there were few really rich Jews left in Europe. The word "wealth" became a relative term when used in the ghetto. It had almost an ironic connotation. A Jew was considered rich only by virtue of the fact that he was perhaps one degree or two *less poor* than the great mass of his pauperized fellow Jews! From a practical point of view, little reliance could be placed on the philanthropy of the small number of wealthy men who did exist. The poor, for the sake of their own survival, had to learn to help one another. The proverb, "The poor help the poor," acquired the bitter but heartening ring of truth. This is also, no doubt, one of the main reasons why the Talmudic teachers of morality translated the urgent need for the practice of mutual aid *from the poor to the poor* into a religious obligation.

The Babylonian Rabbinic jurist, Mar Zutra, rendered this legal opinion: "Even the poor man, who himself is supported by charity, should give charity to those who are in need." And should the poor man be so poor that he has absolutely nothing to give away, he is reminded that he still has the compassionate warmth of his heart left to offer his brother in distress. He is advised to say to him, speaking in the true spirit of tzedakah: "My brother, my heart goes out to you, but I have nothing to give you."

To enable even the poorest to help other poor, the Jews of latter-day Poland established an ingenious device. The communal authorities had a coinage of their own minted which they sold for coin of the realm to the pious. These were just crude bits of brass that were stamped with the Hebrew word *perutah.* (In Talmudic times, the perutah was a coin of the smallest monetary value.) The Jew asking aid from his fellow Jews in Poland would be given a perutah from the charitable, and after he had accumulated a sufficient number of these trifling coins, he would present them to the gabbai (the treasurer of the Jewish community) for exchange into legal tender.

The Marranos of Portugal—those intimidated Conversos to Catholicism who, nevertheless, stubbornly observed the Jewish religion in secret—had a poignant saying: "The name Jew is derived from the fact that we assist one another."

Organized Charity. Perhaps the highest development in the ethical philosophy of benevolence and in the institutional forms of its practice occurred during the Rabbinic period in Judea. At that time, philanthropic activities had become so widespread—as well as urgently necessary for the Jews in the Roman Empire—that they even drew tribute from a Greek religious competitor of the Jews in Athens (*see* MISSIONARIES, JEWISH)—the Christian missionary, Aristides Mareianus (*c.* 125). In his apologia for Christianity which he addressed to the Emperor Antoninus Pius, he observed about the Jews: "They have compassion on the poor; they release [i.e. ransom] captives; they bury the dead; and they do other things similar to these such as are acceptable before God and also well pleasing to man."

Needless to say, the Jewish philosophy and practice of ma'asim tobim—"good works"—were carried over into Christianity through the traditional Jewish teachings of Jesus and the evangelism of the Apostles.

The paramount importance given to works of benevolence by the Jewish religious teachers during the last centuries of the Second Commonwealth let loose a flood of self-injuring actions on the part of many of the generous and devout. The Sages, somewhat alarmed, then began to consider the inherent truth of the adage that *too good is not good at all!* A religious law to curb over-enthusiastic philanthropy seemed to be required for the protection of the kind-hearted against themselves. During the second century B.C.E. a moralist in the Book of Enoch warned: "If a man gives an alms of his heart-murmur [i.e., he gives at the point when he has nothing more to give but his heart-murmur], he commits a double sin: he ruins himself and his contribution."

About three hundred years later, following the bloody crushing of the revolt led by Bar Kochba against the Romans in Judea, an assembly of the foremost rabbis met in Galilee to consider the proper means of alleviating the widespread need and hunger among the people. It was finally resolved: "A man's benefactions should not exceed a fifth of all his possessions. . . . While the giving of charity is obligatory, it has its limits. If a man will give away all he possesses, he will only make a pauper of himself, and that is forbidden."

This ardent feeling for "doing good" overflowed narrow group loyalties to take in other than Jews. While it is true that, when the Jews were fragmentized as a people and dispersed with the ill winds of chance, Jewish charity was wholly designed to help Jews—for what Gentiles were there willing to help them?—nonetheless, Jewish ethical practices were never allowed to relax and to become parochial; they required that all needy non-Jews living among Jews had to receive benevolence *equally* with them. Charity knows neither race nor religion, advised the Talmud. It drew its authority for this view from the Torah: "God loves the stranger. . . . Love ye also the stranger." Under Mishnaic as well as under Biblical law, the Gentile poor were to share with the Jewish poor in the gleanings of the harvest. They were to be given food, shelter, and clothing, when they required them. Their sick were to be visited, aided, and comforted. And when they died, they were to be given decent burial if there was no one of their own to perform this last act of human kindness for them.

In his book about the rites and ceremonies of the Jews, Rabbi Leone da Modena of early seventeenth-century Venice, states: ". . . they do upon all occasions help any object of charity, let him be what he will."

Beginning with the Middle Ages, Jewish charitable societies with wide-ranging fields of specialized welfare service made their appearance in the collective life of Jews everywhere. There was—and still is—no Jewish community in the world, however small, that has not always hummed like a beehive with benevolent projects of every imaginable kind. In the words of the Mishnah, with reference to the social setting of the period preceding the final national tragedy in 70 C.E., there existed in every community many organized societies which directed their efforts to "the practice of charity . . . hospitality to wayfarers, visiting the sick, dowering the brides, attending the dead to the grave . . ."

There also were societies for the care of orphans and the aged; for assisting widows; for waiting on expectant and new mothers before, during, and after childbirth, and engaging wet-nurses for ailing mothers; and for providing medical treatment and medicines for those unable to pay (in later centuries, such societies established hospitals and clinics). Other groups, in response to desperate situations, undertook to collect the unconscionable fines and levies that were constantly being demanded of Jewish communities by the Christian rulers and local municipal councils. Special organizations, at no small risk to themselves, were formed to succor the survivors of massacres and to give Jewish burial to those who had fallen, to give aid to refugees in flight, to extend plague-, fire-, and flood-relief, to ransom captives, and to free slaves by purchase.

There were other specialized charitable societies devoted strictly to religious goals and ritual observance. They provided free mezuzot, Sabbath and Channukah candles, matzot and wine for Passover, oil (and in later ages, candles) for the illumination of synagogues, Houses of Study, and religious schools. There were societies in every community tirelessly working for the support of the educational institutions—the Talmud Torahs and yeshibot—including those in the Holy Land.

Perhaps closest to the hearts of the devout in bygone times was the religious instruction of the young. This was motivated by the national resolve of the Jewish people, one that was continuous since the Rabbinic age, never to allow "the light of the Torah to be diminished" in Israel. To this end, too, there were groups which were exclusively dedicated to the buying (and keeping in repair) of religious works for the libraries of the Houses of Study and the yeshibot.

The scope and intensity of those numerous ventures in organized benevolence—exclusive, it should be kept in mind, of all official communal philanthropies and poor relief—kept pace with the tempo of persecution in various places. For example, in the year 1350 there were in existence in the little French ghetto of Perpignan five societies, each with a distinctive charitable objective. In the seventeenth century, following the Thirty Years' War and Bogdan Chmielnicki's ferocious pogroms in 1648, in which hundreds of thousands of Jews lost their lives in the Ukraine, the number of societies greatly multiplied, so pressing was the need for mutual aid. In the Turkish-Jewish community in Smyrna, at the very same time, a contemporary chronicler noted the existence of seventy societies dedicated to seventy separate charitable tasks. In the city of Rome, late in the seventeenth century, aside from all other organized philanthropic activities, there were seven societies alone for the distribution, in a prescribed area, of clothing, linen, bedding, and warm coverlets—separately to small children, children of school age, women alone, widows, and prisoners.

Collecting for the Poor. The voluntary collector of charity among Jews has been the most admired and, in some instances, also the most disliked or, more truly, *feared,* of individuals. Entering into the homes of the generous, no matter how poor, he always seemed a messenger of righteousness in the service of his unfortunate fellow men. To the miserly and the flint-hearted, on the other hand, he appeared like a specter —an unwelcome reminder of their guilty consciences.

With the bewildering number of charitable projects constantly in progress among Jews—and so many of them lying outside of official communal activities—the collectors of charity were faced with a staggering task. Because there were so many societies, dedicated to every imaginable kind of poor relief, the number of collectors was virtually legion. One might almost say that practically every Jew and his cousin was a collector for some charitable cause or another! Competition for a pitiful coin was keen. It is amazing that, considering the usually fantastic poverty of the Jewish masses, they were able so successfully to pursue their benevolent objectives in such a bewildering variety of directions. Despite the best intentions in the world and the most stringent of personal sacrifices, there simply were not enough coins to be collected from or to go around among the dwellers of the ghetto hovels!

Clearly, under such circumstances, the lot of a charity collector was an unenviable one. His solicitation of funds was marred by much unpleasantness—sometimes by humiliation or even abuse. Nonetheless, out of a holy dedication, the pious did not flinch from their tasks. The mere certainty that they were performing a mitzvah—a good deed—on behalf of the needy, was a sufficient reward for their efforts. Perhaps it was to encourage the sensitive and the faint-hearted among collectors that a Sage of the Talmud offered these words of comfort with this prayerful hope for himself: "May my lot be cast among those who collect charity rather than among those who give it!"

Without any exaggeration, no sacrifice of pride or sensitivity was considered too great for the dedicated collector to make, providing it resulted in a donation. There is the story of a Chasidic tzaddik who once was reproached by his disciple who thought that the holy man was demeaning himself when he solicited a donation from a miserly man. The rabbi laughed, "My dear son," he asked with a wink, "if you want to milk a cow, don't you have to stoop a little?"

It is most engaging to discover that the charity collector's chore of "milking the cow" was valued in Jewish tradition as one of the most exalted forms of charity. Sometimes the role of the collector took on an astonishing character. It is recounted in the Talmud how Rabbi Zechariah, the son-in-law of the Sage, Joshua ben Levi, used to accept charity together with all the indigent. His neighbors were both shocked and amazed. Many muttered unkind words against him; they very well knew that he did not stand in need of public assistance. However, when Rabbi Zechariah died, it was discovered that not only had he not used for himself any of the charity money he had accepted, but he had distributed it secretly among those of the poor who were too proud to ask for public assistance. He had humbled himself in order to protect their pride.

However deeply furrowed may have been the field of benevolence in Jewish life by individual charity and by the semiofficial charity societies, the most effective work in poor-relief in other centuries was done then, just as it is today, by the Jewish community (the kahal) itself. Communal charity was already in existence in Mishnah times among the Jews in Judea, Syria, Babylonia, Egypt, Rome, Cyrenaica, and other far-off places. Each community had a fund called the *kuppah* which was supervised by financial overseers (gabbaim). These officials assessed the wealth—or lack of it—of every individual in the community, levying periodic proportionate tithings of 10 per cent of them in order to cover the needs of all public charitable and religious enterprises. No one was exempted from this taxation—not even the old and the sick, or the women and children.

It is touching to find, in Jewish writings of several centuries ago and in the long memory of the folk, many bitter references to the overseers of charity and to the harsh methods they occasionally adopted—no doubt more often out of desperation than hardheartedness—toward those unable to pay the communal tax. It sometimes happened that the most important household possessions, such as the Sabbath candlesticks, the silver Kiddush cup, or even the bedding, were "sequestrated" by the kahal officials—held, so to speak, in pawn so these officials could exert effective pressure for the payment of taxes in arrears. There are still extant folk songs in Yiddish which berate the communal bigwigs and tax-collectors for their unfeeling hearts toward the desperately poor.

There were a hundred different "voluntary" ways by which the hard-worked kuppah in the community could be replenished. There was no occasion, whether of rejoicing or of sorrowing, of good fortune or of bad, when tzedakah was not collected. Contributions came from fond parents whose "cup [of joy] runneth over," as they celebrated the birth of a child. They gave at a circumcision party, at a Pidyon ha-Ben (the ceremony for the redemption of the first-born son), at a Bar Mitzvah, at a betrothal, at a wedding. The beginning of a hazardous journey was prayerfully marked by a donation, as was the safe arrival at journey's end. Whenever an individual or any member of his family emerged alive from sickness, an epidemic, or a pogrom, he made a charity donation during the service of thanksgiving (in Yiddish: *goimel-benschen*) with the congregation. Even when a man had a bad dream and woke up safe and sound, he often celebrated his joy at being alive with a contribution to the charity fund.

Other sources of revenue for charity were the not unsubstantial "honors" conferred at services in the synagogue on the Sabbath and on holy days during the reading of the Torah. These honors were auctioned off to the highest bidders among the worshipers (*see* TORAH-READING), and the money accruing from them was dedicated to the alleviation of human misery and to the various religious institutions and enterprises of the community.

Then, too, for a variety of reasons, there were charity collections on feast days and on fast days. Yahrzeit (q.v.), the annual memorial day for departed loved ones, was another occasion. Even during week days, and without any specific reason, some congregants would drop coins into the charity-box as they left the synagogue at the conclusion of the prayer service. Often there were several charity-boxes serving several purposes. For example, in the synagogue at Mantua, Italy, in 1630, the worshipers were confronted by the imperious demands of seven separate charity-boxes: one each for the Holy Land, for burial purposes, for the care of the sick and the aged, for dowries for poor brides, for relief of the needy, for the support of the Talmud Torah, and for the redemption of captives.

A memorable line from The Song of Songs, although it referred merely to a lover's devotion, became most fittingly the motto of Jewish collectors of charity in their tireless labors: "I sleep, but my heart waketh."

What if an individual was so penurious that he would not make any donation at all, as so frequently happened? That was, indeed, a bitter pill for the kindhearted to swallow.

The following folk story illustrates what the folk-Jew thought of the illimitable resources of giving after there was nothing more to give.

> When an orphan asylum was in danger of closing down because it lacked a certain sum of money, the rabbi of the community urgently implored the richest man in town to make up the deficit. But the nogid [wealthy man] promptly refused. "I will sell you my share in Paradise if only you will give me the money," pleaded the rabbi out of desperation. The rich man was delighted with the "bargain" and gave him the money. And so the orphan asylum was saved, but the collector was without his portion of bliss in the World-to-Come.
>
> The rabbi's disciples were aghast when they heard of his "deal." They remonstrated with him: "Oh, Rabbi! how could you do a thing like that—you, a holy man who was sure to enter Paradise!" The rabbi replied: "Twice each day I repeat in my prayers: 'Love thy God with all thy heart, with all thy soul, and with all thy possessions.' My sons, I'm only a poor man. What are 'the possessions' with which I can serve God? All that I possess is my share in Paradise, and to serve God's children, the orphans, I am ready to part with even that."

Anonymous Charity. The teachers of Jewish ethics placed great emphasis not only on the need for giving charity, but also on *how to give* and *how not to give*. The delicacy of feeling shown for the unfortunate and the needy, which was a powerful tradition among Jews since Maccabean times, is mirrored in the Rabbinic concern to protect the receivers of charity against the possible arrogance and vulgarity of some of their "benefactors."

The Sages decreed that no act of charity had any religious merit if it was unaccompanied by compassion for a fellow creature in distress. The Talmud makes this point abundantly clear, time and time again, citing numerous Rabbinic opinions and reflections on it. "Even if one speaks only a single kind word to comfort the poor and those who are in distress, he has given in true charity indeed." What did the Torah have to say on the subject? "Because of this [compassionate] word, God will bless you!" However, "compassion" always was more than a mere word to upright Jews. It represented part of their way of life. "Sons of Compassionate Fathers" is one traditional name Jews have called themselves collectively.

The subject of *how not to give* received equally exhaustive treatment in the Talmud. "A man may give charity lavishly, yet, because he gives without brotherly love, he wounds the hearts of the poor," gloomily observed one Disciple of the Wise. Of what use, in a moral sense, were such benefactions? The somber conclusion was that they were worthless since they never even acquired the true character of ordinary charity; that is, they were devoid of all righteousness and justice! However, observed the Rabbis consolingly, "A man may give only a little, but if the sentiment of the heart goes along with it, both he and his giving are blessed, indeed!"

The Sages also took severely to task those who give publicly and ostentatiously to an unfortunate person in order to direct flattering attention to themselves, for the net result is that then they succeed only in humiliating and degrading the object of their "generosity." The Talmud relates how a Rabbi once saw a man give a zuz (a small silver coin) with a munificent gesture to a needy person. The Rabbi rebuked the donor: "Far better if you had given him nothing at all than that the whole world should watch you hand him alms! See what you have done with your charity! You have humiliated the poor man with it!"

Pointedly, with the insensitive among the rich in mind, the Talmud suggested a supplementary prayer for daily recitation: "O God, grant that we may not have to ask help from others. Let not our sustenance depend on their bounty, for though their benevolence is small, the shame they inflict is indeed great." And so, in order to protect the sensitive and the proud, the Rabbis decreed: "A benefaction to the poor must be made privately, with no one else present."

It is recorded that Rabbi Abba was in the habit of helping the proud poor in a singular way. He would tie some money in a kerchief and then proceed to "lose" it in the vicinity of the needy person he wished to help. Mar Ukba, another religious luminary of ancient Babylonia, was careful to slip, unobserved, the sum of four zuzim under the door of a poor neighbor each day. This "technique" of giving became a continuous tradition in Jewish life. It is told of Rabbi Elimelech of Lizhensk, the Chasidic tzaddik of eighteenth-century Galicia, how be would disguise himself as a peasant and would dump a load of firewood, a bag of flour, or a sack of potatoes before a needy widow's door. He would then make good his departure before he could be questioned about it.

The Sages summed up their praise for anonymous giving, thus: "He who gives charity in secret is as great as Moses."

But the requirements of communal benevolence in the more complicated Palestinian society during the third century C.E. led Chiyya bar Abba to counsel: "The best way to give charity is to deposit the money in the collection box. In this way, the giver does not know whom he gives, nor does the poor man know who the giver is."

However severely the miserly or ostentatious givers of tzedakah were lectured by the Rabbis, the characterless takers of charity were not spared either. Censorious sounds the Shulchan Aruch, the sixteenth-century code of Jewish law: "One should always avoid accepting charity and rather roll in misery than depend upon the help of others. And thus our Sages commanded: 'Rather turn your Sabbath into a weekday than be dependent on others.' "

See also BURIAL RITES AND CUSTOMS; FELLOWSHIP IN ISRAEL; HOSPITALITY; HOSPITALS; LAMED-VAV TZADDIKIM; LOANS, FREE; MAN, DIGNITY OF; MUTUAL AID (*under* ETHICAL VALUES, JEWISH); SICK, VISITING THE.

CHAROSET. *See* PASSOVER.

CHASIDIM (Hebrew pl., meaning "the pious"; s. CHASID)

Not since the Rabbinic age began to flower in ancient Judea and Babylonia at the close of the Second Temple period, was the impact of a religious movement on the Jews as great or as profound as that of Chasidism. In less than a century after its founder, Israel Baal Shem, started to preach his philosophy of faith and mission (*c.* 1735), it had succeeded in penetrating deep beneath the surface of Jewish life in every part of Eastern Europe, where the majority of the Jewish people was concentrated. Certainly, Chasidism was able to revive the failing spirit of Jews in a manner entirely new and dynamic in Jewish religious experience. In that sense, it can be said that, historically, it was necessary and possibly inevitable to ensure the moral survival of Slavic Jewry.

By the end of the nineteenth century, at least half of the Jews of the world—three or four millions—could be counted among the fervent adherents of Chasidism. And as for the other Jews—even those who considered themselves its Misnagdim (Opponents)—living as they did in the same environment, they too could not escape being influenced by it in some measure.

In a significant way, Chasidism may be said to have constituted a social-religious revolution. It bore a certain resemblance to the religious insurgency of the Essenes and other nonconformist idealistic sects of latter-day Judea. Whatever its defects—and, objectively, these may be reckoned to have been serious and many—it nevertheless succeeded in accomplishing a great and constructive good. To employ a mixed, and perhaps paradoxical-sounding, metaphor: If it blew like a dust storm that obscured, it also surged up like a flood that cleansed. For that reason, Jewish life became both the better and the worse for Chasidism, but the final balance-sheet would probably show that Jewish life was the better for it.

Perceived through the social filter of the Chasidic movement, the Jewish religion was not designed to be the special preserve of an oligarchy of a learned elite or a handful of Cabalist initiates and superior spirits. It stood, in fact, at the very opposite pole of those groups in its democratic social direction and religious goals. Although cast in new terms to fit the special conditions of the times, it was, to a great extent, only a reaffirmation of the traditional Rabbinic teachings and ethical outlook on faith and worship. Those were completely democratic, vibrant with a warm humanity and unpretentiousness, but they had been sidetracked and supplanted, beginning with the sixteenth century, by the generally arid Talmudic casuistry of the learned and pietistic preoccupation with ritualism which was defacing Jewish religious culture in the Polish and Ukrainian ghettos and robbing it of content.

Chasidism became the sectarian instrumentality by which the empty, formalistic Judaism of that period was transformed into a meaningful, livable religion for the plain Jew of Eastern Europe. By making him aware, in religious terms, of the presence of the divine, the poetical, and the wondrous (even in the most commonplace things), it opened up his inner vi-

Polish Chasid, wearing a shtreiml (the sect's traditional velvet hat trimmed with fox tails), on his way to the synagogue. Pre-Nazi period. (R. Vishniak. Joint Distribution Committee.)

The Lepinker Rebbeh receiving homage and "shulem" (shalom = "peace") greetings from his adherents. Poland, before the Nazi occupation.

sion. He thus was able to establish his identification with God, with all his fellows, and with all creation, notwithstanding the fact that, culturally, he was at the same time taking several steps backward, since he utterly succumbed to Cabalistic mystification, to magic-directed rites, and to a morbid preoccupation with invisible demonic powers.

The immediate and widespread success of Chasidism was due to a number of historical, religious, and social reasons. The fact is incontrovertible that, beginning with the second half of the sixteenth century, the Jews of Europe, and especially the great majority who were living in Poland and its provinces, were submerged in their own "dark ages." State and Church reaction to the insurgent and successful Protestant Reformation had, as a side effect, the intensification of the persecution of the Jews in all Catholic countries. The Jewish masses in Poland, the Western Ukraine, Galicia, Bohemia, and Slovakia, continuously confined in crowded ghettos and deprived of normal productive outlets for their energies, barely managed to survive. They were sunk in a state of indescribable poverty, squalor, and ignorance. A great many sought, and actually found, an illusory refuge in feverish Messianic expectations, in primitive beliefs and superstitions, and in the magical abracadabra manipulated by the wonder-working Cabalists.

The barren state of Jewish religious culture in Eastern Europe during that troubled period was considerably to blame for this mass-retrogression. Prayer had become increasingly more formalistic, observance ever more legalistic and ritual-burdened. The Jewish religion was suffocating from a diminishing moral-emotional content. Torah-learning, too, had become routinized and dry as dust. Both the scholars and the scholarly were principally preoccupied by textual trivialities in the Scriptures and by novelties of Talmudic interpretation, and wasted their time in endless hair-splitting (pilpul).

A judicious eyewitness account of the religious-intellectual climate that prevailed in Poland and Lithuania in the seventeenth century was given by an Italian rabbinical humanist and physician who had been a student of Galileo's in astronomy. Joseph del Medigo noted with gloom: "Deep darkness covers the earth and the ignorance is terrible. Despite the fact that the country is full of yeshibot [Talmudic academies] and *Batey ha-Midrash* [Houses of Study], even the study of the Talmud is very much deteriorated. That is because all those thousands of people that crowd the yeshibot and knock upon the gates of Torah . . . have in mind only mundane things and are prompted by materialistic motives—a livelihood, honor, vanity, etc. They are interested only in careers. . . . All this vileness has devoured everything. The highest and the most important [i.e., the Torah] has become but a secondary thing. . . . Of scientific knowledge they have no inkling. They detest all knowledge. 'God,' they say, 'stands in no need of grammar, rhetoric, mathematics, astronomy, and philosophy. All this worldly wisdom was invented by the Gentiles! One must run away from these people! They might make one stray from the path of righteousness.' "

If this was the unflattering but presumably true portrait of the learned, who possessed both a working knowledge of Hebrew and Aramaic and were well-versed in the literature of the Talmud, how much more dismal must have been the religious-cultural state of the masses? At that time, the majority of Jews in Slavic lands were little more than able to recite their prayers in Hebrew, repeating words which they did not understand, reciting teachings and sentiments that eluded them but which, nonetheless, they accepted on faith as sanctities. It therefore stands to reason that religion made available to the great majority of Jews only few consolations which they were at all able to grasp.

The fertile soil in which Chasidism sprang up luxuriantly was *disaster*. The actual historic conditions of Jewish life in Eastern Europe were as threatening as they were desperate. In 1648, about fifty years before the birth of Israel Baal Shem, the initiator of the Chasidic sect, there had occurred two cataclysmic events which shattered the collective will and the faith of the Jewish people. The first took place during the Ukrainian Cossack uprising against Polish rule led by the hetman Bogdan Chmielnicki. In the course of the struggle, terrible barbarities were perpetrated on the Jews, and some 300,000 were believed to have been massacred. The effect of these atrocities upon the Jewish survivors was prostrating. The simple-minded folk were convinced that the end of the world was already at hand, for they were reminded of the ancient tradition that, when the suffering of the Jewish people should have reached its most desperate point, God—moved by his fatherly love and compassion—would send his earthly messenger, the Messiah—Mashiach ben David—to redeem it.

That very year (1648), as if in direct answer to this wishful thinking, in Izmir (Smyrna), a young Jew of arresting personality and magnetism proclaimed himself the Messiah. He was the Sefaradic Cabalist, Sabbatai Zevi. Because the Jews of his day had the will and a desperate need to be saved from further disaster by supernatural means (since no natural ones were available), he seemed the answer of Heaven to their prayers. Messianic hysteria convulsed European Jewry. Thousands liquidated their affairs and readied themselves for the End of Days.

Then came the shattering disillusionment. The psychologically complicated "Messiah," after a series of melodramatic adventures, actually *betrayed* his followers. Threatened with death by the Turks, he had turned Mohammedan. The effect of his action on the Jewish masses was one of benumbment. They grieved and sank into an even deeper despair than before.

Again, as if in answer to the general grief, a comforter appeared. This was Israel ben Eliezer, called by the superstitious folk "Baal Shem-Tob," meaning "Master of the Good Name." In common Jewish parlance, it meant that he was a Cabalist wonder-worker. He had been born *circa* 1700 (he died about 1760), either in the Ukraine or in Galicia—no one knows for certain. Throughout his youth he had revealed an inclination to solitude and had been possessed by a great love of nature. He had wandered alone through field and forest, communing with God in the poetical-mystical way that was characteristic of him and of other cabalists. It was at such times that he spun his visions of the aspiring soul, of worship through joy, and of the redemption of Israel.

Chasidic tradition described the Baal Shem-Tob variously as a bahelfer (an assistant to a melamed—a teacher of religion to children), as a synagogue sexton or beadle (shammes) in a Galician town, and as a carter of lime and clay in Volhynia. Although his early humble callings exposed him to the ridicule of his learned middle-class opponents, the rationalistic Misnagdim, they nevertheless proved of tremendous advantage to him in his preaching among the common folk, for he spoke their language and articulated their unrequited religious hungers and emotional needs.

Israel Baal Shem, despite his lack of rabbinical status, journeyed from place to place as an itinerant preacher. Everywhere, he proclaimed his mission of love and joy in the most simple terms: "My teaching," said he, "is based on three kinds of love: love of God, love of the Torah, and love of man."

Israel Baal Shem's little synagogue in Miedziboz, the Ukraine.

Grave of Israel Baal Shem (d. 1760) in Miedziboz, the Ukraine.

Polish Chasid of the early 19th century walking with his wife. (Sketch by L. Hollaenderski in Les Israelites de Pologne, *Paris, 1830.)*

It was love of man which led him to his doctrine of joy. God, he declared, was everywhere; He was to be found in all creation. The universe sang with joy for it was the radiant garment in which He wrapped His majesty. The Baal Shem's preaching recalls the mystical doctrine of the sixth-century-B.C.E. Greek philosopher Pythagoras, who called this universal harmony "the music of the Spheres." In the Baal Shem's scheme of thought, everything, including the most commonplace, was in perfect harmony—holy and blessed—for God was of it, and around it, and in it.

Israel Baal Shem was an optimist. He was also an ecstatic mystic—a continuator of the old Jewish Cabalist doctrines and practices. The world he saw was an indescribably wondrous emanation of God. It was full of beauty, melody, and joy. The human being, too, he found potentially beautiful and good and capable of great joy. How could it be otherwise? he asked, since God, the Creator, had put His divine signature on man, His handiwork! From this reasoning, the Baal Shem developed his ringing principle that not lamentation and despair, but a joyful spirit, a cheerful demeanor, and a heart brimming over with faith and hope were God's moral requirements of man, no matter how deep his afflictions. To laugh, to sing, to dance—not for fleeting sensuous pleasure but with the intention (kavanah) of adoring the Almighty—meant to engage in the purest and the highest forms of prayer. Therefore, in worshiping God, what had religious significance was not the prayers one recited or the rites one performed, but only the pure intention and the aspiration of the soul. And these could be wordless and expressed in simple acts of loving-kindness to one's fellow men. By loving man actively, the believer was demonstrating his love for God.

In such an unconventional, emotional philosophy of religion, some of the more sober Rabbinic intellectual values were derogated or even passed over. Reason was subordinated to intuition, and formal prayer made way to the supplication of the heart. The Baal Shem put love of God above all forms of religious worship—even above obligatory Torah-study. In consequence, he scandalized the law-minded Talmudists with his teaching that to do good in life was more meritorious in the eyes of God than to observe punctiliously every one of the mandatory 613 precepts of the Torah. Also to the chagrin of the pious formalists, he contrasted the moving devotion of the heart with the empty casuistry of the intellect. The excessive rationalism of the Talmudic scholars, he charged, was a menace to true religion, which had to do with intuition and feeling and not with a conceited display of pedantry. Satan, too, could rationalize, he gibed, thereby entangling the clever scholar in a web of falsehood and vanity which could but lead to the destruction of his soul.

He extended to the simple and unlettered folk the consolation of his thought that the humble and the pure in heart, no matter how ignorant, poor, or socially despised they might be, had a far greater chance of enjoying the blessings of the World-to-Come than the self-preening Talmudists, puffed up with pride in their learning and the punctiliousness of their religious observances.

The preaching of the Baal Shem acted like sparks on dry stubble. It set the whole Slavic-Jewish world aflame. Disciples—some learned Talmudists among them—flocked to him for illumination and, after they had become initiates, were sent out as preachers. They won many adherents to Chasidism.

The rabbinic authorities and the scholars in Poland, Galicia, and Volhynia condemned the Baal Shem, his doctrines, and his zealous disciples. They branded them as heretical and immoral. In 1772, twelve years after the death of the Baal Shem, in order to put out the "conflagration" of Chasidism that was making headway in Lithuania, the foremost religious authority of the age, Rabbi Elijah ben Solomon of Vilna, celebrated among Jews as the Vilner Gaon, pronounced the solemn formula of excommunication against him and his teachings. Five years later, he ordered the Chasidic writings seized and burned, and forbade all Jews to intermarry with or to have any contact whatsoever with the "heretics." But except in Lithuania, the principal stronghold of rabbinic rationalism, the decree proved to be in vain. Chasidism rolled on like a tidal wave over the Jewish communities of Volhynia and Podolia, and of Galicia, Poland, Bohemia, parts of Hungary, and Slovakia. Nothing that its opponents were able to do could stop its rapid advance.

Unfortunately, like so many other idealistic religious movements, Chasidism, too, carried within itself the seeds of its corruption. The purity of belief and practice which had characterized the movement during the lifetime of its remarkable founder and of some of his early disciples, before long began to show the taints and warpings of institutionalism and careerism, and even of charlatanry and sordid greed.

By the end of the eighteenth century, a new type of Chasidic religious leader began to emerge. He was called either *rebbeh* (rabbi) or *tzaddik*, but principally the latter. The Chasidim, hero-worshippers to the last man, generously thought of their rebbeh also as a tzaddik—a supremely righteous man or saint. Because of his presumed superior spiritual and prophetic powers, they considered him able to act as intercessor—the bridge between their urgent desires and the inscrutable will of God.

This concept of the tzaddik was first clearly formulated by the Baal Shem's foremost and most able disciple, and his successor to the leadership of the sect. This was Dov Ber (1746–1812), popularly called "the Great Maggid" (Preacher). He was revered by the Chasidim not only as a great Cabalist who could perform wonders, but as an erudite Talmudist as well. And there lies the irony! Whereas the guileless Israel Baal Shem himself had restated the old democratic Rabbinic tradition that the worshiper's communion was to be directly with God, Dov Ber began to circumvent it. He institutionalized the Chasidic movement. He conferred upon the tzaddik the supreme religious role. Now the Chasid was even more dependent on his intercession with God than the ancient Judean had been on the priest in the Temple. In consequence, the intimate and spontaneous communion between man and God so fervently preached by the Baal Shem—although it still continued because it had always been a powerful tradition in the Jewish religion—nevertheless, became more restricted for the Chasid. He could no longer function religiously in a complete sense without the mediation of his rebbeh.

Another leading disciple of the Baal Shem, Elimelech of Lizhensk (Lezajsk) in Galicia (1716–86), "improved" upon Dov Ber's doctrine of the tzaddik as mediator. He made the title and the powers dynastic, categorically declaring that "sainthood" was an inborn trait and therefore to be considered hereditary! A tzaddik's elder son usually inherited not only his father's "sainthood" and his official position, but also his frequently lavish income, derived from the contributions brought, in most cases, by very poor but worshipful followers who were prepared to make every material sacrifice for their rebbeh's well-being.

It is a matter of history that hundreds of self-perpetuating dynasties of tzaddikim mushroomed in hundreds of Jewish communities in Eastern Europe. Several of the best known as well as the most affluent were those of Belz, in Galicia;

of Sadagora, in Bukovina; of Ger, in Poland; and of Lubavitsch, in Russia.

The pious Chasid visited his tzaddik at least three times a year. Each time he came, he presented him with a generous "free-will" offering: a pidyon ("redemption" money), for which he received the tzaddik's blessing or counsel. The Chasid also came to see the holy man on special festive occasions or in times of emergency, when he desperately stood in need of intercession with the Almighty. Most frequently, he came to get the tzaddik to bless him with parnosseh (a livelihood)—the pauperized ghetto Jew's everlasting anxiety and nightmare—or to consult him on whether it would be propitious to start a new commercial undertaking (in the majority of cases, this could involve but a picayune financial investment, for in the petty ghetto commerce, there were more traders than customers). In times of sickness and trouble, the rebbeh also was called upon to implore God for mercy and for his succoring hand.

The rebbeh had an ever ready supply of amulets and talismans to take care of every contingency, human lack, frustration, and affliction: amulets for pregnant mothers and barren wives; for those who were haunted by specters, possessed by demons, or persecuted by the Evil Eye; for the sightless, the crippled, the mentally retarded, the lame, and the halt. Upon these amulets and talismans were inscribed in Hebrew protective incantations and Cabalistic formulas to foil the malevolent designs of Satan and his demonic hosts.

Not a few of the tzaddikim lived in ostentatious style, emulating the landed Christian gentry. When they went out for a ride or on a journey, it was, often, in an elegant coach. They usually were followed by a throng of worshipful adherents who hung on their every word and took careful note of every facial expression and gesture, trying to detect in them some hidden mystical meaning.

Hundreds of Chasidim ate at their rebbeh's table, sometimes remaining as his guests for days or weeks at a time, being lodged and fed without cost. Together they worshiped God with prayer and song. They danced with abandon in the mystic circle. The disciples listened with bated breath to their rebbeh's Cabalistic exposition of some verse in the Torah. And together with him, and also in intimate group-communion with one another, in the mystic union of fellowship, they attempted to soar to the dizzy heights of rapture (hitlahabut)—the most characteristic feature of the Chasidic mode of worship.

In the teachings of Chasidism, tremendous emphasis was placed on the creative power of song—as a force to create blessings for life. It was valued as the purest and highest forms of prayer. By means of melody, said the great poet-tzaddik Nachman of Bratzlav (1771–1811), the great-grandson of Israel Baal Shem, God had created the universe; by means of song, the pure in heart could be inspired to the inner vision of prophecy. Because of his supposed spiritual illumination and personal sanctity, the tzaddik was believed to have acquired a knowledge of divine song. Therefore, when he sang, his soul was able to wing its way to the highest reaches of heaven and to perform "miracles and wonders."

Describing the manner in which his Rebbeh Aaron, "the Great Tzaddik" of Karlin (*d.* 1772), sang before his Chasidim, a worshipful disciple recorded: "When our Rebbeh Aaron chants The Song of Songs on the eve of the Sabbath, a great commotion takes place in Heaven. The angelic and seraphic choirs hush their hymning so that they might listen to our Rebbeh Aaron's singing, for its source is the limitless world of song."

Rabbi Israel of Kozienic giving his blessing to a young Chasid, c. 1815.

Whatever its admitted backwardness and undeniably retrogressive features, Chasidism produced a profound religious revolution in its time. It helped to provide the much harassed folk in the old ghetto towns with the moral strength to endure its ordeals. Its continuing creative impact on Jewish culture, even in the areas of secularity such as music, literature, art, the dance, and the theatre, is still apparent today.

As an organized religious movement—and not including its numerous sophisticated but non-observing Neo-Chasidic devotees who are drawn to it for sentimental, mystical, or poetic reasons—Chasidism is still demonstrating a surprising vitality. Its adherents, in many urban centers throughout the world, live grouped around the tzaddikim of their choice, who are, in the main, descendants of well-known Chasidic dynasts from home towns in the "old country." However, the "saints" no longer are expected by their followers to perform any Cabalistic miracles. For it would seem that the wondrous, the childlike-poetic, and the magical have forevermore gone out of Israel Baal Shem's mission of redemption. It is difficult for a belief in the supernatural—natural enough in a bygone period—to rise again in spectral splendor in the nuclear age, especially in the down-to-earth, sophisticated Jewish communities that are to be found in New York, Chicago, Buenos Aires, and London.

See also CABALA; DOCTRINES IN JUDAISM; ESSENES; ETHICAL VALUES, JEWISH; FELLOWSHIP IN ISRAEL; FOLKLORE; FOLK MUSIC AND DANCE; KARAITES; LAMED-VAV TZADDIKIM; PHARISEES; SADDUCEES; SAMARITANS; THERAPEUTAE; ZEALOTS.

CHASIDISM. *See* CHASIDIM.

CHAZZAN (Hebrew s., meaning "cantor"; pl. CHAZZANIM)

It was not until the final phase of the Renaissance—just before the Baroque era descended ornately upon the European arts like a sunburst—that the professional chazzan first came into his own as a performing vocalist in the synagogues of Central and Southern Europe. Until that time, the direction of the prayer service had been entrusted to the baal tefillah—the "master of prayer" or precentor. (This latter post, of course, was only honorific; no remuneration was attached to it.) The precentor stood wrapped in the long folds of his prayer shawl at the lectern before the Holy Ark. He was there as "the advocate of the congregation," intoning the Hebrew liturgy in an informal yet fervent manner. He employed the familiar musical modes, intonations, and hymn tunes that were traditional with the Jews in his particular region. But by the end of the sixteenth century, this amateur though pious folk-pleader no longer was deemed entirely adequate for the congregational service by those worshipers who had acquired a more sophisticated musical taste.

The dissatisfaction with the non-professional precentor might be explained, in part, by the gradual rise, in affluence and also in worldliness and culture, of a sizable class of merchants and traders in the urban ghettos. With their increased wealth and cultural sophistication came also a desire for greater splendor and formal dignity in the performance of the prayer service. The opulence and sensory appeal with which both Catholic and Protestant churches in the cities and towns were conducting their religious services helped nurture this desire among Jews.

Collaterally with these developments, musical taste in most of Christian Europe was undergoing profound changes. Knowledgeable Jews could not help but notice that in the churches, polyphonic, mensurate music, with its rich harmonies and tonal contrasts, was beginning to displace the colorless and dreary plain song of the Middle Ages. Even though the Jews lived segregated in ghetto confines, they were not bypassed by the cultural changes that were taking place all around them. Their artistic standards, too, however unschooled, were becoming more discerning and exacting. Like their Christian contemporaries, they expected from the performance of their precentors, besides spiritual uplift, esthetic and sensory pleasure.

A striking illustration of this change in taste could be seen in the musical achievements of the Jews in Italy in the late Renaissance as they were swept forward into the stream of general culture. Several of the finest schools of music in Italy, during the fifteenth and sixteenth centuries, were conducted in the ghettos of Venice and Ferrara by accomplished Jewish musicians, and even talented young Christians pursued their studies in them. From this musical environment and cultural interchange with Christians was produced a new and very different category of chazzanim for the synagogues of Italy. In performance, they combined the traditional Jewish chants and intonations with the refined taste, vocal style, and rhythmic melodic line of contemporary Italian art-music, which was then setting the most advanced and discriminating standards in Europe.

Perhaps this trend in Jewish liturgical song, epochal in so many ways, can best be understood by reviewing the remarkable career as chazzan in Venice of Salomone Rossi, who bore the tag of "L'Ebreo Mantuano" ("the Jew of Mantua"). In the history of music he is written down as a composer, solo violinist, and tenor (during 1587–1628) at Il Paradiso, the almost legendary ducal court of Vicenzo Gonzaga in Mantua. Here he was active as a distinguished co-worker of Claudio Monteverdi (called by his contemporaries "the glory of our century") in the development of the *ars nova*, the new art of polyphonic music: the so-called Florentine Reform. In his own right as a musical pathfinder, Salomone was one of the first composers in Europe to experiment with musical variations for the new instrumental forms of the sinfonia and trio sonata (*sonata a tre*). He thereby became an immediate musical ancestor of such luminaries as Alessandro and Domenico Scarlatti, Corelli, and Vivaldi. They all used Salomone's compositions, among others, as working models for the development of their own superior creations.

For years, Salomone had been agitating in the ghettos of Venice, Ferrara, Mantua, and Padua for the reform of the musical service of the synagogue, and for the introduction of a choir, and of an organ and other instruments. The opposition from the Ultra-Orthodox traditionalists was unyielding and fierce; they considered the proposals as verging on sacrilege. Nevertheless, Salomone succeeded in winning over to his side the redoubtable humanist and preacher-rabbi of Venice, Leone da Modena. When, in the year 1605, officiating as chazzan in the synagogue of nearby Ferrara, Salomone organized a choir of eight voices to assist him in part-singing his own compositions, written "according to the rules of harmony," a complaint was lodged against him with the Rabbinic Assembly of Venice. Years later (in 1622), in a challenging preface to a collection of Salomone's published compositions for the synagogue, Rabbi Leone recalled with some asperity that earlier controversy:

> We are determined to protect this work from those people who invariably recoil from all progress, who wish to proscribe every useful innovation that they fail to understand. I am taking the opportunity to present here an important document [of 1605] in response to the individual who addressed me on this subject when I was Rabbi at Ferrara. I then wrote the decision for the Rabbinic Assembly of Venice in which I brought demonstrable proof that there was nothing in the Talmud that opposed the introduction of choral song into our synagogues. I did this in order to silence the malevolent detractors. Despite all that the latter may say, I call upon all our faithful to honor, to cultivate and to disseminate in our synagogues the art of choral song to serve Israel. . . .

Probably the first chazzan to leave behind an authenticated record of his cantorial ministry and creativity was Salomone Rossi. In the dedication that he wrote for his published collection of liturgical compositions (mentioned above), bearing the Hebrew title *Ha-Shirim Asher li-Shlomo* ("The Songs of Solomon" [i.e., Salomone]), he stated that his aim in creating them was "to glorify and beautify the songs of King David *according to the rules of music.*" In all, he wrote musical settings to thirty-three hymns, psalms, and prayers. He composed them elaborately for choir and solos in three, four, five, six, seven, and eight parts, and with instrumental accompaniment variously by *chittarone* (a large lute), organ, and *basso continuo*.

Now this event was something entirely novel and without precedent in the history of the synagogue. It had never been the custom for composer-chazzanim to write down the notes of the music they created and sang. Few and far between were those who had gone to the trouble of learning the notation system employed in Western music, let alone acquiring even a rudimentary knowledge of counterpoint and harmony. To a large extent, Jewish liturgical song was handed down, like other forms of folk music, "by ear," from one generation to the next.

That Salomone's cultured voice was not entirely one crying in the wilderness to the unheeding may be inferred from Rabbi Leone's eulogy of him: "In spite of the apathy his co-religionists have for music, he is not discouraged. He has placed his faith in God, and each day he has added to the psalms, prayers, and songs which he has now compiled

This is proof that the faithful have wanted to sing his songs. They have studied them and found them full of charm. Their ears have been caressed in such a manner that they have developed a taste for music."

Even if Salomone's accomplishments remained unique in the history of cantorial music until the nineteenth century, the artistic values that he championed were shared in varying degree by other Italian chazzanim. They too were products of the same cultural milieu; they were motivated toward the same goals by the humanistic spirit of the Renaissance. But regardless of their zeal, their combined efforts to introduce polyphonic and instrumental music into the synagogue bore little fruit. This was entirely due to a caprice of history. The religious and social reaction that set in at that very time–during the Counter Reformation–in Italy and the rest of Europe, brought about an intensification in the persecution of the Jews. Apart from other blighting effects–and these were many–it resulted in the stagnation of Jewish cultural values, including musical art in the synagogue. Metaphorically speaking, the fragrant bloom of the Jewish "Florentine Reform" was nipped in the bud.

Nonetheless, following the axiomatic proposition that no significant intellectual or cultural enterprise of man is ever entirely wasted, it should be noted that a least a few of the innovations introduced by Salomone Rossi and by other Italian chazzanim of his day made a real impact on the synagogical song of Germany, Austria, and Bohemia. This song, however, was a shallow and somewhat debased musical

Salomon Sulzer, the founder of modern European cantorial singing and chief composer for the Ashkenazic synagogue. LEFT

Louis Lewandowski, cantorial composer whose works still enjoy a wide popularity in the musical service of the synagogue. RIGHT

Chazzan Isaac Polack (Reb Itzik Chazzon) of the Great Synagogue in London, middle of the 18th century. BOTTOM LEFT

Sirota, celebrated chazzan of Warsaw, c. 1900. (Jewish Welfare Board.) MIDDLE

Yosele Rosenblatt, the most admired of American cantors, who also sang with the Metropolitan Opera Company in Jacques Halevi's La Juive. BOTTOM RIGHT

expression. Although it managed to preserve some of the hauntingly lovely traditional modes and intonations, it led, finally, to the adoption of a rather wooden and declamatory churchly-style of singing during the nineteenth century, one, by the way, that is still very much in evidence today in some congregations.

All this time, the chazzanim of Eastern Europe did not depart from their traditional, folkloric sacred song. Their music may have been deficient in art values but it remained faithful to the devotional ideas, moods, and nuances of meaning in the prayer texts, and their customary way of singing the ancient ornamental melos was lyrical and full of emotional fervor. That is how it happened that among Slavic Jews there were always found numerous and knowledgeable devotees of cantorial singing who, unlike their more formal and cultured German brethren, were far less impressed with the splendid vocal equipment and the clever artifices of the chazzan than with his innate musicality and his expressive interpretation of the prayers. The memory of an older generation of plain folk, who stemmed from the cities and towns of Lithuania, still glows warmly when recalling the musical exploits of a young chazzan-composer from Vilna. His name was Yoel-David Strashinsky (1816–50), but to his contemporaries he was known only by the endearing Yiddish sobriquet of Dos Vilner Baalhabesil (freely translated as "The Little Gentleman of Vilna"). With his sweet lyrical tenor, muted and expressive of the deepest and most refined emotions, and improvising breathtaking embellishments, around the ancient modal chants, he was reputed to send his hearers, who hung upon his every note, into transports of rapture.

The stylistic differences between the German and Polish chazzanim were explained by the eighteenth-century rabbi of Halberstadt, Germany, Abi Selig Margolius. Born and raised in Poland, he recalled with nostalgia that in his native town of Kalisz, the community chazzan, Reb Burech (Baruch), used to sing the service with such sweetness and feeling that he moved the congregation to tears and melted many sinners to repentance: "Such ability is possessed by the chazzanim in our country [i.e., Poland] only, whereas in other countries, the chazzanim sing with neither melody nor feeling." That is perhaps why, during the eighteenth century, chazzanim from Poland were much in demand in London, Amsterdam, and Prague.

In the musical idioms that the chazzanim of Eastern Europe employed and in the variety of vocal styles they affected right down to the twentieth century, may be discerned a fusion of diverse Jewish and non-Jewish musical currents. It has been found difficult by musicologists who are specialists in the field to disentangle the intertwining strands of regional ethnic melodies in Jewish song. It can be assumed that the stylistc character of cantorial singing and the form and content of the liturgical song it projeced naturally varied according to the prevailing musical patterns and fashions in a given region. But because of the frequent massacres and expulsions that the Jews were made to suffer everywhere, they were always involved in a great deal of migration–a wandering about, a flight from fear and hunger in perpetual and restless movement from city to city and from country to country. It followed inevitably that, under these mercurial conditions, there resulted also a biologic and cultural intermingling of the various Jewish ethnic strains that met in the Polish provinces and in Russia. This, of course, was true too of the blending of different traditional melodies and cantorial styles employed in the service of the synagogue.

In the rich body of liturgical song that had been created for the East European synagogue over the course of many centuries is discernible the impress of diverse musical idioms and patterns that must have stemmed from a number of geographic areas and cultural currents, including even the exotic. In the order of historic time-sequence, there are, first of all, the very beautiful but hard-to-define "Oriental" or "Semitic" Jewish modes, intonations, cantillations, and melodies, handed down, say some musicologists, across many centurie of Jewish vicissitudes. Although supposedly drawn from a common Judean source in Hellenistic times, they, nonetheless, underwent significant changes that were inevitable from acculturation in different parts of the world.

Powerful too was the impact of the Slavonic songs indigenous to the East European region. After the overthrow in 970 C.E. of the fabulous Jewish kingdom of Khazaria, in the Crimea, by the boyars of Kiev, there was a great influx of Khazarian refugees into Russia, Poland, the Ukraine, and Hungary. These Jews, who had been but recently (740 C.E.) converted from paganism, had brought along with them the total ethnic baggage of their distinctive culture, the Oriental songs of their Asian synagogues included. But what those songs were like, or what elements of them were absorbed by the Slavonic Jews, is not ascertainable, for the culture of the Khazar Jews is an utterly vanished one.

Probably the principal contribution to the music of the synagogue in Eastern Europe was made by the Jews of Germany. It must be kept in mind that their influence was exerted only by degrees, over a long process of migration and acculturation. This first began on a mass scale in the period which followed the Black Death–the epidemic in 1348–49 when the Jews of Central Europe were falsely accused of poisoning the wells; as a result, they were subject to massacres and expulsions. Tens of thousands fled for their lives into the Polish provinces. There they implanted among the Slavonic Jews not only their own Jewish-German language–Yiddish–but also their other cultural values, including the songs of the Ashkenazic synagogue.

There were also musical influences stemming from still other ethnic groups of Jews: Spanish-Portuguese, Turkish, Arabian, and Walachian. Evident, in particular, was the stamp of the Sefaradic idiom, which was Spanish-Moorish in character. This rich, melodic element was introduced into the music of the Ashkenazim after the expulsion of hundreds of thousands of Jews from Spain in 1492, when many of them sought a haven in Poland and other Slavic lands, by way of Turkey, Greece, and Bulgaria.

All of these recognizable and separate streams of Jewish melody flowed together and mingled their strains into a common pool of religious song. And, in time, by means of the chemistry of cultural fusion, both the German and East European chazzanim created out of it the related kinds of cantorial singing that are heard today in the synagogues of Europe and the Western Hemisphere.

A Gentile's impression of cantorial art at its best was stated by Franz Liszt. He had gone, while in Vienna, to hear "the famous tenor [Salomon] Sulzer, who served as cantor in the synagogue, and whose reputation is so outstanding. . . . Seldom were we so deeply stirred by emotion as on that evening, so shaken that our soul was entirely given to meditation and to a participation in the service."

This was the very same Sulzer (1804–90), a member of Franz Schubert's circle of musical friends, who, despite modest creative talents, brought on a veritable revolution in the cantorial art of the Ashkenazim. What Salomone Rossi, the Venetian composer-chazzan, had, two hundred years before, tried and so largely failed to do–namely, to reform the musical service of the synagogue "according to the laws of music"–Sulzer accomplished. Without question, the middle of the nineteenth century, culturally and historically, was more propitious for the attempt to bring the folkloric ornamental melos of the synagogue into the orbit of contemporary art-music.

An adherent of the Romantic school, Sulzer blended, both in his arrangement of the musical service and in his vocal performance, much of the emotionalism and introspectiveness which are characteristics of traditional synagogical songs and chants with the melodic idioms, and harmonies popular in contemporary German music. His singing, if not his compositions, drew respectful attention from the most distinguished musicians of the day. To them—as it had to Liszt—it represented a novel esthetic experience augmented by the discovery that there actually existed such a thing as Jewish liturgical music, which, even if it was not comparable with the best in church music, was, nonetheless, very expressive.

Even during his lifetime, Sulzer had already become almost a legend among Jews knowledgeable in chazzanut, the cantorial art of the synagogue. His influence penetrated into the Russian and Polish ghettos. Some of the more adventuresome and perceptive chazzanim there were eager to emerge from their cultural parochialism; they wished to become Europeanized. Consequently, they found very attractive Sulzer's melodic idiom and cultured vocalism that corresponded more to the musical tastes of the new generation of relatively sophisticated worshipers.

Some of the East European chazzanim, serving congregations of the wealthier and the more assimilated, soon began building a cult of imitation around Sulzer's innovations; they also cultivated his oratorio style of singing. Following his lead, they introduced two-, three-, and four-part choral singing into the prayer service. But since they were far less accomplished musically than he and did not possess his musical culture and good taste, their net musical results often proved to be less than successful. Some of the more pretentious cantors even tried to assume Sulzer's air of imposing dignity—one which, apparently, was quite natural to him. They also aped his theatrical way of dressing for the prayer service and manner of wearing his leonine shock of hair: like a mane in the back. To this very day, there are still chazzanim in all parts of the world who, without knowing that the custom is a personal legacy from Salomon Sulzer, sing the liturgy while dressed resplendently in the flowing white robe and miter-like skullcap that he introduced long ago in Vienna, in the days of Franz Schubert!

The chazzanut of the Ashkenazim is an unusual kind of liturgical music; there is no other like it in existence. Although there were, and still are, a number of different vocal styles followed by cantors, each is merely a modification, with its own special embellishments and personality "signature" of the chazzan, of the same evocative goals, the same traditional modal patterns and recurring idioms and conventions. One observation, though, is inescapable: The music patterns are most often keyed in the melancholy minor. That, of course, is a characteristic of all Semitic music, but in the instance of traditional Jewish melody, the pensive mood and the pathos cut deeper. This is evidently due to the macerated psyche of the Jew, upon which has been etched in grief all the tribulation and injustice experienced by his people throughout its long history.

What some musically cultivated listeners frequently find disturbing is the unrestrained emotionalism in much cantorial performance. Yet this should not be surprising, for the intentions of the chazzan are ingenuously transparent. He is required by custom to play his part in the collective drama of the prayer service in a literal manner: as the shaliach tzibbur—the "advocate of the congregation." This is a religious role assigned to him by a tradition which has become sanctified by time and practice. He steps forward as the "defense counsel," so to speak, for the worshipers, who have, through searching self-examination, customarily come to regard themselves as "sinners" and "wrong-doers." As such, they feel plagued by life's ills and tormented by personal shortcomings. The chazzan, if he is genuinely pious, identifies himself so closely with the congregants that he feels himself no more righteous than those backsliders he "defends," and enters wholeheartedly into his role of pleader. Accordingly, he strives to interpret the Hebrew prayer-texts, which give uninhibited tongue to these guilt-feelings, woes, and frustrations, with the umost fidelity and literalness. He tries hard—sometimes even too strenuously—to evoke by means of his singing all the multitudinous moods and nuances of liturgical piety. These run through the entire emotional spectrum of pathos, contrition, repentance, compassion, God's anger, lamentation, despair, tenderness, humility, fidelity, sweet reasonableness, exhortation, laudation, invocation, thanksgiving, adoration, and many other tonalities of faith, self-revelation, and petition.

It has not infrequently been commented upon by discriminating devotees of chazzanut that, beginning with the second half of the nineteenth century, during the era of Jewish emancipation, the hauntingly beautiful modal chants traditional in the synagogue were exchanged for ersatz cantorial display-singing. A deteriorating musical taste was the price exacted for cultural assimilation, for chameleon conformity to the mediocre "religious spirit of the times." Cantorial singing often became distorted by an excessive reliance on tonal embroidery, startling dynamic contrasts, and grand operatic bombast.

A somewhat disconcerting feature for some listeners has been the chazzan's coloratura singing in falsetto. Yet no less eminent an authority on Jewish music than A. Z. Idelsohn was fervent in his praise of this kind of vocalism: "The coloratura in East European chazzanut is like the soul in the body; without it, that chazzanut loses its vitality, its charm, its fascination."

Until recent years, when schools for the study of Jewish liturgical music were established in rabbinical seminaries, there was no cantorical institution in which the aspiring young

Jan Peerce, who, following World War II, became perhaps the most admired operatic tenor in the United States while also enjoying great popularity as a chazzan. (Courtesy of RCA Victor.)

singer could develop his talents and acquire a technical competence in chazzanut. The usual course of training followed the medieval pattern of apprenticeship, wherein the talented boy who possessed a good voice and wished to follow the cantorial calling learned the intricacies of his exacting craft in a hard school: as meshorer (Hebrew, choir singer; pl. meshorerim) to a chazzan. He was usually apprenticed at the age of nine or ten, when he still sang alto or soprano. By the time he reached maturity, he was ready to strike out on a cantorial career of his own.

The meshorer belonged to a most rudimentary sort of choir, if such it can be called at all. It customarily consisted of only two vocalists—a boy soprano, or *"singerl,"* as they called him in Yiddish, and a resounding bass. Such a singerl had been John Braham, who developed into perhaps the most famous operatic tenor of his generation in Europe. He assisted, late in the eighteenth century, in the Bevis Marks Synagogue in London as descant alto to Chazzan Meyer Levin. The latter, following the fashion among opera singers, had Italianized his name for stage purposes to Leoni. Under that pseudonym he sang comic-opera roles to his enthralled listeners at the Drury Lane Theatre during week nights, but on the Sabbath and on Jewish fast and festival days he continued to chant the Hebrew liturgy in the synagogue.

This doubling in musical careers, as chazzan and as opera and concert singer, became quite common after the turn of the twentieth century on both sides of the Atlantic. The most prominent of such vocalists were Hermann Jadlowker, "the German Caruso," and Joseph Schwartz, bass-baritone of the Imperial Opera in Berlin before World War I. Comparable artists today, to list only a few in the United States, are Alexander Kipnis, Jan Peerce, Richard Tucker, and Robert Merrill. This adaptability of the Jewish singer is quite phenomenal; it attests to the intellectual and musical suppleness he displays by standing with each foot planted, so to speak, in a different culture.

But probably the greatest significance that this achievement points up is that the music of the synagogue and the vocal art of the chazzan were all along conditioning Jewish worshipers to a love of serious music. When the opportunity to develop this secular musical interest finally opened up to them, they eagerly grasped it. How else explain the large number of gifted Jewish singers, instrumentalists, composers, conductors, teachers, and musicologists who made their appearance during the first half of the twentieth century and have been, ever since, enriching the total musical culture of mankind?

See also BAAL TEFILLAH; HYMNS OF THE SYNAGOGUE; MUSIC IN THE TEMPLE; MUSICAL ACCENTS; MUSICAL INSTRUMENTS OF THE BIBLE; PRAYER AND WORSHIP; ZEMIROT.

CHAZZANUT. *See* CHAZZAN.

CHEBRAH KADDISHAH. *See* BURIAL RITES AND CUSTOMS.

CHEDER (Hebrew, meaning "room"; pl. CHEDARIM)

When, exactly, the Talmud Torah—the elementary religious school that has been traditional since late Judean time—was transformed into the single-room cheder, is hard to verify. But the latter was an educational institution stamped with a different physiognomy. Very likely, it took the form so well known today to the oldest generation of Jews of East European stock, during the period that has been so aptly described as "the Jewish Dark Ages." This was a period which began with the sixteenth century in the Slavic ghettos and ended only after World War I.

In our time, the cheder has become peculiarly related to the Ultra-Orthodox and Yiddish-speaking milieu. Yet similar forms of the cheder still exist in the backward regions of North Africa and the Islamic countries of the Near and Middle East.

Although it is true that it was not at all uncommon (especially in the smaller communities of Palestine and in the countries of the Jewish Diaspora during Talmudic times) for the children to receive their religious instructions from the teacher (melamed) in his living quarters, the quality of such teaching was, nevertheless, on a much lower instructional level than that which could be obtained in the traditional Talmud Torah. The latter institution, which was a bona fide school, was staffed, as a rule, by several teachers, was better organized, and had better administrative control and class discipline. Its teachers were also better qualified than the melamed, and the place of instruction was, at the least, less unattractive and distracting for the child than the more informal and more haphazard cheder. In addition, the subject matter taught in the Talmud Torah was somewhat broader in content than that of the cheder.

That the curriculum of the cheder was narrow, its learning objectives limited, and its teaching methods antiquated at all times, should be fairly apparent to every person acquainted with its working, for the inclusion of secular subjects was naturally unthinkable. Beginning with the late Middle Ages, the East European rabbis—most of them uncompromising traditionalists—were obsessed by the fear that the study of non-Jewish subjects might have the disastrous effect of drawing Jews closer to their Christian neighbors in a common bond of cultural interest, and such close contact, they were convinced, could only lead, sooner than later, to apostasy from the Jewish faith. This was the dread specter that haunted Jewish life in Russia and Poland at every step.

Such a neurotic fear is easily understood when we examine the historic conditions of Jewish ghetto life, which existed so precariously in the Christian world. For many centuries, the Jews of Europe had been exposed to the violent efforts of the Church to convert them to Christianity. They were forced by the authorities to listen to conversionist sermons delivered in the churches especially for their benefit, only to hear their own faith reviled and be themselves abused and physically maltreated when they resisted "persuasion." It was perfectly natural that, when the pious merely recalled the appalling number of Jewish martyrs who had perished because they abjured baptism, the allurements of the ghetto, stemming from its physical and cultural isolation, seemed irresistibly attractive to them.

Unlike the Talmud Torah, which was free and was supported by the Jewish community, the cheder was a private enterprise of the individual teacher, who charged a seasonal tuition fee for his instruction. The cheder was in the teacher's home, usually a dingy and wretched setting that frequently had some harmful environmental effects on the pupils, notwithstanding the fact that so many of them came from homes that were no more attractive. Just the same, the informality with which the teacher conducted his class was, in certain respects, quite engaging, and it exerted a strong democratizing influence on the children's social attitudes. For six days a week they spent the long school day (eight to ten hours a day in summer, and twelve hours a day in winter) with the melamed and—unavoidably—also with his household, like members of the same family. As a result, they often developed emotional attachments lasting all their lives. This was particularly true where the melamed had a warm, out-

Cheder in old Jerusalem.

"Modernized" cheder in Munkacevo, Hungary.

Melamed (teacher) drilling his pupils in a medieval cheder in Germany. (From an illustrated machzor [festival prayer-book], 13th or 14th century.)

Bahelfer (teacher's assistant) shepherding pupils to cheder in Eastern Europe, end of 19th century. (From a Jewish New Year's card.)

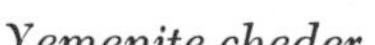

Yemenite cheder.

going nature and was able to win both the respect and affection of the children in his charge. Under those special conditions, he became a sort of second father to them, for actually they spent more of their time with him in the cheder than with their father in the home.

The initiation of the child into the cheder was surrounded with sentimental ceremony and symbolism. In some countries he was considered ready for the cheder at three years of age; in other places at a somewhat later age, but this hardly ever exceeded five. On the Sabbath day before the little boy was to embark on what was to be his unending quest for Torah-learning, he was carried into the synagogue either in the arms of his father or by a worthy Torah scholar, and often by the melamed who was going to teach him. As the small boy stood before the bema, the platform in the center of the synagogue, clutching the protective hand of his father and with the attention of the entire congregation centered upon him, the Sefer Torah (Torah Scroll) was unrolled and the Ten Commandments were read aloud to him, just as if he were standing more than three thousand years before at Mount Sinai together with his ancestors, the ancient Israelites.

Equally symbolic was the more informal ceremony that took place on the first day when he was brought to the cheder. With his father and mother hovering nearby, the melamed pointed out to the child the aleph-bet in the Chumash (Pentateuch). As the boy repeated the names of the Hebrew letters after his teacher, his mother gave him little cakes to munch and put honey in his mouth. This was by way of pedagogically pointing out to him how "sweet" were the sounds of the Hebrew letters of the Torah on his tongue, the music of piety he was to sound until the day he died. At the conclusion of this first lesson, the fond mother clasped him in her arms and rejoiced over her great good fortune, murmuring the prayer of all devoted Jewish parents: that her child should be fulfilled with years in "Torah, marriage, and the performance of good deeds."

In the cheder, the Five Books of Moses (the Torah) constituted the sole textbook for instruction. After the boy had mastered the aleph-bet or alphabet, he would be taught the vowel-points (*see* VOWEL SOUNDS, HEBREW); then he would be shown how to combine the consonants with the vowel points to produce syllables. For several months he conned these lessons together with the other children his age. The pace and the key in which the lesson was pitched were set by the teacher. The children recited rhythmically and in unison in loud, clear trebles and in the familiar cheder singsong, swaying their bodies in accompaniment (*see* TORAH STUDY). At last they were ready for reading the weekly portion of the Torah text, and this they learned with its traditional musical notation system for cantillation (*see* MUSICAL ACCENTS). Soon they were started on the formidable task of translating the Scriptural text word for word into Yiddish, the vernacular of the Jews in Eastern Europe. The learning of the Hebrew words by translating them into the vernacular (whether Aramaic, Greek, Arabic, Spanish, or French) of any country was always traditional in Jewish schools everywhere.

The cheder was arranged physically somewhat like the one-room rural schoolhouse in the United States. The children were grouped for their lessons according to their ages and the extent of their knowledge. While one little group was receiving instruction from the melamed, the others were reviewing or memorizing out loud the lessons they had already learned. This method of learning by constant repetition and vocal review endured as a time-honored tradition among Jews in all countries and in all periods. In Yiddish it was called *chazern* ("to repeat"). To be more specific, there was not just one type of cheder in operation; there were at least two and sometimes even three. Each of these religious schools was accommodated to the learning accomplishments and capacities of the individual boy and the desires of his father. Normally, at the age of nine or ten, when the student had demonstrated that he had already learned all he could in the elementary cheder described above, his father would enroll him in another cheder in which more advanced studies were taught. Here, until the boy became Bar Mitzvah at the age of thirteen, he was instructed and drilled in the less complicated treatises of the Talmud, together wtih their commentaries by Rashi and Abraham ibn Ezra.

See also COMMENTARIES, RABINNICAL; TALMUD, THE; TALMUD TORAH; TORAH STUDY.

CHEREM. *See* EXCOMMUNICATION.

CHET. *See* SIN AND SINNER.

CHETUBIM. *See* BIBLE, THE.

CHIBAT TZIYON. *See* ZIONISM.

CHILDREN, BLESSING OF

One of the most ancient of Jewish religious folkways is the blessing of children by their parents, most generally by the father. The love and tenderness of which it is an index testify to the emotional closeness—a traditional feature of Jewish family life—that has always existed between parents and children.

The role of the father in the Jewish family was, in a number of respects, priestly in character. His periodic blessing of the children was highly esteemed, for it was considered to be endowed by Heaven with unusual spiritual effectiveness. As Jesus ben Sirach declared in the second century B.C.E. in Ecclesiasticus 3:9:

> "The blessing of the father builds houses for the sons;
> The curse of the mother destroys them."

The great significance placed upon the parental blessing is movingly detailed in the Biblical account of the blessing by Isaac. The dramatic details of the conflict between Jacob and Esau to obtain their father's coveted blessing, the deception plotted and advanced by Rebecca for her favorite son, and, finally, the anguish of Esau on discovering that he has been duped out of this all-important privilege, rings out in his grieving outcry to Isaac:

> "Hast thou but one blessing, my father?
> Bless me, even me also, O my father!"
> GENESIS 27:38

This custom of a father blessing his children survived all the tides of change and fortune in Jewish life through the centuries. In an old devotional work written in Yiddish, the *Brantshpiegel*, which was printed in Basel in 1602, the customary procedure of blessing children is described: "Before the children can walk they should be carried on the Sabbath and on the holy days to their father and mother to receive their blessing. After they are able to walk, they should go to them of their own accord, with body bent and with head bowed, to receive the blessing." The blessing, recited accompanied by the laying on of hands on the head, took place either in the synagogue upon the conclusion of the prayer service, or immediately upon arriving home. Over his sons, the father would say, in memory of the words the Patriarch Jacob pronounced when he blessed Joseph's sons: "May God make thee like Ephraim and Manasseh." For daughters, the formula was similar: "May God make thee like Sarah, Rebecca, Rachel, and Leah." This was followed with the recitation of the priestly blessing.

The Patriarch Isaac blesses his son Jacob. (From the Sarajevo Haggadah, Spanish, 13th century.)

Rabbi blesses child in synagogue. Galicia, 19th century. (Painting by Isidor Kaufmann.)

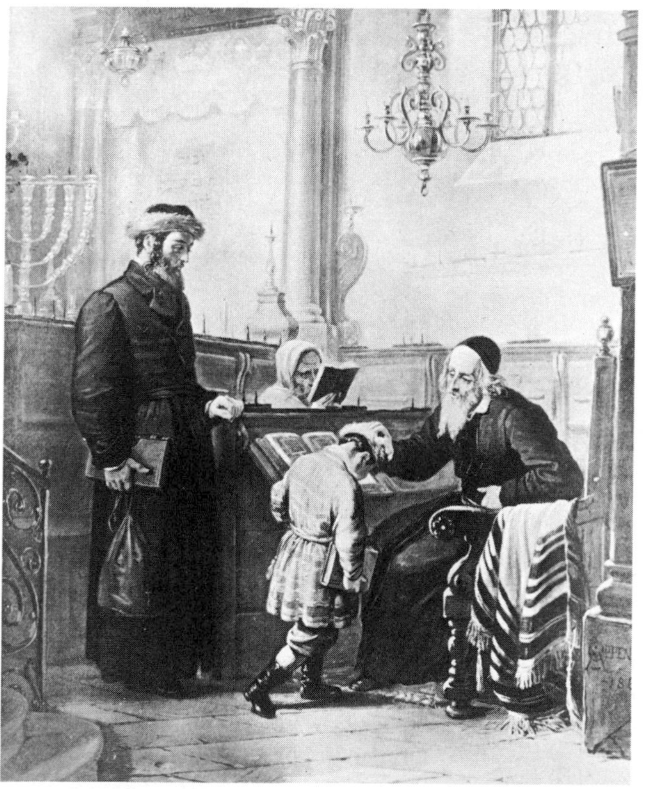

The custom began to decline with the emergence of the Jews into the world from their ghetto isolation, but it is still observed by a number, however dwindling, of traditionalists.

See also PRIESTLY BLESSING.

CHILDREN AND PARENTS. *See* FAMILY RELATIONS, TRADITIONAL PATTERNS OF.

CHOSEN PEOPLE, THE

This expression is derived from *Attah Bechartanu* ("You have chosen us"), which are the opening Hebrew words of a prayer in the liturgy for the Holy Days.

The concept of Israel as an Elect of God is first indicated in the covenant with Abraham, "the first Jew." God had chosen him, and through him all of his descendants down the ages, to be his dedicated "servants." This awesome covenant with God, according to the Book of Exodus, had been reaffirmed by the entire Jewish people before Mount Sinai. It constituted a total consecration–the kind which no people in history, before or since, seems to have entered into with any deity.

The classic statement of this agreement, in the words of God in the Bible, runs thus: "Now, therefore, if ye will hearken unto my voice indeed, and keep My covenant, then ye shall be Mine own treasure from among all peoples; for all the earth is Mine; and ye shall be unto Me a kingdom of priests, and a holy nation." (Exodus 19:5-6.)

What this meant was that, out of its own free will, Israel was dedicating itself to worship God and to serve in the world as the champion of His eternal truth–the Torah. In addition, it solemnly undertook to put the precepts of the Torah into daily practice and, by setting an example in its own righteous national existence, inspire all the other peoples of the earth to embrace the Jewish faith and thereby bring about the redemption of the entire human race.

This universalistic striving of the Jewish people was at the heart of many of its religious beliefs, ethical ideals, and practices, and largely explains the wide appeal and success of Christianity, which took over from Prophetic and Rabbinic Judaism so much of its philosophy of life, as well as many of its social and moral values.

Understandably enough, there has been much confusion and disagreement regarding the concept of the Jews as a chosen people. Two diametrically opposite views have been presented in Jewish religious literature. One holds that the Jews became "the Chosen People" because they "chose" the Torah. The Talmud states: "The Lord offered the Torah to all the peoples, but they refused to accept it, except Israel." In each case, the rejection occurred because the burdens and disadvantages of cleaving to the Torah seemed far greater than the privileges and rewards holding to it might bring.

In a fantasy set in the World-to-Come, the Midrash has the opportunistic Romans, eager for admittance into the Eternal Reward, plead with God: "Let us practice the commandments of the Torah now!" To which, God, amused by their insincerity, bids them: "Go and sit in the succah!" However, the succah is small and discouragingly dingy, and besides, the day is hot. Thereupon, the Romans are overcome by a sincere dislike for the Jewish religion and its uncomfortable practices. And so they angrily leave the succah.

The "yoke of the Torah" was always a popular figure of speech among the pious, and it was a very real yoke too, but to them it seemed woven of roses. Saadia Gaon (882–942), the foremost Jewish religious authority before Maimonides, made the interesting point that, with regard to the concept "chosen," it was not Israel that had been chosen by God but rather His Torah that Israel had chosen. In wordly terms, what profit did this bring to the Jews? asked Saadia. And his answer was: not privileges but duties; not rewards but sacrifices; not pleasure but pain; not peace but only eternal struggle, persecution, and rootlessness.

Saadia's interpretation obviously was an elaboration of the Second (Deutero-) Isaiah's celebrated parable concerning the role of the Jewish people in the world as *the suffering servant of the Lord*. This was the parable that the founders of Christianity had conveniently extracted from its real context and laid claim to as a prophetic reference to Jesus, the "Man of Sorrows" still to come: "He [i.e., Israel] is despised and rejected of men; a man of sorrows. . . . Surely he had borne our griefs. . . . But he was wounded for our transgressions, he was bruised for our iniquities: the chastisement of our peace was upon him; and with his stripes we are healed." (Isaiah 53:3-5)

From Saadia's interpretation it would appear that Israel had not been chosen by God but only *chose to be the chosen people* to fulfill God's plan and to implement His will for the redemption of Israel and of all mankind.

Much obloquy and scorn has been heaped by modern anti-Semites on the concept of "the Chosen People." No doubt the pretensions of certain Jews, who have laid an unjustified emphasis on their own chauvinistically motivated misinterpretations, have added fuel to the fire. For instance, the exalted self-dedication of Israel to the service of God (Isaiah 61:6)—"But ye shall be named the Priests of the Lord"—was interpreted by some Talmudic Rabbis to mean that the Jews were morally superior, which was one reason God had chosen them as his favorites. This pretty conceit evoked these comments of self-praise: "All Jews are holy. . . . All Jews are princes. . . . Only for Israel was the world created. . . . None but Israelites are called the Children of God. . . . None but Israel is beloved by God." And to cite just one modern variation of this ancient theme—and one offered by none other than Georg Brandes, the eminent Danish literary historian: "I maintain that the Jews are the most intelligent of all the peoples on earth."

Much more general in Jewish esteem than "the Chosen People" idea, and running as deep as an underground stream, is the tradition formulated by Saddia Gaon: "All creatures are His creatures, and we may not say that He has taken to Himself one to the exclusion of the other, or to a greater degree than another. . . . For when the Psalmist exclaimed, 'O Lord, the portion of my inheritance and my cup,' did he alone want to possess the Master of the World? . . . We hold that He is the God of all mankind. . . . The worth of each man and his lot are equally precious to Him."

To conclude, far from aiming to build itself up as a superior, an elite, or "master" race, the Jewish people, according to fundamental tradition, was dedicated to bringing all the peoples of the earth into a common brotherhood, bestowing an equal worth upon each—although on Judaism's own idealistic terms—of God, Torah, Justice, and Peace.

See also BROTHERHOOD; GENTILES, JEWISH ATTITUDE TOWARD; MESSIAH, THE.

CHOVEVEI TZIYON. *See* ZIONISM.

CHRIST. *See* CHRISTIANITY, JEWISH ORIGINS OF.

"CHRIST-KILLERS." *See* CHRISTIANITY, JEWISH ORIGINS OF; CHRISTIANS, SERVITUDE OF JEWS TO; CONVERSION OF JEWS; CHURCH AND PERSECUTION; "HOST DESECRATION" CALUMNIES; MASSACRES: THE CRUSADES, THE BLACK DEATH; PERSECUTION IN "MODERN" DRESS; POGROMS IN SLAVIC LANDS; "RITUAL MURDER" SLANDERS; WANDERING JEW.

CHRISTIANITY, JEWISH ORIGINS OF

The remarkable but little known Joseph Kirkisani, a Karaite scholar of Babylonia in the tenth century, even in his time had a correct historical perspective about Jesus and Christianity. He wrote that what Jesus had founded was a *Jewish sect,* but that following Jesus' crucifixion by the Romans, Paul of Tarsus, a Hellenized Jew of Asia Minor, had originated from it a new religion: Christianity. Kirkisani has been borne out in his view in modern times by knowledgeable Christian scholarship, which has demonstrated that Paul achieved his religious transformation by grafting upon the ethical body of Jesus' Jewish teachings—and on his life and death, as well—a whole series of pagan notions, myths, rites, and practices. This was part of a de-Judaizing process which was continued by the four canonical Gospel writers and by other early architects of Gentile Christianity. Nevertheless, the New Testament still remains permeated by Jewish thinking and ethics: The frame may be Gentile, but the picture in it is Jewish.

Absolutely nothing is known about the actual life of Jesus except what is narrated in the Four Gospels by Matthew, Mark, Luke, and John, and in the Acts of the Apostles by Paul (Saul) of Tarsus. It must be kept in mind, however, that these works, which were written in Greek many years after the crucifixion of Jesus (liberal Protestant scholars even date the Gospel by John in the beginning of the second century) were not intended to be histories but inspirational evangels. Quite obviously, as in the instance of the Five Books of Moses (*see* BIBLE, THE), the books of the New Testament were also written, rewritten, and edited by a variety of theological hands in response to different religious convictions as well as the changing practical needs of Christian propaganda in the Greco-Roman (Gentile) world. There is even serious question whether any of the New Testament writers, including Mark, had known Jesus personally. In his book, *The First Christian,* the Protestant scholar A. Powell Davies makes this view very plain: "Nor is it in the least true, as is often thoughtlessly assumed, that the Church was somehow founded upon the New Testament. . . . We might put in that instead of the New Testament producing the Church, the Church produced the New Testament."

It is surely a task beset with hazards and a multitude of difficulties even to attempt a coherent and factual exposition of the life and teachings of Jesus as they are set forth in the Gospels and other Christian writings. The confusion is great and the contradictions are multiplied by the very number of evangelists presenting their separate versions, despite the many similarities in their texts which are explained by New Testament scholars as being due to the fact that the Gospel of Mark was their common source. All four Gospels are so encrusted with non-Jewish elements—with the magical, the demonological, and the miraculous—that it would constitute almost a miracle in itself to be able to separate the objective historical fact from folk-legend and imaginative reconstruction.

Historically oriented New Testament scholars are quick to point out that the fourth-century Church Father, Eusebius of Caesarea, cited the authority of the early-second-century Bishop Papias to the effect that the canonical Gospels were all based, more or less, on notes in Greek taken from the text of Aramaic oral gospel tales and presumed teachings and sayings of Jesus that had been transmitted by word of mouth by Judean followers of Jesus. This would explain the textual similarities in the Gospels of Matthew, Mark, Luke, and John. Actually, New Testament scholars have been unable to solve the perplexing problem of the Four Gospels and their attribution to Apostles who, obviously, had not themselves known Jesus yet were presumed to have been among his twelve intimate disciples!

The alleged Greek notes referred to by Bishop Papias must have had an anti-Jewish bias or they would not have been followed so readily by the Gospel writers, who blamed the Jews for the Crucifixion. How this happened to be, remains also an unsolved mystery, as there were extant other gospels composed by disciples close to Jesus: by James, "the Lord's brother," and by (Simon) Peter. But these were *not* admitted to the New Testament canon when it was closed, early in the third century! This was a definite indication of a schism that had taken place between the Jewish followers of Jesus, who wished to remain Jews although believing that the crucified Jesus was the Messiah and would come again, and the anti-Jewish Gentile-Christians who had been organized by Paul.

The Biblical scholar Millar Burrows comments, in *What Mean These Stones*, on the question of the evolution of the Gospels: of historic fact intertwined with legend:

> That there was a period of oral tradition of the gospel materials is almost universally recognized. Some written record of Jesus' words and works may have been made during his lifetime, but the preservation of the gospel material was doubtles for some time very largely a matter of transmission from mouth to mouth. Many sayings and acts of the Master must have been forgotten; on the other hand, legend was soon at work creating stories and sayings, and many apocryphal gospels were written as time went on.

In ancient religions, and in several modern ones as well, myth-creation was always busily at work. Despite the curious insistence by a number of scholars (the eminent Danish-Jewish literary critic, George Brandes, among them) that Jesus was a myth—that he had never even existed—the reality of Jesus as a man has been almost universally recognized. The very same kind of skepticism had been leveled at the historicity of Moses. No matter whether Jesus was real or only a figment of the inflamed Messianic imagination of some first-century visionaries; it is, nonetheless, possible to extract from the bewildering tangle of Gospel supernaturalism a credible, although slender, outline of his life.

Jesus (in Hebrew: Jeshua or Joshua) was the son of Mary and Joseph, a humble carpenter of Nazareth, in Galilee. Jesus too earned his livelihood as a carpenter (early in the second century, the Palestinian apologist of Christianity, Justin Martyr, noted that in his own day, some of the wooden plowshares that had been made by Jesus were still in circulation among farmers in Galilee). Except for certain unilluminating passages in the Gospel of Luke, there is a hiatus in the biography of Jesus, as detailed in the Gospels until his thirtieth year (some historians place his birth between 8 and 4 B.C.E.), when he was launched on his Messianic preaching career, following his immersion of Essenic initiation by John the Baptist at the river Jordan, near Jericho. He subsequently wandered through all the towns and villages in Galilee, accompanied by his disciples and preaching in the synagogues. (The rabbinical maggid or wandering, moralizing preacher has always been a familiar Jewish folk-type; *see* MAGGID.) In emulation of the Prophets of Israel, Jesus tried to stir with words of fire the slumbering conscience of sinners, that they might repent of their wrongdoing and prepare themselves for the Messiah and the Kingdom of God. He declared: "The time is fulfilled and the Kingdom of God is at hand." As in the preaching of every other Jewish moralist, his homilies were copiously illustrated and enlivened with striking metaphors, parables, and Biblical citations and allusions, in accordance with the elaborative poetical method of the Midrash employed by the preachers in the synagogues. (*See* MIDRASH, *under* TALMUD, THE.)

That Jesus and also his disciples were convinced that he was the Messiah is made abundantly plain, yet at first he was afraid to reveal himself as such, for in his day, the Messianic movements, which were frequent and fierce, often exploded into open, armed rebellion against the Roman overlords of Judea, who promptly crushed them in their usual bloody manner. Not until Jesus preached in Jerusalem, when it was no longer possible to hide his conviction that he was the Messiah, was it made known.

That Jesus should have assumed, by the promptings of some mystical revelation within, that he was the Messiah, was not at all unnatural for the extraordinary times in which he lived. It was a period of great tensions and public excitement, running riot with transcendental ideas, apocalyptic visionings, and End-of-Days delirium. In the desparate climate of Jewish life in Judea during the decades prior to 70 C.E. (when the Temple was destroyed and Jerusalem laid waste by the Romans), the clarion call of the Messianic mission had summoned many an ardent visionary and Jewish patriot to act as God's instrument for Israel's redemption. And they ended, where Jesus had ended—on the cross—for crucifixion was the standard method of execution of criminals employed by the Romans. (*See* MESSIAHS, WOULD-BE.)

Jesus the Jew. Before the nineteenth century, it was unthinkable, in countries where Church and State were interlinked, to refer to Jesus as a Jew. In the inconography of Christianity, he had been thoroughly de-Judaized in appearance in much the same way that the seventh-day Sabbath had been transformed by the Church into Sunday, the Seder metamorphosed into the Eucharist, the Passover festival turned into Easter, and Shabuot into Pentecost. The Jesus-image has been represented in the Church art of various national and ethnic groups according to their own distinctive characteristics. Thus, the Byzantine-Roman–Christians made him in their own image, giving him a Roman "look" in the Byzantine style; the Armenians endowed him with an Armenian appearance; the Spaniards depicted him as a Spaniard; the Anglo-Saxons and Scandinavians delineated him as cool, blond, and blue-eyed; and, not to be outdone, the Ethiopian icons pictured him as a Negro. In short, Jesus has been made to appear all things to all men except what he actually was: *a Judean Jew.*

Even well into the nineteenth century, at the start of an era burgeoning with progress and enlightenment, it still required an adventuresome spirit to say publicly that Jesus had been a human and a Jew. Once, in Catholic and Imperial Vienna, the composer Beethoven, who was a Deist and a Republican by conviction, stopped to watch a religious procession pass by. As he looked on the sea of banners, holy images, and giant crucifixes, he remarked to a friend who was with him how odd it was that so much pomp and ceremony should be expended "on a poor crucified Jew." His observation, overheard by unfriendly ears, was promptly reported to the municipal authorities, who summoned him to defend himself against the charge of "blasphemy."

Nevertheless, the second half of the nineteenth century did witness a break in the dike of Christian fundamentalism so that a spirit of free inquiry was permitted to penetrate into Protestant theology and New Testament scholarship. This made it possible for Julius Wellhausen, a foremost German Biblical scholar, to state quite simply: "Jesus was not a Christian; he was a Jew. He did not preach a new faith."

That this was literally true would be hard to refute, since judging by the words out of his own mouth (as they are recorded in the Gospels) Jesus was a devoutly believing Jew. He himself observed, and also imposed on his disciples, the duty of scrupulously living according to the laws of the Torah. He kept the Sabbath, the festivals and fasts, put on tefillin (phylacteries) at morning prayers, fulfilled the commandments to wear tzitzit (fringes), and observed the laws of kashrut (the dietary laws)—all of which institutions the Gentile-Christians later abolished. More important still, he taught traditional Rabbinic doctrines and ethics, and these, coming from him, sound quite startling in the pagan and anti-Jewish context of Pauline Christianity in the New Testament.

Paradoxically, despite the abuse and scorn supposedly heaped by Jesus in the Gospels on "the scribes, Pharisees and hypocrites," he himself preached the very doctrines that they (the Rabbinic Sages; *see* SAGES, RABBINIC) enunciated. This irreconcilable contradiction has been a source of much embarrassment to fundamentalist Christian scholars.

Their attacking the "scribes, Pharisees and hypocrites" en masse—as a class and not as individuals—reveals the clear intent of the Gospel writers to disparage Pharisaic (Rabbinic) Judaism. They wished to make this out to be merely a variety of soulless religious legalism and the Sages themselves to be merely pettifogging lawyers, formalists outside and hypocrites inside. At the same time, they tried to contrast the noble spirituality of Jesus' teachings with the Pharisees' sole preoccupation with empty law and ritualism. This, as can readily be recognized, was but part of a well-calculated campaign on the part of the New Testament writers to de-Judaize Jewish Christianity, to transform it into a new religion having strong Gentile appeal, for the prospects for gaining converts from among the pagans seemed far more promising than from among the Jews.

The irony of this mode of attack is compounded when it is recalled that Jesus was made by the evangelists to adopt the very caustic attitude that the great majority of Rabbinic Sages themselves were taking against pietists and hypocrites among their colleages. The Talmud referred to them as *Zebuim*—"the Tainted Ones"—"they who preach beautifully but do not act beautifully." They were placed in categories by the Rabbis in witty banter as *the ostentatious Pharisee* "who carries his mitzvot [commandments] on his shoulder"; *the self-preening Pharisee* "who knocks his knees together," saying, "Wait for me—I've got a mitzvah to perform"; *the "bleeding" Pharisee* who, to avoid looking at a woman in order not to get lecherous thoughts, runs helter-skelter against the wall and bloodies his face; *the "Pestle" Pharisee* who, like a pestle in a mortar, walks with downcast eyes in simulated pious meekness, asking: "Tell me of another mitzvah I have to perform!"; and, finally, the Pharisee who is pious *out of fear that God will punish him*. In conclusion, asks the Talmud, "Who are the *genuine* Pharisees?" And the answer it gives sounds like the very opposite of what the Gospels made these Sages out to be: "Those who do the will of their Father in Heaven because they love Him!"

The abusive treatment given to the Rabbinic Sages in the New Testament in alleged utterances made by the tongue of the gentle Jesus is a matter of anti-Semitic fact and was responsible for much of the uncomplimentary thinking about the Jewish religion, about Jews, and—not least—about rabbis, by countless millions of Christians over some seventeen centuries. All one need do is turn to any general dictionary for the meaning of "Pharisee" (which is another word for "Rabbinic Sage"). It defines the term as any strict observer of the outward forms in religion, without the spirit of it; in other words, a hypocrite. The word "Pharisaism"—which really should be synonymous with "Talmudic" or "Rabbinic" Judaism—it explains as hypocrisy in religion or censoriousness or self-righteousness in manners, morals, or religion. The clichés of prejudice and ignorance have had an astonishing persistence through the ages, thereby pouring deadly poison into the bloodstream of civilized life.

Judging even on the basis of the belligerently anti-Jewish bias of the Gospels, written by evangelists *who most likely had not even known Jesus during his lifetime,* Jesus never sought to separate himself from the Jewish community. True, he was apparently a member of an Essenic fellowship that Clement of Alexandria (*c.* 150–215), the Greek Church Father, called "Hemerobaptists" or "Morning Bathers," of whom John the Baptist had been the leader. Jesus felt that his Messianic evangel was meant for the Jews alone. He declared: "I am not sent except to the lost sheep of the House of Israel." The odds are that, had not the ambitious, dynamic, and resourceful Hellenistic Jew, Paul (Saul) of Tarsus, entered upon the scene and gone into the world of the Gentiles, seeking greener pastures for his propaganda, there would have been no Christian religion at all, but only a small, Essenic sect of Jews in Judea who persisted in believing that the crucified Jesus was the Messiah.

The Protestant historian of early Christianity, Morton Enslin, notes that "Christianity was the child of Judaism . . . [which] within a score of years became a Gentile cult . . . adopted new conceptions, took on a totally different character, borrowed from all with which it came in contact." It is perhaps a double irony of history that the bloody mark of Cain which had been stained upon the Jewish forehead for their everlasting shame by "pious" Christian theology, Church, and State for nineteen centuries in order to justify their persecution of the Jews, was done on the pretext that Jews had "rejected" the teachings of Jesus the Messiah. In reality, it was Pauline or Gentile Christianity which "rejected" *Jesus the Jew* and transformed him instead, by the process of deification, into "the Son of God"—a pagan invention of both the Egyptian and Greco-Roman religions.

That both Jesus and his disciples considered that he was the Messiah, "the son of David," does not at all cancel out his self-identification as a Jew who lived in accordance with the religious precepts of the Torah, with the laws of the (Rabbinic) Oral Tradition, and in group-solidarity with the Jewish community. When Jesus was asked, allegedly by a hostile scribe:: "Which is the first commandment of all?" his reply (in Mark 12:28-31) came in the uncompromisingly monotheistic words of the Shema: "The first of all the commandments is, Hear, O Israel; The Lord our God is one Lord: And thou shalt love the Lord thy God with all thy heart, and with all thy soul, and with all thy mind, and with all thy strength: this is the first commandment. And the second is like, namely this, Thou shalt love thy neighbor as thyself. There is none other commandment greater than these." Amusingly enough, the Gospel of John, innocent of the fact that this was a central doctrine of the Torah, had Jesus say (in Chapter 13:34) "A new commandment I give unto you, That ye love one another."

What have we here, if not the quintessential teachings of the Torah, based on the Oneness of God and the love of mankind which represented the foundation and source of Rabbinic (Pharisaic) doctrine and ethics? (*See* ETHICAL VALUES, JEWISH; TALMUD, THE.) As if to underscore the completely Jewish identity of Jesus, he stated categorically (in Matthew 5:17) that it was not at all his intention to found a new religion: "Think not that I am come to destroy the Law [i.e., the Torah], or the Prophets: I am not come to destroy, but to fulfill."

Jesus' whole system of ethics, sometimes even down to the very expressions he used, were drawn from the then current Pharisee teachings and from such apocalyptic-moralistic work by Jews as the Testaments of the Twelve Patriarchs. Yet for nineteen centuries, Christians have sedulously cultivated the myth that the Jews believed in a God of Vengeance and practiced a barbarous "eye-for-an-eye" way of life—that Christianity was the first to project a God of love, compassion, and ethical conduct. It was Paul who had abrogated the laws

A Cabalistic projection of the unity of the three religions (left to right): Islam, Judaism, and Christianity. (From a Hebrew work by the noted Cabalist, Rabbi Jacob Emden [1697–1776] of Altona, Germany.)

One of the fourteen stations along the Via Dolorosa in Old Jerusalem where Christian tradition had Jesus pause to rest when carrying his cross to Calvary for his crucifixion.

of the Torah as being no longer binding for Christians, since, he averred, the truths and revelations of Jesus superseded them in spiritual authority. It should be quite clear to anyone that from a historical point of view, such an assumption is without validity. Jewish religious and moralistic writings *before, during,* and *after* the time of Christ prove this conclusively.

There are innumerable references in the Pentateuch, in the Prophets, in Psalms, in post-Biblical literature, and especially in the Talmud of the Scribes and Pharisees which condemn hatred, vengeance, cruelty, envy, lying, anger, subtlety, and greed, and, conversely, glorify humility, truth, love for one's fellow men, charity, sincerity, gentleness, generosity of spirit, and forgiveness. The ethics of Jesus in almost every instance were Jewish—and Pharisaic and Essenic—and derived from the cardinal Mosaic commandment: "Love thy neighbor as thyself."

To cite only a few examples: The Book of Proverbs, written centuries before the advent of Jesus, tried to establish the moral truth that "The reasonable man is noble, he glories in pardoning injury." The prayer uttered by pious Jews before lying down at night extols this particular virtue for all men: "Master of the World, I pardon every transgression and every wrong done to my person, to my property, to my honor, or to all that I have. Let no one be punished on my account."

A Rabbinical moralist in the Midrash laid down this guiding principle: "Ever shall a man bestow loving-kindness, even on one who does him harm; he shall not be vengeful nor bear a grudge. This is the way of Israel." And although Philo, the first-century Hellenist philosopher-rabbi of Alexandria, had little contact with the Rabbinic Sages of Judea, he nevertheless drank from the same clear spring of traditional Jewish ethics. He taught: "If you ask pardon for your sins, do you also forgive those who have trespassed against you." (*See* THE LORD'S PRAYER of Christians, below.)

The preoccupation of Jesus with penitence, the religious urgency of which he preached wherever he went, was characteristically Messianic and Rabbinic. The genuinely penitent person is extolled in the Talmud as standing on the pinnacle of spiritual perfection: "The just, the perfect, will not be worthy to sit with penitents in the World-to-Come."

Love for one's fellow men, a fundamental Mosaic commandment which formed the core of the Jewish teachings of Jesus, was in harmony with Rabbinic ethics. The Talmud expresses its amazement that Micah, the idolatrous Jew who continued to worship teraphim (presumably these were tribal household gods), yet went unpunished by Heaven. The Talmud says that the angels came before God and said: "See, Lord, the smoke from your altar mingles with that of the offerings to Micah's idols!" And God answered them: "Leave him in peace; he gives his bread to poor wayfarers."

And as for Jesus' preachments about peace, love, justice, and brotherhood—he surely must have been well versed in the Prophet Isaiah's exalted poetic declarations on those themes, and fully cognizant of one of the most celebrated Rabbinic teachings formulated by the Pharisee Scribe, Hillel, which appears in Pirke Abot 1:12 of the Mishnah: "Be of the disciples of Aaron, loving peace and pursuing peace, loving mankind and bringing them near to the Torah."

A recognizable source for many of the preachments of Jesus on love of people is this gentle sermon from the post-Biblical moralistic work, The Testaments of the Twelve Patriarchs written before 100 B.C.E. (see POST-BIBLICAL LITERATURE):

> Love ye therefore one another from the heart; and if a man sin against thee, cast forth the poison of hate and speak peaceably to him, and in thy soul hold not guile; and if he confess and repent, forgive him, lest catching the poison from thee he take to swearing and so thou sin doubly.

This teaching, it is well worth noting, is also found in paraphrased form in Matthew 18:15-35 and Luke 17:3-4—evangels which were composed at least two hundred years later!

The opposition of Jesus to mere formalism in religion, to the observance of the letter of the law while disregarding its spirit, is well illustrated by his exasperated rebuke to a Pharisee critic who had charged him with violating the Sabbath: "the Sabbath was made for man and not man for the Sabbath," and it finds its identical formulation in the teaching of another Pharisee, Simon ben Menasya, who taught: "The Sabbath is given over to you and not you to the Sabbath." The anti-formalistic attitude of the major body of Talmudic Judaism—an approach which was patterned upon the tongue-lashings given by the Prophets to the ritual-obsessed pietists and hypocrites—was the source from which Jesus logically drew his spiritual approach to religion. Yet, in the Gospels it was he who was represented to have been *the initiator* of a new religious and moral philosophy in opposition to Rabbinic legalism.

Moreover, the essence of The Lord's Prayer, which is the supreme expression of the simple Christian's faith, was also extracted from Jewish religious writings, even to using the same figures of speech. In particular, its kinship is most apparent in the ideas and very wordings of the liturgy of the Synagogue, with which Jesus as a devout Jew, must have been thoroughly familiar. The very first words of The Lord's Prayer—"Our Father which art in Heaven—" are a paraphrase of a part of a sentence in the ethical sayings of the Rabbinic Sages (Pharisees!) included in Pirke Abot 5:23: ". . . to do the will of thy Father who is in Heaven." The very concept of "Our Father" (in Hebrew: *Abinu*), in referring to the Deity, is found nowhere else but in Hebrew sources, including the fifth and sixth benedictions of the Shemoneh Esreh (q.v.).

Who can fail to recognize many other parallels, paraphrases, and echoes of The Lord's Prayer in the daily service of the synagogue? "O lead us not into the power of sin, or of transgression, or of scorn. May it be thy will, O Lord my God, and God of my fathers, to deliver me this day, and every day, from arrogant men and from arrogance. . . . Our Father who art in Heaven, show mercy towards us for Thy Great Name's Sake whereby we are called; and fulfill unto us, Lord our God, that which has been written, 'At that time will I bring you in, and at that time will I gather you [i.e., into the Kingdom of God].' "

The Mourner's Kaddish (*see* KADDISH) also points consolingly to the inevitable establishment by the Messiah of the Kingdom of Righteousness:

> Magnified and sanctified be His great Name in the world which He created according to His will. May He establish His Kingdom [*see* KINGDOM OF GOD under MESSIAH, THE,] during your life and during your days, and during the life of all the house of Israel. . . . Amen.

De-Judaizing Jesus. Many ways were found by Paul and later Gentile-oriented founders of Christianity to disassociate Jesus from the Jews and the Jewish religion as far as possible and to bring the new religion into a closer alignment with such

The Sea of Galilee. Here the Apostle Peter plied his trade as a fisherman and, according to Matthew (14:25-29), both he and Jesus miraculously "walked on the water." (Israel Government Tourist Office.)

favored pagan religious doctrines and practices as were dominant in Greco-Roman antiquity. And even though the great majority of modern Christian believers are unaware of this fact, observes A. Powell Davies, the Protestant commentator on Paul's evangelical labors. ". . . he [the scholar] has known all along that *historically*, Christianity is not the religion founded by Jesus. . . ."

Without a doubt, the most dramatic and drastic step taken by Paul was to transform Jesus the Messiah—a Jewish concept—into Jesus, "the Son of God"—a pagan apotheosis that was by no means a mere figure of speech or symbolism but a literally meant conception that was formulated in this famous Gospel declaration by John 3:16: "For God so loved the world, that he gave his only begotten Son, that whosoever believeth in him should not perish, but have everlasting life."

While it is not within the province of this brief excursion into Christianity to examine critically its theological dogmas, nevertheless, it is of genuine pertinence to point out that if, with the exception of some small groups, Jews remained impervious to Christian apostolic allurement, it was entirely because they were undeviating believers in the Oneness—"the Onlyness"—of God. The Pauline conception that God had a son was altogether shocking and unthinkable to them. The same conception was, however, entirely acceptable to pagans in the Hellenistic world, for they had been conditioned to accept such a notion by their own ages-old religious beliefs and practices. In the mythology of the Greeks and the Romans, for a divinity to have offspring by mating with a human being was a commonplace, a well-rooted idea. Zeus-Jupiter, the chief of the gods, was singled out for this extraordinary procreative activity with various daughters of the earth such as Leda, who became the mother of the heroes Castor and Pollux, and Europa (the daughter of a Phoenician king), who bore Minos; Apollo, who fathered Linus with Psamanthe, a virgin daughter of the king of Argos; Pluto, who loved Persephone, etc.

Ultimately, the apotheosizing of Jesus of Nazareth as "the only begotten Son of God" was accompanied by the explanation in the New Testament that God had sent the Holy Ghost down to earth to effect the Immaculate Conception of Mary, the virginal wife of Joseph. This dogma, held sacred by Christians, is reverently enunciated in the teaching of the Roman Catholic Church: "Christ, conceived of the Holy Ghost, was born of the Virgin Mary, who, by divine intervention, remained a virgin before, during, and after the conception and birth." The view shared by several Protestant denominations today is that Jesus was conceived in the womb of the Virgin Mary without a human father.

Historians of comparative religions have been marveling over the strong resemblances which exist between the Christian concept of the Holy Trinity—"the Father, the Son, and the Holy Ghost" and the pattern of divinity that prevailed in the Egyptian religion. It should be noted that one of the most fertile of missionary fields for the early Christian Church was Grecized Egypt, where more than one million Jews lived and where the process of theocrasia (a fusion of the identity of one god with another) had been vastly stimulated by Ptolemy I, who had introduced, *circa* 300 B.C.E., a mixed Greek and Egyptian worship in the Serapeum temple in Alexandria.

The trinitarian arrangement of the deities in ancient Egypt seems to have been traditional. Referring to this design, Samuel Birch, Keeper of Egyptian Antiquities in the British

Tiberias, one of the towns on the Sea of Galilee in an area where Jesus did most of his preaching. (Israel Government Tourist Office.)

Museum during the middle of the nineteenth century, wrote: "In the local worship of Egypt the deities were arranged in local triads; thus at Memphis, Ptah, his wife Merienptah, and their son, Nefer Atum, formed a triad, to which was sometimes added the goddess Bast or Bubastis. At Abydos, the local triad was Osiris [the father], Isis [the mother], and Horus [the son], with [the additional deity] Nephthys, etc."

This divinity pattern appears even more arresting when it is taken into account that the Virgin Mary, too, was accorded an appropriately divine elevation alongside the Father, the Son, and the Holy Ghost of the Christian Trinity, thus duplicating the exact design made by the Egyptian triad, to which a lesser deity was usually added. It should be said, however, that the prestige of the mother of Jesus, far from being evaluated as "lesser," has loomed ever larger with the centuries, ultimately occupying, as in Roman Catholicism, the position of centrality with her son in Christianity. Actually, the identity of Jesus has been so blended with that of the Father as God as to make them appear the same.

Mary has been venerated, worshiped, and extolled as the Mater Dolorosa, the Mother of God, the Mother of the World, and the Queen of Heaven. Of no little associative significance, suggest some scholars, is the fact that also the Egyptian goddess Isis was hailed as the universal Mother and the Queen of Heaven, and her cult, which endured into the sixth century, was the most formidable rival that Christianity had to compete with for converts in Hellenistic Egypt. It has sometimes drawn the startled attention of students of Egyptian art that in many graphic and sculptural representations of Isis, she is shown holding maternally in her lap the divine child Horus; it immediately brings to mind the classic depiction of the Madonna and the child Jesus in Christian religious art.

It should be emphasized that there actually were *two* opposing movements within early Christianity following the crucifixion of Jesus: One was Gentile oriented, declaring itself to be "the true Israel" and the Jews "the false Israel." This was led by the brilliant Paul and this was the one that ultimately triumphed when Constantine imposed it as the state religion of the Roman Empire in the fourth century. The second was the Jewish-oriented movement in Judea that was piloted by Peter (the Elder of the Twelve Apostles) and James ("the Lord's brother"; i.e., literally the brother of Jesus); this, within a short time, disappeared. The several congregations of the Jewish-Christians, which were few in number, resisted every effort by Paul and Barnabas to de-Judaize Jesus. There are leading Christian scholars today who disbelieve that the Epistles of James and Peter, which are included in the New Testament, were actually written by them either in their entirety, or even at all, but for reasons not clearly definable, had been attributed to them in the canon which was closed early in the third century.

The early Christians of Judea who followed Peter and James could not, strictly speaking, be classified as Christians in the Pauline sense. They considered themselves to be Jews. They adhered faithfully to the Jewish religion, observed the Sabbath (on Saturday), kept all the festivals and fast days, circumcised their male infants, ate kosher food, and, like the Pharisees, fasted on Mondays and Thursdays. They prayed in Hebrew and devoted themselves to Torah study, and when, a generation or two later they no longer knew any Hebrew, they studied the Torah in Aquila's Greek translation. Their one sectarian deviation, which resulted in their ostracism as heretics (minim) from the main body of Jewry, was their fervent belief that Jesus was the authentic Messiah whom God

Franciscan monk praying before the ruins of the synagogue of Kfar Nachum, the "Capernaum" of the Gospels, where Jesus proclaimed his Messianic message: "Repent, for the kingdom of heaven is at hand." (Matthew 5:17.) (Israel Government Office of Information.)

Amphitheatre in Caesarea built by the tetrach Herod in honor of Caesar Augustus, c. 22 B.C.E. Here, at the very time that Jesus was preaching, gladiators were fighting wild beasts and each other to the death for the entertainment of Judea's Roman oppressors. (Israel Government Tourist Office.)

the Father—the One God—had sent to redeem Israel, and that although he had died on the cross, he had risen from the grave and would reappear in a Second Coming, whenever God willed it. They completely disavowed the "Son of God" claim made for Jesus; they considered Paul an apostate and rejected his writings. The fact should not be minimized that, when the Jewish revolt against the tyranny of Rome broke out in 132 C.E. under the messianic banner of Bar Kochba, there were sectarian Jewish-Christians who also fought in the ranks.

While the Talmud refers to Christians (without attempting to make any distinction between the Jewish-Christians who adhered to the One God and the Gentile-Christians who worshiped the Trinity) as *Notzrim* (s. *Notzri*) it has not been conclusively established that this name was derived from Nazareth, the Galilean birthplace of Jesus. The early-fourth-century Christian writer Eusebius calls these Jewish-Christians in his *Ecclesiastical History* "Ebionites" (in Hebrew or Aramaic: *Ebionim,* s. *Ebion,* meaning "the Poor"; i.e., those dedicated to poverty). And Eusebius, like his contemporary, Origen, abuses them roundly for denying that Jesus was the Son of God.

During the reign of Trajan (98–117 C.E.), there were some Jewish-Christians who followed the leadership of one Elchasai. They had somewhat different variations in dogma, although they had much in common with the Ebionites in that they stood determinedly in opposition to Gentile Christianity. They too affirmed the existence of One God, and believed that Jesus was human, but a reincarnation of the Prophets of old into whom the Holy Spirit had entered, and that he was the Messiah who was predestined to lead Israel to salvation.

It should be carefully noted that the Judean-Christians, who identified themselves with the Jewish people and who clove to the religion of Israel until the first Nicene Council in 325 placed its seal of approval on the dogma of the Holy Trinity, obtained their theological and inspirational sustenance from writings said to have been derived from the Preachings of Peter (known in Greek as *Kerygmata*). They spurned the New Testament altogether, indicting those Christians "who have rejected Peter's teachings and have attached themselves to the frivolous teachings of the enemy [this was a reference to Gentile Christianity] which is contrary to the law [i.e., the Torah] . . . the Law of God which Moses proclaimed, and to whose eternal duration our Saviour [Jesus] attested when he said: 'Heaven and earth shall pass away but not one jot or tittle shall pass away.'" Rejecting, too, the Pauline claim that Jesus was divine and "the Son of God," the Judean-Christians declared: "Only the God of the Scriptures should be called God. Nor is it lawful to think that there is any other, or to call any other by that name. And if anyone should dare do so, eternal punishment of soul is his."

In the light of these monotheist views, which presumably represent the Christian thinking of Peter and James, it cannot come as a surprise to read in the Koran (written in the seventh century) the crude but forthright rebuke by Mohammed, who was an uncompromising monotheist: "O Jesus, son of Mary, hast thou said unto mankind, 'Take me and my mother as two gods beside God?'" To the Mohammedans, the Prophet of Allah gave this counsel: "Believe, therefore, in God and his Prophets, and say not there are three gods; forbear this, it will be better for you. God is but one God. Far be it from him that he should have a son!"

The theological detachment of Christianity from its Jewish parent seemed to become even more urgent as time went on. There were some Christians, like the sectarian Gnostics, who actively agitated for a *complete* divorcement from the Jewish religion. There was even, during the second century, a determined attempt made by a schismatic group of Gnostics (branded as heretics by the Church) under the leadership of Marcion, to eliminate the Jewish God from the Trinity, the Bible from sacred Christian literature, and all institutions and practices in the Church that could be attributable to Jews.

Even in modern times, there has been a sentiment in certain quarters, although desultory and uninfluential, to make Christianity *Judenrein* (free of Jewish taint). The late Dean W. R. Inge of Westminster, in a sermon he preached in August, 1950, before the Cambridge Conference of the Modern Churchmen's Union, posed this question to the clergy of the Anglican Church: "Do you agree with me that our services are terribly clogged with Judaism?" As indeed they are!

For "unclogging" Christian practice of its Jewish observances there was no dearth of eager theological hands in early times. Until the end of the second century, Easter, the festival which memorializes the resurrection of Christ, was invariably celebrated on the fourtheenth of Nissan—the same day on which the Jewish festival of Passover falls. It took the energetic First Roman Synod, convoked by Pope Victor I (189–198 C.E.) to order the Near Eastern bishops to refrain, under pain of severe penalties, from designating that day for the observance of Easter. The Corpus Juris Civilis of the Emperor Justinian in the sixth century also forbade it. But so persistent was the custom, that in 784, the Second Council of Nicea required of all new converts that they take this oath of abjuration: "We will not . . . celebrate the Passover, the Sabbath, or the other feast days connected with the Jewish religion."

The indefatigable Church historian, Eusebius, noted that during the first three centuries of Christianity, the Jewish Sabbath was observed by the faithful together with "the Lord's Day"—so called in honor of the pagan god Mithras—on Sunday. But upon the conversion of the Roman Emperor Constantine, the First Ecumenical Council of the Church, held in 325 in Nicea, abolished the observance of the Sabbath on Saturday and substituted for it the observance of Sunday as the Sabbath—the day of rest—for Christians. Despite their repudiation of the Jewish Sabbath, so strong was the power of custom and habit, that even on Sundays, well into the sixth century, Christians observed Jewish Sabbath laws against making a fire, cooking, working, riding, etc. So stated the Church Fathers.

The Church itself, in its very concept as a house of prayer, in many of its institutions—the congregation, the chanting of prayers, the singing of the Psalms, the reading of Scripture (Gospels), the antiphonal responses, the congregational "Amen!" and the preaching of a sermon based on a Scriptural text followed by its exposition—all these were adopted from the service of the Synagogue.

In several of their traditional elements, the liturgical texts of the Church, too, were adapted from the Synagogue service in the form in which it existed during the first centuries of Christianity. Some of the same literary sources were drawn from by both; not infrequently, the identical phraseology was used. There could be no more monumental irony than that the congregational reading of the Ten Commandments, which formed a high point in the service of the Synagogue, was introduced into the Church service, and when the Rabbinic Sages during the second century were faced with this staggering development, in order to save the simple-minded and unwary from confusing the synagogue with the church they promptly placed a ban on the public recitation of these central postulates of the Torah of Moses and ordered the Shema read instead!

Other Jewish innovations were adapted by the Church. The Missa Catachumenorum and the Divine Office are said to have been derived from the Jewish liturgy; the Apostolic Letters and exhortations were framed in the hortatory style of the Prophetic writings; and the Te Deum in the Milan creed is practically a translation of the Jewish hymn: "Rejoice, O daughters of Zion!"

Padre Martini, the eighteenth-century composer-musicologist, wrote in his *Storia della Musica* that it was to be expected that the Apostles of Jesus should have incorporated into the church service the synagogue melodies that they had known since earliest childhood. Weren't those the songs that the Levites used to sing in the Temple in Jerusalem? Actually, the Jewish musicologist, A. Z. Idelsohn, has been able to trace a number of melodies, still sung today in the synagogues of the Oriental Jews, which bear striking resemblances to the plain chant of the ancient church.

There is no question but that the Gregorian Chant, which is the most pervasive element in the musical service of Roman Catholicism and the Anglican Rite and which exerted such a profound influence on the development of European music, was also derived, as the musicologist Peter Wagner avers, from the "solo-psalmistry of the synagogue." Another authoritative opinion on this subject is given by the Catholic musicologist, Monsignor Dechevrens in his *Plain Song*: "Gregorian Chant is the music of the Hebrews, and there is for the totality of the Roman Catholic melodies but one modal system, not that of the Greeks, but that of the Hebrews."

To devout Christians, the rite of the Eucharist (Greek, meaning "thanksgiving") is the most awesome and mystical manner of personal communion with Christ. To many of the liberal faithful, it is a symbolic act of personal identification with Jesus, but to most, especially to Catholics and Lutherans, it is meant to be taken in its literal sense. The Lutheran Church, for example, teaches: "Jesus said: 'This is My Body' and 'This is My Blood.' These statements should not be rejected, or explained as merely figurative. The Lutheran Church teaches that the glorified Christ is able to be present with His Body and Blood, wherever the Lord's Supper is celebrated, and to give them in a real way which we cannot understand, along with the bread and wine as a pledge of our forgiveness." As the ethnologists explain: The Eucharist was conceived of as a rite of magical fellowship, or communion with God, by "eating with Him" and also, symbolically, "of Him."

What was "the Lord's Supper"? It is said to have been the last meal that the disciples ate with Jesus before his impending arrest, trial, and Crucifixion. And from the clear-cut statements made in the Synoptic Gospels of Matthew, Mark, and Luke, it actually was the Seder home-service that has been celebrated for three thousand years in every Jewish home on Passover in commemoration of Israel's liberation from the Egyptian Bondage. The Seder's chief ritualistic symbols are the matzot (the unleavened bread which is, in the Eucharist, the wafer) and the arbah kosot (the four ritual cups of wine; *see* PASSOVER). But in what strange manner this symbolic Passover food and drink was metamorphosed by Gentile-Christians into holy sacraments remains unknown.

Scholars of comparative religions have discovered that a strong similarity existed between the conception of the Eucharist and certain sacraments that were employed in the cult of the Persian sun-god Mithras, whose "Mysteries" enjoyed enormous popularity in the Greco-Roman world in the time of Paul of Tarsus. This strange resemblance must have perplexed many people. As if in answer to this bafflement, Justin Martyr, early in the second century, blamed it all on the magical foresight of evil spirits who, knowing that someday in the future Christians would consider this sacrament the holiest in their faith, had taught it centuries before to the idolators "out of memory, in the Mysteries and Initiations of Mithras. For in these likewise, a cup of wine, and bread, are set out with the addition of certain words, in the sacrifice or act of worship of the person about to be initiated." This explanation was given even greater prominence by the authoritative Church Father Tertullian in the third century: "The Devil, whose business it is to to pervert the truth, mimics the exact circumstances of the Divine Sacraments in the Mysteries of Mithras. . . ."

It should serve as a historical footnote that the Church Fathers and priests of Mithras were in fierce opposition to each other until the fourth century, when the emperor Julian the Apostate made an unsuccessful attempt to overthrow Christianity as the state religion of Rome (it had been established as such by his uncle, Constantine) and tried to supplant it with Mithraism. According to Porphyry, the third-century moralistic-philosopher who was an opponent of Christianity, all the Mithraic writings were hunted down and destroyed by the triumphant Church, which fact explains why so very little is known today about the once popular and worldwide religion of Mithras.

Much has been written about the vicarious sacrifice of Jesus on the cross in atonement for all the sins of the world which had accumulated since Adam's Fall. The doctrine of "Original Sin" is one which Judaism does not share with Christianity, yet the very notion of atonement is central to Jewish ethical-religious belief; it is an affirmation of the perfectability of mankind, which learns from its mistakes and corrects them by volitional acts of conscience. Martyrdom (not as atonement) on behalf of others has run a long and heroic course in Jewish history. But to suffer death *deliberately* as an atonement-sacrifice *for others' sins* is not a Jewish notion at all. "May my death be an atonement for all my sins!" This is the abbreviated form of the Viddui—the Jewish confession before death (*see* CONFESSION)—which is designed for the recitation of that dying person whose strength is fast ebbing, but the atonement petitioned is *for one's own sins* and not for anybody else's, inasmuch as Jews believe that each person is responsible *only for his own actions.* The Fourth Book of Maccabees recounts in elegiac cadence the martyrdom of Eleazar who, as he lay dying, pleaded with God: "Be merciful unto Thy people, and let our punishment be a satisfaction on their behalf. Make my blood their purification, and my soul to ransom their souls." But also the kind of atonement mentioned here is not the predetermined (by God) sacrifice of Jesus for the salvation of mankind in his ritual-drama of the Passion and Crucifixion.

Some scholars (among them the great ethnologist, James G. Frazer) have found a number of analogues in ancient religions for the Jesus-tragedy with similar themes of suffering, death, and resurrection. In the mystery-cult of Attis, that divinity of Phrygia (in Asia Minor) was the protagonist in an annual ritual-drama of sacrifice, death, and eternal renewal. He was tied to a tree in effigy, pierced with knives by the priests until "he bled to death," and then buried in the ground. But with the spring blossoming of the earth, Attis arose triumphantly from the dead, amidst the rejoicing of all mankind.

This redemption-theme through the self-sacrifice of a divinity is even more explicitly delineated in the ritual-drama of Osiris, the paramount divinity in the religion of Egypt. In order to atone with his death for the human race and thereby bring it to redemption, Osiris achieved incarnation in human form. It was said that he, like Jesus, had long foreseen the inevitability of his sacrifice, it being recorded in the Egyptian "scriptures," The Book of the Dead: "Osiris knows the day of his sacrifice." His death, by hate and treachery at the hands of the Evil One, Set, was followed by his miraculous resurrection, bringing with it happiness to the human race.

The sacrifice, death, and resurrection of the Greek god Adonis and of the Babylonian divinity Tammuz followed a similar pattern of the eternal renewal of life on the earth in the rites of spring.

The Trial and Crucifixion of Jesus. Almost a hundred years after the crucifixion of Jesus, it was possible in retrospect for several Roman writers to make but the barest reference to it, of such little importance did they regard it. In his work, *The Messiah Jesus and John the Baptist,* Robert Eisler mentions two pagan Roman writers of the second century, Celsus and Sossianus Hierocles, who observed about Jesus that he was "a bandit" and rebel chieftain who had threatened Rome in Judea. Such a view was in line with the official Roman stand taken in several instances of other Jewish "bandits" during the first century. For in the guise of messiahs, those idealistic visionaries who both preceded and followed Jesus, had organized uprisings in Judea against the tyranny of "Edom," i.e., Rome, as a prelude to the End of Days.

Inevitably, the rebellions were crushed in a general slaughter of their participants and their leaders—each of whom had, in turn, been hailed by his followers as "God's Anointed" and as "King of the Jews," and, consequently, as the future ruler of the righteous Kingdom of God—were publicly crucified in order to serve as a warning to the revolutionary-minded among the Jews.

The writings of the Roman historian Tacitus confirm that this was actually the attitude the Roman authorities had toward Jesus and his messianic movement. Although Tacitus was a bitter opponent of the Jews, nevertheless, what he wrote about the execution of Jesus in the *Annals* (*c.* 115 C.E.) sounds persuasively objective and precise from the Roman point of view. He stated: "Christus, the founder of that name, was put to death as a criminal by Pontius Pilate, procurator of Judea in the reign of Tiberius." His crime, said Tacitus, was that he had led a conspiratorial band of criminals who were "opposed to all mankind." But oddly enough, when the famous apologist for Gentile Christianity, Justin Martyr, was berating the Jews for their wickedness only a few years later—merely echoing the opinions and sentiments of the Synoptic Gospels of Mark, Matthew, and Luke, and of the Acts and Epistles of Paul of Tarsus—he told them: "This very Son of God . . . was crucified *under* Pontius Pilate *by* your [Jewish] nation."

The fateful phrase "under Pontius Pilate" entered into the Apostles' Creed. The difference in implications between the two little words "under" and "by" altered irrevocably the destiny of the Jewish people for nineteen centuries, for by means of them, Rome and Pontius Pilate were declared innocent of the murder of Jesus, and the Jews were forevermore branded as fratricides and God-killers. (*See* "HOST DESECRATION" CALUMNIES; "RITUAL MURDER" SLANDERS.)

That Pilate should have been treated so tenderly in the Gospels is indicative of how history is often written (or rewritten) from the writer's own bias, perhaps to promote some special vested interest—in this particular instance, to convert the pagan Romans to Christianity. Every other *contemporary* historical reference to Pilate refutes the Gospels' picture of his "fairness" and remarkable judicious restraint. King Agrippa I of Judea had formally complained to the Emperor Caligula in Rome that the procurator he had sent to Judea was "inflexible, merciless and obstinate." Philo of Alexandria, who was a man of the world as well as a Platonic philosopher and rabbi, and who had met Pilate personally, wrote of him that he was rotten with "corruption, violence, robbery . . . oppression, illegal executions, and never-ending most grievous cruelty."

Yet this was the noble, patrician Roman contrasted—to Pilate's advantage, of course—in the Gospels with the sly, demoniacal, clamoring mob of Jews in Jerusalem. In fact, as time moved on, Pilate's moral stature grew perceptibly; he was heaped by the religious leaders of the early Church with virtues unsuspected. The Church Father Tertullian (*c.* 160–*c.* 230), although he did not deny that Pilate was a pagan, nevertheless called him "a Christian in his own convictions"! Origen (*d. c.* 253), another famous patristic writer, went even farther; he called him a believer: "Pilate confessed that Jesus was the Christ [Messiah]."

Seemingly, the sole aim of this gratuitous "conversion" of the Roman despot was to associate him directly and in a favorable light with Jesus, demonstrating the existence between the two of a sympathetic bond and thereby, by reflection, lending eminent respectability and prestige to Christianity, which was then engaged in the highly competitive missionary field for Roman converts.

Perhaps the greatest single catastrophe that ever befell a nation was the one experienced by the Jewish people in consequence of the inflamatory account given in the Gospels about the trial and crucifixion of Jesus. Was the account true? Much of it has the tragic ring of truth, but there are also elements of verifiable distortion, fantasy, and reconstruction in it, no doubt introduced by the overzealous evangelists to heighten the drama of the events they described as well as to serve the propaganda goals of Gentile Christianity.

Principally, the intention of the gospel writers was to disassociate Jesus from the Jews. This they tried to do by demonstrating in their scriptural texts (in Greek) that not only had Jesus not been hostile to the rule of Rome—witness the statement in Mark 12:17: 'Render to Caesar the things that are Caesar's, and to God the things that are God's"—but that he had been savagely set upon by the Jews, a people, it should be remembered, whom the Roman master-race hated heartily. The Jews were hated because they had been consistently a thorn in the imperial side: They were constantly seething with social unrest and repeatedly rising in armed revolt against Rome under the leadership of such firebrand zealot "messiahs" as Judas the Galilean, his grandson Menachem, Theudas, Benjamin the Egyptian, and the most tragic of all Judean 'messiahs" after Jesus—Simon Bar Kochba. (*See* MESSIAHS, WOULD-BE; ZEALOTS.)

What was the crime that Jesus committed to merit crucifixion? Viewing it in historic perspective, from the Roman point of view, it is quite evident that he was charged by Pontius Pilate, the procurator of Judea, with the identical crime that had been charged against all the other captured "bandits": with sedition. He was accused of attempting an armed uprising as "King of the Jews." The historian Tacitus indicates that Jesus was believed by the Roman authorities to have been the leader of a conspiratorial band. But actually, Jesus had not planned any rebellion at all. While other messianic leaders before him (such as Judas the Galilean) and also after him (Bar Kochba) were fiery actionists, Jesus was, on the contrary, the most pacific and gentlest of quietists. An extreme non-resistance to evil seems to have been even more of a dominant principle with him than it was with Mahatma Ghandi, Jesus preached: "Whosoever smiteth thee on thy right cheek, turn to him the other also." As an Essene, this was a natural attitude for him to take. (*See* ESSENES.)

But the hard-headed Romans decided to leave nothing to chance. If subversion was being planned by Jesus and his followers—and past experience with messianic leaders (*see* ZEALOTS) could lead them to no other supposition—then it would be an act of foresight on their part to nip the conspiracy in the bud in the most decisive and prompt manner. So they crucified Jesus in order to make an example of him—to warn any other would-be "King of the Jews" what end he could expect. The Romans did not at all seem to consider what was the actual implication of that august title; they did not understand that it referred to the Messiah. This can be seen in the "regal" crown of thorns and the derisive sign Pontius Pilate ordered nailed to the cross over the tormented and broken body of the crucified Jesus: JESUS NAZORAEUS REX JUDAEORUM ("Jesus of Nazareth King of the Jews"). That's what the procurator thought of Jesus and that's what he thought of the Jews!

The Gospels, in their treatment of this epic drama, wonderfully written with a simple eloquence and an emotionalism that is genuinely stirring, placed an entirely different emphasis and motivation on its events and the personalities involved. In the Gospel of Matthew (Chapter 27), it was the chief priests and elders of the Jews who "took counsel against Jesus to put him to death. And when they had bound him, they led him away, and delivered him to Pontius Pilate the governor . . ."

As for the High Priest, Caiaphas, and other high Jewish officials who were said to have delivered Jesus to Pontius Pilate for trial with the expectation that he would be condemned to death, they were aristocratic Sadducees (and collaborationists of the Romans [*see* SADDUCEES]). As such, they must have been ready at all times to be the "running dogs"—the collaborationists—of the master-race and to do the will of the proçurator, even if it was to the hurt of their own people.

"And Jesus stood before the governor: and the governor asked him, saying, Art thou the King of the Jews? And Jesus said unto him, Thou Sayest."

So Jesus stood self-condemned; he was destined for a cross on Golgotha. Pontius Pilate, the symbol and instrument in Judea of the omnipotent power of the Emperor Tiberius, even had he wanted to, had no choice but to execute him—a potential rebel against Rome. Every "King of the Jews" before had been crucified by the Romans as a seditionist.

But the Gospels willed it differently. In them it was Pilate who was moved to admiration by the noble humility of Jesus and had no desire to cricify him. It was the custom, the Gospels infer, that during the festival of Passover (no such custom on Passover was ever known or recorded in Jewish literary sources) the procurator graciously would pardon a prisoner for whose life the people would ask. It so happened that "a notable prisoner, called Barabbas" was held in custody at that time. Addressing himself to the multitude, and giving it a broad hint and an even broader opportunity to save the life of Jesus, Pilate said to them: "Whether [whichever] of the twain will ye that I release unto you?" And the people answered—"Barabbas!" "Pilate saith unto them, What shall I do then with Jesus which is called Christ? They all say unto him, Let him be crucified. And the governor said, Why, what evil hath he done? But they cried out the more, saying, Let him be crucified."

When the "saintly" Pilate saw that there was nothing he could do to soften the hard-hearted mob clamoring for Jesus' death, he took water and washed his hands before the multitude, saying, "I am innocent of the blood of this just person: see ye to it. Then answered all the people, and said, His blood be on us, and on our children."

Actually, point out some New Testament scholars, it would be absurd and unrealistic to believe that there was the slightest possibility that the arrogant and despotic Roman procurator, Pontius Pilate, would for one moment have considered *delegating* his own supreme judicial powers to the Jews, whom he despised and distrusted, especially in a case in which the charge was sedition with conspirary to revolt. After all, they stress, was it not the Jews with whom he was constantly struggling? Where would be the sense then of allowing these very Jews (in a howling mob) to pass sentence on an alleged "bandit" leader?

Yet all four narratives of the evangelists—the Gospels of Matthew, Mark, Luke, and John—described in an emotionally inflammable setting, bear down inexorably on one premeditated conclusion: that it was not Pilate but the Jews who, in a frenzy of hatred for Jesus, were responsible for his agony and death on the cross. The diabolical image of the Jews—frightening, cunning, and cruel, as they are collectively depicted—stimulated the imaginative genius of Christian art during the Middle Ages and the Renaissance. The foremost painters and sculptors portrayed the heart-rending scenes along the Via Dolorosa: Jesus being scourged, "the Jews" abusing and leering villainously at him as he dragged his cross to Golgotha, the "Hill of Skulls," and gloating vengefully as they beheld him, hanging shattered, bleeding, and still, nailed to the cross of his martyrdom.

To the Christian who is enlightened and is also knowledgeable about the principles of the Jewish religion and of its moral values, institutions, and practices, such a depiction of the Jews must seem either an absurd libel or a vast distortion. And one need hardly go into the historical record: Christian mobs, howling their hatred for Jews and led by priests holding aloft the cross of the crucified Jesus to "inspire" them, who had preached love and forgiveness, descended murderously upon helpless Jews everywhere in Christendom. For one Jew—Jesus—uncounted millions of his fellow Jews had to pay with their lives in a perpetual Jewish Golgotha.

In his monumental work, *Mission and Expansion of Christianity*, Adolf von Harnack, a prominent leader of liberal German theology, declared with an obvious feeling of regret and contrition:

> Truly, such an injustice as that done by the Gentile Church to Judaism is almost unprecedented in the annals of history. The Gentile Church stripped it of everything; she took away its sacred Book; herself a transformed Judaism, she cut off all connection with the parent religion. The daughter first robbed her mother, then repudiated her.

The question often asked by thoughtful Christians is: What do the Jews themselves think about the trial and crucifixion of Jesus? Do they consider it just? When Moses Mendelssohn (Germany, 1729–86), the philosopher and initiator of the Jewish Enlightenment (Haskalah), was asked the question by the Swiss Protestant theologian, Johann Kaspar Lavater, he replied with an evasion: "How do I know what just or unjust judgments were pronounced seventeen or eighteen hundred years ago by my ancestors?" Especially, he added, since it was not even reasonable to expect that he accept responsibility for the trials and sentences issued by the Prussian law courts in his own day.

Whatever the thoughts and feelings of the great majority of Jews toward the Crucifixion—an act that caused unhealing wounds on their souls and minds and countless generations of suffering and humiliation—the astonishing observation has been made that, although they are, understandably, bitter, they seem to bear no rancor or any desire to "avenge" the terrible wrongs their people experienced because of it. In this attitude of most Jews—which is in the gentle spirit of Jesus himself—can perhaps be seen a vindication of Israel from the libels the Gospel writers wrote against their forefathers.

It should not pass unnoticed that, indicative of the average Jew's desire to let bygones be bygones and to seek fraternal relationships with all Christians of good-will, was the declaration made by the Jewish philosopher-rabbi Maimonides (Spain, 1135–1204), who himself was a victim of bitter persecution at the hands of Mohammedans, in his celebrated code, Mishneh-Torah: "The teachings of the man of Nazareth [i.e., Jesus] and of the man of Ishmael [i.e., Mohammed] who arose after him, help to bring to perfection all mankind, so that they may serve God with one consent. For in that the whole world is full of the words of the Messiah, of the words of the Torah and the Commandments. These words have spread to the ends of the earth, even if many deny their binding character at the present day."

See also BROTHERHOOD; CHURCH AND PERSECUTION; DOCTRINES IN JUDAISM; ESSENES; ETHICAL VALUES, JEWISH; MASSACRES: THE CRUSADES, THE BLACK DEATH; MESSIAH, THE; MISSIONARIES, JEWISH; MONASTICISM, JEWISH; PHARISEES; POST-BIBLICAL LITERATURE; REPENTANCE; TALMUD, THE; THERAPEUTAE; WANDERING JEW.

CHRISTIANS, SERVITUDE OF JEWS TO

The legal groundwork for anti-Semitism as a permanent policy of Christian states was laid by the Emperor Justinian of Byzantium (ruled 527–65 C.E.) in his celebrated code. One clause provided: "They [the Jews] shall enjoy no honors. Their status shall reflect the baseness which in their souls they have elected and desired." Furthermore, his code laid down the principle (later strengthened by the theological decision and restatement of Thomas Aquinas [1224–74], "The Angelic Doctor") of *servitus Judaeorum*—"the servitude of the Jews" to Christians—because the Jews had rejected Jesus as their saviour and had caused his death.

Whatever hardships and tribulations the Jews had to undergo during the Middle Ages simply to survive physically were nothing compared to the mental anguish, the degradation, and the social pariahism to which they were perpetually condemned by religious hatred and bigotry. The Jews were included by the central dogmas of Christianity in the grand design for the redemption of Christians. However, it was with far less than Christian charity that Bernard of Clairvaux, the spiritual mentor of the Second Crusade (who was later sainted), had expatiated thus concerning the "just punishment" to be meted out to the Jews: "They are living symbols for us representing the Lord's Passion. For this are they dispersed to all lands, so that while they pay the just penalty for so great a crime [i.e., the Crucifixion], they may be witnesses for our Christian redemption."

In 1519, during his early period of belligerent criticism against the Church, the then Catholic priest, Martin Luther, derided the doctrine of *servitus Judaeorum*: "Absurd theologians defend hatred for the Jews by claiming that [the members of] the race are slaves of Christendom and the Emperor. . . . What Jew would consent to enter our ranks when he sees the cruelty and enmity we wreak on them—that in our behavior towards them, we less resemble Christians than beasts?"

Continuing the guerrilla warfare against the Church, Luther, who was a past master of unsubtle satire, wrote in his essay, "Jesus Was Born a Jew": "Were I a Jew and saw what blockheads and windbags rule and guide Christendom, I would rather become a pig than a Christian. For they have treated the Jews more like dogs than men. Yet the Jews are kindred and blood brothers of our Saviour. If we are going to boast about the virtues of race, Christ belongs more to them than to us."

When the segregation of the Jews in ghettos was ordered by the Fourth Lateran Council of the Church in 1215, accompanied by the most crushing economic, legal, and civil restrictions (*see* GHETTO), Jews were given the doubtful privilege, granted even to serfs, of owning arms with which to defend themselves. But later they were deprived even of this fundamental medieval right. Being given no place or function in the stratified feudal system, they were obliged to stand outside of it, being thenceforth designated legally as *servi camerae*, "chattels of the [royal] chamber."

The royal charter promulgated on behalf of the Jews in the year 1180 in Angevin England made the following point very clear:

> It should be known that all Jews, wheresoever in the realm they be, ought to be under the guard and protection of the King's liege. Nor ought any of them place himself under any rich man without the King's license; because the Jews themselves and all theirs belong to the King, and if any detain them or their money, let the King, if he will and can, ask it back as if it were his own.

Because they were his personal "property," the king could dispose of the Jews—and did—in any way he saw fit: as a gift, or, in lieu of cash, as payment for some service rendered by a feudal vassal. Sometimes he "sold" them outright or, when he happened to be in need of cash, "pawned" them to a princeling, to a bishop of the Church, to a baron, or even to a municipality. For the "protection" the Jews were to receive, at least theoretically, they were obliged to pay, half to the emperor or king and half to the reigning prince, an annual *opferpfennig*—a "penny"—which, in fact, amounted to considerably more than a penny. The pfennig swelled into a gulden for each Jew over twelve years of age. Jews were also required to pay a special "coronation tax" separately to emperor, king, and prince, when each ascended his throne.

Onerous, to put it mildly, was the payment of the so-called Jewish body-tax which Jewish travelers, as they passed through a city, were forced to pay the local authorities for a military escort to protect them against the many robber bands that infested the medieval city streets, making them unsafe even during daylight. And even in death the Jew was not free from the harassments of the tax-collectors. For then his family had to pay not only 'escort money" on the way *to* the cemetery but a special burial tax *in* the cemetery. For the Jew, it was frightfully expensive to live, but it was equally costly for him to die.

Some Jewish communities were required to pay "special" "imperial" taxes in addition to the "regular" taxes. For instance, in Frankfurt-am-Main, in Germany, the Jews were ordered to supply all the parchment needed by the Emperor's chancellery, all the bedding required by the court, and all the pots and pans for the palace kitchen, as well as specified sums to the imperial officials as a kind of salary or bonus.

Despite the fact that the Jews formed only a tiny part of the general population in the imperial domains, they were, nevertheless, expected to pay the emperor alone 12 per cent of all the taxes received. In addition, they had to pay one-fifth of all city and town taxes. These crushing taxes, special payments, and "gifts" were further increased by the enormous collective fines levied against Jewish communities upon every conceivable pretext, whether on the local, regional, princely, kingly, or imperial level.

Perhaps some thirteen or fourteen centuries ago, when Christianity was still young and its gospel of salvation was still being propagated by "the Church Militant," the Midrash commented ruefully on the incredible tax-burdens of the Jews: "He who works his way through brambles, in detaching himself on one side, only entangles his garment on the other. And such is the case in the [Gentile] land of Esau. Barely has the tax-collector been paid, when the poll tax is demanded. And while this is being collected, the exactor of new tributes makes his appearance."

The realities of this plaint could well have furnished the basis for a bitter passage in another Rabbinical Midrash commentary: "The princes of Edom [Christendom] are covetous of money; they therefore flay Israel alive."

See also ANTI-SEMITISM: THE "RACIAL PURITY" MYTH; CHRISTIANITY, JEWISH ORIGIN OF; CHURCH AND PERSECUTION; COMMUNITY, SELF GOVERNING; CONVERSION OF JEWS; DISPUTATIONS, RELIGIOUS; FEUDAL SOCIETY, POSITION OF THE JEWS IN; "HOST DESECRATION" CALUMNIES; JEWISH OATH, THE; MARRANOS AND THE INQUISITION; MASSACRES: THE CRUSADES, THE BLACK DEATH; MONEYLENDERS; NAZIS, THE; PERSECUTION IN "MODERN" DRESS; POGROMS IN SLAVIC LANDS; "RITUAL MURDER" SLANDERS; SEPARATISM, JEWISH; SHYLOCK MYTH, THE; WANDERING JEW; YELLOW BADGE.

CHRONOLOGY, JEWISH

Jewish chronology has a different historic focus than that of the Christian, Mohammedan, or other religous groups. The chroniclers of the post-Biblical period, as well as the Rabbinic writers and subsequent Jewish scholars, followed a number of primitive, and often discrepant, systems for reckoning chronologic time, variously choosing in an arbitrary manner some epochal event in Jewish history (or, in a number of instances, in myth) from which to start their dating. Thus the different chronological systems began from the Creation, the Flood, the Exodus from Egypt, the beginning of the Babylonian Exile, the Hasmonean Era, the Destruction of the Second Temple, and—by Jews in Islamic countries—from the Hegira, which marked the flight of the Prophet Mohammed from his enemies.

The Biblical writings, of course, had their own inscrutable systems for computing time. The chronicler of the Book of Kings, for example, dated Jewish historic events from the starting point of the Exodus. In that way, he has the erection of the Temple of Solomon take place 480 years after the Israelites' departure from Egypt. Hardly more convincing to the modern historian is the chronology of the most important events in Jewish history that was arranged by the second-century Mishnah Sage, Yoseh ben Halafta. He counted from the Era of Creation and, accordingly, ascribed fancied dates to various Jewish events that were presumed to have taken place from Adam, the first man, to Alexander the Great. Other Rabbinic contemporaries computed time from the Destruction of the Second Temple, in 70 C.E., but this approach was deplored as negativistic and gloomy by the optimistic Tanna (Mishnah teacher) Yochanan ben Zakkai. He asked if it would not have been more appropriate to reckon time from the *building* of the Temple instead of from its *destruction?* But his challenge went unheeded.

Odd as it may seem, the most widely used chronological system—and one fully sanctioned by the Rabbis of the Talmudic age—was adopted from the Syrian Greeks. The Jews, being considerably Hellenized by the start of the Common Era (C.E.), readily accepted the dating method then in general use in the Gentile world around them in the Near East. This was the Seleucidan system: *Cheshbon ha-Yevanim*—"the computation of the Greeks"—which began with the Battle of Gaza in October, 312 B.C.E. The alien acculturation which this acceptance by the Jews represented, aroused bitterness in Yochanan ben Zakkai. He mused: "They [the Jews] were not satisfied to count with their own era [the Biblical], so they started to count according to the era of others [strangers]."

The Seleucidan system demonstrated a remarkable vitality. Jews clung to it for more than one thousand years, until 987, when Sherira Gaon, the religious leader of Babylonian Jewry, decided to return to dating from the time of Creation. This was arbitrarily made to coincide with the year 3760 B.C.E., a point of historic time no modern person could be expected to consider seriously. (Amazingly, the Seleucidan chronology continued among the Jews of Yemen and Saudi Arabia until the twentieth century.) One can, therefore, understand the embarrassment of such a scientifically precise writer as Maimonides (Moses ben Maimon, twelfth century) when he had to mention a date. In order to make himself understood by the Jews of his day, who were variously following different chronologies, he was forced to write as follows in one reference: "In the year 1107 of the Destruction of the Temple, in 1487 of the Seleucidan Era, in 4936 of the Creation . . ."

Today, Orthodox Jews, in the main, still count time from the Creation. But being also down-to-earth realists, they have recognized the need for accommodating themselves to the prevailing dating system used by Christians. On purely religious grounds, they and many other Jews with different Jewish religious affiliations, have felt it wrong somehow to qualify a date as B.C. (before Christ) or A.D. (Anno Domini, i.e., "in the year of [our] Lord"), since such qualification would constitute, *ipso facto*, a symbolic recognition by them of the religious validity and divine nature of Jesus Christ. Nonetheless, in order not to create any confusion with two different sets of dates, and at the same time to be strictly factual and consistent with prevailing usage, it has become customary for English-speaking Jews to write B.C.E. (before the Common Era) for B.C. and C.E. (Common Era) for A.D.

See also CALENDAR, JEWISH.

CHUMASH. *See* BIBLE, THE.

CHUPPAH. *See* MARRIAGE; WEDDING CUSTOMS.

CHURCH AND PERSECUTION

After Constantine the Great (ruled 306–37) had made Christianity the state religion of the Byzantine Empire, its spread elsewhere in Europe was inevitable. Thereupon the systematic and savage persecution of the Jews fanned out in every direction on the continent, but this time with the unimpeachable sanction of the Gospels and under the direction of the Church. Notwithstanding that in his Edict of Toleration, which he had issued in Milan in 313 C.E., Constantine had magnanimously included the sufferance of Jews, he did not grant them civil equality with either Christians or pagans. His stated reason for their exclusion from the rest of society was that they were "a nefarious and perverse sect." And only two years later, he promulgated a series of repressive edicts, including one that forbade Jews to seek converts and another banning their intermarriage with Christians.

All this enmity and hyperemotionalism expressed against the Jews—whatever the precipitating socio-economic and political considerations that lurked behind them—were fed by a strong undercurrent of religious fanaticism. Who can deny that, whatever the cumulative hostility that had been built up against the Jews during pagan Hellenistic times, it received a new and startling factor even more powerful than the lies and fairy tales invented by the Greek, Roman, and Egyptian provocators from the early Christian writings and decrees of the Church.

The religious basis for anti-Semitism in Christendom was derived from the accusation, as it appears in the Gospels and as it was unquestioningly accepted by all Christians, that the Jews were to blame for the crucifixion of Jesus. The epithet "Christ-killer" became a synonym for "Jew," and subsequently was bandied about with unthinking ease through the ages by countless Christians, including popes, theologians, philosophers, and poets. The Gospels, although presumably written by the Disciples, who were born and raised as devout Jews, are, nevertheless, full of overt hostility toward the Jews.

What devout Christian has not been inflamed in his deepest feelings on reading in an uncritical state of mind about the clamor the [Jewish] mob raised before Pontius Pilate, the Roman procurator, for the life of Jesus. "Let him be crucified," they are alleged to have cried. Then, as if to crown its own infamy and make it appear the more unspeakable, the Gospel writer puts these incredible words into the mouths of the shouting mob: "His blood be on us, and on our children." (Matthew 27:25.)

It was principally on this particular passage that the religious anti-Semites of history pounced, nailing it down as the source of supreme sanction for the unremitting persecution of the Jewish people. They argued that the Jews had out of their own mouths condemned themselves with these words, voluntarily accepting their blood-guilt as "Christ-killers," bringing it down on the heads of their children and their children's children for all eternity. Some modern Christian students of the Gospels, reading this passage critically, have come to the conclusion that it is nothing but an editorial comment that was patently inserted into the dialogue of the trial-scene in the Passion-drama of Jesus in order to make the cynicism and the diabolical meanness of the Jewish "mob" appear the more revolting. Certainly, it passes all credibility to believe that the Jews, in screaming their hatred for Jesus before the Roman procurator—the man who was both their oppressor and their relentless enemy—would gleefully accept the mark of Cain for themselves and all their descendants so readily and with such relish!

John Chrysostom (*d.* 407), who was later sainted by the Church, took the lead in harassing the large Hellenized Jewish community in Antioch, Syria. He roundly abused the Jews, saying they were possessed by demons and that their synagogues were serving as rendezvous for devils. During the Feast of Purim in 405, he incited a Christian mob to attack the Jews in their quarter of the city. Taking holy fire from him, Bishop Cyril of Alexandria shortly thereafter led another devout rabble against the Jews of that metropolis. The synagogues were torn down virtually stone from stone in a holy frenzy, and Jewish homes were pillaged. Leaving many dead and wounded behind, the several hundred thousand Jews of Alexandria were driven out, most of them never to return, from the city where their forefathers had settled in the time of Alexander of Macedonia, more than seven hundred years before.

Statue of a woman, symbolizing the Synagogue, standing blindfolded and dejected, the crown of her spiritual glory falling off her head, the Tablets of the Law reversed, the staff of her authority broken. (In the Liebfrauenkirche of Trier [Treves], Germany, c. 1520.)

The American non-Jewish historian, Herbert J. Muller, has correctly observed: "The martyrdom that Christians suffered in their early history was negligible compared with the martyrdom they later inflicted on the Jews . . . The [Christian] victims of the Roman Empire were a few thousand in number . . . Israel cannot number or name its millions of martyrs. . . ."

See also CHRISTIANITY, JEWISH ORIGINS OF; CHRISTIANS, SERVITUDE OF JEWS TO; "HOST DESECRATION" CALUMNIES; MASSACRES: THE CRUSADES, THE BLACK DEATH; PERSECUTION IN "MODERN" DRESS; POGROMS IN SLAVIC LANDS; "RITUAL MURDER" SLANDERS; WANDERING JEW.

CHUTZPAH (Aramaic, meaning "impudence," "brazenness")

Whenever Jews use the word *chutzpah*, it is intended as a term of criticism whose ingredients consist of equal parts of indignation and amazement, spiced with a dash of involuntary admiration that anyone could possibly possess such unmitigated nerve or gall!

The portrait of the righteous Jew, as it emerges from two thousand years of Rabbinic Judaism, endows him in his outward deportment with certain admirable traits. He is delineated as gentle and courteous, modest and bashful. Judah ha-Nasi (Judea, *c.* 135–220), the codifier of the Mishnah, declared impatiently: "The brazen-faced one goes to Gehinnom [Purgatory]; the bashful-faced one to Gan Eden [Paradise]." This saying illustrates the general dislike that has existed among most Jews for that individual who conducts himself with chutzpah. Jewish tradition has much scorn and not a little pity for him—the *chutzpanik*, as he is referred to by Yiddish-speaking folk. He is censured as a rude and coarse fellow, and his offensiveness is recognized as one of the identifying marks of an essentially unethical personality.

The Hebrew description for the person with chutzpah is *azzut-panim* (in Yiddish, it is *azzes-ponim*), which means "brazen-faced." The Talmudic saying goes: "Where there is impudence, there is no human dignity."

At the opposite pole from the chutzpanik, according to the Talmud, stands the gentle, modest person. He is glowingly described as being *boshet-panim*, or "bashful-faced." The implication is that only the righteous individual is capable of feeling "bashfulness," which, in the way it is used, is meant to be the antonym for "forwardness." The Mishnah Fathers accordingly stated: "He who has not boshet-panim–truly his ancestors did not stand at Mount Sinai!"

CIRCUMCISION (in Hebrew: MILAH; also called BRIT (BERIT) MILAH, the "Covenant of Circumcision," or BRIT ABRAHAM, the "Covenant of Abraham")

Circumcision is the rite of removing, by surgical means, the prepuce or foreskin from the penis in order to uncover the glans. It is performed on a male Jewish infant when he is eight days old, unless he is ill. Unlike the rite of baptism in the Christian religion, circumcision has no special sacramental significance. The Schulchan Aruch, the manual of Jewish ritual observance, makes this clear when it declares that even an uncircumcized Jew is a full Jew by birth, although one might add inferentially, hardly a proper one. Circumcision, therefore, is a symbol or a sign, made indelible on the flesh, of the everlasting covenant the God of Israel entered into at the dawn of Jewish history with the Patriarch Abraham, "the first Jew," and through him, with all his descendants forevermore: "And ye shall be circumcized in the flesh of your foreskin; and it shall be a token of the covenant betwixt Me and you." (Genesis 17:11.)

It was not inappropriate, in a rite whose object it was to link each generation with all before it in the symbolic continuity of identity, that the father should have had a leading role. Tribal custom in ancient days required him to act, so to speak, as the priest of the covenant, circumcizing his infant son himself. But with the passing of the centuries and the refining process that the Jewish religion underwent, this task was transferred to a professional circumcizer who held semi-ecclesiastical status. He was called the *mohel.* His specialized surgical skill and the dispatch with which he worked won for him general commendation, even from non-Jewish doctors.

In the literature of the Talmud there are references to another personage, honorary in rank for the occasion, who assisted the mohel by cradling the infant in his lap and holding him firmly during the operation. He went under the name–one obviously Hellenistic in origin–of *sandik* or *sandikos,* as it was phoneticized in the Talmud. This was derived from the Greek *syndikos* (which was in Latin *syndicus*), meaning "patron." When Paul of Tarsus dispensed with circumcision for Christians, he substituted for this ceremony of group identity the Essene rite of baptism, retaining in it the role of the sandik or syndikos. The role of the Christian syndikos was to assist the priest with the child at the baptismal font. The function of the pre-Christian Jewish sandik, down to our own day, has been to assist the mohel in the rite of circumcision.

With their characteristic fondness for verbal variety–due largely to their traditional use of two or even three languages in whatever country they happened to live–the Jews during the Middle Ages adopted two other names for sandik which they used interchangeably with it. One was *Baal Brit* (Master of the Covenant); the other was the German *Gevatter* (godfather). In time, the Jews of Eastern Europe, who had taken over the Yiddish language from the German Jews, adopted this latter name, but in the process of assimilation into their speech, *Gevatter* was transformed into *kvatter.*

Somewhat less prominent in the rite of circumcision was the role of the *kvatterin* (godmother) who, often as not, proved to be the wife of the kvatter. Her function was to fetch the infant on a cushion from his mother's room and to place him in the arms of the mohel. Whereupon, all those present, whether the circumcision was being performed in the synagogue or in the home, chanted joyously with the ancient Psalmist: "Blessed be he that cometh in the name of the Lord!"

To the student of primitive cultures, circumcision does not appear to be a specifically Jewish practice. Undoubtedly, it goes back to the primeval Hebrew past when, like their neighbors–the Egyptians, Phoenicians, Canaanites, and Arabs –the Hebrew tribes performed this same surgical operation on their male children. The Copts of Ethiopia, descendants of an early Christian sect, and the several hundred millions of Mohammedans who adhere to the law of Islam, which carried over this rite of their early Arab ancestors, also practice circumcision today. However, its religious significance among those peoples is not linked to the covenant of Israel. Ethnologists in their field studies have ascertained how widespread the rite and its elaborate ceremonial are among millions of primitive peoples today–the Polynesians, the Mayas of Yucatan, the Indians of Peru and the jungle regions along the Amazon and Orinoco rivers and also among the numerous Negro tribes in Equatorial Africa.

Among all these peoples, the motivation for performing a surgical operation on the genitals of their boys–and in certain instances, as among the Jewish Falashas of Dahomey, on those of their girls as well (i.e., clitoridectomy)–seems complex and obscure. It sometimes, though, bears the character of a sacrificial offering brought to insure fertility or to effect magical protection for the circumcized. But usually–and this holds true for most primitive peoples today–circumcision represents a significant act in the elaborate tribal rite of initiation into manhood at the age of puberty. Because the operation is extremely painful, it is, therefore, considered a test of courage and fortitude for the youngsters if they endure it without a whimper or a trace of fear.

None of these aforementioned elements, though, entered into the Jewish conception and practice of the "Covenant of Abraham." For Jews–whether ancient, medieval, or modern–it was exclusively an act of religious-national consecration to God, Torah, and Israel that began at birth and ended only with death. For the primitive rite of initiation into manhood, the Jewish religious reformers of the Second Temple period substituted the spiritualized symbolism of Bar Mitzvah (q. v.). As a symbolic rite, therefore, the Jewish covenant of circumcision is partly removed from the realm of religion and enters into that of national history. That is because it devolves upon the Jewish national identity and its historical continuity, although it is set in a religious context. The Zohar, the medieval "Scripture" of the Cabalists, epigrammatizes its relative significance thus: "The Lord of the Covenant is God, the Book of the Covenant is the Torah, the Son of the Covenant is the circumcized one."

The practice of the rite of circumcision called forth not only ridicule but hostility from the enemies of the Jews, whether Greeks, Romans, or Christians, principally because circumcision was the most powerful symbol that stamped the Jewish identity, thereby strengthening its stubborn resistance to assimilation. One provocation for the Maccabean revolt in 168 B.C.E. was the decree of the Seleucid king, Antiochus (Epiphanes) IV, forbidding, under the penalty of death, among other fundamental Jewish practices, that of circumcision. As the course of events demonstrated, not only were the Jews ready to fight in defense of this rite but they were also quite willing to die for it *al kiddush ha-Shem* (for the sanctification of God's Name). Likewise with reference to the practice of circumcision, the memory of the Hadrianic persecutions that followed the failure of the bloody uprising under Bar Kochba, in 132 C.E., rankled long in the Jew's consciousness. There is this bitter dialogue in the Talmud concerning the martyrdom of the faithful:

> "Why are you dragged to be stoned?"
> "Because I circumcized my son. . . .
> I only did the will of my Father in Heaven!"

Although, under the Roman Emperor Hadrian, circumcision was punished as a capital crime, under his more enlightened successor, Antoninus Pius, who was mellowed in outlook by his taste for Stoic philosophy, the rite was again allowed for all Jews *born as Jews,* but banned for those *not Jews by birth.* This law may have had a significant impact on the subsequent history of mankind, for it sharply curtailed Jewish missionary efforts. Until that time, and throughout much of the Hellenistic period, Jewish preachers—especially outside Judea—had proven themselves indefatigable missionaries. They were out to win proselytes for the Jewish religion from among the Gentiles. The early Christians, being Jews, also followed this well-established evangelical pattern; Paul in his Epistles addressed himself almost exclusively "to the Gentiles." But the unyielding condition laid down by the Rabbis that, before a proselyte could be admitted into the fellowship of Israel, he first had to undergo the painful (for adults) rite of circumcision, discouraged innumerable prospects who were otherwise greatly drawn to the ethical ideals and social practices of the Jewish faith.

In the first period of the Christian Church, there had been a sort of nip-and-tuck race between Judaism and her daughter religion, Christianity, for winning Gentile adherents in Rome, Greece, North Africa, and the Balkans. A severe blow to Jewish evangelical hopes was dealt by Paul. Basing his stand on the celebrated concept of "the circumcision of the heart" advanced in the Book of Deuteronomy and by the Prophet Jeremiah, he abolished altogether physical circumcision for Christians. This decision, among others that Paul took, weighted the scales of proselytism against the Synagogue in favor of the Church. And with the imperial edict of Antoninus Pius against the circumcision of Roman proselytes to Judaism, which was later reinforced by the even sterner provisions of the Justinian Code, Jewish missionary activities

Rite of Circumcision. (From the Sefer ha-Minhagim, 1695.)

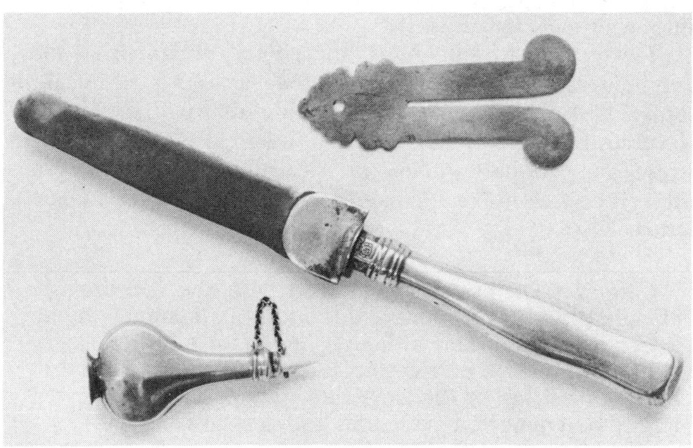

Instruments used in circumcision rite. (Courtesy of Joseph B. Horwitz Judaica Collection, Cleveland.) TOP

Silver platter used in circumcision rite and decorated with the head of Aaron, the high priest. (Courtesy of Joseph B. Horwitz Judaica Collection, Cleveland.) ABOVE

"Bench of Elijah" used during circumcision rite. Germany, 17th century. BELOW

came to an end for all time.

During the Middle Ages, the rite of circumcision must have impressed many an intellectual Jew trained in philosophy, literature, and science as being a throwback to tribal primitivism. We find, for instance, Judah (Yehudah) Halevi, the great poet-philosopher of twelfth-century Spain, admitting as much in his apologetic work on the Jewish religion, *Kuzari*:

> Circumcision has nothing to do with the constitution of social life, yet Abraham, although this commandment is against Nature and although he was a hundred years old, subjected his person and that of his son to it, and it became the sign of the Covenant, that the Divine Power might be connected with him and his descendants. . . .

Some twelve centuries before, the Hellenized philosopher-rabbi Philo had come to the defense of this rite in another way: He attempted to prove that circumcision was an important aid to personal hygiene and health. Many modern physicians, Christian and Jewish, have supported this view. But going even father back in time, the formalistic stress laid by many Jews upon circumcision as a primary religious-national expression, to their neglect of the spiritual and ethical principles of the Torah, led the Prophet Jeremiah to ridicule the belief that there lay any special grace in the surgical act iself. Bitterly he warned: "Behold the days come, saith the Lord, that I will punish all them which are circumcized with the uncircumcized." (Jeremiah: 9:25.) And the Scriptural moralist in whose eyes mere physical circumcision had no special merit, harshly advised, "Circumcize therefore the foreskin of your heart." (Deuteronomy 10:16.)

It is a cultural phenomenon worth pondering that, however neglected other traditional rites and ceremonies of Judaism may be among highly assimilated and even free-thinking Jews of today, the rite of circumcision is, nevertheless, almost universally practiced by them upon their infant sons even as it is on all religious Jews. Some have it done, as they embarrassedly admit, for "hygienic" reasons; others, who are national-minded, because they are dedicated to the preservation of every symbol of the Jewish identity; and still others, because of their reverence and sentiment for an ancient tradition that began with the Patriarch Abraham some four thousand years ago in the Land of Canaan and has continued unceasingly to this very day.

The full significance of the rite of circumcision as a symbol of dedication to the Jewish way of life is pointed up at the climax of the ceremony, when the circumcised child is given his name. The worshipers, in response to the father's recitation of the benediction, chant the resounding finale of supplication on behalf of the infant: "As he has entered into the Covenant, so may he be permitted to enter into the study of the Torah, under the chuppah [the marriage canopy], and into the performance of good deeds."

See also MITZVOT.

CODE, PRIESTLY. *See* PRIESTS.

CODE OF RABBINICAL LAW. *See* SHULCHAN ARUCH.

COHAN, COHANIM. *See* PRIESTS.

COHANIM, BIRKAT. *See* PRIESTLY BLESSING.

COHEN (COHAN), COHANIM. *See* PRIESTS.

COHEN HA-GADOL. *See* HIGH PRIEST.

COMMANDMENTS, TEN. *See* TEN COMMANDMENTS.

COMMENTARIES, RABBINICAL

It is a fact of Jewish cultural history that the quest for truth and understanding, in terms of religious values, rarely faltered throughout three millennia. The central focus for this preoccupation always remained "The Book." Around it went on a continuous activity in examining and re-examining its sacred texts, which the religious revered as constituting divinely revealed truth. A lesser but also very important allied area for this critical investigation and interpretation were the Oral Laws of tradition—the Mishnah—after that code had been canonically fixed in the second century under the editorship of the Patriarch of Judea, Judah ha-Nasi.

These investigations of the Torah text resulted in a great number of written commentaries that aimed at drawing fuller and more precise meaning from the sacred Hebrew texts. The Western mind, unfamiliar with Jewish religious-cultural preoccupations, is hardly capable of grasping the scope and vigor of this analytical activity. A familiar point of comparison, inadequate as it might be, are the thousands of commentaries and analyses that have been written on Shakespeare's plays since the nineteenth century. And yet, although these are worshipfully regarded in the field of secular culture, there certainly have not been any sacred associations with the works of the Bard of Avon!

The relatively undogmatic and open character of Jewish religious thinking made this scholarly investigative work possible, notwithstanding the fact that there were long and intellectually barren periods when the religious thinker was expected to conform without deviation to whatever doctrines and interpretations of Rabbinic laws and ritualism were considered in his time to be sacrosanct and unchangeable.

Not infrequently, these commentaries on the Bible and the Talmud led to discord and controversy because of the presumed "heretical" nature of their views. Two celebrated examples of works that were originally reviled by the bigots as "heretical" were *A Guide to the Perplexed*, by Maimonides (Moses ben Maimon, 1135–1204) and *The Wars of the Lord*, by Gersonides (Levi ben Gerson, 1288–1344), which his detractors cleverly proceeded to rename "The War *Against* the Lord." Despite these and similar exceptions, much difference of opinion was possible in Torah investigation.

The urgent need to clarifiy the Biblical text and to reconcile its seeming inconsistencies and contradictions in statements, in doctrines, and in laws and practices by a reasoning method which scholars call "exegesis," was the principal driving force behind the writing of the commentaries and their study by the pious—rabbis and laity alike.

Ezra the Scribe had set the traditional pattern for all such investigative studies in the middle of the fifth century B.C.E. "For Ezra had set his heart to seek [i. e., to investigate] the Law of the Lord, and to do it, and to teach in Israel statutes and ordinances." In this manner Biblical exegesis was initiated. It was pursued diligently within the limits of knowledge and dialectical skill, by the Scribes (the Soferim) and the Talmudic Sages (the Tannaim and Amoraim who followed the Scribes). During the last phase of the Second Temple period, the synagogue, the House of Study (Bet ha-Midrash), and the Rabbinic academy (yeshibah) were the proving grounds for these intensive investigations and researches. Yet these studies were not written down but were transmitted orally as the revered traditions of the Fathers.

In the first centuries that followed the Destruction of the Temple in 70 C.E., this probing, elaboration, search for illumination, and desire for a religious synthesis resulted in the creation of the monumental Gemara and Midrash literature.

Together with the Mishnah, of which they were elaborating commentaries, they formed that collective Rabbinic work known as the Talmud, which shortly acquired the more descriptive name in Hebrew of *Yam ha-Talmud,* "the Sea of Talmud."

First attempts at a scientific approach to the textual examination of the Bible and the Talmud were made at the great Rabbinical academies of Sura, Pumbeditha, and Nehardea in Babylonia during the so-called Geonic period in the several centuries which preceded the Middle Ages. The time for this new method of research was ripe, and this activity quickly spread from Babylonia to Palestine, North Africa, Moorish Spain, and the Provence. Culturally, the Jews, together with the Arabs and other Hellenistically oriented peoples, were being disciplined both in the logical method employed by the Greek philosophers and in the scientific approach that the Arabs applied to all cultural problems, including those of religion. Searching for the proper intellectual tools with which to pursue their exploration of Scriptural meaning, Jewish rabbinical scholars became philologists; they soon excelled as Hebrew grammarians, lexicographers, and translators.

The most penetrating of these Biblical exegetes and commentators was, without a doubt, Saadia Gaon (882–942), who was head of the Academy (Yeshibah) of Sura in Babylonia. He has often been called "the Father of the Science of Hebrew Philology." A rationalist in method and a humanist in outlook, he had a vast range of intellectual interests to keep him absorbed throughout his busy life. He even translated the Bible into Arabic (for it was that language, and not Hebrew, which the Jews in Islamic lands knew best), and to his translation, he added his own commentary in Arabic. That became an authoritative interpretation of the Bible for Jews everywhere in the world, and even avidly studied by Arab scholars, who applied his methodology of objective, literal exegesis to the Koran and other sacred Mohammedan writings.

Commentaries written in Mishnaic Hebrew were being produced with enthusiasm and much brilliant thinking by rabbinical scholars everywhere, and displayed learning, culture, and considerable ingenuity. A number of schools of Biblical exegesis, proceeding according to different principles, arose in Egypt, Tunis, Morocco, Palestine, Spain, and the Provence. Even in Christian France and Germany, where the Jews were far less advanced culturally, an interest began to awaken in the hitherto neglected fields of philology and grammar, although it never resulted in achievements comparable to those of the Sefaradim and other Arabic-oriented scholars.

The three most influential writers of Biblical commentaries during the Middle Ages were Solomon ben Isaac of Troyes, better known as Rashi (1040–1105), Abraham ben Meir ibn Ezra (1092–1167), and Maimonides. Although probably the least persuasive in its reasoning of all three, Rashi's commentary was, nevertheless, the most widely acclaimed and accepted, in particular by the Ashkenazim.

Rashi had a positive genius for making the most complicated matters seem plain. This was because he possessed an orderly intellect, and his fund of common sense never deserted him even in the deepest casuistical involvements. If to his Biblical and Talmudic analyses he did not consider it necessary to apply in a more than pedestrian way the already existing tools for scientific research—philology, grammar, and history—he more than compensated for this lack by an unusual conciseness of statement, orderly treatment, and simple explanation. Where Maimonides would either express bafflement or else attempt a clarification of some incomprehensible text by philosophical speculation or by means of allegoric reconciliation, Rashi would grapple with the problem in a most disarming way. He was often uncritical, and was prepared to accept every incident, every statement, and even every word in the Torah as being absolutely and literally true. Legends were treated by him as factual events, primitive beliefs as

Last page of Rashi's commentary to the Bible. (From the first Hebrew book printed following the invention of the printing press, Reggio di Calabria, Italy, 1475.)

Rashi's marginal commentary to The Song of Songs. (From an illuminated parchment Bible produced in Brussels, 1310.) CENTER

Nicholas of Lyra (c. 1292–1340), the celebrated Franciscan exegete who declared: "I usually follow Rabbi Solomon [Rashi]." Nicholas supplied Martin Luther in the 16th century with Rashi's system of Biblical interpretation, and for this reason, Nicholas was dubbed by his critics simia Salomonis *"Solomon's ape." It has been remarked that "Rashi made Nicholas of Lyra, and Nicholas of Lyra made Luther." Thus Rashi left his mark on the Protestant Reformation. (From a manuscript of 1402 written in the Franciscan monastery of Pesaro, Italy, now in the John Rylands Library, Manchester, England.)* RIGHT

denoting religious ideas, and superstitious practices for what they naïvely aimed to accomplish.

Rashi's commentary on the Pentateuch became a constant interpretative companion for it, and it has served as the classic model for religious commentaries of every description since his time. Because it, as well as his equally celebrated commentary on the Babylonian Talmud, was studied by all Jews —from small boys to graybeards—as part of their obligatory daily Torah portion, the name of Rashi became almost as familiar and as much a byword in the Jewish home as the names of David the Psalmist, King Solomon, and the Prophet Elijah. The expression "as Rashi says" has been constantly on the lips of all authority-citing Torah-expounders since the twelfth century. It has been traditional for each page of the Hebrew Chumash—the Five Books of Moses—to carry the Rashi commentary on one side and that of Ibn Ezra on the other, although that of Rashi has enjoyed a greater authority among the Ashkenazim. For the average literate Jew, Rashi's commentary certainly was far easier to understand.

Abraham ibn Ezra was not only a great liturgical poet who helped in the creation of the Golden Age of Hebrew Song in Spain; he was a talented Hebrew philologist as well. He was one of the first investigators to introduce into his critical analysis of the Pentateuch certain sound scientific principles, some of which appear to be just as valid today as they were in the twelfth century. He was the first Bible critic to advance the hypothesis, arrived at by the philological-historical method, that there was not just one Prophet Isaiah but two! (This view, so startling to his contemporaries, has been generally accepted by Biblical scholarship, but only in our own day.) Another provocative (for his time) theory of his was that, while Moses was indeed the author of the Torah—the Five Books of Moses—the work must have been *rewritten* later by someone else. This line of reasoning was the only one that could explain some of the incongruities and historical anachronisms, such as the description of the death of Moses—an event which Moses could hardly have chronicled himself! —to be found in them.

Maimonides (Rabbi Mosheh ben Maimon, or "the Rambam," as he was generally called in former times) seemed to have addressed himself in particular to the knowledgeable and intellectual Jews of his day in his *Guide to the Perplexed*, completed in 1109. His main objective in this work was to reconcile inconsistencies that appear in the Bible text, principally those that bear on questions of faith and doctrine. He composed this commentary, said he, for "thinkers whose studies have brought them into collision with religion, and for those who have studied philosophy and have acquired sound knowledge, and who, while firm in religious matters, are perplexed and bewildered on account of the ambiguous and figurative expressions in the holy writings."

Although he was a consistent rationalist, a forthright religious thinker who was endowed to an unusual degree with scientific detachment, he, nonetheless, relied far less on philology and the objective historic method for interpreting Scripture than did, for instance, Ibn Ezra.

His was a complex mind. Although he was an Aristotelian philosopher, he was also a Jewish chacham (see TALMID CHACHAM). He was deeply versed in most branches of Jewish lore yet, curiously, he was also inclined to mysticism. Like Philo and the Cabalists, he sought for hidden or double meanings in the Biblical texts. Sometimes he fell back on the perhaps too facile allegoric method of Philo, the Alexandrian Jewish-Platonist rabbi, in order to explain contradictions. The Torah, argued Maimonides, was not meant to be understood literally; its words, its symbolisms, and its stated ideas carried within them hidden spiritual, moral, and philosophical meanings that, together, composed a harmonious system of eternal truth. For that reason, his commentaries on the Bible as well as on the Mishnah were found to be too elusively abstract and metaphysical by many Jews. A logician of the first order, he perfected his own original method of reconciling the doctrines of religious faith with the dictates of reason. This technique, for which he was celebrated among his many learned admirers—Jews, Mohammedans, and Christians—and for which he was reviled even more enthusiastically by his critics, was eagerly adopted by the medieval Schoolmen of the Church and applied to the doctrinal inconsistencies they met with in their own religion. Alexander of Hales, Albertus Magnus, and especially St. Thomas Aquinas ("the Angelic Doctor") left in their Latin writings words of admiration for "Rabbi Moses."

In later centuries, the intellectual content in commentary literature declined greatly in quality, and also in culture and in breadth of view, although it did increase much in volume. With the seventeenth century, particularly in such backward regions as Poland, Lithuania, the Ukraine, Bohemia, and Russia, the production of religious works, especially commentaries on a single Scriptural writing, became the order of the day. No rabbi could earn any kind of public recognition without first producing "a little commentary" of his own. The overwhelming number of these were characterized by much hairsplitting and the meaningless Talmudic casuistry and mental "thumb-twisting" called *pilpul*. That was, in many instances, nothing but a dreary rehash of scholarly sounding trivia, piously tesselated with Scriptural verses and citations from the Rabbinic Sages and later authorities. Nonetheless, it is claimed that some remarkably fine individual commentary and moralistic writings did appear in Eastern Europe during the seventeenth and eighteenth centuries, for the gift of inspired scholarship and the dedication to ethical ideas, were ever present among "the people of The Book," even in their darkest days.

See also ARABIC-JEWISH "GOLDEN AGE"; RABBINICAL DECISIONS; TALMUD, THE; TOSAFISTS.

COMMUNITY, DUTY TO THE

The Jews learned early in their history that the fate of the individual was irrevocably linked to that of the community. When it prospered, he benefited; conversely, its adversity proved his misfortune. "When the house caves in—woe to the windows!"

The lessons of Jewish experience made clear that, without group solidarity and mutual aid, survival was impossible. The strength of the individual Jew was, therefore, to be found in the collective strength of all Jewry. Hence the Talmudic proverb: "If two dry logs and one wet one are laid together for burning, the flame from the two dry logs will dry and kindle the wet log as well."

Jewish tradition pours scorn on the individual who keeps himself aloof from community affairs. It is, acidly observes one Sage in the Talmud, as if he were saying: "What do the affairs of the community have to do with me?" Why should he get involved in other people's troubles? Smugly he decides: "Let my soul dwell in peace." A more constructive attitude, the Rabbis point out, is one of dedicated social responsibility. This is illustrated by the folk anecdote about Honi ha-Meagel (Honi "the Circle-Drawer"), an Essene teacher of the first century B.C.E., who exclaimed, as he saw an old man plant a carob tree: "Surely you don't expect to live that long! Why, it takes seventy years for a carob tree to bear fruit!" The old man replied: "Did I find the world empty when I came into it? Just as my father planted for me, so I am now planting for my children."

It is this reciprocal regard of the generations, one for the ɔther—egotistical only in the sense of "enlightened self-interest"—that led the Mishnah Sage, Rabban Gamaliel, to present nis altruistic formulation of social service early in the first century C.E.: "All who occupy themselves with the affairs of the community should do it in the name of Heaven, for the nerit of their fathers will sustain them and their righteousness will stand forever."

In a list of the officials who served in the Temple in Jerusalem, the Mishnah included the obscure name of Ben Babai. Who was this "Son of Babai"? He was the custodian of the lamp wicks for the menorot! Although his position was humble and his task of trifling importance, his name was, nevertheless, included, for he too served the community "in the name of Heaven." By including him, the Mishnah Sages were able to emphasize that, exalted or lowly, all service to God was equally important, whether it was performed by the High Priest or by the custodian of the lamp wicks.

In the scale of religious values, the ethical Judaism of two thousand years ago was truly democratic, showing all men to be equal.

See also FELLOWSHIP IN ISRAEL; UNITY OF ISRAEL.

COMMUNITY, SELF-GOVERNING

It is a social-cultural phenomenon of the first magnitude that for some twenty-three centuries—covering by far the greater portion of Jewish recorded history—in all of the far-flung places of the world, Jews constituted a community within a community. Their separate group-existence made necessary a considerable degree of self-government, but it was one which always remained under the firm control of the "host" Gentile society.

This autonomy was, however, like a double-edged sword; it cut both ways. Because it was set apart in a confined area, Jewish existence was allowed to evolve its own ethnic character and foster a separate religious life, language, and culture, and its own institutions. At the same time, it resulted in an increase in Jewish self-consciousness, and an intensification in group identity. This fact was commented upon with grim irony by Ludwig Boerne, the great German-Jewish writer: that when the enemies of the Jews isolated them from the general population and sealed them off hermetically in ghetto prisons like so many criminals or pariahs, they only succeeded in doing the very opposite of what they had intended—they actually helped to preserve the Jews *as Jews;* yet, since hatred is never consistent nor rational, anti-Semites have, ever since the days of the Persian vizier, Haman, charged Jews with being "a peculiar people," separate and exclusive, refusing to mix with Gentiles because they consider themselves superior.

Historically considered, Jews lived in "splendid" isolation in semi-autonomous Jewish communities located within the general communities ever since the fourth century B.C.E., after Alexander the Great had made himself master of the Jewish destiny. Not surprisingly, both the Egyptian Ptolemies and the Seleucidan kings of Syria who emulated Alexander, favored limited self-rule for their subject Jews. The Greco-Roman geographer Strabo noted in the first century C.E. that the Jews in the Egyptian metropolis of Alexandria, who composed about one-third of the general population, were ruled over by their own ethnarchs. These officials "governed their own people and secured the enforcement of laws as the rulers of a free *politeia.*" In addition, the autonomous Jewish community embedded within Alexandria boasted its own legislative and consultative assembly, called a *gerusia,* and even a Jewish tax-collector, the *alabarch!*

Lesyer, the Judenmeister *or parnas (chief of the Jewish community) of Vienna before 1389.* TOP LEFT

Coat of arms of the medieval Jewish community of Judenburg, Styria, in Austria. Jews lived here since Roman times, when the place was known as Idunum. TOP RIGHT

Page from the Minute Book (Pinkes) *of the semiautonomous Jewish Council of the Four Lands (Great Poland, Little Poland, Galicia, and Volhynia). The Council acted as the "Sanhedrin of Poland."* BOTTOM

The communal lockup of the Jewish community of Lemberg (Lvov). (Youth Department, Zionist Organization.)

The Rathaus Town Hall of the Jewish community in Prague. In the foreground is the Altneuschul (the "Old-New Synagogue"). RIGHT

This became the classic pattern, more or less, for all Jewish self-governing communities, not only throughout the Greek and Roman empires but throughout other countries during every subsequent historic period in Europe, even as late as the end of the eighteenth century. This arrangement proved attractive to the rulers of each country where Jews lived because it was the most efficient way of getting the optimum profit out of them with the least expenditure of effort. Certainly, from their point of view, it was more practical to have a central, well-co-ordinated Jewish authority to do their bidding and also to deal with than an unwieldy conglomeration of individual Jews.

Corporate self-government by Jewish communities was particularly useful to the rulers, for the very important purposes both of collecting taxes and of enforcing their laws and decrees in the ghettos. The Jews themselves, involuntary recipients of so much privilege and generosity, were not unaware of their own usefulness to their masters. When, for instance, the Roman governors of the Ionian Islands and Asia Minor, in their characteristically arrogant manner, began harassing the Jewish communities in their charge—they interfered rudely with the time-honored observance of the Sabbath and holy days, and they even attempted to confiscate for the coffers of Rome the traditional half-shekel contribution made by every Jew to the treasury of the Temple in Jerusalem—the Jews, realizing their danger, promptly appealed to the emperor in Rome for his intervention. It is a matter of record that both Julius Caesar and Augustus were persuaded on different occasions, out of realistic considerations, to issue stern orders to their rapacious proconsuls abroad to let the Jews strictly alone, to allow them "to live in accordance with their own laws and the customs of their ancestors."

Less spectacular, and also less troubled, was the history of the large and old established Jewish communities in the Persian Empire under the Sassanid kings, beginning with the third century C.E. Their communal affairs were ruled over by a Jewish official called Resh Galuta (Prince of the Exile) or Exilarch. He was responsible to the government officials for all the Jews. But in strictly religious-cultural matters, it was not to the exilarch but the Geonim, the Rectors of the Rabbinical academies in Sura and Pumbeditha, who exercised supreme authority. This authority they continued to wield even after the conquest of Persia by the Mohammedan caliphs in the eighth century—actually, until the Crusades.

In Spain, self-regulation of the Jewish communities under the Moors was accomplished by means of the *aljama* (from the Arabic world *jama*, meaning "to gather"), which "gathered" taxes for the caliph, preserved order among the Jews, and, in general, acted as the responsible communal authority. How necessary and self-serving the Spanish rulers found autonomous government for the Jews is to be illustrated by the fact that when the Visigothic kings wanted money from the Jews, they neatly clapped a collective tax on each *aljama* and allowed the Jewish leaders the privilege of racking their brains for ways to raise the money by assessing each Jew individually. In the thirteenth century, the Christian kings of Spain authorized each bishop to rule the Jews residing in his diocese—with the aid, of course, of the Jewish elders. The rabbis, the elders, and the religious judges that were chosen by each *aljama de los judíos* first had to be approved by the regional bishop before they were allowed to serve the community.

It was not much different during the Middle Ages in Central Europe. There the Jews, as the feudal kings' personal property (*servi camerae* or *Kammerknecht*), were governed in their communities by a so-called *Judenbischof* (Bishop of the Jews) or *Judenmeister* (Master of the Jews). He was tax collector as well as rabbi, and also enforcer of the oppressor's harsh laws and demands. No wonder some of these Jewish "bishops" were often hated and feared by their fellow Jews.

There is little question but that the most highly developed instrument for Jewish self-government was the *Kahal* (Council) of Poland. This institution was initiated through a charter issued by King Sigismund Augustus, in 1551. A kahal (pl. kahalim) consisted, in most cases, of seven parnasim or elders. They were obliged to rule their communities with an iron hand. This was not, in every instance, because of any misuse of power nor out of callousness for their fellow Jews, but because of the unbearable pressures they were subjected to from the king, the nobility, the Church, and the entire ruthless state apparatus. Unfortunately, the elders frequently included individuals who were either rich or very ambitious, and who often used their power arbitrarily and unjustly.

The responsibilities of the kahal were numerous and far-ranging. They concerned all matters affecting the Jew in relation to the king, the State, and the Church. The kahal appointed the rabbis, the judges (dayyanim), the cantors (chazzanim), the treasurers (gabbaim), the beadles (shammashim), the overseers of charity, the religious teachers (melamedim), the ritual slaughterers (shochtim), etc. It was the duty of the members to see to the construction and the proper maintenance of kahal property: synagogues, Houses of Study, religious schools, bathhouses, slaughterhouses, courthouses, and the communal ovens for baking matzot.

To increase administrative efficiency, all local kahalim were at first organized into five regional kahalim covering Greater Poland, Little Poland, Red Russia (Galicia), the Ukraine (Podolia-Volhynia), and Lithuania. But after a while, the Lithuanian kahal seceded, and the four remaining councils then constituted themselves a federated body or kind of ghetto parliament calling itself the "Kahal of the Four Lands." The Council met yearly at the great Polish fairs. Most important were the sessions held at the Lublin fair. Here inter-kahal disputes on a regional level were settled, new measures for all of Polish Jewry were legislated, and ways and means were examined for countering whatever threats and dangers were being leveled at the Jews by their enemies at the time.

The laws of the realm sharply defined the self-government of the kahalim. The severity or leniency of these laws depended at any given time on the religious climate, on the political situation, and, especially, on the financial requirements of the Polish king, the higher nobles, and the Church. Unless contravened in any instance by specific Polish laws, Rabbinic law was allowed to serve the kahalim as both guide and yardstick in their self-regulation. The Jews were allowed to elect their own officials. Their rabbis and "lawful judges" were permitted to perform marriages, issue divorces, and decide on all questions pertaining to Jewish religious-cultural life. The kahal could also regulate commercial transactions between Jew and Jew and all other avenues of Jewish community relations, as well as individual conduct. But in all serious criminal and civil cases, especially those involving Christians, the Polish authorities stepped in and dealt with the Jews.

Nonetheless, the kahal authorities had certain punitive powers when dealing with such minor malefactors as thieves, embezzlers, disturbers of the peace, and wife-beaters. Judgments included the imposition of money-fines, religious excommunication, and the denial of certain privileges, but corporal punishment was also customary. This took the form, usually, of a light flogging (with a leather strap) or of being chained to the outside wall of the synagogue—the humiliated target of public scorn. On more than one occasion, when the kahal elders found that they were unable to enforce their rulings, they were obliged to call on the Christian authorities for help. This help was always forthcoming, with the natural result that it intensified the bitter feelings of a large section of the Jewish community against their leaders.

While there exists much documentary evidence concerning the frequent abuse of power and acts of outright discrimination by the elders, especially against the weak and the poor—and those, unfortunately, constituted the great majority of the Jews in the ghetto—the rule of the kahal, in its broader and over-all aspects, proved of enormous benefit to Jewish collective existence during the dark and trying period from the sixteenth to the eighteenth centuries in Poland and Russia. As a centralized corporate body, the kahal made possible not only the flowering of Jewish religious culture but also the establishment of many institutional forms of mutual aid and social welfare within the Jewish community. It is a matter of record that the Council of the Four Lands frequently appeared in defense of Polish Jewry before the Diets and the kings themselves, petitioning against harsh decrees, the infringement of religious practices, and the imposition of too crushing taxes and collective fines and levies.

A chronicler of those times, Nathan Hannover, wrote in 1653 of his impression of a session he attended of the Council of the Four Lands: "The Elders . . . reminded one of the Sanhedrin which in ancient days assembled in the Chamber of Hewn Stone in the Temple at Jerusalem. They had jurisdiction over all the Jews of the Kingdom of Poland (which then also included the Ukraine). They issued decrees and made binding decisions, and imposed penalties as they saw fit."

The kahal system of self-rule, of a "state within a state," came legally to an end in 1764, when it was abolished in the Polish provinces by royal decree. Yet the old pattern of communal living and collective management, although modified and ever in flux, was *voluntarily* preserved by the ghetto-enclaves within the cities and towns of Poland and Lithuania.

To the great masses of tradition-bound Jews, communal self-regulation, even without legal status, was an additional guarantee for the continuity of the Jewish religion, Torah culture, and folkways. Of course, as the Jews of Europe advanced more and more toward civil emancipation as the ghetto walls crumbled, they became culturally assimilated, in varying degrees. This process tended to weaken group cohesiveness and the traditional outlook and modes of life. Some saw in this fragmentation the danger of a gradual dissolution of the Jewish identity. Many looked yearningly back to the time when the kahal was in full flower and ghetto life displayed a distinctive physiognomy and a vitality.

The question of assimilation and the abandonment of collective Jewish group-life became the subject of heated debate in Jewish religious and Zionist-nationalist circles at the end of the nineteenth century, and, for that matter, still goes on.

See also GHETTO.

COMPASSION. *See* ETHICAL VALUES, JEWISH.

CONCENTRATION CAMPS. *See* NAZIS, THE.

CONDOLENCE CALL. *See* SHIVAH.

CONFESSION (in Hebrew: VIDDUI)

As the pious Jew lies at the point of death, with all his remaining strength he repeats for the last time the affirmation of his faith. First he utters the Shema, which proclaims the Oneness of God. Then he recites the prayer of Confession (Viddui) for, says the Mishnah, "he is about to suffer the ultimate penalty of the law."

Since the mediation of the rabbi is not required by Jewish belief, the dying person must make his own peace with God and his conscience. He recites the Confession by himself or, if he is too weak to do so, someone else reads the prayer while he repeats after him word for word, even if only with a soundless movement of the lips.

Because the Jew is a realist, he knows that death may overtake him suddenly, without warning. Therefore, nightly, before lying down to sleep, he recites his Confession of sins. And should he be spared and wake again next morning for another day of life, he is glad that he has confessed, for doing so has given him a better knowledge of himself, and this, if he has a sensitive conscience, will lead him to repentance and, finally, to make atonement to any of his fellows he has wronged. He resolves to live more uprightly thereafter.

The Sages declared: "One who confesses his sins has a share in the World-to-Come." Therefore, they believed that the Viddui was not merely created for the moral benefit of the dying but for the spiritual instruction of the living.

Not only does it form a dramatic part of the Yom Kippur liturgy, but its meaning is pondered daily in his prayers by every believing Jew.

CONFIRMATION

The rite of mass-Confirmation was introduced into Reform congregations early in the nineteenth century, the first one taking place in 1810, in Kassel, Germany. In the United States, it was initiated at Temple Emanu-El, in New York, in 1847. However, it took the form then of a group ceremony for boys alone. Although it was a variant of the Orthodox Bar Mitzvah, it dispensed altogether with the traditional wearing of the prayer shawl (tallit) and phylacteries (tefillin) and the reading by the celebrants from the Torah and the Haftarah (the Prophets). In later decades, girls too were drawn into the privileged circle of initiates into religious adulthood that, for so many centuries, had been considered exclusively a male preserve—and still is so regarded by Orthodox Jews—and which could be attained only by the boys on their being Bar Mitzvah.

In preparation for their Confirmation, the boys and girls in Reform (and in some Conservative) congregations are given careful instruction, and must pass an examination as well, in the principles of the Jewish religion, but from the modernized viewpoints of both Liberal or Conservative Judaism. Also, unlike the Bar Mitzvah or Bat Mitzvah, which is observed at the exact age of thirteen, the rite of Confirmation for boys and girls takes place only once annually: during the festival of Shabuot (the Feast of Weeks), commemorating the giving of the Torah to the Jewish people at Mount Sinai. Not the confirmant's age but his or her knowledgeability and understanding of the fundamentals of religious belief and practice are considered essential. It is, therefore, not unusual to find that the confirmants' ages range from twelve to fifteen.

The initiation rites are quite elaborate and are intended to be impressive for the youngsters. There is a procession of the confirmants to the pealing of the organ and the singing of the cantor and the choir. The rabbi offers the boys and girls his priestly blessing, and they in turn take a solemn vow to remain faithful to their religion. Actually, the ceremony is not fixed but varies considerably according to the particular tastes and wishes of each Reform congregation.

Some Orthodox critics have observed rather caustically that the Confirmation ceremony in Reform Judaism bears, externally at least, a certain resemblance to the Confirmation ceremony of Protestant churches. In this, they say, they recognize a precipitate desire to conform: an assimilationist drive to reconcile Jewish tradition, rite, and ceremonial with those prevailing in a world that is predominantly Christian.

See also BAR MITZVAH; BAT MITZVAH.

CONSERVATIVE JUDAISM. *See* JUDAISM IN THE MODERN AGE.

CONVERSION OF JEWS

Conversion by Persuasion. It would, of course, be an oversimplification and also unjust to declare that the Church stood monolithically in religious *enmity* toward the Jews. There were popes and lesser clergy who, unlike those two implacable foes of the Jews, Innocent III (1198–1216) in Rome and Benedict XIII (1394–1423) in Avignon, took a more humane and moderate attitude toward Jewish "separatism." In a time of great public excitement and excesses against the Jews, Pope Martin V (1417–31) issued a bull which was similar to those that had been promulgated earlier by Calixtus II (1119–24) and Gregory IX (1227–41). It solemnly drew to the attention of the faithful these facts:

> WHEREAS The Jews are made in the image and likeness of God and a portion of them will one day be saved; and WHEREAS That they have besought our protection, following in the footsteps of our predecessors, we command that they be not molested in their synagogues; that their laws, rights and customs be not assailed; that they be not baptized by force, constrained to observe Christian festivals, nor to wear badges, and be not hindered in their business relations with Christians.

It is, indeed, a matter of intriguing irony to contemplate the seemingly contradictory approaches to "the Jewish problem" that the Church took during the Middle Ages. On the one hand, it made the most strenuous efforts to effectuate the assimilation and conversion of the Jews to Christianity by pious and gentle means—by persuasion and emotional appeals—so as to bring to an end their religious and ethnic "separatism." On the other hand, it leaped to the diametrically opposite extreme and laid its crushing hand on the Jews *qua* Jews—it made pariahs of them and raised such walls of economic limitations and harassments around their daily life that it made mere physical survival a near miracle. Furthermore, it forced them into ghettos where they remained segregated from the Christian population lest they "contaminate" them, and likewise forced them to wear in human degradation the sugarloaf hat (*Judenhut*) and the yellow badge. Whatever the religious-social and group separatism—a separatism that certainly caused no harm to anyone—that was voluntarily undertaken by the Jews themselves in order to preserve their heritage, the cruel kind of separatism and isolation that was forced on them by Christian society provoked Martin Luther, in his benevolent phase, into savage sarcasm. He presented his own "program for the Christian" treatment of the Jews, one which was emulated by Oliver Cromwell when he allowed the Jews, about a hundred years later, to return to England, and by Roger Williams, in the same century, when he granted religious and civil equality to Jews in the colony of Rhode Island:

> My advice, therefore, is to deal kindly with the Jews and to instruct them in the Scriptures [i.e., the New Testament] so that they come over to us. . . . How can we hope to win them over and improve them if we forbid them to work among us and to trade and mingle with us, and force them into usury! . . . We must welcome them into our midst, permit them to work and trade among us. They will then have an opportunity to witness Christian life and doctrine. Should, however, some of them still remain stubborn—what of it? Not every one of us is a good Christian.

The idea of using persuasion instead of force for conversion—although it was never accompanied by the liberality of Luther's social-economic proposals—was already many centuries old at the time he made them. Pope Gregory "the Great" (590–604) had outlawed acts of violence and persecution against Jews. His stated object was to win over the Jews for Christ both by material inducements and by evangelical persuasion. In order to shield them against the rapacity of the rulers and the fanaticism of many of the clergy, he, it has been said, laid the groundwork for "Letters of Protection"

Jews forced to listen to a conversionist sermon at a special service for them in a church. (Water color by Hieronymus Hess, 18th century. Museum in Basel, Switzerland.)

(*sicut Judaeis*) that were issued to the Jews by a number of popes, beginning with Calixtus II (1119–24), for the safe guarding of their lives and their possessions, and the right to practice the Jewish religion without molestation.

"The Sermons for Conversion" were first introduced by Pope Nicholas II in 1278 and were given binding force in the decree of the Church Council of Basel in 1434. The anti-Pope at Avignon, Benedict XIII, in his bull of 1415, had indicated what the subjects of the conversionist sermons were to be, namely, that "the true Messiah has already come . . . that the heresies, vanities and errors of the Talmud prevent their [i.e., the Jews] knowing the truth . . . that the destruction of the Temple and the city of Jerusalem and the perpetuity of their captivity" had been prophesied by Jesus and other prophets as constituting the just punishment for the Jews' sins and crimes.

In the city of Rome, conversionist sermons were delivered uninterruptedly in certain designated churches until the nineteenth century, a reminder that the barbarous attitudes and practices of mankind have a disheartening durableness.

Conversion by Force: ANUSIM. In Byzantium—the Eastern Roman Empire during the early Christian centuries—Jewish children were forcibly taken away from their parents; they were baptized, placed in monasteries or convents, and instructed in Christian dogmas and observances. The intention, of course, was to wean them away from their Jewish identity. The remarkable fact is that for generations after their forced conversion, these seemingly estranged Jews and their descendants stubbornly kept alive the consciousness of their Jewishness. In different degrees, they remained faithful to Judaism, but secretly. The Hebrew name they bore was *Anusim*—"Those who were compelled." There is reason to believe that the famous Kol Nidre prayer chanted on the eve of Yom Kippur, the Day of Atonement, is a solemn supplication for the remission by Heaven of the forced vows taken by these Anusim during their conversion to Christianity or Islam.

Perhaps the Jews of Spain, among all the Jews in the world, were most exposed to the determined efforts of the Church there to bring them worshiping to the foot of the Cross, whatever means were required for that. The reasons for such an implacable stand are highly complex. Already, in the year 612, the Visigothic Christian king in Spain, Sisebut, tried to baptize "his" Jews by force. He decreed that every Jew who refused to accept baptism was to be given one hundred lashes, shorn of his or her hair, deprived of all possessions, and then expelled from the country.

One ingenious device introduced for discouraging Jews from remaining Jews was inserted in the Visigothic Code (Fuero Juzgo) in 634 C.E. This law forbade Jews, under the penalty of being sold into slavery and of forfeiting all their property, to observe the principal institutions and practices of the Jewish religion: the Sabbath, the festivals, the dietary laws (kashrut), etc. These pressures apparently led to a mass conversion, for only nine years later, a decree was issued prescribing death (by beheading, by the fiery stake, or by stoning) for those caught practicing Judaism secretly.

During the middle of the twelfth century, when the Unitarians (Almohádes) of Islam engaged, from purely religious motives, in a ferocious suppression of both Christianity and the Jewish religion in the Maghreb (Morocco) and in the Mohammedan principalities of Southern Spain, in order to create "a Moslem state for Moslems," the caliph Abdulmumen decided to adopt the old battle cry of the Prophet Mohammed against the Jews of Medina: "Islam or death!" He said to the Jews in his domains: "We can no longer permit you to continue in your unbelief. . . . You have only the choice between Islam and death."

It became the boast of the Moors at that time that "There is no church and no synagogue in our land." Many Jews resisting conversion—even in a nominal form—were slain. But inasmuch as Abdulmumen was not as bloodthirsty as some of the medieval Christian rulers, he was prevailed upon to allow many Jews to leave the country, selling into slavery those who remained. Many who were converted continued as secret Jews (*Anusim*); they were the exact equivalent of those New Christians (Conversos) of fifteenth-century Spain who bore the unflattering name of *Marranos*—"Pigs"—given to them by non-Jewish Catholics.

The Domus Conversorum *at Oxford for the reception of Jewish converts. (Sketch from Skelton's* Oxonia Antiqua.)

The almost total conversion of the Moorish Jews to Islam created a moral crisis in the souls of many. One such anguished convert had asked for an opinion from an unnamed rabbinical authority abroad; the latter replied in the most scathing terms that the only honorable course left for a believing Jew when facing the inevitability of apostasy was to undergo martyrdom *al kiddush ha-Shem* (for the Sanctification of the name [of God]). This rabbinic decision, which was widely circulated among the Anusim who were pseudo converts to Islam, caused the deepest despondency among them. Aroused by this unfeeling fundamentalist condemnation of the unfortunates, the great rabbi-philosopher Maimonides (Moses ben Maimon), at the time being only twenty-five and probably himself a pseudo convert to Islam, countered with his celebrated "Letter on Apostasy" *(Iggeret ha-Shamad)* in 1160.

In it, addressing himself to all Jews who might be placed in jeopardy of their lives because of their religion, he pointed out that the Rabbinic Sages of the second century C.E., Meir and Eleazar, had saved their own lives by feigning conversion to the gods of the Romans during the Hadrianic persecutions. Maimonides commented ironically upon the fact that all that the Mohammedans required of the Jews was to recite the creed of Islam, giving mere lip-service to a formula about the Unity of God that was very similar to the first part of the Shema of the Jewish religion. The Islamic prayer ran: *"La illaha illa Allah, Muhammad rasul Allah!"* ("There is no God but Allah, and Mohammed is the Prophet of Allah!") In answer to this, Mainmonides wrote: "But if a man asks me: 'Shall I be slain or utter the formula of Islam?' my answer is: 'Utter the formula and live!' . . . Indeed, any Jew who, after uttering the Moslem formula, wishes to observe all of the 613 commandments [mitzvot] in the privacy of his home, may do so without hindrance."

It is in this intelligent, rationalistic declaration, and in similar decisions made by other religious authorities during the Middle Ages in Spain and Portugal, that there was created a special intellectual climate for Jews, sanctioning their nominal submission to the empty externals of conversion under extreme duress without in the least being affected in their own moral principles, self-respect, or religious sentiments. This is how so many of the Marranos, those pseudo converts to Christianity, could maintain their Jewish identity in an "underground" way and yet manage to live at peace with themselves, waiting patiently for better days to come and for the opportunity to live openly as professing Jews.

The youthful Maimonides saw one practical way out of the dilemma for himself and his fellow Jews: "The advice I give to myself, to those I love, and to those who ask my opinion, is that we should go forth from these places and go where we can fulfill [the precepts] of the Torah without compulsion and without fear. . . ."

In a summary-account such as this, the telescoping of historic events and religious and social changes is quite an arbitrary but necessary evil. To start perhaps from a chronologically arbitrary point in the history of the Jews in Spain, one could well say that the chief focus (although not the only one) of Christian enmity for the Jewish population in that country was the bloody civil war and the struggle for power that ensued during the fourteenth century in the kingdom of Castile between the reigning monarch, Pedro ("the Cruel"), and Henry de Trastamara, his half-brother, who wished to take his throne away. No question but that the Jews constituted an important element in the conflict. Pedro was well disposed toward his Jewish subjects; he had surrounded himself with so many Jews—physicians, tax-farmers, moneylenders, diplomats, and ministers of state—that his court became known among his enemies as "The Jewish Court." If for no other reason than this, his half-brother Henry nurtured an unholy hatred for the Jews. In the year 1355, Henry's soldiers attacked and pillaged the ghetto of Toledo and massacred 12,000 Jews. An ally of Henry's, the notorious French warrior, Bertrand du Guesclin, ordered his soldiers to round up all Jews and "kill them like sheep if they will not be baptized." And this his soldiers did cheerfully.

In this bloody manner the stage was set for historically more momentous butcheries of Jews. On June 6, 1391, a fateful massacre, led by the Dominican fanatic Ferrand Martinez, vicar-general of Seville and confessor to the Queen, took place in Seville. The result: 4,000 male Jews were slain, the remainder were forcibly converted, and the women and children were sold into slavery. Religious hysteria had been so whipped up that a virtual conflagration of massacres of Jews swept through the cities and towns of Spain and the island of Majorca, following the only partly successful crusade of converting the "Christ-killers." In only three months' time some 50,000 Jews perished.

Only twenty years later, in 1411, the Dominican preacher, Vincent Ferrer (later he was sainted), started out on his crusade to convert the Jews of Castile. Placing himself at the head of a band of fanatical Flagellants *(Penitentes)* and also a mob of ordinary looters and cutthroats, he rushed into the synagogues on the Sabbath at the time when the Jews were assembled for worship. Holding a Torah Scroll with one hand and brandishing menacingly a crucifix (as if it were a sword) with the other, he thundered at them: "Baptism or death!" While there were many thousands who submitted to baptism when faced with this choice, there were also other thousands who, wrapped in their prayer shawls and reciting the Shema, preferred to remain faithful to their religion, and so were slain by the mob. Vincent Ferrer boasted that with his own hands he had baptized 35,000 Jews. However, his "method" of saving souls was condemned in 1414 by the Church Council of Constance.

See also CHRISTIANITY, JEWISH ORIGINS OF; CHURCH AND PERSECUTION; DISPUTATIONS, RELIGIOUS; GHETTO; ISLAM, JEWISH ORIGINS OF; KOL NIDRE; MARRANOS AND THE INQUISITION; PERSECUTION IN "MODERN" DRESS; POGROMS IN SLAVIC LANDS; SEPARATISM, JEWISH; YELLOW BADGE.

CONVERSOS. *See* CONVERSION OF JEWS; MARRANOS AND THE INQUISITION.

COUNCIL OF THE FOUR LANDS. *See* COMMUNITY, SELF-GOVERNING.

COVENANT. *See* ARK OF THE COVENANT; CHOSEN PEOPLE, THE; CIRCUMCISION; SACRIFICE OF ISAAC.

CREED, JEWISH. *See* DOCTRINES IN JUDAISM; JUDAISM IN THE MODERN AGE.

"CROWN OF GLORY." *See* HALO.

CRUCIFIXION. *See* ANTI-SEMITISM; CHRISTIANITY, JEWISH ORIGINS OF; WANDERING JEW.

CRUSADES, THE. *See* MASSACRES: THE CRUSADES, THE BLACK DEATH.

CULTURE, JEWISH. *See* ACCENTS, MUSICAL; ARABIC-JEWISH "GOLDEN AGE"; ART, CEREMONIAL; ART AMONG THE JEWS; BET HA-MIDRASH; BIBLE, THE; CHAZZAN; CHEDER; ENLIGHTENMENT, THE JEWISH; FOLK MUSIC AND DANCE; FOLKLORE; HEBREW LANGUAGE, HISTORY OF THE; HEBREW LITERATURE, MODERN; HYMNS OF THE SYNAGOGUE; JEWISH LANGUAGES; KLEZMER; MERRYMAKERS, TRADITIONAL JEWISH; MUSIC, ANCIENT JEWISH; MUSIC IN THE TEMPLE; MUSICAL INSTRUMENTS OF THE BIBLE; POST-BIBLICAL WRITINGS; PRAYER AND WORSHIP; SYNAGOGUE, THE; TALMUD TORAH; TORAH STUDY; YESHIBAH; YESHIVAH BACHUR; YIDDISH LITERATURE, MODERN; ZEMIROT; ZIONISM.

D

DANCE, FOLK. *See* FOLK MUSIC AND DANCE.

DARSHAN, DARSHANIM. *See* MAGGID.

DAY OF ATONEMENT. *See* YOM KIPPUR.

DAY OF JUDGMENT. *See* DEATH; DOCTRINES IN JUDAISM; GAN EDEN; GEHINNOM; IMMORTALITY; RESURRECTION; REWARD AND PUNISHMENT; SIN AND SINNER; SOUL, THE; WORLD-TO-COME.

DAYS OF AWE. *See* SELICHOT.

DEAD, PRAYER FOR THE. *See* KADDISH.

DEAD SEA SCROLLS

In a class set apart in many ways from other Jewish-Hellenistic writings produced during the Greco-Roman period are the Hebrew manuscripts, written on leather and papyrus and stored in earthen jars, that were accidentally uncovered in 1947 in a cave at Qumran, along the Dead Sea coast. Unquestionably, these documents are an important addition to the meager literature that exists on the Essenes, the Jewish collectivist sect with which Jesus and the Apostles have been linked by many historians. However, the sensational manner of their discovery and their immense exploitation by newspapers, books, and periodicals led to an exaggerated estimate of their historical and religious importance, and also to much fanciful hypothesizing about and an over-evaluation of them. This was especially true of some Biblical scholars who burned with an excess of zeal to link up the data in the Scrolls directly with Jesus and the Apostles and with the origins of early Christianity. Fortunately, further and more dispassionate study of the Scrolls resulted in a more realistic assessment of their contents.

Among these documents some interesting new writings turned up, including a number of "historical" texts: the Book of Hymns (obviously part of the Qumran community's synagogue liturgy), modeled upon the Biblical Psalms, although far less distinguished as verse; the apocalypse—The War Between the Children of Light and the Children of Darkness; and commentaries on the Biblical books of Genesis, Nahum, and Habakkuk. But perhaps the most valuable among all the writings is the Manual of Discipline, containing the laws and regulations that governed the monastic brothers in their daily lives at Qumran.

The Manual increases the scant knowledge previously available only through the writings of the rabbi-philosopher Philo, the historian Josephus, and Pliny the Elder about the Essenes and, inferentially, about the first Christian communities as well. The sectaries lived in a commune (called in Hebrew *ha-Yachad;* literally, "Togetherness") in a setting of monastic seclusion on the shores of the Dead Sea, and in an atmosphere and under conditions expected to stimulate brotherly love and a life of physical and moral purity. Before entering the community, the chaberim (companions; s. chaber) were required to renounce all their worldly ambitions, cease their acquisition of money and material possessions, and abandon the pursuit of all fleshy pleasure, for they deemed all of these things to be but empty vanities, snares to corruption, and stumbling blocks to the fulfillment of the covenant contracted at Mount Sinai between God and Israel.

The dating of the Dead Sea Scrolls is still a matter of controversy. The various estimates that have been advanced by the Biblical specialists range all the way from the second century B.C.E. to the seventh century C.E. One scientific estimate arrived at by W. F. Libby's radioactivity test—the Carbon 14 process—produced the date 33 C.E. But Dr. Libby counseled to subtract or add two centuries "either way." This would set the correct date at either 167 B.C.E. or 233 C.E. And that is where the matter has been left to rest.

See also APOCRYPHA, THE; BIBLE, THE; CHACHMAH; CHRISTIANITY, JEWISH ORIGINS OF; ESSENES; HELLENISTS, JEWISH; MESSIAH, THE; MESSIAHS, WOULD-BE; PHARISEES; POST-BIBLICAL WRITINGS; PSEUDEPIGRAPHA; TAMUD, THE; THERAPEUTAE.

DEATH

In Jewish religious thinking, life and death were one, being merely different aspects of the same reality. They were considered as complementary to each other as night is to day and winter is to summer. They were the turning wheels in the process of creation that never ends. The eleventh-century teacher of ethics, Bachya ibn Pakudah, reflected: "Life and death are brothers; they live in the same house. They are joined to each other and cling together so that they cannot be severed. They are united by the two ends of a frail bridge over which all created things must travel. Life is the entrance; death is the exit."

Because the Jew of tradition did not argue with God concerning the justice of death, but bowed to its inevitable coming as an expression of the divine will, leaving life through its "exit"—death—proved less frightening to him than one would suppose from the display of uninhibited emotionalism surrounding his departure. Death did not appear to the Jew as a dread specter. Rather, it came to lay at rest all grief and pain, to comfort and to fulfill. In the Bible, that was the way it happened to the dying Moses. God came to him, and like a loving father, took his soul away—with a kiss. . . .

The devout Jew of every generation considered himself merely a temporary sojourner, a wayfarer on earth. Death did not mean to him the utter extinction of his being, but the beginning of another phase of it. Life on earth, according to the Sages of the Mishnah, was merely "a corridor" that led into the radiant Hall of Eternal Life. It was this certainty which brought to the believing Jew in the crisis of death a serenity and a resignation. This childlike yet realistic submission of the Jew to the limitations of his fleshly body was most eloquently expressed by God's "afflicted man," Job. In his hour of trial he murmured: "The Lord gave, and the Lord has taken away; blessed be the name of the Lord!" And so, for almost twenty-five centuries, since the time of Job, these Hebrew words of reconciliation between a troubled life and an inscrutable death have been repeated at the open grave each time a Jew is laid to rest.

Clearly enough, the certitudes of faith are governed by their own rules of logic. For the believing Jew, what need was there to grieve and sigh over the dissolution of the body whose "days are as grass" when he was full of the conviction that the life of the soul, liberated by death from its earthly husk, would be incomparably more satisfying and beautiful! Of course, even among believing Jews, there were varying degrees of emphasis placed on acceptance of death. Perhaps the most extreme view was held by the Essenes, the Judean sect from whom Jesus and his disciples drew most of their religious and social doctrines, including their other-worldliness. According to their contemporary, the historian Josephus, the Essenes regarded death with indifference; they trained their spiritual gaze instead upon the pure existence they expected to enter in the World-to-Come.

Certainly, with a different emphasis intended, the Second-century Talmudic teacher, Rabbi Meir Baal ha-Nes, wrote in the margin of his Chumash (Pentateuch): "And it was very good; namely, death." He meant to imply that if life was deemed good, then death should be considered equally so, for were not both part of the Creator's plan for all existence? Each had its own special function and brought its own kind of duties, rewards, and time of fulfillment. This, more or less, remained the traditional view of Jews in the centuries that followed.

These was always, among Jews of former times (more so than in our own), a sense of resignation as they made ready for their departure from the world. For them, the course appeared clearly charted, and the destination–the World-to-Come–certain. Like that saint of eighteenth-century Chasidism, Israel Baal Shem, they were supremely confident that, though they were leaving life through one door, they would come in again through another on the day of the Resurrection. They felt secure in the thought that the departing soul, on leaving its frail envelope of flesh, would wing its way heavenward to nestle at peace in the bosom of God. And so, even though parting from dear ones and saying "finish" to certain cherished pursuits and pleasures proved to be a bitter wrench indeed, for the soul it was no tragedy at all. On the contrary, it was an occasion for joyful reunion with its Creator.

"Away, like a bird, to your nest you will fly!" sang the Hebrew poet Solomon ibn Gabirol nine centuries ago.

See also BURIAL RITES AND CUSTOMS; IMMORTALITY; RESURRECTION; SOUL, THE; WORLD-TO-COME.

DECALOGUE, THE. *See* TEN COMMANDMENTS.

DECISIONS, RABBINICAL. *See* RABBINICAL DECISIONS.

DEDICATION, THE FEAST OF. *See* CHANNUKAH.

DELUGE, THE. *See* BIBLICAL MYTHS, SIGNIFICANCE OF; CHRONOLOGY, JEWISH.

DEMONS. *See* AMULETS; DYBBUK; EVIL EYE.

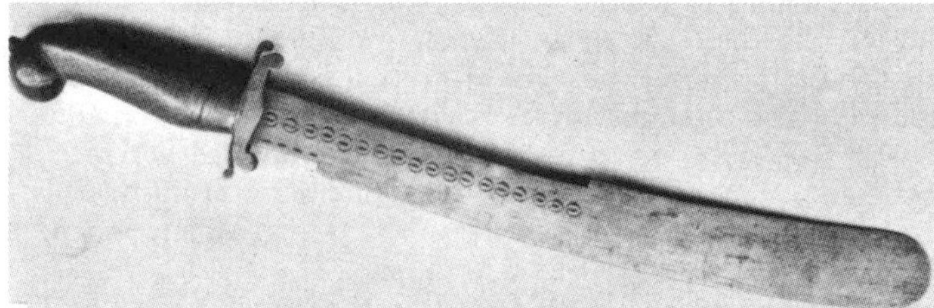

"Revolving" knife for fending off demons from women during childbirth. Germany, 18th century.

Cabalistic amulet to protect women in childbirth against demons.

DERASHAH. *See* SERMON.

DEUTERONOMY, BOOK OF. *See* BIBLE, THE.

DIALECTS, JEWISH. *See* JEWISH LANGUAGES; YIDDISH LANGUAGE, THE.

DIASPORA (Greek, meaning "dispersion" or "scattering"; Hebrew equivalent GALUT and Yiddish GOLUS also carry the more complex connotation of "the Jewish Exile")

As it is commonly used, the word "Diaspora" refers collectively to all the geographic places outside of Judea where Jews settled after their national life had been destroyed by the Romans in 70 C.E. Historically speaking, this is not entirely true; it leads, in fact, to a historical misconception. The plain fact is that before that catastrophic event, the "dispersion" of the Jews had already been in progress for a long time. It had been carried out on a massive scale after the northern Jewish kingdom of Samaria fell before the Assyrian invaders in 721 B.C.E., and the "king of kings," Sargon, began the deportation of tens of thousands of Jews. He sent them either to colonize in selected regions of his far-flung empire, or he had them sold as slaves in the market.

Sargon's imperial successors followed the same course as a policy of state, so that the Jewish population in Palestine was greatly reduced after several centuries. One can get an inkling of the size of these deportations from the boastful cuneiform inscription (now in the British Museum) which is a quotation of the conqueror Sennacherib, celebrating his victory over the army of Judah in 701 B.C.E. It reads: "200,150

Judaea Capta–*"Captive Judea." Roman "victory" coin issued by Titus following the Destruction.*

people, small and large, male and female . . . I brought out of their midst, and I counted them as booty."

Despite those historians who tend to oversimplify events and social forces as if they were generated in a vacuum, the captives whom Nebuchadnezzar led with halters around their necks into Babylonia after he had destroyed Solomon's Temple in Jerusalem, in 586 B.C.E., undoubtedly saw in the land of their captivity large and well-rooted Jewish communities which had been established there since the eighth century. The newcomers, it can be assumed, merely swelled their numbers. About a century later, when the exiles returned from Babylonia to Jerusalem, it was surprising to find, according to the statements of Ezra and Nehemiah, that they consisted of no more than 60,000 individuals. Obviously, then, the majority of the exiles must have chosen to remain in Babylonia, where, after more than twenty-six centuries of uninterrupted residence, some of their descendants still live.

Needless to say, Babylonia did not constitute in those days the entire "Dispersion." It should be noted that, during the national debacle in 586 B.C.E., though thousands of Jewish captives were taken away to Babylonia, there were many Jews, including the Prophet Jeremiah, who were said to have escaped into Egypt. It becomes reasonably certain from this and other statements in the Bible that Jewish settlements must have existed in the land of the Pharaohs for a long time, possibly even before the Bondage; therefore, it is not too unreasonable to assume that not all Jewish slaves had revolted under Moses' leadership and fled from Egypt. We know that during the seventh or sixth century B.C.E., a formidable military colony of Jewish professional soldiers was settled in the Elephantine region of Upper Egypt by one of the Pharaohs in order that they might prevent, from that strategic outpost, an invasion by the threatening Ethiopians. In fact, a central sanctuary–the Temple of Onias–was erected there in the middle of the second century B.C.E. to strengthen the colonists' wavering loyalty to Judaism. This was, according to all references, an impressive sanctuary, equipped with altars, a ministering priesthood, sacrificial offerings, and an elaborateness of ritual which were said to rival those of the Temple in Jerusalem.

It is, therefore, not surprising that, during the time of the Greek and Roman overlordship of Judea and before its final destruction, large Jewish centers of population had been planted in such widely separated places as Babylonia-Persia, Syria, Antioch (in Asia Minor), Rome, Athens, Thessalonica, Bulgaria, Armenia, the Island of Cyprus, Carthage and Cyrenaica (on the North African coast), and in Alexandria and other cities of Egypt. The Hellenistic-Jewish philosopher, Philo, estimated that in his day, early in the first century C.E., when the population of Judea was about three millions, the number of Jews in Egypt alone was more than a million, and it is believed that twice that number of Jews were, during the same time, living in Babylonia-Persia, Cyrenaica, and elsewhere.

Both Jews and Gentiles marveled at the global dispersion of the Jews. Philo wrote: "So populous are the Jews that no one country can hold them, and, therefore, they settle in very many of the most prosperous countries in Europe and Asia, both on the islands and on the mainland."

Fascinating in the extreme is the psychological and emotional relationship of these expatriate communities to the Jewish homeland. Philo attempted to explain this: "And while they hold the Holy City [Jerusalem], where stands the holy Temple of the most high God, to be their Mother-city, yet those [i.e., cities in the Diaspora] which are theirs by inheritance from their fathers, grandfathers, and ancestors . . . are in each case considered by them to be their Fatherland in which they were born and reared." This double attachment of the Jews in the Diaspora–to their Homeland on the one hand and to the lands of their adoption on the other–remarkably resembles that which exists today in the relationship between the Jews living in other countries of the world and the State of Israel.

Curious, indeed, throughout the centuries has been the state of mind of most Jews living outside of Palestine to their millennial separation from the homeland. The very word *Galut*–"Exile"–remains the most eloquent and poignant index to it. The Jews were never reconciled to their dispersion, considering it to be merely a temporary though painfully long interlude. And they waited hopefully for the fateful hour of their restoration to Mount Zion, a happy consummation the pious throughout the ages persisted in believing would come about inevitably–but only with the appearance of the Messiah. The traditional view among the devout has been that the Dispersion of the Jewish people was a judgment of Heaven visited upon them as a collective punishment for the untold sins they had committed against God and man. "On account of our sins," humbly begins an ancient penitential refrain of the Jews, as the tears of regret fall like quiet rain.

Ironically, Christian theology, which, in relation to the Jews, put aside its evangel of love and turned instead vengeful and unforgiving, eagerly seized upon this public confession of wrongdoing by the Jews. It, too–but from entirely different motives–proceeded to justify the wide scattering of the Jewish people and the persecution and suffering meted out to them by good Christians as a punishment from God for their sins. But principally, argued the Church, it was for the most terrible sin of all: for having rejected Jesus as the Messiah and as the son of God. In addition (and this also has been fundamental in Christian doctrine relative to the preordained fate of the Jews), with their total rejection by the whole world and with their suffering and humiliation, they were to serve, in whatever part of the world they had to live, as everlasting witnesses to the divinity of Christ and to the truth of his teachings. St. Augustine piously commented: "Now that they are dispersed through almost all lands and nations, it is through the providence of the One true God."

Some of the Tamudic Sages took an optimistic view of the Galut. They reckoned that it was, indeed, providential that the Jews were so fantastically dispersed all over the globe, for that way, they could never be totally destroyed by their enemies! That view appears ironic in the light of our own times, when German efficiency corralled 6,000,000 Jews from every part of Europe into scientifically run extermination centers, where the Nazis butchered them.

The word *Diaspora* or *Galut* is still widely used today by both Jews and Christians, but no longer, for the most part, with any theological connotations of sin, guilt, or divine retribution. In the majority of countries, Jews have adjusted more or less to their Gentile environment. With the emergence of Israel as a Jewish state on the very site of its ancient but turbulent history, the idea of the Galut in the sense of "Exile" has lost most of its pathos. The ultra-religious, however, still cry out with longing in the synagogue at the close of the prayer-service on the Day of Atonement: "*Leshanah haba'ah bi-Yerushalayim!*" ("Next year in Jerusalem!") But the far more numerous national-minded Jews throughout the world have established close psychological, cultural, and practical ties with the new State of Israel in whose upbuilding they actively participate. Zionists maintain that the "family attachment" between Israel and world Jewry serves as a reassurance to Jews everywhere that they can draw on Israel for at least part of their cultural and spiritual sustenance.

See also ERETZ YISRAEL; FELLOWSHIP IN ISRAEL; UNITY OF ISRAEL; ZIONISM.

DIBBUK. *See* DYBBUK.

DIETARY LAWS (in Hebrew: KASHRUT)

Whereas the word *kasher* or *kosher,* as read in the Biblical text, originally connoted "fit" or "proper" food for consumption, it took on a more specific meaning in the Talmud. There it was employed as the antonym of *terefah* (forbidden) and meant food that was "permitted" by ritual law. In support of these two opposing but unitary concepts of "forbidden" and "permitted," there was developed over a time-span of perhaps more than 2,500 years, a priestly-rabbinic code of dietary laws and regulations that was vast and all inclusive. Thorough familiarity with this dietary code constitutes an essential portion of the rabbi's store of specialized knowledge. In the unique scheme of Jewish life in the medieval ghetto and down to very recent times, the rabbi was occupied much of the time with rendering ritual decisions on what was kasher and what was terefah for the individual households under his religious supervision.

In the view of many critics of the dietary laws, the Jews throughout their history evinced an excessive preoccupation with them. In the scale of religious values, these critics assert, kashrut at worst represents a throwback to the primitive practice of totemism, with its "clean" and "unclean" animals; at best, they say, its ritualistic observance should be only of trivial importance in the context of serious religious values. But to the tradition-minded Jew, the strict observance of the dietary laws is looked upon as an active symbol of Jewish faith and identity, comparable, for example, to circumcision. This estimate of its significance was stated by a Rabbinic Sage almost eighteen centuries ago: "The many rules that regulate the diet of the Jew are intended to test his piety and his love for God."

From the point of view of the traditionalist, the dietary laws are meant without any qualifications to be part of the practical implementation of his belief in Israel's special election to the service of God: "And ye shall be holy unto me; for I the Lord am holy, and have set you apart from the people, that you should be mine." (Leviticus 20:26.) The dietary laws, therefore, must be included among those principal religious folkways which were intended to maintain inviolate the priestly "holiness" of the Jewish people.

Since earliest times, devout Jews have been tormented by the fear of cultural assimilation which might "water down"–or even corrupt–their religious beliefs and the continuity of their identity as Jews. Just as the ancient priestly Scribes and the Talmudic teachers who followed them strove to build a "fence" around the Torah for its preservation, so did they, at the same time, also put up a ritualistic "fence" to guard the existence of the people in their daily thinking, feeling, and practice *as Jews.* Most certainly, among all the "fences" that were put up, the dietary laws, like the practice of circumcision, have proven historically the most formidable and enduring. This is, no doubt, because they involved, on the part of each man, woman, and child, a constant awareness of them throughout the day in the selection, special preparation, cooking, and consumption of food and drink.

Eating and drinking never meant to religious Jews in former times the mere sensual gratification or simple stilling of the pangs of hunger or thirst that they did to other peoples; rather, they constituted a religious rite. This lofty attitude made the Jews even more conscious of their identity. And, naturally, it also gave them the feeling of being "different" from other religions and ethnic groups. The rabbis never seemed to be apologetic or evasive about this attitude, for it was one of the major educational goals of the dietary laws. By means of these laws, they strove to rear up a wall of conscious separation between Jews and the adherents of other religions. When examined objectively, this aim cannot be attributed to any desire for exclusiveness or to any feeling of group superiority or religious chauvinism (as some of the uninformed or malicious have claimed). It needs to be emphasized again and again that the Jews–at least those of former times—considered themselves to be a *dedicated* people. They had a deep conviction that they had been selected by God to serve in the process of history as the human instrument for the fulfillment of his divine plan, not only for the redemption of Israel but of all mankind.

Kosher butcher's sign in Yiddish: "Kosher meat is to be obtained here." Germany, mid-19th century.

It cannot be denied that the unswerving loyalty of the Jews to the practice of the dietary laws had the effect of severely curtailing the social and cultural intercourse between them and non-Jews. Nothing encourages the establishment of friendly relations between individuals more than the experience of eating and drinking together; Rabbinic laws forbade to Jews that sort of social conviviality in the homes of Gentiles out of the certainty that there they would be eating terefah or "forbidden" food. In fact, Jews were prohibited from eating bread that had been baked by a Gentile or even from buying from him wine, milk, and cheese (butter was inexplicably excepted)–foods that could not, of course, be prepared in conformity with the dietary laws.

The reason for the law against breaking bread with non-Jews in their homes was frankly explained in the Talmud: "We should not eat their bread because we may be led thereby to drink their wine. We should not drink their wine because we may be led thereby to intermarry with them, and this will only lead us to worship their gods." But lest this prohibition be considered as representing a "clannish" and "exclusive" attitude towards Gentiles–including Christians, Mohammedans, or any other non-Jews–it should be noted that, during the Middle Ages, the Church Councils became so alarmed (for the very same reasons as the rabbis) by the friendly social relations existing at that time between Jews and Christians, that they restrained the latter, under threat of excommunication and the denial of the Sacrament to them, from any fraternization with Jews. Such "fraternization" included not only eating and drinking with them but even exchanging social visits in their homes.

There was still another major motivation for the introduction of the dietary laws. In a psychological sense, they were meant to serve in the Hellenistic age as a moral discipline. That was a time extravagantly given over to pleasure and sensuality–both of which were values highly prized in the Greco-Roman world. The Rabbis were anxious, by whatever means available, to curb the animal appetites in Jews. Their attitude was that to eat food when hungry or to drink water when thirsty—in other words, to satisfy purely physiologic needs–was just not enough; there had to be a more spiritual motivation for the physical processes. Consequently, they urged upon the faithful the punctilious fulfillment of all the dietary laws and regulations required of every Jew, old and young. This virtually made eating and drinking a form of religious worship, and the "holiness" mood was heightened for the eater when he pronounced the Benediction before eating and recited Grace afterwards.

Seal of shochet (ritual slaughterer). Mannheim, Germany, 1745.

A modified form of this prayer was adapted for Christian use by the Jewish Apostles of Christ, with a similar intention, of course. It should be remembered that, during the first century of Christianity, surface distinctions between Christians and other Jews were not too apparent; Paul of Tarsus, himself born and raised a believing Jew, called (in Acts of the Apostles 21:25) on all converted "Gentiles" (i.e., Romans, Greeks, and other non-Jewish Christians) "to keep themselves from things [animals] offered to idols, and from blood, and from strangled [animals] . . ." Only later, when Christianity began its program of self-purgation from Jewish beliefs and practices, did Christians abandon the observance of the dietary laws. Mohammed, who also adopted many Jewish religious beliefs and customs, declared the pig to be terefah for all true believers.

As long as the Jews of Christian Europe were forcibly isolated in ghettos (beginning with the thirteenth century), the practice of kashrut, down to all its minor details, was scrupulously followed. After they had been accorded status as human beings under the Declaration of the Rights of Man, issued by the National Assembly of the French Revolution in 1789, the abolition of the compulsory ghetto, and with it, the pariah isolation of the Jews, followed rapidly. Yet, strange to relate, although they were now free to leave the wretched ghettos that had served as their communal prisons, they nevertheless continued to huddle there in as close coagulation as ever. No doubt the major reason for this was the desire of the Jews to maintain uninterrupted their religious-cultural group-life, but the communal conditions under which they would be able to obtain kosher meat and to observe the dietary laws was not the least of their considerations in continuing to live close together.

The legal, political, and cultural emancipation of the Jews, which made broad incursions into the traditional patterns of Jewish life in most countries of Europe beginning with the nineteenth century, also effected a steady decline in the observance of the dietary laws. Among the factors responsible for this change, without a doubt, were the progressively loosening ties of religion–mainly due to the secularist spirit of the times, which was in turn motivated by intellectual skepticism and scientific materialism. In the fold of the Jewish religion itself, a deliberate movement away from traditional beliefs and Orthodox practices grew up as Reform or Liberal Judaism. Its position with regard to kashrut was stated bluntly by one of its leaders in the United States, Rabbi David Philipson: "In this country, with our free environment, traditional *Shulchan Aruch* Judaism (i.e., ritual observance) has no place."

The rationalist scientific attack on kashrut was led by Salomon Reinach, the noted archaeologist and historian whose field was Greco-Roman culture. In an impassioned plea to his fellow Jews late in the nineteenth century, he urged that they abandon the dietary laws because, in his opinion, these were merely survivals of practices in "primitive barbarism."

The dispute over the rational validity of the dietary laws also spread to the field of medical science. Even though some eminent medical authorities, including Waldemar Haffkine, who did pioneer research in bubonic plague and cholera in the late nineteenth century, commended the laws of kashrut on hygienic grounds, the majority medical view, however, has seen no such merit in them. Nonetheless, there are a number of health experts today who consider highly praiseworthy the strict requirement for the shochet (ritual slaughterer) to examine the carcass of every animal he has killed for any signs of disease and other pathological conditions. They find additional merit in the fact that meat attested to be kosher by the leaden seal of the mashgiach (the kashrut supervisor) is required to be consumed within a matter of days after the animal is slaughtered, thereby preventing health hazards that result from eating meat which has spoiled.

Under the conditions of decentralized and diffused Jewish group existence in cities and towns today, observance of the dietary laws presents many difficulties–in some ways, even hardships–and for those determined to practice them without compromise, sacrifices, as well. For one thing, a shochet is not always available. In many places it is not possible to obtain or even "import" kosher meat. The difficulties are multiplied for those Jews who live away from home or who travel. Thus the complex and ever shifting character of modern urban living has, in effect, worked not for the strengthening of kashrut observance but, on the contrary, for its gradual weakening. Nonetheless, there are millions of Jews today who still observe the dietary laws to greater or lesser extent.

See also ANIMALS, CLEAN AND UNCLEAN; MEAT, SALTING OF; MEAT AND MILK; SHECHITAH; SHOCHET; TEREFAH.

DIN TORAH. *See* BET DIN.

"DISCIPLES OF THE WISE." *See* TALMUD, THE.

DISPERSION. *See* DIASPORA.

DISPUTATIONS, RELIGIOUS

"Tournaments for God and Faith." One of the chief harassments to which Jews had been subjected by the Church Militant since the fourth century was the unflagging effort by Christians to convert them. There were many sincere though fanatical churchmen and rulers who believed that in the conversion of the Jews, the Church would achieve one of its great spiritual triumphs and in that way would demonstrate to all of mankind the superiority of the Christian faith over the Jewish. Even the most implacable enemy of the Jews, Pope Innocent III (1198–1216), declared his conviction that "as wanderers [*see* WANDERING JEW] ought they to remain upon the earth, until their countenance be filled with shame and they seek the name of Jesus Christ our Lord."

Yet the more the Church tried to convert them, the more passionately the great majority of Jews clung to the religion of their fathers. This state of affairs persisted for centuries after the Middle Ages. Almost twenty years after his benign attitude toward the Jews had made his opponents in the Church wince, Martin Luther, who had since then changed his tune, observed with exasperation: "It is as easy to convert the Jews as the Devil himself!"

There were three principal ways in which the Church and (Christian) State worked for the conversion of the Jews. One was by means of religious disputations ordered by Church or ruler to be held publicly between rabbis and theologians of the Church; another was by means of conversionist sermons delivered by Christian preachers in synagogues and in churches, with the attendance of all Jews above twelve years of age made compulsory; and the third method–probably the most effective–was by the simple expedient of violence or the threat of violence, namely, death.

Characteristic of their age, the religious disputations between rabbis and priests were designated by the medieval Church as "Tournaments for God and Faith." But the title had only ironic implications, for these so-called tournaments held but little of the element of chivalry, the position of the ideological combatants being so flagrantly unequal. Almost always "the verdict" of the judges (variously they were pope, king, prince, prelate, or theologians) went against the Jewish debaters, who were made sport of for the entertainment of those present. Sometimes the verdict carried the most adverse consequences for the practice of the Jewish religion, for the study of the Talmud, for the Jews personally on "trial", and for the community of their fellow Jews living in Christendom.

Among all of these disptuations, several stand out as astonishing public performances which had consequences of harmful historic import for the Jews living in Christian countries. In the year 1240, the king of France ordered a public debate on the Talmud and its alleged anti-Christian teachings to be held between Nicolas Donin, a self-styled "learned" apostate from the Jewish faith, and four eminent rabbis of the country, among whom were the noted Talmudists Rabbi Yechiel of Paris and Rabbi Moses of Coucy. Present at the disputation were the queen, the leading prelates of the Church, and many theologians and members of the royal court. Vainly, Rabbi Yechiel strove to expose Donin's accusations as inventions and slanders. In the end, the Talmud was condemned as an evil, lying work and ordered burned by the Dominican friars in a public ceremony which had all the pomp and drama of a great Church spectacle.

To leave no loophole for the Jews, Donin persuaded Pope Gregory IX–who, as popes during the Middle Ages went, was moderate in his attitude toward Jews–to issue a bull for the burning of the Talmud *everywhere*, and to appoint ecclesiastical inquisitions and censors over other Jewish writings in order to ferret out their "heresies" and "anti-Christian" bias. This institutional practice by the Church was a constant source of grief to Jews for centuries.

Spain, too, initiated religious disputations, but without the excessive fanaticism that accompanied such public debates in the less enlightened countries of Western and Central Europe. In June, 1253, Pablo Christiani, a converted Jewish scholar, prevailed upon the king of Aragon to order Nachmanides (Moses ben Nachman), the famed Talmudist and philosopher, to dispute with him before the royal court and clergy in Barcelona. From the report left behind by Nachmanides, it is plain that he was granted full freedom of speech. So courteous and dignified was his bearing and so sincere his defense, that in presenting him with a gift at the conclusion of the disputation, the king declared that never before had he heard "an unjust cause so nobly defended." Nev-

Disputation between Moses (symbolizing the Synagogue, i.e., Judaism) and St. Peter (representing the Church, or Christianity). Moses is shown wearing the identifying yellow circle and the Judenhut*–the "Jew's hat." Mid-13th century. (Seminary for priests, Bruges, Belgium.)*

The apostate persecutor of the Jews, Johannes Pfefferkorn.

Public disputation between rabbis and Christian theologians. (Woodcut, Germany, 16th century.)

Contra hebreos retinentes li
bros in quibus aliquid con
tra fidem catholicam no
tetur vel scribatur.

ertheless, the Dominicans succeeded in having Nachmanides banished from Spain for blasphemy; he fled for asylum to Jerusalem, where he died.

But with the passage of time, the relatively gentle intellectual climate in Spain changed. The blood-lusting Dominican preacher of Valencia, Vincent Ferrer (who was later sainted), prevailed upon the king of Aragon at the turn of the fifteenth century to "invite" the most learned among the rabbis in the kingdom to a public disputation in Tortosa; the principal subject was to be whether the Messiah had already arrived. Presiding over the debate was (anti-) Pope Benedict XIII of Avignon, and present were also many cardinals, bishops, and a vast audience. Taking part in the disputation was the pope's personal physician–a former rabbi and a convert to Christianity. Among the twenty-two Jewish defenders was the noted Talmudist and philosopher Joseph Albo. This was probably the most remarkable disputation of its kind ever held. It had sixty-nine sessions and lasted twenty-one months.

Naturally, the Jewish disputants were declared the ignominious losers by Benedict XIII. He bade them accept Christian baptism, but this they promptly declined to do. Angered by their refusal, he placed a ban on the study of the Talmud.

See also CONVERSION OF JEWS; KIDDUSH HA-SHEM; KOL NIDRE; MARRANOS AND THE INQUISITION.

DIVORCE (in Hebrew: GET)

The laws in the Bible limited the Jewish woman's social and religious role to the home. While they undoubtedly provided her with certain protections that the women of most other ancient peoples did not possess, they nevertheless placed her in a helpless and dependent position in relation to her husband. In a very literal sense, he was her "lord and master"; he could divorce her at will. The law explicitly stated: ". . . if she find no favor in his eye, because he hath found some unseemly thing in her, . . . he writeth her a bill of divorcement, and give it in her hand and sendeth her out of his house." (Deuteronomy 24:1.)

This was precisely what the Patriarch Abraham did, although in the historic period in which he was presumed to have lived, no bill of divorcement probably was required of him when he sent Hagar and their small son Ishmael out of his encampment to perish in the wilderness. Whether the climax to this cruel episode in the twenty-first chapter of Genesis was written by a latter-day Scriptural moralist we do not know. But certain it is that the Bible story is astonishingly turned into a morality play in which Abraham, although revered as "the first Hebrew," is castigated by implication for

Disputation (in writing) between Johannes Pfefferkorn, a Jewish renegade (the attacker), and the great Christian humanist, Johann Reuchlin (the defender), of the Talmud. Pfefferkorn (left) is depicted holding up the banner of the Christian faith while Reuchlin (right) is shown talking with two tongues (i.e., arguing like a hypocrite). (From Pfefferkorn's Streydtpeuchlin, *1516.)* (TOP)

Papal bull issued by Pope Julius III ordering the burning of all copies of the Talmud. Rome, May 29, 1554. (CENTER)

Polish clerics throwing confiscated Hebrew religious works into the fire. (From Jacob Emden's Sefer Shimmush, *1762.)* (BOTTOM LEFT)

Disputation between a rabbi and a saint of the Church. (From the illustrated Sachsenspiegel *Manuscript of Dresden, 1220* C.E.) (BOTTOM RIGHT)

his heartless act. For God himself sends a succoring angel to the woman who was cast aside to make divine amends to her for the human wrong that had been inflicted on her and her innocent child.

Already, in that early folk memory of Israel, is audible the "still, small voice" of the Hebraic conscience, responsive to injustice and to the unhappy condition of the unwanted wife. From this incident, and from a variety of others found in religious literature, the safe generalization can be drawn that Jewish *practice* with regard to the wife was at all times far more humane and protective than were the laws themselves. These latter were carved in rigid permanence on the Rabbinic statute books despite the fact that changing practice had far outstripped them.

Not long before the Return from the Captivity in Babylonia, the Prophet Malachi took Jewish husbands sharply to task for the arbitrary and cruel way they exercised their masculine right to the bill of divorcement: "The Lord hath been witness between thee and the wife of thy youth . . . she is thy companion and the wife of thy coverant." (Malachi 2:15.)

The moral implications in Malachi's rebuke were ultimately reflected in the restrictions that were enacted during the Second Commonwealth. They were intended to make the basic laws on divorce less intolerable for the wife and more discouraging for her high-handed mate. Divorce was made unprofitable for restless husbands since it first required them to return the dowry the wife had brought them, and also to pay her the marriage settlement that had been agreed upon in the ketubah (the marriage contract).

There were only two absolute grounds for the divorce of a wife by her husband: infidelity or childlessness. The two great rival Rabbinic schools—those of Hillel and Shammai—were at loggerheads on the subject of divorce during the second century C.E. in Judea. The astringent, "zealous" School of Shammai was dead set against divorce on any ground except infidelity, preferring to follow the old Israelite tribal mores. The School of Hillel, on the contrary, was accommodating and easygoing. It advanced this legal proposition: "A wife may be divorced by her husband even if he has nothing against her other than that she spoiled the cooking." To this, the usually sedate Rabbinic Sage Akiba, with unaccustomed levity for him, added: "A husband may even divorce his wife for the sole reason that he has found someone who is prettier than she."

When the subject of what constituted "infidelity" was brought forward, Akiba quite seriously expressed the view that any wife about whose doings there was much scandalous gossip should be divorced even were no proof of infidelity furnished. His Rabbinic colleague, Yochanan ben Nuri, was aghast. "If we accept your opinion, Akiba," he retorted, "not a single daughter of Abraham will be safe with her husband!" How could one proceed legally merely on idle or malicious gossip? he challenged. Didn't the Torah lay down this guideline for the judge: "At the mouth of two witnesses, or at the mouth of three witnesses, shall a matter be established"? (Deuteronomy 19:15.)

Most tragic of all in Jewish life was the lot of the barren woman, for there was nothing to change her condition nor to assuage her sorrow. If after ten years of marriage she remained childless, then her husband, bound by the explicit obligations of his religion to "increase and multiply," was expected to put her aside. To make the blow to the bruised feelings of the rejected wife seem less damaging, her husband, with a fanfare of verbal gallantry from the Rabbinic judges, was declared to be "unworthy of being built up by

Hebrew get (bill of divorce) dated 1088 C.E. *(Discovered in the Cairo Genizah.)*

Divorce Proceedings. 1. Drawing up the get. 2. Reading it aloud. 3. Throwing the get to the husband. 4. Husband throwing the get to the wife. (From Bodenschatz, Kirchliche Verfassung, *Germany, 1748.)*

her," i.e., unworthy of having her bear him children to continue his line. The possibility of remarriage for a wife divorced for childlessness was absolutely nil, since it was prohibited by Rabbinic law. One can well imagine the anguish and despair in the cry of Rachel to her husband, the Patriarch Jacob: "Give me children or else I die!" It was probably often preferable for the childless woman to die than to live unwanted in the world.

There are many moral dicta by the Rabbinic Sages reported in the Talmud. These urge the husband to exercise forebearance and patience in order to preserve family peace, even if he has to contend with a shrewish wife: "There is a substitute for everything, except for the wife of one's youth. . . . A man can find happiness only in his first wife . . . God's very altar sheds tears when a man divorces the wife of his youth."

More than a thousand years later, in the Rhineland town of Worms, Rabbi Eleazar ben Yehudah (*d.* 1238) picked up the moralizing theme of his Rabbinic forerunners and pleaded with the Jewish husband of his day: "When your wife makes your life unendurable for you, there is danger that you will begin to hate her. Then you must pray to the Lord not to give you another wife, but instead to return your wife's heart to you once more in love."

In modern times, the importance of the religious divorce granted by a rabbinical court, except in the State of Israel, has vastly diminished. In our secular society, where there is a complete separation of church and state, the law of the land is paramount. The civil divorce is the only one that is recognized officially. Of course, the traditional Jew who seeks a divorce is not content to have merely a legal dissolution of his marriage; he also wants the releasing sanction of his religion for it. Under reasonable circumstances this is granted to him or to his wife without too great difficulty.

In the old ghetto in former times, when the deterrents of public opinions against divorce were many, and the moral pressures from the rabbi for reconciliation were persistent, the incidence of divorce was small. The Jewish family remained intact to a remarkable degree. But with civil emancipation and the cultural assimilation that inevitably followed, Jews became exposed to the same disruptive social and economic stresses that operated in society generally. From year to year, as in every other segment of the population, the number of divorces among Jews has steadily increased.

See also CHALITZAH; FAMILY, THE JEWISH; FAMILY RELATIONS, TRADITIONAL PATTERNS OF; MARRIAGE; MARRIAGE AND SEX; WEDDING CUSTOMS; WOMAN, THE TREATMENT OF.

DOCTORS. *See* ARABIC-JEWISH "GOLDEN AGE"; HEALERS.

DOCTRINES IN JUDAISM

It is a cause for wonderment that, despite the fierce conservatism Judaism often displayed in matters of religious tradition and the even more marked legalistic rigidity which for long periods of time governed the performance of its numerous rites, it remains perhaps the least dogmatic of the world's religions. How explain this paradox?

It is common knowledge that in Judaism are found no such iron-ribbed articles of faith as, for instance, in Christianity. The Nicene Creed, the Athanasian Creed, the more familiar Apostles' Creed (all composed in the early centuries of the Church), and even the much later Augsburg Confession of the Lutheran Reformation, the Thirty-nine Articles of the Anglican-Episcopal Church, and the Westminster Confession of the Calvinists (Presbyterian)–all aimed to keep the doctrines of their faith authoritative, precise, and unchanging. The objective of each, without exception, was clear: to forestall and silence all potential heresies and non conformism.

It was quite different with regard to the religion of the Jews. Admittedly, its heretics and schismatics were often treated with undue severity–even, not infrequently, with inhumanity–as the melancholy annals about Jewish sects, heretics, and intellectual skeptics make abundantly plain. The threat of excommunication (in Hebrew: *cherem*) always hung ominously over the heads of those who sought to think, believe, and conduct themselves according to the dictates of their conscience and in consonance with the truth as they understood it.

For centuries, beginning with the Middle Ages, in Europe it was a quite common practice for individual rabbis–or, sometimes, a whole group of rabbis–to pronounce the dread formula of anathema against anyone–whether rabbinical or lay scholar–whose doctrinal views or, even, departure from traditional ritual observance, outraged their religious sensibilities. Yet such acts of excommunication were never considered by other religious leaders to be binding or final as a judgment. The classic example of this is furnished by the experience of Maimonides (1135–1204), the foremost Jewish religious thinker of medieval and subsequent times. He succeeded in stirring up a hornet's nest of bigotry with the progressive and rationalistic views he postulated on such doctrinal matters as the Resurrection and Immortality, and on the nature of prophecy. These ran counter, in so many fundamental ways, to sanctified traditional beliefs, that during his lifetime and for several centuries after, his writings were attacked and reviled by certain rabbis as heresies. They were even placed under rabbinical ban in some places. Nonetheless, the religious authority of Maimonides remained undisputed in Jewry during his day and in the centuries that followed. The general reverence in which his genius was held is well illustrated by the charming folk-saying: "From Moses [our Teacher] to Moses [Maimonides] there has been no Moses like Moses!"

The intellectual right to dissent, even from cardinal theological doctrines, was tacitly recognized in Jewish thinking as far back as the time of the Sages of the Talmud. Of course, this liberality of thought was not at all general, nor was it uniform. In various countries, during different historic epochs, and depending on the religious-cultural level of Jewish life, deviators from accepted theological dogma, doctrinal belief, or even ritual practice, were publicly execrated and harshly punished. During the seventeenth century in Amsterdam, the implacable religious fundamentalism that tried to silence their free thinking with the pronouncement of excommunication, drove the science-oriented skeptic, Uriel da Costa (1585–1640), to suicide, and the outstanding philosopher, Baruch Spinoza (1632–77), into banishment from the Jewish community. Yet, one must hasten to add, during much of the time in the history of Judaism, there was apparent a great reluctance on the part of the religious teachers, conditioned to tolerance by their gentle and humane views, to freeze the stream of religious ideas into unalterable doctrine or to punish drastically those who dissented from them.

There is found, in the rabbinic writings created over a time-span of almost two thousand years, much evidence to prove the existence of this mellow religious climate in Jewish life. For example, in Judea, toward the end of its existence as a Jewish state, there took place many fierce disputes on religious doctrine between the two strongest religious-social parties: the conservative Sadducees and the liberal Pharisees. They clashed over the acceptance of such central theological doctrines as the intervention of Providence in human affairs and the immortality of the *body* leading to its resurrection at the End of Days. The Sadducees were skeptical materialists; the Pharisees were ardent supporters of these beliefs.

Similarly, there were interminable intellectual debates during the Middle Ages carried on between the rationalists and the mystics, with the Aristotelian and Neo-Platonic interpreters of Judaism pitted against the anti-philosophical traditionalists and pietists who conceived the Jewish religion to be a body of divinely revealed truths and law, of which the Torah was the sole repository.

The absence of a fixed creed—of a canonical body of doctrinal teachings in the religion of the Jews—is perhaps the most convincing proof of its comparatively undogmatic character. This fact may appear to be paradoxical when observed against the multitudinous laws and regulations which governed the observance of religious rites and ceremonies among the Jews of Russia and Poland since the sixteenth century.

It is no exaggeration to state that, ever since the Pharisee Sage Hillel the Elder taught Jewish ethics to entranced classes of students in Jerusalem in the opening decades of the first century C.E., repeated attempts were made by the Rabbinic teachers—all men of the people and, therefore, concerned with the simplification and popularization of religious knowledge—to reduce the bewildering number of dogmas and principles of the Torah to their ultimate quintessentials. This, no doubt, is what Hillel had in mind when he was asked for an epigrammatic condensation of the entire Torah—and to make his statement as brief as if he were "standing on one foot." The teacher of ethics replied with his celebrated formulation of the Golden Rule (adopted by Jesus in a slightly modified form, one generation later): *"And what is hateful to you, do not do to your fellow men."* To this, Hillel added his own astonishing estimate: "The rest [of the Torah] is merely commentary."

In the years that followed, other teachers of ethics, as recorded in the Talmud, presented their own selections of what they considered the quintessential doctrines of the Torah. Ben Zoma chose the Shema—the affirmation of the unity of God: "Hear, O Israel, the Lord our God, the Lord is One." Citing the words of the Prophet Amos, Simlai selected the Scriptural exhortation: "Seek me and ye shall live." Nachman referred to the Prophet Habakkuk: "And the righteous shall live by his faith." Bar Kappara asked rhetorically: "Which passage contains the essence of the whole Torah?" And he answered his own question: "That which in Proverbs reads: 'In all thy ways acknowledge Him, and He will make level thy path.' "

The selection most beloved among Jews of later times was also the briefest: Rabbi Akiba ben Joseph's "Love thy neighbor as thyself."

But certain principles of religious belief did, nevertheless, crystallize over the centuries, and until the modern period, these were universally accepted by Jews as fundamental and incontestable. It was Maimonides who set himself the difficult task of selecting, formulating, and codifying these, hoping to offset somewhat the almost irresistible pressures—including the threat of death—which were brought to bear upon the Jews of his day to force their conversion to Christianity or Mohammedanism. He wished this abbreviated code of Thirteen Articles to serve as "A Guide to the Perplexed," and to those Jews confused or made wavering by the arguments of church and mosque for apostasy from their faith, as a firm avowal of their own people's beliefs. One could very well say that they came nearest to an approximation of a well-defined creed for the Jewish religion.

THE THIRTEEN ARTICLES

I. I firmly believe that the Creator, blessed be His name, is both Creator and Ruler of all created beings, and that He alone had made, doth make, and ever will make all works of nature.

II. I firmly believe that the Creator, blessed be His name, is One, and no Unity is like His in any form, and that He alone is our God who was, is, and ever will be.

III. I firmly believe that the Creator, blessed be His name, is not a body, and no corporeal relations apply to Him, and that there exists nothing that has any similarity to Him.

IV. I firmly believe that the Creator, blessed be His name, was the first and will also be the last.

V. I firmly believe that the Creator, blessed be His name, is alone worthy of being worshiped, and that no other being is worthy of our worship.

VI. I firmly believe that all the words of the Prophets are true.

VII. I firmly believe that the prophecy of Moses, our Teacher (peace be upon him!) was true, and that he was the Chief of the Prophets, both of those that preceded him and of those that followed him.

VIII. I firmly believe that the Law which we possess now is the same which hath been given to Moses our Teacher (peace be upon him!).

IX. I firmly believe that this Law will not be changed, and that there will be no other Law (or Dispensation) given by the Creator, blessed be His name.

X. I firmly believe that the Creator, blessed be His name, knoweth all the actions of men and all their thoughts, as it is said: "He that fashioneth the hearts of them all; that considereth all their works." (Psalm 33:15.)

XI. I firmly believe that the Creator, blessed be He, rewardeth those who keep his commandments and punisheth those who transgress his commandments.

XII. I firmly believe in the coming of the Messiah, and although he may tarry, I daily hope for his coming.

XIII. I firmly believe that there will take place a revival of the dead at a time which will please the Creator, blessed be His name, and exalted His memorial forever and ever!

About the middle of the fourteenth century, the liturgical poet of Rome, Daniel ben Judah, paraphrased in Hebrew verse the Thirteen Articles of Maimonides. So immediate was the acceptance by the people of the poem "Yigdal," that it was entered into all the prayer books for the festivals, among the Ashkenazim as well as the Sefaradim. It also received a number of musical settings, and became one of the noblest hymns in the liturgy of the synagogue.

See also EPIKOROS; ETHICAL VALUES, JEWISH; EXCOMMUNICATION; GOLDEN RULE, THE.

DOWRY (in both Hebrew and Yiddish: NADAN; derived from the Aramaic NEDUNIA)

Yemenite bride wearing her "dowry."

The dowry is the marriage portion, whether of money, land, house, jewels, or clothing, that a bride brings to her groom. A modern euphemism refers to it delicately as a "wedding present."

Although the custom of dowering the bride was quite general among other peoples, it became fixed among Jews only toward the close of the Second Temple period. At that time, laws regulating it were laid down by the Rabbinic teachers in the Talmud, but later religious authorities modified these with other rulings.

The institution of the Jewish dowry system, examined superficially, could easily be misunderstood as being merely a mercenary arrangement—a "deal." Viewed historically, the opposite conclusion can be reached. The dowry was designed principally as a prop for Jewish national survival. Without it, it would not have been possible for poor girls, the mothers of future generations, to be married, for the young men, with few exceptions, were themselves too poor to support wives on their own limited means. Furthermore, Jewish tradition held that helping a poor girl to marry with even a small dowry was an aid to morality as well as an act of simple humanity.

Rabbinical law required that a father give his daughter at the time of her marriage a part of his possessions, however small, to help her and the youth she wed to establish a household of their own. The minimum money value of the dowry was set at fifty zuzim, a sum barely sufficient for acquiring a few indispensable furnishings or articles of clothing. And when a parent was so poor that he could not provide his daughter with even fifty zuzim, then the communal funds were drawn upon to make up the difference, for it was considered heartless, as the Talmudic folk-saying had it, to allow the poor girl "to sit until her hair turned gray."

The calamities that befell the Jews of Europe during the Crusades led to the formation in every Jewish community of a benevolent society that had as its objective the furnishing of dowries to indigent brides. Unfortunately, money was scarce and poor brides were numerous. In 1618, such a society, active in the city of Rome, had available minimal funds, sufficient to dower only twelve brides at two hundred scudi each. Lots were drawn for these, and those who were unlucky, went away weeping.

Almost two thousand years ago, the Rabbinic sages were already mindful of the corrupting possibilities inherent in dowries. One of them warned: "He who marries for money will have wicked children." A later Yiddish folk-saying expressed similar apprehension: "Dowry and Inheritance go into partnership with the Devil." The Mishnah relates how in Jerusalem, before its final destruction, anxious fathers, with cunning aforethought, would dangle the promise of large dowries temptingly before prospective sons-in-law, only to renege on the promise after the wedding. Therefore, the gloomy view of the Talmud: "There can be no marriage settlement without a quarrel."

There is no question but that, with the deterioration of traditional values and practices in modern Jewish life, the dowry system among certain members of the Jewish middle class (just as among their non-Jewish counterparts) became quite corrupt. Mercenary matches, arranged by the shadchan–the marriage-broker working for his fee on a percentage basis (of the dowry)–resulted in much sordid haggling and mutual deception. Happily, however, the enlightenment and economic equality that Jews now enjoy in many lands no longer require the continuance of the customary dowry for poor brides. Likely as not, their husbands marry them for love alone.

One ancient Talmudic wit referred to girls who wed for love as being married "by the hair of their heads."

See also DIVORCE; MARRIAGE.

DREYFUS CASE, THE

It is worth noting that the French national soil in which the seed of the Dreyfus Case germinated had for a long time been carefully prepared by a coalition of monarchists, clericalists, and high army officers. The monarchists had suffered by the abolition of the throne in 1871 and its supplantation by the Third Republic; the clericalists had suffered a setback when the separation of the Church from the State was proclaimed by a secularist government, and the army officers had suffered in their ambitions because, following the disastrous defeat of the French Army at Sedan in 1870, during the Franco-Prussian War, their obsessive dream of *revanche* against the Prussians was dissipated by the pacific policies of the Republican government.

The emotional amalgam, a well as the pretext for coalescing any potential opposition among the French people against the Third Republic, was provided by the Jews of France. There was nothing new or strange in this choice, for since time immemorial, the Jewish bogey had been raised, sometimes to *attract* and at other times to *distract* from troubling conditions. The Jewish people had thus readily earned the distinction of serving as "the scapegoat of history."

At the time when the Dreyfus furor was raised, in 1894, Jews in all of France numbered less than 75,000–a mere fraction of 1 per cent of the population. But what proved grist for the anti-Semitic mill was the fact that Napoleon's policy of *carrières aux talents* (careers for the gifted) had made it possible for a relatively small number of the Jews in France to achieve success in the professions, the arts, commerce, government, and banking. For this they were never forgiven by the anti-Semites. Consequently, during the Panama Canal scandal (named by the reactionaries "the Republican Scandal"), which broke into public view in 1888, certain shady financial transactions, involving a number of cabinet ministers, leading members of the Chamber of Deputies, and bankers, came to light. The mere fact that several

Captain Alfred Dreyfus, who inadvertently became the victim of the French monarchist-militarist-clericalist plot to use anti-Jewish prejudice to overthrow the Republic of France at the end of the 19th century.

of the bankers implicated were Jews was sufficient to raise the familiar hue and cry by the anti-Semites that the Jewish capitalists and money-changers were dominating the Republic and were corrupting French statesmen and lawmakers with their gold.

This has always been the singular method employed by anti-Semites: to pounce upon any act of wrongdoing (whether actual or merely alleged) of an individual Jew, and then lay the guilt at the door of *all* the Jews. This kind of logic—leaping from the particular to the general—was well illustrated in a conversation once engaged in by Alfonso XI of Castile (*c.* 1350) with a Jew. The king had deplored the fact that the conduct of the Jews in business was "reprehensible." To which the Jew replied by repeating the popular Spanish saying: "If one mouse eats the cheese, people say: 'The mice have eaten it.' "

L'Affaire Dreyfus, in all of its convoluted elements, in plot and counterplot, catapulting from climax to climax, until it achieved the cumulative melodramatic character of a gigantic murder mystery, is too well known to require a detailed account of it here. Every history of France and every encyclopedia contains for the reader interested in all its details the factual narrative of the case, lacking perhaps only the historical and social insights that are needed for a proper understanding of its genesis, its unfoldment, and also its denouement.

The story, in brief, is that of Captain Alfred Dreyfus, a sedate and conservative captain of artillery and also a Jew, who suddenly found himself pulled out of the ranks by his superiors and charged with selling military secrets to the Germans. Precipitately, he was court-martialed, found guilty, and branded a traitor to France. As he was led off to a lifetime of penal servitude on Devil's Island, he cried out: "*Je suis innocent! Vive la France!*" ("I am innocent! Long live France!")

All France applauded: A traitor had been caught and properly punished. The reactionaries, led by the arch anti-Semite Eduard Drumont, the editor of *La Libre Parole* ("Free Speech") made a Roman holiday of the occasion. Dreyfus' conviction proved what they had alleged all along: that the Jews were traitorous by nature, that they dominated and corrupted the life of the nation, and that, if their grip was not loosened, they would soon destroy it.

But some time later, quite by accident, the Chief of the Army Intelligence Bureau, Colonel Picquart, examined certain incriminating documents (the so-called *bordereau*) alleged to have been in Dreyfus' handwriting, and he came to the conclusion that they were forgeries; that, in fact, they had been written by a certain Major Esterhazy, a notoriously debauched officer.

In the line of duty, as he understood it, Picquart reported his discovery to the Chief of the Army General Staff, General Boisdeffre, and to the Minister of War, General Billot. How amazed he was when they curtly ordered him to drop the matter at once! He began to suspect the existence of some sort of plot, but exactly what its nature was he could not guess. Once more he felt it his duty to press for a re-examination of the findings of the court-martial. As if in answer to his efforts, he was immediately removed as Chief of Intelligence and packed off to a dangerous outpost in Tunis, where a rebellion of Arab tribesmen was taking place. Actually Picquart, and not Dreyfus, was the real hero of this tale.

But from this point on, Picquart's scruples of right and conscience were picked up by an increasingly influential section of the French people that was Republican by conviction, including the novelist Émile Zola, and Jean Jaurès, the leader of the Socialists. To drown out their clamor for the reopening of the case, the anti-Semites launched a "patriotic" series of counterattacks. They branded all *Dreyfusards* as traitors to France and calumniators "of the honor of the army." They worked frenziedly to build up a popular hysteria. One religious order even published a daily newspaper, *La Croix* ("The Cross"), in which it relentlessly attacked Dreyfus and all the Jews.

As in a well-ordered melodrama, the plot thickened, the cast of characters multiplied a hundredfold, and the incidents took on fantastic ramifications. Major Esterhazy, upon Picquart's insistence, was court-martialed but acquitted with an ovation; in his turn, Colonel Picquart was imprisoned; his successor, Colonel Henry, then committed suicide, after first confessing his part as a forger in the conspiracy. And to cap the climax, Major Esterhazy himself did an about-face, confessed his guilt, and escaped to Austria. Dreyfus was then fetched from Devil's Island, re-tried, and ultimately freed. As it happens to the hero in every good melodrama, Colonel Picquart became a national hero, was promoted to high rank by the President of the Republic, and then appointed Minister of War.

But the lessons of the Dreyfus Case were, in retrospect, not lost on thinking Frenchmen. They realized that the Jewish factor in the scandal had been purely incidental—a mere diversion, a peg on which to hang a gigantic conspiracy—itself traitorous and unconscionable—by the royalists, the generals, and the clericalists. Hatred for the Jew being an everlastingly inflammable emotion, it had been cunningly utilized by them as the catalyst for a counterrevolution for destroying the Republic and restoring the monarchy that had been abolished in 1871.

See also ANTI-SEMITISM; THE "RACIAL PURITY" MYTH; CHRISTIANS, SERVITUDE OF JEWS TO; CHURCH AND PERSECUTION; MONEYLENDERS; NAZIS, THE; PERSECUTION IN "MODERN" DRESS; SEPARATISM, JEWISH.

DROSHO. *See* SERMON.

DRUNKENNESS AMONG JEWS. *See* INTOXICATION.

DUCHAN, DUCHANEN. *See* PRIESTLY BLESSING.

DYBBUK (DIBBUK) (Hebrew s., meaning a "cleaving to," an "attaching [itself]"; thus, a sinful soul that has taken "possession" of another living body; pl. DYBBUKIM [DIBBUKIM]; GILGUL, GILGULIM had approximately the same meaning).

The belief that the soul of man "transmigrates" from its own body after death into another human body—or even into an animal, fish, bird, insect, tree, or stone—is as old as all primitive animism. Even highly advanced religions have been unable to resist its allure.

Historically, the notion of metempsychosis or transmigration (in Hebrew: *gilgul*), must already have been in general currency among the Jews in the Maccabean Age. That was a time of religious syncretism and cultural diffusion among all the peoples living within the orbit of Hellenism in the Near and Middle East. Where the belief regarding the "wandering" of the soul after death originated, is impossible to tell. The Egyptians subscribed to it; in the Brahman and Buddhist religions it served as a central doctrine; it was a characteristic of the Greek "mystery religions" of Orphism and Pythagoreanism; and it was also fundamental to the Zoroastrian and Mithra cults. These last two left the impress of many of their beliefs on the numerous Jewish communities in Babylonia and Persia. The neo-Platonic philosopher Porphyry (third century) observed that the topmost rank of Zoroastrian Magi or Wise Men "neither kill nor eat any living thing, but practice the long established abstinence from animal food. For in all the highest grades [of Magi] the doctrine of metempsychosis is held, which also is apparent in the mysteries of Mithra."

Now here is the remarkable thing: notwithstanding the fact that nowhere in the Bible nor in the Talmud is there any assertion that the Jews believed in the transmigration of the soul after death (the Rabbinical authorities, being rationalists, were severely opposed to this notion, considering it a superstitution and an expression of idolatry) the belief must, nevertheless, have persisted in the thinking of the mystical sectaries and the common folk. This is strongly suggested by the related fact that the Jewish Apostles in the Gospels ascribed to Jesus the magical power of "casting out" evil spirits (devils or demons) that had taken "possession" of certain living persons. And throughout the history of mankind, a person suffering from mental illness has been said to be "possessed" by an evil spirit.

The concept of gilgul was first developed as a religious doctrine among the Jews by the early Cabalists of medieval Spain and the Provence. It was moralistic in essence: The sins one committed in life had to be expiated for after death by the soul in a "wandering" and torment. The duration of the spiritual odyssey and the degree of suffering were determined by the gravity of one's sins. The soul was not permitted to return to the Infinite Source from whence it came until its period of purgation *on earth* was completed. And so it was forced to wander along its predetermined course, from one body into another, dwelling in an animal or even in an inanimate object until it had returned at long last to its pristine state of purity. "All souls are subject to transmigration," says the medieval "scripture" of the Cabalists, the Zohar, "and men do not know the ways of the Holy One, blessed be He! . . . They are ignorant of the many transmigrations and secret probations which they have to undergo, and of the number of souls and spirits which enter into this world and which do not return to the palace of the Heavenly King. . . ."

Oddly, the doctrine of transmigration as atonement for the sins one has committed on earth was extended by the Cabalists of sixteenth-century Safed, in Palestine, to include the Galut—the dispersion of the Jewish people into its millennial Exile. As the devout admitted in prayer and in lamentation, that supreme catastrophe had occurred as divine punishment "on account of our sins." The persecutions of Israel, its wanderings and sufferings in an inhospitable world, were considered to be its spiritual gilgul which, inexorably, it had to go through in order to atone fully for its sins. Ironically, the anti-Semites seized upon this "confession" of the pure-hearted as one more justification for hounding the Jews, asking with pious hypocrisy, Didn't they themselves testify to their collective wickedness?

The word *dybbuk*, referring, like gilgul, to the sinful transmigrating soul that "takes possession" of another living body, was first mentioned in a Cabalistic Hebrew document dated 1571. It also figured in a legend about the master-Cabalist Isaac ben Solomon Luria (the Ari, 1534–72) of Safed, included in the celebrated Yiddish folk-tale collection, *Maaseh Buch* (1602). Luria's disciple, Chaim Vital, developed the Jewish version of the doctrine of transmigration in a work which he called *The Book of Transmigrations*. Subsequently, generation after generation of Cabalists and Chasidic wonder-workers drew upon this authority to support their teachings and the retelling of bizarre tales about transmigrating dybbukim taking possession of living persons, whom they drove mad.

Once, it is told, the celebrated Ari was on his way to pray at the tomb of a Rabbinic Sage in the company of his disciple, Moses Galante. As they came near their destination, they noticed a crow which was raising a raucous din in a tree. "Did you know Sabbatai the tax-collector?" asked the great Cabalist. "I knew him," the disciple recalled. "He was very cruel to the poor when they were not able to pay their taxes." The Ari observed: "Do you see this croaking bird? Sabbatai's soul lives in it now."

The telling of tales about wandering dybbukim afforded a delightfully chilling pastime for the superstitious folk in the ghettos of Germany, Poland, and Russia, and attracted as well the attention of sophisticated people when S. Ansky's mystical melodrama in Yiddish, *The Dybbuk*, was produced on many stages in Europe and the Americas after World War I. A principal merit of the play was that it was faithfully folkloristic; it focused on the superstitious notions popularly held by the Jewish masses about transmigrating souls. It went into great detail about the Cabalistic rite of exorcism and the formulas of incantation.

The rite of exorcism or "casting out" of a dybbuk was developed during the seventeenth and eighteenth centuries among the practicing Cabalists in Eastern Europe. In substance, a baal Shem (Chasidic wonder-worker) would preside over the proceedings before a minyan (the required quorum of ten male worshipers). The baal Shem would intone the ninety-first Psalm, and then in a stern voice would command the parasitical dybbuk, in the name of God, to leave the body of the "possessed" person and go to his "eternal rest." In the event that the dybbuk proved stubborn or defiant (which was usually the case), the holy man would order that the ram's horn (shofar) be blown; that was the most extreme measure that could be taken against a dybbuk, and it was generally unfailing. A sure sign that the exorcism was effective and that the dybbuk had fled was the appearance of a bloody spot the size of a pinpoint on the little toe of the right foot of the "possessed" person. Another sign was a tiny break in a windowpane in the room where the exorcism had taken place.

A similar technique for driving out evil spirits was also prescribed officially by the Roman Catholic Church in the manual for priests, *De Ordinatione Exorcistarum* ("Ordination of Exorcists").

The most sophisticated comment on the reality of dybbukim was that made by the famous rabbinical humanist of Venice, Leone da Modena (1571–1648). He asked: Why did the all-powerful Deity have to go to all the bother and weird complications of sending a corrupted soul to inhabit and torment another body? Couldn't God have punished the wretch straightaway, while he still inhabited his original body?

See also AMULETS; CABALA; CHASIDIM; REWARD AND PUNISHMENT; SATAN; SHOFAR; SIN AND SINNER; SOUL, THE.

E

EARLOCKS. *See* PE'OT.

ECCLESIASTES, BOOK OF. *See* BIBLE, THE.

ECCLESIASTICUS, BOOK OF. *See* POST-BIBLICAL WRITINGS.

EDEN, GARDEN OF. *See* GAN EDEN.

EDUCATION. *See* BAR MITZVAH; BAT MITZVAH; CHEDER; CONFIRMATION; MELAMED; TALMUD TORAH; TORAH STUDY; YESHIBAH; YESHIBAH BACHUR.

EIGHTEEN BENEDICTIONS. *See* SHEMONEH ESREH.

ENLIGHTENMENT, THE JEWISH (in Hebrew: HASKALAH. The followers of the HASKALAH called themselves MASKILIM [s. MASKIL], meaning "the Enlightened [ones]," from the verse in Daniel 12:3: "And they that are wise [enlightened] shall shine as the brightness of the firmament.")

The Jewish Enlightenment—the Haskalah—was, in reality, a tangential offshoot of the general enlightenment movement in Western Europe during the eighteenth century. That movement had arisen directly as a consequence of the industrial revolution, which was rapidly changing social and economic patterns, bringing the insurgent middle class into the struggle for political power. The numerous members of that class were impatient to achieve their place in the sun, and were determined to displace or to curb the despotism of kings, clerical domination, and the feudal privileges of the nobility. No longer was feudalism operable as an economic system; it was rotted away by the social evils it had spawned.

The new conditions of life under emergent capitalism and the problems which they began to create stimulated the foremost political thinkers and intellectual dissenters during the seventeenth and eighteenth centuries to reexamine rationalistically and critically all class and group relationships hitherto held to be sacrosanct. They reappraised as well the political, moral, and intellectual values that prevailed in the social fabric of their day. Among the leaders of this democratic insurgency were Locke, Bentham, and Priestly in England; Montaigne, Voltaire, and Rousseau in France; Franklin, Paine, and Jefferson in the American Colonies; and Dohm, Lessing, and Herder in Germany.

Out of their bold challenges there gradually began to crystallize a libertarian conception of social and political organization in which the rights of the common man were given prominence. Those values, in great part, became embodied concretely in the French Revolutionary Declaration of the Rights of Man in 1789.

Even though the Jews of Europe had been living for almost a thousand years walled in and apart from Christians in their ghettos, they, too, had everything to gain from this equalitarian ferment and struggle for civil emancipation. They, who had been virtually without rights, standing as pariahs outside the framework of the feudal system, being considered mere chattels for the arbitrary "use" of Christian kings, feudal lords, and the Church, now also appeared likely to become beneficiaries of the general awakening and self-assertion of the masses of Europe.

During the latter part of the eighteenth century, there were quite a few thoughtful middle-class Jews in Europe who were attracted to these advanced political and social views. They had come to the conclusion that, in order for them to share, as Jews, in the benefits of civil emancipation with Christians, it was first necessary that they bring their fellow Jews out of the physical isolation and cultural backwardness of the ghetto.

The Jew with liberal ideas felt a burning shame when he thought of his own socially and civilly inferior status. As an individual, he wished to escape the certain economic straitjacket which had been the Jews' lot since the early centuries of the Holy Roman Empire. He now became convinced that his cultural assimilation within his Christian environment would serve as the key with which to unlock the door that all along had barred him from social acceptance as a human being and as a European. At the same time, he entertained the sober thought that, while the civil emancipation of the Jew might very well come from "without," through the efforts of the more advanced sections of Christian society, it was also just as necessary if not a pre-condition, to emancipate the Jew from "within," so to speak, by indoctrinating him with the knowledge and the values of general Western culture.

In its initial stages, the Jewish Enlightenment was entirely a middle-class movement. Its cultural goals, as well as its immediate benefits, could be shared by but a relatively few among the educated and the well-to-do. The Jewish masses, by and large, remained oblivious to it; they were even hostile to the very idea of cultural assimilation because they considered it to be merely a lure—an open door to apostasy.

The German Haskalah. Historically, the cradle of the Haskalah was in Prussia, and the time of its infancy was the period of the absolutist rule of Frederick II. A sadist who also despised all human beings—and Jews in particular—that cultured cynic had himself been swayed in his youth by the liberal thoughts of Voltaire, D'Alembert, and other French intellectual radicals. Yet, strange to relate, by some ironic contradiction, he actually became the active sponsor of the Jewish Enlightenment.

The reason for Frederick's sudden switchover to patronage of the Jews, whom he had previously persecuted, was rooted in cold, financial calculation. His change of heart occurred because of the manufacturing and commercial needs that were being created by the new industrialism. Prussia's development in these respects lagged far behind that of England, France, and Austria, for it is an astonishing fact that the Germans in Frederick's day displayed neither the talent nor the initiative for technological and industrial enterprise for which they became famous a century later. (The first industries in Germany had been established not by Germans but by French Huguenots.) Frederick's ever unsatisfied hunger for conquest led him, in order to feed his military machine, to seek every possible means for stimulating the introduction of new industries and the establishment of factories. These fitted profitably into the economic planning for his own enrichment and the aggrandizement of Prussian power.

Recognizing realistically the organizing talents and enterprise of the Jewish middle class, the Prussian king ordered his Fiscal (Royal Treasury) to devise ways and means whereby wealthy and capable Jewish businessmen from England, France, Holland, and Austria would be given incentives to settle in Prussia "in order to encourage the growth of commerce, manufactures, and factories." Quite a number of such Jews were indeed persuaded to settle in Prussia because the financial prospects were made so alluring, and they greatly prospered, especially in the textile industry. With sardonic wit Frederick referred to them as "my velvet Jews" or "my silk Jews," etc. It so happened that Moses Mendelssohn, the philosopher, who was also the

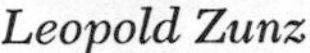

Leopold Zunz

David Friedländer

Solomon Maimon (Portrait by W. Arndt.)

Marcus Herz *Moses Mendelssohn (Portraits by Chodowiecki.)*

Abraham Geiger

Moritz Steinschneider

Heinrich Graetz

King Ferdinand of Hungary visits a modern Jewish School in Presburg, 1830.

initiator of the Jewish Enlightenment movement, was one of Frederick's "silk" Jews.

For the first time, Jewish business entrepreneurs found ample room for the exercise of their talents. Many of the legal restrictions which formerly had kept them in an economic ghetto were lifted by the Prussian king's orders that facilitated their business activities. To stimulate their enterprise and to widen their prospects, it was essential to devise a broad credit system that would make continuous industrial development possible. Consequently, Jewish bankers and merchants were encouraged to play a leading part in the organization of the credit and banking institutions of Prussia, and from there, they moved, before long, into all of the other German states.

The Jewish Enlightenment came into being in the most natural way. While they were engaged in their banking, manufacturing, and export-and-import transactions with Prussia's principal customer, France, it was inevitable that Jewish businessmen, being natively intelligent, wordly, and well-informed, should come into business and even social contact with their French counterparts, many of whom were both liberal thinking and cultured. In this manner, they acquired a strong taste for the French Enlightenment and were eager to pass it on to their fellow Jews.

The founder of the Enlightenment movement among Jews was Moses Mendelssohn (1729–86). He realized that in the general spread of free ideas, laws and institutions—which would involve the exercise of freedom of conscience and a separation of Church and State—Jews, for the first time, would be able to come into their own and stand on an equal footing with Christians. Almost a century later, in observing the rosy social and cultural landscape of Jewish life in Germany, the historian of German literature, Ludwig W. Geiger, saluted Mendelssohn as the Father of the Berlin Haskalah: "And should we be asked who it is that Berlin Jews have to be grateful to for having become members of educated society—whom they have to thank for having become Germans—we will answer, 'Moses Mendelssohn.' "

The "German Plato," as Mendelssohn was called by his admiring Christian contemporaries, was an intellectually honest man. He was sincerely devoted to the liberation of his people from their ghetto isolation, their inferior status in society, and their cultural backwardness. The son of a poverty-stricken Torah scribe (sofer) of Dessau, he exemplified in his own person the synthesis of perhaps the best in Jewish traditional culture with some of the most advanced elements in Western thought. Both Jews and Gentiles saw him in that light; the famous Christian writer and liberal thinker, Gotthold E. Lessing, even modeled his hero, Nathan the Wise, upon Moses Mendelssohn's personality and character.

Mendelssohn had taken very much to heart the wretchedness and stagnation of Jewish life everywhere in Europe. For that reason (to cite his own words) he was resolved to lead "the Jews out of the narrow labyrinth of ritual-theological casuistry onto the broad highway of human culture."

Mendelssohn was successful in gathering around him a circle of Westernized Jewish disciples who saw eye to eye with him on the need of bringing cultural enlightenment to the Jews of Europe. They disseminated his ideas and program by means of the printed word and by the establishment of secularized religious Jewish schools. The first such school—the model in many ways for the Jewish parochial schools of today—was founded in Berlin in 1781. Taught there, besides Bible and Talmud, were German and French, mathematics, geography, and several technical subjects. By such means, the Jewish Enlightenment initiated its practical program of education and propaganda.

Great emphasis was laid by Mendelssohn and his circle on the necessity of displacing Yiddish with German as the vernacular of the Jews so as to bring the latter into cultural alignment with the German people from whom they were standing apart. Therefore, opposition to Yiddish was made a cardinal principle of the Haskalah ideology. As the movement's leaders assayed it, spoken Yiddish was a badge, offensively recognizable to Gentiles, which advertised blatantly the cultural inferiority and pariah role of the Jew.

"Look at our brethren in Poland!" impatiently exclaimed Mendelssohn's close collaborator, the neo-Hebrew poet Naphtali Hartwig Wessely. "They converse with their neighbors in good Polish. . . . What excuse have we [namely, the German Jews] for using our [Yiddish] dialect and jargon?"

With a verve deserving of a better cause, the Jewish Enlightenment, whether in Germany or in Slavic lands, continually belabored Yiddish as a "corrupt jargon" that had worked for the degradation of the Jewish masses and had ruled out all possibilities of progress for them. It was described as "a lingering ghetto ailment," as a speech unworthy of the descendants of the Hebrew Prophets. Obsessed by this *idée fixe,* Mendelssohn completed the exhaustive task in 1780 of translating into German the Hebrew Pentateuch and several other Biblical writings. Following a carefully thought-out strategy, he had transliterated his German text into Hebrew characters, which are also used in writing Yiddish. This gave many thousands of Jews who could read only Yiddish and Hebrew an opportunity—which had never before been afforded them—to learn German. The language was a tool for drawing them closer to the German people and for opening up to them its secular interests and activities.

The Civil Emancipation of German Jews. Weighed in the scales of cultural history, the Haskalah movement succeeded in prying open from within the tightly shut gates of ghetto medievalism in order to let in the light of modern ideas. Some of the early Maskilim or proponents of the Haskalah, in their fight against religious fanaticism among their own people, adopted Voltaire's celebrated battle-cry: *"Ecrasez l'infame!"* ("Crush the villain [i.e., superstition]!") Their numbers grew even greater when the ghettos throughout much of Europe were abolished—in the legal-physical sense—during the decades following the French Revolution in 1789. From that time on, a number of Jews—adherents of the continuing Haskalah—emerged from their squalid ghettos, the *Judengassen* and *Juiveries,* to claim their rightful places in society alongside the Christians.

It was by no means difficult for most of the Haskalah devotees to reconcile their Jewish religious and group loyalties with their other role as Europeans. However, in the complex process of cultural assimilation, there occurred many a casualty of the much maligned Jewish identity. While some of the Maskilim, influenced by the rationalist and skeptical trend of the general Enlightenment in France and England, turned away entirely from their religious affiliation, yet they still managed to retain in varying degrees, and from different motives of sentiment, interest, or conviction, some ties with their cultural and group identity as Jews.

At the same time, there were also many others—particularly among the wealthy and educated Jews—who were solely concerned with and intent on assimilating in every way possible into their non-Jewish environment. This they wished to do not so much out of reasoned conviction but from motives of expediency and practical self-interest, in order that they might enjoy equal status with the Gentiles. Their opportunism often led them to become formal converts to Christianity, for after undergoing baptism, they were permitted both by law and by social custom to pursue unhindered whatever careers they formerly had been denied merely because they were Jews.

Ironically, some of the most distinguished devotees of the Jewish Enlightenment—for example the great poet Heinrich Heine (1797–1856) and the pioneer philosopher of law, Eduard Gans (1798–1839)—were lured by a desire for public careers to submit to conversion. Heine, who had been a religious freethinker, found that his opportunistic act of apostasy never gave him a moment's peace, for he had a sensitive poet's conscience and an honest mind to contend with. Other turncoats were far less troubled.

It has been estimated that, at one time or another, perhaps half of the Jews of Berlin, during the first decades of the nineteenth century, marched to the baptismal font. There is little doubt that, aside from the religious and philosophical considerations which activated Reform Judaism in Germany at that time, another factor in its development was the deep urgency felt by some of its leaders—themselves strong adherents of the Haskalah—to stem the tide to apostasy with a liberalized Judaism that moved in step with the times.

It is an ironic footnote to Moses Mendelssohn's earnest strivings for a modernized Judaism and an enlightened Jewry that his program of reform miscarried completely in the instance of his own social-climbing daughters and sons, including Abraham, the father of the composer Felix (1809–47). All of them became formal converts to Christianity. They had become far more enlightened as Jews and emancipated as Europeans than their religious-observing father had ever expected!

How opportunistic the trend toward the submersion of religious and group-identity among the wealthy and cultivated Jews of the day was may be gathered from the astonishing proposal made in 1799 to a prominent Protestant clergyman by David Friedländer (1750–1834), Mendelssohn's close collaborator and his successor as the leader of the Jewish Enlightenment. In all apparent seriousness, Friedländer announced that he was ready to accept baptism for himself and for all the followers of the Jewish Enlightenment in Berlin, provided they were excused from believing in such cardinal dogmas of Christianity as the Holy Trinity and the Immaculate Conception. The clergyman to whom he had applied, obviously startled by the offer of this "deal," was reported to have berated Friedländer for being a trifler.

The East European Haskalah. From Berlin, the Jewish Enlightenment quickly spread to Galicia, which was geographically the gateway to Poland, White Russia, Lithuania, and the Ukraine. After the partition of Poland, in 1772, 1793, and 1795, Galicia had become an Austrian province. The cities of Lemberg (Lvov), Cracow, Brody, and Tarnopol, which had large Jewish populations, thereupon established commercial and cultural links with both Vienna and Berlin. Under the relatively mild policy of Joseph II, the Jews in all provinces of the Austrian Empire were treated with much greater liberality than those in Poland and Russia.

As a result of the intensive Teutonization program which was carried out by Austria in Galicia, the Jewish merchants, traders, agents, and factors there came into close official and business contact with the thousands of German-speaking Austrian colonists who had settled in Galicia. Many Jews thus learned to speak German. At the same time, many of them became vastly enamored of German secular culture; consequently, they were entirely ripe for the program of the Jewish Enlightenment.

The intellectual leaders of the Berlin Haskalah, in their evangelical zeal, lost no time in establishing an entente cordiale with the most Europeanized among the Galician

Jews. Some of the latter, jibed their critics, then "journeyed to Jerusalem"—i.e., to Berlin—there to drink from the original fount of the Mendelssohnian Enlightenment. They came back to Galicia from their pilgrimage not only dyed-in-the-wool Germanophiles but—even more—devoted adherents of a Hebrew literary revival. The leaders of this neo-Hebraic renaissance were earnest, dedicated men. They wrote, however, in a purple and stilted Biblical style, perhaps too ornate for modern tastes. Nevertheless, what the majority of Galician Maskilim seemed to lack in creative talent they more than compensated for by a singleminded attachment to their cause.

In short order, the Maskilim launched virtriolic attacks on the Talmudic "casuists" and the ritual-obsessed "fanatics." But their strongest fire was reserved for the sectarian Chasidim, who were devoted to the Cabala, to the miraculous, and to an uninhibited religious emotionalism. In broad, derisive strokes, they caricatured the Chasidic rebbehs (the wonder-working rabbis) for their ignorance, greed, and mystical hocus-pocus; their followers they berated for their blind faith and gullibility, and for leading shiftless, unproductive lives.

Everywhere in the countries of Eastern Europe, the Jewish Enlightenment was splitting up into two rival camps. The preponderant one wished to propagate the ideas of the Haskalah to the ghetto Jews in the Hebrew tongue: the language of their forefathers regarded as sacred. The other camp, sparser in the number of its Maskilim, wished, for avowed tactical reasons, to indoctrinate the Jewish masses with liberal ideas by employing Yiddish—popularly referred to as *Jargon*—because that was the only language that the ghetto Jews really understood. There was, understandably, much enmity between the Hebraists and the Yiddishists, even if their goals were indentical.

The religious-minded leaders of the Haskalah in Galicia —and later also in Lithuania, Poland, and Russia—were fully aware of the diversionary assimilationist directions their movement was taking for many of their followers. Early in the nineteenth century, one East European Maskil of the Enlightenment, angered by this assimilationist trend, ridiculed those of his freethinking fellow Maskilim for believing "that Mirabeau and Voltaire represent the last word in wisdom and progress. They scoff at God and his Torah, failing to grasp the truth."

Of all the Jewish communities in Eastern Europe, those in Lithuania furnished the most fertile soil for receiving the seeds of the Enlightenment. For centuries, Lithuanian Jewry had been deeply attached to the Talmudic tradition of learning. It had established the most important yeshivot in Europe, had demonstrated, even within the framework of Orthodoxy, a preference for rationalism and modern ideas. Although mystical Chasidism had swept like a tidal wave over the other Jewries in Slavic lands, it had met with determined resistance in Lithuania. The Vilner Gaon—Rabbi Elijah ben Solomon (1720–97)—who was the greatest single force in Orthodox intellectuality during the eighteenth century—was a vigorous opponent of the Chasidim. He had even found time from his taxing Talmudic labors to study mathematics and astronomy. Probably, and quite unintentionally, with his personal pursuit of secular knowledge he had set the example, had paved the rationalist scientific way for the Haskalah in Lithuania. He did not hesitate to use the cherem (excommunication)—the ultimate punitive weapon of religious fundamentalism—to combat the new mystic heresy, and especially its initiator and leader, Israel Baal Shem.

It was precisely because the Jews of Lithuania (despite the obstacles raised by their poverty) so greatly excelled in Talmudic learning and in rabbinic dialectics, that the intellectual challenges of the Haskalah won many adherents among them, especially among the Yeshivah bachurim (students; *see* YESHIVA BACHUR). In a relatively short time, there were a large number of these enlightened ones who, in their turn, became embattled "enlighteners." They produced minor poets, polemicists, journalists, novelists, translators, and popular writers on scientific subjects. They agitated tirelessly on behalf of the Jewish Enlightenment: in Polish and Russian, a little in Yiddish, but principally in Hebrew. The results of their educational campaign were never spectacular, but they were definitely, though slowly, cumulative and outspreading.

TOP ROW, LEFT TO RIGHT: *Heinrich Heine. (Bust owned by Professor Guido Kisch, New York.) Ludwig Boerne. (Portrait by Moritz Oppenheim.) Gabriel Riesser.*
BOTTOM ROW, LEFT TO RIGHT: *I. B. Levinsohn. Moses Leib Lilienblum. Max Lilienthal.*

The Haskalah in Eastern Europe had a promising beginning when Czar Alexander I (reigned 1801–25), on his ascension to the throne, publicly proclaimed the liberal and humane ideals that he had acquired from his tutor, the French philosopher Jean François de Laharpe. He also announced that it was his intention to ameliorate the wretched condition of the Jews in the Russian Empire. In an ukase promulgated in 1804, he granted to them the right to own land and to farm it, the freedom to establish factories, and the right to follow any trade or calling they wished. Furthermore, he declared qualified Jewish youths thenceforth eligible to enter the gymnasia (high schools) and the universities without restriction.

A new and brilliant era seemed about to begin for the great masses of Jews in Russia, Poland, Lithuania, the Ukraine, and elsewhere. Those Jews who had already fallen under the spell of Moses Mendelssohn and the Berlin Enlightenment, eagerly entered their sons in the various government schools. Fortified with varying degrees of secular education, thousands prospered as merchants, bankers, brokers, agents, manufacturers, doctors, teachers, journalists, and government contractors. Not a few opportunistically joined the Russian Orthodox Church and disappeared in the shuffle.

It was inevitable that the expanded commercial and industrial activities of the Polish and Russian Jews at the turn of the nineteenth century should not only bring them into contact with educated Christians in every country of Europe but also with their fellow Jews in Germany, Austria, Galicia, and Bohemia. No doubt, the chief molding-force of the Haskalah in all the Slavic lands were the Galician Maskilim. One contemporary exponent of the Enlightenment in Russia wrote: "The Jews of the big Galician cities [Lemberg, Cracow, Brody] were the first to be illumined by the light of wisdom that emanated from Mendelssohn and his disciples. And whenever they would come on business to the Russian cities, they would bring with them some spices of their enlightenment and culture. The youth would taste them and their eyes would light up."

In other ways, too, the Galician Haskalah served as the model for the Enlightenment in the Russian Empire. Its new type of Jewish school, in arresting contrast to the traditional Ultra-Orthodox cheder (q.v.), combined the study of the Hebrew Pentateuch, the Talmud, the commentaries of Rashi and of others, and Hebrew grammar with such secular subjects as Polish, Russian, or German, arithmetic, history, and geography. A number of such "advanced" Jewish schools appeared during the first decades of the nineteenth century in the large cities of the Russian Empire.

The cultivation of Hebrew, naturally, remained a central plank in the Haskalah program in the countries of Eastern Europe, notwithstanding that its fortunes either increased or ebbed according to the fluctuations in the Russification of the educated Jewish youth. Nevertheless, nineteenth-century neo-Hebraic literature, attuned to Jewish middle-class values, acquired a small but enthusiastic following among the adherents of Haskalah. Its importance, historically, lay in the fact that, however slight and faltering it may have been as creative writing, it marked out the path for later brilliant productions of modern Hebrew literature. (*See* HEBREW LITERATURE, MODERN.)

It should be remembered that the Haskalah was not just a spirited social movement with a longe-range goal of full civil emancipation for the Jews. It aimed, rather, to bring to an end their economic rootlessness, to give them the long denied opportunities to turn their talents, which had been misspent and diverted into unproductive channels by their enemies, to useful trades and callings and to the cultivation of the soil, from which they had become estranged during centuries of oppression and legal restraint. In short, the Haskalah aimed at endowing the Jew with the stature of a man: with the human dignity of which he had been robbed by a conscienceless world for more than sixteen centuries after the Roman Empire became Christian under Constantine.

One of the most memorable of the European Haskalah's achievements was its organization of societies in the large Jewish centers for the teaching of handicrafts to children to prepare them for productive lives.

At various times—even in czarist Russia, where a virulent type of anti-Semitism had been elevated legally into a state policy (*see* POGROMS IN SLAVIC LANDS)—there were Christian liberals—men of character and influence—who courageously espoused the cause of secular education for the Jews. One such prominent educator, Nikolai I. Pirogov, who was in charge of the Odessa and Kiev school districts, was touched by the devotion of the poor Jewish youth, struggling against great odds to acquire an education. He complained bitterly: "Where are religion, morality, enlightenment, and the modern spirit, when these Jews, who with courage and selfsacrifice engage in the struggle against prejudices centuries old, meet no one here to sympathize with them and to extend a helping hand to them?"

Often the clamor against the existence of these secular-oriented Jewish schools was raised on the one hand by Orthodox traditionalists who dreaded assimilation as the certain path to apostasy, and on the other hand by hate-ridden reactionaries who could not tolerate the thought of Jews being given the same educational opportunities with them. These latter accordingly agitated for the closing of the Jewish secular schools. Their attack was met head on by a prominent Christian educator, who warned: "The abolition of these schools will drive the Jews back to their fanaticism and isolation. It is necessary to make the Jews useful citizens, and I see no other means of achieving this than by educating them."

It would be correct to say that, for all its inconsistencies, its compromises, and its easy accommodations—at least in the early stages of its activity—the Jewish Enlightenment movement gave organization and direction to the aspirations of modern, thinking Jews, just emerging from their ghetto-confinement and too bewildered to know where to begin and where to go. It supplied them at least with some of the tools of intellectual adjustment to a highly complex life. Certainly, it played a vital part in the struggle for civil emancipation.

For many, the Haskalah served as a bridge for joining their unique Jewish identity—whether religious, national, or cultural—with the life and civilization of the Western world.

See also BATLAN; CHASIDIM; CHEDER; GHETTO; HEBREW LITERATURE, MODERN; JUDAISM IN THE MODERN AGE; YESHIBAH; YESHIVAH BACHUR; YIDDISH LITERATURE, MODERN; ZIONISM.

EPIKOROS (APIKOROS) (Hebrew, meaning an "unbeliever," or one who is careless in observing the laws of Judaism; pl. EPIKORSIM (APIKORSIM); from the Greek *Epikoureios,* meaning an "Epicurean")

Epicurus (341–270 B.C.E.) was a Greek philosopher who taught that there is no Providence. He said that the universe is not governed by divine powers but runs of its own accord and by chance. He was widely frowned upon in the Hellenic world both as an atheist (he denied the legitimacy of the gods in the Greek pantheon) and as a hedonist (a lover of pleasure).

Epicureanism, because of its very character, could be popular only among a small circle of intellectual sophisticates. It first struck roots in Jewish life in Hellenistic Alexandria during the third century B.C.E., and was carried over into Judea in the natural course of inter-Jewish cultural exchanges.

The Jewish Epikoros was scorned by the ancient Rabbis as a moral libertine and as one who "denies the fundamental principle of religion." The general ignorance concerning this type of intellectual nonconformist is amusingly indicated in a definition of an Epikoros by Rabbi Joseph that is found in the Talmud: "An Epikoros is one who despises a rabbi . . . or one who says: 'What good do the rabbis do for us? They study Scripture and Mishnah for their own benefit.' "

Among the classes of heretics shut out from the blessings of the World-to-Come, notes the Mishnah, are those who deny that there will be a Resurrection after death, those who deny that the Torah is a Revelation from Heaven, and he who is an Epikoros. An eternity of hellfire was promised the Epikorsim as their portion.

The Epikorsim were quite likely not bona fide atheists but freethinkers. From the many allusions to them found in Jewish religious writings of former centuries, it appears that they were rather vocal skeptics who challenged many cherished Jewish beliefs. They were, unquestionably, scoffers and gadflies who outraged the Rabbis with their clever sophistries and heresies. Thus, Rabbi Eleazar ben Arach urgently counseled his disciples always to be prepared with "what answer to give to the Epikoros."

In the Talmud, the classic personification of the smart-aleck Epikoros was the Biblical character Korah. With malice aforethought—and a straight face, no doubt—he inquired of Moses whether tzitzit (ritual fringes: *see* TZITZIT) were required also on a garment that was blue!

In the more backward periods of Jewish ghetto life, a man was often branded an Epikoros simply for disagreeing with any popularly accepted viewpoint. A good illustration of this is the statement of an early-nineteenth-century European rabbi: "One who doubts or ridicules one word of the Torah or of the Rabbinical authors is an Epikoros in the fullest sense—an unbeliever who has thrown off the yoke [of the Torah]—and there is no hope for him."

ERETZ YISRAEL (Hebrew, meaning "Land of Israel")

In a geographic sense, unquestionably the most passionate, and also the most enduring, love affair in all history has been that which has persisted between the dispersed remnants of the Jewish people and their historical homeland. From the ancient Biblical chronicle itself it would seem that this fervent attachment for Zion has enjoyed a continuity that has been uninterrupted for about four thousand years. It began as far back as the Jewish folk-memory can go in point of time: during the legendary period of the Hebrew Patriarchs—the presumed "Founding Fathers" of Israel. Eretz Yisrael was the name of the "Promised Land" which, according to the Scriptural account, God had guaranteed in the most solemn covenants he entered into with Abraham, Isaac, and Jacob, and subsequently, with Moses and with the Jewish people itself during the theophany at Mount Sinai. The Land of Israel thus has for the Jews a holy and awesome significance.

By the beginning of the eighth century B.C.E., the tradition of the inseparability of the Jewish people with God, the Torah, and Eretz Yisrael had already been fully established. "For out of Zion shall go forth the Torah, and the word of the Lord from Jerusalem," exulted the Prophet Isaiah. Several centuries later, the Prophet of the Babylonian Captivity, Ezekiel, becoming nostalgic for the ancestral homeland, recalled it as *Eretz Chayyim*—"the Land of the Living." He implied thereby that Jews living in Galut—in the Diaspora—could be counted only as being among the dead. (*Bet Chayyim* is one of the Hebrew names for "cemetery.")

It is hardly possible to grasp in its ultimate agony the character of the emotional turmoil in the hearts of the Jewish people after the Temple had been sacked, Jerusalem destroyed, and the Kingdom of Judah ended so ingloriously by the Roman legions of Titus and Vespasian in 70–73 C.E. Thereupon, the Jewish people went into a collective, gigantic, perpetual mourning, banning all luxury, all gaiety, and even the solace afforded by instrumental music. This pall of grief, the Rabbinic Sages said, would be lifted only when the Messiah would come to re-establish the remnants of Israel on Mount Zion.

The realistic and highly intelligent Romans understood only too well the true character of the Jew's love for Eretz Yisrael, and in their own selfish political interests, did everything to curb and frustrate it. The early Church Father Eusebius notes in his *Ecclesiastical History* that, after Bar Kochba's disastrous uprising in 132 against the Romans, the Jews were "strictly forbidden to set foot in the region around Jerusalem, by the formal decree and enactment of [the Roman Emperor] Hadrian, who commanded that they should not, even from a distance, look on their native soil."

Nevertheless, Jews found ways to circumvent the harsh imperial decrees. Maimonides, the twelfth-century rabbi-philosopher of Spain, states that "even after the Destruction [of the Temple], they gathered in Jerusalem on the Festivals, coming from all the surrounding regions."

The longing for the Jewish Homeland continued to be agonizing for the pious. Away from Eretz Yisrael, they felt orphaned and emotionally insecure. Not a few in every generation felt an overwhelming urge to journey to the Holy Land. They went there imbued with the Prophet Ezekiel's affirmative conception: to "live" in the *Land of the Living*. This traditional view is also found expressed in the medieval Cabalistic writing, the Zohar: "It is a great privilege for a man to live in the Holy Land. There the dew of heaven falls upon him in benediction; he sinks his roots deep into its life, which is holy."

Many are the instances cited in Rabbinic and medieval religious literature which dwell on the passionate love for Zion among Jews. In the Talmud, it is chronicled how the noted Rabbinic scholar Ullah had left his home in the Land of Israel and gone to settle among the Jews of Babylonia. As he lay dying and recalled how distant he was then from Eretz Yisrael, he started to weep. His colleagues and his students tried to console him. They pleaded with him: "Do not weep so! We promise faithfully to carry your body to Eretz Yisrael and there bring it to eternal rest." "Of what use will that be to me?" lamented Ullah. "See, I'm losing my jewel [i.e., his soul] in this unclean land!" How he longed, said he, to surrender his soul while nestling in "the lap of my mother [Eretz Yisrael]" and not to have to surrender it while "in the lap of a strange woman [Babylonia]!"

An imaginary depiction of Jerusalem and the Temple. (From a fragment of an illustrated ketubah [marriage contract], Rivarollo, Italy, 1727.)

But though many of the pious wished to settle in the Land of Israel in order to find a greater spiritual meaning for their lives, many more felt a compelling need to go there that they might die on holy soil. This compulsion was no doubt precipitated by the terrible massacres of the Jews by the Crusaders and by the violence that the Church and state of medieval and later times engaged while attempting to bring the Jews to the baptismal font (*see* CONVERSION OF JEWS).

There was much pathos in the journeys to Zion. The "exiles" were like footsore wanderers going home again. Many perished from hunger on the way; others met with death at the hands of robbers, or of fanatical Christians or Mohammedans.

With the sixteenth century, in the wake of the many calamities that had struck at the Jews in Europe, and at a time when they had sunk back into abysmal ignorance and superstition in Eastern Europe, the practical Cabala, with its mystification and numerological mumbo-jumbo, ensnared the minds of tens of thousands of Jews. The return to Eretz Yisrael, which had been a thin but perpetual stream until this time, now turned into a virtual torrent. Large cummunities of pietists formed in Jerusalem, Hebron, Safed, and Tiberias. These settlements were anchored around the Cabalists and "wonder-workers": Isaac Luria ("the ARI"), Joseph Caro, Moses Cordovero, and others.

The zealots of the Return greatly increased in numbers in the second half of the eighteenth century with the mass-arrival of sectarian Chasidim from Poland, Galicia, and the Ukraine, led by their holy rabbis, the tzaddikim. In a mystical sense, the Chasidim were both the inheritors and the continuators of the Cabalist doctrines and outlook and way of life. Probably the most compelling reason for their return was their wish to be buried in the sacred soil of Eretz Yisrael so that, when the Messiah would come and the first trumpet blast announcing the Resurrection would sound, they, the pious, would lose no time in rising from their graves.

The Jewish cemetery in the Valley of Jehoshaphat, at Jerusalem, presents an apalling spectacle. It consists of a forest of graves tumbling over one another. The older tombstones have long since crumbled and disappeared to make way for the advance of the new ones.

A folkway both poetic and poignant in its symbolism, still practiced outside of Eretz Yisrael, is the sprinkling of a little earth from the Holy Land into the open graves of tradition-minded Jews at their burial. It is a vicarious way of satisfying the unrequited yearning of the pious Jew of the Dispersion for being united, in a physical sense, at least, with the Holy Land. That this custom must have originated during the Middle Ages is indicated in the somewhat tentative report by a medieval rabbi: "I have heard that earth from the Holy Land, when it is sprinkled upon the eyes, navel and between the legs of those who die outside of that country, is considered equal to being buried in Eretz Yisrael itself."

There can be little doubt but that cumulative emotional and psychological factors in the religious-national attachment of the Jews to the historic land of their forefathers for so many years determined the inevitable geographic direction Zionism took. The establishment of the State of Israel in Eretz Yisrael in 1948 bears witness to this timeless and enduring love.

See also DIASPORA; MESSIAH; MESSIAHS, WOULD-BE; RESURRECTION; TEMPLE, THE; ZIONISM.

ESSENES (in Hebrew: TZENUIM, meaning, variously, "modest," "chaste," "humble," or "pious" men. Philo, the Hellenistic philosopher-rabbi of Alexandria, thought that it was an Aramaic word signifying "holy." In Yiddish parlance, to this day, a woman answering this description is called a TZENIAH.)

The turbulent, and sometimes catastrophic, events that rent apart the Jewish social-political fabric in Judea in the Seleucidan pre-Maccabean period and reached a bloody climax at the siege of Jerusalem in 70 C.E. by the Romans, gave rise to a phenomenal number of "escapist" religious sects—twenty-four, according to the Talmud.

During that dismal period, the Jews were subjected to every kind of robbery, oppression, suppression, and outrage. These came both from their conquerors—first the Greeks, then the Seleucidan Syrians, and finally the Romans—and from the pliant agents and collaborators of these enemies—the Jewish kinglets of Judea, the corrupt priestly hierarchy of the Temple, and the self-serving class of wealthy landowners and merchants. "From whence will come my aid?" became more than a mere liturgical outcry of the despairing. The helplessness, the utter moral loneliness, of the individual Jew in his own chaotic society could hardly be described better than in the lament of the ancient psalmist: "I look at my right hand, and see, for there is no man that knoweth me; refuge faileth me; no man careth for my soul."

It was in this climate of fear, abandonment, and hopelessness that the Essenes appeared. Some scholars believe that they were Pharisee schismatics who had broken away from their mother-sect because it was no longer capable of responding to the urgency of their religious and social needs. Others think that they were but the religious continuators of the Chasidim (*see* ZEALOTS), the Pious Ones of Maccabean times. Their primary purpose in forming their own sect was to prepare themselves for the coming of the Messiah, a miraculous event which they—like most of their fellow Jews—believed to be imminent. They not only renounced the world with all its joys as a snare and a delusion, but they went the whole way and *separated themselves physically* from the rest of society and from all its conflicts, corruption, and social injustice.

In Jewish-Christian religious history, they constituted the first approach to monasticism, advancing in that direction far closer than the Nazarites (Rechabites) had during the First Temple period.

The Essenes lived in semimonastic brotherhoods, principally along the shores of the Dead Sea and the river banks of the Jordan. "They prefer to live in villages and avoid cities on account of the habitual wickedness of those who inhabit them," testified the first-century philosopher-rabbi Philo, who came to know their communities at first hand. But according to his contemporary, the Jewish historian Josephus, there were also Essenic communities in the cities.

The Essenes ardently wished to hasten the advent of the Redemption and the establishment of the ideal Kingdom of God *on earth* by their own efforts. So they took Levitical (priestly) vows of purity and followed a rigorous regimen. They prayed and fasted much, they bathed frequently and dressed in white. They studied the Scriptures under "true exponents of the Law [Torah]," and practiced self-denial. They devoted each day to achieving a state of spiritual uplift and "holiness" by means of productive labor (which they regarded as a form of religious worship), by refraining from any act of cruelty or injustice, and by drawing closer to their fellow men through love.

According to Josephus' information, there was a total of four thousand Essene probationers and initiates in his day. But they commanded—mostly among the workers and the poor in the towns and cities—a large number of sympathizers who could only go part of the way with them in the pursuit of "holiness" and would not, so to speak, burn all their bridges and separate themselves from society. Josephus, who had himself lived as a probationer for a time in one of their brotherhoods, wrote that they held "all things in common,

Hall in the main building of the Qumran Essenic community near the Dead Sea. (Photo by M. L'abbé J. Starcky of the Centre National de la Recherche Scientifique, Paris.)

so that a rich man enjoys no more of his own wealth than he who has nothing at all."

The Essenes ate together, worked together, and prayed and strove together for self-perfection and moral worthiness. Each member had a daily task, assigned to him by an overseer, to perform. The brothers labored from sunrise to sunset, some cultivating the fields, some as herdsmen and beekeepers; others were occupied with necessary handicrafts. All income was placed in the custody of the steward or treasurer. (It is interesting to note that Judas Iscariot occupied this office in the Essenic brotherhood formed by Jesus, the Apostles, and their followers.) "As lovers of frugality," noted Philo, "they shunned luxury as a disease of both body and soul."

The Essenic brotherhoods were probably the first Jewish communities *to outlaw slavery* from their midst. This was testified to by Philo as an eyewitness: "There is not a single slave among them, but they are all free, serving one another; they condemn masters, not only as representing a system of unrighteousness in opposition to that of equality, but as personifications of wickedness in that they violate the law of nature which made us all brethern, created alike."

Of one piece with this concrete expression of humanitarianism and social justice–since, in Judaism, all avowed principles and beliefs are considered of no value unless put into practice–was their opposition to war and to violence of any kind, including the violence of angry or abusive words. Philo, who was himself a pacifist, noted with admiration: "Among them there is no maker of any weapons of war."

Their practice of mutual aid and concern for the common welfare were unremitting. When the Essenes grew old or sick they were "nursed at the common expense" and cared for by all as if they were "their own parents." Concluded Philo, they "regularly closed their life with an exceedingly prosperous and comfortable old age."

That the Essenes were fanatical in their views and practices and were, therefore, completely dedicated to their mode of life, is a fact beyond dispute. They submitted themselves out of choice to a severe discipline of self-repression, so that they rejected as sinful both the sex impulse and the propagation of the species. Consequently, they remained celibate all their lives. They had several illiberal motives for this view. One was extremely Oriental in its contempt for woman, running contrary to the main Jewish tradition of respect and considerate treatment of woman as developed by the Rabbinic Sages. To quote Philo: "For no Essene takes a wife, because a wife is a selfish creature, excessively jealous and adept at beguiling the morals of her husband and seducing him by her continued impostures." Another feeling was that familial ties and responsibilities shackled a man and kept him from fully serving the brotherhood—a view shared in the New Testament by both Jesus and Paul. "And if children come . . . casting off all shame, she compels him to commit actions which are all hostile to the life of Essenic fellowship. For he who is either fast bound in the love-lures of his wife or under the stress of nature, makes his children his first care, ceases to be the same to others, and, unconsciously, has become a different man and has passed from freedom into slavery."

The reason for the great fascination that the Essenes, their beliefs and practices, and their way of life have had for the modern world is obvious. It is because of their close connections with the beliefs and practices of Jesus and the Apostles, and with the organization of the early Jewish-Christian Church. It is generally agreed that the founder of Christianity and his immediate disciples and followers may have been Essenes originally or, possibly, adherents of the closely related Essenic offshoot, the Morning Bathers or Baptists, who followed the prophetic leadership of John (in Hebrew: Yochanan) the Baptist.

Unusual popular, as well as scholarly, interest was aroused in 1947 with the discovery of the so-called Dead Sea Scrolls in a cave at Qumran, on the northern shore of the *Yam ha-Melach* (Salt Sea), in Palestine. The excitement among scholars was no doubt due to the fact that, although their actual significance was overrated by some enthusiastic theologians, new knowledge was definitely gained from them about the Essenic brotherhoods and, consequently, about the origins of Christianity. The Dead Sea documents corroborate in large part information concerning the beliefs, practices, and organization of those other Jewish sectaries given in other contemporary accounts by the Jewish writers Philo and Josephus and the Roman writer Pliny the Elder.

Singularly enough, the Christian Gospels and other New Testament writings make no mention of the Essenes by name, although they engage in vitriolic attacks on the "Scribes and Pharisees, hypocrites," who, it should be recalled, were the implacable religious opponents of the Essenes as well as of Jesus and his disciples. This unusual fact alone, it has been pointed out by alert commentators, is prima-facie evidence that the reason the Essenes were not mentioned was because they were the sectarian "brothers" of Jesus and the Apostles and, therefore, required no special attention from them.

It has now been quite generally conceded that Christianity owes an enormous debt to the Essenes (and, incidentally, to the Pharisees as well). Not only did it draw its initial adherents from their dedicated ranks, but it retained many of their fundamental doctrines, social attitudes, and ethical values and practices. Some of these were: the certainty that the Messianic Age was about at hand; the practice of baptism and ritual bathing; the pessimistic view that sex, procreation, and the marriage institution were sinful; the extolling of the virtues of poverty, humility, self-abnegation, and nonresistance to evil; and–above all–the proclamation of the redemptive power of love and brotherhood. The "love feast" of the Essenes (*see* CHRISTIANITY, JEWISH ORIGINS OF) and the communion meal (in Greek: *Agape,* as used in I Corinthians 11:20, but translated into English as "the Lord's Supper") of the early Christians, were one and the same. Furthermore, the early Christian brotherhoods, beginning with Jesus and his small band of followers, were organized and governed along Essenic lines: that of utopian communalism in which all the members were equal and each shared everything with the others.

See also ASCETICS, JEWISH; CHRISTIANITY, JEWISH ORIGINS OF; MONASTICISM, JEWISH; PHARISEES; SADDUCEES; SAMARITANS; THERAPUETAE; ZEALOTS.

ETERNAL LIGHT. *See* LAMP, PERPETUAL.

ETHICAL VALUES, JEWISH

The Rabbinic Sages concurred in the belief that "Every human being is equal in worth to the whole world." No similar high estimate of the individual was ever given in other ancient religions.

Perhaps alone among all the peoples, the Jews accorded a genuinely spiritual character to the life of man–*of every man.* Rabbinic teachers of ethics likened the moral nature of the human being to that of his Creator. Consequently, his life on earth was to be a sanctification, because he resembled God in his potential of ethical attributes and in his capacity to exercise free will in his actions.

For the God-intoxicated Jews, the main emphasis in ethics was on altruistic practices. "For all moral principles concern the relation of man to his neighbor," stated Maimonides, the medieval rabbi-savant, who described them as being, "as it were, given to man for the benefit of mankind." In other words, the practice of these principles by each individual was not to be considered optional; it was mandatory!

This definition by Maimonides was in line with the concensus of Talmudic opinion which held that for a man to profess moral principles without trying to put them into practice was not only a mockery, it made him guilty as well of the sin of hypocrisy.

The crux of the matter is this: Ever since Moses taught the moral laws of life to the Jews, they have believed in the perfectibility of individual man and of all society. Hence they have directed both the teaching and practice of morals and ethics toward the achievement of this goal. The wellspring of all moral values, said the Rabbis, was love. It was the primal force, the all-embracing principle of life. The precepts of Moses and of later teachers of religious ethics tirelessly played on this selfsame theme: "Love thy neighbor as thyself." "Hate not thy brother." "Avenge not." "Bear no grudge." "Love the stranger."

To the medieval Jews, standing helpless and mute under the savage assaults made upon them by their enemies and drawing to the fullest from those experiences in disaster a lesson on the spiritual emptiness of worldly power and ambition, the image of the Righteous Man–one dedicated to ideal goals and the pursuit of ethical ways–loomed ever grander and more luminous. The Cabalists, with their other-world directed goals, evaluated the Righteous Man as being immeasurably the most fortunate of all men. Then why, like his Biblical prototype, Job, was he afflicted in his life with greater troubles and sorrows than were the wicked? Like Rabbi Philo of Hellenist Alexandria, the Cabalists took the austere view that the only man who can be considered free is the good man, for he lives by what he thinks and believes, despite the misfortune and persecution his lonely but determined course may bring him.

"Love Thy Neighbor." Akiba ben Joseph, the second-century Mishnah Sage, prized above all others the Scriptural commandment "Love thy neighbor as thyself." He said that it contained the quintessence of the entire Torah because it equated the divine love of God with the earthly love of man, thereby upholding both as the twofold and active duty of righteousness.

In the Talmud, God, cast in the role of the tender Father, is made to say to the Jews: "My sons, my sons, is there anything I ask of you for myself? All I require is that you love one another." This affirmative love-principle became the foundation for subsequent Jewish ethical values from which the teachings of Jesus were derived. "The Temple was destroyed because men hated one another," lamented several Talmudic teachers of ethics who had been eyewitnesses to that national tragedy for their people.

Maimonides, elaborating on this central commandment in the Torah of bearing love for one's "neighbor," whether near or far, also urged "love for the stranger." This was a duty, said he, that stemmed from two positive commandments in Scripture: "First, because he [the stranger] is included in the definition of *neighbor,* and again, because he *is* a stranger, and because the Torah tells us: 'Love ye, therefore, the stranger.'"

Your "Brother's Keeper" (*Kol Yisrael chaverim*). All in Israel are comrades. Thus runs the credo of Jewish group-solidarity that has been uttered with simple conviction by the Jewish folk for two thousand years. With it comes the corollary duty of each brother to protect and watch out for the welfare of the other. Urged Maimonides: "A man ought to speak in praise of his neighbor, and to care for his possessions just as he cares for his own, and as he wishes for his own honor." Conversely, he added: "Whosoever glories in the shame of his fellow has no share in the World-to-Come."

There have always been in evidence among Jews–just as among all peoples–mean and twisted souls who have sought to profit from an injury done to a fellow man. The Scriptures are severe in condemnation of those who, to advance their own selfish ends, place "stumbling blocks before the blind."

At no time, especially during periods of grave stress and persecution, was the informer (in Hebrew-Yiddish: *masser*) absent in Jewish community life. The Talmudic Sages, living in the darkest days of Roman persecution, heaped scorn upon this type of wretch: "He who secretly informs against his fellow man will have no share in the World-to-Come." Also, they could find no terms of opprobrium strong enough to match their revulsion for slanderers, who proved to be a constant menace to community morale, for like termites they undermined the faith that existed between a man and his neighbor. The Rabbis picturesquely called tale-bearing "the dust of slander." The slanderer was classed by them with the murderer. This was because his venom frequently not only destroyed his victim but also took away from him the possibility of earning his livelihood.

Savage in its indignation is this parable in the Talmud told to dramatize the evil of slander.

> One day the members of the animal kingdom will assemble to reproach the serpent: "If the lion rends his prey, it is because he is hungry. If the wolf devours his victim, it is because he must eat. But you, O serpent! what profit do you get from biting others?"
>
> And the serpent, being very clever, will reply: "Am I worse than the slanderer?"

Using precisely the same argument given by the psychologists of today concerning racial and religious prejudice, the Talmudic Sages warned the unthinking against the destructive consequences of slander: "Slander injures these three: the person who is slandered, the one who listens to the slander, and the slanderer himself."

A contrary course to informing was urged by Hillel the Elder: "Let the honor of your fellow man be as dear to you as your own." Thus, every man would be truly his "brothers' keeper," as Scripture advised.

Mutual Aid. Having been turned into sober realists by their historical conditioning, Jews always thought deeply about the plight of the individual standing alone in a chaotic world. Obviously, said the Rabbis, in order to survive, all human beings must practice mutual aid. This statement was not dictated by a desire to further altruism; it grew from a simple realization of enlightened self-interest: It was *necessary* for people to help one another.

The medieval Cabalists held a belief concerning this matter which was remarkable for the advanced social attitude of interdependence it reflected: "Not only do all men rely on one another for mutual aid, but this is practiced also by all the species in nature. The stars and the planets and even the angels support one another!"

The definitive formulation of mutual aid in terms of enlightened self-interest is found in the celebrated aphorism of Hillel two thousand years ago:

> If I am not for myself, who then is for me? And if I am for myself alone, what am I? And if not now, when then?

By means of the art of the parable, the Rabbis of the Talmud sought to illuminate their teachings concerning the interdependence of all people. The Judean Sage, Simeon bar Yochai, told the following story:

> Once a number of men set out to sea. In an idle and mischievous moment, one of the passengers started to bore a hole in the bottom of the boat where he was sitting.
>
> "What are you trying to do?" cried his fellow passengers in alarm.
>
> "What does it concern you what I am doing?" replied the man. "I am not boring a hole under where you are sitting, only under my own place!"
>
> "It may be only under your place," retorted the others. "But should the water fill the boat, it will capsize. Then all of us will drown!"

A problem of far greater moral implication was posed in a Rabbinical controversy that took place in Jerusalem during the second century between Akiba ben Joseph and Ben Paturi. It had to do with this hypothetical situation: Two men are traveling in a desert. Only one of the two has any water left in his gourd. Unfortunately, it is only a little—not sufficient to slake the thirst of both. What is to be done? Should the travelers practice mutual aid and share the water? Then both might perish! But, on the other hand, if only one drinks the water, then his companion is sure to die. Now, notes the Talmud regarding this quandary, both of these travelers are good men. What, in Heaven's name, should they do?

Akiba, always common-sensed and a realist, argued that the prior duty of every person is, naturally, to himself. Therefore, it would be perfectly all right for the man who had some water left in his gourd to try to save his own life by drinking all of it himself. Ben Paturi, an unflinching moralist, strongly objected to such a selfish and heartless course. He said that it was better that both should drink and die, for was it not written in Scripture, "And thy brother shall live with thee"? And if the man with the water found that he couldn't "live" with his brother by sharing it with him, then was it not better that he "die" with him in brotherhood?

Gentle People. To be gentle—not merely in manner, but also in thought, word, outlook, feeling, and action, so that together all formed a harmonious pattern of human personality—this was the traditional Jewish matrix for the Righteous Man. Hillel, who left the impact of his glowing personality and his teaching on most Jews of his time, including Jesus and his disciples, was the archetype of the "gentle Jew" for all the generations. His whole being and conduct, his way of life, his manner of thinking and of speaking were keyed to benevolence and a universal embrace of all mankind. Such descriptives as "a disciple of Hillel" and "peace-loving as Hillel" were used by Jews throughout all ages to evoke the image of a very gentle and good man.

The antonym for "gentle" in traditional Jewish thought is "angry." The angry man was fully execrated in the Bible: "He who gives way to his anger shall be considered in thine eyes as an idolator." What could be the profit in getting angry? asked the Rabbis. And they answered their own question: "His life is no life; his anger is the only profit he has."

There are some individuals, of course, who think they are "wise," but they too get angry. Then Simeon ben Levi chided: "A wise man who gets angry is no longer a wise man!" A Talmudic aphorism injected in a clever play on three Hebrew words makes plain the familiar Jewish attitude toward the angry man: "In three things may a man's character be known: [by his behavior] in his cups (*be-koso*), in his purse (*be-kiso*), and in his anger (*be-ka'aso*).

A "teaching" story is recounted in the Talmud concerning the novel manner in which Judah ha-Nasi (135–220 C.E.), the Patriarch of Judea who compiled the Mishnah, used to transmit ethical values to his students. Once he invited several of his contentious students to dine with him. By his prior order, a platter of two cooked calf's tongues was placed before each of his student-guests. One tongue was well cooked, properly seasoned, and soft; the other was just parboiled, overseasoned, and quite tough. After sampling each tongue, the students with one accord turned their entire attention to the soft, well-seasoned tongues. "My sons," said the Sage, "consider this matter and learn from it: Is it possible that there is anybody here who does not prefer a soft tongue to a tough one? Then let your tongues be 'soft' to one another!"

It was by such teaching methods—through lessons reinforced by parables, wise sayings, and the illustrations of practical experience—that character among Jewish children was molded.

Gentleness in response to provocation and insult was another aspect of the ideal image. Beloved among the folk has been this Talmudic saying: "If others speak evil of you, make no answer." There is no more moving testimonial to the practice of this attitude than a letter that the gentle philosopher-rabbi, Maimonides, wrote to Joseph Aknin, a disciple of his, at a time when he was being abused by the rabbinical bigots of his day:

> I have been much humbled by years and by sorrows. I especially forgive those who try to offend my honor and heap insults upon me. . . . And if someone has been induced to say that I am without religion and good actions, he may say so. And all this, my son, as there is a living God, shall not hurt nor provoke me, even should I have heard it with my own ears, or seen it with my own eyes. . . . On the contrary, I should have humbled myself, and have answered in gentle terms, or been silent, or answered softly or modestly. . . .

The pride and dignity of the human personality, taught the Sages, were not to be lowered by the practices of the gutter. They counseled that it was far better to be counted among those who are reviled than to be among the revilers. And why so? The Sages, the personifications of gentleness, explained: "Curses only curse those who do the cursing."

The Pure in Heart. The anonymous writers of the twenty-four separate books of the Bible were not infrequently poets, and often inspired ones. With breathtaking imagery they referred to the heart as "seeing," as "understanding," or "hearing." By means of this word-alchemy that made the heart the very essence of the human personality, the creators of post-Biblical literature and the Talmud gave to that human organ the dimensions of man's interior universe, involving all of his sensory, emotional, spiritual, and intellectual resources.

The great canonical Prophets and the unknown Psalmists, in their ethical search for the true meanings of life, both listened attentively, as it were, to the murmurings of the human heart.

> Who shall ascend into the mount of the Lord?
> And who shall stand in His holy place?

And the answer came:

> He that hath clean hands and a pure heart.

The Sages of the Talmud taught: "The merciful God asks for but one thing: the heart." All other expressions of homage, of praise and devotion, are deemed inconsequential by him. Did the worshiper wish to bring a gift to God? Only the pure heart was worthy as an offering! The latter-day Cabalists offered a physical explanation for the heart's spiritual primacy. Had not God placed it in the center of the human body, and was it not placed there so that it might govern the body?

"The heart is like the Holy of Holies in the Temple," mused the Cabalistic work, the Zohar. "Yet it consists of two chambers; in one there is healing, in the other–deadly poison." The problem, therefore, was how to eject the poison and leave the heart pure.

"What is the highest good?" asks a Rabbinic catechism. And the answer given is: "To be found pure in the eyes of God and man."

Compassion. *"Ab ha-Rachamim!"* "Father of Compassion!" This is sometimes the emotional form of address the suppliant uses when he speaks to his God in prayer. Compassion has always been extolled by the Rabbinic teachers as one of the divine ethical attributes which it is man's duty to emulate: "Do you pray that God should show you compassion? Then show compassion to your fellow man!"

All benevolence is considered as springing from the sentiment of compassion. "The entire merit in charity is when it is motivated by compassion," taught the Rabbis. To this the Zohar, the "scriptures" of the Cabalists, added: "He who shows compassion to a poor man and revives his soul is as if he himself had been the creator of that soul." Such benevolence is an affirmation of principle as well as a sentiment of humanity in that it prompts a man to give *of himself*–not only of his material possessions–to alleviate a fellow man's suffering or need.

This is the desirable image of the Jew projected by the ancient Sages: "He who feels compassion for the suffering of his fellowmen is a true son of Abraham."

Humility. The archetype of humility was Moses. It is written in Scripture: "And the man Moses was very meek." Moreover, observed the Talmudic Sages concerning the great teacher of Israel: "While wisdom wrought a crown for his head, humility made sandals for his feet."

Perhaps twelve centuries after Moses, Hillel arose to serve for his people as the second human symbol of humility. When someone once rebuked him, charging that for one so exalted he was being too self-effacing, he replied: "My humility is my exaltation."

When Hillel died, the pious of every generation strove to imitate him in humility. "Humble, like Hillel" became a figure of speech for Jewish folk.

However, Hillel did not stand alone in his striving after humility. Humility was also prized as one of the character traits the wise man (the chacham, pl. chachamim) sought to develop in his quest for righteousness. A quaint but pithy catechism in the Talmud presents the relative value of humility in the moral life of man.

> What is the ornament of man?
> The Torah.
> What is the ornament of the Torah?
> Wisdom.
> What is the ornament of Wisdom?
> Humility.
> What is the ornament of Humility?
> Reverence for God.
> What is the ornament of reverence for God?
> Good deeds.
> What is the ornament of good deeds?
> Modesty in performing them.

Many are the sayings that the chachamim uttered in praise of humility. These are some of them:

> "Any man who thinks himself superior to his fellow man is really inferior to him."
>
> "If you have acquired much knowledge in the Torah, do not pride yourself because of it."
>
> "Do not forget that God created the flea before he made man."
>
> "Be humble, for the end of man is worms and maggots."

The Rabbinic teachers of ethics also spun their nets of persuasion over the folk mind by means of allegories and fables. The following pedagogic fable illustrates the virtue of humility.

> The fruit trees were chided once by the shade trees: "Why don't you make a noise in your branches like we do?"
>
> The fruit trees replied: "Why do we have to make a noise? Our fruit speaks loudly enough for us."

As a salutary reminder to the conceited, the Patriarch, Rabbi Judah ha-Nasi, taught with tongue-in-cheek: "When man was first created, he had a tail like other animals. But in order to spare him humiliation, God–blessed be He!–later took his tail away."

There is a medieval parable that for centuries enjoyed a vast popularity among the Jews of the European ghettos. It was written down by the German teacher of ethics, Rabbi Judah ben Asher (1270–1349):

> A wise man was asked: "Why is it that we see you always honoring every man you meet?"
>
> He replied: "I have not yet seen the man in whom I did not discover some merit I do not possess and for which I feel bound to do him honor. If he is old, I say: 'This man must have performed more good deeds than I.' If he is rich, I say: 'This man undoubtedly practiced more benevolence than I.' If he is young, I say: 'I must have sinned more than he.' If he is poor, I say: 'This man certainly must have suffered more than I.' And if he is wise, I say: 'Surely, God's punishment rests lighter on him than on me!' "

The Charitable Spirit. A charitable approach to the faults o[f] others that teaches one to be mellow, understanding, an[d] patient, is a characteristic of all gentle people. This is wha[t] Eleazar ben Samuel of Mayence told his sons and his daugh[t]ers in the testament he left them in 1357. He wrote: "Judg[e] every man charitably, and try your hardest to discover a fa[v]orable explanation for the conduct of others, however su[s]picious they may appear to you." That is classic Jewis[h] thical doctrine, and it all points to the real source of benevo- ence: a love of people.

"Who is a hero?" is the question rhetorically posed in he Sayings of the Fathers (Pirke Abot). And the answer is iven: "He who turns an enemy into a friend."

But the Rabbinical teachers had no illusions about how asy it was to overcome hatred with the power of love. It vas the sober reflection of the great medieval poet, Solomon on Gabirol, that "The space in the eye of a needle is suffi- ient for two friends, but the entire world is not big enough o hold two enemies."

The Talmudic Sages recognized that one source of con- ict in people lay in their irrational impulses. Another fre- uent source was the malicious drive in individuals that omehow deluded them into thinking that by denigrating thers they could elevate themselves. Of this perverseness in onduct, the Rabbis observed ruefully in the Talmud: "There re many people who eat and drink convivially together. Jevertheless, they stab each other with their tongues."

Fully aware of these incongruities in human character nd of the difficulty in overcoming them, the Rabbis ex- orted all individuals of sincerity and good will to exercise a ıoral discipline and bridle their errant thoughts, impulses, nd feelings so that they might avoid the pitfalls of the rational.

orgiveness. Forgiveness, said the ancient Rabbis, was one ctive aspect of love. It called for the exercise by the indi- idual of moral restraint and strength to overcome the petty nd rancorous emotions aroused in him by the hostile conduct f others.

Forgiveness was among the ethical values most extolled y the ancient Scribes and Pharisees—the Rabbinic teachers f ethics who lived during the Second Commonwealth in ıdea. There is no question but that they transmitted their igh regard for the qualities of love for one's neighbor, com- assion, gentleness, mutual aid, purity of heart, and forgive- ess of wrong, into the teachings of Jesus, the Essenic rabbi f Nazareth.

Antedating by about two centuries the founder of Chris- anity in his preachments of love, humility, charity, and for- iveness, is the following exhortation in the Testament of ad: "Love ye one another from the heart; and if a man sin gainst thee, speak peaceably to him . . . and if he repent nd confess, forgive him . . . But [even] if he be shameless nd persisteth in his wrongdoing, even so forgive him."

The duty to forgive was considered to be an essential art of the Jew's moral apparatus, necessary in all of his elations with others. And if the Lord's Prayer of the Chris- ans, which strikes so many exalted sonorities, is represented y many as marking the birth of a new ethos in religion, ıperseding that of the Jews, one need only point to oft- ticulated ancient Jewish beliefs that were cut from the very ame moralistic cloth.

A generation before Jesus appeared upon the Jewish cene, Philo, the rabbi-philosopher of Hellenistic Alexandria, reached to the Jews of his city in Attic Greek: "If you ask ardon [from God] for your sins, do you also forgive those 'ho have trespassed against you? For forgiveness is granted r forgiveness." Similarly, a Rabbinic Sage in the Talmud sserted: "God is my witness that my head has never rested n the pillow before I pardoned all who injured me." To this ery day, before lying down to sleep, traditionally pious Jews ecite this ancient Hebrew declaration in the inward-directed ndertone of private devotion:

> Master of the world! I pardon every transgression and every wrong done to my person, to my property, to my honor, or to all that I have. Let no one be punished on my account.

It has always been the custom—one perhaps unique in all the religious experience of mankind—that on the eve of Yom Kippur, just before the Kol Nidre service commences, the worshipers in synagogues rise in their seats and, with the guilt-laden conscience that is so characteristic of the innocent, appeal tearfully to their fellow worshipers:

> Listen, my masters! I beg forgiveness for all the offenses I may have committed against any of you whether in deed or in word.

Good Manners. In other cultures, good manners have been treated usually as a requirement of etiquette, as a submission in conformity to the prevailing social protocol arrived at either by custom or by entirely arbitrary criteria of "good taste" and "courtesy."

Good manners were a far different matter for Jews in Rabbinic times. Then the emphasis on social manners was ethical in character. The Sages thought about it in this way: Good manners were good morals; bad manners were sinful acts. In past generations, Jews conformed to the social pattern to avoid offending the sensibilities of their fellow men. And so the pious followed the numerous moralistic admonitions against speaking or acting out of perversity, without first weighing the consequences or possible effects their behavior might have on others.

The Pharisee Sage Hillel taught, two thousand years ago: "Do not sit in the midst of those who stand, and do not stand among those who sit. Also do not laugh when others weep, and do not weep when others laugh."

To say or do anything to humiliate another person, no matter how young or old, whether he was illustrious or humble, was condemned as the "shedding of blood." The assumption was that the feelings as well as the flesh of human beings can be made to "bleed," and to hurt with words constituted an indefensible form of violence. The Sages therefore concluded that because wounding with words can leave scars that never heal, "Far better were it for a man to leap into a fiery furnace than to humiliate his fellow man."

The morality of good manners also produced strictures against obscenity and indecent conduct. There was always evident—although less so since the start of the civil emancipation of the Jews in the nineteenth century—an almost consistent refinement or puritanism among the great majority of Jews. To talk about sex or women in a lewd or cynical manner was condemned by religious law as sinful; it was an intrinsic part of Jewish "good manners" to avoid any discussion, no matter how discreet, of such subjects. "Delicacy forbids talking about such things," pointed out the moralists.

The same restraint was observed in social life with respect to the use of coarse language. Making rude references to the human anatomy and to its physiological functions was frowned upon—not that religious Jews could not be direct and outspoken whenever it was required. The Rabbinical moralists cautioned: "Accustom not your lips to vulgar words, for in that too is sin." Ghetto Jews quite often retreated into the employment of euphemisms—the inevitable escape of the "refined" in all cultures—to avoid the dilemma of having to call a spade a spade.

See also ANIMALS, COMPASSION FOR; BROTHERHOOD; CHARITY; COMMUNITY, DUTY TO THE; "EYE FOR AN EYE"; FAMILY, THE; FAMILY RELATIONS, TRADITIONAL PATTERNS OF; FELLOWSHIP IN ISRAEL; FREE WILL; GENTILES, JEWISH ATTITUDE TOWARD; GOLDEN RULE, THE; HOSPITALITY; LABOR, DIGNITY OF; LIFE, JEWISH VIEW OF; LIFE, THE SANCTIFICATION OF; MAN, DIGNITY OF; MESSIAH, THE;

MITZVOT; PHARISEES; POOR, THE; REPENTANCE; REWARD AND PUNISHMENT; TEN COMMANDMENTS; TRUTH, JEWISH CONCEPT OF; UNITY OF ISRAEL; WOMAN, THE TREATMENT OF.

ETHICS OF THE FATHERS. *See* PIRKE ABOT.

ETIQUETTE. *See* ETHICAL VALUES, JEWISH; HOSPITALITY.

ETROG. *See* "FOUR SPECIES, THE."

EVIL EYE (in Hebrew: AYIN HA-RAH)

Since earliest times, the backward among the Jews, like their counterparts among other peoples, believed in the Evil Eye. Together with the Egyptians, the Canaanites, the Babylonians, and others, they drew their superstitious notions from the common reservoir of regional folk-beliefs and practices. In all the religions of antiquity, including those of the Greeks and the Romans, magical and demonic elements predominated; all the phenomena of nature were believed to be impregnated with and governed by the invisible and invincible powers of the spirit world.

The notion—common to all people, the Jews included—was that the power of evil lay in dreadful concentration in the human eye, and that the organ of vision could be employed by a person in diametrically different ways: either constructively, for the purpose of defense; or destructively, for aggression. In the latter case, a mere glance, triggered by the concentrated force of malice or envy in a person's soul, could bring dire grief to the one who was affected.

The significance of the belief among Jews in the destructive power residing in the Evil Eye is underscored by a statement of Rab (Abba Arika), the founder of the great Rabbinic Academy in Sura, Babylonia, during the third century C.E. He claimed that out of every one hundred persons who die, fully ninety-nine perish from the effects of being *looked at evilly*.

Not only were the wicked said to be in possession of the power of the Evil Eye, but also the very righteous. To the latter, it was entrusted by Heaven to be employed as an instrument of justice and of divine retribution. The celebrated Rabbinic mystagogue, Simeon bar Yochai, was said to have been able, with a mere glance, to reduce a wicked person to a heap of dry bones. Such punitive power, too, was exercised, according to the Talmud, by the Tanna (Sage) of the Mishnah, Eliezer ben Hyrcanus. Upon his ejection for heresy from the academy of which he was a member, every object that he looked at was promptly consumed by fire.

Those early Talmudic worthies who showed an interest in the awesome workings of the Evil Eye offered many helpful suggestions to the unwary for their protection. Rab, for instance, warned against standing in the midst of a neighbor's cornfield where the ears had already ripened so as not to look upon it with admiring (i.e., envious) eyes. Bridegrooms, being the objects of intense envy on the part of less fortunate males, had one protection against the Evil Eye: walking backward.

Those persons regarded as most vulnerable to the potential mischief of the Evil Eye were beautiful or gifted children—more especially boys. But since every child—at least in the opinion of his doting parents—is cherished as "beautiful," a most rigorous watch had to be established for warding off the hurtful sorcery that was inherent in every expression of admiration uttered by others. Thus it became the custom for a person speaking admiringly of a child's beauty, goodness, health, or cleverness, to add hurriedly, as he concluded the compliment, the fervent Hebrew-Yiddish exclamation: *"Kein Ayin ha-Rah!"* ("May no Evil Eye harm him!")

Inexhaustible were the specifics employed to protect the child against the Evil Eye. One, considered especially efficacious, was a Habdalah candle lit during the rite to honor the outgoing Sabbath. This would be snuffed out in front of the child's face and the smoke from it blown into his mouth. Also considered effective was the folk custom, followed by many a loving mother, of depositing a crumb of bread and a little salt in her child's pocket (or, during the eight-day Passover festival, a little piece of matzah in place of the bread). Regarded as helpful too against the Evil Eye were the magic circlets of amber beads that little girls wore, and the practice of looking down the left side of one's nose.

An assumption commonly held by the early Gentile-Christians (in contradistinction to the early Jewish-Christians) was that every Jew, because he was believed to be the Devil incarnate and a sorcerer, possessed the magic powers of the Evil Eye. Matters finally reached such a crisis that the Church Council of Elvira (held in the fourth century in Spain) actually promulgated Canon Law 49, which forbade Jews from standing amidst the ripening crops belonging to Christians lest, with their malevolent glances and hypocritical words of blessing, they cause them to rot and wither!

A curious incident that illustrates the general attitude of Christians toward the Jews and their alleged possession of the power of the Evil Eye, was chronicled about the corona-

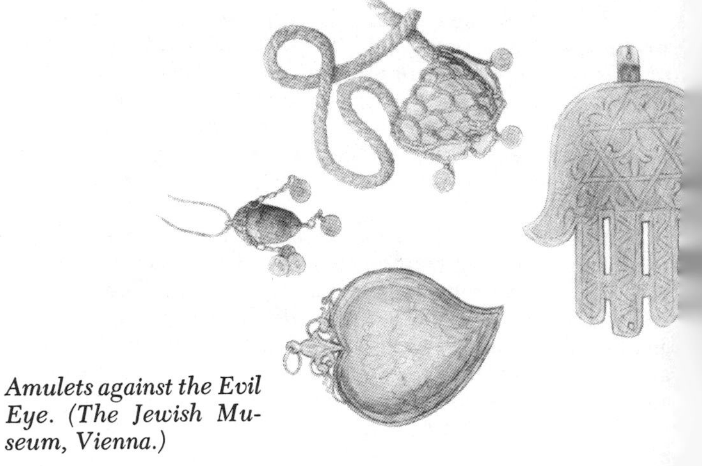

Amulets against the Evil Eye. (The Jewish Museum, Vienna.)

Amulets against the Evil Eye, from early Israelite period, dug up at Gezer.

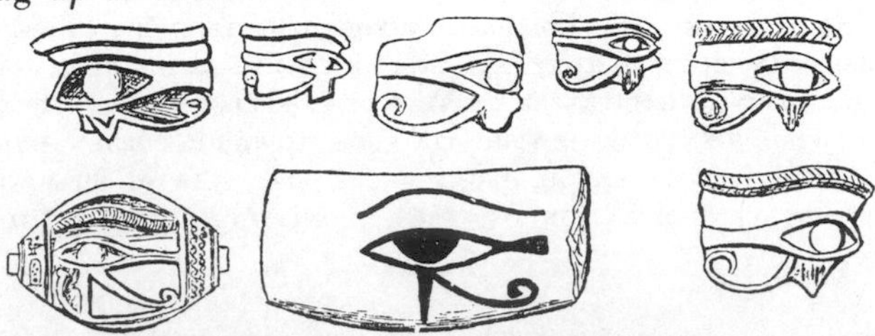

(Left) Cabalistic amulet against epilepsy. (Right) Cabalisti[c] amulet against every kind of sickness. Eastern Europe, 18t[h] century.

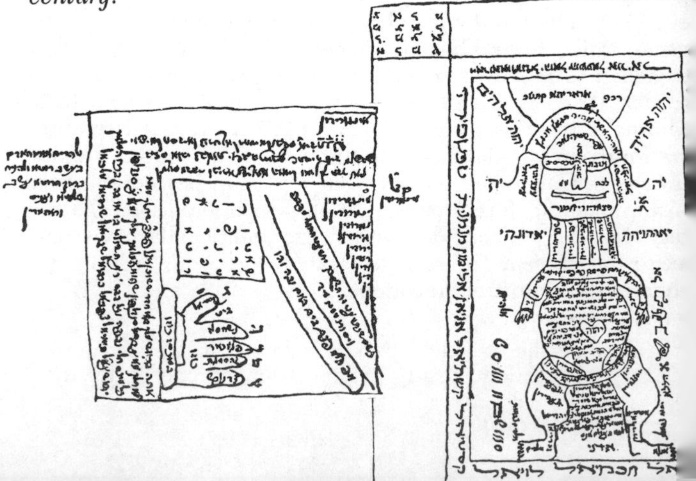

tion of Richard the Lion-hearted in 1189. The Jews of England had sent a delegation to London bearing gifts for the king. But instead of being allowed to attend the coronation ceremonies, they were chased away. It was not thought right that infidel Jews should be allowed to look with their "evil eyes" on the royal crown; they might cause harm to it.

The myth of the Evil Eye was so deeply etched on the consciousness of the German folk that their name for it during the Middle Ages was (and still is) *Judenblick* (Jew's look). The Nuremberg racist laws enacted by Nazi Germany against the Jews had been a long time in the making. . . .

See also AMULETS; DYBBUK; SATAN.

"EVIL INCLINATION," THE. *See* YETZER TOB AND YETZER HA-RAH.

EXCOMMUNICATION (in Hebrew: CHEREM)

The ban of excommunication, which originated as an ecclesiastical instrument of discipline with Ezra and the Scribes during the fifth century B.C.E., became a full-fledged institution during the Talmudic period. Ezra had introduced the ban for the purpose of purifying the Land of Israel from the idolatry into which it had relapsed and from the effects of the mixed marriages which had taken place there during the relatively brief period of the Babylonian Exile. His two main objectives were, firstly, to purge the Jewish religion of its polytheistic and immoral accretions, and secondly, to put up proper safeguards for the preservation in the future of the biological purity of the Jewish people. The disciplinary measures taken were stern and uncompromising, even condemning to death those who deviated, no matter how slightly, from the set path.

When the organization of Jewish society during the Second Temple period had achieved a state of complete theocratic domination, every Jew was expected to align all of his individual interests, religious ideas, and moral conduct with those of the general community. To define these, a set of rigid standards was devised, and to enforce conformity to these standards, the religious authorities instituted the ban of excommunication. There were several kinds of this disciplinary action, varying only in the degree of their severity. The cherem was, in effect, a punishing arm of the religious community, and a highly effective one, at that.

Although the religious teachers during the Second Commonwealth did not exercise the formal authority of the priests in matters of rite and ceremony, they did wield extraordinary disciplinary powers in the special areas of religious belief and moral conduct. They armed the Rabbinical Court (*see* BET DIN) with a formidable array of laws and regulations. Some offenses were automatically punished by excommunication, and this meant the deprivation of certain privileges, public disgrace, and, finally, social ostracism, resulting in the loss of all means of livelihood.

In the microcosmic self-enclosed universe which constituted the automonous Jewish community of later days (especially during medieval and subsequent centuries), the effects of the cherem on the one on whom it was pronounced were totally devastating, for there was no way of escape, no evasion of it possible. However, there was always one doubtfully ameliorating element in this harsh discipline for conformity. By a demonstration of proper repentance, the transgressor could have the ban and its crushing effects removed from himself.

Beginning with the Talmudic Age, there were two principal forms of excommunication: niddui (from the Hebrew *niddah,* meaning "cut off" or "cast out") and "the great cherem." Niddui was imposed by the Bet Din for only thirty days, and only as a punishment for minor religious and moral

Interior of the first Sefaradic synagogue in Amsterdam. Here Uriel da Costa and Baruch Spinoza were excommunicated.

offenses. It was a stern warning to the culprit to mend his ways. He was required to go into formal mourning, as for the dead. He could not bathe nor cut his hair nor wear shoes, but instead had to "walk humbly and speak low" throughout the period of the ban. The only social contact he could have was with the members of his immediate family, but the court had the discretionary power to punish them too, if the excommunicated man did not show a readiness to reform or to comply with the court's decisions. Often enough, if he was obdurate, his children were banned from the religious school, and his wife was not allowed to attend synagogue services.

The offenses for which the niddui was imposed seem surprisingly trivial to the Jew of today. The Talmud lists twenty-four. Among these appear the following: violating the second day of a Holy Day, even if only in a matter determined by custom (minhag) and not by religious law; insulting a messenger of the Rabbinical Court; owning a savage dog or a broken ladder that might cause injury to others.

Of course, the most remarkable in the whole list of "sins" which automatically brought down the niddui on an unfortunate's head was for insulting a rabbi or a scholar, even if he was deceased. The frequency with which this offense was punished by the niddui during the Middle Ages drew this gentle chiding from the twelfth-century sage, Maimonides: "Although the power is given to the scholar to excommunicate a man who had insulted him, it is not praiseworthy for him to employ this means too frequently. He should rather shut his ears to the words of the ignorant. . . . This was the custom of the early pious men, who would not answer when they heard themselves insulted, but would forgive the insolent."

The ban of niddui also required that the person thus punished be anathematized. The curses pronounced in that formula sound somewhat startling to the modern ear.

The early Church, for the identical purpose of religious discipline for conformity, adopted the ban of excommunication and the anathema from the Synagogue. The Apostle Paul, born and raised a Jew, declared fiercely: "If any man love not the Lord Jesus Christ, let him be Anathema Maranatha." (I Corinthians 16:22.)

As formidable as the instrument of excommunication had been among Jews in the days of the Minim (the Judean heretical sects which probably included the early Christians), it grew in severity and in the frequency with which it was imposed during the Middle Ages, when the persecution of the Jews and the efforts to convert them to Christianity became intensified. The slightest deviation from traditional ideas or practices was immediately regarded by the religious and communal leaders as being fraught with the possibility of apostasy, viewed as the very gravest of all sins in the potential of the backsliding Jew. Like the Church, the Synagogue, too, appointed special officials to act as overseers of religious and moral discipline. These were, in a manner of speaking, censors. Their arsenal of punishment was extensive: public humiliation, money-fines, corporal punishment (the traditional thirty-nine stripes), imprisonment, and, finally, the dread imposition of "the great cherem." The last meant expulsion from the Jewish community, thus making of the culprit a pariah, as it were—an untouchable to his own people.

During the Middle Ages, the effects of "the great cherem" on the excommunicate were completely comprehensive and crushing. The ban lasted sometimes for years, sometimes for an entire lifetime. During its period, there was no possibility of human contact with other Jews, not even with the members of the excommunicate's own family who, if they did not promptly renounce and shun him, could themselves be put under a secondary cherem. Thus the ban carried with it the terror of rejection and ejection, and it almost invariably resulted in tragedy for the outcast and his family.

The very rite of excommunication—no one really knows how far back it was instituted—was designed to instill an overwhelming fear of the consequences of heresy in the Jewish community. The entire collective was, therefore, required to witness the ceremony of ostracism, in much the same way that all the personnel of an army unit would be required to witness the punishment of one of its soldiers for a major crime.

The ceremony of the pronouncement of cherem opened with the lighting of candles in the synagogue, as for someone who had died. Then the candles were blown out—a symbolic act of extinguishing the one to be excommunicated from the close-knit collectivity of Israel. The shofar shrilled its harsh execration, and the rabbi, dressed in the white kittel worn on the Day of Atonement, intoned the anathema. The ceremony of excommunication, in spirit if not in the details, was identical with that performed by the Medieval Church.

Perhaps the most tragic instance on record of "the great cherem's" consequences resulted from its pronouncement against the gifted Marrano intellectual, Uriel da Costa (1590–1647). Charged with holding heretical views, he was, after repeated rabbinical warnings, excommunicated. Unable to endure his total isolation from the Jewish community of Amsterdam which was an outcome of the ban he consented to repent publicly of his errors. And so, before the congregation solemnly assembled in the synagogue, he recited a confession of his sins and recanted his heresies. Then he was made to lie down and was scourged with the Scriptural "forty stripes save one." As a fitting climax, he prostrated himself across the synagogue threshold while all the worshipers, as they left the scene of his humiliation, stepped and trampled upon him. Uriel da Costa went home, and after writing down a reaffirmation of his heretical opinions shot himself.

A generation later, it was the destiny of the greatest philosopher that ever sprang from the Jewish people, Baruch Spinoza (1632–77) to be excommunicated by the same angry rigorists in the same synagogue in Amsterdam for his religious and intellectual nonconformism. But the young truth-seeker, possessing a clearer understanding and a firmer character than the unfortunate Da Costa, did not wait for the scourge of the ban to be pronounced upon him (which it was, *in absentia*); instead, he turned away forever from the ghetto, thenceforth to pursue serenely what he called "a life of reason."

It was not only recalcitrant individuals who were made to suffer the severe penalties of "the great cherem" but also entire communities and groups of dissenters. The religious fundamentalists, for example, would excommunicate the religious liberals, and in reciprocity, the liberals would put the fundamentalists under a counter-cherem. That is what happened when the anti-assimilationist religious leader of Barcelona, Solomon Ibn Adret (1235–1310), put under the ban all those Jews under twenty-five years of age who engaged in the "profane study of Greek and Chaldean" writings. In a counteroffensive, the religious champions of general culture put Ibn Adret and his associates under anathemas of their liberal brewing.

The cherem became the absolute weapon in the never-ending struggle of orthodoxy versus liberalism, of traditionalism versus sectarianism, of fixed dogmatism versus heretical ideas. The celebrated eighteenth-century Lithuanian traditionalist, Rabbi Elijah ben Solomon, better known as "the Vilner Gaon," even pronounced the anathemas of the cherem upon the saintly founder of Chasidism, Israel Baal Shem!

The frequent practice of resorting to the excommunication of opponents led to ceaseless strife in the community, and threw into sharp relief the fissures and confusions—religious, social, and intellectual—that, as in other societies, rent the fabric of Jewish group life. Happily, the institution of the cherem died a natural death for, in the enlightened and tolerant religious climate in Jewry today, it can no longer have any validity nor wield any practical effect. But viewed historically, it served in times gone by as a powerful coercive instrument for authoritarian control of Jewish belief, custom, and practice.

EXILE, JEWISH. *See* DIASPORA.

EXODUS, THE. *See* PASSOVER.

EXODUS, BOOK OF. *See* BIBLE, THE.

"EYE FOR AN EYE"

Like all other primitive religious codes developed by the ancient peoples of the Near Middle East, that of the Jews also contained the "law of retaliation." This, in general legal nomenclature, is known as the *lex talionis.*

The Bible defined the principle as well as the character of this law by means of illustrations. It presented a number of concrete kinds of wrongdoing and named for each the punishment to be meted out to fit the crime. For instance: "And he that smiteth any man mortally shall surely be put to death. And he that smiteth a beast mortally shall make it good; life for life. And if a man maim his neighbor; as he hath done, so shall it be done to him: breach for breach, eye for eye, tooth for tooth." (Leviticus 24:17-19.)

The Rabbinic jurists of the Talmud defined the punitive end of this law as a dealing out to everyone who had committed a crime a corresponding "measure for measure"—

The philosopher Baruch Spinoza. (Sculpture by Mark Antokolski.)

Isaac de Fonseca Aboab, Chief Rabbi or Chacham at Amsterdam, who was one of the rabbinic judges in the heresy trial of Baruch Spinoza in 1656.

middah ke-neged middah. "With the same measure of that which you do to others, so shall it be measured out to you," they ruled. This, of course, was not just a Jewish law but the universal law that was operative everywhere in the ancient world. No one seemed to question its validity as a principle of justice.

Nevertheless, the Talmudic legal scholars felt uneasy about it and started to search for "historic" precedents of "measure for measure" retribution in the Bible. They pointed, for example, to the incident when the Egyptians, in the days of the Bondage, plotted to drown the Israelites; in retribution, Heaven decreed that they themselves be drowned. They also underscored an instance of a different kind: Samson, lecherous and irresponsible, had seen fit to follow the seduction of his eyes. His punishment, decreed by God, was that the Philistines pluck out his eyes. They noted that in a third case, Absalom, the unfaithful son of David, who had taken sinful pride in his fine long hair, was also and inexorably given "measure for measure" retribution: While he was fleeing from his pursuing enemies, his hair caught in the thick branches of a tree, so that it was the incidental cause of his death.

Their array of "precedents" was probably an attempt to justify—at least theoretically—the law of retaliation and to quiet the doubts it must have raised in the minds of many Jews who had been nurtured in the morally questioning and humane spirit characteristic of the Talmudic period. This defense by the authorities appears somewhat labored and academic considering that, in actuality, the "eye for an eye" law of retaliation, though it remained formally on the statute books, was to a great extent inoperative in practice. What happened with time was that the refining process in Jewish social and ethical thinking—a development of long duration which began with the Prophets, about the eighth century B.C.E.—reached its high mark only during the last century of the Second Commonwealth.

Even if religious belief and rigid custom opposed any questioning of or tampering with what was revered as the unalterable text of "the revealed truth" of the Bible, so that the law of "measure for measure," enunciated first in Scriptures, had to be retained on the statute books, nevertheless, the humane and morally gentle character of Jewish life and thought called for a far less harsh implementation of it. Leniency, broadmindedness, and forgiveness of wrongs were earnestly recommended by the Rabbinic teachers. Thus, even though the law explicitly prescribed the death sentence for a murderer, the forebearing rabbis conducted court-hearings involving capital crimes with every conceivable kind of procedural hedging, with legalistic obstructions, and a leaning far back in compassion: nor did they make any pretense of hiding their strategy.

It is a matter of record that, long before Mishnaic times, it was rare for anyone in Judea actually to be executed for any major crime. The antipathy of the Sages—those Pharisees much maligned and castigated in the Christian Gospels—toward the death sentence is made plain in this Rabbinic opinion: "A Sanhedrin [namely, the Supreme Court in Jerusalem composed of twenty-three judges sitting in criminal cases] which executes a person once in seven years may be called 'destructive.'" The Sage Eliezer ben Azariah was left dissatisfied with this opinion; he amended it thus: "A Sanhedrin which executes a person once in seventy years can be called 'destructive.'" But perhaps the ultimate humane and passionate regard held by so many Jews for life—even the life of a murderer—can be seen in the concurring opinion expressed by the great teachers Akiba and Tarphon: "Were we members of a Sanhedrin, never would any person be put to death."

Nevertheless, it would be fallacious to think that there were no ardent defenders left among the Jews of "eye for an eye" justice. The Patriarch (President) of the Sanhedrin, Simeon ben Galaliel, retorted to Akiba and Tarphon with the heat of exasperation so reminiscent of the modern defenders of capital punishment: "In that case, you would merely be multiplying the shedders of the blood of Israel!"

There was also demonstrated a similar reluctance to impose harsh sentences for lesser crimes than murder. At the very time that the brutal "eye for an eye" principle of justice was operating unashamedly among other ancient peoples, the Jews devised an ameliorating system of money-fines to expiate damages. This made the "measure for measure" application of the law virtually null and void. The Talmudic law worked out a table of compensating fines to take the place of physical retaliation. For example:

one punch	=	one shekel
one open-handed slap	=	200 zuzim
one back-handed slap or pulling an ear	=	400 zuzim
a kick with the knee	=	3 selas
a kick with the foot	=	5 selas

If the offense resulted in injury or illness, then appropriate damages, as well as compensation for loss of earning power, medical treatment, and other expenses, had to be paid by the defendant.

In view of the fact that one so often hears the philosophy of Jewish law derogated by the uninformed or prejudiced as being as implacable "eye for an eye" justice, its character should be examined in full historic context and—for proper perspective—against the law of retaliation that prevailed in other ancient societies. For instance, the Romans, whose culture and legal philosophy put them near the top of the ladder of civilization in antiquity, maintained a system of punishment of far greater severity than did the Jews. Whereas they would crucify thieves or break or cut off their arms and legs, the Rabbis of Judea merely imposed a fine on such offenders of an additional 100 per cent of the value of what had been stolen.

To bring the coarse reality of life perhaps closer to the truth, in all Christian lands down to the nineteenth century—and, in some places, right down to our own time—the physical torture of prisoners for the purpose of wringing confessions from them was looked upon with complacence as a matter of course. But in Jewish society—even that in which Jesus and his disciples lived and preached—to torture a prisoner charged with a crime, no matter how revolting, was simply unthinkable, and it was sternly prohibited by Rabbinic law.

It is common knowledge that, until the nineteenth century, the debtor's prison was widely esteemed by merchants and statesmen as an institution necessary for the protection of legitimate commerce and honest business practice. Debtor's jails in England and in the American Colonies drew upon them the anathema of all liberal-minded people of their time because of the heartlessness with which they were operated. And even though debtor's jails flourished in Biblical times among the Jews, in enlightened Talmudic law, the repayment of a debt was not regarded as a legal obligation but as an act of consistent morality. Whatever measures were taken for the collection of a debt two thousand years ago were never more drastically punitive than those employed today in so-called civilized countries.

See also ETHICAL VALUES, JEWISH; MONEYLENDERS; SHYLOCK MYTH, THE.

F

FAMILY, THE

The Jewish people always was forced to draw from a reservoir of its inner strength in order to survive the calamities visited upon it in almost every generation. Historical necessity, therefore, gave an urgency and a peculiar emphasis to the ideal of family attachment. It is an undeniable fact that the group identity of the Jews could not have been preserved without the consolations offered by their family life, nor could they have been given a hope for better days without the affirmations of the good that they were able to draw from it. However, the tradition of familial devotion could not have sustained itself, whatever desperate need may have existed for it, were it not for the moral climate of humanity and benevolence generated for centuries by a community existence that was disciplined in the ethical beliefs and practices of the Jewish people. Family love was not an isolated phenomenon by itself but an integral part of the entire culture-pattern of the Jews.

Family love among Jews in the centuries gone by glowed comfortingly for them, like a lamp on a starless night. Whatever the harassments and miseries that awaited them without in a hostile world, in the sanctuary of the home, affection between kinfolk vibrated with an emotionalism that was both warm and tranquilizing. Together with the House of Prayer (Bet ha-Knesset) and the House of Study (Bet ha-Midrash), the home served as a group integrating-agent, as an emotional stabilizer, and as a psychological corrective. It invested the personality of the Jew with the human stature and dignity his enemies tried to deny him.

"In his own household, even the wool-comber is a prince," exulted a Sage of the Talmud.

The evolution of Jewish family mores, ever since the Jews' tribal beginnings several thousand years ago, was a slow but ceaseless process. By the time of the Maccabean revolt, in the second century B.C.E., we already find the historic pattern of the family emerging under the refining impact of the new ethical values that appeared in Jewish life. About two centuries later, in appealing to the ruling class of Rome for a more liberal policy toward the Jews in the Empire, the Jewish historian, Josephus, argued with some asperity and not a little pride: ". . . We must not be treated merely as tolerated aliens simply because we honor our parents, respect old age . . . and strive to maintain family purity in our midst!" Here we already meet with the well-known features of Jewish family life, but dramatically, because this was in an age which elsewhere was degraded by widespread immorality, cruelty, and cynicism.

In the ghettos of Europe, where the Jews were forcibly segregated from their Christian neighbors during the long centuries following the edict of the Fourth Lateran Council in 1215, the stream of life became sluggish and, sometimes, stagnant. It hardly could have been different, because the Jews were cut off from most productive activities by the laws of Church and State and by popular prejudice. Hemmed in not only by the ghetto walls but by implacable persecution, they were reduced to pariah-status. Without being allowed to sink healthy roots into society, how did they ever manage to survive? That is the paradox of all Jewish historic experience. The unexpected happened when the enemies of the Jews shut them up in their ghetto prisons: Unintentionally, they helped preserve the Jews both ethnically and religiously. For, despite all the crippling limitations of their ghetto existence, the Jews, islanded in the ocean of hostility around them, were able to exist semiautonomously and–in a religious and cultural sense–also creatively, within their own little world.

Regardless of the ever present communal differences and squabblings, everybody in the ghetto was molded by the same environmental, institutional, and cultural influences, and was tormented by the same fears and stirred by the same hopes. Despite all that was backward, that was blighting and destructive of body, mind, and spirit in the ghetto, there were, nevertheless, many compensations of a constructive nature. All Jews observed the same religious rites and ceremonies, kept the same festival and fast days, and followed the same folkways, which were a product of their collective living. In varying measure, of course, they shared the same social attitudes and cherished the same ethical practices. Their cohesiveness was a remarkable feature of their community existence. Together, in obligatory perpetual study, they strove to draw wisdom and knowledge from the traditional well of the Torah. They rejoiced together in good fortune and also grieved together and comforted one another in misfortune. The rationale behind this was trenchantly expressed by the popular saying: "Whatever happens to all Israel also happens to Reb [Mr.] Israel."

Not only loyalty to the group and its traditions, but also the stark necessity of their lives, led the Jews to stand firmly together and to practice mutual aid. Whatever the motivation, it resulted in an unusual measure of integration for the individual, the family, the community, and–beyond these–for the Jewish people everywhere. Husbands and wives, parents and children, sisters and brothers–all kinfolk traveled the

Parents and children leaving the synagogue at the end of the service. The great bond that united the members of the Jewish family was their daily pursuit together *of the religious life and of its ethical practices and culture. (From a 14th-century illuminated Hebrew manuscript of Spain.)*

hard road of life together, helping and supporting one another through many vicissitudes.

From the cradle up, the Jewish child was indoctrinated with a comprehensive set of loyalties. First came loyalty to God and the Torah, then to father and mother, and after that to other kin. Next came the loyalty of the family to the community, which, in actuality, was but a constellation of families. Finally, there was the indestructible solidarity of the community with all the hundreds of Jewish communities everywhere. The devotion, self-sacrifice, and filial reverence so widely demonstrated in Jewish family life became a byword in the world. It stands to reason that, under such favorable circumstances, there was only minimal emotional conflict between husband and wife and between parents and children.

That this kind of family relationship no longer exists among Jews to the same extent as previously, qualitatively as well as quantitatively, is self-evident. Many explanations for its decline have been given. But one thing is certain: Jewish life and Jewish community problems are no longer what they used to be. The isolated and culturally self-contained microcosm of the ghetto is no more. The more thoroughly Jews have entered into the general life and culture of the world around them, the more their traditional mores, attitudes, values, and folkways have come to resemble those of other peoples. It is indeed ironic that the deterioration of Jewish family solidarity should have been a concomitant of progress and the emancipation of the Jew!

See also CHALITZAH; DIVORCE; FAMILY RELATIONS, TRADITIONAL PATTERNS OF; ISRAEL, UNITY OF; MARRIAGE; WOMAN, THE TREATMENT OF.

FAMILY RELATIONS, TRADITIONAL PATTERNS OF

The family life of the Jews has always been celebrated in the world for three things: for its solidarity, for its warm emotional attachments, and for the high level of its morality.

Even in our own chaotic age, when the traditional mores and sentiments of familial attachment–not only of the Jews but of Gentiles–have been steadily eroding, a non-Jewish observer of the acculturation of immigrant Jews from the European ghettos into American urban society was led to comment: "The patriarchal family of Biblical times may still be discovered in modern communities. Members of Jewish families seem to be able to maintain greater family solidarity than is shown by many other groups. This may prove to be the greatest contribution of the Jew to modern life."

The degree to which the old pattern of Jewish family relations has survived the disrupting effects of the social and cultural pressures inherent in today's general environment is attributable to the continuing, although admittedly weakening, hold of traditional attitudes, moral ideas, and practices upon the Jews. What are these?

Husband and Wives. The extraordinary concern of the Jewish religion with establishing correct norms for family relationships can be seen in the fact that the Talmud devotes five tractates to the opinions and rulings of the Rabbinic Sages regulating husband-wife relationships. Their major aim, of course, was to insure lasting marital happiness. But they had several other–and just as cogent–goals. Not least among these was the advancement of the common good. "Happiness in the home penetrates into the world outside . . . He who establishes peace in his own family is as if he were establishing it for all Israel," the Sages declared, adding that family happiness and peace could be achieved only by one means: by the power of *love*–love between husband and wife.

Anticipating the thinking of modern child psychologists on the same matter by some seventeen or eighteen centuries, the Rabbinical educators laid down this fundamental principle for family happiness: "He who loves his wife as himself and honors her more than himself, will guide his children along the right path." And like the marriage-counsellors of today, the Sages of ancient Judea and Babylonia perceived that, in homes which are rent by discord between parents, the children suffer irreparable psychic damage. The Talmud warned: "Discord in the home is like rottenness in fruit . . . A home rent by strife will be broken."

"God bless our home," in Jewish symbols of the Ten Commandments and a menorah, made from hair and felt. South Germany, 19th century.

Bokharan mother and son celebrating his Bar Mitzvah. (Israel Government Information Services.)

Recapitulating this Talmudic tradition, the medieval Cabalistic work, the Zohar, presented a definitive formula for achieving family peace: "The wife who receives love from her husband gives him love in return. And if he gives her hatred—she returns hatred." Consequently, in the give-and-take of the marital union, husband and wife were likened by the Rabbis to two candles, the one being kindled by the flame of the other. For that reason, exhorted Hai Gaon (*d.* 1038), the last of the brilliant Rabbinical academicians of Babylonian Jewry: "All your days love the beloved of your youth, and plant your love for her well in her heart."

Because many of the religious teachers of the Jewish people were sober realists, they exhibited a compassionate solicitude for the wife in her position of social inferiority and relative rightlessness in a man's world. Despite the fact that Jewish husbands generally treated their spouses with greater humanity and gentleness than did their non-Jewish contemporaries, the Rabbis directed their teaching and moralizing principally at them, and not at their wives. Some of the fundamental moral principles and ground rules the Sages laid down established the classic pattern of Jewish marital conduct that has been followed for almost two thousand years.

The Jewish Sages of Hellenistic times stressed that it was to the best interests of the husband that he deal justly and kindly with his mate. "If a man is happy, it is mostly because of his wife. . . . Whatever blessing enters his home comes from her."

In an age that among non-Jews was characterized by much cynicism and disrespect for women, Rabbi Eliezer of Mayence (*d.* 1357) urged: "[Wives] must respect their husbands and always be amiable to them. For their part, husbands must honor their wives more than themselves. They must treat them with tenderness and consideration." To act otherwise, in the words of the encyclopedic humanist-scholar, Rabbi Judah ibn Tibbon (twelfth-century Provence), "is the way of contemptible men."

The husband was repeatedly lectured against exercising a too severe authority over his wife. And cruelty, even of the verbal kind, was strictly forbidden. "A man must not make a woman weep, for God counts her tears," admonished the Talmud.

The gentle regard in which most Jewish husbands held their wives is reflected in the stern Rabbinical proscription against wife-beating. This was at the very time when, among Christians and Mohammedans, the periodic chastisement of the wife was looked upon as a quite respectable corrective and a legitimate practice for the master of the household to help him maintain his undisputed authority. Rabbi Meir of Rothenburg (Rhineland, 1220–93) merely repeated what in his time was a well-known fact when he observed: "Jews do not follow the prevailing custom of beating their wives."

Wife-beaters in Jewish community life were publicly disgraced and ostracized until they repented. The Yiddish-writing moralist, Yitzchok ben Eliakum of Prague, evidently outraged by an increase in the mistreatment of wives by some Jewish husbands in that culturally backward period, raged in 1610: "No son of Israel is allowed to beat his wife! This is not fitting for a Jew. It is not a Jewish trait. Moreover, it is a very terrible sin, even more terrible than if he were to beat a man! . . . And even if he only raises his hand to strike her, and yet restrains himself, he is still a wicked man. Under no circumstances must such a wretch be called upon at services to read from the Torah!"

Parents and Sons. If the happiness of the Jewish family devolved upon a harmonious husband-wife relationship, its principal goal was the rearing of upright and pious children—of sons, especially. The frank emphasis on the latter arose because in the traditional religious-social scheme of the Jews, it was the menfolk who were assigned the central and dominant position. Hai Gaon extended these words of comfort to the parents of girl-children: "Do not worry if it is your lot to have a daughter. Trust in God, rejoice, and be glad in your good fortune. Many a daughter is better than a son and a source of joy and happiness to her parents."

In the "ethical" testament that Rabbi Eleazar "the Great" of Worms (*c.* 1050) addressed to his son, he summarized the Jewish parents' main goal: "My son! It is your duty to beget children and to raise them for the study of the Torah. Because of them you will be deemed worthy of eternal life."

This interconnection between the rearing of worthy sons, the study of the Torah (in the estimation of the devout, this was the principal road to righteousness), and the end-reward of the life eternal, formed a revered tradition in the Jewish religion. The universalistic mission of the Jews, in which they were to serve as the instrument of God's will for bringing all the nations in brotherhood to Mount Zion by means of the Torah, demanded their biological continuity. Moreover, it urged Jewish parents, generation upon generation, to prepare their sons for this exalted dedication.

To add moral weight to this supreme duty, the Sages taught the people that in the "creation" of every child there were three partners: his father, his mother, and God. In fact, God was considered to be the principal but "silent" partner in the production of every child, with the parents his active associates. However, they, and not God, were to be held strictly accountable for the "finished" product—a product they wanted to be deemed worthy of the Creator in whose divine image he was believed to have been made.

The paramount importance given in Rabbinic Judaism to the raising of righteous sons and daughters was epitomized in this Talmudic parable.

> When the Israelites were gathered at Mount Sinai to receive the Torah from the hands of Moses, God demanded of them: "You must first give me a guarantee that you will observe the commandments of the Torah."
>
> The Israelites replied: "Our fathers will gurantee that for us."
>
> "No!" protested God, "your fathers were backsliders."
>
> "Then the Prophets will stand guarantee for us," went on the Israelites.
>
> "No!" said God, "they, too, sinned against me."
>
> The Israelites became downcast. Timidly they ventured: "Perhaps our children could be our pledge?"
>
> "Your children!" cried the Creator joyfully, "them I will accept!"
>
> And so he gave the Torah to the Israelites.

There were certain specific obligations that the father had toward his children. He had to provide for them and protect them against all harm. In matters of religion, he was to arrange for the circumcision of his sons and for the "redemption" of his first-born, if he was a male, and have them taught their prayers and the Pentateuch (the Five Books of the Bible) in the holy tongue, Hebrew. If the father was too poor to provide for his sons' religious instruction, then he was required, by whatever exertion and sacrifice of pride it demanded, to borrow the money. Furthermore, each father

A Jewish couple of Warsaw. (Sketch in L. Hollaenderski's Les Israelites de Pologne, *Paris, 1830.)* (LEFT)
Chasidic husband and wife. Jerusalem, early 20th century.

was duty bound to teach his son whatever measure of Torah-learning he himself possessed. This was to be in fulfillment of the Scriptural precept: "And ye shall teach them [the Commandments] to your children."

It is a singular fact that in no other religion has it been a categorical "must" for parents to assume the primary responsibility *as educators* of their own children. Among the Jews, in former times, this task was considered to be an all-important and sacred dedication. "Blessed is the son who has studied [Torah] with his father, and blessed is the father who has instructed his son!" rejoiced an ancient Sage.

The mother, too, had her own special role as educator. Because she spent more time at home with her children than did the father, she was expected to devote herself to the task of helping to mold their characters, disciplining them, and supervising their conduct and religious observances. In different ways and by their own behavior, both father and mother strove to set a proper example for their children in uprightness and piety.

The Rabbinic teachers, over the course of several centuries, developed a philosophy of child-rearing which made concentrated parental attention understandable. A classic principle of education had been formulated as far back as the compilation of the Book of Proverbs and was expressed therein:

> Train up a child in the way he should go:
> And when he is old, he will not depart from it.

In Roman times, the Rabbinic Sages gave their own homely paraphrase of this maxim: "If you do not teach the ox to plow when he is young you will find it hard to teach him when he is fully grown."

The merit of a father was judged within the Jewish community by the kind of children he had raised and by the goals toward which they were directing their lives. Judah ibn Tibbon pleaded with his son: "What is the honor I so dearly wish for? It is to be remembered for good, both in life and in death, because of you, so that others, observing you, may say: 'Blessed be the father who begot this son; blessed be he who raised him!' "

The control and discipline of children was carefully moderated by the gentle precepts the Rabbinic Sages had taught. They furnish an intriguing study in contrast with the legal regulations and customs for parents prevailing among the Romans who were their contemporaries. According to Roman law, as long as the father was alive, he remained absolute master over the actions and the destinies of his sons. Among the Jews, on the other hand, the son, after his marriage, was free to lead an independent life, and provided he conducted himself uprightly and was not guilty of unfilial disrespect, he was not accountable for his actions to his father.

From the earliest years of the Rabbinic age, parents were cautioned against being unreasonably severe with their children, especially in disciplining older sons and daughters. It was pointed out to them that punishment often makes the child bitter and resentful, and might even provoke him into behaving aggressively, thus warping his attitude and ruining him for life. Rather, parents were counseled to show forbearance and to act gently and patiently with a wayward or unheeding child, using reason with him instead of force. Some Rabbinic educators took the view that a parent who inflicted any kind of corporal punishment upon his child was guilty of violating the Scriptural commandment: "Thou shalt not put a stumbling block before the blind." (Leviticus 19:14.) One medieval rabbi went so far in his condemnation of such parents as to observe: "They deserve to be excommunicated for it!"

The Zohar tells in a teaching parable of a father who was grieved because his son was disobedient. He mulled over his problem thus in his mind: "What if I were to punish him–what would I accomplish thereby? If I were to inflict pain on him, it would cause me pain also, and if I were to rebuke him publicly, it would only humiliate him. What then shall I do? I know–I shall plead with him to mind me!"

It became a traditional and quite general practice among the Jews to correct their children not violently, with the rod, but gently, with love, and by reasoning with them. Two maxims in the Talmud became classic guidelines for parents: "Do not threaten a child; either punish him, or forgive him. . . . If you must strike your child, do it with a shoestring."

Such unusual forbearance was by no means the consequence of a maudlin sentimentality or any inclination to pamper children. Like the most advanced child psychologists of our time, the Rabbinic teachers followed the vision of a wholesome family environment in which the child's personality could develop harmoniously, both for his own good and for the good of society. Thus he would be able to respond to his parents' understanding love with a reciprocal attachment that is described in the Talmud: "The child should keep green the memory of his father and mother. When ever he speaks of them, it should be with love and respect."

In Jewish moralistic writings, parents were sternly admonished not to show any favoritism. One ancient psychologist in the Talmud warned: "Remember what happened with Joseph!" In the Bible it is told that Joseph had been his father's, Jacob, favorite, therefore, his brothers were jealous of him, and they hated him with an unforgiving hatred. When the opportunity finally came for settling accounts, they got rid of him.

Rabbi Moses of Evreux (*c.* 1240) commented concerning this problem in child-raising: "Give your love equally to all your children. The great expectations many parents place on favorite children often turn out disappointing, while the one who may have been neglected or rejected, may prove in the end to be the source of their joy."

Children and Parents. Since all human relations, in order to be just, have to be regulated on the principle of reciprocity, the Rabbinic teachers also provided a set of laws and regulations for the conduct of children in relation to their parents.

In the ethical-religious climate of Jewish life in centuries past, the Jewish child was brought up to believe that, next to God, he was to love, revere, and obey his father and mother. He was taught to look upon them as the instruments of God's love for him, for it was in close partnership with God that they had "created" him, and they were devoting their lives to raising him and giving him their tender love and care. The child was constantly being made aware, in the synagogue and in religious school, of the fact that his parents were unselfishly striving to mold his character and teach him to tell the difference between good and bad so that he might grow up to be an upright, knowledgeable, and pious Jew. For, as such, he would in due time be able to find a useful place for himself in the scheme of life.

Did his father and mother claim from him any recompense for the love and devotion that they were lavishing on him? It is significant that the Fifth Commandment makes no mention of the *duty to love* one's parents, since love cannot be "commanded"; it merely bids the child: "Honor thy father and thy mother . . . that thy days may be long . . . upon the land which the Lord thy God giveth thee." (Deuteronomy 5:16.)

Filial piety was a sentiment and an attitude that grew out of the special conditions of Jewish family relations, in which respect and concern on the part of the parents for the personality and the feelings of the child in turn generated in him love and reverence for them. Filial piety also had deep religious overtones. It is stated in the Talmud: "If you honor and revere your father and mother [says God], then you also honor and revere Me. If you distress them and cause them grief, you also distress and grieve Me."

Clearly indicated were the duties to their parents of sons and daughters, regardless of whether they were still children or middle-aged married men and women. Some of these precepts merely constituted moral attitudes, others were of a practical nature and were prescribed to rule their conduct toward parents in a variety of situations.

Children were to be respectful to their parents at all times. They were to listen to a parental rebuke and counsel with "open hearts" and without interrupting, for to contradict a father or mother was considered unspeakably impudent and intolerable. The parents' wishes on matters they felt strongly about were to be honored, even after their death. The manner in which sons and daughters behaved toward or spoke to them was expected to conform to the generally accepted notions of filial respect among Jews. Under no circumstances were the father or mother to be shamed, either by action or failure to act, or by word or gesture, or even a look. "Cursed be he that dishonoreth his father or his mother!" thundered the wrathful Biblical moralist. "And all the people shall say: Amen." (Deuteronomy 27:16.)

Children were expected always to remain scrupulously loyal and devoted to their father and mother, and they were required to submit willingly to parental authority until they married and started families of their own. They were expected to recognize that such authority was being exercised not capriciously or to tyrannize over them, but for their own good.

When they grew to maturity, sons and daughters were duty bound to support their parents to the best of their ability when such aid became necessary. They were to care for them with devotion in sickness and in old age. "My son," wrote Jesus ben Sirach, the great wisdom-teacher of Jerusalem (*c.* early second century, B.C.E.), "help your father in his old age, and do not grieve him as long as he lives, and if his understanding fail, have patience with him."

However, not all Jewish sons and daughters behaved as models of devotion to parents in adversity. These lapses from probity are illustrated by the bitter Jewish folksaying: "One father is able to support ten sons, yet ten sons are not able to support one father."

It was always a popular notion among peoples in the East that wisdom ripened with age and that the chief repositories of it were old people.

> Hear, my son, the instruction of thy father,
> And forsake not the teaching of thy mother;
> For they shall be a chaplet of grace unto thy head,
> And [gold] chains about thy neck.
>
> PROVERBS 1:8-9

Respect, honor, and devotion were expected to be extended in equal measure to one's father and mother–this the Fifth Commandment made mandatory. Even if in former times the Jewish woman was not accorded equal social and

Drawn closer together by their trials and suffering in a German concentration camp, this refugee couple looks trustfully and hopefully into the future. Israel, 1949.

religious status with the man, she did, however, enjoy equality with him in the management of the home and in the rearing of their children. (*See* WOMAN, THE TREATMENT OF.) A mother's wishes had to be obeyed just like a father's, and Rabbinic law equated contemptuous treatment of her with murder and idolatry.

The mother held a central position in keeping the Jewish home together. Often—especially in Europe, during the later centuries—the Jewish family was more matriarchal than patriarchal in character. It was on the mother's frail but determined shoulders that the heavy burdens and anxieties of her loved ones rested, and her efforts on their behalf often represented a triumph of love over discouraging odds. The father, preoccupied with earning a livelihood and an unflagging attention to Torah study and worship, frequently left to the mother the all-important task of rearing the children in rectitude and piety. It is no cause for wonder then that once, on hearing his mother approach, the Talmudic Sage, Joseph, gravely announced to his colleagues: "I must rise, for the Schechinah [God's Presence] is about to enter!"

Mothers-In-Law and Daughters-In-Law. Relations between mothers-in-law and daughters-in-law, at all times and among all peoples a potential source of emotional problems, were no less so among Jews. Yet the Rabbinical moralists made no attempt to ignore or sidetrack this problem as if it did not exist. The deep devotion that existed between Ruth and her mother-in-law, Naomi, in the Biblical romance was always held up as the matchless example of what an in-law relationship could and should become. The folk-pattern of Jewish family mores called for unremitting tact, self-restraint, and a sense of responsibility in efforts to establish a *modus vivendi* by mutual accommodation.

The traditional view on this matter was given by Rabbi Elijah ben Solomon (Lithuania, 1720–97), celebrated among Jews as the Vilner Gaon. In the "ethical testament" that he left behind for the guidance of his family, he wrote:

I also beg my wife to honor my mother in accordance with the prescription of the Torah, especially regarding a widow. It is an indictable offense to distress her, even in the smallest matter. My mother, too, I entreat to live harmoniously with my wife, each bringing happiness to the other by kindly conduct, for this is a prime duty incumbent on all mankind. In the hour of Judgment each one is asked: "Has your conduct toward your fellow men been friendly?" The aim of the Torah, in large part, is to create happiness for mankind. Therefore, let there be no dissension of any kind among all my household, both men and women, but let love and brotherliness reign. In case of offense, forgive one another and, for the sake of God, live in amity. . . . And may the Master of Peace grant you, my dear sons and daughters, my sons-in-law and my brothers, and to all Israel, life and peace!

Brothers and Sisters. The closest ties were expected to be established and preserved, as long as they lived, between all siblings: between brother and brother, brother and sister, and sister and sister. All were required to behave toward one another with mutual affection, devotion, and amity. "How good and how pleasant it is for brothers to dwell together in unity!" rejoiced the ancient Psalmist. In time of trouble the children of the same father and mother were to stand loyally together, and to render each other all necessary assistance. Said the Wise King in the Book of Proverbs: "A brother helped by a brother is like a fortified city."

Grandparents. Grandparents played a very important role in the life-drama of the family. In a very literal sense, they were "associate parents." The traditional view concerning them was expressed in the Talmud (as it were) by an orphaned boy: "Rear me, rear me! I am the son of your daughter!"

The moral responsibility placed upon grandparents to care for and to give their love and protection to their grandchildren was virtually as great as that which devolved upon parents, and this obligation was unquestionably accepted by them in every generation.

Grandfather instructing grandson before his Bar Mitzvah in putting on tefillin. (Painting by Bender, Poland, early 20th century.)

Grandparental blessings on Rosh Hashanah. Galicia, end of 19th century.

"Second parents." Warsaw, late 19th century.

Family idyll, modern Israel.

With the beginning of the Middle Ages in Europe, custom assigned to grandparents a distinctive educative and moral function. They were required to participate with the father and mother in indoctrinating the children with the "right" precepts and practices. Grandmothers helped their granddaughters memorize the most essential prayers and blessings, and extolled for them the shining virtues of truthfulness, modesty, chastity, and piety. The grandfather periodically examined his grandson in his religious studies to ascertain what progress he was making. And when the time for the boy's Bar Mitzvah approached, the grandfather tried to help him in every way possible to acquit himself well in the severe tests he was to be put through (*see* BAR MITZVAH). He drilled him in the correct modal intonation of the weekly portion of the Chumash (Pentateuch) and the Haftarah (the portion from the Prophets) which the boy was to recite aloud in the synagogue before the entire congregation on the Sabbath of his Bar Mitzvah. His grandfather also aided him in the preparation of the customary derashah, the religious discourse with which the Bar Mitzvah would demonstrate to his elders the extent of his Torah-knowledge and his proficiency in Talmudic argumentation. But perhaps his grandfather's principal act of merit (mitzvah), and the one conceded to him by tradition, was to teach the boy the complicated procedures of putting on and taking off the phylacteries (tefillin) before and after the daily morning prayers.

Jewish custom decreed that the grandchildren in their turn comport themselves with the utmost respect and consideration toward their grandparents. This was in line with the extraordinary respect Jews, like all other Eastern peoples, were taught to show the old:

> Thou shalt rise up before the hoary head, and honor the face of the old man. LEVITICUS 19:32

See also CHALITZAH; CIRCUMCISION; DIVORCE; DOWRY; FAMILY, THE; INTERMARRIAGE; KETUBAH; MARRIAGE; MONOGAMY; PIDYON HA-BEN; SHADCHAN; WOMAN, THE TREATMENT OF.

FAMILY TIES. *See* FAMILY RELATIONS, TRADITIONAL PATTERNS OF.

FASTING AND FAST DAYS

At various times in Jewish history, different emphases were placed upon and different meanings were read into the physical act of fasting. Attempting to propitiate a seemingly angry deity by not eating or drinking was, no doubt, one of the principal motivations in primitive thinking. One of the traditional Jewish meanings of fasting—as a symbolic or spiritual act performed by the devout person—was first projected by the Prophets. Because they were neither formalists nor ritual traditionalists but religious-social idealists, they laid the greatest emphasis not on fasting as a mortification of the digestive system, but on the awakening, by means of it, of the individual's slumbering conscience.

The most meaningful and ethical definition of fasting was given by the Second Isaiah—the Prophet of the Babylonian Captivity in the sixth century B.C.E. Rebuking, in the words of God, the literal-minded among the fasters, he chided (58:5):

> Is such the fast that I [God] have chosen,
> The day for a man to afflict his soul?
> Is it to bow down his head as a bulrush,
> And to spread sackcloth and ashes under him?
> Wilt thou call this a fast
> And an acceptable day to the Lord?

What then did God consider to be the true religious function for fasting? This, according to the Prophet, as expressed in Isaiah 58:6-7:

> Is not this the fast that I have chosen?
> To loose the fetters of wickedness,
> To undo the bonds of the yoke,
> And to let the oppressed go free,
> And that ye break every yoke?
> Is it not to deal thy bread to the hungry,
> And that thou bring the poor that are cast out to thy house?

The teachings of the Prophets concerning fasting were further elaborated in their social-ethical goals by the Talmudic Sages. An entire tractate of the Mishnah—Megillat Ta'anit, the Scroll of Fasts—was devoted to an exploration of the subject. It posed three objectives for fasting: repentance, supplication for God's help, and mourning or commemoration.

Fasting leading to repentance was considered meaningful only when it was an act of free will, so it could stimulate in the faster an honest self-examination. Fasting as supplication for God's intervention in time of great trial was most often a collective act. In the troubled history of the Jewish people, who were scattered in ten thousand different places throughout the world, the observance of special fast days occurred but too frequently. These could be ordered by the rabbinic authorities of a single community—or even of an entire country or region—for the purpose of imploring God's aid in averting some harsh decree by Church or State, or to frustrate the plottings of enemies inplacable in their hatred of the Jews. In time of drought, rural communities joined in a fast to bring rain. When pestilence struck, ghetto Jewries fasted to supplicate divine protection. The third major aim of fasting—one that had been instituted by the Prophets—was to recall to the seed of Abraham the many calamities that had befallen them a various times since the Bondage in Egypt.

Alone among all the fast days, Yom Kippur, the Day of Atonement, had received the sanction of the Torah as a commandment. But inasmuch as the perpetuating power of custom is often as great as that of canonical law, a whole series of extra-Scriptural fasts took a firmly rooted place in Jewish religious life.

Held in greatest reverence was the fast of Tishah B'Ab (the Ninth of Ab). This is a day of national grief and contrition that commemorates the Destruction (in 586 B.C.E. and in 70 C.E., respectively) of both the First and the Second Temples in Jerusalem. The implication of this and of other historic commemorative fasts is that if calamities have befallen the Jewish people, it has been, in the words of the liturgy, "on account of our sins"—as punishment from God (*see* TISHAH B'AB).

Another traditional fast day is Tzom Gedaliah (the Fast of Gedaliah). It takes place the day after Rosh Hashanah, and is observed by Orthodox Jews in memory of Gedaliah, surnamed "the Righteous." King Nebuchadnezzar of Babylonia, after he had laid the First Temple in ruins, in 586 B.C.E., had appointed Gedaliah governor of Judah. For reasons unknown, he was assassinated by fellow Jews. In reprisal, there took place a massacre of the Jews.

The fast of Asarah B'Tebet (the Tenth of Tebet) recalls the beginning of the siege of Jerusalem by Nebuchadnezzar. The fast of the Seventeenth of Tammuz commemorates an assortment of national calamities listed in the Talmud. Moses, according to Exodus 32:19, broke the tablets of the Ten Commandments on that day; and on that day also, the daily sacrifices in the Temple were abrogated, Titus successfully made a breach in the walls of Jerusalem during the siege of the city, the Syrian general Atsotomos burned the Scrolls of the Torah, and a pagan idol was set up in the very sanctuary itself on Mount Zion by weak-kneed priests of the

Temple. These were among the reasons that were given by the religious teachers during the Rabbinic Age to explain and justify God's punishment of Israel, when he destroyed the Temple and scattered its people in Exile (*Galut*, in Hebrew) to all the far corners of the earth.

Ta'anit Esther (the Fast of Esther) is observed by the tradition-adhering on the Eve of Purim in grateful memory of the patriotic fast that Queen Esther kept when seeking divine guidance and strength prior to her pleading for the lives of her fellow Jews before her husband, King Ahasueros of Persia.

The eve before Passover is commemorated by the Ultra-Orthodox as Ta'anit Bechorim (the Fast of the First-Born), as an expression of gratitude to God for having spared the first-born of Israel at the time of the slaying of all the first-born of the Egyptians, prior to the Exodus from Egypt by the Israelites.

In the category of commemorative fasting, the presumed anniversaries of the deaths of the Biblical eminences Moses, Aaron, Miriam, Joshua, and Samuel, and of the Rabbinic martyrs who perished at the hands of the Romans (Akiba ben Joseph, the Ten Martyrs, and others) were customarily observed as half-day fasts in former centuries. But these fast days are no longer observed except by a handful of the unyielding tradition-bound.

The personal life of the Jew in the round of his experiences has also included fasting on important occasions, thus giving them a quasi-religious character. Still widely observed in every part of the world is the fast of bride and bridegroom on their wedding day. After a bad dream it was customary in days gone by for the dreamer to protect himself against its threats by expiatory fasting: Ta'anit Chalom (Fast After a Dream). During the Middle Ages and afterward, there were saintly mystics and dedicated pietists who, anxious to hasten the coming of the Messianic age, fasted faithfully in behalf of all Israel on every Monday and Thursday until the day of their death.

Eleazar ben Pedat, the Sage of the Talmud, once declared that the act of fasting was in a way superior to the giving of benevolence, for whereas the ends of charity are accomplished merely by giving money to the needy, through fasting, one gives of oneself to God. However, this line of reasoning was considered too facile a way of excusing a man from dispensing "loving-kindness" to his fellows. And so the Talmud hastened to caution the faster: "The merit of a fast day lies in the benevolence one gives on that occasion."

See also ASCETICS, JEWISH; KIDDUSH HA-SHEM; TISHAH B'AB; YOM KIPPUR.

FEAST DAYS. *See* HOLY DAYS.

FEAST OF BOOTHS, THE. *See* SUCCOT.

FEAST OF DEDICATION, THE. *See* CHANNUKAH.

FEAST OF INGATHERING, THE. *See* SHABUOT.

FEAST OF LIGHTS, THE. *See* CHANNUKAH.

FEAST OF LOTS, THE. *See* PURIM.

FEAST OF WEEKS, THE. *See* SHABUOT.

FELLOWSHIP IN ISRAEL

A revered tradition of ancient origin has it that when the Children of Israel stood at the foot of Mount Sinai to receive the Torah, God made them pledge themselves one for another. From this historic memory stemmed two basic beliefs, the first being that "All Jews are responsible for one another," and the second, that "All Jews are comrades." (*"Kol Yisrael chaverim."*)

The Talmud has a haunting tradition that in the First Temple, built by Solomon, there were two special gates. The one on the right was reserved for bridegrooms; there they would be greeted on the Sabbath day thus: "He who dwells here shall bestow on you the joys of a Father." The gate on the left was reserved for mourners and the afflicted. The former would be greetd thus: "He who dwells here shall bring you comfort," and those who entered to pray for the sick would be consoled with these words: "May the One Who dwells here have compassion upon you!"

But after the Temple was destroyed, the bridegrooms, the mourners, and the petitioners for the sick had to go to the synagogues for prayer. From that time on, all Israel was no longer content merely with extending its good wishes; instead, it rejoiced *together* with the bridegrooms, mourned *together* with the mourners, and prayed *together* with the afflicted.

See also CHARITY; ETHICAL VALUES, JEWISH; UNITY OF ISRAEL.

FESTIVAL OF THE NEW MOON, THE. *See* ROSH CHODESH.

FESTIVALS, JEWISH. *See* HOLY DAYS.

FEUDAL SOCIETY, POSITION OF THE JEWS IN

The legal groundwork for anti-Semitism as a permanent policy of Christian states was laid by the Emperor Justinian of Byzantium (ruled 527–65 C.E.) in his celebrated code. One clause provided: "They [the Jews] shall enjoy no honors. Their status shall reflect the baseness which in their souls they have elected and desired." Furthermore, his code laid down the principle (later strengthened by the theological decision and restatement of Thomas Aquinas [1224–74] "The Angelic Doctor") of *servitus Judaeorum*—"the servitude of the Jews" to Christians—formulated because the Jews had rejected Jesus as their saviour and caused his death.

Whatever hardships and tribulations the Jews had to undergo during the Middle Ages simply to survive physically were as nothing compared to the mental anguish, the degradation, and the social pariahism to which they were perpetually condemned by religious hatred and bigotry. The Jews were included by the central dogmas of Christianity in the grand design for the redemption of Christians. However, it was with far less than Christian charity that Bernard of Clairvaux, the spiritual mentor of the Second Crusade who was later sainted, had expatiated thus concerning the "just punishment" to be meted out to the Jews: "They are living symbols for us representing the Lord's Passion. For this they are dispersed to all lands so that, while they pay the just penalty for so great a crime [that, is, the Crucifixion], they may be witnesses for our Christian redemption."

In 1519, during his early period of belligerent criticism against the Church, the then Catholic priest, Martin Luther, derided the doctrine of *servitus Judaeorum*: "Absurd theologians defend hatred for the Jews by claiming that [the members of] the race are slaves of Christendom and the Emperor. . . . What Jew would consent to enter our ranks when he sees the cruelty and enmity we wreak on them—that in our behavior toward them, we less resemble Christians than beasts!"

Continuing his guerilla warfare against the Church, Luther, who was a past master of unsubtle satire, wrote in his essay, "Jesus was born a Jew": "Were I a Jew and saw what blockheads and windbags rule and guide Christendom, I would rather become a pig than a Christian. For they have treated the Jews more liks dogs than men. Yet the Jews are kindred and blood brothers of our Saviour. If we are going to boast about the virtues of race, Christ belongs more to them than to us."

When the segregation of the Jews in ghettos was ordered by the Fourth Lateran Council of the Church in 1215, accompanied by the most crushing economic legal and civil restrictions, Jews were given the doubtful privilege, granted even to serfs, of owning arms with which to defend themselves. But later they were deprived even of this fundamental medieval right. Having been given no place or function in the stratified feudal system, they were obliged to stand outside of it, being thenceforth designated legally as *servi camerae*, "chattels of the [royal] chamber."

The royal charter promulgated on behalf of the Jews in the year 1180 in Angevin England made the following point very clear:

> It should be known that all Jews, wheresoever in the realm they be, ought to be under the guard and protection of the King's liege. Nor ought any of them place himself under any rich man without the King's license; because the Jews themselves and all theirs belong to the King, and if any detain them or their money, let the King, if he will and can, ask it back as if it were his own.

Because they were his personal "property," the king could dispose of the Jews—and did—in any way he saw fit: as a gift, or, in lieu of cash, as payment for some service rendered by a feudal vassal. Sometimes he "sold" them outright or, when he happened to be in need of cash, "pawned" them to a princeling, to a bishop of the Church, to a baron, or even to a municipality. For the "protection" the Jews were to receive, at least theoretically, they were obliged to pay, half to the emperor or king and half to the reigning prince, an annual opferpfennig—a "penny"—which, in fact, amounted to considerably more than a penny. The pfennig swelled into a gulden for each Jew over twelve years of age. Jews were also required to pay a special "coronation tax" separately to emperor, king, and prince, when each ascended his throne.

Onerous, to put it mildly, was the payment of the so-called Jewish body-tax which Jewish travelers, as they passed through a city, were forced to pay the local authorities for a military escort to protect them against the many robber bands that infested the medieval city streets, making them unsafe even during daylight. And even in death the Jew was not free from the harassments of the tax-collectors. For then his family had to pay not only "escort money" on the way *to* the cemetery but a special burial tax *in* the cemetery. For the Jew, it was frightfully expensive to live, but it was equally costly for him to die.

Jews in procession go out to meet Henry VII, the Holy Roman Emperor, to present to him a Torah Scroll in homage and subservience. Rome, c. 1312.

Bound Jew brought before a Christian judge. (Drawing in the Dresden Sachsenspiegel, *c. 1220.)*

Some Jewish communities were required to pay special "imperial" taxes in addition to the "regular" taxes. For instance, in Frankfurt-am-Main, in Germany, the Jews were ordered to supply all the parchment needed by the emperor's chancellery, all the bedding required by the court, and all the pots and pans for the palace kitchen, as well as specified sums to the imperial officials as a kind of salary or bonus. Despite the fact that the Jews formed only a tiny part of the general population in the imperial domains, they were, nevertheless, expected to pay the emperor alone 12 per cent of all taxes received. In addition, they had to pay one-fifth of all city and town taxes. These crushing taxes, special payments, and "gifts" were further increased by the enormous collective fines levied against Jewish communities upon every conceivable pretext, whether on the local, regional, princely, kingly, or imperial level.

Perhaps some thirteen or fourteen centuries ago, when Chrsitianity was still young and its gospel of salvation was still being propagated by "the Church Militant," the Midrash commented ruefully on the incredible tax-burdens of the Jews:

> He who works his way through brambles, in detaching himself on one side, only entangles his garment on the other. And such is the case in the [Gentile] land of Esau. Barely has the tax-collector been paid, when the poll tax is demanded. And while this is being collected, the exactor of new taxes makes his appearance.

The realities of this plaint could well have furnished the basis for a bitter passage in another Rabbinical Midrash commentary: "The princes of Edom [Christendom] are covetous of money; they therefore flay Israel alive."

See also CONVERSION OF JEWS; GHETTO; MONEYLENDERS; SHYLOCK MYTH, THE; YELLOW BADGE; WANDERING JEW.

FIRST-BORN SON, "REDEMPTION" OF THE. *See* PIDYON HA-BEN.

FIVE BOOKS OF MOSES, THE. *See* BIBLE, THE.

FLOOD, THE. *See* BIBLE, THE; CHRONOLOGY, JEWISH.

FOLK MUSIC AND DANCE

Probably the most vivid definition of a folk song was given by the Russian novelist Nicolai Gogol: "A song is created when the spirit leaps up." Because the Jewish folk were perpetually preoccupied with the spirit, the songs which "leaped up" spontaneously from their souls suffused their lives with beauty and—not least—with truth. And since their existence was drab, gloomy, and threatened from without so much of the time, song—incandescent and lyrical—lit up their sad world with hope and lightened their burden.

Out of the depths of the American black man's despair and need for hope flowed one of the purest streams of folk song: the spirituals; similarly, out of the suffering of the Jew was born a splendor of heartfelt eloquence: folk singing that was unadorned but meaningful. When the French composer, Maurice Ravel, a Basque from the south of France, first heard some Jewish folk songs that included a Sefaradic Kaddish and several Yiddish melodies, he was enchanted: "I was attracted to the strange and haunting beauty of Jewish music. I felt, almost, as though I had been brought into a new musical world when a few authentic Jewish melodies were brought to my notice. I was so bewitched by the mysterious color and exotic charm of those melodies that for weeks I could not get this music out of my mind. Then my imagination was set aflame."

The same life-forces and historic experiences out of which flowed the stream of Jewish folk tales, myths, legends, parables, allegories, fables, anecdotes, quips, and proverbs also was responsible for Jewish folk music, both vocal and instrumental, secular and religious (*see* KLEZMER; HYMNS OF THE SYNAGOGUE; MERRYMAKERS, TRADITIONAL JEWISH; ZEMIROT). The songs, both music and words, have had an enormous range in point of time, in geographic diffusion, and in the employment of different ethnic idioms. No matter where they may have been produced originally, no matter what their borrowings from non-Jewish sources, no matter how variegated their Jewish regional adaptations subsequently, these melodies traveled like fraternal messengers of consolation and glad tidings from the Jews of one country to the Jews of another. Often—and this is particularly true of synagogical chants—they even went around the globe, for it should be kept in mind that Jews constituted a global people through the ages, from the time of their several dispersions in the ancient world.

"It is certain," observed the Russian-Jewish composer, Julius Engel, a pupil of Rimsky-Korsakoff, about Jewish folk songs, "that they are songs which were disseminated among the people by unknown and long-forgotten composers, or else they were actually created by [known] contemporaries, but because of their folk-character they were adopted by the people."

Perhaps it has not fully occurred to some that *Jewish* folk music was created in many tongues: in Hebrew, Aramaic, Arabic, Yiddish, Ladino (Judeo-Castilian), Malayali (the language of Cochin Jews), Greek, and Persian—that is, in as many languages as Jews had Hebraicized, in greater or lesser degree, in order to make them conform to their own religious-cultural needs in whatever country they happened to live in sizable communities for a long period of time. Unique perhaps in all folk music is the strange intertwining of religious and secular elements in both words and melody of many of the Jewish folk songs. This phenomenon, as has already been pointed out, resulted from the fact that Judaism had established a theocratic society in which all human activity was submitted to the dominance of the religious principle, and catered to the needs of the religious community.

Certainly, the Bible itself is replete with enchanting folk songs, although the memory of their melodies has utterly faded, and most of the devout avoid considering them as such. Who can fail to draw the conclusion that the "Song of Moses" in Chapter 15 of the Book of Exodus, written in rude but overpowering cadence, is such a folk song—that it is, in fact, one of the imperishable songs of the Jewish people? One can easily understand how Moses, a genius of the first magnitude, under the excitement and exaltation of the liberation from the Egyptian Bondage, composed on the spot and sang an unforgettable song of triumph and thanksgiving before the children of Israel. And they, in turn, taking fire from him, sang with him. Also, "Miriam, the prophetess, the sister of Aaron, took a timbrel in her hand; and all the women went out after her with timbrels and with dances." And Miriam too sang the "Song of Moses":

Sing ye to the Lord, for He is highly exalted:
The horse and his rider hath He thrown into the sea.

Other folk songs, though primitive in articulation and theme yet versified in an authentic folk-song manner, are the "Song of Lamech," in Genesis 4:23-24; the "Song of Deborah," in Judges 5:1-31; and the "Song of the Well," in Numbers 21:17-18. But most eloquent of them all is the one mentioned in Deuteronomy 31:22: "Moses therefore wrote this song the same day, and taught it the children of Israel." It is indeed startling to think of Moses not only as a lawgiver and leader of men but as a poet! And a gifted poet he was, to be sure, judging from the text of his song in Chapter 32 of Deuteronomy:

Give ear, O ye heavens, and I will speak;
And hear, O earth, the words of my mouth.
My doctrine shall drop as the rain,
My speech shall distil as the dew,
As the small rain upon the tender herb,
And as the showers upon the grass:
Because I will publish the name of the Lord.

The Talmud, which was created during the historic age that followed the end of Judea as a Jewish state in 70 C.E., also contains a number of ingratiating folk songs. One of these having genuine loveliness was quoted by Dimi bar Chinena, the fourth-century Rabbinic Sage of Babylonia: "Thus they [Jews] sing before a bride in the West:

"Her eyes without kohl,
Her face without rouge,
Her hair without curl—
Yet a form full of grace."

It is regrettable that the only well-plowed fields of Jewish folk songs are those in East European countries, and even these songs are far from adequately collected and analyzed. As for the folk songs of the Sefaradim, North African, Beni Israel, Persian, Kurdish, Bokharan, Cochin, and Arab Jews, but the barest surface has yet been scratched by investigators. However, at the present time, there are in progress in Israel a number of valuable surveys by well-trained musicologists and folklorists. The indifference (or ignorance) with which such matters were regarded in the past is well illustrated by a comment made in 1917 by the Sefaradic editor of the Ladino periodical—*La Voz del Pueblo* ("The People's Voice"): "Our [Sefaradic] most popular songs are the charming 'Viejas Romanzas Españolas' ('Old Spanish Love Songs') which the young Jewish maidens sing in the silence of midnight."

Miriam's song and dance of triumph at the Israelite crossing of the Red Sea. (From an illuminated Spanish Haggadah, c. 1200 C.E., *in the British Museum.)*

The parents of bride and groom doing the Machitonim Tanz—*the "In-Laws' Dance"—at the wedding festivities. Late 19th century. (Illustration on a post card by an anonymous folk artist of Galicia.)*

Hadassah Bedach of INBAL, a member of the Yemenite folk-dance group of Israel.

Bokharan Jewish folk dance. (Israel Government Information Services.)

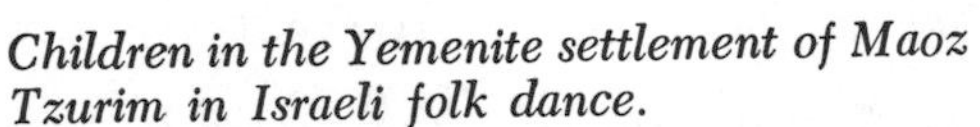

Children in the Yemenite settlement of Maoz Tzurim in Israeli folk dance.

The Koilitch *(Braided Challah) Dance before the bride and groom. Galicia, early 20th century.*

The secular folk songs among the Yiddish-speaking Jews of Germany, Bohemia, Slovakia, Silesia, Lithuania, Poland, White Russia, Galicia, and the Ukraine first began to take a prominent place in the culture of the ghetto during the twilight of the Renaissance. Until that time it had been the religious songs which served predominantly as the folk songs of the Jewish masses. Much to blame for this tardiness in achieving secularization with all the other peoples of Europe was the traditional rabbinic disapproval of secular songs, which held them to be carriers of lasciviousness and immorality, and corruptors of the young. Jews who but indicated the mildest pleasure in love songs were pointedly reminded that Israel, by divine election, had been honored with the mission to make of itself "a holy nation." For this reason Jews were duty bound to occupy their leisure only with morally uplifting song—with the hymns of the synagogue, with the Psalms, and with the Zemirot (the devotional table-songs for the Sabbath and festival days). This constricting attitude largely explains why the musical creativity of the Jews was for so many centuries channeled into pious rather than secular directions.

The Yiddish songs that were sung during the sixteenth and seventeenth centuries by the Jewish folk contemporary with Michelangelo, Shakespeare, and Palestrina, projected every aspect of Jewish life of the time. Some of the lyrics were even frivolous and lightly satirical. Others sounded echoes of early-nineteenth-century romanticism. As if freshly out of a tongue-in-cheek *lied* by Heinrich Heine are these lines from a Yiddish choral-dance of the late Renaissance:

> I'm on fire! My heart's ablaze!
> I cannot put it out!

Not a few of the folk songs were on themes of social criticism and protest. One of these, with the title of "Ein Nyeh Kluglied" ("A New Lament") is full of bitterness toward the ghetto parnas or elder because he locked the gates to keep the horde of vagrant Jewish poor folk (uremihleit) from entering. "*Ach*! dear God!" cry the indigent with indignation, "How can You look on while that *roosheh* [scoundrel or wicked man] mistreats us like that!"

It was only toward the end of the sixteenth century that both religious and secular folk songs which were composed to Hebrew and Yiddish texts first became well defined in their musical as well as poetic forms. In exactly the same way that Jewish folklore falls into such an astonishing variety of categories—and for most of the same reasons—Hebrew and Yiddish folk songs too boast an immense diversity in form, idiom, theme, rhythm, and mood. Their themes well-nigh touch upon everything in the daily experiences of ghetto life. They range from the lullaby and the lisping nursery jingle to the stylized Torah cantillation and the Talmudic study intonation —the celebrated Gemara nigun (pl. nigunim), of which there are many.

What do the Jewish folk songs treat of? They sing of God and of creation, of the World-to-Come and of the Messiah, of Moses the Lawgiver, and of the Patriarchs and the Matriarchs. They also celebrate the joys of living and the anguish of dying; they sing of courtship, love, and marriage; and of the heartbreak in loss or separation. They discourse about attainment and about frustration, about hunger and about loneliness, about faith in people and about disenchantment, about pogroms and about persecution. They sing of work and of the market place, of the House of Study and of the tavern, of good fortune (mazel) and of misfortune (schlimazel), of rationalist Talmudic studies and of the Cabalist mystical ecstasies, of the holy Sabbath and of all the holy days—festivals and fast days—and lamentations, the New Moon, and eternal renewal.

Yiddish folk songs have their own distinctive charm and characteristics. Many are emotional, tender, and introspective. But there are also humorous songs which are touched by the same wry or ironic comicality that distinguishes Jewish folk humor; the melancholy songs bear the same unresigned plaintiveness as do the tales about the medieval Jewish martyrs; only their sorrow is lightened by a lyrical sweetness in the melody.

The great majority of Jewish songs, whether in Hebrew or in Yiddish, in a linguistic combination of both, or in a "macaronic" mixture of Hebrew and Arabic, of Yiddish with Polish or Ukrainian or Russian—oddly, even those that are intended to be expressive of joy and conviviality—are in a minor key. This represents a curious cultural phenomenon and has elicited surprised comment from musicologists and composers. Yet, to one familiar with the long history of Jewish suffering and insecurity, there can be no cause for surprise in this fact. To be sure, Jewish songs in the minor key have strong points of resemblance to Slavic, to Spanish-Moorish, and to Arabic songs, which also are predominantly in the minor. Nonetheless, Jewish songs are penetrated by a special kind of sadness which is hard to describe but which, on closer familiarity with them, one soon learns to recognize as "Jewish."

Curiously, this "Jewishness," which is recognizable in feeling and sensibility, is what furnished the clue to the French composer, Maurice Ravel, for evaluating the uniqueness of Jewish folk songs. He was vastly intrigued by both the words and music of the Yiddish song "Fraygt di Velt an Alteh Kasheh" ("The World Asks an Old Question"). Its argumentative melody, set to quizzical words, sounds like an interior Talmudic soliloquy—philosophical, detached, wryly humorous yet touched with a cosmic sadness, for the question that is asked by its very nature is unanswerable. Therefore, when Ravel arranged the song for orchestra, he gave it the appropriate title "L'Enigme Eternelle."

To the Chasidim (*see* CHASIDIM), the sectarian followers of Rabbi Israel Baal Shem, the great socially motivated mystic of the eighteenth century, song was equivalent to prayer, and because it was devoid of all rhetoric and pretentiousness, it even superseded prayer in spiritual truth and power. It was generally esteemed as "the ladder to the Throne of God." Rabbi Nachman Bratzlaver, the great-grandson of the Baal Shem and a mystic poet of soaring imagination, adopted the magical view about music that was held by the early "seers" of Israel as it is noted in the Bible. He declared: "Music originates in the prophetic spirit; it has the power to raise one to the inspiration of the prophet." (*See* MUSIC, ANCIENT JEWISH.)

The marshalik or badchan, the traditional rhyming merrymaker, does a humorous dance at a wedding. Galicia, early 20th century.

There were many Chasidic rabbis (rebbehs) who considered that words were an impediment to spiritual expression—that they were a wall standing between the communion of the individual and his God. Consequently, numerous Chasidic melodies (nigunim) were sung without words, in somewhat the same manner as the vocalise by Rachmaninoff. While some nigunim, especially the melancholy meditative ones, were merely sung or intoned, the lively and ecstatic ones usually served as vocal obbligati to the famed Chasidic dance in the mystic circle: When a Chasid danced, his every fiber was in movement; he danced with hands, feet, head, eyes, and lips. His every muscle was required to be in motion, with every part of him pulsating to the rhythm, straining to apprehend the divine, in physical, mental, and spiritual exaltation.

There are an astonishing number of Chasidic songs and dances. Many are merely unmusical vulgarizations of nineteenth-century German military marches, Russian gopaks, Polish polkas and mazurkas, and Viennese waltzes—all abstracted from Gentile repertories. But at the same time, there are just as many melodies which, in their totality, probably represent the most distinguished and original element in the musical creation of the Jewish folk. Like their lyrics, Chasidic tunes are steeped in mystical rapture. Many of them employ some of the musical idioms of Moldavian and Walachian folk-tunes, but in their exalted moods, their burning intensity, they are characteristically Chasidic—and Jewish. In what strange way, it is hard to say, but quite a few of these songs have carried over the somber, meditative intonation in the minor key from the traditional liturgy of the Oriental synagogue!

Of a different physiognomy, but revealing in many of its facets a distinctive individuality, is that body of Jewish folk music in Hebrew that was created in the yishuv (the Jewish community of Palestine) and, after the establishment in 1948 of the Jewish state, also in Israel. In the decade before World War I, the handful of songs of the Zionist settlers gave clear utterance to their yearnings and indestructible faith in the survival of the Jewish people, and in its final restoration in its ancient homeland. With the mass-settlement of the land by the new wave of young and purposeful chalutzim (pioneers) in the 1920's, the folk songs took on a fresher and ever more modern and sophisticated character, with many of them extolling the virtues of manual labor and the moral imperative of self-sacrifice in rebuilding Zion.

The young pioneers sang as they worked at building roads, reclaiming swamps, plowing the land, cultivating orange groves and vineyards, and while engaged in hundreds of other manual tasks. All the manifold aspects of their new life and struggles are vividly—and also optimistically—expressed in their popular songs and dances. Musically speaking, many of these songs are characterized by an emotional intensity, by strong rhythmic patterns, and a delivery that is vigorous and spirited. The prolonged struggle of the yishuv in support of the "illegal" immigration of Jews into Palestine (*see* ZIONISM), for gaining political independence from the British Mandatory Government, and for sheer physical survival from the savage attacks and harassment by Arab nationalist bands and marauders, injected a militant spirit into many of the new songs. This dynamic quality, flowing from the increase of Jewish group strength and national solidarity, was given full utterance in the songs of the Haganah (the Jewish armed forces)—songs that emerged from the climactic War for Independence that was fought in 1948 against the invading armies of the six Arab nations.

Because the Jews in present-day Israel came from virtually every Jewish community in the world, it was only natural that there should have occurred a certain fusion of the different musical traditions, idioms, and tastes they brought with them. Out of this intergroup acculturation has rapidly been evolving an easily definable body of Jewish folk songs and folk dances, bearing upon it the authentic stamp of Israeli life and culture. The musical patterns and idioms of the various ethnic groups—principally the Chasidic, Yemenite, Moldavian, German, Iranian, Turkish, Sefaradic-Oriental, Bokharan, Arabic, Moroccan, Algerian, Russian, Polish—are still recognizable.

Israel has become the living storehouse of global Jewish folk-music—a repository of many diverse strains of melody, both sung and played. How long these separate groups will be able to preserve *intact* the characteristic features of their own regional ethnic "Jewish" music is problematical, for the process of intergroup cultural assimilation is very rapid in Israel. Therefore, musicologists are working against time to collect whatever songs they can. It is an astonishing fact that one collector alone has tape-recorded 26,000 melodies among the various Jewish ethnic groups in the country.

It is only too well known how very frustrating it has been for musicologists to attempt to reproduce with exactitude any notation of Oriental music. They have found it virtually impossible to recapture the elusive Oriental pitch, rhythm,

Dancing the horah in an Israeli kibbutz (collective settlement).

and meter; these constitute, to a large extent, another *kind* of music than what Western ears are accustomed to. Some musicians are of the opinion that musical survivals from ancient times are to be found only in so called closed groups—those who lived for thousands of years in virtual isolation from other Jewish groups. Such a distinction has been claimed by the Jews of Kurdistan, Yemen, and Bokhara; they say with conviction that some of the religious songs they sing were chanted by the Levite choirs in the Temple in Jerusalem more than two thousand years ago.

The Dance. The dance among the ancient Jews was an indispensable element in the Temple rites. However, if one is to generalize on the basis of Biblical references to the dance, it was performed chiefly as an expression of popular rejoicing over the triumph of Israel in war. Such was the choral dance of victory performed by Miriam the Prophetess and the Israelite maidens as they sang and danced to celebrate the destruction of Pharaoh's host at the Red Sea. Such, too, was the song and dance of the women of Israel, performed "with timbrels, with joy, and with three-stringed instruments" (I Samuel 18:6) as they met David and Saul, returning victorious from their battle against the Philistines.

The group dances in Biblical times consisted of two principal kinds: the choral dance and the processional dance. The latter, a ritual dance, was performed around the Temple altar in a halting rythmn during the festivals. But the convolutions of the dance became far more animated during the Festival of Water-Drawing on Succot, when a vast throng assembled in the Women's Court of the Temple in Jerusalem, swinging lighted lamps and carrying water-jugs on their shoulders. The Talmud, reminiscing nostalgically about the departed joys of olden times, described the celebration in this wise: "Pious men, and also men of eminence, danced with torches in their hands and sang songs of joy and praise. And the Levites made music with lyre and harp and cymbals and trumpets and countless other instruments." The dancing and singing went on through the night, and only when the trumpets of the Levites announced with a fanfare the arrival of daybreak did they come to an end.

One ancient dance, apparently highly revered by custom, was the so-called Marriage Dance which was performed twice a year—on Yom Kippur and on the fifteenth of Ab, on which day there took place the Feast of Wood-Offering (for the Temple altar). On these two occasions, all the marriageable maidens, dressed in spotless white to denote their chastity, went out to the vineyards to take part in choral dances. And while they danced and sang, the young men looked them over and chose brides from among them. Some ethnologists view this custom as a survival of the primitive practice of marriage by capture. In fact, such bride-snatching by the tribe of Benjamin is described graphically in Judges 21:16-25.

It was the fear of assimilation by the Jews of the "profane" customs and folkways learned from non-Jews that prompted many rabbis, beginning with the Middle Ages and even as late as the twentieth century, to wage a relentless war against dancing. (However, this ban did not apply to the dancing of the Chasidim, which is not considered secular in character but, rather, completely religious—a form of worship. Here only the men dance together.) According to the rabbis' way of thinking, the preservation of the Jewish religion and its moral values could be maintained only by the complete cultural separation of the Jews from the Gentiles.

Yet, whatever stringent means were adopted by the religious and communal authorities of the ghetto to suppress all "profane" pleasures of life, the youths and maidens, nevertheless, persisted in expressing the joys of their springtime to the shock of their elders. In Renaissance Germany, for example, where Christians had instituted the *Tanzhaus* (Dance House), the Jews, too, had to have a similar place for themselves in the ghetto. Originally, during the Middle Ages, the Jewish dance hall was called the *Brutehus* (Bridal House) because Jewish wedding festivities were celebrated there. But when young Jews developed the same passion for dancing that Christians had, the Bridal House was transformed into the Dance House. The Jewish tantzmeister (dancing master) became a popular figure in ghetto life during the sixteenth and seventeenth century. In Italy, for example, where the cultural assimilation of Jews was the most pronounced in Europe, the humanist scholar and rabbi of Venice, Leone da Modena, a man of many casual talents, supplemented his meager income by giving dance instruction. The Jewish youth of Italy at that time danced on every possible occasion: at weddings (traditionally celebrated for an entire week), on joyous religious festivals (Passover, Purim, Channukah, and Simchat Torah), and on Sabbath nights after the Habdalah rite was performed.

As was the custom in those times, the dancers sang in chorus as they advanced in the rhythmic patterns of motion. In a Yiddish choric dance, the young man sang to his dancing partner:

Jung Fräulein, wilt ihr nicht
Mit mir ein Tenzlein tun?

(Young lady, won't you do a dance with me?)

And the reason for his invitation:

Freilich mus ich sein.

(Merry I must be.)

After the Fräulein sang her gracious reply, the young man took his place beside her, and together they went through the measures of the dance with the other couples:

Nun tanzen wir in lieblichen Reien,
Und wellen einander frisch freilich sein.

(And so we dance in charming rows,
And we will be gay together.)

But the "worst"—as seen from the jaundiced perspective of the fundamentalists—has not been told yet, for the young men and women chose to overlook the Biblical admonition against men and women dancing together. "Though hand join in hand, the wicked shall not be unpunished," warned Proverbs 11:21. This also was the attitude of the Sages as expressed in the puritanic Talmudic injunction that "men and women shall neither rejoice nor mourn together." Aparently,

Biblical Shepherd's Dance by members of INBAL, Yemenite folk-dance group of Israel.

in their view, the "hand in hand" situation seemed fraught with the direst possibilities for the morals of Jewish youth. Only the nearest of kin—married couples, parents, and brothers and sisters—were exempted from the prohibition against dancing together. But, as has happened in every generation, the young folks preferred dancing with other than blood relations of the opposite sex.

The dancing of the Cabalists (*see* CABALISTS) and of their continuators, the Chasidim (*see* CHASIDIM), had an entirely different character. In sixteenth-century Safed, the Cabalists and their followers would go in procession, dancing over the hills and valleys of Galilee, to greet the incoming Sabbath Queen (Shabbat ha-Malkah) on Friday afternoon. The religious dancing in the mystic circle (known in Yiddish as the *redl-tantz*), was choreographically primitive, each dancer laying one hand on the shoulder of the dancer before him as, with his other hand, he cupped his face. His head was tilted to the side; his eyes were closed in rapture. The circle whirled round and round in increasing abandonment, moving ever faster and more vehemently, almost literally fulfilling the declaration of Psalm 35:10: "All my bones shall say: 'Lord, who is like unto Thee?' " The authentic Chasidic dance tunes are among the most beautiful and most original in all of Jewish folk-music.

To this day, although with ever diminishing frequency, the old Jewish wedding dances of Eastern Europe are still being performed by die-hard traditionalists everywhere. There is the *Mitzvah* or *Kosher-Tantz,* a "handkerchief dance" performed by close kinfolk of bride and groom; the *Machitonim Tantz* of the in-laws; the *Bubbe's-Tantz*—"Granny's Dance"—which is performed solo by her in honor of the wedded pair; the *Koylitch-Tantz*—"Braided-Bread Dance"—danced by a woman and derived from the Ukrainian peasant dance in which white braided Easter bread (*kulitch*) and a little salt are offered to bride and groom as symbols of hoped-for domestic peace and contentment; the *Broyges-* (or *Royges*) *Tantz*—a handkerchief dance that is a pantomime of quarrel and happy reconciliation. There are also the innumerable instrumental folk divertissements and interludes called *Freilachs* (Merry Tunes) played by the folk-musicians (*Klezmorim*) to sustain the gay mood of the wedding guests.

In Israel, as is natural and appropriate, Jewish folk-dancing, symbolizing national unity and common cultural aspirations, has been flourishing remarkably since 1944, and the country's youth has flocked to dance festivals, wherever they are held. Folk dances in Israel today are primarily based on the dance steps of the Yemenite Jews and of the East European Chasidim. The horah—the simple and universally popular dance-in-the-round—had its formal roots in the Romanian dance by that name; it has traveled far and wide among the Jews of the world and has been taken into the world's repertory of folk-dances.

See also ACCENTS, MUSICAL; FOLKLORE; HYMNS OF THE SYNAGOGUE; KIBBUTZ; KLEZMER; MERRYMAKERS, TRADITIONAL JEWISH; MUSIC, ANCIENT JEWISH; MUSIC IN THE TEMPLE; MUSICAL INSTRUMENTS OF THE BIBLE; PURIM PLAY; ZEMIROT.

FOLKLORE

The creation of folklore is a spontaneous and never ending process; it flows along with the stream of life. In its own terms, folklore is scarcely less authentic and revealing than documented history and, in fact, constitutes for it a complementary body of knowledge.

This intimate relationship of folklore to the historical record—a kinship recognized only in recent decades—is particularly true of Jewish folklore, for Jews, to a great extent—probably to a far greater extent than Christians—live by tradition and culture in the past. As a people with perhaps the longest continuous history of any, they have been creating myths, legends, fables, folktales, parables, allegories, moralistic anecdotes, wise and witty sayings, and folk songs for at least four thousand years. This lore is inextricably woven into the broader tapestry of Jewish culture.

Having been produced in millennial time and with a global span, the corpus of Jewish folklore is exceptionally rich, variegated, and colorful, with the imprint of diverse cultures and historic epochs upon it. It is axiomatic that even after the Jews were forced by the Church to live in ghettos and by the rulers of Islam to crowd into the Arabic equivalent of the ghetto, the mellah, they could never be hermetically sealed off from the ways of life and the cultures of other peoples. In consequence, their folklore, too, was exposed to the effects of acculturation in their non-Jewish environment, as can be seen in the medieval compilation of Yiddish tales known as the *Maaseh Buch;* these, in turn, made a reciprocal impression, with their fantasy, social outlook, and lively storytelling art, on Gentile folklore (for example, a number of stories in the *Arabian Nights* are of Jewish origin). Nevertheless, despite all foreign accretions, Jewish folklore preserved its distinctive physiognomy, being unmistakably stamped with the traditional ethical values and historic experiences of the Jewish people.

It requires little laboring of the point to prove that, because of the mercurial nature of civilization and life, the whole human race serves as the clearinghouse for the diffusion of culture—and also of folklore. While each ethnic group man-

Page from the Hebrew collection of fables, Mashal ha-Kadmoni, *by Isaac ibn Sahula, Brescia, Italy, 1490.*

ages to maintain some of its individuality in cultural expression, nevertheless, it acts simultaneously as "borrower" and "lender" in the complex interchange of folkloric materials.

Take the fable, for example. There are found in the Talmud some 30 fables, several of remarkable subtlety, which have been attributed to the Mishnah Sage Meir (second century C.E.). He was a great teacher of the people and spurned pedantry. Being well read in the literatures of Greece and Rome, he had discovered that the unadorned fable or animal tale could be an effective aid to instruction. The Talmud records—no doubt with considerable accuracy—that he had collected 300 fables. Other talented Jewish fable collectors appeared subsequent to Meir; one of these was Berechiah ha-Nakdan (*c.* 1190, known to his academic colleagues at Oxford as Benedictus le Puncteur ["the Punctuator"]), who issued his Hebrew collection of 107 witty and moralistic *Fox Fables* (*Mishleh Shualim*); another was Joseph ibn Zabara (c. 1200), who compiled *The Book of Delight* (*Sefer Shashuim*). Nevertheless, the "Jewish" fables in these compilations were, by and large, borrowed and freely reworked (sometimes to the point of being unrecognizable) from Hindu and Greek versions. Among the Hindu sources were the Panchatantra, the Mahabharata, and the Jatakas—nativity stories about Buddha which were compiled by Bidpai. The fables adapted from the Greek were by such creators and anthologists as Aesop, Phaedrus, Avianus, Kybises, and Syntipas.

The role of folklore as an indispensable branch of cultural history was emphasized by Sigmund Freud, the founder of psychoanalysis, in *Totem and Taboo*: "Primitive man is known to us . . . through our knowledge of his art, his religion, and his attitude toward life, which we have received either directly or through the medium of legends, myths and fairy tales." It is, without a doubt, through the medium of folklore that the prehistoric and Patriarchal periods of ethnic Hebraic civilization are brought to life for us in the Pentateuch. It is a reasonable assumption that such myths and legends found in the earliest Biblical narratives, as the Creation, the murder of Abel by his brother Cain, the Flood, Abraham's intended sacrifice of Isaac, the "birthright" struggle between Jacob and Esau, and the story of Joseph and his jealous brothers, were already ancient when they were written down (*see* BIBLE, THE).

"Yarn-spinning." Galicia, early 20th century. (Sketch by I. Kaufmann.)

The myths, legends, and folktales of the Jews are held together by a remarkable unity despite their great time-space range. It is noteworthy, for instance, that while American folklore has had a continuous three-hundred-year history of creativity in a unified geographic area, it, nevertheless, can claim a lesser cohesiveness and integration than the folklore of the Jewish people, spread out, in several thousand years of turbulent history over all the five continents!

The greater cohesiveness of Jewish folklore probably is due to the fact that the great bulk of it is anchored in the Hebrew Scriptures and in the literature of the Talmud. It treats of heaven and earth, Gan Eden and Gehinnom (*both of which see*), the spiritual and the supernatural, the rational and the superstitious.

There are to be found in the sacred writings of the Jews myths of all kinds: solar and lunar myths, cosmological and zoological myths. A great number of legends and folktales found in the Talmud tell of human encounters with Satan, demons, and spirits, all being projected as mediators between God and man. In many other tales there passes an imposing procession of Patriarchs and Matriarchs, of Prophets and Sages, of kings and heroes, saints and sinners, rabbis and martyrs, rationalists and mystics. Disturbingly enough, the principal object of many of these tales is to reconcile for the troubled mind of the individual Jew the tragic destiny of the Jewish people with his own trust in God's providence and love. There are other legends whose sole aim, it seems, is to "explain" the seemingly irreconcilable incidents and statements in the Scriptures that baffle the persistently questioning Jew.

There are mystical overtones in most Jewish myths, legends, and folktales. The apprehension of the supernatural, in its most imaginative and poetic facets, often reveals the Jewish genius for fusing the enchantment in dreams with an awareness of reality. Behind all the images projected, behind all incidents recounted, is discernible the Will of God articulated in Jewish ethical terms. This Will is portrayed as being neither inscrutable nor frightening; its intentions are clearly perceived and clearly defined for its human protagonists. The pious Jew believes that God wills his happiness and not his destruction, and since God is the fountainhead of all the ways of righteousness, the individual has only to emulate His ethical attributes in order to achieve redemption and the joy of blessedness.

Gentile scholars and writers have expressed some astonishment at the marked intellectual and sophisticated character of much of Jewish folklore, these being characteristics hard to associate with the naïvetes that usually constitute myth, legend, and folktale. Nevertheless, a salient feature of Jewish folklore is that most frequently it is of an interior and introspective nature. It is intellectual and subtle, moralistic and pious, gentle and emotional, witty and ironic. These qualities alone are enough to endow it with a uniqueness among all other bodies of the world's folklore.

Jews became an intellectual people not because of any innate mental superiority over other peoples, but because of the different nature of their religious patterns and their history. They have cherished and preserved their tradition of learning ever since the fifth century B.C.E., during the age of Ezra the Scribe and the public teaching by the Men of the Great Assembly. In large measure, this tradition sprang from the obligation imposed on all male Jews (who then lived in a theocracy, or priest-state) to study constantly the Scriptures and the Talmud. (*See* TALMUD, THE; TORAH STUDY.) Such an intellectual dedication, sustained in Jewish life generation after generation, century after century, ultimately resulted in a razor-sharpening of wits, in a verbal ease of articulation and argumentation. It also led to a preoccupation with abstract ideas, with philosophical speculations, and—on the negative side—even with dialectical virtuosity as an end in itself.

There is still another significant reason why Jewish folklore has such an intellectual tone. The Rabbinic Sages, during and after the Hellenistic period, actually "created," adapted, and disseminated Jewish legend, fable, allegory, and parable (mashal) by their oral teachings in the yeshibot (Talmudic academies). These stories were ultimately incorporated into the written Talmud—in particular, into the Agada or anecdotal portions of that monumental body of literature, and into the Midrashim (s. Midrash, the commentary elaborations of Biblical texts by the illuminative means of legend, allegory, and parable). In their turn, the Jewish masses, who revered these tales and their Rabbinic sources, in the process of telling and retelling them, embroidered them with their folk fancy and added to them new details, but, nonetheless, managed to preserve intact their moralistic meanings, which were transmitted *as instruction* from one generation to the next.

Instruction in the eternal verities of the Jewish way of life seems to have been a chief motivation of Jewish folklore, being greatly aided by a narrative art that possessed the liveliness, suspense, and color of all Middle Eastern storytelling. It is true that also Hindu and Arab folktales show a similarly ingenious plot inventiveness; they, too, use with much effectiveness the technical devices of action, suspense, and the surprise ending. Yet there is a tangible but subtle difference marking off Jewish tales from theirs. The Jewish tales are very often cerebral—as it were, turned inward—tirelessly pointing a moral for the guidance of man.

Conspicuous in Jewish folklore is the art of the parable (mashal) which is constructed on a particular Biblical passage. In the Rabbis' skilled hands it became a principal instrument of pedagogy. No doubt having intellectual snobs in mind, one Rabbinic Sage cautioned: "Do not despise the parable. With a penny candle one may often find a lost gold coin or a costly pearl. . . ."

Although there are some parables in the Bible also, they are almost overwhelmingly present in post-Biblical writings: in Hellenistic-Jewish literature, in the Judeo-Christian Gospels, in the Talmud, and in medieval and later moralistic works. The exegetical or preaching Midrash of the Talmud is the fullest repository of parables by whose means the religious teachers strove to deepen the understanding of the Jewish folk and to add to its moral improvement.

A characteristic of the Jewish parable is that it is not just a story for entertainment, but it often is wisdom instinct with spirit. It is subtle and imaginative, penetrating to the very heart of an idea or a truth; it is also mellow in its commonsense understanding of both the heights and the limitations of the human being. Hundreds of such ingratiating parables enlivened the sermons of the celebrated itinerant moralist, Rabbi Jacob Krantz (Lithuania, 1740–1805), better known to the folk as Der Dubner Maggid—"The Preacher of Dubno."

It is doubtful if there exists a body of national folklore as dominantly religious and moralistic as the Jewish. Hardly a tale, fable, or parable fails to point an ethical or religious lesson. The Talmudic Sages established a tradition—which in time became fixed—when they employed legends, fables, folktales, parables, and Rabbinic exempla of righteous conduct for the instruction of the people in piety, morals, ethical values, and in the simple wisdom of daily living. This practice was continued unbroken down the many centuries to our own time by rabbis, preachers, and teachers.

Another characteristic of Jewish folklore is that it mirrors the Jew's devotion to his faith, his loyalty to his people, and his keen consciousness of responsibility to his group. The historic experiences of the Jews welded them together in suffering, conditioned them in social awareness because of the compelling need for mutual aid in order to survive. If, in the folktales about the Cabalists and the Chasidim, the wonder-worker or mystic is shown going through the rigors of self-mortification, endless prayer, and painful inner searching for hidden sinfulness, it is not so much because he wishes to elevate himself spiritually for his own heavenly reward, but because he is moved by social idealism to succor his fellow Jews or to help hasten the coming of the Messiah to redeem the Jewish people from its long Exile (Galut) and suffering. It is precisely for this reason that Jewish folklore abounds with Messianic and martyrological tales.

Many Jewish folktales and legends, in whatever historic period they may have originated, are haunted by a deep sadness which somehow rarely deteriorates into self-pity or despair. Almost always this sense of tragedy carries within it the saving-grace of catharsis, of steadfast fidelity; of spiritual triumph even in defeat. This elevated melancholy mood no doubt originated from incessant persecution and wandering, and from a pervasive guilt-feeling. It is the traditional belief of the devout Jew that, if God visits affliction upon the Jewish people, it is on account of its backsliding and infidelity. Nevertheless, this belief is lightened by an indomitable hopefulness (it appears persistently in a great many folktales) that redemption will come some day because "the good God" never abandons those who put their trust in him.

Curiously, the Chasidic rabbis of the eighteenth and nineteenth centuries—even more than the ancient Rabbinic Sages of Judea and Babylonia—employed the legends and tales about the tzaddikim (the holy wonder-workers of their own sect) for the spiritual and moral education of their adherents. Both the strength and the weakeness of institutionalized Chasidism (*see* CHASIDIM) were reflected in them. Many of the tales were childish; they boasted about the supposedly supernatural powers of the wonder-working rabbis, and with bated breath recounted "actual" incidents of their hair-raising performances.

But intermingled with these inane legends, which were related orally before they were gathered into groschen (penny) chapbooks, were tales of an ethical and mystically poetic kind. Many of them, following the Jewish traditional pattern, were of a social character. In the true spirit of Rabbi Israel Baal Shem, the great founder of the Chasidic movement, they extolled the true nobility inherent in the poor, nondescript but warmhearted Jew despite his ignorance of Torah lore, and castigated the haughty, the rich, and the learned for the emptiness of their piety and pretensions, even though they were respected pillars of the community. The folktales and legends, it should be noted, imprinted their lasting influence on modern Jewish literature—especially in the Yiddish and Hebrew writings of Peretz, Anski, and Agnon (*see* YIDDISH LITERATURE, MODERN; HEBREW LITERATURE, MODERN).

Notwithstanding that so much of Jewish folklore is overshadowed by the *Judenschmerz* (the grief-consciousness of being a Jew), it would be a fallacy to assume that Jews are incapable of genuine gaiety or full-bellied laughter. Jews have ever been a robust, life-affirming people. Neither persecution nor grief—nor even life in their dank ghetto-prisons—could keep them from laughing. Laughter to Jews, in the usually difficult circumstance of their lives, was something even more than gaiety, more than mere diversion; it was a kind of medicine without which they could not go on living in their nightmare world. For this very reason Jewish folklore achieves a wonderful intellectual and artistic balance. Light and shade set each other off harmoniously; the grave, pietistic or tragic folktale finds its right counterpoise in the sharp wit and light-heartedness of many a humorous story or witticism.

Jewish folk-humor, as Freud has testified, is quite unique. It is almost never savage or cruel, but sly, ironical, philosophical. It relishes holding up to ridicule or ribbing all aspects of foolishness, boorishness, sanctimonious piety, and virtuous humbug. It exposes with delight the ignorance which preens itself and the pretentiousness that sacrifices the common decencies. In fact, Jewish humor is not often marred by self-righteousness or moralizing, but is tolerant of human frailties

One very unusual characteristic of Jewish folk-humor is its sophisticated but gentle irony. The irony of the Jew is almost all embracing; it takes in all aspects of existence, himself included. This odd national trait of self-irony (the poet Heinrich Heine was the most brilliant example of it) led Freud to remark, in *Wit and Its Relation to the Unconscious:*

> This determination of self-criticism may make clear why it is that a number of the most excellent jokes . . . should have sprung into existence from the soil of Jewish national life. There are stories which were invented by Jews themselves and which are directed by Jewish peculiarities. The Jewish jokes made up by non-Jews are nearly all brutal buffooneries in which the wit is spoiled by the fact that the Jew appears as a comic figure to a stranger. The Jewish jokes which originated with Jews admit this, but they know their real shortcomings as well as their merits. . . . I do not know whether one finds a people that makes so merry unreservedly over its own shortcomings.

See also AMULETS; ANGELS; BIBLE, THE; BURIAL RIGHTS AND CUSTOMS; CABALA; CHASIDIM; DYBBUK; EVIL EYE; GAN EDEN; GEHINNOM; GOLEM, THE; SATAN; WEDDING CUSTOMS.

FORGIVENESS. *See* ETHICAL VALUES, JEWISH.

FOUR CUPS, THE. *See* PASSOVER.

FOUR FRINGES. *See* TZITZIT.

"FOUR QUESTIONS, THE." *See* PASSOVER.

"FOUR SPECIES, THE" (in Hebrew: ARBAH MINIM)

Whatever may have been the religious aspects of its later development, Succot originated as a harvest festival. As such, it was but natural that the fruits of the earth and the greenery of tropical trees should enter in its celebration. "The Four Species," of which the lulab constituted one, formed an essential part of the religious rites during the seven-day festival. Its use had a Biblical sanction: "And ye shall take you on the first day the fruit of goodly trees [interpreted by tradition to mean the etrog], branches of palm trees [the lulab], and boughs of thick trees [in this case, hadassim, or myrtles], and willows of the brook [aravot]; and ye shall rejoice before the Lord your God seven days." (Leviticus 23:40.)

Excepting the etrog, which is a species of citron—but a sweet and aromatic fruit—the other three species—namely, the palm branch, the myrtle (three twigs are used), and the willow (two twigs)—are bound together by rings made of braided palm fiber. The Midrash sought to explain this combination in symbolic terms: "Just as the etrog has taste and a pleasant fragrance, so there are in Israel men who are at the same time learned and pious. Just as the lulab has taste yet is without fragrance, so there are those who are learned but not pious. Just as the myrtle has a pleasing fragrance yet has no taste, so there are men who perform good deeds yet possess no learning. And even as the willow has neither taste nor a pleasant fragrance, so there are men who are neither learned nor do they perform good deeds." However, concluded the Rabbis, who always took a realistic view of human limitations, when all the positive aspects of human beings are combined, like the Four Species, they represent collectively all the requisite virtues.

Another Rabbinic allegory of the lulab ceremony compares the etrog to the heart of man, the lulab to his frame, the myrtle twigs to his eyes, and those of the willow to his lips. The symbolism of this is that, in order to sing the praise of God adequately, it is necessary that the heart, the spine, the eyes, and the lips unite their homage.

In the days of the Second Temple, the lulab rite was performed on each of the seven days of Succot, but only the officiating priests took part in it. All lay-worshipers observed it on the first day of the festival only. But after the Temple was destroyed by the Romans under Titus, the Rabbinic Sage Yochanan ben Zakkai recognized the urgent necessity of strengthening the Jewish religion in every way possible if it was to survive at all. He therefore decreed that all in Israel—and, in particular, all adult males—were to perform the rite of the lulab and on all of the seven days of Succot except on that day which fell on the Sabbath.

What is the significance of this rite? During the recitation of the Hallel service (Psalms 113-18), the worshiper is required to hold the lulab and its attending myrtle and willow twigs in his right hand, and the etrog in his left hand. First he recites the benediction, then, holding his two hands together, he waves the Four Species up and down, forward and backward: north and south, east and west. Thus, in six movements he symbolically encompasses the entire universe in homage to God, who is everywhere, and to his rule, which is eternal. Also, during each day of the festival, upon the completion of Mussaf (the Additional Service), the custom in the traditional synagogue is to open the Ark and to take from it a Sefer Torah (Scroll of the Torah). Then all the worshipers, each holding a lulab and an etrog, march slowly in procession around the bema (reader's desk), chanting the ages-old supplication of Hoshanah (Hosanna):

A Chasid of Jerusalem and his son recite the blessing over the lulab and etrog in their succah festooned with bunches of grapes and other fruits of Israel. (Israel Government Tourist Office.)

Etrog on a copper coin issued in Judea c. 143 B.C.E.*—42* B.C.E. *by Simon Maccabeus.*

Procession with lulab and etrog in the Amsterdam synagogue on Hoshanah Rabbah during the Succot festival. (Engraving by Bernard Picart, 1724.)

Save us, we beseech you, O Lord!
Prosper us, we beseech you, O Lord!

On the seventh and last day of the festival, which is called Hoshanah Rabbah, every scroll of the Torah is taken out of the Ark. The procession forms and seven circuits (Hakafot) are made—this number, of mystic significance, for greater emphasis and as a dramatic climax.

The procession with waving palms is, of course, an ancient Jewish custom. Practiced as a religious rite, it was also used on festive occasions, as when the Temple was reconsecrated by Judah Maccabee. In the Gospel of John (12:12-13) the writer describes a similar procession formed by the followers of Jesus: ". . . when they heard that Jesus was coming to Jerusalem [they] took branches of palm trees, and went forth to meet him, and cried, Hosanna. . . ." And thus a Jewish custom, though modified in form, has been commemorated by Christians for nigh onto two thousand years on Palm Sunday in connection with the most solemn events preceding Easter.

See also SUCCOT; HAKAFOT.

FREE LOANS. *See* LOANS, FREE.

FREE WILL.

The Jews, during the days of the Second Temple, did not subscribe to the religious doctrine (later adopted by Christianity) that sin was "original" and hereditary for all mankind on account of Adam's fall. On the contrary, Jewish teachings denied that man was naturally evil. In the Apocalypse of Baruch, a post-Biblical Jewish work apparently written prior to the rise of Christianity, this optimistic view of the nature of man was colorfully expressed:

> For though Adam first sinned and brought untimely death upon all, yet of those who were born from him, each one of them has prepared for his own soul torment to come, and again each one of them has chosen for himself glories to come. . . . Adam was, therefore, not the cause [i.e., of the downfall] save only of his own soul, but each of us has been the Adam of his soul.

Traditional Judaism never taught the doctrine that salvation for the individual lay in his special election by grace or by a predetermined heavenly decision. In Deuteronomy 30:19 God addresses the Israelites with the challenge that they exercise their free intelligence and moral will: "I call heaven and earth to witness against you this day, that I have set before thee life and death, the blessing and the curse; therefore choose life." The second-century Tanna (Sage) and teacher of ethics, Rabbi Akiba, himself incorporated the essential point of this Mosaic teaching in the Oral Tradition, the Mishnah: "Everything is foreseen [by God], and [nonetheless] freedom of choice is given." (Pirke Abot 3:19.) The "freedom" was the individual's volitional choice to do good or to do evil. God (so stated Yochanan ben Zakkai, the first-century Judean religious authority) can be served only by those who exercise their moral will for doing good *freely*. "He cannot be served by slaves." This opinion was in line with the concept, general among Jews, of the dignity of man, and of its corollary: that, having been made in the image of God, man was to imitate Him by striving to do good and create the perfect and the harmonious in society.

For eight centuries, Jews in every land have repeated word for word the memorable testament about the freedom of the will formulated by the medieval rabbinic-philosopher, Maimonides:

> Every human being is master of his actions, of what he does or leaves undone. If he desires to set out upon the good way and be a righteous person, he is free to do so, and if he desires to set out upon the bad way and be a wicked person, he is also free to do so. . . . Man is the only being in creation—and no other resembles him therein—who by himself and through his own discernment and by his own thinking can differentiate between the good and the evil. . . . Therefore, do not listen to the idle talk of the fools among the heathen and of the stupid among the Jews who say that God decrees for man before he is born whether he shall act uprightly or wickedly. That is not so."

See also DOCTRINES IN JUDAISM; REPENTANCE; REWARD AND PUNISHMENT; SIN AND SINNER; YETZER TOB AND YETZER HA-RAH.

"FRONTLETS." *See* TEFILLIN.

G

GABBAI (Hebrew s., meaning "receiver"; pl. GABBAIM)

The gabbai is the treasurer of the synagogue. He is, so to speak, the "businessman" and holder (usually tight) of the congregational purse-strings. Like the canon in the Church of England, he is the financial administrator, but he is strictly a lay functionary. To be elected to his office, burdensome as it may turn out, is considered a high honor. But in the past, he was not always held in such esteem. In Rabbinic times, in the centuries following the Dispersion, the gabbai was also the tax-collector, which did not make him more popular. In Europe, in later centuries, he was even less admired, for he controlled, to a large extent, the distribution in the ghetto of food, money, and clothing to the indigent poor, and these were appallingly numerous as well as clamorous.

An interesting historical footnote to the office of this functionary; the Christian bishop, during the beginnings of the Church, was originally a gabbai, patterned after the contemporary Jewish model.

GALUT. *See* DIASPORA.

GAN EDEN (Hebrew, meaning "Garden of Eden"; i.e., Paradise)

In one of the minor Midrashim (the pre-medieval elaborations of the Talmud), Gan Eden is described in almost eyewitness detail as having five separate chambers (although other opinions say there are seven) reserved for the various categories of the righteous who receive their heavenly rewards according to their hierarchical order of merit. For example, the third chamber in Gan Eden is supposedly reserved for great Torah scholars, and tradition has it that here all the knotty questions of Torah that baffled them in their studies during their lifetime will at long last be answered, for in Gan Eden "the Holy One, blessed be He, will reveal to them the mysteries of the Torah in the World-to-Come." In fact, according to one tradition, God himself will preside over the Torah-discussions of the Sages, ably assisted by Mosheh Rabbenu, "our Teacher Moses."

Glittering in all its gaudy, innocent glory is the description given of the fifth chamber of Gan Eden: "built of precious stones, gold and silver, and fragrant with the scent of aloes. In front of this chamber flows the river Gihon, and on its banks grow shrubs which give forth aromatic fragrance. There [in the chamber] are couches of gold and couches of silver with fine coverlets upon them for the righteous to take their ease. In the middle stands a canopy made of cedar of Lebanon and constructed in the manner of the Tabernacle, with posts and ornaments of silver."

How does one enter Gan Eden? Through sparkling ruby gates, well guarded by sixty myriads of angels. When the man of righteousness is admitted, these celestial beings first divest him of his shroud (tachrichim). They dress him "in eight robes made of the clouds of glory," then they place a crown upon his head such as is worn by a king. One crown is made of pearls and precious stones; another is of gold. Into his hand they put eight myrtle boughs and, as they shove him gently into the halls of Eternal Life, they say to him: "Go and eat your food in joy!"

As he proceeds to explore the world of his new existence, the righteous one is enchanted. What he sees is like the fullfillment of a poor child's dream of a royal palace. He is first conducted into a vast garden that is everlastingly in bloom. He hears the gurgle of running brooks and breathes the fragrance of eight hundred varietes of roses and myrtles. He is treated like a guest of honor: He is given an enormous room, all to himself and in it he finds four fountains—one of milk, one of wine, one of balsam, and one of honey—from which to refresh himself. Needless to say, the righteous one is much pampered. Sixty angels are assigned to wait on him hand and foot. They coax and wheedle: "Do eat your honey in joy, because you occupied yourself with Torah, which is comparable to honey!" Or they cajole: "Do drink your wine, which has been preserved in the grape from the six days of Creation, because you occupied yourself with Torah, which is comparable to wine. . . ."

The most conscientious among the Rabbinic teachers tried hard to discourage the banal speculations and flights of childish imagination which sought to translate spiritual and ethical values into such crass materialistic objects, thereby entirely nullifying the moral concept of the reward for virtue. Some teachers of religion almost eagerly confessed their own ignorance about the Hereafter. They urged the folk always to keep in mind that no one as yet had come back to earth to say that he had seen the World-to-Come! How was it possible then to describe what "no ear has heard, no eye has seen"? The first-century Tanna, Yochanan ben Zakkai, had pointed out that even the Prophets, whom God had blessed with the inspiration of vision, had not attempted to describe the Hereafter. From this the Sage concluded: "The Almighty alone knows what awaits us in the world beyond the grave!"

Two centuries later, Rab, the foremost religious authority of Babylonian Jewry, grew impatient with the vulgar visualizations of Gan Eden current in his day. Testily he declared that there could not be the slightest resemblance between life on earth and the life to come in Gan Eden. "There is no eating there, no drinking, no begetting of children, no buying, and no selling. There is also no jealousy, no hatred, and no strife. But the righteous, with their crowns of grace [halos] on their heads, sit in the radiance of the Shechinah [the Divine Presence]."

Nine centuries later, in Moorish Spain, the rabbinic-philosopher Maimonides found himself exasperated by the continuing hold on the folk-mind by these notions concerning the heavenly reward. He chided those who were taking them seriously: "To believe so is to act like a school boy who expects nuts and sweets as a reward for doing his lessons. Celestial pleasures cannot be measured or understood by human beings any more than colors can be distinguished by the blind or music can be heard by the deaf." Rather, he held forth anew the ages-old Messianic promise of a Gan Eden *on earth*, to be established when the Redemption would come. By self purgation of all injustice, all hatred, all oppression of man by man, and of fratricidal war, human society could then become worthy of the enjoyment of true blessedness.

This is a legend that the Talmud relates.

> Alexander the Great, the conqueror of the world, at last stood before the gates of Paradise. He knocked.
> "Who is there?" asked the keeper of the gate.
> "It is I, Alexander the Great!"
> "I do not know you. Go away!" replied the gatekeeper, "only the righteous may enter here!"

This legend illustrates well the traditional Jewish view that when a man dies, he can take along with him neither his gold nor his distinction nor his worldly power, because—before God and divine justice—their value is but as dust! Only Torah-learning and a life full of good deeds, like a "pomegranate is full of seeds," survive beyond the grave for man's bliss.

So the Sages taught almost two thousand years ago.

See also DEATH; GEHINNOM; IMMORTALITY; RESURRECTION; REWARD AND PUNISHMENT; SOUL, THE; WORLD-TO-COME.

GAON. *See* GEONIM.

GARDEN OF EDEN. *See* GAN EDEN.

GEDALIAH, FAST OF. *See* FASTING AND FAST DAYS.

GEHENNA. *See* GEHINNOM.

GEHINNOM (Hebrew, meaning "Gehenna"; hence, Hell or Purgatory)

The etymology of the word Gehinnom remains in doubt. Some modern students think that its prefix, *Ge-*, in Hebrew means "Deep Valley," and that *-hinnom* refers to the "lusts" which, in mastering man, cast him down into the darkness of the "Deep Valley." Another more widely held conjecture is that it is the name of a place which in ancient times lay south of Jerusalem: *Ge-Hinnom*, the "Valley of Hinnom." This was also known as the "Accursed Valley" because, in pre-Israelitic days, the Canaanites had sacrificed their children there on the altar of their man-eating god, Moloch. If this surmise is correct, then the association of such a place with the infernal regions could well serve as an index of the moral revulsion the Jews of ancient times felt towards the barbarous practices of their neighbors.

The folklore about Gehinnom is inexhaustible. As to its "geographic" location, which has been widely contested, the Talmud notes: "Gehinnom lies above the earth. Others say it lies behind the Mountains of Darkness." These mountains, in the overawed popular belief, lay in a mythical region far "in the west." Another folk-view was that Gehinnom stretched underneath "the lid of the world." For that reason, it was assumed that darkness originated there, just as light was generated in Gan Eden (Paradise).

The popular belief was that the souls of evildoers and sinners were condemned to live in the everlasting darkness and terror of Gehinnom, a place lit only by the infernal fires that raged and crackled there, each having a heat sixty times greater than that of ordinary fire. Gehinnom reeked with the stench of burning sulphur or brimstone (this, incidentally, was also a characteristic of the Greek Hades). Suffocating, acrid smoke arose from the "Fiery Pit" or "Pool of Fire" in which the wicked, expiating for their misdeeds in life, agonized while the winds of damnation shrieked and howled through the seven descending regions of Gehinnom. It was too late for the wicked who wished to escape their fiery torments —too late for remorse when remorse could no longer avail them! Their punishment was clearly written down in the Talmud: "The Holy One, blessed be He, judges the wicked in Gehinnom for twelve months. At first He afflicts them with itching. After that [He roasts them] with fire. At this they cry out: 'Oh! oh!' and then He torments them with snow. Thereupon, they cry out: 'Woe is me! Woe is me!' "

In Talmudic times there were two differing opinions as to which category of souls would be flung into the Fiery Pit. The School of Shammai (first century B.C.E.; see TALMUD, THE) held that three classes of souls were judged after death: Those who had been perfectly righteous, those who had been completely wicked, and those who were merely "so-so"—namely, a "little" righteous and also a "little" wicked. The names of the righteous were instantly entered into the Book of Judgment; they were considered worthy of Eternal Life without any prior examination. The souls of the wicked were cast down into the dark caverns of Gehinnom to be tormented and finally consumed in the Fiery Pit. As for the "mediocre" sinners, namely, the run-of-the-mill men and women—they were obliged to go down into Gehinnom for a brief period of fiery purgation before being deemed sufficiently worthy of ascending and entering Gan Eden. The disciples of Shammai based these constructions on this prophecy: "Many of them that sleep in the dust of the earth shall awake, some to everlasting life, and some to shame and everlasting contempt." (Daniel 12:2.)

But the School of Hillel, which was contemporary with that of Shammai and was always at loggerheads with it, had a more humane conception of the fate of evildoers in Gehinnom. Because the Hillelites considered God to be compassionate and just, they were sure that after the process of purification by suffering and remorse had been completed for the whole human race, "Gehinnom will cease!" They consoled the backsliding, the confused, and the straying with the assurance that, in the fires of retributive justice, all their impurities would be consumed. In this way there would be fulfilled the promise that the Prophet Zechariah had given Israel: that God "will refine them as silver is refined, and will try them as gold is tried." (Zechariah 13:9.) That being done, the rehabilitated souls would be permitted to enter Gan Eden.

This moral principle, with its implication that the human being is perfectable—a belief fought for so valiantly by Hillel and his devoted adherents—assumed, finally, a central position in the ethics of Talmudic Judaism. "Every man has a share in the World-to-Come" became one of the most beloved of the moral dicta of the Sages of the Mishnah.

What really did the most advanced religious thinkers of that age conceive Gehinnom to be like? A second-century C.E. teacher of considerable profundity, referred to in the Talmud only as Ben Azzai (Son of Azzai), stated his position with almost epigrammatic conciseness.

> "What is the reward of a good deed?
> "The good deed.
> "What is the punishment of a sin?
> "The sin."

The advanced view was that Gehinnom as well as Gan Eden exists *in* man, and is made *by* man alone. Ben Azzai perceived that a logical consequence stems from every human action, good or bad, and in that action lies the reward or the punishment for the doer.

When the School of Hillel said: "Gehinnom will cease," it meant only that *man himself would abolish it* when he became fully worthy by reason of his righteous living.

See also DEATH; GAN EDEN; IMMORTALITY; RESURRECTION; REWARD AND PUNISHMENT; SOUL, THE; WORLD-TO-COME.

The Assyrian abyss Tiamat (called by the Israelites Tohum*). Into this bottomless fiery void, Jews believed, were cast the souls of the wicked. (From Ball's* Light from the East.*)*

GEMARA. *See* TALMUD, THE.

GEMILUT CHASADIM. *See* LOANS, FREE.

GEMILUT CHESED. *See* LOANS, FREE.

GENESIS, BOOK OF. *See* BIBLE, THE.

GENOCIDE. *See* KIDDUSH HA-SHEM; MASSACRES: CRUSADES, BLACK DEATH; NAZIS, THE; PERSECUTION IN MODERN DRESS; POGROMS IN SLAVIC LANDS.

GENTILES, JEWISH ATTITUDE TOWARD

There is a fundamental theme illustrating the way Jews have regarded Gentiles—whether pagans, Christians, Mohammedans, or others. It runs through most of Jewish sacred literature, beginning with the Bible. To a large extent, it has also set the pattern for the attitude toward Christians quite generally expressed in modern secular writing by Jews. The theme is first stated as an absolute moral truth in the form of a Biblical commandment to the Jews: "Love ye therefore the stranger." (Deuteronomy 10:19.)

Such a benevolent attitude stated in the positive terms of "loving" those outside the Jewish fold stands out conspicuously among the narrow parochial practices and teachings of some ancient religions. The Scriptural commandment categorically lays down the law that the stranger living in the midst of the Jewish people was not to be vexed in any way nor oppressed, the tireless reminder being, "for you were strangers in the land of Egypt." This attitude of fraternalism appears in sharp contrast to the chauvinistic group-pride that existed among the neighbors of the Jews in antiquity: The Greeks scorned all non-Greeks as "barbarians"; the Hellenistic Egyptians looked down on the Jews in their midst as being their cultural inferiors; and the Romans, with their customary arrogance, esteemed themselves as "the salt of the earth."

There can be little question but that the gentle regard, the moral concern, and the just treatment of the Gentiles in the midst of Jewish life in Biblical times was due both to the universalism which is stamped so prominently on the religion of the Jews and—not least—to the equalitarian nature of their early social structure. It was possible, therefore, for the Deuteronomist lawgivers to decree concerning the treatment of the non-Jew: "There shall be one law for the native-born and for the stranger who lives among you." (Exodus 12:49.) Not only did Jewish law forbid discrimination to be practiced against the Gentile, but it also forbade his being segregated physically in any way. The Biblical commandment made it perfectly clear that the place where he was to live was one "which he shall choose" himself. Oviously, there were no "ghettos" established for Gentiles in the Jewish society during its independent existence.

The Rabbinic teachers of ethics who flourished during the post-Destruction period (after 70 C.E.), in meditating on the morality of the laws concerning the natural rights and the protection of Gentiles, made many observations on their practical application. These provisions, commented one worthy in the Talmud, resulted from the fact that "the ways of the Torah are the ways of peace." Thus, equally with the Jewish poor in Judea, the Gentile needy were permitted to gather the marginal produce left lying in the fields during the harvesting. And, equally with the needy among the Jews, the Gentile poor were also to receive food and clothing provided by communal funds. To complete this remarkable picture of disinterested loving-kindness, other practices of Jewish benevolence were equally to be extended to cover non-Jews: Their sick were to be visited and given aid and comfort; their dead, where there was no one to give them decent interment, were to be buried by Jews with the same scrupulous care and respect that they would give their own. And—perhaps in imitation of the central principle of the Jewish religion, which is, according to Rabbi Akiba, "Love thy neighbor as thyself," a Talmudic Sage taught: "When a Jew passes a Gentile at work in the field, he should greet him with his brotherly blessing."

Much light on the evolution of this attitude toward non-Jews is thrown by the stated supremacy of the practice of righteousness over all other virtues and dogmas in the Jewish religion. The Talmud contains a great many aphorisms on this. Some of the most famous of these dicta, which helped mold the people's thinking and practice in almost every generation, are these:

> The voice of God at Mount Sinai sounded in all the seventy languages of mankind.
>
> He who hates another human being hates God.
>
> The Gentiles are My handiwork even as the Israelites are my handiwork. Shall I, therefore, destroy the Gentiles for the sake of the Israelites?
>
> The righteous among the Gentiles will have a share in the World-to-Come.

But the same criterion of merit was also applied to the Jew:

> I call upon Heaven and Earth to witness the truth of what I am saying: That: regardless of whether it be a Jew or a Gentile, a man or a woman, a man-servant or a maid-servant, according to the actions of each person does the Shechinah [God's Presence] rest upon him.

Beginning with the persecution of the Jews in Judea—initiated by the Greeks and Romans—there was a rising crescendo of terror through the Middle Ages into the middle of the twentieth century, when the German Nazis slaughtered six millions of Jews, and something new and disturbing was injected into Jewish national feeling: a consciousness of martyrdom, and also of the exaltation stemming from it. With the growth of this terror, a deep bitterness toward anti-Semitic Gentiles became evident among many Jews.

The seventeenth-century Jewish philosopher, Baruch Spinoza, with the thought of all the persecutors of man in mind, made this melancholy and regretful reflection in his *Ethics*: "The heaviest burden that men can lay on us is not that they persecute us with their hatred and scorn, but that they plant hatred and scorn in our souls." But Jews, in their relations with Gentiles, always drew a clear-cut distinction between Gentiles who hated and persecuted them and Gentiles of goodwill and probity. They honored the latter and tried to meet them more than halfway to bridge the artificial chasm that has divided man from his fellow men.

See also ANTI-SEMITISM.

"GENTLE PEOPLE, THE." *See* ETHICAL VALUES, JEWISH.

GEONIM (Hebrew pl., meaning "Excellencies"; s. GAON)
The title of "Gaon" or "Excellency" was bestowed upon each of the rectors of the great Rabbinic academies of Sura and Pumbeditha in pre-Mohammedan Babylonia. World Jewry, from the end of the sixth century to the first half of the eleventh, which has been labeled "the Geonic period," recognized these Geonim as their highest religious authorities, referring doctrinal-ritual disputes of all kinds to them for adjudication. The impact of their legal-religious decisions was deeply felt on Jewish life everywhere. Very understandably, in the state of dismemberment and wide dispersion of the Jewish people, the Geonim represented a great unifying force to whom all Jews looked for religious guidance and reassurance.

The relatively tolerant treatment by the Persian kings of the hundreds of thousands of Jews who had been transplanted from the Land of Israel into the valley of the Tigris and Euphrates rivers in a series of deportations culminating in the Babylonian Captivity in 586 B.C.E., resulted in the development of an autonomous community life for them. (Alexander the Great continued to follow his same benign policy of permitting Jewish communal and religious separatism after he triumphed over the Persians in 311 B.C.E. at the Battle of Arbela.) The government of this vast Jewish community, which at one time was said to have numbered in excess of one million and continued to grow even after the return to Judea of many thousands of exiles under Zerubbabel, Ezra, and Nehemiah, lay in the hands of two officials. One was the Resh Galuta or the Exilarch—"the Prince of the Exile"; he was supposedly a scion of the idealized royal House of David. He officiated as the political, fiscal, and judicial head of the Jewish community. The other functionary was the rabbinical Gaon; he presided over all religious matters exclusively.

The Geonim were men of culture and erudition. Their intellectual attainments became especially notable after Babylonia had fallen to the crusading zeal of Islam (during the seventh century). Under the Abbasid dynasty of caliphs,

Greek-oriented Arab philosophy, poetry, and science came into flower among the Jews. The interchange between Hellenistic-Arab culture and Rabbinic culture was extraordinary and proved very fruitful for both.

By and large, the Geonim were rationalists in their intellectual approach to religious ideas, but they were at the same time also traditionalists. This posed many difficulties for them, since they often were obliged in their decisions (Responsa; *see* RABBINICAL DECISIONS) to try to reconcile various contradictions which appeared between Jewish religious doctrine and practice in other parts of the world.

These centuries were a period of transition and change in many areas, one in which religions clashed for supremacy with a book of Scripture in one hand and a sword in the other. The chaotic times led many Jews to undertake a re-examination of old religious values.

In Babylonia itself, a schismatic conflict took place, with the Karaite sectaries rising in militant and impressive opposition to Rabbinic-traditional Judaism. In addition, the Cabalists with their esoteric mystical teachings pitted themselves against the Hellenistically oriented rationalism of the Babylonian rabbis. The Geonim—including the greatest religious thinker of them all, Saadia ben Joseph, the Gaon of the academy at Sura in 928—led the polemic onslaught against the Karaite insurrectionists and scored the most telling blows.

There is no question but that the Geonim, who themselves were among the important architects of Rabbinic Judaism, gave to the Babylonian Talmud a significance and religious authority that was denied to the Jerusalem Talmud.

See also COMMENTARIES, RABBINICAL; KARAITES; RABBINICAL DECISIONS; TALMUD, THE; YESHIBAH.

GET. *See* DIVORCE.

GHETTO

One of the most baffling words in use concerning Jews has been "ghetto." Its etymology is obscure, and there are many theories about it, but most of them are merely guesses.

The ghetto was first established as a place of enforced residence for Jews by the Fourth Lateran Council, in 1215, but in early Church documents it is referred to not by the name "ghetto" but by the old Byzantine descriptive, *Vicus Judaeorum* (Latin for "Jewish Quarter"). The first settlement bearing the name of "ghetto" actually took place in Venice. By an odd coincidence, it was situated near an iron or cannon foundry, called a *gheta,* in Italian. Furthermore, until relatively modern times, the Jewish quarter elsewhere was not called "ghetto" at all, or by any other name resembling it. In Spain, it went under the name of *Juderia;* in Portugal, *Judiaria;* in France, *Juiverie;* in the Provence, *Carrière des Juifs;* in Germany and Austria, *Judenviertel* or *Judengasse;* and in England, *Jews' Street.* Some philologists even have assumed that the word "ghetto," before its supposed Italianization, was derived from the Hebrew *get* (i.e., "separation" or "divorce"). Other philologists just as persuasively claim it stemmed from the Italian word *borghetto* (quarter). One scholar finds the Tuscan *guitto,* meaning "dirty," convincing; still another, the German *Gitter* (bars).

Whatever its etymology, the physical characteristics of the various ghettos were very often the same. A clear groundplan of the ghetto as an institution appears in one of the earliest references to it—in the preamble to the codex of canonical laws drawn up by the Church Council of Wroclaw (Breslau) under the guidance of Papal Legate Guido in 1266. It expressed the fear that, in view of the fact that the people of Poland had only recently been converted to Christianity, there was an ever present danger that it would "fall an easy prey to the superstitious and evil ways of the Jews living among them. . . . For this reason we [i.e., the Church Council] most strictly enjoin that the Jews residing in the Diocese of Gnesen shall not live side by side with the Christians, but apart, in houses adjoining each other or connected with one another, in some section of the city or town. The section inhabited by Jews shall be separated from the general dwelling place of the Christians by a hedge, a wall, or a ditch."

In the sense of being a compulsory place of residence in the prescribed area of a city, the ghetto into which Jews were herded during the Middle Ages and at later times was a decided innovation. It resembled the mellah of Morocco, Algiers, and Tunisia, into which North African Jews were segregated from the Arabs in the most sordid part of the city so that all contact with them could be avoided; they were apart symbolically as "outlanders" and religious and social rejects from the rest of the population. The average ghetto (to which there were occasional exceptions) was a virtual squalid prison for the Jews; it was intended to be such by those who had created it. It was, as has already been noted, an enclosed area very frequently shut off from the Christian population by one or more walls. In daylight it was closely guarded by an armed Christian watch stationed at the gate, which was called in Church and municipal records by the Latin name: *Porta Judaeorum.* This gate afforded the only means of entering and leaving for the inhabitants of the ghetto and remained under the constant control and surveillance of the local authorities. To add insult to injury, the "prisoners" were required to pay the wages of their "jailers."

The movements of the ghetto dwellers were governed by strict regulations, and if they chose to break any of these, it was at their own peril. Every Jew had to be inside the ghetto enclosure before the sun had set. The gate, of massive proportions, was usually shut after the recitation of the Hail Mary in the churches. At night it was barred and bolted and reinforced with heavy iron chains and locks, exactly like any fortress or prison gate of the period. However, there were times when the high walls and sturdy gates that imprisoned the Jews turned out to be a blessing in disguise, affording them a measure of protection against the fanatical armed mobs that periodically tried to break into the ghetto to kill and rob the inhabitants.

In presumably more enlightened times, in the year 1848 (the year famed for the libertarian revolutions in Europe), a Christian writer of Italy described the ghetto of Rome, which was still legally in existence, in terms that might have fitted its appearance and that of many other ghettos centuries before. He saw it as "a formless heap of hovels and dirty houses, ill-kept; in which a population of nearly four thousand souls vegetates, when half that number could with difficulty live there. The narrow unclean streets, the absence of fresh air, and the filth—the inevitable consequence of such a conglomeration of human beings, wretched, for the most part—renders this hideous quarter neauseating and deadly."

To be sure, not all ghettos were alike, nor were they always considered to be degrading and oppressive by their inhabitants. For that matter, neither were they all established at one time. The earliest were set up in the Roman Catholic countries as a result of the cumulative hostility and mass hysteria among Christians, which had been fed during the Crusades (in the eleventh, twelfth, and thirteenth centuries), and the time of the Black Death (1348–49: *see* ANTI-SEMITISM), by massacres and persecutions of the Jews. It was during this

The Judenplatz *(Jews' Square) and nearby streets in the First* Bezirk *(District) of Vienna. This was the earliest center of Jewish community life in that city. (Houfnagel's view of Vienna, 1609.)*

Gate of Octavius, ancient entrance into the Roman ghetto. (CENTER RIGHT)

Plan of the Roman ghetto, 1640. (From Zeiler's Itineraria Italia.*)* (BOTTOM)

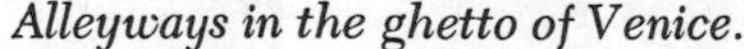

Alleyways in the ghetto of Venice.

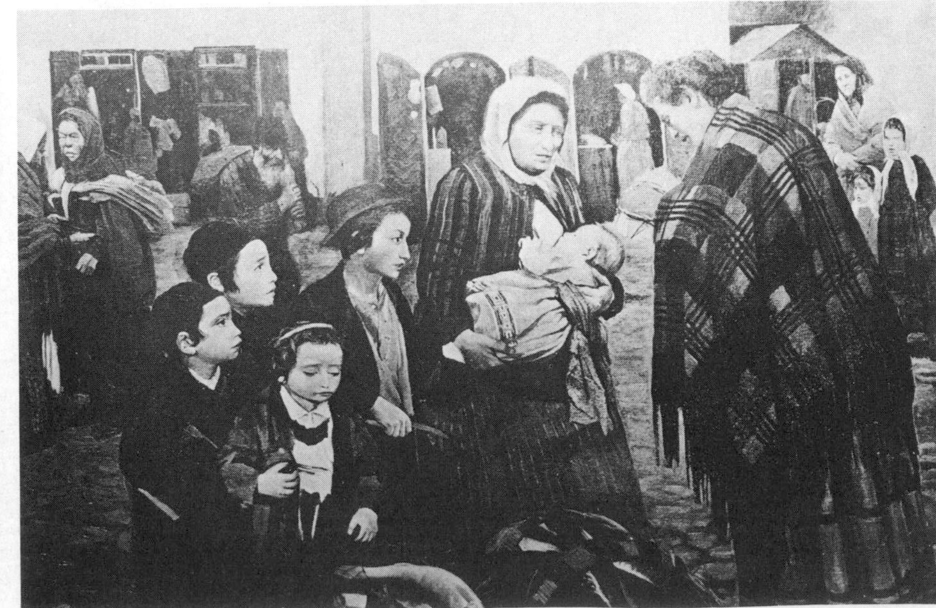

Street in the ghetto of Nikolsburg, Moravia, c. 1900. (UPPER LEFT)

In the ghetto of Cracow, Poland. (Engraving, 1869.) (TOP RIGHT)

Sunday market in the Amsterdam ghetto. (CENTER LEFT)

The marginal all-weather "merchant" in a Pol ish ghetto town. (R. Vishniak, Joint Distribu tion Committee.) (CENTER, MIDDLE ROW)

Knife- and scissors-grinder in a Polish ghett town. (R. Vishniak, Joint Distribution Com mittee.) (CENTER RIGHT)

Selling fish in the market place of a Polis shtetl (small ghetto town), early 20th centur (Painting by Minkowski.) (BOTTOM)

Bagel woman waiting for customers in a Polish ghetto market place. (TOP LEFT)

Market place in a Polish ghetto town. (R. Vishniak, Joint Distribution Committee.) (TOP RIGHT)

Shop-lined street in the Vilna ghetto before the Nazi occupation. (CENTER)

This was "Jews' Street" in Lincoln until the expulsion of the Jews from England in 1290. The stone house on the extreme right was once lived in by the money-lender Aaron (d. 1186). (BOTTOM RIGHT)

The London ghetto area before the expulsion in 1290, on a map of 1586. (BOTTOM LEFT)

period that the latter were driven, in the German states, Austria, Bohemia, Poland, Italy, France, Portugal, and Spain, into walled-off ghettos, in one city after another.

The cry for Jewish blood almost bypassed Russia. This was due, in some measure, to the fact that the state religion there was Russian Orthodox and anti-Jewish agitation had not yet reached the mob level. Whatever pogroms, expulsions, flights, and drastic restrictions the Jews suffered in Russia were first to come in the "Days of Enlightenment" under the latter-day czars, beginning with the eighteenth century. Only in a few places and under exceptional circumstances were they compelled to live in ghettos. Generally speaking, the Russian Jews of former centuries were allowed a limited measure of freedom in their movements. Their merchants and traders enjoyed, most of the time, a relatively secure position, being free to attend fairs, and to transport, sell, and buy merchandise in the open market. Their good fortune was that they were under the special protection of the czars who, ruling over an overwhelmingly peasant and feudal economy having an underdeveloped Russian merchant class, stood greatly in need of the commercial activities and financial skills of the Jews.

True enough, there did exist in Russia the Jewish "Pale of Settlement," which might correctly be described as a vast "geographic ghetto," but that was a relatively modern innovation in segregation. It was first established by law in 1772, and further delimited by statute in 1804, and it permitted Jews to live only in a prescribed area in Russia: in large sections of the Ukraine, in White Russia, in Lithuania, and in those Polish provinces that had been annexed by the Czarina Catherine II in the partition of Poland. The aim in establishing the Pale of Settlement was to keep the "Holy" Russian people (Great Russians, particularly) as racially and religiously *Judenrein* as possible.

The fact should not be ignored that, for centuries, the Jewish quarter in many a Catholic city and town was not, *by law*, a compulsory place of residence for Jews. The respective *Juiverie, Juderia, Judengasse*, and Jew's Street were merely special districts set apart for Jews in urban centers. They stood for a voluntary living together of those who had a great deal in common: religion, ethnic group identity, language, and culture. The stranger feels isolated, and like usually seeks like. By uniting in a community existence—in a community within a community, so to speak—the Jews found they were better able to carry on their traditional way of life, to follow their own folkways and customs, and to preserve their religious-educational and benevolent institutions. From the Jewish point of view, this road led to Jewish survival. However, because living space in the Jewish quarter was limited, and because the authorities usually opposed its expansion, there often took place intolerable overcrowding. And to aggravate the situation, economic and legal restrictions against the Jews, combined with a dismal lack of occupational opportunities for them, led to their widespread pauperization, especially in more recent centuries. As a result, the voluntary ghettos took on some of the unloveliest aspects of the compulsory ghettos.

It took a long time indeed for the medieval ghetto to become universally established in Europe. One principal obstacle was the reluctance of many feudal kings and princes to submit to the decrees of the Church in matters that affected their secular power and material self-interest. For it should not be forgotten that, in the scheme of the feudal system, Jews were considered *servi camerae, kammerknecht*, the "King's chattels" or property. Understandably, the rulers were determined to extract as much profit from "their" Jews as from any other property they owned outright. The imposition

Sunday market in Petticoat Lane, Whitechapel, London, 1908.

Old-clo' market in Petticoat Lane, Whitechapel, London, 1905.

Old Jewish quarter in Salonica, Turkey.

of a ghetto upon any city invariably brought an economic loss to the Christian community and certainly no financial profit to the ruler, for by restricting the Jews' movements, their legal rights, and opportunities for work and trade, the royal exchequeur had less to exact by force or to rob by law and taxation. In consequence, the Church councils, after the decree of 1215—and also a number of popes of fanatical constitution—were obliged repeatedly to reissue and reaffirm earlier decrees and papal bulls concerning the Jews that had either been ignored by the lay rulers or had only been half-heartedly heeded by them.

Strange as it may appear, it was not until 1556, at the height of the reaction which characterized the Counter Reformation, that the city of Rome (the seat of the popes and the very nerve-center of Catholicism) officially established a ghetto. This was done, finally, in response to a papal bull which the implacable enemy of the Jews, Cardinal Carafa, had issued after his election to the papacy as Paul IV in 1555. This bull decreed that "in Rome and in all other cities of the Papal States, the Jews shall live entirely separated from the Christians in a quarter or a street with one entrance and one exit; they shall have but one synagogue, shall build no new synagogue, nor own real estate."

But the secular authorities must fairly well have disregarded the edict. Ten years later, outraged by the apathy

Main street in the "white" Jewstown of the Cochin Jews, along the Malabar coast of India. The synagogue "belltower" may be seen in the background.

Entrances to the mellah of the Jewish cave-dwellers of Medenine, in the Matmata Hills of Tunisia.

A street in the mellah of the city of Algiers.

A street in the mellah of Tetuan, Morocco.

shown to it, Paul IV's successor, Pius IV, convoked the Council of Milan (1565) and issued this challenge: "We sternly demand of the rulers that they designate in the various cities special places in which Jews shall live apart from Christians." This time they obeyed. The existence of the ghetto became irrevocably fixed by state law.

The ghettos of Europe, outside of Russia and Poland, existed for several centuries. The last one, in Rome, was abolished in 1885, after King Victor Emmanuel had extended his rule to take in the Eternal City, one of the Papal States, which he had wrested from the Pope. To this very day, even though the compulsory ghetto as a historic institution has ceased to exist (although it came terrifyingly but briefly to life again during the Nazi domination of Europe), the almost solidly Jewish residential neighborhood in many a large city of the world is still referred to—perhaps gratuitously—as "the ghetto." However factually unprecise, this is said especially of New York's Lower East Side, London's East End, and the Rue de Rivoli locality of Paris.

See also COMMUNITY, SELF-GOVERNING.

Sabbath afternoon in a Moroccan mellah. (Painting by Le Comte du Nouy, 19th century.)

Hester Street on New York's Lower East Side in 1898. (Jacob A. Riis Collection, Museum of the City of New York.)

Preparing horseradish for gefilte fish. New York's East Side, 1904.

The East Side of New York during the 1890's.

Sketches of New York East Side life. (Main scene) 1. Street market on Thursday night at the corner of Essex and Hester streets. (Upper Right) 2. Buying kosher chickens for the Sabbath. 3. The toy vendor. (Bottom Left) 4. Pushcart merchants. Drawing by Durkin in Leslie's Weekly, *1891. (YIVO.)*

Gate (marked by black star in foreground) leading to the medieval ghetto in Strasbourg. (Early 17th-century print.)

Ghetto in Frankfurt, Germany, 19th century.

GILGUL, GILGULIM. *See* DYBBUK.

GOD. *See* BAT KOL; GOD, NAMES OF; MONOTHEISM; SHECHINAH; SHEM HA-MEFORASH.

GOD, IDEAS ABOUT. *See* MONOTHEISM.

GOD, KINGDOM OF. *See* MESSIAH, THE.

GOD, NAMES OF

It is surely ironic that the Jews, who first espoused the conception of the unity of God, should have showered on him a bewildering multitude of names. These have been a subject for not a little puzzled speculation among Biblical historians, philologists, and cultural anthropologists. But all the discussion has resulted in no positive conclusions and too little clarification. Possibly the most reasonable hypothesis presented is that each of the numerous names for God which appears in the Bible merely represents a physical or moral attribute ascribed to him, but couched in human terms.

In trying to explain the reason for the multiplicity of names for God, the third-century Rabbinic teacher, Abba bar Memel, quoted God, as it were, saying to Moses: "When I sit in judgment on the human race, I am called *Elohim.* When I war on evildoers, I am called *Zebaot.* When I recall man's sins, I am called *El Shaddai.* When I have mercy on the world I am called *YHVH.*"

The most frequently mentioned name of God in the Bible —it appears exactly 6,823 times—and the one considered by Jews to be supernal and pre-eminent among all his names, is *Yahveh.* This is the equivalent in English (with vowel-sounds added) of the four Hebrew letters *Yad Hay Vav Hay* or YHVH, which spell out the mystic and ineffable name of God and which may not be pronounced by the pious in their reading except paraphrased as *Adonai* (my Lord). This name—YHVH—is also known as the Tetragrammaton (Shem ha-Meforash).

Among the other names of God: *El,* which finds its Semitic-Assyrian counterpart in the word *Ilu;* and *Elohim,* which, although it has a singular sense, is put bafflingly in the Hebrew plural form. (One philological supposition for this is that it is derived from the Hebrew word meaning "afraid," thus signifying that when man stands before Elohim, it is in fear and trembling.) Appearing with frequency also are the names *El Elion* (Most High God); *Ha-Boreh* (the Creator); El *Elohe Yisrael* (God of Israel); *El Ha-Gibbor* (God the Strong One [or] God the Hero); *Yahveh Elohai Zebaot* (Yahveh, the God of Armies; more commonly referred to in English as "Lord of Hosts"); *Kedosh Yisrael* (Holy One of Israel); *Tsur Yisrael* (Rock of Israel); *Ha-Makom* (literally: "The Place," i.e., the Omnipresent).

In post-Biblical writings God was increasingly referred to as the "Holy One," as "Father in Heaven," and "Our Father Our King"—names the Judeo-Christian writers carried over into New Testament literature. The Rabbinic Sages of the first centuries of the Common Era even called God *Shalom* (Peace). The Cabalists of medieval times added other mystical appellations with numerological significance (*see* CABALA), the one valued as most important being En Sof (Infinite One).

Infinite as well seem to be the names of God given to him by the ancient Jews.

See also SHEM HA-MEFORASH.

GOD AND ISRAEL. *See* CHOSEN PEOPLE, THE; MONOTHEISM.

GOD'S ETHICAL ATTRIBUTES. *See* MONOTHEISM.

GOD, UNITY OF. *See* MONOTHEISM.

GOLDEN MEAN, THE RABBINIC

What careful student of the history of civilization can fail to be struck at every hand by the fact that the process of cultural diffusion and adaptation is incessant among all peoples? This was true even of the Jews, who maintained at all times a greater degree of ethnic and religious separatism than any other group. It becomes quite apparent that the Rabbinic version of the Golden Mean concept—whatever new moralistic overtones it sounded—was cut out of the same thought-pattern as that of the Greeks. And during the Hellenistic age, which ran almost parallel with the period of Rabbinic Judaism, the impact of Greek philosophy upon Jewish intellectuals was indeed profound.

Expert as educators, the ancient Rabbis often used the simple illustrative method to teach abstract or moral ideas to the people. The Golden Mean concept they projected with homely examples: "There are three things of which a little is good but much is an evil: yeast in dough, salt in meat, and indecision in the mind." "There are eight things of which a little is good but much is vexatious: travel, mating, riches, wine, sleep, hot drinks, medicine. . . ."

Like the medical-internists of modern times, the diet-conscious Talmudic teachers of seventeen or eighteen centuries ago prescribed controlled moderation in eating: "Eat one third, drink another third, and the remaining third of your stomach leave empty. Thus, if you should get angry, your stomach will have enough room to expand, and you will be spared an attack of apoplexy."

The practice of the Golden Mean is applicable to every human activity. The arch-champion of moderation was, of course, Moses ben Maimon (Maimonides, 1135–1204). Not only was he the most influential religious authority since the Rabbinic Sages and one of the foremost medical practitioners during the Middle Ages, but he was also an enthusiastic exponent of Aristotelian philosophy. The Golden Mean of the Greeks he restated in Jewish religious terms: "What is the right way is that middle state which is found in all the dispositions of man; namely, that disposition which is equidistant from the two extremes. The Rabbinic Sages of old have therefore directed that a man should always estimate his disposition, and that he should calculate and direct the same so as to keep the intermediate way, to the end that he may preserve a perfect harmony, even in his bodily constitution."

It was to be the moderation of a harmonious balance in all that man did and felt. He was to be neither passionate "nor like a dead man who has no feeling at all," but to follow a middle point between those two extremes. And although as a human being he had to gratify all of his bodily needs in order that he might live, he was to avoid excesses of any kind. Interesting is Maimonides' conception of the well-behaved Jew, one which became a Jewish tradition among Torah scholars and endured in the ghettos for centuries until modern times: ". . . He ought to be neither a jocose nor a gay man, nor a sullen nor a melancholy man, but he should always show a pleasant cheerfulness and a friendly face." The man of moderation Maimonides eulogized as the chacham, (the wise man).

Naturally, the big question was: How should the individual be enabled to achieve this harmonious balance, this Golden Mean? Rabbi Moses ben Maimon suggested that by habituation, by the steady practice of moderation in all things, the individual could become conditioned to the right way. For example, if a man was inclined to behave according to one extreme, "he ought to remove to the opposite extreme and train himself to it for a length of time, until by that means he comes back to the good way—which is the intermediate way. . . ."

See also ASCETICS, JEWISH; FREE WILL; LIFE, JEWISH VIEW OF; PASSIONS, MASTERY OVER; SIN AND SINNER.

GOLDEN RULE, THE

It is widely held that the Jewish saying popularly known as "the Golden Rule" is the one which best typifies the morality and practical idealism of the Jewish religion. There have been several versions of it, all clearly derived from the Biblical commandment, "Thou shalt love thy neighbor as thyself." (Leviticus 19:18.) But the version which gained the most favor was by the Mishnah teacher, Hillel the Elder. He taught love for every human being two generations before Jesus appeared. When an inquiring Gentile asked him to summarize the essence of the Torah, he replied simply: "And what is hateful to you, do not do to your fellow men. The rest [of the Torah] is merely commentary."

The first recognizable form of the saying is found in the Book of Tobit (4:14), which was written in Greek by an unknown Alexandrian Jewish moralist during the second century B.C.E. "And what thou thyself hatest, do to no man." Strikingly similar was the dictum of Philo, the rabbi-philosopher of Alexandria who belonged to the generation just before that of Jesus: "What a man would hate to suffer himself, he must not do to others."

Understandably enough, the Golden Rule, taught by Jesus in a slightly different form, is regarded as the keystone of Christian morality. The Gospel writer Matthew, like Jesus, a Jew, quotes the latter as saying: "Therefore all things whatsoever ye would that men should do to you, do ye even so to them: for this is the law and the prophets." (Matthew 7:12.) The final words—"for this is the law and the prophets"—indicate clearly that the saying refers to a sanctified tradition in Judaism.

Paul Wegener as he appeared in the title role in in UFA's famous German film, The Golem, *in 1920.*

GOLEM, THE

It frequently happens that sophisticated people dismiss legends and folktales out of hand, averring that they are only childish inventions of the superstitious masses. But as every informed student of popular culture eventually discovers, they are the persistent memories that a people preserves of its significant historic experiences, social attitudes, and moral values of the almost forgotten past.

There is no more graphic illustration of this linkage between legend and history than the story of the Golem and the evolutionary process that it went through before it culminated in the epic legend of *The Golem of Prague.* There can hardly be any other reasonable surmise than that this particular legend was the projection of a powerful yearning on the part of the Jewish masses, at a time when their situation in a hostile world had worsened, for a supernatural protector—not God nor one of his ministering angels nor the expected Messiah—to come and save them from the destruction threatened by their blood-lusting, fanatical enemies.

The mystery of "Where do we come from and where do we go?" has always enthralled people. As human control over the forces of nature grew, man became increasingly conscious of his latent powers; he even began to speculate about his own ability to equal, and perhaps even to oppose, the demiurge of creation. It was not such a great conceptional leap from the Prometheus legend, in which man, arrogant in his purposeful knowledge, tried to wrest the elemental secret of fire from the gods, to the mechanical man and chess-player that the ingenious Maelzel made in the early nineteenth century, and thence to the mechanical heart, the mechanical kidney, and the mechanical computer-brain that modern technology has invented.

Like all other peoples, Jews too were intrigued by the idea of creating human beings by other means than normal procreation. Though it is alien to all tenets of traditional

Praying in the Prague cemetery at the grave of Rabbi Judah Löw—"Der Hohe Rabbi Löw"—of Golem legend fame. Prague, 18th century. (Painting.)

Judaism, even appearing sacrilegious by appropriating for man the supreme function belonging only to the Deity, a number of legends in which man tries to encroach on the role of God as the Creator nevertheless appear in Jewish folklore.

The golem (or homunculus) legend in Jewish mythweaving is very old, references about it already being found in the literature of the Talmud which was created during the centuries following the final Dispersion, in 70 C.E. In its simple meaning, the Hebrew word *golem* signifies a mass of inert, shapeless matter, but in the folkloric sense it connotes a lump of clay that was brought to life by the magical and correct use of the Shem ha-Meforash or Tetragrammaton—the ineffable, pre-eminent, and secret name of God, symbolically represented by the four Hebrew consonants of the cryptograph YHVH. (*See* CABALA; GOD, NAMES OF.)

There is little doubt but that the fanciful Talmudic speculations concerning the creation of the first man by God stimulated the proliferation of golem-legends. For instance, there is the following passage in the Talmud, complete with all the "technological" directions for making a golem:

> How was Adam created? In the first hour his dust was collected; in the second his form was created; in the third he became a shapeless mass [golem]; in the fourth his members were joined; in the fifth his apertures were opened; in the sixth he received his soul; in the seventh he stood up on his feet . . .

According to the Agada (the narrative and anecdotal portions of the Talmud) the third-century Babylonian Sage, Rabba, had once created such a golem. This creature was said to have been a man like any other man except that he lacked the power of speech, a faculty which (according to the Jewish folk-belief) God alone could endow. When in a mood of vainglory Rabba sent his golem to call on his Rabbinic colleague Zeira, that Sage quickly discovered the creature's magical origin. Indignantly he returned him to the dust from which he had been made, declaring that the creation of man was God's business.

There is also the legend in the Talmud about the two Rabbinic teachers, Chanina and Oshaya. Every Friday, by means of a mystic formula that only they knew, they would create a three-year-old calf which they roasted and ate on the Sabbath. Reading this remarkable account, Rashi of Troyes (1040–1105), the authoritative Talmudic exegesist and commentator, felt called upon to give the legend both logical veracity and religious sanction. He gave this opinion: "They (Chanina and Oshaya) used to combine the letters of the Name [Shem ha-Meforash] by which the universe was created. This is not to be considered forbidden magic, for the words of God were brought into being through His Holy Name."

Jewish legend even has Rashi's great contemporary, the poet-philosopher of Valencia, Solomon ibn Gabirol (1021–1058), create a maidservant golem. The story runs that when the king heard of it he ordered the Jewish poet to be put to death for practicing black magic, but Ibn Gabirol succeeded in demonstrating to the king's satisfaction that the creature he had made was not human, and forthwith returned her to dust.

Another golem was said to have been fashioned in the twelfth century, at the time of the Crusades in France, by the Cabalist, Rabbi Samuel, father of the famous Judah Chasid, the author of The Book of the Pious (Sefer Chasidim). While it was claimed that he had, like Rabba, succeeded in making a golem, he could not make it talk. Wherever he went, this golem accompanied him as his servant and vigilant bodyguard.

Christian Europe, too, had its own versions of the golem. What else can the medieval legends about Dr. Faustus and the poet Virgil be considered? Even as Rashi believed in the authenticity of the creation of the Rabbinical calf, so did some of the most advanced among Christian thinkers of the Middle Ages believe in the legend about the statue into which the poet Virgil had breathed life and which he compelled to obey his will in various escapades.

By the time of the late Renaissance, legends about golems had become widespread among the Jews of Eastern Europe. The most popular of these was the one about the golem of Chelm, a monster said to have been created in the middle of the sixteenth century by Rabbi Elijah of Chelm, the redoubtable master of "the hidden wisdom." He had brought his golem to life by means of the correct Cabalistic formula of God's secret and ineffable Name, which he supposedly had discovered in the ancient Book of Creation (Sefer Yetzirah). This secret name of God he wrote down on a piece of parchment, placing it in the clay forehead of the golem, which, thereupon instantly came to life. Little did he dream what a monster the creature would turn out to be! When he beheld its frightful aspect and became aware of its lust for destruction, he quickly repented of his folly and concluded that his golem could very well destroy the whole world. So Rabbi Elijah drew forth the piece of parchment containing the Shem from the golem's forehead, and immediately the monster fell to dust.

In 1625, the eminent rabbi-doctor-scientist, Joseph del Medigo, while traveling through Germany, Poland, and Lithuania, took note that "many [golem] legends of this sort are current, particularly in Germany." A hundred years later, in 1718, the credulous German anti-Semitic Orientalist, Johann Jakob Schudt, noted in his *Jüdische Merkwürdigkeiten* ("Jewish Marvels"): "The present-day Polish Jews are notoriously masters of this art, and often make the golem, which they employ in their homes, like *Kobolds* or house spirits, for all sorts of housework."

The golem-legend, however, was far from innocuous in its social effects. When the apostate Jew, Samuel Friedrich Brenz, launched an attack on the Jews of Germany early in the seventeenth century, he raised a great ado in his book *Schlangenbalg* ("Snakeskin") about the Jews' "golem-magic." A Jewish wit, Zalman Zevi of Aufenhausen, made quick reply in German in 1615: "The apostate said that there are those among the Jews who take a lump of clay, fashion it into the figure of a man, and whisper incantations and spells, whereupon the figure lives and moves. In the reply which I wrote to the Christians, I made the turncoat look ridiculous, for I said there that he himself must be fashioned from just such kneaded lumps of clay without any sense or intelligence, and that his father must have been just such a wonder-worker [baal Shem], for as he writes, 'We call such an image a *chomer golem,*' which may be rendered as a 'monstrous ass,' which I say is a perfect description of him. . . . Our fools [golems] are not created out of clay, but are made in their mother's wombs."

It is noteworthy that among the Yiddish-speaking Jews of Central and Eastern Europe, a common synonym for "fool" is *goilem* and even *laymener goilem*—"clay golem."

Certainly the most famous, and also the most enduring, of all golem legends is that of *The Golem of Prague*. Its popular appeal has extended far beyond the confines of Jewish folklore; its monstrous eerie image has stimulated creative expression among writers, cinematographers, composers, sculptors, and painters, not least among these being Franz Kafka, Rainer Maria Rilke, and the Yiddish poet Leivick, who wrote a monumental verse-drama on it. It is also not too difficult to recognize that Mary Shelley had her physiology student, Frankenstein, fashion his terrifying monster, as it were, from the legendary clay of the Golem of Prague.

The legend, which first appeared in print during the seventeenth century in *Nifluot Maharal* ("The Miracles of the Maharal"), recounts how the Dominican friar Thaddeus inflamed the passions of the fanatical Christian mob in Prague with his libel that the Jews followed a religious custom which required them to murder ritually a Christian child and use its blood in the baking of matzot for Passover (*see* RITUAL-MURDER SLANDERS). Soon a champion of the Jews appeared in the person of Rabbi Judah Löw ben Bezalel (*d.* 1609), best known as "The Maharal," but also as "*Der Hohe* [The Eminent] Rabbi Löw." He made desperate attempts to put out the fires of hate with appeals to reason and justice, but to no avail. When the agitation finally had reached floodtide and the annihilation of all Jews seemed imminent, the Maharal called upon Heaven to answer him in a dream how best he could avert the catastrophe that was threatening his people. And the answer came to him in the Cabalistic, alphabetically arranged Hebrew words: *Ato Bra Golem Devuk Hachomer V'tigzar Zedim Chevel Torfeh Yisroel.* ("Create a golem out of clay that will destroy all the enemies of Israel.")

On the second day in the Hebrew month of Adar, in the year 5340 of the Creation (1580 C.E.), at four o'clock in the morning, the Maharal, accompanied by two of his disciples in the "hidden wisdom," went to the river bank of the Moldau and there kneaded out of clay the figure of a man three ells long (the English ell is 45 inches). They modeled for him hands and feet and head, and drew his features in clear human relief. Each of the three made the required seven mystic circuits around the clay figures, reciting in the meantime various incantations. Then, in unison with his disciples, the Maharal intoned (from the Scriptural verse in Genesis 2:7): ". . . and God breathed into his nostrils the breath of life; and man became a living soul."

At this juncture, the Golem opened his eyes and got to his feet. The Maharal and his disciples dressed him in clothes they thought were appropriate for a shammes (sexton or beadle). Then each one, taking a solemn oath not to divulge the secret, returned to the city.

On the way home, the Maharal said to the Golem: "Know that we have created you so that you may protect the Jews, who are defenseless, against their enemies. Your name is Joseph and you will serve me as shammes in the Bet Din [courthouse]. You must obey me no matter what I tell you to do, even should I ask you to jump into fire and water!"

Although the Golem could not speak (for the power of human speech was God's alone to give), he nonetheless understood what the Maharal had said to him. And so, from that time on, the Golem sat in a corner of the courthouse, with expressionless face cupped in his hand, just like a chomer golem who had no thought in his head. Because he behaved like a mute idiot, people winked and began calling him derisively "Yoseleh Golem" (Yoseleh is the Yiddish diminutive for the Hebrew Yosef, or Joseph).

The Maharal ordered Yoseleh Golem to guard the ghetto of Prague, to roam its streets at night, and to be sharply on the lookout for those who might wish to do harm to the Jews. Most of all, he used him in his war against the blood accusations which were then rife in the land and which were causing so much grief to the Jews. Yoseleh Golem's assignment included examining the contents of every passing cart and of every bundle that was carried by the passers-by. Were he but to suspect someone of making preparation for bringing a ritual-murder charge against the Jews (namely, by secretly conveying the body of a dead Christian child with the intention of planting it among the Jews in the ghetto) he was to bind the rogue with his rope and carry him straightway to the city watch in the *Rathaus* or town hall.

A number of years passed and, seeing that not one blood libel was being raised anymore in the Kingdom of Bohemia, the Maharal said to his two faithful disciples: "I have called you to tell you that the Golem is no longer needed."

On the night of Lag B'Omer in the year 5350 of the Creation (1590 E.C.), the Maharal said to the Golem: "Don't sleep tonight in the courthouse, but go up to the attic of the [Altneuschul] synagogue instead and make your bed there."

After midnight, accompanied by his two disciples, the Maharal ascended to the attic of the synagogue and stationed himself before the sleeping giant, the three Cabalists taking their places this time in reverse positions to what they had been when they had created the Golem. Then they started circling around him, making the seven mystic circuits but in the opposite direction, all the while intoning incantations. On the completion of the seventh circuit, the Golem grew rigid in death. Once again he looked like a shapeless lump of clay.

The Maharal and his two disciples took some old discarded prayer shawls (talletim) and wrapped them around the inert Golem. Afterwards, they covered him with thousands upon thousands of loose leaves from old discarded prayer books, so that he was altogether hidden from sight. The task completed, the Maharal and his companions descended from the attic, washed their hands, and uttered prayers of purification, as one usually does after being near a corpse.

One week later, the Maharal had a proclamation posted and read in the Altneuschul, forbidding any Jew, on pain of excommunication, ever to go up to the synagogue attic. So great was the reverence for *Der Hohe* Rabbi Löw that no one did dare to do so. At any rate, there are some believing folk who insist that the Golem is still lying there, waiting for the coming of the Messiah or, perhaps, for the time when new dangers may appear to menace the existence of the Jewish people.

A variant of the Golem legend gives another explanation for the Maharal's decision to return the clay monster to the dust he came from. Although the creature was mighty in strength, supernatural in prescience, and ever alert in following the orders of his Cabalistic creator, so that he saved the Jews of Prague from many a calamity, nonetheless, his creator decided to "unmake" him because he had grown afraid of the creature he had created, for the Golem, waxing drunk with the immense power he was wielding, menaced the entire Jewish community, even trying to bend the Maharal to his will, which had now turned evil and destructive. Thereupon, using the secret gematria of Cabalistic formulas for the second time, the Maharal returned the clay hulk of his creature to its original inanimate condition by withdrawing from its mouth the Shem, the life-creating, ineffable Name of God that he had placed there when first he made him.

The historical link between the Golem legend, the dread of the ritual-murder libel among the Jewish masses, and the Maharal's vigorous defense of the Jews, is plainly indicated in a document that is said to have been discovered in the archives of the Dominican Order in Prague. Rabbi Judah had asked for a public disputation with the monk Thaddeus on the subject of the priest's allegation concerning ritual murder, writing thus to Johann Silvester, Cardinal of Prague: "I demand justice for my oppressed brothers!"

During the disputation, the monk asked the Maharal: "According to the Talmud, do the Jews require the blood of Christians for their Passover festival?"

The Maharal answered: "The use of blood is forbidden by Holy Scriptures. The Talmud neither canceled nor modified this commandment. On the other hand, the Talmud made it even stricter. Those [Rabbinic] Sages who have taught: 'Whoever raises his hand against his neighbor, even if he does not strike him, is an evildoer [Sanhedrin 58 b],' and 'Somewhat greater is the value of human beings, for in order to keep them alive, even the commandments of the Torah may be suspended [Berachot 19 b],' surely could not have authorized the use of human blood, especially when even the blood of animals is forbidden."

One could almost say, so incredible have been the actual occurrences in Jewish history, that, were it not for their tragic reality, they, too, might be considered as but nightmarish legends.

This is the extraordinary significance, with all its symbolic-social implications, of *The Golem of Prague*. It fills in all those intangible elements of life that documented history either overlooks or ignores.

See also CABALA; GOD, NAMES OF; SHEM HA-MEFORASH.

GOLUS. *See* DIASPORA.

"GOOD INCLINATION," THE. *See* YETZER TOB AND YETZER HA-RAH.

GOOD MANNERS. *See* ETHICAL VALUES, JEWISH.

GRACE AFTER MEALS (in Hebrew: BIRKAT HA-MAZON; i.e., "Blessing for the Food")

Jews who follow the Ashkenazic order of prayer call this *Benschen* (Yiddish for "blessing"); the Sefaradim refer to it as *Benedición de la Mesa* (Spanish for "Blessing of the Table"). The pious Jew's custom of expressing thanks to God for the food he eats is founded on the Biblical injunction: "And thou shalt eat and be satisfied, and bless the Lord thy God." (Deuteronomy 8:10.)

The Cabalistic work, the Zohar, directs that this blessing, or Grace After Meals, be recited "with a joyful spirit."

The spirituality of all matter was constantly stressed by the Jewish religious teachers. Food was holy because God had made it. The Talmud points out to the unthinking: "Recollect before you even put a morsel of bread in your mouth, that its preparation required the performance of ten precepts: The grain from which it is made was not sown on the Sabbath nor during the Sabbatical year. Nor was the field in which it was planted plowed during those times. Neither was the mouth of the ox muzzled as he drew the plow. The farmer did not gather for himself the forgotten sheaves and the leftovers. He did not reap the grain in the corners and end-furrows of the field. He gave a little to the Levites. He gave a little to the poor. Finally, he presented as challah to the priests the piece of dough his wife cut off before baking the bread."

Eating, the Rabbis considered to be a religious act because it sustained life—both body and soul. Therefore, they ruled: "It is forbidden man to enjoy anything without pronouncing a benediction." In eating and drinking one experienced the spiritual reality of God's Creation. This transcendental attitude toward food was especially cherished by the Jewish Essenes, the pre-Christian sectaries and personal perfectionists who made preparation for every meal by self-purification—by bathing and putting on clean white raiment. The historian Josephus, who was acquainted with their mode of life at first hand, noted: "They enter the dining room pure, as they would enter a sacred precinct. At the beginning and at the end of the meal, they do honor to God as the sustainer of life." Quite obviously, the grace Christians say *before* meals must be an adaptation of the older Jewish prayer that had been drawn up several hundreds of years before by the Men of the Great Assembly (*see* SCRIBES; TALMUD, THE) in Jerusalem.

It was the desire of the Talmudic Sages to create a lofty spiritual mood during mealtime. Eating was to be on a dignified and refined level, with no quarreling, no coarse levity, no rudeness, no anger expressed during its course. Moreover, since one ate to live and did not live to eat, guzzling and gourmandizing were characterized as gross and sinful. This view did not in any way smack of asceticism; rather it pointed up the Rabbinical view of man's need to exercise an intelligent will over his appetite; one was advised to practice the Golden Mean (moderation) in this area too—by eating and drinking temperately.

Before the meal begins in a Jewish household, it has always been customary for the head of the house to recite this single blessing over bread: "Bessed art Thou, O Lord our God, King of the Universe, who brings forth bread from the earth."

The Mishnah prescribed the saying of Grace After Meals by one single individual on behalf of all those present at the table; however, religious leaders of later generations invited general participation in the recitation of the blessing. And so it was arranged antiphonally, as a dialogue between the leader of the prayer and those who made the responses—at least two males of qualified age to constitute a congregation in miniature.

Interestingly, the Rabbinic teachers, wishing to make the recitation of Grace After Meals universal and easy to comply with, allowed it to be said in the vernacular of the country; the only restriction was that it had to be recited at the table where the meal had been eaten. Among the Yiddish-speaking Ashkenazim, the prelude to Grace is announced by the prayer-leader. (As a matter of etiquette prescribed by tradition, the host is never chosen for this honor when a guest is present at his table.)

PRAYER-LEADER: *Rabosai, mir vellen benschen!* [My masters, we will now say grace!]

THE ASSEMBLED: Blessed be the name of the Lord from this time forth and forever!

PRAYER-LEADER: By permission of the master of this house and my masters and—[*or*] of my father and my masters [if a son is the leader] let us bless Him of Whose bounty we have eaten.

THE ASSEMBLED: Blessed be He of Whose bounty we have eaten and through His goodness we live!

The prayer for Grace After Meals is divided into four sections: The first offers thanksgiving to God "Who feedest the whole world with thy goodness"; the second thanks God for having delivered Israel from the Egyptian Bondage, for having given it the Torah, and for having settled it in the Land of Israel; the third is a supplication for the restoration of Zion, for the coming of the Messiah (the son of David), and for the speedy rebuilding of the Temple. The fourth section, presumably written after the fall of the fortress of Bethar, which marked the total collapse of the Bar Kochba uprising in 131–32 C.E. against the Romans, offers thanks to God for extending to shattered Israel his divine "grace, loving-kindness, mercy and relief . . . blessing and salvation, consolation, sustenance and support. . . ."

There are, in addition, shorter forms of Grace to be recited after eating, even if one has eaten only a slice of cake, or a piece of fruit, or taken a drink of wine or even water. Whatsoever he eats or drinks, it is mandatory for the believing Jew to thank and bless the Creator. It was made traditional for children to recite this abbreviated form of Grace: "Blessed be the Merciful One, King of the Universe."

See also GOLDEN MEAN, THE RABBINIC; PASSIONS, MASTERY OVER.

GRANDPARENTS. *See* FAMILY RELATIONS, TRADITIONAL PATTERNS OF.

H

Habdalah rite. (From Sefer ha-Minhagim *["Book of Customs"], Amsterdam, 1695.)*

The braided candle used in the Habdalah service for the departing Sabbath.

Habdalah rite at the Sabbath's departure. (Etching by Hermann Struck, Berlin, c. 1910.) (LOWER LEFT)

Silver spice-box (in Yiddish: b'somim bix*) in the form of a medieval tower with four turrets. Central or Eastern Europe, 18th century. (Courtesy of Joseph B. Horwitz Judaica Collection, Cleveland.)* (LOWER RIGHT)

HABDALAH (Hebrew, meaning "separation" or "differentiation")

In traditional observance through the centuries, the Habdalah ceremony on Saturday night marked the end of the Sabbath. Just as on the previous day, on Friday at dusk, "Queen Sabbath" (Shabbat ha-Malkah) had been ushered in with a royal fanfare of Cabalistic blessings over lighted candles, with prayer in the synagogue, and, later, at home with the singing of hymns in joyous welcome and the Sanctification rite of Kiddush, so too was the departure of "Her Majesty" marked by ceremony. But this time it was not at all with rejoicing but with regret.

The rite of "separation," like every other kind of separation from a "dearly beloved," was sorrowful in tone. It was charged with mystic symbolism. The medieval Cabalists, being both poets and mystagogues, had planted the notion in Jewish religious thinking of the existence of a Sabbath "over-soul" (a neshamah yeterah) that gave an additional measure of holiness and rapture to the Sabbath—another, an extra, dimension of spirituality. This presumably allowed emotion to overflow in the hearts of the devout so as to increase their bliss for the day. The departure of the Sabbath (so averred the Cabalists) caused the "over-soul" to grieve. The faithful worshipers joined in this unsual—one might call it "abstract"—grief, and in appropriate expressions of it during the Habdalah service. But they took comfort, in a manner symbolic and characteristic of Oriental folkways, by inhaling the aroma of spices (in Hebrew: *besamim*) contained in an ornamental receptacle (most often made of silver) called a "spice box." The Cabalists' "scripture," the Zohar, makes the point that "upon smelling the Habdalah spices, the saddened spirit revives."

Following the terrors met with by Jews in Germany during the Thirty Years' War and in Eastern Europe at the time of the Cossack revolt in 1648, another mood began to pervade the departure of the Sabbath: *inquietude.* Jews felt a biological, economic, and emotional insecurity in the midst of the raging sea of hostility which threatened to engulf them. The ordeals and anxieties of the daily struggle for survival that the Sabbath, with its period of holiness and calm, had set briefly aside for them, loomed large again.

The Habdalah rite was, and still is, performed among the Orthodox by the male head of the family immediately upon his return home from Maariv (the Evening Service) in the synagogue. Before the members of the household gathered around him, he kindles a light: a braided wax candle with a double wick, to recall the torch used in ancient times. Since the kindling of fire was strictly forbidden on the Sabbath in order to discourage the Jews of Biblical and later times from emulating fire-worshiping idolators, the first light struck at the close of the Sabbath constituted a symbolic act of "division," it indicated that the "holy" Sabbath and all the special laws that governed it had come to an end, and that it was permitted once more to resume the "profane" routine of workaday living. It represented, indeed, a sharp transition from the ideal spiritual to mundane reality. This notion is expressed in the benediction which the head of the household recites over an overflowing goblet of wine (or liquor) in the rite: "Blessed art Thou, O Lord our God, King of the Universe, who makes a distinction between holy and profane, between light and darkness, between Israel and the nations, between the seventh day and the six working days."

The kindling of the first light upon the conclusion of the Sabbath has an ancient origin but probably was instituted by the Soferim, the Scribes of Second Temple times who collectively were called "the Men of the Great Assembly" or "the Men of the Great Synagogue," and who established the traditional forms of liturgy and rite for the synagogue and the home. The Rabbinic Sages who were their successors tried to attach to the first light a cosmic symbolism, saying: "The light which God created on the first day lit up the world for man from the time he was made until sundown on the following day, when the darkness that enveloped him filled him with fear. . . . Then God gave him two stones which he rubbed together until fire came. Whereupon he offered a benediction over the fire." This benediction, recited during the Habdalah rite, makes a complete break with the fire-worshipers' animistic conception of fire; it attributes its origin to the First Cause: "Blessed are you, O Lord our God, King of the Universe, who hath created the light of the Fire."

In former centuries, when Jewish community life in Central and Eastern Europe was still colorful, homogeneous, and kept unified by a thoroughgoing religious orthodoxy, the departure of the Sabbath was observed within the ghetto with stirring hymns and with instrumental playing by the klezmorim, the Jewish folk musicians. In the eighteenth and nineteenth centuries, the sectarian Chasidim paid homage to "Queen Sabbath" with rapturous dancing in a mystic circle. In twentieth-century observance by the devout, the Habdalah rite bears but the most pallid resemblance to what it once used to be in the ghettos of Poland and Russia.

See also KIDDUSH; KLEZMER; SABBATH; SABBATH LIGHTS.

HACHNASAT ORCHIM. *See* HOSPITALITY.

HAFTARAH (Hebrew, meaning "conclusion" or "dismissal")

The Haftarah refers to that portion from the Prophetic Writings prescribed as a supplementary reading to the Torah portion for the week. It is cantillated according to a traditional musical mode after the reading from the Torah of the concluding verses of the weekly "portion" or sidrah (pl. sidarot) in the synagogue on the Sabbath and on holy days.

The honorific title that is bestowed on the reader of the Haftarah is *Maftir* (meaning in Hebrew "one who dismisses"). From this designation stems the not unlikely theory that the reading from the Prophets marked the conclusion of the prayer service in Rabbinic times. Then, as now, the Maftir was required to read aloud at least three concluding verses from the Torah sidrah before he launched into the selection from the Haftarah, which varied in length from ten to fifty-two verses. His reading from the sidrah was a symbolic connecting bridge that linked the Torah of Moses and the teachings of the Prophets, one being complementary to the other.

The information given by the Talmudic teachers concerning the traditions were not always precise or enlightening in setting the dates of their institution. The Rabbis, for example, ascribed the origin of Haftarah-reading to Ezra the Scribe, who lived in Judah during the fifth century B.C.E. A more persuasive hypothesis was advanced by a fourteenth-century Spanish rabbi; namely, that the practice had resulted from a ruse to circumvent the incurrence of the death penalty which had been decreed as punishment for all those Jews found reading aloud from the Sefer Torah (Scroll of the Torah) in congregational worship. This decree had been issued by Antiochus (Epiphanes) IV, the Seleucidan Hellenic king of Syria and the conqueror of Judea, who, with his savage suppression of the Jewish religion, had precipitated the Maccabean war of liberation in 168 B.C.E. Reading from the Haftarah was a stratagem to avoid the extreme penalty that would result on public cantillation from the Five Books of Moses, since reading from the Prophetic Writings had not been included in that prohibition. Accordingly, passages from the Prophets containing almost corresponding ideas and making similar implications as the sidarot from the Pentateuch were compiled by the religious authorities in Judea.

Ever after—even though the conditions that had given rise to the public reading from the Haftarah disappeared upon the triumphant conclusion of the Maccabean uprising in 165 B.C.E.—the practice continued as an unbroken tradition to this day.

See also MUSICAL ACCENTS; SIDRAH; TORAH-READING.

HAGANAH. *See* THE BALFOUR DECLARATION (*under* ZIONISM).

HAGGADAH, THE. *See* PASSOVER.

HAGIOGRAPHA. *See* BIBLE, THE.

HAKAFOT (Hebrew, meaning "circuits" or "processions")

Processions in honor of significant religious values and designed to heighten the dramatic effect of certain ceremonies and rites were customary in the Land of Israel in Biblical and post-Biblical times. One of the few ceremonies that has survived the ever-changing circumstances of Jewish life in the Dispersion are the processions that take place on Simchat Torah, the day of "Rejoicing in the Torah." (Sefaradic Jews also make circuits on Hoshanah Rabbah.)

On the evening of this festival of Simchat Torah, when the Mussaf prayer service has been concluded in the synagogue, the doors of the Ark are opened wide, and every Torah Scroll (Sefer Torah), adorned with all its silver ornaments and tiny tinkling bells, is drawn forth and carried amid rejoicing around the synagogue. (In poor or small congregations there may be only one Torah scroll). The first one is usually carried by the cantor or prayer-leader; the other scrolls are borne by the rabbi and other dignitaries during the first circuit of the house of worship.

Tradition calls for at least seven successive circuits, and since Jewish democratic practice provides that every male worshiper be given a chance to carry a Sefer Torah in the procession so that he has an opportunity publicly to rejoice in the possession of the common heritage, if the seven circuits do not suffice to give each male in the congregation, from the most illustrious to the most humble, this chance, additional hakafot are added. Led by the precentor, the line for each successive processions forms and, as it winds its way slowly around the bema (reader's desk) near the center of the synagogue, the worshipers chant the very ancient Hoshanah invocation which begins: "O Lord, save us, we implore You!"

The origin of the seven hakafot has intrigued students of Jewish religious folkways. Undoubtedly, it has an intimate connection with the seven circuits that are made around the bride and groom as they are united in marriage under the chuppah (marriage canopy). Since olden times, the ceremony of hakafot has been viewed by mystics as being symbolic of the marriage rite: The groom is Israel and his beloved bride is the Torah, and their wedding, which took place during the Revelation at Mount Sinai more than three thousand years ago, is commemorated with rejoicing every year and for all eternity on Simchat Torah.

See also SUCCOT.

HALACHAH, HALACHOT. *See* TALMUD, THE.

HALO ("CROWN OF GLORY")

The symbolism of the crown as sovereignty and spiritual grace was very prominent in Jewish religious expression. "The Crown of the Torah" is a case in point. It is the silver ornament with which the Scroll of the Law (Sefer Torah) is beautified. It is, in addition, embroidered in gold thread on both Torah mantle and Ark curtain (parochet). But to the believing Jew, it more particularly represents the spiritual royalty of God's revealed truth that is contained in the words of the Torah.

"In that day shall the Lord of hosts be for a crown of glory, and for a diadem of beauty, unto the residue of his people," preached the Prophet Isaiah (Isaiah 28:5). From this Scriptural text, Rabbi Chaninah drew the image: "God Himself will be a Crown of Glory upon the head of each of the righteous."

This "Crown of Glory" that derived from God and was, in a special sense, expected to come as a reward for exceptional virtue, was implicit in the concept of the Shechinah or "God's Radiance" (*see* SHECHINAH) which was said to "rest" upon the favored righteous as a mark of the favor of heaven. However, inasmuch as representational art had been prohibited to Jews by the Second Commandment of the covenant at Mount Sinai, it remained for Christian art, which had adopted the notion from Jewish belief in the first instance, to depict the "crown of glory"—a halo or nimbus—*visually* over the heads of the Holy Family and Jesus, and the Apostles and all the saints. But the "crown of glory" nevertheless remained a rapturous reality among Jews, even if in fantasy form only. The third-century Babylonian Rabbi, Rab (Abba Arika), merely paraphrased older post-Biblical opinion, both Hellenistic and Talmudic, when he wrote that, in the World-to-Come, "the righteous sit with crowns on their heads and are nourished by the splendor of the Shechinah. . . ."

HASIDEANS. *See* ZEALOTS.

HASKALAH. *See* ENLIGHTENMENT, THE JEWISH; HEBREW LANGUAGE, HISTORY OF THE; HEBREW LITERATURE, MODERN; JUDAISM IN THE MODERN AGE.

HAZKARAT NESHAMAS. *See* BURIAL RITES AND CUSTOMS; YIZKOR.

HEAD COVERING

Eight centuries ago, the rabbi-philosopher Maimonides wrote in his *Guide to the Perplexed:* "The great men among our Sages would not uncover their heads because they believed that God's glory was around them and over them." This belief was based on the benediction recited in the morning prayer: "Blessed be Thou, O Lord, Who crowns Israel with beauty."

Actually, there is no Biblical law or directive for covering the head. To cover one's head with a turban or a skullcap (yarmulkah) as a sign of humility, respect, or reverence has been a widespread custom among many peoples in the Orient, especially among the Hindus, Arabs, and Persians. Jews having originated as an Eastern people, those who follow religious tradition are careful to cover their heads, both when waking and sleeping. The Babylonian rabbi of the fourth century, Chunah ben Joshua, would not walk "four steps" if he was bareheaded, explaining that "The Shechinah [God's Radiance] is above my head."

Applying the approach of modern ethnology, the origin of the practice can be explained somewhat differently. It must have sprung from a tribalistic belief of the early Israelites. Like their neighboring contemporaries, the Jews of ancient times held to a magical notion concerning human hair. For example, the exposure of a woman's hair to the view of strange men was deemed a form of nudity and temptation to sin. The Nazarites of early Biblical times, who took a vow of chastity and sobriety, allegedly derived some of their sanctity and magical powers from their long hair, and the superhuman physical strength of the Nazarite Samson, which is recounted in the Bible, was ascribed to his long hair. In the view of the ancient Jews, one could not trifle with the mysterious demonic powers who were out to do man harm; therefore, the hair could not be uncovered without inviting mischief from them.

In ancient Jewish beliefs there is found stern disapproval of the uncovered head, whether it be of a man or a woman. But the "sin" is compounded by uncovering the head in a consecrated place, like the synagogue or the Bet ha-Midrash (House of Study) or when at prayer or while at Torah study. The pious man has always been exhorted to be on guard against carelessness in this matter. When his head is unavoidably bared, he is forbidden to pronounce the name of God, to recite the Shema, or to read from the Torah. It is always recalled in this connection that, when the high priest entered the Holy of Holies in the Temple in Jerusalem on Yom Kippur, he first had to cover his head with his golden miter.

Christians have often wondered why Jews put their hats on as a sign of reverence while they themselves take their hats off to express the same feeling. Jesus and the early Jewish-Christians, who adhered to this as well as many other

Rabbi Isak Noah Mannheimer, rabbi of the Reform temple in Vienna, wears an adapted yarmulkah. (Lithograph by Adam Sandor Ehrenreich, early 19th century.) (BELOW)

A Lithuanian Jewish family, the man wearing a shtreimel—a velvet-trimmed hat with fox tails. (From L. Hollaenderski's Les Israelites de Pologne, *Paris, 1830.)* (TOP RIGHT)

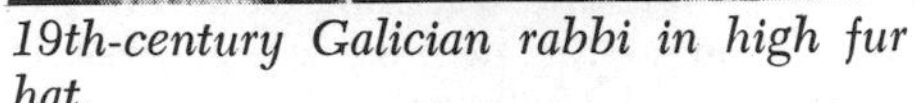

19th-century Galician rabbi in high fur hat.

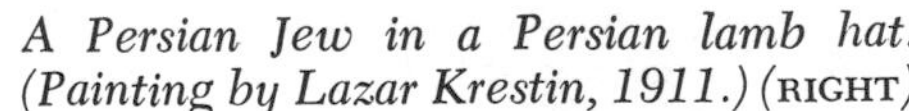

A Persian Jew in a Persian lamb hat. (Painting by Lazar Krestin, 1911.) (RIGHT)

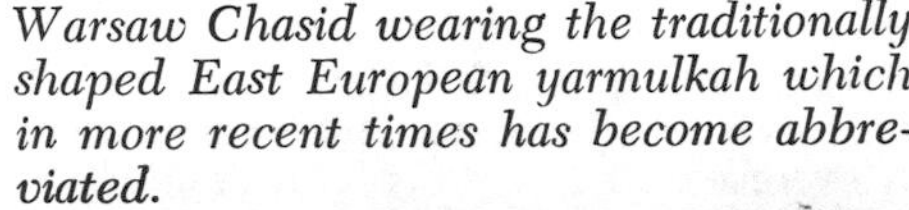

Warsaw Chasid wearing the traditionally shaped East European yarmulkah which in more recent times has become abbreviated.

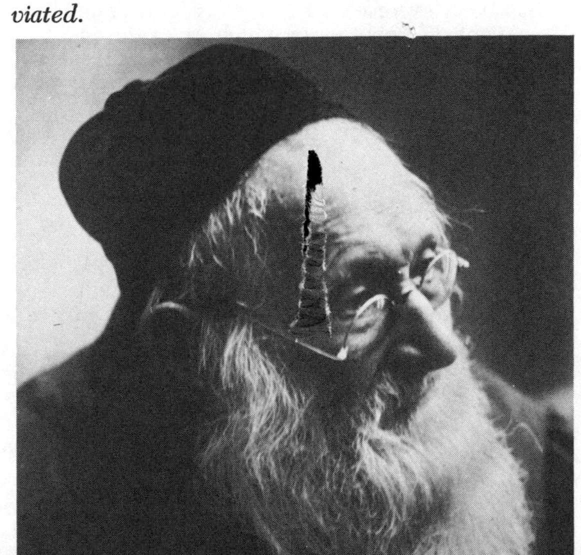

Jewish customs, unquestionably covered their heads when they entered a synagogue or when they engaged in prayer. The origin of the custom of uncovering at prayer among Christians is traceable to Paul (Saul) of Tarsus, himself born a Jew. When he attempted to de-Judaize the new Church he had founded, he concluded that, since the Jews covered their heads, especially at prayer, it was only proper that Christians should do *the very opposite*. He thus cautioned the faithful: "Every man praying or prophesying, having his head covered, dishonoreth his head." (I Corinthians 2:4.)

See also SHEITEL.

Jewish doctor (left) at the head of the bed of the dying Norman king, Wilelmus II, of Sicily (1189); at the foot, with astrolabe in hand, is seated an astrologus *(astrologer). The Jewish doctor was an indispensable functionary at all the royal courts of Europe during the early Middle Ages. (From a 13th-century South Italian manuscript in the City Library, Berne, Switzerland.)*

HEALERS, THE (in Hebrew, pl. ROFEIM; s. ROFEH)

Incessantly, both Jews and Gentiles have expressed wonderment why it is that, in proportion to the general population, there are not only many more Jewish doctors than non-Jewish practitioners, but that, in many instances, they also seem to show a marked affinity for their profession. An astonishing number of Jewish doctors have distinguished themselves as clinicians and medical scientists. The encyclopedic German scientist Virchow, a non-Jew, said to the International Medical Congress in Rome in 1894:

> In early medieval times, it was the Jews and the Arabs who made a definite impression upon the progress of medical science. In our times, Hebrew manuscripts have been brought to light which show with what zeal and learning Jewish physicians of early medieval times were active in the preservation and advancement of medicine. We may, in truth, say that down to these times there can often be discerned this hereditary talent of the Jews which has contributed so much that is great in [medical] science.

While noting this singular aptitude for medicine on the part of many Jews, Virchow did not, however, attempt to furnish any clues to the causative factors behind it. His failure to do so may have been due to the fact that he was not able to observe the phenomenon within the frame of reference of Jewish religious and cultural history—an area of knowledge with which he was not entirely familiar.

It remained for the Italian historian of medicine, Arturo Castiglioni (1874–1953), aided by a knowledgeable understanding of the religious-cultural background against which the Jewish doctors emerged (since he was himself a Jew), to relate their unique dedication to the healing art—at least in part. He noted, in his *History of Medicine:*

> What is particularly notable, and what makes the history of Jewish medicine more interesting, perhaps, than that of other peoples of antiquity, is that one can often observe that [medical] traditions and concepts have been absorbed and, so to speak, filtered through the moral and legislative system of Judaism, and what a decisive role has been exercised in this process of assimilation by the concept of monotheism which gives the Deity the power of healing! As a result of this concept, Hebrew medicine differs from that of all other peoples of antiquity.

The concept of God as the supreme physician is proclaimed in Exodus 15:26—". . . for I am the Lord that healeth thee"—and again, in Deuteronomy 32:39, when speaking through Moses to the children of Israel: ". . . I kill, and I make alive; I have wounded, and I heal . . ."

Notwithstanding that Castiglioni's explanation, as far as it goes, is entirely correct, he somehow failed to make what might be considered the most significant point of all. For the Jewish doctor of former centuries, beginning with post-Exilic times (when an intellectual upsurge and preoccupation with ethics and social ideals absorbed the Jews in Judea, in Babylonia, and throughout the Hellenistic world), the practice of medicine constituted an exalted form of *religious worship*. At the conclusion of his Prayer for Physicians, Maimonides (Rabbi Moses ben Maimon), one of the great rationalistic thinkers and doctors of the Middle Ages, echoed this ancient self-dedication: "O God, Thou hast appointed me to watch over the life and death of Thy creatures; here am I ready for my vocation!"

In his occupational role, the doctor was believed only to be emulating his Creator's moral attribute as the Compassionate Healer of man's sorrows and afflictions. Since, according to the Jewish conception, the healing of illness came from God through the mediation of his "messenger," the doctor, it is not infrequently that in old Jewish religious writings one stumbles across adulatory references to the physician as "God's messenger." In the nomenclature of Jewish supernaturalism, the angels were called "messengers of God," with the Archangel Raphael being honored by the Cabalists as "the messenger of healing" sent by God to the aid of the sick. Thus the believing Jew who was ill combined his hope of being cured by the art of the physician with his supplication to God, in whom he placed all his trust to send him healing. "May God grant you a speedy and complete cure [in Hebrew, a *refuah shelemah*]!" This is the traditional formula of encouragement the sympathetic visitor murmurs as he takes his leave of a sick person. But the latter, however devout he may think himself to be, in a realistic appraisal of his situation, does not fail to follow the advice of his ancient kinsman Jesus ben Sirach (*c.* 200 B.C.E.), the Judean author of the wisdom book Ecclesiasticus: "If you fall ill, cry to the Lord, but also call for the physician, for a sensible man does not neglect the remedies which the earth offers."

That there was believed to exist a close interconnection between the body's health and the principles of morality is amply demonstrated in the literature of the Talmud. Rabbinic doctrine of two thousand years ago did not recognize any cleavage between mind, body, and soul; all three had been wrought by the Creator and endowed with the potential of blending together into a perfect harmony, provided the individual brought his free will into play for the "mastery of his passions" (*see* PASSIONS, MASTERY OVER) and for living uprightly. In some respects, the Rabbinic Sages of old seem to have anticipated that postulate of modern psychosomatic medicine which assumes that bodily illness is very frequently caused (or sharply aggravated) by emotional and psychic distress.

"There is no death without sin," concluded the Talmudic moralists of long ago. One thousand years later, in the twelfth century, the philosopher, rabbi, and medical scientist Maimonides elaborated on this theme by arguing that sickness of the body is brought about not only by excesses and by injurious habits, but *by the violation of good moral principles.* A guilty conscience often results from abuses of the passions (such as anger, envy, hatred, and lust), thereby kindling new fires of affliction for the human being.

The Jewish doctor's medical thinking was steeped in moralistic principles. To succor the sick and to preserve life—these constituted the ultimate expression of piety; love for man was complementary to love for God. Therefore, to treat a very sick patient (Gentile as well as Jew) on the Sabbath was considered not only no violation of that holy day on which all work was forbidden—it was, in fact, esteemed as an act of great merit! No law of humanity ever exceeded in simple nobility the formulation of this oral tradition in the Mishnah (*q.v.* under TALMUD, THE):

> Man was first created as a single individual in order to teach the lesson that, whoever destroys one life, the Torah considers it as if he had destroyed the whole world; and [conversely] *whoever saves one life, it is as if he had saved the whole human race.*

This tradition served as the lodestar for most Jewish doctors in every generation. In his medical "testament" written in 1559, that celebrated Jewish anatomist, internist, and surgeon who was physician to Pope Julius III (and known in the history of medicine as Amatus Lusitanus), stated the principles that guided him in his medical practice:

> I swear by the eternal God and by His ten most holy commandments . . . that I have never, at any time, done anything in my treatments save what inviolate faith has handed down to posterity; that I have never feigned anything, added anything, have changed anything for the sake of gain; that I have always striven after this one thing: namely, that benefit might spread forth to mankind. . . . All men have been considered equal by me of whatever religion they were, whether Jews, Christians or Mohammedans.

Jewish doctor of Constantinople. Turkey, 16th century.

The humanitarian dedication of the Jewish doctor was consistently in harmony with the close-knit Jewish group life, which was distinguished by a climate of moral and religious aspiration. It is of no co-incidental significance that a number of the Rabbinic Sages during the Talmudic age were *also* physicians. The inference is quite clear: Health and hygiene were revered as integral departments of the religious life; since the body was the soul's tenement of flesh and blood, it was the religious obligation of the human being to keep it in a state of health, moral purity, and cleanliness.

The rabbi-doctor, one could say, was the counterpart of the Egyptian priest-doctor who was in the temple-service of the god-doctor Imhotep and the priest-doctor who was attached to the Roman temple of the god of healing, Aesculapius. But one quality distinguished the Jewish doctor from his Gentile contemporaries. Whereas their cultivation of the art of healing was usually not related to any ethical goal but was, in addition, motivated by ritualistic and magical functions *as priests,* he was moved principally by the compassionate desire to alleviate suffering and to preserve human life, which he had been taught by his religion to revere as holy.

Notwithstanding their "pure intention," both the ancient Rabbinic and medieval doctors often became entangled in the thick brush and brambles of superstition and primitivism, features which also characterized the medical practice of the latter-day Egyptians, Greeks, and Romans, and, until the late Renaissance, that of the Christians, as well. The Talmud, although it contains many sound aphorisms, observations, and advice on a variety of ailments, also revels in some of the aberrations of folk-medicine and "old wives'" cures, and gives respectful attention to homeopathic magic and incantations. What especially aroused some of the advanced Rabbinical thinkers was the debasement of the Torah by reciting passages from it with the intention of effecting miraculous cures. Therefore, one Sage sternly admonished, "It is forbidden to cure oneself by means of Scriptural citation."

The religious-moralistic orientation to medicine among the Jews may be seen in the fact that, beginning about the year 1000 and continuing through the Middle Ages, medical and even pharmacological studies were included in the curriculums of the yeshibot (rabbinical seminaries) of Spain, Italy, and North Africa. More than half of the rabbis during that period were, at one and the same time, *also* medical practitioners.

Although it is true that the rabbinical schools gave *some* training to their students in medical theory, it was actually as apprentices to individual Jewish doctors that they acquired their clinical skill. And inasmuch as the physician's calling was very often hereditary—so to speak, "kept in the family"—a father would teach all he knew to his son who assisted him in attending the sick.

The social ideals of professional practice too would be handed down like a precious inheritance from father to son. In the "ethical testament" which he addressed to his young doctor-son, Rabbi Judah ibn Tibbon (Southern France, *b.* 1120–*d. after* 1190), the noted doctor, humanist, scholar, and translator, counseled: "You may accept fees from the rich, but heal the poor without charge." This was part of the traditional pattern of benevolence and concern for the sick poor that most Jewish doctors demonstrated—possibly to an even more marked degree than did Christian physicians, who also were raised in the humanitarian climate of the healing art. No doubt it was a concomitant of the Jewish religious-ethical culture pattern which was applied to every aspect of the Jewish life and activity, in greater or lesser measure.

The purest and most exalted expression of the Jewish doctor's dedication to his calling as healer was given by Maimonides more than eight centuries ago in the private prayer he composed:

> Endow me with strength of heart and mind so that both may be ready to serve the rich and the poor, the good and the wicked, friend and enemy, and that I may never see in the patient anything else but a fellow creature in pain.

That there were also charlatans, incompetents, and money-grubbers among the Jewish doctors goes without saying. But they were scorned by their Jewish fellow practitioners and lampooned in derisive verse by the Hebrew satirists of the Middle Ages and the Renaissance. In fact, even the Talmud records some barbed observations about medical practitioners. That the tradition of treating the poor gratis was considered to be only a mixed blessing can be seen in the folk-saying: "A physician for nothing is worth nothing." The rascality and avarice of some doctors led to the blistering generalization: "The best of physicians is destined for Gehinnom [Purgatory]." Just the same, the Jewish doctor was most frequently a dedicated man, attending the sick and trying to alleviate their pain as "a service to the Lord" and in fulfillment of the commandment: "Thou shalt love thy neighbor as thyself."

There is one ready explanation for the assumption of the physician's calling by the rabbi of former days: It had become a tradition, sacrosanct since the earliest Rabbinic times, when the Temple still crowned the summit of Mount Zion, that no Jew make "a spade of the Torah." To the rabbi-scholar, this meant that he was forbidden to derive any material gain from his ministry. Piety required him to teach or preach or adjudicate or conduct any of the various rites and ceremonies of the Jewish religion without fee or salary. But economic necessity bore down on the dedicated rabbi. The healer's calling, with its labors of brotherly love and compassion for the afflicted, and the rabbi's pre-conditioning by intellectual capacity and training for mastering its intricacies, seemed like the ideal solution to his problem. Besides the religious and humanitarian appeal that the medical calling had for the pious Jew, to many—perhaps less devout—it beckoned with prospects of material reward and of achieving a dignified and superior status in a Gentile society which despised Jews and treated them like pariahs.

Until late medieval times, when qualified Christian doctors began to be graduated in considerable numbers from the medical colleges of Salerno, Bari, Rome, Tarentum, Palermo, and Montpellier—institutions which illustrious Jewish physicians helped found and in which they taught—Jewish doctors virtually held a monoply in all fields of European medicine: in its practice, teaching, experimentation, or writing. Even in catastrophic times for the Jews, Jewish physicians attached to

Paul Ehrlich treating a patient. (Bronze medallion, 1904.)

Amatus Lusitanus (Juan Rodrigo de Castel Branco).

Ephraim Bonus, one of the foremost physicians in Amsterdam during the 17th century. (Etching by Jan Lievens.)

the courts of emperor and caliph, pope and king, archbishop and prince were accorded special protection and enjoyed many privileges denied to their co-religionists. They were even excused from the harsh obligation of wearing the humiliating yellow badge of Jewish identity and the ridiculous sugarloaf *Judenhut*—Jew's hat—and they were also exempted from paying the multitude of special "Jew's taxes" (*see* FEUDAL SOCIETY, POSITION OF THE JEWS IN). Quite obviously, wherever the interest of a ruler was best served, his prejudices were discarded by employing the elastic yardstick of exceptionalism. It is ironic that even under the hammering insistence of the Grand Inquisitor Tomás Torquemada and the Holy Office in Spain, Queen Isabella fought hard, although in vain, as the time grew near for driving out more than a million Jews from her realm in 1492, to keep her Jewish doctors.

An unusual instance of defiance of the Church Militant in Spain, of the invective of Vincent Ferrer, and of the howling mob of pietists whom that "saint" led in the terrible massacres of the Jews in 1391, was shown by John I. Among his royal *familiares* were several Jewish doctors whom he refused to dismiss.

There is little doubt but that the Jewish doctors, standing close to the seat of authority in Mohammedan and Christian lands and often doubling as royal diplomats and ministers—as viziers, treasurers, tax-farmers, etc.—sometimes tried to defend their fellow Jews against the decrees and plots to suppress, rob, expel, or exterminate them. Their intercessions, regardless of whether they were successful or not, brought them the heartfelt gratitude of the Jewish community.

Whether in centuries gone by the Jewish doctor was a rabbi or merely a layman, the very humanitarian nature of his services and of his potential influence made of him a revered figure among the Jews. The religious-ethical tradition of the healing art, coupled so often with an honorable, and also honored, professional career (which could also be lucrative), made medical practice one of the most attractive and glamorous of all callings for Jews. For the doctor's achievements combine altruism with practicality, and constructive social service for the patient with high social status for himself. And, in the final analysis, it also provides him with a good and secure living. In the candid folklore of workaday Jewish life for a Jewish girl "to marry a doctor"—love and romance aside—is usually prized both by her and her parents as a stroke of sound judgment as well as of great good fortune, so deeply rooted is the doctor-reverence in Jewish life! This may help explain why so many young Jews of our day strive so hard to become doctors.

See also ARABIC-JEWISH "GOLDEN AGE"; HOSPITALS; LIFE, JEWISH VIEW OF; MONEYLENDERS; RABBI.

Albert B. Sabin, discoverer of the Sabin oral vaccine for polio. (The National Foundation—March of Dimes.)

HEAVEN. *See* GAN EDEN.

HEBREW ALPHABET (in Hebrew: ALEPH-BET)

The Hebrew aleph-bet is differentiated from our own in that it consists of consonants only (twenty-two in number). It has no vowels, but it does have phonics, indicated by diacritical marks of dots and dashes placed above and below consonants. Of the vowel sounds, five are long and five are short.

Hebrew is a member of the family of languages which philologists call "Semitic," and it derived its alphabet from those ethnic kinsmen and neighbors of the ancient Israelites—the Canaanites—whom the Greeks called "Phoenicians." The probability is that the Jews borrowed not only their alphabet but even the Hebrew language itself, or at least a dialect form of it, from their Semitic-language cousins. The clear inference is that the early Israelites, when they emerged from the mist of prehistoric times, were less developed culturally than the Canaanites.

It should be noted also that the Greeks and Romans—and from them, all European peoples in turn—took their alphabet from the same Canaanite source. In the history of civilization, the invention of the alphabet by the ingenious Canaanites proved to be of far greater significance than the discovery of the wheel, for it provided mankind with the requisite tools for communication, systematic thinking, and creative expression.

Any careful comparison between the Hebrew aleph-bet and the Greek and Latin alphabets, despite the more ornamental design of the Hebrew characters, will reveal their close similarity. Moreover, there is also a close identity between the names and phonics the same letters bear in each alphabet. Thus the Hebrew *aleph* (a) is *alpha* in Greek; *bet* (b) is *beta; gimel* (g) is *gamma; dalet* (d) is *delta; zayin* (z) is *zeta; yod* (i) is *iota; kaph* (k) is *kappa; lamed* (l) is *lambda; mem* (m) is *um; nun* (n) is *nu; pe* (p) is *pi;* and *tav* (t) is *tau.*

At first, not all the letters of the aleph-bet, as we know it today, were in use; the others were added with time. In recent times the discoveries of Biblical archaeologists have added to the slender knowledge available about the early character of Hebrew writing. Inscriptions such as that at the Pool of Siloam in Jerusalem reveal that ancient Hebrew script was angular in character and tended to be cursive; in later times it became more square. Very similar in its appearance to ancient Hebrew script was Moabite writing of the same period. This may be seen in the Mesha Stele (Moabite Stone) on which King Mesha of Moab recorded (*c.* 850 B.C.E.) his military victories over King Ahab of Israel.

Curiously, the Hebrew alphabet with which we are familiar was not derived from the Hebrew alphabet of the early Israelites, but from its sister-language, Aramaic. The latter tongue had displaced Hebrew as the vernacular for the Jews of Judea and Babylonia in post-Exilic times.

There is a rather hazy tradition in the Talmud that it was Ezra the Scribe who introduced Aramaic script to the Jews during the fifth century B.C.E. The inventiveness of the Jewish scribes and copyists in producing different calligraphic styles was considerable. It furnished one of the indirect outlets for artistic creation that had been inhibited in the Jews for several thousand years (until the modern period) by the stern prohibition of the Second Commandment against making "graven images." Some old Hebrew manuscripts still extant reveal a fascinating variety of letter-design set in frameworks of decorative margins, the whole enhanced by exquisite illumination and large initial letters.

When Hebrew and Yiddish books began coming off the printing presses, not long after Gutenberg's epochal invention of movable type (in the fifteenth century), square or block letters were cast. These were tastefully, even artistically, designed, according to the fashion current in a particular European century. Those printed in Italy, with the refined stamp of the Renaissance upon them, were especially beautiful.

See also HEBREW LANGUAGE, HISTORY OF; JEWISH LANGUAGES; YIDDISH LANGUAGE, THE.

HEBREW LANGUAGE, HISTORY OF THE

It is not possible to state precisely when and how Hebrew became the language of the Jewish people. Like the inscrutable Sphinx, the prehistoric ages remain mute with the secrets they hold about the cultural beginnings of the Israelites. All that is known with some degree of certainty is that at the dawn of recorded Jewish history, which is half-obscured by the mists of primitive myth and magic, Hebrew was already the vernacular of the Israelites. But it was only one in a constellation of cognate languages that are called by the philologists "Semitic." These included, among others, Akkadian, Canaanite (or Phoenician), Ugaritic, Aramaic, Ethiopic, and Arabic.

There is no reason to believe that the Hebrew language was invented by the Jews; it had been in existence in the lands of the Fertile Crescent long before the "sons of Abraham" had appeared upon the stage of history (about 2000 B.C.) as a part of a nomadic confederation of related ethnic clans called the "Habiru." Others of their tribal neighbors, such as the Hittites, Philistines, Moabites, and Canaanites, spoke either a similar language or different dialects of it. This conclusion, reached long ago by Semitic scholars, was fortified in the second half of the nineteenth century by philological studies of the inscription on the but recently discovered Mesha Stele, popularly known as the "Moabite Stone." On it the Moabite king Mesha had recorded (*circa* 850 B.C.E.) in language and rhetoric reminiscent of Biblical Hebrew, a summary of the victories he had gained over King Ahab of Israel.

The Hebrew language that the Israelites spoke was not called by that name at all in the Bible. The word *Ivrit* or *Ibrit* ("Hebrew" language) is first met with, but only seldom, in the Talmud, which was compiled several centuries after Judea was no longer the Jewish state. But even in the Talmud the word more frequently used to denote "Hebrew" is the descriptive term *lashon ha-kodesh*, "the sacred language." And it is this name which invariably was used by the religious down the centuries to our own time, when once again it has been displaced by *Ivrit*, the old Talmudic term.

In the Bible itself, Hebrew was clearly referred to by the Prophet Isaiah as "the language of Canaan." "Canaan" was the earliest name for a large section of ancient Palestine that was called "Phoenicia" by the Greeks. There is every reason to believe that originally Hebrew had been the mother-tongue of the Canaanites (i.e., the Phoenicians). It was they who had invented the Semitic alphabet which subsequently served as the "mother" of all alphabets.

It is now practically a historic certainty that, at the time parallel with the Bondage and the Liberation of the Israelite groups that had been settled in Egypt, as narrated in the Bible, other Israelites—their kinsmen, obviously—had been continuously living in Palestine in their own section. This is learned from an unimpeachable historic source: the inscription on a stele in the mortuary temple in Thebes of Pharaoh Merenptah, who died in 1215 B.C.E. In this memorial, the son and successor of Rameses II (who probably was the Pharaoh of the Exodus) recorded his military victories over separate tribal principalities existing at the time in Palestine: Canaan, Ashkelon, Gezer, Yenoam, and—*also Israel.* "Israel is desolated, his seed is not," recount the ancient Egyptian hieroglyphs—the first specific mention of the Jews in ancient records outside of the Biblical chronicle itself.

What language could these non-Egyptian Israelities, living as free men in "the Land of Canaan," have been speaking? From all the facts, there can be only one reasonable surmise: that it was "the language of Canaan"—Hebrew. And even if those Israelites who had been led from Egypt into freedom by Moses and Joshua and were now returning to their original homeland—Israel—no longer understood Hebrew, after the conquest of Canaan they were sure to have re-learned it from their fellow tribesmen who had been living in Israel during the several centuries of the sojourn and enslavement in Egypt.

Local Hebrew dialects and differences in pronunciation were already being noted not too long after the conquest of Canaan had been achieved by the Israelite tribes returning from Egypt. A grim but diverting incident is chronicled in Judges 12:4-7. It is about an intertribal war that was being fought between "the men of Gilead" and "the men of Ephraim." After a successful surprise attack, the men of Gilead started to massacre their prisoners, among whom were many who begged to be spared, swearing that they were not Ephraimites at all. The wily Gileadites thereupon put to them individually a test of pronunciation:

> "Say now 'Shibboleth' "; and if the prisoner said "Sibboleth," for he could not frame to pronounce it right; then they took him, and slew him at the passages of the Jordan. . . .

Apparently thousands of Ephraimites fell into this trap and were slain.

It is true of all languages—Hebrew included—that they never stop growing. Under changing material and cultural conditions, new terms and expressions are invented and loan-words are absorbed from other languages. If the component writings in the Bible, with a probable time-span of more than a thousand years in their composition, seem to show few language differences, it is no doubt because the editors who revised them at a much later age (during the Second Temple period) did so in order to bring them more or less into line with the Hebrew then contemporary.

Examining minutely the Hebrew text of the Bible, philologists have discovered the presence of many loan-words from Egyptian, Hittite, Akkadian, Aramaic, Latin, Greek, Persian, Hindustani, etc. To cite several examples: *pardes*,

	EGYPTIAN		PHOENICIAN	GREEK				GREEK NAMES	LATIN			HEBREW	HEBREW NAMES
1				Α	Α	λ	α	Alpha	A	A	ƌ a a	א	Aleph
2				ϐ	B	B	β	Beta	B	B	B b	ב	Beth
3				7	Γ	Γ	ſ γ	Gamma	<	C	C Ç G g	ג	Gimel
4				Δ	Δ	Δ	δ	Delta	D	D	∂ ∂ d	ד	Daleth
5				∃	E	Є	ε	Epsilon	E	E	e e	ה	He
6				Ϝ	YF		F	(Digamma)	F	F	f f	ו	Vau
7				‡	I	Z	ζ ζ	Zeta	‡	Z	z	ז	Zain
8				日	H	H	h η	Eta	日	H	h h	ח	Cheth
9				⊕	⊙	Θ	θ ϑ	Theta	⊗			ט	Teth
10				≀	I	ι	ι	Iota	I	I	i j	י	Iod
11				K	K	K	κ κ	Kappa	K	K	k	כ	Caph
12				V	Λ	λ	λ	Lambda	L	L	l l	ל	Lamed
13				M	M	M	μ μ	Mu	M	M	m m	מ	Mem
14				N	N	N	μ ν	Nu	N	N	n n	נ	Nun
15				‡	Ξ	Ξ	ξ	Xi	⊞	+	x x	ס	Samech
16				o	O	O	o	Omicron	O			ע	Ain
17				Γ	Γ	Π	π ϖ	Pi	P	P	p	פ	Pe
18				M	M				M			צ	Tzade
19				Φ	Q				Q	Q	q q	ק	Koph
20				P	P	F	ρ ρ	Rho	R	R	r r	ר	Resh
21				≷	Σ	C	c σ	Sigma	S	S	ſ ſ s	ש	Shin
22				T	T	T	τ	Tau	T	T	τ t	ת	Tau
•	I	II	III	IV	V	VI	VII		VIII	IX	X	XI	

Comparison chart of ancient alphabets.

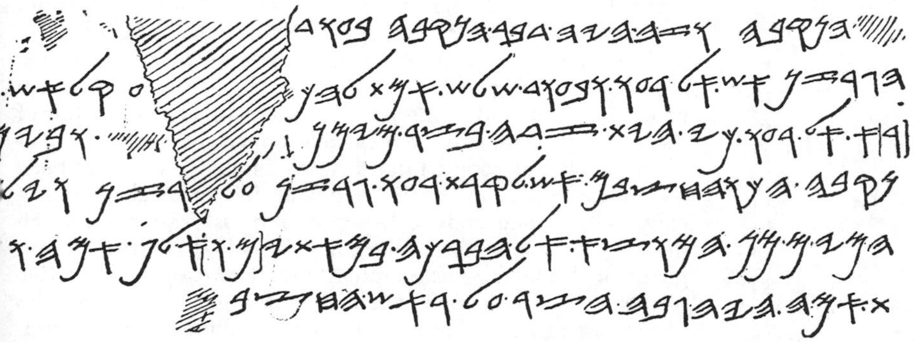

Inscription in Phoenician-Hebrew on the wall of the subterranean Pool of Siloam in Jerusalem, constructed under King Hezekiah to withstand the siege of the Assyrian king Sennacherib (c. 700 B.C.E.), and beneath it, a transcription of the text into modern Hebrew.

הנקבה • וזה • היה • דבר • הנקבה • בעוד
הגרזן • אש • אל • רעו • ובעוד • שלש • אמת • להכ קל • אש • ק
רא • אל • רעו • כי • הית • זדה • בצר • מימן ובים • ה
נקבה • הכו החצבם • אש • לקרת • רעו • גרזן • על • גרזן • וילכו
המים • מן • המוצא • אל • הברכה • במאתים • ואלף • אמה • ומ[א]
ת • אמה • היה • גבה • הצר • על • ראש • החצב[ם]

Square Hebrew Monumental	Medieval Formal Styles	Rabbinic Styles	Cursive Styles	Contemporary (Cursive / Print)

Evolution of the square Hebrew alphabet. (From Diringer: The Story of the Aleph Bet. *Philosophical Library, 1958. © by the World Jewish Congress, London, 1958.)*

Title page of Judah Monis' Hebrew Grammar, *printed in Boston in 1735 for use of Harvard students. It was the first Hebrew grammar published in America. (Rosenbach Collection, American Jewish Historical Society.)*

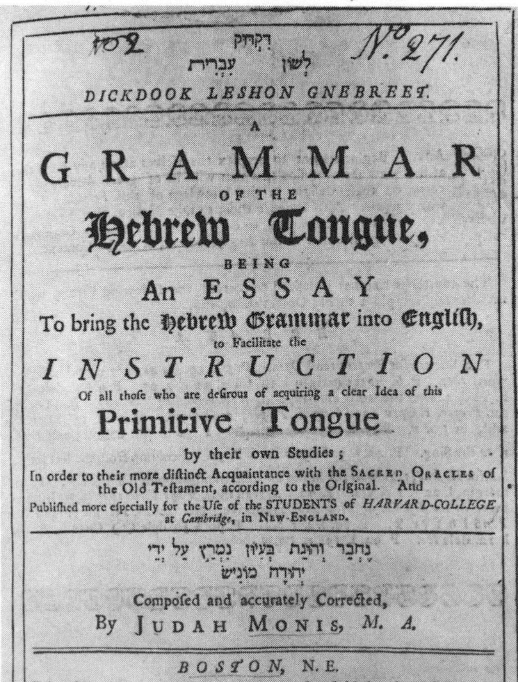

דִּקְדּוּק לְשׁוֹן עִבְרִית

DICKDOOK LESHON GNEBREET.

A

GRAMMAR

OF THE

Hebrew Tongue,

BEING

An ESSAY

To bring the Hebrew Grammar into English,

to Facilitate the

INSTRUCTION

Of all those who are desirous of acquiring a clear Idea of this

Primitive Tongue

by their own Studies;

In order to their more distinct Acquaintance with the SACRED ORACLES of the Old Testament, according to the Original. And

Published more especially for the Use of the STUDENTS of HARVARD-COLLEGE at Cambridge, in NEW-ENGLAND.

נֶחְבַּר וְהוּגַת בְּעִיּוּן נִמְרָץ עַל יְדֵי יְהוּדָה מוֹנִישׁ

Composed and accurately Corrected,

By JUDAH MONIS, M. A.

BOSTON, N. E.

Printed by JONAS GREEN, and are to be Sold by the AUTHOR at his House in Cambridge. MDCCXXXV.

Eliezer Ben Yehudah, the father of the modern Hebrew language.

meaning "orchard" in Hebrew, was an ancient Persian word meaning "garden"; the Hebrew words *kof* and *tukee* are both originally Hindustani, meaning, respectively, "ape" and "parrot."

Heralding the tremendous language-change yet to come in Israel, there appears in the Prophetic writings of Jeremiah, dating from about the time of the Destruction of the First Temple, in 586 B.C.E., an entire verse (10:11) in Aramaic. Aramaic, one of the cognate Semitic tongues, was at that time already the language most widely spoken in the Near and Middle East.

Years later, when Nehemiah, the Jewish cupbearer to King Artaxerxes of Persia, returned to Judah at the head of a contingent of Exiles from Babylonia, he found that Aramaic had been rapidly supplanting Hebrew as the spoken language in the homeland of the Jews. Dirgefully cataloguing the consequences of the numerous intermarriages that had taken place between the Jews who had been left behind in Judah by Nebuchadnezzar, and the Ammonites and Moabites among whom they lived, he lamented: "And their children . . . could not speak in the Jew's language." (Nehemiah 13.24.)

For convenience, the history of Hebrew as a language may be divided into four distinctive phases: Biblical, Mishnaic, Medieval, and Modern. About the language sonorities of the Bible, the eminent French philosopher and Semitic scholar, Ernest Rénan, opined that it was a language that had been beaten out upon an anvil; "A quiver full of steel arrows, a cable with strong coils, a trumpet of brass crashing through the air with two or three sharp notes—such is Hebrew. A language of this kind is not adapted to the expression of scientific results. . . . It is to pour out floods of anger, and utter cries of rage against the abuses of the world, calling the four winds of heaven to the assault of the citadels of evil." But, as is well known, Rénan was a scholar with stubborn prejudices. There are numerous passages to be found in the Prophetic writings, in The Song of Songs, and certainly in many of the Psalms, which, even in translation, are evocative of a lyrical rapture, serenity, and tenderness that have never been excelled in the literature of mankind.

In the period which followed the so-called Biblical age—no more than a century or two before the destruction of the Second Temple by the Romans in 70 C.E.—Mishnaic Hebrew emerged. This was the language in which the Mishnah, the code of Oral Law, was written. It revealed itself to be a language that was more supple and less declamatory, in the sense that Rénan meant, than its Biblical predecessor had been. Its greater flexibility and potential expressiveness, it has been averred, were due not only to the introduction into it of many Aramaic words but also to the Aramaicization of the syntax of Hebrew words. In addition, Mishnaic Hebrew had absorbed several hundred Greek and Latin loan-words and expressions as a result of the Jewish people's acculturation experience with Hellenism under Greece, Seleucidan Syria, Egypt and Rome, beginning with Alexander's conquests in the fourth century B.C.E.

Then, before Mishnaic Hebrew had the time or opportunity to stretch its wings creatively or the Jewish people could initiate a rebirth of a national culture in Hebrew, Jewish life became half-submerged by catastrophic historic events. In 70 C.E., after the Temple in Jerusalem had been sacked and destroyed by the Roman legions, and the Jewish population of the city had been terribly decimated by a combination of starvation and disease and by the appalling number of casualties suffered during the long siege and the mass-slaughter which climaxed it, Mishnaic Hebrew began to die a lingering death. There were two principal causes for its demise: first, the fragmentation and dispersal throughout the world of the Jewish people, and, second, the eventual triumph over Hebrew of Aramaic, which had now become "the Jewish language." In Aramaic were written the Babylonian Talmud and its ancillary elaborating commentaries, the Midrashim. The religious decrees, legal decisions, and opinions of the Geonim (*which see*) of the Babylonian academies, from the sixth to the eleventh centuries, were also composed in Aramaic. Only in the unyielding areas of prayer and Torah-reading did Hebrew, "the sacred language," continue to be used.

The Hebrew language seems to have had the proverbial nine lives; it repeatedly died and was resurrected: It simply refused to remain dead. It constituted a cultural phenomenon probably without parallel in the entire language-history of mankind. The driving force behind its survival was the Jewish religion with its dual dedication to preservation of the Torah and the physical survival of Israel.

Again, during the Middle Ages, there was a revival of Hebrew. It took up where Rabbinic Hebrew had left it many centuries before in a state of near neglect. In the humanistic cultural climate of Hellenistic Arab-Jewish civilization in Islamic countries, it was not unnatural for erudite Jews not only to dream of a Hebrew renascence but also to make strenuous efforts to achieve it. Turning back enthusiastically to the revered, original language-source of their people were a host of remarkably gifted and cultivated men—some even endowed with genius. There were among them philosophers, poets, grammarians, translators, geographers, astronomers, mathematicians, medical scientists, and Biblical exegetes. They were writers who used language with scrupulous restraint, and they strove for precision in their quest for truth. Eminent among them were such encyclopedic thinkers as Isaac Israeli, Moses ben Maimon (Maimonides), Abraham bar Chiyya (Abraham Savasorda), Chasdai Crescas, and Levi ben Gerson (Gersonides). (*See* ARABIC-JEWISH "GOLDEN AGE.")

Perhaps the best literary illustration of this Hebrew revival in the Middle Ages is furnished by the constellation of remarkable philosophical and liturgical poets who flourished in Southern Spain during the eleventh and twelfth centuries. Pre-eminent among these were Solomon ibn Gabirol, Judah (Yehudah) Halevi, Moses ibn Ezra, and Abraham ibn Ezra. Their now famous hymns for the synagogue, their devotional meditations in verse, as well as their love lyrics, still burn with an inner glow and an expressiveness that, in many ways, equal the best poetry to be found in the Hebrew Psalter and the books of Job and Isaiah. The Hebrew language they employed was richer, more varied, and also more subtle, than it had ever been before. Under their deft creative hands, it was able to achieve verbal sonorities and subtle nuances of mood and meaning that had rarely been struck before in Hebrew.

Throughout the medieval period, the Hebrew language continued to grow. The Jewish poets, philosophers, and scientists continued to incorporate, when the need arose, many loan-words from Arabic, Spanish, and Latin. They also invented new words. Their philosophical and scientific writings, especially, called for the invention or the adaptation of a new terminology in order to make meanings more precise.

Despite all these enriching factors that made Hebrew more viable, it still had not become a "living" or spoken language. In line with the bilingual, and even multilingual, pattern of the Jews since ancient times, Hebrew still continued to share with Aramaic and Arabic the distinction of being one of the "Jewish" languages. But, in the meantime, it had succeeded in breaking the shackles of a stubborn tradition which had restricted the use of Hebrew to the composition of sacred literature alone. In medieval Spain, the Provence, and Italy, Hebrew was, for the first time, used in secular compositions: in poetic satires, love lyrics, and poems of mood and sentiment, as well as in scientific works on grammar, lexicography, geography, medicine, astronomy, and mathematics.

Then, sad to say, the Hebrew language once more went into a sharp decline, and it remained in a state of stagnation until the renascence of the Hebrew language and literature in recent decades. Its rapid deterioration was, without a doubt, due to the unsettled conditions—economic, social, and cultural—of Jewish community life. These first began to worsen everywhere in Europe during the catastrophic Crusades; they grew worse during the time of the Black Death (in the fourteenth century) in the countries of North, Central, and Eastern Europe, where the Ashkenazim or Yiddish-speaking Jews were settled. There, because the waves of hatred were mounting and persecution of the Jews was becoming greater, the devout concentrated with an almost desperate intensity on their attachment to Hebrew. Their attachment was to far more than a language, for Hebrew held the key to their sacred religious values, to a knowledge of the Torah, and to communion with God in prayer. It, therefore, assumed for the pious a degree of sanctity that one would not normally associate with a language.

Hebrew was valued traditionally by Jews as one of the principal religious-cultural resources to be tapped for the preservation of Israel and of the Torah. The rabbis and the melamedim (those dedicated elementary teachers of Hebrew and of the Chumash—the Pentateuch) never allowed the folk-Jew to forget that Hebrew was the language in which the Bible had been written and in which Moses had taught their ancestors and the Prophets had preached. For that reason it always retained the name of *lashon ha-kodesh*, "the sacred language." The Jews considered that if it had survived the vicissitudes and determined efforts made for its suppression by the enemies of Israel over several thousand years, beginning with Antiochus Epiphanes, then it was, clearly, not merely a "language" but a "miracle of God." Moreover, it held for them a special meaning in terms of religious nationalism. It constituted a bond linking the past with the present and the present with a glorious promised future that the devout believed would be without end. The Hebrew language thus formed an integral, and even mystical, part of the grand Messianic design of the Jewish people.

The average folk-Jew had a simple conception of the role and functions of Hebrew. He saw it in interconnection with himself and all others Jews who were following a common destiny. Together they wandered a hazardous world over, desperately holding on to Hebrew, not because they had to or were allowed to, but because they *wanted* to. Ghetto mothers, living in the most straitened of circumstances, would, without thought that they were making any great sacrifice, pawn their Sabbath candlesticks, their pillows and featherbeds, so that they might make it possible for their boys to attend cheder (*which see*), there to learn the sacred tongue—the key with which to unlock the treasure: the halls of the Torah.

Still another revival of Hebrew took place during the second half of the eighteenth century. In Germany, the so-called Berlin Enlightenment, led by the philosopher Moses Mendelssohn, initiated the literary revival of Hebrew as part of its movement for the cultural reformation of the German ghetto-Jews. The "enlightened" Jews thought that if those benighted co-religionists of theirs who spoke only Yiddish—"the disgusting jargon of the ghetto"—could be induced to accept German in its place as their daily language, and Biblical Hebrew, the lofty tongue that the Prophets spoke, as their literary language (once it was purified of all "rabbinic medievalism and superstitition"), then it would be possible for them to be accepted as "Europeans."

The Hebrew of the German Enlightenment, particularly after it had spread into Eastern Europe to the "Russifiers" and neo-Hebraists there, was "refined" by artificial and pseudoclassic features, much, for instance, like neo-Greek architecture in the nineteenth century. Instead of continuing where medieval Hebrew had left off, or even from the stopping point of the much earlier Hebrew of the Mishnah, the language virtually leap-frogged—but backward—into Biblical Hebrew. This occurred because the neo-Hebraists wished to return to the "pure" source of the Golden Age of Jewish greatness.

The consequence of this artificial revival of Biblical Hebrew was that, in the rapidly evolving modern age, it constituted an anachronism. In literary expression, it was constituted, in the main, of the repetition and adaptation of Biblical phrases that were familiar to the knowledgeable religious Jew. It bred purple writing, a pseudo-elevated mood, and resounding empty rhetoric. However, the course of history in the Russian Empire and in Poland, and the social and cultural conditions under which Jewish life was being strangulated there, led to surprising results.

In Slavic countries, as is well known, Talmudic learning had been pursued for centuries with a consuming passion, mostly for its own sake and less for the rewards that would be reaped in the World-to-Come. The love for Torah-learning and, collaterally, for "the sacred language," burned more deeply among the poor Jews of the ghettos than in the wealthy and cultured salon-circles of Berlin and Vienna. Many of the leaders of the East European Enlightenment were motivated by a social and cultural idealism in their efforts to transmit and to disseminate the progressive secular learning of the Gentile world among the Yiddish-speaking masses, hoping, in that way, to transform them into modern "Europeans." Their aim was pithily expressed thus by the mid-nineteenth-century Hebrew poet, J. L. Gordon: "Be a Jew at home and a man on the street."

However, the East European "enlighteners" became bitterly disenchanted with the course they had been pursuing when the czarist government, following a genocidal policy only a little less horrible than that of the Third Reich of the Nazis a century or so later, systematically began "to solve the Jewish problem" by means of bloody pogroms. What formerly had been an assimilationist movement, hewing closely to the line of the Berlin Enlightenment with regard to the revival of Hebrew, was rapidly being turned by the unanticipated dictates of history into a cultural instrument for deepening the national consciousness of the Jews in Russia and Poland. One of the early "Founding Fathers" of Zionism, Peretz Smolenskin (1840-84), declared heatedly after the pogroms and the enactment of the punitive May Laws of 1881: "You ask me what good a dead language [i.e., Hebrew] can do for us. I will tell you. It confers honor on us, girds us with strength, unites us into one people. All nations seek to perpetuate their names. All conquered peoples dream of a day when they will regain their independence. We have neither monuments [i.e., national institutions] nor a country at present. Only one relic still remains from the ruins of our ancient glory—the Hebrew language."

A prime mover in the revival of the Hebrew language and culture in Russia and Poland was the philosophical writer, Achad ha-Am (Asher Ginzberg, 1856-1927). He addressed himself primarily to the educated middle-classses with the aim of making them nationally conscious *as Jews*, thereby preparing them for what he called the "Jewish spiritual revival." His efforts, joined with those of others, did bring quick results. A Hebrew literary upsurge took place in the 1880's and '90's. Nevertheless, Hebrew as a spoken language failed to make any appreciable advance. Yiddish still remained the mother-tongue (*mameh-loshen*) of the great majority of Jews. Moreover, a richer and more significant literature was being created in that language by remarkably gifted writers as Mendele Mocher Seforim, Sholom Aleichem, and Yitzchok Leibush Peretz.

However, a new and brilliant phase began for the Hebrew language in Eastern Europe and Palestine in the years preceding World War I, when an entire galaxy of distinguished writers and scholars appeared. Whereas its use formerly had been limited to the Hebrew writer and the Zionist intellectual, now, for the first time, it actually was becoming a "living" tongue for many Jews. Already in the intervening years and until 1948, when the independent Jewish State of Israel was established, Hebrew had become the all-inclusive language of daily living in the Palestine yishuv (community). It was spoken on the street, it served as the language of instruction in the schools, the children prattled it at play, it was being used technically in agriculture, commerce, industry, scientific research, and in all the other areas of social life, culture, and economic activity.

In recent decades, there has been in motion an irresistible, and also understandable, drive to "de-Orientalize" Hebrew: to prune it of many of its archaic Biblical terms and flowery metaphors—a wholesome precondition for allowing successful expression in modern terminology. In this, the indefatigable lexicographer, Eliezer Ben-Yehudah (1858–1922), played a significant part. He dedicated his life with remarkable single-mindedness, from the time of his student days in Russia, to the building up of Hebrew as a modern "living" tongue. But that, he argued stoutly, could not possibly be accomplished except in a concentrated and large-scale Jewish community life in the Land of Israel. An early Zionist, he was among the first "secularist" pioneers to settle there. Before he died, he saw his dream in large measure come true.

Undoubtedly, the necessities of the ever-expanding cultural and material life of the Jewish community in Palestine itself were the principal factors in the rapid development and modernization of the Hebrew language. In response to the urgent need for them in every area, there was a steady outpouring of Hebrew translations of a wide range of foreign works. These included books, monographs, and articles in professional and learned journals, in the areas of literature, philosophy, Biblical scholarship, medicine, the social sciences, the natural sciences, and technology. This vast activity in translation, especially in the sciences and technology, called for the use of precise words and terms. Where no such words and terms existed in Hebrew, they were borrowed outright from Western languages and were adopted by the convenient process of Hebraicizing them.

See also ENLIGHTENMENT, THE JEWISH; HEBREW LITERATURE, MODERN; ZIONISM.

HEBREW LITERATURE, EARLY. *See* ARABIC-JEWISH "GOLDEN AGE"; BIBLE, THE; COMMENTARIES, RABBINICAL; HYMNS OF THE SYNAGOGUE; POST-BIBLICAL WRITINGS; RABBINICAL DECISIONS; SHULCHAN ARUCH; SIDDUR; TALMUD, THE.

HEBREW LITERATURE, MODERN

During the second half of the nineteenth century, and even as late as the outbreak of World War I, in 1914, secular Hebrew writing (as distinct from rabbinic religious works written in Hebrew) could be considered scarcely more than coterie literature. At first, its readers consisted of small but dedicated groups of adherents (virtually all of whom belonged to the educated middle class) of the Jewish Enlightenment—the Haskalah; later they were drawn from the Zionist movement. The appeal this kind of literature had was necessarily limited because the Yiddish-speaking masses, who constituted the great majority of the Jewish people, were devoted to the already established rabbinic writings or to the continuing production of Yiddish literature, which during that period was in its heyday.

Nonetheless, an almost magical change in the fortunes of modern Hebrew literature occurred with the development of the new pioneering Jewish community (yishuv) in Palestine, first under the rule of Turkey and, after that country's defeat in 1918, of Great Britain, the mandatory power. The yishuv, largely a demographic entity whose totality of life was concentrated in one geographic area under the rigorous self-discipline of Zionist goals, revived Hebrew as a living tongue used in everyday life. The mass base (which is the *sine qua non* of every living language) that Hebrew thus acquired gave a tremendous stimulus to lovers of the language to develop in it a secular modern literature.

The Hebrew language and literature, in all of their historic phases, enjoyed the proverbial nine lives. At least three times they appeared to be dying, and yet each time they revived, as it were, miraculously. The first "resurrection" occurred upon the return of the Jewish exiles from Babylonian Captivity to the Land of Israel (in the sixth and fifth centuries B.C.E.), where Aramaic had displaced Hebrew as the "living" Jewish tongue; the second revival took place during the Middle Ages in Spain, Italy, and the Provence; the third happened during the second half of the eighteenth century in Germany, where Europeanized Jewish intellectuals struggled to cast off the gaberdines and *pe'ot* (side curls) of their ghetto backwardness. The last-mentioned revival was at the time of the Haskalah, which the philosopher Moses Mendelssohn had inaugurated (*see* ENLIGHTENMENT, THE JEWISH).

Chronologically speaking, modern Hebrew literature stemmed from the secular program of the Jewish Enlightenment. But here is the literary phenomenon: Because the Maskilim, the adherents of this Enlightenment, had made it a cardinal objective of their program for reviving the ancient cultural grandeur of the Jewish people, they had chosen the Bible to be their source and fount for literary emulation. And since, in rhetorical style, in music, and in cadence neither the Bible nor Biblical Hebrew lent themselves with felicity to the astringent ends of prose, the Haskalah writers displayed a marked preference for composing in Hebrew verse; their prose productions, it is generally agreed, were greatly inferior to their poetry.

The Hebrew writers of the Haskalah had an eminent forerunner in the person of Moses Chayyim Luzzatto of Padua (1707–47), a writer who is sometimes honored as "the Father of modern Hebrew poetry." He composed allegoric dramas and pastoral idylls which in part were patterned on the poetic forms of the Bible, yet at the time time also imitated the Italian verse-dramas of the preceding century.

One of the favorite models for poets of the eighteenth century everywhere in Europe was the charming but highly artificial *Pastor Fido* by Guarini. Luzzatto, being no exception, imitated it in his moralistic Hebrew verse dramas *Migdal Oz* ("The Tower of Strength") and *Leyasharim Tehillah!* ("To the Righteous, Praise!"). In both of these, justice is shown to triumph in the end over the forces of evil. Living in a relatively progressive age and in Italy, and being well read in the literatures of contemporary Europe, Luzzatto achieved, independently from the men of the Berlin Haskalah, his own kind of "enlightenment," notwithstanding that, parallel to it, there ran in him a contradictory drive to the Cabala. His verses, artificial as they may have been, were quite secular in character and as "European" in outlook as that of any Christian writer of his generation in Italy.

The formal revival of Hebrew poetry, however, was sparked by another writer, Naphtali Hartwig Wessely (Germany, 1725–1805), who with Mendelssohn was a co-leader of the Jewish Enlightenment movement. He, too, like Luzzatto, wrote in a strained, declamatory Biblical style—one that was overlaid with a patina of idioms and mannerisms currently fashionable in German poetry. His *Songs of Glory*, an epic poem in twenty cantos about Moses and the Exodus, it has been noted as highly reminiscent of the contemporary epic, *The Messiah*, by Friedrich Klopstock.

This renascence was quickened in an important measure by the appearance of the Hebrew periodical *Ha-Meassef* ("The Gatherer," 1783–1810), which was edited by Mendelssohn's circle of Maskilim or "Enlighteners." A number of writers and scholars contributed to it, the poets producing verses on secular themes. Understandably, this turn to the secular—or, as the traditionalists called it, "the profane"—created a disturbing sensation in Jewish religious ranks, where hitherto only Hebrew poetry of a devout or liturgical character had been deemed acceptable and where any expression of secularism was considered fraught with the danger that it might encourage Jews to stray from the faith. The mere fact that the brilliant freethinker and Deist philosopher, Solomon Maimon (1754—1800), was able to find a forum for his skeptical ideas in *Ha-Meassef* was sufficient reason for some traditionalists to brand this periodical as heretical.

In only a few decades, as one of the affirmative consequences resulting from the issuance of the liberal Code Napoléon, a sizable number of university-educated Jews made their appearance in France, Germany, and Italy. Some of these men, still clinging firmly to their Jewish identity, sought an outlet for their liberal ideas in Hebrew writing, giving the language an even greater impetus toward Europeanization and modernity.

These devotees of the Enlightenment turned their efforts into two major directions: They wrote in Hebrew on non-religious themes, and at the time time carried on scientific researches in the fields of Jewish history and literature—areas in which Leopold Zunz (Germany, 1794–1886) had been the pioneer, even though he wrote in German. The Hebraist Maskilim (like their colleagues in the East European Haskalah, who wrote in Yiddish) were, in principle as well as in pratice, sharp critics and challengers of the religious status quo, of rock-ribbed traditionalism as well as of Chasidic sectarianism. Satire and ridicule, not always used with subtlety, were their principal literary weapons.

Prominent in this polemical campaign against "obscurantism" were Isaac Halevi Satanov (1733–1805), Mendel Levin (1741–1819), and Judah Loeb Benzeeb (1764–1811). They were also the first to speed the linguistic development of Hebrew to such a point that it could compare in literary flexibility and expressiveness with English, French, German, Italian, and Spanish.

Some years later, a group of able scholar-writers, all products of the Haskalah in Galicia, appeared. The most notable among them was Nachman Krochmal (1785–1840), the Hegelian philosopher who applied the approach as well as some of the principles of his German master to a philosophic analysis of the Jewish religion. Others were Solomon J. Rapoport (1790–1867), the gifted rabbi-historian and critical investigator of Judaism; the poets Meir Halevi Letteris (1800–71) and Isaac Erter (1792–1851); and Joseph Perl (1774–1839), the scholar-satirist who, in 1819, published a burlesque on the Chasidic wonder-workers, writing it in a parodied style of Cabalistic obscurity and employing for his model the famous anti-clerical Christian work of the sixteenth century, *The Epistles of Obscure Men.*

Perhaps the outstanding Hebrew writer-poet of that period was Isaac Erter (Galicia, 1792–1851). His career as an "Enlightener" was typical of that followed by most of the secularist writers of the Haskalah. A physician practicing in Lemberg, he waged a kind of guerrilla warfare against the Orthodox chief-rabbi in that city. He used him deliberately as a whipping-boy for his emancipated ideas, satirizing him mercilessly in verse. He also heaped ridicule on the Chasidic wonder-workers for their ignorance and alleged corruption, at the same time making merry over the Chasidim and their superstitious beliefs and practices. Fond of hyperbole and the purple phrase, like so many other writers of the Haskalah, he declared, speaking in the name of the Hebrew language: "I am dead on the tongues of my children, but I still live in their hearts."

The Haskalah employing Hebrew as the language of expression (to be differentiated from the Haskalah that used Yiddish as its language) obviously came as the answer to an imperative cultural need. It found devoted followers among writers in every country of Europe. In Italy, Isaac Samuel Reggio (1784–1855) sought to reconcile the precepts of the Torah with advanced modern ideas. Contemporary with him was another religious modernist, Rachel Morpurgo (1790–1871) whose *Harp of Rachel* was published posthumously in 1890.

However, the greatest development of Hebrew literature was to take place not, as some expected, in Germany or Italy—countries where a thorough assimilation soon made short shrift both of the Jewish Enlightenment and of Hebrew writing; the growth of Hebrew as a language and the creation of a significant literature in it occurred among the teeming Jewish masses in the countries of Eastern Europe. To mention but a few of the best known writers: Abraham Dob Ber Lebensohn (Lithuania, 1789–1878), poet, Hebraist and grammarian, and pioneer Maskil in Lithuania; his son, Micah Joseph Lebensohn (Lithuania, 1828–52), who before his untimely death at the age of twenty-four, wrote lyric poetry in a romantic vein: effusions about the beauty in nature and the nobility of human sentiment; and Abraham Mapu (Russia, 1808–67).

Mapu enjoys the distinction of having written the first novel in Hebrew: *The Painted Vulture.* It was a trite piece of fiction, written with more heat than passion, with more rhetoric than literary skill. Its object was the interminable Haskalah-exposé of the wonder-working holy men of the Chasidim, berating them for their alleged hypocrisy and greed: "They do the deeds of Zimri and claim the reward of Pinehas."

1860

שנה ראשונה.

המליץ

בין עם ישרון והממשלה, בין האמונה וההשכלה.

הוא יהיה לפה לכל דבר הנוגע לכנסת ישראל.

איין צענטראל-ארגאן פיר יודישע אנגעלעגענהייטען.

מאת אלכסנדר צעדערבוים, דאקטאר אהרן יצחק גאלדענבלום.

N° 1.

An 1860 copy of Ha-Melitz *("The Advocate"), the weekly newspaper of the Hebrew Haskalah in Russia, which served as the proving ground for many a young writer and intellectual.*

But a dramatic change took place and a fresh wind began to blow in Hebrew fiction when the uniquely endowed Mendele Mocher Seforim (the pen name of Solomon Abramowitsch) entered the Hebrew literary arena. He caused a virtual revolution; he introduced a quality of down-to-earth realism in the writing of fiction which gave the breath of life to his tales. Forthwith, the finest among the young Hebrew writers decided to follow his standard.

Mendele published in 1868 his first novel in Hebrew, *Fathers and Sons,* quite obviously having in mind the novel by that name from the pen of the Russian writer Ivan Turgenev. Not only is Mendele generally considered to have been "the Grandfather of Yiddish Literature," but by many close students of Hebrew culture he has been dubbed (somewhat grandiloquently perhaps) "the Father of modern Hebrew Literature"—an honorific distinction which, if given credence, represents an astonishing feat—one without parallel in the entire history of world literature.

How Mendele managed to be so active creatively in both Hebrew and Yiddish may partly be explained by the novel fact that after he had written his Yiddish works, he promptly translated them into Hebrew himself! Nevertheless, in the course of his long literary activity, he did produce several original works in Hebrew: *The Judgment of Shalom* (1860), a volume of literary criticism; and the novels *In Stormy Days* (1894) and *The Vale of Tears* (1898).

Whatever the moral imperative of their intentions—and they cannot be questioned—it must be conceded that, up to the time of Mendele Mocher Seforim, the productions of the early Hebrew writers were, for the most part, less than mediocre. The style in vogue then (in some instances it lingered on even into the twentieth century) was belittled, in a later, more sophisticated period, as *melitzah;* namely, it was flowery, stilted, and riddled with Biblical metaphors, linguistic archaisms, and rhetorical flourishes. Undoubtedly, the principal reason why these writers expressed themselves in such an artificial manner was that Hebrew during the nineteenth century was still insufficiently developed as a language to express modern themes, ideas, and emotions in a *modern* way. For this purpose it required a far richer vocabulary, greater elasticity, and simplicity of expression—qualities which neither Biblical nor medieval Hebrew possessed.

A characteristic of most Hebrew writings (and also of Yiddish) is that they have ever been socially conscious in attitude, striking deep overtones of idealism. Such a pattern forms part of the historical and cultural conditioning of the Jewish psyche by ages-old national ethical traditions and practices. It is impressively true that the chief preoccupation of Hebrew writers has been with the survival of their people, with its physical and spiritual regeneration, and, so to speak, with the healing of the many grave wounds and warpings that have been inflicted upon it by persecution, poverty, and social pariahism.

A writer par excellence was Judah Leib (Leon) Gordon (Russia, 1830–92). Of all the poets of the Hebrew Enlightenment he had perhaps the most to say and he said it best. To him, as to all the Maskilim, it seemed that the panacea for all human ills lay in Reason; he advocated sweeping reforms in the religious, social-communal, and educational areas of Jewish life. In 1863 he called upon his fellow Jews in the ghettos to rouse themselves from their backwardness:

Awake, my people! How long will you sleep?
Night has taken flight, the sun is bright;
Awake, lift up your eyes and look about. . . .
English translation by Simon Halkin

What had prompted this "clarion call" was the fact that Gordon had taken seriously the "Great Liberal Reforms" that had been so glibly promised by Czar Alexander II (ruled 1855–81). Like all the other Maskilim, Gordon too was trapped in the meshes of an idealistic romanticism. Elated with the prospects of civil emancipation and equality *under law* for the Jews in the Russian Empire, he composed bucolic idylls that overflowed with optimism and a breathless anticipation; the millenmium was approaching! He counseled his fellow Jews: "Be a Jew at home and a man on the street."

But the realities of history soon sobered up Gordon. Like the two foremost intellectual leaders of the Jewish Enlightenment during that period—Leo Pinsker (*b.* Poland, 1821– *d.* Russia, 1891) and Peretz Smolenskin (*b.* Russia, 1842–*d.* Austria, 1885)—he suffered severe psychic shock when the pogroms of 1881–82 by the "Black Hundreds" broke out. These massacres and other unspeakable atrocities had been engineered in the most cynical manner by the czarist government, and they were quickly followed by the promulgation of the so-called May Laws for the economic, social, and educational suppression of the Jews in the Russian Empire. Gordon's dream for the Russianization (i.e., Europeanization) of the Jews of the ghetto quickly faded. "Enlightenment" as the key which was to unlock the door to the civil emancipation of the Russian and Polish Jews no longer seemed quite as persuasive as before; disenchantment in the objectives of the Haskalah gripped the Maskilim.

Peretz Smolenskin was in complete disagreement with those Maskilim who adopted the slogan (invented for them by J. L. Gordon): "Be a Jew at home and a man on the street." In Smolenskin's opinion (to apply a concept which decades later was described by psychiatrists as "split-personality" or "schizophrenia") this proposed existence of the Jew on two separate planes could only result in confusing the Jewish identity, eventually destroying the psychological center of the Jew. Already he was able to discern its alienating effects:

Faster and faster they are drifting away!

What Smolenskin had in mind, of course, was the necessity of integrating the two elements—of having the Jew and the modern man grow together organically, in a manner of speaking, into a single unity. But as he visualized it, in order to be able to achieve this end, the national and spiritual restoration of the Jewish people had first to take place in Eretz Yisrael, the Land of Israel. What he most wanted, therefore, was to renationalize the Jew of the Diaspora *qua* Jew; namely, to make of him a Zionist, which, for Smolenskin, stood for the equation:

the complete Jew=the complete man

The intellectual impact Smolenskin had on the subsequent course taken by the Hebrew language and literature cannot be overestimated. He, no less than Leo Pinsker with his celebrated manifesto, *Auto-Emancipation* (1882), had given them a Zionist direction and reason for being and urged an all-out campaign to revive the Hebrew language. (*See* HEBREW LANGUAGE, HISTORY OF THE.)

The romantic idealism which marked—and also marred—the Hebrew writings of the Enlightenment (as has already been indicated) had been torn loose from its highflown poetic moorings by the pogroms and the persecutions of the 1880's. But it was not long before a healthy reaction to the resultant state of depression and defeatism took place. It caused a sobering up—a return to the realities of life—brought about by two cultural influences which at first ran parallel to each other but, which, in the end, met in the rich confluence of the new Hebrew culture of Palestine (later, Israel). One trend was that of cultural nationalism; this was a secular movement uniting world Jewry in the common bond of its heritage, and it was led by the philosopher Achad ha-Am (the Hebrew pseudonym, meaning "One of the People," of Asher Ginzberg; *b.* Russia, 1856–*d.* Palestine, 1927). The other stream of influence flowed from the political Zionism fostered by Theodor Herzl (1860–1904).

The quite abstract ideals of the Enlightenment were no longer found tenable or sufficient by the progressions of history; the most gifted among the new generation of Hebrew writers had to find a focus in reality in order to create meaningfully. Just as Smolenskin had not found a complete answer to the problem of the Jewish identity for the modern Jew in the two-level existence that had been proposed by the poet J. L. Gordon, so Achad ha-Am, on his part, could not accept the program of political Zionism advanced by Theodor Herzl as representing the total solution for the Jewish identity and group continuity. Although he readily concurred with Herzl that the establishment of a national Jewish State in Palestine was an indispensable major step that had to be taken to make the rehabilitation of the dismembered Jewish people possible, it was his opinion that such a step was not enough. Instead, the fundamental goal of the program Achad ha-Am outlined was for the inauguration of a Jewish cultural revival and of a spiritual rebirth *within* the Jewish communities throughout the world—a reawakening which could find its stimulus only at the Jewish source: the ethical and social teachings of the Prophets and Rabbinic Sages.

Not that Achad ha-Am ever sought to minimize the imperative need of the Jews to achieve equality and civil emancipation, wherever they lived. What he did perceive, at the same time, were the eroding dangers—dangers inherent in the chameleon varieties of opportunistic assimilation—to the Jewish identity, to the traditional Jewish way of life, and to the preservation of Jewish culture. Part of his solution to the problem was on the practical Zionist level: to settle en masse a Jewish community in Palestine—one which would make a concentrated effort to return to the productive cultivation of the soil, another, was create the necessary climate for the revival of Israel's moral and intellectual greatness. It was only in Eretz Yisrael, he wrote, that the Jews could become a "majority in one land under the heavens, a land where our historical right is unquestionable, requiring no far-fetched proof, and in whose historic atmosphere our truly national existence may develop in keeping with our genius . . . only then may the rest of our people, although scattered in all countries, hope that our national center will imbue them with its spirit, and will give them the strength to live through its life, even though they may be deprived of their national rights, wherever they are."

The English translations of the chief Hebrew writings of Achad ha-Am, in the essay-form he preferred, were *Al Parashat Derachim* ("At the Crossroads"), which was the most influential of his books; *Selected Essays* (1911); *Essays on Zionism and Judaism* (1922); and *Achad ha-Am: Essays, Letters, Memoirs* (1946).

For years Achad ha-Am's ideas made little headway. In fact, they met with cold opposition from many diverse quarters—from the religious, the Haskalah, and the Zionist sectors of Jewish life. A formidable adversary was Micah Joseph Berditchevsky (*b.* Russia, 1865–*d.* Germany, 1921; he wrote also under the pseudonym of Joseph Bin-Gorion). He took his place as the most important exponent in Hebrew letters of secularism, hedonism, and philosophic individualism. His war was against rabbinic traditionalism and spirituality, and this, notwithstanding that he was steeped in Judaic lore, being a most indefatigable and knowledgeable collector of Jewish folktales. Like the great poet Saul Tchernichovsky, whom he influenced, he was impatient with the ritualistic-spiritual single-mindedness of the Jewish people and called for a return to nature, to earthiness and a love of beauty. He was a vigorous polemicist, viewed as the rebel incarnate by the opposing factions, for he was always raising challenging and sometimes disconcerting questions in his critical essays and short stories.

One characteristic example of his philosophic individualism (Berditchevsky, it should be kept in mind, was a disciple of Nietzsche and, consequently, advocated "a transvaluation of all Jewish values") was his comment on the following passage in Pirke Abot (the Mishnah treatise containing the ethical traditions that were compiled by the Rabbinic Fathers): "Rabbi Jacob said: 'He [a Torah scholar] who is walking by the way and cons what he has learned, and then breaks off from his study to say: "How fine is this tree, or how fine is that plowed field," him the Scriptures reckon as if he were guilty of a sin against his own soul!' " To this Berditchevsky tartly added the observation: "I think that only then will the Jews be saved when a new Mishnah will be given them, one which will say: 'If a man were walking by the way and, seeing a fine tree, or a fine plowed field, he turned from them to occupy himself with some other thought, he would be considered guilty of a sin against his own soul.' " And Berditchevsky concludes his anti-Rabbinic sermonette with the demand: "Bring back to us the fine trees and the fine plowed fields—bring back the world to us!"

The vigor with which the "philosopher with the hammer," Berditchevsky, and other Jewish-Nietzschean transvaluators, were agitating for their principles of individualism, precipitated a polemical war among the Hebraist intellectuals in Eastern Europe. Those writers who adhered to the program of the Haskalah and were continually groping their way toward a philosophic system of Judaism—or, in lieu of that, of a Jewish cultural nationalism—were desperately in earnest about what they were thinking or believing. They discussed their views and their differences, pro and con, not only in book and pamphlet form, in lectures and at public debates, but also in the columns of monthly and quarterly periodicals. For example, Achad ha-Am, in magazine articles and essays, charged that Jewish champions of individualism, with their amoral ideas, were only negating traditional Jewish ethics.

Indeed, the principal means found for the advancement of the Hebrew language and literature were the weekly newspapers and the monthly and quarterly literary journals which were published in Russia, Poland, Galicia, Lithuania, and even in the United States. For years these Hebrew periodicals, edited by erudite and skillful writers, constituted the principal forum for the public discussion of crucial problems, and cultural ideologies and trends as they affected the Jewish intellectual. The most important of these periodicals were *Ha-Melitz,* first edited as a weekly in St. Petersburg, beginning in 1860, by the noted Maskil Alexander Zederbaum, and then by Reuben Brainin in 1885, when it was turned into a daily newspaper: *Ha-Tzfirah,* edited by Nachum Sokolow; *Ha-Shiloach,* the monthly issued by Achad ha-Am 1896–1902, and then by Joseph Klausner, beginning with 1903. In the United

Chaim Nachman Bialik. (Portrait by Max Band.)

Saul Tchernichovsky.

David Frishman.

Aaron David Gordon. (Zionist Archives and Library.)

Zalman Schneur

Jacob Cohen

Samuel Joseph Agnon. (Zionist Archives and Library.)

Uri Zvi Greenberg. (Zionist Archives and Library.)

Achad ha-Am.

Peretz Smolenskin.

Hartwig Wessely.

States, Reuben Brainin (who settled in New York in 1916) edited *Ha-Dror* and later *Hatoron;* he was succeeded in the direction of these periodicals by Menachem Ribalow.

Nahum Sokolow (*b.* Poland, 1860–*d.* Palestine, 1936), who in his later years became a world leader of the Zionist movement, was probably the most influential of the editors who helped mold the thinking and tastes of two or three generations of Hebraist intellectuals and readers.

Reuben Brainin (*b.* Russia, 1862–*d.* U.S.A., 1939) who won renown as one of the Founding Fathers of modern Hebrew literature, wrote voluminously in both Hebrew and Yiddish. His collected works in Hebrew alone, which consisted of essays, articles, literary criticism, and biographies of noted Hebrew writers and Zionist leaders, were issued in thirty volumes.

In the movement to modernize the Hebrew language and foster its literature, Joseph Klausner (*b.* Lithuania, 1874–to Israel, 1919) was an indefatigable worker. His *History of Modern Hebrew Literature* (1932) remains a standard work on the subject in several languages. In his writings, he made it plain that he was seeking broader historical perspectives for providing understanding of the life and civilization of the ancient Jewish past. His scholarly studies, *Jesus of Nazareth* (1922) and *From Jesus to Paul* (1925), despite the controversy they stirred up in Jewish religious circles, enjoyed much of a *succès d'estime* among Christian theologians and scholars.

But again to pick up the thread of the historical narrative: In the late 1890's, a group of young writers who in later years were to add much luster to Hebrew literature, found themselves facing a tired old world with the brave new confidence and faith of youth. Among these were David Frishman, Chaim Nachman Bialik, and Saul Tchernichovsky.

An era of militant liberalism and social awareness was then burgeoning in Europe. To these young writers (who were principally poets) and to others like them, the future shone bright with promise for all peoples, including even the oppressed Jews living under czarist autocracy. For the latter, the prospects for civil emancipation and for achieving full equality with all other minority peoples in the Russian Empire proved seductive.

But in the end, unhappily, this sunny promise turned out for the Jews to be only a mirage. Just as the government-inspired massacres of Russian Jews in 1881 had had a traumatic impact on the Hebrew writers and Zionist intellectuals of that time—particularly Smolenskin, Gordon, Achad ha-Am, and Leon Pinsker—so too did the atrocities of the Kishinev pogrom in 1903 and of the other massacres that quickly followed it deal a shattering blow to the impressionable poets Frishman, Bialik, and Tchernichovsky. Moreover, the betrayal of the 1905 Russian Revolution by several of its leaders deepened the despair of these writers and flung them into a defeatist state of mind. Characteristic of their pessimistic reappraisal of life was the poem "O Heaven, You Must Pray for Me," in which its author, Bialik, observed bitterly: "To me the whole world is one gallows!"

Included in the generation of writers and poets who were, perhaps, still too young at the time to express their disenchantment with the world, though they were nonetheless deeply shaken by the same cataclysmic events, were Yaacov Fichman, Jacob Steinberg, Zalman Shneur, David Shimonovitz, and Jacob Cohen (Kahan). Taking note of this significant fact, one cannot be surprised to find that their writings—especially their verse—are overburdened by a sense of tragedy, by feelings of foreboding about dreadful things to come, and by feelings of bitterness and indignation against the persecutors of their people. Not infrequently their poems mirror a desperate inner struggle to overcome their revulsion for the world.

The particular moral problem—that is, whether to accept or reject life with all its seemingly unendurable trials and suffering—a problem with which all thinking Jews, at one time or another and in consequence of the historic experience of their people have had to grapple in the most morbid way—was once given penetrating definition by Baruch Spinoza (Holland, 1632–77). That incomparable Jewish philosopher, who in his own life had successfully achieved a noble serenity by virtue of the triumph of reason although he himself had been the victim of injustice and persecution, commented ruefully: "The heaviest burden that men can lay on us is not that they persecute us with their hatred and scorn but that they thus plant hatred and scorn in our souls."

A pioneer among the modernist Hebrew writers—one versatile in the variety of literary forms in which he worked and perhaps equally facile in all of them—was David Frishman (*b.* Poland, 1862–*d.* Germany, 1922). He wrote in both Hebrew and Yiddish with erudition and satiric wit, producing a small library of novels, novelettes, and short stories (many of them on Biblical themes), numerous lyrical and romantic poems, essays, feuilletons, critical reviews, and literary studies. In addition, he was probably the most prolific translator into Hebrew of world classics. As the most influential critic of Hebrew writing in his time, he had a strong impact on Hebrew literature in the decades before World War I. Being also a scholarly Hebraist, he made substantial contributions to the development of the language. Frishman's youthful essay *Chaos* (1883) stirred up much controversy in the Hebraist circles of the Haskalah because it was an indictment of the bombast and wooden heroics by which the Hebrew writings of that period were disfigured.

The prestige and influence in modern Hebrew literature of the poet Chaim Nachman Bialik (*b.* Russia 1873 [settled in Palestine, 1924]–*d.* Austria, 1934) have been comparable in one essential way with that of Goethe in Weimar: The reverence in which he was held during his lifetime (and for that matter still is held) as the Jewish national poet was that of near idolization—of *the poet as hero.* No such honor by the general consent of the people had been accorded a Jewish poet since Judah (Yehudah) Halevi (Spain, 1085–1140), whom Heinrich Heine, himself a great poet of the nineteenth century, had called "the Prince of Poets." In the Jewish sense, following the tradition of the ancient Prophet-poets of Israel, Bialik was not merely the reigning poet-laureate of his time but the inspired articulator of his people's national ideals, joys, and sorrows.

Two generations of Hebrew-speaking youth in Israel and elsewhere have been reading and reciting his verses, or singing those of his lyrics that have been set to music. One of these poems, "El ha-Tzippor" ("To a Bird") composed when he was eighteen, has achieved the popularity of a folk song. Another such song is "Queen Sabbath," a zemirah (religious song) sung at the festive meal on the eve of the Sabbath, expressing thoughts and sentiments which plumb the depths of the Jew's suffering, giving tongue to his longing for peace even though it be but for one day only: "O bless us with peace, you angels of peace."

Although Bialik wrote exultantly about the affirmative aspects of life, about nature and its beauty, about the raptures of childhood and youthful love, yet it cannot be denied that, in the main, he remained a poet of idealistic pessimism. Even after he had gone to live in Palestine—the Promised Land of his singing—the sense of futility about life that had dogged him all his years, settled upon him like a heavy cloud. Eventually, and to the dismay of his numerous admirers, he put away his poet's harp and fell silent.

Bialik sought fulfillment as Jewish poet and as moralist in his self-elected role of the "Jeremiah of the Jewish Exile (Galut)." Like that ancient prophetic ancestor, Bialik, too, grieved over the luckless fate of his people, chronicling in verse its disasters, frustrations, and warpings through the long night of its ghetto-martyrdom.

Bialik is the Hebrew writer best known to readers of world literature; much of his poetry as well as prose has been translated into English and many other languages. Notwithstanding the inadequacies of translation, his great distinction as a poet has been recognized by those readers—Gentile as well as Jewish—who have no knowledge of Hebrew.

The literary personality of Bialik may be said to have stemmed from two principal sources of influence. The poet was an adherent of the Jewish cultural nationalism expounded by Achad ha-Am. At the same time, the personal mentor of his youth, Mendele Mocher Seforim, had taught him to aspire uncompromisingly toward the highest goals of literary creation. First, imitating Mendele's example, he wrote verses in Yiddish. (No student of Jewish life and culture of Eastern Europe could possibly be surprised by the fact that, beginning with the Haskalah period, a great number of modern Hebrew writers had written much fine verse and fiction in Yiddish. Not only Bialik, but also Frishman, Berditchevsky, Brenner, Schneur, and U. Z. Greenberg displayed this linguistic versatility and attachment to their "mother-tongue" [mameh-loshen].) But before very long, his Hebraist-Zionist principles made Bialik turn to Hebrew, and with a far greater devotion than to Yiddish.

Like many another poet of great gifts, Bialik revealed maturity at a relatively early age. In 1900, when he was twenty-seven, he had already written his celebrated poem "Ha-Matmid" ("The Talmud Student"). The publication of this long poem resulted in his idolization by the Talmud-nurtured youth of the ghettos, for whom it held up a mirror with disturbing images; they saw reflected in it their most painful frustrations. The unending Toraḥ-study of the yeshiva bachurim and their quest for God, even if they did bring them understanding and spiritual illumination, also inflicted upon them a life of utter loneliness, of hunger and alienation from their fellow men. In Bialik's view, this matmid—this perpetual Talmud-student—by a dedication of his own choosing had become his own lifelong prisoner. However in the wretched ghetto-towns of Russia, Poland, Galicia, and Lithuania (wrote the poet), this type of young idealist shone like "a glowing ember amid the ashes."

Only three years later—during the fateful year of the government-sponsored pogrom in Kishinev (in Russia)—Bialik turned to elegizing Jewish group-tribulation. His long poem, "In The City of Slaughter" ("Be'ir ha-Haregah"), was in memoriam for those innocents who had been massacred. At the same time, Bialik leveled a bitter indictment against the survivors because, he charged, lacking courage, they had defaulted in their moral duty of resistance to the murderers of their people.

The dominant note in this particular poem, as well as in the bulk of Bialik's other verse, was tragic and elegiac. Because the indignation that welled-up in his soul was so insupportable, the poet turned it self-maceratingly inward. Following the pattern set by the Hebrew dirges that were composed by the poets of the synagogue for the uncounted thousands of Jewish martyrs who had perished during the Crusades and the Black Death, Bialik cried out to the heavens for retribution on behalf of the slain.

> Remember the martyrs, Lord,
> Remember the cloven infants, Lord.

In the face of the objective fact, who can say that Bialik's spirit was not seared by the acid of hatred? Yet it was not exactly a hatred that is nourished by meanness or one that springs from an insane compulsion for vengeance; the poet's hatred was an austere—even tragic—kind of hatred, one that was touched with the nobility of indignation that can only be felt by an outraged social idealist and patriot toward the persecutors of his people. It should not be overlooked that this same ambivalence of love and hate is inherent in the ethical values of Biblical prophecy and Rabbinic morality.

About the same time that Bialik penned "In the City of Slaughter," he also wrote "The Dead of the Wilderness" ("Metei Midbar"). This is a poem which bristles with violent images and symbolism and concludes with an exhortation by the poet to his fellow Jews to draw upon all their inner resources for insuring the continuity of Jewish group-existence and identity. Significantly, the title of the poem is extracted from the declaration in the Talmud: "Come, and I will show you the dead of the wilderness." Whom did the Rabbinic Sages characterize as the dead? They were those Israelites who, liberated from the Bondage in Egypt, eventually succumbed to the trials and vicissitudes of the long wandering in the Wilderness. Those who perished (the poet makes clear) were sacrificial offerings for the Jewish people. In a mystic strain, he concludes that some day these dead will surely rise again in the Wilderness; they will rise and claim their rightful inheritance to the freedom and the Promised Land that they were denied in death.

Another memorable poem of Bialik's is "The Scroll of Fire" ("Megillat ha-Esh"), which was composed in free-verse style but was part poetry—part prose. Its theme was the bitterness of the unending Jewish Exile (Galut). The poem is built upon the ancient legend which tells how, while the Destruction by the Babylonians of Solomon's Temple was in progress in 586 B.C.E., a mysterious hand reached down and spirited away the fire from the altar. Where did the altar fire go? asks the poet, and then he answers: It was carried off in the minds and hearts of the Jewish captives being led into the Babylonian Exile.

Yet it would be erroneous to assume that Bialik's muse was entirely tragic; during the very same period when he produced his "Poems of Wrath," he also composed lyrics in every variety of mood, color, and tonality. He sang in praise of happiness and youthful love, of sunny fields and shady glens, of green trees and wild flowers in the springtime, of sun and stars, of lovely girls and laughing children. He found the whole universe replete with wonders and the divine spirit. But after he had gone to live permanently in Palestine, the sense of futility about life which had troubled him all his years gradually led him to abandon the writing of poetry. Amidst all the fame and adulation that he was exposed to by hero-worshiping Hebraist readers, Bialik remained sad and aloof.

Although poetry was his forte, Bialik also wrote five long tales, three being included in the volume called in the English version *Aftergrowth.* He was a born storyteller and displayed a decided gift for humor in characterization and invention in plot. He also recast in a poetic modern vein a number of Biblical legends, including some about David and Solomon, which were issued in English under the title *And It Came to Pass.*

It was Bialik's fervent thesis, that, in order for a people to advance into a *creative* national life it had first to recapture its cultural-spiritual past at its source—and also at its best. It was this belief that motivated him to compile, together with his friend Joshua Chaim Ravnitsky, the *Sefer Agada* ("The Book of the Agada," 1908–10). It consisted of Rabbinical aphorisms, teachings, illustrative anecdotes, and legends out of the Talmud, all ethically slanted for the reader's illumination. Bialik strove toward the same goal with his six volumes of *Notes* on Jewish folklore.

Perhaps the most distinguished modern Hebrew poet—with the single exception of Bialik—was Saul Tchernichovsky (*b.* Russia, 1875–*d.* Israel, 1943). Unlike Bialik, who was singularly obsessed by his sense of tragedy and weighed down by the tribulations of the Jewish people, he used his poetic gifts to extoll the sensuous joys of existence.

In his early years, Tchernichovsky followed the same path as Berditchevsky. He was a self-asserted individualist and an iconoclast. Considering himself thoroughly emancipated in his ideas and moral judgments and a citizen of the world, he was determined at first to detour around the mainstream of Jewish grief. His poems, in fact, were a stinging rebuke against the imbalance of the Jewish people as evidenced by their one-sided God-seeking and spirituality, which, he charged, caused them stubbornly to try to live only in the past, thereby glorifying pain and the renunciation of life.

Tchernichovsky proclaimed the primacy of Nature, the pleasure of the senses, and the triumph of laughter over tears. In his deification of the body's beauty and strength, he emerged as a modern Jew with a classic Greek outlook; he was a self-conscious pagan. Not a few recoiled from his approach, considering it alien to the puritanical tradition in Jewish life. His poems, therefore, stirred up a hornet's nest of controversy. In reality, Tchernichovsky was intent on recapturing the joy of the sensory experience which, he complained, had been drained out of the life-pattern of his people by centuries of Gentile oppression and Jewish self-suppression.

But what sobered him up considerably were the atrocities of the Kishinev and other pogroms, and the collapse of the Russian Revolution of 1905. Tchernichovsky's carefree gods and goddesses of fleshly beauty then began to fade from his inner vision. He no longer felt like a hedonistic Greek but only like a member of a persecuted people.

When, finally, he went to settle in Palestine, the dissenter and rebel in him subsided and he became more affirmative in his verses. The spectacle of the pioneering Jewish youth from the ghettos, flocking to Eretz Yisrael, and dedicated to rebuilding it with the toil of their hands, inspired him with hope for a new and wholesome splendor to arise in Jewish life: "For Zion shall be redeemed by the hoe."

But Tchernichovsky's philosophic outlook went far beyond the merely Jewish; he had faith in the redemptive potential of the whole human race. His poem "I Believe" was his retort to the pessimists and the cynics:

Laugh on, laugh on at all the dreams . . .
Laugh on, I still believe in man,
For I still believe in thee.
English translation by REGINALD V. FELDMAN

Tchernichovsky's poetry, though, was not all sensuousness, sweetness, and light; he, too, was forced to face the same moral and social problems that were distressing all Jews, and he reacted strongly to them. His martyr-poems in their historical settings of the Middle Ages, especially *Baruch of Mayence* and *The Martyrs of Dortmund* (the latter written in 1937 and, therefore, gloomy with foreboding on account of the Nazi menace hanging over the Jewish people) are true elegiac poems composed in the spirit of the medieval martyr-elegies—the kinot (s. kinah). Like Levi Yitzchok of Berditchev, the late-eighteenth-century Chasidic tzaddik ("saint"), he, too, raised his voice in reproach to God for not dealing justly and mercifully with the Jewish people.

Among Tchernichovsky's published poetic works are: *Visions and Melodies* (1898), *Sheaf of Sonnets* (1922), *Book of Idylls* (1922), *New Poems* (1924), *The Flute* (children's verse; 1923), *Behold, O Earth* (1940), and the posthumously issued *Stars in Distant Skies.*

Perhaps even more of a hedonist than Berditchevsky and Tchernichovsky was Zalman Schneur (*b.* Russia, 1887–*d.* Israel, 1959). An intellectual like them, he, too, was interested in philosophical ideas; some pretend to find in his poetry evidence of the same Nietzscheism—the glorification of power and iconoclastic no-saying—they displayed. A restless spirit, Schneur was ever seething with intense and contrasting emotions. As a literary creator, he possessed a stormy temperament which he found hard to leash, yet the power and the drama of his interior experiences and thought processes have proven exhilarating to his readers.

Bialik once observed that Schneur was amply endowed with all the five senses: "His poetry abounds in images of vision, sound, taste, smell, and the sensuousness of bodily movement." It was a good augury for the Jewish people, said Bialik, "that our sensual life has been fully resurrected [by such a writer as Schneur]."

Schneur was without question a great poet; his poems possess suppleness, bold imagery, and a pure melodic line. If some of his love-poems sometimes strike a careless, gay cynicism, his martyr-verses resounded with an "out-of-the-depths" grief. The savage, Hitler-like massacre of the Jews in the Ukraine during the years of the Civil War following the Russian Revolution by the White Guardist generals Petlyura, Denikin, and Machno, prompted Schneur to write a series of sonnets that are unmatched in delineative power and indignation except perhaps in "The City of Slaughter" by Bialik.

Virtuosity was a characteristic of Schneur's literary talents. Besides poetry, he also produced a number of novels which are full of vivacity and color. As was to be expected, they are markedly different from the rhetorical abstractions produced by many other contemporary writers of fiction in Hebrew. His characters are earthly and real, and the plots in which they are involved are about everyday life and are convincingly projected.

Like Bialik and some other noted Hebrew writers, Schneur also wrote in Yiddish; his novels and verses in that language possess the same individuality as those in Hebrew. Among his volumes of poetry are *The Songs of Fate* and the verse-cycle that includes *The Hidden Tablets, Under the Sun, Vilna, Melodies of Israel,* and *Under the Strains of the Mandolin.* Among his best-known novels, several of which were translated into English, are *Noah Pandre* (1936), *Noah Pandre's Village* (1938), *Pandre the Strong* (1945), *The People of Shklov* (1944), *Song of the Dnieper* (1945), and *Emperor and Rabbi,* a Yiddish historical novel in five volumes set in the Napoleonic era.

Jacob Cohen (or Kahan as he is also known; *b.* Russia, 1881—*d.* Israel, 1960) was a romantic symbolist, a poet of gentle and restrained pathos; he was modern in outlook, and his verse was stylistically polished. He was a prominent leader in the renascence of the Hebrew language, literature, and culture in Israel.

Cohen's poems—notwithstanding that many of them are on themes extracted from Jewish history, the Bible, and the Talmud—are far less parochial in treatment and outlook than those written by many of his fellow poets in Israel; he attempted to draw from them moral inferences of universal applicability. He wrote symbolic verse-dramas full of rich imagery on subjects taken from the Jewish past; two of these that have been greatly admired are *At the Pyramids* and *The Scroll of Bar Yochai.* He too, like Bialik, Tchernichovsky, and Schneur, was fascinated (in an almost masochistic manner) by martyrological themes. In "The Third Cry," a poem based on the Talmudic account of the various ways the Ten Martyrs perished at the hands of the Romans in the second century C.E. (*see* KIDDUSH HA-SHEM), the poet linked up the fate of those Rabbinical saints with the millions of martyrs slain during the subsequent eighteen centuries. For him the Jewish people collectively appeared as but one martyr.

The romantic Chibat Zion (Love of Zion) movement, which developed in sharp reaction to the Russian pogroms of 1881–82, advocated the return of the Jewish people to Eretz Yisrael and to the soil. The popular image of the restored Jewish homeland in those years was of "a land of milk and honey" where every settler from the East European ghettos would be a farmer sitting under his own fig tree, at peace and unafraid. It was, therefore, not strange that in such an unrealistic mood the Hebrew writings of that period should have reflected this image, and should also have been romantic and loftily Biblical in tone.

Mosheh Smilansky (*b.* Russia, 1874–*d.* Israel, 1953) was one such short-story writer. He was a romantic realist who grappled with actual problems and aspects of the Palestinian-Israeli environment, drawing his knowledge of it from his own long experience as a farm laborer in the Jewish colonies

His tales about Arabs and life in the Arab villages, and especially about the struggles of the Jewish pioneers of his generation, were cast in uncomfortably heroic dimensions colored by his own traditionalist religious outlook. He employed a strained Biblical style which hardly proved a literary asset.

The practice of idealizing reality gradually underwent a change during the period 1905–18, when a new wave of settlers—the "Second Aliyah"—brought to Palestine many educated young men and women, including university students, writers, and other intellectuals who had in the past established an identification with the European labor and socialist movements.

A. D. Gordon (*b.* Russia, 1856–d. Palestine, 1922) was one of them. A follower of Tostoy, he advocated a kind of mystique of labor—a "Religion of Work"—that was to be followed under a collectivist social system. Said he: "A people torn away from Nature and immured [in ghettos] for two thousand years, a people which has adapted itself to every mode of life except to a life of labor—such a people will not again become a living, natural, working people without exerting all of its will."

Gordon reasoned that the individual Jew who exerted himself to be socially productive would be able to develop and fulfill himself at the same time that he would also be advancing the general welfare of the community. But, said Gordon, that community would have to be enlightened, ethical, and ideal-aspiring, for "Without a humane nation there can be no humane man, and we Jews must emphasize this."

The "Religion of Work" preached by Gordon and practiced by his own example in the agricultural collective settlements of Palestine had a uniquely powerful impact on many young Hebrew writers in the Palestinian community. It is precisely in this that the significance of A. D. Gordon lies in his effect on the history of modern Hebrew literature. As the inspirer of the new toiling chalutziut (the militant pioneering spirit in Palestine) and as one of the principal initiators and organizers of the agricultural collective settlements (kvutzot; s. kvutzah) that later developed into the kibbutzim; s. kibbutz, Gordon laid the groundwork for and furnished the writers who followed him with the social ideas and goals for their writing. Gordon's essay, *Religion of Work* ("Da'at ha-Avodah") and his *Letters from Palestine* (1919), in which he expounded his philosophy, were widely read in translation throughout Europe and left their stamp on the thinking of at least two generations of Hebrew writers and—in extension—on an important section of Israel's pioneering society.

Like Berditchevsky, some of whose ideas had made a deep impression upon him, the novelist and short-story writer, Joseph Chaim Brenner (*b.* Russia, 1881–[killed by an Arab mob in Jaffa] Palestine, 1921) was an incorrigible doubter. He questioned everything and everybody—himself, the Jewish character, and the disillusioning reality of his people's experiences in the world. Despite all his intellectual quibbling, he finally came to the conclusion that "In the psychology of young Jews throughout the Diaspora there must emerge a sense of *in spite of it all.*" This phrase, "in spite of it all," became the battle cry of the chalutzim (pioneers; s. chalutz) in their struggle against the British mandatory government in Palestine (*see* ZIONISM). Brenner called for the indomitable "chalutz who is prepared for everything" to fulfill the Jewish national destiny.

Extremely individualistic by temperament, Brenner reveals himself in his novels and stories to be a spiritual flagellant who broods over the inadequacies of human beings because they are remiss in matching their conduct with their avowed ideals. In almost all his works—and they were among the most significant produced by Hebrew writers of his generation—he displays a preoccupation with double-dealing and hypocrisy. This is plainly evident in his novels *Between the Waters, Bereavement and Failure,* and *From Here and There.* Brenner described his literary approach and method as "a simple realism, a realism whose wings are clipped, a creeping realism, a photographic realism." In the final analysis, he was an uncompromising moralist absorbed in the eternal problems of good and evil.

Another distinguished figure in Hebrew fiction is Shmuel Yosef Agnon (the pen name of S. Y. Chachkes, *b.* Galicia, 1888–to Israel, 1909). He is a highly individualistic writer in a quiet but arresting way. He treats reality as would a moralist, and diffuses his storytelling art with Chasidic mysticism and Talmudic lore. But perhaps what characterizes him best is a feeling of nostalgia that displays a pathos for the old forms of Jewish communal existence, piety, and folkways—a vanished life that in his idealization takes on the aspect of some Paradise Lost.

Foremost among his novels (and that best known to non-Hebrew readers because it has been translated into English and other foreign languages) is *The Bridal Canopy.* This describes the life of the Chasidim in Galicia by means of the convoluted storytelling device known both to the Orient and to the Middle Ages in Europe as the "story within a story," each tale being tangential to the main narrative yet illuminative of the central theme. Following the Don Quixote pattern, *The Bridal Canopy* traces the travels of an impecunious Talmudic scholar as he goes from one Jewish community to another in quest of the dowries he must provide for his three marriageable daughters. All along the way, this Talmudic knight-errant, accompanied by his Sancho Panza–style Jewish driver, experiences all kinds of adventures and misadventures, both merry and tragic. The gloom and drabness of Jewish life in the towns and villages of Galicia that Agnon describes are lit up in this work by a spiritual glow which might be said to come from within, being chiefly evoked by the folk-wisdom, the gentle humor, and the compassionateness of plain Jews.

In his novel *In The Heart of the Seas,* Agnon narrates in his customary folkloristic style that is keyed to the awed and miraculous tones of a believing age long gone by of the wondrous journey that a devout company of Galician Chasidim once undertook to Eretz Yisrael—the Promised Land.

To make a re-evaluation of the kind of life he described in the two above-mentioned novels, Agnon revisited his native town in Galicia following the first World War. Upon his return to Palestine he wrote *A Wayfarer for the Night,* which is actually a fictionalized autobiography—a record of his dismay on finding the old Jewish institutions, the ethical practices, and dedicated piety he had known so well in his youth, lying both physically and morally in ruins. This novel might best be characterized as a prose elegy on the death of the shtetl (the homogeneous Jewish village community in Eastern Europe of bygone days).

In the novel *In Days Gone By,* a tale about a young chalutz, the author reveals his penchant for gentle irony and satire in recounting his protagonist's efforts to adjust to his hard new life in Israel. In this and in other later novels and short stories, Agnon left behind him the old world of the ghetto that had already vanished and instead turned with a brave hopefulness to chronicle the struggle for national self-renewal by the Jewish people in Palestine (Israel).

Abraham Abba Kabak (*b.* Russia, 1883–*d.* Palestine, 1944), highly regarded in Israel as a storyteller, always conceived on a monumental scale. *Between Sea and Desert,* a tale in several volumes, treats of Jewish life in Palestine under the rule of Turkey and of the subsequent armed struggle between the Allies and the Central Powers for the possession of Palestine in World War I. Kabak also wrote a trilogy about the sixteenth-century messianic mystic, Solomon Molcho, and a four-volume novel, *The History of a Family,* which, in the manner of Galsworthy's *Forsyte Saga,* follows the fortunes of several generations of a family, who are described in various circumstances and settings in Russia to their eventual settlement in Palestine. Regarded as Kabak's best work is *On the Narrow Path,* a reconstruction of the life and tragedy of Jesus in ancient Judea.

A writer of many facets is Isaac Dov Berkowitz (*b.* Russia, 1885–Israel,), a son-in-law of the famous Yiddish humorist, Sholem Aleichem, many of whose works he translated into Hebrew. Berkowitz, who spent many years in the United States, produced a number of Hebrew and Yiddish novels, short stories, and one-act plays. These dwelt on New York ghetto-life, the Jewish immigrant's problems of adjustment, and the conflicts resulting from cultural assimilation. Probably his best-known work is *Messianic Days,* a novel about an American Jew of Russian origin who, while on a journey to Palestine, suddenly discovers his kinship with the struggle being waged there by the pioneers to rebuild the ancestral homeland. By identifying himself actively with their dedication, he finds a purpose for his hitherto meaningless life.

During his early period, Jacob Steinberg (*b.* Russia, 1886–d. Palestine, 1947) produced short stories, verses, plays, and essays about Ukrainian-Jewish life, much of it of an introspective and skeptical character. But after he had settled in Palestine in 1914, his writings about the new environment became mystical, affirmative, and ecstatic. He was convinced that there existed a spiritual and indestructible bond between the Jew and his ancient homeland.

An individualistic writer of fiction was Deborah Baron (*b.* Russia, 1887–to Israel, 1911). At first she wrote about her early environment in Russia, but later she delineated Palestinian Jewish life. Besides many short stories, she also published six novels.

A much read and admired novelist, short-story writer, and poet was Asher Barash (*b.* Galicia, 1889–*d.* Israel, 1952). During his earlier period, his novels and short stories dealt with the life of the Jews of Galicia. His tales were realistic and touched with the kind of mysticism and religious naturalism often discovered in modern Hebrew writings. Some of his best known books are *Chapters From the Life of Jacob Rudorfer* (1928), *The Gardeners* (1944), and *Before the Gates of Heaven.* The last-mentioned work has for its central character the sole survivor in a pogrom during the savage Chmielnicki uprising in 1648. The hero lays down his life fighting to save the Torah-scrolls in the synagogue from profanation by the rampaging Cossacks.

Even if he cannot be counted among the foremost of contemporary Hebrew novelists, Yehudah Burla (*b.* Palestine, 1886–Israel,) is, nonetheless, a unique literary personality simply because of the Oriental Jewish types that he has created. A Sefaradic Jew himself, he has written about the kind of ethnic Jewish life he knows best—themes about Turkish, Bokharan, Yemenite, and Persian Jews. He has published a trilogy based on the life of Rabbi Yehudah Alkalai. He has also written a novel about Jerusalem Jews from the turn of the twentieth century to the present.

Gershon Shofman (*b. Russia,* 1880–to Israel, 1938) has been a popular writer of fiction with a penchant for dramatizing his themes in brief, vignette-style episodes. He calls these "charcoal sketches." They deal principally with rootless as well as restless types of the Russian Jewish intelligentsia prior to the Russian Revolution of 1917, describing men and women who could not make their proper adjustment to life because of their eternal quibbling, doubting, and indecision. However, some of these "sketches" are too obviously contrived, the better to point up the author's theses.

Avigdor Hameiri (the pen name of Avigdor Feuerstein, *b.* Austria, 1890–to Israel, 1921), has published many short stories as well as novels and verse. The writing for which he undoubtedly will be longest remembered is *The Great Madness,* whose subject-matter stemmed from his unhappy experiences as an officer in the Austrian army during World War I. In it he dwells relentlessly on the horrors and stupidity of war and expatiates on the suffering and indignities inflicted on Jews by Austrian anti-Semites.

With possibly the single exception of Agnon, the most arresting among contemporary writers of fiction in Hebrew is Chaim Hazaz (*b.* Russia, 1897–to Israel, 1931). He is especially noted for his character portrayals, and his range is wide in the choice of types and subject matter. He has written stories on Biblical and Jewish historical themes; one of his dramas, *Beketz ha-Yamim,* which was produced by the Habimah Theatre in Tel Aviv, is centered on the delirium that was unleashed among the desperate Jewish masses by the melodramatic appearance of the would-be Messiah, Sabbatai Zevi (1648). Many of the short stories and novels by Hazaz deal with small-town life of Russian Jews during the Revolution of 1917 and during the civil war which followed. *In Forest Homes* is a novel about Jewish forest-dwellers in the Ukraine; *Under the Shadow of Kingdoms* is a grueling narrative about the desperate flight of some pogrom survivors during the Civil War. A satirical novel about Yemenite Jews has appeared in an English translation under the title of *Mori Said.*

One of the most respected of Israeli novelists and short-story writers is Judah Yaari (*b.* Galicia, 1900–to Israel, 1920). He has written with great force and authenticity about the struggles of the pioneers in the kibbutzim in which he worked as a laborer for many years, thus stamping his stories with the conviction of his personal experiences. His novel *When the Candle Was Burning* drew praise for its depiction of the struggle and the joys and heartbreak felt by the pioneers in Palestine during the difficult period after World War I.

Another delineator of kibbutz life in Israel today is David Maletz (*b.* 1900–). In his novel translated into English in 1950 as *Young Hearts,* he depicts the microcosm of the collective settlement, viewing it through the fulfillments and the disenchantments of those resolute individuals who constitute it. Because of its frank discussion of the problems and conflicts bedeviling a kibbutz, it aroused much controversy.

A novelist of unusual storytelling gifts and one who is very popular in Israel is Yitzchak Shenberg (*b.* Russia, 1905–*d.* Israel, 1957). He wrote realistic fiction about modern Jewish life in Russia and Palestine. Himself a pioneer and farmhand, he wrote stories and novels on various aspects of rural life in Israel. Stories of this genre are included in his collection translated into English as *Under the Fig Tre*[e]. Having a preference for topical and contemporary theme[s], Shenberg published a novel after World War II about sev[en] Jews—six men and a girl—who were caught in the Nazi net [as] they attempted in vain to steal across border after border [to] reach safety in Palestine.

The first Hebrew poets of eminence—Bialik, Tchernichosky, Schneur, and Cohen (Kahan)—had completed their literary lives in Palestine years before the creation of the Sta[te] of Israel in 1948. In consequence, the bulk of their poe[try] had reference to the problems of the Jewish people a[s]

Jewish identity, and to the life-patterns and traditional religious culture of the ghetto. Perhaps the same appraisal, although to a lesser degree, may be applied to the group of poets who both stemmed from and followed them—Yaacov Fichman, Yehudah Karni, David Shimonovitz, and others.

Although these were younger men when they settled in pre-Israel Palestine, they too, drawn by the compelling force of Jewish cultural tradition, looked over their shoulder, as it were, and meditated upon the multi-faceted Jewish past and Jewish lore. Nonetheless, the mainstream of their creativity was directed to the contemporary life of the new Jewish society (yishuv) that was being built in the Jewish Homeland.

A leader in this group of so-called second-generation poets was Yaacov Fichman (*b.* Russia, 1881–*d.* Israel, 1958). Arriving in Palestine from Bessarabia in 1912, he not only produced a significant body of poetry but served as one of the foremost critics for two generations of Hebrew writers. Fichman is a lyrist whose verse often exults with his rediscovery of nature and of the joy and earthiness of living on and from the soil of Israel.

Even on themes of the ancient past, he superimposes modern ideas and values. His poetic soliloquies about Israel Baal-Shem Tob articulate the traditional Jewish passion for redemption in terms of social idealism—for the whole people and not for the individual alone. Although deeply grieved by the Nazi terror and by the world carnage to which it inexorably led, he refused to give up his faith in mankind, holding that although there were many human beasts of prey intent on destroying their fellow beings, there nevertheless remained more people who were ready to work for the happiness of the human race.

Another, if lesser poet, was Yehudah Karni (the pen name of Volovelski; *b.* Russia, 1884–*d.* Israel, 1948). He wrote many fine poems on themes of nature and life in Palestine, the latter touching on various aspects in the tumultuous processes of its rebirth. He published five volumes of verse, but the one for which he was most highly regarded and awarded the Bialik Prize for poetry was *Jerusalem* (1944).

One of the most distinguished poets writing in the Hebrew language, who with his verses about Israel and pioneering in the modern vein helped establish that trend among the younger Hebrew poets, was David Shimonovitz (Shimoni; *b.* Russia, 1886–*d.* Israel, 1956). Although a lyrist, he was inventive in many forms, but especially noted for his "idylls." Shimonovitz placed emphasis on the absolute need for the individual Jew to remove all the walls of consciousness separating him from a communion with nature in Eretz Yisrael.

His idylls expatiate upon the beauties of the Israel landscape in mellifluous cadences. In *Waggoner's Jubilee* he describes his delight on discovering the enchantments of nature in Israel and of his gradual growing into harmony with its earth and sky. Even in his poems about the Cabalists of sixteenth-century Safed, he follows them on their mystical journeys on foot only in order to be able to describe the beauty that lies in the hills of Galilee.

David Frishman, the noted literary critic, first discovered the poet-dramatist Mattitiahu Shoham (the pen name of M. Poliakewicz; Poland, 1893–1937). Shoham's plays in verse on Biblical themes make their implications for the problems and conflicts of our time in the sharply contrasted opposition between good and evil. The poet built his play *Jericho* around the struggle between the idealistic nomad-Israelites and the corrupt agricultural-Canaanites for the possession of the Land of Promise. The drama *Balaam* personifies the encounter between the *positive* protagonist—Moses, "the blesser"—and his *negativist* adversary, "the curser," Balaam. Yet in the end, Balaam, too, has to submit his evil will to the life-demanding need of blessing. *Tyre and Jerusalem* focuses on the clash between two polarities—*moral will* (as symbolized by the Prophet Elijah) and *immoral compulsion* (represented by Queen Jezebel). In 1933–34, during the early Nazi period, Shoham wrote the drama *Thou Shalt Not Make Thee Gods of Iron.* Again his theme was the eternal duality and mutual repulsion of good and evil. Here his two protagonists are the Patriarch Abraham and Gog, the ruthless military leader of the Northern tribes (i.e., the personification of Hitler and his monstrous drive to power and annihilation).

The poetry of Uri Tzvi Greenberg (*b.* Galicia, 1894–to Israel, 1924) is tumultuous; it expresses violent emotions in a violent manner. His poems on themes of Jewish tribulation and bruised national pride are massively constructed, rhetorical, and surging. Often he strikes the stridency of a patriotic chauvinism, a characteristic which reflects his political views, for he is a leader of the rightist Herut Party in Israel. He has often stirred a deep resentment with his savage polemics in verse.

There can be no question of his passionate, indeed fanatical, attachment to the land of Israel and the Jewish people. A nonconformist, he abhors modern urban life and distrusts city dwellers. He is drawn in sympathy only to the chalutzim, who are acting instead of talking, who are breaking stones on the roads, draining marshes, and conquering the unyielding wilderness of the Negev. Greenberg writes in free verse, and his poetry, aside from its scorching intensity, its clarion call to militancy, and its wild lamentation, often brings to mind the uninhibited "open-road" poetry of Walt Whitman.

Greenberg always was a stormy petrel; he intended his poetry to provoke action, not merely to entertain or to elevate. In his *Book of Indictment and Faith* (1937), he took to task the Jewish Agency for counseling the much harrassed Jews of Palestine to practice havlagah (self-restraint) in their desperate contest with the British Mandatory Government and the embattled Arab nationalists. Consistent with this political philosophy, he advocated that Jewish youth be mobilized to defend the national interest. Following the Nazi butchery of the six million Jews, he published the volume *The Streets of the River,* in which, with his characteristic verbal ferocity, he commemorated the tragic events that had overwhelmed his people.

Far different from Greenberg in temperament, social philosophy, style, and poetic form was Yitzchak Lamdan (*b.* Russia, 1899–*d.* Israel, 1956). He can be said to have personified the poet of the unyielding spirit of pioneering (chalutziut) in Palestine-Israel. His poetry is distinguished by a luminosity of dedication. Unlike Greenberg, he avoids self-dramatization. In his long verse-cycle *Masada* (1927), which has enjoyed continuously great popularity, he tries to link the efforts of the chalutzim of his generation to establish in Israel a last refuge for the Jewish people with the heroic last stand of the defenders of the fortress of Masada. The latter, situated on the Dead Sea, was the site of the final military engagement fought against the besieging Roman legions, after the Temple in Jerusalem was destroyed, in the first century C.E.

One of the most talented and respected of Hebrew poets in Israel, Abraham Shlonsky (*b.* Russia, 1900–to Israel, 1913), has written on themes that eulogize the spiritual and social motivations of pioneering. Upon his arrival in Israel, he became first a road-laborer and later a working member of a kibbutz. He has sung about the joys and dignity of work and, in particular, about the conquest of the soil in the interests of the national reconstruction of Israel. Not a few of his poems have been set to music and are popular in Israel. Inescapably, like so many other Hebrew writers, he evinces an affinity for tragic themes that mirror the Jewish people's historic experiences. Like so many other sensitive Jews, he suffered psychic shock following the catastrophe that consumed one-third of the Jewish people in the Nazi furnaces.

It is a cultural oddity that there have been very few women writers of verse in Hebrew, although such a lack is hard to find in other literatures. However, there have been two highly regarded women poets in Israel. Rachel (the pen name of Rachel Bluvstein, *b.* Russia, 1890–*d.* Israel, 1931) was a social idealist who came to Palestine in 1909 to pioneer in a farm-settlement. She fell in love with the countryside and with the rustic life of the chalutzim, glorying in their preparatory labors for the restoration of the Jewish people to a life on the land in its ancestral home. Although she was confined to her bed by tuberculosis for years before her death, she wrote lyrics in which she sang in muted tones of things closest to her heart. One song, titled "Dawn," which ultimately achieved the popularity of a folksong in Israel, expresses her resignation to the premature death which she knew awaited her.

> Be this my lot, until I be undone:
> Dust of thy road, my land, and thy
> Grain waving golden in the sun.
>
> *Translated by* ABRAHAM M. KLEIN

As the most prominent Hebrew woman poet, Leah Goldberg (*b.* Lithuania, 1911–to Israel, 1935) is attracted to themes about nature, showing a strong preference for the modified sonnet form devised by Rainer Maria Rilke, the great poet of pre-Hitler Germany whose mother was Jewish. She has published several volumes of essays and poems, and also a collection of children's verse. Leah Goldberg has been preoccupied with that inexhaustible theme of all Hebrew poets—the miracle of the perpetual self-renewal of the Jewish people, always rising like a phoenix reborn from its ashes.

In Israel today, a number of the poems of S. Shalom (the pen name of Shalom Joseph Shapira; *b.* Galicia, 1905–to Israel, 1922) are widely sung. This is because, as a lyrist, his verses have an innate musicality. Being a Neo-Chasid and a devotee of the traditional Jewish past, he imparts to much of his writing—short stories as well as poems—a mystical-religious mood. He writes simply and folkloristically, but the over-all impression is often of grief-consciousness and tragedy. He has a predilection for the ballad and the sonnet forms, and has translated into Hebrew all of Shakespeare's sonnets. His *Book of Poems and Sonnets* is a popular collection in Israel. Other works of Shalom are *On Ben Peleh, Galilean Diary,* and *Face to Face*—a volume of poems for which he was awarded the Bialik Prize for Poetry in 1941.

A popular Hebrew poet during the struggle for the independence of Israel was Nathan Alterman (*b.* Poland, 1910–Israel,). In the War of Liberation against the Arab invaders in 1948, his battle verses prominently printed in the daily newspapers, helped fire patriotic fervor among the Jewish defenders. An original stylist in his particular field of composition, he was the originator of the brief political and social verse-commentary in Hebrew which lent itself to humorous and often satirical treatment. Of the several volumes he has authored, *The Seventh Column* has been perhaps the most successful.

There have been, of course, a number of Hebrew poets, novelists, and scholars in the United States, Canada, Latin America, and Europe, but a necessarily brief outline such as this permits only the sketchiest reference to them. By and large, they had no decisive impact on the development of Hebrew literature. The presence in the United States for a number of years after World War I, of a Hebrew writers' circle, which included such influential Hebraists as Reuben Brainin and I. D. Berkowitz, stimulated a Hebrew revival but on a relatively small scale. In the United States and Canada, where it was not possible for Hebrew to flourish as a "living" language, Hebrew literature remained at best a coterie-literature read by a relatively small group of Zionist enthusiasts. Having had their cultural roots in the East European ghettos, these Hebrew writers, like their Yiddish writer-colleagues, drew their literary materials from the reservoir of Jewish life and its heritage of the past. Yet, in time and rather tentatively, themes indigenous to the American scene began to appear in Hebrew writing.

Among these Hebrew writers in the United States have been the poet Menachem Mendel Dolitzky (*b.* Poland, 1856–*d.* U.S.A., 1930); the poet and critic Simon Ginzburg (*b.* Russia, 1891–*d.* Palestine, 1943); Chaim Abraham Friedland (*b.* Lithuania, 1891–*d.* U.S.A., 1939), short-story writer and poet; Israel Efros (*b.* Russia, 1890–Israel,), scholar and poet; Eisik Silberschlag (*b.* Galicia, 1903–), critic, essayist, poet; Hillel Bavli (*b.* Lithuania, 1893–1961), essayist and poet; Simon Halkin (*b.* Russia, 1899–to Israel, 1948), poet, novelist, literary historian, and translator; Yochanan Tversky (*b.* Russia, 1904–to Israel, 1948), historical novelist.

There is, what has been called, for want of a better description, *Sabra* or indigenous Israeli literature. It dates from the War of Liberation in 1948 and the establishment of the State of Israel. Sabra writers (native-born Israelis are nicknamed *Sabras* after the fruit of the Israeli cactus of that name) of the current generation evince all the well-known characteristics associated with the name: they are young, brash, down-to-earth, and self-confident. As native-born "prickly pears" they have had fewer traditions to bind them and fewer styles to imitate. Irreverent and utterly unorthodox (in the sense of literary preconceptions), they have found themselves quite free to seek new ways, to cultivate new styles, to develop a new rhetoric, so to speak, for their portrayal of Israeli life.

It may be considered significant that most of these talented Sabra writers have lived on a kibbutz at some time or another and, consequently, have acquired a Socialist orientation of one variety or another. And because many of them have also fought in the Palmach—the commando corps of the Israeli Army during the patriotic war against the Arab invaders—they are less inclined toward the "universalism," romanticism, pacifism, and mysticism that marked the older Hebrew writers and are attracted more to a hard-bitten realism and militant nationalism. Their experiences are strongly reflected in the novels, stories, and poems they have been writing.

One of the most gifted among the Sabra writers and a naturalist in his style is Mosheh Shamir (*b.* Palestine, 1921–Israel,). He has been attracted to historical themes, having already published a novel about the chameleon kinglet of Judea, Alexander Jannaeus, who preferred appearing like a Greek to being a Jew. He also wrote *In His Own Hands* (1951), a biographical novel in memory of his brother, who fell in the crucial battle of the Jerusalem Road during the war with the Arabs.

Other Sabra writers of novels and short stories who have drawn attention are Nathan Schacham, whose two cellections of short stories about kibbutz life were followed by a novel about the Palmach commandos—*Always We* (1952); Yigal Mosenson, the author of the novel *In the Wastes of the Negev;* S. Yizhar, whose novel *Far Down the Negev* describes the epic search for water by the young pioneers of the Negev wilderness; and Yonat and Alexander Sened, whose novel *Land Without Shade* (1950), in which an entire kibbutz is made the protagonist, describes the determined struggle against all odds of a small number of young people of both sexes to establish an outpost of Jewish national life in the hostile wilderness.

The new crop of still undeveloped Sabra-poets in Israel, although they have not as yet found their authentic voices, touch on virtually every aspect of experience in the internal life of their country. They have written poems which commemorate heroic exploits during the guerrilla-fighting against British colonial rule and, later, in military combat against the Arab invaders. They have written on political and social subjects, sensitively reacting to the totality of Jewish life in the homeland, not omitting the Israeli landscape and its unique beauties.

See also ENLIGHTENMENT, THE JEWISH; HEBREW LANGUAGE, HISTORY OF THE; YIDDISH LITERATURE, MODERN.

HEBREW VOWEL-SOUNDS. *See* VOWEL-SOUNDS, HEBREW.

"HEBREWS," "ISRAELITES," "JEWS"

The earliest beginnings of all peoples, having invariably occurred before the dawn of their history, are shrouded in mystery; their reality is romanticized and distorted by myth and contradictory statements. The outline of Jewish origins is also blurred. This may partly be explained by the fact that the Bible is the sole written source of information for the opening act in the Jewish life-drama, and as history, the Bible has proven to be not an entirely reliable record. Its narrative portions are an admixture of the real with the supernatural, of the historical with the legendary, of poetic fantasy with the nightmarish fears obsessing the primitive mind. And the whole again is confused by the irreconcilable contradictions of its chronology, statements of alleged fact, and events invariably telescoping their occurrence in point of time. These, of course, are characteristics of all scriptural chronicles, whether of the Assyrians, Babylonians, Egyptians, Greeks, Romans, or others.

Nevertheless, in the face of so much obscurity and confusion, the scholar of modern times has, in some significant areas, succeeded in creating a logical order out of the chaos. He has come to his task armed with the formidable tools of scientific research and methods. Illuminating in recent decades have been the studies of the Biblical archaeologists, Semitic philologists, and cultural anthropologists, supported by collateral findings made by the historians of comparative religions and cultures of peoples who, four or five thousand years ago, lived side by side with the most ancient Jews on the outskirts of the so-called Fertile Crescent in the Near and Middle East. True, their conclusions or, sometimes, mere hypotheses have often been in sharp disagreement with one another, each bristling with a multitude of reservations, qualifications, and speculative ifs, buts, and perhapses. Just the same, certain assumptions, although provisionally made, have emerged which have won wide acceptance among specialists in the field of Biblical studies. One of these is the belief that the earliest Jews, who in the Biblical chronicle went under the name of Hebrew, are to be identified with the Habiru or Hapiru.

Who were these Habiru? They were warrior nomads and shepherds. Was it the pangs of hunger? Was it a massive social upheaval or irresistible pressures from predatory enemies that sent hordes of the nomadic tribes then inhabiting the grazing lands of Central Asia fleeing in receding and advancing migratory waves of panic across half that continent almost four thousand years ago? It is virtually agreed that Habiru was not the name of any specific race or of a constellation of tribes or a single ethnic group. It was merely an ancient Semitic term for nomads—men with no fixed homes, wandering shepherds who led a primitive and hazardous existence. To survive, they were forced to form tribal federations, to be warlike and predatory so they could overcome their enemies and rob them of their flocks.

Numerous inscriptions have been found in non-Jewish sources of that era which contain references to the Habiru and which show them to have been migratorially active from the middle of the third millennium B.C.E. to almost the end of the second millennium B.C.E. These inscriptions testify to the existence of political and social groupings of Habiru in various parts of Western Asia, first in the Mesopotamian region, then in Asia Minor, in Syria and Palestine, and, finally, in Egypt.

That the Patriarchs, the "Founding Fathers" of the Jewish people, were Habiru or similar nomads is quite plain from the Bible narrative which relates their doings and movements. It was formerly thought that the word *Ivri* (or *Ibri*), which has been translated into English as "Hebrew," meant a "crossing over" (i.e., the crossing over of one who came from the other side of the Euphrates River). Possibly this indicates a connection with the original locale of the Habiru, who formed part of the Semitic-language constellation in Asia.

"Arami obed abi!" ("A wandering Aramean was my father!") was the persistent and pensive autobiographic recollection by the Jew regarding his past. These words (in Deuteronomy 26:5) also opened the prayer which was recited in the Temple of Jerusalem at the time of offering the first fruits of the harvest (bikkurim). This was when the Jew had already long been settled as a tiller of the soil and a town dweller. Most suggestive of "Abraham the Hebrew," who is so designated in Genesis 14:13, is the non-Jewish inscription which recounts the story of a certain chieftain, Tettish the Habiru. It is remarkably similar to the narrative of Abraham's activities. Like the Hebrew Patriarch, Tettish moved from place to place in search of water-wells and grazing land for his flocks, and, like Abraham and other successful chieftains, he fought and overpowered other clans and tribes and took away all their possessions as booty. Just as Abraham had laid the foundation for the future power of Israel, so did Tettish the Habiru for his numerous descendants. His grandson ultimately became ruler of a tribal kingdom in Northern Syria.

The pattern of life and destiny was much the same for all the Habiru groups in the Semitic constellation.

It has been pretty well established that late in the seventeenth century B.C.E., the Hyksos, a mighty Semitic confederation of "shepherd kings," began pouring southwestward from Central Asia in an irresistible tide of invasion. They actually conquered Egypt and ruled it for 120 years. The unorganized Habiru clans and tribes, it is believed, finding themselves in the dangerous path of the invaders, fled precipitately before

The face of an ancient Israelite, shaped into a stone pitcher. Probably from the period of the Judges. Unearthed in Bet Shemesh, Israel.

them, trying to get out of their way. Among these Habiru may have been the Patriarch (Chieftain) Jacob, who, with his large household of some seventy souls, when he felt the effects of a famine, sought food and refuge in Egypt. He settled in the Land of Goshen, on the eastern fringe of the fertile Nile Delta. After a sojourn of 430 years, according to the Biblical chronicle, his numerous descendants were enslaved. This took place, seemingly, in the fourteenth century B.C.E. Finally (the not-too-certain date of 1230 has been established as a possible time for this occurrence), the Hebrews revolted against the Pharaohs and succeded in fighting their way out of Egypt. They then started out on their long trek back to the land of their origin, Canaan, in Palestine.

It was at about this juncture in the history of the Jews that the name Hebrew disappeared from the Biblical record. (Interestingly the word Habiru also was dropped from non-Jewish inscriptions almost at the same time.) The name Israelite now took the place of Hebrew. This changeover from one identifying name to another is explained naïvely in the earlier legend (in Genesis 32:29) concerning a physical encounter—an all-night wrestling match—between the Patriarch Jacob and an angel. Having triumphed, Jacob extracts from the helpless angel this curious and mysterious blessing: "Thy name shall be called no more Jacob, but Israel; for thou hast striven with God and with men and hast prevailed."

Although all those Jews who regard every word in the Bible as incontrovertibly true interpret the legend literally and point to it as the source of origin for the names Israel and Israelite, the objective historian of today is on a surer footing when he turns to a non-Jewish "official" source for factual verification. The earliest reference to the designation Israelite was found not too many decades ago in the inscription on a stele put up for Pharaoh Merneptah in his mortuary temple at Thebes. In this inscription, in which the Egyptian king celebrates his victories over the tribal kingdoms of Palestine, he itemizes:

> Canaan is plundered . . .
> Carried away is Ashkelon.
> Gezer is taken.
> Yenoam is no more.
> Israel is desolated, his seed is not.

As Merneptah died in 1215 B.C.E.—some historians believe that he and not his predecessor, Rameses II, was the actual Pharaoah of the Exodus with whom Moses contended—obviously, the inscription cannot refer to the Israelites who were, presumably, still slaves in Egypt and had not as yet revolted, but to *other* Israelites who were established in Canaan as a recognizable ethnic group of tribes occupying a distinctive geographic area called "Israel" by Merneptah. This, therefore, leaves the whole problem of the ethnic origin of the Israelites and of the "Promised Land" in Canaan as hitherto understood in a state of unresolved confusion, but pregnant with unexplored possibilities, which future researchers will perhaps help to clear up. All this merely points up the fact that, despite the facile use of the terms "Hebrew" and "Israelite," little of a precise nature is actually known about them.

But even though the historic roots of the people called Hebrews and Israelites remain still obscure, this is not at all the case with the third and final designation of ethnic identity; Jew. This word, of course, is the English derivation of the medieval French word *juieu*, which, in turn, came from the Latin *Judaeus*—a "Judean," i.e., one who was a native of Judea. Judea was the name the Romans gave to Judah (Yehudah), the southern Jewish kingdom which they conquered and suppressed, finally, in 70 C.E.

In the Book of Esther, dating back to a still unidentified period in the history of the Persian empire, Jews, even though they had long been culturally assimilated and were natives of the country, were identified merely as a religious group who followed the faith of the God of Israel. In the broader definition of today, it is considered sufficient that a "Jew" be ethnically of Jewish descent; he does not have to be religious in order to be identified as such.

HELL. *See* GEHINNOM.

HELLENISTS, JEWISH

In addition to the Apocrypha and Pseudepigrapha, there was still another category of writings produced by Jews who had assimilated in depth Hellenistic culture in the Greco-Roman period. These works had nothing about them of oracular seer-declaiming "revelations"; most often they were written in the measured style and reasoning method of men who by education and culture had been disciplined in philosophical argumentation. By and large, their works (some of those extant are but mere fragments and constitute only a small number of a much larger body of lost, destroyed, or mutilated writings) consist of apologetic religious "histories" composed in the allegorizing Hellenistic manner, mystical-moralistic works about the Jewish religion, philosophical disquisitions (especially by the first-century rabbinic-philosopher, Philo), and even a snatch of verse-drama (like the Homeric works) about the Exodus, written by the poet Ezekielos of Alexandria.

One of the over-all aims of these writings was to validate the proposition that the ethical monotheism of the Jews was superior to animistic paganism. Another was to demonstrate, at the same time (by a tortured kind of reasoning), that the teachings of Moses had been "adopted" by the great Greek philosophers: Plato, Aristotle, Pythagoras, Epicurus, and the Stoics.

The religious-cultural need for this kind of Jewish "propaganda" literature in the Greek language seemed to have been of historic urgency. First of all, the religious and intellectual leaders of the Egyptian and other Hellenized Jews (so many of whom were but recent and, therefore, insecure, proselytes to Judaism) were forced by the strenuous and open competition between Judaism and the Greco-Roman and Eastern "mystery" religions to resort to militantly defensive measures. But just as compelling a reason for the production of such wrtings was the fact that, in the Hellenistic climate of cultural fusion and of dissolving religious beliefs and loyatlies, there were many Jews who had begun to question the worthiness of their own faith. In fact, Philo referred ruefully to those of his fellow Jews living in the Greco-Roman milieu who had cultivated "a dislike of the institutions of our fathers and make it their constant study to denounce and decry the Laws."

To add to these problems, there was the menace implicit in the agitation that was being fomented against the Jews of Egypt by such rabble-rousers as Manethon, the Egyptian temple scribe of Thebes, and Lysimachus, Apollonius Molon, Posidonius, and Chaeremon. Also the great burgeoning in size and in influence of the Jewish communities in the Mediterranean area, largely from their accretion of great numbers of proselytes, furnished more fuel for the anti-Semitic fires. (Philo stated that there were more than one million Jews in Egypt; there were perhaps two or three million more in other Greek-speaking regions—in Syria, Asia Minor, Cyreneica, Libya, Greece, and Rome.)

The great successes of contemporary Jewish missionary efforts led Philo to rejoice: "They [the Laws of Moses] attract and win the attention of all, of barbarians [the Greeks called all non-Greeks 'barbarians'], of Greeks, of dwellers on this mainland, of nations of the East and West, of Europe and Asia, and of the whole inhabited world from end to end."

Perhaps the principal objective of the Jewish-Hellenistic writers was to stiffen the line of those Jewish believers, especially among the recent converts, who had begun to waver in their religious loyalties—to try to raise their morale and to reassure them that, in spite of all the slanders and libels of the enemies of the Jews, who were derogating them as "barbarians" and "aliens," they, *as Jews*, should consider themselves to be every bit as "good Greeks" as the best among the Hellenes.

Accordingly, Philo and other writers, from the second century B.C.E. to the second century C.E., engaged in a spirited campaign—a self-deluded one, it might appear to many moderns—to demonstrate to both Jews and Gentiles that all the great ideas in Greek philosophy and all the noble principles current in Hellas had been *originally* drawn from the Jewish Bible.

In his fanciful didactic *Life of Moses*, the Alexandrian historian Artapanus (second century B.C.E.) made that great leader out to be a Greek (in contrast to Sigmund Freud, who made of him an Egyptian). Artapanus did not content himself with half-measures; he bestowed on Moses the classic Greek name of Musaeus, and claimed that he had been the teacher of Orpheus; to add further to the prestige of Musaeus, he attributed to him the invention of military science, navigation, architecture, philosophy, and even hieroglyphics!

In the employment of such fables Artapanus did not stand alone among the Jewish Hellenists. For instance, in the Letter of Aristeas (written in the second century B.C.E.), which is a fulsome panegyric to the Jewish religion, its author contended that the Greek philosophers had merely "copied" Moses and derived their "inspiration" from him. Aristeas' contemporary, Aristobulus of Panaeus, specifically charged the Greek philosopher Plato and the early Greek mystic Pythagoras with plagiarizing from the Jewish Scriptures. This odd notion apparently took deep root among the Hellenized Jews, for after the Destruction of the Second Temple in 70 C.E., the historian Josephus also strained to show that there was a link between Greek genius and the Jewish religion. Pridefully he stated: "Our earliest imitators were the Greek philosophers, who, though ostensibly observing the laws of their own countries, yet in their conduct and philosophy were Moses' disciples, holding similar views about God."

All that we possess today—mostly fragments and abstracts—of these writings of the Jewish Hellenist intellectuals, we owe to their preservation—almost providential, it may be added—first by the encyclopedic Greek scholar, Alexander of Miletus (105–40 B.C.E.) and later by the Church Fathers Clement of Alexandria (*d. c.* 215 C.E.) and Eusebius (fourth century). Although it may at first glance seem strange that Jewish writings were ignored by the Jews but preserved and honored by the Christians, it came about because patristic scholars operated under the curious misapprehension that those writings were among the earliest Christian religious and historical works. In fact, Philo, who was the rabbi of the Great Synagogue in Alexandria, was officially revered as one of the first Church Fathers; it was not until the end of the sixteenth century that the Italian Jewish humanist, Azariah dei Rossi, rediscovered Philo for what he actually was: a devout Jew!

It goes without saying that almost all of the Jewish "histories" produced by the Jewish Hellenists—including those by Demetrius, Eupolemus, Artapanus, Justus of Tiberias, Thillus, and Jason of Cyrene (from whose five-volume work the second Book of Maccabees was extracted by a later editor)—were but minor works, judged either as history or as literature. They, like most histories in Hellenistic antiquity, abounded with incredible inventions, fables, and archaisms. The Jewish historian of that time of real stature was Josephus Flavius. He was the philo-Roman politician and military leader who had been branded by the Jews of his day as a traitor, for he had gone over to the Roman side during the catastrophic siege of Jerusalem in the patriotic revolt of the people, and had helped Titus capture the city. The memory of his defection was made more bitter and unforgiving because of what followed: the terrible carnage of the defenders, the razing of the Temple, and the destruction of the Jewish state.

Josephus' version of the uprising of 66–70 C.E. is chronicled in his autobiography (*Vita*) and in his *History of The Jewish War*. Despite their obvious contradictions and his undisguised bias in favor of the Romans, despite his conscienceless disparagement of the revolt and its leaders, and the self-exculpation he attempts of his own treachery, dressing it up in reasonable and even idealistic terms, those two works, nevertheless, remain invaluable and fascinating as records of that tumultuous period in Jewish history. There certainly are extant no other works like them.

Valuable too, although for a different reason, was his monumental history, *The Antiquities of the Jews*, a chronicle from the Creation to the outbreak of the revolt against Rome in 66 C.E., which became a world-classic. Perhaps the chief foundation for the enduring fame of Josephus as historian was the exceptional reverence in which his writings were held by the Church since early times. This was because he had been almost a contemporary of Jesus and the Apostles in Judea. His chronicles (so it is judged by many modern scholars, both Christians and Jews) were altered textually at an early period in Christian times by overzealous propagandists of the Church in order to provide historic corroboration for the mission of Jesus as the Christ or Messiah, since no other *contemporary* "outside" historic testimony for it existed.

The most eminent of all the Jewish Hellenists was Philo (*c.* 20 B.C.E.–*c.* 40 C.E.). Because of the exclusive interest that the Christian Church evinced in his theology—which resulted in his being ignored by the rabbis—Philo's true greatness was overlooked until recent decades. There is little question but that his like as a philosopher of ethics in Jewish religious terms was not seen until the appearance of Baruch Spinoza, some sixteen centuries later. Each had the same concern with reason and truth, although each viewed them within the context of different intellectual values. The tag of "God-intoxicated," which a French writer affixed to Spinoza, could have been applied to Philo as well. Like the philosopher of Amsterdam, Philo too believed in the intellectual love of God and in man's perfectability, seeing him as "a relative and kinsman of God because of his reason. . . . Every man, as regards his mind, is related to the divine reason, for he is an impress or fragment of that blessed nature." This was by no means a statement unusual for Philo. It was the golden thread of a personal spirituality which he deeply felt and drew through everything he wrote.

One interesting thing to observe is that Philo was not an "original" philosopher. The only thinking he ever developed into a kind of system was his philosophy of the Jewish religion. He was really a strong Platonist and a Pythagorean, more a philosophical writer than a writer of philosophy. As a writer, too, his work was stamped with his unique literary individuality. He was a poet writing about religion in philosophical prose. Probably no writer during the Hellenistic Age, whether Jew or Gentile, could compare with him as a pellucid literary stylist. He employed the most sensitive imagery to express his ideas, sentiments, and moods.

As a rabbinic sage—a role which was integral in his physiognomy as a philosopher—Philo concentrated his efforts on interpreting the teachings of the Bible to his Grecized fellow Jews. As a logician–mystic though he was—he was faced with inconsistencies and primitivism in many Scriptural passages. These he tried to reconcile or to explain away by means of the allegorical or symbolic methods which the contemporary Stoics applied to the texts of the Homeric lays in order to explain their myths and logical incongruities.

Philo contended—not only as a philosopher but also as a rabbinic sage (he is not to be confused with the Rabbinic Sages of the Talmud), that the Pentateuch contained hidden meanings which were projected symbolically in mystic form. For him the story in Genesis about the temptation of Adam and Eve in the Garden of Eden was intended to connote *virtue* which God had implanted in the heart of man. In the same way, the Sabbath meant *peace of the soul;* the fratricide Cain symbolized *sin,* and the intended Sacrifice of Isaac by his father Abraham stood for *faith.*

This allegorizing method of Scriptural interpretation Philo employed in all of his writings. His principal and most interesting Jewish works are *The Life of Moses, Allegorical Commentary to Genesis, Questions and Answers to Genesis and Exodus;* and the Commentary on the Five Books of Moses. Philo also produced historic works that treated of the bitter persecution of the Jews during the imperial reigns of Tiberius (14–37 C.E.) and Caligula (37–41), and two pieces —"Against Flaccus" and "The Embassy to Gaius"—that he wrote to answer the anti-Semitic attacks made by Gentile contemporaries of his. These works demonstrate clearly that Philo's religious-ethical phisosophy was not as "abstract" as some scholars have tried to make out but armed him with the moral imperative to act on behalf of truth, his religion, and his people, when those were endangered.

An early nineteenth-century scholar of the Jewish Enlightenment or Haskalah, Nachman Krochmal (1785–1840), made this acute observation about Philo: "He uses Scripture as a sort of clay which he molds to convey his philosophical ideas." But this is only half the truth. The other half is that, by every count, Philo was a devout Jew, perceiving the tenets of his religion through the prisms of Platonism and Greek mystical philosophy.

The mere thought is full of irony: that the patristic historian Eusebius and other theologians of early Christianity like Clement and Origen should have thought Philo to have been the first of the Church Fathers. Perhaps even more wry is the knowledge that he profoundly influenced Christian theology and yet left no trace of his thinking on Jewish religious and intellectual history.

Here it is appropriate to take note that Philo's books, together with other writings by Jewish Hellenists, including most of the works designated as Pseudepigrapha, were placed under the ban by the Rabbinic Sages. They seemed to have had no choice: The Christian Church had adopted them as its own. Perhaps that, by itself, would not have had so decisive an affect on the Rabbinical rejection, inasmuch as the Bible also (in its Greek Septuagint version) had been made part of the Scriptures of Jewish Christianity. But the historical fact of the matter was that the New Testament (especially the apocalypses and the propagandistic-missionary books) had been "patterned" after Jewish-Hellenistic writings, not only in some of their thinking, which was frowned upon by the Rabbis as being "heretical," but also in their literary styles: the parables, the familiar Greco-Jewish similes, and Messianic allusions, even to the very expressions.

See also APOCRYPHA; CHRISTIANITY, JEWISH ORIGINS OF; PSEUDEPIGRAPHA; THERAPEUTAE.

HERZL, THEODOR. *See* THEODOR HERZL (*under* ZIONISM).

"HIDDEN WISDOM, THE." *See* CABALA.

HIGH HOLY DAYS. *See* ROSH HASHANAH; SELICHOT; YOM KIPPUR.

HIGH PRIEST (in Hebrew: COHEN HA-GADOL)

The high priest ruled over the orders of priests and Levites which, during the Second Temple period, were said to have more than twenty thousand members in Judea. These constituted a highly stratified organization run on the lines of a well-graduated hierarchy.

The first high priest was Aaron, the brother of Moses. The family dynasty he founded supplied the high priests and other leading priests for many generations thereafter.

Like a king at his coronation, the high priest too was anointed. The vestments and ceremonial insignia that he wore became traditional of his office: the triple crown, the Urim and the Thummim (a mysterious sacerdotal object that he wore like a breastplate, suspended from his neck). His daily vestments, as befitted his supreme priestly dignity, were resplendent with gold and precious stones. On Yom Kippur, he alone was allowed to enter the inner sanctuary of the Holy of Holies, there to make atonement for the sins of his own house and for those of all the people of Israel by offering the sacrifice in person instead of through a ministering subordinate. In later centuries, the high priest sometimes served also as the presiding judge of the Sanhedrin, the supreme legislative-religious-judicial body of seventy-one elders.

In the entire history of the Jewish people, until the Destruction of the Second Temple, there were only eighty-two high priests. Some of them, backed by the proliferating institution of the priesthood, exercised a power and influence in political-social matters as great and sometimes even greater than that of the king. That is the reason why some modern historians have been led to label the Jewish society that was established during the First and Second Commonwealth a "priest-state." Nonetheless, in the almost continuous struggle for power between the high priests and the kings, the royal despots of Israel and Judah quite frequently were able to force the high priests to serve as their pliant tools. Copying them, both the Seleucid king of Syria, Antiochus IV, and the various legates of Rome in Syria-Judea manipulated the office of the high priest with considerable political skill. In consequence, the history of the high priesthood in the Greco-Roman period was replete with scandals, with Temple "palace" intrigues, and even with outright murder of or by the high priest. With the exception of a small

Representation of the high priest, adorned with crown and wearing the prognosticating Urim and Thummim. (From an illuminated Hebrew Bible manuscript c. *1288. The British Museum.)*

number who were distinguished by high moral integrity and dedication in their roles as the religious leaders of the people, many of the high priests lost all odor of sanctity and disinterestedness. The Jewish masses transferred the reverence which should have been the due of the high priests to the Rabbinic teachers who had, collectively over centuries, created the ethical-religious literature called the Talmud.

It should be noted that the office of pope in the Roman Catholic hierarchy is closely modeled upon that of the high priest in Jerusalem.

See also PRIESTS; LEVITES; TEMPLE, THE; YOM KIPPUR.

HOLY DAYS

See the individual entries for information on these special days. SABBATH, THE. *See also* CHAZZAN; CHILDREN, BLESSING OF; HABDALAH; HAFTARAH; HYMNS OF THE SYNAGOGUE; KIDDUSH; PIRKE ABOT (*under* TALMUD, THE); SABBATH LIGHTS; SERMON; SHABBES GOY; SIDDUR; SIDRAH; TEITSCH-CHUMASH; TORAH-READING; ZEMIROT.

Festivals of Liberation.

CHANNUKAH (The Feast of Lights or Feast of Dedication). Marks the triumph of the Maccabean uprising. *See also* CHANNUKAH LAMP.

PASSOVER (PESACH). Marks the Exodus from Egypt. *See also* ART, CEREMONIAL; CHAD GADYA; KITTEL.

PURIM (The Feast of Lots). Marks the rout of Haman and the Persian enemies of the Jews. *See also* ART, CEREMONIAL; PURIM PLAY.

Commemorative Festivals.

HOSHANAH RABBAH. *See* HAKAFOT; SUCCOT.

SHABUOT (The Feast of Weeks). Marks the giving of the Torah to Israel at Mount Sinai.

SHEMINI ATZERET. *See* SUCCOT.

SIMCHAT TORAH. *See* HAKAFOT; SUCCOT.

SUCCOT (The Feast of Tabernacles). In Memory of Israel's forty years of wandering in the wilderness.

High Holy Days (YAMIM NORAIM: The Days of Awe and Repentance).

ROSH HASHANAH (The New Year).

YOM KIPPUR (The Day of Atonement).

Fast Days.

TISHAH B'AB (The Ninth of Ab). A day of mourning for the Destruction of the Temple.

YOM KIPPUR. *See above.*

See also FASTING AND FAST DAYS.

Nature Festivals.

CHAMISHAH ASAR BI'SHEBAT. (The Fifteenth of Shebat; the New Year of the Trees).

LAG B'OMER (The Counting of the Omer: The Students' Festival).

ROSH CHODESH (The Festival of the New Moon).

Pilgrim Festivals.

PASSOVER. *See above.*

SHABUOT. *See above.*

SUCCOT. *See above.*

HOLY LAND. *See* ERETZ YISRAEL.

HOLY SPIRIT (in Hebrew: RUACH HA-KODESH)

The Holy Spirit, according to Jewish tradition, rests upon the God-seeker as a sign of divine grace and love. It is but another form of the mediating powers of God in relation to man and is somewhat similar in meaning and function to the Shechinah (Divine Presence), with which mystical term it is sometimes used interchangeably in the Bible and—more frequently—in Rabbinic writings.

The concept of *ruach*—"spirit"—in Jewish religious thought is closely related to "breath," i.e., the breath of God. Because the breath of life is given by the Creator, and because all creatures that live, breathe, they are regarded as being animated by the Holy Spirit. "The Spirit of God hath made me, and the breath of the Almighty hath given me life." (Job 33:4.) And this divine emanation, stated a Mishnah Sage, does not recognize the barriers of formal religion, of nation, or of race; in the days of the Messiah, when redemption will come, the radiance of the Holy Spirit will rest equally upon Jews and Gentiles, upon men and women, upon free men and slaves.

By its power, said the Rabbis, the Hebrew Prophets were able to foretell future events and to give utterance to God's instructions and will. And when the well of prophetic inspiration had dried up with the last of the Minor Prophets and prophecy had ceased altogether in Israel, the Holy Spirit, comments the Talmud sadly, felt bereaved and returned to its abode in Heaven.

When the Christian religion was founded, among the many beliefs it borrowed from Judaism was that of the Holy Spirit, a term which appears about ninety times in the literature of the New Testament. However, in Christian theology the concept was accorded a far greater importance; it was made part of the Trinity, the Godhead in which the Father, the Son, and the Holy Ghost (i.e., the Holy Spirit) occupied equal positions.

Not at all surprisingly, the symbol of the Christian Holy Spirit is the same as that of the Jewish—a dove.

See also BAT KOL; SHECHINAH.

"HOLY VESSELS." *See* TORAH ORNAMENTS.

HOSHANAH RABBAH. *See* HAKAFOT; SUCCOT.

HOSPITALITY (in Hebrew: HACHNASAT ORCHIM)

The moral roots of hospitality may be found in mankind's practical need for survival. Because this need was such an urgent and ever present reality in the life of the Jew, he learned for his self-protection to develop the social virtue of mutual aid, of which hospitality to the poor and the wayfarer was but one among many facets.

The earliest Hebrews and Israelites, it is made clear in the Biblical chronicles, were "wandering Arameans"—pastoral nomads. The daily uncertainties of their existence, especially in the matter of finding shelter, food, and water with which to sustain life in the wilderness, led them, out of sheer self-interest, to the practice of hospitality. *Today* it was their obligation to provide for the simple physical needs of the stranger. But being rolling stones themselves, *tomorrow* it might very well be their turn, as footsore, hungry wayfarers, to have it extended to them.

Certainly, the practice of hospitality has never been a specifically Jewish tradition; it is also a characteristic of other peoples. The Bible records incident after incident in which warm and even life-saving hospitality was lavished by "heathens" on the nomadic heroes of Israel. The most notable examples of what the Talmud describes as acts of "loving-kindness" were those shown by the idolator Laban to the Patriarch Jacob, by the Midianite priest Jethro to Moses (who later became his son-in-law), and by Rahab to the men whom Joshua had sent "to spy out" the Land of Canaan.

Of course, the classic protagonist of the ideal of hospitality was the Patriarch Abraham. Each generation of Jews, for perhaps four thousand years of uninterrupted history, strove to model its attitude to the stranger, to the lonely, and to the rejected upon the pattern of Abraham's wholehearted hospitality. The mere fact that the ideal of hospitality sprang from the primeval conditions of nomadic tribalism made it endure so much the more as a powerful tradition in Jewish life—and this even after the pastoral economy had made way for the settled agricultural society during the First Commonwealth.

The need for fraternal helpfulness became even more urgent with the increase of social inequalities and the growth of poverty in the century just before the final fall of Judea. These and other aspects of mutual aid dominated the discussions of the Rabbinic teachers of ethics for generations. The effect of their opinions on the public practice of benevolence was startling, standing perhaps as the greatest milestone since the preachments of the Prophets in the evolution of Jewish social ethics.

Illustrative of the concern of Jews for their needy fellows was a touching custom observed widely in Jerusalem, and one that most likely also prevailed everywhere else in Israel at that time, for it is suggestive of a national tradition. It called for the householders to set out little flags, whenever eating-time arrived, as a method of informing all and sundry—the poor, the hungry, and any strangers who happened to be passing by—that the meal was about to be served and they were welcome to enter and take their places as guests. In the view of the Rabbinic Sages, it was most meritorious for would-be hosts to linger over their meals in order to give more time for the needy to seek them out.

The Talmud made the observation that it was not so much *how lavishly* or *how well* a host entertained his guest as *how much of himself* he put into the act. For this reason, the illustrious Tanna of the Mishnah, Akiba, would himself prepare the bed of a wayfarer in order to honor him. From this it can be deduced that the amenities of Jewish tradition and of the ethical teachings of the Rabbis did not make the course of the hospitable host any too easy. The fact is that they imposed on him a specified discipline of conduct—one far more thoroughgoing than what was required of his guest. First of all, he had to act graciously and display a cheerful countenance. At table, because of the Rabbinic reminder: "He who eats of another's bread is afraid to look at him," he had to show the utmost discretion and delicacy in order that he might not be suspected of stinting on the food or of "watching" his guest as he ate, lest thereby he embarrass him and curb his appetite.

Children, too, were taught not merely by the formal rules of etiquette, but by example, to behave with warm hospitality to the stranger and the needy person. They were instructed how to greet them at the door, and were rehearsed in the courteous manners with which they were to conduct them into the house, to set food before them, and, finally, to bed them.

Commencing with the Middle Ages, when persecution and innumerable vexations were set in full play against the Jews, it seems incontrovertible that, without the universal Jewish practice of hospitality, untold thousands of wayfarers, refugees in flight, victims of massacres, and the rootless and economically footloose, would have perished. Thus, in the blighted and impoverished Jewish communities of Eastern Europe, the custom arose centuries ago that every Sabbath Eve, upon the conclusion of the prayer service in the synagogue, the worshipers would invite any stranger to be their honored guest for the Sabbath and to draw warmth for himself from the warmth of the family circle. In this way they fulfilled the precept of the Mishnah Fathers that urged the righteous: "Let the poor be members of your household."

See also BROTHERHOOD; CHARITY; ETHICAL VALUES, JEWISH; FELLOWSHIP IN ISRAEL; HOSPITALS.

HOSPITALS (in Hebrew: S. BET CHOLIM)

The highest form of charity, the Sages of the Talmud taught, was "the benevolence of love," namely, the giving *of one's self* to the needy. Daily repeated in the service of the synagogue is this declaration from the Mishnah. "These are the things, the fruits of which a man enjoys in this world, while the stock remains for him in the World-to-Come." Among those "things" enumerated is "the benevolence of love" extended to the sick.

There is no evidence to show that hospitals existed among Jews of Biblical times to care for the sick. The institution most closely resembling them was the lazaretto for lepers, the Bet ha-Chofshit. King Azariah, when he was stricken with leprosy (as told in II Kings 15:5), and King Uzziah, likewise stricken (as we learn from II Chronicles 26:21), "dwelt in a house set apart."

Despite the paucity of documentation in the matter, it is plausible to conjecture there must have existed in post-Biblical times an institution of some kind for the lodging and care of the Jewish sick, especially of strangers, refugees in flight, and the homeless. This is clearly implied in one of the letters of St. Jerome (fourth century). Contradicting the claim which certain writers of Church history make—that the hospital was a Christian institution born of the compassion for suffering man inherent only in Christianity—is the description St. Jerome gives of Fabiola, a Christian matron of Rome, who had established a hospital for the poor. He praises her as "translating the terebinth of Abraham to Ausonian shores." (The Jewish Patriarch had built a hospice for travelers under a terebinth tree in Beersheba.)

The first clear reference made to the existence of Jewish hospitals in the Rhineland appeared in the town register of Cologne at the end of the eleventh century. And in Ratisbon, a deed drawn up in 1010 made reference to the existence there of a *domus hospitale judaeorum.* The existence of another hospital was recorded in Trier in 1422, one in Ulm in 1499, and in Berlin in the mid-fifteenth century. No description exists of this type of institution, but it was known as the Bet Hekdesh l'Aniim (The House Consecrated to the Needy), and was popularly referred to as "the Hekdesh." The Jewish communal inn or guesthouse, such as the Jews' Inn in England and the Auberge Juive in France, was usually the place where Jewish travelers lodged and the sick stayed, but private care for the latter was generally preferred.

It was the duty of every Jewish community, no matter how small, to provide lodging, food, and care for the sick, whether its own or strangers to the community. Where there was no Jews' Inn or Hekdesh—and small villages were often without them—the sick were assigned to the care of private families. (To care for the sick was a religious-social obligation mandatory for every Jew, rich and poor alike.) Of course, Jewish doctors rendered service without fee to the poor-sick, in accordance with Jewish traditional practice. Judah ibn Tibbon (the Provence, twelfth century) restated this general practice in the testament he wrote for the guidance of his young doctor-son: "You may accept fees from the rich, but heal the poor without charge." In times of epidemic, as during the Black Death, in 1348–49, Jews everywhere risked their lives in order to tend the stricken. It was part of the moral philosophy of Judaism.

The first hospitals—in the modern sense—for the Jewish sick were established fairly late, and by the Sefaradim. The Bet Cholim in London was founded in 1747 by Portuguese Jews; the Krankenhaus in Berlin in 1753; the Jewish Hospital in Metz at the close of the eighteenth century. In the United States, the earliest Jewish hospital was The Jews' Hospital, established in 1852 in New York; in 1871 its name was changed to Mount Sinai Hospital and it was transformed into a non-sectarian institution. In Philadelphia, the Hebrew Hospital (today part of the Albert Einstein Medical Center) was founded in 1864.

One reason for the establishment of such specifically Jewish institutions was revealed by a noted physician, Dr. Joshua I. Cohen, at the laying of the cornerstone of the Asylum for Israelites in Baltimore in 1866: "Many of us know the instances in which our poor co-religionists, stricken down upon the bed of sickness in the hands of strangers, have been greatly annoyed and their last moments embittered by the obtrusion of sentiments in the vain attempt to draw them away from the God of their fathers." There were, of course, other contributing reasons: In a Jewish hospital it was possible to supply kosher food to patients and to make readily available to them the rites and consolations of the Jewish religion. In addition, it gave Jewish physicians, who were often denied the right to practice in the general or Christian denominational hospitals, a place of their own.

Since the last century, Jewish hospitals have been established in many large cities in the United States, but they are operated on strictly non-sectarian lines. Their medical services and scientific research are rated among the best in the country.

"HOST DESECRATION" CALUMNIES

The eminent philosopher, Alfred North Whitehead, has observed: "Jewish history, beyond all histories, is composed of tragedies." There are so many tragedies that it is not possible to list them all; it is a grim chronicle written repetitiously, *ad nauseam*, in blood and anguish. The writing of history is usually not motivated in the historian by moral considerations or by a concern for establishing the truth but by partisan interest and bias chiefly. One can with justice state that the Jewish people's fate in the world has not received any but cavalier, indifferent, or the most cursory treatment in the works of most modern historians. As the Jewish-Austrian writer, Stefan Zweig, once mused bitterly: "History has no time to be just. . . . She keeps her eyes fixed on the victors, and leaves the vanquished in the shadows."

This axiomatic statement is fully corroborated by the number and variety of libels and myths that have been invented about the Jewish people in order to prove their inborn wickedness. Almost two thousand years ago, a Rabbinic Sage, full of the grief-consciousness of being a Jew, punned cheerlessly in Hebrew: "*Sinai* awakens *sina* [hatred]!" And there has been no time or place ever since which has been free of this hatred, for each generation has successively and successfully indoctrinated the next with its aberrated notions of and primitive emotions against the Jews.

One of the most persistent accusations leveled at Jews during the Middle Ages was that of Host-desecration. This charge quite obviously stemmed from the tragic fiction that the Jews were "Christ-killers." Not enough that they were blamed for the Crucifixion of Jesus: They were also condemned for supposedly nurturing in their hearts an undying hatred of him. This diabolical obsession gave the Jews (so reasoned their calumniators) a compulsion to continue ad infinitum *the act of Crucifixion* even if only in symbolic form; that is, by their secret desecration of the Host—the consecrated wafer which represents the body of Christ in the Roman Catholic mass. There are hundreds of instances on record, in practically every country in Europe in which Jews were accused of this weird anti-Christian crime. In almost every instance the holy wafer was presumed to have been stolen from the church altar by a Jew, or by a Christian whom the Jew had corrupted with money. Popular hysteria, fed by the fulminations of deranged bigots and self-serving demagogues, pictured the Jews as being in the midst of a fiendish orgy, gleefully and cruelly piercing, burning, and defiling the holy wafer, vicariously crucifying Jesus over and over again. And where else could it take place but in the holy sanctuary of the synagogue, right before the Ark of the Law! Some of the most estimable and best educated Christians considered Host-desecration to be a normative "sacred" Jewish rite!

The libel of Host-desecration first arose after Pope Innocent III, at the time of the Fourth Lateran Council in 1215, gave official recognition to the dogma of Transubstantiation. This doctrine meant that, when the Christian worshiper was drinking from the wine of the Holy Sacrament at church, he was considered to be drinking of the blood of Christ—in a symbolic sense, of course—and that by eating the holy wafer—the Host—which the priest put into his mouth, he was partaking of the very body of Christ.

The stock accusation by the priests was that the Jews "pierced" the holy wafer, i.e., inflicted the stigmata of crucifixion on the body of Christ with sharp knives, needles, or other pointed objects. It was the popular Christian belief that every time the Jews pierced the wafer it miraculously began to bleed, as if from the very wounds of the crucified Christ. Many of the clergy encouraged beliefs in this "miracle," averring that it was the intention of Heaven to bring the Jews' secret crime into the open so that stern punishment might be meted out to the enemies of Christ.

Whenever the charge of Host-desecration occurred, it inflamed Christian mobs to riot and resulted in a general massacre of the Jews, in burnings and mass-expulsions, in the collective payment by the Jewish community of enormous fines, and, more often than can be imagined, in the confiscation of Jewish possessions.

There were always those who had a great deal to gain from these calamities when they were visited upon the Jews. Quite often, on the site of a destroyed synagogue, a Christian chapel would be consecrated to commemorate the "miracle." This was the case with the Ratisbon synagogue (in Germany). In Deggendorf, a town on the Danube, following the alleged Host-desecration of 1337, the chapel and shrine of the Holy Sepulcher were erected on the site of the destroyed synagogue. Miraculous cures of the sick, the lame, and the halt were constantly being reported by imaginative pilgrims visiting this holy place. Perhaps the most impressive miracle of all was the official declaration issued by the ruling prince, Hein-

Woodcut depicting the popular Christian myth that Jews periodically and secretly performed in their synagogues the vicarious crucifixion of Jesus by piercing with knives the Hosts (Holy Communion wafers) stolen from churches. Lübeck, Germany, 1492.

Burning of Jews at Passau, Germany, in 1477, on the false accusation that they desecrated the Host. Contemporary woodcut. (RIGHT)

rich of Landshut (fourteenth century), which released all Christians in his domain from their legal obligation to pay their debts to Jews. Furthermore, the prince even lavished praise upon his subjects for "burning and exterminating our Jews of Deggendorf"—and himself devoutly pocketed the money of the massacred Jews and seized their possessions as an act of justice.

Probably the charge of Host-desecration which resulted in the greatest catastrophe occurred in 1298 in the Franconian town of Röttingen where the Jews were accused of stealing a holy wafer from the church altar and crushing it with diabolical glee in a mortar. Led by the master-builder Rindfleisch, who announced that God had chosen him to kill all the Jews, a mob howled its bloody way through all the Jewish communities of Germany and Austria, gathering like an avalanche numerous recruits as it rolled along. It was estimated that in a period of only six months, they wiped out 146 Jewish communities, killing, burning, raping, and pillaging as they went. More than 100,000 Jews were slain—a staggering number even for those days.

See also CHRISTIANITY, JEWISH ORIGINS OF; CHURCH AND PERSECUTION; CONVERSION OF JEWS; DISPUTATIONS, RELIGIOUS; FEUDAL SOCIETY, POSITION OF THE JEWS IN; KIDDUSH HA-SHEM; KOL NIDRE; MARRANOS AND THE INQUISITION; MASSACRES: THE CRUSADES, THE BLACK DEATH; MONEYLENDERS; NAZIS, THE; PERSECUTION IN "MODERN" DRESS; POGROMS IN SLAVIC LANDS; "RITUAL MURDER" SLANDERS; SHYLOCK MYTH, THE; WANDERING JEW.

HOUSE OF STUDY. *See* BET HA-MIDRASH.

HUMILITY. *See* ETHICAL VALUES, JEWISH.

HUSBANDS AND WIVES. *See* FAMILY RELATIONS, TRADITIONAL PATTERNS OF.

HYMNS OF THE SYNAGOGUE

It may come as a surprise to many to discover that much in Hebrew psalmody that is sung today in the synagogue was not originally composed by Jews. This bafflement becomes compounded when one considers the unusual musicality of the Jew, which has had full expression since the nineteenth century in all sectors of musical activity.

Perplexing too is the fact that during the ninth century Jews had already worked out a musical notation system of their own which they called *ta'amim,* or "accents." While it may have been primitive and inadequate as a system, it certainly was no less advanced than the Byzantine neumes employed as notations in the pre-medieval Church during the period when the musical culture of the Church was no richer in its resources than was the synagogue. As a matter of historic fact, the Church was then still holding on to some of the modal chants and intonations that had been inherited, as part of fixed tradition, from the early Jewish-Christian sectaries. The Gregorian chants, as even leading Christian musicologists concede, were close adaptations of the ancient Torah-chanting modes of the synagogue.

And yet, here is the puzzlement: Why was the liturgical music of the Church able to make such extraordinary progress in its development while that of the synagogue stood still?

During the Byzantine and Middle ages, Christian musical theorists were encouraged by the Church to develop the rudimentary notation system of neumes. Those efforts culminated in the notation system devised by Guido d'Arezzo, an eleventh-century Benedictine monk. By introducing the musical staff, steps and intervals, and *solfeggio,* he effected a cultural revolution of the first magnitude. From that time on, Western music, with giant strides, moved forward toward significant achievements.

Unfortunately, Jewish music did not fare so well. What were the reasons for its stagnation? The rabbinical humanist of sixteenth-century Venice, Leone da Modena, lamented: "It was our Exile, our Dispersion over the face of the globe, our incredible persecution which have depressed us, that necessarily have led to the decadence and to our neglect of the arts and the sciences. . . . Therefore, in this age we have been obliged to borrow from other peoples: to borrow their music, to adapt from it our religious chants."

One other significant reason for the anomalous position of Jewish liturgical music Leone failed to state. That was, that the unyielding granite of tradition upon which Jewish musical creativeness broke was the obsessive, self-macerating drive in the shattered Jewish people. In an excess of love and devotion—one so admirable in its moral sense yet so regrettable in its cultural consequences—the Jewish people imposed on itself until the coming of the Messiah "a perpetual mourning" for the Temple in Jerusalem that had been destroyed by the Romans in the year 70 C.E. The commemorative program of never ending grief brought from the very beginning a Rabbinic ban against all choral and instrumental music in any house of prayer. Why so? Because they had been the glory of the sanctuary on Mount Zion which had been laid waste. This prohibition will help explain why the art of music, on purely negativistic religious grounds, was allowed to languish and wither on the vine in the synagogue.

Thus, Jews were obliged to borrow or adapt their hymn tunes from the peoples in whose midst they lived. All kinds of tunes were grist for their musical mill: folk, drinking, and love songs; dances—even Church hymns. They would have adapted some of this music even under normal circumstances (many Christians hymn tunes were also the product of the natural process of cultural diffusion). But wasn't this *"borrowing"* an act of impiety? Many rabbis of this period seemed to think as Martin Luther did when, in drawing upon German folk-tunes for his church chorales, he said that he saw "no reason why the Devil should have all the beautiful tunes."

During the Middle Ages, this practice of "borrowing" music had created a source of intense anxiety for the rabbis. They perceived in it the seeds of religious assimilation, fearing that, through it some Jews would eventually end up in apostasy. Therefore, some of the leading religious authorities issued sharp strictures against the singing of Hebrew prayer texts to "profane" tunes.

However, apparently not all were agreed upon this matter, for we find an interesting notation in the medieval communal records of the Jews of Worms. The reference is to Simeon ben Isaac Abun (Simeon the Great), the famous liturgical poet-rabbi of the eleventh century. One night, in a dream, he had heard the strains of a haunting melody. When he awoke he said that he had heard a song of the angels. The fact that the tune had been "revealed" to him while asleep he interpreted as a command from Heaven to use it for a hymn that he had written. But strange to relate, the ethereal melody that the angels had sung for him in his sleep turned out to be the Church tune called "Magdala"!

One century later, Judah Chasid of Regensburg, the religious authority for the Jews of the Rhineland, forbade them to learn any hymn tunes from Christians or to teach them their own. There were Jews, he declared with a sense of shock, who were even being taught to sing Christian tunes from Church missals! At the very same time, and for the very same reasons, the Church authorities were distressed because they felt Christians were being undermined in their faith by singing Jewish tunes. Accordingly, in 1197, Odo, the Archbishop of the Rhineland, issued a ban against what apparently must have been a quite common practice: priests learning the songs of the synagogue from Jews.

A foremost contender against the invasion of the synagogue by the secular tunes of Mohammedans and Christians was the religious luminary of twelfth-century Spain, Maimonides. In his "Responsum on Music," he stated this rabbinical opinion: "Secular music is to be prohibited because it arouses lust and wickedness. Music of a religious character and music leading to ethical wisdom [alone] is permitted." The great difficulty of his position was: By what criteria of judgment could the sacred tunes be sifted from the profane (or secular)? These were the twin horns of the musical dilemma that frustrated all efforts by the rabbis to regulate synagogue song. And it was exactly the same problem that plagued the Church. But the Protestants, following the lead of Martin Luther, gave no thought whatsoever to the source or origin of the hymn tunes they "borrowed" or adapted.

What gave impetus to this "alien" trend in Jewish religious song was the renascence of Hebrew devotional poetry during the early Middle Ages. The art of versification was an indispensable cultural accomplishment for every young rabbi and scholar. The composition of thousands of devotional poems (in Hebrew: *piyyutim*, s. *piyyut*) called for popular tunes to match them, since they were intended for singing, but regional musical tastes also had to be considered; manifestly, the Jews of Medina and Baghdad had little in common with those of Avignon and Regensburg. And so, like Martin Luther, the rabbinical poets turned to the broad field of Christian and Moslem popular and folk music. Most of the tunes they borrowed, by the very nature of the folklore process of acculturation, they adapted for their own special needs, and in the reworking, endowed them with the indefinable ethnic group feeling and idiom which transformed them, to a certain extent, into what could justifiably be called "Jewish" melodies.

Rabbi Simon Duran (Majorca, 1361–1444) commented upon this custom of tune-adaptation, saying that, in each locality, the chazzanim (cantors) adapted tunes that were popular among the Gentiles in whose midst they lived. Certain vastly popular liturgical poems, like the Sabbath hymn, "Adon Olam" ("Lord of the World"), written by an unknown medieval poet, and "Lechah Dodi" ("Come My Beloved"), the inaugural hymn for the Eve of the Sabbath by Solomon Halevi Alkabez (Palestinian Cabalist, sixteenth century), have been sung to innumerable tunes by Jews in practically every part of the world. The latter hymn, it is claimed by the musicologist A. Z. Idelsohn (1882–1938), has been set to some two thousand different tunes!

In Spain, the hymn tunes adapted by the synagogue generally were Mohammedan-Moorish or Spanish-Christian in character. The original titles of some of those *canciones* can hardly give one a clue as to why they were selected to articulate the aspirations of the sin-obsessed and God-intoxicated Jews of the Middle Ages; for instance: "Señora" ("Madam"); "Tres Colores en Una" ("Three Colors in One"); "Porqué No Me Hablan?" ("Why Don't You Speak to Me?"). The Hebrew liturgists of France took over such a famous chanson of the troubadours as "L'Homme Armée" ("The Warrior") and the popular folk-tune "Les Filles de Tarascon" ("The Girls of Tarascon"). The naive melody customarily used for singing "Chad Gadya" ("An Only Kid"), the "nursery rhyme" that is included in the Seder, the Passover home prayer service, is of medieval Provençal origin.

The story was the same in Italy. The chazzanim in that country had a special fondness for the melodious *gondolieras* and swooning love songs, and these they somehow made compatible with sentiments of repentance and adoration of God. A rabbi of Verona in the eighteenth century expressed mortification over the fact that in Italian synagogues, the sacred Hebrew verses were being hymned to the melodies of lascivious songs and dances of tavern and carnival.

An objective examination of the old Ashkenazic hymns—some of which are still deeply loved by the Jewish masses—shows the clear influence of German folk song upon them. To cite just a few examples, the Channukah hymn "Ma'oz Tzur" ("Rock of Ages") that is sung by Jews all over the world is, in reality, but a reworking of Martin Luther's famous chorale, "Nun Freut euch Ihr lieben Christen" ("Rejoice, Dear Christians"), which was itself adapted by Luther from the German folk song, the "Benzenauer" battle hymn. And "Addir Hu," ("The Mighty One"), a hymn of the Passover Seder service, represents a thematic composite of two sixteenth-century popular German songs: "Marias Wiegenlied" ("Mary's Cradlesong") and "Pilgerlied" ("Pilgrim's Song"). The tune of the Sabbath and festival hymn "En Kelohenu" ("None Like Our God") is a rather insipid mid-nineteenth-century creation in German folk-song style.

To indicate how completely unconcerned the German chazzanim were with the musical sources that they tapped for the synagogue, one has only to listen to the Ashkenazic musical version of the Yom Kippur hymn, "El Norah Alilah" ("God, Mighty in Thy Deeds"). It recalls immediately Martin Luther's most celebrated hymn, "Eine Feste Burg ist unser Gott" ("A Mighty Fortress Is Our Lord").

There is no question but that, in addition to some of the above-mentioned tunes, which eventually became "traditional" and which the chazzanim in East European Slavic countries inherited for their psalmody, in more recent times they exploited still other non-Jewish musical sources. They adapted shepherd tunes from Walalchia, Polish folk-songs and dances, Ukrainian gypsy melodies, etc.

Jewish hymn melodies, indeed, were a strange conglomeration of dissimilarities—the result of a busy and often ingenious cooking in many musical pots. Sometimes, what came out of those pots was a tasteless stew; but just as often, in the magical process of transmutation wrought by the cultural genius of the people, some of the base metal which they had "borrowed" they turned into the pure gold of beauty and eloquence. One such example is the imperishable "Kol Nidre" hymn (*see* KOL NIDRE), chanted in all the synagogues of the world on the eve of Yom Kippur, the Day of Atonement. Another is the ancient Judean hymn which the kedoshim (those Jews perishing as martyrs at the hands of their enemies) always sang in a final affirmation of their faith before death. The twelfth-century poet-rabbi, Ephraim ben Jacob, in chronicling the martyrdom by burning in 1171 of more than thirty Jewish men and women at Blois, in France, noted: ". . . as the flames mounted high, the martyrs began to sing in unison a melody that began softly but ended with a full voice. The Christian people came and asked us: 'What kind of song is this for we have never heard such a sweet melody?' We knew it well, for it was the song: 'It is our duty to praise the Lord.'" ("Alenu le'Shabe'ach.")

See also BAAL TEFILLAH; CHAZZAN; KOL NIDRE; MUSIC, ANCIENT JEWISH; MUSICAL ACCENTS; PRAYER AND WORSHIP; ZEMIROT.

I

IMMIGRATION. *See* CONVERSION OF JEWS; FOLK MUSIC AND DANCE; HEBREW LITERATURE, MODERN; KIBBUTZ; MARRANOS AND THE INQUISITION; MASSACRES; PERSECUTION IN "MODERN DRESS"; POGROMS IN SLAVIC LANDS; YIDDISH LITERATURE, MODERN; ZIONISM.

IMMORTALITY

Immortality is a central doctrine in Jewish religious belief.

Without it, the allied beliefs of the Resurrection, Reward and Punishment, and of the World-to-Come could not hold any meaning. The Bible itself affords only a few clues to its historic development, although we do find the germ of the idea that the soul survives after death in various Scriptural passages, especially in Psalms.

There is little question but that Jews must have been influenced in their thinking concerning life beyond the grave by the Egyptians of Hellenistic times in Alexandria, and by the Persians during the period of the Captivity in Babylonia. But apparently it was not until the Second Temple period (perhaps during the third or fourth century B.C.E.) that a belief in the soul's immortality took firm root, for, presumably, this belief was not in currency among Jews when the Book of Job was written. This we can see in the fact that, in his direst tribulations, the anguished Job is not even offered by his argumentative friends the solace and the hope of the soul's immortality and the reward of the just in the World-to-Come to compensate for the unmerited sufferings he had to endure in life.

Moses ben Nachman (Nachmanides) of Catalonia, a foremost religious authority of the thirteenth century, extended this solace and hope of immortality to the persecuted Jews of his day. The soul of man—"the lamp of God"—said he, could never go out no matter what happened to the body. It was part of the soul of God; it belonged to Him, and to Him alone it had to return. By the Will of God it was fashioned in immortality, because, for Israel's sake and for that of all mankind, it had to aspire continuously, without rest and without abatement, to an ever higher and purer form of existence. Said the Sages: "The righteous climb from strength to strength, from one stage of existence to an ever higher one."

Centuries before Nachmanides, the Rabbinic teachers of Judea and Babylonia had speculated on the course the soul had to take in its climb to perfection. "The Talmidai Chachamim [the Disciples of the Wise]," wrote the Talmud, "find rest neither in this world nor in the World-to-Come." The personal identity of the soul, they stated, always remains, even after death and the falling away of the body. Its individual destiny continues on unbroken, being determined only by the actions of the person himself, involving his whole being, both body and soul. Whatever reward or punishment is to be the lot of the individual soul will be determined on the Day of Judgment by the Tribunal of Heaven.

The burning question for the religious Jew always was: In what state would God find his soul when it stood before the Judgment Seat in the End of Days? Therefore, the ancient Midrash exhorted man to remember: "Even as the soul is pure when it enters the body, in the very same condition of purity must man return it to his Creator." "Purity" was but another way of saying "holiness," and "holiness" was a principal attribute of God. All-pervasive in Jewish religious thinking and living was the ideal of purity-holiness.

See also RESURRECTION; REWARD AND PUNISHMENT; SOUL, THE; WORLD-TO-COME.

IN-LAWS. *See* FAMILY RELATIONS, TRADITIONAL PATTERNS OF.

INQUISITION. *See* CONVERSION OF JEWS; MARRANOS AND THE INQUISITION.

INTERMARRIAGE

The notion that there is such a biological condition as "racial purity"—a conceit which not a few Jews would like to believe in as representing one of the proofs of the moral incorruptability of the Jew and of his devotion to his in-group Jewish identity—has been proven by historians and anthropologists to be completely a myth. As long ago as the Captivity in Babylonia, in the fifth century B.C.E., the Prophet Ezekiel tried to refresh the hazy recollection of those among his fellow Jews who were taking pride in their alleged superiority with this satirical reminder: "Thus saith the Lord God unto Jerusalem: 'Thine origin and thy nativity is of the land of the Canaanite; the Amorite was thy father, and thy mother was a Hittite.'" (Ezekiel 16:3.)

It must be remembered that if Mosaic Law was opposed to mixed marriages, it was not on biologic but on purely religious grounds; the Jews were motivated by the fear that, through intermarriage, many of them would be absorbed into the alien religions of their mates. Stringent, therefore, are the prohibitions in the Bible, and also in the Talmud, against intermarriage. Possibly the strongest is that given in Deuteronomy 7:1–3; it enjoins the Israelite, prior to his conquest of Canaan, against choosing a mate belonging to any of the tribal peoples among whom he is destined to live. Singled out for particular mention are the Hittites, the Girgashites, the Amorites, the Canaanites, the Perizzites, the Hivites, and the Jebusites. ". . . Neither shalt thou make marriages with them: thy daughter thou shalt not give unto his son, nor his daughter shalt thou take unto thy son." The reason for this prohibition was because (warned God) "he [namely, the alien peoples] will turn away thy sons from following Me, that they may serve other gods."

Despite this Scriptural ban, the very thing that it aimed to avoid came to pass. Once the Israelites had conquered Canaan, they proceeded to take mates from among the indigenous tribes with whom they mingled. From an ethnic point of view, this was not unnatural, for the non-Israelites happened to be closely related to their conquerors in language, culture, and folkways.

One has only to read the earlier Biblical narratives to discover with what matter of factness the Israelite chroniclers made mention of these mixed marriages into which even some of the most illustrious among their people had entered. To cite just a few notable instances: The Patriarch Abraham, who is traditionally regarded as "the first Jew," wedded the Egyptian woman Hagar; his grandson Jacob took two non-Jewish wives, Bilhah and Zilpah; Jacob's sons Reuben, Simeon, and Judah married Canaanite women. Of his other sons, Dan married a Moabite, Zebulon a Midianite, and Joseph—according to tradition—the Egyptian woman Asenath. To understand even more the widespread custom of intermarriage it is necessary to mention that the greatest Israelite of all, Moses, had married Zipporah, the daughter of the Midianite priest and idolator Jethro.

Even centuries of collective ethnic living *as Israelites* in their historic homeland did not seem to alter this common practice of intermarriage. King David married Maccah, daughter of the king of Geshur, and she bore him Absalom. David also wedded Bathsheba, the former wife of Uriah the Hittite, and she was probably no Israelite herself. She became the mother of Solomon.

Of all worthies in the polygamous Jewish society of those times, Solomon was by far the most intermarried. Censorious and indignant sounds the lament of the latter-day Biblical chronicler in noting these dubious marital activities of the "Wise King," for he "loved many foreign women, besides the daughter of Pharoah, women of the Moabites, Ammonites, Edomites, Zidonians and Hittites; of the nations concerning which the Lord said unto the children of Israel: 'Ye shall not go among them, neither shall they come among you; for surely they will turn away your heart after their gods; Solomon did cleave unto these in love." (I Kings 11:1-2.)

And so it is to be seen that even the sacrosanct force of the Law of Moses and the additional pressures for conforming to the rigorous discipline of tribal custom were insufficient to curb the inclinations of many of the Israelites toward other peoples when they were choosing mates for themselves. It was only at a much later time, when an authoritarian theocracy had been imposed upon the Jewish people by Ezra the Scribe, in the fifth century B.C.E., that mixed marriages almost ceased. This occurred, according to the Biblical account, with dramatic suddenness, under circumstances that were indeed remarkable and without precedent in Jewish history.

For when Ezra led his sizable contingent of returning exiles from Babylonia to Jerusalem in 458 B.C.E. he found that, in little more than a century, not only many plain Jewish folk but also priests and Levites had intermarried with Gentile women ". . . so that the holy seed had mingled themselves with the people of the land." Because of this—which Ezra considered an overwhelming national catastrophe—he went into mourning, as for the dead. He rent his garments, plucked out the hair of his beard and head, and he lamented. He then called upon the people assembled in the Temple court to repeat after him this solemn oath: "to put away all the [non-Jewish] wives and such [children] as are born of them." (Ezra 10:3.)

This drastic measure, which was harshly followed through among thousands of intermarried families, had the most shocking effect on the whole people. There was a great outcry against Ezra's inhumanity, which he had sanctified by invoking the name of God. Many Jews were driven out of the land of Judah. Others fled for refuge to Samaria, where they joined the rejected sectarian Samaritans and became, they and their descendants, separated from the Jewish people forever. Needless to say, Ezra's horror of mixed marriages was soon translated into canon law and endured for a long time. Such marriages were afterward contracted under penalty of death or, at best, banishment from Judah.

The aversion to intermarriage grew into a deeply rooted tradition, and although it lapsed in the assimilationist climate of Hellenistic-Jewish society, it came militantly to life again during the Middle Ages in Europe, Africa, and Asia. To be sure, intermarriages did take place on a massive scale in the Greco-Roman period. Then, through missionary zeal, thousands upon thousands of converts were won over to the Jewish religion, and there was a great increase in the Jewish population because of the children that resulted from these intermarriages.

With the ascendancy of Christianity, and, later, during the early Middle Ages in Europe, intermarriages between Jews and Christians must have occurred far more frequently than is generally suspected. This is not a verifiable fact but it can be guessed at from the numerous enactments of the rabbinic authorities as well as from the decrees issued by the bishops of the Church sternly forbidding mixed marriages as constituting not only a grave sin but a crime. In many places, Christian authorities made this "crime" punishable by death. The harsh edicts repeatedly issued against intermarriage with Jews by the Church councils, beginning with that of Chalcedon in 388, remain eloquent testimony to this.

With the increasing emancipation of the Jew from his ghetto isolation and his gradual integration into Western life and culture in the nineteenth century, the rate of intermarriage once more was on the ascendancy. It increased from decade to decade, but particularly in France, Germany, Austria, Switzerland, Italy, and the Scandinavian countries. The noted Jewish religious scholar, Solomon Schechter (1850–1915), once commented with bitter irony on the alleged fact that the number of Jews lost to their religion and people by voluntary intermarriage was greater than the number driven to the baptismal font by persecution or the threat of immediate death. In Germany, during the decades before the advent of Hitler and the Nazis, intermarriage had been taking place on a large scale, especially among Jews living in urban centers. In Berlin alone more than half of all marriages contracted by Jews were with Gentiles. Although statistics on this subject are a slender reed on which to rest any assumption, it is well known that in the United States also, the rate of mixed marriages has been steadily rising. This fact is even truer of the Soviet Union and other Communist countries, where the grip of the Jewish religion and the Jewish identity has been rapidly weakening.

Everywhere, except in the State of Israel, Jewish religious and cultural identities have, in varying degree, been steadily loosening, and the problem of intermarriage is one that has been perturbing Jewish communities and religious leaders everywhere. Orthodox Jews have taken a militant stand against mixed marriages. The strict traditionalists find Gentile mates unacceptable even if they are willing to become converts to Judaism. A representative view on this by Orthodoxy is that expressed by the late Chief Rabbi of England, J. H. Hertz (1872–1946): "In our days, in conditions that are world's asunder from those in Canaan of old, intermarriage is no less fatal to the continued existence of Israel."

However, a new and perhaps more realistic attitude has been developing in late years on this question. The Jewish religious leadership in the United States, including Orthodox, Conservative, and Reform, has begun to realize that mixed marriages in this modern age cannot be prevented simply by invoking religious prohibitions or by emotional appeals to group loyalty. Consequently, it has been seeking for a strategic position from which to channelize the trend of fusion *not away from* the Jewish fold but *into it.*

The year 1959 was witness to an extraordinary historical anachronism: the launching of a Jewish missionary movement in Chicago. Some Jewish critics of this effort thought that this might lead to even more intermarriages. But its proponents stoutly maintained that, inasmuch as the *sine qua non* for these intermarriages was prior conversion to the Jewish faith by the Gentile mate, all the gain of the Jewish missionary effort was for Judaism and the Jewish people. Not since the great missionary movement in Hellenistic days had Jews taken up religious propaganda for gaining new adherents.

In addition to seeking converts, its spokesmen averred, the new movement had still another aim: to inform non-Jews of the fundamental principles of the Jewish religion concerning God, man, and society as they are taught in the Bible and in Jewish tradition. Thus the end goal was to "unite all the people of the world in a commitment to the one Universal God and the Brotherhood of Man." Here is found once more a recapitulation of the ancient Jewish belief in its religious-historic mission of universalism, of bringing all the peoples of the earth into one fold—of transforming the synagogue into "a house of prayer for all peoples."

See also MISSIONARIES, JEWISH.

INTOXICATION

The history of the Jews reveals that they have never been teetotalers. But neither have they been drunkards. In Rabbinic Judaism, the Golden Mean (*see* GOLDEN MEAN, THE RABBINIC) was ever held up as an ideal for the guidance of sensual appetites. True, there were always ascetics among Jews—the ancient Nazarites, for example—who regarded pleasure, and strong drink in particular, as a snare of Satan.

Folk sayings derogatory of drink are found frequently in Rabbinic literature: "Wine brings lamentation into the world." "Wine ends in blood." "The [forbidden] tree from which Adam ate was the grapevine, for there is nothing which brings trouble upon a man as much as wine."

However, drink in moderation found greater support than abstention from drink among the Talmudic Sages. They did not merely tolerate a little drink; in fact, they encouraged it. "There is no gaiety without wine." "Chief of all medicines am I, Wine."

Nonetheless, religious teachers did frown upon the winebibber. "The prayer of the drunkard is an abomination," was one Rabbinic opinion.

If drink in excess was thought bad for the man, it was deemed altogether unthinkable for the woman. "One cup of wine is good for a woman. Two degrade her. Three make her act lewdly. Four cause her to lose all self-respect and her sense of shame."

An ancient Jewish legend relates how the Prophet Elijah appeared once in disguise before a rabbi who, ostensibly, had been drinking. He chided him: "Don't get drunk, and you won't fall into sin."

It has been widely, and even favorably, commented upon that there are fewer drunkards to be found among Jews than among other peoples. This fact testifies to the relatively greater puritanical character of Jewish life and upbringing, and to the abstemious habits Jews have developed in keeping with the teachings of the Jewish religion. Nevertheless, this holds less true today than it did a generation or two ago, when Jews were not so assimilated as they are today. In our general culture of today it is perhaps inevitable that the traditional Jewish mores should break down or, at best, be revised to suit the new circumstances. The change has come about in a natural way. The social and business requirements of middle-class and professional Jews, for example, have forced them to conform with the general social patterns of Gentile behavior and modes of entertainment, including drinking. They are, accordingly, consuming greater amounts of intoxicating drinks than ever before. The same trend, if to a much lesser degree, is also observable among Jewish workers and small shopkeepers.

ISLAM, ANTI-SEMITISM IN. *See* ISLAM, JEWISH ORIGINS OF

ISLAM, JEWISH ORIGINS OF

Like Christianity, the religion of the Mohammedans, which bears the name of Islam (meaning, in Arabic, "submission to the Will of God"), is also to be considered, in its way, a daughter-religion of Judaism. The reasons for Mohammed's selection of the Jewish religion to serve as the model, inspiration, and source from which to draw for his new monotheistic faith the seminal ideas–its doctrines, beliefs, rites, laws, ceremonials, institutions, and even nomenclature–will always appear strange and not entirely clear. Writers about Islam have endlessly conjectured about his reasons, but never conclusively, for they are anomalous. Christianity was, so to speak, "biologically" a daughter-religion of Judaism that sprang out of its loins in a natural way, for its founder had been a Jew, but what could attract an illiterate camel-driver of Mecca, even though he was a genius in organization and leadership, to the Jewish religion so he would wish to adopt it, *and the Jews with it?* An astonishing situation, indeed, regardless of whether it was brought about by religious conviction in Mohammed or, as some cynics maintain, from cunning expediency.

The historic circumstances early in the seventh century C.E., preparatory to Mohammed's intended embrace of Jews and Judaism, are very odd. When the Prophet of Allah tried to interest his fellow Arabs of Mecca in Allah and in his own eminence as Allah's Prophet they only laughed at him, and he had to run for his life to Medina. In that chief city of Arabia were living numerous Jews, who formed the most cultured and influential section of the population. Mohammed had counted, apparently wrongly, that a great number of them would eagerly flock to his standard and accept him as the Prophet of Allah since, as he saw it, they, too as well as he, were following the same God and religion. He preached to them as a "prophet" of Israel in a grandiloquent style that he assumed was rabbinical. But when the Jews of Medina, close knit in their powerful tribal organization of Bani Koreish and Bani Koreiza, proceeded to expose his brand of Torah as ignorant and fraudulent twaddle, the Prophet of Allah turned furiously away from them and against them with the passionate vehemence of a rejected suitor.

The English scholar of Islam, Alfred Guillaume, has remarked how astonishingly obsessed the Koran shows Mohammed to have been with the Jews: "He can never let them alone: appeal, argument, rebuke, denunciation, and cursing are successively addressed to them. They are never to be ignored."

In the end, Mohammed declared a holy war–a jihad–against the Jews. He avenged himself upon them with fire and sword for the ridicule they had heaped upon him. Although the Jewish settlements in the northern oases of Arabia were numerous and strongly fortified, he, nonetheless, managed to overcome them by a combination of craft and ferocious attack, forcing many thousands of Jews to dig their own graves in long trenches, where they were decapitated and mutilated.

It is intriguing, on perusing the early suras or verse chapters in the Koran (its name means, in Arabic, "Proclamation") that Mohammed, during the trying years in Mecca, had dictated to his secretary, Zayyid (for he himself could not write), to find hardly a trace of Jewish influence in them. But since the Koran charts, as it progresses, a telltale course of the different stages of development in the Prophet's thinking, it shows that his preoccupation with Judaism and his wooing of the Jews occurred during his fateful residence in Medina.

On objective considerations, it can be concluded that Islam is a purer form of monotheism than Christianity. Islam's proclamation incessantly rings out: *La illaha illa Allah!*–"There is no god but God!" Although the Prophet of God wooed the Christians of Arabia after the Jews had snubbed him (he even included Jesus in his variegated company of the "true prophets" of Allah, and declared the Gospels to be sacred writings for the Mohammedan), he, nevertheless, attacked the Trinitarians (Christians who worshiped "the Father, the Son, and the Holy Ghost") as idolators; he denied flatly that Jesus was "the begotten son of God." He constantly went out of his way to stress the Oneness of Allah.

> God is One,
> The Self-Existent;
> He begets not and is not begotten.

The Islamic confession of faith is a free adaptation of the Hebrew Shema: "Hear, O Israel, the Lord our God the Lord is One!" The Arabic Shahadah proclaims in much the same manner and spirit: "There is no god but Allah, and Mohammed is his Prophet . . . I believe in Allah, in His angels, in His Scriptures, in His Prophets, in the future life, in the divine decree [in respect to] the good as well as [to] the bad, and in the Resurrection of the dead."

Mohammed also believed in the imminence of the Day of Judgment (in Hebrew: *Yom ha-Din;* he called it [in Arabic] *Yaum al-Din*). He believed in Paradise and in its fleshly rewards, in Gehinnom (Gehenna) and in its fiery pits. Like the Providence of God over Israel, the Providence of Allah was ever spread out protectingly over the Mohammedan. The Jew eulogized God in Hebrew as *El Rachamim*—"God the Compassionate"; Allah was likewise described in Arabic as *Al-Rachim*—"the Compassionate." The sacred formula of Islam, recited tirelessly before each of the 114 suras of the Koran, runs: "In the name of Allah, the Compassionate, the Merciful . . ." One might say He was the same God but in another, although a cognate, language.

At first, Mohammed preached that the Hebrew "Taurat"—i.e., the Torah—was also to be revered as the Scriptures of Islam, and that the Koran, which Allah had revealed to him through the Angel Gabriel, was just an integral part of the Taurat. As in Judaism, there existed in Islam a duality of revelation and law. Furthermore, the complementary relationship between Bible and Mishnah (the code of Oral Tradition) was equated in Islam by the Koran and Hadith (oral tradition)—a resemblance hardly to be considered a mere coincidence. To go one step beyond this unavoidable comparison: Even as there have been thousands of Hebrew commentaries written on the Bible, so too have there been written thousands of Arabic commentaries on the Koran. The dedicated study of the Koran and of the traditions of Islam has always been a marked characteristic of Mohammedan ecclesiastics: mullahs, theologians, and scholars, although never as universal an activity as it has been among Jews in the past.

Mohammed drew Islam's doctrines, traditions, and laws from the chief Jewish sources—from the Bible, the Apocrypha, and the Talmud—but he did not do so directly, only tangentially and folkloristically, for, it must be recalled, *Mohammed could not read.* He probably had gained his smattering of Jewish knowledge from the Jews of Medina chiefly from listening to their moralistic anecdotes about the Rabbinic Sages culled from the Agada and to the legends and elaborations from the Midrash about the Biblical eminences. He apparently was not a too careful listener, or his memory was faulty, because much that he heard became confused in his mind and, in his later reworking of these tales they issued forth in a garbled and sometimes weird hodge-podge.

Like Jesus before him, Mohammed had not the slightest intention of setting out deliberately to found a new religion. He declared that there was only one true religion, and it had been in existence since the beginning of Creation; that it had been revealed to all the Prophets since Adam (the latter, too, he included among the Prophets). When the Jews of Medina, as they listened to his preaching, asked him to tell them succinctly what he believed in, Mohammed answered: "We believe in God, and in what has been revealed to us [i.e., the Koran], and in what was revealed to Abraham and Ishmael and Isaac and Jacob and in the Twelve Tribes, and in what was given to Moses and to Jesus, and what was given to the Prophets by their Lord. We make no difference between them, and we are resigned to Him."

The Koran makes constant use of Biblical materials, incidents, legends, and personalities. The stories of the Pentateuch and the legends about the Prophets, as retold in the Midrash, furnished Mohammed with the necessary springboards for the projection of his own religious views and moral values. He dwells on the story of Creation, Adam and Eve in the Garden of Eden and their Fall, Cain and the murder of Abel, the Flood and Noah and the Ark, Abraham and the idols, the destruction of Sodom, Ishmael and the Angel, Joseph and his brothers, etc.

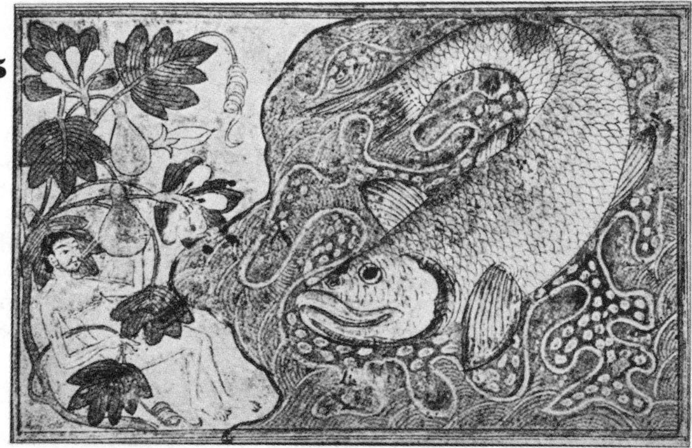

The Biblical legend of Jonah and the whale in a Mohammedan graphic description, following the story told in Suras 10, 37, and 68 of the Koran. (From an Arabic manuscript of 1306 in the Edinburgh University Library.)

The strict monotheism of Mohammed and Islam is visible in this motto on the walls of the Alhambra; "Wa la Ghalib ila Allah!"—"There is no king but God!" (From Granada, Past and Bygone, *by A. F. Calvert, London.)*

In the process of reworking the materials, however, the events and personalities became confused for him. The story of the Bondage in Egypt and of the Exodus is recounted in sura 28 of the Koran in an almost comical jumble. There Haman is described as Pharaoh's minister; Moses is hopelessly confused with Jacob, and works for eight years to win his wife; furthermore, Pharaoh commands the Israelite slaves to make bricks "so that I may make a lofty building, so as to become acquainted with the God of Moses," to which Mohammed hastens to add his own opinion about the king of Egypt: "though, indeed, I think he is a liar." The same deficient memory the Prophet also strained on behalf of Miriam, the sister of Moses; he discovers her suddenly as "the mother of Jesus."

But, however mistaken he might have been about Biblical details, Mohammed had the certainty that he himself was the last and the greatest of all the Prophets. He had the conviction that his mission to the world had been divinely appointed by Allah. To Omar, who later succeeded him as caliph of Islam, he once modestly confided: "If Moses were alive and knew my prophecy, he would follow me."

In religious laws, institutions, ceremonials, rites, and customs, Islam, too, drew from the Jewish reservoir of the Pentateuch, Talmud, and later traditions. Concerning the character and the institutions of the Mosque, it can be said that the Synagogue left a deeper mark on it than it had on the Church. This definitely has reference to Islamic prayer: Its all-absorbing concentration, called *niyya* in Arabic, was the equivalent of the Hebrew kavanah—the ecstatic elevation of the soul while wrapped in supplication and communion with the Deity. The evening service of the mosque, for example, is called Maghrib, resembling the Hebrew Maariv. The leader of prayer for the Islamic congregation had the identical mission of the Jewish shaliach tzibbur; he too was "the messenger of the congregation," interceding with God for the worshippers and the Mohammedan congregational responses were also similar to those in the synagogue service.

At the beginning of his preaching in Medina, obviously having his gaining the goodwill of the Jews in mind, Mohammed had chosen Jerusalem as his "holy city" and, at the direction of the Angel Gabriel, Allah's personal messenger, he made that city his *Kibla*–i.e., the direction in which he and all the faithful turned their faces while at prayer. But when the Jews of Medina scorned him, the Angel Gabriel paid him opportunely another visit and ordered him to change the *Kibla* from Jerusalem to Mecca!

The spiritual-religious guise of the rabbi is discernible underneath the turban of the Islamic mullah, mufti, and imam. They also issue decisions and opinions on matters of Islamic law; and just like the rabbis, they have developed a dialectical casuistry in their reasoning. The early Arab theologians issued Responsa on canon law in frank imitation of the Babylonian Geonim (*See* GEONIM; RABBINICAL DECISIONS). This similarity in approach and method to legal-theological problems–for both were produced by the necessity of reconciling contradictions and inconsistencies appearing in the scriptural texts of Bible or Koran–led to a similar intellectual development for both during the Byzantine and Middle Ages, when they lived in geographical and cultural contiguity in Islamic countries (*see* ARABIC-JEWISH "GOLDEN AGE").

There is also a strong similarity in the dietary laws of the two religions; both make a distinction between "clean" and "unclean" animals. Swine's flesh is sternly forbidden to Mohammedans as it is to Jews; so, also, is the drinking of blood and the eating of the flesh of animals that have been strangled, wounded, accidentally killed, or stricken with illness. Some of the laws and regulations that govern Jewish shechitah (ritual slaughtering) also apply to Mohammedans; and among the latter, Allah's name must be uttered before severing the jugular vein of the animal.

Pilgrimages, fasting, and the giving of charity have been highly regarded traditionally by both Jews and Mohammedans. Pilgrimages to Mecca were merely a substitution for the three "pilgrim" festivals to Jerusalem that Jews used to make in Temple days. To add a patina of antiquity and sanctity to the pilgrimage to Mecca, Mohammed declared that the *Kaaba,* the sanctuary in that city, had been built by none else than the Patriarch Abraham. At first Mohammed had instituted a Day of Atonement; he called it *Ashura* and, very appropriately, it was observed, like the Jewish Yom Kippur, on the tenth day of the Hebrew month of Tishri. But when he failed to induce the Jews to accept him as the Prophet of God, he angrily abolished Ashura. Thenceforth, all fasting was transferred to the entire pilgrimage month of Ramadhan, when the faithful, still following the Jewish custom, abstain from food and drink from sunrise to sunset each day but feast at night.

There can be no end to the religious-cultural inventory in Islam of Jewish impact and borrowing. There is the doctrine of Repentance and Atonement which holds a position of centrality in both faiths. The Hebrew doctrine of Zechut Abot (Merit of the Fathers, *which see*) also became a revered tradition among the Mohammedans. Like the Jews, the Mohammedans too observe the laws of purity and "cleanliness" derived from the Levitical regulations in the Bible. Arabs also practice circumcision, and as among the Jews, this rite is performed at birth and not at puberty, as it was among other ancient peoples and as it is among some primitive tribes today as a rite of initiation into manhood.

It is worth noting that there is ritual washing and bathing among Mohammedans, as there is among Orthodox Jews. And, finally, the marriage and divorce laws of Islam are practically all derived from their Jewish counterparts, although the attitude of Jews toward the woman and their treatment of her have been more moral, more humane, and on a more advanced plane.

Anti-Semitism in Islam. It will sound paradoxical to apply the term "anti-Semites" to the Arabs, who regard themselves as descendants of Abraham's son Ishmael, for this view makes them "blood relations" of the Jews. Moreover, Arabs are linguistically and ethnically as Semitic as the Jews. But the causes and traditions for their animus against their Jewish "cousins" differ from those found in the anti-Semitic syndrome of Christians. Although the Jews were not considered "Mohammed-killers," the Arabs' hostility to them was based on the fact that they had spurned Mohammed as the Prophet of God, and for that reason he waged a jihad or holy war against them. It is reasonable to suppose, of course, that the Christian example of the persecution of the Jews–and the reasons and myths invented to justify it–also percolated to a degree into Islamic folk-belief and practice, but most of the time the animus was expressed in a much milder form than by Christians; the Mohammedans and the Jews had a lot more in common religiously and culturally.

The religious sanction for disliking Jews was first given by the Prophet of Allah himself: He charged them, in the early suras of the Koran, with hating "true believers," and therefore he counseled his adherents to hold the Jews at arm's length. The establishment of the segregated mellah (the Arabic equivalent of the European ghetto) was one of the ultimate consequences of this tension; the tradition became fixed among the faithful that "God's anger rests" on the Jews.

But after Islam's great triumphs in the seventh century, the Prophet advised a gentler and more tolerant attitude toward both Jew and Christian: "Whoever wrongs a Christian or a Jew, against him shall I myself appear to accuse on Judgment Day." From then on, the treatment of Jews by the Arabs even increased in mildness until the twelfth century.

Nonetheless, Mohammed had many grievances against the Jews. Principally, he accused them of falsification in the Hebrew text of the Bible; supposedly, they had suppressed passages which predicted his coming as the Prophet of God. What he may have had in mind was the Christian theologian's claim that certain verses in Isaiah had foretold the Messianic mission of Jesus, and so he felt a grievous lack of a like distinction for himself.

Among the "traditions" handed down through the centuries is one which holds that in the End of Days the "true believers" will battle the Jews wherever they will find them. Cunningly, the Jews will then hide behind rocks. Thereupon the rocks will cry out warningly to the faithful of Allah: "O Muslim, a Jew is hiding behind me! Strike him dead!"

Echoing a mythic belief held by Christians in the Middle Ages about Jewish evil intentions toward them, the Arabs have been fond of saying: "Never is a Jew alone with a Muslim without his planning how he might kill him." Mohammed himself, perhaps smarting from the memory of the ridicule the Jews had heaped on his "rabbinical" sermons, which he delivered to them in Medina, accused the Jews of employing circumlocutions or slurring Arabic expressions to mask their derision for Islam and all true believers. One remarkable example he gave: When the Jews give the customary greeting to an Arab–"*Salaam alaykum!*" ("Peace to you!")–they mumble it quickly, but what they are actually saying is "*Saam alaykum!*" ("Poison to you!")

There have occurred–since Mohammed had set the stage for them–innumerable atrocities against the Jews in Arab lands: torture, imprisonment, beatings, rape, murder, robbery, mutilation, and a great many massacres far too gruesome to describe. In recent decades, with the emergence of independent Arab states cutting loose from the colonial oppression of centuries, the wild explosions of nationalism ac companying the process of liberation have created a climate of crisis and fear for Jews in those countries. The chief source of hostility has not been religious or ethnic, but *political*—the war to the death proclaimed by the leaders of Arab countries on Zionism and the State of Israel. One result of this anti-Jewish persecution and the feeling of insecurity it has engendered has been the mass emigration of Jews from Arab countries, and the principal beneficiary of this new exodus has been Israel, where hundreds of thousands of Jews have been settled since 1948.

See also ANIMALS, "CLEAN" AND "UNCLEAN"; ANTI-SEMITISM; BIBLE, THE; CHRISTIANITY, JEWISH ORIGINS OF; COMMENTARIES, RABBINICAL; DIETARY LAWS; DIVORCE; MARRIAGE; MONOTHEISM; PRAYER AND WORSHIP; SYNAGOGUE, THE; TALMUD, THE; TORAH-READING; TORAH STUDY.

ISRAEL, CHILDREN OF. *See* CHOSEN PEOPLE, THE; "HEBREWS," "ISRAELITES," "JEWS."

ISRAEL, FELLOWSHIP IN. *See* FELLOWSHIP IN ISRAEL.

ISRAEL, LAND OF. *See* ERETZ YISRAEL.

ISRAEL, LOVE FOR. *See* ERETZ YISRAEL.

ISRAEL, STATE OF. *See* ZIONISM.

ISRAEL, UNITY OF. *See* UNITY OF ISRAEL.

ISRAELITES. *See* "HEBREWS," "ISRAELITES," "JEWS."

J

JERUSALEM TALMUD. *See* TALMUD, THE.

JESUS. *See* CHRISTIANITY, JEWISH ORIGINS OF.

JEWISH ASCETICS. *See* ASCETICS, JEWISH.

JEWISH ATTITUDE TOWARD GENTILES. *See* GENTILES, JEWISH ATTITUDE TOWARD.

JEWISH BADGE. *See* YELLOW BADGE.

JEWISH CALENDAR. *See* CALENDAR, JEWISH.

JEWISH CHRONOLOGY. *See* CHRONOLOGY, JEWISH.

JEWISH CIVILIZATION, SOME ARCHITECTS OF. *See* SOME ARCHITECTS OF JEWISH CIVILIZATION.

JEWISH CONCEPT OF TRUTH. *See* TRUTH, JEWISH CONCEPT OF.

JEWISH CREED. *See* DOCTRINES IN JUDAISM; JUDAISM IN THE MODERN AGE.

JEWISH DIALECTS. See JEWISH LANGUAGES; YIDDISH LANGUAGE, THE

JEWISH ENLIGHTENMENT, THE. *See* ENLIGHTENMENT, THE JEWISH; HEBREW LANGUAGE, HISTORY OF THE; HEBREW LITERATURE, MODERN.

JEWISH ENTERTAINERS. *See* KLEZMER; MERRYMAKERS, TRADITIONAL JEWISH.

JEWISH ETHICAL VALUES. *See* ETHICAL VALUES, JEWISH.

JEWISH FAMILY, THE. *See* FAMILY, THE.

JEWISH FESTIVALS. *See* HOLY DAYS.

JEWISH HELLENISTS. *See* HELLENISTS, JEWISH.

JEWISH LANGUAGES

There exists a widespread misconception about the languages that may be reckoned as "Jewish." It is quite generally believed that there have been only two: Hebrew and Yiddish. Actually there have been others, and the reasons are of considerable cultural and historic interest.

It is true that Hebrew was the mother-tongue of the early Jews until the Destruction of the Temple of Solomon in 586 B.C.E. But when the exiles returned from the Captivity in Babylonia less than a hundred years later, they were faced with the fact that the vernacular in the land of Israel no longer was Hebrew but Aramaic. (The latter was then the common tongue throughout the entire Near East.) One of the reasons for this change was that the Babylonian conquerors had disrupted the normal flow of Jewish life by discouraging its ethnic cultural forms and by colonizing among the Jews, for calculated political reasons, large numbers of Aramaic-speaking non-Jews with whom many had proceeded to intermarry. But Aramaic must have had wide currency among the Jews even before then because it was the main language, both commercial and diplomatic, in all the countries of the Near East and Mesopotamia.

To be sure, Hebrew was still prized as the "sacred tongue" (lashon ha-kodesh), and while almost every Jew was familiar with it to some degree, it was used, from this time on, only for religious worship and for Torah-reading and study. There was even a Rabbinic prohibition introduced against the recitation of prayer in Aramaic. But despite this, a few prayers which had originally been composed in Aramaic achieved such overwhelming popularity that they were incorporated in the Hebrew prayer book. These Aramaic prayers are the Kaddish (the prayer for the dead), Kol Nidre ("All the Vows," chanted in the synagogue at the opening of the Yom Kippur service), and the Akdamut hymn (sung on Shabuot or Pentecost, the Feast of Weeks).

In their complicated history over many centuries in different parts of the world, the Jews evolved a special approach to their adoption of foreign languages. During the Middle Ages, at a time when illiteracy was almost general among Christians (except for a small class of scholars and priests) in Europe, most Jews were literate. At the very least, the Jewish "man in the street" was able to read Hebrew because the daily observances of his religion required that minimal language competence from him.

In medieval Germany, where the Jews adopted German as their vernacular, they began to write it—but in the characters of the Hebrew alphabet, which they already knew; they seemed to feel an antipathy for the "monkish" Latin letters. Then—after the ghettos were officially established by the papal bull issued by Innocent III in 1215—under the special requirements and conditions of Jewish ghetto-life, the original Old and Middle High German of the Jews, influenced by Hebrew phonetics and the incorporation of Hebrew words and idioms into ordinary speech, combined to evolve into a distinctive but *different* Germanic language—Yiddish—written in Hebrew characters. And as Yiddish spread from Germany into Poland, Russia, and other countries of Eastern Europe, it assimilated other language ingredients and added them to the German which formed its base. Some philologists have tentatively estimated that Yiddish, as it is spoken today, is comprised of about 70 per cent German, 20 per cent Hebrew, and 10 per cent Polish, Russian, Romanian, Hungarian, etc.

Judeo-Arabic too had a vogue in Mohammedan countries (including those of Mesopotamia, Arabia, and North Africa, as well as Moorish Spain) as extensive as and for even a longer period of time than did Yiddish. Surprisingly enough, after the final Dispersion, in 70 C.E., as the centuries advanced, Arabic and not Aramaic became the spoken language of the majority of Jews. It was also the literary language in which many of the foremost Jewish scholars, philosophers, scientists, and poets composed their works (*see* ARABIC-JEWISH "GOLDEN AGE"), even though Hebrew remained the language of religious worship and Torah study. It should not be overlooked that, living in the midst of the world of Islam, some of the principal creators of Jewish culture in the Middle Ages, such as Saadia Gaon, Solomon ibn Gabirol, and Maimonides, wrote their principal religious and

Yiddish (Judeo-German) Kol Nidre text in Hebrew characters. (From a machzor [festival prayer-book] printed in Cracow in 1571.)

Judeo-Persian manuscript page. The text is in Persian, the characters are Hebrew. Persia, 1660.

ספר
חובת הלבבות
בויניציאה
Nella Stamperia Bragadina
Con Licenza de' Superiori

Ladino (Judeo-Spanish) text in Hebrew characters of Bachya ibn Pakudah's ethical work, Chobot ha-Lebabot *("The Duties of the Heart"). Venice, 17th century.*

משלי שלמה
בויניציאה
Appresso i Clar. Sig. Pietro
e Lorenzo Bragadin.

Title page of the Book of Proverbs in Judeo-Italian. The language is Italian but the characters are Hebrew. Venice, 1617.

Arabic page written in Hebrew chara[cters] (Judeo-Arabic) of the original Paris m[anu]script of Chobot ha-Lebabot *("The D[uties] of the Heart") by Bachya ibn Pakudah.*

philosophical works *in Arabic* and not in Hebrew, although they used the characters of the Hebrew aleph-bet.

A similar language pattern was followed by the Jews of Spain after their expulsion from that country in 1492. By the time they had found asylum in the Mohammedan countries of North Africa and in Turkey, Greece, and Bulgaria, they were already writing their native Spanish with Hebrew characters. This old-new Spanish language, in the course of time, and because of accretions deriving from the cultural experiences of the refugees when they settled in various countries, became enriched with all kinds of foreign words and expressions: Turkish, Italian, Greek, Arabic–even Slavonic. The Castilian language of these Sefaradic Jews is called Ladino (or, sometimes, Spaniolish). In most respects, Ladino has not gone through such marked changes as, for instance, Spanish, in its Latin-American environment since the Conquest.

Judeo-Greek had long been spoken in Christian Byzantium and in early medieval times. However, although today it is still written in Hebrew characters, it shows that it has absorbed only a very few Hebrew words and expressions. On the other hand, Judeo-Italian evolved into much more of a "Jewish" language than Judeo-Greek. This was because each region of Italy had its own Italian dialect, or *parlata.* Consequently, during the Renaissance, Jews coming into one part of Italy from another found it easier to communicate with the Jews there in their own vernacular: Judeo-Italian. It is an odd fact that, although most Italian Jews in other centuries could neither read nor write Italian in Latin characters, they were, nevertheless, able to do so in Hebrew characters. They produced in Judeo-Italian translations of the Bible, prayer books, and religious as well as secular poetry.

There is even a Judeo-Persian language; it is spoken by the Jews in Iran, and different dialects of it are current among Jews in all of Central Asia. Many of the Jews of Bokhara in the Soviet Union still speak an ancient Tadjik dialect of the Persian language-family into which, long ago, was incorporated a number of Hebrew and Aramaic words and idioms. The Mountain Jews, who, according to their tradition, have lived in the Caucasus since Second Temple times, speak Farsi-Tat. This is a Persian dialect which they have enriched with Biblical Hebrew words and expressions. It is not without cultural interest that in their relatively obscure dialect they have been able to develop an interesting "Jewish" folk-literature.

See also HEBREW ALPHABET; HEBREW LANGUAGE, HISTORY OF THE; YIDDISH LANGUAGE, THE.

JEWISH LAW. *See* LAW, JEWISH.

JEWISH LITERATURE, MEDIEVAL AND RENAISSANCE. *See* ARABIC-JEWISH "GOLDEN AGE."

JEWISH LOAN SOCIETIES. *See* LOANS, FREE.

JEWISH MERRYMAKERS. *See* KLEZMER; MERRYMAKERS, TRADITIONAL JEWISH.

JEWISH MISSIONARIES. *See* MISSIONARIES, JEWISH.

JEWISH MONASTICISM. *See* MONASTICISM, JEWISH.

JEWISH NAMES. *See* NAMES, JEWISH.

JEWISH NATIONAL FUND. *See* THEODOR HERZL (*under* ZIONISM).

JEWISH OATH, THE. *See* OATH, THE JEWISH.

JEWISH ORIGINS OF CHRISTIANITY. *See* CHRISTIANITY, JEWISH ORIGINS OF.

JEWISH RELIGIOUS DIVISIONS. *See* JUDAISM IN THE MODERN AGE.

JEWISH RITES AND CUSTOMS. *See* BAR MITZVAH; BAT MITZVAH; BURIAL RITES AND CUSTOMS; CIRCUMCISION; CONFIRMATION; DIETARY LAWS; HOLY DAYS; JUDAISM IN THE MODERN AGE; PIDYON HA-BEN; SHECHITAH; WEDDING CUSTOMS.

JEWISH SEPARATISM. *See* SEPARATISM, JEWISH.

"JEWISH STAR." *See* MAGEN DAVID.

JEWISH TEACHERS AND THINKERS. *See* SOME ARCHITECTS OF JEWISH CIVILIZATION.

JEWISH VIEW OF LIFE. *See* LIFE, JEWISH VIEW OF.

JEWS. *See* "HEBREWS," "ISRAELITES," "JEWS."

JEWS, SERVITUDE OF TO CHRISTIANS. *See* FEUDAL SOCIETY, POSITION OF THE JEWS IN..

JEWS AND GENTILES. *See* GENTILES, JEWISH ATTITUDE TOWARD.

JEWS IN FEUDAL SOCIETY. *See* FEUDAL SOCIETY, POSITION OF THE JEWS IN.

JOB, BOOK OF. *See* BIBLE, THE.

JUBILEE (in Hebrew: YOBEL, meaning a "jubilating" or "exulting")

It is significant that, in the earliest centuries of the existence of the Jews as a people in the Land of Israel, their social morality was superior to that of their descendants of later times in a number of ways. The Israelites had begun their group existence as a tribal society untrammeled by the complexities and complications that inevitably arise from the existence of different social strata and conflicting vested interests. Theirs was a society libertarian in outlook, and it practiced an equality in social and property rights which was made easier to maintain because of the simple pastoral-agricultural economy under which it existed. The society that the Mosaic Laws envisioned has often been described by sociologists as having been built along the lines of a primitive socialism. The institution of the Jubilee is perhaps its most striking feature.

According to the Biblical account, which describes the origin of the Jubilee and its several socio-economic purposes, God had instructed Moses on Mount Sinai that on the tenth day of the seventh month (i.e., on Yom Kippur, the Day of Atonement) of every fiftieth year, the Year of Jubilee was to be celebrated, and it was to be proclaimed with the loud blowing of the shofar throughout the land. "And ye shall hallow the fiftieth year, and proclaim liberty throughout the land unto all the inhabitants thereof; it shall be a jubilee unto you." (Leviticus 25:10.)

At the core of the idea of the Jubilee–and, incidentally, of all agrarian reforms in the Biblical era–was the Mosaic doctrine that all things and all creatures that were in the world did not belong to men at all *but to God alone,* for He had created them. Since the land belonged to God alone, it was to be distributed equally among men–"leased," as it were, to all who wished to cultivate it. To prevent the rise of big estates through land-grabbing practices by the lawless and the powerful and the inevitable expropriation of the small farmers whenever they happened to default to their creditors, the Biblical law, in the austere words of God to Moses, stated: "The land shall not be sold in perpetuity, for the land is Mine." (Leviticus 25:23.) In consequence, after fifty years of ownership, the land a farmer had tilled had to be returned to the state for reassignment to someone else.

The remission of all indebtedness, too, played an important part in the program of the Jubilee, which had been designed for the protection of the poor farmer and farm laborer. Every man indentured or imprisoned for non-payment of his debts, or for any other reason whatsoever, was to be released and restored to his family in the Year of Jubilee.

Hardly less in social implication was the commandment tersely worded: ". . . ye shall return every man unto his possession." (Leviticus 25:13.) This required the return of farm homes to the original owners who might have been forced to mortgage them. It also directed the return of all other possessions of the poor that might be held in pledge by the creditor.

The social purpose of the Jubilee enactment, it must be stated, was not unique with the Jews. Other semi-pastoral Near Eastern peoples with a primitive agricultural economy followed at various times a similar practice, but with them it constituted merely an occasional venture into agrarian reform; it was not the permanent institution that the Israelites had established with the Jubilee. There is even extant a curious Babylonian inscription of a royal decree announcing the cancellation of all debts.

The hard historic fact is that the provisions of the Jubilee were not always observed, especially under the more highly developed agricultural economy of the Land of Israel in later centuries. New social stratifications developed that soon were in conflict with one another. This is made abundantly plain by the Prophets' impassioned attacks on the various kings of Israel and Judah from the ninth to the sixth centuries B.C.E. Their preachments also were unsparing of the rapacious land owners who were "swallowing up" the small holdings of the peasantry, of an accommodating priesthood which looked the other way, and of the emerging merchant class in the towns and cities which, by corrupt means, was growing richer while the poor were growing poorer. From Chapter 5 in the chronicle of Nehemiah, for example, it is learned that during the fifth century B.C.E. the expropriation of the landholdings and homes of small farmers who had fallen into debt represented a rampant social evil which not even the legal and religious protections provided by Mosaic Law were able to halt. Only Nehemiah's own iron-willed authority was successful in curbing it.

See also LOVE THY NEIGHBOR (*under* ETHICAL VALUES, JEWISH); THE PROPHETS (*under* BIBLE, THE); POOR, THE; SLAVERY AND THE SLAVE; SABBATICAL YEAR.

JUDAH, LION OF. *See* LION OF JUDAH.

JUDAIZERS. *See* CONVERSION OF JEWS; MARRANOS AND THE INQUISITION.

JUDAISM, DOCTRINES IN. *See* DOCTRINES IN JUDAISM.

JUDAISM IN THE MODERN AGE

To the student of the Jewish religion who brings to it an objective historical approach, it becomes apparent that, like all other religions, Judaism has been subject to the inexorable laws of evolutionary, and sometimes even revolutionary, change. All preconceived notions to the contrary, it has never been completely unitary, has never remained static or monolithic.

Aside from all the dissenting sects—and these were numerous in the long history of the Jewish religion—there were always many "re-evaluators" at work. Possessed of inquiring and reflective minds, they were, not unnaturally, assailed by doubts concerning one or another doctrine. They tried hard to reconcile faith with reason, and the ceremonial and ritual observances with the dictates of conscience and practicality.

Religious tradition itself, no matter how hallowed it had become in time, did not remain frozen; mutations were always occurring. They assumed distinctive forms in each historic age and regional Jewish culture. One can draw this inference merely from the fact that the orthodoxy of the medieval Spanish or North African Jew was not quite like the orthodoxy of the medieval German or Bohemian Jew. Neither was the eighteenth-century orthodoxy of the rationalist rabbinic authority, Rabbi Elijah of Vilna (the Vilner Gaon), quite the same as the orthodoxy of his contemporary, Israel Baal Shem, the founder of mystic Chasidism. Furthermore, it may even be conjectured that what passes today for "Torah-true" orthodoxy in the United States would have been stigmatized as heresy by the East European great-grandfathers of its devout adherents.

One of the possible explanations for this state of flux in Judaism is that Jews, unlike the followers of some other religions, have been less bound by fixed dogmas. Not all Jews submitted readily to a literal interpretation of the "revealed truth" in the Torah. As far back as eighteen centuries ago, it was already recognized by some Rabbinic Sages in Judea that, like all human institutions and intellectual systems, religion too has an organic development. The dynamics of the historic process to which it is subject and the emergence of new conditions of life necessarily produce changes in both its structure and content. Cognizant of this, the Talmud directed: "If you live in the generation of Rabban Gamaliel, do according to the precepts of Rabban Gamaliel—and if you live in the generation of Rabbi Yoseh, do according to the precepts of Rabbi Yoseh."

Each age placed a different emphasis on the values of the Jewish religion. For example, nowhere does the Torah (the Pentateuch) mention anything about the Resurrection or the Hereafter, as the ancient Sadducees correctly pointed out. Yet these religious concepts were ultimately included by the Pharisee Sages among the *cardinal doctrines* of Judaism! To cite another instance: During the Second Temple period, the main religious emphasis in worship was placed upon the priestly cult of sacrifice. Yet in the Talmudic age which followed upon the Destruction of the national sanctuary, the emphasis in Rabbinic Judaism was dramatically shifted to a comprehensive definition of the entire range of ethical conduct, to prayer, and to Torah study!

One of the most urgent contentions by religious Jews who are not in the Ultra-Orthodox fold is that in certain areas of belief and observance, the Judaism of bygone ages no longer has the same organic function to perform within the altered context of modern living. They maintain that it is not enough for the Jewish religion to be exclusively nourished by its heritage of the past. They consider partly outmoded the codes of both ancient and medieval laws that hitherto have regulated the rites, ceremonies, and personal behavior of Jews. They argue that since they are obliged to live realistically in the present and to submit to the influences and pressures of their Gentile environment, they cannot help but make certain adjustments that they believe are necessary for the survival of the Jewish religion and identity in a changing world. Conditions of modern life, they plead, often clash with the categorical imperatives of some observances in traditional Judaism that had their origins in a remote period.

The industrial revolution of the eighteenth and nineteenth centuries had a stunning impact on the Jewish religion and on Jewish life generally by the vast economic, social, cultural, and political changes it precipitated in the Western world. The civil emancipation of the Jews, first begun by the American Revolution in 1776 and closely followed in the French Revolution by the decree of 1791 (*see* GHETTO), had resulted in the slow but certain breakdown of the ghetto-isolation of the Jews and of their religious and cultural particularism. More and more Jews were becoming assimilated Europeans. They were eager both for a secular education and to take their place in society on an equal footing with Gentiles. The Jewish Enlightenment (Haskalah) that resulted, however, had the effect of a double-edged sword; it cut both ways: while it worked for "modernization," it also led to assimilation and, in many instances, to alienation from the Jewish group life and identity.

There were knowledgeable Jews in the ghetto who, having acquired a greater or lesser measure of secular culture, suddenly discovered that they could no longer conscientiously cleave to some of the sanctified traditional beliefs, rites, ceremonies, and forms of worship, or even the manner of their performance. In Germany, the Scandinavian countries, Bohemia, France, Holland, and Hungary, a religious-cultural struggle (*Kulturkampf*) was being fought between the rebels of the Enlightenment and the defenders of the Orthodox status quo. In the Slavic countries, where the great majority of the world's Jews were living, the *Kulturkampf* was waged considerably less strongly; Orthodox conformity was the rule.

Apart from the battle stood the unprincipled opportunists, fleeing chameleon-like from the burdens and handicaps of their Jewish identity into conversion or intermarriage. But there were also serious-minded and principled secularists who were seeking no advantage for themselves but merely wished to follow Baruch Spinoza's example when he rejected blind faith for reason and theology for science (*see* EXCOMMUNICATION). These individuals virtually divorced themselves from their Jewish identity and disappeared from the Jewish scene in the shuffle of history.

In between were those Jews who, while ardently desiring to become full-fledged, educated Europeans, were nevertheless imbued with strong religious sentiments; they were determined to maintain their old ties of group-kinship and association. Yet, although they wished to remain Jews, still enough they were anxious to avoid being trapped by any conflict of reason and conscience. The traditionalists, in their own minds, were firmly convinced that the modernists were either insincere or else misguided in the marriage of convenience they sought to contract between Torah and Gentile culture. They interpreted this as a philistine desire to blend unobtrusively into the accepted patterns of their Christian environment in order that they might earn thereby a tolerated status of social respectability—the pre-condition for carving out for themselves successful careers and a secure existence in a hostile society.

But, as has happened within all the other religions of mankind, neither controversy nor sectarian feuding prevented the divisive process of denominationalism from running its full course in present-day Jewish religion. Yet it must be emphasized that there exists much greater unity among the various branches of Judaism than, for instance, among those in Christianity. This, without question, is chiefly due to the fact that, although what may separate the various groups of Jews in religious matters remains unbridgeable, yet there is one inescapable reality that draws them close together: their identity *as Jews*. In this identity are included special group-interests and loyalties: the heritage of a rich Jewish culture, common folkways and ethical values, the support of Jewish philanthropic enterprises, a fervent attachment to the Jewish State of Israel, and—by no means least, in the words of the sober declaration of Benjamin Franklin—the need to "either stand together or hang separately" in their self-defense against the slanders and plottings of the anti-Semites.

Orthodox Judaism. At least half of all observing Jews today are either "Orthodox" or "Orthodox"-oriented. The dictionary meaning of the word "orthodox" is "sound of opinion or doctrine." This description has been applied to themselves at various times by adherents of all dominant religious sects or churches when they have wished to contrast themselves with their sectarian competitors, whom they usually label—intending no compliment—as "heterodox," or "possessing a false faith."

Before the beginning of the nineteenth century, the word or even connotation "Orthodox" was entirely unknown among Jews. There was no need for this kind of qualification since everybody in the ghetto was "Orthodox." Those few individuals who dissented in any radical way from traditionalism were simply not tolerated. True enough, during the eighteenth century, a sectarian feud did develop between the Chasidim—the Cabalistic-minded ecstatics—and the Misnagdim—their opponents who were Talmudic rationalists. Yet both of these rival groupings were Orthodox in doctrine as well as in ritual observance. They differed principally in their concepts about the nature of religious experience and the approach to worship.

The term "Orthodox" is believed to have been employed for the first time in 1806 to designate "traditional" Judaism. It was used by the French Jew, Abraham Furtado, who was president of the Assembly of Jewish Notables which Napoleon had convened in Paris that year for considering ways and means of "Europeanizing" the ghetto Jews. It was picked up by the early advocates of Reform Judaism in Germany and applied by them to the traditionalists. Yet there were many in the ranks of Orthodoxy in Germany who, for the same reasons as the pioneers of Reform but to a much lesser degree, felt impelled to seek a working accommodation with the new spirit of the times (*Zeitgeist*).

The chief rabbinic protagonists of Modern Orthodoxy were Samson Raphael Hirsch (1808–88) and Israel Hildesheimer (1820–99). Their program called for "unconditional agreement with the culture of the present era; harmony between Judaism and science, but also unconditional steadfastness in the faith and traditions of Judaism." Rabbi Hirsch made this position clear in 1836 when he stated that he was advocating no synthesis or intellectual reconciliation between traditional Judaism and the secular culture of the West. The latter was to remain subordinate to the former. The immutable precepts of the Torah and the institutions of Judaism were to serve as absolute rule and guide for the enlightened Jew in his quest for modernity.

There is no question but that of all the divisions in contemporary Judaism, Orthodoxy has the most clear-cut and the least involved ideology and program. It is a well-defined, delimited, and unified religious system. Its adherents revere all its dogmas, doctrines, statutes, and commandments (the 613 mitzvot) as fixed and unalterable. Nothing may be added, nothing taken away. Said the Talmud: "Whosoever denies that the whole Torah—the Oral as well as the Written—was given by God to Moses on [Mount] Sinai, is a heretic!"

The reason for this sacrosanct regard is self-evident: Orthodoxy is postulated on the principle that both the Written and Oral Laws were divinely revealed. Even such an independent philosopher and rabbinical authority as Maimonides (twelfth century, Spain) asserted that the laws of the Torah were immutable and were meant to last forever. This idea he included as a cardinal dogma of the Jewish religion in his celebrated Thirteen Articles (*see* DOCTRINES OF JUDAISM). He interpreted literally the prohibition of Deuteronomy 4:2: "Ye shall not add unto the word which I command you, neither shall ye diminish from it." To this task, as faithful textual guardians of the teachings of the Torah, the ancient Masorite scholars devoted their talents and lives (*see* MASORAH).

Orthodox Judaism, being traditionalistic and Bible-oriented, is theocratic. Therefore, in its world outlook and in its embrace of all the departments of living, both religious and secular, it is a total system. Nothing is left out, nothing overlooked. Until this day, the sixteenth-century ritual-legal code, the Shulchan Aruch, has provided Orthodox Jews with clearly prescribed and authoritative norms of religious observance and moral conduct. Thus the devout have been disciplined in the traditional way of life by a systematic daily regimen of prayer, Torah study, religious symbolism, rite, ceremony, folk custom, and standards of personal behavior.

Historically considered, Orthodoxy has been the most durable—and certainly the one least affected by the tides of change—among Jewish sects since the Rabbinic Age. Yet, in its strong desire to maintain its position of primacy in the competitive denominational Judaism of modern times, and in direct response to the pressures from the non-Jewish environment, it has had to make some far-reaching—and, not infrequently, also unhappy—concessions.

Orthodox Jews in the United States, however, are not all of one mind. The aura of "immutability" that was created around traditional Judaism so painstakingly over such a long period of time has not stood up too firmly. Since reform is only a relative concept of change, whether in extent or in depth, Orthodoxy, too, has undergone inevitable mutations. Today, there are really three separate categories of the Orthodox: the Ultra-Orthodox, the uncompromising fundamentalists who might still be living in the Middle Ages; the Modern or Neo-Orthodox, who have a liberal orientation, and finally, the sectarian Chasidim, who live in a mystical otherworldly microcosm of their own (see CHASIDIM).

The Ultra-Orthodox, as well as most of the Chasidim, are, for all practical considerations, outside the mainstream of

Professor Martin Buber, initiator of the Neo-Chasidic intellectual trend with ethical existentialist implications. (Photo by Gertrude Samuels. American Friends of the Hebrew University.)

Professor Mordecai Kaplan, founder of the American Society for the Advancement of Judaism and leader of the Reconstructionist movement of Judaism. (Jewish Theological Seminary of America.) (TOP)

Professor Solomon Schechter, who was the chief architect in America of the Conservative philosophy of Judaism. (Jewish Theological Seminary of America.) (CENTER)

Dr. Kaufmann Kohler, who led the Reform movement in Amer can Judaism for many years. (LEFT)

Rabbi Samson Raphael Hirsch, the 19th-century pioneer Germany of Modern or Neo-Orthodoxy. (RIGHT)

Jewish life and are regarded by the majority of Jews as cultural anachronisms. Their separatist way of life and unyielding religious philosophy have been criticized as being survivals of Jewish medievalism completely out of harmony with modern life. By and large, the Ultra-Orthodox have rejected Zionism; thus they are in constant collision with the secularist State of Israel. Like Jews of former times, they pin all their hopes for the redemption and restoration of the Jewish people upon the coming of the Messiah–an eventuality about which they have not the slightest doubt.

The main body of Orthodox Jews in America, describes itself as "Modern." In some beliefs and in many observances its adherents are worlds apart from both the Ultra-Orthodox and many of the Chasidim. This is particularly true of their concept of *the Jews as a people* (Klal Yisrael). These Modern Orthodox are fervently Zionist, even though they believe in the Messianic redemption. To be sure, they have made certain compromises, but in the matter of religious observances only. By and large, these have constituted minor "adjustments" to the realities of modern living rather than a surrender of religious belief or principle. For instance, few Modern Orthodox, unlike the Ultra-Orthodox and the Chasidim, wear beards, and none at all wear side curls (pe'ot or payess). Nor do they dress in the long black coats and hats that the East European traditionalists have worn for centuries. Their wives, too, do not wear the wig (sheitel) customary for married women since the Middle Ages.

Yet in most of their beliefs and ritual observances, these divisions of American Orthodoxy are in agreement. They unquestioningly accept the authority not only of the Bible and the Talmud, but also of the medieval and later codes such as the Shulchan Aruch, the commentaries of Rashi and Abraham ibn Ezra, and the legal opinions rendered in the Responsa (*see* RABBINICAL DECISIONS) to challenging questions by illustrious rabbinic authorities down through the centuries. They observe with remarkable scrupulosity the Sabbath and all the holy days on the Jewish religious calendar. They are faithful to the dietary laws (kashrut) and the Levitical laws governing personal and family "purity" or morals. They voluntarily accept the decisions of the rabbinical courts on matters to which the laws of the Torah apply without conflicting with the law of the land. They maintain separate religious educational institutions: the Bet ha-Midrash, the Talmud Torah, the yeshivah.

On the Sabbath and on holy days, Orthodox worshipers observe the ban on riding in any conveyance; they walk wherever they go. Following ancient custom, men and women sit in separate sections of the synagogue at prayer service–either the men sit downstairs and the women sit in a curtained balcony, or the women sit in the main synagogue but behind a latticed screen. In the synagogue, the men are required to wear a tallit (prayer shawl) and to cover the head with either a yarmulkah (skullcap) or hat. In addition, it is mandatory, and has been, ever since Biblical times, for all Orthodox male Jews over thirteen years of age to put on tefillin (phylacteries) at prayer every weekday morning, whether in the synagogue or in private devotions.

The rise of Jewish suburbia around metropolitan centers has created a new kind of middle-class Orthodoxy in America. Its members are usually affluent, and frequently well educated, sophisticated, and even country-clubbish. The synagogue in the suburbs is often combined with a community center where studies in Jewish religion and culture are mingled with social diversions and communal and philanthropic projects.

It is, no doubt, a clear sign of changing times that the trend in Modern Orthodoxy since World War I has steadily been to synthesize traditional "Torah-true" Jewish values with modern, secular culture. But its chief goal still is the transmission of knowledge and the cherished pattern of life to the young in order that the traditional faith may serve as the continuing legacy of the Jewish people down through the generations.

Reform Judaism. At the opposite pole of Orthodox Judaism in the United States and in other countries today stands Reform Judaism, also called "Liberal" or "Progressive" Judaism.

As an organized movement attempting the formulation of a system of religious philosophy "suitable for modern Jews," it began in Germany in the second decade of the nineteenth century. It was this geographical accident of birth which gave Reform Judaism its distinctive Germanic coloration, even in the United States, to which it was brought by German immigrants. However, its central postulates stemmed directly from the Jewish Enlightenment (in Hebrew: *Haskalah;* in German: *Aufklärung*). That movement, initiated by Moses Mendelssohn, "the German Plato," and his circle of Teutonized Jewish intellectuals during the last quarter of the eighteenth century, was an assimilationist one, and was a demonstration of the hunger for secular culture and Europeanization felt by certain Jews in England, France, Germany, Austria, and the Scandinavian countries. Largely, it appeared as a natural consequence of the industrial revolution which was then making possible the rapid emergence of a small but quite affluent Jewish mercantile class.

It was these latter Jews who first began to wage a determined struggle for civil emancipation in the countries where they lived. Many of them, being wealthy and having already acquired a considerable measure of European culture, were straining hard to be accepted on an equal footing with Gentiles in every area of life. A revealing description of the rapid tempo in assimilation–and to a certain extent also of the social acceptance–of middle-class Jews into their German-Gentile environment was given by a Christian writer in 1779:

> There are very rich Jews in Berlin. Some possess factories, though most of them are in trade. Their deportment, especially those who have enjoyed a good education, is refined and pleasing. . . . Many of them dress their hair like Christians and clothe themselves as we do. Their upper-class, or those who have been raised upon enlightened principles, associate freely with Christians and share their amusements–above all the theatre, where on Saturday nights they occupy most of the *parterre.* More than ever they are given to reading, and the theatre and periodicals have developed among them a love of literature as well as talented writers. Their womenfolk devour the latest novels: indeed their fair sex–and what beauty they can boast!–play a great role in Berlin.

There were many who, like Moses Mendelssohn, were sincere assimilationists. To them, aside from all other considerations they may have had, a social and cultural *rapprochement* with Gentiles and with Gentile ways appeared to be the one possible road leading to freedom from ghetto-segregation, rightlessness, and backwardness. In the opinion of the Westernized Jewish intellectuals, it was necessary that every barrier keeping Jews apart from Christians to be removed if the civil emancipation of the Jews was to be realized. Once and for all, Jews had to abandon their religious-cultural "exclusiveness" and to cease being a "peculiar" people! The way they looked at it, traditional Judaism was too exotic, too "Oriental"; it smacked too much of the despised ghetto, about which they could feel nothing but shame, and its rites, customs, ceremonies, and manners—or lack of manners (but this was really informality!) were distasteful to well-bred and emotionally starched German-Christians. The Europeanized Jews, consequently, considered it imperative to "reform" and "modernize" Jewish theology according to the intellectual terms of eighteenth-century rationalism. Likewise, they thought it just as important to bring the rites and ceremonies of the synagogue into line with the decorum and esthetic forms observed in the Christian church.

Although the term "Reform" was not yet formally in use during his time, Mendelssohn's rationalistic approach in his interpretation of the Bible text was made the cornerstone for organized Reform Judaism several decades later. He had furnished the Liberal movement with its definitive theological principle in his book *Jerusalem* (published in 1783). He had stated there: "I acknowledge no immutable truths but such as are not only conceivable to human understanding but also admit of being demonstrated and warranted by the human faculties."

Mendelssohn, as the leading spokesman for rationalism among the educated Jews, had paved the way to Reform by urging them not to stand aloof from the culture of the Gentile society in whose midst they lived. He was perhaps the first Jew to advocate combining "liberal" Jewish religious studies with a secular European education for Jewish children. Actually he was instrumental in the establishment of schools with such a curriculum. Significantly, these bore the motto: "For Culture and Humanity." Like all Jewish Enlighteners—Maskilim—Mendelssohn stressed the importance of employing the national vernacular in religious worship and study, for there were few who still knew any Hebrew. In his instance, the vernacular happened to be the German language. This idea of his, too, was adopted by Reform Judaism a few decades later.

Curiously—and this has always been charged against Mendelssohn as an inconsistency of logic—although he was the rationalist "Father of Reform Judaism," which itself denied that the Torah was divinely revealed truth, nonetheless he was an uncompromising traditionalist in all matters of rite and observance, declaring that they were part of a "revealed legislation." He, therefore, scrupulously kept the Sabbath, observed the dietary laws in his home, and put on the tallit and tefillin every weekday during morning prayer. How different was the approach of early Reform practitioners! They abolished the use of tefillin and of tzitzit (ritual fringes). And when the first Liberal temple was dedicated in Hamburg in 1818 by Rabbi Israel Jacobson, not only was the sermon delivered in German, but the hymns, composed in German, were sung to German Protestant chorale-tunes with organ accompaniment played by a Christian organist!

Still other innovations—all aimed at eliminating "Oriental" features from the synagogue service—quickly followed these reforms. Men and women no longer sat apart, as they did in Orthodox synagogues, but occupied family pews. The men, in a break with tradition, sat bareheaded. The ancient custom of reciting most of the prayers aloud with uninhibited fervor was discarded in the Reform congregation; there prayer had to be reverently subdued, or even silent. Proper decorum had to be observed. In the musical part of the service, the traditional "Oriental" intonations and modes were eliminated, and a mixed choir of male and female singers formed the choral background of the cantor's *bel canto* art to the accompaniment of a pealing organ.

Listening once to the Reform prayer-service in the Berlin temple, the early-nineteenth-century Protestant philosopher-theologian, Friedrich Schleiermacher, was filled with amazement. He commented that, apparently, an ancient historical pattern was being reversed. Whereas Jesus and the Apostles had borrowed for Christianity so many doctrinal, institutional, and liturgical elements from the Jewish religion, Reform Judaism was reciprocating the compliment by borrowing many practices from modern Protestantism. In this impression he was seconded in 1823 by the great poet of Germany, Heinrich Heine. With his customary acidulous wit he observed about the adherents of Reform Judaism that what they apparently wanted was "to give Judaism some new stage scenery . . ." and to set up "an Evangelical [Protestant] Christianity under a Jewish firm name, for they even required that their rabbi, like the Lutheran minister, should wear "a white clerical neckband instead of a beard." And apropos of the Biblical commandment that every Jew should wear a beard, the poet scoffed with conscious self-irony: "We Jews no longer have the strength of character to wear a beard [or] to fast. . . ."

The early leaders of Reform Judaism were not nonplused by such disparaging characterizations. The historian Heinrich Graetz (1817–91), who was a champion of Reform Judaism, tried to justify dispensing with the traditional rites and ceremonies that were clung to with such tenacity by the Orthodox. He stated: "The Prophets and Sages did not regard sacrifice or ritual as the fundamental and determining thing in Judaism."

Reform Judaism met with determined resistance from the majority of German Jews, for they were either oriented toward Modern Orthodoxy or divorced altogether from any kind of Jewish identity. Moreover, it made but little headway in the East European communities which had stood for centuries as the impregnable citadels of traditionalism. Only in the liberal democratic climate of the United States—the crucible in which many diverse culture patterns were being dissolved and interacting—was Reform Judaism able to make steady advances. Here its adherents at first were, almost exclusively, German-speaking Jews, immigrants who had only recently arrived from Germany, Austria, Hungary, and Bohemia, and its first congregations were formed in the principal centers of German-Jewish settlement: in the North, the South, and the Middle West.

During the 1870's, the number of congregations had so far increased that it was considered necessary to find a common program of principles to guide them along a clearly defined course of Liberal faith and practice. This goal was accomplished in 1885, at the Pittsburgh Conference of Reform Judaism, with the issuance of a Platform which consisted of ten "Acts." In Act 5, opposition was stated to the observance of the "Mosaic-rabbinic laws on diet, purity and dress," customs which were declared to be obsolete and ineffective for modern Jews in that they "would obstruct rather than enhance moral and spiritual elevation."

In its Platform, also, the considered attitude of American Reform Judaism toward the questions of Jewish nationalism and Zionism, which were then agitating American Jews, was one of open hostility, and this notwithstanding the fact that several of its most eminent rabbinic leaders had expressed strong pro-Zionist sentiments. Among the latter leaders were Marcus Jastrow, Gustav Gottheil, and Bernard Felsenthal, whose anti-slavery sermons had stirred the Jews of Chicago just before the outbreak of the Civil War. Act 6 gave the following formulation: "Israel's Messianic hope relates to the establishment of the authority of peace, truth, justice and love among men." This merely reaffirmed the Prophetic ideals contained in the Reform doctrine of the universalistic "mission of Israel" to be carried out among all the peoples of the earth and against national separatism. Consequently, the logic of this position made an anti-Zionist stand inescapable. Bluntly, the Reform Platform concluded: "No return to Palestine is expected, nor the re-institution there of a Jewish state."

From that time on, and in spite of frequent opposition to it in its own fold, the Reform movement took the position that Judaism was solely a religion and that the only valid tie that could exist between Jews was that of their being "co-religionists." Its anti-Zionism through the years was fervent and frequently sounded. It turned its back on all aspects of Jewish secular and national culture as being too parochial and separatist, and showed no interest in the nineteenth-century revival of the Hebrew language and literature.

But a dramatic change in attitude took place during the Hitler era, when the terrors unleashed by the Nazis against the Jews of Europe shocked all American Jews, regardless of whether they were Orthodox, Conservative, Reform, or agnostics or unbelievers, into a state of painful awareness of the common destiny of the Jewish people. The old, departmentalized doctrine that Jews were merely being "co-religionists" no longer seemed to have any meaning to the majority of Reform Judaism. Although the movement as such never formally declared for the Zionist principle, leaving that decision to be made freely by the individual adherent or by an entire congregation, yet it repeatedly endorsed the extension of all possible material aid and moral support to the new State of Israel, to its development, its absorption of immigrants, and to fraternal and cultural ties with it.

Furthermore, rather than, with time, moving still farther away from traditional forms of religious rites and ceremonials, American Reform Judaism has retraced some of its steps to its ancient source. More prayers are recited in Hebrew and more traditional melodies are included in the musical part of the Reform service; the Kiddush rite of sanctification for Sabbath and the festivals has been reintroduced in the home; in the temple, the shofar is blown on Rosh Hashanah and the Megillah (the Scroll of the Book of Esther) is intoned on Purim. With the rise in Jewish consciousness, an impressive emphasis is being laid on Jewish cultural values.

Even the ethnic origins of Reform membership are greatly different. It is no longer considered of any importance in the average Reform congregation whether a member stems from German, Lithuanian, Romanian, Polish, or Russian stock. In many temples, in fact, the majority of congregants are of East European derivation. Neither are the old class-distinctions of wealth and social standing in evidence in any but a few of the diehard "snob" temples—"the rich men's clubs," as a prominent Reform rabbi once satirized them.

Yet there are still quite a number of Reform "fundamentalists." An influential group of these functions apart from the main body of Reform Judaism, belligerently and polemically, as The American Council for Judaism. It is fiercely anti-Zionist and anti-Israel and clamors for a return of Liberal Judaism to the Pittsburgh Platform of 1885, reaffirming that "Judaism is a religion of universal values—not a nationality." It rejects the notion that "Jews constitute a 'race,' or a 'nation apart,' or a 'culture.'" The way the Council views it, Jews are Americans who differ only from other Americans in that they attend their own houses of worship.

Quite the opposite is true of a large group in the American Reform movement. It aims to follow the tradition laid down in the years prior to the Civil War by the eminent Abolitionist-Reform rabbis of that period—David Einhorn, Liebman Adler, and Bernhard Felsenthal—who all denounced the institution of slavery in sermons from the pulpit.

This philosophy of social commitment and involvement by the synagogue was eulogized thus after World War II by Dr. Maurice N. Eisendrath: "Reform Judaism has revitalized the passion for social justice which lies at the heart of the Jewish tradition . . . it has created a living and relevant faith which draws upon the creativity of modern life in a democratic setting." This view of a religion playing its active part in the problems of our society was demonstrated vividly in 1961–62, when a number of young Reform rabbis joined some of their Christian ministerial colleagues in anti-segregation demonstrations as Freedom Riders in the Deep South, and together with them, went to jail for their principles.

Conservative Judaism. The imprecision of labels is ironically implied in the designation "Conservative Jews." Objectively considered, these religious "conservatives" are actually "liberals," since their deviations from Orthodox Judaism have been just part of the normal process of change or "reform." But they are far less "reformed" than the adherents of Reform Judaism. As has been indicated above, "Reform" is a loose concept; it differs among the several branches of organized Judaism only in degree. Even Orthodox Judaism experienced its own "reform" during the first half of the nineteenth century in Germany, France, and England as "Neo-" or "Modern" Orthodoxy.

The name "Conservative Judaism" apparently originated from the formulation that was given it by the "Moderate Reform" advocate, Zacharias Frankel, in his program for "Positive Historical Judaism," proposed in the middle of the nineteenth century in Breslau, where he presided over the Jewish Theological Seminary. He defined "Positive Historical Judaism" as "Reform tempered by Conservatism." And such it has remained in essence, holding on to the malaprop label of "Conservative Judaism" in order to distinguish it from Reform Judaism.

In the institutionalized Jewish religion of our time, Conservative Judaism occupies the middle ground between Modern Orthodoxy and Liberal Reform Judaism. It considers the first to be too "orthodox" and the second too "reformed." In short, Conservative Judaism is at the same time moderately orthodox and moderately reformed. But in the matter of its religious philosophy, it shares with Reform Judaism one central principle. This was stated by Leopold Zunz, the pioneer of modern Jewish studies, about one hundred and fifty years ago in Berlin. He had said that his aim was "to harmonize historical Judaism with modern science." One concrete example of the application of this guide-rule has been Messianism. While it is true that Conservative Judaism confidently expects that the Kingdom of God (*see* MESSIAH, THE) will ultimately be established in righteousness and justice *on earth,* it places no credence in the concept of a personal supernatural redeemer as envisaged by the Orthodox. It even considers the establishment of the State of Israel to be a practical step toward the realization of that hope and dream for the redemption of the Jewish people and of all mankind.

To be consistent in its critical-historical approach to Jewish religious values, Conservative Judaism was obliged to disassociate itself from a central doctrine of Orthodox Judaism. This is that the Torah (Pentateuch) constitutes the eternal verities and laws of life that had been "revealed" by God to Moses so that it was to be considered sacrosanct and unalterable, and binding upon the Jew in every word and in every teaching for all time and under all circumstances. The stand taken by Conservative Judaism has been that life is fluid and conditions are incessantly changing, thus requiring reinterpretation and adjustment.

Conservative Judaism has also disagreed with what it views as the uncritical submission by the Orthodox to the authority of the Oral Law and its subsequent elaborations by the Talmudic Sages and later rabbis. With reference to this, the late Professor Louis Ginzberg (1873–1953), a foremost intellectual exponent of the Conservative point of view, coined the epigram: ". . . the doctrine of the immutability of the Torah must not be confounded with immobility." Other like-minded rabbinical scholars have shared his conviction that, to survive, the Jewish religion must not remain static, for the historical process is dynamic and demands change. They agree that the modern scientific age, having established its own intellectual standards, demands of the Jewish religion both a reformulation and a revision of some of its beliefs and practices.

Professor Solomon Schechter (1850–1915), the foremost theoretical expositor of Conservative philosophy during the years before World War I, justified this new approach to the Jewish religion on the plea that "Holy Writ, as well as history . . . teaches that the law of Moses was never fully and absolutely put into practice. Liberty was always given to the great teachers of every generation to make modifications and innovations in harmony with the spirit of existing institutions."

In the decades since his death, there has taken place a continuous reappraisal of the Conservative position. Nothing completely definitive has yet emerged from the search for a clear-cut system of Jewish religious thought and practice, and perhaps it never can. Only the general direction has been charted: to retain as many as possible of the traditional beliefs, rites, ceremonies, and practices but with the proviso that they successfully stand the test of relevancy to our contemporary culture, and that they do not conflict with the scientific postulates and findings of the modern age.

These dissents and qualifications aside, Conservative Judaism makes mandatory submission to the authority of the Biblical precepts and the Rabbinic Law. However, such adherence is made contingent on whether they are responsive to the modern requirements of Jewish life.

It is in the altered circumstances of modern living that Conservative Judaism claims it has found validation for its many revisions of ritual observance and practice. In principle, it has rejected no tradition, no law, no symbol; it has sought only to modify them or to be reasonably selective. It does not consider all of the traditional minutiae of observance as binding. For example, Conservative Jews do not feel that they have violated the Sabbath ordinances against making a fire or doing any manner of work merely by pressing a light switch to create illumination, or by using a house elevator, or even by eating before going to the synagogue for prayer. Applicable to all observance is the Conservative attitude that it is not the *letter* but the *spirit* of a rite or law that has the most religious meaning. Ceremonialism and ritualism are considered significant only insofar as they clearly symbolize to the worshiper a religious or an ethical value.

The Conservative Jews have also dispensed with such customs as separating the sexes in the synagogue, an arrangement which only the Orthodox still follow. A great measure of equality of the woman with the man in social and religious spheres is accorded recognition by seating them side by side during the prayer service.

On the other hand, the importance of ceremonial and ritual symbolism is given great emphasis in Conservative Judaism. "The poetry of life," is the way it is characterized by Dr. Robert Gordis. The Conservative attitude toward circumcision is exactly what it is for the Orthodox: Circumcision is *mandatory*. Equally obligatory is the observance of the dietary laws (kashrut), although in practice it turns out to be less rigid than for the Orthodox. To cite one example: while the latter may eat no food whatsoever in other than a strictly kosher home or restaurant, the rule is somewhat relaxed for the Conservative adherent. Where kosher meat foods are not available, he may eat dairy dishes and fish.

Like the Orthodox Jew, he too is required to observe all the festivals and fast days, to celebrate the Seder home-service with festal joy on Passover, and to sit amidst the rustic greenery of the Succah on Succot, the Feast of Booths. He is expected to put on a tallit (prayer shawl) at prayer, and phylacteries (tefillin) during morning devotions on weekdays, to wear a hat or skullcap in the temple, to recite the appropriate blessings at table before eating, and to say Grace upon the conclusion of the meal.

Just as traditional is his observance of the three daily services, but his prayers are recited in both Hebrew and English. The shofar of ram's horn of Biblical antiquity is blown on Rosh Hashanah (in some Conservative temples, just as in Reform congregations, the organ has been introduced); candles are lit on the eve of the Sabbath and holy days in the home; the Kiddush rite (the prayer of sanctification over wine) is recited on the Sabbath and holy days; and the Habdalah service (the symbolic "Separation" of the "sacred"—the Sabbath—from the "profane"—the weekdays) is performed on Saturday night in the synagogue as well as in the home.

A distinguishing element in the Conservative position, receiving far greater emphasis than in Orthodoxy and Reform, has been its attempt to establish a synthesis between Judaism as a religion and Jewish culture and Jewish national aspirations. In line with this, it has sponsored parochial day schools and has taken a fervent stand for Zionism. This latter was stimulated, no doubt, by the ideas of Achad ha-Am (the pseudonym of Asher Ginzberg; *b.* Russia, 1856), the philosophical proponent of "cultural Zionism." During his lifetime —until his death in Palestine in 1927—he had advocated the preservation of the progressive elements of the Jewish heritage, among which he included its rich religious and secular culture and all those timeless values found in the ethics of Prophetic and Talmudic Judaism.

But he took into consideration the objective fact that since the year 70 C.E., the Jews had been not a national but a global people. He therefore proposed that in each country where they lived the Jews should nurture separately their Jewish cultural heritage, all the while maintaining the closest possible ties with the ancient homeland in Palestine (which later became Israel), which should serve as the spiritual-cultural center for all the Jews of the world.

Defining the scope of Conservative Judaism, Louis Ginzberg once wrote: "It is national and universal, individual and social, legal and mystic, dogmatic and practical at once, yet it has unity and individuality."

The Conservative branch of Judaism has enjoyed a remarkable growth in recent years. In 1961 it claimed upward of one million adherents in more than seven hundred congregations throughout the United States and Canada.

Reconstructionism. Since the traumatic experiences of the Hitler era and the devastations of World War II, Conservative Judaism has been evolving in a more "liberal" direction than formerly—a little more away from Orthodoxy and somewhat closer to Reform Judaism. This trend, in considerable part, has been due to the religious-intellectual ferment introduced by Dr. Mordecai Kaplan and his "Reconstruction" movement. Dr. Kaplan, in his challenging reinterpretations of the Jewish religion, culture, and identity, has conceived of Judaism as an evolving religious civilization, and not just a separate department to Jewish life. Namely, he has defined Judaism as a religion as well as a culture, an ethnic identity as well as a Jewish concept of "peoplehood." Like Zacharias Frankel, Solomon Schechter, and Louis Ginzberg, he too considers that, since life is constantly evolving and taking on new forms, the hallowed Jewish past has meaning only if it can be made to fit into the spiritual goals and intellectual needs of the modern Jew. He has intimated that religious faith cannot constitute an absolute; rather, it must be related, in the concrete terms of life, to the perpetually evolving experiences of mankind.

See also DOCTRINES IN JUDAISM; ENLIGHTENMENT, THE JEWISH; ETHICAL VALUES, JEWISH; SABBATH, THE; SABBATH LIGHTS.

JUDGMENT, DAY OF. *See* DEATH; DOCTRINES IN JUDAISM; GAN EDEN; GEHINNOM; IMMORTALITY; RESURRECTION; REWARD AND PUNISHMENT; SIN AND SINNER; SOUL, THE; WORLD-TO-COME.

JUSTICE. *See* ETHICAL VALUES, JEWISH; "EYE FOR AN EYE"; JUBILEE; LAW, JEWISH; PROPHETS (*under* BIBLE, THE); SLAVERY AND THE SLAVE; SOCIAL JUSTICE.

K

KABBALAT SHABBAT. *See* SABBATH, THE.

KADDISH (Aramaic equivalent of the Hebrew word KADDOSH, meaning "holy")

After the Shema, the affirmation of God's Unity, the Kaddish is revered as the most sacred of all Jewish prayers. Why does it inspire in believing Jews such reverence? This feeling, in varying degree, applies even to many who have become estranged from the traditional way of Jewish life. They may only infrequently—or no longer—be attending the synagogue; they may even have given up observance of the Sabbath and holy days and of the rites and customs symbolic of the Jewish faith. Nonetheless, when death occurs within the immediate family, they hasten to a synagogue to recite the Kaddish to the responsive chanting of the congregation of Israel. At this time—in the hour of his deepest grief—as at no other time does the individual Jew, lonely and insecure in the world, feel his closeness to other Jews.

When it is considered that the male mourner is traditionally required by religious law and custom to recite the Kaddish at three separate prayer services each day in the week except on the Sabbath, and for the duration of an eleven-month period, whether he is in good health or in poor, whether it is in the heat of summer or in the cold of winter, whether the synagogue is close at hand or at a distance, then the real measure of importance the Kaddish holds for most Jews may be readily understood. In the complicated life of modern times, to observe the saying of the Kaddish consistently, calls for unavoidable sacrifices in time, effort, convenience, and material self-interest.

On first examination, the Kaddish appears puzzling. By common acceptance, it is the Jewish prayer for the dead. Yet where is there one word concerning death in it? For the mourner who recites it on behalf of the deceased, it is, presumably, an expression of bereavement. But where in the prayer is there struck a single note of grief? The confusion increases when the view of the Rabbis of the Talmud is considered: that the recitation of the Kaddish is, in effect, an act of intercession for the soul of the departed. Yet, strange to relate, nowhere in the prayer is there even a hint of imploring God's mercy—of asking him to alter or soften his judgment. Neither is there any reference to the World-to-Come, nor to the rewards or punishments awaiting the soul there. But most baffling of all—the name of the departed is not even mentioned!

Why then is this prayer called *Kaddish Yatom,* "the Orphan's Kaddish"?

Judged by its text alone, the Kaddish is thoroughly mystifying. But when it is examined in the context of Jewish religious thinking, it appears as no riddle at all. Quite the contrary; it then impresses one as being perfectly logical—even appropriate. The great reverence in which it is held is undoubtedly due to the fact that it is also a *doxology,* a chant of praise to God. It extolls his greatness and hallows his name. However, the special significance of the Kaddish, which goes back to the time of the Destruction of the First Temple, in 586 B.C.E., is that it gives utterance, both declamatory and poignant, to the bittersweet yearning of the devout for the redemption of Israel and of all mankind from suffering, oppression, and the horrors of war. It wings its supplication to the "Throne of Mercy" for the establishment of God's "Kingdom during your lifetime . . . and during the lifetime of the entire household of Israel, speedily and soon! And so say ye: 'Amen.'"

With the word "Kingdom," the Kaddish makes reference to the Kingdom of God (*see* MESSIAH, THE) which the pious expect will be established *on earth* when the Messiah comes. The ideal of "God's Kingdom" was the Jewish dream of Utopia. It was to be a society harmonious and perfect in righteousness, in the practice of social justice, and in the establishment of universal peace. The Prophet Isaiah first projected this dream in a vision of ineffable gentleness and love for mankind; several of the poets and mystics of Biblical times, whose writings are included in the extra-Scriptural anthology, the Apocrypha, rhapsodized upon it; the Sages of the Talmud gave it ethical content; and, finally, the latter-day Cabalists embroidered it with their ardent fancies for the plain folk in order to give them hope for their ultimate redemption.

Thus, as a prayer for the dead, the Kaddish represents a moral triumph for the mourner. For it gives utterance to no human woe, nor does it impose any demands or entreaties for God's love and mercy on behalf of the soul of the departed. Instead, it transforms the mourner's moan of personal grief into a chant of sanctification for the Creator, thereby elevating narrow concern with self into yearning for a better life for all. In this manner, what always appears as the negative element in mourning becomes transmuted into something positive and uplifting.

The recitation of the Kaddish is of the very essence of religious drama. It may be said only in public prayer when at least a minyan (a quorum of ten male worshipers)is present The text, which is in Aramaic except for the last sentence (which is in Hebrew), is intoned according to one or another in a number of musical modes that have been traditional with Jewish ethnic groupings in various parts of the world. The arrangement, like a Bach cantata, is that of soloist and choir; together they weave a prayer-pattern of exaltation. The mourner, as the soloist, recites the Kaddish. He is symbolically projected as the individual Jew who, in the awesome presence of death, chooses to reaffirm his creed of faith. The worshipers, constituting the choir, intone the brief responses, thus placing their fervent seal of approval upon this creed in testimony for the universal congregation of Israel. In this manner, mourner and worshipers take flame from each other, spark releasing spark in their moment of striving for religious illumination. The Rabbis of old considered that the climax of the Kaddish was reached when mourner and worshipers to-

Recitation of the Kaddish by Chief Rabbi Unterman of Israel at the funeral of President Chaim Weizmann. (Israel Office of Information.)

gether intertwined their voices in these words of sanctification: "Let His great Name be blessed forever and for all eternity!" The Midrash comments that, upon the utterance of these words, "the Holy One forgives!"

At all times it was the ardent dream of fathers and mothers to raise up sons who, fortified with Torah-learning and Jewish traditional practices, would walk in the path of righteousness. They were to be links in the continuing chain of the Jewish identity. Such parents felt emotionally secure in the knowledge that, when they passed on "to their eternal reward," their sons would faithfully recite the Kaddish for them—a crowning blessing to mark the end of their lives! The reciters of the Kaddish would thus demonstrate in a symbolic way before God and the congregation of Israel how devoted they were as sons, and what careful upbringing they had received in Torah, in virtue, and in fidelity. This by itself was considered sufficient to merit the pardon of Heaven for the deceased—for all his sins and strayings in the blind alleys of life. And so it came about that in latter-day Yiddish, the word "Kaddish" was used to refer not only to the prayer itself but, in mock endearment, also to a son who was expected to recite it for his father and mother. With what tenderness and rejoicing parents of former times would exclaim in a folk-formula at the birth of a male child: "God be praised for giving us a Kaddish!"

But what if the departed was left with daughters only? In "a man's world," however more humane and gentle than others Jewish men were to their womanfolk, this was deemed a cruel misfortune, indeed! Generally observed was the custom that women were not to recite the Kaddish. Yet this view was by no means unanimously held by the religious authorities. Two dissenters of great eminence were Joseph Caro, the sixteenth-century Palestinian compiler of the Shulchan Aruch, the authoritative code of Jewish law, and his contemporary, Moses Isserles of Cracow. They took a decidely broader and more humane approach than their rabbinic colleagues, holding that where there was no surviving son, it was perfectly proper—even desirable—for a daughter to recite the Kaddish. Especially meritorious was considered the act of the individual who, although no kin of the deceased, yet out of an altruistic desire to follow the precept "love thy neighbor as thyself" undertook the onerous duty of reciting the Kaddish for him or her throughout the long period of mourning.

It can be said that the dilemma of the childless was the most intolerable of all. That is poignantly illustrated in the Talmud, which relates an incident concerning the illustrious Tanna, Yochanan ben Zakkai, when he was at the point of death. When the Roman legions had laid waste the sanctuary on Mount Zion in 70 C.E., it was he who took the lead in building a new kind of "holy of holies" for his people: that of the school and of Torah-learning. In destroying the fatherland of the Jews, Titus had intended to orphan them in the world, but Yochanan led them instead into the indestructible fatherland of the mind and the spirit. Yet now, at the point of saying farewell to life, he, "the Father of Israel," suddenly began to feel unutterably childless and barren! A great sorrow fell upon him. His tears began to flow. In vain his devoted disciples tried to comfort him.

"Woe is me!" Yochanan lamented. "My sons died in their youth! Now there will be no one to recite the Kaddish for me when I am gone!"

"Aren't we your sons?" asked his disciples reproachfully.

How and when did the Kaddish originate? Actually no single individual composed it, nor was it written at one time. It grew organically, over centuries of groping by the rabbis, from the time of the Talmudic age, before it evolved in its final form as we know it today.

It is perhaps of more than passing interest that the main element of the Kaddish should have been adapted into the Christian liturgy from the beginning. This was quite natural, for Jesus, the Apostles, and the other early Christians were believing Jews. It goes without saying that, like all other Jews, they too recited what was an earlier version of the Kaddish in their public worship. For the Jewish-Christians, this prayer held more than ordinary significance; they believed that its Messianic passage referred specifically to Jesus. Thus, that part of the Kaddish which is the doxology became, in the Latin Mass of the Roman Church, the Gloria and the Sanctus. The Messianic portion—that which concerns the establishment of the Kingdom of God—was closely paraphrased in the Paternoster (The Lord's Prayer), which is considered by Christians as the most sacred among all their prayers.

See also BURIAL RITES AND CUSTOMS; DEATH; MESSIAH, THE; UNITY OF ISRAEL.

KAHAL, KAHALIM. *See* COMMUNITY, SELF-GOVERNING.

KANNA, KANNAIM. *See* ZEALOTS.

KAPPARAH. *See* YOM KIPPUR.

KARAIM. *See* KARAITES.

KARAITES (in Hebrew: KARAIM, from the word MIKRAH, meaning "Scripture"; namely, "Followers of Scripture")

In 1263, the French Dominican Thomas of Cantimpré noted: ". . . all Eastern [i.e., Karaite] Jews consider as heretics and excommunicate those Jews who, against the Law of Moses and the Prophets, obtain and copy this book which is called the Talmud."

This, in essence, represented the principal sectarian view of the Karaites. Strict Torah-literalists, they stood, first of all, in opposition to the Oral Tradition and to the multitudinous extra-Biblical laws, regulations, and guiding opinions that had been developed in Rabbinic Judaism; and, second of all, they opposed the Talmud itself, which was a codex and an exposition of all of the above. Anan ben David, the Babylonian founder of Karaism, in 760 C.E. established this central religious guideline for himself and for his followers: "I will search dilligently in the Torah [ie., the Pentateuch], and I will not rely on my own opinion."

In their interpretation of the Bible, the Karaites (or Ananites, as they were sometimes called) diverged sharply from the symbolic and allegoric method that was universally used by their Talmudic opponents, the adherents of the Rab-

Karaite Synagogue at Odessa, Russia, late 19th century.

bis, who were referred to as Rabbanites. The Karaites applied a critical method, many centuries in advance of their time, to the study of the Scriptures, approximating in many ways the one that is now being employed by advanced Biblical scholars. The medieval Karaite scholars—and they were, beginning with the brilliant Anan ben David, numerous and well schooled in Greek and Arabic philosophy, science, and literature—are said to have been the first to introduce the objective tools of philology and Hebrew grammar into Biblical studies. Some of the writers of the nineteenth century, in particular Salomon Munk and Abraham Geiger, were of the opinion that the Karaites were better able to apply these scientific methods to Biblical lore because they were free of the authority of Rabbinic tradition and of the maze of its legal-ritualistic regulations.

As was the case with the Samaritans, who until our time had not received in Jewish writings even a modicum of objective and fair treatment concerning their religious beliefs and practices, so it was too with the schismatic sect of Karaites. Nothing but hostility toward them has marked and marred rabbinic writings. Heretical movements in any faith unleash acrimony and conflict and leave a residue of bitterness lasting for a very long time in the memory of those who

Karaites of the Crimea, believed to be descendants of the Khazars. (From La Russie, *by Le Comte La Fite de Pelleport, Paris, 1862.)*

are hurt. They usually stir up the most heated passions, which lead to disagreeable consequences. The religious wars that convulsed Christendom in Europe furnish the classic example of this.

The set-to was a noisy one from the very beginning. The Rabbanites, being in the overwhelming majority, sprang to the attack against the heretics with all the intellectual, verbal, and emotional weapons in their arsenal. The Karaites were personally reviled and their activities and intentions were misrepresented. Even that profound rabbinic thinker and man of considerable genius, Saadia al-Fayyumi, the Gaon (Rector) of the Academy of Sura in Babylonia, began writing at the age of twenty-three, in 915, a series of blistering polemics against Anan ben David and the "heretical" principles of Karaism. The emotions he stirred up with his attacks on the Karaites were so violent that the Karaites even made an attempt to assassinate him.

Apparently (all the pertinent facts, unfortunately, are not available) the success of the Karaites as missionaries and propagandists for their sect must have appeared too substantial and threatening to the main body of Jewry, for there was a continuous stream of accusations being leveled against them. They were charged, for example, with being corrupt, venal, and unscrupulous in their conduct. Following the pattern of the ancient Jewish indictment against the Samaritans, the Rabbanites also alleged that the Karaites served as informers for the Mohammedan enemies of the Jews.

How deep were the spiritual macerations on both sides in this religious civil war may be deduced from two contradictory appraisals of Anan ben David. The first evaluation was made in 1161 by one of the most distinguished of all Spanish rabbinical thinkers, Abraham ibn Daud. Customarily of a philosophical and gentle turn of mind, he astonishes with the violent flare-up of his feelings when he but mentions the founder of Karaism: "Anan and Saul, his son—may the names of the wicked rot!" The very opposite approach was taken by a worshipful Karaite scholar of Lithuania in 1757. His portrait of Anan was painted in luminous colors. He conceived him to be "a saintly and pious man. He was the greatest and most prominent scholar of all the Jewish Sages." And as if this praise were not sufficiently honorific, he goes on to add with palpable awe and Messianic suggestiveness: "He was a patrician prince, sprung from the seed of David the King, peace be unto him!"

The Karaites, who were very numerous in Islamic countries during the Middle Ages, were entirely capable of trading insult for insult with their traditionalist adversaries. According to one student of Karaite literature, D. S. Margoliouth (1885–1940), the Karaite verbal counterattack was even more offensive than the abuse of the Rabbanites. "In virulence and obscenity it exceeds anything of the sort I have ever seen; the manifesto of the Spaniards at the time of the Armada comes near it."

The Karaites claimed, but without any historical proof to support this claim, their direct descent from the Sadducees who had flourished during the Second Temple period in Judea. At least for their first several centuries and up to the time of their greatest creativity—the period of the eleventh and twelfth centuries—the Karaite sectaries observed the Priestly Code of Purity. This was done partly to identify with the Sadducees, who had formed the backbone of the priesthood.

It was inevitable that the Karaites practice austerities and renounce all sensory pleasures, for being a Messianic-oriented sect, their daily lives were directed to a preparation for the final Redemption. They had an ascetic dedication to the end that, so long as they remained in Exile (Galut) away from the sacred Land of Israel, they would observe perpetual mourning for the Temple that was no more, by not eating meat nor drinking wine. Friday night, which is the eve of the Jewish Sabbath, was sat through by them in total darkness, in fulfillment of the Scriptural prohibition in Exodus 35:3—"Ye shall kindle no fire throughout your habitations upon the Sabbath day"—which, incidentally, had also been observed by the Samaritans and Sadducees. Throughout many centuries, perhaps the most dramatic single contrast that was visible externally between the Karaites and the main body of Jewry was the total darkness in which the Karaite homes were enveloped while standing in the very midst of the festive, Sabbath-lit Jewish homes in the ghettos and mellahs.

In more recent times, the ascetic practices of the Karaites began to diminish, and so did their traditional intellectualism and their intense piety. Their isolation became more difficult and depressing as their numbers declined. Little contact was permitted them with other Jews out of fear of sectarian seduction. Yet, as in the instance of Ezra's decree against intermarriage with the Samaritan heretics, non-Karaites were forbidden by rabbinic decrees from intermarrying with them.

Perhaps the most ironic footnote to the history of the Karaites across twelve centuries of embattled faith and fruitless debate with the main body of Jewry was that written in blood by the Nazis during World War II. The Karaites, who in the Soviet Union then numbered ten thousand, suffered the same impartial fate as other Jews: They were "liquidated" in the incinerators and gas chambers of Hitler. At least in a common death, grim and ravening and free at last from sectarian passions and injustice, they were accorded their rightful kinship as Jews by those who had scorned them.

See also CHASIDIM; EPIKOROS; ESSENES; PHARISEES, SADDUCEES; SAMARITANS; THERAPEUTAE; ZEALOTS.

KARPAS. *See* PASSOVER.

KASHER. *See* DIETARY LAWS.

KASHRUT. *See* ANIMALS, "CLEAN AND UNCLEAN"; DIETARY LAWS; MEAT, SALTING OF; MEAT AND MILK; SHECHITAH; SHOCHET.

KEHILLAH. *See* COMMUNITY, SELF-GOVERNING.

KELEH KODESH. *See* TORAH ORNAMENTS.

KEMIAH, KEMIOT. *See* AMULETS.

KEREN KAYEMET. *See* THEODOR HERZL (*under* ZIONISM).

KERIAH. *See* BURIAL RITES AND CUSTOMS.

KERIAT TORAH, KERIAT HA-TORAH. *See* TORAH-READING.

KETUBAH (Hebrew s., meaning "marriage agreement"; pl. KETUBOT; in Yiddish: K'SUBAH)

It is an ancient Jewish custom that before bride and groom go under the chuppah (the canopy under which the marriage rite is performed), the ketubah—the agreement which stipulates the dowry terms and related practical matters—is read to them by the officiating rabbi. It is then signed and properly witnessed.

Superficially viewed, the intrusion of such an agreement into the marriage ceremony might strike one unpleasantly, as something perhaps sordid and mercenary, like a bill of sale that is drawn up by lawyers and then notarized before one can take possession of a house or merchandise. But in actuality, seen in perspective in its ancient historical and social setting, when the male among all peoples enjoyed almost arbitrary powers and privileges in the family organization, this marriage agreement, in a concrete sort of way, represented a bill of rights for the Jewish woman. One of its legal stipulations, for example, guaranteed her vested interests in her husband's estate in the event of his prior decease. Even more, her dower rights were fully protected in the event that her husband, whether justifiably or not, divorced her. In fact, many an incipient divorce was nipped in the bud when

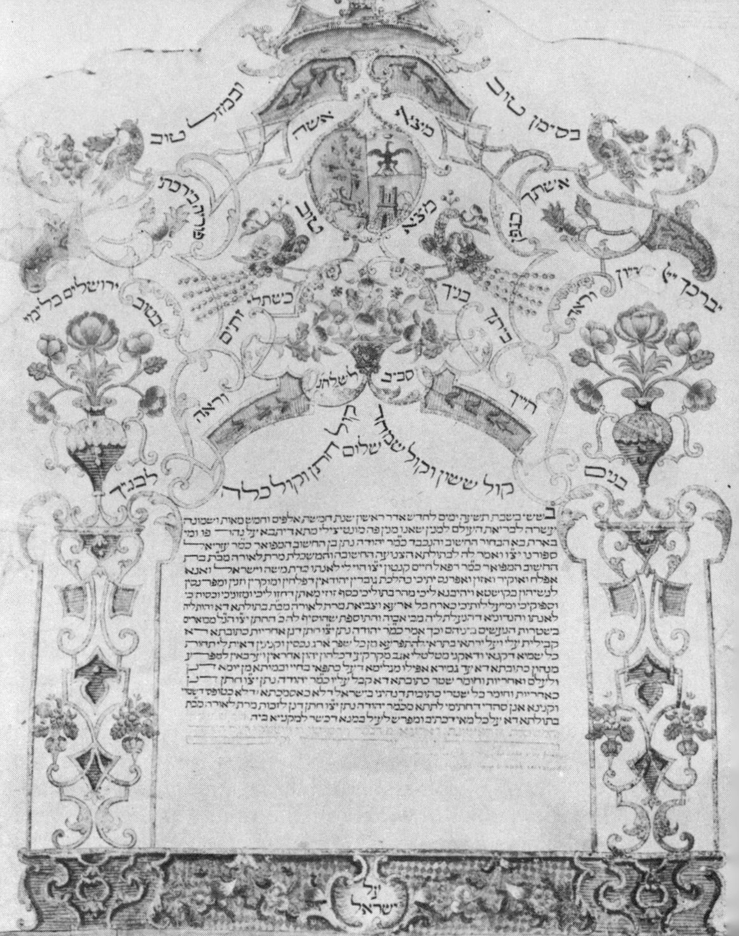

Illuminated parchment ketubah (marriage contract) of the 18t century with colored decorations typical of that period. (Courte of Joseph B. Horwitz Judaica Collection, Cleveland.)

the husband was actually faced with the sometime severe penalties of the ketubah's provisions for financial compensation to the wife if there *was* a divorce! The legal requirement for returning her dowry to a wife in the event of separation seemed too painful for some men—especially those with not too flourishing means—to contemplate.

It becomes abundantly clear that the marriage agreement came into being as a result of an evolving social ethos in which the status of the woman, generally low among all peoples, was raised in Jewish life by guaranteeing her material rights in the marital union. In that revolutionary way she graduated from being a mere "thing" or chattel in the structure of her society into a human being whose moral stature and economic rights had to be respected.

It should, nevertheless, be noted that, as a legal instrument, the ketubah seems to have marked a falling in line by Jewish jurisprudence with the Roman marriage-contract of that time, which afforded legal and property protection to the Jewish woman. No doubt, of the greatest importance in the Jewish marriage contract, next to the stipulations concerning the dowry, was the expressly stated provision that, in the event of the husband's death, the dowry the widow had brought him as a bride, aside from her other rightful claims, be repaid to her from the estate.

But the real motivation behind the ketubah was a social and moral one. It is to be found in the solemn oath of marital obligation the groom takes before his bride, their respective families, and the wedding guests as witnesses assembled: "I shall work for you, honor you, support and maintain you, in accordance with the custom of Jewish husbands who, in truth work for their wives and honor them, and support and maintain them."

Until the eighteenth century, the ketubah consisted of a sheet of parchment on which the Aramaic text was illuminated by a border design. But after that time it was mass produced and printed on paper. Its design became overornate and most undistinguished. The folk art the hand-drawn ketubah represented in former centuries varied with the cultural level of the Jewish community in each region. In the countries of Eastern Europe, where life remained culturally backward in certain respects, the ketubah was simple and virtually without decoration. But in Spain, the Provence, and Italy, where the arts flourished during the Renaissance in the general community, the ketubot, quite naturally reflecting that trend, were lovely and decorative. One can say with justification that, the farther back in the time of the Renaissance, the more exquisitely designed and tastefully colored they were. Quite often, the central design motif then was that of bride and groom, with the symbolic Tree of Life (*see* TORAH ORNAMENTS) blossoming reassuringly between them.

See also DOWRY, THE; FAMILY, THE; HUSBANDS AND WIVES (*under* FAMILY RELATIONS, TRADITIONAL PATTERNS OF); MARRIAGE; WEDDING CUSTOMS.

KETUBIM. *See* BIBLE, THE.

KIBBUTZ (Hebrew s., meaning "group," "collective"; pl. KIBBUTZIM)

Like the kvutzah (pl. kvutzot), the smaller type of collective settlement from which it evolved, the kibbutz operates according to principles of a fused ideology which combines Zionist ideals with a socialistic mode of organization. The kibbutzim—they are banded together for mutual aid in separate federations according to different political philosophies and economic methods—regard themselves as the first "seedlings" from which ultimately will develop a fully grown co-operative or collectivist society in Israel.

The kibbutz has an intriguing history. Because of its dramatic rise since 1909, when it began as the kvutzah, founded by the youthful idealists who lived and worked in it, and because of its relatively successful ability to maintain itself in the face of innumerable physical and material hardships and dangers, it has captured both the imagination and the admiration of the entire world. Today (in 1964) there are in Israel several hundred kibbutzim of different political and ethnic stripes with perhaps a total population of 100,000. Although this number constitutes less than 5 per cent of all the people in Israel, yet in terms of social significance and group achievement for the Jewish Homeland, they do not have a peer. Their special and often heroic role in the defense of the country at their strategic frontier outposts has drawn much attention to them. From all parts of the world, sociologists, economists, psychologists, and educators have been coming to observe and study them at first hand. A number of Asian and newly created African states have even used the kibbutz as the model for setting up their own variants.

The establishment by the so-called Romny Group of the first kvutzah marked a turning point in the agricultural development of Jewish Palestine. Until that time, whatever farming was being done by Jews was in the colonies that had been established by the Chibat Zion (Love of Zion) movement during the 1880's and 1890's in such Bilu settlements as Petach Tikvah, Rehovot, and Rosh Pinah (*see* ZIONISM). But since the Bilu-ites were afflicted with what could be described as "Biblical romanticism"—i.e., they visioned themselves sitting (as the Prophet dreamed) each man under his own fig tree and grapevine, "unafraid" and at peace with his fellow men) they, consequently, floundered in their practical undertakings and, in order to survive, called for help from the Jewish philanthropists.

Edmond de Rothschild and Maurice de Hirsch, both barons, both fabulously rich, and both exceedingly charitable men, responded not only with financial assistance for the colonies but also with "managers" who turned out to be autocrats. Rothschild was a truly munificent patron; he helped found new colonies for the settlers, built houses and planted vineyards for them, pressed their grapes in his own Carmel winery at Rishon-le-Zion, and even bought their produce at generously fixed prices. When, finally, he grew tired of the incessant bickering between them and his managers, he transferred the pious duty (mitzvah) of benevolence to the warm-hearted Baron de Hirsch, who founded for this purpose the Jewish Colonization Association (ICA) in 1899. But the managers appointed by both barons, despite the best intentions in the world, had succeeded only in corrupting the integrity of the Bilu idealists. With colonialist master-race obsession, they induced the colonists to give up working themselves and to hire fellah (Arab peasant) labor, which was to be bought very cheaply.

It was under these morally unwholesome and antisocial conditions of agricultural development of Jewish Palestine that the immediate precursor (and in some ways the model) of the kibbutz—the small collective settlement or kvutzah—came into being.

In the second wave of East European chalutzim (1902–14) were hundreds of idealistic and intelligent young men and women (among them were David Ben-Gurion and Yitzchak Ben-Zvi, subsequently and respectively Prime Minister and President of the State of Israel) who had come to Palestine with the definite intention of becoming tillers of the soil. Many of them had been students or workers who had taken part in the revolutionary struggle in Russia against czarist oppression and had been attached to Socialist groups of varying views. But when they tried to get jobs in the colonies, they usually met with cold refusal, for by urban training and schooling, as well as by the expectation of higher wages, they were completely disadvantaged in work competition with the hardy Arab peasants—the "hired hands" of Jewish colonization.

The situation they faced was almost impossible of solution. The problem obtruded: How could a former Jewish intellectual or professional manage to eat according to the minimal dietary standards of the West on daily earnings of from three to five piasters (the equivalent in those years of less than fifty cents in American money)? Furthermore, under such impossible conditions of existence, it was out of the question even to think of raising a family! The prospects looked dismal, indeed, but the solution suddenly emerged from the very impasse itself.

Before World War I, noted economist and single-taxer Franz Oppenheimer (*b.* Germany, 1864–*d.* U.S.A. 1943) experimented with a pilot settlement-project at Lake Kinneret (the Sea of Galilee); this was a co-operative village for which the Jewish National Fund had purchased the land, and it was directed by a farm-manager who had been schooled in scientific methods. But when the undertaking collapsed—in part because the manager's guaranteed salary swallowed up the co-operators' "profits" and then some—a group of six of these intellectual young immigrants, who were referred to as "the Romny Group," persuaded Oppenheimer to let them take over "the Village" and run it as a small "family" collective (kvutzah). They wished to run it along lines which were the very opposite of the prevailing "colonialist" methods in Jewish settlement farming that relied so much on the exploitation of cheap Arab labor. They declared: "*We must work the land ourselves* and produce such crops as will enable us to be self-sufficient to a maximum degree."

Then and there, in 1909, was founded Deganiya, the first Socialist-Zionist kvutzah in Palestine; it served as the model for all other kvutzot that followed and, ultimately, of the kibbutzim, as well.

A very important factor in the enthusiasm and tenacity of the young chalutzim (pioneers) who came to work in Deganiya (in order to keep it *en famille*, they limited its membership to twenty-five persons; therefore it was necessary to establish two additional nearby kvutzot—Deganiya Bet [B] and Deganiya Gimmel [C] were the teachings on the Religion of Work and the personal example set by the Socialist and (in part) Tolstoyan mystic, Aaron David Gordon (*b.* Russia, 1856–*d.* Palestine, 1922). Gordon was a utopian Socialist (this kind of socialism was much in vogue during the nineteenth century) in that he preached that the good life was possible only in working with one's hands in a collective system, and—most important of all—in agricultural pursuits. He considered that the recovery of the Jewish people from its wounds and warpings through its centuries of persecution and estrangement from nature could not be effected before it first returned to a healthy and productive life on the soil. The analogy that perhaps could be drawn from Gordon's conviction is the story of Antaeus, in Greek mythology; he was invincible as long as he kept his feet firmly on the earth.

Some other ideological influences also entered into the shaping of the collective settlements. These included, most particularly, the writings of Ber Borochov (Russia, 1881–1917), which had a strong appeal for the young Socialist intellectuals. Borochov was largely responsible for the founding of the Poale Zion (Labor Zionist) movement and its more militant Marxist offshoot, Hashomer Hatzair (The Young Watchman) with its federation, Kibbutz Artzi, consisting of a hundred or more collectives in Israel.

The socio-economic principle on which the kvutzah operated was indicated in the formula "From each according to his ability; to each as much as to his neighbor."

After World War I, with chalutziot (pioneering) accelerated once more by a new wave of arrivals from Eastern Europe, the family-type kvutzah no longer could suffice. In 1921, the ground plan for the first kibbutz as an elaboration of the kvutzah was drawn up by Shlomo (Lavi) Lefkovitz, the leader of the collective Ein Harod. He defined the problem in this manner:

> The small collective—the kvutzah—cannot bring out an individual's capacities to the full; it limits his horizon and does not allow his spirit to attain its loftiest heights. Public services, such as education of the children and cultural activities, can achieve a high level only in a large settlement. We must create a source of livelihood in every kvutzah for the largest number of immigrants; this can only be achieved by combining industry and crafts with agriculture. In this way the kvutzah can become a self-supporting, self-sufficient economic unit, supplying almost all the needs of its inhabitants. This will make it possible, too, for the kvutzah to free itself from the capitalist economy of the towns and the exploitation that goes with it.

Generally speaking, the design of the kibbutz, which itself was established on land given in trust to its members by the Jewish National Fund, followed Lavi's definition. Membership in it merely required adherence to the objectives of Zionism and to the general socio-economic principles of the collective (kibbutz) idea. Outside of that, the kibbutz was unencumbered by adherence to any particular political theory or domination by an organization. Anyone, whatever his opinions, was welcomed.

In 1927, all the kibbutzim united to form the Kibbutz Hameuchad (The United Kibbutz Federation) for the purpose of facilitating in every way possible the development of each settlement economically, culturally, and educationally, and to furnish loans through the facilities of a central bank to its member-collectives. However, as could be expected, several dissident groups formed within it under different ideological and political auspices. The cold war that began between East and West after World War II in the late 1940's

A settlement of fishermen established in 1937 on the Sea of Galilee. (Histadrut House.)

Field-workers in a new farm-settlement in Israel.

Members of a new kibbutz drawing a water pipeline through the Negev desert in southern Israel. (U.N.)

Yotvata, a collective settlement in the Negev desert. (Israel Office of Information.)

The moshav Nahalal in the Valley of Jezreel, built with great hardship on former swampland and designed uniquely for tactical defense against possible Arab attack. (Israel Office of Information.)

A kibbutz member standing guard against possible Arab attackers.

also became a bone of bitter contention in the Kibbutz Federation, and it soon resulted in a parting of the ways between the factions. In fact, the results were nearly calamitous, for not only were kibbutzim breaking up, but, frequently, individual families were rent by fierce ideological partisanship that set children against parents or even wife against husband.

In 1951, the kibbutzim began to reorganize. The Social-Democratic faction which adhered to Mapai (the Labor Party of Israel) seceded from Kibbutz Hameuchad and formed its own pro-Western Ichud Hakvutzot Vehakibbutzim (The Union of Co-operative Settlements). The Marxist (and frequently pro-Soviet) kibbutzim joined Kibbutz Artzi (the organization that had first been formed by five kibbutzim in 1928), which was the collectivist arm of the Hashomer Hatzair movement; its members, before being accepted, usually received prior agricultural training on the hachsharah (preparation farm) operated by the organization in several countries. The religious kibbutzim banded together into the Kibbutz Dati federation principally made up of Hapoel Hamizrachi (The Religious Worker) members from the labor wing of the Orthodox Mizrachi Zionist movement.

Whatever differences may separate them in their ideologies, structural forms, social, moral, or religious attitudes, or even in their methods of work, fundamentally, all kibbutzim possess strong similarities. Each kibbutz is a voluntary and self-governing group that collectively passes judgment on the suitableness or desirability of anyone applying to join it. The land which the kibbutz cultivates does not belong to it but was purchased by the Jewish National Fund as a permanent possession of the Jewish nation, in an approach modeled after the Biblical declaration about land ownership: "The earth is Mine, sayeth the Lord." No member of a kibbutz has any proprietary right or share in it, for it must be remembered that the kibbutz is not a collective partnership. Should the kibbutznik (member of the kibbutz) at any time, even after many years of association with it, decide to leave the kibbutz, he carries nothing away with him. All his material rights and privileges come to an end with his departure, except for what fraternal financial assistance he may receive from the kibbutz for his outside adjustment. During his stay, he is not subject to any discipline other than the moral pressure from his fellow kibbutzniks and to no punishment for infraction of the group's laws and regulations other than being requested to leave. This is an index of the ethical standard of relationships required for successful and civilized group life.

The kibbutz is usually structured on a general assembly, on several administrators, and on working committees. The general assembly, consisting of every adult member, is completely democratic in the manner in which it carries on its discussions and in the way it reaches decisions. It holds weekly meetings and decides by majority vote on all questions. The administrative secretariat, depending on the size of the kibbutz, consists of three to seven executives such as an agricultural manager, an assigner of work tasks, a treasurer, a secretary, a bookkeeper, etc. The work committees are chosen by the general assembly to assist the various executives in carrying out their responsibilities. Thus there are engaged in the kibbutz a variety of committees for management and work-planning, and for school, health, and cultural activities. Generally, more than half the members of any kibbutz are deeply involved in one or another of its operational activities. This is in harmony with the principal objective of the kibbutz idea: collective and co-operative living.

The average, fully developed kibbutz, which combines agriculture with light industry, consists of about one hundred family units, although, of course, there are also members who are single. Its relatively large population on the village scale enables it to carry on mixed or intensive farming on a reasonably profitable basis; at least there is less of a financial risk involved for the kibbutz if, instead of one crop, it raises six, should the harvest in one or two of them turn out to be poor or fail altogether. Furthermore, the great variety of work afforded in such a settlement—in field, physical plant, and factory—secures for its members more evenly distributed employment all the year round.

Mechanization of farm work, possible only in the larger settlement, proves an important advantage to production and efficiency. There usually are five main agricultural activities: the cultivation of field crops, the raising of fodder for the livestock, truck gardening, poultry and egg production, and dairying. Some kibbutzim also have ponds in which they raise fish as an extra "crop," or grow flowers and shrubs for commercial sale, or have apiaries.

A spearhead of modernism, in spite of its poverty and external shabbiness, the average kibbutz has served as a clinical laboratory for agricultural research and the application to actual farm work of the latest scientific methods. It has been experimenting with new crops, chemical fertilizers, the selection of hardier and more disease-resistant plants, the improvement of livestock—cattle, sheep, goats, and poultry—and has contributed much in agrotechnical innovations. Each kibbutz has its own shops for the repair of machinery and tools and for carpentry and metalwork. The small factory it usually operates to take up the slack of farm work accounts for about one-third of the total income of the kibbutz and thus helps balance the budget, which otherwise would not be accomplished.

The several federations of kibbutzim, which originated from the compelling need felt by the individual collectives for greater mutual aid in order to survive, have helped sustain each of their member settlements by all kinds of co-operative services—in marketing, in the wholesale purchase of feed, fertilizers, tools, supplies, and food, in the common use of expensive farm machinery (such as harvesting combines), and in the granting of loans at a low rate of interest. Of considerable assistance to all the kibbutzim have been the transport co-operatives which operate hundreds of trucks. Indispensable, too, have been the cultural and educational collaborations between the kibbutzim—activities that are co-ordinated by their central organizations.

The life in a kibbutz is characterized by a familial relationship—there may be dissension, as in every family, but there is also a closely knit fellowship among its members; whether all of their relationships are personally agreeable to them or not, they, perforce, must rely on one another for the common welfare.

The physical accomodations and other arrangements in most kibbutzim are often of a primitive and rudimentary kind—the emphasis is never on appearances, or on comfort, but on the realities of the work and the need for making practical progress. There is little or no individual housekeeping to do. Since the women, who constitute about half of the membership, also have to work in field, plant, and factory, the problem of obviating the need for most housekeeping is in large measure solved by having a communally operated kitchen, dining room, and laundry. Unmarried kibbutzniks usually live in general dormitories, but married couples occupy individual rooms or, in the more affluent kibbutzim, tiny separate dwellings or apartments.

Children in the kibbutz live together in special quarters of their own; after school is recessed, they spend several hours with their parents, but then return to sleep in their own dormitory. Their education and upbringing, notwithstanding the inferior state of the school plant and inadequate books and supplies, is of a remarkably high order. It has called forth both astonishment and admiration from foreign educators and psychologists who constantly keep coming to observe the educational phenomenon. Schooling, of twelve years' obligatory duration, is from nursery to the end of high school, and is thoroughly integrated with all the practical and cultural activities in the kibbutz. Thus, education and life are made to appear to the child as one organic whole.

Although the kibbutz is, in varying degrees, socialistic in its organization and goals, nevertheless, it stimulated the development of other forms of agricultural enterprise, but in less collectivist directions. Second only to the kibbutz in the number of its settlements (also on land furnished by the Jewish National Fund) and in the size of its membership is the moshav ovdim (the workers' or smallholders' co-operative; [pl.] moshavim ovdim). In the moshav, each family owns an individual plot. On part of this, it builds a home; what remains, it cultivates in any manner it chooses.

In the moshav too are present some of the collectivist features of the kibbutz, for its members own, co-operatively, several kinds of expensive farm machinery: tractors, combines, incubators, and cold-storage facilities.

Far less numerous in its settlements than the moshav ovdim is the moshav (meshek) shitufi ([pl.] moshavim shitufim). Its land, like that of the kibbutz, is worked collectively, yet it offers even more latitude to the individual settler than does the moshav ovdim. Like the latter, it too lays primary emphasis on separate family life (as opposed to the collective group-life in the kibbutz).

Yet all forms of settlement—kibbutz, moshav ovdim, and moshav shitufi—use the same co-operative institutions established by Histadrut (the General Labor Federation) for marketing products, purchasing supplies, and obtaining financial credit, and all use the comprehensive medical services of the Kupat Cholim (Medical Fund).

It is noteworthy that each of the kibbutz federations carries on an intensive educational and cultural program for its adult members. For example, in order to obtain a uniform philosophy and methods of education in terms of its own ideology, Kibbutz Artzi, the federation of Hashomer Hatzair, conducts for its membership its own teachers' seminary and an adult-education "university." Whether the kibbutzim in each federation have a prosperous physical appearance or only a shabby one, they, nevertheless, possess libraries. The kibbutzim regularly feature recitals and concerts of fine music (in how many villages in the world can one hear the competent performance by players of chamber music?), and lectures on vital themes followed by lively informal discussions. Then, too, many a kibbutz boasts an art collection, or it outfits, for the benefit of its children, a tiny, natural history museum.

Whether these kibbutzim, which are but little islands of co-operative enterprise in a sea of capitalistic economy, can go on for long, sustained by their own determined and self-sacrificing efforts and without receiving substantial assistance, remains an unanswered and moot question. Already a disturbing element has entered into the total picture: The lack of educational opportunities and the hard life in the kibbutz has prompted a great many youths, although born and raised in the collective, to leave for the brighter prospects of the cities. As yet, the exodus has not reached dangerous proportions, but neither has it been stemmed, and the future remains unpredictable.

Moreover, the establishment of new kibbutzim has not been keeping pace with the increase of the general Jewish population. Not only was the potential reserve of idealistic Zionist youth destroyed by the Germans in the death camps in the 1940's, but the great majority of new immigrants, coming from the Arab countries and being largely uneducated, backward, and conditioned by their former lives to a preference for petty huckstering and peddling, are not at all attracted by the prospect of "working for nothing" in the kibbutzim.

See also HEBREW LITERATURE, MODERN; ZIONISM.

KIDDUSH (Hebrew, meaning "sanctification")

The "holiness" theme, like that of "righteousness," has been central in the development of Jewish religious thinking. It stems from one of the attributes Jews have ascribed to God, who in Scripture (Leviticus 11:44) commands them: "Sanctify yourselves, therefore, and be ye holy, for I am holy." Much in the rites, ceremonies, symbolism, prayers, and religious literature of the Jews dwells almost obsessively on the primacy of holiness in Jewish life; this emphasis, naturally, was carried over into Christianity by the Jewish founders of that religion.

The religious teachers of the Second Temple period wished to impress upon the people that the observance of the Sabbath was not to be regarded in an empty formalistic way. It had to be endowed, they urged, with the raptures of an inner spiritual experience. Therefore, they instituted the ceremony and prayer of the Kiddush.

The Kiddush is principally associated with the eve of the Sabbath—Friday night. "Remember the Sabbath day to sanctify it," runs the Biblical injunction in Exodus 20:8. But the Kiddush is also repeated by the religious traditionalists on Saturday before beginning the midday Sabbath meal, as well as on Rosh Hashanah and on the three Pilgrim festivals—Passover, Shabuot, and Succot.

Although the Kiddush is performed in non-Orthodox congregations by the chazzan (cantor) in the synagogue at the conclusion of the Sabbath prayer service on Friday night, it remains essentially a family rite, with the father performing as the celebrant "priest" as soon as he returns from the synagogue service, and the other members of the family constituting, as it were, a congregation of "worshipers." As the family sits around the table, prior to beginning the Sabbath meal, the head of the household fills the traditional Kiddush goblet with a special "sacramental" wine, made of "fruit of the vine": grapes or raisins. Rising before the hushed house-

Three 18th-century Kiddush goblets. Germany.

hold, he lifts his goblet and recites the prayer of sanctification. This is a composite of a passage from Genesis 2:1-3 which relates, in the epic of Creation how God rested from his labors of fashioning the universe on the Sabbath day—"And God blessed the seventh day and hallowed it"—followed by the two customary blessings: the one always pronounced before drinking wine, and the other extolling God for having hallowed Israel with the commandments—"and in love and favor He has given us the holy Sabbath as an inheritance, a memorial of the Creation . . . and in remembrance of the departure from Egypt." The reciter raises the goblet to his lips and sips from it. He then passes it in turn to all the members of the household, beginning deferentially with the mother, then to the oldest and down to the youngest child, and each one takes a symbolic sip of the wine. By this collective act they achieve an indefinable religious communion.

One is led to wonder what precise relationship there was —and there must have been one—between the sip of wine from the Kiddush cup of sanctification and the sip of wine from the first chalice of the Eucharist taken by the early Jewish-Christians. Almost certainly, the latter had derived their rite, in its initial form at least, from the love-feast (*see* ESSENES) or communion-meal of the Jewish sectarian Essenes. At the same time, one also cannot help but note that the Kiddush ceremony had much in common with the rite of the ancient Greeks and Romans, who drank a libation to their gods—a sacrificial act—before beginning a family meal or a public banquet. The high priest in Jerusalem, too, as he stood in the Temple Court on Yom Kippur, was required by time-honored custom to ceremonially offer a libation of wine while brazen cymbals clashed and massed choirs of Levites sang to the accompaniment of stringed and woodwind instruments. Many are the threads—though they often remain invisible—that link the customs and beliefs of one people with those of other peoples. This helps prove that the principle of the diffusion of all cultures is a basic factor in civilization.

In the numerous Jewish communities in Babylonia, because grape-growing was limited and wine was, therefore, costly (in Judea, where vineyards were abundant, wine was cheap), the lack of wine presented a serious difficulty for the performance of the Kiddush ceremony. The Rabbinic teachers of Babylonia were finally, led to rule, out of necessity, that inasmuch as the Sabbath was given to man for him to enjoy and not to add to his burdens, and since the only reason for drinking wine (even if only a symbolic sip) was because, in the words of the Psalmist, it "maketh glad the heart of man," therefore a combination of fruit juices and sweetened barley water could be substituted for the wine. Still another ritualistic accomodation had to be made in the ghettos of Eastern Europe many centuries later because the poverty there was so extreme. In those homes where the use of wine was prohibited because of its cost, the rabbis readily gave permission for the Kiddush to be recited over the challot (white loaves of bread) that are traditionally required for the Sabbath or a festival meal.

In medieval Europe, after the chazzan had taken his sip from the Kiddush goblet, it was the custom for a Talmud Torah boy to ascend to the bema (the reader's platform) and also take a sip, thus symbolically drinking the wine for the entire congregation assembled. In Conservative and Reform congregations in America in recent years, girls also have been accorded this honor, which is really an act of indoctrination in religious rite and ceremony.

See also ART, CEREMONIAL; SABBATH, THE.

KIDDUSH HA-CHAYYIM. *See* LIFE, THE SANCTIFICATION OF.

KIDDUSH HA-SHEM (Hebrew, meaning "sanctification of the Name")

Of all martyrologies, that of the Jewish people has not had its like in the annals of mankind. It is probably the longest in duration of time, and the vastest—if not also the most appalling—record of man's savagery toward his own kind.

For those Jews who under the strongest duress remained steadfast to the end in their loyalty to their religion and group-identity, the martyrdom that resulted could be counted simply as an act of faith, carrying with it its own solace and moral reward. In the traditional scale of Jewish religious values there was no category of piety that was considered equal to that of the martyr. There was no act of righteousness or heroism that was deemed comparable to that of bringing one's own life as a "burnt-offering" for the sanctification of the Name of God, in loyalty to the Torah, and in defense of the Jewish people.

The martyrdom of the Jews of Trent, falsely accused in 1475 of murdering a Christian child. Contemporary woodcut.

The burning alive of German Jews. (Woodcut by Wohlgemuth in Weltchronik *by Schedel, Nuremberg, 1493.)*

Listing of the martyrs in the old Mainz Memorbuch *(begun in 1250), recording the names of the hundreds of Mainz Jews who perished since the first Crusade, in 1096. Until the Hitler era, these martyrs' names were recited in the town's synagogue on every Sabbath as an everlasting memorial.*

The burning of a Jewish child after his forearms and forelegs were chopped off. (From an illustrated Hebrew manuscript written by Isaac ben Simcha, Germany, 15th century. Hamburg State Library.)

Throughout the centuries, and in whichever country Jews happened to be living, they were constantly being harrassed by the thousand and one pressures—explicit as well as implicit —of a hostile society. Those pressures were brought to induce them to abandon their religion, their ethnic identity, and their cultural separatism. For the individual Jew the choice was never an easy one; it induced in him an inner turmoil and a crisis of conscience.

The test of loyalty to the Jew's group identity was measured by the resistance that he offered to all attempts to lure him from his faith. The weak and the irresolute, understandably, could not muster the moral strength requisite for resolving their dilemma. Many, terrorized by the threat of death—which often was the only alternative to apostasy—sought physical safety in conversion and in the cultural obliteration of their Jewish identity.

Clifford's Tower at York, England, where in 1190 the total Jewish population of the town perished in a suicidal pact rather than fall into the hands of the besieging mob. (Engraving by Joseph Halfpenny, York, 1807.)

The murder and burning of German Jews in a synagogue. (From an illustrated Hebrew manuscript by Isaac ben Simcha, 15th century. Hamburg State Library.)

But—and this is the remarkable fact—the great majority of Jews, scornfully described as "stiff-necked" by medieval Christian churchmen, remained unyielding. They preferred to live by principle—and to die by it as well, if need be. The great second-century Mishnah Sage, Akiba ben Joseph, openly defied the Roman decree which made the teaching of the Torah a capital crime. A grimly humorous saying of his was: "If you have to hang, let it be from a high tree." The high tree he chose for himself—as did uncounted thousands as well—was to die as a martyr: al kiddush ha-Shem.

What first gave impetus to the martyr-dedication of the Jews in Judea was the attempt made by Antiochus IV, the Seleucidan king of Syria, to convert them by force to the Greek religion. According to the ancient Jewish chroniclers of Maccabees I and II, Antiochus had decreed that "all [peoples] should be one people" and that everyone should obey his laws. The resulting campaign of terror led to the Maccabean uprising in 168 B.C.E.

The first concrete mention of Jewish martyrs is found in the sixth chapter of the Second Book of Maccabees. It recounts, in the cadence of a deep emotionalism, the story of the ninety-year-old sofer (scribe) Eleazar, who had resisted all the efforts of the Hellenic Syrians to force him to eat pork. To make an example of him, the Syrians placed him on the rack, and he was tortured until he died. Commented the Greek-writing Jewish chronicler: "And thus this man died, leaving his death for an example of noble courage and a memorial of virtue, not only unto young men, but unto all his nation."

Without a doubt, the most moving story of fidelity recorded in the Second Book of Maccabees—and perhaps embroidered a bit by the devout folk-memory intent on glorifying its heroes—was that of the martyrdom of the widow Hannah and her seven sons. Antiochus had them brought before him, and he commanded them to bow down and worship him—"the god visible"—and all the other gods of Greece. Answered the eldest son: "God forbid that I should bow before your image! Our Torah commands us: 'I am the Lord thy God,' and I, for one, will worship none other." And so he was tortured to death in the sight of his mother and his six brothers. One by one Hannah's sons scorned the king's wishes and chose death to the betrayal of their faith. Even the youngest, a mere boy, defied Antiochus when his turn came, saying: "I will obey the commandment of the Torah that was given to our fathers by Moses." And so he too perished.

The passionate revivalism that inflamed the Jewish spirit during the Maccabean period was an attempt to reach the grass roots and cleanse the Jewish religion and culture of its accomodating Hellenistic accretions, and begin a return to the puritanism of Moses and the Prophets. This revivalism furnished the proper climate of fervency for martyr dedication.

Two centuries later, about 90 C.E., after the Romans had crushed Judea and had razed to the ground the Temple in Jerusalem so that the Jewish people no longer possessed either a psychological center or a national sanctuary, a Rabbinic synod was hastily convoked at Lydda. It laid down, among others, this law: "All negative commandments [mitzvot] of the Torah, except those which pertain to idolatry, adultery, and murder, may be violated if there is any danger of losing one's life." Specifically, they singled out idolatry, which meant renegacy from the faith. In contrast to the religious concept of kiddush ha-Shem (the sanctification of the Name [of God]), apostasy was stigmatized as chillul ha-Shem (the profanation of the Name). By promulgating this fundamental revision of religious law, the Synod of Lydda established a tradition which became fixed and sacrosanct for all the ensuing centuries. It made martyrdom out of devotion to God, to the commandments of the Torah, and to Israel a categorical imperative.

How well this tradition governed the conduct of ordinary Jews can be ascertained in the innumerable examples cited by the Byzantine and medieval chronicles. The onerous conditions of Jewish life in Christian and Mohammedan lands often posed some desperate choices. One of these, for example, considered what was to be the behavior of Jewish women when they were being threatened with rape during the all-too-frequent anti-Semitic riots and massacres. The concensus of rabbinical judgment, based on the earlier decision of the Synod of Lydda with regard to adultery, was implacable and brief: "Die, rather!"

Not all the Talmudic Sages supported the principle of the obligation of martyrdom as an alternative to forcible apostasy. The second-century Rabbinic teacher Papus, for example, even rebuked his friend and colleague Akiba for his suicidal rashness in openly violating the Roman decree that banned the teaching of the Torah. His contemporary, the Sage Ishmael, also strongly dissented from the view of the majority of those religious authorities, including Akiba, who eulogized the act of martyrdom as the stairway of grace leading to Heaven. In an opinion that recalls the decision of Maimonides on the same desperate question a thousand years later, this Judean Rabbi—although he himself only a short time afterward perished as one of the Ten Martyrs—took the unpopular position that, in order to save one's life, it was normally permissible to worship idols.

Maimonides emphasized in his celebrated "Letter to the Jews of Yemen," in 1172, that submission to conversion was to be motivated not by expediency, cowardice, or lack of religious principle, but by considered strategy. He maintained that, from a moral point of view, it was permissible under duress to give lip service to the worship of idols while reserving in one's mind and heart secret devotion to God, strengthened in this ordeal of conscience by the hope of someday being able to openly avow again the faith of Israel. This line of reasoning unquestionably must have been followed by the many thousands of Conversos of Spain and Portugal who, while openly performing as Catholics through dread of the Holy Inquisition, lived as Jews secretly and thus ran the risk of being burned at the stake. (*See* CHRISTIANITY, JEWISH ORIGINS OF; CONVERSION OF JEWS; ISLAM, JEWISH ORIGINS OF.)

The majority view of the medieval rabbis—Maimonides' dissent notwithstanding—ardently supported the Lydda decision of 90 C.E. To die for one's faith was considered the supreme spiritual blessing. By dwelling on the rewards to be given in the World-to-Come to those who died for the sanctification of the Name, they made the torments of martyrdom seem less agonizing. Jewish writings of that time and some of the liturgical hymns of the synagogue (that still endure) point out that, in viewing the heavenly bliss to come, the martyrs were consoled and became reconciled to death. Certainly, no preachment ever had the moral impact that was set by example in action. This is well illustrated by the conduct of the Ten Martyrs, who perished at the hands of the Romans during the Hadrianic reign of terror which followed the drowning in blood of the Bar Kochba revolt, in 135 C.E.

The Ten Martyrs were ten Rabbinic teachers of Judea. They included Akiba ben Joseph and Ishmael (the latter Sage had previously defended the right of the individual to apostatize under extreme duress from the enemy). All of these ten had disobeyed the Roman decree which made punishable by death the observance of the Sabbath and other holy days, the study and teaching of the Torah, and the performance of the rite of circumcision. And since they had made no attempt to conceal their acts, they were condemned to die.

One of the ten, Chanina ben Teradion, had been found teaching the Torah. Fitting the punishment to his "crime," the Romans wrapped him in the parchment scroll of a Sefer

Torah (Scroll of the Torah) and burned him alive at the stake. Just as terrible, if not more so, was the end of Akiba ben Joseph, who had been the "soul" of the Bar Kochba uprising. The Romans imprisoned him in the fortress of Caesarea and tortured him without letup, tearing the flesh off his body with a sharp-pronged iron "comb." By dying (murmured Akiba to his disciples as his end drew near) he had at last found the most exalted way of affirming his belief in God and of fulfilling that commandment of the Torah which said: "Thou shalt love the Lord the God with all thy soul."

There are a number of moralistic anecdotes in Talmudic literature which describe the manner in which the Ten Martyrs perished and record the lofty sentiments they expressed before death. These served as a high emotional point in the indoctrination of the Jewish youth in every generation, holding up for their emulation the example in steadfastness of their illustrious ancestors. It became customary, beginning with the Byzantine period, when the forced conversion of Jews to Christianity had become commonplace, that during the Mussaf (the Additional Morning [prayer] Service on the Day of Atonement), the congregation would recite in unison a dirge which commemorated the ordeals of the Ten Martyrs.

On reading the chronicles and folk tales about the martyrs of the Maccabean and Talmudic periods, one is made aware of the fact that they bear a close resemblance to stories about the early Christian martyrs. There is a historic-cultural explanation for this parallelism. It should be kept in mind that the sectarian followers of Jesus, until the institutional and theological separation of Christianity from the Jewish religion during the second century, were devout Jews. They too, in common with all other Jews, nurtured as part of their religious heritage the example and the emotionalism of the early martyrs of their people—Eleazar the Scribe, Hannah and her seven sons, and the Ten Martyrs.

The Jewish acts of martyrdom reached mass proportions in Western Europe during the Middle Ages. A certain Rabbi Amitai, who lived in the Italian town of Oria about the year 900, recorded that many a French rabbi, when faced with the threat of forced conversion, preferred to burn himself and his students alive. This pattern of self-destruction became quite common in many Jewish communities during the time of the Crusades.

The blood-curdling trials of the times were commemorated in verse by the rabbinical liturgists of the synagogue. One Hebrew elegy, composed by an otherwise unidentified poet, Eleazar, described the variety of ways in which those who resisted baptism perished.

> Thy faithful sons, whom Thou in love hast owned,
> Behold! are strangled, burnt and racked and stoned
> Are broken on the wheel, like felons hung;
> Or, living, into noisome charnels flung.

Notwithstanding the fact that the Jewish religious laws against suicide and infanticide were implacably stern, the medieval rabbinic authorities abrogated them in the crucial concern of dying for the sanctification of the Name. They considered it morally more tenable and forgiveable to die by one's own innocent hand than to submit like sheep to the slaughter before the threat of the enemy: "If Jews ye still remain, ye die!"

In Mayence on May 27, 1095, the entire Jewish community, when besieged by the Crusaders in the palace of Archbishop Ruthard, performed the rite of mass-suicide. According to a Jewish chronicler of the event, they cried out at the moment of parting from life: "Happy are we to do His will! Happy is he who is slain, dying for the unity of His Name, and prepared to enter the World-to-Come, there to dwell in the heavenly fellowship of the righteous, with Rabbi Akiba and his colleagues—the pillars of the universe who perished for His Name's sake!"

Everywhere it was the same: in England, France, Austria, Italy Spain, and especially in the some 350 Jewish communities of Germany. Numerous congregations—men, women, and children together—locked themselves in their synagogues, to which they set fire, and perished together, with the Shema fervent on their lips. In the English town of York, for instance, all the Jews committed suicide in Clifford's Tower rather than submit to the conversion clamored for by the besieging mob without. Before they died (on March 17, 1190), they listened to the last sermon of their rabbi, Yom-Tob of Joigny. He said to them: "God, whose decisions are inscrutable, desires that we should die for our holy religion. Death is at hand, unless you prefer, for a short span of life, to be unfaithful to your faith. As we must prefer a glorious death to a shameful life, it is advisable that we take our choice of the most honorable and noblest mode of death. The life which our Creator has given us we will render back to Him with our own hands. This example many pious men and congregations have given in ancient and recent times."

In the Jewish communities of the Rhineland, it became the custom to honor the memory of local martyrs on the fast of the Ninth of Ab (Tishah B'Ab), which commemorates the Destruction of the Temple in Jerusalem. Each congregation kept its own list of martyrs in a *Memorbuch* ("Memorial Book"). The German-Christian writer Schüdt noted in the seventeenth century that the Sefaradic Jews of Amsterdam "have their own books of martyrs in which they entered the names of those who were burned for the sake of their faith, and many Jews are marvelously steadfast when they face the Inquisition."

But, as should be quite apparent, not all Jews who perished at the hands of their enemies were accorded the alternative of conversion to being killed. The vast holocausts of virtually uncounted numbers of Jews that occurred in Christian and Mohammedan countries—for whatever "justifying" reasons and pretexts—or even without the pretension of a pretext—from the pious massacres of the Crusaders through the cold-blooded extermination centers of the German Nazis, have been commemorated by the Jewish people as kedoshim (martyrs). The devout have always regarded their deaths as an affirmation of the unbreakable covenant that exists between God and Israel and between the individual Jew and his group identity.

See also ANTI-SEMITISM; CHOSEN PEOPLE, THE; CONVERSION OF JEWS; IMMORTALITY; MARRANOS AND THE INQUISITION; MASSACRES: THE CRUSADERS, THE BLACK DEATH; MERIT OF THE FATHERS; SHEMA, THE; SACRIFICE OF ISAAC; UNITY OF ISRAEL.

KINGDOM OF GOD. *See* MESSIAH, THE.

KITTEL

In former times, male adult Jews wore, on certain specified occasions of religious worship, a loose white robe with flowing folds, long wide sleeves, and a girdle of the same material tied in a knot around the waist. With it he also wore a white yarmulkah (skullcap). The robe was called a kittel. The word probably originated among the medieval Jews of Eastern Germany. (The Jews of Western Germany called this robe a *sargenes,* referring to the word *sarg* or coffin, i.e. a shroud, but this name is no longer in use.)

Today the kittel is customarily worn by the head of the traditional household as he presides over the Seder services on Passover. The kittel is also worn by adult male worshipers in Orthodox synagogues on Rosh Hashanah and Yom Kippur, the reason being, some scholars say, because the kittel, made of white material, symbolizes purity—the spiritual objective of

The white shroudlike garment that the male adult worshiper wears in penitence on Yom Kippur in the Orthodox synagogue. (Painting by L. Pilichowski.)

the repentance and atonement that characterize the worshipers' self-accounting on these holy days.

Maimonides (the twelfth-century rabbi-philosopher of Spain) gives a different and equally plausible interpretation of this custom. He says that the kittel is worn on the above-specified occasions to remind careless men that death awaits them and that there is a need, therefore, to abandon all ways of folly. The correctness of this view is strengthened by the fact that, in the Rhineland, beginning with the Middle Ages, the kittel often ended its life as tachrichim, i.e., the shroud in which the pious were dressed for their eternal rest.

See also BURIAL RITES AND CUSTOMS.

KLEZMER (Yiddish, meaning "Jewish folk-instrumentalist"; pl. KLEZMORIM; derived from the Hebrew KLEI-ZEMER, meaning "musical instruments")

Klezmorim were the Jewish folk-musicians among the Ashkenazim. Strictly speaking, they were instrumentalists who first appeared upon the recorded scene in Central and Eastern Europe in the late Middle Ages and during the early Renaissance.

As was the case with graphic representation of the human figure in art, music during the Diaspora suffered a near blackout, but for an entirely different reason. This was because, after the Destruction of the Second Temple in Jerusalem in 70 C.E., Rabbinic law had put a damper of perpetual mourning upon all merriment and frivolity. Nonetheless, there were exceptions to the ban; music and dance were sanctioned by the medieval religious authorities on such special occasions as weddings, Purim revelries, or the dedication of a synagogue. Until the nineteenth century, in the city of Prague and in certain German communities, it was the custom for klezmer bands to play traditional airs and solemn introspective airs just before the Friday night prayer-service began. This was supposed to deepen the solemnity of the Sabbath as well as to usher in the Sabbath Bride (Shabbat ha-Malkah) by paying homage to her with stirring music—a Cabalistic notion, no doubt. Many synagogues even had special ornamented wall-cases built as repositories for the musical instruments which the congregation owned.

The klezmorim were, by temperament, restless and emotionally unstable individuals. The economic uncertainties of

A band of three generations of klezmorim (folk musicians). The calling of klezmer was usually hereditary, being handed down from father to son. Russia, early 20th century (YIVO).

Jewish folk musicians of North Africa.

Klezmorim at the head of two wedding processions—one for the groom and the other for the bride. (From Kirchner's Jüdisches Ceremoniel, *1726.)*

Jewish lute-player performs at wedding ceremony. (Illustration to a text in Hebrew script of the marriage rite in a rabbinical manual. Germany, 1590.)

their calling and the need to earn a livelihood where they could only aggravated their wanderlust. Finding that their own home towns were frequently too limited in opportunities, many took to the road. They journeyed on foot or in peasant carts from town to town and from village to village, wherever Jews lived in community, in hopeful search of work. Their earnings were, most of the time, lean and unpredictable. They visited all the great fairs which Jewish traders frequented—in Leipzig, Danzig, and Lublin. They played at weddings and other festivities. In fact, many Christian noblemen and landowners preferred their playing to that of Gentile bands and hired them to provide the dance music for their balls and banquets.

The average klezmer band was a small ensemble, usually of three or four string and/or woodwind instrumentalists. Few of the players were able to read from notes; they played by ear. Before the nineteenth century, there was little opportunity for a German, Russian, or Polish Jew to obtain any formal musical schooling. Thus, among the klezmorim, fathers taught their skills and chosen instruments to their sons as a sort of family inheritance. Klezmer art—and folk art it surely was—developed its own distinctive musical traditions, styles, and folklore. Undeniably, many of these musicians must have been richly endowed, but they wasted their talents in the barren soil of a constricted Jewish existence. Notably, competent klezmorim had the ability, like jazz men of today, to harmonize spontaneously and, according to several nineteenth-century Gentile composers and musicologists, also correctly. It is of some interest that, while Johann Sebastian Bach was organist and musical director at the Thomaskirche in Leipzig, he visited outlying Jewish settlements on several occasions in order to listen to what he called "the pretty little tunes" that the klezmer bands there played.

The klezmorim performed on almost every kind of musical instrument that was in use in their time and country. But they seemed to show a partiality for all string and woodwind instruments: for the violin, viola, cello, and bass fiddle; for the flageolet, clarinet, and flute.

There were always individual klezmorim who preferred to work independently; that way, they had less temperamental involvement and could wander freely wherever they wished. The instrument most of these solitary individualists favored was, inexplicably, the dulcimer or cembalo, called, in Yiddish as well as in German, *Hackbrett*. This was a flat instrument with strings, played percussively with two padded hammers. Some of these cembalists (the name Zimbalist, borne by the famous violinist, obviously originated with a klezmer ancestor who had played the cembalo) achieved an arresting skill on this instrument. There were not a few who enjoyed wide renown during the late eighteenth and early nineteenth centuries. About one of these, Michel Guzikov, a sensational gaberdined, skullcapped, and earlocked cembalo-player from Poland who also played on a "straw and wood fiddle" of his own invention, the composer Felix Mendelssohn wrote, in 1836: "He is quite a phenomenon, inferior to no virtuoso in the world . . . the man is a true genius."

Patently, the musical compass of the klezmorim was narrow. They were, in the fullest sense of the term, folk musicians. Their repertory was limited to folk dances and on-the-spot improvisations on folk tunes. There were not a few potentially gifted composers among them—many of the traditional Yiddish folk songs and dance tunes were created by them—but their creative efforts were, generally, sadly circumscribed by their lack of formal musical training and general culture.

The presence of klezmorim was deemed by folk custom to be indispensable at Jewish weddings, no matter how impecunious the parents of the bride might be, for they "put a soul," so to speak, into the festivities with their playing. The music they performed was both joyous and sad: lilting dances alternating with inward-turned melodic reveries. These tunes bore upon them the stamp of recognizable non-Jewish folk-idioms and followed conventional forms taken from Polish, German, Russian, Hungarian, Walachian, and Moldavian popular sources. But remarkably, too, they retained, despite all the borrowings from sources extraneous to the Jewish group-culture of the ghetto, an indefinable expressiveness, and over-all bitter-sweet plaintiveness in a minor key that even Gentile musicologists and composers identified as uniquely "Jewish" in character.

As has been true of other Jewish traditional callings, folkways, and institutions, notwithstanding the fact that Jews of today have become sophisticated and less dependent on the culture patterns of the past, and, in addition, have assimilated the musical culture of the West, some klezmorim are still functioning in tradition-conscious Jewish circles. Even in such widely divergent places as New York, London, Cape Town, and Mexico City, it is still customary that at traditional Jewish weddings klezmer folk-music be played, if not by klezmorim themselves, at least by a musical ensemble that is acquainted with the old tunes. But needless to observe, the resultant musical product is often presented in a garbled and tasteless form, "jazzed-up" beyond recognition in many instances. It lacks the musicality, the authenticity, and, most of all, the sincerity, of a people's musical utterance that once sprang spontaneously from the creative soil of life itself.

KOL NIDRE (Aramaic, meaning "All Vows")

Just before the sun sets and the eve of Yom Kippur begins, the synagogues throughout the world resound to the chanting by the cantor (chazzan) of "Kol Nidre." And as he sings the ancient hymn—first in a pianissimo, then, a second time, in a louder voice, and, finally, for the third time, in a triumphant fortissimo—the worshipers, with bowed head and contemplative mien, recite the Aramaic text in an undertone. This is the way it has been done traditionally ever since the sixth or seventh century, when, it is believed, the Kol Nidre rite was first introduced into the liturgy for the Day of Atonement.

The ritual begins when the precentor in his white robe —a symbol of Levitical purity—takes his place before the Ark of the Law. He stands there in the role of shaliach tzibbur—"the messenger of the congregation"—to plead the cause of his "clients" before God the Judge. Two elders of the congregation take up positions on either side of him, each with a Torah Scroll clasped in his arms. Prayer shawls thrown cowl-like over their faces, all three then enact their part in the extraordinary little drama as official "clerks," making pronouncement for a tribunal that is only symbolic.

In the most solemn manner—all three reciting in unison —they promulgate before the assembled worshipers the following dispensation:

> By the authority of the Court on high, and by the authority of the Court below, by the permission of God —blessed be He!—and by the permission of this holy congregation, we hold it lawful to pray with the transgressors.

Three times in succession the three "clerks" of the "Court" repeat this ruling, in keeping with the legal procedure for annulment laid down by the rabbis of old. That recitation being concluded, the chazzan begins the chanting of the Kol Nidre hymn to an ancient melody of unknown origin.

The melody is quietly declamatory, grave yet also plaintive. It discourses, in the interior dialogue of song, on the many unarticulated sorrows and regrets that the conscience of the human being must always wrestle with. Three times, according to rabbinical prescription, the leader of prayer repeats the chant. And as the chazzan sings, night begins to fall.

Generation after generation of the pious has fallen under the strange spell of the Kol Nidre melody. Perceptive Gentiles, hearing it sung in the proper setting of the synagogue, have also been stirred by it. Beethoven used a melodic excerpt from the Kol Nidre in the eight opening bars of his Quartet in C sharp minor, Opus 131, to set the grave interior mood for the work. When Leo Tolstoy first heard the Kol Nidre sung in a synagogue in Russia, he was so deeply affected that he subsequently described it as the saddest, yet the most uplifting, of all the melodies he had ever heard. It was one, said he, "that echoes the story of the great martrydom of a grief-stricken nation."

What is it in the Kol Nidre hymn that endows it with such a primary religious importance for Jews, that produces such an emotion-charged atmosphere in the synagogue? There are several reasons to explain it, and also one persuasive hypothesis. For one thing, to the devout it is not just a hymn but a deeply felt religious experience, for it brings the guilt-burdened individual into a closer communion with "the still small voice" of his conscience. Kol Nidre also serves as the dramatic prelude to the Day of Atonement, which always has been venerated by believers as the most awesome of holy days in the Jewish calendar. It sets the appropriate expiatory tone for the suppliant in the silent accounting that he is to render, in the ensuing twenty-four hours, of his conduct in the year gone by, and in the sincere repentance his self-examination is expected to awaken within him. Another reason, without doubt, is the emotionally evocative power of the melody itself. It lays bare all the pathos and discomfiture of the human being at his awareness of vows that have been broken, of obligations that have not been kept, and of ideal values and loyalties that have been betrayed. All this notwithstanding, it yet seems to affirm at the end the desire, equally natural in the individual, to retrace his erring steps and to make amends for wrongdoing.

And so, year in and year out, the Kol Nidre hymn is sung on the eve of Yom Kippur. Yet it never seems to lose its appeal to true believers, in whom it induces a state of uplift and emotional release.

Just the same, there still remains a certain puzzlement that anyone, searching for the meaning and intention of Kol Nidre in text and in rite, has to face. While the melody itself possesses—despite the numerous revisions and alterations it must have gone through in the course of centuries—a wonderful clarity, the Aramaic text, which is nothing but a dry legal formula of archaic rabbinic vintage, unfortunately does not fit it; thus it represents a sort of *non sequitur*. The text reads:

> All vows [kol nidre], obligations, oaths, and anathemas, whether called *konam, konas*, or by any other name, which we may vow, or swear, or pledge, or whereby we may be found, from this Day of Atonement until the next (whose happy coming we await), we do repent. May they be deemed absolved, forgiven, annulled, and void, and made of no effect; they shall not bind us nor have power over us. The vows shall not be reckoned vows, the obligations shall not be obligatory; nor the oaths be oaths.

The traditional interpretation of this curious Aramaic text, which is, undoubtedly, the correct one, has been that *it literally means what it states.* This is the explanation that is given: Remiss all year 'round in fulfilling the many obligations, promises, and vows that he has voluntarily made *to God*, the individual, *ipso facto*, becomes a "transgressor." Perhaps he was overimpulsive in entering with the Deity into those generous but difficult-to-fulfill commitments. Possibly he is only a "backslider," a "weak vessel." All the same, the apology runs, how can he be expected to go on living without the ameliorating annulment of his broken vows and unheeded obligations which, if allowed to accumulate, can only lead him into the fiery torments of Gehinnom (Purgatory). (It should be noted here that always, from Biblical times on, extraordinary emphasis in Jewish religious practice was given to vows and promises, and their infraction was regarded as a grave sin.)

Let it not be supposed, however, that this curious innovation, so similar to the absolution and the special dispensation practices of the Roman Catholic Church, ever met with the wholehearted approval of the foremost rabbinic authorities. During the ninth century, Natronai, the Gaon of Sura in Babylonia, noted: "It is not the custom either in the two [Rabbinical] academies [in Sura and Pumbeditha] or in these parts to annul vows. Neither on Rosh Hashanah nor on Yom Kippur is Kol Nidre recited, though we have heard that it is recited in other lands. But we never saw or heard the like from our fathers."

In explaining the reason for the rabbinical opposition in Babylonia to its recitation, Natronai wrote caustically (and also logically): "Of what use is an annulment to a man who makes the condition after he has taken a vow that it is to be void?" Nevertheless, the force of custom proved more formidable than all the rabbinical frowns and decisions from many illustrious quarters. And so the rite of Kol Nidre continued to prevail throughout the world except in Babylonia, Algeria, and Catalonia, where it never became part of the liturgy.

But the fog of bafflement about Kol Nidre is lifted by a persuasive hypothesis. Though it is true that at first Kol Nidre stood solely for the annulment of religious vows and commitments made voluntarily to God, it suddenly underwent a dramatic transformation. The process was similar to that which turned the primitive rites of spring among the Hebrews after the Exodus from Egypt into the Passover Feast of Liberation. The historic clue to this change we discover in an examination of the legal formula permitting "transgressors" to worship on Yom Kippur with the congregation, which is recited by the chazzan and the two congregational dignitaries immediately prior to the chanting of Kol Nidre. This formula was introduced by the religious authority of the Rhineland, Meir of Rothenburg, who died a martyr's death in 1293.

Some scholars are agreed that during the Middle Ages and later, the "permission" proclamation that precedes Kol Nidre concealed behind its matter-of-fact legalistic formula a national Jewish tragedy which, at the same time, presented a desperate problem—relative to their survival—to the Jewish communities. It was that of the forced conversion of Jews, which was being achieved en masse under the threat of imminent death. These considerable losses from the Jewish fold had begun with the persecutions and massacres by the Byzantine Empire and Church, in the eighth century. When Rabbi Meir introduced the reading of the above-mentioned formula, it was at a time when tens of thousands had already perished while resisting baptism at the hands of the Crusaders. However, many thousands more had managed to save their lives by conformity in conversion.

Later on, during the Spanish persecutions of 1391 and the wholesale massacres carried out in the synagogues by that bloodthirsty "saint," Vincent Ferrer, the compassionate provisions of Kol Nidre were used to reconcile with their brother-Jews many thousands of the Conversos in Spain and the Cristãos Novos in Portugal. Many of these, although they conformed outwardly to Christianity, secretly clung to the faith of their forefathers with the dogged fervor of the guilt-conscious. Beginning with the thirteenth century, Kol Nidre became the supreme penitential prayer and rite of reconciliation with the Jewish religion and their people of all the many unfortunates who had involutarily broken their vows and pledges to their God.

But the religious convolutions and the historical complexities confusing the implications of the Kol Nidre rite do not end here. An entirely new development occurred at an unverified juncture in Jewish history during the Middle Ages. All we know of this is that the traditional religious oath a Jew was wont to take in the civil courts of Christendom no longer was acceptable. In its stead, he had to take an utterly barbarous and degrading oath—the *more Judaico*, the "Jewish oath (q.v.)"—that had been substituted by the Christian authorities.

In addition, the text of the Kol Nidre had become a notorious *cause-célèbre*. Many were the ordeals that the Jews had to endure thereafter and until very recent times on its account. To cite only one example, in June of 1240, in a forced disputation held before Louis IX, king of France, and an assembly of Christian theologians and clerics, the apostate Jew of La Rochelle, Nicolas Donin, challenged Rabbi Yechiel of Paris and three other French rabbis to defend not only a series of accusations against the Talmud, but also the charge that the Kol Nidre formula absolved the Jew from all moral guilt in breaking his oath when dealing with Christians. Rabbi Yechiel and his three "co-defendants" successfully proved with "book, chapter, and verse" from rabbinic decisions that the Kol Nidre dispensation had no bearing whatsoever on any obligations undertaken or on vows or promises a Jew made to others, including Christians; it had reference only to those vows that had been *pledged voluntarily by the individual to God*. The main authority cited by the defense as proof of this was the statement in the Mishnah, the Hebrew code of Oral Law: "Yom Kippur atones only for the transgressions of man in his relation to God; but for transgressions between man and man, there is no expiation on Yom Kippur until the wrongful act has been rectified."

But since false ideas have a greater attraction and durability than does the truth among the prejudiced, the uninformed, and the malicious, the perverted notion of the Jew as a cynical creature who, like Shakespeare's caricatured projection of Shylock, is always making promises and entering into agreements, only to break them when his self-interests require it, became a stereotype and a catchword for the Jew-baiters in every century. That this is so was well demonstrated by the personal humiliation that Rabbi Manasseh ben Israel of Amsterdam experienced in London in 1655, when he appeared before the hostile commission which the Lord Protector, Oliver Cromwell, had appointed to question the desirability of readmitting Jews into England, from which they had been expelled by Edward I in 1290. The commission put to him the old provocative question: How can a Christian trust the word of a Jew when his religion gives him the dispensation (in Kol Nidre) to violate it at will?

As recently as 1857, the czarist government, acting on numerous complaints it had received from Christians on the same issue, ordered Jewish religious authorities in the Russian Empire to have printed in all prayer books for the High Holy Days (machzorim), as a preface to Kol Nidre, a statement making it perfectly clear that the vows mentioned in the hymn were entirely religious and had nothing whatsoever to do with any *person*, but only *with God*.

The Reform wing of Judaism, about a hundred years ago, dispensed altogether with the recitation of the Kol Nidre text on the grounds both that this would avoid incitement by the anti-Semites and that the Aramaic text of Kol Nidre was anachronistic and obsolete for all practical purposes for the modern Jew. However, it did refuse to part with the beautiful Kol Nidre melody which is, after all, the soul of the prayer. It is interesting to note that, in the trend toward greater traditionalism, the Kol Nidre prayer has been reintroduced in the Reform Yom Kippur service.

See also CHAZZAN; FOLK MUSIC AND DANCE; HYMNS OF THE SYNAGOGUE; MUSIC, ANCIENT JEWISH; MUSICAL ACCENTS; YOM KIPPUR; ZEMIROT.

KOSHER. *See* DIETARY LAWS.

K'SUBAH. *See* KETUBAH.

KVATTER, KVATTERIN. *See* CIRCUMCISION.

KVUTZAH, KVUTZOT. *See* KIBBUTZ.

L

LABOR, DIGNITY OF

In the simple agricultural society of Judea, even during the final and more complicated period of the Second Commonwealth, and despite the superficial veneer of Greco-Roman sophistication and the prosperity of the big landowners and the middle and upper classes in urban areas, the economy was centered around labor: farmers and farmhands in the country, and artisans and unskilled workers in the towns. It was, therefore, not surprising that there emerged a remarkable attitude among the common people which invested productive labor with a great dignity. It is true that other societies having a similar state of social development and the same kind of economy as Judea took a diametrically opposite attitude toward work. This was due, in the main, to the fact that they were slavocracies—societies that were sustained by the unpaid labor of numerous slaves. In consequence, in those countries, labor was equated with bondage, so it was fit only for the slave, and the "indignity of labor" rather than the "dignity of labor" was popularly stressed.

Among the Jews, in particular during the final period of the Second Temple and the Talmudic era which followed it, the ideals of social justice preached so eloquently—although in vain—by the Prophets of former times, reached through the teaching of the Rabbinic Sages to a broad and popular level of acceptance. In the equalitarian climate of Jewish life at that time there was no place for slavery. Although some modified and limited forms of it stubbornly survived, troubling thereby the conscience of many a sensitive Jew, the right to engage in work—whether manual or intellectual—was regarded not only as a necessity but as a moral privilege by freeborn Jews.

The Rabbinic teachers conceived of God as a toiler himself. Was he not represented in the drama of Genesis as a worker who had labored with love and wisdom at his divine and tremendous task of Creation for six days, and rested from it, as every devout Jew did subsequently, on the seventh day—the Sabbath? The Jewish view was that God had made man in his own image and man was, accordingly, a co-worker of God; the dignity of work was also his measure of importance in the scheme in the world. Therefore the ancient Rabbinic maxim: "He who is productive so that the world's work might go on, has a share in God's labor of creation."

This high evaluation of work as a religious-moral act—and as a social necessity, to boot—is expressed in numerous maxims of the Talmud. Some of the best known, pondered over by the Jewish generations in history, are these: "God permits his Shechinah [Divine Presence] to rest on Israel only when it works." "'I will bless thee and increase thy seed,' God had told [the Patriarch] Isaac. Nonetheless, Isaac set to work and planted. How well he knew that blessings fall only on the work of one's own hands!"

It was in line with this down-to-earth conclusion that a remarkable tradition was established by the early Rabbinic teachers. This glorified work as the sustainer of life and the preserver of the ideal objectives of the Torah. With few exceptions, all of the Talmudic Sages worked at trades, and no calling was deemed too lowly for them to engage in so long as it permitted them to be socially useful and honorable. "Acquire an occupation together with your dedication to the Torah," they counseled. The second-century Patriarch, Rabban Gamaliel, explained the wisdom of this advice thus: "A fine thing indeed is the study of the Torah when it is combined with an occupation, for the labor demanded by both

A former leader of the underground fighters against the Nazis in Galicia working with a drill in Israel.

Woman worker in Maoz Tzurim, a settlement in Israel, at the seemingly endless task of clearing the land of stones.

of them leaves neither time nor thought for sinning."

Since the ancient religious teachers of Judea remained loyal to the principle of not making "a spade of the Torah" for material profit, they accepted no remuneration for their teaching, but tried instead to eke out a living by working at useful trades. Abba Joseph was a construction worker; Chiyya bar Abba, a carpenter; Yitzchak Nappacha, a smith; Abba bar Zmina, a tailor; Abba Hoshea, a laundryman; and Joseph Zeidna made fishing-nets. The great Hillel, who undoubtedly served as the model for ethical conduct and exalted religious principle on whom Jesus of Nazareth patterned himself a generation later, was a simple woodchopper who peddled his humble commodity to passers-by on the streets of Jerusalem before he entered the Academy to lecture. Likewise, his famous Rabbinic opponent, Shammai, worked as a land-surveyor. Yochanan ha-Sandler, as his name implies, was a maker of sandals; Abba Hilkiah was a farmhand, and Resh Lakish was a watchman in a vineyard.

Those teachers, for the instruction and guidance of youth, tirelessly expatiated on the wholesome virtues of labor. Some of their pithy sayings were absorbed into the anonymity of folk wisdom: "If I won't work I won't eat." "He who has a trade is like a woman who has a husband." "Glorious work! It warms as well as nourishes those who are engaged in it!" "Teach your son a trade if you do not wish him to become a robber." "No work is disgraceful, no matter how lowly." "A man dies quickly if he has nothing to do." "Flay a carcass in the street and earn your living that way, but don't say: 'I am a superior person and work is beneath my dignity.'"

Unhappily, the drastic edicts of both Church and State in Europe, beginning with the Middle Ages, forbidding Jews—already practically incarcerated in ghettos—to work at most trades and occupations, resulted in a decline of their traditional respect for productive work. They were forced, by and large, into a few socially despised callings and into marginal trades which Christians disliked. Later, in the predominantly merchant-class milieu of Jewish life during the eighteenth and nineteenth centuries, to work with one's hands was considered, if not something to be ashamed of, certainly no social distinction. This attitude still exists today among many middle-class Jews. But in the most recent decades, with the advances of technology, there has been, among Jewish youth, an ever growing respect for work, in the more highly skilled trades especially. In fact, in modern Israel, a virtual "religion of labor," stemming from the urgent requirement of pioneering on the land for the upbuilding of the country and the regeneration of Jewish national life in it, has developed.

See also ESSENES; FELLOWSHIP IN ISRAEL; JUBILEE; LIFE, SANCTIFICATION OF; MAN, DIGNITY OF; MOSES; PASSOVER; PROPHETS (*under* BIBLE, THE); SLAVERY AND THE SLAVE; SOCIAL JUSTICE; THERAPEUTAE; TORAH; UNITY OF ISRAEL.

LADINO. *See* JEWISH LANGUAGES.

LAG B'OMER

On the thirty-third day (the numerical value of the two Hebrew consonants *lamed* and *gimmel,* which form the Hebrew word *Lag,* is thirty-three) of the "counting of the omer," which begins on the second day of Passover, the festival of Lag B'Omer is celebrated. This coincides with the eighteenth day of the Hebrew month of Iyar (which usually fell about May 1), a date of no little ethnological significance, as we shall soon see. The significance given in Rabbinic as well as in Biblical times to the curious rite of "counting the omer," on which this agricultural festival of Lag B'Omer is based, shows how deeply impressed the folk-mind was with it. Even today, although Jewish life can hardly be described as being of an agricultural nature, the custom of "counting the omer" is still observed by the Orthodox.

On the second day of the Hebrew month of Nissan (March-April), it was the time-honored custom in the ancient Land of Israel to bring an omer (a specific measure for grain) of barley, from which bread was commonly made, as a sacrificial "wave-offering" on the Temple altar. Not until that was done could a single Jew eat the bread made of the new harvest. The gathering of this omer of barley was surrounded with an elaborate ceremonial. Three devout and trustworthy men were appointed by the Sanhedrin, the supreme religious-judicial body of the nation, to proceed to a specified field outside of Jerusalem, there to harvest the grain required for the "wave-offering." It was in festal triumph that they returned, carrying their basket with the barley into the Temple court. Here it was ground fine and then sifted through thirteen sieves.

An omer-measure of the purified flour was then presented to the Temple priest who was to officiate at the altar over the "wave-offering." He poured fine oil and frankincense upon it, and then commenced the ceremony of "waving." He grasped the basket containing the flour in his hands and swung it before him, "waving" it backward and forward; this was to prevent the blowing of unfavorable winds upon the land. "Waving" the basket up and down was intended as a specific against the falling of too much dew on the crops. The priest concluded the rite by throwing a handful of the flour into the altar fire as "a new meal-offering unto the Lord." The flour that was left was mixed with leaven and immediately baked into two loaves and then ritually eaten by the priests.

Several different theories have been advanced at various times to explain the origin of Lag B'Omer—a celebration which has, outwardly, more the character of a folk festival than of a holy day and one that is internally, in its concept, more pagan than it is Jewish. One ancient Rabbinic teacher ventured this perhaps not too convincing explanation: that early in the second century, a deadly pestilence broke out in the great school of Akiba and carried off hundreds of his students. Only on the thirty-third day of counting the omer did the epidemic cease. In thanksgiving for being spared, the survivors marked the day with festivities. And so Lag B'Omer afterward came to be known as "the Students' Festival."

Still another commentator in the Talmud presumed to see the matter allegorically. He said that with the one omer of barley brought on the altar of the Temple as a "wave offering," the entire people of Israel was symbolically repaying God for the miraculous omer of manna which he allowed every Israelite to gather in the Wilderness (after the Exodus) in order to preserve him from death by starvation.

Melamedim (teachers) and cheder boys armed with toy rifles (although the usual custom is for them to carry bows and arrows) celebrate Lag B'Omer in Polish fields and woods.

Somehow, Lag B'Omer was adopted by the Cabalists of the late Middle Ages as their own special holy day. This was because that day also marked the anniversary of the death of Simeon bar Yochai, the second-century Judean Tanna of the Mishnah to whom an uncertain tradition has ascribed the authorship of the Zohar, the "bible" of the Cabalists. The custom therefore arose (and it is one, incidentally, that is still flourishing today in modern Israel) for the Jews of medieval Palestine to gather on the night before Lag B'Omer in Meron, in Upper Galilee, at the supposed tomb of Simeon bar Yochai to pay honor to his memory. They celebrated throughout the long night by lighting bonfires and dancing and singing around them until daybreak. A fact probably unknown to the Jews of those times—and to those of today, as well—is that the lighting of bonfires and the wild singing and dancing around them stemmed from a custom that originated among the Christian masses in various parts of Europe. Moreover, it took place at about the same time of year—the eve of May first—as Lag B'Omer; in medieval Germany it was called *Walpurgisnacht* (Witches' Sabbath). Its primary aim was to frighten away the demons and witches from doing harm to the livestock on the farms.

It also became the custom in the East European towns and villages for the Talmud Torah and cheder boys, accompanied by their teachers, to march in procession, singing, into the woods on Lag B'Omer and there shoot with toy bows and arrows. The reason for the ghetto children's engaging in this strange sport, according to the pious, was that the bow symbolized the ark of the wondrous rainbow that would appear in the sky on the day of the Messiah's coming. But this, naturally, was merely a bit of allegorizing to explain away a difficulty, for since the practice of shooting with bow and arrows on the first of May was general among Christians in medieval Europe, what were the little cheder boys shooting at anyway with their bows and arrows? The answer is that Jews had merely adopted the Christian custom around them—although without any practical need for its application—of shooting at invisible demons and witches who (so the popular peasant superstition ran) wished to harm the growing crops in the fields.

To emphasize even more the accretion of non-Jewish customs into European Jewish practices beginning with the Middle Ages, a number of prohibitions strikingly similar to those provided for the forty days of the Christian Lenten season (which also occurs in the springtime) were introduced into the first thirty-two days of the counting of the omer. Principal among the Jewish prohibitions were those against solemnizing a marriage, cutting or trimming the hair, putting on new clothes, listening to non-religious music, and making merry. These mortifications and austerities, especially the ban on marriage, represent a common practice among many peoples, ancient as well as modern, in primitive as well as in advanced societies, during the transition period of infertility between two seasons in an agricultural year. Mating between humans was forbidden as being infelicitous at a time when the earth itself bore no fruit. The pagan Romans also had tabooed marriages during the month of May, and Christians, having at an early stage adopted many of the Roman ways, proscribed marriages during Lent, which occurred about a month earlier. The adoption of the same custom by medieval Jewry is another proof of how irresistible is the diffusion of cultures, which recognizes no boundaries or racial origins or religious dispensations. Every faith of mankind bears upon it the marks of a wide syncretism: indiscriminate religious borrowings from every conceivable source.

LAMED-VAV TZADDIKIM (Hebrew, meaning "Thirty-six Saints"; s. —— TZADDIK; in Yiddish: LAMED-VAVNIKS)

Although there has always been a tradition of reverence among Jews for righteous men who set an example in probity for their fellow men, the saint, as he is conceived of in Christianity, was never a feature of Jewish religious belief and practice until the time of the medieval Cabalists and their continuators of a later time, the Chasidic tzaddikim. In its Biblical reference, the word *tzaddik* denoted a man of ultimate righteousness. No supernatural powers, however, were ascribed to him. His principal reward, as indicated in the Rabbinic discussions of the Talmud, was that he brought his fellow men closer to a love of God, to the Torah, and to the ways of righteousness.

Yet, somehow, there did arise the strange and beautiful myth of the Thirty-six Saints. In keeping with the traditional Jewish understanding of virtue, which is cast in humility and modesty and does not tolerate the preenings of vanity and the posture of self-righteousness, these saints did not even know that they *were* saints. But the hand of God, according to the Cabalistic notion, was presumed to work mysteriously through them. These thirty-six had neither name nor specific personality; even so, upon their selfless righteousness alone, the folk belief ran, the world was able to endure.

The legend was apparently constructed upon a fanciful statement by the Babylonian Talmudic teacher Abbayah in the fourth century: "In each generation there are in the world not less than thirty-six righteous individuals [tzaddikim]. Upon them rests the Presence of God [the Shechinah]." The medieval Cabalists developed this idea with all their famed ingenuity. On a numerological interpretation (gematria) of a few Hebrew letters they made the calculation that there were thirty-six such saints in the Land of Israel, and that there were, in addition, thirty-six also distributed among the Jews of the Diaspora.

Many have been the wonder-tales and folk legends recounting the miracles performed by these nameless tzaddikim. They are described consistently as fitting into a single pattern. In their outer guise they appear as men leading insignificant lives—as humble workers, ignorant peasants, or homeless wanderers—but within, they are illuminated by God's grace as by a secret and wondrous light. Only when the Jewish people or one of its communities is placed in dire danger by its enemies does one of these Lamed-vav Tzaddikim unobtrusively appear as the messenger of God to do his will and to succor his children without their even suspecting it. Once the task is completed (so runs the folk belief) the Lamed-vavnik, fearing that he will be thanked and exposed for what he really is and has done, flees from the scene, because if he *is* found out, his wonder-working powers cease and all his spiritual distinction in righteousness vanishes forever.

In this portraiture of the Lamed-vavniks in selfless and dedicated love for the Jewish people the poetic moralists found wide scope for teaching to the folk the object lesson that the righteous deed, when it is performed for its own sake and without vanity or a desire for recognition, constitutes its own true and satisfying reward. No doubt, the myth of these saints, with their mysterious ways and luminous moral stature, contributed much to the practice, widespread among Jews of other generations, of performing acts of benevolence *in secret* and with modesty.

See also CHARITY; ETHICAL VALUES, JEWISH.

LAMENTATIONS, BOOK OF. *See* BIBLE, THE.

LAMP, CHANNUKAH. *See* CHANNUKAH LAMP.

LAMP, PERPETUAL (in Hebrew: NER TAMID)

The Perpetual Lamp or Eternal Light which today burns electrically before the Ark of the Law in every synagogue in the world, is but a lineal descendant of the oil lamp which occupied the place of honor on the central stem of the seven-

LANGUAGES, JEWISH. See JEWISH LANGUAGES.

LASHON HA-KODESH. See HEBREW LANGUAGE, HISTORY OF THE.

LAVER

As among the Hindu Brahmans and Chinese Taoists, physical purity was regarded by the Jews of ancient times as a pre-condition for spiritual holiness. Washing, bathing, and cleanliness played a prominent role in Jewish "holiness" rites and, indirectly, brought the people of Israel a greater measure of health than was enjoyed by some other peoples.

Frequent ritualistic washing and bathing were required of the Cohanim (priests) as far back as the days of the portable Tabernacle, in the nomadic period of the Israelites' wandering. It was required of Aaron, the High Priest, and his sons that before entering the sanctuary, they wash their hands and feet with water contained in a brass vessel (a layer), for they had to be in a state of bodily purity before they could sacrifice at the altar. At a much later period, in the Temple built by Solomon, in which worship was made elaborate with ceremony and Oriental splendor, ten large lavers were pro-

Perpetual Lamp. (Courtesy of Joseph B. Horwitz Judaica Collection, Cleveland.)

branched menorah in the Jerusalem Temple. While the lamps on the other six branches were lit only at night, the central one was never allowed to go out. That is how it came by its name of "Perpetual Lamp."

Perhaps it may not be viewed as merely coincidental by students of comparative religion that perpetual lamps or fires were also employed in other peoples' worship. A perpetual holy fire burned in the sanctuary of the famed Temple of Vesta, in Rome, tended faithfully by priestesses called Vestal Virgins. An altar lamp also burns all the time in some Christian churches, a custom inherited from the synagogue.

The Perpetual Lamp traditionally is made of glass and is held in an ornamental metal frame which is usually circular in form. Like the conventional chandelier, it is suspended from the ceiling by means of rods or chains and its customary place is directly before the Ark. To it is ascribed much symbolic significance. When a new house of prayer is dedicated, the two most impressive parts in the rites are the depositing of the Scrolls of the Torah in the Ark and the ceremony of kindling the Perpetual Lamp. The institution of the latter is based on the Scriptural directive: "Command the children of Israel . . . to cause a lamp to burn continually." (Leviticus 24:2.)

The Jewish religion, creating its own system of symbolism, drew an intimate association between the unfaltering light of the Ner Tamid with the Torah resting in the Aron ha-Kodesh (the Holy Ark) in front of it. "For the commandment is a lamp and the teaching [i.e., The Torah] is light," is the declaration in the Book of Proverbs (6:23). The Talmudic Sages seized upon this poetic imagery and elaborated on it in this fashion: The Perpetual Lamp symbolized God's promise that he would always abide with his people Israel; thus the lamp flame stood for the radiance of the Divine Presence (the Shechinah), which, in the days of Zion's vanished glory, hovered over the Holy of Holies in the Temple sanctuary.

The continuous self-dedication of the Jewish people since the Revelation at Mount Sinai to the preservation of the Torah and to the fulfillment of its precepts was to be compared, said the Sages, to a light that can never be extinguished.

LANGUAGE, HEBREW. See ENLIGHTENMENT, THE JEWISH; HEBREW ALPHABET; HEBREW LANGUAGE, HISTORY OF THE.

LANGUAGE, YIDDISH. See ENLIGHTENMENT, THE JEWISH; JEWISH LANGUAGES; YIDDISH LANGUAGE, THE.

Stone laver once used in the synagogue of Kfar Nachum (known to Christians as Capernaum), where Jesus preached. Judea, 2nd century B.C.E. *(American Friends of the Hebrew University.)*

Laver on a brass coin minted during the Bar Kochba revolt against Rome, 132–35 C.E. (LEFT)

Laver on the seal of Aaron ben Moshke ha-Levi (Moshe the Levite) of Lvov (Lemberg), 1654. (RIGHT)

vided for the ritual purification of the priests by their Levitical attendants. When the rites were simplified in the Second Temple, beginning with the fifth century B.C.E., one large laver—the "sea of brass"—was found to be sufficient.

With the burning of the Temple by the Romans in 70 C.E., every Jew was reminded by the Rabbis that he belonged to a "nation of priests" and was, therefore, expected to make himself holy to God. In this way, he took over the "holiness" office held by the priesthood since the time of Aaron. This innovation, in religious and social terms, was revolutionary in character and possibly without precedent in the history of religions. With priestly sacrifice—an aristocratic prerogative vested in a small class—at last making way for the democratic practice of personal prayer without the need of an intercessor or mediator, the rite of purification before worship became the responsibility of every single Jew. Before he could enter the pure portals of prayer, he had first to wash his hands.

Today, metal lavers are still in wide use, but in Orthodox synagogues only, and they are simply and inexpensively made. Those congregations that are intent on tradition usually use such lavers that show, in relief, two priestly hands appropriately raised in blessing.

See also BATHING; MIKVAH.

Laver on the tombstone of Moses ben Israel Tchor (d. *1656*) *in the Prague cemetery. The laver served as the traditional identification symbol of the Levite.*

"LAW, THE." *See* BIBLE, THE.

LAW, JEWISH

Like all religions which, by their very nature, are growing systems of belief and observance, the Jewish religion, too, since earliest times, continued to evolve its code of laws and regulations. These laws not only were designed to prescribe and to govern all forms of religious belief and worship—the ritual and ceremonial in particular—but also were to serve as guide for the spiritual life and the moral conduct of the individual.

If to some observers the Jewish religion appears to be weighted down by an overelaborate code bristling with innumerable injunctions, prohibitions, statutes, and regulations, it is mainly because ancient Jewish society, from its very beginnings, constituted a quite unique political system: *a theocracy.* It was a God-ruled corporate body in which all departments of life and culture—namely, the political, civil, social, ethical, and even certain aspects of economic activity—that ordinarily, among other peoples, have been considered to possess a secular character, were directed and controlled by a corpus of religious laws. This code, according to the Biblical statement, was assumed to have had a divine authorship and, therefore, was implicit with an authority that was not to be questioned. The latter fact will explain why religious Jews through the ages showed such an astonishing devotion to the fulfillment of the laws of the Torah.

It is, unquestionably, a fallacy to conceive of the Jewish law as constituting, both juridically and morally, a unified and monolithic system. From the critical-historical point of view, it represents what may be described as a "palimpsest"—a code that is a composite of many codes, of one layer of laws and attitudes superimposed upon another layer, and that one upon still other layers, thus amalgamating those of the most primitive times with later ones of more advanced periods. It should be noted that nowhere in sacred or historic Jewish writings is there specific mention made of a chronological point in time at which a specific law was first introduced. And so it came to pass that the most backward and the most exalted, the most primitive and also the most enlightened laws, do appear, uncritically and without distinction between them, side by side in the monumental corpus of Jewish law.

It should be quite apparent to the modern student of the Jewish religion that its development process was organic and continuous through the centuries. The drawing up of the legal code paralleled and was part of the compilation of the Bible by its ancient editors—Ezra and the Scribes. They retained for inclusion in the Torah what presumably were revered prehistoric traditions from Israelitish tribal times, and they also included certain archaic narratives and passages which they had culled from then already obsolete and discarded Jewish Scriptural works. They interspersed these anthologically with far more advanced religious ideas and writings that were products of later ages. In exactly the same way in which the Scriptures were compiled, Jewish law too embodied elements drawn from a number of diverse and often conflicting older codes.

After the Bible canon had been finally closed during the first century C.E., the Rabbinic Sages (Tannaim) compiled the Mishnah code of Oral Traditions and Laws (*see* MISHNAH *under* TALMUD) to supplement and elaborate the fundamental laws that had already been included in the Five Books of Moses. But inasmuch as all legal philosophies do undergo revisions with time, and new laws—or modifications of old ones, and, occasionally, annulments of obsolete ones—are required by the changing circumstances of life, the Jewish law constantly was enlarged with new accretions. In this organic process, medieval and later religious authorities continued to add their own opinions and decisions to those laws already in existence. Many of these—for instance, Rabbenu Gershom's ("Our Teacher" Gershom ben Yehudah, 960–1040) decree abolishing polygamy about the year 1000—were also transmuted by virtue of their popular acceptance into religious laws binding to Jews everywhere.

In the ages-old traditional view, the laws of Moses are considered to have been divinely given on Mount Sinai to Moses, who wrote them down on two tablets of stone "with the finger of God" for the government and guidance of the Children of Israel. But the more objective Biblical scholarship of today has concluded that the Mosaic Code is merely a composite of at least four separate Biblical codes that were compiled at different times. These are the Book of the Covenant (in Exodus), the laws in Deuteronomy, the so-called Holiness Code in Leviticus, and, finally, the Priestly Code, which consists of portions of Genesis, Exodus, Leviticus, and Numbers.

One important fact not to be overlooked is like the legal systems in other religions, that of the Jews was not entirely original in a number of important respects, although its overall moral and ethical philosophy establishes it as perhaps the most unique religious legal code in the history of ancient civilizations. Quite apparently, Moses, as well as other unnamed Israelite lawgivers, showed no hesitation in borrowing or in adapting the laws of other peoples for the moral or practical ends of Jewish life. Some of the laws were derived from the codes of the Egyptians, the Babylonians, the Assyrians, and the Canaanites.

It is well known to modern scholarship that several of the Ten Commandments appear, in the same order in which they are presented in the Bible, in Chapter 125 of the Egyptian Book of the Dead. This is a scriptural work containing remarkable ritualistic verses, composed by anonymous Egyptian poet-priests in the service of the death-cult of Osiris beginning about the fifteenth century B.C.E. Since this time coincided, it is generally assumed, with the Jewish Bondage in Egypt, some Biblical scholars conjecture, whether rightly or mistakenly, that the germinal ideas of the Ten Commandments had, to some extent, been borrowed by Moses from the existing texts of the Egyptians, with which he was familiar. To a lesser degree than was formerly claimed by Biblical scholars, this kind of indebtedness would also hold true of several laws appearing in the Babylonian Code of Hammurabi (*c.* 1700 B.C.E.)

At a far later time (during the Hellenistic period), the highly developed Greek and Roman laws made an additional impact on the Jewish code. It is unquestionably significant that in the Talmud there have been found, paraphrased phonetically, some seventy Greek legal terms, and a small number of Latin ones as well. It should be interpreted perhaps as a cultural irony that, so long as the Jews were able to live in their own political state within a theocratic society, remaining relatively unmolested by their enemies, the authority of the Jewish law was less effective than during the storm-and-stress period which followed the national disaster of Zion laid in ruins. During the Talmudic era that began then, there took place not only a remarkable activity in the revision and the multiplication of the Jewish laws, but also a fervently awakened interest among the faithful in observing them.

This religious-historical phenomenon might be explained in great part by the fact that, with the destruction of the Jewish state and the dispersion of the Jewish people, the preservation of the Jewish religion and the continuance of the Jewish group identity were considered to be impossible without the observance of certain religious practices. These included the continual study of the Torah and of Oral Law, the fulfillment of the 613 Biblical commandments, the strict observance of all the rites and ceremonies of the Jewish religion, and—not least—the acceptance by all Jews everywhere in the world of the supreme authority of the Jewish law.

The Sages of the Talmud tirelessly taught that the laws of the Torah which governed all aspects of man's moral conduct, the doctrines and dogmas of the Jewish faith, and the prescribed performance of the various rites and ceremonies in all their minutiae, were eternal and immutable. They declared that these had been given by an all-loving and omniscient God to Moses and the Prophets for the illumination and the service of Israel, that they might prepare in holiness and righteousness for the redemptive coming of the Messiah and the restoration of the scattered remnants of Israel to Mount Zion. Being mostly sober realists, and understanding that most people require personal incentives for much of what they are asked to do, the Rabbis of old held out the promise that dedicated observance of all the commandments and laws of the Torah would assure the individual, when his time came to depart from this life, a share of celestial bliss in the World-to-Come.

With the advent of the Middle Ages in Europe, a deadening preoccupation with the minutiae of observance of every law governing religious worship, ritual, and ceremony led to the introduction of many new laws by a multitude of rabbis in the widely separated Jewish communities of Southern, Central, and Eastern Europe. The number of laws by this time had grown so vast, cumbersome, and bewildering, even to the rabbis, that a number of attempts were made to gather and systematize them. Maimonides (the twelfth-century rabbi-philosopher of Spain) himself compiled a monumental and expository code of all the accumulated Jewish laws of the centuries in his Mishneh Torah. However, it turned out to be too elaborate and philosophical for popular and practical guidance. Later and less intellectual rabbinic savants produced less complex and, therefore, more workable codes. The most influential of these manuals were the Arbah Turim (The Four Rows) by Jacob ben Asher (Spain, *d.* 1340) and the Shulchan Aruch (The Set Table) by Joseph Caro (1488–1575), the Safed Cabalist. The latter code, to this day, still wields enormous authority among Orthodox Jews everywhere.

This law-mindedness led at certain times to damaging excesses in pietism and to rigid formalistic worship. This was especially the case in the backward ghettos of Eastern Europe after the Counter Reformation period. Obsessive concern with legalistic trivia had always been present in certain areas of Jewish religious life. The Prophets of old had ridiculed the empty forms of ritualism, castigating them as an evasion of the spiritual and ethical objectives of the Torah. The first-century Tanna, Antigonos of Soko, lashed out at the legalistic *quid pro quo* worshiper who dutifully set himself to the formidable task of performing all of the 613 positive and negative commandments contained in the Torah in exchange for his expectation of heavenly reward. Antigonus chided: "Be not like servants who serve their master for reward, but like those who perform their duties without thought of recompense." (Pirke Abot 1:3.)

What really was the religious and social philosophy behind Jewish law, as Rabbinic Judaism expounded it? A Sage of the Talmud gave the answer: "The laws of the Torah were handed down that men should live by them and not die because of them."

With the modern era, deep fissures became noticeable in the authority that Jewish law had wielded until that time. In the semiautonomous European ghetto established in the midst of Christian society, and in its Arabian and North African equivalent, the mellah, the effectiveness of Rabbinic law was made possible largely by the segregated life of the Jewish communities. But when the Jews were charged, by groups hostile to them, with being nothing but an alien, exclusive group that preferred to be ruled by its own laws, which violated the laws of the land, the rabbis, sensing the great danger that hung over them, hastened to promulgate in clarification a new legal formula which remained ever after operative for Jews everywhere. This stated that "The law of the country is the *law*." (*"Dinah d'malchutah dinah."*)

One of the social fruits of the French Revolution in 1789 was that the Jews were allowed to acquire, although only gradually, certain measures of civil, social, economic, and political equality. With the increasing emancipation and cultural enlightenment that resulted, and with the breakdown of ghetto isolation and the opportunity afforded Jews to become

Europeanized, the supreme authority of the Jewish law not unexpectedly began to decline, slowly at first, but with an accelerated tempo at the turn of the twentieth century.

It is well known that both Conservative and Reform programs of Judaism have made sharp downward revisions in their observance of the traditional Jewish laws–in particular, of those that govern rites and ceremonies. Generally, Orthodox Jews in varying degree still strive to remain steadfast in their adherence to Jewish law. However, they are often frustrated in their intentions and are forced, because of the pressures–economic, social, and cultural–of their Gentile environment, of which they are also a part, to compromise and make unwilling concessions. The law of the land, in so many ways different from the provisions of ancient Jewish law, of course reigns supreme. The only relatively free area of observance, according to the dictates of Rabbinic law, lies strictly in religious worship and practice, in Torah study, and in holding on to certain cherished folkways, symbols, and customs.

See also DOCTRINES IN JUDAISM; MITZVOT; TEN COMMANDMENTS.

"LAW OF RETALIATION." *See* "EYE FOR AN EYE."

LEARNING, IDEAL OF. *See* TORAH STUDY.

LEARNING, LOVE OF. *See* BET HA-MIDRASH; CHACHMAH; SAGES, RABBINIC; TALMUD; TORAH STUDY; YESHIBAH; YESHIVAH BACHUR.

LEAVEN, REMOVAL OF. *See* PASSOVER.

LETZ, LAYTZIM. *See* MERRYMAKERS, TRADITIONAL JEWISH.

LEVIRATE MARRIAGE. *See* CHALITZAH.

LEVI, LEVIIM. *See* LEVITES.

LEVITES (in Hebrew: pl. LEVIIM; s. LEVI)

Before the sixth century B.C.E., when Nebuchadnezzar destroyed the First Temple and led the flower of Jewish youth into the Captivity in Babylonia, the Levites were considered the equals of the priests (Cohanim; s. Cohen). The words "priest" and "Levite" had been until that time practically interchangeable, for the entire tribe of Levi, including Moses and Aaron, had been specially named to serve as the Jewish priesthood: ". . . and the Levites shall be Mine." (Numbers 3:12.)

But upon the return of the first contingent from the Captivity, in 538 B.C.E., the priesthood was reorganized according to a plan that had been prepared during the Exile by the Prophet Ezekiel. And from that time on, the Levites became a distinct group of Temple officials and servants holding a far lesser rank than the priests. They were responsible for all the menial and minor administrative work in the Temple; they were in charge of the priestly vestments and the Temple treasures; they policed the gates and guarded the musical instruments. In addition, they functioned as the musicians in the Temple–both as instrumentalists and as singers in the massed choirs that were employed in the elaborate religious services. Whereas in former times they had shared with all other priests in the first fruits, in the sacrifices and gift offerings, and in the tithes collected from each Jew for the support of the Temple, during the Second Temple period they were excluded from sharing in these interests, which were, by and large, appropriated by the hierarchy of the priesthood itself that, ever after, jealously guarded its great powers and privileges.

Toward the end of the Maccabean era, in the second century B.C.E., when the moral tone of the priesthood had been sharply altered for the worse, a social-economic snobbery, which at first had been built on caste feeling, was turned into *a religious tradition* by the priests themselves. This took place in spite of the democratic revolution that had been achieved by the Rabbinic Sages with their ethical teachings in the social and religious life of the people. In the matter of religious protocol or "precedent," the priests, with the self-assurance of those holding the upper hand, claimed to be superior to the Levites. The Levites, in turn, held themselves to be better than the common garden-variety of Jews who constituted about 99 per cent of the entire Jewish people. Amusingly, these latter, for the purpose of being differentiated from the priests and the Levites, came to be called, by an odd kind of illogic, "Israelites"!

See also HIGH PRIEST; MUSIC IN THE TEMPLE; PRIESTS; TEMPLE, THE.

LEVITICUS, BOOK OF. *See* BIBLE, THE.

"LIBERAL" JUDAISM. *See* JUDAISM IN THE MODERN AGE.

LIFE, JEWISH VIEW OF

The rationalism that became traditional among Jews during the Second Temple era resulted in an affirmation of life that was earthy, wholesome, and balanced, in direct contrast to the religious thinking, steeped in pessimism and a fear of life, which then prevailed among the people living in the countries of the Fertile Crescent. In the sixth century B.C.E., Ezekiel, the Prophet of the Babylonian Captivity, had with a few memorable words fixed the point of religious belief for Israel, contrasting its philosophy of life with the cult of death in other religions. God speaks: "I have no pleasure in the death of him that dieth, wherefor turn yourself and live!"

Centuries later, the Rabbinic "teachers of wisdom" in Judea and Babylonia took up this Prophetic manifesto for a dedication *to* life and *away* from death with renewed zeal. In the Hebrew Amidah prayer, recited for two thousand years in all synagogues on Rosh Hashanah, runs the invocation:

> Remember us for life, O King, you who take delight in life!
> Inscribe us in the Book of Life, for your sake, O living God!

But nothing written by the ancient Rabbis sounds as all-embracing and earthy–as throbbing with a warm and generous humanity–as the last of the Seven Benedictions which are recited during the marriage rite:

> Blessed art Thou, O Lord our God, King of the Universe, who has created joy and gladness, bridegroom and bride, mirth and exaltation, pleasure and delight, love, brotherhood, peace, and fellowship!

The down-to-earth pre-Christian teacher of ethics, Hillel, taught that the world becomes real to us only through the medium of our minds and of our bodily senses. His penetrating aphorism—the very reverse of the motto by the seventeenth-century French philosopher Descartes: "I think, therefore I am"—was: "If I am here—all are; if I am not here—who is?" He believed implicitly that the total life of man, sensory as well as intellectual, was reality, and death was its negation. Therefore, the prescription of the Talmud: For every single breath a human being takes, he should offer thanks to his Creator.

Having accepted the objective fact of his biologic existence, the all-absorbing problem of the Jew became: How should he live? What should he do, and what goals was he to set himself for his life? The Biblical view—and, even more strongly—the Rabbinic, was that God had created man in his own divine image to live uprightly, but that man himself had, unfortunately, by his inventions of folly and wickedness, worked for his own corruption.

Why did that calamitous condition in the life of man have to arise? asked the baffled moralists in the Talmud. Who or what was to blame? Was it the bodily senses? Was it the soul? Fascinated by the enigma, the Sages dwelled long and intently upon the possible implications in the phrase from Leviticus: "If a soul sin . . ." The Midrash notes concerning these words that "the school of Rabbi Ishmael [Jerusalem, second century] taught . . . in the World-to-Come, the Holy One, blessed be He, asks the soul of man: 'Why have you sinned?' And the soul replies: 'Lord of the World . . . it is the body, and not I, that has sinned. This can be proven by the fact that ever since I left the body I have become as pure as a bird that wings through the air!' Then God asks the body: 'Why have you sinned?' And the body answers: 'Lord of the World, I have committed no sin! It is the soul that has sinned. This can be proven by the fact that ever since the soul left me, I have been lying silent like a stone in my grave!' What does the Holy One, blessed be He, do? He once more unites the body with the soul, and then he punishes them *both.*"

This remarkable passage is but one of a number of similar observations which attempt to make the logical point that body and soul are to be considered a single entity, and, being inseparable, are to be held jointly accountable for the conduct of the individual.

In the tenth century, the humanistic religious authority, Saadia Gaon, the rector of the Rabbinic Academy in Sura, Babylonia, went to great lengths to lay down anew the principle that the body and the soul were both creations of God, and that each was, consequently, in its own way, "spiritual." He extolled the divine wisdom which had led God to effect the union of the body with the soul. By itself, he pointed out, the soul remained incapable of action, and this, obviously, was the reason why God had joined it with the body, which *could* act.

To the charge by the Rabbinical ascetics that the body was full of corruption and that it would have been better for the soul if God had allowed it to exist by itself so that it could have remained "free from sin, impurity, and suffering," Saadia retorted: "We declare that there is nothing impure about the human body! On the contrary, it is perfectly pure, for impurity is a condition whose existence is neither apparent to the senses nor discoverable by means of reason. It is known to us only from the religious law which has declared certain human secretions to be impure after their separation from the body. But so long as they are still *within* the body one cannot consider them impure unless one presumes to lay down the law for himself. We, therefore, denounce such a view as monstrous, and we will not accept it as law!"

From such teachings as Saadia's there developed an outlook on life that readily accepted nature and man's biological as well as spiritual role in it. Only the ascetic escapists among Jews continued to revile the body and the senses as evil. The mainstream of Jewish religious culture, however, pursued through the many centuries the quest for physical well-being and sensory delight measured by the Golden Mean. This would explain why it is that the art of healing and the calling of the physician were so highly prized by the Jews in every age, and possibly to a greater extent than by any other people in history. It is more significant that until modern times, Jewish physicians were also, in numerous instances, rabbis. To keep the body—the fleshly tenement of the immortal soul that God had blessed man with—in perfect health became a dedication of piety. The religious literature of the Jews shows them to have been vastly preoccupied with medical questions, personal hygiene, diet, and sex morality. And to what end? To the glorification of God and the sanctification of life.

About one hundred years before the Destruction of Jerusalem, the unknown poet who composed the pseudepigraphic work, the Wisdom of Solomon, addressed the Deity with this ecstatic salutation:

> O sovereign God, thou Lover of Life!

See also ARABIC-JEWISH "GOLDEN AGE"; ASCETICS, JEWISH; FREE WILL; GOLDEN MEAN, THE RABBINIC; HEALERS; MONASTICISM, JEWISH; PASSIONS, MASTERY OVER; SOUL, THE.

LIFE, THE SANCTIFICATION OF (in Hebrew: KIDDUSH HA-CHAYYIM)

A Sage of the Talmud said: "The object of the Torah is the preservation of life, and not its destruction."

Life was deemed good and perfectible in Jewish religious thinking, and it was considered the greatest wickedness to destroy it, for God had made it, and he animated the lifeless flesh with a soul that was of his "breath."

Beginning with the Sixth of the Ten Commandments, "Thou shalt not murder," the Jewish people were conditioned by their ethically evolving religion to abhor war and to eschew violence and to have reverence for life—*all* life, not just that of a Jew. "Every human being is equal in worth to all Creation," Rabbi Nehemiah taught.

At the convocation of the religious assembly urgently called in Lydda at the time of the bitter persecutions by the Roman Emperor Hadrian, the Rabbis solemnly warned all in Israel that no Jew was to attempt to save his life by compromising another person. It was the Babylonian Sage, Rabba ben Joseph (fourth century, C.E.) who, when a certain man asked what he should do because his life was threatened if he did not carry out the murder of another man, tartly replied: "Be killed and kill not! Who has told you that your blood is redder than his? Perhaps his blood is redder!"

The fundamental reason for the Scriptural injunction against violence and the shedding of a fellow creature's blood appears in Genesis 9:6:

> . . . for in the image of God made He man.

Cain slays his brother Abel. (Marble frieze by Jacopo della Quercia, Bologna, Italy.)

LION OF JUDAH

The graphic emblem of the royal house of David was a lion, the "king of the beasts." This ancient symbol of supreme power and majesty was probably acquired from the imperial Assyrians and Babylonians, in whose sculpture it figured as a central motif. Perhaps because of its identification with the Jewish Psalmist-king, it was universally tolerated by the rabbis for use in representational art—in sculpture as well as in painting.

The earliest delineation of a lion extant appears on a seal of Shema, minister of Jeroboam, king of Judah (933 B.C.E.–912 B.C.E.); yet, during the sixteenth century, the question of whether its use as decoration in the synagogue was permissible, was posed in a rabbinical dispute—again the ancient fear of idolatry! (*See* ART AMONG THE JEWS.)

In the decoration of the synagogue, the lion has been used variously: in sculpture, mural-painting, wood-carving in relief, and, most of all, in embroidery. Two lions couchant sometimes served as the bottom supports for the Ark of the Law. Lions rampant have always supported the crowned wooden or stone tablets of the Ten Commandments placed on top of the Ark. They have also been used frequently for decorative purposes on the silver Crown or Breastplate of the Torah, and on the embroidered or appliquéd velvet or silk Torah Mantle or Ark curtain (parochet).

Lion of Judah on the seal of Shema, minister to Jeroboam, king of Judah (933 B.C.E.*–912* B.C.E.*). Dug up at Megiddo.*

LITERATURE. *See* ARABIC-JEWISH "GOLDEN AGE"; BIBLE, THE; CABALA; COMMENTARIES, RABBINICAL; ENLIGHTENMENT, THE JEWISH; HEBREW LITERATURE, MODERN; POST-BIBLICAL WRITINGS; RABBINICAL DECISIONS: SHULCHAN ARUCH; SIDDUR; TALMUD, THE; YIDDISH LITERATURE, MODERN; ZEMIROT; ZOHAR (*under* CABALA).

LITURGICAL MUSIC. *See* HYMNS OF THE SYNAGOGUE; MUSIC, ANCIENT JEWISH; MUSIC IN THE TEMPLE.

LITURGY. *See* PRAYER AND WORSHIP; PRAYER SERVICE; SIDDUR.

LOAN SOCIETIES, JEWISH. *See* LOANS, FREE.

LOANS, FREE (in Hebrew: pl. GEMILUT CHASADIM; S. GEMILUT CHESED)

The Jewish philosophy of tzedakah (charity) takes in the entire spectrum of benevolence. Among the great concerns of the Rabbinic Sages was not only the amelioration of the wants of the poor but also the *prevention of poverty itself* in individual cases. These aims were reinforced as well by their humane regard for the bruised sensibilities of many receivers of benevolence; the Rabbis wished to spare them the possible loss of their self-respect.

For that reason, the Talmud taught that *to help a man to help himself* constituted the highest moral good. It is written: "In the scale of charity, the highest is to grasp a man who is falling and to keep him from falling and becoming a public charge by offering him a gift, a loan, a business partnership, or by finding employment for him." And among the acts of charity ("charity" in the dignified sense of "loving-kindness"), the most glowing praise was reserved by the Sages for the interest-free loan: "Kinder is he who lends than he who gives." The second-century teacher of ethics, Ishmael, taught: "If a man is ashamed to ask you for help, 'open' to him with these words: 'My son, maybe you need a loan?' "

True enough, it was expected that all such loans would be repaid. Yet, where the continued impoverishment of a borrower made him an involuntary defaulter and, therefore, caused him grief, the Rabbis strongly recommended a humane and realistic course for the creditor. They ruled that loans "must never be collected" from the very poor or the unfortunate. Elaborating on this idea, Judah Chasid, the great rabbinical moralist of the Rhineland (*d.* 1217), counseled: "If you have lent money to a poor man who is unable to repay it when you see him approach, turn quickly away, lest he think that you are about to ask him for money."

The pride and human dignity inculcated in the masses of the Jewish people by such ethical teachings and practices—in addition to their imperative need for mutual aid in order to survive in a hostile world—made the free-loan society a vital and traditional institution in the Jewish community everywhere since the Talmudic era.

During the first decade of the twentieth century in the United States, at a time when all public and private charity-agencies were complaining that their funds were being depleted by the great number of needy immigrant families, they were also expressing wonderment at the small number of immigrant Jews applying to them for assistance. The inquiring social workers soon enough found the answer to this puzzle: They ascribed it, in great part, to the dedicated work of "the Jewish free-loan and benevolent aid societies" that had been founded by the poor immigrants themselves for the purpose of rendering dignified mutual assistance to their landsleit (fellow Jews hailing from the same town in "the old country"). On New York's Lower East Side, which contained, before World War I, the principal concentration of Jewish immigrants in this country, free-loan societies were literally numbered in the hundreds.

Today, exclusive of the free-loan service performed by Jewish philanthropic agencies, there are still a number of free-loan societies in operation among the Jewish poor in large cities in the United States and Canada, but their scope is necessarily limited. Immigration virtually ceased in the United States when the restrictive quota laws were enacted in the 1920's. And the great majority of those Jews who had arrived prior to that time had already become adjusted economically. However, there has always been a large number of indigent or needy Jews requiring assistance. To these applicants, when they are unable to avail themselves of the lending services of commercial banks and finance companies, the traditional Jewish free-loan practice still serves as a crutch —no matter how slender and fragile it may be—upon which they can lean.

See also CHARITY; FELLOWSHIP IN ISRAEL; MAN, DIGNITY OF.

LOVE THY NEIGHBOR. *See* ETHICAL VALUES, JEWISH.

LULAB. *See* "FOUR SPECIES, THE"; SUCCOT.

M

MACCABEES. *See* CHANNUKAH; CHANNUKAH LAMP; POST-BIBLICAL WRITINGS.

The "Star of David" in the form of an amulet with Cabalistic words and names to protect an expectant mother and her child against witchcraft, the Evil Eye, and demons.

MACHZOR. *See* ROSH HASHANAH; SIDDUR.

MAGEN DAVID

Although the Magen David—the "Star of David" or "Jewish Star"—has been universally used in modern times by Jews and their enemies alike as a graphic symbol of Jewish national identity, this was not at all the case in earlier Jewish historic periods. Then the representation of the seven-branched menorah served as the traditional pictorial motif. Nowhere in the post-Biblical Hebrew writings—not even in the vast literature of the Babylonian and Jerusalem Talmud—is the Magen David (a hexagram formed by two equilateral triangles) mentioned or even described in any way. True, one can find that motif worked into the architectural ornamentation of the Hellenistic synagogue at Capernaum (Kfar Nachum), described in the Christian Gospels as the scene of Jesus' preachings; the same motif is also engraved on a third-century Jewish tombstone excavated in Tarentum, in Italy. But these examples are exceptional.

There is every evidence that the Magen David as a Jewish symbol first became noticeable when the Karaites (*which see*) and the practical Cabalists (*see* CABALA) of Europe introduced it in the late Middle Ages. Its widespread popularity was fostered by latter-day Cabalists who made it the central geometric design on protective amulets and talismans.

With the turn of this century, the Magen David was adopted by the Zionists as the Jewish national symbol, and although it still remains that, it is interesting to note that the State of Israel has returned to the ancient traditional Jewish identity symbol—the menorah—as a decoration on its official seal.

MAGGID (Hebrew s., meaning "preacher"; pl. MAGGIDIM; similar to DARSHAN; pl. DARSHANIM)

Until relatively recent times, Jewish life was centered in religion, which permeated practically every area of its thought and activity. Accordingly, there were required many different kinds of specialized ecclesiastical and semiecclesiastical officials to minister to the numerous spiritual, intellectual, and purely ritualistic needs of the Jewish community. The rabbi was chiefly preoccupied with clarifying or deciding ritual questions—with interpreting Jewish law as it directly applied to the exigencies of daily life and also checking its violations—and, above all, with furthering the study of the Torah in the congregation; but he, strangely enough, was not expected to preach. For that purpose there were available two other religious functionaries, the darshan and the maggid. Although, in effect, these two were closely related professionally, there, however, did exist marked differences between them.

The darshan was himself a rabbi; he was both Torah-learned and skilled in Talmudic dialectics, and his sermons, always in Hebrew, were required to be scholarly expositions and searching interpretations of Biblical and Talmudic texts. A paid official of the community, he usually preached on Sabbath afternoons in the synagogue.

The maggid, on the other hand, was, in matters of scholarship, of a lower order; he was a popular and (most commonly) itinerant preacher. He felt close to the plain folk and addressed himself to them—mainly in emotional terms—on their own limited intellectual level. In the countries of Eastern Europe, he preached in the Yiddish vernacular instead of in the sacred Hebrew. Except for the occasional

The "Star of David" surmounting pylons at the funeral of Chaim Weizmann, the first President of Israel. (Israel Office of Information.)

Jews assembled in the synagogue to hear a religious discourse by a maggid. (From the Sefer ha-Minhagim, 1695.)

"city maggid" who held an appointive and paid office, he was but infrequently a community functionary, and then non-salaried. For his meager livelihood he had to rely upon the unpredictable generosity and appreciation of his audiences.

During the Middle Ages, and down almost to our own day, when Jewish community life went through one emotional and physical crisis after another, the maggid assumed a very significant role—that of a wandering preacher, trudging along interminable and hazardous roads in the fulfillment of his self-appointed tasks. He journeyed on horseback, by wagon, or on foot, from village to village, from town to town, a shabby-looking but dedicated man who loved his people. He attempted—not always successfully—to illuminate in the simplest of terms the basic problems of faith and conduct. In reality, he was a teacher of Jewish law and morality in a revivalist sort of way. But he was also, ofttimes, a comforter of the plain folk when they felt overwhelmed by their persecutors and their unending troubles. Always, in concluding his preaching, he held out for his audiences the ultimate promise and the unfading hope of the Messiah's coming and of the Redemption that he would bring. It is certain that, among the creators of folk culture and the preservers among the people of ethical Jewish values, the humble wandering maggid played an important role—one which cannot be ignored by the historian of Jewish life.

There were two principal schools of maggidim, although both had many characteristics in common. The first, and numerically the largest, consisted of "awakeners." They were popularly called "terror maggidim" because they were "fire and brimstone" preachers who threatened the miserable sinner (and who wasn't one?) with the torments of Gehinnom (Purgatory). They thundered and they lightened, and with tear-filled eyes and breaking voices, exhorted their hearers to repentance. Their vogue in Slavic countries, from the sixteenth century up until World War I, could be principally explained by the physical wretchedness, the ignorance, and the insecurity of life in the ghetto. One of the most famous representatives of these "terror maggidim" was Moses Isaac (1828–1900), the Kelmer Maggid of Poland.

In sharp contrast to this type of fire-eating preachers were the "gentle maggidim." These were companionable souls. They were humane, good-humoredly folksy, full of earthy wisdom, and benevolent in their attitude toward backsliders and sinners because they understood human weaknesses. They had two unerring darts in their preaching quiver: one was an emotional style of delivery which deeply moved their audiences; the other was the skill with which they managed to weave into their moralizing an inexhaustible number of humorous quips, jokes, and parables, distilled from the many centuries of Jewish folk laughter, irony, and despair. The most celebrated exponent of the "gentle maggidim" was Rabbi Jacob Krantz (Lithuania, 1740–1804), better known as the Dubner Maggid. His use of wise and witty parables prompted the philosopher Moses Mendelssohn, who heard him preach, to call him "the Jewish Aesop."

MALACH, MALACHIM. *See* ANGELS.

MAN, DIGNITY OF

"Where is the center of the world?" asked the Sages.

"Where every human being stands—*there* is the center of the world," was the answer.

The philosophical meaning of this is that the whole universe is mirrored in each individual, and it takes on reality only in his consciousness; without him, all creation would be, as it were, non-existent. For that reason, the Midrash counsels: "Each person must respect himself and say with dignity: 'God created the world on my account.'"

That the institution of the Sabbath was set up not only to enable man to rest from his toil but also to allow him to regain his human dignity and his soul through serenity and reflection on that holy day can be seen in the following anecdote concerning Rabbi Zvi Elimelech, the Chasidic tzaddik of eighteenth-century Galicia. It was his custom never to go to sleep on the eve of the Sabbath. Instead, he whiled away the hours of the night in pious song and mystic dance. Asked to give the reason for this extraordinary conduct, he replied with this parable: "The Emperor Joseph I of Austria used to sleep very little. He said, 'I am the Emperor only when I am awake.' It is the same with us Jews. On the Sabbath, every Jew is a king, no matter how wretched his condition. Wouldn't it be a pity to sleep away our royalty like that?"

MANNERS. *See* ETHICAL VALUES, JEWISH.

MANTLE, SEFER TORAH. *See* TORAH ORNAMENTS.

MAROR. *See* PASSOVER.

MARRANOS AND THE INQUISITION

From a juridical point of view, the canon law of the Church treated professing "stiff-necked" Jews as infidels, generally offering them a choice between conversion or death. But the Jewish Conversos—the New Christians who had renounced the Jewish religion and undergone baptism and, accordingly, been received into "the true faith"—now became exposed to all the hazards resulting from either conscious or unconscious relapses into their old Jewish conditioning in matters of belief, tradition, observance, and custom.

Heresy in former centuries was, more often than not, punishable by prison, torture, and death. The authoritarian Church during the Middle Ages had been painfully involved in the suppression of heresy and heretics within its own fold; it had had to deal with such sectarian dissenters as the Arians Albigenses, Waldenses, etc. But the Jewish New Christian or Marrano, when discovered in any manner as a secret relapser (*Judaizante*), was regarded and also punished as a heretic by the Church. From all this it may be conjectured that it was possibly harder—if that is at all conceivable—to be a "new" Christian than an old Jew.

Both Spain and Portugal were full of Conversos, for every time some mass-crusade against the Jewish religion was started (an occurrence of far greater frequency than is gen

An auto-da-fé *of Marranos held with great pomp and ecclesiastical ceremony by the Inquisition at the enclave of Goa in India. (Engraving by Bernard Picart, c. 1725.)*

erally suspected) the weak-kneed, the opportunistic, those not too firm in their religious convictions, and, of course, those who followed the counsel of Maimonides (*see* CONVERSION OF JEWS), flocked to the baptismal font. In the instance of many however, their conversion was spurious, as the bulls by Popes Clement VI (1342–52) and Boniface IX (1389–1404) made plain when they forbade forced conversions.

As the entire history of anti-Semitism shows, there always entered into its composition other than purely religious or doctrinal determinants; more important than these were economic, social, racial, and cultural considerations. For instance, in Spain and Portugal, the influx of former Jews into the open stream of religious, economic, and national life had introduced a powerful new element of competition to old Christians in entrenched places. Before long, the Conversos occupied numerous important positions at court, in the military forces, in the professions, in finance and commerce, and—perhaps most arrestingly—in the Church itself, where they accounted for some of the foremost prelates, preachers, and theologians. The religious orders too attracted many scholarly Conversos because of the protected, quiet, and contemplative life they afforded.

Without a doubt, this vigorous exercise of their talents by former Jews poisoned the atmosphere against them in the Iberian countries. The Spanish Church, gradually at first, and even in the face of opposition from several popes, ultimately reached the conclusion that no New Christian—however exemplary his Christian conduct might be or how high his rank (quite a number had been ennobled) or how exalted his ecclesiastical eminence—was to be trusted. Moreover, to allow the Conversos or their descendants to intermarry with tried and true Christians would only contaminate *the racial stream.*

It is here that one crosses the ominous threshold of the same racist doctrine that six centuries later was to be made a cornerstone of German life under Nazi rule. The twentieth-century Germans called it *Rasserein;* the fourteenth-century Spaniards named it *limpieza,* but both terms bear the same unscientific connotation of "racial purity." The argument of the Spanish Church was the same as the irrational rationale of the modern Germans: that the "impurity" in the Jew was that of "bad blood"—*mala sangre*; that the evil was biological and, therefore, endemic in the "race" itself. Thereupon, the hawklike surveillance of New Christians in every detail of their life and conduct commenced.

Every Christian was called upon to observe the doings of the Conversos; even the latter, under pain of the harshest penalties, were ordered to report any deviation from correct Catholic conduct of their fellow Conversos. To make the detection of heresy easier for the faithful, a manual for the use of the Holy Office was prepared by the Inquisitor, Bernardo Guidonis. These were some of the ways of identifying the "Judaizing heresy": wearing clean and festive attire on the Sabbath and Holy Days; lighting Sabbath lamps; cooking the meat for the Sabbath *cholent* on Friday; observing the prescribed Jewish fasts and, in addition, on Yom Kippur, the Day of Atonement, "asking pardon of one another in the Jewish manner"; reciting Hebrew prayers with face turned to the wall; kashering (making kosher) meat and slaughtering animals "as the Jews do"; circumcising male children; reciting a berachah (benediction) before eating; "pouring water from jars and pitchers when someone has died"; turning the dying toward the wall; etc.

It was to be expected, in an atmosphere so charged with hate, violence, and intimidation, that informers eager for reward or praise, should rise everywhere to furnish the Church with information—fictional as well as factual—about the heretical views of the Conversos. By a treacherous ruse, thousands of Marranos or New Christians, promised full forgiveness by the Church if they would only confess their "Judaizing" lapses, stepped forward and confessed voluntarily, only to discover that they had been lured into a trap. In addition, many Conversos under torture, implicated others, and these, in their turn, were stretched on the rack to implicate still others in an ever widening circle of betrayal and violence.

It began, in a formal sense, in the year 1449 with the promulgation of the Sentencia Estatuo in Toledo. This legal document declared that it was impossible to trust the fidelity of the Conversos whether in relation to Christian doctrine, to the Church, or to Christians. Consequently, it imposed serious restrictions upon them, both civilly and economically. For the first time the doctrine of *limpieza* (purity of blood) was stressed in a legal instrument.

The pope of that time, Nicholas V, was outraged. He issued a bull denouncing the action by the authorities in Toledo, and reaffirmed the ancient democratic practice of the Church which had established for *all* Christians, whatever their origins, their full equality in Christ. But the Pope's decree was ignored.

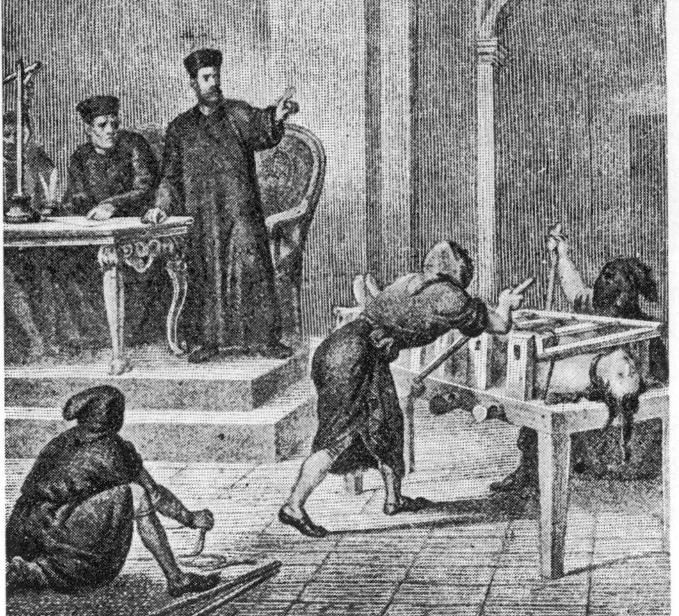

Tribunal of the Spanish Inquisition in Mexico City applies torture to Francisca de Carabajal to extract a confession, 1590. (From Palacio's El Libro Rojo.)

In 1480, tribunals of the Holy Office (Inquisition) were established in Spain by the Cortes (Parliament) at Toledo for the examination and prosecution of Conversos. (This, of course, was not the first time that the ecclesiastical inquisitors of heretics [*Inquisitio haereticae*] were empowered to expose, suppress, and punish heresy and unbelief. The Dominican Order had such tribunals in operation as far back as 1237.) Under the implacable direction of the Grand Inquisitor, Tomás de Torquemada, the confessor to Queen Isabella and the known descendant of a Jewish grandmother (a genealogical fact which throws peculiar psychopathologic light on his ruthlessness toward Jews), the Inquisition began to operate on an enormous, man-devouring scale. Many thousands of suspected "Judaizers" were arrested and flung into dungeons, there to wait in agonizing suspense for their turn to be tried (and tortured) by the courts of the Holy Office.

The trials of the Marranos—and these included many Church scholars, priests and friars, hidalgos, and grandees—were not just routine hearings; they were invariably marked by tragedy, betrayal, and a river of blood. Those who declined to make full confession or to implicate others were put to the torture, and the ingenuity of the pious sadists were fully taxed to create new and more agonizing torments for breaking the will of the stubborn. All this was done in order to accomplish the "holy aim" of the Church. Carved into the stone over the gateway to the Palace of the Inquisition was a Biblical inscription in Latin that was a combination of two Scriptural verses: "Arise, O Lord; judge Thine own cause, and capture for us the foxes." Who were the "foxes?" The Marranos of course.

Amazingly enough, there were thousands who remained firm under torture, dying in tight-lipped agony in the flames of the *auto-da-fé*—"the act of faith," as the Church so euphemistically chose to describe their murder. It took on all the theatricality of a religious spectacle, and like the morality play performed in the medieval churches, it was intended by the Holy Office to strengthen the Christian fidelity of the great crowds who assembled to witness the burning. Besides, the terrible spectacle was also designed to serve as a chilling warning to the vacillating and to the heretically disposed among the Conversos.

To the sound of the chanting priests, and amidst the full display of the Church's panoply of power, the relapsed Marranos were led into an arena especially constructed for the purpose. The heretics wore the *sanbenito* (the penitent's tunic of sackcloth) and carried lighted tapers in their hands. For the last time the priests came forward and exhorted them to confess their relapses into Judaism, promising the sincerely repentant of the Church's forgiveness.

Many did confess, and their abject contrition saved them from the fiery stake—the *quemadero*. But others remained obdurate and refused to confess. What had they to confess? They were being falsely accused by malicious or mercenary informers! Still others proudly declared themselves to be unregenerate in their devotion to the God of Israel and the Torah of Moses, and then tearfully prepared for the end. And as the flames licked upward, enveloping their flesh, they expired, reciting the Hebrew Shema: "Hear, O Israel, the Lord our God, the Lord is One!"

It was the noted Anglican scholar and theologian, R. Travers Herford who, with obvious reference to Christian persecution of the Jew, made this melancholy notation in his study, *Judaism in the New Testament Period:* "The Cross is the lineal ancestor of the stake and the gallows; and the Chief Priests, if they ceased to function after the fall of Jerusalem, have had their imitators in Christian Europe."

During the sixteen years of Torquemada's blood-and-iron rule of the Holy Office, a virtual reign of terror gripped the million or so Jews and Marranos of Spain. A great number of Marranos perished at his direction, as did Moorish and Christian heretics also. He burned 2,000 heretics and imprisoned and ruined 100,000 others. Many were condemned to rot in the Inquisition's dungeons.

For more than three centuries the *autos-da-fé* blazed throughout Spain, Majorca, Portugal, the Provence, Mexico, Peru, Goa in India, and other places. Despite the forces of enlightenment working against its bestial practice during the seventeenth and eighteenth centuries, the power of the Holy Office remained unbroken. This fact drew the bitter reflection from the French philosophical writer, Montesquieu, in 1738: "If in days to come anyone should ever dare to say that the people of Europe were civilized in the century in which we are now living, you [the Holy Office] will be cited as proof that they were barbarians."

An unrepentant Marrano in sanbenito *attire weeps as he walks to his death in an* auto-da-fé. *(Engraving by Bernard Picart, early 18th century.)*

The Grand Inquisitor Torquemada finally reached the conclusion that it was virtually impossible to suppress Judaizing among the Marranos; it was first necessary to remove the source of the contagion altogether. As confessor to Queen Isabella, he was able to persuade her and her husband Ferdinand that the expulsion of all Jews from Spain was necessary in order to quarantine the Christian faith of the Conversos against the Jewish heresy and so assure the greater glory of the Church and Christianity. On March 31, 1492, Ferdinand and Isabella signed the edict of expulsion, and the Jews were allowed four months to prepare for their departure from Spain.

In his diary, Christopher Columbus entered this notation: "In the same month in which Their Majesties issued the edict that all Jews should be driven out of the kingdom and its territories, in the same month they gave me the order to undertake with sufficient men my expedition of discovery to the Indies."

The convolutions of history and the destinies of human beings mesh in the most singular way, as Columbus so significantly observed: While he was sailing forth to discover the New World, the great Jewish community of Spain—one that had wrought such a wondrous Golden Age of Jewish civilization for seven centuries—came to a disastrous end.

See also ANTI-SEMITISM: THE "RACIAL PURITY" MYTH; CHRISTIANITY, JEWISH ORIGINS OF; CHRISTIANS, SERVITUDE OF JEWS TO; CHURCH AND PERSECUTION; CONVERSION OF JEWS; DISPUTATIONS, RELIGIOUS; KOL NIDRE; NAZIS, THE; SEPARATISM, JEWISH; WANDERING JEW.

MARRIAGE

In Biblical Hebrew there was no word for "bachelor." That such a word did not exist is proof *ipso facto* that there was no need for it. Quite obviously, the very idea of *not marrying* was unthinkable to the Jew of ancient days. Centuries later, the Talmud ventured the commiserating opinion that "An unmarried man lives without good, without a helper, without joy, without blessing, and, finally, without atonement." During the Talmudic period, when the forms of traditional Jewish life were feeling the disorienting impact of Greco-Roman ways, there must have been some bachelor-minded, fancy-free sophisticates who, the Rabbis felt, required needling into matrimony.

The question naturally arises: How did it happen that its passionate devotion to the institution of marriage burgeoned up probably more strongly in the Jewish consciousness than in any other? Also, what were the historical and religious reasons that led to the Biblical injunction: "Be fruitful and multiply and replenish the earth"? And why was it that this commandment was given first place among all of the 613 precepts in the Torah?

There are a number of substantial reasons for this extraordinary emphasis, two of them religious. One stems from the Jewish concept that Creation is a ceaseless process in eternity and that mankind is duty bound to help God in the fulfillment of this primary objective of existence through procreation in marriage. The other, and undoubtedly the more formidable, reason is that Jews considered themselves to be a people with a mission—"a nation of priests." They had acquired this distinction, the Bible states, by divine election, reinforced by the solemn covenant into which they (the Children of Israel), under Moses, had entered during the Revelation at Mount Sinai. God himself had consecrated them to keep the Torah and its commandments, and they had sworn to hand down this heritage of law and morality to their children and to their children's children forevermore. Furthermore, they had agreed to serve as the instrument of God's Will on earth, as "a light unto the nations," and to bring all mankind worshiping to Mount Zion.

Obviously, these goals required not only the preservation but also the increase of the Jewish people. The Jews could not do without the Torah and the Torah needed the Jews for the fulfillment of the divine purpose. Without the Torah the Jews would not be Jews; without the Jews the Torah would remain orphaned in an inhospitable world. Then, marriage—God's sancitified institution—was the answer: the way to create more Jews who could preserve and transmit the "revealed truth."

In former times, and not so long ago at that, it was customary to set up the chuppah (the wedding canopy) under the open sky. This was done in order to fulfill symbolically the Scriptural verse detailing God's promise to the Patriarch Abraham: "Thus shall thy children be, like the stars of heaven." And while the bride's wedding attendants were adjusting her veil before the ceremony, they intoned the ancient Hebraic wish for fertility: "O sister, be thou a mother of tens of thousands!"

The need for such exceptional fertility, for such a long view of the yet unborn generations, could pragmatically be justified by the recurring crises in Jewish group-life. The strenuous circumstances under which the Jews of the Biblical period had to carry on their national existence in the Land of Israel for more than one thousand years made a steady increase in population a matter of self-preservation, both militarily and economically. The population was constantly being decimated by invasions, wars, raids, and deportations, and the almost unfailing incidence of pestilence, failure of crops, and migrations of the restless to other lands in search of greener pastures. During the Middle Ages, when the globally dispersed Jews began to feel the full brunt of persecution, untold numbers perished in massacres, under torture, in prisons, and, often, on the highways during flight to nonexistent places of safety elsewhere. These losses were further augmented by the conversion under duress of many thousands to Christianity and Islam. Thus, at all times, there was a desperate urgency felt by Jews for replenishing their dwindling population, and the birth of a child—most particularly of a son, who would assure the biologic continuance of his line—brought joy not only to the parents but also to the entire Jewish community, which saw in him a gain and a reassurance for Israel undying.

All this may have had something to do with the coining in early Rabbinic times of the Hebrew word *kiddushin*—"sanctities"—to mean the marriage ceremony. This characterization makes it abundantly plain that the Jews, who were then living in the midst of Greco-Roman civilization, regarded matrimony as "a sacred union." Their attitude was a contradiction to that of the Romans, who made slighting reference to "the marriage yoke" because they saw husband and wife as "yoked" together in *conjugium*. By contrast, the Jewish bride was "consecrated" to her groom, and she became holy to him by virtue of the act of consecration. As a consequence, his relations with her for the duration of the marriage, both as his wife and as the mother of his children, were expected to conform to high standards. He was held accountable for his treatment of her to God and the Jewish community.

Far different were the views of the ascetic Judean sectaries such as the Essenes and the early Jewish-Christians who derived from them. Himself a Jew, the celibate-minded Paul of Tarsus felt repugnance for the institution of marriage: "The children of the world," he sadly mused, "take in marriage and are taken in marriage, but those who will be deemed worthy of gaining the other world, and of resurrec-

Bride and groom with the Tree of Life between them. The bride is wearing the yellow badge and the groom the Judenhut—*"Jew's hat"—the anti-Semitic signs imposed on Jews to mark their identity. (Miniature from a 14th-century machzor [festival prayer-book] manuscript. Leipzig University Library.)*

tion, they will not take in marriage, nor permit themselves to be given in marriage." The enduring monastic trend in Christianity is ascribable to the disfavor with which its founders viewed matrimony, looking upon it as a snare of Satan.

Yet in Paul's time, the great majority of his fellow Jews gave to marriage a moral value equated with the highest aspirations of mankind. This idealized conception, shared in subsequent Christian thought and practice, is well brought out in the Jewish wedding rites. As bride and groom stand under the chuppah, the seventh of the seven benedictions that are recited makes this ancient affirmation of a life that is potentially good:

> Blessed art thou O Lord our God, King of the Universe, who hast created joy and gladness, bridegroom and bride, mirth and exaltation, pleasure and delight, love, brotherhood, peace, and fellowship.

The chief ingredients indicated by Rabbinic law for the Jewish marriage were mutual respect, devotion, chaste conduct, and kindness. These were counted among the "duties of the heart," that truly definitive name which was sometimes given in the Middle Ages to the corpus of Jewish ethical beliefs and practices. The folk-Jew, with neither sophistication nor sophistry to confuse him, undertook the performance of his marital duties with a religious dedication. It was his way of striving to fulfill what he considered to be the Will of God.

Upon the fathers, in post-Biblical times, there devolved the all-important duty of selecting mates for their sons and daughters. But in the end, the decision of choice was left to the young people themselves. In particular, veto power was vested in the bride-to-be. The Talmudic teachers were soberly aware of the woman's relative helplessness in a man's world and, for that reason, if for no other, they were determined to give her every protection in free choice of a mate. Safeguards in the form of Rabbinic legal opinions and ethical dicta which helped shape the moral climate of Jewish life, upheld her human rights and feelings against the possibility of parental coercion. The rabbis thus conceded to woman her inalienable right to be proven wrong in her judgment. "To choose the right kind of mate is as difficult a task as dividing the Red Sea," mused a Sage in the Talmud.

It was made mandatory in Rabbinic law that prior consent had to be given by the marriageable girl to her father's selection of a husband for her. "A man must not betroth his daughter while she is still a minor," warned Rab, the great religious authority of Babylonian Jewry in the third century. No parent had the right to act precipitately in the matter. Neither was he to exert any pressure upon her in making up her mind. "He must wait until she reaches her majority." At that time, when she was expected to be better able to exercise mature judgment, her father was to ask her in a forthright manner whether out of her own free will she was ready to wed the man he had chosen for her. If she said "no," the match was off. And if she said "yes," her answer had to be explicit: *"This is the man I love."*

The Sages had revulsion for those who married from cold calculation. "He who marries for money will have wicked children," states the Talmud with withering directness. This remark reveals keen psychological insight. For in a home which is founded on mercenary interests, there can be no love —only constant strife. The children in it usually grow up with personality disorders and a distorted view of life.

Akiba, the Tanna of the second century, went even farther in the defense of the love-marriage. He himself had been the hero of an affecting love idyll. While serving as a shepherd to Kalba Sabua, the richest man in Judea, he fell in love with his master's daughter. Although he was illiterate at the time and in the eyes of the world of little account, she, nonetheless, returned his love and left the house of her father to share with him a life of privation and struggle. It is the claim of folk-legend that it was her selfless love and encouragement that turned the shepherd Akiba into the crown and glory of Torah-learning. Consequently, in touching on the subject of marital love, it is understandable that Akiba should have expressed himself with special feeling: "The man who marries a woman he does not love violates five sacred commandments: Thou shalt not kill. Thou shalt not seek vengeance. Thou shalt not bear a grudge. Thou shalt love thy neighbor as thyself . . . and that thy brother may live with thee." How did he deduce all these to be true of a money-motivated marriage? Akiba explained: "If a man hates his wife, he *wishes* she were dead." He was, therefore, said Akiba, morally a murderer! For in the moral philosophy of the Jew, there was but a narrow margin of difference between the evil thought itself and the act to which it could lead.

The ideal of the love marriage, "consecrated . . . in accordance with the laws of Moses and of Israel," became the theme of many medieval Hebrew poets. An early wedding-song that was sung by the worshipers in the synagogue on the Sabbath in honor of a newly wedded youth, eulogized the unfading joys that well up from the requited heart:

> Rejoice, O bridegroom, in the wife of your youth, your comrade,
> Let your heart be merry now, and when you shall grow old
> Sons to your sons shall you see: your old age's crown;
> Sons who shall prosper and work in place of their pious sires,

Your days in good shall be spent, your years in pleasantness.
Floweth your peace as a stream, riseth your worth as its waves.

But with the intensification of the suffering of the Jews during the Middle Ages, concern with love-marriages lessened perceptibly. The contemporary point of view held that to indulge young people freely in the inclinations of their hearts was a luxury the evil times could ill afford. The harsh realities demanded *practical*—not sentimental—marriages. The dominant need of the Jews, it was felt, was for survival as a religious entity and this meant physical preservation as a people. Therefore, the shadchan (marriage broker) acquired a new prominence, for he arranged matings without any superfluous "choosiness," objections, or delays. A rabbi of the eleventh century reflected the new illiberal view when he chronicled with approval: "It is the custom for all Jewish girls . . . to leave the arrangement of their marriage in the hands of their fathers. Nor are they indelicate or impudent enough to express their own fancies, as much as to say: 'I want to marry such-and-such a one.'"

Early marriages (at puberty) for girls, although practiced by all Eastern peoples, did not become general among Jews until the Middle Ages. A reason for this (one weighing heavily with anxious parents) was the moral protection that early marriage provided for their little daughters in a period of widespread atrocity against the Jews. Rabbi Peretz of Corbeil (*d. c.* 1295) noted that "the prohibition against child-marriages in the Talmud applied only to the period when many Jewish families were settled in the same town. Now [after the massacres by the Crusaders], however, when our numbers are reduced and our people are scattered, we are in the habit of marrying off our girls under the age of twelve. . . ."

This unhappy custom persisted for centuries. In Eastern Europe it survived far into the nineteenth century. The folk-memory stored up grievances against the loveless child-marriage and parental tyranny. Many a Yiddish folk song dirgefully recalls the desolation of the first and the cruelties of the latter. This harsh trend notwithstanding, compassion for youth and anxious concern for the happiness of their children prompted many parents, themselves so often the victims of the same soulless practice, to disregard it. The sentiment of love between man and woman could not be suppressed by practical considerations nor even by the interdiction of custom.

See also FAMILY, THE; FAMILY RELATIONS, TRADITIONAL PATTERNS OF; KETUBAH; MONOGAMY; SHADCHAN; WEDDING CUSTOMS.

MARRIAGE, LEVIRATE. *See* CHALITZAH.

MARRIAGE AGREEMENT. *See* KETUBAH.

MARRIAGE AND SEX

Generally speaking, the Jews of former times were puritanical, but they were not prudish. They were frank but never coarse. Theirs was a realistic acceptance of sex, but not in the hedonistic and often depraved sense of the Greeks and the Romans, who pursued it as a pleasurable end in itself. The Jews were inveterate moralists, constantly scrutinizing every one of their actions, thoughts, and feelings with the microscope of the Hebraic conscience. This did not add to the comfort of their existence, but it helped to clarify matters and leave them reasonably unambiguous.

The Jews developed a philosophy of life that had a unified and fairly consistent character, carved out of the granite of a complete moral system. They created no false dualism between the mysteries of heaven and the realities of the earth; they believed one grand cosmic unity reigned in the universe. In traditional Jewish belief (that of the mystics excepted), there existed no actual separation between body and soul. "The soul is Thine, and the body too is Thy handiwork," the pious intoned in prayer. Therefore, in harmony with this view, the power of procreation was revered as the holy instrumentality with which God had endowed all his creatures for the sole purpose of continuing and "collaborating" with him in his work of unending Creation.

The logical mind of the devout Jew inquired: Was the sexual impulse merely a snare of evil, would the Almighty have bestowed it on his children that it might lead them astray, to their destruction? On the contrary. The Jew believed that if carnal passion led to lust and immorality, it did so because evil resided in the sinner alone and was due to his wanton abuse and misuse of his God-given sexual powers.

The first-century C.E. Jewish historian Josephus tried to explain the puritanism of the Jews to the Romans: "The Law (i.e. the Torah) does not give its sanction to any sexual relations except to the natural union of husband and wife." However, he failed to present the traditional view with exactitude, nor did he take realistic notice of the force of custom—nor, in fact, of biology itself, which often superseded the authority or law—when he went on to add that this religious sanction was "only for the procreation of children."

A less suppressive recognition of the psychosexual nature of the human being led the Rabbinic Sages in the Talmud to adopt a more humane approach. They instituted regulations that both enlarged and modified those found in the Bible—regulations which made clear what was permitted and what was forbidden in the intimacies between the sexes. With the utmost frankness and solicitude they spelled out the marital "rights" and "duties" of husband and wife for their guidance to greater compatibility and domestic happiness.

One of the original determinants of sexual morality among the Jews in ancient times, and one stated clearly in the Laws of Moses, was the need to insulate Jewish life against the immorality of neighboring peoples represented first by the orgiastic cults of Baal and Astarte among the Canaanites, and later by the obscenities of the Greek mysteries and the Roman Saturnalia. For that reason the relations of the sexes were sanctioned and regulated by both the Jewish religion and the laws of the Jewish state (which, one must keep in mind, was one integrated whole—a theocracy or God-governed state) so that they achieved a status of relative "holiness" and also a high degree of social responsibility. This pattern of sexual morality became fixed, in its essential features, for all ensuing generations of Jews with, of course, the inevitable moral lapses and revisions that stemmed from the influences of the non-Jewish environment to which the dispersed Jews were exposed in various regions and during different cultural periods.

The practice of adultery in ancient Jewish society was regarded with horror and apprehension. Moses, the Prophets, and the Talmudic Sages saw in it an ever present threat to the moral integrity of the individual and to the preservation of Israel as "a holy nation." Therefore, the imperious prohibition of the Seventh Commandment of the Decalogue: "Thou shalt not commit adultery," reinforced by the special warning sounded in the Tenth Commandment: "Thou shalt not covet thy neighbor's wife."

So sternly set was the moral-social conscience of Jews against adultery that, during the Hadrianic reign of terror, some thirteen centuries following the Covenant at Mount Sinai, a synod of Rabbinic Sages of Judea decreed: "If a man is told: 'Commit this sin and so live,' it is permitted him to sin and thereby save his life. But there are three exceptions: the commission of the sins of idolatry, adultery, and murder." Death, declared the Sages, was to be considered preferable to these.

Under the Rabbinic laws, which were but elaborations and outgrowths of the Scriptural commandments, the adulterer, whether man or woman, was abhorred as a rebel against God's rule of the world and was denigrated as a violator of the sexual forces of life which the Rabbis deemed to be holy and inviolable. "Not merely one who sins with his body is called an adulterer, but also he who sins with his eyes," was the opinion of one ancient Rabbinic moralist.

Harsh and relentless sounds the Biblical prescription for the punishment of the unfaithful wife and her lover, or of any man and a maid found guilty of adultery: ". . . they shall both of them die. . . . So shalt thou put away the evil from Israel." The manner of their execution, dictated by the morality of tribalistic justice (which, incidentally, was also observed by the most culturally advanced peoples settled in the Fertile Crescent during the reign of the Judges and the early kings of Israel), called for stoning, burning, or strangulation.

The savagery of this "punishment to fit the crime" in the more humane and ethically conditioned climate of Jewish society during the Talmudic age, was viewed as shocking and excessive. The Rabbinic Sages, made compassionate as well as melancholy by the compulsive drive of the human frailties, began systematically to hedge the Biblical law with all kinds of legal reservations and pleas of exceptionalism in order to bypass the death penalty. For example, one Rabbinic law introduced the novel and obviously obstructionist proviso that the adulterous woman could not be put to death *unless* it was conclusively proven that, before she had engaged in the sinful relationship, she was fully acquainted with the Scriptural commandment against adultery!

The execution of adulterers ceased and the law requiring it fell into obsolescence at the close of the Second Temple period, after the Roman conquerors of Judea abolished the Sanhedrin and took away from the Jewish courts the judicial instrument of capital punishment. One solace remained for the betrayed husband: He could promptly obtain a divorce from his unfaithful spouse. In fact, Rabbinic law *insisted* upon it: "A woman who has committed adultery must be divorced."

The chastity ideal was integral to the Levitical purity code. While the scrupulous observance of the laws of this code (*see* BIBLE, THE) was mandatory for the priests (*q.v.*) because all Israel had entered into the Covenant with God at Mount Sinai to serve him as "a nation of priests," in certain significant (if lesser) ways the code also had application for them. "Ye shall be holy; for I the Lord your God am Holy," God is quoted (in Leviticus 19:2) as commanding the Israelites to fulfill the terms of their compact with him. And it is related, in the Biblical legend about Joseph in Egypt (Genesis 39:9), that when Zuleika, his master's wanton wife, tried to seduce him, the chaste youth cried out: "How can I do this great wickedness, and sin against God?"

The moral law of the Jewish religion required unconditional chastity, i.e., the complete sexual abstinence of the unmarried of both sexes. From earliest time on, as soon as boys and girls became aware of their sexuality, they were drilled in the exercise of self-mastery over their passions. Masturbation and even "lustful thoughts" were included among the forbidden sexual offenses. Maimonides, the rabbinical philosopher of the twelfth century who was also a celebrated doctor, counseled, in his *Guide to the Perplexed*, a diversionary stratagem for reachieving calm: "We [men] must turn our minds to other thoughts." He recommended hastening to the Bet ha-Midrash (House of Study) to cool overheated desires with draughts of Torah lore.

No doubt the best-conceived-of plan for the preservation of chastity among the youth was the well-tried custom of marrying them off at a tender age to keep them out of the way of temptation. The Talmud defines the ideal husband and father as one who "leads his sons and daughters in the right path and arranges for their marriage soon after puberty." The usual age for marriage was sixteen or eighteen for a boy, and about twelve or thirteen for a girl.

The vast decimation by massacre of the Jewish population in Western and Central Europe during the Middle Ages made the biological preservation of the Jewish people appear to the survivors even more urgent than before. Every religious and communal dedication was made toward as early marriage as possible, even though premature mating brought on a spate of new and complex social, economic, physical, emotional, and psychological problems. It was only with the partial breakdown of ghetto isolation in the middle of the nineteenth century that the ancient custom of early marriages was abandonded.

Although the Jewish youth of former times was impressively more chaste than the youth of other peoples, nevertheless the incidence of seduction and of moral lapses was frequent enough to alert the anxious eyes of parents and the rabbinical authorities to the danger. Even betrothed couples were enjoined from having any sexual intimacy whatsoever until after the wedding ceremony. As late as the eighteenth century—and in Ultra-Orthodox circles to this day—embracing and kissing were strictly forbidden to the engaged pair. Since temptation was ever present, to prevent any accident arising from too close proximity, the foremost Rabbinic authority of third century Babylonian Jewry, Rab (Abba Arika), issued a ban on a groom's living in the home of his future father-in-law.

The premarital conditioning of the Jewish boy and girl to chastity constituted a religious as well as a moral imperative. The youth grew up in a social environment that expected every single member in the Jewish community, both male and female, to exercise a rigorous sexual self-discipline. Any blatant departure from the norms of moral conduct fixed by Jewish law, custom, and the rabbinic authorities was promptly pounced upon, and its transgressors were punished. The chastity of youth, which demanded complete sexual continence, was looked upon as the prelude in moral indoctrination for the chastity of marriage. This conception of married chastity was a spiritualized yet earthy sexuality, but one devoid of grossness and lewdness.

The Babylonian savant and rabbinical authority of the tenth century, Saadia Gaon, took the view that " . . . man should have no [sexual] desire except for his wife, that he may love her and she may love him." Married love for the Jewish pious had the character of a sacrament, for its religious-social goal was the raising of a family, thereby to perpetuate collective Israel and to do the will of God. Cohabitation was not only a marital right but also a religious duty in which, by every Rabbinical sanction, the wife had an equal privilege with her husband. Nevertheless, many were the reminders and the strictures laid down by the religious teachers against the sins of lechery in home life. Maimonides gave this counsel to the married: "We must keep the golden mean [*q.v.*] in everything. We must not be excessive in [sexual] love, but neither must we suppress it entirely, for the Torah commands: 'Be fruitful and multiply.' [Genesis 1:22]."

To be childless was considered a major calamity, for the religious duty of procreation stood central in the Jewish institution of marriage. Divorce of the wife was mandatory after ten years of failure to conceive. But just as great a source of worry as infertility were the problems presented by uncontrolled fertility. The Rabbinic Sages of post-Destruction times possessed considerable knowledge of medicine and hygiene (*see* HEALERS, THE). They were alert to the dangers—physical, moral, and social—that were posed by certain types of pregnancies. Taking into account the bitterly controversial problem of birth-control and abortions in our culture today, it should be a source of surprise that almost two thousand years ago the enlightened Rabbinic Sages sanctioned the termination of pregnancies for clearly specified reasons.

The Talmud stated: "There are three classes of women who should employ an *absorbent* [contraceptive: the nature of which is left unexplained]: a minor, a pregnant woman, and a nursing mother. A minor, lest pregnancy prove fatal to her; a pregnant woman, lest [involuntary] miscarriage result; and a mother who nurses, lest she become pregnant again and be forced to [prematurely] wean her child so that it dies."

Polygamy in the ancient world was commonplace, and not a few Jews practiced polygamy. There never seemed to be a consensus of agreement in ancient times among the Jews on the desirability or the morality of this practice. True enough, in later centuries some Rabbinic opinions accomodated themselves opportunistically to the toleration of this primitive survival in Jewish life: "A man may wed as many wives as he pleases," and "He may not marry more than four."

But there were other legal approaches whose aim was to discourage the taking of plural wives. The protection of women, quite helpless in a male-dominated society, was obviously intended by this Rabbinic ruling of the third-century Sage, Ami: "If, after taking an additional wife, a man's first wife asks for a divorce, he must grant it to her." During the Talmudic age, in an Aramaic paraphrase and elaboration of Ruth 4:6, in which, when Boaz asks Elimelech's kinsman to marry Ruth the Moabitess, the offer is declined with the monogamous plea: " . . . I have a wife and have no right to take another in addition to her, lest she be a disturbance in my house and destroy my peace. Redeem [i.e. marry] thou, for thou hast no wife."

It was purely an academic measure that Rabbenu Gershom, "The Light of the Exile" (Germany, 960–1040), took when he issued his decree against plural wives; except among certain rich Jews in Arab lands, polygamy was virtually nonexistent in Jewry by the year 1000.

At no time was prostitution tolerated within the Jewish fold. This was in enforcement of the Biblical prohibition (in Deuteronomy 23:18): "There shall be no harlot of the daughters of Israel." Maimonides explained that this Scriptural interdiction was made out of fear that the immoral practice, so universally indulged in by all the peoples of the Fertile Crescent, would destroy the sentiments of love and devotion that prevailed in the Jewish family. He added: "Another important object in prohibiting prostitution is to restrain excessive and continual lust, for lust increases with the variety of its objects."

It has been a cause for great surprise to many observers that the traditional patterns of morality and marital behavior among the Jews have been able to retain at least some of their most distinguishable features in our own day. And this survival has taken place in spite of the drastic revisions that the cultural assimilation of the Jews and the disintegrating moral values in modern society have made inevitable for them.

Since Jews form an integral part of the general population today, they too have been exposed to the personality corrosions and emotional instabilities of a world in chaos. It would be foolish to pretend that Jewish religious, moral, ethical, and familial standards are what they used to be during the Middle Ages or even at the turn of the twentieth century. Many Jews have absorbed the value-systems of their environment for better or worse. This is reflected in these observable facts: traditional Jewish family solidarity has declined; discord and marital infidelity have been increasing, as can be judged by the steady rise in the number of Jewish divorces; and the morals of Jewish youth have been deteriorating, thus causing anguish to parents and anxiety to religious and lay leaders of the Jewish community.

Nevertheless, it is recognized by objective investigators that the Jewish family, compared with the non-Jewish family, is more stable and cohesive, that infidelity between Jewish husbands and wives occurs with less frequency, and that Jewish adolescents, by and large, seem to exercise greater self-restraint than do their non-Jewish contemporaries. (This may be borne out by the statistics which show that there are proportionately fewer children born out of wedlock to Jewish than to non-Jewish mothers.)

What is it that has preserved, even if only in attenuated forms, the traditional Jewish values of moral conduct and marital fidelity? A decisive factor has been the long historical conditioning of the Jews to marital fidelity by their ancestral way of life.

Even those Jews who are only casually religious or secularist or who may have chosen to alienate themselves entirely from the Jewish identity and cultural heritage continue to live as the beneficiaries of traditional Jewish morality. They imbibed it, so to speak, with their mother's milk and their father's prodding. The example set by both parents in rectitude, devotion to each other, and self-mastery over the passions became, unconsciously, the matrix for their own future behavior.

See also FAMILY, THE; FAMILY RELATIONS, TRADITIONAL PATTERNS OF; MONOGAMY; WOMAN, THE TREATMENT OF.

MARRIAGE BROKER. *See* SHADCHAN.

MARSHALIK. *See* MERRYMAKERS, TRADITIONAL JEWISH.

MARTYRS. *See* KIDDUSH HA-SHEM.

MASHGIACH. *See* DIETARY LAWS.

MASHIACH. *See* MESSIAH, THE; MESSIAHS, WOULD-BE.

MASKIL, MASKILIM. *See* ENLIGHTENMENT, THE JEWISH.

MASORAH (Hebrew, meaning "fetter" or "tradition"; namely, "to hand down")

The traditional view concerning the sanctity and the unalterable character of the Hebrew text of the Bible, to which the Rabbinic Sages as well as later religious scholars subscribed and to the guardianship of which many had devoted their lives, is indicated in a certain passage in the Talmud. It tells how copyists constantly sat, in the Temple Court in Jerusalem during the Second Commonwealth, before an authoritative copy of the Bible that had been carefully preserved and, with the utmost care, reproduced it, letter by letter, to make certain that no error crept into their work through carelessness. Interestingly, as an extra precaution against mistakes, there was appointed a special group of Temple officials—Rabbinical Scribes—whose function it was to study each text minutely, to point out errors to the copyists, if any did occur, and to pass or reject their completed work. This unflagging watchfulness, probably unparalleled in cultural history with regard to any other written text, was proudly pointed up by the Jewish-Hellenistic defenders of Judaism—by Aristeas in the third century B.C.E. in his famous "Letter"; by Philo (the philosopher-rabbi of Alexandria, 20 B.C.E.–50 C.E.) in his *Political Constitution of the Jews,* and by Josephus (Judea-Rome, 37–105 C.E.) in his polemic *Against Apion.*

The arduous efforts made by the Jewish religious authorities to safeguard the Scriptural text against any changes or errors began immediately after the Bible canon had been finished and closed, as late, presumably, as the first century C.E. There was, of course, a sound reason behind this passion for absolute uniformity of the Bible text. Following the institution by Ezra and the Scribes of obligatory and universal study of the Torah, the feverish preparation of many manuscript copies of the Pentateuch was begun. Copies were circulated not only in Judea, but also among the Jewish settlements that had been long established in Syria, Babylonia, Greece, Rome, Asia Minor, North Africa, and elsewhere. Because there was such a great dispersion of the Jewish people, the religious teachers called for the utmost diligence in preventing the corruption of the Bible text, whether by deliberate error or by mere inattentiveness in the process of transcription.

This minute and thorough examination of the Scriptural text during the Talmudic age was referred to as the "Masorah"; the guardians of the Biblical tradition were called "Masorites"; and the "purified" text, after it had finally been concluded—and the one now in universal use—became known as the "Masoretic" Bible.

The academies of Sura and Pumbeditha in Babylonia opened special institutes for the critical study of the Masorah beginning with the sixth century but the collective studies of a long line of dedicated scholars, most of whom remain unknown, were accomplished over a time-span of some seventeen centuries, from about 300 B.C.E. to 1425 C.E. All of their labors are summed up in condensed critical notes or glosses. These they wrote down on each page of the Bible text, either in the margins, between the columns, between the lines, or around initial words. Ultimately, the critical notes of the Masorah were collated and produced by copyists as independent works. But these, quite obviously, are too involved and technical to have much meaning for any except the Biblical specialists.

The Masorites had a passionate concern with their special statistics. They went into a bizarre counting successively of the letters, words, verses, sections, and chapters in each Scriptural writing and in all the twenty-four books of the Bible. They itemized all the words that began with a certain letter or combination of letters. They also counted the number of times every single word appeared in the Bible text. Certain modern scholars of a challenging but prosaic bent of mind have not been ready to accept the lofty view that all this vast bookkeeping was engaged in wholly out of a dedicated regard for a purified Bible text. They suggest that it may have been prompted by a need, on the part of the copyists, to establish an objective basis for computing the remuneration for their professional labors.

During the ninth century, the Masoretic scholars in the academy of Tiberias, Palestine, perfected a system of vowel-points for the proper vocalization of the Torah text, and with it also the musical accent symbols (in Hebrew: *ta'amim*). These "accents" constituted, in a rather flexible way, a music notation system for the cantillation of the Hebrew text during the public reading from the Pentateuch in the synagogue on the Sabbath and holy days.

See also BIBLE, THE; MUSICAL ACCENTS; TORAH-READING; VOWEL SOUNDS, HEBREW; YESHIBAH.

MASORETIC BIBLE. *See* MASORAH.

MASSACRES

The Crusades. There was hardly a time during the Middle Ages when the Jews were not under harsh attack from feudal king, baron, pope, bishop, or "preaching friar." And whenever these attacks were made on religious grounds, the Jews had sufficient cause to tremble for their lives; it was a sure sign that those in positions of power were casting covetous eyes on their money, their homes, and their possessions. This greed, of course, was never nakedly exposed to public view but was always dressed up in pious sentiments and high-sounding legality.

There are an astonishing number of instances on record in which hatred for the Jew was accompanied by an undisguised love of Jewish money, and this love, for the sake of respectability, was delicately blended with the incense of faith and Christian morality. Thoughtful Jews, turned into sober realists by the tactics of their enemies, had no illusions about this. The Knights of the Cross, for instance, as they descended upon the Jews in the Rhineland towns in order to avenge their alleged blood-guilt against the saviour of the Christians, did not forget to raise the compelling cry: *"Hab hab."* (In Old German, *hab hab* meant nothing more spiritual than "Give give!")

Beginning with the First Crusade (there were actually five) in 1096, religious hysteria was fully whipped up against the Jews in Europe. By that time, hatred of the Jews had already received official sanction; and it had already, for a long time, been written into the canon law of the Church. It also had been made a part of their state policy by Christian rulers everywhere. Its general practice, carried over from one century to the next with an unabating ardor, led Martin Luther in the sixteenth century—using the mistreatment of the Jews as a stick with which to beat the Church—to gibe: "If it is a mark of a good Christian to hate the Jews, what excellent Christians all of us are!"

Hatred of the Jew served as a ready incendiary torch which could be lighted profitably at all times for the purpose of diverting the attention of the Christian masses from the misery of their daily lives in the inhumane feudal society. Jews were convenient scapegoats against whom the rulers could incite the anger of their subjects—an anger which otherwise might have been directed destructively against themselves! Thus, almost every private grief and every public calamity could be conveniently charged against the Jew, of whom the popular image was sedulously cultivated that he literally was a son of the Devil and the Antichrist incarnate.

The First Crusade marked a startling change in the fortunes of the Jews in Christian Europe. For one thing, it precipitated a genocidal slaughter of them on a staggering scale. The call to the Christian faithful for a holy crusade against the Mohammedan "infidels" who were then ruling Palestine, "the Holy Land," was issued by Pope Urban II on November 26, 1095, at Clermont. By the following summer, a host of some 200,000 knights, men-at-arms, priests, burghers, peasants, and artisans had assembled in France in order to march against the Saracens (Arabs). Under Peter the Hermit's impassioned verbal lashing, the religious hysteria of the Crusaders mounted. Peter told them that, since Jews were as much infidels as the Saracens but were near at hand while the Mohammedans were far off, they might as well begin their holy crusade for Christ without delay by killing Jews—a sure way, said Peter, for the Crusaders to earn for themselves salvation.

First in France, then in England, the Crusaders massacred the Jews wherever they found them. From there the tide of violence rolled on, without interference from Church or State, into Germany, Austria, and elsewhere in Europe. Everywhere the Knights of the Cross called out to the Jews: "Christ-killers, embrace the Cross or die!"

The Crusaders accomplished their goriest deeds in the Franco-German Rhineland, northern France, and Lorraine; the numerous Jewish communities in the Provence largely escaped their fury. During the Third Crusade, in part due to the exertions of the renegade Jew Nicolas Donin of La Rochelle, who had become a Franciscan monk, the Crusaders blazed another bloody trail, this time through Brittany, Poitou, and Anjou. In Anjou alone 3,000 Jews were killed and 500 were forced into baptism.

Many Jews saved their lives either through flight, or by undergoing baptism, but most, marvelous to relate, freely chose death. Entire communities destroyed themselves in mass-pacts of suicide. Jewish mothers killed their own children, or, clasping them in their arms, leaped with them to a watery grave in the Rhine. Thousands of other Jews, seeking sanctuary and spiritual consolation in the synagogues, were burned alive by the Crusaders.

After the atrocities perpetrated on the Jews during the Fifth Crusade (in the Thirteenth century) Pope Gregory IX protested to "St." Louis (Louis IX), the king of France, about the knightly deeds of his Crusaders: "Their excesses are horrible and outrageous, an offense against God and a dishonor to the [papal] Holy Chair through whose privileges the Jews are protected." Similarly, Innocent IV, emulating Gregory IX, a few years later expressed his revulsion for the conduct of the Knights of the Cross in the Rhineland; he called on the German bishops to halt the carnage and forbid all persecution of the Jews. How well these bishops "protected" the Jews may be seen in one of several similar incidents—in the kind of "protection" that Archbishop Ruthard of Mayence (Mainz) gave to the numerous Jews in his city: He invited them to take refuge in his palace, where they could conveniently be slaughtered by their enemies. When the massacre was over, 1300 bodies—men, women, and children—were carried out of the archepiscopal palace.

In vain, during the Second Crusade, did Bernard of Clairvaux, who was deeply shocked by the bestiality of the Knights of the Cross, try to put out the fires that he himself had helped light, but his pleas against violence toward the Jews went unheeded. The incitements of his colleagues in muscular Christianity—Peter of Cluny and the monk Rudolph—successfully drowned out his moderating voice; the first even declared that death was too good a punishment for the Jews and that Heaven had ordained that they be 'reserved for great ignominy, for an existence more bitter than death."

This view, implacable and vengeful, was indeed so general among the medieval theologians of the Church that Alfonso X's famous Castilian code, Las Siete Partidas, stated that "the reason the Church, the emperors, the kings and other princes suffer the Jews to live among the Christians is this: that they might always live in captivity and thus be a reminder to all men that they are descended from the lineage of those who crucified our Lord Jesus Christ."

The Black Death: Jews as "Poisoners" of Christians. There was hardly an imaginable crime in the catalogue of human wickedness of which the Jews were not judged to be guilty. When the terrible plague, the Black Death, killed off a great part of the Christian and Jewish population of Western and Central Europe in 1348–49, the Jews were promptly blamed for it. They were accused, by general agreement, of having poisoned the wells and rivers—a charge which drew forth this bitter cry from the liturgical poet, Baruch:

> They shout, "The springs are charged with death,
> With poison charged by you, ye foes,
> That ye might compass our destruction!"

Many Jews were put on the rack and, under torture, allegedly "confessed" to "the truth" of their monstrous crime. One incident, characteristic of a thousand others, occurred in the town of Chillon on Lake Geneva. There a Jewish surgeon, Valavigny of Thonon, was arrested and tortured on September 15, 1348—on the Day of Atonement. When the pain became unendurable he made "a full confession" that implicated Jacob Pascate of Toledo. While on a visit to Chambéry, related the doctor, the Spanish "poisoner," together with the local rabbi, Peyret, and a rich Jew, Aboget, had given him a leather bag containing a substantial amount of poison. He was instructed to divide the poison among several Jews, and was furnished letters of instruction to them. Accordingly, "admitted" the surgeon, he and four accomplices, one being a woman, went about casting the poison into a number of wells, etc.

Under torture, all of the latter admitted their part in the grizzly proceedings and were killed. To the inhabitants of the region, these confessions were tantamount to clear guilt. They raged through the Jewish communities along Lake Geneva and the duchy of Savoy with sword and torch, killing every Jew they found, setting fire to their houses—but making sure to loot them first of their possessions. The destruction swept like a conflagration through all of Switzerland and thence throughout all the countries of the Holy Roman Empire.

In Germany alone armed mobs wiped out physically more than 350 Jewish communities. What the total carnage added up to is hard to estimate. Many tens of thousands of Jews—men, women, and children—were, in the words of a contemporary Christian chronicler, "murdered, drowned, burned, broken on the wheel, hanged, exterminated, strangled, burned alive, and tortured to death." How madness and savagery on such a staggering scale could have been engineered in the first place, became the subject of grim speculation among humane Christian thinkers of that dark period. The contemporary Alsatian chronicler, Closener of Strasbourg, sardonically concluded from his examination of all the events that *"their possessions were the poison* which caused the death of the Jews . . ."

See also ANTI-SEMITISM: THE "RACIAL PURITY" MYTH; CHRISTIANITY, JEWISH ORIGINS OF; CHURCH AND PERSECUTION; CONVERSION OF JEWS; DISPUTATIONS, RELIGIOUS; GENOCIDE; "HOST DESECRATION" CALUMNIES; ISLAM, JEWISH ORIGINS OF; KIDDUSH HA-SHEM; KOL NIDRE; MARRANOS AND THE INQUISITION; MONEY-LENDERS; NAZIS, THE; PERSECUTION IN "MODERN" DRESS; POGROMS IN SLAVIC LANDS; "RITUAL MURDER" SLANDERS; WANDERING JEW; YELLOW BADGE.

MATCHMAKER. *See* SHADCHAN.

MATZAH, MATZOT. *See* PASSOVER.

MATZEBAH, MATZEBOT. *See* TOMBSTONES.

"MAY LAWS." *See* POGROMS IN SLAVIC LANDS.

MEAT, KASHERING OF. *See* MEAT, SALTING OF.

MEAT, SALTING OF (in Hebrew: MELICHAH)

The legendary aspect of the Jewish dietary laws (kashrut) is fascinating to the modern student of folkways. It is suggestive of some intriguing historical hypotheses concerning the dietary beliefs and practices of the primeval Hebrews. For in the Biblical narrative about the Creation, recounting the events that took place on the sixth day after God had fashioned man "in His own image," we hear God saying to Adam, the first man: "Behold, I have given you every herb yielding seed, which is upon the face of all the earth, and every tree, in which is the fruit of a tree yielding seed—to you it shall be for food." (Genesis 1:29.)

Remarkably, nothing is mentioned here at all about animals, birds, or fish to serve as food, the Bible tells us only that man was to hold "dominion" over them. This Biblical legend was amplified in a poetic-ethical manner by the Rabbinic teachers in the literature of the Midrash. They sighed nostalgically for that Golden Age of early man, long before the time of the Sin-Flood, when Adam and Eve still lived in a pristine state of innocence and purity, and ate only uncontaminating fruits and vegetables. It was only after the Flood, in the days of Noah, when the human species had proven itself to be unworthy of grace (thus observed the ancient Rabbis) that its members began to eat meat and fish. The Sages felt this to be a clear reference to the spiritually corrupting character of the carnivorous diet.

Now what do we find here? Merely a definition of the vegetarian "purity cult" of the Brahmanic religion, rooted, no doubt, in still more venerable forms of totem animal-worship. The Brahmans maintained for several thousands of years—and still do to this very day—that eating meat and fish pollutes and corrupts not only the body of man but also his soul. It is, indeed, possible that in the hoary folk-memory of the ancient Hebrews, there lingered persistently the impact of the very same taboos against every kind of animal food. Permission for eating meat, according to the Biblical account, was granted man only with the proviso that he not drink or eat the blood. "I will set My face," says God, in Leviticus 17:10, "against that soul that eateth blood."

An important element in the dietary laws may not be understood without a knowledge of the supernatural notion that the early Jews held concerning blood. Here again we come across a primitive belief that was common to many ancient religions—one which, incidentally, is also shared by some primitive societies of our time.

It must have been noted by early man that when blood flowed profusely in a hemorrhage or from a wound, unconsciousness or death resulted. It is, therefore, most suggestive to find that when the Biblical writers wished to say "kill," they used the phrase "to shed blood." Why? Because even the earliest thinking man was aware that the blood, whether in a human being or in an animal, constituted the mysterious life-essence. Therefore, blood was declared to be a "sacred" substance and taboo, or strictly forbidden, for human consumption: "For the life of the flesh is in the blood." (Leviticus 17:11.) The blood could be used for sacrifical purposes only. The rationale for this is also in Leviticus 17:11, when God speaks to Israel: "I have given it [i.e., the blood] to you upon the altar to make atonement for your souls; for it is the blood that maketh atonement by reason of the life."

In a remarkable passage in his *Guide to the Perplexed*, the medieval philosopher-rabbi-medical scientist, Maimonides (Moses ben Maimon), discusses the justification for the ritual prohibition against blood, but from another angle. His comments startle because they carry the same authentic ring as that of modern anthropological investigation. The ancient idolators, the Sabaeans, he notes, believed that by eating the blood of an animal, a man succeeded in achieving "something in common with the spirits which join him and tell him of future events." Still other idolators, writes Maimonides, would collect the blood of an animal in a pot and eat "of the flesh of that beast while sitting around the blood." This they did because they believed that the spirits would come and eat of the blood while they were eating the flesh. In this way, by dining together, "love, brotherhood, and friendship with the spirits were established," so that they derived certain beneficial magical results. This rite, concluded Maimonides, only led "to the worship of spirits." Therefore, the Torah prohibited the eating or drinking of animal blood, considering the act an expression of idolatry. Hence God's stern warning, "I will set my face against that soul that eateth blood."

With this supreme religious dictate—a commandment directly from God—the elimination of blood from meat (called in Yiddish *kashern*) was rigorously required before the meat could be cooked or roasted, and it has remained an unchanging practice among the observant for several thousand years.

Drawing the blood out of meat is accomplished in three successive stages. First the meat is soaked in cold water for half an hour; this is to open the pores and allow the blood to seep out. Then the meat is placed on a slanting and/or slotted board to drain. Following this, it is sprinkled thickly with salt on all its exposed surfaces and left for an hour. In the case of poultry, the entrails are removed before the kashering process is begun and the neck artery is removed before the bird is salted (this must be done inside as well as out). In the final operation, the meat is thoroughly washed under a freely flowing faucet, then rinsed in cold clean water.

However, meat that will be broiled requires only a light sprinkling of salt, since the fire can be relied upon to burn up all the blood.

Liver is never put through the preliminary soaking process. It must be first washed, then salted, then broiled and washed again.

See also ANIMALS, "CLEAN" AND "UNCLEAN"; DIETARY LAWS; MEAT AND MILK; SHECHITAH; SHOCHET; TEREFAH.

MEAT AND MILK (in Hebrew: BASAR B'CHALAB; in Yiddish: MILCHIG AND FLAISHIG)

The reasons for the many ritualistic prohibitions and regulations against mixing meat with milk or any other dairy foods (those containing milk or milk products) remain obscure. The Rabbinic Sages were themselves unable to explain them on rational grounds. The philosopher-rabbi of twelfth-century Spain, Maimonides (Moses ben Maimon), made the astute guess that this mixing, whether in cooking, handling, or eating, "was probably forbidden because it somehow was associated with idolatory, forming perhaps part of the rites at a heathen festival." He deduced this from the fact that three separate times in the books of Exodus and Deuteronomy the Bible states the prohibition in exactly the same explicit words: "Thou shalt not seethe a kid in its mother's milk."

So strictly, and with such scrupulousness, was this ban made to work that the laws of the Talmud even went to the length of warning: "The *taste* of forbidden food is as forbidden as the food itself. Consequently, the observant were ordered to keep those pots in which meat was cooked separate from those used for the preparation of milk or other dairy foods. Similarly, dishes and other eating utensils were also to be kept separate. Thus, in every home in which the laws of kashrut are observed, there have to be two complete sets of cooking and eating utensils.

The strictly observing Jew waits at least six hours after eating meat before partaking of dairy foods. But after eating dairy foods, he needs to wait only one hour before eating meat, for this shorter time-lapse is considered long enough to get the "taste" of milk out of the mouth. In past centuries, much of a rabbi's time, thought, and energy were taken up with rendering decisions on the dilemmas of the pious concerning milchig and flaishig. To give just one concrete example: If a chicken leg, or any piece of meat, were to fall by accident into a pot containing milk, even though it was removed immediately, it was the general rule that both the milk and the meat thereby became terefah, or ritually "unfit" to be eaten. This was because the "taste" of one lingered in the other.

There is still a third category of foods, called *parveh*, covered by the dietary laws. This is a kind of neutral area between meat and dairy foods. It includes such items as fish (but only those that are ritually "permitted"; i.e., those having scales), fruits, and vegetables. Parveh foods may be cooked and eaten with, before, or after a meal that is meat or dairy.

See also ANIMALS, "CLEAN" AND "UNCLEAN"; DIETARY LAWS; SHECHITAH; SHOCHET; TEREFAH.

MEGILLAH. *See* PURIM.

MELAMED (Hebrew, meaning "teacher"—specifically, a teacher of children; pl. MELAMEDIM)

The melamed was the teacher who ran the single-room cheder, the religious primary school that was traditional in the ghettos of Eastern Europe from the time of the Middle Ages. Because of the peculiar circumstances under which he had to function as an educator, he could not help being a drudge. In fact, he was an unprotected slavey who found it necessary to toil and moil in the vineyard of the Lord from a little after dawn until shortly before midnight. Tirelessly, he had to drill his little, unheeding charges in the aleph-bet (the Hebrew alphabet), in the Five Books of Moses (the Pentateuch), in the daily prayers, and in the recitation of the Shema and the customary blessings in Hebrew.

Most of the time, the melamed was a maladjusted and also an inadequate Torah scholar. He had no special talent for getting on in the world; his ingrained conscience and his daily conditioning in meekness proved to be stumbling blocks for him. Because there were, in practically every sizable Jewish community, so many scholars who were expert in Jewish religious lore, there were, unhappily, not enough paying and prestige-laden rabbinical and semireligious posts available for all those contending for them. Among this plenitude of knowledgeable men, those who were less brilliantly endowed,—or, possibly, only lacked vigorous elbows!—had to be content with "the leavings." These were generally the minor but, nevertheless, very necessary religious callings.

The career of melamed was one of the last refuges left to inept Jewish religious scholars. It was, in the majority

The melamed's (teacher's) official visit to collect tuition: The father quizzes the child on the Hebrew alphabet. Russia, late 19th century. (Painting.)

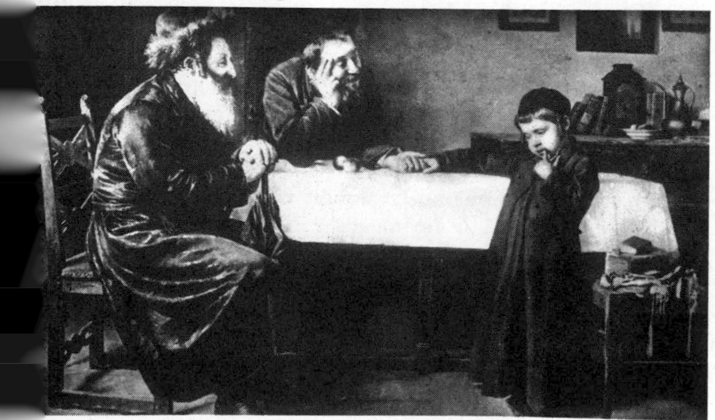

The medieval melamed. (From a 14th-century German illuminated manuscript of the Pentateuch. The British Museum.)

of cases, a career which, little by little, caused the overworked and underpaid teacher to sink into a state of economic and emotional wretchedness from which he could but rarely, as from quicksand, pull himself out.

"Without luck—like a melamed," runs a saying in Yiddish. This is perhaps equivalent to the modern disparaging American quip: "He who can, does; he who can't, becomes a teacher."

Since he was required by Jewish communal regulations to agree that he would not engage in any other occupation so as to be free to devote himself entirely to the exhausting business and the long hours of his cheder, the melamed, who sustained himself and his family only from seasonal tuition fees—not a few of which were never or entirely paid to him—led a fitful hand-to-mouth existence. Too often he was forced to stand in abject docility before the parents of his pupils, and sometimes even before his very pupils, pleading for the funds due him.

But by and large, there was no more upright and truly dedicated an individual in the ghetto then the melamed. His very poverty, drudgery, and schlimazl helplessness frequently acted as a shield for him against the unlikely possibility of corruption. Sometimes, the melamed turned to his unremunerative calling of teaching children because he was a pious man who responded readily to the everlasting shofar-call of Jewish tradition to "build a fence" for the protection of the Torah by planting its redemptive seed in the minds of the children. But there is no doubt that many individuals became melamedim because they were occupational misfits who clutched at any straw, however fragile, that would let them remain alive and feed their families.

It cannot be denied that, often as not, the melamed had but a limited knowledge of the subjects he taught in the cheder. For that reason, it became the custom that, when a pupil had exhausted the teaching capacity of one melamed, his father would set him to graze in the seemingly greener pasture of another melamed—one who was able to teach him more in the same field of knowledge or who specialized in such subjects as Hebrew grammar and Talmudic studies.

During the nineteenth century in Russia and Poland, when the cheder was exposed to the frontal attacks of the Maskilim, "the Enlightened" ones among the Jewish intelligentsia, the old-fashioned "unenlightened" melamed served as a convenient whipping boy. Under the prodding of the Maskilim, the Imperial State Council of Russia, in its report in 1840 to Czar Nicholas I, witheringly characterized the melamedim as "a class of domestic teachers immersed in profoundest ignorance and superstition. . . . Under the influence of these fanatics the children imbibe pernicious notions of intolerance towards other peoples."

To a certain extent, this characterization was not without truth. In his ghetto-setting of cultural isolation, of unswerving religious Ultra-Orthodoxy, the melamed very often stood out in the community as a symbol of the unprogressive status quo and as a deterrent to the Europeanization and emancipation of the Jews. The more advanced and worldly among his fellow Jews consequently regarded him as the last-ditch perpetuator of "medievalism" in Jewish life. In actuality, the Ministry of Public Instruction of the Czarist government attempted in 1856 to suppress the twenty thousand melamedim teaching in White Russia, the Ukraine, Poland, and Lithuania, but the melamedim, with the united strength of all the millions of the faithful behind them, countered with passive resistance. They simply refused to be abolished! Recognizing by 1879 that it was battling a lost cause, the all-powerful imperial government, as much as admitting that it had suffered a humiliating defeat at the hands of the down-to-the-capote melamedim, issued a special ukase ordering that thenceforth they were not to be molested.

What the embattled disciples of the Jewish Enlightenment (the Haskalah) and the *force majeure* of the czar's government could not accomplish, the natural pressures of cultural progress in a changing world effected. Today—and this also holds especially true for the United States, Canada, the British Commonwealth, Israel, and Latin America—the melamed, together with his dingy one-room cheder, has virtually disappeared. Only a relative handful among the diehards and the sectarian Chasidim still hold on to him and what he stands for. To find the melamed today in many cities of the United States, it is necessary to look carefully, but it is possible to discover him there, functioning in approximately the same manner that he did in Cracow, Vilna, and Prague during the nineteenth century. Neither he, his traditional curriculum, nor his method of teaching has altered too much, even though the overwhelming mass of Jews has undergone enormous changes culturally.

On the American scene, in addition to running his cheder in his own home or in rented premises, the melamed coaches Bar Mitzvah boys from Ultra-Orthodox homes for six months to a year in the religious knowledge required for that important occasion. Several facts are discernible: The melamed today is no longer as meek and bowed down as his prototype of former times, he is a lot more worldly and assimilated, and he is, usually, no longer as pious. But he still remains, in a large measure, devoted to the essential goals of his ancient calling.

See also CHEDER; TALMUD TORAH.

MELICHAH. *See* MEAT, SALTING OF.

MEMORIAL LIGHT. *See* YAHRZEIT.

MEMORIAL SERVICE. *See* YAHRZEIT.

MEN OF THE GREAT ASSEMBLY (MEN OF THE GREAT SYNAGOGUE). *See* BET HA-MIDRASH; BIBLE, THE; HABDALAH; MONOTHEISM; PHARISEES; POST-BIBLICAL WRITINGS; SANHEDRIN; SCRIBES; SHEMONEH ESREH; SOFER; TALMUD, THE.

MENORAH (Hebrew s., meaning "candelabrum," "lamp stand"; pl. MENOROT)

The first menorah presumably was fashioned for the Tabernacle in the Wilderness by the artist-craftsman, Bezalel, upon the precise instructions of Moses. The Bible states unequivocally that the shape of the menorah and its design and details were inspired by a revelation from on high. Bezalel "made the candlestick of pure gold: of beaten work made he the candlestick; even its base, and its cups, its knops, and its flowers were one piece with it." (Exodus 37:17.) In the menorah there were seven lamps in all: one central stem, and three branches foliating from each side. On the main stem there were four calices which were shaped like almond blossoms; there were also three each on the six branches. Each of the seven had a lamp bowl which was removed daily by the priests for cleaning, for trimming or renewing the wick, and for refilling with oil. The menorah was impressively large, pure gold, and highly decorative in its design.

We have a remarkably clear representation of this menorah depicted on the bas-relief on the Arch of Titus in Rome and on Judean coins minted during Roman rule. The Bible recounts that, when Solomon was building the Temple, he had King Hiram of Tyre make for him ten menorot. The original one, made by Bezalel when the Children of Israel were in the wilderness, he placed in their midst. When the destruction of the Temple was imminent, the priests concealed Bezalel's menorah, and from that day forward, it was never seen again.

Oddly enough, there are some Bible scholars who believe that the detailed description of the Mosaic menorah, given in chapters 25 and 37 of the Book of Exodus, does actually not describe Bezalel's menorah but the one which is reproduced in the sculptural frieze on the Arch of Titus. For it is their view that the description as well as the entire Book of Exodus were written during Second Temple days, and that in the writing, probably an older Scriptural work was revised.

Of course, fire and illumination have always played important parts in religious rites. "The Sacred Flame" had its own special adaptation in Jewish Temple worship on Mount Zion, typified by the menorah.

"Glorify ye the Lord in the region of light," bade the Prophet Isaiah (24:15). The word "light," as used in the Bible and by the Rabbinic writers, had great symbolic significance. It resulted in the institution of a number of religious rites and practices in which light was a significant element; i.e., the Sabbath lamp and candles in the home, the Perpetual Lamp (Ner Tamid) placed before the Ark in the synagogue, and finally, in Yom Kippur and yahrzeit candles (as a memorial for the dead). It is by no means a co-incidence that in this matter of light too Christian church custom patterned itself on the older Jewish models when it introduced the altar lamp and the votive lamp and candle.

Numerous are the references in Jewish religious litera

Menorah illustration on an illuminated Hebrew Bible manuscript. Germany, 13th century.

ture concerning light. "The light of God is the soul of man" (Proverbs 20:27); ". . . in Thy light do we see light" (Psalms 36:10); "[not sun, nor moon] but the Lord, shall be unto thee an everlasting light" (Isaiah 60:19). The righteous were called "the generation of light." We find similar references in the Synoptic Gospels and in several of the Epistles of Paul. Light, too, was a symbol of the Torah. A Sage of the Talmud interpreted this concept, as if God were speaking:

> "If you will faithfully keep My light burning in your soul, I shall preserve your light. If you will kindle My light in the sanctuary [i.e., the Temple menorah], I shall kindle the great light for you in the World-to-Come."

This association of the soul of man with light was first made by Jewish religious thinkers before the Christian era began.

Many attempts have been made to give symbolic meaning to the menorah. The medieval Cabalistic writing, the Zohar, saw it this way: The oil was the Torah, the light was the Shechinah (Divine Presence), and the wick was Israel. One view was that they symbolized the seven heavens; another, expressed by the Jewish historian Josephus, was that "now the seven lamps signified the seven planets" which were lit up by the light of God. There also was the notion that the central stem and lamp of the menorah stood for the Holy Sabbath, and that the six branches stemming from it were the homaging six weekdays, and that all together represented the time-duration of Creation.

When the Second Temple was destroyed, the menorah, and not the Magen David—"Star of David"—as so many erroneously believe, became the principal decorative art symbol of the Jewish faith. It appeared on Hellenistic sarcophagi lids and on ossuaries (those curious funerary bone-caskets).

Menorah on a brown and violet glass flagon (containing either oil for the synagogue lamps or sacramental wine for the Sabbath Kiddush). Hellenistic design, 1st century C.E.

The menorah was reintroduced in 1948 as the national symbol of the Jewish people and identity in Israel. (BELOW) *The inauguration of Yitzchak Ben-Zvi as the second President of Israel on December 10, 1952. (Israel Office of Information.)*

It was sculptured in relief on the façades and over the doorways of some early synagogues. It was even painted on Jewish tombs in the catacombs of Rome, and carved into the rock walls of Judean burial catacombs.

The reason why the seven-branched menorah was never employed as a ritual vessel or ornament until modern times was because of the Rabbinic prohibition against the reproduction and use of any of the Temple vessels. Consequently, in the home, it was the Sabbath lamp and the conventional candlestick that supplied the illumination on religious and festive occasions for more than two thousand years.

See also ART, CEREMONIAL; CHANNUKAH LAMP; LAMP, PERPETUAL; MAGEN DAVID; SABBATH LIGHTS; YAHRZEIT.

MERIT OF THE FATHERS (in Hebrew: ZECHUT ABOT)

In the prayer that he composed for the synagogue service and which he called "Shield and Quickener," the great Gaon of Sura, Saadia (882–942), hymned this praise to God: "He remembers the loving-kindnesses of the fathers, and answers the children in time of their distress . . . because of the Merit of their Fathers.

At first glance, the concept of "Merit of the Fathers" may prove puzzling to the modern student of the Jewish religion. For although it reveals no traces of the ancestor worship characteristic of some other ancient religions, it nonetheless does show a deep *reverencing* of ancestors.

It is a fundamental principle rooted deeply in the ethical rationalism of Prophetic and Rabbinic Judaism that the individual believer stands independently in a personal relationship with his Deity. He requires neither prophet nor saint nor rabbi to act as his go-between, to intercede for him with God. Whatever merit he is expected to earn during his lifetime for his "heavenly reward" has to be achieved by his own piety and good deeds. Nevertheless, the concept of obtaining grace through the Merit of the Fathers—which, quite obviously, runs counter to the cardinal principle of self-redemption through works of righteousness—remains also very influential in Jewish religious thinking.

In a manner of speaking, the Merit of the Fathers stands as a concession by religion to the puny weakness of man, who remains aware that he cannot always help himself or pull himself up to a state of grace by his own bootstraps or feel with real conviction that he can win the favors of Heaven merely because he "deserves" them. For wherever the individual's communion with God seemed to himself feeble, or where his own moral achievements struck him as being inadequate, he turned to morally superior, even supernatural, mediating powers to succor him. During the Talmudic era, and in times subsequent to that, whenever disaster threatened the Jewish collective or a particular individual, the Jews proceeded to implore the intercession of the spirits of those who had been recognized as morally illustrious in Israel. Most frequently invoked were the spirits of the Patriarchs and the Matriarchs, slumbering through the millennia in the Cave of Machpelah until the arrival of the End of Days. Distressed Jewish women in particular would call upon "Mother Rachel" for help; their menfolk showed a preference for "Father Abraham," for "I will bless thee for the sake of Abraham, My servant" God is quoted as saying (in Genesis).

After these worthies, it was customary to invoke the intercession of the Tzaddikim. These were the martyred saints and the Sages who, over the turbulent course of the centuries, had remained steadfast in defense of the one God, the Torah, and the Jewish people. Last to be called upon, though not least in the procession of ancestral merit, were the souls of the legions of fathers and mothers and of grandfathers and grandmothers. Because their kin called on them for help in their hour of trouble or danger, it suggested that, to the reverent descendants, the beloved deceased—whatever may have been the actual merits of their deeds of piety and righteousness in life—had most assuredly entered into the bliss of celestial Eden and were already part of the godly company of Tzaddikim.

It is well to remember that filial piety has always been intense among Jews, often overwhelming objective criteria of judgment. In Jewish life, righteous ancestors constituted, so to speak, royal "crowns" for their descendants. Thus, to become a worthy ancestor—worthy "for the sake of the children" and of the children's children, became, for many Jews, a driving ideal. The third century Sage Ze'ira, the little saint "with the burnt feet," composed a private prayer which he uttered daily: "O Lord, our God, may it be Your will that we keep from sin and not stand before our fathers in shame and disgrace because of our actions."

Behind the whole idea (of Merit of the Fathers) there flows a deep undercurrent of collective responsibility. Its sources are the ethical concepts of mutual aid and of the fellowship and unity of all Jews. Rabbinic morality pro-

Man reciting Tillim (Psalms) at the graves of ancestors in the cemetery of Lodz, Poland, under the Nazi occupation. (Photo taken by a Nazi soldier.)

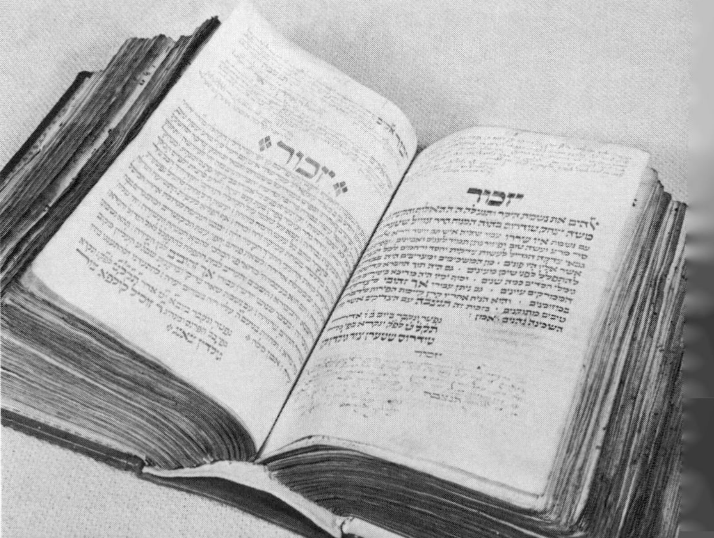

Memorbuch *(Memorial Book) of the Frankfurt ghetto, 1626–1900. (American Friends of the Hebrew University.)*

claimed this doctrine with epigrammatic brevity: "All Jews are responsible for one another." The life of the individual was not considered his alone to lead; all lives and all destinies were seen as meshed and bound together inextricably in a historic chain of continuity without end. Concerning righteous ancestors, the Sages of the Talmud—some of whom were indeed poets of life as well as teachers of ethics and ritualism—declared by means of a parabolic analogy: "As a living grapevine is supported by a prop though it is of dead wood, so is Israel supported by the Merit of the Fathers, even though they lie still in death."

In every century and in all places wherever Jews lived, the souls of the ancestors were prayerfully invoked for their intercession in time of great danger, when life was threatened either by intolerable persecution or by epidemic, or when a loved one was mortally ill. The plain folk would hasten to the Jewish cemetery and there, standing before the graves of their ancestors, would implore their mediation for God's mercy.

Although the essence of the principle of Zechut Abot is moralistic—that "the seeds of virtue germinate and bear fruit" for all—still there were "wise" ancients who perceived the danger to "the good life" inherent in an excessive reliance by the individual upon the merits of his or her ancestors. An unknown Rabbinic teacher of ethics is quoted in the Midrash as having said, while, so to speak, shaking a warning finger: "No man can share in the joys of the World-to-Come merely because of the Merit of his Fathers!" On the contrary, he urged, each individual must prove himself to be deserving by the merit of his own deeds of loving-kindness and uprightness in his dealings with others.

See also GAN EDEN; PARENTS AND CHILDREN (*under* FAMILY RELATIONS, TRADITIONAL PATTERNS OF); REWARD AND PUNISHMENT.

MERRYMAKERS, TRADITIONAL JEWISH

There were always merrymakers in Jewish life. Never was it possible to suppress the folk-will to joy and laughter. Even during the most depressing times, gaiety served as a wholesome corrective and also as a defense against persecution and suffering. It was always a timely reminder to the Jew that life was inherently good, no matter how great its trials, and that one must never abandon hope for the coming of a better day.

During the Rabbinic period, under the stresses of Roman oppression and at the height of the most intense intellectual preoccupation with problems of faith and moral conduct in the history of the Jewish people, the *duty* of merriment was observed as a moral imperative. It was even praised by some of the same Rabbinic teachers who, themselves plain and earthy individuals full of amiability, had, nonetheless, laid down stern prohibitions against licentiousness and rude behavior. The humanitarian spirit then prevailing was such that, to brighten the downcast spirit of a fellow man or to divert him even momentarily from his grief, was considered a most meritorious act. Thus it is not strange to read in the Talmud of the two Jews who introduce themselves by saying: "We are merrymakers and we try to cheer up the sorrowful. Whenever we see two men at odds with each other we seek [by means of waggery] to make peace between them."

During the Succot water-drawing festival at the Temple in Jerusalem, the Patriarch Simeon ben Gamaliel, in honor of the occasion, diverted the great multitude of pilgrims with the juggling of eight lighted torches. Whenever the second-century teacher, Yehudah bar Ilai, would see a wedding procession on the street, he would take up a palm branch and dance gaily before the bride, singing in homage of her: "O beautiful, O virtuous bride!"

Singing Jews wearing funny masks. Italy, 17th century.

Humorous extravaganza rendered extemporaneously by a marshalik at a Chasidic wedding in Galicia. Illustration on a picture post card. (YIVO.)

Shpielmann and Letz. The sanity of laughter was also invoked during the most trying period of medieval persecutions. There were Jewish counterparts of gleemen or merry-andrews professionally active in Central Europe. Like their German prototypes, the *Spielleute,* they were also called *shpielleute* (s. *shpielmann,* i.e., "player" or "musician"). Among the Jews they were also called by the more familiar Hebrew name of *laytzim* (s. *letz,* which means "jester" or "clown").

Whether the performing functions of the shpielleute were also combined with those of the laytzim remains unclear. It was their function to divert the guests at weddings, Bar Mitzvot, and other family festivities with a variety of both serious and light entertainment. They sought to arouse merriment with their ready quips and insolent spoofings, always extemporizing, and in clever Yiddish doggerel rhymes, too. Some of these merry-andrews were adept as tumblers, or performed comical dances, or cavorted about, clowning madly. What the Christian gleemen did outside, they tried to duplicate inside the ghetto.

Among the more prized of their entertaining accomplishments—and in this the shpielleute greatly excelled—was their talent as instrumentalists (in Yiddish: s. *klezmer*, pl. *klezmorim;* from the Hebrew *klei-zemer*, meaning "musical instruments") on lute, harp, viol, dulcimer, and flageolet. The songs they sang were sometimes just a shade lusty and broad, in a pattern borrowed from their Christian medieval environment.

Of course, some of the rabbis, with the traditional conditioning of Torah scholars, did not like these Jewish entertainers at all. They were constantly giving them tongue-lashings. In the thirteenth-century Rhineland, for example, the religious authorities condemned all Jewish merrymakers as "rhyming fools" and "impious scoffers." But just the same, the shpielleute and laytzim enjoyed a lively popularity among the common folk. The merriment they created came as a grateful relief from the excessive gravity and piety with which Jewish life was burdened in that age.

A number of these Jewish merry-andrews were, no doubt, men of genuine talent. Some had considerable Torah-learning, and they, accordingly, drew heavily on the Bible and the Talmud for the songs they composed and sang. They were genuine folk poets and folk singers. In response to popular demand they also "performed" the epic poems of the day, based on themes of love and chivalry. They sang them in Yiddish paraphrases that were written in the customary ottava rima. Such, for instance, were the "Artis Hof" ("King Arthur's Court"), "Dietrich von Bern," and the "Hildebrandtlied."

These Yiddish troubadours half-sang, half-declaimed in a kind of *recitativo* and according to a specified musical mode or melody indentified separately for each chivalric lay. No longer cavorting jesters on these occasions, they were expected to evoke by their singing art and pantomine the various moods of poignancy, the heroic, and the romantic.

Following the terrors of the Thirty Years' War, which were multiplied by massacres perpetrated by Chmielnicki's Cossack hordes in 1648 (*see* POGROMS IN SLAVIC LANDS), the spirit of fun largely vanished from the life of the ghetto. The gloom was intensified by sharp rabbinical interdictions against the "sins of frivolity." A rabbi of that time, David Levi, warned: "A sin most grievous is to engage laytzim to amuse the guests with jests built on verses from the Holy Torah and other sacred writings. Happy is the man who keeps away from such [blasphemers]!"

Marshalik. During the period of the German Renaissance, there emerged in the Yiddish-speaking communities a new type of entertainer—the *marshalik.* He was the Jewish counterpart of the stage official by that name who was traditional in the folk-theatre of Germany. In his merrymaking activities he had an affinity with the shpielmann and the letz, and possibly he represented in himself just another aspect of the same protean actor-singer-jester personality.

During the late sixteenth century, the Purim folk-play or Biblical extravaganza that was the customary presentation among German and Polish Jews had taken on the character of the German Shrovetide carnival play—the *Fastnachtsspiel.* It also showed a resemblance to certain Christian morality plays of even an earlier period. These Yiddish productions, like their Christian models, were presided over by a master of ceremonies. He acted as the *deus ex machina* of the action of the play. He ushered the actors on stage and off stage with comical grimaces and flourishes. He introduced them and commented upon their characters, their motives, and their dilemmas in loud humorous asides to the audience. This stage worthy was the marshalik (from the Middle High German word *Marschall,* meaning "marshal"). It is a reasonable surmise that some of the Purim plays in Yiddish (only a few have survived) were written by such folk poets.

Invariably, the marshalik played the buffoon and wisecracking improvisator, rattling off his doggeral rhymes and quips for the amusement of his appreciative audience. For instance, in the seventeenth-century *Ahashveroshpiel,* a folk-drollery about Ahasueros, the king of Persia, and his Jewish queen, Esther, the marshalik appeared dressed up in the cap and bells and gaudy plummage of a jester. He bounced on stage with jingling bells and a caper to introduce the actors behind him with this salutation in doggeral verse to the audience:

> Greetings, dear friends!
> May God bring you a good Purim!
> I've come here with my jangle [of bells]
> To introduce to you the king's young men!

Badchan. Like the shpielmann and marshalik, the *badchan* (pl. *badchanim*) was a folk bard. He ribbed and lampooned the guests present at weddings, Bar Mitzvot, and other festivities with extemporized quips and rhyming jests. There is reason to believe that the badchan and the marshalik were merely interchangeable names used by the Yiddish folk for the same waggish merrymaker.

Although, during the Renaissance in Germany, the badchan was a communal personage meriting a dignified standing, and appreciated because of his gay wit, comic songs, and capers, and as a consoler and distractor from the sorrows of ghetto life, in later, more decadent, times (beginning with the Counter Reformation in the sixteenth century), he greatly declined in prestige. From then on he was given the same scant respect that was accorded to wandering stage players. Nonetheless he remained ever beloved and esteemed by the plain folk, and his professional services were regarded as indispensable at all festivities.

Despite the fact that the badchan, together with the greater part of Jewish culture and folkways, disappeared from Germany and Austria about the middle of the nineteenth century, he continued to flourish in the other and even larger Yiddish-speaking centers—in Poland, Galicia, Bohemia, Slovakia, Lithuania, Rumania, the Ukraine, and White Russia. In passing, one might note that some of the badchanim, men of genuine though undeveloped poetic talent, were the creators of many Yiddish folk songs, both lyrics and perhaps also the music, that are still very much alive today.

To all intents and purposes, the badchan has disappeared from the stage of contemporary Jewish life. Occasionally, however, he can still be met with among the Yiddish-oriented Ultra-Orthodox in some of the large Jewish population concentrations—in New York, London, and Jerusalem. But even among these he has become somewhat of an anachronism. His quips and doggerel rhymes which formerly delighted Jewish gatherings now are listened to with only the mildest of interest by wedding guests already conditioned to different cultural tastes by the values of the modern age.

See also KLEZMER.

MESSIAH, THE (in Hebrew: MASHIACH, literally meaning the "Anointed," but actually referring to a "Saviour" or "Redeemer")

One of the most enduring and pervasive beliefs in the Jewish religion has been the doctrine of the Messiah. Other peoples avowing different religions who were contemporaries of the Jews in the Biblical Age (i.e., the Egyptians, the Babylonians, the Persians, the Greeks, and the Romans) also entertained various notions about a "redeemer," but their ideas were fundamentally different in the primitive forms they took and in the scope and character of their idealizations; they possessed neither the social goals nor the moral commitments of the Jewish projection.

The Jewish concept of a Messiah as a human, God-elected Redeemer for Israel—and, coincidentally, for all of mankind through the intermediation of Israel—was gradual in its evolution. As was to be expected, because of its mystical character and supernatural goals, it remained shadowy in outline. Its early origins lie half-concealed, due to the fact that no unitary or fully developed conception of the Messiah was ever rendered in ancient Jewish writings. Yet his image in our own day lies smothered under an avalanche of scholarly speculations and sectarian theological interpretations by Christians and Jews alike. The visionings of the Prophets and the many esoteric hints dropped by the writers of eschatological works—apocalypses which treat of the Resurrection and the Day of Judgment—have made it difficult to treat very concretely of the Messiah, his personality, his attributes, his goals, and the time and the manner of his appearance.

Despite this confusion, a definite though blurred image of him somehow does emerge from the welter of overheated fancies, esoteric notions, wild-eyed prophecies and folk legends that have been accumulating about him for nigh to three thousand years among Jews. It pictures him as God's Messenger—the human instrumentality of the Divine Will—who will, at the appointed hour, be sent by God to redeem Israel from its overlong martyrdom of suffering, humiliation, and oppression. It is said also that in the course of fulfilling his divinely appointed mission, he will prove himself to be the greatest of all the Prophets of righteousness in the illustrious line which began with Moses in Egypt.

The predetermined mission of the Messiah was definitive and clear: the establishment of God's Kingdom *on earth* (not *in Heaven*, as the Christians have it) when brotherhood, peace, and justice would usher in the eternal Sabbath for Israel, and for the rest of mankind as well, provided it accepted the belief in One God and his Torah. Enthused the Prophets and the mystics, the coming of the Messiah would usher in a perfect time—a time of unity and fulfillment for both man and beast.

The Prophet Elijah, as the forerunner of the Messiah, comes riding to Jerusalem on horseback and blowing on the shofar of the Redemption. (Illumination from a 15th-century machzor [festival prayer-book] manuscript. Hamburg State Library.)

Preceded on foot by the Prophet Elijah blowing upon the shofar of the Redemption, the Messiah, on horseback, is ready to enter Jerusalem. (Woodcut from a Venetian Haggadah, 1629.)

And the wolf shall dwell with the lamb,
And the leopard shall lie down with the kid;
And the calf and the young lion and the fatling together;
And a little child shall lead them.

The Kingdom of God. The establishment of the Kingdom of God *on earth* (mentioned above) was envisioned by the Prophets of Israel as the principal goal of the Messiah. It was expected to be realized in the Age of Righteousness which God's Messenger of the Redemption would usher into the world.

Almost every people of ancient times, when faced with the bitter frustrations of life, spun for itself a dreamlike Utopia to yearn for, a "golden age" to await. The Kingdom of God, as it was generally conceived by the Prophets, projected such a "golden age" for the Jewish people. But since that age was conceived of as neither national nor parochial, but universal in scope, it also drew into its embrace all the other peoples and races of mankind.

Although many peoples, as a consequence of their numerous vicissitudes and struggles for survival, acquired a tragic sense of life, it is doubtful whether any equalled in intensity the grief-consciousness of the Jews at having been so rejected and persecuted by the rest of the world. Israel saw itself as standing weak and helpless before the Juggernaut onset of its enemies—in turn: Egypt, Assyria, Babylonia, Persia, Greece, Syria, and Rome. Because of its small size and the misfortune of its geographic location—vital in the strategic considerations of the ancient world powers because it served as a land corridor which linked Europe, Africa, and Asia—it was constantly being invaded and its people subjugated, robbed, degraded, and oppressed. Therefore, many Jews came to abandon all hope of extricating themselves from their plight by their own efforts.

One need only read the sacred literature of the Jews—whether it be the Bible, the post-Biblical writings, the Talmud, the rabbinical works of the Middle Ages, or the prayers of the synagogue—to note the constant reiteration of the elegiac theme: "Bondmen were we unto Pharaoh in Egypt." Only the intervention of God by means of miracles—they believed that such miracles had been worked by God many times before to aid their ancestors since the Bondage of Israel in Egypt—could assure their survival.

Throne in a niche in the early-18th-century synagogue of Carpentras, France, reserved for the Prophet Elijah on his expected appearance as the herald of the Messiah.

Under these extraordinary circumstances, it was natural for the Jews to weave a dream-play out of idealistic gossamer about the Messianic kingdom in which all existence would be reshaped to respond to the heart's desire, and in which every grief would be assuaged, every hunger would be stilled, and every moral value be made triumphant. During the eighth century B.C.E., when Isaiah ben Amoz projected his image of the Righteous Kingdom, he struck music of an awesome kind.

And it shall come to pass in the end of days,
That the mountain of the Lord's house shall be
established as the top of the mountains,
And shall be exalted above the hills;
And all nations shall flow into it.
And many peoples shall go and say:
"Come ye, and let us go up to the mountain
of the Lord,
To the house of the God of Jacob;
And he will teach us of His ways,
And we will walk in His paths."
For out of Zion shall go forth the law,
And the word of the Lord from Jerusalem,
And He shall judge between the nations,
And shall decide for many peoples;
And they shall beat their swords into plowshares,
And their spears into pruning-hooks;
Nation shall not lift up sword against nation,
Neither shall they learn war anymore.

ISAIAH 2:2-4

Two centuries after Isaiah, while grieving for Israel and for the whole human race in the Captivity of Babylonia, the Prophet Ezekiel had a vision about the blessings that the Messianic era had in store for mankind. The "evil beasts," he foretold, would disappear from the earth. Who were those "beasts"? They were (he said) war, violence, and social injustice. The yoke of oppression would be broken, and the Jewish people would be delivered out of the hands of those who felt free to enslave them.

And they shall no more be a prey to the nations . . .
but they shall dwell safely, and none shall make
them afraid.

EZEKIEL 34:28

In this fantasy of reconstruction of man's life on earth, rejected and harassed Israel was filled with the mystic certainty that its career in history would end in a blaze of glory. It would be much admired and sought after by the other nations (which all along had scorned and persecuted it) because it had been elected by God to serve as his instrument of redemption for mankind. "In the days of the Messiah," jubilated the Mishnah Sage, Yoseh ben Chalafta, "the Gentiles will flock to Israel as converts." Jerusalem would then become the capital of the entire world.

The medieval rabbinic savant, Maimonides, expressed in the Mishneh Torah the general view of believing Jews concerning the Kingdom of God: "In that era, there shall be neither famine nor war, neither jealousy nor strife. Blessings will be abundant, comforts within the reach of all. The one preoccupation of the whole world will be to know God."

The Messiah As Man. At all times Jews thought that the Messiah would be a man of flesh and blood like themselves. In the Jew Tryphon's disputation with the Christian apologist of the second century, Justin Martyr, challenging the latter's assertion that the Messiah had already appeared in the divine person of Jesus—"the Son of God"—he countered: "We [Jews] all expect that the Messiah will come into being as a man from among men." (*See* CHRISTIANITY, JEWISH ORIGINS OF.)

It was on this crucial disagreement that the relations between Jews and Christians broke and foundered. The steadfast refusal of the Jews to concede that the Messiah had already come in the person of their fellow Jew, Jesus of Nazareth, and to proceed after such affirmation to the baptismal font, brought down upon them from that time forward and through the centuries that followed untold calamities and persecution.

Following the breakaway from Judaism in the second century of the sectarian (Jewish) Essenes, with their subsequent Gentile orientation and overt hostility to Judaism, their institutional organization as a separate religion (Christianity), and, finally, their deviation from the strict monotheism of the Jews through their adoption of the concept of the Holy Trinity, the Talmud issued this grave warning to the Jewish faithful: "If a man says 'I am God,' he lies; if he says, 'I am the son of God,' he will rue it; and if he says, 'I shall ascend to heaven,' he will surely fail."

The idea of a human saviour who, at the bidding of God, would appear to succor Israel in time of supreme crisis, was very old, indeed. This is clearly indicated in the chronicle of the devout Nehemiah, the post-Exilic governor of Judah in the middle of the fifth century B.C.E. Addressing himself prayerfully to God, he reminded Him: ". . . and in the time of their trouble, when they cried unto Thee, Thou heardest from Heaven; and according to Thy manifold mercies Thou gavest them saviours who might save them out of the hand of their adversaries." (Nehemiah 9:27.)

Who might have been those "saviours" to whom Nehemiah had reference? In his day there must have already existed a common folk belief concerning them. In the Midrash commentary to the Book of Psalms, the Talmud cites the listing of such saviours by the Sage Yochanan. He had noted that, when the Israelites were oppressed in the Egyptian House of Bondage, Moses had been their liberator. And when, during their Captivity in Babylon, they were pining for the sanctuary on Mount Zion, Zerubbabel, a prince of Davidic lineage, had led them back to the Land of Israel. Also, when they were threatened with extermination by Haman in Persia, Esther and Mordecai had saved their lives. Then again, when they were being ground down by the Seleucidan tyrant Antiochus, who had defiled their Temple in Jerusalem and had tried to extirpate the Jewish religion, the Hasmonean priest-hero, Judah the Maccabee, had led them to freedom. The popular image of all of these "saviours," in a cumulative though amorphous way, had implanted the seed of Messianic expectations in the folk-thinking.

The Messiah, according to the Rabbinic construction of him, would eclipse all of the heroic leaders and saints (tzaddikim). Furthermore, he would be impelled in the performance of his mission of redemption by the spirit and power of prophecy. "The Messiah will be a very great Prophet, greater than all the Prophets with the exception of Moses," wrote Maimonides upon the appearance in 1172 of a messianic pretender in Yemen. ". . . It is one of the known conditions with us [Jews] that every prophet must have reached mental perfection before God endows him with prophecy. For it is a fundamental principle with us that prophecy settles only upon a man who is wise, mighty, and rich; that is, he is mighty in self-mastery and he is rich in knowledge. But when a man arises who is not renowned for wisdom, claiming to be a prophet, we do not believe him. How much less do we believe an ignoramus who claims to be the Messiah."

Strange to relate, not one but two widely differing portrayals of the Messiah appear in Jewish religious writings. Sometimes the two seem to fuse, borrowing characteristics one from the other until they become virtually indistinguishable.

The earlier one—morally purer than the later but more utopian and less realistic for all that—was first projected by the visionary genius of Isaiah ben Amoz in the eighth century B.C.E. He prophesied that the Messiah would be "a shoot out of the stock of Jesse," namely, a descendant of David, the Psalmist-king. Thus he was named Mashiach ben David (Messiah Son of David). Whether Isaiah himself had originated this legendary notion or had merely repeated what was already a folk belief in his day, is not clear. But one thing is certain: The memory of Israel's greatest power and glory, as personified by the rule of David and his son Solomon, but which it soon lost, always haunted the Jewish people, who idealized and romanticized that too-brief period as its "Golden Age." And so, it was expected that when the Messiah would make his appearance as "the anointed of the Lord," he would restore the departed splendor of Israel—in an even more wondrous and perfect form: not with material wealth and physical power but as the "Kingdom of God." All of Israel's intellectual, spiritual, and moral resources were to be dedicated to the building of this righteous society, this "Kingdom of God."

Isaiah's vision of the Messiah Son of David, pictured him as resolute and gentle, wise and just, pure in heart and invincible in spiritual power, solely motivated by a love for mankind—*all* mankind—and by the desire to establish enduring peace and justice in the world.

> But with righteousness shall he judge the poor,
> And decide with equity for the meek and the land . . .
> They shall not hurt nor destroy
> In all My holy mountain.
>
> ISAIAH 11:4, 9

But before long there began to emerge a new image of the Messiah. Essentially, he retained all the moral qualities attributed to the original image. But much had happened—and was still happening—to the Jewish people since the days of Isaiah. First the Assyrian and Babylonian invaders had rolled over the Land of Israel like a blight, destroying the Temple and carrying off the flower of its youth into Captivity. Several centuries later, it was the turn of the Greek, the Syrian, and the Roman armies to trample upon Judah and to drench its soil with the blood of its sons. It was an age of national woe and humiliation and, therefore, of emotional insecurity and much wishful thinking.

The new conception of the Messiah bore the stamp of this prolonged crisis. Whereas the Messiah son of David had originally been pictured as a gentle, pacific, prophet-king, the later Messiah was delineated as an implacable warrior-hero, champion of the downtrodden Jewish people. It was expected that, because he would hold God's mandate, he would eventually succeed in crushing all of his people's persecutors.

The author of the Apocalypse of Baruch (written *c.* 70 B.C.E.) rejoiced when he envisioned the destruction of the Roman tyrants. He saw in it an act of divine retribution: "The enemy persecuted you, and so shall you see his destruction speedily."

This same characterization of the Messiah was also found in the visionary Book of Daniel (written *c.* 200 B.C.E.), in the Book of Enoch (written *c.* 100 B.C.E.), and in other post-Biblical apocalypses. The prophet Daniel disguised the Messianic hope in the curious allegory of the Four Great Beasts (cited in the Book of Daniel, Chapter 7). These were the four great world empires (Babylonia, Persia, Greece, and

Rome) whose shadow had fallen on the Jewish people. Their "dominion was taken away" from them and "given to the people of the saints of the Most High."

New ideas, esoteric and mystical, although transformed and adapted, had gradually been infiltrating into Jewish religious thinking since the Captivity began in Babylonia in 586 B.C.E. These had been drawn from a variety of contemporary sources, principally from the religions of Babylonia, Persia, and latterday Egypt. As was to be expected, they were heavily fraught with supernaturalism. Both Ezekiel, the Prophet of the sixth-century B.C.E., and the unknown author of the visionary Book of Enoch outlined in remarkable detail the earth-shaking and heaven-storming events that were expected to precede the Resurrection and the Last Judgment, and the terrifying portents and upheavals in nature that would be a prelude to the End of Days. The host of imitators that followed them during the Hellenistic age strengthened these beliefs.

These apocalyptic authors, not satisfied with having introduced their new ideas into the Jewish religion, went about conveniently blending them with the Messianic expectations in currency at those times. Dramatically, they drew a sharp contrast between the two ages—the present Kingdom of Satan and the Kingdom of God that the Messiah would in the future establish on earth. As the post-Biblical writer of the Assumption of Moses confidently believed: "And then His Kingdom shall appear throughout all His creation, and then Satan shall be no more."

In all this welter of speculation and fantasy about the End of Days (which Jews generally believed to be imminent), there were not merely two differently characterized Messiahs but separately personalized ones that became pronounced. Besides the idealistic image that had been projected by Isaiah—that of the Mashiach ben David—another—the warrior-hero representation—took place. He was refered to as Mashiach ben Yosef (Messiah son of Joseph), who would judge and chastise all sinners and destroy the wicked, and with them all evil; i.e., Satan. It is possible to perceive in the martial character and intentions of the Mashiach ben Yosef an adaptation of the dualistic opposition that appears in the (Persian) Zoroastrian religion. This is a reference to the climactic encounter of arms between Ormuzd (the principle of life and light) and Ahriman (the principle of death and darkness; i.e., Satan), from which life and light emerge triumphant.

This mythic individual was expected to lead an army of Jews against their oppressors, the wicked kings of Gog and Magog, who together served as a thinly disguised allegorization of the Romans. In the imagination of the folk, this Warrior of the Lord, mounted on a white charger and with sword flashing in the sun, would ride into battle at the head of his people. It would be the last armed clash on earth, and although legend required that the Mashiach ben Yosef be slain in the fighting, it was foretold that the army of the Jews would be victorious, and the Mashiach ben David would then make his appearance and usher in the millennium.

However Jews may have differed in their concepts of the Messiah, on one related matter they did not disagree at all. Tradition cast the Prophet Elijah in the wondrous role of the herald who would precede the Messiah, and the plain folk of every generation knew that when Elijah would be seen jogging along on a white ass and blowing upon the shofar of the Messiah, then the Redemption of Israel would be at hand.

Why Elijah, "the Prophet of the Lord" who had thundered his rebukes at his enemies in the ninth century B.C.E., was cast in this particular role is not easy to explain; the plain folk has its own criteria of taste and selection. Although the significance of Elijah in the cosmic drama of the Messianic Kingdom is only secondary, to the Jewish folk he nonetheless seemed far more real and lovable than the Messiah himself, who at best remained a somewhat remote figure, an awe-inspiring abstraction.

No doubt, what contributed to making Elijah "real" to the plain Jew was the humanizing process of the many legends that were woven about his personality. Another consideration was the Biblical myth that he had not died but, in fact, had been "translated" to Heaven directly and *alive,* swept aloft by a whirlwind in a chariot of fire. And so, because he had not died and been buried like an ordinary human being (even Moses, the incomparable Prophet, had died), it became traditional to consider him immortal. The medieval Cabalists even elevated him to the rank of an archangel. Thus many supernatural powers were ascribed to him that would enable him to move about with the greatest of ease, both in Heaven among the angels and the saints of God, and on earth among human beings, unhindered not by time nor space, nor by circumstance. The folk believed that whenever he chose, he could take on human shape, and he could vanish just as mysteriously. His disguises were inexhaustible, for, as the protector of the weak, the poor, and the sorely beset, his humility required of him that he move among men unrecognized.

Jewish folk-fancy has pictured Elijah with all the affectionate details of informality. He is portrayed in legend as a benign old Jew, a sort of beloved great-uncle with a flowing gray beard, poorly dressed, and trudging along his solitary way, always with a wanderer's knapsack slung over his shoulder, on his missions of tireless kindness on behalf of the unfortunate. Sometimes, he was endowed by the people's generous fancy with the supernatural attributes of the Messiah himself.

Elijah was first linked directly with the Messiah by the Prophet Malachi:

> Behold, I will send you
> Elijah the Prophet
> Before the coming
> Of the great and terrible day of the Lord.
>
> MALACHI 3:23

From this Biblical passage was drawn the Rabbinic tradition suggestive of wondrous events and miracles to come: "In the second year of the reign of Achaziah, Elijah became hidden and was seen no more, until King Messiah shall come, when again he will be seen."

The Signs of the Messiah. During the two centuries before the Destruction of the Second Temple, Messianic hysteria gripped the Jews of Judea and the foreign settlements. The early Rabbinic mystics became tangled up in fantastic speculations concerning the coming of the Messiah. Impatient were the questions raised by the commonalty of Jews. When would he appear? How would one be able to recognize him? Where was he living in concealment, biding his time until the appointed hour? Moreover, what would be the specific signs and portents that would forewarn of his imminent arrival?

Not a few among the contemporary Jewish writers of visions and revelations having to do with the End of Days strained mightily to supply answers to these questions. Not a few of them allowed their imaginations to run wild. Weird in the extreme were the incidents of horror and desolation which they foretold would be the prelude to the Messianic era. Suddenly all the laws of nature would be reversed. In picturesque idiom, the writers gave a name to the travails and calamities that would descend upon man, beast, bird, fish, and all other created things. They called these calamities "the birth-pangs of the Messiah." They said blood would ooze from trees; the very stones would cry out. There would be heard the terrible clash of swords by myriad hosts of warriors who would be battling in the clouds. And beholding and hearing all that, mankind would be affrighted.

In his apocalypse or revelation, Baruch undertook to describe the circumstances and to indicate the signs that would herald the arrival of the Messiah:

> This, then, shall be the sign—when amazement shall seize the inhabitants of the earth, and they shall fall into great torments. And it shall come to pass when they shall say in their thoughts by reason of their great tribulation: "The Almighty remembers the earth no more." And it shall come to pass when they shall despair, then will the time [of the Messiah] awake!

This line of reasoning was perpetuated in Rabbinic thinking by a statement made by the religious authority of the first century C.E., Yochanan ben Zakkai. He mused that it would, paradoxically enough, get better for Israel only when the worst should have occurred!

There naturally was a variety of opinion among those tireless intellectual speculators, the Rabbinic Sages of the Talmud, concerning the circumstances and the events that would lead to the arrival of the Messiah. Rabbi Eliezer said: "If all Israel repent for only one single day, it shall be redeemed." Musing on this belief, Rabbi Judah ha-Nasi, the compiler of the Mishnah, grew morose: How could one expect all of the people to repent unless they were first crushed by their afflictions?

A tradition arose during the time of the Roman oppression of Judea that, at the hour appointed by the inscrutable will of God, the Messiah would be found at the main gate of the city of Rome. He would be sitting there among the poor, the sick, and the outcast—all the most wretched—indistinguishable from them all, crouching, disfigured as a leper, nursing his wounds and sores. For it was thus, according to a remarkable legend in the Talmud, that the Sage Joshua ben Levi saw him in a dream.

> "Peace be to you, O Master!" Joshua greeted him.
> "Peace be to you, son of Levi."
> "O Master, when will you come with the Redemption?"
> "Today," answered the Messiah briefly.
> Overjoyed, the Sage went away. He waited for him all day, but in vain.
> The following day, Joshua ben Levi met the Prophet Elijah. He said to him, aggrieved: "He—the Messiah—did not speak truthfully. He told me he would come *today*. But *today* has already passed, and he hasn't come."
> The Prophet Elijah replied: "When the Messiah said to you today, he only had in mind the words of the Psalmist [Psalms 98:7], 'Today, if ye but hearken to His Voice.'"

In this ancient moralistic story is mirrored a characteristic of Jewish folklore, which seizes hold of a single Scriptural metaphor—or even word—and weaves meaningful parables around it. For example, the odd notion that the Messiah would be afflicted with leprosy while waiting in Rome for God's bidding to reveal himself to Israel, was imaginatively constructed upon one word contained in Chapter 53:4 of the Second Isaiah: "Surely he hath borne our griefs and carried our sorrows; yet we did esteem him a leper, smitten of God and afflicted."

Here, too, is postulated the doctrine of the *Suffering Messiah*—a Jewish idea that profoundly colored the early Christian image of Jesus and his crucifixion as a vicarious sacrifice for the sins of the world. In the Talmud, there is found an expository passage on the Mashiach ben David in the guise of a leper. He bears his burden of pain and grief meekly and with patience. He does this in order that the compassionate God, taking note of his suffering as an expiation for the collective sins of the Jewish people, would hasten to redeem it.

Interestingly, the same Talmudic passage observes that when the Messiah will perceive that God is also anguished by the misbehavior of Israel, he will become reconciled to his own sorrows. The Rabbis comment thereon: "If the Master Himself suffers so grievously, what right does he—the Messiah, His servant—have to complain?"

The odd notion that the total repentance of Israel was required as a precondition for bringing in the Redemption was turned into a solemn rite by the Cabalists of Safed, Palestine, in the sixteenth century. Daily at midnight, and garbed in the black of mourning, they gathered in their synagogues for a special prayer-service. Seated on the bare floor, in the manner of penitents on the Ninth of Ab (Tishah B'Ab, the fast day that commemorates the Destruction of the Temple in Jerusalem), they recited litanies and lamentations over the downfall of Israel. At the conclusion of this service they recited the Viddui (the Jewish Confession of sins customarily recited before death). This they did in expiation for the sins of all Jews that, they were certain, were holding back the Messiah and the Redemption.

That not all religious thinkers in the Rabbinic Age required the repentance of all Jews before the Redemption could come is indicated in numerous passages in Talmudic literature. One such statement compares the potential of the Jewish people to both the dust and the stars, declaring that if Israel falls, it sinks into the dust; if it rises, it soars to the stars. But this, asserts the Talmud, is the paradox: when Israel sinks into the lowest depths of despair, it is providentially lifted up!

With this line of reasoning the great majority of the Jewish people chose to console itself: The Messiah would surely come—being sent as a gift and a token of God's unbounded love for Israel—at the juncture when it would experience the ultimate in grief and hopelessness. "O add up the sum of the poverty of Israel and its suffering and hasten its Redemption!" prayed one Talmudic Sage.

During his unending trials in a world stained with the guilt of hate, the pious Jew never surrendered his certainty that the Messiah would eventually come. This belief helped sustain him in his resistance to the almost unbearable pressures that were being brought to bear upon him to abandon his faith and his group-identity. What if the Messiah hadn't appeared yet? he would reply to the taunts of his Christian enemies. So he would come someday! But come he would, even if the exact time of his coming remained concealed.

A parable is related in the Talmud about a king who dearly loved his wife, but had to leave her to go on a distant journey. While on his way, he wrote to her that he would soon return. But after that letter he was not heard from again. His wife grieved and wept for him. "Your beloved will never return; he has forgotten you," said her companions to her. "You must marry again." But she uttered not a word. She took out her letter and read it again, and again, taking comfort in her beloved's promise that he would return to her one day. Similarly, observed the Talmudic weaver of moralistic allegories, the peoples of the earth taunt the Jews: "Come! Abandon your faith and be like us! Your Messiah will never come!" But Israel turns to its ancient covenant with God and reads in it for the thousandth time his promise to return to his beloved some day. And reading it, the Jews are comforted.

The twelfth in the Thirteen Articles of the faith that were formulated by the medieval rabbi-philosopher Maimonides and that have been recited by the devout ever since, reads as follows:

> I believe [*Ani Ma'amin*] with complete faith that the Messiah will come, and although he may tarry, yet each day I will wait for his coming.

These Hebrew words an unknown but devout minstrel in one of the human slaughterhouses of the German Nazis combined with a tune he wrote. This is now tragically famous as the martyr-hymn "Ani Ma'amin." Many of the six million Jews who perished under the Nazis in the 1940's in Europe went to their death triumphantly, singing this affirmation of the Redemption. It has been added to the Passover Seder service.

It would be unrealistic to imagine, in this scientific age in which ghetto separatism lingers on only as a fading historic memory, either that *all* Jews still believe in a Messiah or that their conception of him is the same as their forefathers'. More than a century ago, Joseph Perl, a leader of the Jewish Enlightenment (the Haskalah) in Galicia, although himself a traditionalist in religious belief and observance, nevertheless advocated a modern and rationalistic approach to the doctrine of the Messiah. He summarized his ideas in a memorandum that he addressed to the Austrian government: ". . . the truly educated Jews by no means picture the Messiah as a *real* personality. They see in him only a symbol of ideas of the Redemption and universal peace which await their realization when Israel, freed of all oppression, will be accepted into the family of nations."

This, too, is the way progressive-minded Jews regard the Messianic concept today. A noted religious thinker, Mordecai Kaplan of the Jewish Theological Seminary of America, has observed that to the educated modern person it is unthinkable that any human being, no matter how exalted in character or how richly endowed with intellectual powers, merits serving as the instrument of God's intentions for bringing in the Millennium on earth.

However, there is no question but that to millions of Orthodox Jews today, the personalized image of the Messiah is still very real. To them he is no mere symbol or idealized abstraction. In only a few respects do they deviate at all from the views and expectations concerning him that have been handed down since post-Exilic times from parents to children in an unbroken chain of indoctrination. At the same time, other millions of believing Jews who have adopted the Conservative and Reform philosophies of Judaism, although they may invoke or make reference to the Messiah in their prayers, nonetheless conceive of him mostly as a symbol of a more perfect world of men. Rather than dwelling on the supernatural and mythic notions sanctified by tradition, they emphasize instead the Messianic ideals of social justice, moral righteousness, and universal peace as taught by Moses and preached by the Prophets. The attainment of these ends among men and in society, they aver, has been assigned to the Jewish people since ancient days as its religious mission and social dedication.

See also CHOSEN PEOPLE, THE; CHRISTIANITY, JEWISH ORIGINS OF; KADDISH; MESSIAHS, WOULD-BE; MONOTHEISM; PEACE, JEWISH CONCEPT OF; PASSOVER; PROPHETS (*under* BIBLE, THE); POST-BIBLICAL WRITINGS; REPENTANCE; RESURRECTION.

MESSIAHS, WOULD-BE

One of the most fascinating quests, and one even more enigmatic and romantically strange than the search for the Golden Fleece conducted by the Greek Argonauts, has been the Jews' ardent search for the Messiah. It can be said, without danger of exaggeration, that of all the religious beliefs and preoccupations of the Jews in their history, the Messianic dream was the one that most strongly imprinted itself on the Jewish mind and character and hence most greatly shaped the people's conduct. Without its conditioning, the psychic physiognomy of the Jew would have been entirely different.

There were many claimants to the role of Messiah in the course of two thousand years of Jewish history. The plain folk, devout and completely convinced in what they were taught by their religious teachers concerning the Messiah, found numerous "authoritative" signs and assurances of the inevitability of the Redemption in the preachments of the Prophets, in the visionings of the post-Biblical apocalyptic writers, and in the teachings of the Talmudic Sages. Despite the many contradictions and confusions present in those speculations, certain central ideas received general acceptance. One of those root-ideas was expressed in the supplication by Nehemiah in the fifth century B.C.E. . . . "and in the time of their trouble, when they cried unto Thee, Thou heardest from heaven; and according to Thy manifold mercies, Thou gavest them saviours who might save them out of the hands of their adversaries." (Nehemiah 9:28.) As such, indeed, were regarded the liberators and heroes of the people: Moses, David, and Judah the Maccabee.

National troubles, catastrophes, and persecution were the quickeners of the fever of Messianism; an idealistic religiosity lent it spirituality and emotional drive. Several centuries later, like day-dreaming children, the Jews, who were groaning under the juggernaut of Roman tyranny, were emotionally ready for any miraculous solutions to the afflictions of an unjust and topsy-turvy life. Since natural means, considering the military and political weakness of the Jewish State, had failed to succor them, they wishfully were prepared to achieve an ideal harmony and justice in society by the mediation of a supernatural agency.

The popular notion that the emergence in Jewish religious history of Jesus as the *Christos* (the Greek word for the Hebrew *Mashiach*, meaning "Messiah," "Saviour," or "Redeemer") was a unique occurrence among the Jews is, of course, an incorrect one. There were not a few individuals in the same century who dramatically stepped forward and announced to a breathless Jewry—each on his own behalf—that he was the Mashiach, the Redeemer of Israel. Now the extraordinary thing about these first-century claimants for Messianic distinction was that each served as a rallying point for Jewish revolt against Roman rule. Unlike Jesus, who was an Essene pacifist and a non-resister to evil, the other "messiahs" of that period were, without exception, militant firebrands and patriots; they were leaders of the Zealots (q.v.) who formed an influential wing of the sectarian Pharisees. Quite obviously, the tragic events that pursued Jesus to his execution on the cross at Golgotha, stemmed from the historic fact that the would-be messiahs who preceeded him were insurrectionary leaders who managed to inflict severe losses in casualties and prestige upon the Roman legions sent to Judea to suppress them.

There can be no doubt that *all* of the "messiahs" who appeared among the Jews in the tumultuous Roman times were extraordinary men. They were dedicated idealistically, even fanatically, to their religion, yet at the same time, they were inflamed by a patriotic love for their oppressed people which led them to attempt to throw off the Imperial Roman yoke. A factual but acidulous account of them was given by the noted Jewish historian of that time, Josephus, who, as a collaborationist with Rome, went to great lengths to pour fire and brimstone on all Jewish patriots. He raged in his *Antiquities of the Jews:*

> Another group of men also sprang up . . . who destroyed the peace of the city [Jerusalem]. . . . For they were deceivers and deluders of the people, and under pretense of divine illumination, were for innovations and changes, and prevailed on the multitude to act like madmen, and went before them in the wilderness, pretending that God would there show them signs of liberation.

The attempt by Josephus to disparage the rebels either as criminals or as religious maniacs did not suceed. The first of these messiahs of whom Josephus wrote was Judas of Galilee, who led an uprising in 6 C.E. About him and his followers Josephus grudgingly conceded: "They have an inviolable attachment to liberty and they say that God is to be their only Ruler and Lord."

In the year 44, another rebel-messiah came forward. He was Theudas. Conceiving himself to be a prophet in the tradition of Moses, he led a multitude of his followers to the banks of the Jordan with the promise that he would there demonstrate his prophetic powers by dividing the waters so he could lead them dry shod across to the other shore, just as Moses had their ancestors at the Red Sea. Sensing trouble, the Roman procurator dispatched horsemen after them. Many were slain, and those who remained were taken prisoner. Theudas himself was crucified—this was the customary Roman way of executing criminals—and then beheaded.

At some time between 55 and 60 C.E. there appeared a mysterious messiah-warrior known only as Benjamin the Egyptian. He sparked once more the fire of revolt in the people, and proclaimed himself the "Messiah"—"the anointed of the Lord." To his thirty thousand embattled followers, whom he assembled on the Mount of Olives in Jerusalem, he announced that, with his God-given powers, he would make the walls of the city tumble down, just as Joshua had the walls of Jericho, and then they would enter the Holy City in triumph. But he apparently did not figure on the probability that the procurator Felix would march against him with his legions, as indeed he did. Many of Benjamin's followers were killed, but he himself managed to make his escape.

Only a year or two later, another rebel-messiah, his name today unknown, took up his crusading standard against the Romans. He persuaded his adherents to go with him into the wilderness where, according to Josephus, he promised that they would find their "deliverance and freedom from their misery."

A new type of messiah appeared in the year 67 C.E., when the war with the Romans (which finally led to the destruction of the Jewish State four years later) had broken out. This was the fiery Zealot leader Menachem, the grandson of Judas the Galilean. He, too, proclaimed himself "Messiah," and he organized his Zealot followers in a successful surprise attack on the important fortress of Masada. Obtaining weapons there, he armed his men and marched on Jerusalem, capturing the key fortress of Antonia from its defending garrison. But what actually happened after that to his enterprise and to himself remains unknown.

It does seem, though, that the classic pattern for the Messiah had become well-set by this time; he had to be a prophet-warrior. The last great figure in this category was Simeon Bar Kochba, who organized the rebellion against the Emperor Hadrian in 132-35 C.E. It had been provoked by the imperial decrees which had for their aim the breakup of the Jews as a people and as a religious entity. It was Akiba ben Joseph, the most influential of all Rabbinic Sages, who hailed Bar Kochba as the Messiah. He based his recognition of him on the Scriptural verse: "There shall come forth a star [Bar Kochba means "son of a Star"] out of Jacob, and a scepter shall rise out of Israel, and shall smite through the corner of Moab." Akiba's fervent pronouncement provoked this scoffing retort from his skeptical-minded Rabbinic colleague, Yochanan ben Torta: "O Akiba! Before the son of David will appear, grass will sprout on your cheeks!"

For three years the struggle against the Romans lasted, with a staggering loss of Jewish lives—580,000 were killed in battle, and this was in addition to the many thousands more who died of pestilence and starvation. When it was over, the Roman historian, Dio Cassius, commented laconically: "All of Judea became almost a desert." The fortress of Bethar, the last stronghold of the rebellion, fell in 135, and Bar Kochba perished with it.

Whatever the catastrophes that resulted from each messianic adventure, the Jews, practically without a dissenting voice, remained steadfast in their faith that, out of God's infinite compassion and love for Israel, he would, in the fulfillment of time, send it a Saviour, an event that had been foretold by so many Prophets and Sages of Israel. Nourished by

A bundle of Bar Kochba letters written in Hebrew on papyrus between 132 and 135 C.E. and discovered in a Judean Desert cave near the Dead Sea by Professor Yigael Yadin and his Hebrew University archaeological expedition in 1961. (American Friends of the Hebrew University.)

The opening line of this letter by Bar Kochba (Kosiba), the Messianic leader of the uprising against Rome in 132 C.E., reads: "From Shimon Bar Kosiba to the men of En-gedi, to Masabala and to Yehonatan Bar Ba'ayan—peace! You sit, eat, and drink from the property of the House of Israel, and care nothing for your brothers." (American Friends of the Hebrew University.)

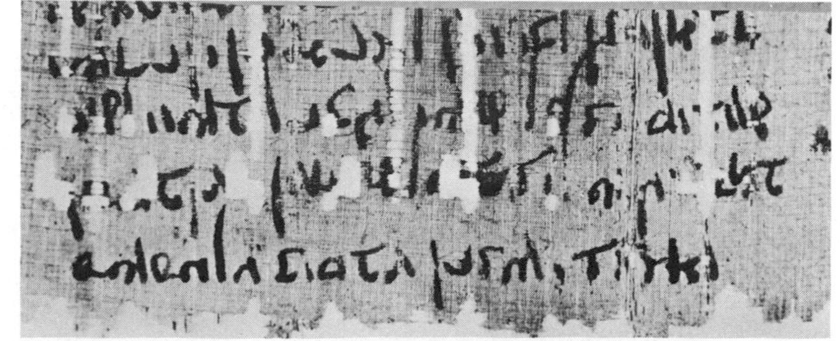

Professor Yigael Yadin (right) watching the expert operation of Professor James Biberkraut at the Hebrew University as he skillfully unravels the bundle of Bar Kochba letters found in a Judean Desert Cave. (American Friends of the Hebrew University.)

national despair and insecurity, the Messianic hope seemed at various times to be just on the verge of being fulfilled. Invariably, each prophetic promise by the would-be saviours ended in bitter disappointment.

To the religious Jew, during the long centuries of the Galut—the Exile in Dispersion—the expectation that the Messiah would soon come riding on his white horse while the Prophet Elijah, as his herald, would precede him, blowing upon the shofar of the Redemption, was anything but a dream. It was a holy certainty which he never questioned. The mystics and the writers of apocalyptic visions, who believed that the End of Days was imminent, engaged in feverish speculations. They got lost in irrational calculations about the coming of the Messiah based merely on the authority of certain Scriptural verses having but the remotest and the most innocent connection with their obsessive subject. A Talmudic authority of the first century raged against that variety of mental acrobatics. He declared that too much preoccupation with the matter was causing unrest and a morbid excitement among the people.

The strictures drawn sharply by some religious teachers against these excesses of fantasy could not stem the popular, and, for that matter, even the Rabbinic, fascination for the subject. One of the many arbitrary dates set for the coming of the Messiah was the year 440. As if in response to this general anticipation, a self-proclaimed "Messiah" suddenly appeared in 431 on the island of Crete. His name was Moses and, like the first Moses, he announced himself ready to lead the dispersed remnants of Israel back to the land of their forefathers. Mastered by the same delusion that had condemned the messianic adventure of Theudas to disaster in the year 44, he also assured his followers that, by means of his supreme prophetic powers, he would be able to lead them dry shod to Eretz Yisrael (the Land of Israel) across the Mediterranean Sea—a feat even greater than Moses had performed at the Red Sea, which is a much narrower body of water. On reaching the Mediterranean, his numerous disciples unquestioningly walked into sea. The contemporary Byzantine Church historian, Socrates Scholasticus, noted that many of the disciples were drowned. But the "Messiah" Moses himself disappeared.

The intensified persecutions of the medieval Jews, which resulted from the religious hysteria of the Crusades, saw a lively increase in Messianic claimants. Maimonides mentioned one who had appeared in the south of France but who was killed—how and why it is not known—in 1087. In 1117 another "Messiah" revealed himself to the Jews in Cordova, and still another in Fez about a decade later. But of all these saviours—whether they were self-deluded visionaries or merely adventurers—the first to arrest general Jewish attention was David Alroy. A native of Kurdistan, Persia, he proclaimed himself "the Messiah" about 1160. He assured his followers that God had sent him to free the Jews from the yoke of Islam and to effect their ingathering in the land of their forefathers. He assembled a nondescript army which was soon enough crushed in battle. In the end, Alroy was murdered while asleep.

The imaginative Jews of Yemen were especially susceptible to the Messianic fever. Time and again there appeared among them wild-eyed seers who announced themselves either as "the Messiah" or as his "forerunner." The Yemenite Jews proved enthusiastic, and also unquestioning, followers. When the attention of Maimonides was drawn to the appearance in 1172 in Yemen of a forerunner or herald of the Messiah, he replied in his characteristically common-sense manner, in his famous "Letter to Yemen." He ridiculed all Messianic speculations as futile and irrational, and Messianic claimants as either swindlers or madmen. Twenty years later, in response to a query on that matter by the Jews of Marseilles, he gave as his opinion that "that poor man, although he appeared to be well enough and God fearing, was demented and altogether ignorant. Everything he said or did was either a lie or an illusion."

The ardor with which the esoteric Cabala, combining Jewish Biblical lore and ethics with primitive occultism and numerological magic, was studied during the Middle Ages, only added a new intoxicating ingredient to the Messianic brew. The first of a string of Cabalist-"Messiahs" was Abraham Abulafia, who won notice in the latter half of the thirteenth century. He first drew public attention to himself when he declared his intention of calling on Pope Nicholas II in Rome to effect his conversion to the Jewish religion by means of his secret Cabalistic powers. When the Church authorities in Rome got wind of his plans, they flung him into a dungeon. Believed to be insane, he was finally released, only to turn up again in Messina, Sicily, where he once again announced himself as "the Messiah"; he claimed there that God had spoken to him "face to face," just as He had with Moses. Though he found many adherents among the ignorant and the emotionally unstable, he was publicly branded as a swindler by Solomon ben Adret, a leading rabbi of the day.

Only a few years later, in 1295, another Cabalist, Nissim ben Abraham, presented himself as "the Messiah" in Avila, Spain. He fixed the last day of the Jewish month of Tammuz of that year as the time when he would inaugurate the Messianic age. All those who believed in him started fasting; they gave their possessions and money away, and waited impatiently for the apocalyptic day to arrive. A mercenary impostor, he was eventually exposed, and so he prudently and quietly disappeared. In bitter disenchantment, many of his followers became Christians.

This incident was duplicated, but on a much larger scale, in 1502 in Germany. There the Cabalist Asher Lämmlein had assumed the role of Elijah, the forerunner of the Messiah. He declared 1502 to be the year in which the Saviour would appear. But the inevitable disillusionment to which this led once more resulted in numerous defections from the faith.

Only one generation later, the mystic Cabalists, by

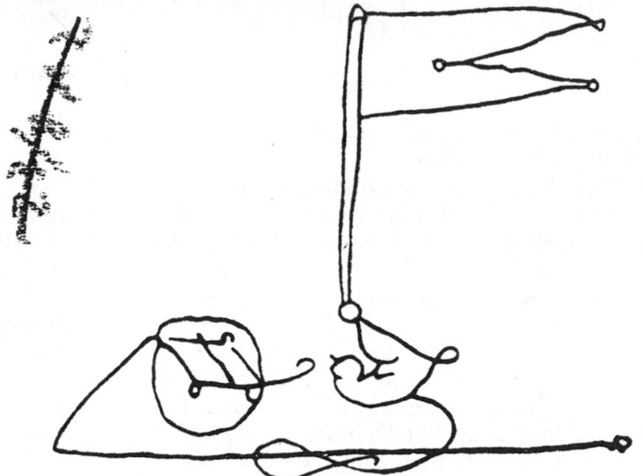

The Cabalistic signature of Solomon Molcho with the Messianic pennant of the Redemption. 1527.

means of their numerological reckoning, had reached with absolute certainty the conclusion that the Messianic era was about to be ushered in. As if by coincidence, in the year 1528 there suddenly appeared out of the east a romantic-looking, self-styled "prince" by the name of David Reubeni. He had come, said he, as the envoy plenipotentiary and extraordinary of his brother Joseph, the ruler of the Jewish kingdom Khaibar, in Arabia. He subsequently made a series of sensational appearances at the royal courts of Europe. On behalf of the Jews of Khaibar, he proposed separately to the Pope in Rome, to the Emperor Charles V, and to King João III of Portugal, a military alliance against the Turks.

The very theatricality of his appearance in Portugal, backed by the Pope's enthusiastic recommendation, excited the wildest interest in him among thousands of Marranos or New Christians, who had been hiding their Jewish loyalties under a pretented Catholicism through dread of the Inquisition. It was a hope for succor by a divine intenvention that prompted them, desperate because of their plight and religious guilt-feelings, to flock to Reubeni and to hail him as "the Messiah." The leader of this "Messianic recognition" among the Marrano Jews of Portugal was the brilliant but mentally unbalanced young intellectual, Diego Pires (1500–32), who under the name of Solomon Molcho, had returned openly to the Jewish fold, despite the dangers, and had become a devotee of the "practical" Cabala.

It was obvious that Reubeni had no intention of playing the Messianic role; he understood only too well the mortal danger in which it would place him—and all the Marranos as well—did the Holy Inquisition of the Church learn of this pretension. But despite the vehemence of his disclaimer that he was "the Messiah," the obsessed Molcho and his Marrano followers would not let go of him. The furor this whole affair aroused eventually led to both Molcho's and Reubeni's imprisonment, trial by the Inquisition, and death.

Nevertheless, the Messianic delirium among the wishful-thinking, the despairing, and the emotionally disturbed, raged on unabated. In fact, it kept on rising in a crescendo of compulsive hysteria. Once again, in 1648, the Cabalists triumphantly were proclaiming that, according to their numerological calculations, *that very year* would see the occurrence of the Redemption. They played up certain popularly held notions. They pointed "convincingly" to the frightful calamities that were then being visited upon the Jews as demonstrable "signs" from Heaven that the Messianic age was about to burst upon them. They emphasized the fact that the Thirty Years' War, in which the Jews of Germany had suffered so grievously, had just come to an end. Infinitely worse, the Cossack and Tatar insurgents, led in their rebellion against their Polish overlords by their hetman, Bogdan Chmielnicki, were still not finished with their side-excursion of mass-slaughtering hundreds of thousands of Jews in the Ukraine, in Poland, and in Galicia. An awareness of all this horror, rolling like a tidal wave of despair over the surviving Jews of Europe, made the Cabalists' fantasies appear entirely credible to the pious.

It was a time of backwardness and intellectual stagnation—their "Dark Ages"—for the Jews of Europe, who from childhood on had been thoroughly indoctrinated with the Messiah-lore, taught how to "recognize" all the "signs"—all the "birth-pangs" of the Mashiach and the Redemption.

Under these desperate circumstances it was not surprising that another self-convinced "Messiah" should make his appearance in answer to the clamor of the bewildered Jews for divine and immediate help. This "Redeemer," possessed of a magnetic personality, was a youth of twenty-one, and his name was Sabbatai Zevi (in Yiddish: Shabsai Tzvi; 1626–76). He had studied the Cabala in his native city of Izmir (Smyrna) and was well versed in every aspect of esoteric Messianic lore. With supreme self-confidence, he announced himself in 1648 as the "Messiah ben David." The Rabbinic Assembly of Smyrna, horrified by his "blasphemous" pretensions, issued against him its most severe excommunication and ordered him to leave the community at once.

But Sabbatai's mere announcement that he was "the Mashiach" unleashed a hitherto unheard of religious hysteria among all the backward elements in the ghettos of Europe.

This popular excitement was intensified when Sabbatai Zevi's claims were championed by Nathan of Gaza. He was an energetic Cabalist-initiate who had elected himself the "forerunner of the Messiah"—the part assigned by legend and tradition to the Prophet Elijah, who was expected to descend from Heaven for that purpose. Nathan wrote grandiloquent pronouncements and issued prophetic-sounding manifestos which he sent by messengers to all the far-flung Jewish communities of Europe, the Near East, and Northern Africa. He exhorted all Jews everywhere to confess their sins, to do penance, and to prepare themselves for the approaching Kingdom of God by renouncing the corrupting goods of the world.

Wherever Sabbatai went, great crowds of hysterical men and women assembled to pay him royal homage as "the Lord's

Execution by the Turks in Sofia in 1680 of Nathan of Gaza (Nathan Ghazzati), the Messianic "prophet" who was the forerunner of Sabbatai Zevi. (From a contemporary engraving).

anointed." Waving palm and myrtle branches (this was also the way the followers of Jesus had greeted his entry into Jerusalem), they met him everywhere with the shout: "Hail to our King Messiah!"

This madness spread like a forest fire. Thousands of devout adherents—Ashkenazim as well as Sefaradim, and also Oriental Jews—flocked to Sabbatai's Messianic standard. Excited deputations arrived from distant countries with worshipful messages and costly gifts for "the Redeemer." Entire communities started preparing themselves for the advent of the Messianic era, at which time Sabbatai Zevi promised he would lead them in triumphal procession to Mount Zion.

A Christian writer in the Ukraine, an eyewitness to the event he was reporting, noted with astonishment: "Some [Jews] abandoned their houses and property. They refused to do any work whatsoever, claiming that the Messiah would soon arrive and would carry them off in a cloud to Jerusalem. Others fasted for days, denying food even to their little ones."

Perhaps "the Messiah" somewhat overdid his boasting when he announced to his followers in 1665 that, in the following year, he would go to Adrianople and drive the Sultan of Turkey, who was also the ruler of the Holy Land, off his throne. Then, he promised, he personally would lead the dispersed remnants of Israel back to Mount Zion, to establish there the Kingdom of God that the Prophets of old had foretold.

But when Sabbatai arrived in Adrianople, the Turkish authorities promptly clapped him in chains and threw him into a dungeon in the fortress of Abydos. Yet, so indestructible was the faith of his followers, that they did not feel the least bit discouraged by his imprisonment. On the contrary, they interpreted the incident as merely being the fulfillment of the the Prophet Isaiah's description of "the suffering Messiah," whom men would despise, mistreat, and persecute before they would be ready to acknowledge him. They actually were confident that the Sultan could do Sabbatai, the "chosen" of God, no physical harm. And so thousands everywhere, while waiting for his expected release, readied themselves for the impending world-shaking climax.

The climax came, but it was not in the awe-inspiring manner that his believers had expected. When Sabbatai Zevi was faced by the Turkish authorities' choice of either becoming a convert to Islam or else suffering decapitation, the "anointed of the Lord" thought well enough of his head to turn Mohammedan.

The shock and disillusionment among the great mass of his adherents after this act of betrayal can be well imagined. They execrated his name and prayed that it should be blotted out forever from the memory of man. Nonetheless, so great was his hypnotic effect on some, that notwithstanding full objective proof of his perfidy, they continued to believe in him and in his "Messianic" election by God. Paradoxically, they even tried to rationalize away his misconduct by all kinds of mystical exegesis and followed his example. The sectarian Mohammedan Dönmeh in Turkey are the present-day descendants of those unyielding adherents of the seventeenth century.

True enough, there appeared several other messianic visionaries and adventurers after Sabbatai Zevi's undoing. But they proved to be ineffectual. This was because the wounds of disenchantment among the Jews after their experience with "the Messiah of Izmir" were so deep and lingering.

Like Judas Iscariot in Christian verbal symbolism, Sabbatai Zevi's name too entered into the vocabulary of contempt among the Yiddish folk in Eastern Europe. The term *shabsaitzvinik* is still being used by the Ultra-Orthodox to describe a religious charlatan, blasphemer, and humbug.

See also CHRISTIANITY, JEWISH ORIGINS OF; CONVERSION OF JEWS; MARRANOS AND THE INQUISITION; MESSIAH, THE; POGROMS IN SLAVIC LANDS.

MEZUZAH (Hebrew s., meaning "doorpost"; pl. MEZUZOT)

Since ancient times, the pious Jew has regarded the mezuzah, like the tefillin (phylacteries) and the tzitzit (ritual fringes), as a symbol of the Jewish faith worthy of the same reverence. The mezuzah is a tubular case of wood, glass, or metal, usually three or four inches in length and containing a small, rectangular piece of parchment, on which, in twenty-two lines, are inscribed in Hebrew the Biblical passages from Deuteronomy (6:4-9 and 11:13-21) which form part of the Shema. It has a small opening near the top to reveal on the reverse side of the parchment the word *Shaddai*, one of the mystical names of God.

The mezuzah, following the Biblical injunction, "And thou shalt write them on the doorposts of thy house and

A 17th-century German engraver's interpretation of the Messianic visions experienced by Sabbatai Zevi.

Delicately wrought mezuzah, showing one of the Hebrew names of God – Shaddai – in the opening. (Courtesy of Joseph B. Horwitz Judaica Collection, Cleveland.)

within thy gates," is nailed in a slanting position on the upper part of the right doorpost at the entrance of the dwelling. Each time he leaves or enters the house, the pious Jew kisses the mezuzah by touching the exposed word Shaddai with the tips of his fingers, which he then presses reverently to his lips, reciting, "May God keep [watch over] my going out and my coming in from now and evermore."

Perhaps the most profoundly religious meaning of the symbolism of the mezuzah was expressed by the great philosopher-rabbi of the Middle Ages, Moses ben Maimon (Maimonides):

> By the commandment of the mezuzah, man is reminded, when entering or departing, of God's Unity, and is stirred into love for him. He is awakened from his slumber and from his vain worldly thoughts to the knowledge that no thing endures in eternity like knowledge of the "Rock of the World." This contemplation brings him back to himself and leads him on to the right path.

Some rabbis in Talmudic and medieval times not as enlightened as Maimonides lent their authority to a far less spiritual conception. They regarded the mezuzah as an amulet against demons, a symbol of God watching over their worldly affairs. This magical notion about the mezuzah is illustrated in several "teaching" anecdotes in the Talmud concerning such Rabbinic luminaries as Judah ha-Nasi and Onkelos.

It is told of the former that, Artaban, the pagan king of Parthia, sent him a gift of a splendid pearl. The Rabbinic Sage responded with a gift of his own—a mezuzah. Outraged by this seeming mockery of him, the king angrily rebuked the Patriarch: "Just see how you insult me! I sent you a gift of great value, and how do you reciprocate?—with a trifle of no value!"

Judah hastened to explain: "What you say is undoubtedly true, but you must consider that the gift you sent me is so costly that I will have to guard it. On the other hand, the gift I gave you *will guard you,* even when you are asleep!"

"In the popular mind," comments the Rev. Dr. A. Cohen in *Everyman's Talmud,* ". . . the mezuzah became an amulet which assured one of the Divine protection." This view is widely concurred in by Jewish scholars. Professor Abraham Z. Idelsohn in *Ceremonies of Judaism* makes the observation: "Just as tzitzit and tefillin originated as charms to protect the body from evil spirits, so also to the mezuzah was ascribed the power of warding off from the house all harm from without. And just as into the former two objects a higher religious conception was later read, so also new meaning was given the mezuzah. The Cabalists, for example, added upon the parchment scroll angels' names, Cabalistic formulas, and graphic symbols, which greatly aroused Maimonides. He condemned them for turning the mezuzah into an amulet for their selfish interests, thus debasing "the fulfillment of a great commandment which has for its end the remembrance of the Unity of God and the love and worship of Him."

The idea behind the mezuzah is not uniquely Jewish. Some other religions make use of like objects. For instance, the ancient Egyptians followed a similar custom, but their emphasis was placed on the magical protective powers of the inscription. Mohammedans, too, inscribe the name of Allah and verses from the Koran over their doors and windows to assure themselves of divine protection.

See also AMULETS.

MIDDAH, MIDDOT. *See* TALMUD, THE.

MIDRASH. *See* TALMUD, THE.

MIGRATIONS OF THE JEWS. *See* DIASPORA; MARRANOS AND THE INQUISITION; MASSACRES: THE CRUSADES AND THE BLACK DEATH; PASSOVER; POGROMS IN SLAVIC LANDS; TEMPLE, THE.

MIKVAH (MIKVEH) (Hebrew, meaning "a collection of water"; namely, a ritual pool or a bathhouse)

The ritual bath or mikvah for many centuries served as one of the physical props of daily ghetto existence. The Jewish woman was traditionally required to go to the mikvah for purposes of religious purification following her menstrual periods and after childbirth and under other specified circumstances. Today, in the inevitably relaxed climate of Jewish religious observance, only the most strictly traditional among the Orthodox women attend the mikvah.

In the ghetto, the mikvah was almost as ubiquitous and as indispensable to religious life as the synagogue, the House of Study (Bet ha-Midrash), the Talmud Torah, and the consecrated cemetery. In fact, every Jewish community was obliged by rabbinical law to maintain a mikvah. If in more recent times in Eastern Europe the women's mikvah sometimes also served as a communal bathhouse for the menfolk, this was perhaps because the straitened circumstances of the local Jews did not also allow them to build and maintain a separate bathhouse for the men. (The latter was a public convenience which had only a hygienic and not a ritualistic character and consequently was not mandatory.) Nonetheless, most sizeable communities since the Middle Ages maintained separately a mikvah for the women and a bathhouse for the men.

In the Latin records of the medieval Church, the Jews' bathhouse was consistently described as the *balneum Judaeorum,* but no reference was apparently made to the mikvah. Possibly one good reason why the Jewish bathhouse for men came into existence in European countries was because both State and Church authorities had sternly prohibited Jews from bathing in the rivers, lakes, and streams, lest they "defile" the waters for Christian bathers.

Astonishingly numerous have been the rabbinical laws and regulations concerning both the physical plant and operation of the mikvah as well as those governing the rite of bathing and its participants. Almost two thousand years ago, the Mishnah Sages devoted an entire tractate to the subject. Exhaustive too in instructions was the sixteenth-century religious manual, the Shulchan Aruch. The mikvah had to be constructed according to rigidly indicated specifications. The work was to be supervised by a rabbi "great in the study of the Torah and in the fear of God." The pool proper was to be filled with not less than 120 gallons of running water and was to be deep enough for complete immersion. The ritual bathing itself was very simple. While standing in the water, the woman bather was required to recite the following benediction in Hebrew: "Blessed art Thou, O Lord our God, King of the Universe, who has sanctified us with Thy

Mikveh (ritual bath). Germany, early 18th century.

commandments and has commanded us concerning the immersion."

Whatever its ritualistic import—and it may be merely a survival of the primitive "purity cult" of the prehistoric Hebrews and later Israelites—the compulsory and periodic bathing of the Jewish woman in the mikvah in former times, when personal hygiene was regarded as of little importance in the non-Jewish world, had a most salutary effect on her health as well as on the health of her family and of the Jewish community in general. In the modern world, where the Jewish woman is provided not only with an enlightened viewpoint and with adequate medical knowledge of personal hygiene but also with bathtubs and showers, except for the most hard-core traditionalists among her sisters, she can see no special benefit accruing to her either in physical cleanliness or in spiritual purification through immersion in the mikvah.

MILAH. *See* CIRCUMCISION.

MILK AND MEAT. *See* MEAT AND MILK.

MINHAG. *See* ASHKENAZIM; PRAYER AND WORSHIP; SEFARADIM.

MINYAN (Hebrew, meaning "count," hence a quorum of ten male worshipers—the number required for holding public prayer)

The institution of the minyan was derived during late Second Temple days from the verse of the Psalmist Asaph: "God standeth in the congregation of the mighty [i.e., men mighty in faith]." (Psalms 82:1.) The Talmud observes: "He who prays with the congregation, his prayer will be answered." And the reason for this: "The Shechinah [God's Presence or Radiance] rests upon ten men when they join together in prayer."

The spiritual superiority of congregational prayer over private devotions was a notion the ancient Rabbis advanced with much conviction. In addition, they felt it created a religious and emotional bond that helped preserve the consciousness of group identity.

The minyan of ten required for public prayer was quite likely built upon the "rulers of ten," the smallest unit in the clan structure that Moses had organized among the Israelite tribes (as discerned in Exodus 18:25). During the Middle Ages, the custom was for each congregation to appoint honorary "minyan-men" who obligated themselves to assemble for all prayer services throughout the year. Sometimes the "minyan-men" were paid, but only poor yeshivah bachurim (Talmud students) and batlanim (men without trade or occupation) who were glad to combine the performance of pious duty with the satisfaction of their hunger, were paid. The twelfth-century rabbi-philosopher of Spain, Maimonides, observed that the intention of this practice of paying the minyan-men, which was even noted in the Jerusalem Talmud, "was that there should be in every place ten men appointed to serve the public well, so that should any communal or religious affair need their attention, they would leave their work and hasten to the synagogue."

See also BURIAL RITES AND CUSTOMS; PRAYER AND WORSHIP; PRAYER SERVICE.

MISHNAH. *See* TALMUD, THE.

MISHNEH TORAH. *See* ARABIC-JEWISH "GOLDEN AGE"; COMMENTARIES, RABBINICAL.

MISNAGED, MISNAGDIM. *See* CHASIDIM.

MISSIONARIES, JEWISH

That there were active Jewish religious missionaries twenty-two centuries ago might perhaps come as a surprise to those who have been accustomed to think of missionaries as being exclusively Christian. The missionary role, observed within the context of Jewish religious beliefs, must have come quite naturally to devout Jews, especially during Hellenistic times, when the overcast sky of Jewish life was convulsed, rent, and illuminated by the lighting of Messianic expectation and the thunder of Judgment Day a-coming. Jews believed they had a special part to play in the imminent redemption of all mankind. They had the absolute conviction—drawn by them from the Bible—that God had most specifically chosen them to serve as "a light for the nations" in order to unite all peoples around the Torah. The exalted objective of this mission was even represented by several Rabbinic teachers as full justification for the Destruction of the Temple and the final Dispersion in 70 C.E. of the Jewish people by the Romans.

In the third century, the Judean moralist, Eleazar ben Pedat, tried to comfort the dispersed remnants of Israel by convincing them that the national catastrophe had not come upon them as divine punishment. Said he: "The Holy One, blessed be He, sent Israel into Exile among the nations only for the purpose of gaining converts."

But Jewish missionaries were active long before the advent of Christianity. An especially vigorous propaganda movement for the Jewish religion had been carried out in the Greco-Roman world during the early Hellenistic era by numerous unprofessional evangelists. These were dedicated zealots, both men and women, who were not unlike Jesus, the Apostles, and Paul of Tarsus. They roamed through all the Mediterranean countries, preaching, teaching, and proselytizing everywhere—in Rome, Greece, Syria (including Antioch), Asia Minor, in North Africa (in Carthage and Cyrenaica), and in other places where substantial Jewish colonies had already long been established. Their successes inevitably stirred up hornets' nests of opposition. This was true especially in Rome, which had had its hands more than full for years, fighting to keep the constantly insurrectionary Judeans subjugated. Even the Roman philosopher Seneca, a man famed for his stoic virtue and temperate outlook, was roused to unphilosophical anger and invective by these Jewish efforts. "The customs of that most criminal nation have gained such strength that they have now been received in all lands; the conquered have given laws to the conquerors," he wrote.

In Rome, as elsewhere, the Jewish missionaries not only won over full proselytes, but they also attracted many thousands of semiproselytes or sympathizers of the Jewish religion, who were called *Metuens*—"devout persons." Although the Metuens observed the Sabbath as a day of rest, attended the synagogue, and listened to the expositions there on the principles of the Torah by the preachers, yet they were not quite ready to go all the way and become converts. Their Judaism was one of degree. An effective discouragement to full conversion was the Rabbinic insistence that every male proselyte had first to submit to the rite of circumcision, a most painful ordeal for adults. This explains why so many more women than men became full proselytes.

Many were the reasons why so many Gentiles embraced Judaism. Part of the explanation lies in the unifying effects Greek culture and language had on the whole Mediterranean world. Because the peoples spoke a common tongue and in many ways possessed similar Hellenistic cultural values, they were brought closer together, and a greater understanding resulted, thus, many preconceived and erroneous notions held by one people regarding another, withered. It was only natural, under such conditions, that each people should borrow from the others in matters of religion, culture, and folkways. This was a period of religious and cultural fusion. Consequently, the Jewish missionaries found their objective not too difficult to attain.

Still another reason for Jewish missionary efforts was demographic. The various invasions of Judea during the Second Commonwealth by Egypt, Greece, Seleucidan Syria, and Rome resulted in constant deportations and resettlements of numerous Jews, not only from Judea itself but from other Jewish colonies abroad. For instance, the "Letter of Aristeas," written by the Jew Aristeas, recounts how, after Ptolemy had completed his conquest of Judea in 301 B.C.E., he deported 100,000 Jews to Egypt and colonized them there in various parts. In addition to such military deportations, there later also took place a large-scale voluntary movement by individual emigrants to foreign lands, especially since Jewish colonies already existed in all parts of the known world. This traffic resulted quite naturally in a lively cultural and economic interchange.

The numerous Jewish settlements in the Diaspora served as bases of operation for the Jewish missionary movement, which, in a phenomenal way, brought large increases in the Jewish population in every land. For these social statistics we have the testimony of the Roman geographer Strabo (*c.* 63 B.C.E.–24 C.E.): "It is not easy to find any place in the habitable world that has not yet received this nation and in which it has not made its power felt."

But the "power" of which Strabo spoke lay principally in the domain of Jewish religious beliefs and ethical practices, for, all in all, the Jews of the world in Strabo's day numbered only from four to six millions. The Greco-Roman slave system was fast disintegrating because of its social evils, cruelties, and economic senselessness. Everywhere, the thoughtful average Roman beheld widespread public corruption and inequities, the ready use of violence, and the resort to plunder and war which were all part of the state policy of their rulers. The vaunted "superior" civilizations of first the Greeks and then the Romans, each of whom, quick to despise everyone else as "barbarians," considered themselves the "master race," had become well rotted with cynicism and immorality. Many Romans, those of the nobility included, being brought into closer contact with Jewish thought and practice, were greatly attracted by the egalitarian and gentle humane features in the Jewish religion and community life. Slaves, especially, were susceptible to the Jewish missionary appeal because they were readily accepted as proselytes and were treated by the Jews if not all at once as equals, at least as human beings, not only as objects to be exploited or bought and sold, like merchandise, for profit.

The unknown Egyptian Jewish woman evangelist of the third century B.C.E. who composed the Third Sibylline Oracle, well expressed the universal goal of all other Jewish missionaries in Hellenistic times when she announced in lofty words: "The Children of Israel shall mark out the path of life to all mortals, for they are the interpreters of God, exalted by Him and bearing a great joy to all mankind!"

The dynamic "mission" of Israel to the Gentiles in Greco-Roman times had been both sparked and greatly aided by the extensive Jewish propaganda literature written in Greek and employing Greek ideas and the familiar Greek terminology and literary allusions. Most influential among these writings in gaining converts were The Wisdom of Solomon, the Book of Ecclesiasticus by Jesus ben Sirach, the Fourth Book of Maccabees, the Sybilline Oracles, and the writings of the philosopher-rabbi of Alexandria, Philo, and the Jewish historian Josephus. Pursuing their missionary ends, these writers extolled the principles and practices of Judaism. Conversely, they tried to lay bare what they regarded to be the fallacies and the moral limitations of the Greco-Roman religion, which, charged Philo, was full of lying inventions. For that reason, he noted, many Gentiles "became sincere worshipers of the truth and gave themselves up to the practice of the purest piety."

Such bold and vehement attacks on the state religion of the "master race" naturally aroused great resentment in Rome as well as in Alexandria. The literati in those great centers wrote many lampoons and diatribes freely misrepresenting and satirizing Jewish religious ideas, customs, and character traits. The most blistering attacks may be found in the writings of Cicero, Horace, Martial, Juvenal, Ovid, and Tacitus.

This Jewish missionary movement, so successful for several centuries in winning converts, both full proselytes and "sympathizers," continued unabated until the time when Christian missionaries entered the field as competitors. They, however, at first had not too much success. But with the ascendancy of the Church and the establishment of Christianity as the state religion by Constantine (in the fourth century), the Jews were driven out of the missionary field entirely in the territories of the Holy Roman Empire and shifted their proselytizing labors into other geographic regions. In Arabia, for example, they made numerous converts. When Mohammed finally came upon the religious scene in the seventh century, he already found in that region a number of powerful tribes that had been converted to the Jewish religion centuries before by the Jews of Yemen. And during the eighth century, another great missionary triumph was scored by the Jews in the vast Khazar kingdom (in the Volga and Don region of Russia), when its ruler, Bulan, together with many of his people, embraced Judaism. They built many synagogues; they learned Hebrew and studied Rabbinic literature under the tutelage of teachers imported from the old Jewish centers.

While it is true that many individual Gentiles even after that time became proselytes, it proved dangerous for any Jew known to have had a hand in converting them. A decree issued in 1235 by the Church Council of Tarragona, in Spain, ruled that any Jew trying to convert a Christian was to be killed and his property and money taken away from him. In addition, the entire Jewish community to which he belonged was to pay a heavy collective fine. Similar stringent steps were taken in states throughout Christendom, so that all Jewish missionary efforts finally ceased.

See also CONVERSION OF JEWS; INTERMARRIAGE; MARRANOS AND THE INQUISITION.

MITZVAH. *See* MITZVOT.

MITZVOT (Hebrew pl. meaning "commandments" or "precepts"; s. MITZVAH; also refers to meritorious or benevolent acts)

With the Rabbinic age, there was general agreement that the number of basic laws, including commandments, statutes, ordinances, and precepts of the Torah, was 613. (In Hebrew common usage these are called *Taryag Mitzvot.*) Following the established pattern of the Ten Commandments, these 613 are also arranged in two categories. The positive or obligatory ones, which are prefaced with the words "Thou shalt," add up to 248; the negative prohibitions, beginning with the words "Thou shalt not," are 365 in number.

To anyone examining these mitzvot, it becomes clear that the Jewish conception of "law" is not the conventional one, neither in character nor in philosophy. It is, in fact, very elastic, and embraces all kinds of values: legal, moral, ethical, social, economic, political, theological, ceremonial, and ritualistic. In short, the Biblical mitzvot make direct reference to the total fabric of Jewish life. This is a unique characteristic which could prevail only in the God-ruled or theocratic Jewish society.

In their larger meaning, the mitzvot constitute, as the novelist Israel Zangwill (1864–1926) so aptly once described them, "a sacred sociology."

The devotion displayed by the plain Jew in his observance of these Biblical commandments remained one of the distinguishing features of the Jewish people in the world. The Jew accepted, without doubt or cavil, the conviction that God was the author of the commandments and that He had personally revealed them to Moses for the instruction—and, consequently, for the salvation—of Israel. To be sure, modern Biblical criticism takes another view; namely, that they were the outgrowth of a long historical development and that, in many ways, they represented a fusion of many religious-social streams and tendencies. Historians aver that this process never really has ceased. Change being a constant in all existence, it was inevitable also that the Biblical precepts would be enlarged and revised by later generations of rabbis.

A clear distinction in the degree of their authority was established between the mitzvot of the Bible and their Rabbinic elaborations and additions. The first kind had to be scrupulously observed; for the latter category a certain freedom for dissent and a latitude in observance was permitted. This flexibility was necessary and inevitable because of differing regional customs in matters of rites and ceremonies which were found to be almost impossible to overcome, even by drastic rabbinic decrees, such a deep hold did they have on the people.

The religious authority of Spain and North Africa, Isaac ben Sheshet (1326–1408), in an opinion he handed down concerning the enforcement of rabbinic regulations, made this point very clear: "We must not presume that such restrictions were fixed Rabbinical ordinances which were meant not to be changed. On the contrary, they were made originally only to meet the [changed] conditions of generations, places and times."

Even though these rabbinic additions and revisions of the Biblical mitzvot added to the already staggering burden of religious practices incumbent on observant Jews, in no way did they diminish the fervor and conscientiousness of performance of the traditionalists. One of the daily prayers in the siddur (the prayer book) reveals the ingenuous attitude of the sincerely pious toward the mitzvot. It runs: "Happy indeed are we! How goodly is our portion! How pleasant our lot! How beautiful our heritage!" For the performance of even one of the lesser mitzvot was considered to be a forward step in the development of a habit which would lead eventually to the performance by the individual of all the other mitzvot.

The more advanced religious thinkers among the Jews, being fully aware that the minutiae of observance could lead only to a sterile formalism in worship, went to great lengths in their teaching to underscore the point that what was of paramount importance was the *moral* value of observance and not its external expression. One Talmudic moralist commented: "How preferable it is to fulfill a [moral] commandment than to light a lamp before God!" Emulating the strictures handed down by the Prophets of old against those businesslike pietists who, by their religious observance, wished, in a manner of speaking, "to make a deal" with God in order to obtain for themselves Eternal Life, one Talmudic Sage remarked scathingly: "Of greater merit is a sin committed with a good intention than a mitzvah performed without it!"

The rewards of salvation, noted Maimonides (the twelfth-century rabbi-philosopher), would be merited alone by him who, even if he performed but one of the 613 commandments, was impelled to perform that one not from any motive of self-interest whatever but "for its own sake, from a sentiment of love."

See also ETHICAL VALUES, JEWISH; LAW, JEWISH; REWARD AND PUNISHMENT; WORLD-TO-COME.

MIZRACH (Hebrew, meaning "east" or "sunrise")

Many were the ways in which the Jew expressed his deeply religious and emotional attachment to the Jewish motherland, especially after the Destruction of the Temple in Jerusalem. One of these was by following the custom—when it originated, no one knows—of hanging a mizrach (a framed picture) on one of the walls of his home. Such a picture hung in every House of Study (Bet ha-Midrash) and in every synagogue in front of the bema (the reading desk). Its sole function was to indicate to the worshipers where lay the direction of Jerusalem, and toward it the pious turned their faces in prayer.

That this was a very ancient custom may be inferred from the Book of Daniel, in which it is stated (in Chapter 6:11) that that Prophet of Babylonian Jewry opened the windows "in his upper chamber toward Jerusalem—and he kneeled upon his knees three times a day, and prayed, and gave thanks before his God . . ." In later times, a Rabbinic decision made this practice general among Jews: "One who dwells outside the land of Israel should turn [in prayer] toward Jerusalem; he who lives in Israel should turn toward Jerusalem; he who lives in Jerusalem should turn toward the Temple; and he who stands within the Temple should turn toward the Holy of Holies." Thus, the Jews living to the east of Jerusalem—in Babylonia, Persia, Arabia, etc.—turned to the west in prayer; similarly those living to the west—as in the countries of Europe—turned to the east.

The mizrach, which only two or three generations ago could have been found in almost every Jewish religious household but today is almost non-existent, was often engraved with Scriptural verses arranged fancifully in the shape of a seven-branched menorah or of a deer (in Hebrew: *tzvi*). Perhaps the most favored of Biblical rubrics for the mizrach was the third verse from Psalm 113:

Mizrach (painted). Alsace, mid-19th century.

Mizrach (embroidered and appliquéd). Alsace, second half of 19th century.

From the rising of the sun unto the going down thereof,
The Lord's name is to be praised.

Although naïve in conception and of negligible artistic worth, the mizrach engravings, illustrative of Biblical incidents and drawn in vignettes, were, to the plain Jew of the folk, eloquent with memories of treasured historic events of the Jewish people. Their subjects varied; they delineated with undisguised sentimentality the Temple in Jerusalem, the Sacrifice of Isaac, the Exodus, Moses either striking the rock or receiving the Ten Commandments, Jacob blessing his grandsons, King Solomon sitting in judgment, King David playing on his harp, the mourning of the Exiles by the waters of Babylon.

See also ART, CEREMONIAL.

MOHAMMED. *See* ISLAM, JEWISH ORIGINS OF.

MOHAMMEDANISM. *See* ISLAM, JEWISH ORIGINS OF.

MOHEL. *See* CIRCUMCISION.

MONASTICISM, JEWISH

The last act in the drama of Judea as the Jewish state and national homeland was played out in an atmosphere of official terror, oppression, and treachery. The suffering of the great mass of Jews had seemingly reached the bottom of the abyss. Where and to whom were they to turn for help or redress? Their own ruling class had become the pliant tool of Imperial Rome and its agent for collaborating in the political suppression and robbing of the Jewish people. Not only the present but the future too appeared totally grim and hopeless. Then, suddenly, there became discernible a startling trend toward mysticism; a sizable number of religious sects with an escape-from-reality coloration sprang into being. The primary purpose of some of them (the Talmud notes that before the Destruction of the Temple, in 70 C.E., there were twenty-four different sects in existence) was to prepare for what they were certain was the imminent coming of the Messiah and his establishment of the righteous Kingdom of God *on earth.*

The sectaries best known to the modern student of that historic period are, of course, the Essenes in Judea, the New Covenanters in Damascus, and the Hellenized Therapeutae in Egypt. All of these not only renounced the world and such of its "illusory" joys as power, possessions, and pleasure, but they also wished to separate themselves from the rest of society and, consequently, from its attendant evils, griefs, and conflicts. By leading morally pure and dedicated lives in special communes or brotherhoods, by engaging in much prayer, Torah study and daily toil, and by scrupulously refraining from any act of injustice toward their fellow men, they hoped to hasten the final Redemption by the Messiah.

Some of these sectarian groups were formed into monastic orders whose members were anxious to remove themselves entirely from the tumultuous and dissonant life of the cities into the hush of the countryside or of the wilderness, where they could strive, unmolested, to achieve holiness, serenity of mind, and a state of spiritual grace.

Such a brotherhood, presumably Essenic, must have been the one that was established at the site of Qumran, on the shores of the Dead Sea, in whose vicinity were accidentally discovered in 1947 the Dead Sea Scrolls (q.v.). The likelihood even exists that it was this identical Jewish monastery which the Roman naturalist, Pliny the Elder, visited nineteen centuries ago. He wrote, in his *Natural History,* that the community there was "remarkable beyond all other tribes [i.e., sects] in the whole world, as it has no women and has renounced all sexual desire, has no money and has only palm-trees for company. Day by day the throng of refugees is recruited to an equal number of numerous accessions of persons tired of life and drawn thither by the waves of fortune to adopt their manners."

Philo, the first-century philosopher-rabbi of Alexandria, who had visited and studied the Essenes at first hand, wrote of them that, by renouncing pleasure, worldliness, and all social intercourse, they hoped to realize their quest for God, virtue, and wisdom. Those living in the monastic brotherhoods observed sexual continence and were opposed to marriage and procreation. They ever strove for priestly purity, especially through frequent bathing and the wearing of clean white apparel, and they tried to follow, in all their actions, a life of holiness and righteousness. Renouncing the tyranny of money and possessions as snares that could lead only to evil, they contributed all material wealth to the common treasury when they entered the brotherhood; there they gave themselves over to self-supporting hard labor in field and workshop. Their leisure time they devoted to prayer, to Torah study, and to spiritual meditation. Eating too was considered to be a form of worship, and they ate their food in silence and meditation.

It would seem from Philo's references to his own inclinations, that he too hungered after the contemplative, ascetic, and monastic life. There undoubtedly must also have been other "sensitive" Jews in those days who were attracted by this escapist utopian mode of living who, nevertheless, did not join one or another of the sects—perhaps because they lacked the requisite courage, or circumstances in their lives over which they had no control prevented them from making the ultimate decision: from, so to speak, burning their worldly bridges behind them.

Apparently, the Jewish monastic brotherhoods (and those of the Essenes in particular) served as the original source of inspiration as well as the pattern for Jesus and his disciples and for the early Jewish-Christians, when they established their first monastic communities. This historic-religious fact might prove somewhat startling today to Jews and Christians both; they might find it hard to visualize Jews as monks—and particularly that their appearance on the historic scene antedated the rise of monasticism in the Church!

Even more monastic and withdrawn from the world than the Essenic communes were the Egyptian-Jewish monks and nuns belonging to the sectarian order of Therapeutae (perhaps meaning "Healers [of their own souls]," from the Greek word for "physicians"). Their monastery was situated on a hill overlooking Lake Mareotis, south of Alexandria. Philo, who during the first decades of the first century C.E. visited these "physicians," noted in his religious-philosophical treatise, "On the Contemplative Life," that each of them occupied a separate cell called a *monasterium*. There they performed their private devotions and, like the Christian monks and nuns of later times, observed austerities, kept prayer-vigils, and performed acts of physical self-mortification. They were abstemious; like Buddhist monks, they ate no meat and drank no intoxicating beverages. They remained sexually continent all their lives and followed a strict discipline in ascetic self-suppression. They were well supplied with sacred books, and devoted much of their time to the study of the Torah (in the Greek or Septuagint version, for few Egyptian Jews knew Hebrew) and to the chanting of the Psalms. They also sang hymns (which no longer exist) composed by their own liturgical poets. These were probably similar to those found among the Dead Sea Scrolls.

The germinal ideas and ideals of Jewish monasticism were apparent in some of the pietistic views expressed by the Pharisee teachers concerning the best way of serving God. There is a saying of a Mishnah Father which describes the kind of existence the student of the Torah is fated for and which illuminates the ascetic trend in certain areas of Jewish religious thinking: "A crust of bread with salt you must eat, sleep upon the ground, and endure a life of hardship while you toil in the Torah." The life of the world was found by some Rabbinic teachers to be corrupt and to have few redeeming virtues. For the good man it was a vale of tears from whose griefs and burdens he could escape only in devoted Torah study and religious worship, with the pious expectation of making himself worthy in the end of a share of bliss in the only "real" world—the World-to-Come.

With the Dispersion, in 70 C.E., the fever of monasticism rapidly died out. This was perhaps due to the fact that the mainstream of Jewish religious tradition, as developed in Talmudic Judaism, flowed on along a rationalistic and affirmative course; it held to the conviction that man was by nature perfectable and that life on earth was good and was to be enjoyed. And although the medieval Cabalists observed austerities and practiced mortifications of the flesh as part of their ascetic ideal, believing that self-purgation was necessary to attain freedom from carnal despotism, they never really separated themselves from the mainstream of Jewish life. Unlike the ancient Essenes, New Covenanters, and Therapeutae, they formed no monastic communities.

See also ASCETICS, JEWISH; ESSENES; POST-BIBLICAL WRITINGS; THERAPEUTAE.

MONEYLENDERS

Biblical law stands in uncompromising opposition not only to usury, but to charging any interest at all on loans. "Take thou no interest of him or increase," sternly admonishes the Biblical moralist in Leviticus 25:36. Rabbinic teachings of the Talmudic age equally expressed a revulsion for the profit-seeking moneylender. It compared him unflatteringly with the murderer, saying that in the Hereafter, each of those "shedders of blood" would be unable to make sufficient atonement for his crimes.

In the developing values of Jewish ethics, the conception of practical benevolence was constantly being extended and refined. Lending money to others was regarded merely as another form of "loving-kindness." In fact, the Talmud raises severe strictures against the lender's taking any interest whatsoever on loans of any kind. The repayment of a loan was not considered part of a business transaction but, rather, a moral obligation.

Despite the outright Scriptural prohibition against them, however, professional moneylenders most certainly did exist in ancient Judea, nor could they be suppressed. They extracted high rates of interest from the needy, in hard times, especially. Their sordid preying on the poor aroused the indignation of the Sages of the Talmud, who pointed with incredulity to their naked greed: "Behold the folly of the usurer! Were a man to call him a scoundrel, he would surely fight with him to the death. Nonetheless, out of his own free will, he takes up writing materials and, in the presence of witnesses, proceeds to write himself down as a rascal and as a blasphemer of the God of Israel."

It is a grim irony of history that the Jews, perhaps the only people of ancient times whose religious laws and ethical practices *condemned* usury and made a social reprobate of the usurer, should have been the very ones to be forced into that sordid calling and be branded, reviled, and harassed as heartless, grasping "usurers" by their Christian enemies. From the Middle Ages on, it became proverbial (for that matter, it still is, among many Gentiles), when the word "Jew" was mentioned, immediately to conjure up the repellent, stereotyped image of a moneylender: a kind of human spider who deviously spun his web of greed, in which he caught his Christian victims, wringing from them a conscienceless rate of interest. The epithets "Jew" and "usurer" took on a synonomous meaning, aided, no doubt, by the fact that Bernard of Clairvaux, the religious mentor of the Second Crusade, had coined the French word *judaizare* to mean "usury." And no less eminent a writer than Sir Francis Bacon (sixteenth century) urged in his essay *Of Usury* that all usurers (in this case, Christians, for in his day there were no Jews allowed in England) should be forced to wear a recognizable mark of their shameful occupation; viz., "orange-tawny bonnets [the familiar identifying color Jews were required to wear during the Middle Ages before their expulsion from England in 1290] because they do *judaize*."

This rubber-stamped caricature of the Jew, which has been clung to so tenaciously even to our own day, had, of course, historic roots. In feudal society, the Jews were considered and treated as "outlanders." Being social outcasts, they had no legal, social, or economic status, but were juridically classified as *servi camerae* or Kammerknecht—"the king's servants" or "chattels." Like all personal property, they could be transferred, pawned, or sold outright by the rulers, the higher barons, and the princes of the Church. Their opportunities for earning a livelihood were painfully limited. Though it is true that their circumstances may have varied in different places and from one century to another, yet certain conditions that were constant handicapped Jews everywhere. They could not belong to Christian trade or merchant guilds nor could they form their own (except in Prague, where there were a few Jewish artisan guilds); they could own neither house nor land, and they were strictly enjoined from engaging in farming.

For limited periods of time they were tolerated as doctors, and in this profession they excelled. But when the medical schools of Europe began turning out sufficient numbers of competent Christian doctors, the Church officially placed the papal ban on Jewish healers for Christian patients, and the field of medicine too was practically closed to Jews. Unhappily, occupations which still remained open to Jews by law were limited to the despised "coarse" or "marginal" trades such as junk-dealing, street-hawking, the buying of old clothes and bones, and—lastly and most hazardously—moneylending, moneychanging, and pawnbroking, all three being usually united in one establishment.

Not only were the vast majority of ghetto dwellers not moneylenders, they were extremely poor, scratching out an uncertain livelihood by working at marginal trades like that of this "old clo'" man on New York's East Side. About 1900.

Until the Third Lateran Council of 1179 passed a decree against it, moneylending had been a highly profitable activity of the Church itself. But after passage of the decree, lending at interest (or "usury," as it was called then) was prohibited by canon law for all Christians. The theological reasoning behind this was that engaging in usury was a threefold sin: It was a violation of natural law, since, unlike the owning of a field that was cultivated, a house, or a workshop producing useful things, moneylending was a barren activity. Moreover, it worked against the social welfare in that it imposed cruel hardship upon the poor, who were, too often, its doubtful beneficiaries. Had not a Biblical injunction specifically outlawed the practice in protective concern for the economically submerged and helpless part of society?

To implement the Lateran Council edict, one Church council after another threatened violators with a denial of the consolation of the sacraments and of Christian burial. The curb was effective only to some extent, because the profits from usury were so great that many Christian moneylenders continued either to ignore or to defy the ban and the reprisals threatened by the Church.

The Church, which aimed, through this edict against moneylending, to curb the abuses attendant on the conscienceless extortion of the poor by the rapacious lender, inadvertently hit a snag. The Church's action was initiated from generous ethical and religious motives, but it failed to take cognizance of the realities and historic developments. What had made the moneylenders—whatever the sordid aspects of their traffic—during the late Middle Ages more necessary than ever before was the silent, almost imperceptible, revolution that was taking place in the economy and social structure of feudal Europe. The primitive system of barter was making way for a more efficient money-economy, and a new middle class, fighting energetically for its rightful place in the sun, was emerging in the cities and towns. With the rapid growth of manufacturing, commerce became an international affair, and by the fourteenth century, profit-seeking enterprises urgently needed "liquid capital": money. For this, the moneylenders—the bankers of feudal society—were found indispensable. They were indispensable, likewise, for the rulers and great barons of Europe, for they made it possible for them to live in ostentation and luxury, to equip and maintain armies, and to launch navies so they could fight expensive wars. Business records of moneylending activities during the Middle Ages and Renaissance that are still extant all point to the great importance of moneylenders in turning the wheels of the wasteful robber-system of feudalism.

"Starr" of Aaron of Lincoln, dated 1181, showing Aaron's Hebrew signature on the receipt, in Latin, for part payment from Richard Malebys, the organizer of the York Massacre in 1190.

No less necessary than the large loans detailed above, although unrecorded, by and large, in history, were the innumerable small loans extended to the plain people. Great numbers of these, driven to desperation by their poverty, sought brief and illusory relief from the spiderous moneylenders, to whom they pawned their pitiable household and personal possessions for small advances of money. But now that the Church had sternly forbidden Christians to engage in moneylending, how would the poor manage?

At this critical juncture, entered the Jews (and in Spain, the Moors, as well) upon the scene. They stepped forward to fill the commercial vacuum being created by the Church prohibition. Conveniently, the Christian authorities exempted the Jews from the provisions of the ban. Why? Because, unlike Christians, who could look forward to achieving salvation—provided they repented in time—the Jews, belonging to an economically depressed and deprived group, treated consistently as enemy aliens in their own native lands, were considered already accursed since they had rejected Jesus as the Messiah. And so, because they were damned anyway, the sin of usury could hardly increase their total wickedness, which was, according to the Church, abysmal.

Let it be said that the Jews did not always become moneylenders of their own free will. Numerous were the instances when they entered this (for them) new calling, either through coercion, as in England before their expulsion in 1290, or by the unexpected benevolence displayed in a formal "invitation" from king and baron, from pope, bishop, or municipal authorities. For despite the edict of the Church, the lucrative business of lending money proved too alluring for those Christians long active in the field for them to abandon it without a struggle. This was particularly true of the Christian moneylenders from Lombardy and Tuscany, who were notorious for their unrestrained greed. (Their methods so incensed the poet Dante that he dispatched them in his *Inferno*—although with but vicarious satisfaction—down to the seventh and lowest purgatory.) The nefarious practices of these Lombards had been a public scandal for such a long time that in 1409, the Merchants Guild of Brindisi—and this is only one of numerous instances—urgently petitioned the authorities to allow the Jewish moneylenders, who had previously been expelled from the town, to return in order that "the greed of the Christian usurers be checked."

It is curious that in Venice, during the Renaissance, where there were active both Christian and Jewish moneylenders, the former were permitted to charge as much as 40 per cent interest on loans, but the latter, at the risk of heavy fine, imprisonment, or explusion, were forbidden to take more than 5 per cent. This strange "discrimination" was noted by Thomas Wilson when he complained in his "Discourse on Usury" (written in 1572) that England had done great economic injury to herself when she had permanently expelled the Jews: "Go where you will through Christendom and you shall have of the Jews under ten [per cent] in the hundred, yea, sometimes for five, whereas our English usurers exceed all God's mercy."

In the light of these observations, the portrayal by Shakespeare of the Jewish moneylender, Shylock, in *The Merchant of Venice* as a merciless bloodsucker, appears, historically speaking, to be not only incorrect but, from the moral point of view, a dismal slander.

It is perhaps superfluous to observe that Jewish moneylenders were hated by those to whom they lent money not only because of the downright inconvenience of having to pay back the loans plus high interest—not only because they *were* hateful moneylenders—but because they were *also Jews*. The myth of the Jew as a moral monster had been sedulously built up through the centuries by Christians playing on religious bigotry, ignorance, and the need for a ready scapegoat they could blame for all the troubles and crimes that took place in society. Actually, at no time did the Jewish moneylenders constitute more than a small group—and then one only secondary in importance to the infinitely larger and more affluent Christian moneylenders, even during the period when the Church ban was technically in force.

It should also be kept in mind that the overwhelming number of Jews in Europe were *not* moneylenders. For the most part, they remained economically rootless and wretchedly poor, so to speak living off one another in submarginal ways.

The notion, quite generally held, even by the knowledgeable, that the Jewish moneylenders, could in buzzard fashion, lay down their own conditions governing the borrowers' collateral of pledged and/or pawned possessions or property and charge whatever interest "the traffic would bear," is almost completely a myth. The true fact is that the rate of interest was fixed by contract beforehand by the authorities and by the Christian moneylenders themselves. In Prague, the law read: "The Jews may take interest at the rate of five pfennig in the mark, six pfennig in the pound, and one pfennig in thirty." They had neither free rein for their alleged cupidity nor possible arena for it. They had to keep account books which were closely examined. And not only were they required to pay the ruling powers a giant share of their profits for the privilege of lending money, but, as soon as a fortune was amassed by a Jewish lender, most of it quickly found its way, by a variety of confiscatory actions, levies, "contributions," fines, and "taxes," into a well-ordered, descending hierarchy of bottomless pockets.

Quite frequently, the contract between a Jewish moneylender and an individual ruler or a municipality, in its final outcome, turned out to be merely of one-sided benefit. While the Jew, with the threat of the most horrendous penalties hanging over him, was expected to abide strictly by the rules and terms agreed upon, the authorities involved, by summary action, often rearranged matters to suit themselves. The latter also took a surprisingly lenient view when Chris-

Jewish moneylender at his calculating device (abacus?) being solicited for a loan by a Christian peasant. Augsburg, Germany, 1531.

Polish Jewish moneylender and currency dealer, 1841. (The Jewish Museum.)

tian borrowers of rank or wealth chose to revise unilaterally—in their own favor, of course—the conditions under which they had obtained their loans from the Jewish moneylenders, or even to default on their repayment altogether.

Common enough, too, was the practice of some ruling princes who, wishing to curry favor with their subjects, for whatever political ends, would declare a general moratorium on all debts to Jewish moneylenders. Perhaps the most notorious instance of this took place when the Crusaders left to fight the infidel Saracens in the Holy Land. By special dispensation of Church and State, the "Soldiers of Christ" were freed from the moral and legal obligation of repaying the loans they had gotten from "the Jew-usurers." In the final reckoning, moneylending, as a career for Jews, proved to be, most of the time, a will-of-the-wisp and near-distastrous calling.

Violent attacks on Jewish moneylenders grew both in extent and intensity after the Black Death epidemic and its aftermath of acute suffering among the Christian survivors. The onslaughts were led by Franciscan and Dominican friars, the most blood-lusting of them being the Italian Franciscans John of Capistrano (1386–1456), the Papal Inquisitor who was honored as "the Scourge of the Jews," and Bernardino de Feltre (1439–94) whom Pope Gregory XIII revered as a prophet. The near-contemporary Jewish writer, Joseph Colon, added this observation to his chronicle of these tumultuous happenings: "Thirty years ago conditions were better until the preachers [Franciscan monks] appeared in great numbers. They were a scourge to Israel. Each day they wished to destroy us, so that our lives and possessions were in constant jeopardy." This continuous agitation against the Jewish "usurers" furnished ready pretexts for massacres and riots.

Moneylending for the Jew brought other occupational hazards as well. Powerful debtors often threw the Jewish lender into prison or, on occasion and more conveniently, murdered him when he had the temerity to demand repayment or even ask for the interest on the loan. In Slavic countries—and this happened only too frequently and as recently as the nineteenth century—whenever a landowner or a tradesman wished to default on his loan to a Jew, all he had to do was to incite his neighbors with an outcry against the "Jew-usurer." A number of pogroms were sparked that way.

When, in the midde of the fifteenth century, the Church decided to re-enter the lucrative field of moneylending, Pope Leo X prudently nullified the three-hundred-year-old edict against the sin of usury. He no longer gave it that uncomplimentary designation but referred to it as a "holy work," since its ostensible purpose was to help the poor. The moneylending, moneychanging, and pawnbroking establishments which the Church opened everywhere, were given the lofty name of *Monti di Pieta*, namely, "Mounts of Piety." Yet, need for the private moneylenders was still present. Soon, however, the irrepressible Lombards pushed out most of the Jewish moneylenders from the field of large-scale loans, where the latter had never really been too prominent. With a few notable exceptions, Jewish moneylenders thenceforth engaged only in small loans against pledged articles. When the modern banking system came into being, they drifted, in a quite natural way, into pawnbroking, which always was a traditional department of moneylending.

See also CHARITY; CHURCH AND PERSECUTION; ENLIGHTENMENT, THE JEWISH; GHETTO; LOANS, FREE; MASSACRES; NAZIS, THE; PERSECUTION IN "MODERN" DRESS; POGROMS IN SLAVIC LANDS; SHYLOCK MYTH, THE.

MONOGAMY

"When in Rome, do as the Romans do," is an adage that well reflects the pressure of custom upon individuals for conformity. Its application to the institution of marriage among Jews demonstrates how, living in a society in which polygamy was generally practiced, it was hardly possible for them also not to conform and be polygamous, especially since there was no Bibical law forbidding polygamy.

That the Hebrews and Israelites had practiced polygamy for centuries during the earlier periods of Jewish history may be plainly seen in the Biblical narrative about the Patriarchs Abraham, Isaac, and Jacob. Each had more than one wife—a statistical fact which is mentioned with the utmost simplicity by the Scriptural chronicler.

Until the return of the captives from the Babylonian Exile, beginning with 538 B.C.E., the institution of marriage among Jews had many features in common with the same institution in the Assyrian-Babylonian empire. No one in that age presumed to question the legal and moral justification for having plural wives; women were merely chattels and were classified as "property." Custom dictated that there be one principal wife and one or more additional ones of lesser marital rank (these were actually concubines). The Bible did not question the morality of Abraham who, while being wedded to Sarah, "married" Hagar, who held only a subsidiary marital status. The same held true of Jacob who, although married to two principal wives—Rachel and Leah—took Bilhah and Zilpah as secondary wives or concubines—a relationship that, in the morality of society today, is hard to reconcile with marriage.

It is fairly certain from an attentive study of the Bible that, in time, the practice of polygamy came to be looked upon with disfavor by Jewish religious leaders. This attitude crystallized with the steady development of a Jewish moral philosophy which embraced all human relations, that of marriage included. It may be noticed more sharply after Ezra and the Scribes had successfully instituted their religious reformation in Judah, and moral scruples about the possession of more than one wife made their appearance in Jewish religious writings. Initial signs of these misgivings are discovered in the older Scriptural works upon which Ezra and the Scribes possibly may have superimposed some of their own more advanced social and moral views. The Book of Genesis, for example, contains (in Chapter 2:24) a statement which clearly implies that the marital union should be consummat-

Grave of Rabbenu Gershom (960–1040)—"The Light of the Exile"—who issued the ban against polygamy. Mainz cemetery, Germany.

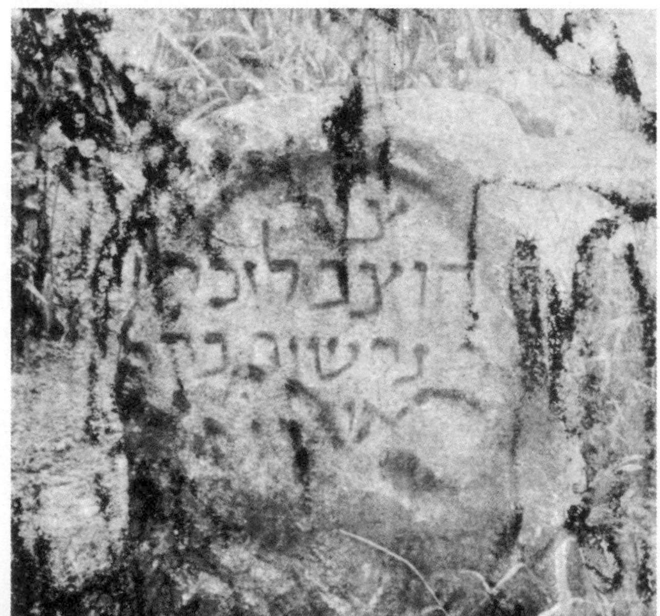

ed with one woman only: "Therefore shall a man leave his father and mother and shall cleave unto his wife, and they shall be one flesh." And in Deuteronomy 17:17, the polygamous relationship is censured as a moral evil: "Neither shall he multiply wives unto himself."

Especially noticeable is the emergence of the preference for monogamy expressed in the Wisdom Literature of the Bible and in the Apocrypha. The most memorable is the famous eulogy to the good wife and mother–commonly known as "A Woman of Valor"–in Proverbs 31:30-13. It should also be noted that in the Book of Job, probably a work of contemporary composition, its tragic hero is married to only one woman. By no means to be overlooked is the fact that the high priest in Jerusalem was not permitted to have more than one wife.

It has been argued quite convincingly that polygamy was discouraged among the Jews by ringing it about in the Bible with certain vested property-and-inheritance stipulations to protect the wife and her children; thus, only the kings, the nobility, and the rich could afford the "luxury" of having several wives at one time. For that reason, it was possible for a Christian contemporary of the Rabbinic Sages in the second century, Justin Martyr, to observe–although without any attempt at criticism–that the wealthy Jews of his day were allowed by Jewish custom to have as many as four or five wives at one time.

It was not until about the year 1000 that a great rabbinical synod was convoked in the town of Worms in the Franco-German Rhineland, to take action on the problem of polygamy. Under the leadership of the foremost religious authority of the day, Rabbenu Gershom ("Our Teacher" Gershom ben Judah, 960–1040), who was worshipfully referred to by the pious as "the Light of the Exile," a prohibition against polygamy, validated on legal, moral, and humanitarian grounds, was enacted. Those Jews ignoring the prohibition were declared by the synod to be subject to the extreme penalty of rabbinic excommunication.

However, the authority of this law–although ultramontane almost everywhere in the Christian West, where it took no great effort on the part of the Jews to conform to the prevailing institution of the monogamous marriage–did not extend into Mohammedan countries in the Near and Middle East and into Moorish Spain. In those places, as is well known, the harem was a long-established institution that had been fully sanctioned by the teachings and example of the Prophet Mohammed and by the Islamic scriptures, the Koran. In those regions, the Jews, like their non-Jewish neighbors, practiced polygamy as a matter of course. Although the philosopher-rabbi Maimonides (twelfth century), residing in a Mohammedan environment (Spain), was himself married to only one woman, he tolerantly observed that, at least theoretically, on the basis of Biblical and Rabbinic law, it was permissible for a Jew to have as many wives as he pleased–on condition, of course, that he was able to provide properly for them.

Not all Jews in the Arabic milieu were in agreement with Maimonides; they soon began to feel the religious-social pressures from the rest of the Jews in the world. It was not long before the ketubah (the marriage agreement) carried a clause wherein the groom solemnly swore that, in the lifetime of the woman he was taking to wife, he would not wed another. Nevertheless, in Near Eastern lands, there were prosperous Jews who, until very recent years, were content to enjoy the vexations as well as the pleasures of more than one wife.

See also FAMILY, THE; KETUBAH; MARRIAGE; MARRIAGE AND SEX; WOMAN, THE TREATMENT OF.

MONOTHEISM

Only a very few ideas in the history of human progress have had as decisive an effect on the course of civilization as Jewish *ethical* monotheism. The great majority of knowledgeable people is in agreement on the fact that the epochal contribution of the Jews to the religious thought of the world was their development of the One God idea. Just the same, the Jews were neither the only people, nor even the first one, to attempt to grope their uncertain way from animism to polytheism to monolatry (henotheism), through the tangled jungles of fetishism, taboos, and magic, and from there to go on in search of one Supreme Being.

In actuality, an approximate form of monotheism was achieved in Egypt by Akhenaton (Amenophis IV, of the Eighteenth Dynasty) *c.* 1370 B.C.E. which was about 150 years before Moses, and by Zoroaster in Persia, during the tenth century B.C.E. Yet neither of their religions could compare with the monotheism that was developed by Moses and by his known and unknown continuators, whose ideas were blended with his in the Torah.

The true significance of the Jewish contribution was that, after having reached the conclusion that there was only One God, the Jews had gone on to universalize and spiritualize their conception of him in socially idealistic and ethical terms. Not that spiritual ideas and moral standards were lacking in either Akhenaton's Aton-religion or in Zoroastrianism. It was only that the Jews advanced much farther and more significantly in that direction–primarily, no doubt, because the circumstances of their group-life and history made it possible. Having conceived of God as a Moral Being who possessed all the perfections and the ideal attributes of holiness, righteousness, truth, justice, love, and mercy, they proceeded from there with consequential logic to the formulation of the next postulate. This was that, since man had been created by God in His divine image, man was duty bound to emulate Him in the practice of all His virtues. The Imitation of God (in Latin: *Imitatione Dei*) became an ardent striving, first in the Jewish religion and then in Christianity.

The ancient Midrash eloquently defined this supreme responsibility of man: "To love God and to cleave to Him means to try to be like Him. Even as He is just, so must you be just; even as He is merciful, so must you extend mercy; and even as He is the God of Truth, so must you be truthful."

In the millennial process of growth and refinement, the Jews were able to develop during the centuries of the Prophetic and Rabbinic ages a comprehensive system of spiritual and intellectual ideas: morals, laws, and ethics for governing the conduct of their lives both individually and collectively. A unitary, *just* God (they thought) had to be equated with a unitary, *just* human race, which He had created, in order to validate the moral purpose of existence. So–probably for the first time in history–there was enunciated a doctrine which affirmed the equality and the brotherhood of mankind: one that was complementary to the central doctrine of the Jewish religion–the Fatherhood of God. "Have we not all one Father?" asked Malachi, the Prophet of universalism. "Hath not One God created us? Why do we deal treacherously every man against his brother?" (Malachi 2:10.)

The ethical monotheism of the Jews gave a fresh direction to religious aspiration and to moral and social thinking.

There is reason to believe that, at least in some ancient religions, there were, broadly speaking, recognizable not one but two or more distinct levels of religious comprehension

Stone altar or upright pillar (matzebah) excavated at Ras Shamra, in southern Syria. Contemporary with the Age of the Patriarchs (probably 2000 B.C.E–1700 B.C.E.). "And Jacob set up a pillar in the place where He spoke with Him, a pillar of stone, and he poured out a drink-offering thereon, and poured oil thereon." (Genesis 35:14.)

and sensibility. In these religions, the great mass of believers was kept ignorant and submissive to priestly authority. The manner of their upbringing must have been such that it made them want to follow unquestioningly along the well-trodden road of their overinstitutionalized religion–one that was ridden with the notions, rites, and practices of primitive barbarism.

Yet at the very same time there were to be found among these animists a small number of thinking individuals who, with strength of character and a passion for truth, stood in their religious ideas far above and in advance of their benighted age. Such nonconformist thinkers–the great Egyptian reformer-king Akhenaton is the first to come to mind–were powerless to move their fellow-religionists from their backwardness and inertia. Of these men there may remain little more than a haunting memory–perhaps a few hieroglyphic or cuneiform inscriptions or a handful of delicate verses–to remind one that their ardent efforts, like chance comets, flashed for a brief moment across the darkened sky.

It was different, however, in the instance of the "One God" idealists among the ancient Israelites. What the factors were that made them succeed where other iconoclasts failed remain conjectural because of the paucity of extant data. Yet, without doubt, some of the reasons for explaining the ultimate triumph of ethical monotheism are to be found in the Bible itself.

First of all, there was the all-around greatness of Moses. Armed with a heroic will, he followed an inner light which never seemed to grow dim for him. And–what is most rare in dedicated idealists and dreamers–he possessed a genius for practical leadership and an organizational skill of such remarkable character that before he died, he was able to turn his dream into a reality. His supreme achievement was that he was able to transform what had been originally a horde of runaway slaves and "a mixed multitude," sunk in ignorance and barbarism, into a reasonably homogeneous people submitting to the discipline of a superior religious-moral code. And if, as actually happened, following the conquest of Canaan and the establishment of the despotic monarchial system, Israel's leaders allowed the standard of ethical monotheism that they had inherited from Moses to fall from their listless hands and thus bring about a general retreat into religious primitivism, the Prophets came forward to raise it high again. They did not lay it down even in the face of the most bitter persecution. In fact, they extended and deepened the spiritual and social teachings of Moses; they laid down the broad base from which, centuries later, Ezra, the Men of the Great Assembly and the Rabbinic Sages (*see* TALMUD, THE) could build what has been declared to be the purest system of ethical monotheism ever evolved.

It was, indeed, a great distance in religious ideas, spiritual values, and moral laws and sentiments that Israel traversed since its resettlement in Canaan. Even during the entire period of Solomon's Temple (down to 586 B.C.E.) the general conception of God was primitive and antithetical to Mosaic and Prophetic teachings. The Deity was endowed then with both the flattering and unflattering characteristics of humans (anthropomorphisms). He was regarded as the tribal "Lord of Hosts" whose Holy Ark, in which He was supposed to dwell, was carried as a palladium into battle by his special votaries, the Israelites, to assure their victory over the enemy. There could be no doubt of it: He was a terror-inspiring God bearing a close resemblance to Baal and Moloch. It must have been an early psalmist who created this frightening image of YHVH (the not-to-be-pronounced Name of God):

> Then the earth did shake and quake,
> The foundations also of the mountains did tremble;
> They were shaken, because he was wroth.
> Smoke arose up in his nostrils,
> And fire out of his mouth did devour;
> Coals flamed forth from him.
>
> PSALMS 18:8-9

It was a far cry from this symbolic projection of God as a mighty and angry idol to the loving Father of Mankind portrayed by the Prophet Micah (late in the eighth century B.C.E.). This selfsame God is speaking: "And what the Lord doth require of thee, only to do justly, and to love mercy, and to walk humbly with thy God." (Micah 6:8.)

An ancient Egyptian bringing the "first fruits" of his produce as offering to the Asherah (holy tree). Tree-worship was common in most religions. ". . . and throw down the altar of Baal that thy father hath, and cut down the Asherah that is by it . . ." (Judges 6:25.)

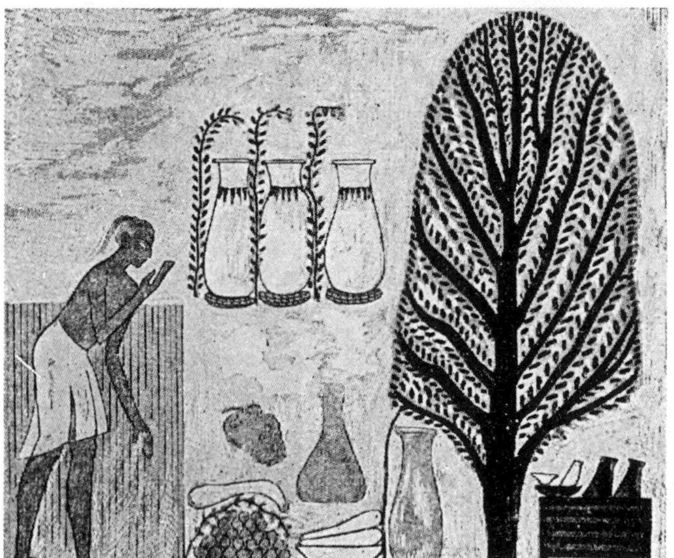

The Mishnah teacher Akiba (60-135 C.E.) used to say: "Beloved is man, for he was created in the image of God, and it was by a special sign of God's love that he came to know it." (Pirke Abot.)

It is axiomatic that the moral ideas and ideal values of the Jewish religion were not created in a vacuum but in a cultural continuum. It took more than one thousand years of dedicated striving–of retrogression as well as advance, since progress never moves in a straight line toward its goals–until the high peak of Rabbinic Judaism was reached just before the Destruction of the Second Temple in 70 C.E.

But in measuring the advances that were made, it becomes unavoidable to note also the many retreats to primitivism. The latter occurred more often in Jewish history than is sometimes realized. Though some among the devout find it distasteful to be reminded of these lapses by their ancient Israelite ancestors, yet the Bible itself, ever steadfast to the truth, makes careful note, as of matters of the greatest moment, of these barbarisms or backslidings, even though painful. For the modern person, to know what the early and less flattering stages were in the evolution of the Jewish religion is to appreciate to the fullest extent the Jewish achievement in ethical monotheism.

It goes without saying that at some remote period in their history, all the most advanced peoples of today evolved from a state of barbaric culture closely resembling that of primitive peoples of today. According to all the proofs found in the Bible, including those discovered in recent times by Biblical archaeologists, the Jews, too, passed through a comparable evolution. The Jewish Scriptures, points out James G. Frazer, the great English anthropologist, contain "many references to beliefs and practices that can hardly be explained except on the supposition that they are rudimentary survivals from a far lower level of culture." Among such survivals he lists "the sacrifice of the first-born . . . and the custom of the scapegoat."

The unfolding of Jewish religious ideas–and in particular of the different group-conceptions of God–were intimately bound up with the changing forms of the social organization and economic systems of Israel. During the relatively uninvolved nomadic period, when the group-economy had a pastoral character, the majority of Israelites were apparently as completely animistic as their equally primitive neighbors, the Moabites, Amorites, Canaanites, etc. They, too, were held in thrall by the mysterious forces in nature and stood in fear of the invisible powers which, they were certain, infested all creation and which they strove to placate by every material and magical means possible. They worshiped fetishes and brought numerous sacrifices, human as well as animal and vegetable. They practiced divination, performed magic, and observed rigid tribal taboos in the manner of all undeveloped peoples.

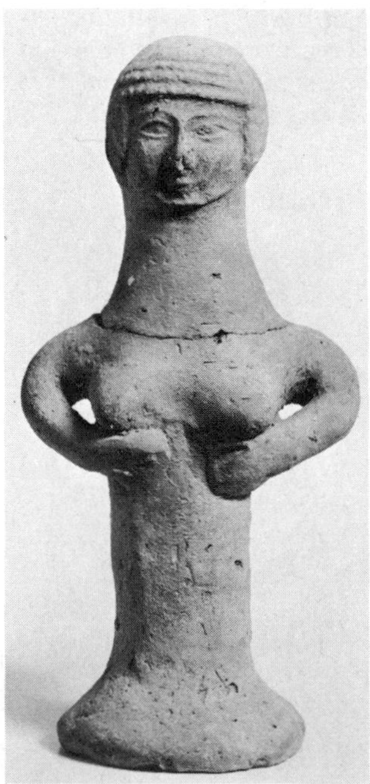

Earthenware figurine, dug up in Palestine, of Astarte (in Hebrew: Ashtoret), the love and fertility goddess of the Phoenicians. Many among the ancient Israelites worshipped Ashtoret at the same time that they sacrificed to YHVH as chief among the gods. Palestine, 1000 B.C.E.–586 B.C.E. (The Metropolitan Museum of Art.)

In the normal process of social and cultural development, after the Israelites (and their neighbors) had finally settled down to an agricultural existence and to the development of town life, they found the necessary conditions for moving forward from animism to polytheism, the religion of many gods. But into the latter they also carried over many of their earlier superstitious beliefs and barbarous practices, as can be readily ascertained by reading the Scriptural texts.

The modern Bible student, armed with some knowledge of comparative religion and anthropology and having an awareness of the continuous process of cultural diffusion, is bound to come to a significant conclusion. It is that, in the course of its long and unbroken history, the Jewish people accumulated a miscellany of highly variegated beliefs, moral values, rites, ceremonies, myths, and folkways. Many of those it created by itself out of the historic circumstances and special character of Jewish group existence, just as a silkworm draws its unique being out of its own cocoon. But there were many others which, in normal cultural interchange, it either borrowed in their entirety or adapted from the beliefs and practices of its animistic and polytheistic neighbors in the Fertile Crescent.

Like geologic rock formations, these disparate elements in the early Jewish religion lay bare some baffling, and often contradictory, strata of development. They did not necessarily emerge, as many people believe, in a well-defined and chronologically ordered sequence. For such is the paradox of history: Ideas—whether intellectual, religious, social, or ethical—do *not necessarily* advance in unbroken progression from a lower to a higher level. Often enough—as the sharp decline during the First Temple period of the ethical monotheism that had been taught by Moses and the Prophets illustrates—they zigzag in a curiously erratic manner, moving forward during one historic period only to recede in the next, but after that, happily, advancing again.

It is possible to reconstruct from numerous passages in the Bible about fetish- and idol-worship (expressed in terms of prohibition, admonition, exhortation, and condemnation) what the character of Jewish religion may have been like until the beginning of the Babylonian Captivity in 586 B.C.E. We find, for example, that the early Israelites in the Patriarchal period were devoted to teraphim (these, conjecturally, were images of family gods—possibly analogous to the lares and penates of the Romans). They worshiped sacred stones (in Hebrew: *matzebot*; s. *matzebah*); totems; sacred groves (*asherim*; s. *asherah*), and individual trees like the terebinth. In this respect they certainly were no different than their primitive non-Israelite contemporaries. It was in vain that the Prophet Hosea derided the asherim as stocks of wood and the Prophet Jeremiah reproached Israel for worshiping every green tree.

One of the primitive practices most condemned in Deuteronomy was the setting up of "holy" stones or pillars—matzebot—on "high places." This form of fetishistic worship was common not only among Israel's immediate neighbors—the Canaanites, Moabites, and Philistines—but also among the culturally far more advanced Greeks and Romans as late as the Hellenistic Age! It was such a stone monolith that the Patriarch Jacob, perhaps two thousand years earlier, after awakening from his celebrated dream, had erected in commemoration of his experience. He anointed the pillar with oil and there, where he believed he had had his dreams, established the Bethel sanctuary, which was to serve as "God's House." Just before World War I, at the site of the Canaanite sanctuaries of Gezer and Taanach, archaeologists found similar rude stone monoliths. These had holes on top or in the side, ostensibly for receiving libations of oil and the blood of sacrifices.

Primitive beliefs and practices, as noted in the Bible, continued to blur the outlines of the Jewish religion up to the time of the Babylonian conquest in 586 B.C.E., and in some areas, even later. Seemingly, only a dedicated but small minority had followed the lead of the Prophets in their preachments of a spiritual and ethical monotheism. Where the rulers and the accomodating priests and "official" prophets led, there the ignorant and inert majority blindly followed.

In the interregnum between the conquest of Canaan by the Israelites (on their returning from their Bondage in Egypt) and their consolidation into a more or less cohesive people, the old Mosaic ethical monotheism, oriented to broadly democratic aims, went into a sharp decline. It finally succumbed to the cultural influences—many of them debased and antisocial—of the regional environment and of the unsettling conditions that the royal despotism of Solomon had helped create. Parvenu in their love of ostentation, the Israelite kings were eager to imitate all the other "arrived" religions in the Fertile Crescent.

Solomon, in particular, had a passion for duplicating in his domain all the external splendors and elaborate ritualism of the national religions of Egypt, Babylonia, and Canaan (Phoenicia). With the borrowed skills of the craftsmen of Hiram, king of Tyre, he built his magnificent Temple on Mount Zion. This, both architecturally and in the large priestly establishment it maintained, was closely patterned after the sanctuaries of other Near Eastern peoples. Among the Israelites, the new upper classes of big landowners and the rich merchants also had set their hearts on aping their counterparts abroad in their life of luxury and ease and in the practice of their religion. And so, besides worshiping the God of Israel's Covenant—YHVH—as their national god, they also genuflected and adored, raised up altars and offered sacrifices to the bewildering number of the "fashionable" gods and fetishes which abounded among their polytheistic neighbors.

This kind of loyalty divided between YHVH and the gods of other peoples was unabashedly demonstrated by King Solomon. Once he had established the splendid Temple in Jerusalem dedicated to the worship of the God of Israel, he showed no qualms in erecting nearby sanctuaries to other gods. The chronicler of the Book of Kings, writing several centuries later, was bitter and censorious about this betrayal.

Other religions during the First Temple period, being based on primitive nature-worship and on the propitiation of the gods and the invisible spirits through sacrifices—a practice common to all pastoral and agricultural peoples of ancient times—consisted in the main of festivals and revels that were marked by many sacrifices and fertility rites. They were celebrated with much eating, drinking, wild dancing, and making joyous music "before the god." The pagan divinities were taken over and incorporated into the worship of Israel, so that in time, the conception of YHVH and of such "chief" gods of other peoples as Baal, Chemosh, Milkom, and Moloch became both fused and confused for the Israelites. This created a major religious and moral problem for the Prophets, who were horrified eyewitnesses to this corruption of the Jewish faith.

During the entire period of the First Temple, except among a minority of stubborn, nonconformist monotheists, the role of YHVH in the religion of Israel was merely that of a national god: the favorite and chief deity in a well-populated pantheon of lesser divinities, comparable, for instance, to the role of "the greatest of the gods," Zeus, in the religion of the Greeks. Hence Jeremiah's lament as late in Israel's history as the beginning of the sixth century B.C.E.: "according to the number of thy cities are thy gods, O Judah."

There were calf and bull worship in the older Israelite sanctuaries of Bethel, Dan, and Beersheba. The cult of the snake-god, Neshushtan—"the brazen serpent"—found its many votaries in Judah until the reformer-king Hezekiah (720–692 B.C.E.) ordered it uprooted. And on the very same altar in the Temple consecrated to the God of Israel, there were also slaughtered holocausts of "fattened beasts" to the sun-gods Milkom of Ammon and Chemosh of Moab.

Occupying an even more exalted position in the pantheon of the Israelite monolatrists were the gods of the Canaanites: the fertility divinity Baal and his female consort Ashtoreth (Astarte). And not least among them was Moloch, the fire-god perpetually belching flame—and the insatiable lover of the burning flesh of children "passing through the fire" in sacrificial offering to him.

The Prophets, who for their times were advanced religious and social thinkers as well as deeply humane, were horrified by the bestial practice of human sacrifice. Centuries before they had begun to appear as "the troublers of Israel," Jephthah, one of the ruler judges following the Conquest of Canaan, had sacrificed his only daughter to the God of Israel in a celebration of a military victory against the Ammonites; Samuel "the Seer" had hacked in a sacrificial manner the body of Agag before God; David, the sensitive poet-king, had handed the seven sons of Saul to the Gibeonites "to hang them up unto the god." Jeremiah bitterly accused the elders and priests of his day for having filled "this place [Hinnom] with the blood of innocents; and have built the high places of Baal to burn their sons in the fire for burnt offerings."

At least on two occasions in pre-Exilic times, determined efforts had been made to purge *by force* the old Mosaic religion of Israel of its many fetishistic and polytheistic aberrations. The first attempt had been made during Hezekiah's reign, but it was short lived. The second and last cleansing was performed by Hezekiah's great-grandson, Josiah. In the year 621 B.C.E., when the Temple was undergoing repairs, the High Priest, Hilkiah, discovered a copy of the long forgotten Book of the Covenant. Instantly Josiah, then a youth of twenty, was filled with a burning zeal for restoring the abandoned religion of the one God that had been taught by Moses and preached by Amos, Hosea, Isaiah, and Micah. Placing torches and axes into the hands of the people "he began to purge Judah and Jerusalem . . . And they broke down the altars of the Baalim . . . and the sun-images, that were on high above them, he hewed down; and the Asherim, and the graven images, and the molten images, he broke in pieces and made dust of them . . ." (II Chronicles 34:3-4.)

How successful Josiah was in his crusade to restore to Israel the monotheistic faith of its forefathers can be inferred from the fact that only twenty-five years later, after Zedekiah had become king of Judah (in 596 B.C.E.), the Biblical chronicler mournfully noted again that "all the chiefs of the priests, and the people, transgressed very greatly after all the abominations of the nations; and they polluted the house of the Lord . . ." (II Chronicles 36:14.)

By what reasoning could the Patriarch Abraham (*c.* 2000 B.C.E.), by tradition designated as "the first Jew," have arrived at his concept of One God? The Mesopotamian world he lived in was sunk in the most abysmal demon- and fetish-worship. Yet in the light of present knowledge about ancient primitive religions, his "discovery" cannot be reckoned an anomaly. Anthropologists, by correlating their numerous separate findings, have ascertained that among certain Australian food-gathering peoples, just as among North American Indians, there emerged notions about the existence of One God at the very same time that the vast majority were sunk in animistic beliefs and practices.

The anthropologist Paul Radin has observed that logical and symbolical thoughts are equally present in the capacity of primitive and advanced peoples, notwithstanding that the latter possess far more knowledge. To cite just one actual instance: the early Indian chronicler of pre-Columbian Mexico, Ixtlilxochitl, told of a poet-king who worshiped a Supreme Being even though the people brought sacrifices to two thousand gods in the Nahua religion. Among the names he gave his One God were "Lord, Master of Heaven and Earth and the Land of the Dead," and "Creator of Life."

Disregarding the legendary folklore that both adorns and confuses the narratives about the Patiarch Abraham and Moses, the Pentateuch nevertheless convincingly describes their mental processes and religious ideas. This holds especially true of Moses, who was immeasurably more advanced, religiously and intellectually, than Abraham. The Scriptural account of his ordeals and conflicts in the midst of the primitivism and mutinous spirit of the Israelite tribes and the "mixed multitude" of non-Israelite slaves who joined their rebellion and their journey through a wilderness of the mind as well as a wilderness of sand and rock on the way to the Promised Land, only underscores the more the pathos of Moses' intellectual and spiritual loneliness.

Without doubt—considering the extent of his intellectual powers—Moses *could* have arrived independently at the conception of One God as the First Cause who existed "from everlasting to everlasting." But judging from the way all significant systems of thought begin, this was hardly likely; even a supreme genius like Moses could not have ideated in an intellectual vacuum. There had to be a connection between his own original thinking and certain relatively advanced monotheistic notions that had been circulating in his native Egypt for many centuries. For example, only about 150 years before Moses is presumed to have experienced the theophany of the Burning Bush on Mount Horeb, Akhenaton had apostrophised Aton, the solar disc, as the symbol of the One Universal God:

> O One! Mighty One! Of myriad
> forms and aspects!
> O Thou Eternal! Thou Perfect!
> Thou Only One!
>
> *From* "The Coming Forth by Day,"
> *in* THE BOOK OF THE DEAD

But it should be noted that Akhenaton was not the first Egyptian monotheist. His ideas were merely the culmination of the efforts by a long line of priest-scribes who extended as far back, it is believed by historians, as 3500 B.C.E., to arrive at a unitarian conception of God and Nature. True enough, the monotheistic vision of Akhenaton was spiritualized; it was suffused by the soft glow of poetic mysticism; but it was almost entirely abstracted. It had little relevance to the practical life of man on earth. It remained for Moses to draw his "One God" ideal into the daily existence and the strivings of human beings for a better and nobler life. The question of whether Moses was actually an Egyptian, as the great Jewish psychologist Sigmund Freud hypothesized, or an Israelite, as the Bible and Jewish tradition categorically state, is academic. Whatever his ethnic origin, the "One God" image he envisioned became indelibly fixed in the Jewish consciousness. After thirty-two centuries of high-tide and ebb-tide in the fortunes of the Jewish people, the faithful—whether in New York or Bombay, London or Buenos Aires, Rome or Haifa—daily raise their voices in the recital of Moses' fervent proclamation of the Shema—the creed of ethical monotheism:

> HEAR, O ISRAEL: THE LORD OUR GOD, THE LORD IS ONE!
> And thou shalt love the Lord thy God with all thy heart, and with all thy soul, and with all thy might. And these words, which I command thee this day, shall be upon thy heart; and thou shalt teach them diligently unto thy children, and shalt talk of them when thou sittest in thy house, and when thou walkest by the way, and when thou liest down, and when thou risest up.
>
> DEUTERONOMY 6:4–6

See also ARK OF THE COVENANT; BIBLE, THE; CHOSEN PEOPLE, THE; DOCTRINES IN JUDAISM; ETHICAL VALUES, JEWISH; LIFE, JEWISH VIEW OF; LIFE, THE SANCTIFICATION OF; SAGES, RABBINIC; TEN COMMANDMENTS; THEOCRACY.

MORE JUDAICO. *See* OATH, THE JEWISH.

MOSES (in Hebrew: MOSHEH)

It should be noted that, until the most recent decades, the meaning of the name Moses had followed the Biblical rendering: "drawn from the water." The Scriptural narrative recounts that, when Pharaoah's daughter went down to the Nile to bathe, she found the "ark of bulrushes" with an infant boy in it. She decided to adopt him and named him Moses. Why Moses? "Because I drew him out of the water," the Biblical chronicler has her explain.

But her reason did not convince the philologists. In late years, almost in a consensus, the most reputable scholars have agreed that Moses was not the Egyptian but the Greek version of that name; originally it must have been Mesu or Mosè, meaning "a child," but when the Septuagint, the Greek version of the Hebrew Bible, was being prepared in Alexandria (*c.* 250 B.C.E.) during the reign of Ptolemy Philadelphus, a final *s* was added to the Egyptian Mosè, thus making it read Moses.

Even if it is conceded that Moses was an Egyptian name, the Biblical scholars have not been able to agree with any degree of finality as to the ethnic identity of Moses himself—was he *really* an Israelite or only a cultured upper-class Egyptian who had espoused the cause of the oppressed Israelite slaves? Sigmund Freud, the founder of psychoanalysis, firmly took the latter view and, in *Moses and Monotheism,* advanced the hypothesis that Moses was either an Egyptian prince or a priest of high rank, but definitely not an Israelite.

Whatever historic merit such theorizing may or may not have, never for one moment have devout Jews doubted that Moses was an Israelite, that he was the son of slave-parents (Jochebed and Amram, of the tribe of Levi), and that, by the guiding hand of Providence, he had been "drawn from the water" as an infant by Pharaoh's daughter, who adopted and raised him so that he could follow his destiny to become the supreme lawgiver of mankind.

To many historians and Bible critics Moses appears more real and significant as an abiding influence on Jewish life and culture than as a historic personality. What really is known about him? Only what is written in the Pentateuch. But for the inquiring person whose outlook is scientifically

Moses presents the Torah to the Israelites at Mount Sinai. (Illumination from the Sarajevo Haggadah manuscript, Spanish, 13th century.)

oriented, it is enough to consider that Moses left his indelible and continuing signature on the Jewish mind, spirit, and way of life. A perceptive modern philosopher of Jewish civilization, Achad ha-Am, gave felicitous expression to this thought:

> I care not whether this man Moses really existed; whether his life and his activity really correspond to our traditional account of him; whether he was really the savior of Israel and gave his people the Torah in the form in which it is preserved among us . . . For even if you [Bible critics] succeeded in demonstrating conclusively that the man Moses never existed, or that he was not such a man as we supposed, you would not thereby detract one jot from the historic reality of the ideal Moses—the Moses who has been our leader, not only for forty years in the Wilderness of Sinai, but for thousands of years in all the wildernesses in which we have wandered since the Exodus.

For the individual who chooses to follow the criteria of istorical investigation, the image of Moses as it emerges om the Pentateuch seems to be blended of both mythic and esh-and-blood elements. But where fact begins and myth ıkes over is to a great extent conjectural and often controersial. Moses could hardly have been "invented"! If he is to e considered as myth, then so should the Bondage of Israel Egypt, the Exodus, and the Wandering in the Wilderness. ut of the morass of legends and incidents of the miraculous at are present in the Biblical narrative about Moses, it ould appear that, in the main, the events recounted are, cording to all the laws of probability, authentic.

There are many happenings and actions involving Moses at have the indubitable ring of reality. Psychologically edible is the incident in which, inflamed with indignation, slays the Egyptian taskmaster for mistreating the helpless ves, or when later, in mounting tension, he organizes the slave-revolt and leads the fleeing Israelites out of Egypt into freedom. Credible, too, is the inevitability of his collisions during the Wandering with the mutineers and backsliding idolators, and with unscrupulous demagogues like Korach, who are able to confuse the ignorant, the weak-minded, and the frightened Israelites who were but recently groaning in the House of Bondage.

The gratitude that the common people expresses for its supremely great men is shown forcefully in the legendary aura with which it surrounds their lives and works. Underneath the shimmer of the supernatural and the magical in the Moses epic lies the essence of *the fact,* its reality and truth. It would be hard to deny that many a legend has its starting point in a historic event or personality; it is not just woven from the gossamer of dreams or from the inventions of idle fancy, nor is its principle intention to be diverting, entertaining, or moralizing. It may be said to be a restatement of the more prosaic historic fact, but expressed in the glowing terms of folk understanding and imagination.

The approach of the Scriptural narrative to the life, actions, and teachings of Moses resembles in every essential way those taken in other ancient chronicles about such hero-founders of their religions as Zoroaster, Buddha, and Jesus. Like the folk sagas about them, the Moses epic, too, is glorified, intertwined, and embroidered with so many strands of the legendary, the awesome, and the magical, that for many realistic-minded persons, it has obscured what might be presumed to have been the image of the *real* Moses. Nevertheless, to the discerning, all the awesome and supernatural events recounted in the Bible narrative only partially succeed in blurring the human outline of the man Moses, at least for no longer than the mists of the summit of Sinai obscured him from the sight of the Children of Israel after

Moses breaks the Tablets of the Commandments before the idolatrous Israelites. (Painting by Lesser Ury, Germany, 19th century.)

he had ascended the mountain to speak "face to face" with God. "How small Sinai appears when Moses stands on its summit!" remarked the poet Heinrich Heine.

To the entranced Jewish folk of all the ages and in all climes, there never seemed to be anything either mysterious or puzzling about Moses. Every word written in the Torah concerning their liberator, lawgiver, and teacher appeared true and vividly real for them. Neither was there anything about his personality to overawe them. How could a child be overawed by his loving father? To the persecuted Jewish people—rootless human beings feeling the need for emotional as well as physical security—Moses appeared as a powerful father-image. He was the indomitable, the wise, the righteous, the comforting father who had been protectingly, in times of crisis, like a shield and a buckler for their ancestors, the Children of Israel, and had led them into freedom when they were slaves in Egypt. And whenever God had lost patience with them on account of their backsliding into idolatry and bestiality, Moses had stood between them and His wrath and had pleaded their wretched cause for them—his straying sheep.

Perhaps it was not inappropriate, therefore, that in the Biblical narrative and in the Midrash legends, Moses should have been made out to be a gentle shepherd, one pure in heart, to whom, while he was tending his flock of sheep on the slopes of Mount Horeb, God revealed Himself in the burning thorn bush. This image of Moses as the faithful shepherd of his flock was, not at all surprisingly, superimposed many hundreds of years later on the Jesus-image by the early Jewish-Christians, so powerfully appealing had it been to the Jewish people for twelve centuries previously.

In the esteem of the pious, Moses was "the greatest of all the Prophets." The Talmudic scholar of Spain, Rabbi Moses ben Nachman (also known as Nachmanides, 1195–1270) eulogized him thus: "The Mishnah teaches: 'Be very humble in spirit.' Even Mosheh Rabbenu—peace be upon him!—was praised for this quality, as is written: 'And the man Mosheh was very meek.' It is also on account of the merit of his meekness that the Torah was given to Israel *through him,* and that he was called the teacher of all the Prophets."

Often the plain folk marveled that one so marked out for supreme eminence by the will of God, so perfect in intellect and character, and so unselfish in the service of others as Moses, should have remained the meekest of men!

Moses was called in Hebrew an *anav*—"a humble person" —and the faithful have always been called upon to emulate him in this virtue. God, too, was described by the Rabbinic Sages as an Anav, and they quoted Him as saying: "I cannot live in the same world with the proud and the arrogant." The Talmudic teachers also declared that God had chosen "the meekest of men, Moses, to give the Torah to Israel, because the sandal of the Torah is humility." But most of the time, for some thirty-two centuries, the Jewish folk have referred to Moses with the reverent affection of disciples for their master as Mosheh Rabbenu—"Moses our Teacher," for he actually was their teacher, having given them what they treasured as their brightest inheritance—the Torah.

For Jews, the archetype of the perfect, the righteous, man was traditionally held to be Moses. Two thousand years ago, Philo, the Hellenized philosopher-rabbi of first-century Alexandria, in his sermonic eulogy in Greek on "Moses' Humanity and Justice," marveled that he was "not like some of those who thrust themselves into a position of power by means of arms and engines of war and strength of infantry, cavalry and navy, but on account of his goodness and his nobility of conduct and the universal benevolence which he never failed to show." Furthermore, added Philo, Moses was a selfless ruler who sought no benefit for himself or for his two sons, neither of whom he gave any position of power nor made them his successor. He remained steadfast to the dedication of his life, which was "to benefit his subjects, and, in all that he said or did, to further their interests and neglect no opportunity which would advance the common well-being."

Any attempt to evaluate or particularize the personal contributions made by Moses to his people and to its religion would seem to be both unnecessary and impossible to accomplish. It would be unnecessary because the *entire* Bible and the faith of Israel are overwhelming testimonials to them; it would also be impossible because the ascription of the Mosaic Code in toto to Moses alone would be unconvincing to any but Scriptural literalists and religious fundamentalists.

It was due to his perceptive genius that Moses was able, against the general tide of primitivism, nature and demon worship, to project the concept of pure monotheism—a unitary conception of the universe as the harmonious creation of the One God who ruled over it. But it is perhaps of even greater historic significance in the religious and intellectual history of mankind that he was the great pathfinder in humanizing and spiritualizing monotheism by translating it into laws of social justice and ethical conduct in a civilizing process which was courageously continued and further developed by the Prophets and the Rabbinic Sages.

To this day, after thirty-two centuries, Moses remains an exemplar of social morality, law, and justice not only to the adherents of three world religions—Christianity, Islam, and Judaism—but also to countless millions of the religiously uncommitted or even downright skeptics and unbelievers. His greatness transcends the sectarian limits of theological dogma or institutional separatism. By his intellectual power and moral will, and with his organizational genius to serve both, he was able to hammer a self-respecting people out of a brutalized conglomeration of former slaves. He taught them to abide by a system of morality and law—not a philosophical or utopian system like that described in Plato's theorizing blueprint for an ideal Republic of *superiors,* but one realistic and practical enough to enable the people who lived by it to cope with the daily problems of living: working, suffering, and striving to create under it a happier and more just society of *equals.* Therein lies his achievement in the history of human progress.

See also ARK OF THE COVENANT; BAT KOL; BIBLE, THE; ETHICAL VALUES, JEWISH; GAN EDEN; HEBREW LANGUAGE, HISTORY OF THE; ISLAM, JEWISH ORIGINS OF; JUBILIEE; LAW, JEWISH; MARRIAGE; MESSIAH, THE; MESSIAHS, WOULD-BE; MITZVOT; MIZRACH; MONOTHEISM; PASSOVER; PEACE, JEWISH CONCEPT OF; POST-BIBLICAL WRITINGS; PRAYER AND WORSHIP; RABBI; SABBATH; SANHEDRIN; SHABUOT; SHECHINAH; SHOFAR; SIDRAH; SOCIAL JUSTICE; SUCCOT; TALMUD, THE; TEMPLE, THE; TEN COMMANDMENTS; TORAH-READING.

MOSHAV, MOSHAVIM. *See* KIBBUTZ.

MOSHEH RABBENU. *See* MOSES.

MOTHERS-IN-LAW AND DAUGHTERS-IN-LAW. *See* FAMILY RELATIONS, TRADITIONAL PATTERNS OF.

MOURNER'S PRAYER. *See* KADDISH.

MOURNING CUSTOMS. *See* BURIAL RITES AND CUSTOMS; KITTEL; SHIVAH.

MUSIC, ANCIENT JEWISH

Among the Jews in Biblical times, music had two principal functions to perform. One was ritualistic, and sought to heighten emotionally the religious symbolism of the sacrificial service in the Temple on Mount Zion; the other was directed purely to magical and supernatural ends. In the early periof Jewish history, music was closely linked with prophecy and was employed by the professional school of prophets (who were, unlike the lofty-minded canonical Prophets, little more than soothsayers) to bring themselves into a state of inspired ecstasy before foretelling the future. The Greek soothsayers also relied on the Dionysian influence of music to waft them into a prophetic trance.

The Bible relates that, when Elisha wished to prophesize, he demanded: "But now bring me a minstrel." That was done. "And it came to pass, when the minstrel played, that the hand of the Lord came upon him." (II Kings 3:15.) In a far less elevated mood was King Saul when he met a prophet-band "coming down from the high place with a psaltery, and a timbrel, and a pipe, and a harp, before them." As he listened to their playing, he experienced what might be described as a divine seizure—". . . and the spirit of God came mightily upon him, and he prophesied among them." (I Samuel 10:10-11.)

The notion that music possesses magical powers has been widespread in all cultures. The best-known example is that of Orpheus in Greek mythology; he, it was said, could tame wild beasts and subdue the very demons guarding the portals of Hades with the magic of his lyre-playing. The most general application of music as magic among many peoples was in the treatment of mental illness. That was because of a popular notion that mental illness was caused by evil spirits or devils who had entered and possessed the body of the afflicted person. It was believed that to cure him all that was necessary was to drive out the demons, either by exorcism or by the magic power of music. The Christian Gospels cite many instances in which Jesus was said to have driven out "devils" from the mentally tormented.

Music was a time-honored therapy for mental illness and was used as such almost universally by all the ancients. Thus, it should be noted that it was not merely the whim of a manic-depressive despot that made King Saul command young David to play the harp for him: "And it came to pass, when the [evil] spirit from God was upon Saul, that David took the harp, and played with his hand; so Saul found relief, and it was well with him, and the evil spirit departed from him." (I Samuel 16:23.)

Evil spirits could also be driven away by bells, jinglers, or tambourines. One illuminated medieval Hebrew manuscript shows a lute-player in a doctor's anteroom waiting to be called in "to play away" the mental affliction of a patient being examined.

It is conjectured by some musicologists that the ancient Jews adopted the seven sacred modes that the Babylonians and Assyrians had employed in their temple liturgy. With the performance of those modes—each of which was believed to have a mystical affinity with a particular celestial body such as the sun, the moon, or the stars—the desired effects of what anthropologists call "sympathetic magic" could be achieved. The alleged curing of illness thus was accomplished on this harmonic principle of "like with like"; namely, of the performance of a specific musical mode for a specific ailment. According to Abraham ibn Ezra, the celebrated Biblical commentarian and liturgical poet of twelfth-century Spain, David, the shepherd-harpist, was able to cure Saul's mental illness by means of sympathetic magic: "He knew the star by which the music should be regulated."

No concrete trace of the seven modal melodies has yet been found. All we have to go by are the frustrating superscriptions that are attached to those Hebrew psalms that were meant to be sung to instrumental accompaniment in the Temple service.

It is interesting to discover, from a reference by the Greek philosopher Plato, that the Greeks also borrowed their modal system from the same reservoir of Eastern song. Proof of this assumption, although it is only circumstantial, is strengthened by the observation of Rabbi Philo of Alexandria (first century) that the Greek mystical philosopher Pythagoras had drawn his two celebrated doctrines of the Harmony of the Spheres and of the Ethos from the Chaldeans. The Pythagorean Ethos was a system of melodic modes each of which, when performed for the purpose of "sympathetic magic," could overcome such depressing passions as melancholia, grief, and anger. There is more than a likelihood that one of these modes had been played by David on the harp to relieve Saul's manic depression.

See also MUSIC IN THE TEMPLE; MUSICAL ACCENTS; MUSICAL INSTRUMENTS OF THE BIBLE.

MUSIC, BIBLICAL. *See* LEVITES; MUSIC, ANCIENT JEWISH; MUSIC IN THE TEMPLE; MUSICAL ACCENTS; MUSICAL INSTRUMENTS OF THE BIBLE.

MUSIC, FOLK. *See* FOLK MUSIC AND DANCE.

MUSIC, LITURGICAL. *See* HYMNS OF THE SYNAGOGUE; LEVITES; MUSIC, ANCIENT JEWISH; MUSIC IN THE TEMPLE; MUSICAL ACCENTS; MUSICAL INSTRUMENTS OF THE BIBLE.

MUSIC OF THE SYNAGOGUE. *See* CHAZZAN; HYMNS OF THE SYNAGOGUE.

MUSIC IN THE TEMPLE

Ever since the Destruction of the Temple in Jerusalem in 70 C.E., the remnants of the Jewish faithful, in whatever part of the world they may have been dispersed, were haunted by the almost legendary folk-memory of its musical service. The image they had of it was graphically reconstructed for them by descriptive passages in the Scriptures, Jesus ben Sirach's wisdom book, Ecclesiasticus, and in the Talmud. The Levites, who were the Temple musicians, sang to the accompaniment of various instruments:

> Give thanks unto the Lord with harp,
> Sing praises unto Him with the psaltery of ten strings.
> Sing unto Him a new song;
> Play skillfully amid shouts of joy.
>
> PSALMS 33:2-3

Obviously, one must not expect from that ancient period a tonal art and expressiveness on a level comparable to the one familiar to modern musical sophisticates. Among no people in the ancient world, including the culturally advanced Egyptians and the Greeks, had music reached a high stage of development by modern standards. This was also true of the Jews. When the Temple of Solomon was being consecrated (sometime during the tenth century B.C.E.), the musical service for the occasion was described (in II Chronicles 5:12-14) in this wise:

> . . . also the Levites who were the singers, all of them even Asaph, Heman, Jeduthun and their sons and their brethren, arrayed in fine linen, with cymbals and psalteries and harps, stood at the east end of the altar, and with them a hundred and twenty priests sounding with trumpets—it came even to pass, when the trumpeters and singers were as one, to make one sound to be heard in praising and thanking the Lord . . . the glory of the Lord filled the house of God.

It is quite certain that the Levites sang in unison, for that was customary then. There were apparently two choirs which faced each other and sang alternately in antiphonal performance. In one of the cuneiform tablets discovered at Tell el'Amarna, in Egypt, there is documentary proof that the closest neighbors of the Jews—the Canaanites—followed a similar liturgical practice, and that at a time long before Solomon's Temple had been built.

While about half of the 150 hymns included in the Book of Psalms were designed (as their superscriptions and instructions indicate), to be sung with instrumental accompaniment by the Levite choirs in the Temple service on Mount Zion, and while there is even a basis for the belief that each was to be sung to a specified musical mode well known to the Jews at that time, not even a hint remains of what those melodies or intonations were.

In Rabbinic tradition, which the folk piously made its own, it was David—the harpist, composer, poet, and king—who was revered as the inspired genius of Jewish song. He was presumed to have founded a school of liturgical music for the training of the Levites in singing and in instrumental playing. (This, of course, was in prophetic anticipation of the Temple that his son and successor Solomon was yet to build.) Still another tradition tells of a school that Solomon had established in Jerusalem for the training of four thousand Levite singers and instrumentalists.

The musicians of the Temple were organized into twenty-four guilds, according to the instruments they played—whether the kinnor (lyre), tzeltzelim (cymbals), chalil (pipe), or chatzotzerah (trumpet). They were instructed and rehearsed by twelve "masters" over whom there was a chief-master, who conducted the final performance. "And Chenaniah, chief of the Levites, was over the song; he was master in the song, because he was skillful." (I Chronicles 15:22.) In the final period of the Second Temple, a boy's choir was added to give a different timbre and quality to the choral singing.

The Temple music was particularly impressive during the three great "pilgrim festivals" of Pesach (Passover), Shabuot (the Feast of Weeks), and Succot (the Feast of Tabernacles), when thousands of Jews from the most distant places in the Diaspora journeyed to Jerusalem, there to reaffirm their ties to God and Israel at the national sanctuary on Mount Zion.

Of one of these festivals the Talmud has left a glowing account: "Whoever has not witnessed the joy of the Festival of Water-Drawing [during Succot] has seen no joy in his life." On the night of the first day of Succot, a vast assembly of worshipers would swarm into the Women's Court of the Temple enclosure. Each one carried a lighted torch and a water jug. "The pious folk, and illustrious men as well, danced with torches in their hands, singing hymns of praise and songs of joy, whie the Levites made music with psaltery, harp, cymbals, trumpets, and many other instruments."

See also LEVITES; MUSIC, ANCIENT JEWISH; MUSICAL INSTRUMENTS OF THE BIBLE.

MUSICAL ACCENTS (in Hebrew: TA'AMIM, literally meaning "tastes"; sometimes called NEGINOT, meaning "notes" or "melodies").

Music among the Jews, since the most remote historic times, was intimately associated with religious worship. It was revered as a divine art because it was believed able to stir the souls of those who sang or heard it into rapture and to bring them emotionally into a closer communion with God.

In the epochal centuries of Jewish self-discovery, religiously and culturally, during the Second Commonwealth, the need for heightening the impact upon the worshipers of the Hebrew Scriptural texts and of the prayers led to the introduction of music into the service of the synagogue. The public "reading" of the weekly portion from the Torah and of the accompanying selection from the Prophetic writings, the Haftarah (q.v.), was not just "reading" but a chanting that some musicologists believe was in monotone plain song style.

The Babylonian Talmud made this Rabbinic stricture about the dry-as-dust formalists: "He who reads from the Torah without sweetness, and studies it without a melody, of such as him the Prophet Ezekiel says [quoting God]: 'And I also have given them laws that are not good.'"

During the Second Temple period, certain fixed musical modes were introduced for the purpose of cantillating the various Scriptural books. Some of these modal patterns were, in time, forgotten. Later on, the students and scholars of the Mishnah and Gemara were also required to intone their recitations from these texts in the course of their Torah studies and discussions. These "study modes" were similar to the musical pattern used for the modulation of the Torah and Haftarah. But when the Jews became so widely dispersed, it was natural for different modes to be adopted in different regions, and modes that were traditional in some communities were disregarded in others. Thus was born a diversity of musical expression.

The modes for Scriptural intonation had originated at various undetermined prehistoric times. They had been handed down orally from generation to generation, for no musical notation system existed among the Jews in those early periods any more than it did among the contemporary Hindus, Egyptians, or Greeks. During the first years of the Talmudic era, when the Hellenistic cultural influence was making itself felt in a very marked manner among Jews, Greek musical modes and idioms were freely borrowed and adapted to the religious needs of the synagogue musical service. (This process of acculturation was afterward probably reversed, as is plainly discernible in the resemblance the Jewish ta'amim bear to the Greek prosodia of the second century.) It took the Jewish scholars, after ceaseless study and correction of a confused musical tradition, until the ninth century to develop a workable system of musical notation. This was achieved, at long last, by the Yeshibah of Tiberias, under the direction of the great grammarian Aaron ben Asher, who had also established the correct vowel points for the

Bible text (Codex Petropolitanus) of 916 C.E., *showing the earliest extant superlinear vocalization.*

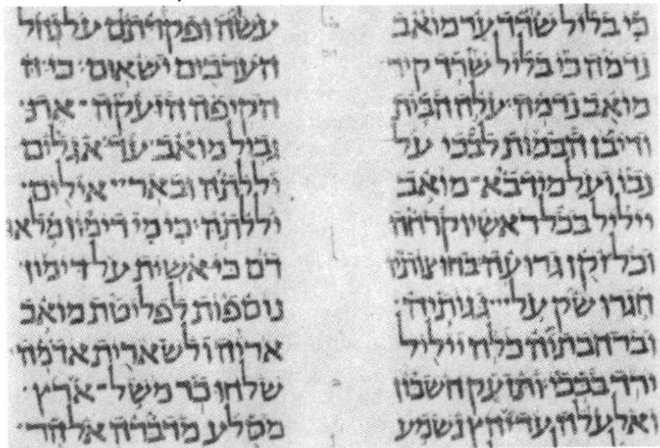

The German humanist Johann Reuchlin's attempt to translate the Hebrew musical accents into approximate Western musical notation. (From De Accentibus, *Germany, 1518.)*

vocalization of the Bible text. Aaron wrote a treatise explaining the intention and meaning of his symbols of notation; these have been called, ever since, "the Tiberian System."

Cantillation of the Torah and the Haftarah by means of the accent marks placed above and below the Hebrew syllables may be described as a form of musical declamation: a fusion of speech with melody. To those familiar with the early history of Western music, the ta'amim or Hebrew accents bear a striking resemblance to the neumes, the system of musical "signs" first employed by the Byzantine Church.

Curiously enough, and for whatever cultural significance the fact may have, the neumes appeared at the same time as the ta'amim—in the ninth century. Both represented rudimentary and inexact systems of notation for plain song. The Hebrew symbols were merely the wispiest of hints or directions to the reader or cantillator. They "suggested" to him where he was to raise, lower, or sustain his voice, or where he was to make a long pause or a short one. It is certain that this system of notation could mean little or nothing to anyone not initiated *orally* beforehand in traditional cantillation, for the emphasis was not at all on the music but on the syllables of the Hebrew words in the text; whatever rhythm there was came from the syllables alone in the cantillation. In time, tropes or groups of notes were developed for the ornamentation of the more significant syllables to give musical emphasis to and enhance the text. Then, with the introduction during the Baroque period of the more self-conscious and more sophisticated style of singing in the German and Slavic synagogues, the relatively simple and bare plain song of the traditional style became overlaid with rococo grace-notes, trills, and quavers.

Actually, the ta'amim indicated no precise tonal, time, and dynamic values. There was no order to the sequence of the sounds; the reader-cantillator was not bound by any rules. He just improvised, merely raising, lowering, and sustaining his notes, and pausing as the signs directed him to do. However, he did maintain the pattern of the mode which he had *learned* to cantillate according to the oral tradition. Where the ta'amim are found wanting, in the historical perspective of Western music's development, is in their failure, present in all early notation systems, to indicate the individual notes, to give their different values, and to establish correct intervals. Moreover, the ta'amim had neither scale nor rhythm. These latter were first elaborated by the Benedictine monk of the eleventh century, Guido d'Arrezzo.

A variety of forms of Jewish cantillations made their appearance in different countries of the world, ostensibly in accordance with different currents of Jewish musical tradition. The indigenous musical idiom of each region infiltrated, to some degree, into the Jewish cantillations. There are a large variety of modes, extant—German-Ashkenazic and Slavic-Ashkenazic, Sefaradic, Persian, Baghdad, Arabian, Egyptian, and Moorish—and each style shows unmistakably the employment of local musical idioms. It has been remarked by students of comparative liturgical music that several of the traditional modes still used for the Biblical cantillation in the synagogue are also found in currency in the Catholic Church. The Viennese composer and musicologist Egon Wellesz, a specialist in the music of the Byzantine Church, has pointed out anent one of its cantillations of third-century vintage, that "this kind of cantillation is typical of early Christian liturgical singing, which is derived from the singing of the psalms in the Jewish liturgy; it came down to us virtually unchanged, both in the practice of the Jews in the Middle East and in the Eastern and Western Churches."

The Gregorian plain chant, introduced during the sixth century in the Roman Catholic Church, also reveals its great indebtedness to early Jewish cantillation. Here again, one is obliged to assume that the cantillation modes were adopted by the early Jewish-Christians from the common traditional source: the synagogue. There can be no doubt but that some of the Judean modes presumed by the musicologists to antedate the rise of Christianity were employed by Jesus and the Apostles when they cantillated, as all pious Jews did and still do, from the Torah.

Thoughtful traditionalists who treasure the cultural heritage of the Jewish people are filled with melancholy forebodings that time and the historic tide of change will ultimately bring an end to cantillation. Some Reform congregations discarded the ancient practice long ago, but the Orthodox and Conservative adherents still faithfully cantillate from the Scriptures. As if to insure the preservation of the tradition and the technical knowledge of its performance, cantillation is taught to the children in many religious schools. Bar Mitzvah boys in traditionally oriented synagogues are required to cantillate from the Torah according to the accents before all the worshipers.

See also FOLK MUSIC AND DANCE; HYMNS OF THE SYNAGOGUE; MUSIC IN THE TEMPLE; TORAH-READING.

MUSICAL INSTRUMENTS OF THE BIBLE

Like so many other ethnic and religious groups, the ancient Greeks were vainglorious about their cultural accomplishments. They claimed for their music not only a superiority in quality over all others but also priority in originating it for the human race. They attributed the invention of the art of music to Apollo, the reed-pipes to Pan, and the lyre to Mercury. The ancient Israelites were quite as unreticent when they claimed that "the father of all such as handle the harp and the organ" was Jubal, the son of Lamech (Genesis 4:21). And if Orpheus was honored by the Greeks as the very genius of music, equally revered by the Jews was David, the harpist-Psalmist.

There is ample evidence—but much of it only circumstantial—that the ancient Jews played on the same or similar instruments that were in use among their neighbors. Unfortunately, while we possess considerable archaeological evidence in painting, sculpture, and inscriptions concerning the musicians and the musical instruments of the Assyrians, Egyptians, and other Near Eastern peoples, this is hardly the case with the Jews of that period. In most recent years, archaeologists have unearthed at Meggido, in Israel, two remarkable graphic portrayals of musicians. These go back to the Chalcolithic Period of the Bronze Age, two to three thousand

A kinnor-playing Israelite (?). (From an Egyptian wall-painting.)

years before King David. One of them is the figure of a woman harpist that a primitive artist had scratched out on the pavement; the other is that of a woman shown playing the chalil (the double-pipe).

The employment of instrumental music as an intrinsic part of Jewish religious worship is indicated in a narrative passage in the Book of Daniel (3:4-5). That Prophet recounts how Nebuchadnezzar, the king of Babylonia, had set up a golden image in the city of Babylon, and for the ceremony of dedication had assembled many of his dignitaries. Before them came a herald who cried out: "To you it is commanded . . . that at what time ye hear the sound of the horn, pipe, harp, trigon, psaltery, bagpipe, and all kinds of music, ye fall down and worship the golden image!" There is every reason to suppose that a similar intimate relationship existed between the performance of the Levites on musical instruments and the requirements of the liturgy in the Temple in Jerusalem.

Manifestly, the principal source of information about the musical instruments played by the ancient Jews is the Bible. That Jewish musicians must have achieved a high degree of competence in their performance is indicated in the memorial that was left by that redoubtable Assyrian conqueror, Sennacherib. He boasted that, as part of the booty that he claimed, the Jewish King Hezekiah had sent to him in Nineveh "male and female musicians." And this was no idle boast, for there is extant in sculptured relief the Assyrian figurative representation of three Jewish musicians, each one carrying a kinnor (lyre), and being guarded as captives by an armed Assyrian soldier bringing up the rear.

Probably the musical instrument for which Jewish performers were most celebrated in the ancient Near East was the kinnor. But this was by no means a specifically Jewish instrument; it seems to have been quite in general use among the peoples of the Mediterrean world. But for some reason the Jews had developed such an attachment to that instrument that they could not conceive of it as being anything but their own. In the Bible it is claimed that it was Jubal who invented the kinnor; in later times the kinnor was described as "King David's harp." But the kinnor was no harp at all; it was really a lyre, such as the Greek played. The great English ethnologist, Sir James Fraser, notes that a similar instrument, which was called a kinyra, was popular among the Greeks. Certain musicologists choose to identify the kinnor of the Jews with the kithara of the Greeks.

Jewish captives (probably Levite musicians) playing the kinnor, guarded by Babylonian warrior. (From a Babylonian bas-relief.)

The kinnor had a curved, yoke-shaped frame, and its strings were attached from horizontal crossbars. This can be seen in a representation of it on one of the coins that was minted in 132-35 C.E., during Bar Kochba's short-lived rule of Judea. Josephus, the Jewish historian of the first century, stated that the kinnor had ten strings, and that it was plucked with a plectron. Musicologists have surmised from this that the instrument must have had a range of two octaves. Abraham ibn Ezra, the twelfth-century Spanish Biblical scholar and poet, described the kinnor, which no doubt he must have seen, as having a semicircular shape, giving the impression of a menorah. Oddly enough, the eminent Jewish musicologist, Curt Sachs, when he examined representations of the kithara (the Greek equivalent of the kinnor), on a variety of Greek, Cretan, and Phoenician vases, recognized the correctness of Ibn Ezra's observation. Probably following the mystical scheme of the seven sacred modes (*see* MUSIC, ANCIENT JEWISH), so widely diffused in the ancient philosophy and practice of music, of pairing "like with like" in the exercise of sympathetic magic, the kinnor was designated by the Jews as the instrument to express the specific "mode of joy."

Another musical instrument frequently referred to in the Bible was the nebel (usually identified as the psaltery). Saadia Gaon, the great rabbinical encyclopedist of the tenth century, identified it as being the same as the Greek psalterion. It was a lyre rather than a harp, was larger than the kinnor, and vertical and angular in shape. It had ten strings which were plucked by the fingers instead of by a plectron, as in the instance of the kinnor.

The chalil, an oboe-like double-reed pipe which is pictured on a Bar Kochba coin of the second century, was in universal use in the ancient Mediterranean world. It was a simple bucolic instrument that produced a plaintive liquid sound. The Talmud states: "The pipe is called *chalil* because its sound is sweet [chalah]." The chalil was played at the dedication of the Second Temple in the sixth century B.C.E. For some reason, possibly because it was also played by the folk for pleasure, it was used in the musical service during the sacrificial rites before the altar in the Second Temple only twelve times a year, during the three "pilgrim festivals": Pesach (Passover), Shabuot (the Feast of Weeks), and Succot (the Feast of Tabernacles).

An instrument with pronounced magical powers that could win God's assistance was the chatzotzerah (trumpet). The Egyptians, as did other peoples living in the Fertile Crescent, so regarded it. Whenever the help of the God Osiris of the nether world was invoked, it was accompanied by the blowing of a trumpet. On the Arch of Titus in Rome there is the famous sculptured relief depicting the looting Romans carrying off the Temple vessels of gold, after the Destruction in 70 C.E. Among these sacred objects are two golden trumpets: long straight tubes looking very much like the trumpets that are pictured in Egyptian wall paintings. It was customary, when the Israelites moved from place to place in the Wilderness, that the Ark of the Lord be preceded by seven trumpeters blowing a protective fanfare on their golden horns.

The trumpet's importance is also recognized in these instructions that God gave Moses: "And if ye go to war in your land against the enemy that oppresseth you, then ye shall blow an alarm with the trumpets, and ye shall be remembered before your God, and ye shall be saved from your enemies. . ."

In addition to frame-drums, cymbals, timbrels, clappers, rattles, jinglers, and other rhythm-accenting musical instruments, there was the formidable magrephah (an instrument that was identical with the hydraulos, the Greek water-organ). Generation upon generation of Jews persisted in the claim that it was their ancestors who had invented the organ. The

Kinnor with six strings. Design on a coin issued by Simon the Nasi.

The Golden Trumpets (right) of the Temple in Jerusalem. (From the engraving by Pietro Santo Bartoli (1635–1700), reproducing the triumphal procession of the Romans with the Temple spoils on the sculptured reliefs of the Arch of Titus, Rome.)

Rabbinic Sages debated the question of whether the magrephah had actually been played during the Temple service, the second-century Patriarch, Simeon ben Gamaliel, denied that it ever had. That controversy notwithstanding, the tractate Tamid of the Babylonian Talmud had this to say: "One of the servants of the Temple [i.e., a Levite musician] took the magrephah and sounded it between the porch and the altar. . . . The priest who heard its sound knew that his brother-priests had entered to worship, and he hastened and came. The Levite who heard its sound knew that his brother Levites had entered to sing, and he hastened and came."

Piecing together references about the magrephah in another tractate of the Talmud, Arakin, some musicologists conjecture that there must have been two different types of organs played in the Temple. The one described above in the tractate Tamid as being played to summon the Temple priests and the Levites to the sacrificial service, is believed to have been the Greek hydraulos, a pulsatile instrument; the one discussed in the tractate Arakin was plainly a pneumatic pipe-organ worked by twin bellows, a prototype of the kind in use today. It contained within a box ten reed-pipes with ten holes in each; some were long and thick, others short and thin.

In giving a mechanical description of this instrument on the basis of the information found in the Talmud, the Renaissance physician-humanist of Mantua, Abraham Portaleone, made plain that "the magrephah of Arakin" was a performing instrument. "So the magrephah emitted, quite conveniently, all the hundred sounds of which our rabbis speak, distinct from one another, due to thickness and fineness of length and shortness of the reed-pipes, and the distance of the holes in them from the first hole to the tenth."

After the Temple was destroyed, the Rabbis decreed a prohibition against the playing in any synagogue of the organ and other musical instruments that had been used by the Levites in the service of the sanctuary. The ban was intended to demonstrate the grief of the Jewish people, who were directed to enter into a perpetual mourning for Zion which was not to end until the Messiah would come and the Temple would be rebuilt. That original ban, particularly against the organ, was greatly reinforced during the period of the Byzantine persecutions of the Jews, when the pressures for their conversion that were brought to bear on them grew ever more ferocious. Because the organ had become an indispensable musical instrument of the Church, Jewish religious authorities concluded that it had no rightful place in the synagogue. They felt that, were the organ to be played during the service of the synagogue, as it was during Mass in the churches, it might lead to a blurring of external differences and the separation that existed between the houses of worship of the two rival religions—it might even result in renegacy from the faith under the threat of death. Jewish religious leaders lived in dread of the possible spread of apostasy.

Ironic, indeed, is the fact, gleaned from the early history of Christianity, that when the introduction of the organ into the churches was being considered, some Church Fathers opposed the step. Their contention was that it was "a Jewish instrument" and might help seduce some Christians to "the hateful religion"—Judaism.

To this day, the organ is unwelcome in Orthodox synagogues, but about the middle of the nineteenth century, its use in the temple became one of the hallmarks of the Reform movement.

See also LEVITES; MUSIC, ANCIENT JEWISH; MUSIC IN THE TEMPLE.

MUTUAL AID. *See* BURIAL RITES AND CUSTOMS; CHARITY; ETHICAL VALUES, JEWISH; GOLDEN RULE, THE; HOSPITALITY; HOSPITALS; SICK, VISITING THE.

MYTHS, BIBLICAL, SIGNIFICANCE OF. *See* BIBLE, THE.

N

NADAN. *See* DOWRY.

NAMES, JEWISH

Wherever they lived, at all times, Jews assumed names commonly in use among the general population, or they adapted their former names to blend with them. In Biblical times in the Land of Israel, Jewish names followed a simple patriarchal pattern; for example: Joshua ben (son of) Nun or Isaiah ben (son of) Amoz. No matter what strange alterations Hebrew names subsequently underwent, religiously, this form has been preserved over three thousand years to our own day. Thus a man's name today for civil or legal purposes may be Nathan Ausubel, but for all religious purposes he is recorded or mentioned as Nissen ben Yisroel (Nathan son of Israel), the name given him at birth.

Certainly, not all Jewish names have been of Hebrew origin. Even the names Moses (Mosheh) is not Hebrew but Egyptian. When the Judean exiles were resettled in Babylonia by their conquerors, the old Biblical Hebrew names quickly made way for local ones. Mordecai is not a Hebrew name, but Babylonian; it is a form of the name Marduk—one of the principal Babylonian gods. Likewise, Mordecai's celebrated kinswoman (the heroine of Purim) was called Esther, after the Phoenician goddess of procreation and love, Astarte, although her Hebrew name was Hadassah. When the first contingent of Exiles returned in 538 B.C.E. to Judah, they were led by two Jewish princes who bore not Hebrew but Babylonian names: Sheshbazzar and Zerubbabel.

In every century and in every country, Jews have changed or adapted their names to fit the culture. During the last period of the Second Temple in Judea and in other regions which bore the impact of Hellenistic culture, even Jewish princes, high priests, and Rabbinic Sages assumed such impeccably Greek names as Alexander, Hyrkanos, Lysimachos, Jason, Demetrios, and Antigonos. And in Rome, "they did as the Romans." Jews adopted such Latin names as Rufus, Drusus, Sallustius, and Justinus. Often the "going over" from the original Hebrew name into the language of the specific country was a literal translation; Tzaddok (Just) became Justus; Jedidah (Love) turned into Philo, and Nathaneel (God's Gift) was equated by Theodorus.

While traditional Jewish names persisted in Arabic-speaking Mohammedan countries and in Moorish Spain, such first names, for instance, as Maimuni (Maimon) and Saadia, borne by the two most illustrious Jewish religious thinkers of the Middle Ages, were distinctively Arabic. The Hebrew word *ben* (son), linking personal name with patronymic, also was Arabicized into *ibn,* thus: Solomon ibn Gabirol and Abraham ibn Ezra.

In medieval times, as well as in later centuries, the personal names of Jews in Germany became German: Süsskind (Sweet Child); Gans, Wolf, Hirsch, Beer (all animal names) for men; Genendl, Frometl, Kreindl for women. What made these acquire the character of traditional names was that, over the course of many generations, Jews persisted in giving them to their children—and this, strange to relate, centuries after the Germans had abandoned them! French Jews did the same. In medieval France, Jewish male children were given such names as Vives, Bonfil, and Deulecress, and girls were named Fleur-de-Lis, Belaset, and Précieuse. Old Hebrew names found their approximate equivalents in French: Obadiah (Servant of the Lord) became Cerfdieu, Elchanan (God-Given) turned into Dieudoné, and Isaiah (Salvation of the Lord) was transformed, appropriately, into Dieusalt.

The manner in which so-called traditional Jewish names survived through the centuries has often puzzled people. It can be said that, in great part, this was due to the old Jewish custom of naming a child after a deceased person. This resulted in the seeming popularity of a given name in a certain geographic area, as can be seen from the genealogical tree that was drawn up by the medieval French rabbi, Meshullam ben Moses. He was able to trace his descent in an unbroken line for fourteen generations, over a time period of about three hundred and fifty years. Beginning with himself and going backward, the lineage showed Meshullam ben Moses ben Ithiel ben Moses ben Kalonymos ben Meshullam ben Kalonymos ben Moses ben Kalonymos ben Ithiel ben Moses ben Meshullam ben Ithiel ben Meshullam. These fourteen generations of men in paternal descent bore only *four* names!

By the middle of the eighteen century, when the walls of the European ghettos began to crumble under the political, economic, and social changes brought about by the industrial revolution, the cultural movement among Jews called "the Enlightenment" (Haskalah) came into being in Central Europe. From that time on, it became the custom among Jews for them to take on family names like all other Europeans. When Moses (Mosheh) ben Mendel (Menachem) came to Berlin from Dessau, he translated his already previously altered patronymic into German, and thus identified himself as Moses Mendelssohn (Moses son of Mendel). This family name-taking marked an important phase in the rapid emergence of the Jew as a European.

A generation or two later, the Austrian Emperor, Joseph II, issued a decree ordering all Jews in the Empire to take on fixed family names, because—in the old "Moses ben Mendel" days—it had not been possible to keep continuous official records of Jews. The Austrian authorities proceeded to register all the Jews in the Empire under their new surnames. There were, however, many tradition-bound Jews who resisted this effort to Europeanize them, and although they eventually had to bow before superior force, they found some solace in the fact that at birth every Jewish child was still given and all his life retained a Hebrew name which tied him, through his father, to his ancestors. This name was used on certan religious occasions, such as his being called to read aloud from the Torah Scroll in the synagogue.

Traditionally, since the nineteenth century, the epitaph on a Jewish tombstone bears both the Hebrew religious name as well as the civil name of the deceased.

In Central and East European countries, the state authorities, during the late eighteenth and early nineteenth centuries were often guilty of a sadistic practice. On numerous occasions, they arbitrarily registered Jews under the most outrageous surnames despite the anguished protests of their victims. They inscribed them under such ridiculous names as Kuh (Cow), Kalb (Calf), Eselskopf (Donkey-Head), Bronfin (Brandy), Schnappser (Whiskey-Guzzler), Taschengreifer (Pickpocket), Fresser (Glutton), Shtinker, and other such names. It was only after much humiliation, trouble, and legal expense in subsequent generations that their descendants were able to free themselves from these odious names.

Jewish family names, since the eighteenth century, have very often been place-names; for instance Oppenheimer, for a man from the town of Oppenheim; Wilner, for a man from Wilna; likewise, Berliner, Warschauer, Wiener, Krakauer, Lemberger, Goldberger, Greenberger, etc. Sometimes the family names referred to a country or a people, as in Franzos, Franco, Frankel, Hollander, Deutsch, Pollak, Italiäner, Navarro, Oestreicher, etc. In the same way in Italy, the names Montefiore, Romano, Romanelli, Mortara, Modena, etc., all refer to a man from a particular city.

As among other peoples, many Jews adopted names that had reference to their trades or callings, which were often passed on from generation to generation in the same family: Wechsler (Money-Changer), Aptheker (Druggist), Schneider (Tailor), Schuster (Shoemaker), Schechter or Schacter ([from the Hebrew] Shochet! [Ritual Slaughterer]). Chazzan or Chasan (Yiddish for "Cantor") had its equivalent in other languages too: in German, Cantor or Kantor; in Italian, Cantarini; and in Dutch, Voorsanger. Especially fertile in variations were names built upon genealogical pride: Cohen (Priest) and Levi (Levite). The name Cohen has a number of variants: Cohn, Kohn, Kahn, Kahan, Kahana, Kahanowsky, Kahanovich, Kagan, etc. All individuals bearing these names claim descent from the Temple priests of Biblical times. Even greater inventiveness has been shown with regard to variants of the name Levi: Halevi, Levie, Levy, Lavey, Lev, Levene, Leven, Levien, Levenson, Levin, Levine, Le Vine, Levinsky, Levitt, Levitsky, Levinsohn, Levinthal, Levison, Lewey, Lewin, Lewisohn, Lewinson, Lewis, Leb, Loeb, Lobel, Lebe[illegible] Loew, Loewi, Lofy, Lowie, Lovy, Low, Loewenstein.

The tendency to Americanize, Anglicize, Hispanicize, [illegible] Germanize Jewish names has long been evident. Often th[e] name-change, in varying degree, has some connection wit[h] the original, whether in meaning or in phonetics. One is, there[-]fore, no longer safe trying to determine Jewish identity mere[-]ly on the basis of a name. This irresistibly brings to min[d] Shakespeare's disparaging quip: "What's in a name?" Mo[st] people will be ready to agree that a name is merely a hand[le] for the convenience of identification.

NAZARITES. *See* HEAD COVERING; INTOXICATION.

NAZIS, THE

The Nazi terror under Adolf Hitler against the Jews did not begin as it is averred, after World War I and as a popular reaction to the national humiliation suffered by the German people following the imposition upon it of the onerous Versailles peace terms. It had its origin long, long before and was actually, for the Jews in Germany, the ripe fruit of a thousand years of blood-red blooming. Nazism in Germany was a tradition of pious and respectable standing. Its lineage was illustrious, for it counted among its venerable ancestors the Crusaders, the preaching friars, the butchers of the Black Death, and the mass-murderers Rindfleisch, Armleder, Fettmilch, to name only a few. (*See* MASSACRES: THE CRUSADES and BLACK DEATH.)

The exact line of demarcation between "medieval" anti-Semitism and "modern" anti-Semitism is impossible to determine, for, in truth, both equally belong to the Dark Ages, and their deeds, as well as their words, have created their own chamber of horrors that, on close scrutiny, make a mockery of any pretensions to civilization and progress.

There can be found no better illustration for this conclusion than the astonishing turnabout that Martin Luther, the founder of the Protestant Reformation, took after some twenty years' of courageously belaboring the Catholic Church for its "cruel" and "un-Christian" treatment of the Jews. Seeing that "the damned rejected race" could not be won over to "the true faith" by persuasion, Christian "patience," and gentleness, he finally counseled a different course of action to his adherents in the manifesto, Concerning the Jews and Their Lies (1544). This is a document which all students of history will recognize as being a blueprint (except for the religious implications it makes) of Adolf Hitler's genocidal program "for the final liquidation of the Jewish problem." Luther wrote:

> Set their synagogues on fire, and whatever does not burn up should be covered or spread over with dirt so that no one man may ever be able to see a cinder or stone of it. . . . Their homes should likewise be broken down and destroyed. . . . They shall be put under one roof, or in a stable, like gypsies, in order that they may realize that they are not masters in our land, as they boast, but miserable captives—as they complain of us before God with bitter wailing. They should be deprived of their prayer-books and Talmuds in which such idolatry, lies, cursing and blasphemy are taught. . . . Their rabbis must be forbidden to teach under the threat of death.

(How diametrically opposite to Luther's were the fair-minded opinions about the Jews and the Talmud of the outstanding Protestant scholar and humanist, Johann Reuchlin, who expressed his views about sixty years later in a controversy with the notorious apostate Jew, Pfefferkorn [*see* TALMUD, THE].)

Luther's now beligerent hatred of the Jews became a standard fixture of Protestant theology until the nineteenth century, when liberal Protestant thinking began working out its own "reformation" and searching of conscience with regard to the Jews. Consequently, it gradually rejected Luther's violent notions and feelings as being incompatible with Christian teachings and ethics.

Nonetheless, so inflamed did Protestant passions against the Jews in Germany continue to be that, more than two hundred years after Luther's appeal to terror, they did not spare even "the Plato of Germany"—Moses Mendelssohn, the grandfather of the composer Felix Mendelssohn. In a letter in 1780 to a friend, a monk of the Benedictine Order, the philosopher unburdened himself of his sorrow:

> Everywhere in this so-called tolerant land, I live so isolated through real intolerance, so beset on every side, that out of love for my own children, I lock myself up in a silk factory, as in a cloister. In the evening, I take a walk with my wife and children. "Father," asks one of the innocents, "why does that fellow yell after us? Why do they throw stones at us? What have we done to them?" "Yes, dear Father," says another [child]. "They always follow us in the streets and scream at us: 'Jews! Jews!' Father, do these people think it is a disgrace to be a Jew? And why does it matter to them?" Ah, I close my eyes, stifle a sigh inwardly, and exclaim: "Poor humanity! You have indeed brought things to a sorry pass!"

The Jews of Europe had to wait some fifteen hundred years before they were officially accorded their equality *as human beings* with all other men. It was the libertarian French Revolution, taking fire from the American Revolution in 1776, that extolled reason above dogma, "the rights of man" above the rights of kings and nobles, and freedom of conscience above subservience to an authoritarian Church, that liberated the Jews from their ghetto-prison. On September 28, 1791—a red-letter day in both French and Jewish history—the National Assembly, sitting in Paris, granted by decree equal rights to the Jews, declaring "that the Jews enjoy the privileges of full citizens."

However, this was not accomplished before the defeat of the clericalist onslaught against the decree by the leaders of the Revolution: Mirabeau, Robespierre, the Abbé Grégoire, and Clermont-Tonnerre. The last-mentioned deputy gave the Assembly this reassurance: "To Jews as human beings—everything; to Jews as a people—nothing!" His intention, he averred, was to make them Frenchmen first, yet at the same time enable them to practice their religion without abuse or molestation, since that was a matter of private conscience.

The process of becoming Frenchmen for many Jews was so rapid, that, according to the eminent Franco-Jewish scholar Joseph Reinach: "After 1791 it was no longer proper to speak of the 'Jews of France' but only of 'French citizens professing the Jewish religion.'"

The Napoleonic Code which followed gave more substantial legal form to the decree voted by the National Assembly. But when Napoleon's star set at the Battle of Waterloo in 1815, the countries which he had taken by conquest scrapped the code. The Prussian Landtag (Diet), which under his prodding had granted civil equality to the Jews of Prussia, promptly invalidated the measure as an aberration of liberalism.

Following the monarchistic Reaction in Europe to the French Revolution, a camarilla which had been organized as the "Holy Alliance" by the Congress of Vienna in 1814–15, the Jews again were burdened with some of the familiar humiliating restrictions that had originated during the Middle Ages. The demagogues and rabble-rousers once more made their public appearance in Germany and in 1879 whipped up the lowest dregs of the population to attack the Jews in Bamberg, Carlsruhe, Mannheim, Heidelberg, Würzburg, Hamburg, and Frankfort-am-Main. As the mobs rioted, beating up Jews and looting the Jewish quarters of those cities, they raised in chorus the hoot the Crusaders used to give six centuries before when they fell upon the Jews—"*Hab hab!*" ("Give give!") Only this time the modern "crusaders" gave it a slight phonetic alteration but with a big difference in meaning—"*hep hep!*" (the combined initial letters of the Latin words *Hierosolyma est perdita!* "Jerusalem is destroyed!") This catcall became the favorite cry of the anti-Semitic mobs on the

Rioting, killing, and looting by German mob led by Vincent Fettmilch in the Frankfort-am-Main ghetto on August 22, 1614. (Engraving in Chronica *by H. M. Gottfried, Germany, 1642.)*

rampage everywhere in Europe during the nineteenth century, and again in the 1930's by the Nazi storm troopers in their murderous assaults on the Jews. But the followers of Hitler added it to still another war cry—the blood-curdling "*Judaverrecke!*" ("Perish, Judah!")

Prelude to Slaughter. Almost two decades have passed (in 1964) since the end of the Nazi regime in 1945. Nevertheless, it is still difficult to discuss dispassionately this nightmarish chapter in contemporary history, especially where it concerns the Jews—not only those in Germany but in all Europe. Nor is it possible, as yet, to assess objectively all the consequences to mankind resulting from the flood of evil and calamity let loose by the Nazis; they engulfed the world in the most devastating war in history, and caused the death of some 25,000,000 people of whom 6,000,000 were Jews. Reading these neatly rounded, statistical estimates of corpses that once were human beings, it is not possible to visualize the enormity of the agony and the crime. It is an understatement to say that the Nazi terror undermined civilization and set in motion a series of terribly disruptive forces which have still to run their demonic course in history.

In the eyes of the world, but mistakenly so, it was one man alone—Adolf Hitler—who generated the Nazi (National Socialist Party) holocaust. Actually, in the first years of his propagandizing, Hitler was only a marionette who ranted, strutted, and grimaced while the German General Staff, the *Junker* barons, and the great Ruhr industrialists pulled the political strings. From the very beginning, Jews were given a suspicious prominence as targets of the rabble-rousing of the Nazis; seven out of the twenty-five points in their program dealt exclusively with the Jews. The Nazis nakedly proclaimed at the very outset their racist objectives: ". . . no Jew can be considered a fellow countryman."

In the late 1920's, the Nazis flooded Germany with obscene posters, stickers, and anti-Semitic leaflets of the gutter variety. Well-organized Nazi mobs roamed through the streets shouting, "*Judaverrecke!*" ("Perish, Judah!") The contagion spread swiftly. On November 7, 1923, the *Berliner Tageblatt* took note: "Not only have Jewish shops been plundered and Jews sought out in their homes, but some of them have had their clothes torn from their backs and have been chased naked through the streets while a jeering mob ran after them and beat them."

Many thoughtful, decent Germans were quite mystified as well as appalled at the spread of this agitation. They could not grasp the demagogic intention of the Nazis in selecting the Jews as "the racial enemy." Yet the official pronouncements of Hitler, Goering, and Goebbels all during this time openly stated their motive for "honoring" the Jews in this manner. In the Nazi party pamphlet, *Hitler's Official Program*, it was declared with cynical frankness: "Anti-Semitism is, in a sense, the emotional foundation of our movement."

Hitler beat on all the drums of hate. To the gutter-mob he held out the bright prospect of looting the Jews of their "gold" and possessions. To those who still smarted under the disgrace of national defeat in 1918 he kept repeating incessantly that if Germany lost the war, it was only because the "Marxian-democratic-liberal-capitalistic Jews" had stabbed the country in the back in order to aid its enemies. In fact, in a speech he delivered in April, 1923, he charged that the Jews had caused the war. They had brought it on, he said, because they were diabolically determined to destroy all of Aryan civilization. He charged too that the Jews, with that end in mind, had "invented" democracy and the Weimar Constitution (this had been drawn up by Hugo Preuss, a Jew who was the German Minister of Justice). "What are the Jewish aims?" asked Hitler rhetorically. And he answered himself: "To spread their invisible State as a supreme tyranny over all the other states in the whole world."

When the Reichswehr generals, the Ruhr industrialists, and the *Junker* landowners were persuaded that the time was ripe for it, they brought Hitler and his National Socialist Party to power. They accomplished this long-hoped-for end on January 30, 1933, with the complaisance of the titular figurehead of the Weimar Republic, the aged national hero, Field Marshal von Hindenburg.

In the course of the thirteen years of furious and benumbing propaganda before their seizure of power, the Nazis had succeeded in making overt and muscular anti-Semitism appear not only respectable but even patriotic to millions of frustrated and embittered Germans. Now, as Fuehrer of the Reich, Hitler's very word became law, and he encountered little difficulty in making his program "acceptable" even to those Germans who had at first felt revulsion for him but who, finally, were intimidated into acquiescence.

Torture, mutilation, and murder of Jews in Vienna following the burning alive (center) of the converted Jew Ferdinand Franz Engelberger, who, at the climactic moment before death, recanted and declared himself a Jew at heart. (Copper engraving. Vienna, 1642.)

Title page of Martin Luther's attack on the Jews and the Jewish religion: About the Jews and Their Lies, *Wittenberg, Germany, 1543.*

As soon as the Nazis came to power, they started a campaign of suppression–the same repeated by them several years later in all the countries they occupied–which followed a well-defined pattern. They systematically expelled Jews from all public places: from theatres, concert halls, museums, and parks. They also strictly forbade Jews to have any social contact with Gentiles. Any infringement of these orders was severely punished, and to make sure that they were obeyed, police and storm troopers would raid all public places in search of Jews.

Step by step, with micrometer precision, the Nazis proceeded to eliminate the Jews from every area of German economic, social, and cultural activity. On April 1, 1933, the boycott of Jewish business establishments began officially. Jewish doctors, dentists, and lawyers found posted on their doors the official warning: "*Achtung!* A Jew! Visits are prohibited!" Germans who disobeyed the injunction were harshly punished. Many were severely beaten, some were given prison sentences, others lost their jobs. In April, 1935, the government ordered Jewish children expelled from all the schools in Germany.

Dr. Joseph Goebbels, the Minister of Propaganda, put the matter quite bluntly in an interview he gave to a London journalist on July 7, 1935: "'Jewry must perish!' has been our battle cry for the last fourteen years. Then let it perish at last!"

Genocide. At no time, even during the years before they came to power, did the Nazis attempt to conceal their ultimate intention of exterminating all the Jews in the world. The speeches of Hitler and of his "Jewish specialists," Dr. Alfred Rosenberg and Julius Streicher, were shrill with this murderous decision. Even the storm troopers' marching songs in the early 1920's were crazed paeans to the prospect of Jewish blood gushing in rivers–a sort of criminal sadists' Walpurgis Night to celebrate the ascendancy over mankind of the Aryan-German master-race. But there were few normal-minded people who were ready to believe that such a monstrous plan was being contemplated; only a small number of knowledgeable Gentiles took these threats seriously. Then, on September 15, 1935, the Nuremberg Racial Laws were promulgated in line with the "racial purity" obsession of the Nazis. These laws established the guideline that anyone who had more than one-quarter Jewish "blood" in his veins was not to be considered German and was to be ejected from German national life.

Even though the assassination of a minor Nazi embassy official in Paris by a seventeen-year-old Jewish boy was followed by a retaliatory pogrom in Germany on November 7, 1938, the Allied world still did not believe that Hitler's intentions where the Jews were concerned were so implacably murderous and far-reaching. In fact, even after the German army invaded the Soviet Union in 1941 and during that summer massacred some 200,000 Jews in Minsk, Vitebsk, Grodno, Bialystok, Brest-Litovsk, Berdichev, and other cities, and an additional 250,000 in towns and cities of the Ukraine, including Kiev and Kharkov, there were still many people so unsophisticated in their knowledge of the world power-struggle then being waged that they scoffed at the mere notion that Hitler was planning *the total extermination* of the Jewish people. Oddly, these skeptics did not believe this even after Hitler himself formally declared it to be his state policy in a speech he delivered before a National Socialist Party rally on January 30, 1942.

By September, 1941, it had become plain to many discerning people that there were terrible developments afoot; there had begun the systematic deportation of Jews into concentration and labor camps especially built for them in Poland and in Nazi-occupied Soviet territory. True, during the 1930's–the preparatory or "cold pogrom" period–concentration camps had been erected in Buchenwald, Dachau, Sachsenhausen, and Oranienburg, but they were used principally to house such political opponents of the Nazi regime as Catholics, Communists, Liberals, and Socialists. But after the blitz had extended the Nazi grip over most of the countries of Europe, Hitler and his Gestapo chief, Heinrich Himmler, decided that, with the bulk of the Jews of Europe already "rounded up," it was time to proceed with their extermination, which should take place in an orderly, businesslike way. With the genius for organization and efficiency for which the German people are famous, the Nazis embarked on their genocidal project as if they were establishing new smelting plants and coke ovens in the industrial Ruhr, employing for it the latest technological advances.

For various reasons, Hitler and his advisers thought it both prudent and efficient to establish most of the death factories for the Jews in out-of-the-way places, mainly in

The German word Jude *(Jew) was daubed on almost every Jewish shop and professional shingle, and all their owners were earmarked for total boycott during the initial stage of the Nazi take-over in Germany, in April, 1933. (YIVO.)*

Poland: in Oświeçim (Auschwitz), Birkenau, Maidenek, Treblinka, Bergen-Belsen (this last in Germany), to name only a few. The "raw material" for these plants–dazed Jewish humanity herded together from all parts of Europe–arrived, packed to suffocation, in trainloads and truck convoys.

While large-scale killings had gone on before in the concentration camps, these had not yet taken on a conveyor-belt character for the production of corpses. How nightmarish and shocking in its details the vast program of extermination, interrupted only by the crushing defeats of the Nazis by the Allied armies, became can be seen in the official indictment that was presented before the International Tribunal for Nazi War Criminals convened in Nuremberg in October, 1945:

> The murders and ill-treatment were carried out by diverse means, including shooting, hanging, gassing, starvation, gross overcrowding, systematic under-nutrition, systematic imposition of labor tasks beyond the strength of those ordered to carry them out, inadequate provision of surgical and medical services, kickings, beatings, brutality and torture of all kinds . . . Along with adults, the Nazi conspirators mercilessly destroyed even children. They killed them, with their parents, in groups and alone. They killed them in children's homes and hospitals, burying the living in the graves, throwing rato flames, stabbing them with bayonets, poisoning them, conducting experiments upon them, extracting their blood for use of the German army, throwing them into prison and Gestapo torture chambers and concentration camps, where the children died from hunger, torture and epidemic disease.

In the extermination camp in Chelmno, 1,135,000 Jews were slaughtered; in the Maidenek camp near Lublin, 750,000 Jews were killed; in Oświeçim and its subsidiary plants, almost 4,000,000 Jewish lives were snuffed out. The register of the slain in the electric crematoria of Birkenau–a typical example–reads like a carefully itemized bookkeeping account of an industrial firm; the plant first gassed, then burned, 6,000 Jews *every single day.*

The tragedy of an individual human being can become understandable to another only if the latter can identify himself personally with it. But how is it possible to grasp the total tragedy of 6,000,000 murdered Jews? It is a grief so vast, an act so shocking, that it leaves one appalled, benumbed, and self-protectingly cold. The normal imagination cannot assimilate, cannot focus, on the reality of criminal acts executed on such a *statistical* scale. This kind of reaction was officially expressed by the English General Sir Douglas Brownrigg when he visited the Breendonck Death Camp in Belgium after the Nazis had fled: "It is difficult to make a normal person believe that such abnormalities could exist today in so-called civilized Europe. I almost wonder whether I should not have been a little skeptical had I not seen things for myself."

The Sleepwalkers and the Fighters. Why didn't the Jews fight back more than they did? That is the question that is so often asked with an emotional intensity and an incredulity that demands an answer. If the question is asked by a Jew, it is often motivated by a feeling of shame, of deeply injured group self-esteem; if the question is asked by a Gentile, sometimes it is tinged with scorn, but more frequently with bafflement. Really, then, why didn't the Jews fight back, seeing that they had nothing to lose? Why did they allow themselves to be led most of the time into the Nazi gas-chambers like sheep to the slaughter?

To be sure, there were a great number of occasions when Jews, whether in organized groups or as individuals, chose to resist in whatever way they could and with whatever means they could find, to give blow for blow, to take life for life. It happened in heroic uprisings at the Warsaw, Vilna, Bialystok, Cracow, Lvov, Tarnopol, and other ghettos. They also took place in the death camps at Sobibor, Poniatowka and Treblinka, where it was almost impossible to make even the most guarded attempt to plan an uprising because of the constant and efficient surveillance by the Germans and the presence of informers among the prisoners themselves. In the notorious Treblinka camp, for instance, although weakened by systematic starvation and overwork, the Jewish slave-laborers on August 2, 1943, launched carefully planned attacks on all the key points of the internal defense system. So bold, so perfectly swift and synchronized was their operation that they quickly overpowered and killed the guards. After burning the entire camp to the ground, the prisoners fled to the woods, but only a few managed to escape recapture and certain death.

Yet in the over-all frame of reference of the 6,000,000 Jews who perished, those were but isolated instances of resistance, for it would seem that the great majority of Jews went to their deaths neither sorrowing that they were leaving this precious thing called life nor rejoicing that their agony would soon be at an end. They entered the gas chambers, or faced the firing squads or dug their own graves like sleepwalkers, only partly aware of what was happening to them. This is the inevitable conclusion one reaches from reading some of the thousands upon thousands of letters, memoirs, official Nazi reports, and other documentary evidence about the greatest crime in history–evidence that has survived those who perished.

The thought springs readily to mind that, had the victims only brought themselves to believe that the nightmarish plan for their total annihilation–a plan that was being blared forth much of the time on all the official trumpets of Nazi hatred–was something actually real and impending, there would have occurred many many more acts of resistance regardless of whether the outcome could have altered the hopeless situation.

Actually, there were few Allied statesmen, diplomats, journalists, and intellectuals in Europe, in the United States and in other countries who gave much, if any, credence to the Nazi genocidal announcements, notwithstanding that their sources of reliable information and appraisal of the situation were far greater than those of the trapped Jews in

Polish Jew having his beard plucked out by the roots with a forceps by a "humorous" Nazi soldier before an appreciative audience on a Berlin Street. (Photo loaned by Lester.)

lated in the camps. They could not give credence to them—as so many of them later stated—because they believed only deranged criminal minds were capable of conceiving a genocidal plan that was so bestial and ghastly.

The Battle of the Warsaw Ghetto. The events that took place in Warsaw prior to the battle of the ghetto there well illustrat the general disbelief regarding the Nazis' intentions. In that Polish metropolis, the Gestapo had systematically, by means of suprise raids and dragnets, corralled all the Jews of the city and its suburbs into a new compulsory ghetto which was carved out of the old one and sealed off tightly from the rest of the city by a high brick wall that was heavily guarded.

On November 15, 1939, after the last Jews had finally been brought into the Warsaw ghetto, the round-up operation was declared by the Germans to be officially completed. A population count at that time showed there were 433,000 men, women, and children concentrated in the small area of the ghetto. The Nazi governor of the city announced without ceremony: "We will destroy this tribe! They will disappear from hunger and wretchedness."

Hunger, organized along the well-known German technological lines, was employed as the first deadly weapon of extermination. Contagious diseases, resulting from the indescribable overcrowding, also killed off hundreds daily. But his was not all: The governor then inaugurated a reign of error which raged day after day and which was calculated o have a cumulative bad psychological effect on the Jews because it created an atmosphere of general hysteria, of near paralysis which would discourage any thought of organized esistance.

Here too is visible another Nazi psychological device for ranquilizing the suspicion of the condemned—the employment of a pliant Jewish Council (*Judenrat*), some of whose members had been appointed by the Gestapo itself from among the well-known and wealthy Jews of Warsaw. By means of "in-group" intimidation and repression, and sometimes by the most bare-faced deception, the *Judenrat* helped keep the Jewish population "in order" for the Gestapo. It supplied the Germans with the required slave-labor gangs, submitted to them secret reports about all grumblers and potential mutineers, and fulfilled the quotas of deportees required for the gas chambers. Striking a tragic note of exceptional character was the unexpected suicide of the president of the *Judenrat;* he apparently could no longer live with himself while playing toady and shepherd-dog to the murderers of his people.

Most interesting was the technique that the Nazis employed in getting the Jews to go "willingly" to their deaths. The first deportations from Warsaw to the extermination centers at Treblinka, Oświęcim, Maidenek, and Bergen-Belsen took place toward the end of July, 1942. A proclamation was posted on the street corners in the ghetto, ordering all Jews, except those working in war plants, to register for immediate and happier "resettlement" in another part of the country. The German authorities went through the pretense of organizing them into labor groups, sorting them out according to their separate trades. But few, if any, suspected the true nature of their destination. Old people and children were shipped out first in daily contingents of 2,000. That number was soon stepped up to 10,000 and finally to 20,000 a day.

During a brief pause in this "resettlement" operation, an egotistical kind of hope burgeoned crazily again among the Warsaw Jews. The general belief was that "the practical Germans" merely wanted "to get rid of" the non-productive Jews; those with industrial trade skills would be spared. Strange, how self-deceiving human beings can be! Although with their own eyes the Jews saw hundreds of their fellows being summarily shot every day on the street by the Nazi soldiers and the *Januks* (the collaborationist Ukrainian and Lithuanian guards), and although they afterwards watched the corpses being taken away in carts and saw them buried in unmarked mass-graves, like carrion, nonetheless, they deluded themselves (the wish no doubt serving as the father to the thought) that they themselves would be saved. They willed themselves to believe in the possibility of miracles, at least where they, the still living, were concerned.

But even if the great majority of Warsaw Jews willed to deceive themselves, there were many clear-thinking young men and women who were able to draw the proper inferences from the Nazi actions. It can be safely stated, on the basis of corroborating data acquired at a later date, that it was neither despair nor an unwholesome hunger for martyrdom which led these youths to prepare for an uprising. Theirs was a calculating and carefully planned act of retribution. Although at first, because of sharp political and religious cleavages, they were unable to unite their combat units against their deadly foes, when the first blood-curdling accounts of the mass-extermination of the Jews in the death camps were brought to the ghetto by Polish and Jewish underground messengers, they had a sobering but also unifying effect on the ghetto fighters. Their bickering promptly ceased, and after a hurried conference, the Jewish Fighting Organization came into being and hastened to make ready for the uprising, which began in April, 1943.

Art gallery, owned by a Jew, closed and guarded against customers by a Nazi storm trooper in the early Hitler period. (YIVO.)

In flames from the German bombardment, a Jewish fighter leaps to his death. (Photo by S.S. General Stupnagel, commander of the besieging Nazis. YIVO.)

Entire Jewish families forced out of bunkers by German troops. (Photo by S.S. General Stupnagel, commander of the besieging Nazis. YIVO.)

There are few battles in the history of mankind that can compare with the fantastically unequal struggle which marked the Battle of the Warsaw Ghetto. On one side was drawn up the unlimited panzered might of the German Army, the Gestapo, and the collaborationist *Januks.* Pitted against them stood the last remnants of Warsaw's starving Jews–some 40,000 emaciated and physically exhausted civilians who were led in battle by small combat units of the Jewish Fighting Organization, which altogether consisted of several thousand men and women. Food supplies to the ghetto had been cut off. The Jews were wretchedly armed. Worse yet, since they were confined to a small area within the ghetto, they were unable to maneuver around the enemy. Nevertheless, they succeeded in holding the Nazi army under Gestapo General Jurgen Stroop at bay for forty-two days! Almost every one of the Warsaw fighters perished in the end, but like their blinded ancestor, Samson, they brought down with them to their death some 5,000 of the hated enemy.

Nazi officers enter into the ghetto ablaze from the German bombardment. (Photo by S.S. General Stupnagel, commander of the besieging Nazi division. YIVO.)

The Tlomacka Synagogue in Warsaw, blown up by the Nazis. (YIVO.)

Jewish last-stand fighters driven out of their bunker and sho several minutes later by the Germans. (Photo by S.S. Genera Stupnagel, commander of the besieging Nazis. YIVO.)

Global Hate: Poland, Romania, Austria, etc. Those who thought that the chauvinistic Nazis were interested only in purifying "Germany for the Germans" were soon to discover their error. As the Nazi youth formations goose-stepped throughout the land, they sang confidently: "Today Germany [is ours]—tomorrow, the world!" With this objective in mind, Hitler and his ministers were resolved to make of anti-Semitism an effective weapon for global conquest. The Fuehrer once boasted to Hermann Rauschning of Danzig, an old associate: "You will see how little time we shall need in order to upset the ideas and criteria of the whole world, simply and purely by attacking Judaism."

The Nazis beamed a steady propaganda barrage over short-wave radio to every country in the world. Through this means and also through motion pictures, newsletters, periodicals, books, and millions of leaflets, which they fed free to all foreign sympathizers and anti-Semitic organizations, they obtained a firm foothold in many countries. By pounding away tirelessly on the single synthetic theme of "the Jewish Bolshevist and capitalistic menace," they made a great part of the Western World racist-conscious. The image of the Jew they were building up on a vast global scale was that of a monster of evil, stretching out his tentacles into each country to strangle it.

The plague of Jew-baiting that swept the world beginning with 1933 soon reached epidemic proportions. There were indigenous Nazi-patterned parties formed everywhere: in Norway, under Vikdun Quisling; in England, under Sir Oswald Mosley; in Quebec, under Adrien Arcand; in South Africa, under Dr. Daniel Malan, who later became Prime Minister.

Most powerful was the Nazi influence in Romania. There fascism triumphed in 1937 when King Carol, himself a pro-Nazi, made Octavian Goga, the anti-Semitic leader of the Iron Guard, head of the government. During his brief stay in power, Goga and his Iron Guard followed the Nazi anti-Semitic blueprint in almost every detail. Goga's successor, Miron Christea, the Patriarch of the Romanian Orthodox Church, declared in 1938: "The Jews are sucking the marrow from the bones of the nation." His ultra-clericalist government completed the legal, economic, and cultural strangulation of Romanian Jewry, numbering more than 800,000.

The anti-Semites of Poland, who were sitting in the saddle of power and who, long before the Nazis appeared in Germany, had shown themselves to be past masters in the art of baiting Jews, required neither mentoring nor inspiration from the German Nazis on how to deal with "their Jews." When Marshal Josef Pilsudski seized power in Poland in 1926 by a coup d'état, although he still gave lip service to his "socialist principles" by abolishing all anti-Jewish laws, he, nevertheless, accomodated himself to "unofficial" Jew-baiting, an activity in which both government authorities and the political leaders engaged enthusiastically. The economic crisis at the time made expedient the maltreatment of the Jews, who had always served as the traditional scapegoats for the misery of the Christian masses.

The new anti-Semitism in Poland proved most aggressive in the professions, in the universities, in government departments, and especially in business and commerce. Hardest hit were the Jewish shopkeepers, the middlemen, and the small manufacturers against whom the "cold pogrom" raged. Major political factors in this virulent agitation during the middle 1930's were the Endeks (National Democrats) and the Naras (National Radicals). Another well-organized "cold pogrom," later copied by the Nazis, began to operate in all fields of activity; it led to privation and ruin for many of the 3,000,000 Polish Jews who were declared to be *aliens*, not Poles! For if a livelihood was to be drawn from industry, trade, or commerce, did it not rightly belong to Poles? was the question Poles asked everywhere.

The elimination of the Jews from the economic and public life of Poland thus became a patriotic and even religious cause, with both the government and the Church sanctioning the crusade. The government-owned radio constantly blared forth its appeals to the Polish people to boycott Jewish business establishments. Ignacy Mościcki, the President of the republic, and Marshal Edward Śmigly-Rydz militantly led this campaign. Leaders from most political parties made demagogic and slanderous attacks on the Jews from the rostrum of the Sejm (Parliament) and a concerted campaign of legal and financial restrictions was introduced. The anti-Jewish hysteria soon overflowed into the schools and into all fields of cultural life. "Ghetto-benches" were legalized in all the classrooms by the Minister of Education.

The impoverishment of the Jewish population of Poland spread like a fungus disease; it was hardly possible for Jews to obtain employment outside of enterprises owned by Jews, and these were rapidly closing down. In large industrial cen-

Beaten up and tortured by Munich Nazis, this Jew complained to the police and was promptly paraded by them through the streets carrying the sign: "I will never again ask protection from the police." (YIVO.)

ters, especially in the textile city of Lodz, the pauperization of the Jewish population grew rapidly. Most of the 3,000,000 Jews were now faced with the grim prospect of starvation. From 1918–34, 404,000 Polish Jews left their native land. Hundreds of thousands more were also anxious to leave but either they lacked the means for emigration or they found the gates of other countries barred to them.

Thus, when the Nazis took power in Germany in 1933, the Poles found that making their political and social programs mesh with that of Germany provided no difficulties. Jubilantly, the Polish government, through its Foreign Minister, Josef Beck, a "Pilsudski colonel," established "fraternal" relations with Germany. The "cold" or economic pogrom which had been in operation in Poland for years threatened to become "hot." Incidents of violence, permitted and even encouraged by the authorities, flared up everywhere. The Church even gave its religious sanction to the economic and cultural expulsion of the Jews from Polish life. In his pastoral letter of 1936, the primate of Poland, Cardinal Hlond, advised all Catholics: "It is also true that the Jews are committing frauds, practicing usury and dealing in white slavery . . . one does well to prefer his own kind in commercial dealings, and to avoid Jewish stores and Jewish stalls in the markets."

Polish Jews conveyed to a concentration camp by Nazis at the beginning of the German occupation of Poland in 1939. (YIVO.)

Gate to the Auschwitz (Oswieçim) death camp in Poland, where almost 4,000,000 Jews perished in the crematoria and gas chambers. The sign in German carried the sardonic encouragement to those who entered: Arbeit macht Frei!—*"Work Makes Free!" (YIVO.)*

Jews in a concentration camp digging their own graves while guarded by a Nazi soldier. (Photo loaned by Lester.)

Muscular anti-Semitism was also raging in Austria several years before Hitler came actively to the attention of the world. After World War I, following the dismemberment of the Austro-Hungarian Empire, the Jews again began serving their tiresome historic role as scapegoats. In Vienna, General Ludendorff, the darling of Kaiser Wilhelm of Germany and the Pan-German reactionaries, instructed the clericalist party of Christian Socialists to organize street brawls and riots against the Jews. It was his violent and demagogic inflammation of the public mind in Vienna against the Jews which originally had inspired his great admirer, Hitler, to emulate him in the way of a fuehrer. In the years which followed, with the blessing of the Church, under the rule of the Christian Socialists, led by the Chancellor of Austria, Monsignor Seipel, and later under the clerico-Fascists Prince Starhemberg and Chancellor Dollfuss, a "pious" and "patriotic" cold pogrom was waged in Austria against the Jews in the same way as in Poland—in public life, in business, in the profes-

Jews in a concentration camp, under German guard, digging a mass grave for their massacred brothers. (Photo loaned by Lester.)

Final retribution: leading Nazi defendants at the Nuremberg War Crimes Trial (in 1945) which ended in their conviction. (U. S. Army Photograph.)

sions, and in the universities of Vienna and Graz. The Nazis found the most fertile field for their sowing of fascism outside of Germany in Austria.

While all this was taking place, there was also an upsurge of organized terrorism against the Jews in Hungary, where the reactionary monarchist, Admiral Horthy, had battled his way to power leading his shock troops of the so-called Awakening Magyars. They "awakened" by beating and murdering Jews on trains, on the streets, and in the parks. They threw Jewish passers-by into the Danube and bodily kicked Jewish students out of the universities and colleges. The Jewish communities were completely terrorized; there was no one to whom they could turn for help. And under Horthy's successors, upon the coming of Hitler to power, the anti-Semitic pattern was much expanded and expressed even more violently.

See also ANTI-SEMITISM: THE "RACIAL PURITY" MYTH; CHURCH AND PERSECUTION; COMMUNITY, SELF-GOVERNING; CONVERSION OF JEWS; DISPUTATIONS, RELIGIOUS; DREYFUS CASE, THE; FEUDAL SOCIETY, POSITION OF THE JEWS IN; GHETTO; "HOST DESECRATION" CALUMNIES; KIDDUSH HA-SHEM; KOL NIDRE; MARRANOS AND THE INQUISITION; MASSACRES; MONEYLENDERS; OATH, THE JEWISH; PERSECUTION IN "MODERN" DRESS; POGROMS IN SLAVIC LANDS; "RITUAL MURDER" SLANDERS; SEPARATISM, JEWISH; SHYLOCK MYTH, THE; WANDERING JEW; YELLOW BADGE.

NEBIIM. *See* PROPHETS (*under* BIBLE, THE).

NEFESH. *See* SOUL, THE.

NEGINOT. *See* MUSICAL ACCENTS.

NEILAH. *See* YOM KIPPUR.

NER TAMID. *See* LAMP, PERPETUAL.

NESHAMAH. *See* SOUL, THE.

NESHAMAH YETERAH. *See* HABDALAH.

NEW COVENANTERS. *See* MONASTICISM, JEWISH.

NEW MOON, BLESSING OF THE

There are a number of survivals in the Jewish religion of animism or nature-worship. Imperceptibly, the more primitive conceptions of divinity fused with the ethical ideas and practices of enlightened Judaism. The merging, for example, of the rite to the Babylonian moon-deity, Sin, with later Jewish religious practice, is made arrestingly clear in the Blessing of the New Moon still recited today by Orthodox Jews.

In very ancient times, among the Babylonians, and equally among the tribalistic Israelites, the worshipers followed the curious custom of paying homage to the moon by leaping and dancing toward it. So close to idolatry did this seem to the Jewish religious teachers that, in the days of Ezra and the Scribes, this custom was finally abolished and a modified rite was substituted. This required the Jewish worshiper to rise on tip-toe three times in succession, and with his face upturned toward the moon under the open sky, to recite: "As I dance toward you, but yet cannot touch you, so shall none of my evil-plotting enemies be able to touch me." The symbolism of this custom is curiously associated with that of another still in vogue among the Ultra-Orthodox—that of shaking out one's outer garments at the ceremony, in the pantomine of "shooing" away one's enemies. Primitive symbolism and magic practice somehow have found subterranean ways of enduring in all religions. This part of the ceremony of blessing the moon, which requires at least a quorum of ten (a minyan), ends with the worshipers greeting one another heartily, saying: *"Shalom aleichem! . . . Aleichem shalom!"* ("Peace [Good luck] . . . to us and to all in Israel!")

However, the actual text of the Blessing of the New Moon, as it was first recited by the Talmudic Sages about two thousand years ago and as it is still recited today by the religious traditionalists, employs a poetic-exalted symbolism which reads, in part: "And He ordered the moon to renew itself as a crown of beauty over those He sustained from childhood [i.e., Israel] and as a symbol that they too will be regenerated in time to come. . . . Praise be the Lord Who renews the moon!"

See also ROSH CHODESH.

Blessing of the New Moon. (Etching by Lionel Reiss.)

NEW MOON, FESTIVAL OF THE. *See* ROSH CHODESH.

NEW TESTAMENT. *See* APOCRYPHA; CHRISTIANITY, JEWISH ORIGINS OF; DEAD SEA SCROLLS; POST-BIBLICAL WRITINGS; PSEUDEPIGRAPHA.

NEW YEAR. *See* ROSH HASHANAH.

NINTH OF AB. *See* TISHAH B'AB.

NUMBERS, BOOK OF. *See* BIBLE, THE.

NUMERUS CLAUSUS. *See* THE UNITED STATES (*under* PERSECUTION IN "MODERN" DRESS).

NUREMBERG RACIAL LAWS. *See* GENOCIDE (*under* NAZIS, THE); PERSECUTION IN "MODERN" DRESS.

NUSACH. *See* ASHKENAZIM; PRAYER AND WORSHIP; PRAYER SERVICE; SEFARADIM.

O

OATH, THE JEWISH

Whatever rights Jews possessed after the Church decree of 1215 were either nominal or trifling. An index to their legal position in Christian society lay in the *More Judaico* ("Oath according to the Jews' custom"). This humiliating oath was to be recited before a Christian judge by order of the otherwise humane Emperor Charlemagne. In some places, before taking this oath, the Jew was required to put a wreath of thorns on his head in damning memory of the crucifixion of Jesus—the "hereditary" crime with which the Jew was always charged. Standing ankle-deep in water (in pointed scorn for his having rejected Christian baptism), he was forced to recite aloud: "In the name of the Lord Zebaot I swear truthfully . . . But if I swear falsely, may my descendants be cursed, may I grope along the wall like a blind man . . . at the same time, may the earth open up and swallow me as it did Dathan and Abiram."

Even more humiliating, if possible, were the circumstances under which the oath was for centuries taken in the kingdom of Saxony. There the Jew had to stand on the skin of a sow, an animal sternly forbidden to a pious Jew by ritual law as being the most unclean in the animal kingdom. In Silesia even more sport was made of the Jew when he appeared in a Christian court; there it was required that he recite the text of the *More Judaico* while struggling to keep his precarious balance on a rickety stool from which one leg had been removed. All this he did while wrapped in his tallit (prayer shawl) and wearing the ridiculous sugarloaf hat that the Fourth Lateran Council had mockingly made obligatory for all Jews in order that they might properly be identified as such by Christians.

See also CHRISTIANS, SERVITUDE OF JEWS TO; CHURCH AND PERSECUTION; CONVERSION OF JEWS; WANDERING JEW; YELLOW BADGE.

Jew kneeling before a Christian judge in Augsburg while reciting the humiliating More Judaico—*"the Jews' oath." Germany, 1509.*

Jew of Breslau, Silesia, taking the medieval "Jews' oath" (More Judaico) *in court. His breast is bare and his right hand is on the text of the Ten Commandments in an open Hebrew Pentateuch. He takes the oath while standing on the skin of a sow in mockery of the Jewish religious prohibition against eating pork. (Engraving. Breslau, 17th century.)*

OLAM HA-BAH. *See* WORLD-TO-COME.

OMER, COUNTING OF THE. *See* LAG B'OMER; PASSOVER.

ONE GOD, CONCEPT OF. *See* MONOTHEISM.

ONEG SHABBAT. *See* SABBATH.

ORAL LAW(S). *See* MISHNAH (*under* TALMUD, THE).

ORAL TRADITION(S). *See* MISHNAH (*under* TALMUD, THE).

ORDINATION. *See* RABBI.

ORTHODOX JUDAISM. *See* JUDAISM IN THE MODERN AGE.

P

PALE OF SETTLEMENT. *See* PERSECUTION IN "MODERN" DRESS; POGROMS IN SLAVIC LANDS.

PALESTINIAN TALMUD. *See* TALMUD, THE.

PARADISE. *See* GAN EDEN.

PARENTS AND CHILDREN. *See* FAMILY RELATIONS, TRADITIONAL PATTERNS OF.

PAROCHET. *See* ARK CURTAIN.

PASSIONS, MASTERY OVER

The Talmudic Sages, dedicated teachers of the people, worked for the enlargement and deepening in the Jewish consciousness of ethical values. Being humanists as well as humanitarians, many of them approached the problem of the passions with objectivity and restraint. They argued that, since men were to be considered neither angels nor demons but only creatures of flesh and blood, their turbulent emotions, their often irrational desires, and the complex inner drives that led them to act, could be regarded as being natural to the human personality. The liberal-minded Rabbis thought that it was highly unrealistic to expect anyone to eradicate or fully suppress his passions; the best that could be hoped for was that the individual himself impose a discipline of moderation over them, in harmony with the moral laws of the Torah.

It was by no means remarkable that Greek philosophical ideas—and even terminology—should have infiltrated into Jewish thought when the Jews, living under the hegemony of the Greco-Roman empires, both in Judea and in their populous foreign settlements, experienced the impact of Hellenistic culture. These influences can be plainly discerned in post-Biblical writings and in the literature of the Talmud, which was created in the historic epoch that followed. It is not possible to doubt that the Rabbinic teachings on man's mastery over his passions—a major objective of Jewish thought and practice—owed much to the ideas of the Stoic philosophers whose central postulate was expressed in the axiom by Epictetus: "No man is free who is not master of himself." Philo (the Platonic philosopher of first-century Hellenistic Alexandria) and the Rabbinic Sages of Judea and Babylonia expressed the very same idea in similar words.

There is the ironic reference in the Talmud to the "strong man," Samson, who slew the Philistines "with the jawbone of an ass." Yes, indeed, Samson was able to kill lions, destroy the armies of the Philistines, and raze their cities. But, asks the Rabbinical commentator witheringly: could he master his lust? Not at all! Why? Because "Samson followed his eyes." What was meant by this was that not he himself but his lusting eyes were his master; therefore, in the end, carrying out the sentence of Heaven, the Philistines gouged out his offending eyes—"his master"—that had led him into the gravest sin. The moral of this and similar preachments was that if man wished to become a creature worthy of self-respect and of the divine image in which he was made, it was incumbent on him "to place a bridle upon his passions."

See also ASCETICS, JEWISH; FREE WILL; GOLDEN MEAN, THE RABBINIC; LIFE, JEWISH VIEW OF; REWARD AND PUNISHMENT; SATAN; SIN AND SINNER; YETZER TOB AND YETZER HA-RAH.

Miniature from illuminated parchment manuscript of the Hebrew Pentateuch. Brussels, 1310.

PASSOVER (in Hebrew: PESACH, meaning to "pass over," to "spare")

The most beloved of all Jewish holy days is the festival of Passover. Symbolically, in its most meaningful sense, it represents a cherished traditional Jewish value—a love of freedom. That is the reason why, in the religious literature of the Jews, the festival is referred to pridefully as "the Season of Our Freedom."

The memory of the Bondage in Egypt, although it occurred at least thirty-two centuries ago, has continued to rankle in the macerated consciousness of the Jew. In reality, he has never considered—except for the Golden Age of his people's greatness in the Land of Israel—that the Bondage ever came to an end. This idea is touchingly projected in the Aramaic prayer at the Seder (the home-service that opens the celebration of Passover); this states the theme of the holy day like the opening chorus in a Greek tragedy. As the head of the household, robed in his white kittel and skullcap, and acting on this occasion as the celebrant-priest, gravely raises the tray with the three ceremonial matzot and shows them to the assembled company, he intones in the minor key of well-remembered sorrows: "Behold! This is as the bread of affliction that our fathers ate in the land of Egypt . . . Now we are here—may we be next year in the land of Israel! Now we are slaves—may we be free men in the year to come!"

The poignancy of this prayer is self-revealing. It was composed not too long after the Romans had brought the Jewish national existence in Judea to an end in 70 C.E. Thereafter, driven from their homeland, the dispersed remnants of the Jewish people considered themselves to be living in perpetual "Exile"—Galut—and this fact continuously haunted Jews in whatever country they found themselves. How could they forget it? Most of the time they were struggling for sheer physical survival in the midst of a Gentile hostility that was aggressive, and with the Middle Ages, ever worsening. They were, everlastingly, the victims of social scorn and religious oppression, and were denied even the most elementary of human rights. The ancient liturgist in the Passover Haggadah tried to express the sense of humiliation and rejection that Jews felt when they regarded their status as outcasts in society. Therefore, grim was his reminder: "*Now* we are slaves . . ."

Because of the tormented fate of the Jew throughout history, the observance of Passover since the Middle Ages was suffused with a deep melancholia—this despite the outer festive gaiety and songs of thanksgiving. Raising his commemorative goblet of wine—one of the traditional Four Cups (Arbah Kosot) drunk in the course of the Seder, the maggid—the narrator of the service, who is usually the father and head of the household—intones: "Not just one man has risen against us to destroy us, but in every generation have men risen against us to destroy us. But the Holy One—blessed be He—delivers us always from their hand."

The devout, however, do not too often allow themselves the luxury of despair. They take heart as they listen to the reading of the narrative; they note the many "miracles and wonders" that their God wrought for their ancestors when he liberated them from their Bondage in Egypt. "And the Lord brought us forth out of Egypt with a mighty hand, and with an outstretched arm, and with great terribleness, and with signs, and with wonders. And he hath brought us into this place and hath given us this land [Israel], a land flowing with milk and honey." (Deuteronomy 26:8-9.)

And so it has been a firm tradition since the days of the Mishnah Sages, after the destruction of the Second Temple, that Jewish families throughout the world gather for the performance of the Seder home-service on the first two nights of the eight-day festival. Together (on innumerable occasions in the past, in times of calamity and anti-Jewish agitation, they sat around the festal table in very fear of their lives) they relive, by means of symbolic rites, by the somber narration of the Haggadah, by the offering of prayers and the hymning in unison of their thanksgiving, the most unforgettable episode in their long, long history.

In this saga—part history and part folk legend—of the happy ending and the fulfillment of their forefathers' dream in the Promised Land, they found, over the centuries, the sustaining hope and promise for their own ultimate deliverance from oppression and grief. That precisely was the principal motive for the institution of the Seder home-service by the Patriarch Rabban Gamaliel, late in the first century. He decreed: "In every generation each one should regard himself as if he too had departed from Egypt. It was not our forefathers alone that the Holy One redeemed on that occasion, but through them, us too."

Yet there is no basis for the assumption that Passover had always held such lofty libertarian significance. Until the initiation of drastic religious reforms by Hezekiah, king of

Preparations for the Seder feast. (Woodcut from the Sefer ha-Minhagim, 1695.)

The baking of matzah. (Woodcut from the Sefer ha-Minhagim, 1695).

Judah, (720–692 B.C.E.), at a time when the First Temple period was advancing to its disastrous close, the commemoration of Passover as a festival of spring consisted of primitive rites having nothing in common with the monotheistic religion introduced by Moses in the thirteenth century B.C.E. Even during the considerably more advanced epoch of the Second Temple, Passover represented an incongruous composite of several much older festivals, each having a different rationale and distinctive rites, but all blended together.

Closely linked with the celebration of the Passover festival in the Pentateuch, and referred to in a manner suggesting that they were to be regarded as one and the same, are the Festival of Abib and the Festival of Matzot. Where one begins and the other ends within the conceptual context of Passover is hard to say.

The Festival of Abib (*Abib* in Hebrew means "greening" or "spring") held for the ancient Israelites the same supernatural significance that the Festival of Spring had for the Sumerians, Assyrians, Babylonians, Canaanites, Greeks, and many other peoples who were their contemporaries. The rites of Abib, judging from those observed in other religious festivals commemorating spring, probably constituted a continuous orgiastic revelry in which the fertility cult dominated. But the unseemly and licentious elements were entirely eliminated by the puritanical religious revolution that was effectuated in the middle of the fifth century B.C.E. by Ezra and Nehemiah and completed by the Scribes and the Rabbinic Sages in the centuries that followed.

One agricultural feature in the spring festival was retained from olden times. That was the sacrificial offering of the first sheaf of barley that the farmers brought to the Temple in Jerusalem on the second day of Passover in fulfillment of the Scriptual commandment: "The choicest of the first fruits of thy land thou shalt bring into the house of the Lord thy God." (Exodus 23:19.) It clearly had no "historic" connection with the events connected with Passover. Abib was merely a seasonal harvest festival for the propitiation of the Deity, in order to insure his favor for the success of future crops. Before the people could begin eating the bread made of barley—their principal food staple—they first had to bring the required offerings to the priests at the Temple altar amidst impressive rites and ringing psalmody. (*See* LAG B'OMER.)

In the course of blending religious values and rites—the consequence of historic changes and the evolution of Jewish culture through many centuries—the Festival of Abib seems to have been merged at some unspecified time with the Festival of Unleavened Bread (Festival of Matzot). This may have occurred coincidentally or have been arranged for greater convenience. The origin of the Festival of Unleavened Bread, however, remains not entirely clear. It drew its authority from a Biblical statute which, it should be made clear, is mentioned (in Exodus 23:15) with no special reference to Passover: "The feast of unleavened bread shalt thou keep; seven days shalt thou eat unleavened, as I commanded thee, at the time appointed in the month of Abib [i.e., the month of "Spring"], for in it thou camest out of Egypt." In short, the Israelites had come out of Egypt coincidentally with the Festival of Unleavened bread, which was observed in the month of Spring. And all the ingenious hypothesizing by the Biblical specialists has left the matter still hanging in much the same bafflement.

Here is the crux of the matter: The utterly disproportionate attention given in the Five Books of Moses to the subject of the prohibition of leaven (chametz) persuasively points to the likelihood that it had been a powerful ritual taboo in the religion of the Israelites, and as such it continued, so extraordinary was the devotion of religious Jews to their customs.

The reasoning behind this prohibition or taboo still remains somewhat of an enigma. How important it was considered in the Biblical age is amply proven by the extreme punitive measure that was taken against violators. "Seven days shall ye eat unleavened bread; even howbeit the first day ye shall put away leaven out of your houses: for whosoever eateth leavened bread from the first day until the seventh day, that soul shall be cut off from Israel." (Exodus 12:15.)

Although it is only suggested obliquely, the Bible implies that the eating of leaven, under certain circumstances, constituted a violation of a taboo. One such reference, among several, is found in the covenant itself. It categorically gives this directive to the priests: "You shall not offer the blood of my sacrifice with leavened bread." Obviously, this sacerdotal regulation had no connection with Passover but with the

Preparing knaydlach (matzah balls) for cooking. Alsace, 19th century. (Drawing by Alphonse Lévy.)

The symbolic Search for Leaven (Bedikat Chametz) on the night preceding Passover Eve (the 14th day of Nissan). (Engraving by Bernard Picart, 1723.)

ritual practice of "eating the sacrifice" in general. It thus became a sacrosanct custom—one that was scrupulously observed for a thousand years, during the First and the Second Temple periods—for the priests to eat ritually *only* unleavened bread (matzah) with the flesh and the blood of the animal sacrifices. Perhaps it was in order to rationalize the observance of this primitive taboo that the medieval Cabalists, leaning heavily on allegory and symbolism, described leaven as being a corrupting element in the dough. They also said, figuratively speaking, that it was the symbol of the Yetzer ha-Rah, the Inclination to Evil which is concealed deep in the heart of man.

The question arises again: Why did the Bible make mandatory and why did it bristle with such severity concerning the eating of matzah on Passover instead of bread that was leavened? The premedieval rabbis of the Geonic age, who helped write the Haggadah for Passover, were ingenuous in their explanation: "This matzah that we eat—what is its reason? It is because there was no time for the dough of our ancestors to become leavened. . . ." Namely, because they were leaving Egypt in a great hurry, the Israelites had no time to wait until the dough with leaven in it would rise for baking their bread. It strains credulity that for such a trivial reason, even if it is historically true, the Festival of Unleavened Bread should have been instituted for seven days, and that it carried with it the dire threat of cutting off from the community of Israel anyone who ate leaven during that period!

There is, of course, a direct connection between the eating of matzot on Passover and the Biblical commandment requiring every household to sacrifice a lamb or a kid—"a yearling without blemish"—on the fourteenth day of Nissan. This was to commemorate the day when God had spared the first-born of the Israelite slaves but had slain the first-born of their Egyptian masters. This act of God's justice—rewarding his faithful followers and punishing their enemies—was accomplished by the magical means of the blood-rite, a practice common in primitive religions, both ancient and modern.

> And ye shall take a bunch of hyssop, and dip it in the blood [i.e., the blood of the paschal or Pesach lamb] that is in the basin, and strike the lintel and the two side posts with the blood that is in the basin; and none of you shall go out of the door of his house until the morning. For the Lord will pass through to smite the Egyptians; and when He sees the blood . . . the Lord will *pass over* the door, and will not suffer the destroyer [i.e., the Angel of Death] to come in unto your houses to smite you.
>
> EXODUS 12:22-23

That is how Passover got its name as well as its descriptive—"Night of Watching"—for on that night, the devout believe, God holds vigil over Israel to protect it: "This is the Night of Watching . . . of the Lord for all the children of Israel throughout all generations."

In the view of some scholars, the possibility is not ruled out that the sacrifice of the paschal lamb and the blood-rite which accompanied it had a much greater antiquity than the Bondage in Egypt. But over the course of the primeval centuries, it was absorbed, like the Festival of Abib and the Festival of Unleavened Bread, into the historical concept of Passover. Still, of all this no positive proof can be brought forward; these are merely logical inferences and conjectures.

Originally, the Passover festival was limited to the Night of Watching, when the ritual eating of the paschal sacrifice was observed: "And they shall eat the flesh in that night [i.e., the fourteenth of Nissan], roast with fire, and unleavened bread; with bitter herbs they shall eat it . . . its head with its legs and with the inwards thereof. And ye shall let nothing of it remain until the morning; but that which remaineth of it until the morning ye shall burn with fire." (Exodus 12:8-10.) Moreover, it was to be eaten in haste, with "loins girded" and staff in hand, as the Israelites themselves had been when they departed from Egypt.

Seder Service. (Miniatures from an illuminated Haggadah manuscript, Germany, 15th century.)

Matzah-cover, woolen cross-stitch. Germany, mid-19th century. Besides the benediction over the matzah, the Hebrew words list the various "edible symbols" required for the Seder service.

How far the Passover concept itself wandered with "staff in hand" through the centuries may be judged by its several transformations and fusions. The Biblical commandment strictly confined *to the family* the commemorating sacrificial feast of the paschal lamb, the unleavened bread, and the bitter herbs. No outsider was permitted to participate in this magical family rite. How different it was when the home-service of the Seder was introduced in the first century! Then a new spirituality entered into the celebration of the festival and the primitivism of the old rites was allegorized into new meanings—religious, ethical, and social. In the prefatory declaration with which the father narrator commences the reading of the Haggadah, a fraternal invitation is issued to all who may hear it: "Let all who are hungry enter and eat thereof; and all who are needy come and celebrate the Passover!"

The Search for Leaven (in Hebrew: BEDIKAT CHAMETZ). It has been a custom since an unspecified period in ancient times that on the night preceding the Eve of Passover, the ceremony of Bedikat Chametz take place in each Jewish home where tradition is observed. The head of the household makes a diligent search in all possible places for overlooked crumbs of chametz (bread which is leavened). This is to make sure the house is rid of *all* leavened bread throughout the eight days of Passover, when only matzah—unleavened bread—may be eaten.

It is customary for the diligent searcher to equip himself with a candle, a wooden spoon, and a whisk made of several chicken or goose feathers tied together. At the outset, symbolic of his "search," he "hides" a few crumbs at a starting point on a window sill. During his rounds, he "finds" the crumbs and brushes them ceremoniously into the spoon, pronouncing while doing so the benediction: "Blessed be Thou . . . who has commanded us to remove the leaven." The following morning, the leaven he has put aside is burnt.

Illustration of one of "the Ten Plagues of Egypt," from a 13th-century Haggadah manuscript. (Hamburg State Library.)

The four types of questioners about the Israelites' Exodus from Egypt mentioned in the Haggadah (left to right): the uninformed child, the fool, the wicked man (warrior), and the sage (scholar). (Illustration from an old Haggadah.)

A bewildering number of rabbinic regulations affecting the disposal of chametz had to be observed by the devout, for its presence in the house during the festival was considered an absolute defilement. Jewish communal laws in the old ghetto were severe about such laxness. If any violation was discovered, harsh punishment followed, including the imposition of the symbolic thirty-nine "stripes" or lashes on the violator. This too tends to corroborate the probability of the original existence of a taboo against leaven that had been initiated from a fear of collective punishment of the entire community for the "sin" of an individual.

So thoroughgoing were the cleansing operations for chametz, that all kitchen utensils and silver had to be given a meticulous scouring with hot water, burning with fire, or vigorous scrubbing with sand.

The Seder (Hebrew, meaning "order"; hence, "order of service"). The festival of Passover begins on the eve of the fourteenth day of Nissan (March-April) and lasts eight days, the eighth day having been added during the Middle Ages. (The Jews of modern Israel as well as of Reform congregations observe only seven.) The first two days and the last two are traditionally observed as full holy days; the intermediate ones are considered only half-holy days.

The advent of the festival is marked by elaborate preparations. (This was particularly true in former times, when life in the ghetto was intensely religious in character and the Jewish community was more integrated, single minded and ritual observing.) Special dishes, silver, and pots and pans are used for the entire period. There are special wine-decanters, silver matzah trays, and embroidered matzah covers, special goblets for the Kiddush or sanctification, made usually of silver, brass, or glass. The table, too, around which the entire family gathers for the Seder service and the feast which follows the reading of the first part of the Haggadah, is made as festive and beautiful as both means and taste permit.

For the performance of the rites of the Seder, a number of symbolic foods are required: a z'roah (shank-bone of roast lamb), to recall to the worshipers the paschal lamb that was sacrificed in ancient times; a beitzah (roasted egg)—one of several allegoric explanations given for its inclusion by the rabbis is that the egg, usually a Jewish symbol of the Resurrection and Immortality, also stands for Israel: the longer you cook it, the harder and more indestructible it becomes; a piece of maror ("bitter herbs"—i.e., horseradish), to recall the bitterness of life during the Bondage in Egypt; a dish of salt water; a sprig of karpas (parsley); a mound of charoset

Galician family celebrating the Exodus of their ancestors from Egyptian Bondage. 19th century.

(a mixture of ground apples, raisins, almonds, cinnamon, and wine) that symbolizes the brick and the mortar that Israel's enslaved ancestors had been forced to make in Egypt; and chazeres (a piece of horseradish). All of these foods are put on a special Passover plate which is placed over the three covered ceremonial matzot employed during the service.

The members of the family are gathered at the festal table around the father-narrator. He reclines in demonstrative "ease" on cushions placed at his left side. This ceremonial custom, in imitation of the patrician manner of banqueting customary in Greco-Roman times, began in the first century, when the Seder was introduced; it was meant to symbolize the free status of the Jew. Each participant in the service has a full goblet of wine, and there is a special cup, reserved for the Prophet Elijah that is given the place of honor in the center of the table. It is placed there for him in the confident expectation that the Messiah, of whom he is to be the herald, will "speedily" make his appearance.

The ceremonial act of opening wide the street door at a certain juncture in the Seder service "to let Elijah in" was, on the surface, but a childlike notion, an innocent invention of folklore, since Elijah was popularly considered to be the supreme master of the miracle. Actually, this custom had a more realistic motive. Even since the eleventh century, and even as late as the twentieth, the Blood Accusation was constantly being leveled at the Jews. This was a slanderous charge that, as Passover approached, Jews murdered Christians in order to drain their blood, which they baked into their matzot and also drank ritualistically during the Seder, pretending it was wine.

There was hardly a time or a country in Christian Europe in which Jews did not stand mortally in fear of their lives on account of the frequency of this accusation which erupted more than once into massacres. (*See* "RITUAL MURDER" SLANDERS.) It seems reasonable to assume that this odd custom of opening the door for Elijah was one way of making plain to Christian neighbors that no such bloodthirsty rites were being performed by the Jews. The rabbis, desperately anxious to allay the mass-hysteria of the Christian populace that was being whipped up by rabble-rousers and fanatical priests, banned the use of red wine for the mandatory drinking of the Four Cups during the Seder. Thus, until modern times, only white or raisin wine was permitted for sacramental purposes, even for the cup of sanctification (Kiddush) drunk on the Sabbath!

The ceremony of drinking the Four Cups to denote festivity had been arbitrarily introduced by the Rabbinic

Reading the Haggadah narrative about the Israelites' Bondage and Liberation from Egypt more than 3,000 years ago. Tel-Aviv, 1960. (Israel Office of Information.)

Passover celebration unlike any other celebrated among Jews is that of the 30,000 Portuguese Marranos, accidentally discovered by the mining engineer, Samuel Schwarz, in 1919. Outwardly living as Roman Catholics for several centuries following their forced conversion, they have now formally integrated themselves into the Jewish community of Portugal.

Sages. They justified that number by four Hebrew verbs which appear in Exodus 6:6-7 describing the liberation of the Israelites from the Egyptian Bondage: "bring out," "deliver," "redeem," and "take." One curious custom has always baffled people: Why it is that, during the recital of the Ten Plagues from the Haggadah, as each one is read off, the worshipers spill a little wine from their cups. The reason, declared the Rabbis, was to caution the ethically conditioned Jew through this symbolic act not to rejoice too much–not to drink the cup of triumph to its full in recalling the misfortunes that God had visited upon Israel's ancient oppressors, the Egyptians. The spilling of the wine was to serve as a sober reminder to the Jew that he should not feel vengeful toward his enemies nor gloat over their downfall. The Rabbis cited for their authority Proverbs 24:17: "Rejoice not when thine enemy falleth."

It is related in the Talmud in the form of a teaching parable that, when the angels wanted to join in the "Song of the Sea," which Moses had composed and the Israelites sang in triumph at the crossing of the Red Sea, God hushed them: "What? My children [i.e., the Egyptians] are perishing in the sea and you want to sing!"

The Seder today still is a family celebration, just as it was during the Biblical Age. But the primitive connotations tied in with the observance of the blood-rite of the paschal lamb no longer are present. Besides its commemoration of the freeing of ancient Israel from slavery, the Seder, by implication, celebrates the homely virtues of love and devotion between relations. In the disruptive complexities of today's urban living, when so many parents and their married sons and daughters no longer reside in the same community, and thus "grow away" from one another, the Seder still remains a symbol of family unity. It is, at least, a good reason for a once-a-year "gathering of the clan" around the festal table, with the attendant renewal of familial ties.

The Haggadah. The Hebrew word *haggadah* means a "telling" or "tale." The custom of narrating the historic events of the Bondage and the Liberation, of which Passover is the commemoration, was ordained in the Scriptural commandment: "And thou shalt tell thy son in the day, saying: It is because of that which the Lord did for me when I came forth out of Egypt." (Exodus 13.8.)

The narration by the father-celebrant is dramatized by an effective pedagogic device: The youngest child or participant in the Seder service directs to him "Four Questions" (in Hebrew: *Arbah Kushyot* or *Arbah Sh'elot* or in Yiddish: *Di Feer Kashes*). These queries, which are recited out of the Haggadah in Hebrew and, in many Orthodox homes of East European derivation are also repeated. in Yiddish, ask the father to explain the reasons why ceremonial customs are different on the Seder night from other nights in the year. The father responds with the ageless retelling of the events of the Exodus that begins: "Slaves were we unto Pharaoh in Egypt."

The Haggadah is the book of the Passover Seder service. It combines in anthological form narrative excerpts from the Biblical Book of Exodus interspersed with discussions and interpretive opinions from the literature of the Talmud: the Mishnah, the Gemara, and the Midrash. For contrast, and to heighten and deepen the meaning of the festival, it also contains appropriate prayers, psalms, and special Passover hymns written by medieval liturgists. At the close, two "nursery" jingles (*see* CHAD GADYA) are introduced to arrest the straying attention of the small children during the long Seder service, which usually goes on until late in the evening.

Although some of the prayers in the Haggadah were already in general currency before the Destruction of the Second Temple, the Haggadah in the form in which it is known today first took shape during the second century. It represents a true folk creation, for it took on new accretions in every age after that. Its first appearance as a separate prayer collection occurred during the thirteenth century. Next to the Bible itself, it has been translated into more languages than any other Jewish religious work. Since the Middle Ages, it has gone into many hundreds of editions. One may judge the continuing hold of the work upon rabbinical scholars from the fact that the Vilna edition (published in 1892) of the Haggadah carried 115 commentaries!

Before the introduction of printing by Gutenberg in the fifteenth century, Haggadot were written by copyists, many of whom were genuine calligraphic experts. The Hebrew lettering, conceived in a most creative way, was exquisitely drawn, and the illuminations and illustrations were, in a number of instances, executed imaginatively and in the most engaging tradition of folk-art. Primitive, crude, and inexpert most of them may have been in technique, but they communicated their deeply felt conviction about the subjects they delineated.

The illustrations depicted Biblical incidents beginning with the Creation, but most of them dealt with the dramatic events of the Bondage, the Exodus, the wandering in the Wilderness, and the covenant at Sinai. These were preceded by genre portrayals of the customs relating to the celebration of the Passover, of the Four Sons (the Wise Son, the Wicked Son, the Simple-Minded Son, and He Who Doesn't Know Enough to Ask) in the Haggadah parable and, at the end, of the Prophet Elijah blowing the shofar to herald the coming of the Messiah, with the Temple and the city of Jerusalem standing radiant in their restored glory on Mount Zion.

Of the approximately two dozen medieval and Renaissance Haggadah manuscripts still extant, no doubt the most original and beautiful from the standpoint of art, are the "Sarajevo Haggadah," the "Second Haggadah" in the Germanic Museum of Nuremberg, the "Darmstadt Haggadah," and the "Crawford Haggadah" in the John Rylands Library in Manchester, England. All of these illuminated Haggadot were produced during the thirteenth and fourteenth centuries in Europe by unknown artist-scribes.

When the printing of Hebrew books began, illustrated Haggadot, because of the relative cheapness of reproduction,

Passover plate decorated with an incident from the Bible. Moses appears before Pharaoh, pleading with him "to let my people go." (Courtesy of Joseph B. Horwitz Judaica Collection, Cleveland.)

became the vogue. Perhaps the first of these was the magnificent "Prague Haggadah," which appeared in 1526. It was done in German Renaissance style, was profusely adorned with fine wood engravings which consisted of elaborate figured borders, capital and initial letters, and illustrations of both Biblical and contemporary scenes of Jewish life. Despite the Scriptural commandment against the reproduction of graven images, the human figure was freely employed in all of the more than four hundred illustrated Haggadot extant.

See also ART AMONG THE JEWS; ART, CEREMONIAL; MOSES.

PAYESS. *See* PE'OT.

PEACE, JEWISH CONCEPT OF

As unique in its comprehensive scope as it is in its depth is the Jewish conception of peace (in Hebrew: *shalom*). No conventional definition can possibly do it full justice. In the view of the ancient Rabbinic teachers of ethics, peace did not stand merely for "an absence of war" nor even an act of reconciliation between hostile contenders. That approach, at best, suggested a static condition, and a compromise of accommodation. On the contrary, in the traditional Jewish view, peace represented the total ethics of benevolence toward life, a dynamic striving for a universal harmony. It was a moral radiation outward from the mind and the volition of the individual, motivated by the active principles of human brotherhood, social justice, and truth. Such a peace was many faceted and all embracing, extending in a moral continuum from the individual to his family, from the family to the community, from the community to all in Israel, and, finally, from Israel to all of mankind in a grand envelopment of brotherhood and righteousness.

Two thousand years ago—a generation before Jesus of Nazareth—Hillel the Sage taught in Jerusalem: "Be among the disciples of Aaron; love peace and strive for peace; love people and acquaint them with the noble teachings of the Torah." Even more explicit in declaring peace to be inextricably linked up with every other aspect of morality was the teaching during the second century C.E. of Simeon ben Gamaliel: "The world rests on three foundations: on justice, on truth, and on peace. All three are one, for where there is justice there is also truth and there is peace."

The Jewish advocacy of all-inclusive peace in human existence had its roots in the central religious doctrine of *Kiddush ha-Chayyim*, the "Sanctification of Life." It rested on the foundation of the Scriptural reminder ". . . at the hand of every man's brother will I require the life of man. He that sheddeth the blood of man, by man shall his blood be shed; for in the image of God made He man." (Genesis 9:5-6.)

Peace was considered to be a universal law as well as a universal necessity; it transcended all narrow religious and sectarian barriers. A Rabbinic Sage exclaimed: "Wonderful is peace! Even if it dwells among idolators, no evil can come near them." Among the panegyrics uttered for the ideal of peace, proclaiming it as the natural law of universal harmony and balance, is this one by an ancient Talmudic teacher: "Great is peace! For peace is to the world what leaven is to the dough. Had God not placed peace on earth, the sword and the wild beasts would have devoured all of mankind."

How to avoid conflict between nations became the all-consuming preoccupation of the Jewish religious moralists. They concluded that only by the exercise of reason, restraint, and good will would man be able to escape the abyss that yawned for him. Not only, they were at pains to point out, was war waged for selfish materialistic ends, but it was the ultimate in evil, running counter to the moral conscience of mankind.

The Sages of the Talmud found corroboration for their indictment of war in the Prophet Isaiah's conciliatory plea to the corrupt society of his day: "Come, let us reason together!" Elaborating on that theme, they coined a saying that became one of the most beloved of the folk ever after: "One mountain and another can never get together, but one man and another can." The real problem then was how to get "one man and another" together so that they would have an opportunity to reason away their differences. The inference was clear: Once that was accomplished, the Prophet Isaiah's rapturous envisioning of peace for the human race would be closer to realization:

> And they shall beat their swords into plowshares,
> And their spears into pruning-hooks;
> Nation shall not lift up sword against nation,
> Neither shall they learn war any more.
>
> ISAIAH 2:4

The ideal of brotherhood and one of its corollaries—peace—the Jews found supported by the Biblical commandment in Deuteronomy 23:8: "Thou shalt not hate an Edomite, for he is thy brother; thou shalt not hate an Egyptian, because thou wast a stranger in his land."

No idea has been woven into the warp and woof of Jewish thought and sentiment as much as that of "peace." This word, together with all the many ethical tonalities that it sounds for the attuned inner ear of the Jew, appears in all Jewish religious writings, in the prayers, and in everyday folk-usage more frequently than any other. This is a fact of tremendous cultural significance. Merely to cite a few examples will suffice for the purpose of illustration.

One of the names of God mentioned in the Scriptures is Adonai Shalom, "Lord of Peace." Among the most frequently met-with Jewish masculine names are Shalom, Sholem, and Shelomoh—all meaning "Peace." Since Judean times, the usual Jewish greeting has been "*Shalom*!" or "*Shalom aleichem!*" ("Peace be to you!") Said the Rabbinic Sage Joshua ben Levi in the third century: "Therefore, he who loves peace runs after peace; he offers peace and he answers peace. . . . Great is peace, in that all benedictions and all the prayers conclude with the word 'peace.' We end the reading of the Shema with 'peace' and pray, 'Spread over us the tabernacle of Thy peace!' The Priestly Benediction ends with 'peace . . . and give thee peace.' And the Eighteen Benedictions [Shemoneh Esreh] also conclude with 'Blessed be thou, O Master of Peace!' "

"The shedding of blood," whether it referred to war, to murder, or to merely giving offense to a fellow man, thereby "wounding him in his soul," was sternly interdicted. The moral aversion to such acts among the Jews rested on the central theological doctrine that God had created man in His own divine image. The social-moral principle inferred from this was that "every human being is equal in worth to the whole world." Violence, even of the mildest verbal kind, was frowned upon by the Rabbis as being criminal: "He who raises a threatening hand against a fellow man is to be considered wicked."

Most touching in this regard was the high reverence in which the folk held Moses' brother Aaron. This was not only because he was the brother of Mosheh Rabbenu, ("Our Teacher Moses") nor because he was the first high priest, but because a worshipful tradition ascribed to him the exalted role of "peacemaker." The Talmud states: "Aaron strove to make peace between men, to divert them from doing evil to each other by gentleness and reason."

Often a man who loved peace was called "a disciple of Hillel." This was in grateful memory of the benevolent example which that ancient Sage had set, early in the first century, for all the generations.

See also LIFE, THE SANCTIFICATION OF.

PENITENTIAL DAYS. *See* SELICHOT.

PENTATEUCH, THE. *See* BIBLE, THE.

PENTECOST. *See* SHABUOT.

"PEOPLE OF THE BOOK, THE." *See* BIBLE, THE.

PE'OT (Hebrew pl., meaning "sides," "curls," "locks of hair"; hence, "side earlocks"; s. PE'AH; in Yiddish: PAYESS)

Pe'ot (earlocks) have been worn, one on each side of the face, by some male Jews, regardless of their age, since most ancient times. They were a distinguishing feature of the Jew's appearance. The custom of wearing *pe'ot* presumably was based on Leviticus 19:27, the same Biblical passage which forbade the rounding of the head and beard. The ancient Rabbis decreed that the pe'ot, like the hair of the head, be worn unclipped and untrimmed. A minor controversy arose among the rabbis of Spain during the Middle Ages as to whether it was permissible to trim pe'ot. The enlightened rabbi, Maimonides (Moses ben Maimon, twelfth century), was led to throw the weight of his authority upon

Jews of Cracow with the traditional pe'ot or side-locks. 19th century. (YIVO.)

the side of the "liberals"; he could see nothing wrong in such a "trivial" modification of the Biblical commandment.

It is indeed odd that the pe'ot became as much an object of persecution, beginning with the Middle Ages, as the Jews themselves. There is no question but that, at all times, the overwhelming majority of Jews remained loyal to their earlocks, whatever the hostile pressures from without. In 1845, when the ruthless Czar Nicholas I issued an ukase forbidding Jews to wear pe'ot as well as the gaberdine, shtreimel (the fur-trimmed Sabbath hat), etc., the pious throughout the Russian Empire held out grimly against the *force majeure* applied by the imperial government, which soon had to abandon its order.

It is clear that the "giveaway" pe'ot, in the harassment of the centuries, became for many a Jew a prideful and stiff-necked affirmation of his identity.

At crucial periods during the various assimilationist processes in Jewish history, the wearing of pe'ot represented, in a manner of speaking, a declaration of war by the traditionalists against the defaulters. In the United States, during the great immigration tide from Eastern Europe during 1881–1914, the problem of whether to wear pe'ot became very acute. Immigrants wearing pe'ot met with pressures even from "enlightened" sources, as well as with ridicule–and sometimes molestation–from anti-Semites. Some faltered and hid their pe'ot behind their ears to make them less obvious. Still others were driven to discard them entirely, and the beard as well. Such weakness in many of the believing was quite understandable, yet for many a sincere believer it presented a grave problem of conscience, with resulting feelings of shame and guilt.

However, it need hardly be added that, among the majority of those who discarded beard and pe'ot the decision to do so created no emotional disturbance, for they had simply ceased believing in their religious validity.

See also BEARD.

PERPETUAL LAMP. *See* LAMP, PERPETUAL.

PERSECUTION IN "MODERN" DRESS

In the United States. The Nazi tentacles reached out even into the United States during the 1930's. Here, as everywhere else in the world, there were already in existence anti-Semitic organizations and individuals eager to be allied with the Nazis, who, as everyone could see, were steadily advancing to a position of world supremacy.

The pattern of anti-Semitism had been but slowly emerging in the United States, taking shape only at the end of the nineteenth century and in the years prior to World War I. Formerly, organized prejudice and discrimination toward Jews had been of little significance, but with the economic dislocations and repeated crises which resulted from the rapid industrial transformation of rural America, they turned virulent. Whenever a Jew committed a crime, the word "Jew" was sure to figure prominently in the press accounts. Stickers and posters with the rubric NO DOGS AND JEWS ALLOWED HERE blossomed out on city lamp posts and walls and at conspicuous places at seaside resorts. On the stage–first in burlesque and vaudeville, and later in the silent movies–the Jew was caricatured as being either comic or evil, he was presented often as moneylender, pawnbroker, or fence for thieves. The noun "Jew" was turned into a verb; i.e., "He jewed me," or "I jewed the price down." Also entering into common parlance were the offensive tags "Jew-boy," "Jew-girl," "Shylock," and "Fagin."

The rude awakening of American Jews to the existence of anti-Semitism in the United States first occurred in 1913. In that year, Brooklyn-born Leo Frank, a twenty-nine-year-old Jewish superintendent of a pencil factory in Atlanta,

Leo Frank, seated near his wife, in court in Atlanta, Georgia, during his trial on the charge of murdering a Christian girl. He was found guilty and condemned to death, but was hanged instead by a lynch mob. (Anti-Defamation League.)

Georgia, was charged with criminal assault and the murder of a fourteen-year-old Gentile girl whose body had been found mutilated and secreted in the cellar of the factory where Frank worked.

Prior to and during the court trial, the yellow press of Georgia and the rabble-rousers were whipping up a genuine hysteria among the ignorant and hoodlum elements, harping incessantly on the fact that Frank was both a northerner and a Jew, so that the outcome was a foregone conclusion: Leo Frank was sentenced to hang. Outside the courthouse and the prison where he was confined the mob chanted: "Hang the Jew!" But the governor of Georgia, John Slaton, stood firm against the clamor. Because he was convinced of Frank's innocence (ten years later the real murderer confessed) the governor commuted the death sentence to life imprisonment, giving this reason for his clemency: "Two thousand years ago, another governor [Pilate] washed his hands . . . and turned a Jew [Jesus] over to a mob. For two thousand years, that governor's name has been a curse. If today another Jew were lying in his grave because I had failed to do my duty, I would all through life find his blood on my hands, and must consider myself an assassin through cowardice."

Convinced that his life was being threatened, Governor Slaton fled the state. Then, with the unspoken consent of the authorities, the mob entered the prison and in the most brutal manner dragged out the prisoner and strung him up on a tree. Next day, in the notorious newspaper *The Jeffersonian*, published in Atlanta by Thomas E. Watson, there appeared this brief warning: "Jew libertines, take notice!"

However, this lynching had one salutary consequence: It awoke Jews with a start to the realization that they could no longer remain quiescent. One direct result was the founding of the Anti-Defamation League for combating prejudice and discrimination in the United States. This was organized by the Jewish fraternal order B'nai B'rith.

The war's end in 1918 had brought about an acute economic crisis in the United States, a depression which was acerbated by a widespread bellicose society that sought relief from its tensions in aggressive and lawless acts against weak minorities. Most prominent in this vigilante hate movement was the Ku Klux Klan, which boasted a membership of 4,000,000. The Klan burned crosses before synagogues and Jewish homes and shops in an attempt to drive their owners

John M. Slayton, governor of Georgia during the trial and conviction of Leo Frank as the brutal murderer of a Christian girl. After reviewing the trial records, the Governor, as an act of simple justice, found the condemned man innocent and pardoned him; he then resigned, and left the state. (Anti-Defamation League.)

out of town. Henry Ford's Jew-baiting *Dearborn Independent* did much to spread the myth of the "International Jew" so ardently fostered by German and other anti-Semitic writers, and disseminated the slanders of the *Protocols of the Elders of Zion,* a proven forgery. (Some years later, Ford, realizing his error, issued a public apology to the Jews.)

This agitation against the Jews had regrettable effects and contaminated certain areas of American business, commercial, and educational life. An undisguised effort was made by President A. L. Lowell of Harvard to restrict the admission of Jewish students into the colleges of the university, especially into the medical school, by means of the numerus clausus (the percentage norm).

Nine national Jewish organizations, including B'nai B'rith, the American Jewish Congress, and the American Jewish Committee, decided to counterattack. They succeeded in exposing the *Protocols* as a fraud and aroused many Americans to the fact that anti-Semitism could become a divisive and antisocial force in the life of the nation. Numerous Christians, including President Woodrow Wilson and his predecessor at the White House, William Howard Taft, denounced the agitation as dangerous and disruptive of the American traditions of racial and religious equality, and the Federal Council of Churches of Christ also condemned the anti-Semitic movement as anti-Christian and evil. No small part in the recession of aggressive anti-Semitism in the United States was played by the era of prosperity that set in during the mid-twenties, but this lasted for only a few years, until the Great Depression exploded in 1929; then privation and insecurity began once more to spawn an aggressive hatred toward the Jews.

The Nazi propaganda machine recognized its rare opportunity. Its anti-Semitic appeal in the United States was directed by its American arm, the German-American Bund,

A swastika "calling card" of American Fascists, left at the door of a synagogue in Atlanta. Hundreds of such anti-Semitic desecrations occurred in various cities and towns of the United States during the Hitler period and still continue to take place (in the 1960's). (Anti-Defamation League.)

under its Fuehrer, Fritz Kuhn, to struggling small businessmen and shopkeepers, to the unemployed, and to the emotionally unstable and the ignorant. It found a large number of anti-Semitic groups flourishing from coast to coast with which to mesh in the role of "co-ordinator" and supplier of badly needed funds and of printed literature. The programs and methods of all those groups were very much alike, some of the best-known were the Silver Shirts, the Black Legion, the Christian Crusaders, the Knights of the Camelia, American Vigilantes, Defenders of the Christian Faith, and the Christian Mobilizers. But the most formidable of all was the Christian Front, which was led by Father Charles E. Coughlin—"the radio priest" who was also the publisher of the magazine *Social Justice.*

These organizations virtually flooded the country with provocative and often libelous and obscene periodicals, leaflets, posters, and stickers in which the Jew was caricatured. The entire country was in a turmoil as a result of these ac tivities, eliciting from Justice Frank Murphy of the Unitec States Supreme Court an appeal to the nation "to recogniz and combat hateful propaganda against American citizens o Jewish descent as a powerful secret Nazi weapon—powerfu because it has been deliberately spread to this country wher no Nazi invading force has been able to set foot, and secre because victims so inoculated are often unconscious of th source from which it comes."

So long as Hitler and Nazi Germany appeared to b triumphant in the war, the Fascist demagogues in the Unite States continued to daydream about their own ultimate as sumption of power, but with the military defeat of German in 1945 and the world-wide revulsion against Nazi ideas an practices, the would-be fuehrers of America lost much c their mass-influence. However, the poison that they had in jected into the thoughts and feelings of many Gentiles towar the Jews remained. There are still organizations, self-style "Christian" and "patriotic," which, in their programs, pe iodicals, pamphlets, and leaflets, continue to vilify Jew Jewish practices, and Jewish community life. "Anti-Semitis changes its forms and its intensity, but it does not disa

Convention in Cleveland during the 1930's for uniting American fascist organizations. (Left to right): Rev. Gerald L. K. Smith, who headed the Share-the-Wealth faction in the Huey P. Long political machine; Father Charles Coughlin, the leader of the Christian Front movement among Roman Catholics; and Dr. Francis E. Townsend, the author of the so-called Townsend Recovery Plan. (Wide World Photo; Anti-Defamation League.)

pear," commented Dore Schary, the chairman of the Anti-Defamation League, in 1963. ". . . We will do with it what we've always done. Where we find prejudice we fight it. That's a commitment you make as an American and as a Jew."

Discrimination against Jews in the United States is still commonly practiced, but to a noticeably less degree than heretofore. It occurs in employment in private industry, in "restricted" housing, in admission to certain colleges and universities, and in the exclusion of rich Jews from membership in country clubs. Naturally, because of the existence of anti-discrimination laws and fair-employment practice rules in a number of states, discrimination is most often covert, calling for circumspect maneuvering to avoid complications.

Anti-Semitism in the United States, observe sociologists, is endemic to the life of the country, as it is elsewhere in the world. Discriminaton, both of the overt and the covert varieties, is even now (in 1964) widely practiced, although it is less noticeable than before. Jews still find it difficult to get employment in a great number of large national corporations and in banks and insurance companies. A study in 1962 of 1,065 hotels and motels in the United States, Canada, and the West Indies revealed that more than 22 per cent, excluded Jews by one means or another; in 780 of 1,152 country and social clubs in the United States, their religion kept out Jews from membership; 75 of 340 employers in San Francisco frankly admitted their opposition to hiring Jews; of 844 top officials in eight of the largest commercial banks in New York City—where more than 2,000,000 Jews live—only 30 were Jews. Not least—the admission of Jewish students to professional colleges still operates "unofficially" according to the old numerus clausus or quota plan. And lastly, social and cultural anti-Semitism in many "refined" and respectable areas of American life raises enough barriers against Jews to make only the most insensitive and opportunistic attempt to break through them.

In the Soviet Union. The history of the discouragement (in many instances of downright suppression) of the Jewish religion, culture, and group-identity in the U.S.S.R. has diverged in some of the most essential ways from that experienced by Jews in capitalist countries. In the latter, the hostility stems most often from the bigotry of a competing religion, from economic rivalry (or resentment), and from racist notions; in the Soviet Union this opposition, although often tinged with the above elements of classic anti-Semitism, stems largely from certain Marxist ideological premises which consider the fostering of Jewish religious beliefs and practices and of a separatist culture to be inconsistent with the goals of a "godless" Socialist society which strives for monolithic unity. But whatever the justifying reasons given by the Soviet government for this repressive course of action against its almost 3,000,000 citizens of Jewish birth, it has been bitterly condemned both in the Soviet Union and abroad as constituting a state policy of anti-Semitism.

Jews have long been conditioned by their history to interpret as acts of anti-Semitism all attempts made to suppress or restrict any of their religious practices, their sacred books, and their group-identity. At all times—and the times were many—beginning with the efforts in 168 B.C.E. by Antiochus (Epiphanes) IV, the Seleucid despot, to destroy the national identity of the Jews and to force them to renounce their religion, the Jews considered such a move to be the supreme expression of persecution. Regardless of whether the stated reasons for this repression previously stemmed from the bigotry of a competing religion (i.e., Greek paganism, Christianity, or Islam), or, as it is explained in the Soviet Union, from the antireligious and antinationalist zeal of Marxist-Leninist socialism—religious Jews have viewed the end results as being the same.

Actually, the Russian Revolution brought to an end the most outrageous instrument of Czarist oppression—the pogrom. Only a few days after the Bolsheviks had seized power (in 1917), they promulgated the Declaration of the Rights of the Peoples of Russia, which announced the "abolition of all national and national-religious prejudices and restrictions, and the full development of national minorities and ethnic groups." In this general benevolence the Jews of the Soviet Union also were to share. When the still undefeated czarist remnants, the Slavophile "White Guards," made anti-Semitism an important rallying point in their counter revolutionary crusade, and then followed up their agitation with pogroms in the geographic areas they controlled, the Council of People's Commissars, under the signature of Nicolai Lenin, issued a decree on August 9, 1918, declaring:

> Any kind of hatred against any nation is inadmissible and shameful. . . . The Council of People's Commissars instructs all Soviet deputies to take uncompromising measures to tear out the anti-Semitic movement by the roots. Pogromists and pogrom-agitators are outside the law.

The Soviet government then initiated a large-scale program of education among the Russian people against anti-Semitism in the Red Army, in the press, in the factories, and in the schools. But the carrying out of this task was far from easy, because for centuries the Russian people had been nurtured on the poison of hatred for the Jews.

Infinitely more calamitous for Russian Jews than the brutal treatment they were given by the White Guards during the Civil War years were their experiences during the same period in the Ukraine. Many were butchered by General Denikin's "Whites"; others were set upon with mounting savagery by the marauding nationalist insurgents of the "Ukraine Directory" under the command of the Cossack generals Petlura, Skoropadsky, and Machno.

No one really knows how many of the total Jewish population of about 1,250,000 in the Ukraine were slain. But it is conservatively estimated that 200,000 perished and several hundred thousand Jewish children were left orphaned. The savagery finally came to an end in 1922 with the defeat of the White Guards and the Ukrainian nationalists. Although thenceforth Jews were promised full protection by the Soviet government—even anti-Semitic remarks were made punishable by law—the nightmarish experiences which they had undergone filled many Jews with disquietude for the future. Consequently, there was an extensive emigration of Jews from the Ukraine in the early 1920's to the United States, Latin America, Palestine, Australia, and South Africa.

From its very beginning, the Soviet Union had adopted as its guiding motto in matters of religious belief this dictum of Karl Marx, the ideological founder of socialism: "Religion is the opium of the people." This declaration succinctly expressed the Communist attitude toward religion, because the principles of Marxism, which are based on a materialist philosophy of history, reject all aspects of theology and the supernatural. Consistent with this view, the Soviet Government sponsored a nationwide campaign by the Young Communist "League of Militant Atheists" against all religions, including the Jewish. And so, besides having to wrestle with the problems of economic and psychological adjustment to the new conditions of Soviet society, the religious Jews were also forced to cope with the well-nigh shattering challenges to their religious faith, identity, and conscience.

Juridically, this antireligious crusade was based on the general principle later incorporated as Article 4 in the 1925 Constitution: "For the purpose of assuring real liberty of conscience to the workers, the church is separated from the state, and the school from the church; and the right of all citizens to practice freely any religious belief or to engage in antireligious propaganda, remains inviolate." True enough, the League of Militant Atheists found complete freedom and also the means to carry on its antireligious propaganda, but this kind of freedom was completely denied to the religious; it was a one-sided arrangement.

To wage ideological war against the Jewish religion the Jewish Young Communists (Comsomols) organized their own agitational unit, The League of Militant Jewish Atheists. It was especially combative during the 1921–23 period, when middle-class Jews were drifting back into urban private trade, which was then permitted under the temporary New Economic Policy (NEP). But freedom of worship remained unaffected, nor were any of the congregations interfered with.

As time went on, however, it became clear that the primary objective of the antireligious campaign was to wean the Jewish youth from its religion and, conversely, to draw it closer to the Communist movement. With this end in mind, all religious groups, including the Jewish, were forbidden to give institutional religious instruction to anyone under eighteen years of age. Instruction to older youths (in the post-eighteen group) was allowed with the proviso that it be given at home either by their parents or by a private tutor.

Patently, it was hard for the Jewish religious community to reconcile itself to such a narrowing scope of activity; it ran counter to all its cultural traditions and historical conditioning for 2,500 years. To the pious Jew, the religious (and also religious-cultural) education of the young was considered to be the most sacred of all trusts and obligations. On it he pinned his hope for the survival of the Jewish religion and, in large measure, for the continuity of his Jewish identity. The separation of "the school from the church" led automatically to the abolition of all parochial schools on the grounds that they were incompatible with the principles of "Socialist education" in Soviet society. For the Orthodox Jews—and these were in the great majority—it meant the end of the traditional cheder (q.v.), the Talmud Torah (q.v.), and the yeshivah (q.v.), with all the implications about the dissolving religious values resulting from such a loss.

Many Jews were determined to resist what they considered a fundamental encroachment on their way of life. The outlawed cheder began to operate clandestinely, despite the grief it brought to its initiators. The stream of Jewish religious life continued to flow, for the most part erratically and sluggishly, much of it in the open, with grudging official sanction, but some of it subterranean and illegal. The majority of synagogue buildings, like the churches, were expropriated and converted into worker's clubs, libraries, and "houses of culture," but it was chiefly the loss of a great number of its youth to atheism and communism that struck the Jewish religious community its most grievous blow.

In November 1962, the English language weekly, *The Moscow News,* attempted to explain the decline of the Jewish religion in the Soviet Union: "True, the number of [Jewish] believers is gradually diminishing, but this is not the outcome of administrative measures, but is due to the fact that materialistic concepts [of Marxism-Leninism] are gaining the upper hand over the idealistic conceptions."

Religious-cultural autonomy for the Jewish communities had been customary for many centuries, the institution of the kahal (the administrative organ of Jewish self-rule in the ghetto; *see* COMMUNITY, SELF-GOVERNING) was suddenly ordered dissolved by the Soviet government, being considered a survival of feudal czarism that was entirely superfluous in a Socialist society. One of the major functions of the kahal had been to collect communal taxes for the support of Jewish religious, educational, and charitable institutions; the collection and the dispensing of tzedakah (charity) had ever been regarded as a paramount duty in the social-religious practice of the Jews. Now the government declared it to be no longer necessary since that function had been taken over by the state welfare services and the various ministries.

Still another cause for official resentment against Soviet Jews was that they evinced unmistakable Zionist sympathies; after the founding of the State of Israel in 1948, many did not even attempt to conceal their group-pride and elation. "In many cities," wrote Harrison E. Salisbury in *The New York Times* on February 8, 1962, "Soviet Jews have demonstratively welcomed Israeli diplomats. In Leningrad, for example, during the celebration of Simhat Torah three years ago [1959], about 4,000 Jews turned out and serenaded an

Bombing of the Jewish Community House in Atlanta in October, 1958. Photo by Bill Young of the Atlanta Journal-Constitution. (*Anti-Defamation League.*)

A Nazi-type caricature in an anti-religious book, Judaism Without Varnish, *published in Kiev in 1963 under the auspices of the Ukrainian Academy of Sciences. The description reads: "During the years of the Hitlerite occupation, the Zionist leaders served the Fascists." The book was officially repudiated and soon withdrawn.*

Israeli diplomat. The next year 7,000 Jews appeared, and last October [1961] between 8,000 and 12,000. This kind of display alarms Soviet security officials."

Throughout the 1920's and the 1930's, the Soviet government repeatedly condemned the world Zionist movement as a covert agent of British imperialism, with which it was linked under the Palestine Mandate. This appraisal had already been made by Joseph Stalin four years before the Revolution. He had then characterized Zionism as "a reactionary and nationalist movement recruiting its followers from among the Jewish petty and middle bourgeoisie, business employees, artisans, and the more backward sections of the Jewish workers. Its aim is to organize a Jewish bourgeois state in Palestine, and it endeavors to isolate the Jewish working-class masses from the general struggle of the proletariat."

With this definitive declaration to guide it, the Soviet government proceeded to ban all Zionist activity. The leaders of Russian Zionism stubbornly maintained their Jewish nationalist position, even in the face of official interdiction, with the result that several were executed as counterrevolutionists, and a large number were imprisoned or exiled to remote parts of the Soviet Union. Also the Hebrew language and literature fell as casualties in the class war; the famous Hebrew Habimah Theatre (in Moscow) was ordered closed in 1924.

Nevertheless, when the political prospects of Zionism changed after World War II and the Jews of Palestine began to wage a war of liberation against "British imperialism," they received open encouragement from the Soviet Union as well as desperately needed arms from Communist Czechoslovakia. In fact, the first country to extend *de jure* diplomatic recognition to the newly founded State of Israel was the U.S.S.R. This benevolent attitude continued so long as the Israeli government maintained a neutralist position in the cold war, but no sooner did Israel abandon this policy for one of closer collaboration with the West, and especially with the United States, then the old harassment of Zionists and Zionism was resumed by the Soviet government, but this time with greater vigor than ever before.

There began to appear increasingly uncomplimentary references in the Soviet press to "Jewish bourgeois nationalism," to "Zionism," and to "cosmopolitanism"–the last no doubt was a satirical gibe leveled at the Soviet Jews' sympathy and identification with their fellow Jews throughout the world. Early in 1949, the cultural ax fell. The Jewish Anti-Fascist Committee, formed during the Second World War for uniting all Jews in the world in the struggle against the Nazis, was dissolved without any explanation. In quick order, there followed the closing down of a variety of Jewish educational and cultural institutions which hitherto had been sponsored and supported by the government: the Yiddish state-book-publishing houses, the Yiddish-language newspapers, periodicals, schools, theatres, clubs, etc. Leading Yiddish writers such as David Bergelson, Itzig Feffer, Der Nistor, David Hofstein, Leib Kwitko, Peretz Markish, I. Kushnerov, and O. Schvartzman, among others well known outside the Soviet Union, fell completely silent and disappeared. No one knew why, nor did anyone know their whereabouts. Only when Nikita Khrushchev had made his startling "revelations" in 1956 was it learned what had happened to them: They all had been shot.

Charges that the Soviet government was persecuting its Jews and was discriminating against them in every avenue of life continued to be raised by Jews abroad. In a resolution that the Central Conference of American Rabbis adopted on June 22, 1962, the Soviet Union was condemned for its efforts to "liquidate" Judaism and to assimilate Jews by means of social and economic pressures:

> The arrest, conviction and execution of lay leaders of synagogues; the repeated anti-Semitic expressions in the Soviet press; the restrictions suffered by Jews make impossible any organizational and communal contact with their co-religionists in other parts of the world; and the denial of religious articles, such as Bibles, prayerbooks, prayer shawls, and matzohs, are matters seriously disturbing to our conference.

Not all Jews, however, were convinced that the discrimination shown to Jews represented an official Soviet policy of anti-Semitism. Dr. Nahum Goldmann, head of the Jewish Agency and President of the World Zionist Organization, said in February, 1963, that "it is untrue to characterize the [Soviet] Government as anti-Semitic." What he found gravely wrong was "the denial to the Jewish community of the same facilities accorded other religious and national minorities." Most crucial of all, he stressed, was the crisis being faced by the Jews of the Soviet Union in their efforts to maintain and develop their own communal and cultural life. "If there is anti-Jewish discrimination," commented in agreement Max Bressler, the then President of the Zionist Organization of America, "it stems from other sources [than governmental anti-Semitism], most probably from a misconception of what constitutes Jewish nationality, or Judaism, combined with a political aversion for Israel."

Four survivors of the pogrom in Slovetchna, the Ukraine, 1919. (YIVO.)

Persecution in "Modern" Dress

Trial of Schwartzbard (in prisoner's dock, RIGHT*) in the Court of Assizes, Paris, in 1927 for shooting the pogromist Petlura on a Paris street in retribution for his mass-slaughter of Ukrainian Jews. (YIVO.)*

The Prospects For Eliminating Anti-Semitism. Anti-Semitism—it has often been asserted—is merely a disease of ignorance. Therefore, the advice has been: Step up education and culture among the masses and it is sure to disappear. This kind of "therapy" recommended for those afflicted with the virus of hate and prejudice is directly traceable to the popular romantic view that progress and civilization, powered by their own internal dynamics, move in an uninterrupted line of advance. But ever since the Nazi *Schrecklichkeit* (horribleness) engulfed the Jewish people, a far less sanguine outlook has emerged.

A question commonly posed in bafflement asks: Prior to the ghastly years of 1932–45, was there a people in the world with higher cultural traditions, with an educational preparation for life superior to that of the Germans? Nevertheless, the bestiality of the jungle seized hold of its spirit and corrupted it, and even threatened to swallow up with it the rest of mankind. Ironically, many of the best minds in Germany, among them scientists, educators, writers, composers, artists, and philosophers, were ready, even eager, to serve as Hitler's "Professors," and worked hard to cover up the naked savagery of the Nazi performance with "intellectual" and "cultural" fig leaves.

Like some deadly contagious disease–and as such it is regarded by many historians, sociologists, and psychologists—anti-Semitism has become endemic in the feelings and thought-processes of many peoples in every type of social system. Although, as a result of patient medical research and the implementation of its curative discoveries with the necessary social controls, a number of deadly diseases which afflicted the body in the past have been eliminated, this has not at all been possible with regard to anti-Semitism. As a social disease it is so complex, so enmeshed in all the pathologic conditions and problems that plague nations of Western civilization, that no *single* cure, prophylaxis, or control is possible. This is the dilemma for both society and the Jews in the foreseeable future.

Anti-Semitism has been running rampant for some two thousand years, waxing or receding in extent or in intensity and modifying or changing its character or direction according to the demands of different circumstances. But it has always remained largely uninhibited, whether by the humane precepts of Christianity, by the enactment of laws, or by fervid appeals directed to their fellow men by the keepers of the moral conscience. When, during the Good Friday services at St. Peter's Cathedral in Rome in 1963, the late Pope John XXIII interrupted the recitation of a prayer at the altar in order to have the celebrant priest omit from his Latin text the time-revered phrase "perfidious Jews," the entire world sat up in astonishment, and the Jews were moved and grateful. Such a thing had never happened in the entire history of the Church!

Yet, however significant and far reaching in its impact this symbolic act of breaking with the past by a great-hearted and courageous pope was, its implications must have given pause to many thoughtful Jews and Christians. This is the paradox it presented: If in the year 1963, less than two decades after the slaughter of 6,000,000 Jews by the Nazis, a world-sensation was caused merely by the elimination of one scurrilous adjective from a Christian prayer that had been recited with fervor on every single Good Friday for more than a thousand years in all the Catholic churches, then how unfathomably deep must this prejudice toward the Jews still be today?

The commonly held view that progress *always* moves forward in a straight line has been losing some of its persuasiveness since World War II and the invention of thermonuclear weapons. Not infrequently–certainly where it concerns anti-Semitism–the progression of history can be measured only by the kind of satirical command that is given to the Sabine Women as they advanced to battle in Andreyev's play by that name: "Two steps forward–three steps backward–march!"

Possibly, as some objective observers of the human scene believe, mankind is being unreasonably impatient with whatever social and moral progress it is making; but it does inch forward even if only slowly and painfully and sometimes, imperceptibly. In his book *Man Against Himself*, the American psychiatrist Karl A. Menninger tried to make this point: "When we remember that in the calendar of time 'civilized' human beings are only a few seconds removed from the cannibal and a few minutes removed from the

Ukrainian soldiers of the Cossack Ataman Zelioni's army posing with the tallit-wrapped Jews they had massacred on the road from Bohuslav to Tarastcha on August 10, 1919. (YIVO.)

beasts, it will not be surprising to discover that in the unconscious, cannibalism is not yet extinct."

Some people might even consider anti-Semitism to be a disguised or sublimated form of cannibalism in which "the enemy" is eaten ritually for one's own self-aggrandizement. But whereas there exists a universal revulsion and horror in mankind for devouring the flesh and drinking the blood of fellow humans, leading, as Dr. Menninger has suggested, to their repression into the subconscious, no such scruples seem to hamper the exercise of anti-Semitic aggression, regardless of the variety of forms it takes, whether brutally, as a compulsive desire to hurt or kill Jews, or merely as a refined intellectual disparagement of them.

In the perfectionist scheme of human striving–a design that is so awesomely discernible in the history of homo sapiens–the ultimate control of anti-Semitism, if not its eradication, is not at all outside the realm of possibility. Even its most recent decline in some countries, though this decline may not be permanent, offers a measure of hopefulness. Yet, in the full sobriety of historic experience, ranging over two thousand years, one should–although never surrendering to despair–still keep realistically in mind the possibility that should the cold north winds start blowing, the wolves may howl again.

More than three thousand years ago, the Israelites heard from their teacher Moses this exhortation: "Love thy neighbor as thyself." Many among the Jews since that time, having become conditioned in their outlook by their traditional exercise in ethical thinking, feeling, and conduct, actually tried to love their "neighbors" as themselves. Unfortunately, their neighbors did not always wish to reciprocate this love. More than a thousand years after Moses taught, the Talmud recounted how Israel complained plaintively to God: "Behold, on Succot we bring seventy sacrifices [on the Temple altar] for the welfare of the seventy nations of the world because of our love for them. Should they not return our love? Yet they hate us!"

See also ANTI-SEMITISM: THE "RACIAL PURITY" MYTH; CHURCH AND PERSECUTION; DREYFUS CASE, THE; "HOST DESECRATION" CALUMNIES; NAZIS, THE; POGROMS IN SLAVIC LANDS; "RITUAL MURDER" SLANDERS.

PERUKE. *See* SHEITEL.

PERUSHIM. *See* PHARISEES.

PESACH. *See* PASSOVER.

PHARISEES (in Hebrew: PERUSHIM, meaning "Separated Ones"; i.e., those who had taken the Levitical [priestly] vow of purity which kept them apart from others)

The anonymous author of II Maccabees, who evidently was a Pharisee Scribe of the second century B.C.E., announced the equalitarian objective of the Pharisees like a clarion-call to salvation: "Unto all are given the Kingdom, the Priesthood, and the Heritage!" By the "Kingdom" he meant the righteous Kingdom of God which was to be established *on earth* by the Messiah; by the "Priesthood" was indicated the possibility (since Israel considered itself "a nation of priests" through its consecration to God and the Torah) for each individual Jew to worship God and to commune with him in prayer directly–without priestly intercession; by the "Heritage" was meant the Torah and all the extra-Biblical laws, traditions, customs, rites, and ceremonies that had been accumulated, preserved, and handed down orally from generation to generation since Moses.

The Pharisees, who were the democratic inheritors of the religious ideas of the "Men of the Great Synagogue," (*see* TALMUD, THE), also adopted as their motto the obligation to "raise up many disciples and build a fence around the Torah." When they finally succeeded, under the leadership of Simeon ben Shetach, in wresting control of the Sanhedrin from the priestly aristocratic Sadducees about 150 years before the Destruction of the Second Temple, they proclaimed to the people that the Torah was the heritage not just of the priestly elite, but also of every single person "in the congregation of Jacob." Accordingly, they established what amounted to obligatory universal and free religious education for the young in every Jewish community–an event unprecedented in all history and one that was not duplicated anywhere until the introduction of free elementary schools in the United States during the nineteenth century.

The democratic innovations of the Pharisees met with determined and well-organized resistance from their patrician opponents, the Sadducees. The latter constituted the hierarchy of the Temple priests. They also formed the hereditary ruling-class and the landed gentry, and furnished the Judean army with its commanders. Absolutists in their notions concerning the use of power and authority, they were, fittingly, fundamentalists in matters of religion. They were Scriptural literalists who, being fearful of change, considered only the Five Books of Moses as canonical, and their own arbitrary decrees, issued through the Sanhedrin (the supreme religious-legislative-judicial tribunal composed of seventy-one members)–which they dominated most of the time–to have supplemental force.

The social composition of the Pharisees did not always follow rigid class-lines; not a few of them were men of wealth and influence. Yet the greatest number had humble origins; they came from the poor masses and earned their daily bread not from their teaching, which they did "for the sake of Heaven," but from work at ordinary trades, thereby investing productive labor with a moral dignity it had never possessed before in Jewish life nor, for that matter, in any other people's life. They spoke the language of the ordinary folk and became emotionally identified with its many trials and aspirations. Understandably, the upper-class Hellenized Sadducees feared and despised the Pharisees. They resented them especially for electing themselves the social sponsors and religious mentors of the *hoi polloi,* whom they considered the rabble.

There can be but little doubt that the bitter struggle for supremacy in Jewish society between the aristocratic Sadducees and the plebian Pharisees had a strong economic aspect. The Sadducees, entrenched in all important positions of authority in the Temple and in the State, had large vested interests to defend–principally in the Temple treasury. This consisted not only of a sizable part of the country's farm produce, not only of the steady income from "sin," "thank," "redemption," and other offerings made at the altar, but also of the vast accumulation of funds from the half-shekel contribution that every Jew–in Judea and also in all the Jewish settlements throughout the world–was required each year to send to the sanctuary in Jerusalem, both for the support of this large ecclesiastical establishment and for the maintainance of the government and the army.

It is patently an oversimplification to define the stubborn conflict that continued for three hundred years between the two major ideological groupings in Judea as merely a "sectarian wrangle" between the Sadducean Biblical literalists and the Pharisaic-Rabbinical traditionalists.

The Greek word *Pharisaios* is first found in latter-day Jewish-Greek writings: in the historical books by Josephus and in the New Testament. The Talmud, composed in Aramaic, treats extensively of the Pharisees (Perushim) and of their public activities, opinions, principles, and practices. For it must not be forgotten that Rabbinic Judaism, as it is codified and expounded in the literature of the Talmud, was the creative product of the Pharisees collectively. And so, in a large measure, the Talmud remains, for the student of the Jewish religion, a graphic self-portrait of them, of their values, and of their way of thinking.

Although there is no actual mention of the Pharisees by name either in the books of the Apocrypha or in any other work of post-Biblical literature, nevertheless, the essence of Pharisaism is easily discovered in those writings. It is not too difficult to trace the fundamental beliefs, attitudes, and practices of the Pharisees to the religious-ethnic separatism which had been conceived of and decreed for the Jews by Ezra and the Soferim (Scribes)—"the Men of the Great Synagogue" who had compiled the Bible canon. This isolation, possible only in such a theocratic society as Israel's, had been implemented by means of an implacable religious discipline and law enforcement. It had a twofold goal: on the one hand, the scrupulous preservation of the Torah—both its teachings and its laws—possible only by a constant watch against the taint of pagan influences that might seep in from without; and, on the other hand, the maintenance, by stern prohibitions against intermarriage, of biologically pure ethnic stock. The events which had led to the struggle with and expulsion of the Samaritans from the main body of the Jewish people during the fifth century B.C.E. by Ezra and Nehemiah, had apparently determined this uncompromising stand.

Yet, only about two centuries later, after the Greeks had made themselves masters of Judea, the defensive separating walls that the Scribes had interposed between the Jewish people and the rest of mankind began to show dangerous breaks. These were caused by the inroads of Hellenistic culture which, with the military-political conquest of the Mediterranean world by Alexander of Macedon and his successors, were then being made among many peoples. They left a strong imprint, even on those Jews who resisted them. All elements of Greek culture—language, dress, manners, sports, and pastimes—even the adoption of Greek proper names in place of Hebrew and Aramaic ones—cropped up in the Jewish pattern of life. The full impact of this cultural diffusion on the Jews may be gauged by the fact that even that very Judean Scribe (of the third century B.C.E.) who traditionally is considered to have been the first of the Pharisees or "Separated Ones"—who themselves had come into being primarily to keep the "poison" of Hellenism from contaminating "the well of Judah"—bore the Greek name of Antigonos of Soko!

It became both fashionable and expedient for the ambitious Jewish ruling class, the higher ranks of Temple priests, the generals, and the rich landowners to toady to the Greek "master race" and to de-Judaize themselves as much as possible. If they embraced Hellenism, it was by no means out of cultural conviction or in response to a humanistic taste. Rather—as all centemporary writings, Jewish as well as Greek, clearly bear out, they sought to don a spurious Greek identity for self-serving ends alone, and in the process, they did not hesitate to collaborate or to curry favor with the foreign oppressors of their own people—even to the point of carrying out harsh orders against their fellow Jews—so long as they might be allowed to maintain their own position and wealth.

There were, notwithstanding, many who bitterly opposed the Greek incursions into Jewish religious belief and culture, regarding their acceptance as a betrayal of the Jewish faith and identity. The adherents of this opposition took on the name of Chasidim—"the Pious." In order to differentiate them from the modern Chasidim who derive from East European sectaries, some historians refer to these Chasidim of the Maccabean era by the Greek name of Hasideans or Assideans.

The struggle between the Hellenist upper-class opportunists and the patriotic pietists, the Hasideans, was at least temporarily resolved by the religious-libertarian uprising of the Hasideans that took place in 168 B.C.E. under the leadership of the priestly Hasmonean Maccabees. It was fought, on the one hand, against the political-military oppression of Antiochus (Epiphanes) IV, the Seleucidan king of Syria, and on the other hand, against the subversion of Judaism by cultural Hellenism. The revolt succeeded in achieving both objectives, but not conclusively. After only three decades of religious and cultural "cleansing" of Jewish life, the Hasmonean rulers and high priests of Judea became drunk with power and forgot all about their earlier Hasidean principles. They quickly succumbed to the attractions of Hellenism themselves, and in so doing, betrayed what their fathers had been fighting for only a generation before!

Once more the ideological and power struggle between the religious traditionalists and the Hellenistic assimilationists in Judea was resumed. But this time it led to the crystallization of two opposing classes which found form in the organization of the Sadducees and Pharisees into sects.

The Pharisee initiates were organized into sectarian companies, each called in Hebrew a *chaburah* (fellowship or brotherhood). They accordingly addressed each other as chaber (pl. chaberim)—i.e., "brother" or "comrade." Actually, on the evidence available, it would seem that they were relatively few in any generation; it has been estimated that there were only five to ten thousand Pharisees in their entire history, spanning two centuries. They counted in their brotherhoods scribes, juridical experts, teachers of ethics and morality, liturgists, and expounders and interpreters of religious doctrines and ritual laws. It is strangely ironic that these Rabbinic sectarians, with so many of whose religious views and ethical values Jesus was in agreement, should have fared so badly in the literature of the New Testament (*see* CHRISTIANITY, JEWISH ORIGINS OF). The repeated abuse in the Gospels, with words hardly credible as coming from the lips of such a devout and gentle Jew as Jesus was described to have been, is concentrated in the stinging rebuke "Scribes, Pharisees, hypocrites!" In Luke 11.39, we read: "Now do ye Pharisees make clean the outside of the cup and the platter; but your inward part is full of ravening and wickedness."

The Pharisees continued the work of the Scribes in the exposition, analysis, and reinterpretation of the Biblical laws. Finding some of these laws either so outdated as not to conform to the exigencies following an historic change, they revised some of them, elaborated others, and even added to them new extensions of their own. *In toto*, their amalgamation of the sacrosanct Biblical laws with Rabbinic teachings and regulations formed the bedrock of the Talmudic Judaism that grew up following the Destruction of the Temple in 70 C.E.

In a very significant way, Pharisaism comprised a religious-social revolution. It worked for the inner transformation of Jewish life through the already existing democratic and universal institutions of the synagogue and the House of Study. Its effects were felt not only in Judea, but in the remotest places in the then known world, where, with a mere minyan of ten Jews (the required quorum for holding public worship), Jewish congregational and institutional life could be initiated.

It is a fact that it was the Rabbinic Sages—Pharisees for the greater part, who, in keeping with their dedication "to build a fence around the Torah"—in other words, to successfully maintain the group-separatism and the purity of the Jewish religion against the threat of change and the inroads of alien influences—made a thorough inventory of all the mitzvot, the commandments and the laws contained in the Five Books of Moses. They discovered that there were 613 such mitzvot (in Hebrew: *Taryag Mitzvot*). To keep them fixed and inviolable, the Pharisee Sages decided that these precepts were to constitute "the fence around the Torah"—a fence consisting of 613 indestructible "palings": doctrinal, ethical, moral, legal, and ritualistic. Of them, 248 were affirmative laws directing the people "what to do"; the remaining 365 were "negative" precepts, consisting of prohibitions. Each of these mitzvot the Pharisee Sages ringed around defensively with the heavy armament of Rabbinic sanctions and regulations: "ifs," "buts," "hows," and "whens" of their own making. This, in part, explains why the Talmud contains, in addition to the many exalted and elightened Rabbinic discussions by the latter-day Pharisees, many dreary hair-splitting casuistries. (This fruitless type of mental thumb-twisting acrobatics, known as *pilpul,* drew forth from an exasperated Sage in debate with a legalistic colleague the ironic retort: "Aren't you from [the Academy of] Pumbeditha, where they draw an elephant through the eye of a needle?")

Perhaps the truest epitome of Pharisee teachings is the celebrated Pharisee maxim found in the Talmud to guide the seeker after righteousness: "Take upon yourself the yoke of the Kingdom of God; let the fear of God be your judge and guide; and deal with one another according to the dictates of love."

There is little doubt but that the observance of all the 613 commandments found in the Torah proved very onerous for the Jew who was determined to practice his religion conscientiously and consistently. Many, to be sure, in whom the spirit was willing although the flesh was weak, murmured against the imposition of such a grievous and constant burden. Scrupulous performance of the commandments consumed much time, effort, thought, and feeling, necessarily distracting from the other urgent tasks of daily existence. Yet, it is an awe-inspiring, historic fact that the great majority of Jews, for at least two thousand years, faithfully observed even the minutiae of all these commandments. In Rabbinic literature, the burden of the dedicated performance of the 613 commandments was triumphantly described as "the yoke of the Torah," but one to be worn with pride and joy for it was to be valued as the sum of all the good.

See also ESSENES; KARAITES; SADDUCEES; SAMARITANS; THERAPEUTAE; ZEALOTS.

PHILOSOPHERS. *See* ARABIC-JEWISH "GOLDEN AGE"; BIBLE, THE; MOSES; POST-BIBLICAL WRITINGS; SOME ARCHITECTS OF JEWISH CIVILIZATION; TALMUD, THE; THERAPEUTAE.

PHYLACTERIES. *See* TEFILLIN.

PIDYON HA-BEN (Hebrew, meaning "Redemption" [or "Ransom"] of the Son")

When the first-born male infant in a Jewish family passes the thirtieth day of his life, he is arbitrarily assigned the role of non-speaking but leading actor in an unusual and even puzzling ritual drama, which, however, ends to the complete satisfaction of all concerned. This rite, performed since time immemorial, is the Pidyon ha-Ben. The symbolic action and the fixed dialogue recited before an assembly made up of relatives, friends, and other invited guests, who collectively stand by in the guise of witnesses, take place between the infant boy's father and a Cohen, a Jew of priestly descent, who acts during this rite as the official representative of the priesthood of ancient days. (*See* PRIESTS; LEVITES.)

The rite, which is performed in the home, commences with the father handing over his first-born son to the Cohen. As he does this, he recites the following formula in Hebrew: "This, my first-born, is the first-born of his mother, and the Holy One, blessed be He, has given us the commandment to redeem him." The commandment is categorically stated in the Book of Numbers (18:15-16): ". . . the first-born of man shalt thou surely redeem, and the firstling of unclean beasts shalt thou redeem." The redemption fee is fixed by Scripture at "five shekels of silver." (In the United States the fee has by custom been fixed at five dollars, payable in silver; in Great Britain, at fifteen shillings. The sum usually goes to some charity.)

The dialogue then proceeds:

COHEN: Which would you rather have: give me your first-born son—the first-born of his mother—or redeem him for five shekels [or selaim], which you are bound to give according to the Torah?

FATHER: I want rather to redeem my son. And here you have the value of his redemption which I'm obliged to give according to the Torah.

The Cohen accepts the redemption money and restores the child to his father who, rejoicing at this accomplishment, recites two benedictions of Talmudic authorship, offering thanksgiving to God for having given Israel the commandment to redeem the first-born son. The Cohen then places the money upon the head of the child and recites: *"This* instead of *that, this* in commutation for *that, this* in remission of *that."* And he goes on with the traditional formula which utters the fervent hope that even as the child this day has received his redemption, so may he be destined, when he grows up, to enter into a dedication to the "Torah, Chuppah [marriage], and good deeds," the three most prized values in the life of the Jewish man. Then, over a goblet of wine, the Cohen recites the benediction and the prayer for God's protection, favor, and peace in a life of righteousness for the redeemed infant.

The question that has long puzzled many thoughtful Jews and Christians, is: What is the first-born male child being redeemed *from*? One tradition attempts to explain the rite of redemption as being performed in commemoration of that time during the Israelite Bondage when "the Lord slew all the first-born in the land of Egypt [but] . . . spared the first-born of the Israelites." The same tradition holds that because of this providential act of mercy and protection, all in Israel for all the generations to come were commanded to consecrate their first-born sons to God; they belonged to him because he had spared their lives. This "belonging" was interpreted to mean that all the first-born males were to be consecrated to the personal service of God in his Temple in Jerusalem. There is even a Talmudic tradition that, until the time when the building of the sanctuary in Jerusalem had been completed, the priesthood which ministered to the Children of Israel in the Wilderness was composed of first-born sons, but that thereafter, it drew its priestly personnel for the Temple solely from the tribe of Levi. And to help support the vast priesthood, as well as to become legally and ritualistically released from the obligation of serving as priests, the first-born sons were redeemed by their fathers for five shekels in the ceremony of the Pidyon ha-Ben.

However, it is not possible, from the point of view of ethnology, to evade certain assumptions in connection with this rite. From all the references made directly or indirectly concerning it in the Bible, we discover a kind of cultural

The redemption of the first-born son in the ceremony called Pidyon ha-Ben. (Engraving by Bernard Picart, 1722.)

palimpsest—the presence of layer upon layer, superimposed one upon the other, from the various stages of development of Jewish society and its religion during its millennial history. These divergent elements, in fugal dissonance, seem to be disconcertingly present in many Jewish beliefs, rites, and ceremonies. Sometimes they almost incongruously combine the most primitive with the most advanced ideas concerning religious worship and human relations.

The primitive origin of this redemption drama is clearly indicated in the Book of Exodus, which chronicles how God bade Moses say in his name: "Sanctify unto Me all the first-born, whatsoever openeth the womb among the children of Israel, both of man and of beast it is Mine." Read in the context of this peremptory declaration—a primitive concept and a practice, incidentally, found in other religions, that of the Greeks included—the first-born son, presumably being the most prized, shared with a first-born animal as well as with the first fruits of the field and the orchard, the character of a divine sacrifice with which to propitiate God and win his favor for the good of the whole group.

Brass Pidyon ha-Ben plate. Danzig, 18th century.

Nonetheless, in the ancient world of peoples and religions, the Israelites made a unique contribution to moral progress. They were the first to abolish human sacrifices, and they engaged thereafter in a relentless war against its reappearance in their midst. This is made abundantly plain in the stern Biblical prohibitions against it, not the least of which is seen in the moralizing drama of the Sacrifice of Isaac, recounted so movingly in Chapter 22 of the Book of Genesis. Abraham's substitution of the ram for his first-born son, Isaac, as a sacrificial offering to God is suggestive of the final liberation of the early Israelites from that nightmarish practice. It establishes as moral law the humanitarian idea that the life of man is sacred and must not be taken away.

It must certainly be true that "the redemption" of the first-born son was at a much later date directly connected with his obligatory priestly service in the Temple in Jerusalem. But there can be little doubt that when it came, it was as the climax to a long and stubborn struggle to substitute service of the first-born through priestly ministration for a sacrifice to God on the altar. The survival of the rite of the Pidyon ha-Ben, even after there was no longer any need for "redemption," since the priesthood of the Jews came to an end with the Destruction of the Temple in Jerusalem nineteen centuries ago, is an amazing demonstration of the hold religious tradition and custom have exerted on the minds of the Jewish people.

PILGRIM FESTIVALS. *See* MUSIC IN THE TEMPLE; MUSICAL INSTRUMENTS OF THE BIBLE; PASSOVER; SHABUOT; SUCCOT.

PIRKE ABOT. *See* MISHNAH (*under* TALMUD).

PIYYUT, PIYYUTIM. *See* HYMNS OF THE SYNAGOGUE.

PLAGUES, TEN. *See* PASSOVER.

POETS. *See* ARABIC-JEWISH "GOLDEN AGE"; HEBREW LITERATURE, MODERN; YIDDISH LITERATURE, MODERN.

POETS, LITURGICAL. *See* ARABIC-JEWISH "GOLDEN AGE"; HYMNS OF THE SYNAGOGUE.

POGROMS IN SLAVIC LANDS

Medieval Russia and Its Jews. In every country of Christian Europe except in the Slavic East, during the Middle Ages and in later centuries as well, the persecution of the Jewish population followed almost the same grim pattern of extortions, executions, and expulsions, of ritual-murder and Host-desecration libels, of irresistable economic and social pressures for conversion to Christianity, and of actual baptism effected by brute-force and violence. In addition, the Jews were open prey to floggings, robbery, rapine, imprisonment, torture, and even to the ultimate weapon employed by feudal society—the massacre.

In all of these departments of illegality and inhumanity, the boyars, czars, and priests of old Russia were far less expert than the Knights of the Cross in Western and Central Europe and the Dominican hunters of heresy in Spain and Portugal. At the very time when Jews in other lands were being herded like cattle into pens called "ghettos," the then relatively small Jewish population of Slavonic Russia remained unsegregated, free in its movements, and enjoying not a few legal and economic rights. They could trade without hindrance and own property and belong to the merchant guilds. There were but few massacres, no expulsions, no forced conversions and ritual-murder slanders. The Crusader and "Christ-killer" hysteria had somehow bypassed Russia, and so its Jews were not, at least at first, the victims of massacres on religious grounds.

However, an event of a grave character occurred about the year 1500; it was referred to as the "Novgorod Judaizing Heresy," and had some far-reaching consequences. Two prominent Orthodox priests of Novgorod, Denis and Alexius, became converts of the Jewish religion and went about the country preaching and proselytizing for their new faith. They made so many converts, especially among the nobility at the court in Moscow, that in 1504 a special Church Synod decreed that all "Judaized heretics" were to be mercilessly hunted down and burned at the stake.

Because of the religious hysteria prevailing at the time, the superstitious Russian masses, who had hardly ever seen any Jews, began to fear them greatly, thinking of them as sorcerers and "children of the Devil." The fear and aversion for them was indeed so great and general that, in 1526, the ambassador of Muscovy in Rome declared: "The Muscovite [Russian] people dread no one more than the Jews, and do not admit them into their borders." This may help explain why, at a time when there were several million Jews living in the provinces of Roman Catholic Poland, there were so few in Orthodox Russia; this population lack was, however, remedied later.

Needless to say, the Russian czars were just as superstitious and frightened of the "sons of the Devil" as their most ignorant muzhiks. When Ivan IV ("the Terrible") received a request from the king of Poland in 1550 asking that he permit Jewish merchants from (Polish) Lithuania to attend the Russian fairs, the czar with severity replied: "It is not convenient to allow Jews to come to Russia with their goods, since many evils result from them. For they import poisonous herbs into the realm and lead Russians astray from Christianity."

A century later, when Czar Alexis annexed Lithuania, where a great many Jews lived, the Russian soldiers proceeded to plunder and then to exterminate them. They drove the remaining Jews from Vilna, Mogilev, and other towns into the Russian interior.

But the Jewish problem for the Czars became progressively complex and difficult to cope with, when first, Russia swallowed up large parts of Poland and the Ukraine—regions with dense Jewish populations—and, finally, after the three Polish partitions of 1772, 1793, and 1795 had brought under Russian rule some 900,000 Jews. Nevertheless, although they belonged to a special category of the despised and the rejected and felt painfully the whiplash of legal and economic restrictions and disabilities, yet the Jews in Russia, compared with the martyred Jews of Western and Central Europe, led a relatively tranquil existence.

Persecution in Poland. By contrast with the tormented existence the Jews led in other Christian countries, their lot in the vast Polish domains during the Middle Ages and in the several centuries which followed was not unbearable. Even the animus directed against them as "Christ-killers" was not of the virulent variety that was met with elsewhere in Christendom. This relative mildness was chiefly due to the fact that, until the end of the tenth century, Poland was a pagan land, and Lithuania, which was then part of Poland, had not accepted Christianity until the time of King Yaghello (1386-1434); he, upon his conversion to the Christian faith, emulated the example set by Constantine in the Roman Empire during the fourth century, and forced the new religion on all of his subjects.

But there was possibly another and more cogent reason for the less harsh treatment of the Jews in medieval Poland (which included the greater part of the Ukraine, Great Poland, Little Poland, Lithuania, Silesia, and Galicia ("Red Russia"). The early kings of Poland were troubled by a breakdown of their feudal economy which had been brought about by the material devastation of their domains and the decimation and impoverishment of the people in constant wars with the Tatars. Therefore, they were anxious to do whatever possible to rebuild their country and thereby recoup their depleted treasuries. For this crucial task Jewish traders, shopkeepers, and moneylenders (*see* MONEYLENDERS) were urgently required.

The Cossack hetman, Bogdan Chmielnicki. Although less efficient than Hitler, he managed to exterminate hundreds of thousands of Ukrainian Jews in the revolt he led against Polish rule in 1648.

In the year 1264, Boleslav the Pious issued the Statute of Kalisz for governing the Polish Jews, many of whom had sought a haven in Poland after fleeing for their lives from the Crusaders, from the ritual-murder nightmares, the well-poisoning slanders, and other grizzly terrors that had been fabricated against them in Western and Central Europe. In this celebrated charter—the only one of its kind in the history of Christendom and one which had been promulgated with the consent of the "estates" or organizations of nobles and burghers—the king made plain his resolve to give the same protection to Jews as to Christians, and to guarantee to them full freedom of worship. Moreover, he forbade Christians on pain of severe punishment to desecrate, to injure, or to wreck the Jews' synagogues, religious schools, or cemeteries. The Jews were to be secure in their persons and possessions, were to be free to go anywhere and engage in whatever trade they chose without interference or molestation. The charter also stated that if a Christian witnessed an attack on a Jew, it was his simple duty to come to the Jew's aid. Moreover, it sternly warned Christians not to bring the ritual-murder accusation against any Jew for it declared such a charge to be without foundation.

Casimir III ("the Great"; ruled 1333–70) extended the rights, privileges, and protections granted to the Jews by the Statute of Kalisz. Most of those included in his charter of 1334 were of an economic nature. However—and most important of all—he granted to the Jews a greater measure of communal self-rule (autonomy) than they had ever enjoyed before in the Polish lands. This proved most significant for the continuity of Jewish ethnic, religious, and cultural life in Poland. With simple candor Casimir exposed the practical motive behind his benevolence, declaring: "We desire that the Jews whom we wish to protect in our own interest, as well as in the interest of the Royal Treasury, should feel comforted in our beneficent reign." In consequence, the Polish regions beckoned irresistibly to hundreds of thousands of desperate Jews attempting to flee from the bloody horrors of the five Crusades, the Black Death, the Hussite wars (religious wars in Bohemia), and the genocidal slaughter led by such criminal rabble-rousers as Rindfleisch and Armleder.

But it was not too long before the epidemic of religious hatred, obsessive pietism, and violence, fanning out in every direction, from France, Germany, Spain, and other countries penetrated into Poland. Some German traders—the traditional and unforgiving business rivals of the Jewish merchants in Poland during the Middle Ages and the Reformation—frequently instigated ritual-murder and Host-desecration accusations against the Polish Jews. In the superstitious and pietistic climate of Poland in those days, the consequences of these slanders were almost always catastrophic for the Jews. During Easter Week of 1407, when the religious hysteria awakened by the memories of the Crucifixion became most acute, a mob of looters and cutthroats, incited by the German traders and led by a local priest, roared through the Cracow ghetto, sparing the lives only of those who promptly submitted to baptism. This choice offered to the Jew—"Baptism or death"—became the tragic pattern for the centuries which followed.

Haidamak pogromists of the 18th century feasting while they string up a Jew on a tree. A contemporary engraving.

During the fifteenth century, living conditions for the Jews in Poland, Lithuania, the Ukraine, and Galicia had become as intolerable as they were in other Christian countries. The regional church councils periodically issued anti-Jewish decrees which forbade Jews to have any social intercourse with Christians (a prohibition that obviously would have been unnecessary had countless Christians not been well disposed toward Jews) and forced them to pay a special Jews' tax for the support of the churches. To give the matter a pious flavor as well as to allow wide latitude to the priests in determining the rate of the Jews' tax, the law stipulated that the amount of the tax could be fixed at a sum equal to the "losses" inflicted by the Jews upon the Christians—a very elastic conception. Furthermore, as in other parts of Europe, the Church laws forced the Jews into ghettos and obliged them to wear, for their greater humiliation, the yellow badge on their outer garments identifying them as Jews.

A new and complicating factor now entered the already bedeviled life of the Polish, Lithuanian, Galician, Silesian, and Ukrainian Jews: the organized assembly of the nobility called the *Shlakhta*. Like the earlier feudal barons of England, the Polish nobles, too, frequently challenged the absolute rule of their king. Because they were well organized, their influence in state policy soon made itself felt—to the injury of the Jews. On the one hand, the king and a small group of the highest nobles required the services of the Jews as moneylenders, as tax- and cutom-collectors, as lessees and operators of the salt mines, and as merchants and agents in foreign lands for the sale of surplus grain, lumber, wool, and hides. On the other hand, and opposed to them in economic interest, were extensive sections of the lesser nobles who were excluded from the all-powerful ruling circle around the king. These lesser nobles became allied with the Church, the disgruntled German business rivals of the Jews, and the native Polish merchant and artisan guilds against the Jews.

It was between these two upper and lower millstones of aristocratic class conflict that the Jews of Poland were caught and crushed. Supported by the Shlakhta, the Church rose up in arms against the Charter of Privileges to the Jews; the Archbishop of Cracow, Oleshnicki, felt strong enough to fling this challenge at Casimir IV: "Do not imagine that in matters touching the Christian religion you are at liberty to pass any law you please. No one is great and strong enough to put down all opposition to himself when the interest of the faith [Christianity] are at stake."

Intimidated by this formidable opposition, the king did a *volte-face* and backed down. He canceled the charter to the Jews with the lame excuse that he now recognized that it was "equally opposed to divine and temporal laws."

This policy bore bitter fruit immediately. Riots and massacres took place in Cracow, Lvov (Lemberg), Posen, and other cities. In 1495, under the pressures of both Church and Shlakhta, all Jews were expelled from their well-rooted communities in Lithuania—from Grodno, Brest, Pinsk, and Troki. The king, with becoming piety, confiscated their property and, in order to win the Shlakhta's good will, shared the spoils with it.

But the Jews were readmitted to the country six years later, only this time under crippling economic handicaps and discriminatory laws. Jewish merchants were permitted to engage in fewer and fewer trades and businesses, and were forced to sell fewer articles in fewer places and at fewer fairs. The Jewish tradesmen in Lvov, for instance, could sell only cloth, wax, furs, and horned cattle. This process of economic strangulation—of the "cold pogrom"—became the national pattern for Polish Jewry ever after. The wry Yiddish folk-saying: "How does a Jew make a living? He claws his way up the wall!" must have originated under such constricting conditions.

Perhaps the nearest "practical" approximation in history to Hitler's grizzly project for the extermination of *all* Jews was initiated in 1648 by the Cossack hetman, Bogdan Chmielnicki, who led a Ukrainian uprising against Polish feudal rule. Judging superficially, he saw Jews serving as stewards on the estates of the Polish nobility—acting as their financial agents and factors, tax-collectors, and moneylenders—people he hated as much as he did the Polish gentry. A historian who lived in that period recorded: "The most terrible cruelty, however, was shown towards the Jews. They were destined to utter annihilation, and the slightest pity shown to them was looked upon as treason. Scrolls of the Law were taken out of the synagogues by the Cossacks, who danced on them while drinking vodka. After this, the Jews were laid down upon them and butchered without mercy. Thousands of Jewish infants were thrown into wells or buried alive."

Many Jews fled to the illusory safety of the fortified towns which Polish troops were defending, but instead of safety they found there only a ready tomb, for the Poles gave them neither protection nor solace. Massacres on a vast scale took place wherever the Ukrainian insurgents went. It has been estimated that in that year and a half of Cossack terror, the number of Jews slain was between two hundred and four hundred thousand.

If in their despair and ignorance the Cossacks considered the Jews to be their enemies, working together with the Polish overlords, the Poles in their turn and by the most savage of ironies accused the Jews of plotting against them with the Swedes during the latters' invasion of White Russia and Lithuania in 1654. One chronicler of the time described the plight of the Jew, placed between the Cossacks and the Poles, as that of a man who, when he "runs away from a lion . . . meets a bear." The Poles proceeded to exterminate every Jew they could find in more than seven hundred communities, slaying without mercy, torturing the old for "hidden Jewish gold," violating the women, and braining the infants.

During the first half of the eighteenth century, armed bands of serfs called *Haidamaks* rose in revolt against the despotic Polish feudal landowners. They raged with fire and sword through the same territory that Chmielnicki had laid desolate a century before; they, too, tortured, slaughtered, and mutilated an uncounted number of Jews.

All these horrible experiences at the hands of the Cossacks and Haidamaks left unhealing wounds on the consciousness and the inner life of East European Jews, not only when they happened, but for all the succeeding generations.

Modern Russia and its Jews. About the very time that the French National Assembly and the Declaration of the Rights of Man were bestowing equal citizenship on the Jews of France, a forbidding though invisible wall of anti-Semitic separation began to rise all around the Jewish communities of Russia, the Ukraine, Lithuania, and Poland. Beginning with the year 1772, the Jews were forbidden residence in any place outside of the communities in which they were already living; this geographic straitjacket became known as the "Jewish Pale of Settlement." The limits of this immense ghetto were more precisely defined by statute in 1804, and those Jews who had the temerity to venture beyond its confines were arrested by the police and punished, unless, of course, they were protected by the special travel and residence permits which only a limited number were able to obtain from the government.

Czar Alexander I (ruled 1801-25), who had started out his reign with a liberal policy for all the Russian peoples—

Old synagogue in Bendzin, Poland, built as a "fortress" behind whose thick stone walls the Jews could defend themselves whenever attacked. To the left stands another defensive stronghold: the ruins of a medieval castle. (YIVO.)

a policy which included the improvement of the conditions of the Jews, giving them the right to own land and to till the soil, to follow whatever trades they wished, and to attend all schools on the same footing with other Russians—eventually became frightened by his own liberal policy lest it bring on a revolution. Accordingly, he soon began to abrogate all the reforms he had introduced for the Russian people, including those for the benefit of the Jews. The latter received summary orders to leave the villages and the countryside where large numbers had settled as farmers and innkeepers; thereafter, they were allowed to live only in the towns and cities. Alexander's successor as czar, Nicholas I, constricted the area of the Pale of Settlement even more. Under the new ruler, the Jews were driven out in 1827 from all the villages in the District of Grodno, in 1829 from the villages on the shores of the Baltic and Black Seas, and in 1830 from all the numerous settlements in the Kiev region. Prince N. Golitsyn, a man of humane feeling, was distressed by the manner of their expulsion: "In the dead of winter, half-naked Jews were driven from their homes into the towns. Many were crowded together in quarters that gave them no breathing space. The others, ill-sheltered, were left exposed to the bitter cold."

When the hordes of refugees flooded the towns within the Jewish Pale, they caused frightful overcrowding and a situation of near panic. The new difficult conditions, aggravated by already existing anti-Jewish restrictions in commerce and in the trades, resulted in an intolerable competition and widespread unemployment. A vast army of unskilled, shiftless, and maladjusted elements—luftmenschen (s. luftmensch) "men of air"—quickly sprang up. In the mad scramble for physical survival, they were found pitifully inadequate, thereby turning into "superfluous" men. The luftmensch thenceforth remained an enduring type in Slavic ghetto life.

The religious fanaticism of the czar was shrewdly worked upon by his advisers and brought about a most calamitous situation for the Jews of the empire at that time. In 1827, Nicholas established a compulsory army service period for Jewish recruits; this was designated as "the Jewish Cantonist System." It demanded of all Jewish communities that they furnish the army with specified levies of Jewish boys from twelve to eighteen years of age. Unfortunately and incredibly, when there were not enough youths to fill the quotas of such cantonists, they were rounded out with children of seven and even of six years. To prevent their children being taken away, parents concealed their boys and would not bring them voluntarily to the communal officials. In consequence, a nightmarish type of ghetto official was created out of the direst need for the protection of the Jewish community against severe reprisals. This was the *chapper* (the "snatcher" or "kidnaper"). The chapper would prowl the streets and literally "snatch" little boys and carry them off, frightened and sobbing, many of them never to be reunited with their fathers and mothers again. The people's macerated memory of their "lost children," of the chapper's ghoulish deeds, and of the sad fate which lay ahead of the *Nikolaevske-soldaten* (Yiddish, meaning "Nicholas' soldiers") has been preserved in many a dirgeful folk song.

The well-reasoned plan behind this weird cantonist system was that, by tearing away little boys from their families and their Jewish religious environment and by keeping them in the army for twenty-five years, they would become weaned from their identity and would become so Russified that they would be more amenable to efforts to convert them to the Russian Orthodox faith.

One czar succeeded another, yet almost the same grim pattern of persecution and harassment of the Jews was followed. The expression "in darkest Russia" became a figure of speech in a number of languages, including English. Under the sponsorship of the Slavophile chauvinists whose political creed was centered in the concept of "Holy Mother Russia," of the Russian government working behind the scenes, of the Orthodox Church which gave its religious sanction, and of Alexander II personally, anti-Semitism in the Russian Empire became a well-organized and respectable movement.

The first pogrom under these august auspices occurred in Odessa in 1871. The whole civilized world shuddered when in due time the actual facts became known. Ten years after its occurrence, six revolutionists succeeded in assassinating the czar. Because one of the terrorists was a Jewish girl, Chasia Helfman, the new czar, Alexander III, goaded on by his Slavophile advisers to preserve "Russia for the Russians," marked out the Jews for special retribution—by liquidation. Thus, immediately after his coronation during Easter Week in 1881, a pogrom was "engineered" in Elizavetgrad. From there the terror spread out fanwise into Kiev and Odessa. In the Kiev region alone there were pogroms in forty-eight towns. From there the epidemic of violence and bloodshed moved

Caricature by the French graphic satirist, Honoré Daumier, depicting the real motive of Tzar Nicholas I in persecuting the Jews in the Russian empire. Paris, 1855.

Expulsion of the Jews from the village of Tedolsk, c. 1870, in the general action taken by the Czarist government to drive all Jews out of the Russian countryside.

Pogrom in a Russian city by the Slavophile Black Hundreds sponsored by the czarist government. (Lithograph by Max Liebermann, Berlin, before World War I.)

into the districts of Volhynia, Podolia, Chernigov, and Poltava, where it raged all of that year. There was also a massacre in Warsaw. As was to be expected, the czar, the government, the Orthodox Church, and the Slavophiles disclaimed any responsibility for the massacres. As a matter of fact, tart official comment was that the Jews had only themselves to blame for their misfortunes because of the way they had "preyed" upon the Russian people.

A decisive influence on Alexander III's thinking about the Jews was the pietist, Pobiedonostsev, the Procurator of the Holy Synod of the Church who was also the leader of the Slavophiles. He regarded the modern democratic spirit and all intellectual enlightenment as "leprous" diseases with which "the vulgar" new bourgeoisie was infecting all of European society, the Jews being the worst of all these pestilential carriers. Therefore, aided by a subservient press, he and other leading Slavophiles, including the Minister of the Interior, Count Ignatiev, demanded the severest suppression of the Jews in the Empire.

On May 3, 1882, the government promulgated the so-called May Laws. These were harsh restrictions and disabilities which really constituted "pogrom by law" on a national scale. They were intended to bring a quick and total solution to the troublesome Jewish problem. Pobiedonostsev had worked out a formula for the liquidation of the millions of Jews in the Russian Empire. It was arithmetically very neat: one-third of the Jewish population was to be absorbed by conversion; one-third was to be ejected by emigration, and one-third was to be exterminated by starvation.

Soon the Russian, Polish, and Lithuanian Jews began to reel from these crushing blows; panic seized them. They wanted to flee the country while there was still time. When the imperial government opened the gates to Jewish emigration, about 1,300,000 poured through from 1881 to 1918 in a flood comparable to the Exodus from Egypt. Most of the immigrants went to the United States, but many settled in England, Germany, France, Holland, Switzerland, and other countries. Many more would have left had they been able to scrape together the passage money, for the masses of Jews in czarist Russia, it should be kept in mind, were desperately poor. In 1892, the Belgian historian Errera noted: "There are in Russia only ten to fifteen thousand Jews who possess any certain means of existence. As to the masses, they have nothing." Conditions had grown so critical after the economic noose had been tightened around the neck of Russian Jewry, that to maintain themselves and their families, Jewish workers and petty tradesmen had to labor from fifteen to twenty hours daily, living on a diet consisting principally of bread, a few potatoes, and a herring—the poor man's chicken.

Czar Nicholas II (ruled 1894–1917), the last of the Romanoff despots, continued the repressive and brutal measures of his imperial predecessors in Russia, Poland, and Lithuania. The well-established internal political policy of blaming everything on the Jews also proved expedient for him and his ministers. When the ritual-murder circus performed around the Jews was found insufficient to distract the Russian masses from their hunger and rage against their oppression, there was always cynical recourse to the pogrom. During "the four pogrom years," beginning in 1903 with the Kishinev slaughter, 410,098 Jews fled for their lives from Russia to the United States.

After the debacle of the Revolution of 1905 against czarist absolutism, when the government-sponsored Slavophile Black Hundreds (League of the Russian People) raged, unhindered by the police or army, through the ghettos, intent on exterminating all the Jews, the foremost literary men of Russia were dismayed by the butchery. Tolstoy, Korolenko, Sologub, Andreyev, and Gorky appealed to the conscience and humanity of the Russian people to put an end to the savagery. But their appeals were promptly suppressed by the government as subversive. It was only in February, 1917, that the czarist despotism was overthrown by the Russian Revolution and a liberal Republic was established.

See also ANTI-SEMITISM: THE "RACIAL PURITY" MYTH; CHRISTIANITY, JEWISH ORIGINS OF; CHURCH AND PERSECUTION; COMMUNITY, SELF-GOVERNING; CONVERSION OF JEWS; DISPUTATIONS, RELIGIOUS; FEUDAL SOCIETY, POSITION OF THE JEWS IN; GHETTO; "HOST DESECRATION" CALUMNIES; JEWISH OATH, THE; SEPARATISM, JEWISH; MASSACRES: THE CRUSADES, THE BLACK DEATH; MONEY-LENDERS; NAZIS, THE; PERSECUTION IN "MODERN" DRESS; "RITUAL MURDER" SLANDERS; SEPARATISM, JEWISH; WANDERING JEW; YELLOW BADGE.

POLAND, JEWS IN. *See* POGROMS IN SLAVIC LANDS; PERSECUTION IN "MODERN DRESS."

POOR, THE

A commentary in the Talmud interprets one Biblical passage thus: "It is written: 'If you lend money to any of my people.' Asked Israel of the Holy One—blessed be He!—'Who are your people?' To this God answered: 'The poor are my people,' for it is stated in the Torah: 'The Lord has comforted His people, and has compassion upon His afflicted.'"

If the poor were declared to be God's children and his special wards, the rich and the powerful certainly did not share in His favor, judging by the scorn and occasional pity expressed for them in the Scriptures, the post-Biblical writings, and the vast Talmudic literature. The medieval philosopher-rabbi, Moses ben Maimon (Maimonides), hazarded an explanation for this attitude of disrespect, which he shared.

"It is to be feared that those who become great in riches and comfort generally fall into the vices of insolence and haughtiness, and abandon all good principles." Maimonides regarded the acquisitive compulsion in human beings with gloom. The Sages had asked with conundrum irony why it was that the rich man could be compared to a weasel. And the answer given was that just as a weasel accumulates and doesn't know why, so also does the rich man hoard and doesn't know what for. To this Maimonides added his own somber reflection: "It is in the nature of man to strive to gain money and to increase it; and it is his great desire to add to his wealth and honor that is the chief source of misery for man."

This misery, the Prophets charged, resulted from the greed and rapacity of the rich.

> It is ye that have eaten up the vineyard;
> The spoil of the poor is in your houses;
> What mean ye that ye crush My people
> And grind the face of the poor?
>
> ISAIAH 3:14-15

It was different in the Golden Age of Moses and the Judges. The tribalistic society of Israel they had molded and ruled was unencumbered by excessive worldly goods and relatively unhampered by social inequalities. The good of the people and the welfare of the individual were considered to be the worthiest goals of society. There was to be no oppression of class by class, for had the Israelites themselves once not groaned in the Egyptian Bondage? Why then should they wish to oppress their own kind in freedom? Moses had taught them the doctrine of the brotherhood of man: "Thou shalt love thy neighbor as thyself." For that reason, every Israelite was obligated to be his brother's keeper, to protect him, and to support him when he was feeling faint. The Scriptural commandment, therefore, advised: "And if thy brother be waxen poor with thee . . . Thou shalt surely open thine hand unto thy poor and needy brother." This equation prompted the following triumphant commentary from the Sages in the Talmud: "It is not written 'the poor man' but 'thy brother,' in order to show that both of them are one and the same!"

In the social democracy of tribal Israel, before the imposition of the monarchial system by Saul, every effort was made by the Elders to protect the weak from the oppression of the strong, and to prevent the strong from becoming still stronger. The legislation passing under the generic term "Mosaic"—regardless in what historic period it arose—undertook to preserve the equilibrium of ancient Jewish society in terms of morality and simple humanity. To prevent the swallowing up of the small holdings of the farmer by the land-greedy rich, the Scriptural declaration stated bluntly in the name of God: "The land is Mine." Therefore, it could not be owned in perpetuity; the time limit it could be owned was fifty years, after which it reverted back "to the Lord," that is, to the God-governed state. (*See* JUBILEE.)

There also was what might perhaps best be described as a compulsory sharing of the most urgent necessities of life of the "haves" with the "have-nots." For the relief of the poor in distress, it was decreed that a tithe of the produce of the fields be left over for them by the harvesters as gleanings.

The taking of interest on loans to the poor was branded as a crime against man and as a sin against God. Nor was the collection of these loans to be pressed; every such indebtedness was wiped out automatically every seventh year—the Sabbatical year. There were also laws and regulations to insure the humane and just treatment of workers, of servants, of slaves, and of other non-Jews—considerations virtually unknown, except in isolated instances, in the brutal dog-eat-dog world of antiquity. Widows and orphans and other categories of the unfortunate were taken under the special protection of the community in conformity with the doctrine that all Jews were members of one fellowship.

But this tender regard for the poor and the suffering gradually began to fade from Jewish life under the corrupt rule of the kings, when a sizable class of "new rich" appeared. This was composed of hereditary princes and nobles, of big landowners, usurers, speculators in grain, wealthy merchants, bribe-taking judges, political priests, and yes-saying "prophets." Now the struggle between the classes was drawn: the landlords against the landless, the rich against the poor. The great "Wisdom"-writer, Jesus ben Sirach (c. 200 B.C.E.), asked this rhetorical question in Ecclesiasticus:

> What fellowship shall wolf have with the lamb? . . .
> And so is the rich unto a man that is destitute.

In the last centuries of the Second Temple period, the formerly primitive agricultural economy gradually changed, became more complex, more commercial. It was bedeviled by contradictions and problems. For example, the great estates—the latifundia—had rapidly been swallowing up the land of the numerous smallholders who, in consequence, became uprooted. There appeared a large class of idle and hungry farm workers who roamed the countryside like locusts, finding no place to lay their heads. Harsh taxes and the debtor's prisons (debts no longer were forgiven the poor on the seventh year), voluntary (indentured) servitude on the part of the desperate, and the forced labor of tens of thousands of the people by command of the king—all these social evils were compounded by the horrors of interminable wars. And so the poor became ever poorer and also more discouraged. The Prophets rebuked the ruling class but they were persecuted as a result. There was no one to turn to for aid but God. Poignant in the midst of the social turmoil sounded the affirmation of the Psalmist:

> I know that the Lord will maintain the cause of the poor,
> And the right of the needy.
>
> PSALMS 140:13

When Judea lay prostrate under the iron heel of the imperial legions of Rome, aided and abetted by the Jewish collaborationists who nominally ruled the nation, the lot of the poor had become even more desperate. And so, idealistic brotherhoods, composed of escapists from the injustice and cruelty of life, went into monastic retreats everywhere. Such were the Essenes, the New Covenanters, the unidentified community at Qumran which left the Dead Sea Scrolls behind, and the small band of disciples and adherents of Jesus of Nazareth.

Bitter are the reflections of some of the Pharisee rabbis (the Sages of the Talmud) who observed those tragic events and the suffering and humiliation of the people. They saw no reason for glorifying poverty as a moral virtue. "A poor man is a dead man," said one. "Dirt is the name of the Angel of Poverty," ventured another. It was the Mishnah Tanna, Resh Lakish, who seemed to plumb the very depths of the poor Jew's misery and helplessness. "When a man goes out into the field and meets the bailiff, it is as though he had met a lion. When he enters the town and is stopped by the tax collector, it is as though he had met a bear. And when he enters his home and finds his sons and daughters devoured by hunger, it is as though he had been bitten by a serpent."

The poor themselves expressed their feelings in sardonic folk-witticisms. The Talmud quotes them: "They eat and we say grace." "One beats the bush and the other catches the bird."

Yet there were many Talmudic Sages who, like Jesus of Nazareth and his disciples, were of the opinion that the affliction of poverty was a blessing in disguise. They wished to see the poor as "God's people," as the meek preservers of the tested and proven virtues of Torah morality in contrast to the arrogant rich who, they believed, being "shackled to gold and silver," were violating the mitzvot in a life of avarice, vice, and luxury. Says the Talmud: "God wished to give Israel the best possible gift, but He could find nothing more precious to give it than poverty." "Poverty is becoming to Jews like a red ribbon to a white horse."

The Book of Tobit, a work included in the Apocrypha and written several centuries before the Talmudic era, already took the same attitude toward poverty—i.e., that it was a moral virtue. Old Tobit counseled his son: "And fear not, my child, because we have become poor; thou has much wealth if thou fear God and avoid every kind of sin and do the things which are good in the sight of the Lord thy God."

Curiously, the Hebrew word-concept meaning "poor," according to close students of the Talmud, finds more synonyms in subtle shadings of difference than the same word does in other languages. This linguistic fact readily testifies to the "poverty consciousness" of Jews. In the Talmud alone are found these words for "poor": *ani* (to afflict); *ebion* (to want); *misken* (impoverished); *rash* (landless); *dal* (empty-handed); *dak* (beaten down); *mak* (reduced); *halek* (homeless); etc. It can be no accident that the Hebrew word for the non-Jewish concept of "charity" is *tzedakah*, which means "righteousness" and also "justice" i.e., "justice to the poor" and not just "alms" or "benevolence." The fraternal care of the poor, the weak, the sick, and the needy was a fundamental obligation of social justice in Jewish group life, and so it has remained to this day.

See also BROTHERHOOD; CHARITY; ESSENES; ETHICAL VALUES, JEWISH; FELLOWSHIP IN ISRAEL; LABOR, DIGNITY OF; LIFE, SANCTIFICATION OF; MAN, DIGNITY OF; MOSES; LOANS, FREE; PASSOVER; PROPHETS (*under* BIBLE, THE); SLAVERY AND THE SLAVE; THERAPEUTAE; TORAH, THE (*under* BIBLE, THE); UNITY OF ISRAEL.

POST-BIBLICAL WRITINGS

During the final centuries of the semiautonomous Jewish society of Judea, which came to an end in 70 C.E., literary activity was both lively and fertile. It was carried on in all the three contemporary "Jewish" languages—Hebrew, Aramaic, and Greek. These facts, of course, run counter to the popular notion that, until the time of the historian Josephus (first century) and following the second century C.E., when the Mishnah was compiled in Hebrew by the Rabbinic Sages, and the New Testament was written by the Judeo-Christian evangelists in Greek, the entire period—in a creative sense—was intellectually barren except for the production of the Bible.

Certainly, from about 200 B.C.E. to the end of the first century of the Common Era, religious writings, which were keyed to the lofty mood and sonorous rhetoric of similarly patterned works in the Hebrew Scriptures, had poured from the quills of many gifted men in Judea and the Jewish communities throughout the Hellenistic Diaspora. These works had been written by a variety of "prophets," visionaries, chroniclers, poets, evangelists, apologists, storytellers, and initiates in "the hidden wisdom."

Actually, only a relatively small number of these extra-Biblical and post-Biblical Jewish writings have survived the caprices of history and sectarian religious wranglings. It happened that some of these were preserved for posterity quite fortuitously in Hebrew, Greek, or Aramaic versions, not just because of any recognition that they possessed some special merit or sanctity that was found lacking in other writings that were neglected, denigrated, or even warred upon by the religious authorities of their time.

Not too much, however, is known about this matter. Some books were suppressed, according to testimony in the Talmud, because they were written by such religiously "outlawed" sectaries (minim) as the Samaritans, Gnostics, and Christians. (They had been branded by the Rabbinical Sages as heretical.) Other works, also pretending a Scriptural character, had been frowned upon as being potentially subversive of Jewish religious doctrines and traditions. They were considered tainted with alien notions, for they employed abstruse symbolism and terminology and projected a conception of life and the universe that sometimes was closer to the ideas of the Greek Pythagoras and the Persian magis than to Moses and Isaiah. Into the limbo of this religious disapproval of the Sages had been consigned—not in every instance too consistently or judiciously, even according to Rabbinical criteria—all the allegorical, mystical, and magical writings that the Jewish Hellenists had composed.

The marriage of polyglot Greek-Oriental decadence with Messianic and Judgment Day Judaism, which was morbid and fevered in its own right, produced some exotic literary

Two miniatures from a Hebrew Bible manuscript (c. 1288) depicting the entrapment and slaying of Holofernes by the Jewish national heroine, Judith of Bethulia. These events are described in the Book of Judith of the Apocrypha. (The British Museum.)

The Hellenistic Jewish historian Josephus (anachronistically wearing the medieval black Judenhut *or "Jew's hat") in an audience with the Emperor Vespasian. (From a Latin manuscript of the 13th century in the Landesbibliothek, Fulda, Germany.)*

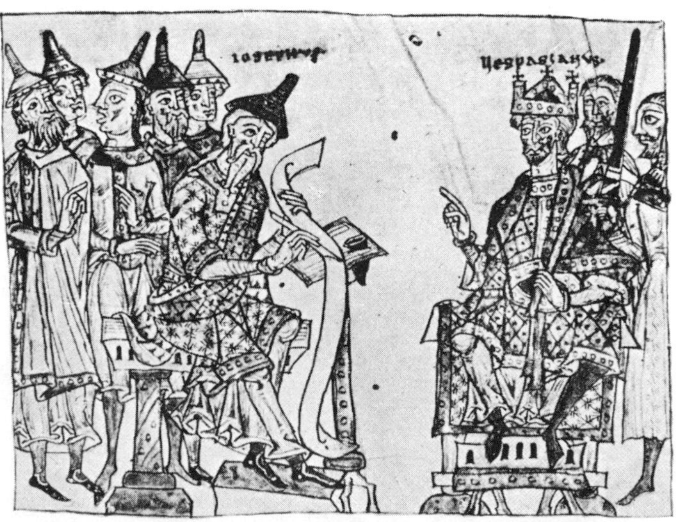

Tobit bids farewell to his son, illustrating an incident in the Book of Tobit. (Drawing by Rembrandt.)

Cave at Qumran near the Dead Sea where the famed Dead Sea Scrolls were discovered in jars. (American Friends of the Hebrew University.)

Professor James Biberkraut of the Hebrew University unrolling a Dead Sea Scroll and studying its text. (American Friends of the Hebrew University.)

blooms. Living in a milieu like Alexandria, which had displaced Athens, as the world-metropolis, one in which were intermingled a great many ethnic strains and which was characterized by a remarkable measure of religious-cultural receptivity and, consequently, of fusion—the Jewish religious intellectuals had absorbed a great many of the magical and theosophical elements from Greek-Egyptian-Persian mysticism. By means of the chemism of the irrational, they were able to blend them with the doctrines and values then current in the Jewish religion, as well as with not entirely relevant Greek philosophical speculations, into a sort of esoteric system.

The Dead Sea Scroll of the Book of Isaiah discovered in a cave at Qumran near the Dead Sea. (American Friends of the Hebrew University.)

All the Jewish religious writings in Hellenistic antiquity became a source of contention between the Rabbinic teachers of Judea who followed tradition and their assimilated and more sophisticated counterparts among the Hellenists. It was not merely a question of writing about Judaism in Greek instead of in the hieratical Hebrew, or even of developing different customs or of producing different nuances in religious beliefs. From a historical-cultural point of view, the controversy turned out to be much more serious than that; it marked, in a concrete sense, clear signs of a parting of the ways between the two opposing cultural trends in the faith of Israel.

See also APOCRYPHA; BIBLE, THE; CHACHMAH; CHRISTIANITY JEWISH ORIGINS OF; DEAD SEA SCROLLS; ESSENES; HELLENISTS, JEWISH; MESSIAH, THE; MESSIAHS, WOULD-BE; PHARISEES; PSEUDEPIGRAPHA; SADUCEES; THERAPEUTAE.

PRAYER, THE CHARACTER OF JEWISH. *See* PRAYER AND WORSHIP.

PRAYER, THE JEW'S POSTURE AT. *See* PRAYER AND WORSHIP.

PRAYER AND WORSHIP

The Character of Jewish Prayer. What a people collectively thinks about itself (discounting the natural tendency toward group self-flattery) is probably far more correct than what outsiders, with but inadequate information and insights, believe to be true. Not long after Judea had fallen (in 70 C.E.) and had ceased to exist as the political-religious homeland of the Jews, an appraisal of the Jewish national drive for power was expressed by a Rabbinic Sage: "While other peoples rely on the might of their arms, Israel's weapon is prayer."

This spiritualized concept of Israel's power-quest in the world—a point of view that was continuously being developed and deepened in ethical and social terms by the idealistic Rabbinic teachers of Roman times—was quite in harmony with the over-all traditional religious outlook that had been developing during the Second Commonwealth. This was: that human life, having been created by God, was therefore sacred, and that man, in order to justify morally his presence in the world, was duty bound to aspire to a nobler existence. Prayer, assured the Rabbis, was the ladder of aspiration upon which man was able to climb to heaven to commune directly with God. One quaint Talmudic fancy even described God as revealing himself to Moses on Mount Sinai in the guise of a baal tefillah (leader of congregational prayer), wrapped in his tallit or prayer shawl. This was so he could teach man the way to pray and to impress upon him the great significance of prayer. God himself was cited as uttering this prayer: "O that My mercy shall prevail over My justice!"

Such an exalted view of prayer, however, represented but the flowering of Prophetic and, at a later period, of Rabbinic Judaism. For a long time, especially in earlier centuries Jews, together with all other ancient peoples, had but a primitive conception of the end-purpose of prayer. The student of Jewish culture and religion has no choice but to recognize certain sober facts. In the course of its long history, the Jewish people accumulated a highly variegated body of religious beliefs, moral values, ethical practices, myths, customs, rites—and also a multitude of prayers. Many of these, spun, so to speak, from its own religious cocoon, it created by itself, from historic necessity and from the special character that Jewish life happened to have at a given time and place. There were still others that, in normal cultural interchange, it borrowed or adapted from the religions of its neighbors—the Egyptians, Babylonians, Caananites, Greeks, Persians, etc.—to fit its own requirements, fusing them imperceptibly with its own.

Like geologic rock formations the disparate elements that are to be found in the Jewish religion (and in its prayer-values as well) expose different, and often contradictory, strata of development. But these developments did not necessarily emerge, as many people believe, in chronological time-sequence.

It is one of the paradoxes of history that intellectual, social, and ethical ideas do not at all times advance, as it were, in a well-ordered progression from lower to higher values. Quite often they have taken a curious zig-zag course: They may have moved forward during one historic period only to recede in the one which followed. To cite just one illustration of this: What a world of difference lies between the poetic and spiritually exalted character of the Hebrew Psalms composed perhaps twenty-five hundred years ago as liturgical hymns and devotional prayers, and the Satan-and-angel infested prayers, incantations, and exorcisms which were composed by the medieval and later Cabalists! To be sure, both of these varieties of supplication must be considered bona fide prayers, but where the Psalms are an authentic religious expression, the Cabalistic incantations and exorcisms rely principally on the vocal recitation or the writing down of *the proper formulas;* without question, these latter have the abracadabra character of all primitive magic.

It should be remembered, though, that in the cultural history of mankind, both religion and magic have represented alternative methods by which worshipers, regardless of what primitive or sophisticated civilizational level they were on, have attempted to achieve natural ends that stood outside of natural means. Thus, the cultural Spanish-Jewish religious philosopher, Joseph Albo (d. 1444), stated categorically: "Pious men . . . can change the laws of nature by prayer." But his mystical view of the miraculous power of prayer was far removed from the attitude of the "practical" school of Cabalists which held that all one had to do was discover and recite *the correct magic formulas* to get the right results.

Magic being merely irrational wishful thinking about material things and physical situations—a daydreaming infantile tendency found in such a large portion of mankind—it has been inevitable that strong elements of it have survived in the prayer-literatures and rituals of all religions, side by side with spiritually elevated articulations.

Judging from many of the Hebrew prayer-texts, one would, without question, know that this was also true of the Jewish religion. This polarity or opposition is plainly seen in the primitive character of certain prayers that are found in those portions of the Bible that were composed earlier. Purportedly, these supplications were related to the patriarchal or tribal period of Israelite history. Those were the prayers of materialistic-minded suppliants who wished to enter into a kind of *quid pro quo* arrangement with the Deity. In a religious-moral sense, they were not freer from primitive notions concerning God than the prayers of their non-Israelite contemporaries whose gods were death, the moon, the bull, the lightning, and the corn, among others.

One arresting example of this kind of early Israelite prayer is found in the Scriptural narrative of the Patriarch Jacob's flight from the vengeance of his brother Esau, whose birthright as the eldest son Jacob had taken from him "with guile." Frightened by the thought of his pursuer, Jacob cried to God: "Deliver me, I pray Thee, from the hand of my brother, from the hand of Esau; for I fear him, lest he come and smite me . . ." (Genesis 32:12.)

This supplication of Jacob contains a classic feature of all protection-begging prayers recited against enemies, and it is found abundantly in the prayers of every religion. Considerations of morality or truth do not enter here. The petitioner ingenuously believes that God will serve him at all times as his steadfast and invincible ally simply because he believes in him and prays to him and offers homage and material gifts to him.

The reverse of Jacob's plea for divine protection was that for vengeance uttered before his death by the blinded Israelite strongman, Samson, while he was "making sport" before the Philistines in their temple of Dagon. "O Lord God," he implored," . . . strengthen me, I pray Thee . . . that I may be this once avenged of the Philistines for my two eyes." (Judges 16:28.)

But since peoples, just like individuals, grow toward maturity in gradual cultural stages, so ideas about prayer in time acquired greater spiritual stature. Beginning with the great Prophets, at the close of the First Temple period, there took place an intellectual, spiritual, and ethical revolution in the Jewish religion. From this point on, living uprightly

"Prayer." (Painting by Sheva Ausubel.)

and working to ensure peace and justice in the world were considered to be infinitely more important as religious values than animal sacrifices, gift offerings to God, and prayer.

The Rabbinic Sages, even at the time when the Second Temple still was standing, were teaching the same values and elaborating upon them. They taught that it was "the cry of the heart" to God, the prayer of the afflicted and the sorrow-laden—not the mere mechanical recitation of prayer texts—that was heard by the Creator.

In some Jewish ethical writings, prayer mystically assumed other than verbal forms. Jesus ben Sirach (c. 200 B.C.E.), being a philosopher, a poet, and a worldly man, in his Wisdom Book, Ecclesiasticus (38:34), took an even broader and more poetical view of prayer. He eulogized as a high form of prayer all productive labors because they were of use and benefit to mankind. Of conscientious artisans and workers, he sang:

> But they will maintain the fabric of the world,
> And in the handiwork of their craft is their prayer.

Certain medieval Cabalists, alike with the Rabbinic Sages, placed the major emphasis on good deeds. Intensely ethics-conscious, they taught that acts of loving-kindness and brotherly benevolence were among the highest forms of prayer. The Rhineland mystic, Judah Chasid (*d.* 1217), in his Book of the Pious (Sefer Chasidim), lamented that the prayers of many an individual go unheeded because he has callousy turned away from the crying need of the poor and from the suffering of the afflicted, thereby making a mockery of the supreme commandment of the Torah: "Thou shalt love they neighbor as thyself."

It is plainly evident that, generally, men and women pray for themselves alone and for their personal goals. Certain religious teachers and liturgists, being human and, therefore, sometimes also narrow-minded and only formalistically pious themselves, encouraged a self-seeking trend in prayer among the unthinking. This would perhaps explain why it is that there are found in the prayer and devotional books of Jews several supplications that sound transparently frank in their self-seeking ends. These prayers give pitiful utterance to the vast range of unappeased human hungers, fears, and frustrations. Through them, the worshiper implores that he be granted good health and prosperity; he petitions for protection against illness, suffering, poverty, and death.

The great Rashi of Troyes, who flourished in the Rhineland during the eleventh century and who was the principal religious authority among the Ashkenazim of that and subsequent ages, somberly warned: "The person who trades with God, as it were: 'I will pray to You, and in return You send me what I want,' is a gross and insolent sinner."

That primitive barter arrangement with the Deity was denounced in the same manner by the Talmudic Sages a thousand years before Rashi. They had warned the unthinking against trying to serve God and/or doing good for a reward, for this was treating him exactly, they said, like a servant working for hire.

Many were the strictures drawn in Rabbinic discussions against the flattery and verbose adulation of God. It is related in the Talmud that a certain baal tefillah began to intone, "O great, O Almighty, O Awesome, O Exalted, O Merciful, O True, O Omniscient, O Omnipotent . . .!" And when the precentor paused to catch his breath, the Rabbinic Sage, Chanina, who was sitting among the worshipers, quickly cut in: "Are you through showering praise on the Lord?"

A fundamental tradition in the Jewish religion has been that prayer is a simple *duty of the heart*; therefore, it requires the utmost mental concentration to reach an understanding of its inner meanings. The medieval teacher of ethics in the Rhineland, Eleazer of Worms (1170–1238), in his moralistic work The Book of the Perfumer, urged upon the worshiper: "Before you utter a single word of prayer, think of its meaning . . . If a worldly thought occurs to you while at prayer, fall silent and wait until you've brought your mind back into a state of awe toward the Creator."

It was always traditional that prayers should be recited in Hebrew. This was because Hebrew was revered as the "sacred tongue," and this is precisely the name in Hebrew—*lashon ha-kodesh*—that identifies it as a language. The objective fact, however, is that, with the return from the Babylonian Captivity in the sixth century B.C.E., a linguistic revolution took place among the Jews of Judah. Not Hebrew but Aramaic, the language very similar to it which was the lingua franca of the entire Middle East, had become the vernacular of the masses. This problem of variance in languages led to efforts (which turned out to be entirely fruitless) on the part of some religious teachers to sanction public prayer-services in Aramaic, since that and not Hebrew was the language that the majority of the Jewish people understood. The proponents of this reform in public worship argued that it was more important for the suppliant to *understand* the meaning of the prayers than just to render a mechanical recitation of the words the prayer contained. This prompted an irate traditionalist of the third century C.E. to warn, "He who prays in Aramaic will get no help from the angels, because they do not understand Aramaic."

Needless to say, Hebrew and not Aramaic continued to be employed as the sacred language for prayer and Torah-study in Judea, Babylonia, and other centers of Jewish life. But in the Hellenistic world, especially in Egypt, there is conclusive evidence that Greek finally displaced the lashon ha-kodesh as the obligatory language of prayer.

This language "heresy" flamed up anew at various times in different regions. Toward the end of the twelfth century, the German Cabalist, Judah Chasid, urged the adoption of Yiddish as the language of prayer among the Ashkenazim. He put it bluntly: "If the mind does not know what the lips are saying, prayer is no prayer." Even more forthright was the position taken by the East European sectarians, the Chasidim, during the eighteenth and nineteenth centuries. Rabbi Nachman Bratzlaver (Nachman of Bratzlav), the grandson of the Baal Shem, who had been the founder of this mystical movement, preached that any man should be able to "pour out his heart to God in a free and intimate manner and in the language familiar to him—in his mother tongue. In our country [Poland] this is *mameh-loshen* [literally: 'mother tongue,' i.e., Yiddish]. The average person has little knowledge of Hebrew and it is, therefore, difficult for him to express himself fluently in it. That is why, often, when the prayers are recited in Hebrew, the ears do not understand what the lips are saying."

It is common knowledge that, in modern times, praying in Hebrew has gone through a similar linguistic crisis among Jews in various parts of the world. Although praying in the lashon ha-kodesh still is *de rigueur*, even in the order of service of Reform Jews, it is noticeable that praying in the vernacular–no matter what the language is–is becoming increasingly popular, especially in the United States, England, and other English-speaking countries.

The Jew's Posture at Prayer. The posture assumed by Jews at prayer has never remained consistently the same. It has undergone some remarkable changes and, ironically, on several occasions it took an *opposite* direction from the posture of prayer being observed at the time by the dominant non-Jewish religions.

In modern times, except in Mohammedan countries, where cross-legged squatting is the customary way of sitting, prayer in the synagogue is for the most part recited by the worshipers while they are seated on benches or chairs. An exception is made during the recitation of the most solemn portion of the prayer service, the Eighteen Blessings (Shemoneh Esreh), which is read silently while standing.

The Jews in ancient times certainly prayed in a different manner. Moses is described as praying with hands outstretched in supplication (Exodus 9:29). As late as the time of Isaiah ben Amoz, during the first half of the eight century B.C.E., that mode of worship was still in vogue.

> And when ye spread forth your hands,
> I will hide Mine eyes from you.
>
> ISAIAH 1:15

It is not difficult to visualize this posture at prayer: One has only to turn to a certain Egyptian wall-painting, contemporary with early Israelite history, which depicts Egyptians at prayer, to see it graphically illustrated.

This posture changed entirely beginning with the Captivity in Babylonia. Just as the Jews there were influenced in other of their religious ideas, customs, and folkways by the Babylonians, so were they also influenced to adopt the Babylonian posture at prayer. Accordingly, the worshiper kneeled and prostrated himself during worship as a sign of complete submission. The posture is illustrated on a number of sculptured bas-reliefs of that historic period. Particularly arresting is the figure of the captive Jewish king Jehu (*c.* 842 B.C.E.), depicted on the Black Column of King Shalmaneser of Babylonia now in the British Museum. He is shown in a position combining kneeling with abject prostration, and with his face touching the ground, an attitude suggesting two things: supplication for his life and submission to the authority of he "King of Kings." It would have been natural for the Jews of that period to assume this posture at prayer simply as a sign of their submission to God, the Ruler of the Universe, and it is not unreasonable to assume that, at a much later period, during the time of the Second Temple in Jerusalem, this posture had already become traditional in Jewish prayer. The Talmud tangentially records that, when the worshipers in the Temple were making the above-described obeisance, they also kissed the Temple floor in adoration.

It has also been commonly assumed that folding the hands in prayer is exclusively a Christian custom. This is not the historical fact at all. As early as the post-Exilic period, when Jews prayed, *they folded their hands*, and they observed this custom for several centuries even after it had been adopted by Christians. The Talmud relates how the Babylonian Sage, Rabba (Abba ben Joseph, *c.* 280–352), used to pray with his hands folded.

In the days of Jesus, the Jews, when at prayer, in addition to folding their hands, observed three postures: kneeling, prostration, and standing. Quite naturally, being Jews, Jesus and his Apostles also practiced this mode of prayer. But this soon was modified when, under the direction of Paul of Tarsus, Christianity step by step abandoned its identity with the synagogue and its institutions and rites. Since standing at prayer was, during Paul's time, still associated in the Jewish-Christian mind with the most solemn part of the synagogue service–the repetition of the Shemoneh Esreh–standing at prayer became, logically, the posture adopted and used for several centuries in the early Church, as the Church Father, Tertullian, testified. It was only later that kneeling at prayer was first introduced into Christian worship. When this crucial point was reached–and it occurred at a time when the harsh persecution of the Jews by the triumphant Church was in progress in the Holy Roman Empire–the Rabbis decreed that Jews were to discontinue their ancient custom of kneeling at prayer since their oppressors and the enemies of their faith were doing the same thing. Since Christians folded their hands, in prayer, Jews, thenceforth, were to abandon this practice also.

The Rabbis considered that the ruthless pressures for the conversion of the Jews by the Church required this ritualistic disassociation, but they did, however, approve a symbolic retention of kneeling. Maimonides' son Abraham (thirteenth century) gave it as his rabbinical opinion that "the worshiper should kneel once after having finished his prayers." The performance of this symbolic act was for centuries faithfully observed by the Jews of Palestine, Babylonia, North Africa, and other Oriental communities. It is still followed today by the Yemenite Jews.

As for the tradition-observing Orthodox Jews of Europe and elsewhere, since medieval times they have been making one full prostration (which includes kneeling) in the synagogue on Rosh Hashanah, and four prostrations during the Yom Kippur service, but they do not kneel or prostrate themselves at any other time. Many Jews who conform to the Liberal (Reform) practices of Judaism have discarded this custom entirely.

PRAYER BOOK. *See* SIDDUR.

PRAYER FOR THE DEAD. *See* KADDISH.

PRAYER SERVICE (in Hebrew: ABODAH)

The congregational service of the synagogue has had a venerable history. Its development has been continuous to our own time, but its chrysalis stage is to be looked for in the liturgy of the Temple in Jerusalem. At that point it already had taken a thousand years or more for its evolution in form and content.

Almost nothing is known of the character of public worship in the Temple of Solomon which was destroyed by the Babylonians in 586 B.C.E. One thing is certain though: that besides the massed choral chanting of the psalms by the Levites to instrumental accompaniment, there was also a prayer service. But that merely held a subordinate position to the sacrificial rites, which were paramount and central. The ceremonial institutions of the early Israelites, while they frequently struck tones of arresting spirituality, did not at all disdain to employ the theatrical props familiar to all polytheistic religions that could turn a rite into drama, a spectacle of ecclesiastical splendor full of magical meanings and suggestive symbolism.

The Israelite priests were dressed in the symbolic white of purity, and the high priest glittered in his mitered crown and in the jeweled Urim and Thummim—the legendary breastplate that he is presumed by some scholars to have used for divination. The priests performed the sacrifices, intoned prayers, and served as mediators between God and man. They offered to the Deity a staggering holocaust of fattened animals in the names of their donors, and accepted for him propitiating gifts of produce according to the prescriptions of Scripture. The "gifts" included, besides the regular sacrifices, the urgent sacrifices of atonement, the offerings for the remission of sins, the offerings of gratitude: the meal-offerings, the incense offerings, and the first-fruit offerings.

In the view of the Prophets, these exercises in official piety constituted but an empty and barbarous ritualism that was wholly devoid of spiritual grace. For the lay-worshipers had little to do at the Temple services but to act as supernumeraries in the religious drama enacted for them by the priests. All that was required of them was to listen and genuflect and, at specified times, to utter such brief congregational responses as "Amen" and "Hosannah" to the drone of the prayers of the officiating priests.

That public prayer, although of a subsidiary nature in connection with the cult of sacrifices, had some importance even then may be inferred from the Prophet Isaiah ben Amoz' scorching rebuke in the eighth century B.C.E.:

And when ye spread forth your hands,
I will hide Mine eyes from you;
Yea, when ye make many prayers,
I will not hear;
Your hands are full of blood.

ISAIAH 1:15

Prayer played an increasingly important role during the period of the Second Temple after that sanctuary had been rebuilt by the exiles who returned from Babylonia at the end of the sixth century B.C.E. During the relatively brief Captivity (of less than a century), when they were separated from their only permitted national "House of the Lord" in Jerusalem so that their priesthood could no longer function, and because the Prophet Ezekiel sternly vetoed—despite the popular clamor for it—the erection of a new temple in Babylonia, the Jews no longer could bring the customary sacrifices of bullocks, sheep, and goats. It was natural for them, under those circumstances, to seek other outlets for religious expression. They were finally ready to receive the ethical and social teachings of the pre-Exilic Prophets which had been so far in advance of their time. These teachings at last made enough of an impact on the consciousness of the Jews to remold—although slowly—their religious beliefs and practices, and guided them to a more spiritualized conception of God and forms of worship than they had held hitherto: "So will we substitute for the sacrifice of bullocks with the offering of our lips."

During the troubled existence of the Second Temple, although the primitive cult of sacrifice was continued, it was on a lesser scale than before. The blood of slaughtered beasts, sprinkled upon the sacrificial altar of the sanctuary, was found more and more repugnant to the religious sensibilities of intelligent believers. Incense offerings became more frequent as a substitute. The rabbi-teacher of the Torah gradually took the place of the priest, whose role as intermediary between God and man no longer was deemed absolutely necessary, and the priest, who hitherto had occupied a dominant and unchallenged position in religion as well as in society, began to lose ground in public esteem.

Prayer service in a Spanish synagogue. (Miniature from a 14th-century Hebrew manuscript. The British Museum.)

Numerous synagogues began to appear everywhere, not only in the cities, towns, and villages of Judea but also in the scattered Jewish communities abroad—in Egypt, North Africa, Arabia, Syria, Rome, Greece, and elsewhere. It was, therefore, possible for Philo, the Hellenized philosopher-rabbi of Alexandria, who flourished in the half-century before the Destruction of the Second Temple, to state that "though the worshipers bring nothing else, in bringing themselves they offer the best sacrifices, the full and truly perfect oblation, as they honor with hymns and thanksgivings their Benefactor and Saviour—God."

Because custom is always resistant to change, the sacrificial rites and ceremonies still continued in the Temple on Mount Zion, but with the liturgy increasingly more prominent. At both morning and evening sacrifices, the priests and Levites would intone benedictions of praise and thanksgiving; as in former times, the sacrificial rites were accompanied by the singing of psalms and the playing on a variety of stringed, brass, woodwind, and percussion instruments by the Levites. At the morning sacrifice the priests recited the Ten Commandments (this practice was later abandoned by the Rabbinic Sages) and the Shema (the affirmation of God's Oneness which is the most revered prayer in the liturgy). After the "Men of the Great Synagogue" (*see* TALMUD, THE) had introduced them, the Shemoneh Esreh were also recited by the Temple priests. The reading from the Torah was another daily institution of worship—in fact, the climactic part of the service.

In one of its descriptive references to the liturgy that was followed in the latter-day service of the Second Temple, the Mishnah, the corpus of the Oral Tradition (*see* MISHNAH, *under* TALMUD) of post-Exilic Judaism, noted that the chief Temple officer at Jerusalem, who was a sort of conductor or master of ceremonies for public worship, began the formal order of the morning prayer-service that accompanied the sacrifices with the hortatory call: "*Barechu et Adonai!*" ("Bless ye the Lord!") Thereupon, the great multitude of worshipers, which usually assembled at all services in the inner and outer courts of the sanctuary, cried out responsively: "Amen!" There were several other responses given by the worshipers to different prayers, such as "Hosannah!" (*Hoshahnah* = "Save us, I pray!") and "Blessed be the Lord!" But the prayers and benedictions themselves were recited by the priests and Levites alone. Except for the brief responses and doxologies of "praisings," the congregation remained mute.

When the Temple in Jerusalem finally was put to the torch by the Roman besiegers under Titus, in 70 C. E., the elaborate system of sacrifices and gift-offerings which had endured for a thousand years came to an end. Then it was that the synagogue, "the house of prayer," which had already been in existence for several centuries, and which, in fact, was the only religious institution known in history until that time devoted *completely* to worship by prayer, took its place. Congregational prayer was but a spiritualized paraphrase and an elaboration of the three daily sacrificial services that were conducted in the Temple. A reference in the Book of Daniel–a work which was believed, to have been composed less than three centuries before the Destruction–already indicates that the synagogue liturgy was modeled upon lines that followed the Temple service. ". . . and he [Daniel] kneeled upon his knees three times a day, and prayed, and gave thanks before his God, as he did aforetime." (6:11.)

Even if the unyielding character of Jewish religious tradition is taken into consideration, the question that intrigues the student of the Hebrew liturgy remains. Why did the Rabbinic Sages institute three services–neither less nor more–daily? The answer to this is a somber one, and it can only be understood within the context of Jewish historical experience. It is conjectured that, when Rabban Gamaliel II became Nasi, or Patriarch of the Jews in Judea, two or three decades after the Destruction of the Temple, he was appalled by the excessive religious and patriotic grief of the people over the loss of their sanctuary and their national independence. It was, in part, to help assuage their mourning that he instituted the three daily prayer-services, symbolic of the sacrificial rites that had been observed in the Temple.

The three prayer-services of the synagogue were Shacharit (the Morning Service), Minchah (the Afternoon Service), and Ma'arib (the Evening Service). While the Minchah Service had originally been conducted at noon in the Temple, right after the midday sacrifices, the Rabbinic Sages, for some unknown reason and at some unspecified date, shifted the time of observance to sunset. The first notice of this change in the Talmud is found in the observation by the third-century teacher, Yochanan ben Nappachah: "It is meritorious to pray at twilight." And so it has remained ever since for the traditionalists.

An "Additional Service," the Mussaf, is recited immediately following the Morning Service on the Sabbath, on festivals, and on the occasion of the New Moon. This, too, was instituted during Rabbinic times in remembrance of the "Additional Sacrifice" which had been brought by the priests in the Temple on those holy days.

The formulary of the congregational service, as well as its ceremonial regulations, was constantly being revised and added to by the Rabbinic Sages. The liturgy was enormously developed and elaborated under the direction of four Geonim or Rectors of the Rabbinical Academy in Sura, Babylonia: by Cohen Tzedek (845), Mar Shalom (849), and Natronai (853). The crowning event of all these efforts was the completion by the Gaon Amram in 856 of the first comprehensive prayerbook–the siddur (*see* SIDDUR). By the time of Maimonides, in the twelfth century, there were already in general use among the Jews of the world two major liturgies: that of the Sefaradim (used in Babylonia, Persia, Egypt, Morocco, Spain, Portugal, and the Provence) and that of the Ashkenazim (used in Northern France, Germany, Austria, and Bohemia). In subsequent times, still other regional liturgies were compiled and became separately associated with the Turkish, Polish, Italian, Roman, Yemenite, and North African rites. Although they differed somewhat in arrangement and selection of prayers, the differences were fairly minor, representing local custom and taste; in their literary and devotional construction, the liturgies were very similar to one another. Each drew from a common reservoir of devotional poems (piyyutim; s. piyyut), most of which had been composed during the Middle Ages by genuinely gifted poets. These liturgical verses consisted of pious meditations, supplications, penitential self-examination, laments of regret, martyr-elegies, and paeans of adoration and thanksgiving to God.

The Jewish philosophy of prayer, since the end of the cultural isolation of the ghetto, has undergone great change. It has become far less traditional and more formal–even more attenuated in its religious emotionalism. The need for adjusting the liturgy to the assimilated and more liberal tastes of modern Jews, who, in most instances, hold a more

Prayer service in the old synagogue at Fürth, Germany, 1705.

Prayer service at an unidentified synagogue in France, c. 1810.

scientifically orientated view of God, society, and the individual, has led to an extensive revamping and modification not only in text and in language (the vernacular in every country has gradually been displacing much of the sacred Hebrew) but also in the rites and ceremonies. The separate liturgies of the Orthodox, Chasidic, Conservative, Reform, and Reconstructionist congregations in the United States are eloquent illustrations of this adjustment.

That the fervency and the dedicated spirit of the worshipers of olden times have become lessened today may be noted in the disappearance of two cherished old folkways. About one of these it is stated in the Talmud that the devout would "pray before prayer"–spending considerable time in silent supplication and meditation in order to make mind and mood receptive for communion with God during the congregational service. One such prayer by an eighteenth-century Chasidic saint of Poland is a shining model of disinterested piety: "Lord of the Universe! I ask for neither Your Paradise, nor Your Bliss in the World-to-Come! All I desire is You and You alone!" Another tradition, universally cherished by Jews for countless generations and urged upon all worshipers by the Rabbinic Sages, was always to go to the synagogue in a hurry, but to leave it slowly and regretfully.

No doubt, the most arresting feature of the Jewish prayer-service is the social philosophy behind collective worship. Stated the Talmud: "He who prays with the congregation shall have his prayer granted." Why so? Wouldn't the worshiper be able to accomplish the same ends if he prayed *alone*? The Rabbis commented: As the worshiper joins his supplications with those of his fellow Jews, he is not selfishly praying for himelf alone; he is performing a significant moral and social act inasmuch as he is also praying *for the collective good*. Thus, he is drawn closer in the bonds of brotherhood and religious exaltation to his fellow men.

Part of the congregation at a prayer service in the Great Synagogue of Bokhara, Russia, 19th century.

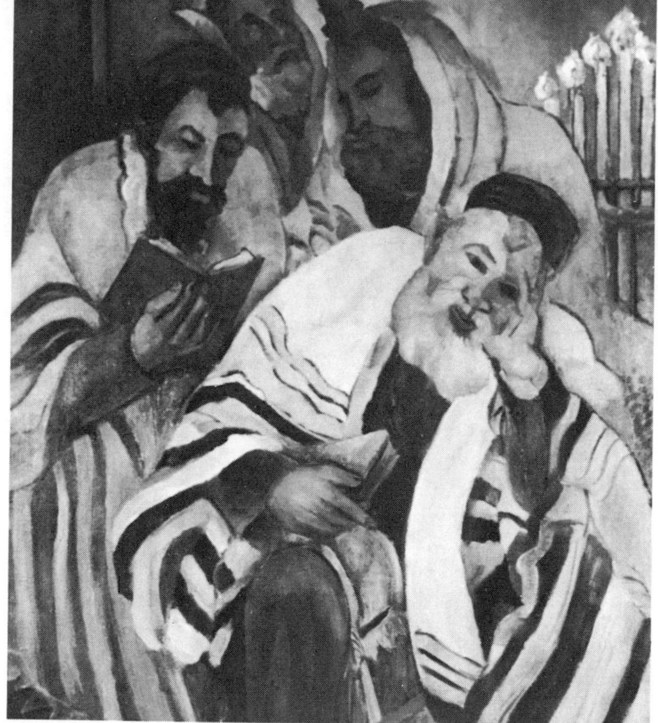

Prayer service of a Lower East Side congregation in New York. (Painting by Sheva Ausubel, 1935.)

It is noteworthy that Jewish prayers are but seldom couched in the first person singular. Most of the time they say "we" and "us" and speak of "our sins." This is of considerable social significance, for the Jew was always prompted by his religious ideals as well as by the course of his people's historic experience to think in terms of *all Israel* and not of himself alone.

See also ASHKENAZIM; BAAL TEFILLAH; CHAZZAN; FELLOWSHIP IN ISRAEL; HYMNS OF THE SYNAGOGUE; LAVER; MINYAN; SEFARADIM; SELICHOT; SHEMA, THE; SHEMONEH ESREH; SIDDUR; SYNAGOGUE; UNITY OF ISRAEL.

PRAYER SHAWL. *See* TALLIT.

PRAYERS. *See* BAAL TEFILLAH; BAR MITZVAH; BAT MITZVAH; CABALA; CANDLE-LIGHTING; CHASIDIM; CHILDREN, BLESSING OF; HABDALAH; HYMNS OF THE SYNAGOGUE; KADDISH; KIDDUSH; KOL NIDRE; PASSOVER; PRAYER SERVICE; PRIESTLY BLESSING; ROSH CHODESH; ROSH HASHANA; SELICHOT; SHEMA, THE; SHEMONEH ESREH; SIDDUR; TEFILLIN; YIZKOR; YOM KIPPUR.

PRIESTLY BLESSING (in Hebrew: BIRKAT COHANIM; in Yiddish, the act of blessing is called DUCHANEN, from the Hebrew DUCHAN, meaning the platform from which the priests pronounced the blessing)

This impressive rite goes back to the Temple service in Jerusalem. Rabbinic opinion presumes that it was first instituted by Moses in the Wilderness when God commanded him (Numbers 6:23): "Speak unto Aaron and his sons, saying, On this wise ye shall bless the children of Israel. . . ."

The formula of this priestly blessing consisted of only fifteen words in Hebrew, although in the less concise English translation it reads: "The Lord bless thee and keep thee; the Lord make His face to shine upon thee, and be gracious unto thee; the Lord lift up His countenance upon thee, and give thee peace."

The words of the benediction, as they are intoned today by the genealogical descendants of the priests who served in the Temple, are exactly the same as they were then. There they were chanted to an ancient ecclestiastical mode, and it is believed by musicologists that some of the musical idioms still in use in the priestly benediction may be traceable to this venerable source. Most of the melodies to which the blessing is sung in the synagogues of Eastern Europe and the Americas are of seventeenth and eighteenth-century composition; however, the Spanish and Portuguese Jews chant a melody of Moorish character which attests to its even greater age.

In the elaborate service of the Temple, the benediction was intoned by the priests every day, and at the four separate services on Yom Kippur. After the Temple's Destruction, the priestly blessing became an important element in the liturgy of the synagogue. Today, the custom is to duchan on the festivals and on the High Holy Days, provided they do not coincide with Sabbath. In modern Israel alone, as in ancient Israel, is the priestly blessing pronounced at the daily morning services.

Before the rite is performed, the priests have to purify themselves both in body and soul. They first are required to fulfill the Biblical injunction (in Psalms 134:2): "Lift up your hands in holiness and bless ye the Lord." The priests or Cohanim (s. cohan or cohen) first wash their hands over which the Levites pour water from the ritual laver, then they remove their shoes, just as Moses did before God's Presence. They then advance solemnly toward the Ark and take up their positions on the steps before it, each covering his head in his tallit (prayer shawl). While chanting the blessing, the priests are not allowed to look at their own hands, neither are the worshipers allowed to look at the priestly hands. This is on account of an ancient folk-belief, recorded in the Talmud, that at the moment when the hands of the cohanim are upraised in the benediction, the "Radiance of God"– the Shechinah–rests upon them, and it could "have a blinding effect on the eyes that looked upon them." Countless generations of Jews were nurtured on this fear of blindness as a punishment for the impiety of looking, and so they shut their eyes tight and buried their heads deep in their prayer books during the rite.

The precentor (baal tefillah) who leads the services cries out the awesome summons to the priests to commence: "*Cohanim!*" The priests turn and face the congregation. They raise their hands over their heads, palms facing downward. Then, putting their thumbs tip to tip, they join the first fingers with the second, and the third with the fourth fingers. In this arrangement the fingers are so separated that they form openings through which, so tradition has it, the blessed Radiance of the Shechinah streams down upon the praying throng. The priests intone: "Blessed be Thou, O Lord our God, King of the Universe, Who has sanctified us with the holiness of Aaron and has commanded us to bless Thy people Israel in love." The precentor then recites for the Cohanim the fifteen-word formula of the blessing, and they intone it after him. And as they chant, they sway toward all sides of the house of prayer, straining to enfold all the worshipers in their benediction.

Priestly blessing. (From an illustrated [printed] Pentateuch of Prague, dated 1537.)

PRIESTLY CODE. *See* PRIESTS.

PRIESTS (in Hebrew: pl. COHANIM; S. COHAN or COHEN)

By the time that the First Temple had been completed by King Solomon, *circa* 959 B.C.E., there already existed a mediating priestly caste that was drawn exclusively from the tribe of Levi and was separated from the rest of the people by the aloofness of their ecclesiastical role and by the "laws of purity" (Levitical laws) they had to observe. From the Bible itself we learn that, in the theocracy that Moses had created for the total rule of Israelite society, the priesthood was intended to play a dominant, if not a predominant, role. Its influence and power increased rather than diminished five centuries later during the Second Temple period, when its functions were broadened to include religious instruction in various forms.

"The priest's lips should keep knowledge, and they [the people] should seek the law at his mouth," declared Malachi the Prophet.

There was nothing unusual in the fact that Jews required a priesthood for the institutional practice of their religion and for mediation with God. This constituted, then as now, an essential feature in the practice of all religions.

Before the Temple of Solomon had risen in Jerusalem, there were already several Israelite sanctuaries in existence: the portable Tabernacle in the Wilderness, and the "House of God" first at Shiloh and then at Nob. In each of these holy places, Israelite priests officiated over the rites and performed the sacrifices. It was not at all remarkable if, in that primitive stage of Jewish religious development, these Cohanim should have been barely distinguishable from the Egyptian, Babylonian, and Canaanite priests of their time, being little more than shamans in the modern ethnologist's vocabulary. Like the Greeks, the Cohanim consulted oracles. The Bible makes perfectly plain that the teraphim and "the graven image of the ephod" (Judges 18:18) were consulted by the priests for divination and augury, as were, similarly, the Urim and Thummin, those mysterious, unverified sacred objects worn by the high priest, presumably as part of his sacerdotal breastplate, for the purpose of obtaining divine guidance.

There is a strange ring of authenticity in the Biblical account which describes the preliminaries to the "divine election" of Joshua to succeed Moses as the supreme leader of the tribes of Israel. God instructs Moses to stand Joshua "before Eleazar the priest, who shall inquire for him by the judgment of the Urim before the Lord." (Numbers 27:21.) Presumably, the verdict of the Urim was in Joshua's favor, for Moses "laid his hands upon him, and gave him a charge, as the Lord spoke by the hand of Moses." It is surprising to find, though, that as late as Ezra's personal ministry of religious reform, in the fifth century B.C.E., there existed such a religious "throwback" as consulting the oracle to determine the genealogical register of certain priests in order to establish their ethnic "purity." These priests were told (in Ezra 2:63) "that they should not eat of the most holy things, till there stood up a priest with Urim and Thummim [with which to divine the truth]."

Since the pre-Temple sanctuary of Bethel was a rather primitive institution, it performed no elaborate ritual, and so the number of its priests was relatively small. Their principal function, besides divining and sacrificing, was guarding the Ark of the Lord, the priestly vestments, and the sacred vessels. But the unsettled conditions of Jewish life in that age—a time marked by incessant warring with enemy-neighbors—most memorably the Philistines—and aggravated by almost continuous intertribal fighting and squabbling—were certainly not conducive to any orderly, meaningful, or consistent functioning of the priesthood. The appointment of the high priest and of the other chief priests was often motivated by political considerations, and was of doubtful morality or of Scriptural legality. It is amazing to find, for instance, that both David and Solomon, arrogant in their absolute royal power, sometimes performed the priestly functions themselves! At the dedication of the Temple that the "Wise King" (Solomon) had built in Jerusalem, he himself acted in the capacity of High Priest! Quite apparently, the priesthood in Solomon's day had not yet been able to entrench itself in relation to the royal power in a political as well as religious sense. This, however, it succeeded in doing soon thereafter, when it solidified all of its vested interests in religion into a single monopoly, which also involved a portion of all sacrifices, the extensive "first-fruits," gift-offerings, and the individual annual tithes of a half-shekel exacted from the entire people for the support of the Temple.

The priests, each with his own special function and arranged into twenty-four separate orders, expounded the ritual and other Scriptural laws in the Temple Courts for the benefit of the people. They alone were privileged to bring the numerous sacrifices and gift offerings on the Temple altar. They conducted the elaborate liturgical and ceremonial services in the Temple during the three "pilgrim festivals" of Passover, Shabuot, and Succot. They also exercised their traditional function as judges. Not the least important of their duties was standing guard in all matters concerning ritualistic purity, whether in clothing, in body, in food and drink, or in moral conduct.

It is, of course, well known to the modern student of comparative religion that the cult of purity was a familiar aspect of many ancient religions—most strikingly of the Brahman, the Egyptian, and the Babylonian. Characteristically, if purity consciousness among the Israelites made perhaps a broader and deeper penetration into their religious practice than it did among other faiths, it was mainly because of the crystallization among them of the idea that they had been chosen by God to serve him as "a nation of priests." The logic behind this national assumption of the purity cult was simplicity itself. The argument ran: Since every Jew was "a priest" by divine election in a spiritual sense, then he, too, had to observe the priestly purity laws, as did the members of the professional priesthood. Of course, it was not expected of him to follow them out in such an inclusive manner as the priests, for the latter had definite sacerdotal functions and commitments which required them to observe most stringently the rules of Levitical purity which had been especially drawn up for them.

It is not possible to underscore sufficiently the preoccupation of the Mosaic law with the highly complicated problem of maintaining purity in the daily life of the people, but most especially that of the priests. The Book of Leviticus, as well as sections in Genesis, Exodus, and Numbers, give great prominence to the laws governing the priestly life and conduct. This Priestly Code required that the priest have no physical deformity and that he be of proven irreproachable moral character. While he, like every other male adult, was required by religious law to marry, he could not take a divorced woman as his wife, nor could he touch a corpse, or even come in the physical contact with anyone who had done so. To this day, the Cohen (the Jew who claims to draw his line of descent from the ancient priesthood) is considered "defiled" by the religious if he but enters a cemetery. This kind of "secondary" defilement is also guarded against by the Brahmans in India today, but appallingly, there the taboo is directed not against corpses but against seventy millions of human beings—the "Untouchables" who occupy the lowest rung in the caste system of the Hindus.

The hieratic priesthood lasted as long as the Temple did; it came to an end with Destruction of the Temple by the Romans in 70 C.E. Touching in the extreme and testifying to the indestructible faith of the Jewish people in the ultimate restoration on Mount Zion, are the Rabbinic laws which declare that even though the Temple in Jerusalem is but a ruin and all the ministering priests are vanished, their direct male descendants, down to the end of time, yet must maintain the same Levitical purity; they must preserve their pedigree unstained. And the reason for it? When the Messiah arrives with the Redemption and raises a new and more wonderful Temple for the worship of God on Mount Zion, they—the descendants of the Cohanim—are expected to be morally and spiritually ready and worthy to assume the priestly offices that their forefathers were forced to drop nineteen centuries before.

Today, in all the synagogues of the world, only those Jewish males who are Cohanim or priests (the names Cohen, Cahan, Kahn, Kohn, Kahan, Cahen, Kagan, Kogen, Kaganovitch, etc., indicate priestly descent although a Cohen can also bear any other name) are privileged to recite the Priestly Blessing while standing before the Ark of the Torah. They are honored in another way too; they are given precedence in the public reading from the Torah: The opening passage from the weekly portion—and often the concluding one as well—are reserved for cantillation by a Cohen, if one is present at the service.

See also PRIESTLY BLESSING; TEMPLE, THE; TORAH-READING.

PROGRESSIVE JUDAISM. *See* JUDAISM IN THE MODERN AGE.

PROPHETIC WRITINGS. *See* BIBLE, THE.

PROPHETS, THE. *See* BIBLE, THE; MONOTHEISM.

PROSELYTES. *See* CHRISTIANITY, JEWISH ORIGINS OF; CONVERSION OF JEWS; MISSIONARIES, JEWISH.

PROVERBS, BOOK OF. *See* BIBLE, THE.

PSALMS, THE. *See* BIBLE, THE.

PSEUDEPIGRAPHA

There are extant a considerable number of Jewish writings, designated collectively as Pseudepigrapha, which were also produced during the brilliant era of Jewish Hellenism. Although these did not enter (for Hellenized Jews) into the sanctified category of the Apocrypha in the Greek Septuagint Bible, nonetheless, they ran parallel with those fourteen favored writings. Whatever their intrinsic merit, they help reproduce much of the Jewish religious-intellectual climate of the age; the same historic cultural period generated them as it did the Apocrypha. In their general religious and ideational tenor, and also stylistically and linguistically, both groups of writings had much in common.

Most of the Pseudepigraphic works had the character of apocalypses—divine "revelations" concerning the Messianic age, the Resurrection, and the Last Judgment—which is why they are also known as the Apocalyptic Books. They fed the ecstatic visionary mood and the morbid yearnings for the supernatural and the miraculous of many contemporary Jews. These believed that the End of Days was imminent and that it would be consummated by a series of awe-inspiring events unprecedented in the experience of mankind that would result in the raising up of Israel—for so long bowed down and long-suffering—which would then triumph by Messianic intervention over its powerful enemies. It would emerge from the final conflict shining and resplendent in spiritual and moral glory while all the heathen peoples of the earth, the Greeks included, would hasten to close ranks with it in the worship of the one true God.

These writings, like those in the Apocrypha, are inaccurately termed. Modern Biblical scholarship of another generation had ineptly classified them as Pseudepigrapha, and as such they have remained. That word connotes that they were falsely attributed productions. But the prefix "pseudo-," in their instance, by no means implies that there is a falsification or deception intended by the writer upon the reader. Their name rather is derived from an ancient Eastern literary device whereby a writing was magnified in importance and prestige-value by ascribing its authorship to some illustrious and universally revered personage.

This device, too, had been followed, if not directly by name then by traditional ascription, in the case of several of the works in the Bible. The Psalter has been referred to frequently as "The Psalms of David" when it actually was an anthology of verse-hymns which had been composed by a number of liturgical poets over many centuries. All modern evidence to the contrary, The Song of Songs, Proverbs, and Ecclesiastes have been attributed to King Solomon, and Job and Lamentations to the Prophet Jeremiah. The Apocrypha too followed this common pattern of "pseudo"-attribution, as can be seen from the titles of The Wisdom of Solomon, the Book of Baruch, and the Prayer of Manasseh. In the same way, most of the Apocalypses were ascribed to exalted Biblical personages. Yet the very anonymity of their authors lends these works a moral dignity and conviction which must have motivated their writing in the first place.

There is the Book of Enoch, for instance. Composed originally in Hebrew (about 200 B.C.E.), it was translated into Greek one or two generations before the appearance of Jesus of Nazareth. The protagonist of the work, Enoch, who had "walked with God," was the antedeluvian ancestor of the human race. The Book of Genesis describes him as the son of Cain and the father of Methuselah. The Biblical myth has it that, because of his righteousness, he escaped the inconvenient necessity of dying and was "translated" *alive* to heaven. "And Enoch walked with God, and he was not, for God took him." (Genesis 5:24.) And so, out of love and compassion for his descendants, he "revealed" to them in the Book of Enoch all the miraculous things he had seen and heard in the World-to-Come.

With all the supporting details, he described for their benefit the architecture and the inhabitants of the Seven Heavens, the glories of Gan Eden (Paradise) and the terrors of Gehinnom (Gehenna or Purgatory), the battle-array of Satan and his hosts of demons, and the myth of the Fallen Angels and their sad fate. In dream-visions of dread import he told of the impending world-drama: the final cataclysm, the coming of the Messiah, the establishment by him of the righteous Kingdom of God, the Resurrection of the dead, the Last Judgment, and the unending bliss of the righteous in the millenmium, when death and suffering would be abolished. The impress of this work upon the thinking, and even language, of the New Testament cannot be overestimated. (*See* CHRISTIANITY, JEWISH ORIGINS OF.)

Another work of historic significance in connection with Christianity was the Testaments of the Twelves Patriarchs. This book was both a serial apocalypse and a body of religious moralistic preachments. The "Patriarchs" were the sons of Jacob whom the latter-day Jews of the Hellenistic Age, reverencing their remote ancestors, had elevated to exalted moral eminence. Each of the twelve Patriarchs "spoke out" in his personal Testament in fatherly grieved denunciation of his descendants. Each foresaw with the far gaze of a prophet that his descendants would practice evils learned from every people on earth, and would, because of their sins, be punished with many troubles and much grief. But each of the Patriarchs, being the loving "father" of his "children," reached out to Israel with words of comfort glowing with the promise of ultimate redemption. Surely, the God of love and compassion would speedily send the Messiah to save them from their enemies and to rule over them in the Kingdom of Righteousness!

The Patriarchs, patterning themselves upon the prophecies of Isaiah and Micah, spun a wondrous vision of the millennium, when all war and every manner of strife would be banished forever and when oppression and social injustice would cease. They predicted too that when that blessed juncture would be achieved, then the righteous—the saints of God—would enter *Gan Eden,* there to bask in the radiance of God's Shechinah (Divine Presence) and to eat of the fruit of bliss that grows only on the Tree of Eternal Life.

It should be emphasized that, like many other Jewish post-Biblical documents, the Testaments, too, were tampered with by overzealous Christian propagandists—a fact that has been noted by Christian Biblical scholars. Because the purpose of the alteration in the text was to marshal "prophetic" testimony in Jewish sacred writings that would foretell the coming of Jesus *as the Christ* or Messiah (this was the case also with the Book of Enoch and many another Hellenistic Jewish writing), the Rabbinic Sages put the Testaments under the ban.

The vexing problems posed for the Rabbinic authorities in Judea by the religious writings of the Hellenized Jews is well illustrated by the Pseduepigraphic Sibylline Oracles. These were produced over a considerable period of time (beginning with the second century B.C.E.) in Alexandria. The author (some say there were more than one), presumed to be a Hellenized Jewess, described herself as a missionary of "the High God." Her aim, which was unequivocally stated by her, was to convert the Greeks and other Gentiles to the Jewish religion. Obviously, she had adopted the elevated role of sibyl in order to make her prophecies and invocations more acceptable to the tastes and religious conventions in the Hellenic world. She wished to communicate with it on its own familiar terms, so she issued her "revelations" in the oracular fashion of the classic Greek sibyls who prophesied at Delphi.

In her Oracles the Jewish Sibyl recounted the supernatural history of Israel. She also extolled the virtues of the Jewish religion. Confidently she declaimed her belief in Israel's universalistic mission: "The children of Israel shall mark out the path of life to all mortals, for they are the interpreters of God, exalted by Him, and bearing a great joy to all mankind." She also predicted the downfall of the great pagan empires, which she described as being full of evil, corruption, and social oppression. Like other preachers of apocalypses, she, too, foretold the coming of the Messiah and the subsequent rule of righteousness in a world that would be free from poverty, suffering, pain, war, and injustice. Her conviction was that, seeing how great were the rewards and the bliss of Israel in its worship of the One God, all the heathen nations of their accord would flock to Zion to be redeemed.

An interesting fact about the Sibylline Oracles is that they proved so effective an instrument of propaganda for the Jewish religion that the early Christian missionaries decided to adopt and adapt them for their own use. On the one hand, they interpolated into them passages "predicting" the coming of Jesus as the Messiah. On the other hand, they added to them oracles of frankly Christian evangelism. For that reason it is quite difficult to disentangle the threads of the Jewish original from the Christian additions. But some good did, after all, derive for the Jews from this tampering: It was primarily *because* of these Christian additions that the Sibylline Oracles have been preserved.

There are a number of other Jewish-Greek apocalypses, chronicles, and missionary writings. However interesting they may be from a historical or religious-cultural point of view, they are of but minor importance as literature. Among the most interesting are the following writings, all produced during a time-span of three–four centuries (from the second century B.C.E. to the middle of the second century C.E.): The Letter of Aristeas, The Assumption of Moses, The Apocalypse of Baruch, The Book of Jubilees (known also as The Apocalypse of Moses), The Psalms of Solomon, the Third and Fourth Books of Maccabees (the Fourth contains the celebrated philosophical discourse "On the Supremacy of Pious Reason over the Passions"), the apocalyptic-moral preachments of The Testament of Adam and Eve, The Testament of Abraham, The Testaments of Isaac and Jacob, The Testament of Solomon, and The Testament of Job.

See also APOCRYPHA, THE; BIBLE, THE; CHACHMAH; CHRISTIANITY, JEWISH ORIGINS OF; DEAD SEA SCROLLS; ESSENES; HELLENISTS, JEWISH; MESSIAH, THE; MESSIAHS, WOULD-BE; PHARISEES; POST-BIBLICAL WRITINGS; TALMUD, THE; THERAPEUTAE.

PULPIT (in Hebrew: AMUD)

The wide variations in Jewish religious practice—caused mostly by geographic separation and exposure to the regional influences of non-Jewish cultures—affected not only the manner of worship (in Hebrew: *minhag*) but styles in synagogue architecture. Thus there was never any uniformity in the place from which the precentor, who could be either the cantor (chazzan) or prayer-leader (baal tefillah) led the worshipers in the religious service. In the Oriental and Sefaradic congregations, the precentor stood on the bema (*which see*) or almemor, but in the Central and East European synagogues of the Ashkenazim, he took his place at the lectern, customarily standing directly in front or at the right of the

Amud or pulpit for the chazzan (cantor) or baal tefillah (prayer leader), in the synagogue at Modena, Italy. Dated 1472. (Musée Cluny, Paris.)

Ark, with his back to the worshipers. This prayer desk or pulpit was called the *amud* and, in addition to the bema, was an independent structural unit made of wood or, sometimes, of stone.

This use of the amud and not the bema for conducting public prayer was grounded in a curious rabbinic tradition that had arisen in medieval Germany. It held that the prayer-leader, who served as the shaliach tzibbur (the congregation's emissary before God) was obliged to fulfill the supplicating words of the Psalmist: "Out of the depths I cry unto Thee, O Lord!" (Psalms 130:1.) To comply, in a symbolic sense, with the prayer-leader's calling to God "from the depths," the amud was introduced as an additional piece of synagogue furniture in Germany and in the countries of Eastern Europe, and it was sunk one step below the synagogue level.

Custom also established that the mizrach (the framed and illustrated indicator of the direction in which Jerusalem lay) be hung directly in front of the amud, and that it be inscribed with such appropriate Scriptural verses as "Know before Whom you are standing," or the equally popular "I behold my Lord before me always."

See also MIZRACH.

PUNISHMENT AND REWARD. *See* REWARD AND PUNISHMENT.

PURE IN HEART, THE. *See* ETHICAL VALUES, JEWISH.

PURGATORY. *See* GEHINNOM.

PURIM

The "justification" for celebrating Purim as a holy day—one that commemorates the deliverance of the Jewish people throughout the Persian Empire from a plot hatched by Haman, the chief minister of King Ahasueros, to exterminate it—rests entirely on events that are chronicled in the Book of Esther. Even though this Biblical narrative, which the Jews familiarly call The Megillah (The Scroll), was represented by its author as authentic history, few modern scholars are ready to accept it uncritically as such, for the annals of ancient Persia, despite a most thorough ransacking by research scholars, have turned up no corroborating evidence of this Scroll's historicity. Nor is mention even found of a Persian king bearing the name of Ahasueros. Following a theoretical line of internal evidence in the Book of Esther, some scholars concede the possibility that Ahasueros might have been Xerxes I, "the Great" (ruled 486–465 B.C.E.). Other writers merely point out, for the sake of the record, that in the Septuagint (the Greek version of the Bible that was translated in the third century B.C.E.) Ahasueros was identified as Artaxerxes II (404–359 B.C.E.). The first-century Jewish historian, Josephus, insisted on the identification as a fact.

Even if little has been accomplished in trying to establish the historical actuality of Ahasueros, still less success has met all attempt to verify the alleged historic events connected with Haman's plot against the Jews. Nor has a shred of plausible proof been found to indicate that the other principal characters in the Biblical melodrama—Vashti, Esther, Mordecai, and Haman—were real personages. The belief among scholars—even the most romantic of antiquarian reconstructors—is that these events and characters are purely fictitious, and that, furthermore, as a plot, the narrative is too neatly contrived to be accorded credibility.

At the same time, there are students of comparative religion who have taken the unsentimental position that the writing of the Book of Esther, as well as the fact of its inclusion in the Bible canon, represented merely a Jewish "rationalization" to give authority and sanction to the celebration of Purim—a pagan carnival that the Jews could in no wise be persuaded to abandon. It is argued that the formal institution of this festival among the Jews, presumably during the Maccabean era in the second century B.C.E., may have been prompted by the realization among Jewish religious leaders that its observance was already an accomplished fact and that the only way to control it was by adopting it.

Purim, claim the cultural anthropologists, was actually the New Year festival of the Babylonians—the day on which the fate of each individual, for good or for ill, was determined in a kind of celestial lottery by the Babylonian gods, ruled over by Marduk, the chief god. The Babylonian word for "lot" was *pur* (pl. *purim*). Therefore, because the gods cast lots, Purim was "the Feast of Lots." But in the Book of Esther, a literary switch took place. Instead of the gods deciding the fate of human beings, it was Haman, the archenemy of the Jews, surnamed by pious Jews *ha-Rashah*—"the Wicked"—who "cast lots" to determine by divination what day would be most propitious for exterminating all the Jews in the 127 provinces of the empire, "from India even unto Ethiopia."

To the lay-reader it must hardly seem credible that the Jewish people, so shortly after the alleged historic event of its national deliverance had taken place, should have chosen to initiate a commemoration of it, if it was merely a contrivance of fiction! Tradition among Jews has always been scrupulously preserved in the national memory. Consequently, the Jewish folk-memory is, in a manner of speaking, a "historic record" hard to counterfeit. Whatever the folkoristic embroideries that are superimposed on the narrative of Esther, the reasonable likelihood is that the timely foiling of a plot to exterminate the Jewish people was an actual historic fact. For that very reason it was commemorated by the Jews with joyous celebration. Before saying positively that the story is made up out of the whole cloth of fancy, one should call to mind that in 1870, when almost the entire world of Greek scholarship dozed smugly in its belief that the *Iliad* by Homer was pure mythic saga, the city of Troy was dug out of the earth by Heinrich Schliemann on the very site Homer had indicated—at Ilium!

But regardless of whether the events on which the festival of Purim is based are to be regarded as authentic or merely as part of a neatly contrived historical novel bristling with oriental divertissements and extravaganzas, with plot and counterplot, devout Jews during the past twenty-two centuries have serenely accepted every word in the Book of Esther as being unquestionably true and divinely inspired. To them, the hateful image of Haman, who had plotted the destruction of their ancestors, had as much flesh-and-blood reality as that of Adolph Hitler has for the Jews of today. Haman was the embodiment of every criminally obsessed anti-Semite in history, and there have been many such in the dismal experience of the Jews. Beginning with the Mid-

Traditional tomb of Esther and Mordecai in Iran (Persia).

dle Ages, there were instituted a large number of "special" Purims. These were celebrated in various places in commemoration of the Jews' deliverance from one or another local "Haman."

What makes the central event in the Book of Esther seem so convincingly real is the genocidal mania and cunning plotting of Haman against the Jews. To win approval for his diabolical plan, Haman, in his well-argued brief before King Ahasueros, brings forward all the familiar clichés about Jewish separatism that have been used by anti-Semites in every age. Says he: "There is a certain people scattered abroad and dispersed among the peoples in all the provinces of thy kingdom; and their laws are diverse from those of every people, neither keep they the king's laws; therefore, it profiteth not the king to suffer them. If it please the king, let it be written that they be destroyed."

Haman was ready now for the final and clinching argument. "And I will pay ten thousand talents of silver into . . . the king's treasuries," he promised. The king was convinced; he gave his consent. A decree was drawn up in his name by Haman and copies sent by swift courier to the governors of the 127 provinces, ordering the massacre of all Jews–men, women, and children–on the thirteenth day of the month of Adar (February-March). "And in every province . . . there was great mourning among the Jews, and fasting, and weeping, and wailing; and many lay in sackcloth and ashes."

But it was the wondrous design–whether of Providence or of the author of the Book of Esther–to have Mordecai the Jew, whom Haman hated so, discover the plot in time. He appealed to his cousin, Queen Esther, whose own Jewish identity and her kinship to Mordecai she had kept a secret from the king, to intercede with him for the lives of her people.

Scenes from the Book of Esther depicted in folk style and executed in a piece of embroidery in cross-stitch. Palestine, 19th century. (The Jewish Museum.)

Accordingly, she laid a skillful countertrap for the trapper Haman. In the end, she succeeded in exposing his perfidy before her husband, the king. Because it was not possible for the king to reverse a decree, he issued another royal command, giving the Jews throughout the empire arms to defend themselves. On the thirteenth day of Adar, which was the date set for the general massacre, the Jews, instead of being exterminated, leaped to the attack. They routed their enemies in the characteristically gory fashion of the East.

The personal fate of Haman is recorded in the exultant words of the meditation that is read on Purim in the synagogue:

> A wicked man, an arrogant offshoot of the seed of Amalek, rose up against us. Insolent in his riches, he digged himself a pit, and his own greatness laid him a snare. In his mind he thought to entrap, but was himself entrapped; he sought to destroy, but was himself speedily destroyed . . . he made him a gallows, and was himself hanged thereon.

Just as in a medieval morality play, the events behind the festival of Purim celebrate God's Providence in protecting the innocent and, conversely, in punishing the wicked.

How did the Jews celebrate Purim in former times? Being only a secular holiday, although with the ultimate sanction of religion, Purim took on the character of a carnival. Masquerading, merriment, and mummery were freely engaged in. Graybeards for that one day shed the grave burden of their piety and years. They put aside their dignity and played the buffoon. They sang, they danced, and they clowned their way through the day. There are some modern writers who claim to see strong points of resemblance between Purim and the celebrations of the medieval Carnival in Rome and the English Shrove Tuesday and Twelfth-night. That observation, no doubt, is justified, for the Carnival in Christian Europe, in its essentials, was merely a continuance, under new religious auspices and some modifications, of the same old pagan revels.

Purim observances in premedieval times probably were far more uninhibited than they became later. Under the watchful puritanical control of the rabbis, after the formal institution of Purim in the Hebrew calendar in the second century B.C.E., its orgiastic elements were prohibited. Yet, despite its "purification," Purim ever remained sufficiently gay and convivial to make the Jews living in dank, sunless ghettos look eagerly forward to its coming every year. It was a day of rejoicing *together,* like members of the same family, exchanging, gifts (*shalachmoness*), usually consisting of fruits, sweets, and wine.

The Haman-rattle (variously called gregger *or* grahger *or* Hamanklapper *in Yiddish). Poland, 19th century. For centuries it has been the merry custom for Jewish children to grind this noisemaker at every mention of Haman's name during the public reading of the Megillah (the Book of Esther) in the synagogue on Purim. (The Jewish Museum.)*

Masked ball celebrating the festival of Purim. Amsterdam, 1780. (Alfred Rubin Collection, London.)

The great se'udah or feast on Purim was, like the Passover Seder banquet, one of the most memorable gastronomical occasions of the year in the Jewish home. Eating, drinking, and unrestrained merrymaking were highly commended by folk custom. Only once during the year—on Purim—it was not merely permitted but in fact made obligatory for every male adult to drink such a large quantity of wine that (in the indulgent words of the rabbis), during the reading aloud in the synagogue from the Megillah, it would no longer be possible for him to distinguish "Cursed be Haman" from "Blessed be Mordecai!" In short, Jews were encouraged to get pleasantly "illuminated," but not riotously drunk. Everything was permitted on Purim—that is, everything except disorderly, scandalous, and licentious conduct, any sign of which was sternly suppressed by the Jewish communal authorities.

The Purim observances, for the strictly Orthodox, begin on the thirteenth of Adar, one day before Purim, with a solemn fast—Ta'anit Esther (the Fast of Esther). For it was by fasting that the ancient Jews, led by Queen Esther, girded themselves against the massacre that had been ordered and sought the protection of God in the impending ordeal.

Purim is considered to be a minor festival. The Rabbinic explanation for its somewhat slighting assessment is that the name of God does not appear even once in the Book of Esther, nor does the chronicle contain the record of a single miracle. But why a holiday celebrating such a supreme national deliverance was deemed less significant than one with a religious content has not been explained. However, having incorporated the Book of Esther into the sacred Bible canon, the Rabbinical authorities felt it incumbent upon them to provide it with a fitting religious observance. Thus they decreed that the Megillah be read aloud, following the prayer service, for every man, woman, and child to hear: once in the morning and once in the evening. Before the chazzan or some other reader commences the cantillation of the Hebrew text (each geographic region has its own "traditional" intonation), it is customary, in lieu of a sacrificial offering, to donate "as a gift" for the needy the currency equivalent of the half-shekel that Jews of ancient times were required to send each year to the Temple treasury in Jerusalem.

The folkways and manners which, at least since medieval times, have accompanied the public recital in the synagogue of the Megillah, are in line with the boisterous character of the Purim carnival, for gay carnival it unquestionably is! Each time the reader pronounces the name of Haman, it is customary to respond, especially in the case of children, by making as loud and as raucous a noise as possible. In the seventeenth century, the inquisitive Samuel Pepys noted in his Diary that, when he visited the London synagogue on Purim, he was almost deafened by the noise. It has always been the same in Orthodox synagogues everywhere: The children stamp their feet, beat on their seats, pound on pots and pans they bring from home, blow horns, and grind rattlers (in Yiddish: *drehers* or *greggers*) to execrate the memory of the man who tried to destroy their forefathers. It was the custom in ancient Persia, and also in Italy during the Middle Ages, for a reveling crowd of youngsters first to hang and then to burn an effigy of Haman amidst shrieks and derisive hoots.

It is written in the ancient Midrash: "While all the festivals may [some day] become annulled, Purim will never disappear." Why so? The unknown commentator made his inference quite clear: Until the coming of the Messiah, Jews will remain faithful to their God and to their people. Therefore, there will always rise up Hamans who will plot to destroy them. And by the same token, there will always be justification for celebrating Purim—if for nothing else, then to demonstrate that Israel is indestructible.

See also PURIM PLAY.

Playing merry tunes in the streets of the Prague ghetto in honor of Purim, 1741.

"Jonah and the Whale" float in a Purim celebration in modern Israel. (Israel Government Tourist Office.)

The Megillah (Scroll of the Book of Esther). Engraved by Salomone d'Italia. Italy, 17th century. (The Jewish Museum.)

Closing chorus from the popular Yiddish Purim play Achashverosh Shpiel. *Note the klezmorim (folk instrumentalists) at the right. Warsaw, 17th century.*

PURIM PLAY (in Yiddish: PURIM SHPIEL)

On Purim, as early as the fourteenth century, the Jews of Germany took part in masquerades built around the subject of Haman's plot to exterminate the Jews of Persia (*see* PURIM). The revelers often dressed up as fools in cap and bells and blew on raucous horns. No one in particular wrote the dialogue, which was in Yiddish; the lines were improvised; thus, no text has survived because none was written down. These Purim mummers were no respecters of persons; they even ridiculed with mock solemnity the rabbis and the community bigwigs. Every license was permitted on this, the jolliest of all Jewish holy days. In true carnival spirit, men wearing grotesque masks dressed up as women, and women dressed up as men.

By the sixteenth century, the Purim play in Germany had taken on the character of the *Fastnachtspiel* (Shrovetide carnival play). A contemporary Yiddish chronicler recorded that on Purim the Jews went to the *Tanzhaus* (community dance and wedding hall) to be diverted by the Yiddish play *Tab Yeklein, Sein Weib Kendlein, un Seineh Zvei Zindlech Fein* ("Tab Yeklein, his wife Kendlein, and his two fine sons").

The best known of these Purim plays, patched together with doggerel verse and interspersed with popular Jewish folk-tunes, were *Ahashueroshshpiel* ("The Play about King Ahasueros"), printed in 1708; *David and Goliath;* and *Mekirat Yossef* ("The Sale of Joseph"). At the first public performance of the last-mentioned play in the *Tanzhaus* of Frankfurt in 1713 during the festival of Purim, all the parts—female as well as male—were played by yeshivah bachurim (Talmud students).

Although written in the slapstick style of the clown-comedies so popular in Germany, these plays were entirely free of the vulgar and the suggestive that characterized the former. *The Sale of Joseph* became so popular that it drew a great number of Christians to the Jewish *Tanzhaus*. Finally, the city watch had to post two men with firearms at the doors to keep off the crowds. While Joseph, Potiphar, and Zuleika were played with mock seriousness by the Talmud students, real comic relief was furnished by the merry-andrew, Pickleherring, Potiphar's servant. He proved such a hilarious attraction that, in order to preserve the peace, the city authorities forbade the play's further performance. Thenceforth, it proved a prime favorite with Jewish audiences in Eastern Europe until the turn of the twentieth century.

Whatever inferior level of Jewish culture the Purim play represented, it did give utterance to the robust will to song, laughter, and optimism of the East European Jews in one of the most depressing periods in their history. And however primitive and absurd in dramatic form, dialogue, and content it was, it did lay the groundwork for the modern Yiddish play and theatre.

See also PURIM; THEATRE, OPPOSITION TO.

R

RABBANITES. *See* KARAITES.

RABBI (Hebrew, meaning "teacher")

Each historic period for more than two thousand years placed its own cultural stamp on the character of the rabbinate and on the official functions of the rabbi. Yet, although these were never quite the same, there were certain traditions and characteristics that always remained unchanging.

The principal image of the rabbi in every century has been that of teacher in the precepts of the Torah and in their fulfillment in daily practice. The precedent and the beau ideal of this traditional figure was the greatest teacher of all: Moses. In every generation the Jews have lovingly referred to him as Mosheh Rabbenu—"Our Teacher Moses." But almost as great an impact on the Jewish folk-mind was made by the Rabbinic Sages in the centuries following the Dispersion. As teachers, they created collectively the monumental literature and culture of Talmudic Judaism. They laid down the guiding principle that it was not enough merely to be a Torah scholar; a man had to justify his learning by sharing it with others perhaps less knowledgeable or less fortunate than himself but being, in any case, in quest or in need of religious-moral illumination. Such was the dedication of the rabbi from the time he first appeared on the Jewish scene.

To go even further: Belief in God, Torah study, prayer, and ritual observance were never considered in traditional Jewish belief as constituting all that there was to piety. Faith and precepts were regarded as only the beginning. They were to lead to their justifying end, which was the constant practice in good deeds! In the ancient Jewish view, therefore, the best way of teaching piety and the moral values of the Torah was by personal example. And so the rabbi was expected to light the uncertain way not only to the fear, knowledge, and love of God but to the Torah, to daily worship, and, through the labyrinth of ritual observance, also to the highest good of all—to righteous living. All this he was expected to do not with any material or heavenly reward in mind but simply for its own sake. This fundamental dedication to Torah study and

Rabbi

Torah-teaching, for layman as well as for rabbi, was called in Hebrew *Torah li-Shema* (or . . . *Lishmoh*, meaning "Torah study for its own sake") and it became a driving national ideal during the late Second Temple period. To a remarkable extent, it also generated among the great mass of Jews in every subsequent century and in every country throughout the world, wherever they lived in communities, an altruistic dedication-drive to learning.

The earliest rabbis—and these appeared during the last three centuries of Judea's existence as a Jewish state—were not religious professionals at all. The rabbinate represented then no official office and it brought no emolument at all. The rabbi was merely a religious leader esteemed as spiritually and intellectually privileged: a self-dedicated teacher and guide of the Torah to his fellow Jews. Even Torah-learning as a claim to superiority was frowned upon as a posture of empty vanity. The religious enthusiasm which flowed from the universal and obligatory Torah-study among the people, beginning with the ministry of Ezra and the Scribes, also made unthinkable the exploitation of Torah scholarship for material ends. The Rabbinic Sages drew up for themselves the ethical principle that no one was to use the Torah "as a spade" with which to dig for himself either a living or a worldly career.

This material disinterestedness of the early rabbi in the dedication to his calling was described symbolically and in flowery terms by Rabbi Yochanan ben Zakkai, the religious leader of Palestinian Jewry during the first century: "The rabbi should appear as clean and as pure as an angel." In naïve correspondence with this conception, the custom arose for rabbis to wear spotless white robes. At a perhaps less dedicated time, early in the tenth century, the foremost Babylonian rabbi and teacher of his generation, Sherirah Gaon, looked back nostalgically to that Golden Age of Rabbinic innocence: "The more ancient generations [of rabbis], however, which were far superior, had no such titles as Rabban, Rabbi, or Rab, for either the Babylonian or Palestinian Sages. This is evident from the fact that Hillel, who came from Babylonia, did not bear the title Rabban [Chief Rabbi] before his name . . . some of the Sages are called simply by their names without any title, thus: Simon the Just, Antigonos of Soko, and Yoseh ben Yochanan."

The honorific title of Rabbi, which in the beginning was granted by ordination with the laying on of hands, was introduced by Yochanan ben Zakkai during the first century in Judea. The Babylonian academies, too, followed this method of ordination, but instead of Rabbi they bestowed the title Rab and also its equivalent, Mar. The distinctive title Rabban was carried only by the presidents (the Patriarchs) of the Sanhedrin, i.e., Rabban Gamaliel.

And even these honorific titles, which were merely given to add to the worldly prestige and weight of the religious instruction by the teachers of Torah, carried with them, in most cases, no material awards. The trades and callings by which the Talmudic Sages earned their daily bread in order to avoid using the Torah "as a spade" were held up to successive generations of Jewish youth as shining examples of disinterested devotion to sacred values: They were reminded that the great teacher of ethics, Hillel, chopped wood for a living, that Shammai was a land-surveyor; Ishmael, a simple tanner; Chanina, a cobbler; Chuna, a water-carrier; Abba Hoshaiah washed clothes for pay; Isaac Nappacha was a smith; Yochanan ha-Sandler, a sandal-maker; etc. Certainly no snobbery of any kind was tolerated with regard to a rabbi's class origin, educational background, and material circumstances. Even Resh Lakish, who formerly had followed the unsavory calling of a gladiator for the entertainment of the Romans but who, in time, repented, was accord-

David Nieto, Sefaradic rabbi, doctor, and mathematician of London during the 17th century.

Chief Rabbi Meyer Stern, head of the Ashkenazim in Amsterdam, 1674–99. (Contemporary engraving.)

Chief Rabbi David Simonsen of Copenhagen, Denmark. Early 20th century.

Ashkenazic rabbi of Jerusalem. (Drawing by S. Kischinevsky, 1901.)

Portrait of a rabbi of Amsterdam, 17th century. (By Rembrandt.

Jonathan Eybeschutz (c.1690–1764), Chief Rabbi of Altona, Germany. Drawn by Elimelech Filter, the physician.

ed the same respectful attention in the Talmud as the saintly Akiba.

In that age and in the many centuries which followed, the rabbi, unlike the Catholic priest, was for most of the time no mediating agent between man's desires and God's favors. In the religious and moral sense of "worthiness," neither his learning nor his rabbinical distinction necessarily placed him in any way above the layman, all other things being equal. To be sure, once the practical Cabalists of the sixteenth century and their later continuators, the Chasidic rebbes or tzaddikim (the holy "wonder-workers" who were their leaders) appeared on the Jewish scene, they sought to effect natural ends through supernatural means. Then rabbinical mediation became, among large groups of European Jewry, a powerful force in religious life. But this represented a phenomenon in the history of Jewish religious experience; the democratic and rationalistic tradition in Judaism, which spurned rabbinic mediation between God and the common man, remained dominant at most times. This distinction was predicated on the moral proposition that all human beings were children of God; consequently, they stood as equals before Him, to be judged only by the degree of righteousness in their faith and works. The only privileged of God, in the final analysis, were the righteous. And even the humble man, the unlettered, and the sinner required no intercession from anyone in order to achieve that distinction; he could bring it about through his own efforts.

True enough, the Sanhedrin, composed of seventy-one Elders sitting in ancient Jerusalem, wielded supreme religious authority for several centuries over world Jewry. Also, and to a lesser degree, the Rectors (Geonim) of the Babylonian Talmudic academies at Sura and Pumbeditha did the same. But commencing with the late Middle Ages, supreme religious authority had withered away except for the great personal influence wielded by such religious luminaries as Rabbenu Gershom of Metz, Maimonides, Rashi, and Jacob ben Asher. In everyday practice and in his religious-juridical decisions, each rabbi was allowed wide latitude in interpreting Jewish law and tradition, although this liberalism could not help but create unhappy situations for continuous rabbinical disagreement and controversy. It was this legalistic wrangling which led ultimately to the production of a number of religious codes, aimed at standardizing religious law and regulation, rite and practice. The Shulchan Aruch (the Spread Table), the ritual code compiled by the Cabalist Joseph Caro (Palestine, 1488–1575), won widest acceptance and has served as a guide for Orthodox rabbis ever since.

The rabbinical salary, for all its pitiful meagerness, became an inevitable actuality in the thirteenth century under the increasingly complicated conditions of Jewish ghetto-existence. Then it was no longer physically possible for the rabbi to perform his many duties and functions, no matter how dedicated an individual he was, unless his living was first assured, for the rabbinate, in the course of time, had become more complex, and the functions of the rabbi more numerous and time-consuming. To indicate merely some of his most important activities, the rabbi expounded the Torah texts and their meanings before scholarly adults in the synagogue and in the House of Study (Bet ha-Midrash) and settled learned disputes among them. He supervised and took the leading part in the religious education of the young. In addition, he was constantly on the alert against ritual violations–such, for instance, as concerned the dietary laws and Sabbath observance. Also, he was obliged to render decisions daily on innumerable matters religious, civil, and communal. He officiated at circumcisions, at the "Redemption" of the First-Born (see PIDYON HA-BEN), and on the occasion of a Bar Mitzvah. He blessed, married, and buried, and–except where there was a dayyan (rabbinical judge) or Rabbinic Court (Bet Din) in the community–arbitrated in divorce proceedings and cases of ordinary civil litigation. Criminal cases were, with rare exceptions, out of his jurisdiction in both Christian and Mohammedan countries.

It stands to reason that, although the rabbi of today is the inheritor of many revered rabbinical traditions and practices, he is also a product of the modern age in terms of the general culture of contemporary society. Except among the Orthodox rabbis, who are the least changing of all, ritual matters no longer present such consuming problems as they did in previous times. The rabbi–to a certain extent even the Orthodox one–no longer is expected to demonstrate exceptional prowess in Torah-learning, although he is required to have scholarly interests and a reasonable fund of knowledge in the Jewish religion and in its literature. Even if his sermon is expected to be knowledgeable in its Scriptural and Rabbinic allusions, it remains, in the main, inspirational in character and popular in delivery.

Quite naturally, there are real differences between the rabbis affiliated with the various religious groupings: Ultra-Orthodox, Orthodox, Conservative, Reform, and Chasidic. Like the Christian clergyman, the modern rabbi too has certain pastoral duties to perform. He must visit the sick, console mourners, and, in the more fashionable congregations, even give "pastoral psychotherapy" to the emotionally and mentally troubled. Also, in an age of skepticism and assimilation, he acts, in a very literal sense, as "a guide to the perplexed." And, as if this were not enough, he is entrusted with the practical and multi-faceted administration of his congregation. Necessity requires him also to be a leader of the Jewish community, of Zionist and philanthropic affairs. In addition, he must play his public part, side by side with priest

Sefaradic rabbi in Jerusalem. (Painting by Sheva Ausubel, 1930.)

Rabbi Robert E. Goldburg of the Reform Congregation Mishkan Israel, New Haven, Conn. (Photo by Samuel Kravitt.)

and clergyman, in the various interreligious and general community affairs—a social-cultural phenomenon of the twentieth century.

In former times, all that was necessary in order to become a rabbi was to be an accomplished Torah scholar, a man of good moral character, and of exemplary piety. Upon undergoing a searching examination by a noted Torah scholar and religious authority, he was, if successful, granted ordination (in Hebrew: *semichah*). But when the ghetto Jew finally emerged as a "European," the rabbi had to show himself to be a man of broader culture and worldliness than his predecessor and well versed in general non-Jewish scholarship. Today he is usually a graduate first of a general college and then of a yeshivah or a rabbinical seminary.

By and large, like the Christian clergyman, the rabbi considers himself a religious professional and the rabbinate his career. He is usually well-paid and occupies a respected position both in the Jewish and in the general communities. If less saintly and dedicated or less learned in Torah-matters than the rabbi of olden times, he is, however, more sophisticated and certainly more adapted to the complex requirements of modern Jewish life in a rapidly changing world.

RABBINIC ACADEMIES. *See* YESHIBAH.

RABBINIC GOLDEN MEAN, THE. *See* GOLDEN MEAN, THE RABBINIC.

RABBINIC SAGES. *See* SAGES, RABBINIC.

RABBINICAL COMMENTARIES. *See* COMMENTARIES, RABBINICAL.

RABBINICAL DECISIONS (in Hebrew: SHE'ALOT U-TESHUBOT, meaning, literally, "questions and answers"; often referred to as "Responsa")

While the fundamental authority in religious matters for the Jew has always been the Bible (and, in ancillary way, the Talmud, too) the relative freedom from dogmatism in Jewish religious thinking left the door open for greater clarification and for revision in conformity with historic changes and the emergence of new conditions of life. Despite the imperious rule of tradition and religious custom among the Jews, there were always internal as well as external pressures that called for further illumination and authoritative guidance in all matters pertaining to Jewish belief and practice.

With the completion of the Mishnah in the second century under the editorship of Judah ha-Nasi, the Patriarch of Judea, there began a reappraisal of Jewish law in all of its component departments. The Gemara and Midrash of the Talmud constituted the first phase, and they were followed by the vast commentary literature written by the Geonim of Babylonia and later by the medieval rabbis. But one of the most influential media for the elaboration and illumination of the laws was the unique system of rabbinical She'alot u-Teshubot—of questions and answers called by the Latin term *Responsa* in English and in other European languages. These had a time-range of some seventeen centuries. The essence of five of them is incorporated in the Halacha, the legal portions of the discussions in the Gemara of the Talmud; the remainder are to be found in the more than one thousand individual collections of Responsa which are still extant. When we consider the historic circumstances of Jewish life—the flights, the expulsions, and massacres in which untold treasures of the Jewish creative genius, as well as untold thousands of dedicated Torah-scholars, were ruthlessly destroyed—the mere survival of such a large number of Responsa compilations is a cause for astonishment.

It was quite the normal procedure for lesser scholar-rabbis, being uncertain in their own minds about the operation or meaning of particular religious laws and their interpretations, to address themselves deferrentially to higher rabbinical luminaries for clarification and authoritative decision. They laid before them questions about dogmas of faith, aspects of ritualism, the composition of the liturgy, various problems of ethical conduct, commercial transactions involving religious duties, dilemmas produced by the calendar (*see* CALENDAR, JEWISH), philosophic impasses, Messianic speculations, involvements of marital relations, and almost every other conceivable matter about which doubt and confusion could arise for the law-conscious Jews in the daily existence of the Jewish community.

These questions and their answers fall chronologically into two major divisions: Rishonim (The First Ones) and Acheronim (The Later Ones). The answers of the first category contain those that were written from the time of the codification of the Mishnah, in the second century, to the publication of Joseph Caro's Shulchan Aruch, in the sixteenth century. The second division consists of those which appeared subsequently. To the questions presented to the religious authorities for clarification or decision, the answers, more often than not, were considered neither absolute nor binding. By and large they were merely advisory opinions. They attempted to clarify complex or doubtful legal-ritual matters with the aid of a greater knowledge of religious literature or by more precise definition. Usually the question that was raised concerned a point of specific doubt or a novel situation, as in the following instance.

Part of a Responsum by Maimonides, in his own hand. Egypt, 12th century. (The British Museum.)

In the year 1160, when Maimonides (Moses ben Maimon) was a rabbi in Fez, Egypt, he received a sorely troubling question from a correspondent. It posed this problem: What was a God-fearing Jew to do if he was threatened with death unless he submitted to conversion to an alien faith? This letter came at a time when Mohammedan evangelical zeal for making new "true believers" was accompanied by the threat of certain decapitation for the unwilling. Although he was only twenty-five at the time, Maimonides already displayed much worldliness and a compassionate understanding of the torment of conscience those of his fellow creatures were undergoing when faced with such a decision. He answered in his now famous Letter Concerning Apostasy. In it he counseled prudence and simulated submission to conversion, stating that the victim of other men's savagery was to resign himself to wait hopefully for a more tolerant day when he would be able to return to the Jewish fold. Far from recommending conversion or renegacy to attain safety as an end in itself, the great religious thinker and rationalist brought his celebrated common sense and humanity to bear upon the dilemma.

It is claimed that literally hundreds of thousands of such Responsa were written since Mishnah times. Often those decisions or opinions contradicted one another, with one authority blithely refuting the other. But disagreements between authorities were rarely harsh. They were couched in courteous and even chivalrous language–an intellectual tradition derived from the Judean Sages. The rabbinical questioner would address himself to his superior in authority (who might, nevertheless, not be his superior in knowledge) in this wise: "May our teacher [be pleased to] instruct us in this . . ." And the authority, who might very well deserve his distinction, would perhaps modestly respond: "I am not worthy that you should lay your doubts before me . . . but the opinion of your pupil is . . ."

During the Talmudic era, the Responsa were written in Aramaic; in Geonic or premedieval times they were composed in Hebrew or Arabic, as well as Aramaic; during the Middle Ages, they were written in either Hebrew or Arabic. From that time until the modern period, the custom was to compose them in Hebrew only. For the Ashkenazim, those Yiddish-speaking Jews settled in North, Central, and Eastern Europe, the most authoritative Responsa, which were consulted by rabbis for many centuries, were those written by the French rabbi, Solomon ben Isaac of Troyes, better known as Rashi (1040–1105). And after him came the Tosafists, so named because of the critical "additions" (tosafot) that they appended to his decisions and opinions.

Other precedent-establishing opinions were those written by Meir of Rothenburg (1215–93) and Asher ben Yechiel (1250–1328). For the Spanish Sefaradim and the Jews of Asia and North Africa, the most significant Responsa were those written during the twelfth century by Maimonides (Moses ben Maimon) and about a hundred years later by Nachmanides (Moses ben Nachman).

See also COMMENTARIES, RABBINICAL; SHULCHAN ARUCH; TOSAFISTS; TALMUD, THE.

RABBINICAL LAW, CODE OF. *See* SHULCHAN ARUCH.

"RACIAL PURITY" MYTH. *See* ANTI-SEMITISM; MARRANOS AND THE INQUISITION; NAZIS, THE; PERSECUTION IN "MODERN DRESS."

RECONSTRUCTIONISM. *See* JUDAISM IN THE MODERN AGE.

"REDEMPTION" OF THE FIRST-BORN SON. *See* PIDYON HA-BEN.

REFORM JUDAISM. *See* JUDAISM IN THE MODERN AGE.

RELIGIOUS DISPUTATIONS. *See* DISPUTATIONS, RELIGIOUS.

RELIGIOUS PRINCIPLES. *See* DOCTRINES IN JUDAISM; JUDAISM IN THE MODERN AGE.

RELIGIOUS SYMBOLS. *See* CIRCUMCISION; MEZUZAH; TEFILLIN; TZITZIT.

REPENTANCE (in Hebrew: TESHUBAH; in Yiddish: TSHUVEH) The Jewish religion, holding to the conviction that man is both redeemable and capable of self-perfection, adopted the doctrinal view of free will, which held that every human being could make a voluntary choice between good and evil conduct. In such a scheme of alternatives, not even the most dismal sinner was to be considered irredeemable; true repentance was the road to salvation for each individual without exception.

There is a remarkable statement in the Talmud that *all* Jews are fated to enter Paradise. How could it be otherwise? Where was there the Jew, asked the Sages–even the most hardened of sinners–who did not make his peace with God by repenting of his sins at the time of his departure from the world? Even if an individual was already standing at the very gates of Gehinnom (Gehenna) there was still time for him to repent. The truly pious, commented the medieval Cabalistic work, the Zohar, "are those who look upon each day that comes as if it were the very last day of their lives. Therefore, they repent of their sins." And it went on to emphasize the urgency of genuine self-reformation: "Repent while you are still young, before your Evil Inclination (Yetzer ha-Rah) grows old!"

The Jewish religious teachers based their stand in this matter upon the axiomatic truth that all men–even the most righteous–are, without a single exception, sinners. But repentance has the miraculous power of being able to transmute the baser feelings of man into the most noble. "Great is repentance," exulted the Talmudic Sages, "it transforms sin into virtue. . . . The righteous are unworthy of standing in the place of sincere penitents!"

It has been generally assumed among religious Jews that no person can sincerely repent of his wrongdoing without first making a stern self-accounting. Each person is believed to be endowed with a rational intelligence; each has the ability to look within himself with honest eyes. The Rabbis held that a single twinge of awakened conscience could work as a better corrective than the severest flogging; therefore, they declared: "He who examines his conduct and meditates upon it is his own benefactor."

Indeed, so obsessive was the febrile Jewish conscience with regard to one's own wrongdoing that, during the Middle Ages, there was apparent a very marked tendency among many Jews toward excessive feelings of guilt. Alarmed by this self-condemnation, the foremost religious thinker of that age, Maimonides, addressed himself to his fellow Jews with these words of consolation: "Do not think meanly of yourselves, and do not despair of [achieving] perfection." The recapitulation by the Jews in their penitential prayers of the contrite refrain, "we have trespassed . . . on account of our many transgressions," ironically, in the words of a medieval Jewish writer, led their enemies to mock: "The Jews must be more wicked than the other peoples, for their prophets, their preachers, their leaders, are all reproaching them with their failings."

The process of reaching a pure state of mind and spirit before one could become truly repentant was not an easy one. The formula for it the Jews of every generation found in the outcry of the anguished Psalmist: "Out of the depths I cry unto Thee, O Lord!" (Psalms 130:1.) Similar was the advice given in Lamentations 2:19: "Pour out thy heart like water."

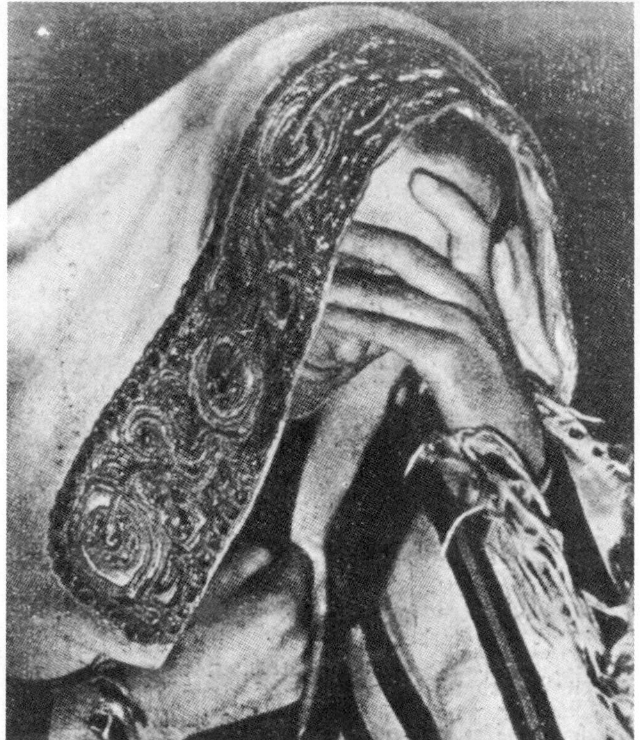

Reciting the prayer of confession of one's sins, ending on the high note of repentance, in the synagogue on Yom Kippur, the Day of Atonement.

A certain teacher of ethics, cited in the Midrash, used a poetic analogy to stress the primacy of the "broken heart" in any successful search for truth about oneself. Said he: Just as the rose, while it bursts into bloom, strains its "heart" toward the light (toward Heaven), so must man emulate the rose, reaching upward to God with his heart in penance.

There was one evil, though, warned the Rabbis, that the honest individual had to beware of: formal repentance through lip-service. The Talmud, paraphrasing the distinction made by the Prophets of old between righteous conduct and a sterile mechanical piety, taught that neither putting on sackcloth and ashes nor fasting and mortifying the flesh can redeem man. The only true repentance, said they, is the *repentance of the heart* leading to the performance of good deeds *for their own sake*—not as atonement.

See also FREE WILL; PASSIONS, MASTERY OVER; REWARD AND PUNISHMENT; SIN AND SINNER; YETZER TOB AND YETZER HA-RAH.

RESPONSA. *See* RABBINICAL DECISIONS.

RESURRECTION

Daily, at his devotions, the pious Jew recites this benediction: "You sustain the living with loving kindness, you revive the dead with great mercy . . . you keep faith with them that sleep in the dust . . . yes, faithful are you to revive the dead! Blessed are you, O Lord, who revives the dead!"

This, the second of the "Eighteen Benedictions" (Shemoneh Esreh) composed, it is presumed, during the final period of the Second Temple, gives utterance to the doctrine of the Resurrection, one which both Christianity and Islam adopted from their Jewish mother-religion. It expresses the certainty that, when the Messiah will come, the dead will *physically* rise up again and be reanimated by the individual souls which had been theirs in life.

The belief in the Resurrection has occupied a central position in Jewish religious thought. For the pious it has served as the connecting link between the world of reality and the supernatural world of the Hereafter. Maimonides made it the last of the Thirteen Articles of Faith which he drew up to serve as guiding principles of the Jewish religion. Without it, the Sages gravely warned, no redemption could be possible for the believing Jew, nor could there be any expectation of a divine reward or punishment, of an incentive for virtue and of a restraint upon wrongdoing. In fact, without it, belief in the immortality of the soul and in the World-to-Come would be impossible.

And so, generation after generation of believers has steadfastly clung to the assurance that, at some future period in Jewish history—when, exactly, would be determined by God in his own time—the Messiah would appear to usher in the "Time of Redemption"—the establishment of the Kingdom of God *on earth,* to occur at the end of the Messiah's expected rule: the four hundred years signifying that the final act of God's work of Creation will have been accomplished. Thereupon, in a blaze of celestial drama, the Last Judgment of the human race will take place. The accumulated souls that in life had inhabited the bodies of the dead since time immemorial will be summoned by the Almighty to return to them. Then the lifeless will stir, and the dead will awaken and rise up again!

Because Jewish religious ideas were exposed, in a remarkable measure, to critical analysis, they never quite froze into arbitrary dogma. On the subject of the immortality of the soul and of the Resurrection there was sharp disagreement among Jews. The most bitter dispute during the Greco-Roman epoch took place between the Sadducees and the Pharisees. These two groups then represented the mainstreams of Jewish religion, culture, and society. The Sadducees, aristocratic assimilationists who had absorbed Greek materialist ideas, held that both body and soul perished at the moment of death; for them, the grave marked the end of human existence. The poet, Jesus Ben Sirach (about 200 B.C.E.), presumably a Sadducee himself, chided the Pharisees:

When the dead is at rest
Let his memory rest!

The Pharisees, on the other hand, represented the liberal and less sophisticated trends in Jewish life. They were close to the people. From their more numerous ranks came the majority of Rabbinic teachers whose humane views and discussions comprise the greater part of "the Sea of the Talmud." The nature of the debate between the Sadducees and the Pharisees is well illustrated by this incident related in the Talmud.

Once a Sadducee came to Gebiha ben Pesisa, a Pharisee scholar, and asked him: "If everyone who lives must someday die, how is it possible for you to say that the dead will rise again?" Gebiha replied: "How much more reason is there for those who once have lived to reappear in life than for those who have never even existed before and yet are constantly being born in the world!"

Apparently this answer did not satisfy all the skeptics, for almost one thousand years later, we find the foremost religious philosopher of that age, Saadia Gaon (Babylonia, 882–942), trying to answer the same objection with a scientific analogy about ". . . fire, which is quick to burn, yet only separates the parts of a thing, so that each part rejoins its element, and the earthly part becomes dust; but it [the fire] does not destroy anything . . ." From this it would follow, said he, that even in life the body undergoes numerous physical changes through growth, illness, and the aging process. Was it implausible then to assume that the reunion of the body with its soul at the time of the Resurrection might take on an entirely new form, one hitherto unrevealed to man who, at best, knows so little?

Of course, besides the skeptics and the materialists, there were also the Ultra-Orthodox and the literal minded. The latter never doubted, never wavered in any of their be-

Graphic illustration by a Jewish artist of the Prophet Ezekiel's vision of the Resurrection at the End of Days. (From Hellenistic frescoes in the synagogue of Dura-Europas, Syria, 3rd century C.E. *Courtesy of Yale University Art Gallery.)*

liefs. They required no logical proof for anything. Such a one was Rabbi Jeremiah of the fourth century. He left the following instructions for his burial: He was to be laid to rest, beautifully dressed in a linen coat, with fine stockings and slippers on his feet. A good strong staff was to be placed at his side so that, when the first shofar blast announcing the Redemption would be sounded, he would be ready to rise quickly from his grave and, taking up his staff, follow the Messiah, "God's Anointed," to Mount Zion.

All religious ideas advance in slow stages of development. This fact also held true with regard to the origins of the Jewish doctrine of the Resurrection. Jews had lived for a very long time among peoples engaged in nature-worship (the Egyptians, the Babylonians, the Canaanites). Consequently, it was not possible for them to be unmindful of pagan fertility cults and of the rites with which these peoples celebrated the rebirth of their gods—in particular that of the Babylonian god Tammuz—each springtime. Therein, unconsciously absorbed, was perhaps the germ-idea of the Jewish religious concept of the Resurrection. But because the most dedicated elements among the ancient Jews made conscious efforts *not* to believe and *not* to do whatever idolators believed or did, those ideas and practices had a lesser impact on Jewish life than one would normally expect. The specifically Jewish idea of the World-to-Come did not crystallize until centuries later.

In those sections of the Bible that are presumably of earlier composition, there are found stray references, vague and shadowy at best, of a belief in the physical survival of the individual after death. They consist of the most rudimentary elements of primitive magic. From them it would appear that all that could survive of a dead person were his bones, his blood, and his name. It was believed these somehow would find a new existence in a place called She'ol. Nothing was said of the soul. This Jewish netherworld bore some resemblance to the Egyptian Underworld and to the Hades of the Greeks. She'ol is described in the Bible as a world that is immersed in everlasting "darkness" and "forgetfulness." By no stretch of the imagination could She'ol be regarded as the "World-to-Come."

There cannot be the slightest doubt that, when Isaiah first advanced the idea of the Resurrection in prophecy, he did not have in mind merely the survival of the individual beyond death. Rather, he addressed himself concerning this matter not to the individual Jew, but to the whole Jewish nation, living poor and oppressed and waiting with dread for the crushing juggernaut of Assyria to roll over it. He wished to comfort it beforehand, to gird it with strength against a darkening future, and to arm it with hope against its despair. "Thy dead shall live, thy bodies shall arise!" he proclaimed to the people. Then jubilantly he cried out: "Awake and sing, ye that dwell in the dust!" If in this world they suffered tribulations, in the World-to-Come, for which the Resurrection was to serve as a mere prelude, they would be recompensed and comforted by a just and all-knowing God.

It was also, unquestionably, the national and religious survival of Israel that the Prophet Ezekiel had principally in mind when he foretold, in the name of God, several centuries later in Babylonia: "Behold, I will open your graves, and cause you to come up out of your graves, O my people!"

Even in later Jewish teachings, although the survival of the individual Jew beyond the grave was given its due importance, it was considered secondary to the necessity that the Jew remain an eternal people. And the reason for this: As God's chosen instrument of salvation for all mankind, as "a nation of priests," consecrated by him in an awesome covenant at Mount Sinai, Israel undying was to serve as "a light unto the nations."

See also DEATH; GAN EDEN; GEHINNOM; IMMORTALITY; MESSIAH, THE; SOUL, THE; WORLD-TO-COME.

REWARD AND PUNISHMENT

The very notion of divine reward for good behavior and punishment for misconduct stems from a primitive and childlike conception of morality. In their development toward a more ethical and rational system of values, the Jews, like other peoples with a long experience in history, carried over and preserved some of their more crude beliefs about reward and punishment. Such, for instance, was the certainty of the ingenuous that in the World-to-Come, in the banqueting halls of Paradise, the righteous, coming into their reward, would forevermore gourmandize on "wild ox" and the flesh of "leviathan" preserved in brine, washing them down with "wine preserved in the grape since the sixth day of Creation." Conversely, the wicked, consigned by their sins to Gehinnom, would be broiled in Hell's fires until they had been sufficiently purged of their corruption.

This *quid pro quo* attitude on the part of the formalistically pious that is present in every religion of mankind had been evident among sizable sections of the Jewish people since its tribalistic beginnings. The literal-minded, always the most rigorous of ritual observers, held the view that, if they took pains to perform faithfully all of the 613 Scriptural commandments (mitzvot), they were assured of their proper reward in the World-to-Come.

This very popular consideration was forthrightly expressed by a noted codifier of the ritual law, Rabbi Judah ben Asher (Germany, 1270–1349). He urged upon his readers: "Consider also that man is a sojourner on earth. His days are counted and he does not know their number. Nor does he know when he will be summoned before the King of Kings to render account for all he has done. He should, therefore, perform all the good deeds he can. Let no commandment be too small in his sight, for there is no limit to the reward he will receive for it. In the World-to-Come, when the Lord, blessed be His name, pays the righteous their reward, the righteous man will ask in astonishment: 'Why do I receive such a big reward?' And he will be told: 'It is because on such and such a day you performed such and such a good deed.' Whereupon he will sigh [incredulously] and exclaim: 'For a trifling thing as this I get such a big reward! Woe to the days that I wasted and did not occupy myself with good works!' "

Among the advanced religious thinkers, for more than two thousand years, this conception of the heavenly reward for the righteous was frowned upon and declared to be degrading. Antigonos of Soko (possibly the first of the Pharisee teachers), who flourished in Judea during the second century B.C.E., is quoted in the Sayings of the Fathers (Pirke Abot): "Do not be like servants who work for their master only in the expectation of reward." Maimonides, the twelfth-century rabbi-philosopher of Spain, had even harsher strictures to make about those traders in piety who wished to make a "deal" with God: "And, indeed, no one serves the Lord after this manner except vulgar men, women, and children, those who are trained to serve God out of fear [of punishment] . . ." or out of greediness for a reward.

There is also extant in religious literature a remarkable body of rabbinic questioning that, in a mood of skepticism, tried to reconcile the logical incongruities observed in connection with the way Providence meted out reward and punishment to good and to evil men. The fundamental challenge had first been raised in the Book of Job. Why did the righteous suffer and the wicked prosper in the world? In the tenth century, some fifteen hundred years after the compiling of this work, the philosopher-rabbi Saadia Gaon, who was the foremost religious authority of his age, restated the melancholy theme of Job: "Moreover, we see that unbelievers live in happiness and believers suffer misery in this world." He brought forward the most classic illustration in Jewish historic experience for this observation. He asked: Could there have been a more righteous man than Moses? God had spoken face-to-face with him on Mount Sinai. Nonetheless, the incomparable Moses was not privileged to enjoy the fruits of his striving—to enter into his just reward, the Promised Land. Why? Where was God's justice? The answer to this—the only one that the deeply devout but intellectually troubled Saadia could give in order to reconcile the life of man with the seemingly contradictory workings of Providence—was: "The conclusion, therefore, cannot be avoided that to both classes [i.e., to the 'happy' unbelievers and to the 'miserable' believers] a second place is allotted [in the World-to-Come] where truth and justice will decide their [ultimate] fate." And with regard to Moses: His reward, added Saadia, although denied to him in his early life, would be given to him in full measure on the Day of Judgment.

Job and Saadia to the contrary, some of the most enlightened of the Rabbinic moralists spurned all such materialistic quibbling. They denounced reward and punishment on "a something for something" barter-basis as being unworthy of the spiritual life of man. One of the first on record to do so was the Hellenistic philosopher-rabbi of Alexandria, Philo Judaeus, an older contemporary of Jesus. In his treatise, "On Honor to Parents," he stated with awesome simplicity: "For wisdom itself is the reward of wisdom; and justice, and each of the other virtues, is its own reward." Extracting the selfsame truth from Jewish traditional teachings, a Talmudic Sage of a later generation taught: "The reward of a good deed is the good deed; the punishment of a sin is the sin."

See also GAN EDEN; GEHINNOM; SIN AND SINNER; WORLD-TO-COME.

RICH AND POOR. *See* CHARITY; JUBILEE; POOR, THE; PROPHETS (*under* BIBLE, THE); SOCIAL JUSTICE.

RITUAL BATHING. *See* MIKVAH.

"RITUAL MURDER" SLANDERS

Bernardino de Feltre (1439–94), the eloquent Franciscan preacher, once raised his voice in warning: "Let Christian parents keep a watchful eye on their children, lest the Jews steal, maltreat, or crucify them!" Hearing this, the Jews trembled because they knew from bitter experience that the sadistic wish of the friar was the father of his thought, which the superstitious mob always was ready to put into action.

A blood-relation, in a manner of speaking, of the Host-desecration (q.v.) myth, but of greater potential danger, was the ritual-murder libel. It, too, originated from the "Christ-killer" fiction and involved the shedding of Christian blood. It was popularly believed that the "ritual murder" of a Christian child by Jews was required of them by their "revenge-lusting" religion to re-enact the crucifixion of Jesus. During this, the Jews supposedly drained the blood of the murdered child-victim into a basin, and—so the superstition persisted—they then not only used it ritually in the baking of matzot for Passover, but they also drank it ritually from their wine cups with appropriate prayers in the course of the Passover Seder service, for only in that way could they get rid of the "Jewish stench" (*foetor Judaicus*) that allegedly emanated from the pores of every Jewish body!

These folk-fantasies, with their potential for infinite mischief, disgusted Martin Luther, who declared them to be both ridiculous and wicked. Said he: "So long as we use violence and slander, saying that they use the blood of Christians to get rid of their stench and other nonsense of a similar nature, and treat them like dogs, what can we expect of them?"

Not in condonation of the genocidal crimes by Christians during the Middle Ages but in informative explanation of their background, it should be pointed out that certain features of the ritual-murder charge were already present in the anti-Jewish propaganda of antiquity. These alleged "crimes," which furnished the foundations on which the Christian "blood-madness" was superimposed, were not leveled by certain Greek and Roman writers against the Jews from religious motives but rather for political reasons, chiefly from nationalistic chagrin and animus against a little people that was rebellious against Rome and was considered to be provokingly upstart and unyielding.

The pre-Christian Roman writer, Democritus, made the statement that it was the custom of the Jews in Jerusalem every seven years to seize and bind some visiting stranger and, laying him upon the altar in the sanctuary of the Temple, offer him as a sacrifice to the God of Israel in a frenzy of hacking and slashing. The first-century-C.E. Greek anti-Semite, Apion, not only repeated this fairy tale but embellished it with all sorts of corroborative details and variations, saying that the Jews would seize "a Greek foreigner, and fatten him thus every year, and then lead him to a certain woods and kill him, and sacrifice with their accustomed solemnities, and taste of his entrails, and take an oath upon

Mendel Beilis in the prisoner's dock during his criminal trial in a 1913 Russian court on the charge of the ritual murder of a Christian boy. (Water color by Leo Brodaty. Contemporary.)

Scene in which a Christian, allegedly slain by Jews for ritual purposes, is miraculously brought to life by means of a crucifix. Outraged Christians learning of the crime from him, are shown (left) killing the Jews. (From Les Miracles de Nostre Dame *by Jean Mielot. France, 15th century.)*

thus sacrificing a Greek, that they would ever be at enmity with the Greeks."

Only in one accusation by a Roman writer is there any mention made of blood. Dio Cassius, the late-second-century "historian" in describing the uprising of the North African Jews against Roman rule and in order to expose the savagery of the Jews, noted: "The Jews were destroying both Greeks and Romans. They ate [ritually] the flesh of their victims, made belts for themselves out of their entrails, and anointed themselves with their blood."

The first case of a ritual-murder accusation on record is that of William of Norwich in 1144. The boy had mysteriously disappeared and an alarm was raised. An apostate Jew, Theobald of Cambridge, went before the authorities and charged the Jews with having murdered the boy. He swore that it was an ancient Jewish custom to sacrifice an innocent Christian child during the Passover festival—that representatives of the Jews throughout the world had assembled for that purpose in Narbonne, France. They had cast lots, he said, and the "honor" for performing the ritual murder had fallen to the Jews of Norwich in England. When the body of little William was finally found, there was no evidence of murder, so no one was punished. However, the boy was declared a martyr and was subsequently sainted; a memorial chapel and shrine were erected in his honor in his native town.

One of the earliest ritual-murder accusations was brought in Blois, France, in 1171. It resulted in the mass burning-alive of the Jews in that town. Then the blood-myth spread to Germany, where it reached epidemic proportions. It moved first through the towns of Franconia, then through Bavaria, and from there into neighboring Austria, Bohemia, and other countries of Europe. (It is worthwhile to consider that in German religious texts, both during the Middle Ages and centuries later, a favorite description of Jews was *Kindermörderische Juden* ["children-murdering Jews"]). This violence troubled some of the rulers and princes of the Church. Where, they asked, would these bloody excesses lead?

Although the ritual-murder libel cropped up periodically in England after the Norwich incident, it was not until 1255 that another such incident—this one involving a little Christian boy named Hugh—occurred in the town of Lincoln. It had fantastic consequences, for it resulted, in 1290, *in the expulsion of all the Jews from England*. This ban against them remained in effect for four centuries, until Oliver Cromwell readmitted them in 1656.

But nowhere has the account of the "crucifixion" of little Hugh been rendered with more authentic horror than in the *Historia Major* by Matthew Paris, the famous English chronicler who lived at that time:

> . . . about the feast of Peter and Paul, the Jews of Lincoln stole a child called Hugh, being eight years old; and when they had nourished him, in the most secret chamber, with milk and other childish aliments, they sent to almost all the cities of England wherein the Jews lived, that, in contempt and reproach of Jesus Christ, they should be present at their sacrifice at Lincoln . . . And coming together, they appointed one Lincoln Jew for the Judge, as if it were for Pilate. By whose judgment by the consent of all, the child is afflicted with sundry tórments. He is whipped even unto blood and lividness, crowned with thorns, wearied with spitting and strikings . . . and after they had derided him in diverse manner, they crucified him."

The report of little Hugh's "crucifixion" let loose an indescribable hysteria among the English population. To prevent disorders, the authorities arrested all Jews of Lincoln. When, soon thereafter, they found the body of the murdered child in the well of the Jew, Jopin, where it is believed it had been secretly deposited by the real murderers, the Jew was put to the torture. To bring an end to his torment, he confessed whatever he was asked to confess. Besides Jopin, eighteen leading Jews of the town were publicly hanged and twenty others were imprisoned in the Tower of London.

Meantime, the body of little Hugh was borne amidst great pomp and solemnity to the cathedral for burial. Thousands of the devout subsequently came to worship at the shrine erected over the tomb of "St. Hugh of Lincoln."

Pope Innocent III and the Fourth Lateran Council of the Church in 1215 did nothing to stem the outrages against the Jews—massacres stemming from the ritual-murder hoax. If anything, the harsh anti-Jewish repressions they enacted only poured more oil on the flames. It remained for the human Pope Innocent IV not only to challenge the savagery with which the Jews were treated, but to brand as a fraud the so called proof that Jews practiced ritual murder. In his bu of 1245, he forbade Christians to bring the blood accusation against any Jew because it was groundless and a mockery of Christ's teachings. Pope Gregory X found it necessary to reassert in another bull in 1274 the prohibition of his predecessor. Other popes as well denounced the hoax in official decrees of the Church. Unfortunately, they were not always listened to by prelate, priest, and friar, and only for brief periods was it possible to stem the outrages.

There were few secular rulers who took a firm stand against the ritual-murder madness. When they did take action against it, it was less on moral or legal grounds and more from a fear that the great frequency of riot and bloodshed might ultimately weaken their own authority. These actually were also the considerations behind the ban against the ritual-murder charge issued separately by the German Emperor Frederick II (ruled 1194–1250), and by the Austrian Emperor Rudolph of Hapsburg in 1275.

Most interestingly, following a massacre of the Jews at Fulda in 1235 on the accusation that they had murdered the five children of a Christian miller in order to use their blood for curing their own diseases, Frederick II convoked a tribunal of noted Church scholars to make a thorough inquiry into the truth of the charge that Jews found it necessary to use Christian blood. They came to the following conclusion—a conclusion remarkable in the reliability of the factual information and most impressive in its objectivity, inasmuch as renegades from the Jewish religion assisted in the drawing up of it—and presented it in a report to the emperor:

> Neither the Old nor the New Testament states that the Jews have a lust for human blood: on the contrary, it is expressly stated in the Bible, in the laws of Moses, and in Jewish ordinances designated in Hebrew as *The Talmud*, that they should not defile themselves with blood. Those to whom even the taste of animal blood is forbidden, surely cannot thirst for the blood of human beings—(1) because of the horror of the thing (2) because it is forbidden by Nature (3) because of the human tie that also binds the Jews to the Christians (4) because they would not wilfully imperil their lives and property.

Upon reading the report by the doctors of the Church, Frederick II affixed to it the imperial seal and signature and appended his own decision:

> For these reasons we have decided, with the general consent of the governing princes, to exonerate the Jews of the district [Fulda] from the grave crime with which they have been charged, and to declare the remainder of the Jews in Germany free from all suspicion.

It is significant for the history of the Jews in Slavic lands that the ritual-murder accusation was not always welcomed there. Casimir IV, who had given asylum in Poland to many refugee Jews who had fled from Germany during the late fifteenth century, had decreed that any Christian who brought the charge of ritual-murder against Jews *and could not prove it conclusively* was to be put to death.

Were it not for the bizarre fact that the ritual-murder hoax cropped up like a recurring nightmare through the centuries which followed (there was hardly a generation or a country which was not treated to the grizzly spectacle) there would be little point in detailing anew so many of these melodramatic incidents. But, like "Shakespeare in modern dress," the blood-libel strutted its ghoulish antics before the footlights of history, attired in the latest fashion, adapting itself to contemporary situations, tastes, and emphases in each century. It often was enough for a Christian child to get lost or to drown unnoticed for a hue and cry to be raised against the Jews. This actually happened in the United States. In the year 1928, in the town of Massena, New York, a Christian child disappeared. It is sufficient to say that in certain church circles, in the back alleys of the town, and in the local press, the ritual-murder hoax, though already doddering with age, once more was trotted out against the handful of Jews in the town. Nothing terrible, of course, happened; after all, it was the twentieth century, and in the United States, too!

Yet the nightmarish lie was again given credibility during the Nazi period in Germany. The two leading fascist newspapers—*Der Stuermer* and the *West-Deutscher Völkischer Beobachter*—harped continuously on the alleged Jewish practice of ritual murder (of Christian children). The former publication, specializing in anti-Semitic canards and obscenities under the editorship of Julius Streicher, even carried a caricature which showed a villainous-looking rabbi sucking the blood from the veins of an "Aryan" child!

The Mendel Beilis Trial. A most stunning event, judging from its effect on public opinion, was the trial in Russia of the Jew Mendel Beilis, in 1913, on a ritual-murder charge. (Next to the historic but politically motivated *L'Affaire Dreyfus* in France, which had been enacted less than two decades before, this was the chief Jewish *cause-célèbre* of modern times. Fortunately, the pressures from an outraged world-conscience helped avert what might have been a calamitous blow to the seven million Jews then living in the Russian Empire.)

The czarist government was in constant and notorious need of diversionary excitement to siphon off the revolutionary restlessness of its oppressed masses. It followed its well-established policy of blaming everything on the Jews. Ritual-murder hoaxes against the Jews, with their circus distraction for the unthinking, were being brought with increasing frequency during the reign of the last of the Romanoff despots, Nicholas II (1894–1917). These provocations either stimulated the general hatred for the Jews among the ignorant masses or they led to a natural climax in government-inspired pogroms through the officially sponsored Slavophile "League of the Russia People," better known with revulsion as the "Black Hundreds."

On March 25, 1911, Andrei Yushinsky, a twelve-year-old Christian boy, was found brutally murdered in a cave on the outskirts of Kiev. He had forty-seven knife wounds in his body. Several days before the body had even been discovered, there were sinister rumors that the Jews had committed a ritual-murder upon the missing boy. A medical autopsy made later upon the body, according to the official record, purportedly revealed that all the blood had been drained from the victim's veins.

At this juncture, the leading newspaper of the Black Hundreds in St. Petersburg entered the affair; it charged the Chasidim with the ritual murder of little Andrei. The cry of outrage it raised was picked up by the chauvinist Slavophiles in the Duma, the quasi parliament of czarist Russia. The "crime" had been providentally committed just at the time when the reactionaries needed a cudgel with which to beat the liberals, who were waging a determined battle in the Duma to abolish the Jewish Pale of Settlement, that geographic area of Russia to which Jews were restricted.

The crime was pinned by the agents of the Black Hundreds on Beilis, the black-bearded superintendent of a brick kiln in a Kiev suburb. Two habitual drunkards were brought forward to testify that they had seen "a man with a black beard" kidnap the boy on the street, and promptly identified Beilis as that man.

But, astonishingly enough, as in the instance of Colonel Picquart in the Dreyfus case, the chief of the Secret Police of Kiev, Mitschuk, was also an incorruptible official. Upon thorough investigation of the crime, he concluded that it was no ritual murder at all. On the contrary, it was his opinion that a band of Gentile criminals had tortured the Christian boy to death because he had been foolhardy enough to go to the police and inform against them.

For thirty-four days Beilis' trial dragged on in Kiev, capturing the headlines of the world press and creating great turmoil among Jews everywhere because of the terrible implications hanging on the outcome of the hearings. The life of the defendant hung literally by a hair, for the czar, his ministers, the members of the court, influential elements in the Russian Orthodox Church, large sections of the ignorant and fanatical Russian masses, and—not least—important newspapers in the country, were fully convinced of the guilt of Mendel Beilis. The accused Jew was at the mercy of a hysterical and arbitrary court, and in constant danger from threatening mobs (several unsuccessful attempts had been made on his life).

The denouement of this dangerously played melodrama was almost as incredible as its origin had been. Under withering cross-examination by the defense counsel, the accusing witnesses broke down and retracted their charges. Later, the leader of the criminal band, Vera Cheberiak, confessed her guilt. Under the circumstances, the jury and the judges were forced, with open reluctance, to acquit Beilis, who then emigrated to the United States.

See also ANTI-SEMITISM: THE "RACIAL PURITY" MYTH; CHRISTIANITY, JEWISH ORIGINS OF; CHURCH AND PERSECUTION; CONVERSION OF JEWS; DISPUTATIONS, RELIGIOUS; DREYFUS CASE, THE; "HOST DESECRATION" CALUMNIES; KIDDUSH HA-SHEM; KOL NIDRE; MARRANOS AND THE INQUISITION; MASSACRES: THE CRUSADES, THE BLACK DEATH; NAZIS, THE; PERSECUTION IN "MODERN" DRESS; POGROMS IN SLAVIC LANDS; WANDERING JEW.

RITUAL SLAUGHTERER. *See* SHOCHET.

RITUAL SLAUGHTERING. *See* SHECHITAH.

ROSH CHODESH (Hebrew, meaning "head [or first] of the month"; hence, "Festival of the New Moon")

In early Biblical times, the emergence of the new crescent moon, signalizing the beginning of the Jewish lunar month, was celebrated as a minor festival. Its appearance was accompanied by much fanfare and drama, by the blowing of the shofar, and by the flashing of fire signals from peak to peak, bearing far and wide the message that the new month was begun.

Together with the Sabbath, Rosh Chodesh was endowed by tradition with great sanctity. In First Temple days, it was celebrated by special sacrifices and prayer and by a cessation of all work. We know that this festival was observed as far back as the time of King Saul; for it is mentioned in I Samuel 20:18-24. The Prophet Isaiah also notes that in his day a festive meal was enjoyed in each household on Rosh Chodesh. The great sanctity in which the day was held may be seen in the satire the Prophet Amos wrote concerning the greedy merchants of Judah in the eighth century B.C.E.: "When will the new moon be gone that we may sell grain, and the Sabbath that we may set forth corn?"

The rite of sanctification that marked the beginning of Rosh Chodesh (and that was called in Hebrew *Kiddush ha-Chodesh*) was performed originally by the high priest himself in the Temple court; in later centuries, it was performed by the president of the Sandedrin, the highest religious and judicial body in Jewish theocratic society. He would pronounce before the assembled worshipers: "The new moon is herewith consecrated!" To which the throng would respond with emphasis: "It is consecrated!"

Students of comparative religion and of the folklore of religion are of the opinion that the festival of Rosh Chodesh is a survival of the moon worship of the Babylonian deity named Sîn. For many centuries the early Israelites, beginning with Abraham, "the first Jew," were living in those centers in which moon and sun worship were practiced, and so the tradition, naturally, became enmeshed in the monotheistic fabric of the Jewish religion. What reason might have rejected thus became hallowed by custom.

Although the importance of Rosh Chodesh as a holy day receded before the primacy given to the Sabbath after the Destruction of the Second Temple, it nevertheless has retained the characater of a half-holy day, and is thus given festive celebration, but among Orthodox observers only.

On the Sabbath which precedes Rosh Chodesh, special prayers are recited in the synagogue. The beginning of the month is then announced by the chazzan (cantor). Hallel (the "Hallelujah" Psalms), offering praise and thanksgiving to God, are recited, and there is reading from the Sefer Torah just begore the Mussaf service.

See also CALENDAR, JEWISH; NEW MOON, BLESSING OF THE.

ROSH HASHANAH (Hebrew, meaning, literally, "Head of the Year"; thus, "New Year")

It stands as a tribute to the progressive character of the Jews as a people that when they first took up the observance of rites, ceremonies, and holy days in their primitive state of culture, by dint of much reflection and idealistic striving they evolved them in the course of the many centuries into ethical and religious values of a high order. Even though they may have continued with the primitive *forms* of worship, this was only because they wished to preserve that which was already familiar to the people. However, they gave these forms a new and meaningful *content*, like pouring new wine into old bottles.

Notwithstanding that Rosh Hashanah is called the "Jewish New Year," its institution showed no concern with the calendar. It occurs, not—as one would expect—on the first day of the first month of the Hebrew month of Nissan (March-April), but on the first day of the seventh month of Tishri (September-October). This dating, although appearing illogical to modern thinking, nevertheless had a direct relevance to the history of this holy day, which, to the devout, appears as second only to Yom Kippur, the Day of Atonement, in significance and solemnity.

Rosh Hashanah, like most other Jewish holy days, originated in a primitive culture that was set in a pastoral-agricultural economy in which magic, myth, and incantation were familiar features of religious belief and practice. And since early Jewish culture was within the constellation of that of Babylonia, which dominated the civilization of the entire Near and Middle East, Rosh Hashanah followed, in its main outline, the "Day of Judgment" of the Babylonians, who considered it to be their New Year. The Babylonians believed that on that day there took place an awesome convocation of all their deities in the great Temple of Marduk, the chief god in Babylon. They assembled there on every New Year to "renew" the world and to pass judgment on human beings, and then inscribed the fate of each individual for the ensuing year on a "tablet of destiny."

The name Rosh Hashanah was not the one that had been originally used by the Jews to designate this day of judgment that followed the Babylonian pattern. Actually, the first mention of Rosh Hashanah is found in the Mishnah, the code of the Oral Tradition which was first compiled in the second century. Before that time, Rosh Hashanah bore other names. Among the earliest were probably Yom ha-Zikaron (Day of Remembrance) and Yom ha-Din (Day of Judgment). These names are very revealing because they are thoroughly Babylonian in concept. The first name—Yom ha-Zikaron—was a reference to the belief shared by many Near and Middle Eastern polytheists that on that day (in the words of the Rosh Hashanah prayer) God remembers "each man's deeds and destiny, his works and ways, his thoughts and schemes, his imaginings and achievements." This "remembrance" was extended to include God's judging not only of individuals but also of the nations of the world: "which of them is destined to the sword and which to peace, which to famine and which to plenty." Here, in this idea, we find the genesis of the Jewish apocalyptic concept of the Last Judgment which was taken over by Christianity.

Trembling before the dread possibilities of this annual judgment of God, the devout Jew, accordingly, sent his supplication to him on Rosh Hashanah to "remember" him with kindness, to show him mercy, and to grant him salvation. Why God should show any wretched sinner these considerations is argued with eloquence in the liturgy for Rosh Hashanah. It was principally to be in memory of the covenant that he had entered into with the Jews' great ancestor, Abraham, "the first Jew," on Mount Moriah—an outcome of the stirring ordeal of faith represented in the intended sacrifice of Isaac by his loving father. The devout worshiper implores his God to "consider the binding with which Abraham, our father, bound his son Isaac on the altar, how he suppressed his compassion in order to perform Your will with a perfect heart . . . O remember the binding of Isaac this day in mercy to his seed!"

Perhaps the oldest name found in the Bible (in Numbers 29:1) for Rosh Hashanah is Yom Teruah (the Day of Blowing the Horn). This primitive musical rite, based on a very ancient tradition, captures the most dramatic attention in the entire religious service of Rosh Hashanah. (*See* SHOFAR.) Numerous theories about the use of the shofar during the Rosh Hashanah service have been advanced by ancient Rabbinical writers: They have stated that the blowing of the shofar in ancient Israel served as the clarion call to war; it was blown also to prod the devout into repentance because Divine Judgment of him was at hand; it was meant to recall to Israel the covenant at Mount Sinai. Strangely the Talmud itself provides the reason that is most acceptable to the anthropologist. It states that the shofar is blown in order to confuse and drive away malevolent Satan and his hosts of evil spirits who strain to prejudice God's judgment against sinners.

The most generally accepted interpretation today was expressed by Maimonides, the religious philosopher of the twelfth century. He stated that the only reason for blowing the shofar in the synagogue was to make urgent the repentance of the individual. The shofar blares forth its piercing notes as if it were sounding in great alarm: "Sleepers, awake! Reflect upon your actions! Remember your Creator and turn back to him in repentance! Do not be among those who, while they grasp at shadows, miss that which is real, and waste their lives in pursuit of empty things that can neither bring them profit nor deliver them . . . Sleepers awake! Look after your souls! Reflect upon your actions!"

In the evolution of the concept of Rosh Hashanah, its "New Year" aspect went through a gradual transformation. While the date for its formal observance remained fixed and immutable, religiously, it was no longer deemed a matter to be confined by the calendar to one holy day in the year. The inference was that every time an individual turned his gaze within and illumined his conduct with the lamp of conscience, with the result that he repented of his errors—*that* was the real Rosh Hashanah! It became the New Year for a new life. The transformation of Rosh Hashanah thus became complete. From being at first a "Day of Remembrance" for God about man, it had become a day of remembrance for man about God and the soul-baring accounting he was to give Him of his conduct.

This emergent new meaning is illustrated by the massive devotional preparation that was required of the devout before the advent of Rosh Hashanah. The Rabbinic Sages of post-Destruction times, being penetrating philosophers of education, did not conclude that the mere formal observation of Rosh Hashanah in synagogue devotions was sufficient to bring an individual in one fell swoop to true repentance. Rather, they conceived repentance to be a state of mind and of feeling, a spiritual illumination which had to grow on one through much reflection. Each person, they said, in order to achieve that state of elevation on Rosh Hashanah, had first to prepare himself, by means of extended prayer, introspection, and—even more—by the daily practice among his fellow men of acts of loving-kindness (in Hebrew: *gemilut chasadim*).

The blowing of the shofar on Rosh Hashanah in the Portuguese Synagogue of Amsterdam. (Engraving by Bernard Picart, 1723.)

Accordingly, for the entire month of Ellul, which precedes Rosh Hashanah, the pious man was expected to busy himself with the bookkeeping of his soul. He had to examine himself unflinchingly, scrutinize every one of his actions with scrupulous detachment, and check them, item by item, against each of the 613 Scriptural commandments (mitzvot) to find out where he had been remiss, or what moral laws he had violated. Among the devout it was (and to an extent it still is) the custom on those preliminary thirty days of self-purgation to meditate and to keep grave silence, to study Torah and to recite penitential prayers, to intone hymns from the Hebrew psalter and to supplicate without cease for God's forgiveness.

The Chasidim of Poland relate how once, as their sainted tzaddik, Rabbi Levi Yitzchak of Berditchev (early nineteenth century) was standing at the window, he saw a Christian cobbler coming down the street and calling: "Shoes to mend! Any shoes to mend?" When he saw the holy man, he asked him with a smile: "Anything to mend?"

Did he have anything to mend? Levi Yitzchak thought hard, then suddenly he was filled with dismay. "Ah, woe is me, woe is me!" he wailed to himself. "Rosh Hashanah is almost here and I have been neglecting to mend my soul!"

One strange thing about Rosh Hashanah: although it is the solemn "Day of Judgment," nevertheless, it has not been made a fast day, like Yom Kippur. On the contrary, it calls for a feast (se'udah) during which a special custom is observed: Each person at the festal table dips a piece of challah or a slice of apple into a dish of honey and, before eating it, recites this undimming hope and prayer: "May it be Thy will that a good and sweet year be renewed for us!"

The Jew of the generations was an irrepressible optimist. He felt certain that God would, in judging him, like a loving father temper justice with mercy. The Talmud holds out the promise: "And God will say to Israel, even to all mankind: 'My children, today, on Rosh Hashanah, I look upon all of you as if you had been created for the first time."

Repentance and its corollary, self-renewal, form the ethical theme of the Jewish New Year.

See also FREE WILL; REPENTANCE; REWARD AND PUNISHMENT; SELICHOT; SIN AND SINNER: TASHLICH.

RUACH HA-KODESH. *See* HOLY SPIRIT.

RUSSIA, JEWS IN. *See* ENLIGHTENMENT, THE JEWISH; HEBREW LITERATURE, MODERN; PERSECUTION IN "MODERN" DRESS; POGROMS IN SLAVIC LANDS; YIDDISH LITERATURE, MODERN; ZIONISM.

S

SABBATH (in Hebrew: SHABBAT, meaning "cessation" or "rest"; in Yiddish: SHABBES)

Among the holy days of the Jews, with the exception of Yom Kippur (the Day of Atonement), the Sabbath is revered as the most sacred and inviolable. The very frequency of its appearance and the many pleasurable associations it evokes have made it the most beloved institution in the Jewish religion. It was the modern exponent of Jewish cultural nationalism, Achad ha-Am (the pen name of Asher Ginzberg, 1856–1927), who coined the epigram which became famous not merely because it was witty but because it was true: "More than the Jews have kept the Sabbath, the Sabbath has kept the Jews."

From the point of view of the historian of religion, the day has served as one of the chief bonds of unity for the Jews throughout their millennial history. "It is a sign between me and the children of Israel for ever," the Bible has God say of the Sabbath (in Exodus 31:17). And ever since Moses taught this doctrine to the Israelites in the Wilderness, their descendants have clung to the conviction that the Sabbath would endure as an institution until the end of time. Maimonides, the rabbinic philosopher of the twelfth century, concluded: "The Sabbath is an eternal covenant between us and the Holy One–blessed be He!"

According to Jewish tradition, God blessed and hallowed the Sabbath, the seventh day on which he rested after he had completed his work of Creation. And so, in commemoration of that epochal event, the day was named Shabbat (which in Hebrew means "rested"). But there is still another tradition which gives a historical reason for its observance: "And thou shalt remember that thou wast a servant in the land of Egypt, and the Lord thy God brought thee out thence by a mighty hand and by an outstretched arm; therefore the Lord thy God commanded thee to keep the Sabbath day." (Deuteronomy 5:15.)

This was the rationale presented by the Rabbinic Sages for the obligation of keeping the Sabbath: Because the imitation of God in all of his moral attributes was the measure of conduct recommended for the pious man, therefore, in the matter of Sabbath-observance as well, the example of the Creator was to be held up for the inspiration of the devout. Since God, who never grows weary, rested from his labors on the seventh day, how much more reason was there for frail man, who tires so easily, to lay down his work on the Holy Sabbath! So argued the Sages of the Talmud. This "rest" was of a moral-spiritual import. It was part of Israel's covenant with God at Mount Sinai, comprising the essence of the Fourth Commandment in the Decalogue: ". . . the seventh day is a sabbath unto the Lord thy God." (Exodus 20:10.)

At its most advanced stage of development, the Sabbath represents in its symbolism one of the highest expressions of social ethics among the Jews. It reaffirms the Mosaic principle that, no matter how poor, how downtrodden, or how rejected a man may be in the world, on the Sabbath day he achieves a great dignity and moral stature. Nature has endowed him with human rights that far transcend all property rights and the artificiality of social status. And in order to protect these rights, the Lord himself steps forward to champion them. The Sabbath is the assertion in religious-social terms of the rights of man before God.

The Jews' observance of the Sabbath often aroused the hostility–and sometimes the ridicule–of the anti-Semites in Greco-Roman times. The first-century Alexandrian rabble-rouser, Apion, gave this "real" historic reason for its institution: "When the Jews had traveled a six days' journey [in the Wilderness], they had buboes in their groins; and on this account it was that they rested on the seventh day . . . and called that day the Sabbath, for that malady of buboes in their groins was named *Sabbatosis* by the Egyptians."

The Latin poet-satirists Horace, Martial, and Juvenal also jeered at the Sabbath. However, it is quite clear that their scorn had an economic basis. The Roman society of their time, which boasted that it was such an advanced civilization, was built on the toil of millions of slaves. The mere notion of a seventh day of rest for helots filled the cultured gentry with both horror and mirth. Furthermore, as is so well-documented by contemporary records, the astonishing success that the ethical preachments of the Jewish missionaries (and later of the Jewish-Christians) were finding among many patrician Romans already surfeited with the cruelties and social injustices of the slavocracy under which they lived, filled the upholders of the status quo with alarm. Juvenal gibed at those "Judaized" Romans:

> Some Romans spring from a father who reveres the Sabbath,

Adore nothing but clouds and the divinity of heaven . . .
Trained to despise the laws of the Romans,
They maintain and revere the laws of the Jews
Which Moses had transmitted in his mystic tome . . .
Blame the father, to whom each seventh day
Is idle, and disconnected from the duties of life."
(GIFFORD'S *translation*)

The Stoic philosopher, Seneca, being a far more serious man than the light-headed mocker Juvenal, took greatly to heart the attraction that the Sabbath seemed to hold for so many of his fellow Romans. The Jewish day of rest, he wrote, was a form of robbing oneself: "This most outrageous people . . . by taking out every seventh day lose almost a seventh part of their own life in inactivity, and many matters which are urgent at the same time suffer from not being attended to." Gloomily, and not without some truth, he mused that "the conquered [the Jews] have given laws to their conquerors [the Romans]."

There is this poetic allegory in the Talmud concerning the Sabbath: The six days of the week stood joined together. Only the Sabbath day was left standing solitary and apart. The Sabbath became plaintive in protest: Why was it so discriminated against? God comforted it: If the Sabbath stood apart from the other days of the week so, for that matter, did Israel stand isolated in its faith among the other peoples of the world. It was meant as a distinction, not as a punishment. Moreover, the Sabbath would never be alone, for were it not wedded to Israel, who would treasure it forever?

The question of the origin of the Jewish Sabbath has never been fully resolved by modern scholars. A widely held view first suggested in 1873 by the eminent Protestant Biblical scholar Franz Delitzsch was that it had been adapted, although on weekly cycles supposedly to correspond with the four lunar phases, from the full-moon festival of the ancient Babylonians called Shabbattu or Shapattu. The meaning of this word was "to cease" or to come "to rest," and it referred to that phase when the moon had reached the juncture of its highest increase. In the moon-cult of the Assyro-Babylonian god Sîn, inviolable taboos had been imposed against the performance of all labor and trading on this day. In primitive animism, such activities on a taboo day (one is still observed among a number of African tribes) were regarded not only as unpropitious and ill-fated but as might even bring down on the head of the violator the wrath of the offended god. In one respect alone the Israelite Sabbath resembled the Babylonian Shabattu: in its strict and numerous prohibitions. The Scriptural commandment for the keeping of the Sabbath was explicit and all inclusive: It was against the performance of any kind of work whatsoever. It cautioned the Israelite that ". . . in it [the Sabbath] thou shalt not do any manner of work, [neither] thou, nor thy son, nor thy daughter, nor thy man-servant, nor thy maid-servant, nor thy cattle, nor thy stranger [i.e., the non-Jew] that is within thy gates . . ." (Exodus 20:10.)

It was not until the Babylonian Exile (sixth century B.C.E.) that the Sabbath evolved, simultaneously with the synagogue, into a great religious institution. Then the day of rest afforded the Jewish captives, orphaned from their homeland, the opportunity to meet in community worship and to read aloud from the Hebrew sacred writings they had brought with them. It is noteworthy that by the time of the Maccabean uprising, in 168 B.C.E., the observance of the Sabbath bristled with so many ordinances, regulations, and prohibitions, that Jewish soldiers would not fight on the Sabbath day even in self-defense. This fact became well known to the enemy generals, records Josephus, the Jewish historian of the

Recitation of the Kiddush by the head of the household upon his return home from the Friday night prayer service. (Drawing by Regina Mundlak. Eastern Europe, early 20th century.)

first century, and they gleefully took advantage of this scruple of the Jews.

The ancient Mishnah, which is the repository of the Oral Tradition of the Jewish religion, canonically laid down the design for Sabbath observances. It specifically prohibited thirty-nine principal activities. These must be viewed in the context of contemporary economic life in Judea, which was then simple and predominantly agricultural. Among the categories of labor and activity that were banned on the Sabbath were plowing, sowing, harvesting, constructing or tearing down (buildings), spinning, weaving, sewing, hunting, butchering, hammering, cooking, baking, writing, making a fire or putting one out, carrying burdens, etc. These categories, in turn, were enormously expanded during the Middle Ages and in later times.

An extreme approach to the minutiae of Sabbath observance is illustrated by the prohibition against tying or untying even two threads, because that, too, constituted "labor". "It is forbidden to tear or twine even threads or hairs . . . A knot . . . is likewise forbidden to be untied. In case of pain it may be loosened through a Gentile." (*See* SHABBES GOY.) Neither, in the old ghetto days, was it permitted that anyone carry the least burden–even if only a handkerchief. (Human ingenuity eventually circumvented the restriction concerning the carrying of a handkerchief by an amusing stratagem. It became the folk custom to tie or pin the handkerchief to a garment, thus making it appear to be an intrinsic part of it!) The exigencies of ghetto confinement also led to an easement in the ancient law against walking beyond the rabbinically permitted "Sabbath limit" (Techum Shabbat). A mythic "legal" arrangement called an *erub* was introduced to extend community boundaries for the Sabbath by two thousand ells. Thus the devout had more room in which to move around.

Judging by the passages in the Talmud written in defense of the bewildering number of Sabbath laws (consisting of both prohibitions and obligatory observances), one can deduce that they must have aroused considerable discontent. Apparently some thought them to be too much of a burden. "Have I given you the Sabbath in order to injure you?" asked God of Israel, according to the allegorizing Talmud. "No, I have given it to you for your good!" Certainly, pleaded the Rabbinic Sages, the Sabbath was not to be considered a liability but an asset, inasmuch as man's observance of it resulted in his spiritual and intellectual enrichment. Moreover, was it not also a boon to him physically in that it afforded him rest from toil and, at least for a day, surcease from care? "The Sabbath was created to bring mankind rest, peace of mind, and contentment."

The Talmudic teacher of the first century C.E., Chanina, had urged that the Sabbath be celebrated in a joyous spirit. This view, except for the Essenes (*which see*), who extended their austerely ascetic practices even into the Sabbath, became the customary one. During the third century, the pious in Judea would welcome the arrival of the Sabbath with joyous song and with the recitation of psalms of praise. The Rabbinical mystics referred to the holy day poetically as "Queen Sabbath" (in Hebrew: *Shabbat ha-Malkah*) and "the Sabbath Bride," and greeted it with tokens of homage and tender joy —sentiments considered appropriate to welcome a royal bride. In a manner of speaking, this spirit of joyful celebration for the Sabbath became, in the Middle Ages, the "central doctrine" for the Cabalists, and it continued in that vein for their continuators, the latter-day Chasidim of Eastern Europe.

The medieval Cabalists conceived of the Sabbath as a divine incorporeal being who dwelt in the Seventh Heaven within the radiance of the Divine Presence (the Shechinah). Every Friday at sundown—so their mystical fancy noted in the Zohar (the "scriptures" of the Cabalists)—she would descend from Heaven, girded with beauty, enveloped in holiness, and scented with the fragrance of Paradise (for "The Sabbath is a foretaste of Eden," says the Talmud). No sooner did her feet rest upon the earth than all grief and care fled from the heart of Israel, ever faithful in its Sabbath observance, and peace and joy reigned.

Such is the refrain of the celebrated Friday night hymn, "Lechah Dodi," which was composed by the Safed Cabalist, Rabbi Shelomoh Halevi Alkabez, in the year 1540, and has been sung—so it is claimed by marveling musicologists—to some *two thousand* different musical settings in the synagogues and Jewish homes of the world!

Come forth, my friend, the Bride to meet,
Come, O my friend, the Sabbath greet!

A Jew, writing in 1700 in Venice, observed with keen appreciation: "The Sabbath is received with great joy and with pleasant songs and hymns; and in several communities choral singing [to the accompaniment of] string and wind instruments is employed. The reason for it is that the Sabbath should be received with joy; the divine Shechinah dwells among us only when we are joyous."

Much has been made by Christian writers of the saying of Jesus as recorded in the Gospels: "The Sabbath was made for man and not man for the Sabbath." This humane view of the founder of Christianity has been employed for drawing a dramatic contrast with the legalistic formalism charged against the Pharisees (the creators of Rabbinic Judaism) in the Gospels. Yet this humane attitude of Jesus was precisely the same as that held by many contemporary Pharisee teachers of religion. Quite obviously, since Jesus flourished as an observing Jew in the Pharisee-Essene milieu of Judea, he must have derived his attitudes from it. The fact is that Simon ben Menasyah, a Pharisee teacher, states this very saying of Jesus in the Talmud and in only slightly different form: "The Sabbath was handed over to you, not you to the Sabbath."

Though the Jewish people had its full share of bigots and literalists who strictly observed the letter of the law—who were more concerned with mechanical performance of the minutiae of observance than with their spiritual or ethical import—yet the dominant approach to them in Rabbinic Judaism was humane, sincerely devout, and informal. Examples of the piety of the heart rather than of the piety of the tongue were marshaled by the Rabbinic Sages as examples of true Sabbath devotion. In time, all Sabbath observances and rites were spiritualized by being given symbolic and ethical meanings. Humanity was placed above all law. The Sages of the Talmud taught: "When life is in danger, it is one's duty to violate the Law. . . . You may violate the Sabbath in order that thereby a sick person may live to observe many Sabbaths." And if by any chance it happened that a pietist in a ghetto community chose to place Sabbath observance above the duty of helping the sick or those in mortal danger of their lives, he ran the risk of being branded a hypocrite and a sinner by his fellow Jews.

Even the preparation and the eating of the three meals (each of which was obligatory) on the Sabbath were endowed with spiritual meanings. The folk was convinced that there was a very special taste to be found in eating on that day which increased the pleasure of the experience. What was that special taste? The Rabbis of old, with didactic wit, called it "Sabbath observance." The Talmudic mystic Simeon taught: "They who eat the three Sabbath meals in a spirit of holiness enter into a state of blessedness."

It became a fixed custom during the latter days of the Second Temple period for the male head of the household also to take part on Friday in the preparation of the three Sabbath meals. Either he shopped for the food or he cooked one or more dishes. He performed these humble tasks to symbolize his personal homage to the "royal" guest—the "Sabbath Queen"—about to enter his home.

It is related in the Talmud that whenever Friday came around, the two Rabbinic Sages, Ammi and Assi, would go to market to make their purchases for the Sabbath. On one occasion, when they were chided for doing this, they retorted: "Would we have done less if Rabbi Yochanan [Yochanan ben Zakkai, the illustrious Rabbinic authority of the first century] were our guest?"

During the Greco-Roman age, there was quite general agreement among Jews that the Sabbath was to be honored by every possible means—spiritually, mentally, and also physically. It became the custom for the individual to gratify even his sense of smell on that day by inhaling either incense or the fragrance of flowers and aromatic plants in order to increase his "delight in the Sabbath"—Oneg Shabbat—that celebrated the creation of God's fragrant world.

The Talmud recounts how once, during the Hadrianic persecutions of the Jews and their religion in Judea, when the Sage Simeon bar Yochai and his son Eleazar emerged from

The Shterntuch *(pearl coronet worn by the middle-class Jewish woman to the synagogue on the Sabbath and on Festivals. Poland, 19th century. (Courtesy of Joseph B. Horwitz Judaica Collection, Cleveland.)*

their hiding place in a cave on Friday afternoon, they were astonished to see coming toward them an old man, seemingly tranquil and unconcerned about the Romans' harsh ban against Sabbath observance. He was clutching a bunch of fragrant myrtles in each hand.

"For what purpose are the myrtles?" Simeon asked him.

"I will smell them in honor of the Sabbath," replied the old man.

"Wouldn't one bunch be enough? Why must you have two?"

"No!" answered the old man. "One bunch I will smell in honor of 'Remember the Sabbath day [Exodus 20:8]'; the other will be in honor of 'Observe the Sabbath day [Deuteronomy 5:12].' "

"Just see!" exulted Simeon to his son, "How faithfully the Jews are keeping God's commandments!"

The ancient Rabbis believed that on the Sabbath the Jew undergoes a transformation both from without and from within. He not only bathes and puts on festive garments to welcome Queen Sabbath; his personality also undergoes purgation and a change. "The expression on a man's face is different on the Sabbath than on a weekday." Why so? Sabbath observance, explained the Talmud, opens up for the devout person new sources of holiness and spirituality. According to the medieval Cabalists, the pious man acquires an "extra-soul" or "over-soul"—neshamah yeterah—the possession of which endows him with a higher wisdom. It makes him forget all anxieties, frustrations, and sorrows. The soul is suffused with an ineffable joy and becomes aware of the divine spirit in the universe.

One tradition that rests on foundations which were already ancient in the days of Philo of Alexandria (*b.* 20 B.C.E.) was that the Sabbath was to be hallowed by Torah study and by pious reflection on the moral truths of the Jewish religion. Philo wrote that Moses had required of the Israelites that, as they journeyed through the Wilderness, they "assemble in the same place on these seventh days and, sitting together in a respectful and orderly manner, hear the laws read so that none should be ignorant of them. . . . But some priest who is present, or one of the elders, reads the holy laws to them and expounds them point by point until about the late afternoon, when they depart, having gained both expert knowledge of the holy laws and a considerable advance in piety."

Torah study always was the most valued of all forms of Sabbath afternoon worship. The Cabalists said that it put man in touch with his highest being. There is little question but that the weekly day of rest created the physical possibility, the mental relaxation, and the mood for a systematic pursuit of religious learning on a massive community scale. This fact explains the reason why, during the Middle Ages, when illiteracy was quite the general rule among the Christian masses, there was hardly an unlettered Jew to be found in the ghettos. The Jewish religion had made it obligatory for every boy, however poor his parents were, to learn at the very least how to read the "sacred tongue" (lashon ha-Kodesh)—Hebrew.

The observance of the Sabbath commences late on Friday afternoon, not later than eighteen minutes before sunset. At such time, the mistress of the home lights the Sabbath candles and recites the appropriate benediction over them. In Judea, during the Second Temple period—and also in foreign Jewish settlements in the centuries which followed the Dispersion—the kindling of lights became the ceremonious prelude for ushering in the Sabbath. At spaced intervals, a communal trumpeter would blow a total of six blasts of proclamation. At the first note, the tillers in the fields would lay aside their work and hasten to their homes to get ready for the holy day. The second blast warned the villagers or townspeople to cease their labors. At the third call the women had to bring to an end their household preparations and promptly commence the kindling of the Sabbath lamp. The final three notes of the trumpet were sounded together in a kind of fanfare, announcing that the day of rest had finally begun and that its holy peace was not to be "profaned" by further work or unseemly activity. It is an interesting footnote to history that this ancient Judean custom of blowing warning signals on the trumpet before the Sabbath's arrival has been revived in modern Israel.

Lighting the Sabbath lamp or candles has never been considered an isolated cermony; it comes as the climax to all the Sabbath preparations in the home. Custom dictates that the table be set in as festive and attractive a way as possible in order to honor Queen Sabbath. With all appropriate ceremony a white cloth is spread; in some countries freshly cut flowers in a vase are placed upon it. At the head of the table are laid the two traditional Sabbath loaves or challot (in Yiddish: challes), which are covered by an embroidered cloth. (In former generations—and not so long ago at that, in the countries of Eastern Europe, the hand-stitching or embroidery on the challah-coverlet [like that on the matzah coverlet for

Cholent (shalet) ovens for keeping warm Sabbath foods cooked on Friday. (Engraving in Kirchliche Verfassung *by Bodenschatz, Germany, 1748.)*

Passover] represented a homely kind of Jewish folk-art. It was cultivated by well-brought-up young girls as an artistic accomplishment, and was presumed to bolster their chances for making a fine marriage.) Next to the challot on the Sabbath table is placed a decanter of sacramental wine and a small Kiddush goblet (in Yiddish: a *becher*) or "cup of sanctification."

The medieval Cabalists, pursuing the hidden mysteries of faith, warned the pious in the Zohar: "When Queen Sabbath enters a home on Friday night and finds no festive arrangement prepared in her honor, no light kindled, no table set properly with white cloth, challot, and sacramental wine, she says sadly: 'This is not a Jewish home, for there is no holiness in it!'"

Once all the preparation are completed, the housewife, however poor, puts on her best Sabbath clothes, and adorns herself with whatever trinkets she may have in honor of the royal guest she expects imminently to enter her home. And because acts of benevolence on behalf of the poor and suffering have always been included by Jews as one of the modes of religious worship, before the housewife lights the candles, she puts aside some money for tzedakah—whether for charity, for the support of the synagogue, or for some Jewish educational institution. In recent decades this art of tzedakah often also included a contribution to the Jewish National Fund to help reclaim the soil of Israel.

This performance of a seemingly trifling act of benevolence before the candle-lighting ceremony is not to be underestimated because, in the scheme of Jewish religious-ethical values, it is of fundamental importance. One must bear in mind that the poverty of Jews in the East European ghettos was desperate indeed. Yet, unfailingly, the devout wife and mother, before she felt herself to be spiritually ready to start lighting the Sabbath candles, would first drop a few coins—often desperately needed to buy bread for her children—into her Meir Baal ha-Nes pushkah. This pushkah—her private charity coin-box—was reverently named after Rabbi Meir, the Rabbinic Sage and fable-writer of the Talmud, whose acts of loving kindness for the poor had earned for him the surname of "Miracle-Worker" (Baal ha-Nes) among the folk.

It has been the custom for the head of the household, upon his return from the Sabbath Eve services in the synagogue, to bless his children with the same blessing that the Patriarch Jacob had uttered over his grandsons, Ephraim and Manasseh (*see* CHILDREN, BLESSING OF), and then to recite the Kiddush benediction over a goblet of sacramental wine.

Since earliest times, it has also been a revered custom for worshipers, at the conclusion of the Friday night prayer-service in the synagogue, to invite some poor man—whether he be a homeless stranger or just a passing traveler—to come home and to sit as an honored guest in the bosom of the family at the Sabbath table. This act of "loving-kindness" was practiced by even the poorest. What if the Sabbath meal was necessarily skimpy and the bed they were able to provide, hard? Nevertheless, they tried to compensate for this lack with the warmth of brotherhood they extended to a fellow Jew, roaming solitary in an otherwise inhospitable world. For all Jews, whether from near or far, whether friend or stranger, were considered kinsmen, to be cherished and heartened.

The most affecting part of the traditional Sabbath Eve home-service is the husband's singing in honor of his wife of the hymn "Eshes Chayil" (literally meaning "A Woman of Valor" but actually translated as "A Good Woman"). This is a song culled from the Book of Proverbs that is a eulogy to the Jewish wife and mother, extolling her role within the family in ideal terms. It reveals how much higher, so much of the time, the position of the woman was among the Jews than among other peoples.

Kugel (noodle or bread-suet pudding), a traditional Sabbath dish eaten by Central and East European Jews. (Sketch by Alphonse Lévy, Alsace, 1880's.)

> Strength and dignity are her clothing . . .
> She openeth her mouth with wisdom;
> And the law of kindness is on her tongue . . .
> Her children rise up, and call her blessed;
> Her husband also, and he praiseth her.
>
> PROVERBS 31:25-28

In Eastern and Central European countries, certain foods became traditional for the feast (se'udah) on the eve of the Sabbath. It was customary to eat not only the braided challah, but gefilteh (stuffed) fish, lokshen (noodles) in chicken broth, and tzimmes (a sweet side dish or dessert). Upon returning from the synagogue the following morning, the family gathered for the Sabbath noon feast. The main dish this time was the traditional tcholent or shalet, a name derived from the French *chaleur*, meaning heat or warmth. (*See* YIDDISH LANGUAGE.) Tcholent usually consisted of potted meat and vegetables cooked on Friday (since, according to the Biblical law, no cooking is allowed on the Sabbath) and placed in a special warming oven to simmer overnight. Another traditional Sabbath dish was *kugel* (German for "ball" or "sphere"), a noodle or bread pudding. (It should be kept in mind that foods traditionally eaten by Jews on various holy days were originally merely adaptations of regional dishes popular among Gentiles. It would be frustrating to attempt to prove that they had actually originated among Jews. For example the braided challah [often called in Yiddish *koiletch*] which is eaten on the Sabbath is a recognizable variant of the Russian Orthodox *kulitch*, the braided white bread that is customarily served during Easter week.)

The prayer services that are held in the synagogue on the morning of the Sabbath are elaborate with supplication, rite, song, and ceremony. Except for certain later accretions and modifications in the liturgy, they are much unchanged from what they were in 856, when Amram Gaon, the rector of the great Rabbinic Academy in Sura, Babylonia, compiled the first comprehensive Hebrew prayer-book or siddur (which see).

The high point in the Sabbath morning devotions is reached with the public reading of the sidrah (the weekly portion from the Torah). This is followed by the reading of applicable selections from the Haftarah (the Prophetic Writings). (*See* HAFTARAH; SIDRAH; TORAH-READING.) Except

Embroidered challah-cover showing the Hebrew blessing over bread. Germany, before 1850.

in Reform congregations, it is traditional for the readers to cantillate the Hebrew text according to certain modal intonations.

Since Rabbinic times, the afternoon of the Sabbath has traditionally been spent by the pious in the synagogue in devotional reading or in group study of sacred texts, with some time given over to silent reflection upon the teachings in Pirke Abot (the Chapters of the Fathers), called briefly Perek (Chapter) by East European Jews. This is a compilation of ethical aphorisms and traditions forming a tractate of the Mishnah, the ancient code of Oral Law. Parts of it are read aloud from the Sabbath following Passover (in the spring) to the Sabbath before Rosh Hashanah (at the end of summer).

At home, too, on Sabbath afternoons fathers would read and discuss with their children the moral sayings of their ancestors from Perek, helping them to draw the right lessons from them. By including this work in the Sabbath devotions, the Rabbinic Sages wished to keep the minds of the devout constantly preoccupied with the problems and challenges of ethical conduct.

The womenfolk in Germany and Slavic lands, starting with the late sixteenth century, were also supplied by rabbinical popularizers of religious culture with devotional reading for the Sabbath and other holy days. Because very few of them were taught the Hebrew language, a special body of moralistic literature written in the vernacular Yiddish was created especially for them. Certainly, the most beloved and universally read of all these writings was the Teitsch-Chumash, the Yiddish translation of the Pentateuch that was prepared by Yitzchak Yanova (*d.* 1628 in Prague). The work was enriched in its margins with all kinds of pious reflections, anecdotes from the Talmud, and moralizing parables and allegories. Oddly enough, this unpretentious work, composed in a language considered by many of the religious to be only a "jargon" and almost "profane," proved to be one of the supreme educators of the Jewish folk in Central and Eastern Europe. For one thing, it constituted a democratic innovation of great social importance: It permitted the woman, hitherto restricted in so many ways–particularly educationally–to learn Biblical history and Jewish ethics, and to share in the religious and cultural life of her people. Almost immediately upon its appearance, the Teitsch-Chumash became a treasured *household* book. For almost four centuries it served as the Jewish mother's manual for bringing up her children in the ethical and religious values of their ancestors.

In former times, the departure of the Sabbath evoked a genuine feeling of regret in the poor folk because it meant a resumption of the daily struggle for existence. The life of the Jew in the ghetto was almost always hard, full of unpredictable griefs, persecution, and harrassments–even if there were some joys to compensate for them–and an almost complete lack of opportunity made it difficult for him to earn a stable livelihood.

The very economics governing Sabbath observance were of vast importance to the dwellers in the ghetto for at least two days in the week; Thursday and Friday were devoted almost exclusively to trade in food, clothing, and household goods that would normally be required for the celebration of the Sabbath. It has been said that at least half of the Jewish population in Poland until World War II managed to eke out a living from this Sabbath "industry," however marginal it was.

From the vantage point of Sabbath tranquility, the other days of the week seemed utterly gray and discouraging. It was in this pensive mood that the Jew of other times sang the Sabbath song:

> Light and rejoicing to Israel,
> Sabbath, the soother of sorrows,
> Comfort of downtrodden Israel,
> Healing the hearts that were broken.
> Banish despair! Here is hope come!

The Sabbath draws to a close at sundown, after Ma'arib (the evening service in the synagogue) with the Habdalah service–the rite of "Separation" which is repeated later in the home. A candle is lit. Then, filling a goblet to overflowing with wine, the celebrant intones a prayer with the appropriate blessings, after which he opens the spice box reserved for use during the Habdalah ceremony. He smells the spices and pronouncs the benediction over them. This smelling of the spices is a symbolic act. It is a wishful prayer that the week which lies ahead may be free from care and trouble–that it may be as sweet smelling as the spices, that it delight the heart and sustain the spirit with courage in all of its trials.

In his last years, the great Hebrew poet, Chaim Nachman Bialik (1873–1934) introduced into Palestine the custom of holding an Oneg Shabbat. For this, many Jews would gather for cultural and social pastimes considered fitting to the spirit of the day. These assemblies would conclude with communal

Children at play on the Sabbath in the shtetl (small town) of Tellitz, before World War II.

singing of Zemirot (Sabbath "table songs") and of folk songs. Today, Oneg Shabbat gatherings are held everywhere on Friday night in synagogues following the prayer service.

It may be noted as of cultural significance that it was the custom of the great second-century Mishnah Father and fable-writer, Meir, to lecture in diverting fashion to the women–who were completely unlettered in those days–on matters of Torah and ethics every Friday evening in the synagogue. That might be considered the beginning of the Oneg Shabbat custom.

Sabbath Ceremonial Art. In post-Biblical times, the Jewish housewife used a simple oil lamp for Sabbath illumination. This was made of baked clay, molded in a primitive design with several spouts or openings. It was the conventional kind in use among the contemporary Romans, and examples of it have turned up frequently during archaeological diggings of ancient sites in Palestine.

The Mishnah lists the varieties of oils that were declared by the Rabbinic Sages to be ritually permissable for the lighting of the Sabbath lamp. These included sesame, nut, fish, colocynth, tar, and olive oil. Wicks for the Sabbath lamp could be made only of one material–flax. The reasons for this delimiting selectivity remain obscure. However, it has been proven that during subsequent historic periods and in all the regions of the world where Jews were dispersed, the materials and the character of their Sabbath illumination were those currently in vogue among Gentiles in any given region. If the Jews held on to forms of illumination that were already outmoded among Christians who went on to adopt new ones, it was only because Jews, having been psychologically conditioned by their uprootedness and being, consequently, insecure, had a passionate desire for permanence and continuity. In part, this may explain why Jews have always evinced such an extraordinary fidelity to custom and tradition.

It is unfortunate that the precarious and fluctuating tides of Jewish destiny made the preservation of Jewish artifacts and objects of ceremonial art so extremely uncertain and difficult. The farther back in time, the rarer such objects become. Actually, there never existed just one kind of Sabbath lamp that ultimately became traditional for all Jews; there were only regional ones that were used for limited time-spans only.

One such lamp with which many Jews are still familiar was the *Judenstern* ("Jewish star"). Its use was already widespread by the end of the fifteenth century, but because it had been treasured as a family heirloom among the Jews of Germany, quite a number of star-lamps are still to be found, although they are no longer in use.

Lighting the Sabbath Lamp. (From Sefer ha-Minhagim *[Book of Customs], Amsterdam, 1695.)*

Like a chandelier, the *Judenstern* hung suspended from the ceiling; it was lowered for lighting by means of a rachet. It earned its named from its pointed radial spouts, which were eight or nine in number. The spouts were filled with oil and were supplied with small floating wicks made of flax. A drip-bowl, which formed part of the general design of the lamp, protected against any possible overflow of oil.

Most of the star-lamps were wrought of copper or brass, but the wealthy and more fastidious Jews showed a preference for silver. Silver star-lamps were of superior craftsmanship, being elaborately ornamented with all manner of decorative conceits–even medieval bell-towers, which were built in several stages or galleries. Frequently they were enlivened with tiny tinkling bells and knights in shining armor, all worked in *repoussé* with considerable skill.

A new means of Sabbath illumination–the individual candlestick fashioned of brass or of silver–was introduced in Europe early in the eighteenth century, and quickly began to make its appearance in Jewish homes. This occurred when wax candles had become relatively cheap to manufacture and

Grandfather examining grandson on what he has learned during the week in cheder while mother holds ready the boy's reward—a plate of Shabbes-oybs *(Sabbath fruit). (Painting by I. Kauffmann. Galicia, 19th century.)*

so had made possible the displacement of the oil lamp for festive lighting. From that time on, the custom was followed of kindling candles instead of a lamp to usher in the Sabbath. At least two were mandatory, but it was considered more relevant, in a symbolic sense, to burn one candle in supplication for the welfare of each child in the family. This was in line with the statement in the Talmud which declared, "The soul is the candle of the Lord."

Because the sanctification of the Sabbath is a religious rite, Rabbinic tradition has required that the Kiddush cup from which the sacramental wine is sipped by the celebrant head of the household be perfect in condition, shape, and workmanship. Any disfigurement, dent, or crack, especially along the goblet's rim, disqualifies it from use, according to ritual law.

Like all other ceremonial objects related to the performance of the rites of the Jewish religion, Kiddush cups too were required to be as lovely as possible. Most were made of brass, fewer of silver. In Italian cities, during the Renaissance period, many were of fine Venetian glass, although the ostentatious among the wealthy showed a partiality for gold goblets. Following medieval custom, the base of the Kiddush cup, like that of other ceremonial art objects made of metal, was frequently engraved with a Biblical verse such as the benediction recited over the wine: "Blessed art Thou, O Lord our God, King of the Universe, who createst the fruit of the vine." But the favorite inscription has been the Scriptural commandment: "Remember the Sabbath day to keep it holy."

The style of workmanship on the Kiddush cup quite naturally varied with each region and period. Those examples still extant (unfortunately, there are none more antique than post-Renaissance), were made either in one of a variety of techniques or in a combination of two or more: *repoussé*, cast, engraved, or gilded.

A diverting and seemingly inexhaustible source for the Jewish silversmith's folk art was the spice box (in Hebrew-German: *b'samim buchs;* in Hebrew-Yiddish: *b'sumim biks*). The spice box, as noted earlier, is employed during the Habdalah rite that marks the "separation" of the holy Sabbath from the six profane weekdays. The craftsmen in metal lavished upon the spice box, which stirred their imaginations and encouraged their skills, a wonderful profusion of forms and ornamentation. The earliest extant examples are of either Moorish or Spanish-Moorish design, taking the shape of a minaret. In time, the influence of the church bell-tower made itself evident in the spice boxes produced by the Jewish silversmiths of Germany, France, and Italy. Still other types of spice boxes appeared several centuries ago in the countries of Eastern Europe. Unstylized, they often were in the shape of apples, pears, fish, carts, or petaled flowers entwined with leaves and tendrils.

See also ART, CEREMONIAL; CHAZZAN; HABDALAH; HYMNS OF THE SYNAGOGUE; KIDDUSH; PRAYER AND WORSHIP; SABBATH LIGHTS; SERMON; SYNAGOGUE; TEITSCH-CHUMASH; TORAH STUDY; ZEMIROT.

SABBATH LIGHTS

As among all Eastern peoples, bright illumination has always been a feature of Jewish celebrations, holy days, and festivities. "Honor the Lord with light," urged the Prophet Isaiah (24:15) in the eighth century before the Common Era. But it is quite likely that the mandatory rite of kindling the Sabbath lights was introduced by the Pharisees while the Second Temple still stood in Jerusalem.

The Sages of the Talmud held that festive lamps, lit on Friday just before sundown and at a fixed time computed astronomically for each Sabbath of the year, helped sanctify the incoming day of rest and added to its splendor. They imagined God saying, as it were, to the Jewish wife and mother: "If you will kindle the Sabbath lights, I will reveal to you the lights of Zion redeemed."

This rite is one of the relatively few *positive* commandments (*see* MITZVOT) the Jewish religion traditionally imposed on the married woman. But in the folk view, it bears more of the character of a religious privilege than of a duty. For at the moment of its performance, the woman acquires the ministering character of a priestess–the priestess of the home. It is quite likely that the ancient teachers of Israel wished to underscore thereby for the Jewish people the great importance of the woman in family life as the preserver of

Rite of kindling the Sabbath lights–the special religious prerogative of the wife and mother. Eastern Europe. (Drawing by Rahel Szalit, c. 1920.)

Jewish clay lamps in the Roman style of the 3rd–4th centuries with the religious symbol of the menorah in their centers.

Orthodox functionary in an Israeli city riding through the streets in a half-truck announces the exact time for the lighting of the Sabbath candles.

its moral purity and as the guide for her children in the ways of right conduct.

The Cabalists of the Middle Ages, who felt impelled to endow every religious idea, rite, and custom with mystical-ethical meanings, observed that, even as Torah-study served as a source of spiritual illumination for the man, so did the rite of kindling the Sabbath lamp serve the woman as a light for her soul in the darkness of the world. They therefore urged upon her that, before performing the rite, she strive for a preparatory spiritual pose, reflecting upon the symbolic significance of the physical act of illumination, and thus, understanding it, allow her soul to become flooded with the beatitude of true piety.

Also of Cabalistic origin is this traditional symbolic practice: Immediately after lighting the Sabbath lamp or candles, the woman is required to close her eyes and place her palms or fingers over them, the better to shut out the light and the physical reminders of the worldly life. Thus, sightlessly, and with an inner concentration, she recites silently—as it were, to God and herself alone—the words of the Hebrew benediction: "Blessed art thou, O Lord our God, King of the Universe, Who has sanctified us by Thy commandments, and has commanded us to kindle the Sabbath lights." Folk custom has also dictated that, either before or after her recitation of this blessing, she is to supplicate God with the wordless prayer of her heart for the health, honor, and peace of her husband and her children.

No aspect of the religious experience among Jews has evoked a deeper sentiment than the simple poetic ceremony of kindling the Sabbath lights. Because, in its symbolic meaning, it stands for the moral purity and steadfastness of Jewish family life, there is no subject in modern Jewish genre art which has been as frequently, or as lovingly, delineated. In fact, even many women who are non-observing in most matters of religious practice, still light the Sabbath candles every Friday at dusk, doing it, as they often say, "for the sake of the children"—as a reminder to them of their Jewish identity and their national-cultural heritage.

See also SABBATH.

SABBATICAL YEAR (in Hebrew: SHEMITAH; i.e., "release") The Levitical (priestly) law provided that every seventh year there should be a "sabbath"—a year of "solemn rest" for the soil in the Land of Israel. Inviolate was the commandment: "Thou shalt neither sow thy field, nor prune thy vineyard." (Leviticus 25:4.) The sabbatical year began on Rosh Hashanah and lasted until the following Rosh Hashanah. Ancient Rabbinic law provided exile from Judea as punishment for infraction of the laws of shemitah.

While it is presumed that this "sabbath of the soil" was intended to restore the soil's fertility, which was continuously being sapped during the previous six years, the economic and social effects of having the nation's land lie fallow for one entire year must have been disastrous to the economy of Judea as a whole and the poor masses in particular. This must have been the case especially in the complicated Judean society of the Second Commonwealth, for it can be accepted almost as a matter of certainty that the farmers with small land-holdings (who constituted the great majority of agricultural producers) would have been unable to set aside from their seasonal meager crops enough of a surplus to provide themselves, their families, and their livestock with food for a whole year. How they managed to survive is a puzzling question to the historian.

After he had established his overlordship of Judah, Alexander the Great—who, as world-conquerors go, often behaved like a civilized and far-sighted man—readily grasped the nature of the economic crisis that the sabbatical year was creating for the Jewish poor. He accordingly exempted the Jews from paying the land-tax during that lean year. Far less considerate were the greedy Roman proconsuls of a later time. During the third century, they used force and threats of severe punishment to extract the land-tax from the people at the time of the sabbatical year. That this "milking" had a near catastrophic effect on the poor Jews can be seen in the proclamation that Yannai (called Rabbah), a chief Rabbinic authority of the time, issued abrogating this Levitical law.

The annulment of the law of shemitah had an interesting side-effect: It virtually brought to an end the related "sabbath for debts." For the sabbatical year had also been a time during which all money-debts, in accordance with Levitical law, were declared annulled. At all times, during the Second Temple period, poor Jews remained in dread of the threat hanging over them of bondage, indenture, or imprisonment in the event that they could not pay their debts. The humane and ethical ideas that had developed in the period of storm and stress about the time of the Maccabean uprising, must have led naturally to the legal-religious sanction for the annulment of loans and debts. So, in a way, the seventh or sabbatical year really represented a statute of limitations. Unintentionally, it also constituted a primitive form of business bankruptcy. During the tumultuous final period of the Judean state, which was rent by social and economic injustice and by class-conflict between poor and rich, the establishment of a sabbatical year for loans and debts must have seemed to the contemporary religious leaders of Jewry one way of ameliorating the suffering of the people. The law, by wiping the debt-slate clean, prevented the harassment and cruel treatment of the impecunious that had disastrous results to family life and social welfare, and it gave the poor man another chance to start his life hopefully again.

Yet it was inevitable that the general annulment of debts should, sooner or later, come to a halt, since, in the final analysis, it was found to be both impracticable and unjust. For the automatic cancellation of all debts every seventh year ensured financial ruin for many creditors and helped destroy the economic fabric of the country, which was predominantly agricultural.

Considering that the Bible describes the law of shemitah as a commandment issued directly to Moses at Mount Sinai by God himself, it becomes clear why the Rabbis of the Talmud, rather shamefaced and unhappy about their task, counseled the pious: "He who pays his debts in the sabbatical year has the approval of the Sages [Chachamim]."

See also JUBILEE.

SABRA. *See* ZIONISM.

SACRIFICE OF ISAAC (in Hebrew: AKEDAH)

To the sophisticated, believing Jew of modern times, the Biblical story about the binding and the intended sacrifice of the boy Isaac by his father, the Patriarch Abraham, gives the impression of being an ancient Jewish morality play. But to the pious Jews of uncounted generations back, it was more than merely an affecting morality tale; it carried over through its narrative drama the certitude of a spiritual reality—of an inner revelation that always lingered in their consciousness and one which neither the passage of time nor the remoteness of distance could dim. A great deal of the religious thinking and moral feeling of the Jewish people was shaped and colored by it. No other single incident or teaching of the Bible, with the exception of the awesome drama in which was set the giving of the Torah to Israel at Mount Sinai, had such an overwhelming effect on the emotions of the Jewish faithful.

In order to properly appreciate the moral and religious implications of the Akedah, one must first examine its recounting in Chapter 22 of the Book of Genesis. The narrative reveals how God, seemingly in a capricious mood, and entirely without giving Abraham any prior hint or warning as to his baffling intention, bids him take his only son Isaac—"whom thou lovest"—to a mountaintop in the land of Moriah "and offer him there for a burnt-offering." This astonishing command, so imperiously issued to him, must have sorely perplexed Abraham, as indeed it did countless other true believers in the four thousand years that followed. The universal bafflement was: What was God's purpose in demanding this sacrifice anyway? Had not he himself blessed Abraham, "His servant," with a loving son to comfort him in his old age? Furthermore, had not God, only a little while before that, promised Abraham that "in Isaac shall seed be called to thee" (meaning that his line would be perpetuated through him)? Now, by all rules of common sense, wasn't God contradicting himself completely? Wasn't he forgetting his promise to Abraham and, in addition, bidding him to commit murder, thereby requiring him to violate the law of morality as well as to negate his natural parental feeling and every dictate of reason?

But to return to the Scriptural narrative. Without betraying any expression of shock or outrage—emotions which would have been natural to him under the trying circumstances—Abraham, according to the Bible account, without in the slightest demurring or attempting to argue the point with God, proceeded to obey him. With a self-control hardly human, he led his son to the mountaintop, and there he "took the wood of the burnt-offering and laid it upon Isaac, his son; and he took in his hand the fire and the [sacrificial] knife . . ."

To add to the heartrending pathos of the situation, the boy Isaac, unsuspecting of his father's grisly intention, is led to express his surprise ingenuously: "My father . . . !" he calls out to Abraham. "And he [Abraham] said, 'Here am I, my son!' And he [Isaac] said: 'Behold the fire and the wood; but where is the lamb for a burnt-offering?'" To this question Abraham replied cryptically and evasively: "'God will provide Himself the lamb for a burnt-offering, my son.'" (Genesis 22:7-8.) Then, as Abraham grasped the knife for the sacrificial plunge, the unexpected happened: God stayed the hand of Abraham through one of His angels, who called out: "Lay not thy hand upon the lad, neither do thou anything to cause injury unto him; for now I know that thou art a God-fearing man, seeing that thou hast not withheld thy son, thine only son, from Me."

At the conclusion of this incident, Abraham offered up a ram, which he saw "caught in the thicket by his horns," as a burnt-offering in substitution for his son. Thus arose the primitive Jewish concepts of the scapegoat and of vicarious sacrifice—notions that, centuries later, profoundly affected the Christian image of Jesus and furnished an explanation of his death as being in atonement for the sins of the world.

The Biblical chronicler drew the requisite moral from this extraordinary incident: "And God tried Abraham." He tried him in his faith, and as generations of the pious concluded gratefully, their noble ancestor was not found wanting in fidelity. Joyfully and with unquestioning humility he had submitted to the will to God and had consented to serve as the instrument of his purpose, whatever grief it entailed for himself.

Still another moralistic conclusion was extracted from the climactic resolution of the story: God had chosen this means to demonstrate that he did not stand in any need of nor would he require—in fact, he would not allow—a human sacrifice to be offered in worship to him, considering the faith of the believer to be enough.

Tearfully emotional and touching was the reponse of the plain Jewish folk to this morality drama, glorifying the act of faith as standing higher than reason, dogma, love, and humanity. Jewish tradition and legend resound with this Akedah music. The literature of the Talmud, like later rabbinic writings (particularly the medieval liturgical hymns of the synagogue) dwelt lovingly and exaltingly on the theme of the Akedah. Fervently and tirelessly they sent winging the supplication to the Throne of Mercy that, in recalling the sacrifice of Isaac, God would be moved by love to forgive his people their sins. The great Rab (Abba Arika), who watched over the religious life of third-century Babylonian Jewry, composed a prayer which ultimately was incorporated into the afternoon synagogue service for Rosh Hashanah:

> Our God and God of our fathers, let us be remembered by You for good: grant us a judgment of salvation and mercy from Your heavens, the heavens of old; and remember in our favor, O Lord our God, the covenant and the loving-kindness and the oath which You swore to our father Abraham on Mount Moriah! Consider the binding of his son Isaac upon the altar, when he suppressed his [parental] love in order to do Your will with a full heart! In the same way, may Your love overcome Your wrath against us . . .

The daily morning prayers (Shacharit) also include the plea to God that, by recalling the Akedah, he extend his forgiveness to transgressors. For centuries, beginning with the Middle Ages, a special Akedah hymn was sung on each day during the "Season of Penitence"—the Days of Awe (*see* SELICHOT). In reference to it, the fourteenth-century codifier of the Jewish law, Jacob ben Asher, stated that the traditional melody to which it was sung but which has since been forgotten was known as the Akedah-tune.

The tradition was fixed by the Rabbis in the Talmud that, in awesome and grateful memory of Abraham's trial and the triumphant affirmation of his faith in God, the twenty-second Chapter of Genesis be recited in every synagogue on Rosh Hashanah at the time when the first blast of the shofar was sounded. (It became the custom in the Sefaradic synagogues for the worshipers to chant a hymn before the blowing of the shofar. This hymn, composed by Judah ben Samuel ibn Abbas, a liturgical poet who flourished in Fez, Egypt, during the twelfth century, is actually a versified narrative in ballad form of the Akedah story.)

Sacrifice of Isaac. Note the "scapegoat" near Isaac—the Biblical moralist's substitute for human sacrifice. (From an illuminated Hebrew manuscript of the Mishneh Torah by Maimonides, 1296.)

This rampant ram (with head and legs of gold) which was found in an ancient grave in Ur, the native city of Abraham, recalls the miraculous appearance of a "scapegoat" before the latter during his intended sacrifice of his son. "And Abraham lifted up his eyes and looked, and behold behind him a ram caught in the thicket by his horns." (Genesis 22:13.) (Museum of the University of Pennsylvania.)

But the Akedah had an impact expressed far more tragically than just in prayer and worship. For, with the persecutions initiated in Judea by the Romans under the Emperor Hadrian in the second century C.E., and followed by those of a later period in Byzantium and then in Western and Central Europe during the Middle Ages, an appalling martyrology arose in Jewish life. To the Jewish masses, the Akedah served, quite understandably, as a consolation in adversity and as a model for emulation in conduct, and Isaac was given a legendary stature as the prototype of the gentle, unflinching martyr, who was prepared to lose his life if he could thereby serve the will of God. During the Crusades, when hundreds of thousands of Jews fell victim to the religious fanaticism, blood-lust, and greed of the Knights of the Cross, the example set by Abraham and Isaae was turned into a ghastly inspiration by the devout, who resisted conversion at whatever cost. In numerous towns in England and in the Rhineland, fathers with their own trembling hands slaughtered their children in order to save them from the certain baptism that would be their fate if they fell into the clutches of their persecutors.

Some modern students of the Bible read the narrative of the Akedah as if it had been intended to serve as a dramatic teaching, to shock the ancient Jews into a revulsion against child sacrifice, a savage religious practice common among most of Israel's ancient neighbors. That it was not possible for Jewish life, even down to comparatively late Biblical times, to eradicate entirely from itself all traces of this barbarous rite in worship, may be seen in the fact that among the reforms which King Josiah instituted, *c.* 621 B.C.E., after the discovery of a long-lost Scriptural writing (presumably Deuteronomy), was the prohibition against human sacrifice. He decreed that "no man might make his son or daughter to pass through the fire [of the Babylonian god] Moloch." Presumably this marked the end of the matter, for the ethical advances made by Judaism in subsequent centuries led to the universal acceptance by Jews of the central principle of belief that because man was created in the divine image, the life of every human being is sacred and must not be wantonly destroyed.

SADDUCEES (in Hebrew: TZADOKIM)

The Sadducees—so their tradition stated—were the descendants and followers of the priest Tzadok who, when David fought to make himself master over the two Jewish kingdoms of Judah and Israel, threw in his lot with him. Victorious, David rewarded Tzadok for his devoted partisanship with the high priesthood some time around the year 1000 B.C.E.

The Sadducees played a dual role in Judea during the Second Commonwealth. They constituted the priestly hierarcy and they also formed the ruling-class. From their patrician ranks came all the principal military commanders. Realists in politics and fundamentalists in their religion, they ever remained jealous of their leading positions in the Temple priesthood and of their control of the state; they were, at all times, ready to employ every means to maintain their power and preserve their prerogatives.

These objectives made it necessary—mostly—for practical reasons that they perpetuate the religious *status quo.* Thus, when Rabbinic Judaism (Pharisaism), which was merely an extension and elaboration of Prophetic Judaism, began to unfold during the last phase of the Second Temple period, the Sadducean oligarchy opposed it as representing a direct threat to Sadducean vested interests. That was because the Pharisee Scribes and teachers were attempting to democratize the Jewish religion, to spiritualize its beliefs, and to invest its hitherto primitive rites with an ethical content. In other words, they were teaching the plain folk that communication with God required no mediation by any elite, whether priest, rabbi, or saint; instead, they stressed the validity of *direct* communion by means of prayer (with the "still, small voice" of conscience), and by seeking justice, living uprightly, and loving mankind.

The greater the influence of the Rabbis grew over the people, the more aroused the Sadducees became and the more opposed to them. Not least among the reasons for their hostility was the fact that the immensely rich Temple treasury, which they controlled, was being placed in jeopardy by the new teachings. Thus they were precipitated into an uncompromising war against the Pharisees.

One of the most crucial areas of conflict lay in doctrinal differences. The Sadducees represented themselves to be uncompromising champions of the Mosaic Law; the teachings of the Pharisees they ridiculed as "heresies." Because they tightly confined all religious authority within the texts of the Five Books of Moses, they carried on a continuous and acrimonious debate with the Pharisees, especially over the teachings by the latter on Immortality and the Resurrection. The Sadducees were implacably opposed to the "alien" beliefs expressed by the Pharisees. They denounced them as being in violation of the teachings of Moses, for nowhere in the Torah, they averred–and correctly so–was there any authority for them.

The only information available today on the Sadducees is limited to what is written about them in the Talmud and in the works of the first-century Judean historian Josephus reporting the ideological clashes they engaged in with their Pharisee opponents. But inasmuch as the Talmud was written, compiled, and edited by the Pharisee Scribes and their Rabbinic continuators and since Josephus was a self-declared Pharisee sympathizer, it woud be too much to expect an unbiased or favorable presentation in either of these sources of the Sadducean views. The suspicion even arises that, when the Pharisees finally wrested control of the religious life of the people from the Sadducees, they suppressed their writings, which must have been considerable; whatever else they may have been, the Sadducees were intellectual, worldly, and probably articulate. This much can be judged from the reports in the Talmud about their disputes with the less cultured, if more idealistic, Pharisees. The Wisdom Book Ecclesiasticus, written (*c.* 200 B.C.E.) by the gifted Sadducean poet Jesus Ben Sirach, is very revealing of the religious outlook and social and world-views of the best among the priestly patricians of Judea.

Probably the contumely–no doubt justly deserved–in which the Sadducees have been held, was due to their unconscionable grasping for power at the expense of the people. Their political program was always aligned opportunistically with the voracious empires of the age which held Judea vassal. The implied philosophy of the Sadducees was that it was more profitable to hunt with the hunters than to run with the hares. For that reason–although there must have been other reasons that were less reprehensible–they tried hard to become thoroughgoing Hellenists. Because of their open and sycophantic collaboration with the enemies and oppressors of Israel, which started under the Greeks, then continued under the Seleucidan Syrians and the Romans, the Jewish masses hated and despised them.

The conflict between the patrician Sadducees and the plebeian Pharisees–aside from the doctrinal differences at issue–was political and social in character. Their groupings represented opposing class-interests, and their tug of war continued until the debacle of the heroic Bar Kochba revolt against the Romans in 135 C.E. However, the secular and religious power of the Sadducees had been shattered effectively before that, in 70 C.E. (at the time of the Destruction of the Temple), and it had been buried in the charred rubble of the Temple edifice and in the political ruins of the Jewish state.

See also ESSENES; IMMORTALITY; KARAITES; PHARISEES; RESURRECTION; SAMARITANS; THEAPEUTAE; ZEALOTS.

SAGES, RABBINIC (in Hebrew: TALMIDAI CHACHAMIM; i.e., "Disciples of the Wise")

The term "Sages" or "Rabbinic Sages," whenever it is used in English, is merely a reference to the Talmidai Chachamim–those religious teachers of Rabbinic times who laid down the foundation and erected the structure of Jewish tradition. It was not in character with their consecrated calling that they should themselves assume the immodest name of Chachamim–"Sages"; rather, it was the pious of later generations, who held them in such reverence, who bestowed on them that flattering title.

Actually, the English rendition of Talmidai Chachamim as "Sages" is incorrect. The Hebrew designation, literally translated, means "Disciples of the Wise," and that–not "Sages," which implies arrogant pretensions so foreign to Jewish tradition–is what they considered themselves to be. The so-called Sages never were content to rest smug in their wisdom, but perpetually tried to enlarge and deepen it. Often the Talmud recounts how some of these Sages were content to "sit at the feet" of the more sentient among their disciples!

The Talmidai Chachamim, quite obviously, had much in common with the Gurus of the Hindus, the Magi of the Persians, the "Wise Men" of Chaldea, and–not least–the Greek philosophers. All of these thinkers and teachers, in their own special ways, were dedicated to intellectual-moral ends and, excepting the Greek philosophers, who were secular minded, to the formulation, codification, and elucidation of religious beliefs and the laws governing rites and ceremonies.

Proof that some of the Greek philosophers were fully aware of the teaching activities and the thinking of the Talmidai Chachamim is found in one of the writings of the early Church Father, Clement of Alexandria. He gives what is presumably a verbatim quotation from an unknown narrative by the Greek philosopher Clearchus of Soli concerning an encounter his master, Aristotle, once had with a remarkably "wise" Syrian Jew. This Jew, in the supposedly exact words of Aristotle, "not only spoke Greek, but had the soul of a Greek. During my stay in Asia, he . . . came to converse with me and some other scholars to test our learning. But as one who had been intimate with many cultivated persons, it was rather he who imparted to us something of his own." And this, it must be remembered, must have occurred some three hundred years before the Tannaim (the Fathers of the Mishnah or Oral Law, whom we refer to in English as the "Rabbinic Sages") began their teaching activity.

Obviously, the pursuit of wisdom had a very old tradition in Israel. There must have been priestly schools of wisdom in Israel long before the Babylonian Exile took place in 586 B.C.E. And those "wise" men among the Jews, in an ethnic-cultural sense, must have laid the groundwork for or even created much of the Wisdom Literature that later on appeared in the Bible canon and in the writings that were included in the Apocrypha and in the Pseudepigrapha.

The pursuit of wisdom has always been a cumulative process in which each generation, as if paying compound interest on the capital, adds its own contribution to the understanding of mankind.

See also CHACHMAH; MASORAH; PHARISEES; SCRIBES; TALMUD, THE; TORAH STUDY.

SAMARITANS (in Hebrew: SHOMRONIM, i.e., inhabitants of Shomria or Samaria)

The Samaritans were not so much a dissident sect in Judaism as a tragic accident of history. They had not come by their separatism initially as a result of avowing any new religious principle or because of doctrinal differences with other Jews, but as a consequence of social rejection. Our knowledge about them is not altogether trustworthy since it is derived from such sources belligerently hostile to them, as the Book of Ezra, the Talmud, the writings of the first-century historian, Josephus, and the derivative account by the early Church Father, Epiphanius.

The history of the Samaritans was created in a climate of conflict. In 720 B.C.E., the northern kingdom of Israel, which was subsequently renamed Samaria by its conquerors, was overrun by the army of the Assyrian king, Sargon II. To take the place of the many thousands of Jews who had perished in the fighting or had been carried off as captives to Medea and to other parts of Mesopotamia—"peoples from the lands that I had conquered I settled therein." These words Sargon ordered recorded on a cuneiform tablet now in the British Museum.

The fusion of diverse ethnic groupings, colonized arbitrarily in a particular geographic area, was part of the political program devised by the astute empire-builders of Assyria and Babylonia. Their sole aim was to "unhinge" the population of every conquered people by robbing it of its leaders and its most valuable elements so that its subjugation would be made easier and be more enduring. The inevitable process of assimilation of the main body of the Jews that had been left in Samaria, first by King Sargon and later by King Ashurbannipal, with the foreign groups—such as the Cuthaeans, Babylonians, Elamites, and Shushanites—that had been transplanted into their midst, resulted in drastic biologic and religious modifications of the Jewish ethnic pattern.

In the meantime, the Babylonian kings, by military means, had wrested away the world-power from the Assyrians. In 586 B.C.E., the Babylonian ruler, Nebuchadnezzar, completed the reconquest of the southern Jewish kingdom of Judah. Destroying the Temple that Solomon had built in Jerusalem, he deported the flower of the Jewish population for colonization in the Euphrates Valley.

The Samaritans appeared on the stage of Jewish history in a sudden and wholly unexpected situation. When the first returning band of Babylonian Jewish exiles, led by Zerubbabel, was permitted by King Cyrus of Persia to return to Jerusalem in 536 B.C.E., its members immediately set about accomplishing the rebuilding of the ruined Temple. Then came down from the north a deputation of Samaritans and said to them: "Let us build with you; for we seek your God, as ye do." But their offer of assistance was scornfully rejected: "Ye have nothing to do with us to build a house unto our God." Rejected from participating *as Jews* in the rebuilding of the sanctuary on Mount Zion, the Samaritans became bitter and plotted to settle the score with the exiles. According to the chronicler in the Book of Ezra, the Samaritans "weakened the hands of the people of Judah, and harried them while they were building, and hired counsellors to frustrate their purpose."

This rejection of the Samaritans as brother-Jews by the returned exiles had serious consequences of a religious and political nature for both groups. Incensed by what they considered an injustice and humiliation, the Samaritans sent written petitions and complaints (according to the testimony in the Book of Ezra, they contained nothing but calumnies accusing the returned exiles of the most heinous and seditious crimes) to the royal court at Nineveh. By these inflammatory means they succeeded in having the construction of the Temple halted for eight years.

Some decades later, in the year 458, when Ezra the Scribe and Nehemiah arrived in Jerusalem from Babylonia at the head of another important contingent of returning exiles, they found the religious biologic situation (i.e., intermarriage and cultural and religious assimilation) relating to the Samaritans even more "alarming," according to their puritan views, than it had been to Zerubbabel, for intermarriage between the Samaritans and the returned exiles had been widespread. Armed with the authority for the direction of Jewish affairs vested in them by King Artaxerxes of Persia, Ezra and Nehemiah decreed invalid all marriages that had been contracted with Samaritans. Ezra proceeded to take even harsher measures: He drove out of the congregation of Israel all those who had intermarried with Samaritans or were the seed of such a union, and in addition, barred them from all religious and social intercourse with other Jews.

The many thousands of intermarried couples and their children now found themselves in the tragic position of social and religious outcasts. And these decrees, which had resulted in great suffering for those families that were affected by them, stirred up in them an enduring hatred against those responsible for them. A kind of guerrilla civil war ensued.

The high priest of the rapidly dwindling sect of Samaritans, with their tenderly guarded Sefer Torah.

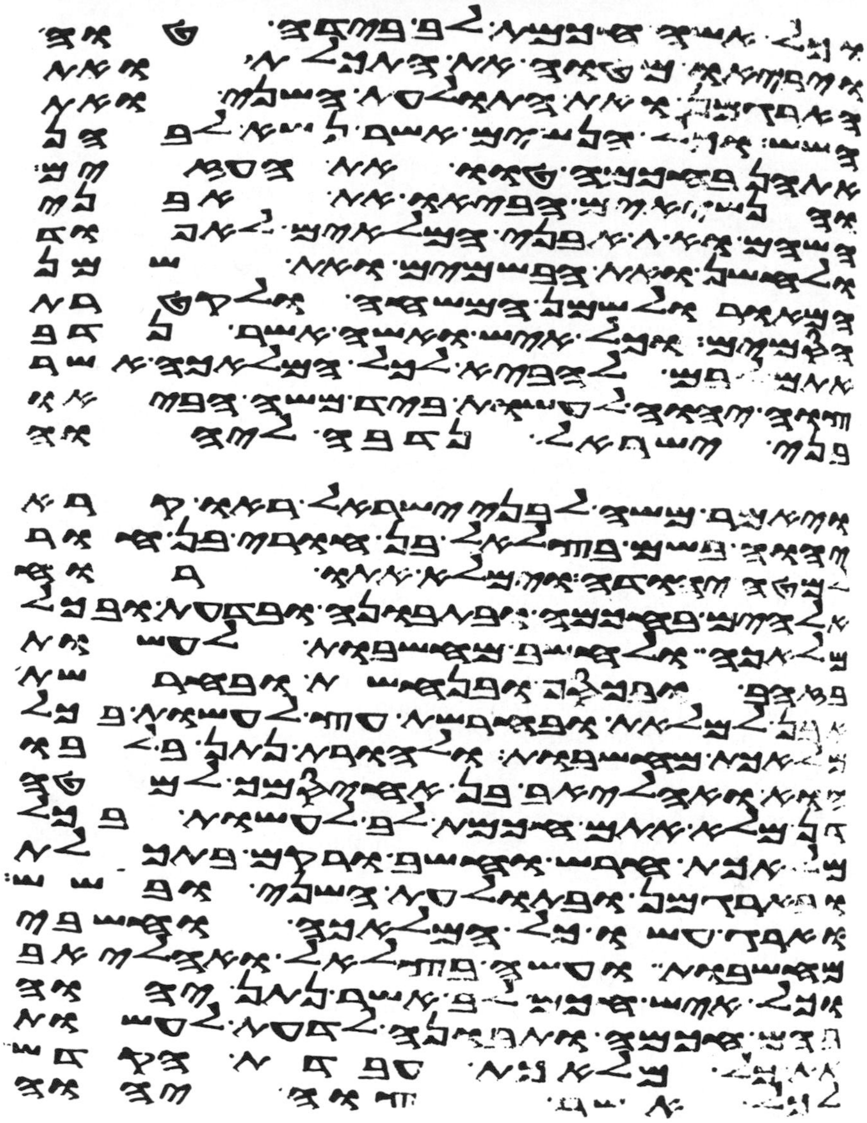

Page from a Samaritan Pentateuch manuscript. Damascus (?), 1485. (American Friends of the Hebrew University.)

With a building tool in one hand and a weapon in the other, according to the narrative of the Book of Ezra, the "pure" Jews labored at the construction of the walls of Jerusalem while fighting off the surprise attacks of the "impure" Jews—the Samaritans.

In an institutional sense, the sectarian differentiation of the Samaritans from the main body of Jews took place when, following their rejection, they built their own temple on Mount Gerizim, at Shechem (today known as Nablus), upon the reputed site of Bethel, the first Israelite sanctuary built during the Patriarchal Age.

The Samaritan conception of the Jewish religion, observed in the historical setting of its own time, was hardly distinguishable from that of the other Jews. It was centered in the belief in one God and in the Torah. Its credal affirmation ran as follows:

> My faith is in You, YHVH [i.e., 'Yahveh,' the letter symbols of the secret and awesome name of God that was never to be pronounced]; and in Moses, son of Amram, Your servant; and in the Holy Torah; and in Mount Gerizim Bethel; and in the Day of Vengeance [i.e., 'Punishment'] and Reward."

To the often heard charge that the Samaritans were rejected as Jews because they had absorbed pagan beliefs—a claim which was undoubtedly true—it must also be pointed out that at no time was the Jewish religion free from idolatrous borrowings. Ezra and the Scribes and the other exiles returning from the Captivity had brought back with them the rather "un-Jewish" belief in angels and demons—notions that they had absorbed from the religion of the Persians.

At the historic juncture when the Samaritans were forced to shift for themselves as a sectarian group, the only Scriptural writings that had been canonized were the Five Books of Moses and the sixth one, the Book of Joshua. These sacred texts the Samaritans preserved scrupulously. Although some two-and-a-half millennia of hatred and ostracism have kept the Samaritans apart from the Jews, a comparison of their Hebrew text of the Torah with that of the Jews reveals but minor word-differences and a number of interpolations that the Samaritans introduced for buttressing their own special pleading. Amusingly, both the Samaritans and the Jews of Talmudic times were led by a belligerent partisan spirit to call each other's Torah text forged and full of errors!

Whatever it is possible to say in extenuation of the Samaritans' conduct toward the Jews, who had made them the victims of an unthinking fanaticism, it becomes quite clear that the force of historic events drove the Samaritans into political alignments and conspiracies which were, at the most charitable evaluation, opportunistic and unscrupulous. As far as they were concerned, their desperate struggle with the Jews was necessary simply for their survival as a group. Their notion of justice was violent retaliation for the injustices they believed they had suffered; it was the primitive one the early Israelites used before they had developed an ethical consciousness and a system of law—"an eye for an eye and a tooth for a tooth."

After Antiochus (Epiphanes) IV of Syria had invaded Judea—an event which led to the Maccabean uprising in 168 B.C.E.—the Samaritans had, conveniently and hypocritically (so it was alleged), supported his pro-Hellenist campaign of de-Judaizing the Jews. They even were induced, out of unprincipled group self-interest, to rededicate their Temple Bethel on Mount Gerizim to the service of the chief Greek god, Zeus. In the light of such doings, if the accusation was accurate, then it was quite understandable why, four decades later, the Hasmonean Zealot ruler, John Hyrcanus, laid waste to their sanctuary on Mount Gerizim.

However much they disliked the Samaritans, even their enemies were respectful of the fortitude and courage they displayed in defense of their religion. They suffered martyrdom perhaps just as gladly as the Jews had in the service of the same God and the same Torah. It was the sadistic Roman procurator Pilate—that worthy so flatteringly presented in the Gospel story—who, as the Samaritans were worshiping on Mount Gerizim, slaughtered them without mercy, obliging the Roman legate in Antioch to recall him in haste. Perhaps it should be remembered that in the Great War which the militant Zealots sparked in 67 C.E. against Roman tyranny, not a few Samaritans perished with the Jews as they fought side by side against their common enemy. It is, indeed, a historic irony that, although the Samaritans had not been allowed to help in the building of the Temple, they did not have to ask anybody's permission to lay down their lives for it at its Destruction.

The Jews during Roman times quite realistically had a keen mistrust of the Samaritans and they kept them at arm's length. Time itself widened the gap between them. The Rabbinic Sages who created Talmudic Judaism waged a relentless war against them, principally on religious-moral grounds. They tried to restrict all Jewish contact with them in a manner that was both severe and, often, unfair. The Talmud cites the second-century teacher Meir as handing down this juridical opinion: "If an ox belonging to a Samaritan gores the ox of an Israelite . . . the Samaritan must pay for the damage." However, if the situation were reversed: "If the ox of an Israelite gores the ox of a Samaritan, then the Jewish owner goes free [namely, does not have to pay]."

The Samaritans, when the Jewish state of Judea was still in existence, were not allowed to own any fixed property, to raise crops, to own stands of timber, or to buy their sheep from Jews. "This is the principle," states the Talmud, "they are not to be treated in any matter in which they are open to suspicion." And this thread of suspicion runs very painfully through the historic memory of the Jews. The old chronicles are full of bitter references to Samaritan betrayals and double-dealings in the service of the enemies of Israel.

"When shall we receive the Samaritans?" asked the ancient Rabbis. And their answer was: "When they shall renounce Mount Gerizim and acknowledge Jerusalem and believe in the Resurrection of the dead." But the Samaritans, although they were the rejected step-brothers of the Jews, were perhaps just as stiff-necked in their religious loyalties. It is worthy of thought: Many centuries have passed, but the Samaritans still have not renounced Mount Gerizim. Now they are almost extinct as a people. In 1950 there were two hundred of them alive at the optimum—just enough to constitute an archaeological oddity for Biblical scholars to wonder how they had ever managed to keep "alive" their identity for so long.

Samaritans of today observe the Passover Festival in a prayer service on their holy Mount Gerizim, where, following the Biblical prescription, Paschal lambs are slaughtered, roasted, and promptly eaten by the standing worshipers. (Photo., 1921.)

See also ESSENES; KARAITES; PHARISEES; SADDUCEES; THERAPEUTAE; ZEALOTS.

"SANCTIFICATION OF THE NAME." *See* KIDDUSH HA-SHEM.

SANDIK. *See* CIRCUMCISION.

SANHEDRIN (Hebraicized form of the Greek word *Synedrion*, meaning "Assembly")

When the religious revival launched during the fifth century B.C.E. by Ezra and continued later by the Men of the Great Assembly had lost its fervency, and the brilliant period of the soferim (scribes and teachers) had come to an end, there was a vacuum left in Jewish religious authority that had to be filled. Accordingly, the official institution of the Great Sanhedrin (Sanhedrin ha-Gedolah) took place in Jerusalem. The exact date it first convened is not known for certain, although the Talmud states it was after the last of the Men of the Great Assembly, Simon the Just, had died (third century B.C.E.). Presumably it is the High Priest of that name who is meant.

Although there is a great deal of reference to the Sanhedrin in ancient Jewish writings recording the kind of laws it legislated or abrogated and the political and ritual questions it had to decide, nothing really precise is known concerning it. In fact, there exists much contradictory information about the way its members were chosen and even of its composition. The information found in the Talmud and in the account given by the Jewish historian Josephus, in the first century C.E., do not at all seem to square. From the facts furnished by both of these literary sources, there seems to emerge a reasonable inference that there may have been not one but two different bodies called Sanhedrin: one completely political (i.e., legislative and judicial in function); the other solely occupied with questions pertaining to religion. Of course, being oriented to the cultural values of Rome, Josephus was principally interested in presenting to his Gentile readers the political-legal aspect of Jewish history and society. He treats of the Great Sanhedrin as if it constituted solely a legislative-judicial body—a supreme tribunal as well as a political council of state.

The possibility also exists that there may have been one Great Sanhedrin consisting of two separate panels of Elders (Zekenim): one given over exclusively to deliberating all matters of religion; the other making civil laws and sitting as an appeals court in criminal cases.

It should be recalled, according to the Biblical account, that in his rule of the Children of Israel, Moses was assisted by seventy Elders: "Gather unto me seventy . . . elders of Israel." (Numbers 11:16.) It is certainly remarkable that about a thousand years later, a religious-judicial institution that had been founded by Moses should have been revived in Judea. Then, too, the Sanhedrin consisted of seventy Elders, with the Patriarch or Nasi (Prince) constituting, like Moses, the seventy-first member and presiding justice.

Entrance to the underground rock tombs of the Sanhedrin in Jerusalem, c. 1st century C.E. *(Israel Government Tourist Office.)*

Niches hewn out of the rock in the tombs of the Sanhedrin in Jerusalem, c. 1st century C.E. *Stone coffins of the deceased Rabbi-jurists were deposited there. (Israel Government Information Services.)*

The Sanhedrin was, from all the evidence, mainly an upper-class body. It was composed for the most part of members of the nobility and of the higher Temple priests, identified as belonging, by and large, to the Sadducees, the political-religious party that was the ruling class. The Talmud even makes a clear reference to the Sanhedrin as "the Court of the Sadducees." Whatever democratic-minded Pharises were among these seventy-one Elders formed only a small minority. Their debates with the Sadducees were often sharp and acrimonious, for that dominant group quite frequently acted against the best interest of the Jewish people and for the benefit of the Romans. Also the attitude of accommodation by the Sadducees toward the assimilationist inroads of Greek and Roman ideas, ways, and fashions into Jewish life and religion caused violent disputes between them and the Pharisee members of the Sanhedrin, who remained uncompromising religious traditionalists and were the democratic continuators of Ezra and the Scribes.

Inasmuch as Rome always took a realistic approach in safeguarding its political interests, when it took over the rule of Judea, it reassessed the wisdom of allowing the Great Sanhedrin to continue to function as a political-judicial instrument of popular self-government. As a result, in 57 B.C.E.,

Gabinius, the Roman governor of Syria-Judea, had the Sanhedrin stripped of all its non-religious powers. Gabinius then proceeded to establish five separate councils—one for each of the five administrative districts of the country. These sat in Jerusalem, Gadara, Hamath, Jericho, and Sepphoris, and served merely as auxiliary oppressive instruments in facilitating Roman rule over the unresigned Jews.

See also BET DIN; "EYE FOR AN EYE"; PHARISEES.

SATAN

If primitive man was frightened by death, he stood in even greater terror of life. For him the universe was haunted by myriads of hostile intangible forces, demons and evil spirits, devils and hobgoblins. His terror was increased because these forces remained invisible but were omnipresent. Much of his conscious existence was devoted to the placation of these all-powerful, supernatural enemies. Possibly because of his inability to cope with the forces in nature or to understand them to any extent, he invented angels and demons to give design to the perplexing drama of his life.

In this respect the Jews were no different from other peoples. They populated the universe for themselves with those magical nebulous creatures whose vast empire was ruled over by Satan, that tireless and infinitely resourceful adversary who always worked to ensnare their souls. Wherever man lived, worked, struggled, and suffered, there was Satan, invisible at his side, insinuating evil thoughts into his mind which, sooner or later, he was bound to put into action.

According to Jewish theology, Satan was as singleminded in his efforts to stir up the inclination for evil (Yetzer ha-Rah) in man as God and his ministering angels were in inspiring the redemptive good in each individual. Satan was at once a hard-bitten realist and a philosophical cynic, mocking at man's hypocritical pretentions to virtue and operating on the basic premise that whatever human beings did or wished to do sprang from motives of crass self-interest. Nowhere in ancient Jewish writings was this characterization by Satan of man drawn in such acid lines as in the astonishing prologue to the Book of Job.

For a proper understanding of the significance of Satan's role in the Jewish religion and folk belief, this prologue has to be read attentively. If anything, it clearly reveals that the questioning mind of the ancient Jew was already obsessed with the paradox of why it was necessary for God, the all-powerful and infinitely wise Creator of everything in the universe, to introduce into the life of man such a destructive antagonist as Satan to torment and frustrate him in his quest for virtue. In the explanation offered in the Book of Job, Satan is depicted not as a devil but as one of the principal angels of God! For God was equally the creator of good and evil.

> I form the light, and create darkness;
> I make peace, and create evil.
>
> ISAIAH 45:7

In post-Biblical literature, the evolution of the concept of Satan in connection with the problems of good and evil shows that the portraiture as presented in Job remained central. If Satan was sent by God to tempt and harass confused and weak human beings, it was not to destroy them but *to test them*—to prove their virtue the hard way. This resulted from a certain dualistic conception the Jews adapted from the Parsees in Iran: that virtue, without first being tried by the temptations of evil, proved but a fragile reed.

Under how many names this Angel of Temptation passed in the classical religious literature of the Jews! Most often he was called Satan or Satanel. He also went under the name of Ashmedai (Asmodeus). But his most terror-inspiring role was as Samael, the Angel of Death. In God's original plan, man was to live forever in the innocent bliss of Eden, but because of the Fall of Adam and Eve from grace and the moral corruption that rotted the human species thereafter, God abruptly changed his intention. Bitter was this lamentation of the unknown author of The Wisdom of Solomon during the second century B.C.E.: "Although God created man for incorruption, and made him in the image of his own proper being . . . by the envy of Satan death entered into the world" (2:24).

In the cosmic tragedy of the Fall, Satan had played the sinister role of the serpent-tempter. Ostensibly, he was to blame for all the misfortunes that befell the human race and for all the evils that beset it. But the morally conscious and conscience-burdened Jew of ancient days looked within and made a shocking discovery. It was that Satan was not *outside* of himself but within, was an integral part of his own complex being. From this followed his recognition that in all his thoughts, feelings, and actions man was being torn between two opposing forces: the Yetzer Tob (the inclination to Good) and the Yetzer ha-Rah (the inclination to Evil). His conclusion was that Satan could be overcome only by his devotion to the commandments of the Torah and by a life of consistent righteousness.

A folk myth of Rabbinic origin describes Satan as "the Angel of Strife," namely, strife within the mind of man himself. For that reason, whenever the shofar—the call to repentance and good deeds—is sounded in the synagogue on Rosh Hashanah, it is said that Satan flees in confusion, for all his archangelic eminence! This defeat is one which he considers ignominious, and it causes him—the genius of cynicism—to weep in abject grief!

The universal belief among the pious was that, if the commandments of the Torah that God had given Israel were fulfilled *by all Jews*, then the Messiah would come and there would be an end to the terror that Satan had brought into the world. Accompanying the Messianic expectation was the notion that, with the final defeat of Satan, Eternal Life in a cloudless Eden would once again be the blessing for all mankind.

To the superstitious and simple-minded among the Jews, however, Satan was not conceived of with any ethical implications. To them he appeared vastly real, as a terribly feared and hated being. With rude literalness—and that too has been an observable facet in the Jewish religious kaleidescope, the Jews incorporated both his name and the dreaded thought of him in the Cabalistic incantations and on the amulets and talismans they used and implicitly believed in. The fact is that the name of Satan even appears in the morning prayers and in the Blessing of the New Moon.

If Satan cut such a significant figure in the Jewish world of the supernatural, he occupied an even more influential position in derivative Christian religious thinking and folk beliefs. In the New Testament, Satan and the cohorts of evil spirits who do his bidding are represented by the Judeo-Christian writers as forming an all-enveloping cosmic force and determinant in the moral conduct of individuals. "Casting out the Devil" from the possessed became an important magical function ascribed by the Apostles to Jesus. The Devil appears in Christian scriptural writings under a number of names, such as Satan, Adversary, the Enemy, the Accuser, the Old Serpent, the Great Dragon, Beelzebub, Belial. Also, the worst of all possible roles in Christian theology is assigned to him; he is represented as the Antichrist, the unscrupulous enemy of man, striving with might and main to prevent the second coming of "the Messiah Jesus." This notion of the Antichrist probably is derived from a well-known post-Biblical Hebrew writing called The Sayings of Rabbi Eliezer. It is told therein how, when God showed the Messiah to Satan, the latter "trembled, fell upon his face, and cried out: 'Truly, this is the Messiah who shall cast me and all the princes of the demons down into Gehinnom!"

See also AMULETS; ANGELS; EVIL EYE; GEHINNOM; PASSIONS, MASTERY OVER; SIN AND SINNERS; YETZER TOB AND YETZER HA-RAH.

SAYINGS OF THE FATHERS. *See* MISHNAH (under TALMUD).

SCHOLARS. *See* ARABIC-JEWISH "GOLDEN AGE"; BIBLE, THE; CHACHMAH; SAGES, RABBINIC; SOME ARCHITECTS OF JEWISH CIVILIZATION; TALMID CHACHAM; TALMUD, THE.

SCIENTISTS, EARLY JEWISH. *See* ARABIC-JEWISH "GOLDEN AGE"; HEALERS, THE.

SCRIBES (In Hebrew: SOFERIM; s. SOFER)

Ezra and those writer-scholars who were associated with him during the fifth century B.C.E. in compiling, codifying, revising, and editing the twenty-four books of the Bible and, in addition, in teaching and interpreting their Hebrew texts to the Jewish people, were called Soferim or Scribes. Some modern historians, rightly or mistakenly, have identified them as members of that select religious-intellectual circle called "the Men of the Great Synagogue" or "the Men of the Great Assembly." These Elders flourished in the Kingdom of Judah from the middle of the fifth century B.C.E. to the time of the High Priest Simon the Just—a little less than two centuries.

In a very literal sense, just as the Christian monks in medieval Europe were considered bookish men because they knew how to read and write, so were the Soferim distinguished in their day for possessing the same abilities. In the popular mind, to know how to read and write was equivalent to being "wise." (Ezra himself was dignified in the Bible as "a ready scribe in the Law of Moses.") Until the period of these Scribes, the supervision and the teaching of religion and the various Hebrew Scriptural writings that concerned them lay exclusively in the hands of the priests who, as in all other religions, served as the mediators between man and God. Theirs was an esoteric body of religious knowledge, replete with magical elements and with a dramatic array of Temple sacrifices, rites, and ceremonies to beguile the unlettered worshipers, whose role in religion was, to a large extent, a passive one, and emotionally arid besides. In the frame of reference of the lofty teachings of the Prophets, this kind of religious primitivism and formalistic worship appeared utterly inconsistent and frustrating, lacking in that intellectual cohesion and moral content it was first to acquire several hundred years later.

The innovations introduced by Ezra and the Scribes to the Jewish people amounted to a virtual religious, social, and cultural revolution. This "revolution" had come about in a phenomenal manner, but partly as a result of the national disaster suffered by the Jewish people at the hands of their Babylonian conquerers in the sixth century B.C.E. While in captivity in Babylonia, they had undergone an intellectual metamorphosis which had altered and refined their entire world outlook. For one thing, during their exile, many Jews had broadened their culture, had become conversant with the religious literary and historical writings and with the legal codes of the Babylonians. Having lost, through their own negligence and apathy, the thread of their own troubled history and cultural values, they began to appreciate more what it would mean to gather and safeguard all Jewish historical, literary, and legal records—an intellectual activity in which the more cultured Babylonians had showed them the way. Under the stimulation of this new-found cultural awakening, some of the best minds among the exiles began to ponder the written corpus of their own history, religion, and laws, including the Oral Traditions that had survived concerning them. They soon discovered that these were in a state of utter chaos and contradition, and required close critical analysis, editorial sifting, revision, ordering, and final codification before they could present to any extent a cohesive unity.

The principle concern of Ezra and the Scribes was to collate the scattered and random Scriptural documents into an anthologized and canonical arrangement. They carefully scrutinized and finally selected individual Hebrew writings of a religious or devotional character and, where necessary, apparently revised, interpolated, and edited them to bring them into closer line with their own advanced ideas. In order to preserve in unaltered permanence the Torah they had thus compiled, they instituted a remarkable system of textual "guards" around the Scriptures (*see* MASORAH). Also, they became dedicated to the task of making as many correct copies as possible of the Torah, and at the same time they began the systematic codification of religious tradition or Oral Law. This, in the second century of the Common Era, culminated in the completion of the Mishnah, the central work of the entire literature of the Talmud.

The Scribes started their great religious-educational ministry by teaching the fundamental principles of the Torah to the people and then by explaining it to them, chapter by chapter, verse by verse. "And they read in the book, in the Law of God, distinctly; and they gave the sense, and caused them to understand the reading." (Nehemiah 8:8.) Since the fundamental concern of the Scribes was to perpetuate for all time the knowledge of what they revered as the "revealed truths" of the Torah, they therefore made Torah study obligatory, initiating for this purpose what was probably the first democratic and free public school system in history, one that remained unknown to the rest of the world until its introduction in the United States early in the nineteenth century. In setting this up, the Scribes succeeded in undermining the exclusive, privileged position of the aristocratic priesthood, whose members finally were forced to make way for the humble but dedicated Rabbinic teachers whose cultural as well as religious influence remained undisputed.

Some critics of the religious-educational work of Ezra and the other Scribes, while conceding that it constituted a democratic revolution without parallel in history because it encouraged religion to be practiced directly by every individual Jew without the intervention of a mediator, point out what they nevertheless regard as a serious negative element. They claim that the "freezing" into an immutable form of the Scriptural texts and of the religious laws, rites, and practices in the complete theocracy established by Ezra and the Scribes had a stultifying effect on the basic rites and practices, with the result that religious observance became rigid and unchanging tradition.

See also BIBLE, THE; MASORAH; RABBI; SOFER; TALMUD, THE; THEOCRACY; TORAH STUDY.

SEARCH FOR LEAVEN. *See* PASSOVER.

SEDER, THE. *See* PASSOVER.

SEDREH. *See* SIDRAH.

SEFARADIM (Hebrew pl.; s. SEFARADI)

The word Sefaradim is derived from the Biblical Sefarad, the name of an unidentified country to which Jewish exiles were said to have been brought from Jerusalem and in which they were colonized. Medieval Jewish scholars were certain that

Sefarad was the ancient name for Spain and Portugal. In consequence, following their Expulsion from Spain in 1492, the Jews who had come from the Iberian peninsula, as well as their descendants, were called Sefaradim.

As a regional group living under different environmental and historic conditions from the Ashkenazim of Central and East European countries, the Sefaradim developed their own recognizable ethnic cultural physiognomy. To the student of the Jewish religion, however, the designation Sefarad has another meaning, entirely unrelated, the geographic and ethnic group character. It represents a specific order of prayer—of customary rites and ceremonies—called the Minhag Sefarad, and it differs in various particulars from that of the Minhag Ashkenaz, observed in their synagogues by the Jews of German, Polish, and Russian stock.

The Sefaradim cling to a persuasive tradition that both their pronunciation of Hebrew, which is quite different from that of the Ashkenazim, and their liturgy as well, originated with the Geonim of the Talmudic academies of Babylonia. Their text and order of prayer (nusach) are said to be based on the Siddur of Amram.

It is an oddity in Jewish religious history that the Chasidic sect, the revivalist cabalistic-mystic movement which shook Ashkenazic Jewry to its depths during the second half of the eighteenth century, discarded the Minhag Ashkenaz for the Minhag Sefarad. This was due to the fact that they drew many of their mystical notions as well as some ritual customs and practices from the Palestinian and Turkish Cabalists, who were Sefaradim. In consequence, Chasidism represents a remarkable fusion of religious-cultural elements from both branches of European Jewry.

Settlements of Sefaradim are found today in most countries of the world, although they are far less numerous than those of the Ashkenazim. Responding to the natural desire of all mankind to group itself like with like, the Sefaradim (the same holds true of the Ashkenazim) lived almost entirely apart from other Jews for almost five centuries in their own religious and social communities; until the Nazi period they but rarely intermarried with the Jews of Germany and Slavic countries. No doubt they were held together in their ethnic separatism by the definable and the intangible bonds of common historic experiences, the same regional manner of worship, their vernacular Jewish language (Ladino), and a group-culture rich in Moorish-Iberian folkways and customs differing in many ways from those of the Ashkenazim.

Although of minor import, since both of these wings of Jewry are religiously and culturally rooted in the same Torah and Rabbinic laws, in Jewish ethical values and traditions, some of the differences that can be noted between them were, no doubt, produced by diverse environmental and cultural influences.

One interesting divergence in the two liturgies as they developed during the Middle Ages was revealed in the taste and quality of the devotional poems (in Hebrew: *piyyutim*, s. *piyyut*) each rite incorporated in its prayer books. The liturgy of the Ashkenazim was strongly partial to the fervently expressive but crudely versified piyyutim of Eleazar ben Kalir, a Palestinian poet of the eighth or ninth century; that of the Sefaradim of Spain, Portugal, and the Provence, was enriched with stirring and evocative piyyutim by the great Hebrew master-singers of the Arabic-Jewish Golden Age (q.v.): Solomon ibn Gabirol, Judah (Yehudah) Halevi, Abraham ibn Ezra, and Moses ibn Ezra. However, the Ashkenazim, although less discriminating in their literary standards than the more sophisticated and knowledgeable Sefaradim, eventually succumbed to the beauty and the spirituality of these Sefaradic poems and entered many into their prayer books.

A matter of some oddity is the contrasting treatment accorded the Kol Nidre (q.v.) prayer on Yom Kippur Eve by the Sefaradim and Ashkenazim. For centuries among the Ashkenazim it has been sung by the chazzan to a hauntingly expressive melody, one which Beethoven introduced into one of his last quartets, whereas in Catalonia, among the Sefaradim, the Kol Nidre was at first entirely absent from the prayer-service. Although it was in later times introduced into the Sefaradic machzor, however, it was not sung but intoned.

An amusing difference in the manner of reciting the prayers was noted by the famous codifier of Jewish laws Jacob ben Asher (*d.* Spain, 1340). Said he: "The children of Sefarad cast down their eyes when they pronounce *kadosh, kadosh, kadosh!* [holy, holy, holy!] while the children of Ashkenaz turn their eyes upwards as they raise their bodies." The Sefaradim lowered their eyes because they were filled with awe by the mere thought of God's holiness; the Ashkenazim raised them to heaven for the identical reason. Another example of differences between them was cited by Jacob Mölln, the German rabbinical authority of the fourteenth century. He stated that at an Ashkenazic wedding, to recall to the groom at the height of his rejoicing that the Temple in Jerusalem had been destroyed (in 70 C.E.)—a catastrophe which remained the bitterest single memory in the grief-consciousness of the Jewish devout—ashes of mourning were sprinkled on his head; endowed with the same symbolic meaning of mourning was the Sefaradic custom of placing an olive wreath on the groom's head.

Rigidly observed for many centuries has been the custom of the Ashkenazim of naming their children *only* after deceased parents or grandparents; the Sefaradim follow the divergent custom of naming the child after a *living* grandparent or parent. The Ashkenaz form of congratulation at weddings is the well-known *"mazel-tov"* (good luck"); the Sefarad formula is *be' siman tob* ([may it be] in good season).

Burial customs are also diverse. In former times (much less so today) it was the practice among the Sefaradim to solemnly blow the shofar during the rite of taharah (the washing the body before interment), but this custom was unknown among the Ashkenazim. During the Middle Ages, at the time of the Crusaders' massacres of the Jews, when the despair of the Jewish communities in the Rhineland reached such a point that it seemed they must resign themselves to inevitable extermination, those who did survive touchingly offered, as a last consolation to those who perished, a little earth brought from the Holy Land. This was cast into the graves before they were closed to affirm the indestructible Jewish certainty that, when the Resurrection would come, the martyred dead would rise again to life eternal. Before very long the Iberian Jews, although they had been spared the terrors of the Knights of the Cross, adopted this custom of placing a sack of such earth in the graves and cling to it to this day.

No Jewish ethnic group ever remained long insulated from other Jewish ethnic groups; Ashkenazim and Sefaradim, in the natural interplay of a common identity, a common heritage, and a common historic destiny, left deep religious and cultural imprints, one on the other.

Today's Sefaradic communities and congregations are to be found principally in Turkey, Greece, Bulgaria, Yugoslavia, Asia Minor, Israel, North Africa, England, Holland, the United States, and Latin-American countries. Many Sefaradim are descendants of those Spanish and Portuguese Jews who were expelled from their native countries upon their refusal to become apostates from their religion. But still others claim descent from the Marranos, those "New Christians" who, despite their formal conversion to Catholicism under duress, secretly practiced, in defiance of the Inquisition, Jewish rites and ceremonies in their native Spain and Portugal until the opportunity came for them to escape to Mohammedan and Protestant lands where they were allowed to live openly as Jews again.

The Sefaradim, in contrast to the Ashkenazim for whom, by and large, Yiddish is the vernacular, employ Ladino as their group "Jewish" language. Written in cursive Hebrew characters, it consists mainly of Castilian flavored with Turkish, Arabic, and Greek words and idioms. In addition to Castilian, the principal language ingredient is Hebrew, employing Biblical, Talmudic, and later rabbinical nomenclature and expressions. By adding Hebrew case endings, prefixes, and suffixes, Ladino Hebraicised many Spanish words, and vice versa.

See also ASHKENAZIM; CONVERSION OF JEWS; JEWISH LANGUAGES; KOL NIDRE; MARRANOS AND THE INQUISITION; PRAYER AND WORSHIP; SIDDUR.

SEFER TORAH. *See* TORAH SCROLL.

SEFIROT, THE TEN. *See* CABALA.

SELF-MASTERY. *See* PASSIONS, MASTERY OVER.

SELICHOT (Hebrew pl.; S. SELICHAH, meaning "he forgave")

The Selichot are penitential prayers usually written in verse form and dating from the seventh century. They are supplications to God for forgiveness, and each worshiper, when reciting them, presents himself before the judgment of Heaven as a humble petitioner, fully conscious of being a sinner and unworthy of God's compassion—which he implores, nevertheless.

There are many such prayers found in the siddur (daily prayer-book) and machzor (prayer book for holy days), and they are turned to for succor during every crisis by the religious traditionalist. He recites them to obtain divine help in time of grief and suffering and to ward off any calamity—even death—that may threaten him, his family, and his community in time of war and massacre, conflagration and hunger, pestilence and persecution. The Selichot have ever been a crutch and solace to the Jew of faith.

Principally, however, the Selichot are reserved as fuel of moral introspection for the Yamim Noraim—the "Days of Awe" that begin on the first day of the Jewish month of Tishri (on Rosh Hashanah) and end ten days later on the Day of Atonement (Yom Kippur). In many Orthodox congregations, Selichot are recited every day before dawn for an additional one or two weeks preceding Rosh Hashanah, in order to help create in the individual the proper mood for honest self-examination for the Days of Awe, when the alarum of the shofar tries to awaken his slumbering conscience with thoughts of regret and repentance.

Since ancient days, it has been the custom for Jews to rise from sleep at midnight during the Days of Awe in order to hasten to the house of prayer for the recitation of the Selichot. In the small towns and also in the city ghettos of Eastern Europe, they would be awakened by the shammes (the beadle of the synagogue) as he made the rounds from house to house. He would knock loudly three times upon the door with his wooden klapper, intoning in Yiddish to the singsong of a traditional melody: "O Israel! O holy people! Awake! Rouse yourselves! Get up for the service of the Creator!

This rising at midnight for communion with God found Biblical authority in the words of the Psalmist: "At midnight I will rise to give thanks unto Thee." (Psalms 119:62.) The custom was observed most faithfully of all by the mystics—the Cabalists and their continuators, the Chasidim. A Hebrew writer during the time of the Lutheran Reformation gave this explanation for midnight prayer: "And the Holy One hears the prayers that one utters at midnight . . . and He answers them, because that is the hour of divine good-will when the Holy One, blessed be He, is reminded of the Destruction of the Temple and of the Exile of Israel among the nations. Therefore, He has compassion on them and is merciful to them."

Perhaps most revealing, in an ethical sense, is the fact that, in former times, the man chosen by the congregation to lead it in the Selichot supplications was regarded as its "defense counsel" before God. To merit this appointment, he first had to declare himself as being free of all hatred, resentment, and prejudice, and found, in the judgment of the elders, in truth to be so. This moral requirement of the pleader was laid down in a rabbinical decision by Meir ben Isaac Katzenellenbogen (1482–1565) of Padua, Italy: "He must say explicitly that he will include his enemy in his prayer, the same as every other man."

The purgation of the spirit from all its impurities was the aim of the Selichot in order that it might lead the sinner to full repentance. The themes of the Selichot are varied, but they principally are broodings upon individual man's personal worthlessness, which shows that the flesh is weak and the spirit not always willing. They are confessions of moral weakness and of straying, cries of despair "out of the depths," made in the certainty that God will be moved to grant pardon for sins committed and faith not kept. Yet, quite characteristically, Jewish ethical tradition requires that the individual suppliant should not raise too great a clamor for his guilt-laden soul alone. There are many Selichot that also implore forgiveness from God for *all* Jews, that plead with him to redeem Israel and to put an end to the Exile and to the martyrdom of the faithful: "Remember the covenant with Abraham and the binding of Isaac," beseeches Rabbenu Gershom (tenth century), "the Light of the Exile," in the most solemn of all Selichot, which is recited on Rosh Hashanah, "and lead back the seed of Jacob from Exile! Help us for the sake of Thy Name! We have wandered from one exile to another, yet we have never forsaken the Torah."

The literature of Hebrew Selichot is vast, with a time-range of a thousand years, and only partly explored. Several thousands, written by hundreds of poets in many lands, are extant. Some have exceptional beauty *as poetry*, having been written by the truly great poets of medieval Spain: Solomon ibn Gabirol, Judah (Yehudah) Halevi, Moses ibn Ezra, and Abraham ibn Ezra. Almost all are charged with a deep emotionalism appropriate to prayers of introspection and regret. Their styles of versification are naturally varied, being drawn or adapted from the contemporary verse patterns of the nations in which their writers lived. Thus, the influences of non-Jewish cultures—Byzantine, Persian, Syrian, Arabian, and the like—are strongly in evidence.

The Selichot represent an impressive body of Jewish religious poetry, one that grapples with the problems of moral conduct with a gravity unequaled perhaps in all of world literature.

See also HYMNS OF THE SYNAGOGUE; PRAYER AND WORSHIP; REPENTANCE; SIN AND SINNER.

SEMICHAH. *See* RABBI.

SEPARATISM, JEWISH

In the tangle of many reasons that might explain the enmity of many non-Jews for Jews, one reason in particular must not be overlooked—that of xenophobia. As used in psychiatry, the term denotes an irrational fear of strangers.

The explanation for this disquietude is not too hard to find. Speaking historically, no religious group has ever appeared as strange or as disturbingly different to the unthinking, the uninformed, and the prejudiced as the Jews. The historic fact is that, while living as a small, persecuted minority in the midst of other peoples during their long Dispersion (which began in 70 C.E.), the Jews led, more or less, a *separatist* existence; sometimes they were a semiautonomous religious-ethnic community, at other times they were accorded official recognition as a quasi-ecclesiastical "congregation." Their distinctive status—that of a nonconformist group standing outside of the general social-cultural structure—naturally marked them as a "peculiar," "stand-offish," and "stiff-necked" people and, concomitantly, often drew the hostile conclusion from their enemies that they were also "alien" and "unassimilable."

The real explanation for their separatism was, of course, not understood by non-Jews until modern times—and then only by enlightened persons—when the historical method was introduced into the study of religion and culture. The new approach made it plain that the Jewish religion had originated in what was a theocratic or God-governed society, where every single aspect of human existence—whether economic, social, intellectual, bodily, or spiritual—was strictly subordinated to the commandments, laws, regulations, and traditions of the Torah. Jewish believers were perhaps different from every other kind of believer in the extent and intensity of their religious-group identity: This was a *dual* identity, one simultaneously of religion and of peoplehood—complementary concepts based on the all-embracing covenant declared in the Bible to have been established between God and Israel at Mount Sinai in the days of Moses. On that occasion, in accepting the Torah, the Jews were said to have solemnly dedicated themselves to serve their God as "a nation of priests" forevermore. And so—the better to preserve their religious identity, group cohesiveness, and quasi-priestly "purity"—the Jews stood apart: "After the doings of the land of Egypt, wherein ye dwelt, shall ye not do; and after the doings of the land of Canaan, whither I bring you, shall ye not do; neither shall ye walk in their statutes." (Leviticus 18:3.)

The reasons for this separatism were well understood by Hecataeus of Abdera, the Greek historian of the fourth century B.C.E. He wrote that Moses had given the Jews laws and customs which were different from those of other peoples, and that he had done this in order to keep them apart as a nation so that they might be preserved inviolably as such.

However, such knowledgeable insight as that of Hecataeus was only too rarely in evidence among non-Jews. The fact is that Jewish "separatism" offered a justification and a pretext to many a rabble-rouser and greedy ruler for oppressing and robbing the Jews. Even in the Book of Esther (3:8-9), in the Bible, the royal vizier, Haman, in asking King Ahasueros' permission to exterminate all the Jews in Persia, presented this same argument, but in distorted form:

> There is a certain people scattered abroad and dispersed among the peoples in all the provinces of thy kingdom; and their laws are diverse from those of every people; neither keep they the king's laws; therefore it profiteth not the king to suffer them. If it please the king, let it be written that they be destroyed. . . .

This type of enmity toward Jews became a virtual stereotype during the Hellenistic phase of Roman antiquity. In the first century C.E., for example, the Greek rhetorician, Apollonius Molon, drew the derisive refutation from the Judean historian, Josephus, for being "one of those crazy fools" who condemned the Jews for staying aloof from "persons with other preconceived ideas about God, and for declining to associate with those who have chosen to adopt a different mode of life." That this reserve was nothing unusual, declared Josephus, could be seen in the fact that many Greeks also stood aloof from close contact with strangers: "The Lacedaemonians [Spartans] made a practice of expelling foreigners and would not allow their own citizens to travel abroad" for fear that their laws and their morals might become corrupted.

One century later, that thorough reprobate—the Roman satirical poet, Juvenal, who was, actually, no worse than his fellow wits, Horace and Martial, made short shrift of the truth when, with seeming sincerity, he detailed certain "barbarous" ways of the Jews: "They become accustomed to despise Roman laws, and study, observe and revere only the Jewish laws—whatever Moses had handed down in a secret volume [the Torah!]; namely, to refuse to show a traveler the way unless he is a coreligionist, or to lead anyone to a drinking-place unless he is circumcised."

All the Roman, Egyptian, and Greek satirists and pamphleteers of the period concentrated on one theme: the pernicious social separatism and religious particularism of the Jews. Their provocation had persuasive grounds; of all religious groupings in the vast Hellenistic world, only the Jews stubbornly refused to submit themselves to the process of religious fusion. True, they had become Greco-Romans linguistically, intellectually, culturally, in appearance, and even in name, but they were steadfast in their refusal to abandon the Jewish religion. Their granite-like resistance and alleged group-clannishness shocked the celebrated orator-politician Cicero (first century B.C.E.) to such a degree that he became—and remained—irrationally, violently and—not entirely without calculation—an enemy of the Jews. "You know very well how numerous that class [Jews] is, with what unanimity they act, and what strength they exhibit in the political meetings," orated he, hardly with disinterestedness, in *pro Flacco*. He emphasized, too, the religious and cultural gulf that divided the Romans from the Jews: "Our ancestral institutions are as different from theirs as they well can be. Now, however, there surely can be all the less obligation upon us to respect Jewish religious observances when that nation has demonstrated in arms [i.e., in uprisings against Rome] what its feelings are toward Rome, and has made clear how far it enjoyed divine protection by the fact that it has been conquered, scattered, enslaved."

The repeated and always costly Jewish uprisings against Rome in Judea and in other Jewish settlements in the Diaspora such as Antioch, Libya, and the Greek cities, proved humiliating in the extreme to the pride of the patricians who belonged to the "master race" of the Caesars. Enmity for the Jews, therefore, found a fertile soil for growth in the Roman Empire.

But the Roman resentment of the Jews was not the only source of anti-Semitism in antiquity. One might say that hatred of the Jew in Hellenistic Egypt antedated even that of Rome, although under Roman hegemony it was accentuated. The world-metropolis, Alexandria, only superficially Grecized but profoundly decadent, was the chief hotbed of the infection. Not a little of this hostility was engendered by the issuance of the Bible in the Greek Septuagint translation and by such Jewish missionary, polemical, and apocalyptic writings that were composed in the Greek language as the Fourth Book of Maccabees, The Wisdom of Solomon, The Book of Esdras, The Testaments of the Twelve Patriarchs, and The Sibylline Oracles. In all of these agitational works, the God of Israel and the Jewish way of life leading to salvation were extolled to the detriment of the pagan gods and the pagan way of life.

It might be said that in Rome the various notions about

the wickedness of the Jews and the spirit of hatred for them had been implanted and nurtured by the intellectuals: the historians, the orators, the philosophers (even Seneca, the Stoic moralist), and the poets—in short, the so-called "choice spirits." But it was in Alexandria that anti-Semitism first bloomed from the grass roots.

Although, in the city of Rome—notwithstanding what Cicero had observed concerning its supposed political power and influence—the Jewish community never occupied the privileged status it did in Egypt under the Romans (especially in Alexandria, where the Jews composed more than a third of the population, and their cultural, social, economic, political, and legal position was superior to that of the native Egyptian masses, who remained backward and immersed in animistic religious worship and practices), here, too, the Jews succeeded in obtaining their religious, legal, and political rights only by dint of rigorous and collective self-assertion. Yet always they were regarded as "aliens," and, always, they stood in an inferior relationship to those Alexandrians of Greek or Roman descent. They were able, however, to practice their religion without molestation; they built fine synagogues and observed the Sabbath, the dietary laws, and the rite of circumcision. Furthermore, they were well organized as a separate, semiautonomous community with all of its supporting institutions. They even had their own traditional courts presided over by rabbinical judges.

Once again, Jewish religious and communal separatism served as the peg on which the anti-Semites could hang their calculated distortions, misrepresentations, and libels. In the third century B.C.E., Manetho, an Egyptian who was the high priest of the Greek temple at Heliopolis and also court historian to the early Ptolemaic kings, concocted a "history" of the Israelite Bondage in Egypt in which, among many other weird observations, he ridiculed the claim of the Jews that they had fought their way into freedom, countering it with the assertion that they had actually been *expelled* from Egypt because they were afflicted with leprosy and scrofula!

It is a wry commentary on the reliability of historical writings, and no less a source for amazement, that the famous Roman historian, Tacitus, should have chosen to adopt some of the fictions of Manetho in the fifth book of his *History*. He even concluded that the laws of the Jews are "hostile to men and calculated to inspire the Jew with hatred and opposition to the rest of mankind . . . the first instruction they [the Jewish children] receive is to despise the [Roman] gods, to forswear their country, to forget father, mother, and children."

Amusingly enough, one century later, the Greek Mnaseas circulated, under the pretense of enlightened religious criticism, the no less ridiculous fiction that became widespread during that era: that an ass's head was enshrined in the Holy of Holies of the Temple in Jerusalem because the Jews worshiped it as the most sacred symbol of their religion!

A dramatic juncture in the history of the struggle of the Jews in behalf of their religious and group identity was reached in 168 B.C.E., when the Hasmonean priestly family, the Maccabees, sparked their successful revolt against the Greek Seleucidan despot Antiochus (Epiphanes) IV. Whether this epic encounter between the Jewish patriots and the foreign overlord—an event that is commemorated annually in the Feast of Lights, Channukah—was provoked by Antiochus' personal hatred of the Jews or of the Jewish religion, is not altogether clear. At any rate, if his harsh decrees against Jewish religious practices are to be classified as authentic anti-Semitism, which they may very well have been, they should be accompanied by the additional explanation that Antiochus seemed to have had something else in mind than merely giving vent to his animus.

It should be remembered that Antiochus was a ruler with a totalitarian conception of governing, implacably determined to force all the peoples he conquered to conform to the Greek way of life in order that he should be able to hold them the more easily in subjection. As the Jewish Scroll of Antiochus recounts, the Seleucidan king issued a decree *"that all should be one people, and that each should forsake his own laws."* This, it is obvious, was his principal, even if not the only, motive for having ordered the Jews to end their worship in the Temple and to give up offering sacrifices to the God of Israel. He also required them to break *demonstratively* with their religious laws and observances: that they "should profane the Sabbath and feasts and pollute the sanctuary . . . should build altars and temples and shrines for idols; and should sacrifice swine's flesh . . . and that they should leave their sons uncircumcised." And as for him who did not obey "the word of the king, he shall die!" In the face of this threat the Jews decided that, if they *had* to die, they would do so defending their most sacred values, which they did, and triumphantly.

Although every previous manifestation of hatred toward the more than a million Jewish inhabitants of Egypt had been in character mostly agitational, whipped up by self-serving rabble-rousers and literary hacks, it suddenly took an ominous turn after the insane Caligula became emperor of Rome in 37 C.E. He insisted, basing his claim to divinity on firm Roman tradition, that he was a god, and as such, was to be worshiped by all his subjects; he therefore ordered the Jews to put up a statue to him in the Temple sanctuary in Jerusalem and in every one of their numerous synagogues throughout the Roman Empire. Naturally, the Jews refused, for to comply would have been a cardinal blasphemy—one violating the awesome Second Commandment against idolatry.

The then Roman Governor of Egypt, Flaccus, who was no friend of the Jews, thereupon made the most of their quiet but firm resistance. He gave free rein to the Egyptian demagogues to inflame popular passions. What occurred was only inevitable: Bloody riots ensued in 38 C.E. and several times subsequently, and each time Flaccus penalized *the Jews* heavily for the singular crime of being the victims of mob violence! These riots constituted the first bona fide massacres in Jewish history and set the stage for numerous others that soon followed. Each time Jewish armed rebellion against Roman tyranny flared up anew, it was more fierce; each time it ended in a struggle that was virtually to the death.

During the early rule of the Romans in Judea, the Jews felt the conqueror's mailed fist bear down crushingly on their political and economic life; yet in matters purely religious, the Jews both in and away from their homeland, in their many settlements throughout the Empire and even in the city of Rome, enjoyed considerable freedom of worship. But all this began to change several decades before the final Dispersion in 70 C.E., when anti-Jewish feeling spread like a forest fire.

Persecution of the Jews by the Romans on a systematic basis started during the reign of the Emperor Tiberius; in the year 19 C.E., he had ordered the expulsion of all Jews from Rome. From that time on, repressive measures were increasingly imposed. For example, in Judea, the Sanhedrin, the supreme religious-legislative-judicial council of the Jews, composed of seventy-one leading priests and elders, found itself stripped of many of its traditional functions and powers. The Jewish kinglets of Judea who were placed over the people by the conqueror were little more than tax-collectors and assistants to the Roman procurator resident in Jerusalem; they served as willing tools of the foreign despots, helping to keep the Jewish people cowed and submissive.

Over the course of the more than hundred years following, there were many abortive and bloody revolts aimed at driving out the Romans from Judea, the most terrible of them being the siege of Jerusalem, in 69–70 C.E., in which more than a million Jews perished. The frequency of these rebellions, which culminated with the collapse of the Bar Kochba uprising in 132–35 C.E., and the savagery of the Roman reprisals against the Jewish population, left wounds that never healed. Moreover, they indelibly stamped the national Jewish psyche with bitterness and concomitantly helped strew the dragon's teeth of anti-Semitism in the vengeful Roman world. From then on, the Jews were pursued by an inexorable hatred —one which Christianity, as the state religion of Rome, later inherited and, in some significant ways, even deepened and extended.

See also ANTI-SEMITISM: THE "RACIAL PURITY" MYTH; APOCRYPHA; CHANNUKAH; CHURCH AND PERSECUTION; CONVERSION OF JEWS; DIASPORA; GHETTO; MISSIONARIES, JEWISH; NAZIS, THE; PERSECUTION IN "MODERN" DRESS; POGROMS IN SLAVIC LANDS; POST-BIBLICAL WRITINGS; PSEUDEPIGRAPHA.

SERMON (in Hebrew: DERASHAH; from it comes DARSHAN, meaning "preacher")

The institution of the sermon as an integral part of the Sabbath service in the synagogue or in the House of Study (Bet ha-Midrash) came into being after the Exiles' return from Babylonia. That was at a time when Torah study had assumed the universal character of a national-religious dedication. In effect, the sermon served as a primary source of popular adult education as well as a spiritual illumination for the Jewish people. The philosopher-rabbi Philo of Alexandria (first century B.C.E.) noted that the sermon, delivered in Greek, constituted one of the highlights of Sabbath worship in Hellenistic Egypt.

It was quite natural that preaching should have acquired increasing importance after the Temple cult on Mount Zion with its elaborate sacrifices and dramatic musical service came to an end (together with the Jewish state) in 70 C.E. Unusual emphasis was laid by all the Christian Gospel writers about that time on the institution of preaching. In actuality, Jesus of Nazareth and Paul of Tarsus had been indefatigable itinerant preachers (maggidim), expounding their sectarian (Essenic) religious views in the synagogues in traditional Jewish homiletic style.

Naturally, many of the synagogue sermons delivered by the regular preachers (darshanim) were scholarly. They were meant to be although they often degenerated into pedantry and dry-as-dust casuistry. The sermons of the itinerant maggidim were far less learned but, by the same token, more comprehensible and diverting to the taste of simple folk. During the Middle Ages and the early Renaissance, the sermons of the preachers of the Spanish, Provençal, and Italian Jews were naturally on a higher intellectual plane than those of their fellow religionists in Central and Eastern Europe, since their culture and degree of enlightenment were greatly superior as well. Because, in the world of Yiddish-speaking Jewry, incessant persecution and community uprooting had forced it to remain culturally backward, the sermons of its preachers were largely of an undistinguished order, although having a high ethical content. Either its maggidim were fervently pious and moralistic, or they aimed to dazzle with their virtuosity, so their sermons became merely a display for their vanity of learning, and the ethical values of which they preached were smothered in a downpour of Biblical references and citations from rabbinic authorities.

It became customary in medieval Europe for the sermon to be delivered from the almemor or raised platform in the center of the synagogue on Sabbath mornings and on the mornings of holy days, after the reading from the weekly portion of the Torah had taken place. But in Germany and in the Polish provinces, beginning with the seventeenth century, the sermon, having no connection with the prayer service but designed purely for illumination and moral uplift, would be preached during midafternoon. Traditionally, the preacher spoke in Hebrew, but with the later rise of the wandering maggidim who ministered to the small communities of town and village, the Yiddish vernacular was substituted in order to be more intelligible to the majority of listeners, who had little more than a reading knowledge of the sacred Hebrew tongue.

Like everything else in Jewish life, the form of the sermon, if not its contents or the language in which it was cast, has been in a state of flux ever since the end of the eighteenth century, when the ghetto walls and the isolation they enforced began to crumble. The quest for conformity to modern life in general naturally led to a number of accomodations. The influence of the Protestant sermon can be plainly seen today in both the construction and the technique of synagogue sermon composition and delivery. In the United States and in other English-speaking countries, the sermon is given in English, except in the Ultra-Orthodox Ashkenazic congregations, where the force of ghetto custom is so unyielding that the preaching is invariably done in Yiddish.

See also MAGGID.

SE'UDAH, SE'UDOT. *See* PURIM; ROSH HASHANAH; SABBATH; ZEMIROT.

SEX IN MARRIAGE. *See* MARRIAGE AND SEX.

SHABBAT, SHABBES. *See* SABBATH.

SHABBES GOY (Yiddish, meaning literally [a] "Sabbath Gentile")

The institution of the Shabbes goy, in which a Gentile is engaged to attend on the Sabbath in the Jewish household to several minor services specifically forbidden to the Jew by ritual law because it considered them a desecration of the day of rest, was peculiar to the East European Ashkenazim alone. It originated from the strict Sabbath prohibition against engaging in any kind of physical labor or exertion. The chores the Shabbes goy was asked to do were of the simplest kind, and included kindling a fire in the oven, fetching water from the well, removing the Sabbath candlesticks from the table, and, most particularly, extinguishing the candles or lamp on Friday night.

It was characteristic of the Shabbes goy that he was one of the most needy or least employable Gentiles in the community. The traditional reward for his slight labors was a large slice of white challah with, sometimes, a glass of brandy or a piece of gefilteh fish. In many instances, he would be paid a few coppers when the Sabbath was over.

It should, however, be noted in all objectivity that, despite the intense religiosity or even fanaticism of the East European ghetto Jew, his arranging for a Shabbes goy appears to be a violation of Rabbinic law. For the Talmudic teachers, at least, frowned upon the practice of hiring a Gentile to do the kind of work a Jew was himself enjoined from doing on the Sabbath. They declared: "To ask a Gentile to do work on the Sabbath is still a violation of the laws of the Sabbath."

It is intriguing to discover that in Czarist Russia, the country which once contained the largest Jewish population in the world and where the Shabbes goy had become a famil iar figure in the life of the ghetto, two of these shabbes goyim ultimately achieved world renown. These were Maxim Gorky, the writer, and Feodor Chaliapin, the basso. Each of them publicly mentioned or wrote, without any self-consciousness and some amusement, about this "distinction" of being a shabbes goy in his youthful days.

See also SABBATH.

SHABUOT (Hebrew pl., meaning "weeks"; thus: the "Feast of Weeks")

The recollection by the Jewish people of the consecration by God of their ancestors as "a holy people" at Mount Sinai, when Moses presented it with the covenant of the Torah, was made indelible by Jewish tradition in the two-day festival of Shabuot. In descriptive commemoration of that epochal event, this holy day is often referred to as *Zeman Matan Toratenu*–"the Season of the giving [to us] of [our] Torah."

Like a number of other Jewish festivals with a deeply religious and ethnic-national content, Shabuot, too, had an agricultural origin going much farther back than the Exodus from Egypt. This is indicated by another ancient name it bears: Chag ha-Bikkurim–the "Festival of the First Fruits." The Hellenistic Jews of Egypt, who spoke only Greek after the third century B.C.E., called Shabuot "Pentecost" (from the Greek *Pente Kostus,* meaning "fiftieth") because it was observed fifty days after the offering of the barley-sheaf made in the Temple in Jerusalem on the second day of Passover. Thus Shabuot was celebrated on the sixth day of Sivan (May-June).

The Rabbinic Sages, wishing to inspirit this harvest-festival with a higher religious meaning, concluded that the departure of the Israelites from Bondage in Egypt was, in reality, only the *prelude* to their liberation and not its *realization,* for the former slaves could not really be considered free, said the Rabbis in a striking paradox, until they had voluntarily taken upon themselves the liberating "yoke of the Torah." And it was the joyful acceptance by Israel of these very "fetters of freedom" on Shabuot, they said, which made that holy day the ageless anniversary of Israel's liberation from the slavery of mind and spirit.

Procession of singing kibbutz children bearing "first fruits" on Chag ha-Bikkurim (the Festival of First Fruits), during the holiday of Shabuot in Israel.

While the Temple still stood, Shabuot was observed as the second of three annual "pilgrim-festivals." It's culmination came at the sanctuary altar in Jerusalem with the offering of the first fruits of the summer harvest. When the time drew near for bringing these first fruits to the Temple, bands of pilgrims from every part of Judea and from many Jewish settlements abroad would fill the highways that led to Mount Zion. No doubt referring to the final period of the Second Temple, the Mishnah gives this vivid description of the festive spirit of these pilgrims, carrying their harvest burdens to the sanctuary altar:

> The people in the villages assemble in the principal town of their district. They pass the night in the open streets. At the break of dawn their leader calls out: "Arise! Let us go up to Zion to the House of our God!" All along the way these pilgrims sing psalms in unison, the favorite one being: "I Was Glad When They Said Unto Me, Let Us Go Unto the House of the Lord."

In modern Israel, Chag ha-Bikkurim—the Biblical festival on which the first fruits of the produce were brought to Jerusalem as Temple-offerings—has been transformed into a national demonstration of achievement by the agricultural settlements.

Those who came from nearby villages brought offerings of fresh figs and grapes. Those, however, who came from a distance, carried dried figs and raisins. As the procession wound its way among the hills that lay before Jerusalem, it was preceded by an ox, festively adorned: Its horns were overlaid with gold, and a wreath of olive leaves crowned its head. The pilgrims were bringing this animal for a sacrifice upon the Temple altar. All along the way to Jerusalem, the chalil (the double-reed pipe) sounded joyously. At the city gates, the procession halted, and the pilgrims were met by priests who led them with ceremony into the Temple precincts to the sound of the fluting of the pipes.

In later times, when the synagogue had taken the place of the Temple for congregational worship, the harvest rites were perpetuated during the festival in a symbolic manner only, and homes as well as synagogues were decorated with greenery and flowers. In every other way, the festival was stripped of its original primitive character and endowed with a new religious meaning. Thenceforth, it was observed as the day on which Israel had received the Torah from Mosheh Rabbenu, "Our Teacher Moses," at the foot of Mount Sinai. Today, in Israeli farm villages and kibbutzim (collective settlements), first fruits of the summer harvest are brought as communal displays of achievement.

In the synagogue on this festival of Israel's consecration to the service of God, the Book of Ruth is read aloud. The Sages considered the story that it tells appropriate for the occasion not only because it has a summer harvest setting, but because of the moral it teaches. Its emotional climax is reached when the Moabitess Ruth, upon her Jewish husband's death, refuses to part from her mother-in-law, Naomi, saying to her: "Entreat me not to leave thee, and to return from following after thee; for whither thou goest, I will go; and where thou lodgest, I will lodge; thy people shall be my people and thy God my God." (Ruth 1:16.)

The moral of this demonstration of total devotion was always being driven home to the Jewish devout in every generation. The Rabbis, marveling greatly, reasoned thus: If Ruth, a pagan woman of Moab, was capable of such a perfect act of faith and of cleaving to the Jewish people, how much more eager should Israelites themselves be to renew the covenant their forefathers had made with God at Mount Sinai!

Beginning with the Middle Ages, this Shabuot theme of consecration to the Torah was carried over into the field of child education. It became customary for parents to start their small boys in cheder (the religious school) on this festival. The symbolic meaning of the occasion was explained thus to the children: They were told that, by taking this first step in Torah-learning, they, too, were standing, as it were, side by side with their ancestors before the Lord at Mount Sinai. Fond parents were made conscious of the fact that the offerings they were bringing to God were the most precious of "first fruits" in all of Israel's harvest. From that custom there developed still another–one of only recent date: It is that of the group-confirmation of boys and girls in Reform and Conservative synagogues on this festival.

SHADCHAN (Yiddish, meaning "marriage broker")

The shadchan is the professional Jewish matchmaker or matrimonial agent. The calling of shadchan was already followed in twelfth-century Europe. In fact, in a more limited way, it was a clearly defined activity during the Talmudic period, for there are Rabbinic decisions regulating the shadchan's fees so as to avoid later misunderstandings. But it was during the Crusades, when so much of Jewish community life in Western and Central Europe was either destroyed or uprooted by expulsions and flights and—worst of all—by the decimation of the Jewish population through hundreds of massacres, that there arose a compelling need for the services of the shadchan. It was considered that, if the Jews were to survive under the incessant blows of their enemies either as a religious entity or as a people, their increase biologically was urgent. But its accomplishment had to be in keeping with the uncompromising religious and moral laws of "Moses and Israel," which meant through marriage only with Jews.

Under these unusual circumstances, the shadchan was required to be a dedicated man. The practice of matchmaking often involved grave risks to life and limb, for the shadchan had to journey, uneasily at all times, from town to town, through hostile territory, without any protection, in furtherance of his "holy work." So he served, at various times, as one of the few physical links connecting the widely scattered and insecure Jewish communities.

It is of interest that, during the Crusades and for several centuries thereafter, noted Torah scholars and rabbis acted as matchmakers. One example is that of the celebrated Torah scholar, Jacob Mölln (1365–1427), better known as Maharil. Rabbi of Mayence (Mainz), in the Rhineland, he undertook the part-time calling of shadchan as a labor of humanity and as an act of devotion to his people.

It is to be noted that, in the period directly preceding the modern era, when Jewish life in the ghetto had turned stagnant under constant persecution and repression, the ethical stature of the shadchan often declined as well. In the moralistic literature (written both in Hebrew and Yiddish) of the seventeenth century, he is enthusiastically roasted over the coals for his avarice and lack of conscience. With pointed sarcasm he is reminded that, in former times, not greedy hucksters like himself but high-minded rabbis were privileged to be matchmakers "for the sake of Heaven." At least one reason for the moral decline of the profession of shadchan was the fact that it was composed mainly of individuals with unstable characters and possessing no fixed occupation; they

An old-fashioned shadchan in a Russian Jewish community. Late 19th century.

were the ones most easily tempted into the highly speculative undertaking of matchmaking as a means of livelihood.

The average shadchan, to do him justice, was an honest intermediary–if you like, a broker or businessman who felt he was giving value for value. He had the reasonable expectation, therefore, of a fair fee for his services, and his commission–one previously agreed upon by all parties concerned–consisted of a small percentage of the dowry the bride brought with her. In the society of long ago, which was almost devoid of "modern" notions like "romantic" love and "marriage for love," the shadchan served a practical and useful function as a go-between.

Today, the shadchan, as a free-lance matrimonial agent, is rapidly disappearing, except in Orthodox circles. Changing culture patterns and the circumstances of modern life require of matchmaking that it operate with far greater delicacy and dignity. Even the contemporary businesslike matrimonial agency with its cold-blooded filing system and "consulting psychologist" has had to make way for less offensive and more "spontaneous" ways of matchmaking. These include the groups operated euphemistically as "social" or "cultural" clubs and as "friendship" circles. They certainly are more artful and discreet in their manner of bringing marriageable people together without hurting sensibilities. But in effect, the old-fashioned *shadchan* with his little black address book, his umbrella, his jovial talkativeness, his genius for exaggeration and for bringing together "a flea with an elephant (as the Yiddish saying goes)," did the very same thing, but he did it a little more straightforwardly.

See also DOWRY; MARRIAGE; WEDDING CUSTOMS.

SHALACHMONESS. *See* PURIM.

SHALIACH TZIBBUR. *See* BAAL TEFILLAH.

SHALOM. *See* PEACE, JEWISH CONCEPT OF.

SHAMMES (Yiddish; in Hebrew: SHAMMASH, meaning "servant")

The shammes is exactly what his name implies: the "servant" of the synagogue and of the congregation. In our day, he combines in his office some of the functions of the Christian verger, sexton, and beadle. He is both caretaker and general congregational factotum. Not a few of his tasks are of a menial character. He is expected to keep the synagogue swept, dusted, and in repair, and during the cold weather, also heated. All of the synagogue's properties, such as decorations and furnishings, including the Scrolls of the Torah and their silver ornaments, prayer books, and various ceremonial vessels and objects, are placed in his special custody.

The shammes was already a well-defined synagogue official during the Talmudic period, eighteen centuries ago. He was even then the communal messenger and slavey, ready to carry out the bidding or decisions of all the community's dignitaries. Beginning with the Middle Ages, he was obliged to transact much of the congregational business in his diversified capacities as executive assistant to the rabbi, the dayyan (judge), the parnas (president), and the gabbai (treasurer). He was the personification of the arm of the Jewish communal law; he saw to it that the orders and decisions of the Bet Din (the religious court) were carried out to the letter, and he also administered, under the limited Jewish self-government in the ghetto, the one kind of corporal punishment empowered the communal authorities by rabbinic law–"stripes" upon the backs of the most serious offenders.

In bygone days, the shammes also had the duty of announcing the exact arrival of the Sabbath, when all work and trading was to cease. He did this in earliest times by blowing the ram's horn or shofar; at a later period, during the Talmudic ages, he blew six blasts on a trumpet; and finally, beginning with the sixteenth century, he announced the arrival of the Sabbath by rapping several times with his wooden knocker (schulklopfer) on the door of each Jewish household, at the same time crying: *"In shul herein!"* or *"In shul arein!"* ("To the synagogue!")

A shammes calling to morning prayer–"Arise, Jews! To the service of the Creator!"–while he knocks loudly with a hammer on the shutters of each Jewish home in town. Poland, early 20th century.

But there were more "elevated" duties which kept him busy and harassed from early morning until late at night. For example, he collected membership dues and pledged contributions; he made all announcements of a congregational nature from the bema (synagogue platform); he summoned plaintiffs, .defendants, and witnesses before the Bet Din. If death struck a family, he was indispensable in making all arrangements pertaining to the funeral and burial, and he was invariably responsible for rounding up a minyan (the required quorum of ten worshipers for holding public prayer services) for the house in mourning. Similarly, in the celebration of all the important festivities and rites in the congregation–circumcision, Pidyon ha-Ben (Redemption of the First-Born), Bar Mitzvah, betrothal (tena'im), and wedding, he played a leading, though practically unnoticed, part in the proceedings. Perhaps to add a little melancholy glory to his harassed existence, whenever the cantor (chazzan) was vocally indisposed and there was no one else qualified to take his place, the shammes had the duty and honor of leading the congregation in prayer.

To top everything, he not only was required to be "strong as a lion and fleet as a hart" in the tireless service of the Lord and of the congregational bigwigs, he had to be something of a Torah scholar besides. Nevertheless, although he was endowed with multitudinous "talents" and worked to near exhaustion by his unending tasks, he remained, like most vergers, sextons, and beadles in the Christian churches, scandalously underpaid.

In our time, in pace with the changing historic scene, some of the functions of the shammes have sharply changed. In fact, the very word shammes is becoming somewhat archaic. Now, often as not, he prefers to masquerade under the churchly name of "sexton," and even has an assistant, who is more overworked than himself, to do the daily chores.

SHAS. *See* MISHNAH (*under* TALMUD, THE).

SHE'ALOT U-TESHUBOT. *See* RABBINICAL DECISIONS.

SHECHINAH (Hebrew, meaning literally "[the] Dwelling"; i.e., God's Presence or Radiance)

The term *Shechinah* was sometimes used interchangeably with the word God. It signified that he "dwelt" in or "rested" upon —so the expression went—those whose righteousness merited his favor, whether an individual, a community, or the entire Jewish people. When the conception of God reached that stage of development (in the days of the Second Temple) and it was deemed no longer proper to refer to him and to his attributes in anthropomorphic—i.e., physical—terms, as one would to a human being, the more abstract and symbolic term Shechinah was invented as a substitute.

Some scholars presume to see a striking connection between the concept of the Shechinah and the later Neo-Platonic idea of Logos—"the Word"—which Philo introduced into Jewish philosophical thinking and which was taken over with even greater emphasis in Christianity by several of its Hellenistic Jewish architects. The Gospel of John, for instance, opens with these suggestive words: "In the beginning was the Word, and the Word was with God, and the Word was God."

In the scheme of the Neo-Platonic doctrine of emanations or mediating powers, such concepts concerning the Deity as the Shechinah (God's "Presence"), the Holy Spirit (called in Christianity "the Holy Ghost"), and the Bat Kol ("the Daughter of the Voice," namely, God's Voice), proved very useful. What the essential differences among these terms were have never been satisfactorily established; they have often been used interchangeably and rather vaguely, as in the case with all mystical notions.

Tradition has it that the radiance of the Shechinah, with its untold blessings, "rests" upon all those who are pious and righteous. It appears, wrote the ancient Rabbis, in the midst of at least a minyan of worshipers when they pray in congregation, and of two or more Jews when they engage in Torah study, or on a man when he recites the Shema. It is said also to rest upon the chaste, the benevolent, and the hospitable, and upon husband and wife when they live in peace and harmony. The Shechinah, the Rabbis further said, appeared before Moses in the theophany of the Burning Bush; it rested upon the Tabernacle in the Wilderness on the day of its dedication, and in the Holy of Holies in the Temple at Jerusalem; and it has illuminated the bliss of the tzaddikim (saints) in the World-to-Come ever since.

Some Talmudic Sages conceived of the Shechinah as a spiritual essence of indescribable beauty and exalting effect. Their more literal-minded colleagues translated it into physical terms as a light and radiance. Its approach, they averred, was announced by a tinkling sound, like that of some ethereal bell. One legend even described the dying Moses as being lovingly enfolded in the "wings" of the Shechinah.

After the Destruction of the Second Temple (in 70 C.E.), the "Shechinah in Exile" became a haunting concept in Jewish thinking. The Talmud states that wherever the Jewish people go, the Shechinah follows. In not so remote times, a curious custom arose among East European Jewry: It was called in Yiddish *Golus uprechten.* Saintly men, as an expression of penance for all Israel, "went into Exile [Golus]." They wandered from town to town as mendicants and as mourners in order that they might share the "Exile of the Shechinah" and thereby hasten the end of the "Exile of Israel."

It is an interesting fact that Rabbi Elijah, the renowned Vilner Gaon, "went into Exile" when he was twenty, in 1740, and did not end it until eight years later.

See also BAT KOL; HALO; HOLY SPIRIT.

SHECHITAH (Hebrew, meaning "[ritual] slaughtering")

According to the dietary laws, it is not enough for certain species of animals to be classified as "clean" and, therefore, "permitted" for consumption as food by tradition observing Jews; it is also necessary that they be slaughtered in the prescribed ritualistic manner by a thoroughly trained, semireligious functionary: the shochet. The laws and regulations governing every detail of shechitah are exhaustive. Even though the Bible makes no special prescriptions for them, these laws must have evolved in the form of traditions since ancient times, being finally codified in the Talmud and expanded by rabbinic rulings since the Middle Ages.

Much public controversy has raged in recent times around the practice of shechitah. In almost every country it has served as a convenient springboard for attacks by anti-Semites who, in accordance with their familiar techniques, have not hesitated to distort and to misrepresent the objective facts concerning it. It is odd that in such countries with liberal traditions as Norway and Switzerland, in the years directly before World War II, the practice of shechitah was prohibited by law on the grounds that it constituted an act of "cruelty to animals." The aim of the anti-Semites, who were behind the enactment of this ban, palpably was to play on the sincere and humane sentiments of all animals-lovers, who, be it said, were not too well acquainted with the methods of shechitah. They wished to make capital out of the misconceptions regarding the practice that might arise on the part of well-meaning people by building up the rationale that the Jews are basically a cruel people. This slander was fostered zealously ever since the Middle Ages by enemies of the Jews. By the inferential method, they wished to tie it up to the supreme libel of all: that Jews were "Christ-killers." Nazi Germany made full capital out of the public row over shechitah to whip up popular prejudice against Jews.

These are the simple facts of shechitah: Whatever elements of primitive survival it may still hold, its primary intention was humanitarian. The Jewish religion sternly forbade the cruel treatment of animals. For instance, there were Biblical injunctions against the killing of an animal and its young at the same time, and against the practice, common among Israel's early neighbors, of chopping or tearing off a limb from a live animal for eating. The foremost Jewish religious authority since the Rabbinic Age, Maimonides (Moses ben Maimon, Spain, twelfth century), expounded on this point: "Since the need of procuring food necessitates the slaying of animals, the law enjoins that the death of the animal should be the easiest."

The practice of Jewish ritual-slaughtering greatly intrigued an impressive number of nineteenth-century physiologists, biologists, surgeons, and dietitians. Some important studies were made of it, and many among the investigators, who included those foremost Gentile scientists Lister, Virchow, and Vogt, concluded that shechitah not only was not cruel, but that, in fact, it was *the most humane and painless method* of slaughtering animals and one superior to non-Jewish methods such as anesthetizing, electrocuting, and knocking unconscious with a blow. For in shechitah, by one swift, clean stroke of the shochet's knife, the animal's jugular vein, windpipe, and gullet were promptly severed. The great gush of blood that resulted caused anemia of the brain and almost instantly rendered the animal unconscious and without sensation.

The investigators found, too, that from the point of hygiene, shechitah had much to recommend it, for the complete draining off of the blood enabled the meat to remain fresh longer. In this way, it was less open to bacteria forming with the resulting putrefaction, ptomaines, and other toxic matters. Biochemical examination of muscle tissue in animals slaughtered according to shechitah has convinced some investigators of its lower toxicity.

See also ANIMALS, "CLEAN" AND "UNCLEAN"; DIETARY LAWS; MEAT AND MILK; SHOCHET; TEREFAH.

SHEITEL (Yiddish, meaning "wig"; pl. SHEITLEN; sometimes also called PERUK, from the French *perruque*)

The sheitel is made either of false hair or, sometimes, from that hair clipped from the wearer's own head. The sheitel came into vogue probably during the late Middle Ages among the Central and East European Jews. According to one supposition, it must have originated from the desire of Jewish men to protect their wives against violation by Christian mobs in times of anti-Jewish excesses, and it followed logically from an old Jewish folk belief that the hair of a woman, like her voice, was endowed with an irresistible sexual attraction for the male—a view which was shared by the Church. This correlated with the taboo which forbade pious males to recite their prayers or to study Torah in a place where they could look upon a woman's uncovered hair.

This attitude is first discovered in the literature of the Talmud. The ancient Rabbis demanded strict observance of the custom that married women cover their hair at all times in order to eliminate it as a source of temptation to strange men. In the Mishnah, this custom is referred to as a "Jewish ordinance." In fact, for a married woman to appear in public with uncovered hair was considered sufficient grounds for divorce. The early Church Father, Tertullian, observed that it

Fruit vendors (East European) wearing the traditional sheitel of the married woman over their cropped hair. (Drawing by Regina Mundlak, Berlin, c. 1900.)

was possible to tell that a Jewish woman was married by the manner in which her hair was covered. Unmarried Jewish girls wore their hair braided and were not obliged to cover it by headdress, shawl, or veil.

Though there appears to have been no objection on the part of the medieval rabbis to the then new custom of clipping or shaving the head of a woman at the time of her marriage, the introduction of the sheitel did meet with considerable opposition. Originally, the sheitel was worn only during the Sabbath, on holy days, and on festive occasions, at times when no danger threatened the ghetto. It was undoubtedly meant to serve as compensation to the woman for the loss of her own hair. Therefore, there were some rabbinic moralists who contrasted the vanity of the Jewish women, which led them to wear sheitlen instead of simple shawls or kerchiefs, with the modesty and austere piety of the Christian nuns, who willingly covered their shorn heads not with wigs but rather in the manner required by custom of Jewish women! Needless to say, the Jewish women suffered by this comparison.

The sheitel, in short, was never required on religious grounds; it was adopted merely to satisfy feminine vanity. But custom is enduring. Concerning it, the rabbis were divided in their opinions. The eminent Moses Isserles (Poland, sixteenth century) viewed with disfavor the wearing of the sheitel, as did the religious authority Rabbi Moses Sofer (Czechoslovakia, eighteenth century) and his famous disciple, Akiba Eger. They found nothing in Jewish law and tradition—or, for that matter, in rabbinic decisions—that required a married woman to wear the sheitel. It was, they believed, an outmoded custom sanctified only by time and observance. Beginning with the nineteenth century, women in Eastern Europe began to wear their sheitlen in public but without the head-covering hitherto required. Well-to-do matrons started a new fashion, dressing their wigs in a variety of styles to make their appearance less unattractive.

All this time, in the Sefaradic and Oriental Jewish communities, the sheitel had never been adopted; instead, only a shawl, veil, or turban-like headdress was worn to cover the natural hair. Today, even among women of East European stock, the wearing of the sheitel is an oddity, seen only among the ever diminishing number of the Ultra-Orthodox.

SHELOSHIM. *See* BURIAL RITES AND CUSTOMS; SHIVAH.

SHEM HA-MEFORASH (Hebrew for "Tetragrammaton," which in Greek means "the four letters"; i.e., YHVH—those constituting the mystic name of God and pronounced Yahveh in English)

All religions have their special areas of mystery. One of these in the Jewish religion concerns the mystic name of God, and this was deemed so ineffably holy that it was utterable, and, therefore, kept secret. The folk imagination at fever pitch endowed the utterance of this name with the most miraculous powers. Its pronunciation was considered in Jewish tradition an intrusion into the divine mysteries and thus an unforgivable sacrilege. The privilege of learning how YHVH was to be pronounced literally was accorded only to a small number of the esoteric "elect" of heaven.

It is known, of course, that among the Jews, God was referred to by many names. But with regard to the Shem ha-Meforash, the Oral Tradition in the Mishnah laid down the rule: "In the sanctuary, the name of God is to be pronounced in the Priestly Benediction as it is written: *YHVH* [the English equivalent of the Hebrew letters *Yad Hay Vav Hay*]; but outside the sanctuary it must be paraphrased and pronounced as *Adonai* [generally, *Adoshem—'my Lord'*]."

During the time when the Temple still stood, the High Priest went up on the Day of Atonement—the most solemn occasion of public worship in the entire year—into the Holy of Holies to recite the Confession of Sins (Viddui) before all the people and the priests and Levites assembled. On that occasion, he and he alone was privileged to utter the awesome and mysterious name of God in the authentic manner. And when the worshipers heard him pronounce it, a great awe fell upon them, and they prostrated themselves and chanted fervently: "Praised be the glorious Name of His Kingdom forever and ever!" Then the priests and the Levites, accompanied by instrumental music, rolled forth a mighty doxology of homage.

It appears from references in post-Biblical and Talmudic literature that in Second Temple times, there were not a few religious notables who had received instruction in how to pronounce the Shem ha-Meforash. "In former times, the Name was taught to all," notes the Talmud mournfully, "but when immorality increased, it was reserved for the [select] pious alone."

It is odd that, by the second half of the twelfth century, the foremost religious authority of the Middle Ages, Moses Maimonides, stated that he had no knowledge of how the Shem ha-Meforash was to be pronounced. But some of the practical Cabalists and "wonder-workers" of the sixteenth and seventeenth centuries claimed that they had rediscovered the "secret." With the spread of Cabalistic notions and mystical practices, an inflamed folk-fancy, as articulated in numerous legends and myths, conceived of the Shem ha-Meforash as an instrument for working miracles; for instance, raising the dead, or flying to heaven to learn its secret and returning alive. By utilizing the mystic powers contained in the name of YHVH, the famous sixteenth-century Cabalist, the *Hohe* Rabbi Judah Löw of Prague, was reputed by folk legend to have infused the breath of life and human will into a lifeless lump of clay—the humunculus called a *golem* (*which see*).

It should be noted here that although the Hebrew Bible uses the Tetragrammation YHVH most frequently of all the names for God, Christian theologians, who had an inadequate knowledge of Hebrew punctuation and vowel-phonics, substituted for it, beginning with the year 1518, a distorted form of Yahveh; namely, Jehovah.

See also GOD, NAMES OF.

SHEMA, THE

At the very heart of Judaism lies the Shema, the fervent declaration of the Unity or Oneness of God:

> Hear, O Israel: the Lord our God, the Lord is One!
> And thou shalt love the Lord thy God with all thy heart, and with all thy soul, and with all thy might. And these words, which I command thee this day, shall be upon thy heart, and thou shalt teach them diligently unto thy children, and shalt talk of them when thou sittest in thy house, and when thou walkest by the way, and when thou liest down, and when thou risest up.
> DEUTERONOMY 6:4-7

This is the Jewish prayer most often recited, an affirmation most insistently made by the pious from childhood until death. Over the course of the centuries, from the days of the Sages on, as soon as a child began to speak, he was taught to repeat daily, with the utmost awe and reverence, the ringing Hebrew words of the Shema until he knew them by heart. He continued to repeat them twice a day in his prayers throughout all the days of his life. And the Shema was his last conscious utterance as he lay dying. Later, this declaration was elaborated and became a fundamental part of the daily prayer service, both morning and night. However, in time of danger or at the point of death, the recitation of the first verse cited above—or even only its first two Hebrew words, *Shema Yisrael*—have been considered sufficient by the religious teachers of Israel, since in Jewish belief, the intention is what matters most.

A luminous illustration of this devotion to the Shema is recorded in the Talmud concerning the death of Rabbi Akiba, who was the inspiration of the Bar Kochba revolt against the Romans. When the rebellion had been crushed (in 135 C.E.) in a sea of blood, the Romans put the Sage to the torture. When his torments had become unbearable and he realized that he was dying, Akiba turned his eyes to heaven and with all his remaining strength cried out: "Hear, O Israel: the Lord our God, the Lord is One." And when he reached the word "One," he stubbornly hung on to it, lovingly continued to murmur it, refused to surrender it, and died on it.

Countless martyrs since then have repeated the Shema with traditional fervor as they perished at the hands of the enemies of the Jewish people. Yet, curiously, the Shema does not evoke any grim or desperate feeling in the believing Jew, but only the joy of dedication. This is triumphantly expressed in one of the morning prayers, the Ashrei:

> Happy are we! How goodly is our portion, how pleasant our lot and how beautiful our heritage! Happy are we who, early and late, morning and evening, twice every day, declare: "Hear, O Israel! The Lord our God, the Lord is One."

SHEMINI ATZERET. *See* SUCCOT.

SHEMITAH. *See* SABBATICAL YEAR.

SHEMONEH ESREH (Hebrew prayer meaning "Eighteen Benedictions"; also known as the AMIDAH—"Standing"—since it is recited while standing)

Shemoneh Esreh is the name by which the Ashkenazim refer to this prayer; the Sefaradim call it the Amidah.

The Eighteen Benedictions constitute a central part of the liturgy and are considered of the utmost sanctity. They are recited by the worshipers in an undertone, while standing during all the three daily prayer services as well as during those on the Sabbath and holy days. To extend the benefit of the prayer to everyone in the congregation, the precentor or prayer-leader repeats it in a loud voice, thus acting as the petitioner before God for the blind, the deaf, the mute, and the illiterate. Each time he utters the name of God, the congregation responds with a fervent "Blessed be He and blessed be His Name," and, at the end of each blessing, with a loud "Amen!"

The custom of reciting the benedictions in an undertone was already well-established at the opening of the Talmudic Age. It was instituted in order to permit earnest and intimate communion by the worshiper with his own conscience and with his God. This was in marked contrast to the congregational practice generally followed of reciting the prayers in a loud, emotion-charged voice. Concerning this unusual exception, an ancient rabbi commented that as distant, exalted, and overwhelming as the Ruler of the Universe may be, yet when the most insignificant human being but murmurs a supplication to Him, He turns to listen to him with the affectionate attention of a dear friend to whom one whispers a confidence. The medieval religious authority of Spanish Jewry, Moses ben Nachman (Nachmanides, 1195–1270), counseled his son: "During the recitation of the Eighteen Benedictions, you should erase all worldly matters from your mind. Instead, fix your thoughts on the prayer with the utmost concentration. Prepare and purify your heart and mind before God, blessed be He! Thereby your prayer will be pure, clean, untainted, full of devotion, and acceptable to the Holy One, blessed be His Name. . . ."

Somewhat different was the reason given by the Talmudic Sage, Rabbi Jonah. He was in the habit of reciting the Eighteen Benedictions in an undertone, but he did this only while at prayer in the synagogue because he did not wish to disturb his fellow worshipers. However, when he prayed at home, he recited the Benedictions in a loud voice, for he was anxious that the holy words should penetrate into the consciousness of his growing sons.

There is a Talmudic tradition that the Eighteen Blessings were composed by 120 elders—the Men of the Great Synagogue (*see* MASORAH)—beginning with the fourth century B.C.E. The first three blessings, on Messianic themes, were probably drawn up during the Maccabean era; the others, conceivably, in Persian and later Hellenistic times. While several of the eighteen constituted a part of the liturgy in the Temple, they were taken over into the synagogue prayer service after the Destruction of the Second Temple in 70 C.E. The final editing of all the blessings was done by Simon, the head of the celebrated academy at Yahneh, in Judea, at the bidding of the Patriarch Gamaliel II, about 100 C.E. Curiously, the "Eighteen" Benedictions are really nineteen, the one that is twelfth in the order of recitation having been added at a later time to help counteract the disturbing agitation carried on by so-called heretics (in Hebrew: *minim*), principally the newly emerging Jewish-Christians and other schismatic sects which departed from some of the basic tenets of Judaism.

The themes of the Eighteen Benedictions, in the religious terms of the age that produced them, are widely inclusive. They praise God's ideal attributes. They plead for the well-being of Israel and for the granting of God's protection against its enemies. They pray for wisdom and repentance, for deliverance from trouble, sickness, and poverty. They give utterance to the unfading dream of the Jewish people for the eventual ingathering in Zion of its scattered remnants throughout the world, for the coming of the Messiah, for Jerusalem rebuilt, and the Temple and its rites restored. Finally, as is characteristic of Jewish prayer, they reach a climax in an ardent expression of longing for peace.

See also PEACE, JEWISH CONCEPT OF; PRAYER AND WORSHIP; SIDDUR.

SHIVAH (Hebrew, meaning "seven"; the name given to the seven days mourning for the dead)

For seven days mourners are directed by religious law to observe shivah, a private sorrowing in the home for a deceased person by his or her survivors, which begins upon the return of the mourning family from the funeral. This period of grief, set into a ritualistic pattern, is incumbent upon the closest of kin only for the loss of father or mother, wife or husband, son or daughter, brother or sister.

Immediately upon reaching home, the members of the family are required to take off their shoes. There is a puzzling prohibition against the wearing of leather shoes by the mourners; there is a strong possibility that it has no religious significance but might have been a taboo originally. The bereaved put on slippers, but only the kind made of cloth, and seat themselves on low benches or stools. In Mohammedan countries, the mourners sit on the bare floor, which was one of the ancient Israelite ways of showing grief. The author of the Book of Nehemiah, writing (in Chapter 1, Verse 4) about the middle of the fifth century B.C.E., chronicles: ". . . I sat down and wept, and mourned certain days; and I fasted and prayed before the God of heaven . . ."

The duty of mourning and its consolation are symbolized at the beginning of shivah by placing before the bereaved a dish containing a little ashes and an egg. The ashes are a survival of the Biblical custom of strewing ashes on the head as an expression of deepest grief; the egg is a reassurance to the living of immortality. For just as the egg has a rounded shape, so, in the cycle of life and death, the mystic circle will finally be completed when the Resurrection will take place in the End of Days.

Some of the observances and folkways surrounding the mourners during shivah have perplexed ethnologists. The close of kin are forbidden to do any work (minor household chores excepted), to attend to business, bathe, wear finery and/or freshly laundered garments, cut their hair or shave, perfume themselves, laugh and play, and attend festivities or the theatre. In religious matters, except for reading from the elegiac Book of Job and Lamentations, they may not engage in Torah study or publicly read the weekly portion from the Torah in the synagogue on the Sabbath and on such festivals when remission from mourning is granted. Neither are they to recite a benediction, extend greetings, nor, in turn, accept greetings from callers, politely reminding them that they are mourners and may not do so.

The day of the funeral is a fast day for the members of the family, but upon its conclusion the "mourner's meal of consolation" is served. For some puzzling reason, this may be prepared only by neighbors and not by kinfolk. It bears a striking resemblance to the Irish wake in that it is designed, by means of food and drink, to buoy up the drooping spirits of the bereaved. The mourner's meal, symbolic in content, is limited to dry bread, lentils or peas, and hard-boiled eggs. Also ten cups of wine are indicated for those able to drink them: three cups before the "meal of consolation," three cups during, and four cups after eating.

Whether the mourner's meal actually succeeds in cheering up the sorrowing is doubtful. The Talmud, however, counsels the bereaved not to mourn excessively nor too self-tormentingly. According to Rabbinic protocol, these are the "appropriate" measures of grief: the first three days should be devoted to "weeping," and the remaining four days of shivah to "lamentation"; during the entire thirty days of deep mourning called *sheloshim* (thirty)—which also includes the seven days of shivah—the mourners must wear shabby clothes and let their hair grow. In medieval times, black was worn for the whole Jewish year of general mourning. But latter-day rabbis, motivated by the fear that imitating Christian ways might lead to apostasy from the faith, banned black attire for mourners.

The duty of comforting mourners has been deeply etched in the moral consciousness of Jews by repetitive emphasis in religious writings and by constant practice. The Sages exhorted the kindhearted: "The Holy One—bessed be He—comforted those who mourned, as it is written [Genesis 25:11]: 'And it came to pass after the death of Abraham, that God blessed Isaac his son.' Therefore, do likewise: comfort those who mourn."

As in the case of every other department in the total group-life of the Jews, an important place among the institutions established for practicing humanity, mutual aid, and "loving-kindness" was reserved in former times for the "Society to Comfort Mourners." Every Jewish community and every sizable congregation since Talmudic times had one. Its members went calling on every family saddened by death, and they brought with them the modest tokens of condolence

—tempting delicacies of food and drink. Asked Jesus ben Sirach, almost three centuries before the Destruction:

> Shall not the dew assuage heat?
> So is a compassionate word better than a gift.
> ECCLESIASTICUS 18:16

And the kindest word of all that each caller brought with him to the mourners was one that was first uttered in Judea during the second century: "*Tisnechomu!*" ("Be comforted!")

However, in the East European ghettos, every man, woman, and child who was acquainted either with the deceased or with his survivors would behave like an ex-officio member of the "Society to Comfort Mourners." Unobtrusive was their shivah call, in keeping with tradition. All conversation with the mourners, except for some appropriate words of praise about the deceased, was tacitly avoided. And on leaving the house of mourning, each visitor would express the same fraternal hope that had been sounded at the funeral: "May God comfort you together with all who mourn for Zion and Jerusalem!"

During the entire seven days of shivah, except on the Sabbath, the mourners may not leave the house. Since the menfolk cannot attend services in the synagogue for the purpose of reciting the Kaddish (the mourners prayer), the custom has been for a minyan (a quorum of ten worshipers) to meet at the house of mourning twice daily in order to pray with the bereaved and to render them any service that may be required.

A much modified form of shivah is observed today in Reform congregations, the period itself being reduced to three days. As far back as 1846, the Breslau Conference of Liberal Judaism made a break with the traditional observance of mourning. It passed this resolution for the guidance of its adherents: "The custom of tearing a rent in the clothes, letting the hair grow, sitting on the floor, removing the leather covering of the feet, and the prohibition to wash, bathe, or tender greetings, having lost all meaning and religious validity in our day, and being repulsive to our religious feelings, should be abolished."

See also BURIAL CLOTHES; BURIAL RITES AND CUSTOMS; DEATH; IMMORTALITY; KADDISH; RESURRECTION; SOUL, THE.

SHOCHET (Hebrew, meaning "[ritual] slaughterer")

In Jewish religious practice, the shochet has not been just a slaughterer of animals to supply kosher meat for the pious, but a semi-ecclesiastical functionary of a specialized kind. He slaughters animals for food according to humane and clearly prescribed religious laws and regulations. His knowledge of these laws must be thorough, and his work is under the close scrutiny of the rabbinic authorities.

This, however, was not true in Biblical times. There was no calling of professional shochet then. Every adult—unless declared mentally ill—who was conversant with the rudimentary laws of ritual slaughtering, was allowed to kill for food animals that were included among these "clean" and fit for human consumption.

Very unusual is the fact that, for a long time in medieval Europe, Jewish women were also allowed to act as ritual slaughterers. When the Jewish "Dark Ages" closed in on ghetto life during the sixteenth century, this privilege, as well as others, was taken away from the woman, as can be seen from the numerous strictures against her participation in religious life contained in the definitive sixteenth-century ritual code, the Shulchan Aruch.

The shochet in some ways had to be a superior person. He was required to be physically healthy and his piety was expected to be unimpeachable. His character too had to pas[s] searching scrutiny. Moreover, he was expected to demon[-]strate, prior to his appointment to the office of shochet, [a] capacity for moral responsibility and to prove that he wa[s] painstaking in his professional duties. His Torah knowledge[,] too, had to be extensive, inasmuch as he had to learn all b[y] heart the information available concerning "clean" and "un[-]clean" animals, animal pathology and disease, and all th[e] minute directions regulating ritual slaughtering from the Ta[l-]mud, from rabbinic discussions and decisions, and from th[e] various Jewish codes which blue-printed such matters. Bu[t] in addition to this book learning, he had to obtain practic[al] skill as a shochet by apprenticeship to a qualified, experience[d] shochet. At last, when he passed his theoretical and practic[al]

The iron branding-seal of the shochet, used to guarantee that the animal slaughtered was killed according to all the ritual prescriptions of rabbinical law and practice. Alsace, 18th century.

Shochet, adhering to the humane Jewish ritual laws o[n] slaughtering, severs the jugular vein of a cow in order t[o] make its death quicker and less painful. (Engraving. Ger[-]many, 18th century.)

examination by a rabbi, he was vested with the authority to follow his calling as shochet.

In the past he was a functionary of the Jewish community and he was paid an annual salary. But such is no longer the case. The shochet today is largely a "free-lance" slaughterer and makes his own commercial arrangements for his services with meat-packing houses and private clients.

See also SHECHITAH.

SHOFAR

The shofar, or ram's horn, is the only ancient musical instrument still used in the rites of the synagogue. Why is the horn of a ram chosen to serve as the shofar? It is to recall to the pious listener the matchless act of fidelity to God in the binding of Isaac when Abraham, by providential intercession, was permitted to spare his son and to substitute a ram for the sacrifice. (*See* SACRIFICE OF ISAAC.) Jewish law forbids the use of a shofar made from the horn of a cow or of an ox because that might bring to mind the faithlessness of Israel, when it turned away from God to worship the Golden Calf after the departure from Egypt.

The shofar, usually ten to twelve inches long, is also required to be curved as a symbol of the contrite heart which is bent in repentance.

In Biblical times, the role of the shofar was prominent in both religious and public affairs of Israel. Like the conch shell still in use among certain primitive peoples, the shofar sounded the clarion call to battle. It was also blown to proclaim the time of the New Moon and fast and feast days, to alert the people to national dangers, and to bring the glad tidings of peace. A fanfare announced the coronation of a new king or the convocation of solemn assemblies, and when blown by watchmen guarding the battlements, reassured the inhabitants of a city of their security. In addition, the shofar was blown to herald the approach of the Ark of the Lord, the advent of the Sabbatical Year, and at the end of every forty-nine years, the Jubilee.

But most important, after Israel lost its Palestinian homeland, was the rite of blowing the shofar in the synagogue on Rosh Hashanah. The reason for this practice was given in the Midrash: When Moses went up for the second time to the summit of Mount Sinai in order to receive "the Tablets of the Law and the commandments" from God, the shofar was blown so that its shrill, awesome blasts would remind the children of Israel that they were not to fall again into idolatrous practices, as they had during the first absence of Moses on the Mount. And so, of all solemn occasions during the year, Rosh Hashanah was chosen by the teachers of Israel to commemorate the supreme religious-historic experience of the Jewish people: its consecration to the Torah at the foot of Mount Sinai more than three thousand years ago. In the Bible, Rosh Hashanah is described as "the Day of Blowing the Shofar."

But unlike its use in more primitive times, the shofar no longer sounds the alarm of war; it only exhorts the spiritual warriors to battle firmly against sin and backsliding. It aims to awaken the conscience and to induce a searching of the heart and mind, a moral self-accounting called in Hebrew *cheshbon ha-nefesh*.

Maimonides, the medieval rabbi-philosopher, interpreted the sounds of the shofar in this manner: They seemed to be calling: "Sleepers, awake! Awake from your sleep and rouse yourselves from your lethargy! Examine your actions and turn to repentance! Remember your Creator, O you who forget the truth in the trifles of the hour, who stray all your lives after vain things which can neither profit nor deliver you!"

The shofar-blower, who is required to be a man of singular piety and purity of conduct, goes by the Hebrew

The baal tekiah (shofar-blower) calls the worshipers to repentance in the synagogue on Rosh Hashanah. The accompanying benediction: "Blessed art Thou, O Lord, Who in mercy hearkenest to the shofar sounds of Thy people, Israel." (Illumination in a machzor [festival prayer-book] of the 14th century.)

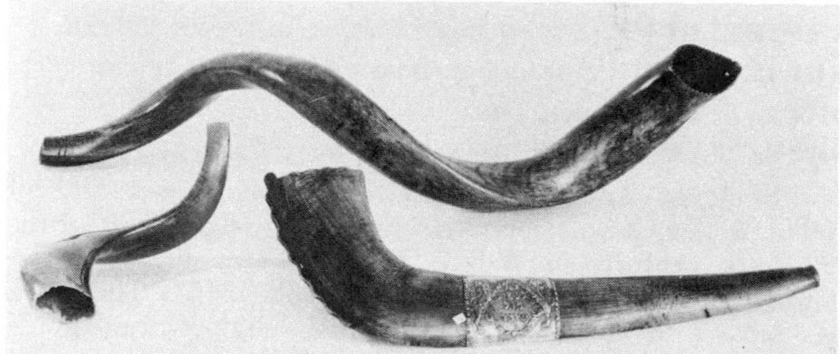

The shape of the shofar, fashioned from the horn of a ram, depends on the original formation of the horn. (Courtesy of Joseph B. Horwitz Judaica Collection, Cleveland.)

This shofar, made from a conch shell and said to be 3,000 years old, was discovered by the archaeologist Yigael Yadin in Israel. (American Friends of the Hebrew University.)

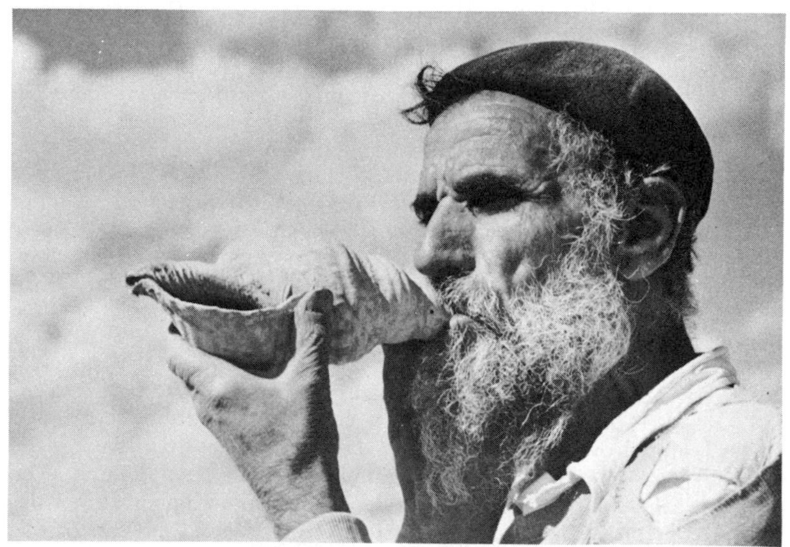

name of *baal tekiah.* He does not blow upon his instrument until directed to do so by another participant in the rite—"a prompter" called the *makri,* who, often as not, is the rabbi of the congregation. There are three prescribed sound clusters (tekiot) which are blown either individually or in combination. These are: the *tekiah,* a deep blast which ends abruptly; the *teruah,* a staccato treble; and *shebarim,* a rising and falling tremolo sound. The concluding blast, longer than all the others, is the *tekiah gedolah* (big tekiah).

The following is the musical formula of the ten tekiot, repeated three times (to make thirty in all) for emphasis:

> tekiah; shebarim-teruah; tekiah; tekiah-shebarim-tekiah; tekiah-teruah-tekiah.

These thirty tekiot are sounded in series: once after the reading from the Sefer Torah (Torah Scroll), again during the Mussaf prayers, and a third time at the conclusion of the service, when ten additional tekiot are blown, to total one hundred in all for the holy day.

Whatever reasons the Jewish religious teachers and chroniclers have given for the institution of the rite of shofar-blowing, some modern Bible scholars and ethnologists hew to the theory that, when it originated among the Jews in primitive times, it was for the single purpose of terrifying and driving away evil spirits.

SHOMRONIM. *See* SAMARITANS.

SHPIELLEUTE. *See* MERRYMAKERS, TRADITIONAL JEWISH.

SHPIELMANN. *See* MERRYMAKERS, TRADITIONAL JEWISH.

SHUL. *See* SYNAGOGUE, THE.

SHULCHAN ARUCH (Hebrew, meaning "[the] Set-Table")

The Shulchan Aruch is the title of a systematized code of Rabbinic law. It was compiled during the second half of the sixteenth century in Safed, Palestine, by the Cabalist-scholar Joseph ben Ephraim Caro (1488–1575). This work has proved to be the most influential religious-ritual guide among the Orthodox Jews of the world since then. The enormous authority it enjoyed in the past—and in a limited way still does—was due largely to the intellectual-cultural stagnation that had set in among European Jews with the Counter Reformation and the increasing repression of Jewish life in Christian society almost everywhere.

In his famous code, Caro attempted to reconcile the differences in all existing ritual codes produced by various rabbinic schools of thought and then weld them into one authoritative manual to serve world Jewry. He largely succeeded in this objective by means of accomodation and compromise. The manner in which he selected the laws, regulations, and decisions for his manual was most interesting. He would compare the codes of three of the most revered authorities in medieval religious law—Isaac ben Jacob Alfasi (1013–1103), Moses ben Maimon (Maimonides, 1135-1204), and Asher ben Yechiel (1250–1328). When he found two out of these three rabbinic savants in agreement on a particular regulation, he accepted it without further argument. However, if the three differed but he discovered that later rabbinic views upheld a decision of even one of his three authorities, he adopted that one too.

It should not be thought that the Shulchan Aruch was readily accepted as the authoritative code. Its initial appearance aroused heated controversy, and the rabbinical battle raged over it for at least a century. This was particularly the case among the Ashkenazim in Germany and Poland. The Shulchan Aruch was severely attacked by religious authorities in those countries and, as if in refutation of Caro's work, the rabbis there produced their own codifications.

By the middle of the seventeenth century, the authority of the Shulchan Aruch had become world wide. It was accepted in particular by the Sefaradic and the Oriental Jews, and starting with the eighteenth century, by the sectarian Chasidim of Eastern Europe as well. There appeared at different times a number of independent religious thinkers who were caustic in their criticism of it, charging it with being an arbitrary and undiscriminating compilation. One of the most unyielding critics of the Shulchan Aruch was the famous Talmudic scholar Elijah ben Solomon (1720–97), the Vilner Gaon.

It stands to reason that, with the steady advances made within the ghettos toward the Europeanization of the Jews in the nineteenth century, a running war was waged against the authority of the Shulchan Aruch by the Maskilim (the champions of the Haskalah or Jewish Enlightenment), by the assimilationist freethinkers, and by the leaders of the newly emerging Reform Judaism. All of these disparate elements were united on one proposition: that Caro's code of ritual laws and regulations was an anachronism in the modern world and was serving as a citadel for medievalism in Jewish religious life.

Nevertheless, the Shulchan Aruch enjoyed a continuing reverence among traditionalists, in particular among the modern Ultra-Orthodox and the sectarian Chasidim.

See also DIETARY LAWS; LAW, JEWISH; MITZVOT.

SHYLOCK MYTH, THE

The Spread and Development of the Myth. Since the first centuries of the Christian era, the motivational power for the propaganda-war of hatred waged against the Jews was drawn from a number of image-symbols. These were very familiar to the masses of Europe. Significantly, some of them had a definite ideational or emotional link with the Gospel accounts of the betrayal and crucifixion of Jesus.

The most potent of those employed to inflame the passions of the unthinking and the ignorant were, and still are, several notorious stereotypes. First and foremost was the denigrating characterization of the Jews, en masse and in perpetuity, as "Christ-killers." This epithet was incessantly shrilled by fanatical preachers and demagogues to incite Christian mobs to acts of violence and pillage in the ghetto. Another was to equate the word Jew with the odious name of Judas Iscariot, the hypocritical, avaricious disciple of Jesus who had betrayed him for "thirty pieces of silver." Still another was the provocative spectral fiction of Joseph Cartaphilus, the "Wandering Jew." The medieval legend of which he was the "hero" explained that, because he had mocked at Jesus in his anguish as he was dragging his cross to his execution, a curse like the mark of Cain was placed upon him by Jesus; it was that he was never to die and was never to find rest through the ages until Jesus would come again. (*See* WANDERING JEW.)

To these and other gargoylish symbols of alleged Jewish depravity, it became the doubtful distinction of Shakespeare to add still another. This he did in 1594 with his creation of the character of Shylock, a repulsive caricature of the Jewish moneylender, in his so-called comedy *The Merchant of Venice.*

The bewildering plot that involves Shylock in the action of *The Merchant of Venice* is, briefly, this. In the trivial matter of a wager that he has to honor, Antonio, a sporting Christian merchant of Venice, cajoles the Jewish moneylender, Shylock, into advancing him three thousand ducats. The implausible legal agreement they enter into is that, in the event that Antonio should fail to repay the loan by a certain date, the Jewish moneylender has the right to demand a pound of flesh, cut from Antonio's body as punishment.

Amusingly, this "pound of flesh" device of Shakespeare drew a scornful guffaw from the poet Coleridge in his *Table Talk.* Banal as it may have appeared to him, it was hardly original with the Bard. It had had a long "literary" history before that in England, cropping up in a number of medieval writings, including a tale in the *Gesta Romanorum,* the most widely read collection of popular stories in Europe. However, it was no Jewish moneylender who figured here, but an avaricious Christian merchant from whom a lovesick knight had borrowed one thousand florins. The two had signed an agreement which included the "pound of flesh" rigamorale. Then, when the knight defaulted on the agreement, the money lender dragged him into court. But the verdict of the judges was almost identical with that pronounced in *The Merchant of Venice*: ". . . the knighte bonde [bound] him never by letter, but that the merchant should have power to kitte [cut] his fleshe from the boons [bones], but there was no covenant made of shedding of blode [blood]. . ."

Shakespeare, without doubt, must also have been familiar with the popular "Ballad of the Jew Gernutus, or, The Jew of Venice." In Percy's famous collection, *Reliques of Ancient*

Rudolf Schildkraut, famous Yiddish actor, in the role of Shylock in Shakespeare's The Merchant of Venice, *which Max Reinhardt staged in a German production in Berlin during the 1920's.*

Poetry, this folk ballad is described in a superscription as "a new song showing the crueltie of Gernutus, a Jew, who, lending to a Merchant a hundred crowns, would have a pound of flesh, because he could not pay him at the time appointed."

For the purposes of Shakespeare's melodramatics, Antonio, too, is conveniently made to default in his repayment of the loan to Shylock, the Jewish moneylender. And so, in accordance with the ghoulish stipulation of their contract, Shylock insists on carving his pound of flesh out of his Christian victim's body. However in the end the satanic "Jew usurer" is foiled in his thirst for human blood and vengeance. The *deus ex machina* of his downfall proves to be the beautiful Portia, Antonio's absurdly improbable female defense counsel. She appears in court—disguised as a man!—and by a legalistic stratagem considered by the Bard of Avon himself a brilliant coup of pleading, she declares to the judges that Shylock is standing self-condemned before them. For while she concedes that his claim to a pound of Antonio's flesh is valid legally, she goes on to ask how, in cutting out the flesh to which he is entitled, Shylock can avoid spilling even one drop of her client's blood—a contingency which had not been considered in the contract. Suffice it that this challenge throws Shylock into utter confusion; he is trapped at last by his own "villainy."

The Doge of Venice proceeds to condemn Shylock to death upon the justification that he had plotted to shed the blood of an innocent Christian. But setting an example in Christian mercy, he spares Shylock's life. However, this is only on condition that the three thousand ducats the Jew has claimed from Antonio are forfeit, and that he assigns half of his ill-gotten fortune to Antonio. Then, to add insult to injury, the Venetian prince orders Shylock forthwith to become a Christian and, at the same time, to give his parental blessing to the marriage of his only daughter—who had deserted her father!—to her Christian suitor. And so the final curtain falls on what Shakespeare intended to be a general glee and satisfaction in the audience produced by Shylock's comical writhing in anguish and chagrin.

Had Shylock remained merely a spidery villain in a melodrama or stage burlesque, even though Shakespeare drew him artistically with the impermissible broad strokes of contempt, ridicule, and slapstick, the problem would have been relatively simple; comment about his characterization, whether in praise or in blame, would have belonged strictly in the province of literary psychology or dramatic criticism. Unfortunately, the matter turned out far differently than is usually the case with a fictional character, no matter how eminent its creator. As it actually happened, Shylock leaped out of the cardboard trappings (in an almost literal sense) on the stage of make-believe. Like the protagonist-automaton in the Jewish legend of the clay Golem of Prague, he became menacingly real—perhaps a little too real—for the comfort of Jews or the conscience of sensitive Christians.

It is no exaggeration to say that the image of Shylock occupies an important place in the history of cultural anti-Semitism. In the English-speaking world, Shylock has come to embody the reason for hatred of the Jew. Whatever may have motivated Shakespeare in creating him, he succeeded—as he obviously had intended—in presenting Shylock as a verminous creature, a composite of several classic anti-Semitic stereotypes. From the "Christ-killer" and "Wandering Jew" images he had borrowed a compulsive vengefulness and a capacity for gloating, traits which supposedly were intrinsic in the Jewish character. He also endowed his Jewish moneylender of Venice with the cold avariciousness, unctuousness, and treachery made odious to Christians by the example of Judas Iscariot.

The fact cannot be overlooked that, if *The Merchant of Venice* has been played so often on the stages of the world and has been revered as a classic of English dramatic literature (for generations it was required reading for older schoolchildren in English-speaking countries) it has hardly been because of its intrinsic merits. Rather, the contrary is true. Objective literary and dramatic criticism have placed it among the synthetic and labored trivialities of Shakespeare. One can only assume that it has enjoyed such a vast popularity in the past because it pandered to the base prejudices of the malicious and unthinking.

In the hate-riven world of today, the word "Shylock," which has been widely adopted into all the languages of the Western world, has become a figurative term for avaricious and ruthless dealing. Worse, it is sometimes used—without the user's ever giving it a second thought—as a contemptuous synonym for "Jew." There are Gentiles—and for complex psychological reasons, not a few Jews also—who, when they wish to show their contempt for some sharp-dealing, heartless individual, point him out with the often well-meant warning: "Watch out for him—he's a Shylock!" Therein lies the sinister power of anti-social images, symbols, slogans, and catchwords. Repeated often enough and by enough people, they are in time accorded general acceptance and thereby sanctioned as representing the truth.

It is futile, and also unnecessarily apologetic for Shakespearean devotees to pretend that, in writing *The Merchant of Venice,* the Bard of Avon, like Zeus who carelessly "nodded," had merely suffered a lapse in the humanity and honest thinking so characteristic of him in all his other works. The truth rather lies in the unavoidable fact that, in his dislike of the Jews and incapacity for an unbiased judgment of them, Shakespeare was utterly sincere. Neither did he try to pretend anything else. In his prejudices against the Jews he was merely echoing the unobjective and sometimes barbarous views of his literary precursors and contemporaries in England. They, too—including William Langland, Matthew Paris, Geoffrey Chaucer, Christopher Marlowe, Francis Bacon, Thomas Dekker, Thomas Middleton, and John Fletcher—wrote contemptuously and slanderously about the Jews.

The Shylock-image and the weird "pound of flesh" device with which it is associated in most educated people's minds find their roots in medieval English history, social conditions, and culture. Their genesis and development furnish a striking illustration of how anti-Semitic myths have been invented and propagated, to the everlasting grief of the Jews and the shame of Gentiles. The fact that Shakespeare lent his genius to such dismal ends merely fortifies the melancholy adage that even the gods have clay feet.

Certainly, the hostility toward the Jews in England (of which Shakespeare was the cultural legatee) had not arisen all at once or from one special cause. It had taken centuries of inflaming by the combined efforts of fanatics, rabble-rousers, and the more respectable agencies of indoctrination of Church and State. In this "holy war" against a helpless minority, Christian hatred of the Jews was legitimized and accorded full religious and moral sanction. On numerous occasions, it also winked piously whenever massacre, rapine, and pillage by mobs made a shambles of every Jew Street in England.

The Jewish Moneylender in England. One of the most effective incitations worked up against the Jews of England during the Middle Ages was that there were many "usurers" or moneylenders among them. This was unquestionably true, and it had come about in a remarkable way. For in their perpetual struggle with the rebellious barons, who were fighting to obtain more power for themselves, the kings of feudal England were compelled to turn to the moneylenders to raise the money they required for fighting their wars as well as for operating the different administrative departments of the state apparatus. But by a cruel twist of history, since Christians had been forbidden in 1179 by the Church edict of the Third Lateran Council to engage in the "sinful" trade of "usure"—as the charging of any interest on loans was termed then—only Jews, considered to be unregenerate "sons of the Devil," were allowed to perform the imperative moneylending function in feudal society. And this was particularly true in Angevin England.

As a matter of fact, the various kinds of medieval England greatly encouraged the growth of this despised trade among the Jews in every way they could. The more money the Jews would make from their moneylending, moneychanging, and pawnbroking transactions (the latter were also conducted by moneylenders), the more profitable it was bound to turn out to be in the end for the Jews' Exchequer, which was merely an administrative department of the King's Exchequer.

The Jewish moneylenders were required by their licenses to advance loans to the English nobles, to the town councils, and to the Church itself, against the deposit of proper pledges. But always they acted in the official capacity of *agents* for the Crown and were held tight in its iron control. It can be assumed that the royal and baronial thirst for the money of the "Jew usurers" remained always unquenchable. By a variety of stratagems, both legal and extralegal, by the imposition of special communal levies, heavy fines, and outright confiscation on trumped-up charges, the moneylender's "clients" managed quickly to relieve the Jews of their "sinful" burden.

When Aaron of Lincoln died in 1186, it was after a long period as head of a Jewish "combine" of moneylenders that had helped the Church to finance the construction of nine Cistercian monasteries, the cathedrals of Lincoln and Peterborough, and the Abbey of St. Albans. Aaron was said to have boasted that, when a Christian saint (i.e., his relics) went homeless, he, Aaron the Jew, built a home for him! In the inflammatory anti-Jewish agitation which took place in his lifetime, he and other Jewish moneylenders were reviled as "sons of the Devil." (After his death, the Jew's Exchequer promptly confiscated the fortune he had amassed in his lifetime and expended it in fighting the king's war against France.) The mere fact that Christian churches were dependent for their financing on Jewish moneylenders, intensified the already existing feeling of outrage among the English against them. The word "Jew" became synonymous with "usurer." It was usually uttered by Christians with the same revulsion that is directed against a moral leper.

A source of special apprehension for the Jewish moneylenders was their rigidly controlled dealings with the nobles, the clergy, and the rich burghers. The fervent hostility evinced by these classes most of the time had a materialistic basis. It stemmed from the fact that the Crown, in order "to protect" the pecuniary interests (its own) of the "King's chattels" (as the Jews were designated by feudal law) required of all Christian borrowers that they furnish pledges adequate for covering their loans. For these deposits of collateral the moneylenders were strictly accountable to the "Exchequer of the Jews."

Consequently, whether they liked it or not, the moneylenders in England were compelled to accept a great miscellany of pledged goods and property. This, as they had already learned before—to their sorrow—was fraught with the gravest physical danger to themselves and even to the entire Jewish community. Such pledges often consisted of baronial castles, country manors, suits of armor, and even the next year's corn crop. The clergy sometimes offered pledges of the church-plate, altar vessels and priestly vestments. Perhaps the strangest collateral of all was furnished by Bishop Nigel of Ely in the twelfth century: He deposited with the Jewish moneylenders the *relics of a saint!* Logically, it had to be the clergy and the nobles who were the principal inciters against the Jews in England during the Middle Ages.

But the resentment was strongest and, in consequence, most threatening among the lowest social strata, and in particular among the serfs, who were suffering cruelly under feudal oppression. Their inciters, in order to divert the serf's attention from their real troubles, now furnished them with an additional grievance against the helpless scapegoat.

Furthermore, the religious hysteria that convulsed England during the Crusades dangerously aggravated the situation for the Jews. The fabrication and spread of a report in 1144 that the Jews had "ritually" murdered young William of Norwich in order to drink his blood during the Passover Seder service, and a similar slander cooked up a century later involving a boy called Little Hugh of Lincoln (see CHURCH AND PERSECUTION; "RITUAL-MURDER" SLANDERS) unleashed a mob violence of the most savage kind. Then, when the barons rose in revolt against the king in 1215 and again in 1264, they massacred several thousand Jews in London, Canterbury, and Northampton.

The climax to the moneylending activities of the Jews was reached in 1275. Seeing how profitable the "sinful" moneylending business had become, the Church throughout Europe relaxed its century-old edict forbidding Christians to engage in "usury," and the Jewish moneylenders were displaced by the Caorsini, who had formerly been the collectors of the Pope's revenues. Jewish history in England during the Middle Ages came abruptly to an end in 1290 and some sixteen thousand Jews who had survived the final massacres were expelled from the country.

In the four centuries which followed, the English people had virtually no physical contact with Jews. Their principal knowledge of them was drawn either from anti-Jewish writings or from a vague but persistent folk-memory. The Jew as they "knew" him was a stereotyped image, further distorted by unbridled fancy and fear and a blind hatred. A terrifying bogey had been built up in the popular mind—that of a cunning monster who trafficked with the Devil and who, in his ancient hatred of "Our Lord and Saviour, Jesus Christ," conspired to rob and destroy honest Christians.

For the Englishman of the later Renaissance and Elizabethan periods, the Jew possessed no human physiognomy at all; he was visualized as a demon out of a nightmare. This conception of him was nurtured by a steady stream of literary libels of native English authorship and by foreign writings which had appeared in translation in England. Generation after generation of the English sang scurrilous popular ballads in a great many versions, such as "Sir Hugh and the Jew's Daughter" and "The Ballad of the Jew Gernutus." In the fourteenth century, the great Chaucer himself—who, like Shakespeare two centuries later, shared the hatreds and prejudices of his age—helped perpetuate the blood-curdling anti-Jewish myths among the "cultured" classes. In the "Prioress Tale" of the *Canterbury Tales,* taking up the ever popular theme of the martyrdom of "Little Hugh," he played on the heartstrings of the ignorant and unthinking with a lurid recital of the manner in which the Jews allegedly had enticed and then secretly murdered for ghoulish ritual purposes the eight-year-old Christian innocent as he went by piously singing the protective hymn "Alma Redemptoris Mater." In passing, Chaucer did not neglect to pay his poetic respects to the Jewish moneylender—that Satanic specter of the Middle Ages:

> For foule usure and lucre of vileynye,
> Hateful to Crist and to his compaignye . . .

This, approximately, was the popular image of the Jew during the Elizabethan period. With but very few exceptions, it was held universally by the common folk as well as by such sophisticated intellectuals as Shakespeare and Marlowe. For both these writers it came to real life, and in the most astonishing manner, in the year 1594. Then, a certain Doctor Rodrigo Lopez, a Portugese Jew who had been converted to Catholicism and who was chief court physician to Queen Elizabeth, was suddenly arrested and put in chains at the behest of his former patron, the Earl of Essex. It was charged that he, together with several Christian Portugese accomplices, had plotted to poison the queen for the convenience of the king of Spain. In payment for this little service, if it was successful, he was to receive the sum of fifty thousand ducats.

When Lopez was put to the torture on the rack, he made a full confession. He revealed the details of his dazzling virtuosity in playing his double loyalties to the queen of England and to the king of Spain, manipulating one against the other, but for his own mercenary ends. Whether his own confession under torture or the fact that his confederates implicated him in their confessions, also made under torture, can be considered valid, has been seriously questioned by several legal scholars in England.

Innocent or guilty, the sensational revelations made in the courtroom during his public trial made his case a *cause célèbre* in England. The judges damned Lopez in the most abusive terms as "that vile Jew . . . wiley and covetous . . . the perjured and murderous Jewish doctor." The Lord Chief Justice Coke, the foremost English jurist of the Elizabethan period, declared that, legally as well as morally, the Jews were to be regarded as the natural enemies of Christians. There could be "no peace between them, as with the Devil whose subjects they are, and the Christians."

So great was the popular commotion whipped up by the trial and the subsequent execution of Lopez, that the enterprising playwright Marlowe, eager to turn the general excitement to his own profit, quickly wrote *The Jew of Malta.* This turned out to be such a financial success on the stage that his less adroit but infinitely more gifted rival in the contemporary theatre, Shakespeare, felt himself challenged to undertake a production of his own on the same theme. His play, *The Merchant of Venice,* scored an even greater success and put Marlowe's banal caricature of the Jew in the shade. Several of the more objective historians of the Elizabethan stage in recent times have concluded, although with understandable reluctance, that the immortal but needy Bard was impelled by opportunistic considerations to capitalize on the rabid anti-Semitic feeling of the times.

In certain stock aspects of slapstick melodrama, the characterization of Shylock closely resembled that of Barabbas sketched in such venom by Marlowe in *The Jew of Malta.* In other respects—since Shakespeare, the profound prober of motivation, could not help being Shakespeare—Shylock as the hateful Jewish moneylender was charitably endowed with some of the credible reactions of a human being, however depraved he might be. But even with his superior and psychologically more persuasive approach, Shylock nonetheless emerged as a monster of cruelty. In its over-all effect, the play itself is a slander directed against all Jews. The classic anti-Semitic thesis of the Jew's alleged vengefulness reinforced by money-lust was fully corroborated by the villainies that Shakespeare piled up against Shylock, even though he made a half-hearted effort to make his conduct believable.

The Barabbas of Marlowe's depiction was obsessed by his hatred for Christians; his thirst for vengeance was maniacal:

> I am not of the tribe of Levi, I,
> That can so soon forget an injury,
> We Jews can fawn like spaniels when we please
> And when we grin we bite.

Shakespeare's Shylock utters virtually the same sentiment concerning Antonio:

> I hate him for he is a Christian . . .
> Cursed be my tribe if I forgive him.

The assumption that it was improbable for a profound thinker like Shakespeare to nurture a genuine hatred for the Jew is naïve and does not take into consideration the complexities of the human being and the Zeitgeist—the spirit of the times—in his culture. For that matter, Shakespeare was followed by a number of other great creators—Voltaire and Richard Wagner, for example—who were also rabid anti-Semites. It is a tragic truth affecting many deified geniuses —and Shakespeare perhaps most of all—that the literary idolatry which surrounds them in many quarters makes their works sacrosanct against any truly critical and objective analysis. The least of Shakespeare's plays, however inferior and unworthy of his great art they may be, and among which *The Merchant of Venice* has been frequently counted, are reverenced as immortal classics and as revelations of the eternal verities.

In this Shakespearolatry an entire school of literary exegesis has sprung up to "explain away" the incongruities, the malice, and the antisocial claptrap that Shakespeare poured into his characterization of Shylock. That urbane nineteenth-century critic of English letters, William Hazlitt, preferred to believe that the Bard's "real" intention in drawing his caricature of Shylock was to dramatize for Englishmen the deplorable moral and social consequences of Christian hatred and mistreatment of the Jew. Shakespeare's projection he interpreted as that of a man who was "no less sinned against than sinning." But this generous evaluation, unfortunately, has difficulty in standing up against all the shafts of ridicule and contempt that Shakespeare, to the very end of the play, shoots into his groveling unprincipled gargoyle of a Jew.

It has been remarked by Shakespearean scholars that not infrequently since the second half of the nineteenth century —as in the stage interpretations by Sir Henry Irving, Adolph Sonnenthal, Jacob Adler, and Rudolf Schildkraut, of whom the last three were Jews—the portrayal of the Jewish money-lender struck some compassionate, and even tragic, overtones. But their humane reconstruction of the character was presented only to conform with the modern liberal outlook. In part, it was also a calculated attempt to soften an offensive and implausible caricature. When it is read in the cold

Rowlandson's caricature of "A Jew Broker," a conception he derived from the stylized stage delineation of Shylock. London, 18th century.

print, the characterization of Shylock emerges in all its malevolent nakedness. Furthermore, the intentions of Shakespeare are clearly revealed in the early stage-directions. These require that the actor who plays the part of Shylock be "made up" to look like the anti-Semitic stereotype in fashion then. He is to have a large hooked nose, look unkempt and dirty in his gaberdine, and conduct himself in a wheedling, cringing, and devious manner. And it was precisely that conception which became standard—and has so remained to this very day—for the part in Shakespearean repertory.

A footnote for the recent history of *The Merchant of Venice* in the United States is required. It starkly illuminates how, under certain circumstances, a work of literature can be utilized as a weapon of destruction if its theme is antisocial.

With the rise to power of Hitler and the Nazis in Germany in 1932, their savage anti-Semitic propaganda found sympathetic reverberations in the United States during the critical depression years. Powerful organizations of a socially menacing character, led by rabble-rousers and "patrioteers," mushroomed during the 1930's. Among the defamatory image-symbols of the Jews, designed to stir up an aggressive hatred of them among the unthinking and the desperate, was the Shylock-slander of Shakespeare. It was projected in a number of disguised forms, chief among which was the spidery bogey of the "international Jew-banker."

In this combustible socio-political setting, many thoughtful Americans—both Christians and Jews—were filled with apprehension. They awoke to the insidiousness of such a hate-propaganda vehicle as *The Merchant of Venice* on the stage. Considered even more dangerous, because of its possible impact on the impressionable and uninformed minds of adolescents, was the fact that it had been made required reading in English courses in many of the high schools. In a vigorous campaign of public enlightenment on the pros and cons of the issue, the Anti-Defamation League of B'nai B'rith was instrumental in having *The Merchant of Venice* voluntarily dropped from high school curricula throughout the United States and Canada.

See also MONEYLENDERS.

SIBLING RELATIONSHIPS. *See* FAMILY RELATIONS, TRADITIONAL PATTERNS OF.

SICK, VISITING THE (in Hebrew: BIKKUR CHOLIM)

Upon the return of the Jews from the Captivity in Babylonia, the social and economic problems in the re-established Judean society multiplied and constantly grew more acute. From these conditions of crisis, the concept of mutual aid deepened among the people and the practical expressions of it greatly increased. Visiting the sick and the afflicted in order to render assistance and to speak words of consolation to them was given unusual prominence. "Do not delay visiting a man who is sick," urged the "Wisdom"-writer, Jesus ben Sirach, in the second century B.C.E. The Talmudic Sages, in the centuries that followed, tried to impress upon the devout that "he who visits a sick person helps him to live longer."

It was considered morally incumbent upon every person to visit the sick at every opportunity and to give them whatever material or personal service was necessary. The nature of this help was specifically indicated; it included providing food and medicines, and feeding, dressing, and caring for the bedridden, especially if there were no kin or friends to do these things. Equally important, the visitors were expected to do everything in their power to cheer up the sick, and by a concrete demonstration of fraternal concern and sympathy encourage them to hope for complete and rapid recovery. In keeping with these attitudes, the traditional Hebrew phrase

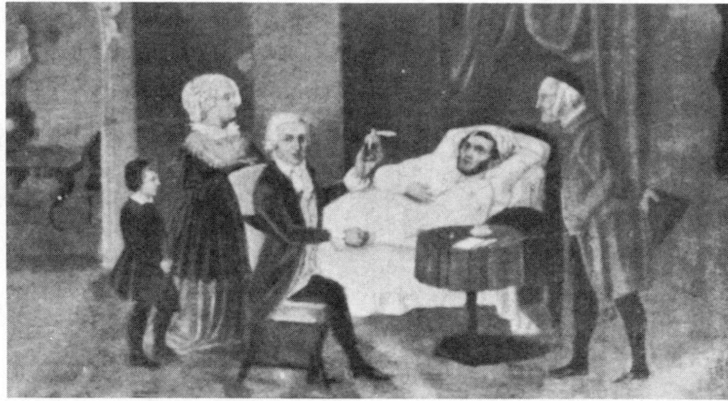

Visiting the sick. (Painting of the late 18th century, by an unknown artist, belonged to the Chebrah Kaddishah Society [Holy Brotherhood] of Prague.)

with which one took leave of the sick was *"Refuah shelemah!"* ("May God grant you a speedy and complete recovery!")

It has been frequently noted by Jewish religious writers that a visit to a sick or helpless person always raises his spirits. In fact, it is related in the Talmud that, as the third-century Rabbis Judah and his father Chiyya were taking their leave of a blind Torah-scholar to whom they had paid such a visit, he blessed them thus: "You have come to see one who cannot see. May it be you merit to see him who sees but is not seen!"

It became the custom during the Middle Ages in Europe to visit the sick immediately after the conclusion of the Sabbath morning service in the synagogue. On entering the sickroom, the visitor's greeting, prescribed by the Talmud, was to be: "May good health be yours!" And on leaving, he was to say to the sick man: "Today is the Sabbath day, and we are forbidden to offer tearful prayer on your behalf. But have confidence that you will recover soon. Believe in God's infinite compassion, and let this holy day bring you peace!"

The Rabbinic Sages warned that acts of benevolence and humanity should have no narrow sectarian interpretation or motive: "Visit the sick of the Gentiles along with the sick of Israel." With the confinement of the Jews in ghettos by decision of the Lateran Council of the Church in 1215, societies with the special dedication of visiting and caring for the sick were formed in every Jewish community throughout Europe. Rare, indeed, was the instance when this simple demonstration of human kinship and compassion was not forthcoming to a sick person. Even in our own depersonalized times, when it has been the fate of many a humanitarian practice either to go into a decline or disappear, or, just as

Brass charity-box for supplying funds to the Society for Visiting the Sick (Bikkur Cholim). 18th century.

likely, to take on new and more effective organizational forms, the identification of the individual Jew with the sick in terms of direct "personal" service still remans a powerful, binding force in Jewish life.

See also BURIAL CUSTOMS; HOSPITALS.

SIDDUR (Hebrew s., from the word SEDER, meaning "order"; thus, the "order of prayer" or the "prayer book" itself; pl. SIDDURIM)

The siddur is the Jewish book of common prayer for every day in the week and for the Sabbath. But it cannot be regarded as just one unified production. Actually it constitutes a monumental anthology of both congregational and private prayers that are applicable to every religious need and situation in the life-cycle of the Jew. It comprises the liturgical and devotional creations of many minds and of a variety of religious outlooks. Truly, it is an omnium gatherum of diverse literary materials that were shaped in the many forms and styles evocative of many culture-periods. Those were culled from a number of sacred writings; they include selections and paraphrases from the Pentateuch, the Prophets, and the Psalms; extracts from the Mishnah and the Gemara; and verse-hymns by the liturgical Hebrew poets of the Middle Ages, including those great rabbinic lyricists of Mohammedan Spain, Solomon ibn Gabirol, Judah (Yehudah) Halevi, and Abraham and Moses ibn Ezra. In addition, the siddur contains benedictions, brief praisings (doxologies), special prayers for every rite, and a miscellany of devotional poems.

The fact is that there have been compiled, as an inevitable consequence of the world-wide dispersion of the Jewish people, not just one siddur but many siddurim. Each among a number of regional Jewries and at different times created its own siddur. This clearly was done in order to satisfy its desire for a special kind of congregational worship that would project its own religious feelings and cultural tastes. However, whatever the textual variations or differences in custom, the fundamental matrix, hallowed by tradition since the time of the Talmudic Sages, remained the same in all siddurim.

The first siddur, with the order of prayer and with all the regulations and traditions indicated, was arranged by the Geonim or Rectors of the famed Rabbinic Academy of Sura in Babylonia during the Byzantine Age. Successively, each Gaon continued the work of liturgical compiling of his predecessor: First there was Cohen Tzedek in 845, then Mar Shalom in 849, and Natronai in 853. Finally, the momentous work was completed by Amram Gaon in 856.

The Siddur of Amram was universally used by Jews for several hundred years. This, said Rashi (France, 1040–1105), the foremost religious authority among the Ashkenazim of Europe, was because "all our customs follow Babylonian tradition." But shortly thereafter, at the time of the Crusades, the influence of the Geonim of Sura began to decline. The Jewish communities in various parts of the Diaspora then felt free to follow their own liturgical inclinations. Different traditions, rites, and customs (pl. minhagim; s. minhag) in certain religious matters had crystallized, in the meantime, in a number of far-flung places, and the disparate orders of prayer called for revised prayer books for each region. Quite a few siddurim appeared during the Middle Ages, each compilation being identified according to its geographic location and its special minhag. Thus there were the Italian Minhag, the Spanish Minhag, the Castilian, the Byzantine (Romaniya), the Roman, etc.

The most widely used of all the prayer books in later centuries were those developed by the Ashkenazim (the Jews of Central and Eastern Europe) in accordance with the Minhag Ashkenaz, and the Minhag Sefarad, which served

Evening Service

OF

ROSHASHANAH,

AND

KIPPUR.

OR

The BEGINNING of the YEAR,

AND

The DAY of ATONEMENT.

NEW-YORK:

Printed by *W. Weyman*, in *Broad-Street*, MDCCLXI.

First English translation of the machzor (festival prayer-book) in the American Colonies. New York, 1761. (Rosenbach Collection, American Jewish Historical Society.)

It was the festival prayer-book rather than the daily book of prayer upon which were lavished the decorative arts of the Hebrew calligrapher and illuminator. Illuminations from a medieval machzor manuscript, Germany, 13th–14th centuries.

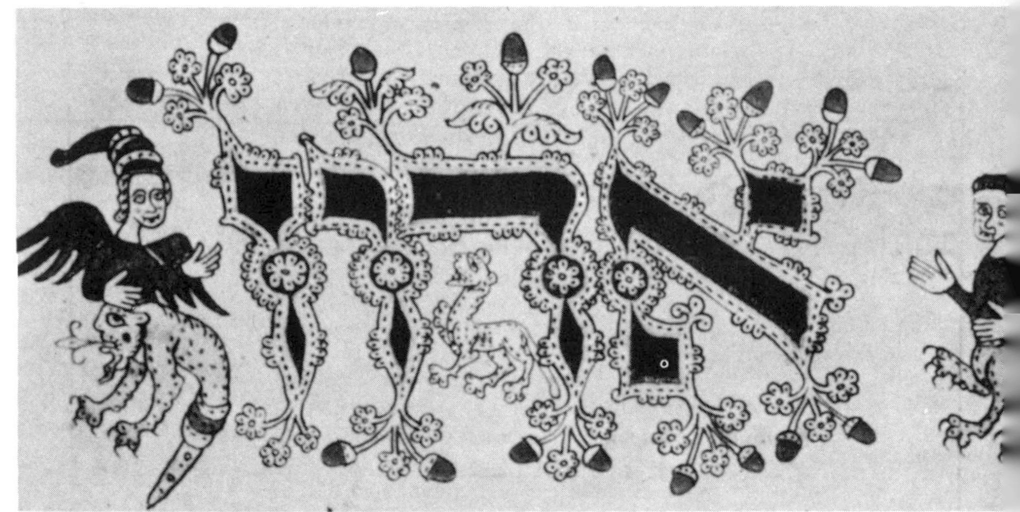

the Jews of Spain, Portugal, the Provence, Greece, Turkey, North Africa, the Middle East, etc. The Sefaradim arranged theirs after the Babylonian model of Amram Gaon. The Ashkenazim, on the other hand, followed the liturgical pattern that had been developed separately in the Holy Land. Their first prayer book was the Vitry Machzor (the latter word means "cycle" in Hebrew), and it contained festival and other holy day prayers and liturgical poems, but not the daily and Sabbath prayers which were included in the siddur. It was compiled *c.* 1100 in France by Simchah ben Samuel of Vitry, a disciple of the great commentarian Rashi of Troyes. It was arranged in chapters, according to the yearly cycle of holy days, and also had reference to such special occasions in the life of the individual as marriage, burial, and mourning.

In the course of time, literary materials from one siddur found their way into the others. There was nothing either fixed or canonical about the book of Jewish common prayer; it grew luxuriantly, and freely, revealing all the kaleidescopic facets of global Jewish culture. The mere fact that the sectarian Chasidim of eighteenth-century Austrian Galicia, the Ukraine, and Poland—Ashkenazim all—adopted, as a matter of preference and legacy from the Palestinian Cabalists, the Sefaradic Rite, is an indication of the cultural give-and-take existing among the various ethnic groupings of Jews. But in reality, whatever differences there were among the prayer-compilations, they were entirely of secondary significance, for the identical pattern and the principal textual ingredients were to be found in all of them, grouped around the Shema

Illuminated Hebrew word from a 14th-century machzor (festival prayer-book) manuscript. (Japanisches Palais, Dresden.)

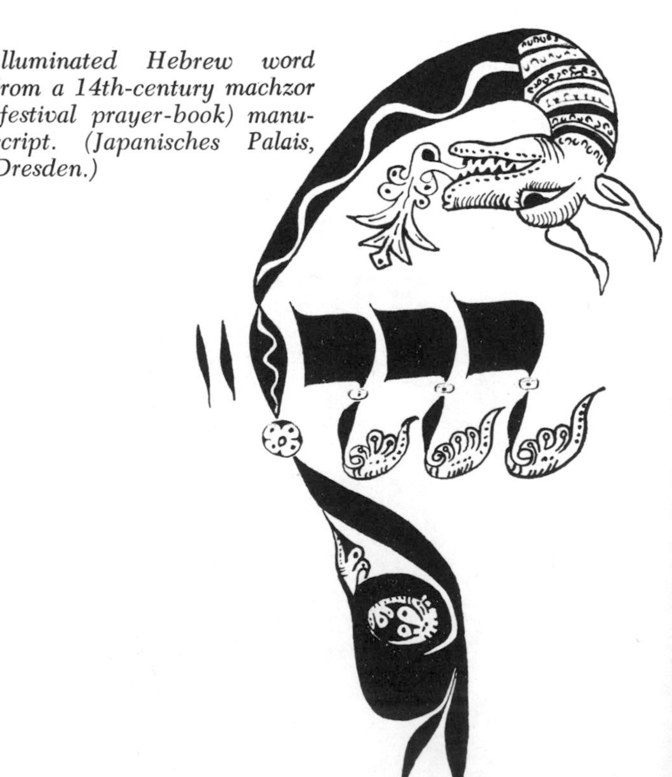

Illuminated page from a machzor (festival prayer-book) of 1272 that in pre-Nazis days belonged to the Rashi Synagogue in Worms, Germany.

Handwrought silver and partly gilded covers used for binding either siddur (prayer book) or Chumash (Pentateuch). Amsterdam, 18th century. (Courtesy of Joseph B. Horwitz Judaica Collection, Cleveland.)

(the affirmation of God's Oneness) and the Shemoneh Esreh (Eighteen Benedictions, also called the Amidah).

By the sixteenth century, when Jewish books were already being printed in Europe, the numerous additions to the prayers had made the siddur so bulky that it was found more convenient to print it in two volumes. Thereafter, the daily and Sabbath prayers were kept in the siddur; the festival and other holy day prayers were issued separately as the machzor.

The fragmentation of Jewish life, occurring with the breakdown of ghetto isolation during the nineteenth century, brought about not only divisions in religious groupings and observance, but also a number of new siddurim, revised and accomodated to the needs of the changing modern age. The Jewish rabbinical scholar, Solomon Schechter (1847–1915), observed wryly that "at a time when *all* Jews prayed, one prayer-book sufficed their needs. Now, when far less Jews pray, more and more prayer-books are required."

The first new English prayer book in the United States was the one produced by the Reform or Liberal congregations in 1895: The Union Prayer Book. With the years, it underwent much revision, so that it might conform the better to the changing religious outlook and the literary tastes of this most "advanced" branch of contemporary Judaism. Reconstructionism, the small but influential religious group founded by Dr. Mordecai M. Kaplan, published in 1945 its own Sabbath Prayer Book with parallel Hebrew and English texts. While it retained "the classical framework of the service" and adhered "to the fundamental teachings of that tradition concerning God, man and the world," it eliminated all prayers which referred to the ancient doctrines of Revelation, Retribution, Resurrection, and other beliefs it considered unacceptable to the scientifically oriented thinking of our time. Also the several divisions in contemporary Orthodoxy in the United States made their own rearrangements of the traditional prayer book. The latest was that issued by the Rabbinical Council of America in 1960, with Dr. David de Sola Pool as editor and translator. Hitherto, the standard prayer book for American Orthodox worshipers was the one that had been sponsored for English Jews by the British rabbinate, in particular the version by S. Singer in 1890 and the revised edition of it prepared by Dr. Joseph H. Hertz in 1941 and republished in the United States in 1948.

See also ASHKENAZIM; JUDAISM IN THE MODERN AGE; PRAYER AND WORSHIP; SEFARADIM; SHEMA, THE; SHEMONEH ESREH; SYNAGOGUE.

SIDE CURLS. *See* PE'OT.

SIDRAH (SEDREH) (Hebrew, s. meaning "order" or "arrangement"; thus, the weekly portion or lesson from the Pentateuch; pl. SIDROT)

The custom of reading publicly from the Five Books of Moses during the synagogue service on every Sabbath day, which in former times was accomplished in three Jewish calendar years but in recent centuries in only one, made it necessary that the Pentateuch be divided into weekly portions. Each of the Biblical selections which was fixed for reading on a particular Sabbath was called a *sidrah* by the Ashkenazim and a *parashah* by the Sefaradim.

In the Scroll of the Law, which contains the Five Books of Moses, there are fifty-four such sidrot. The first, which begins with the narrative of the Creation in the first chapter of the Book of Genesis, is read on the first Sabbath that follows Succot, the Feast of Tabernacles. The final portion is read aloud on the festival of Simchat Torah, when believing Jews everywhere rejoice over what they regard as their incalculable good fortune in possessing the Torah. The sidrah for this special occasion is Chapter 33 of Deuteronomy. On a note of high emotion, it begins: "And this is the blessing, wherewith Moses the man of God blessed the children of Israel before his death."

SIMCHAT TORAH. *See* HAKAFOT; SUCCOT; TORAH-READING.

SIN AND SINNER

The ethically conditioned Jew of tradition, like all men of his type among other peoples, was ceaselessly engaged in explaining his conduct and motives to his conscience. This kind of stocktaking resulted in an intellectual humility where the search for truth was concerned. And so the devout Jew

Table inserted in a 13th-century illuminated Hebrew manuscript of the Pentateuch, indicating the order of some of the weekly portions to be read.

often took a dim view of his own virtue; he could not afford the luxury of self-esteem. By the same consideration, he was inclined to be tolerant of the sins and misdeeds of others. Jewish moralists–especially those who wrote down their painful ruminations about human folly and error during the Middle Ages and in the centuries which followed–deplored the fact that all human beings were cast from the same mold of perverseness and contradiction. The Evil as well as the Good, they perceived, flowed from the same baffling source–the human nature of man.

Rabbi Meir, the rueful Sage of the fourth century, once grew disconsolate when he tried to understand his own actions. "Woe is me from my Maker, and woe is me from my own nature!" he lamented. This was a recognition, which he shared with other enlightened religious thinkers of the Talmudic period, that in his own human personality were to be

The temptation of Adam and Eve and their fall from divine grace. (From an illuminated Hebrew manuscript of the Mishneh Torah by Maimonides, 1296.)

found the seeds of his moral imperfection. A restatement about this misfortune endemic in man's character was attempted by the medieval French codifier of rabbinic law, Moses of Coucy: "It is because man is half-angel and half-beast that such a bitter conflict takes place in his inner life."

But not always was sin regarded by Jews as being utterly calamitous. There was in currency in the Talmudic age a perfectly charming folk-belief that not even the tzaddik (the holy man of God) would be privileged to enter into his eternal reward in Eden if, God forbid, the Recording Angel, that infallible bookkeeper of heaven, should find in his accounts not a single entry that he had ever sinned. But how could such a miracle possibly happen? The Sages noted with gentle irony: "No man is to be considered holy until death has come to silence the Evil Inclination [*see* YETZER TOB AND YETZER HA-RAH] within him, and he has been laid in the grave with the crown of peace upon his head."

In order to discourage self-righteousness and hypocrisy among the devout, an anonymous Rabbinic moralist spun a scathing parable on the Biblical theme of the First Sin. It was, of course, the traditional Jewish view that on account of Adam's Fall (when he and Eve had eaten of the fruit of forbidden knowledge), death had come into the world. It happened once (the rabbi began his parable), that certain righteous persons of later generations came running to Adam. They pointed accusing fingers at him. "So it is you, Adam, who are to blame for the fact that we all must die!" they cried. "What do you want of me?" replied Adam plaintively. "It is true . . . I committed one sin! But who, O righteous ones, is there among you who has not been guilty of many sins?"

The Jewish definitions of "sin" and "sinner" embraced the whole dreary catalogue of meanness and wrongdoing that no creature but the human being is capable of. It stands to reason that no system of morals can constitute an absolute; each people or religion evolves its own special views, laws, and myths concerning good and evil, sin and the sinner, reward and punishment. And these too do not remain static but undergo changes with time, circumstance, and influences from without.

The Jewish historical record concerning sin began with the imperious "thou shalt nots" of the Ten Commandments at the dawning of the Jewish religion. The Prophets and the Rabbinic Sages amplified and added to them, and the codifiers of the rites and ceremonies during the Middle Ages and subsequent times merely continued the awesome process of inventorying and classifying them, raising about each of the 613 mitzvot (Scriptural commandments) the protective walls of a multiplicity of rules and regulations. And to violate even one of these constituted a sin.

The unimaginative and the literal-minded among the devout cultivated a piety that was excessively formalistic. It was governed at every step by a deadening conformism and legalism. Nevertheless, it has been claimed that the scrupulous observance on the part of the tradition-following Jew of all the ritualistic minutiae of worship had its positive usefulness for him: It habituated him to doing, to reflecting upon, and to feeling about every religious and ethical precept he was required to fulfill.

The religious teachers of the Talmudic era were sound educational psychologists. They had an abiding belief in the power of habit to condition the individual either to do good or to do evil, depending toward which goal it was directed. Famed among the Jewish folk was the Rabbinic axiom:

> When a man does *one more* good deed–
> He becomes righteous.
> When a man does *one more* evil deed–
> He becomes evil.

Akiba ben Joseph, the foremost Tanna of the Mishnah, observed: "At first sin is as thin as a thread in a spider's web, but in the end it gets to be as thick as a cart rope."

Just as pithy was the whimsical declaration of the Babylonian teacher Chuna on the habit-forming character of sin:

> "When a man has committed a sin once or twice, it is permitted him."
> "Permitted! How can you say such a thing?" asked a colleague, aghast.
> "Ah!" replied Chuna, "At least, to the sinner himself, it appears to be permitted."

Again it must be underscored that it is the traditional Jewish scorn of self-righteousness–one, incidentally, which Jesus of Nazareth also had derived from his Jewish upbringing and milieu–that leads to a mellowed understanding of the sinner and stirs a compassion for his self-abandonment. Precisely because sinning is a major activity of mankind–some sin more, some sin less–and the Evil Inclination impartially casts its snares for the holy rabbi as well as for the hardened criminal, the Wise King was impelled to note regretfully in Ecclesiastes: "There is not a just man upon earth that doeth good and sinneth not."

The Jewish religion, following the teachings of the Prophets, never rejected sinners. The enlightened Sages, like their fellow Jew Jesus, left no doubt about that in their utterances that are recorded in the Talmud. "Let sin, not sinners, disappear from the earth." "A Jew who sins is still a Jew."

Said Rabbi Meir: "Regardless of whether they are righteous or sinners, all men are included among the sons of God. Men are sometimes referred to in the Torah as 'foolish sons,' or 'unfaithful sons,' or 'wicked sons,' but they are called 'sons' nonetheless."

Self-correction by the sinner rather than smug moralizing or anathematizing by the holier-than-thou, was deemed by the Rabbis the most effective way of combating the Evil Inclination. Every man–and every man is a sinner–if he only wants to, is capable of looking within, of answering to his conscience, of examining his actions and his motives. More, the power of repentance is always at hand, if only man has the necessary will to change.

The Rabbinic teachers of ethics, being also pragmatists, tried to appeal to the self-interest of the sinner in urging that he abandon his unprofitable course. Using a pungent comparison, the Talmud likened the sinner to a man who eats

The symbol of human depravity (according to the Bible), the city of Sodom was destroyed by angels as an act of divine retribution. Today, on its ancient site near the Dead Sea, stands a perfectly incorruptible branch of the post office of Israel. (Israel Government Tourist Office.)

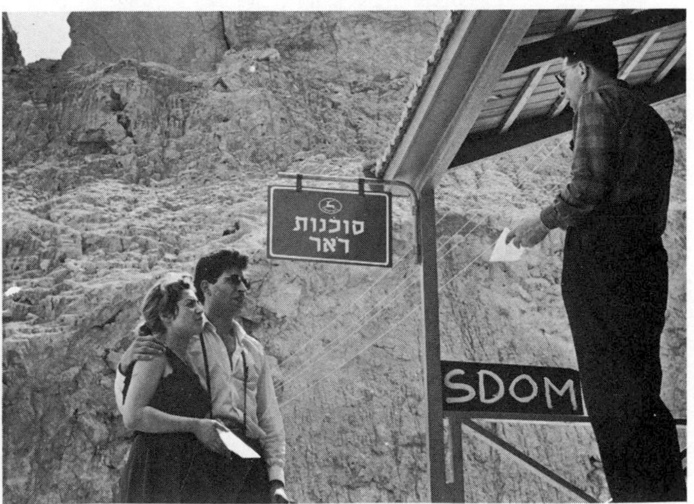

garlic, for while it is true that the eater himself is not at all disturbed by the aroma, his breath, nonetheless, becomes offensive to others. So the folksy Sage, no doubt with a roguish twinkle, put the challenging question: "Shall he go on eating more garlic and become still more repulsive?"

See also FREE WILL; PASSIONS, MASTERY OVER; REPENTANCE; REWARD AND PUNISHMENT; SATAN; YETZER TOB AND YETZER HARAH.

SINNER. *See* SIN AND SINNER.

SISTERS AND BROTHERS. *See* FAMILY RELATIONS, TRADITIONAL PATTERNS OF.

SLAUGHTERER, RITUAL. *See* SHOCHET.

SLAUGHTERING, RITUAL. *See* SHECHITAH.

SLAVERY AND THE SLAVE

When the Jews first emerged as a people in the Land of Israel about three thousand years ago, the institution of slavery was common in all contemporary societies. It was accorded everywhere a status of respectability. It was sanctified by religion, given permanence by custom, and made authoritative by the coercive organs of the state. No one–at least not on record–arose to question its morality. Only a few advanced thinkers, like Hammurabi in Babylonia, a few priest-poets of Egypt, and the Greek dramatist Euripides, were at all disturbed by the savagery inherent in human bondage.

The ironic fact is that the most towering of Greek thinkers, Plato and Aristotle (fifth and fourth centuries B.C.E.), attempted to justify slavery on logical, natural, and even moral grounds. Plato erected the entire physical structure of his ideal utopia (*The Republic*) on the toil of slaves who were to constitute the broad base for his social-economic pyramid at whose top an elite of "free and equal" Athenians would live virtuously, comfortably, and harmoniously. Plato's illustrious pupil, Aristotle, also seemed unperturbed in his conscience when he declared: "Slavery is a law of nature which is advantageous and just." In support of this thesis he even spun a fine "philosophical" web of thirteen arguments.

A diametrically opposite view was advanced by the unknown Jewish author of the Book of Job. That great poet and implacable moralist undoubtedly was a near contemporary of Plato and Aristotle. But his intellectual conditioning had been different from theirs, not so much in fine-spun *sophistries* as in ethics. Job was rooted in the moral values taught by Moses and enlarged by the Prophets. For that reason, he was able to raise the question of questions which challenged unequivocally the morality of human bondage:

> Did not He that made me in the womb make him?
> And did not One fashion us in the womb?
>
> JOB 31:15

Yet it would be incorrect to assume that either the Biblical or the later Rabbinic law went the whole way to work for abolition of the slave system. This it did not do–or, conceivably, from a practical point of view, could not do–because slavery was so deeply woven into the entire economic and social fabric of the ancient world. Notwithstanding this, the Jewish approach to the problem was markedly different from that of the Egyptians, Assyrians, Babylonians, Persians, Phoenicians, Greeks, and Romans. Those societies–whatever may have been their significant cultural contributions to ancient civilization–were still but brutal slavocracies. In their scheme of things, the bondman or bondwoman was nothing but *a thing*–a barterable chattel like a camel or a sheep. In the history of moral and social progress, the efforts of the Jews to expose the evils of slavery, to curb it, and, at the same time, to ameliorate the hard lot of the slave, will always serve as milestones. By according the unfortunate the protection (even if not always effective) of the religious-civil law, it endowed him with human stature and human rights–something virtually unprovided elsewhere for the slave in ancient society. Not without justification did the Frenchman Alexis de Tocqueville, in commenting on the triumphs of the American and French revolutions, write in the nineteenth century: "Liberty, in all its conflicts, has had the Bible for its cradle and its source of authority."

In his analysis, *The Divine Commandments,* Maimonides had stressed that the Mosaic laws which refer to the slave "prescribe only acts of pity, compassion and kindness." But the fact is that the Bible gives no sanction to the enslavement of one man by another, even though it is the Jews alone about whom it particularizes. The antislavery intention of the Biblical law (as it affects the Jews) is unmistakable. Speaking to Moses, in Leviticus 25:42, God says: "For they are My servants whom I brought forth out of the land of Egypt; they shall not be sold as bondmen."

Unfortunately, the pages of history have only too often revealed the wide gap that exists between the principle that is avowed and its actual practice. What noble doctrines the Bible enunciated, what just laws it laid down in consonance with those principles! But beginning with the establishment of the monarchy, the ruling classes of Israel and of Judah found it more convenient or profitable to ignore them. As the social and economic troubles mounted for the oppressed people–in a great measure these stemmed from the creation of the latifundia, the big landed estates that were being built up by the fraud and coercion of the powerful and the rich–many thousands among the tillers of the soil, the smallholders, were expropriated–"swallowed up," as the Prophet so vividly described it.

Despite the Levitical injunction against the selling of Jews into slavery, II Kings 4:1 reveals that it had become the practice in the kingdom of Israel to "seize" and to sell into slavery the sons and daughters of defaulting debtors. In this terrifying passage, a mother runs to Elisha the Prophet, crying: "Thy servant my husband is dead . . . the creditor is come to take unto him my two children to be bondmen."

There must have been times when the traffic in slaves had become so savage and unbridled, that the intervention of the religious law was demanded. The Scriptures accordingly decreed: "If a man be found stealing any of his brethren of the children of Israel, and he deal with him as a slave, and sell him; then that thief shall die; so shall thou put away the evil from the midst of thee." (Deuteronomy 24:7.)

If most methods of perpetuating the slave-system in Israel were devious and illegal, there was one which was "lawful" and, probably for that very reason, more commonly practiced. This was the practice, prevalent among many of the landless and impoverished who were hopelessly in debt and desperate because they had no other choice left them except to starve to death, of *voluntarily* entering into indentured servitude. This meant that they literally "sold" themselves and/or their wives, sons, and daughters as "servants" to the big landowners, the rich merchants, or the usurers.

Despite the laws of Moses, which sternly forbade the enslavement of one Jew by another, and nothwithstanding the pleading of the Prophets that the rich and the wielders of power put an end to the shameful system because it constituted a sin against God's commandments and a violation of the natural rights of man, this form of voluntary bondage, like a stubborn malignancy, continued for a long time to afflict Jewish society. It persisted even following the Dispersion, in 70 C.E., when Judea ceased to be a Jewish state. Rabbi Akiba, appalled by the widespread misery of indentured servitude, was then obliged to reaffirm and reinforce the authority of the Levitical law with new anti-slavery measures. He spurned the very idea of a Jewish slave; to him it was unthinkable and revolting. Said he: "The poorest man in Israel must be considered a patrician who has lost his possessions; for they are all descendants of Abraham, Isaac, and Jacob."

The treatment of the slave, whether involuntary or indentured, obviously negated all the humane and equalitarian provisions of the Mosaic laws and the enactments made by the Judges during the relatively brief period of Israel's social democracy. Unable to abolish the evil of slavery, later priestly legists (whose laws and statutes are believed by Biblical scholars to have been incorporated into the Five Books of Moses) gave their recognition–even though unresigned–to the harsh realities. Their feeling in the matter seemed to be this: Since they were unable to prevent slavery, at least they could try to curb it and, in some respects, perhaps even to humanize it, if slavery could at all be humanized. The anonymous compilers of the code of Deuteronomy decreed (15:12), therefore, that the involuntary slave–that is, the one who had been sold into slavery by others–"shall serve thee

Document of the manumission of a slave, dated 1087 and found in the Cairo Genizah (congregational repository for Hebrew writings mutilated or no longer in use).

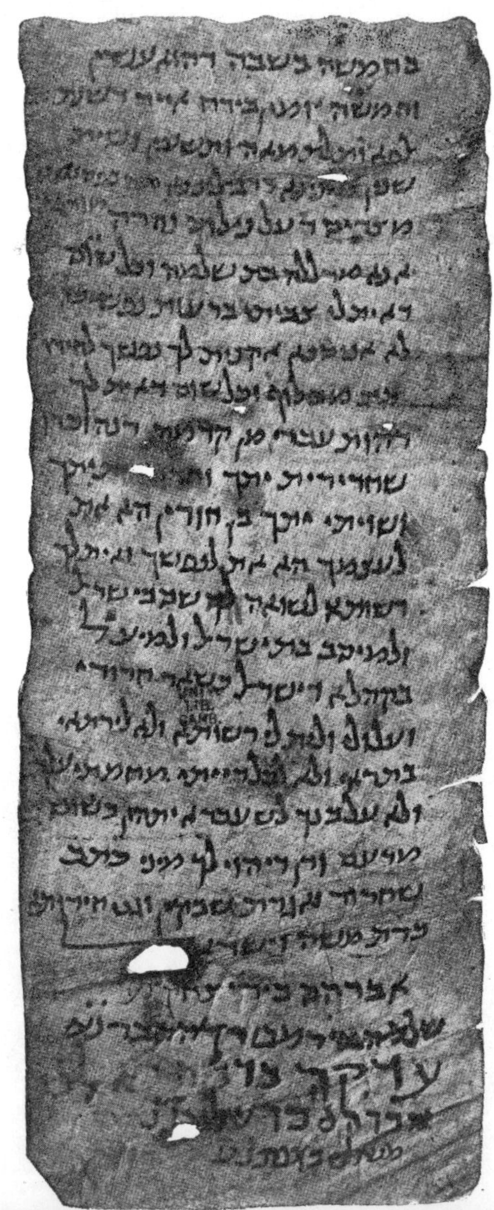

six years; and in the seventh year thou shalt let him go free from thee."

As for the indentured servant (who was, in effect, a slave)–the one who, out of his own free will, had sold himself to a master in order to escape from the despair of his poverty–this was the admonition: "And if thy brother be waxen poor with thee, and sell himself unto thee, thou shalt not make him to serve as a bondservant. As a hired servant, and as a settler, he shall be with thee; he shall serve with thee unto the year of Jubilee. Then shall he go out from thee, he and his children with him, and shall return unto his own family. . ." (Leviticus 25:39-41.)

The horror that the great majority of Jews has always had of slavery was nurtured by Israel's own history. The memory of the Bondage in Egypt, even though it took place more than thirty-two centuries ago, has been like a raw wound in the recollection of the people. The lesson in social morality learned from that national tragedy left a deep impact on the thinking and feeling of all generations of Jews since. It has been kept fresh in their consciousness century after century and year after year on Passover by their celebration of their ancestors' liberation under Moses. As they sit down to the Seder home-service, fused together, even if briefly, by the glow of familial affection and the binding ties of religious and ethnic memories, they begin chanting to a traditional mode in the minor:

> Slaves were we to Pharaoh in Egypt; and the Lord our God brought us out of there with a strong hand and an outstretched arm. And had the Holy One (blessed be He!) not brought our fathers out of Egypt, then we, and our children, and our children's children, would still be slaves to a Pharaoh in Egypt.

The very thought of one Jew being enslaved by another macerated the moral conscience of those holding fast to the covenant of the Torah. Their deeply felt need was to ameliorate the hard lot of the unfortunates. The Levitical lawgiver warned that ". . . over your brethren the children of Israel ye shall not rule, one over another with rigour." And the reason given, reiterated in several places elsewhere in the Bible: "For unto Me the children of Israel are servants; they are My servants whom I brought forth out of the land of Egypt."

Already, in the period of the First Temple, pagan as well as Jewish slaves were protected by special laws against the possibility of brutality at the hands of their Jewish owners. The Jewish master who killed a slave, regardless of whether the slave was Jew or pagan, was to be punished with death, as if he were an ordinary murderer. But among the Romans, until very late times, a master could slay his slave and not be accountable for it. For lesser acts of violence, stated the law of the Torah, the slave was to be given his freedom unconditionally: "And if a man smite the eye of his bondman, or the eye of his bondwoman, and destroy it, he shall let him go free for his eye's sake. And if he smite out his bondsman's tooth, or his bondwoman's tooth, he shall let him go free for his tooth's sake." It was the opinion of Philo, the Alexandrian philosophical moralist, that the slave who was the victim of such cruelty deserved his freedom on simple grounds of humanity, for a master who would inflict such injury upon him was fully capable of hurting him still more or even of killing him outright.

Commenting on the protection extended by the same law of the Torah to non-Jewish slaves, Maimonides wrote: "It is an act of mercy to give liberty to a Canaanite [a generic term for a non-Jew] slave for the loss of one of his limbs, in order that he should not suffer from slavery and illness at the same time." In most respects, the humane treatment demanded by the law for the pagan slave was identical with that for the Jewish slave.

At every opportunity, the Rabbinic Sages extolled the giving to the slave of his freedom as an act of the very highest merit, and in laws and opinions affecting him, they seized upon every convenient pretext to manipulate his liberation. They greatly encouraged the practice of redeeming slaves by purchase. Philo, who flourished one generation before Jesus–and whose teachings and reflections, mirroring the moral climate of Jewish life in that tumultuous age, were entered into the Gospels of Christianity one cenury later–in his role as a rabbi counseled the Jewish devout: "Behave well to your slaves, as you pray to God that he should behave toward you. For as we hear them so shall we be heard, and as we treat them, so shall we be treated. Let us show compassion for compassion, so that we may receive like for like in return."

A thousand years later, Maimonides too stressed the mitzvah of taking a benevolent and compassionate attitude toward the slave. But in his day it was the Gentile slave who was meant, for the custom of Jew taking Jew into servitude no longer was tolerated in Jewish life, having come to an end a thousand years before. Rabbi Moses thus wrote: "It is not sufficient to help those who are in need of our assistance [i.e., the Gentile slaves]. We must look after their interests, be kind to them, and not hurt their feelings by words."

Philo had written, in his discussion of the excellencies of the Jewish law, that it established the moral principle that "children must not be parted from their parents even if you have them as captives, nor a wife separated from her husband even if you are her owner by lawful purchase." What this statement points up so starkly is that more than eighteen centuries after Philo had made it, it was still a common pracice among slaveholders in the United States to break up slave families in order to sell them, separating husband from wife and children from parents so that never again did they meet. It is sad to realize that progress, as measured in terms of chronological time alone, is too often an illusion. For instance, relate the words of the ancient Deuteronomist of the Torah, in which he outlines the duty of the free Jew toward the runaway slave, to what was actually the law in the slave-South of the United States in the nineteenth century: "Thou shalt not deliver unto his master a bondman that is escaped from his master unto thee; he shall dwell with thee, in the midst of thee, in the place which he shall choose within one of thy gates, where it liketh him best; thou shalt not wrong him." (Deuteronomy 23:16-17.)

Commenting on this injunction not to return the runaway slave to his master and stressing the principle of acting as one's brother's keeper, Maimonides stated: "There is a large class of law in our Torah, the sole purpose of which is to fill our hearts with pity for the poor and infirm, to teach us never to hurt their feelings, nor wantonly to vex the helpless. Mercy, likewise, is the object of the ordinance, 'Thou shalt not deliver unto his master the slave that is fled from his scourge.'"

Despite his unenviable status and deprivation of freedom, the slave did not live outside but inside the Jewish family circle; he too was made to rest from his labors on the Sabbath. The Talmud called upon the slave-owner: "Do not eat fine bread while you feed coarse bread to your bondservant. Do not drink old wine while you give him new wine. Do not sleep on soft cushions while you let him lie on straw." Did such tender treatment really make a slave of the slave? With consummate irony, and also not a little of satisfaction, the Talmud adds parenthetically: "This is why people say: 'He who buys a Jewish slave buys himself a master.'"

Those non-Jewish male slaves who had undergone circumcision were allowed to become part of the Jewish community, although they actually held an inferior status religiously, civilly, and socially. Not infrequently they were freed, converted, and intermarried with Jews. In time they became fully absorbed into the Jewish ethnic stream since, in the traditional Jewish view, no shame was attached to being a slave.

It is no doubt significant that there was no word in Biblical or Mishnah Hebrew to denote the status of "freed slave," yet the Greek and Latin languages had such words. From this and other curious indications it can be inferred that in Jewish thinking there was no hereditary taint associated with being a slave. Rather, it was considered more a personal misfortune; it was an inequality that had come about by sheer accident. In any case, it was only a temporary state and, God willing, one that would some day be terminated. That would be accomplished either by redemption through money purchase, by manumission voluntarily arranged by the master, or, at the very worst, by waiting patiently for the arrival of the Year of Release (after the sixth year of servitude) or the Year of Jubilee (the fiftieth year).

Giving a slave his freedom was deemed a voluntary act of piety and loving-kindness. It became a common practice during the Greco-Roman period not only in Judea but in all foreign Jewish settlements. The owner of a slave or the archisynagogos (the equivalent of the parnas or president of the congregation) would usually announce the liberation from the bema (the synagogue platform) to the approbation of the Sabbath worshipers.

The sectarian Jewish grouping—the Essenes and the Zealots—following the priestly example of the pre-Maccabean Hasideans, not only kept no slaves but dedicated themselves to the special task of buying the freedom of slaves from their masters. It may be properly construed from what Philo wrote about the contemporary (with him) Essenes how general the aversion to slavery must have been among the Jews during the Second Temple period. He had noted: "There is not a single slave among them, but they are all free, serving one another; they condemn masters not only for representing a system of unrighteousness in opposition to that of equality, but as personifications of wickedness in that they violate the law of nature which made us all brethren, created alike."

This was hardly a unique view nor was it limited to those monastic idealists of Judea. For Philo wrote further, about another Jewish monastic fellowship, the Greek-oriented Therapeutae established near Alexandria: "They do not have slaves to wait upon them as they consider that the ownership of servants [i.e. slaves] is entirely against nature. For nature has born all men to be free, but the wrongful and covetous acts of some who pursued that source of evil—inequality—have imposed their yoke and invested the stronger with power over the weaker."

Even if the abhorrence of slavery was so general among the advanced segments of the Jewish people that it subsequently, in all future times, became a dominant tradition, the fact should not, however, be overlooked that pro-slavery bias was not negligible. At the very time that the Mishnah Sage, Akiba ben Joseph, was vigorously pressing for acceptance of his antislavery measures—as, for instance, the abolishment of the shameful status of concubine of the female slave to her master—among the Jews under the slavocratic noses of the Roman masters of Judea, his eminent Rabbinical colleague, Yoseh the Galilean, moved perhaps by aristocratic bias, opposed him. His attitude, shared by many Jews, was a frankly materialistic one. He considered that slaves constituted *real property;* therefore, he wished to maintain the institution of slavery at all costs for the profit and the support of the upper classes. In view of this, it is not surprising to learn of the hard-bitten "guideline" that another Tanna of the Mishnah, the wealthy Eliezer ben Hyrcanus, upon the death of his female slave rendered to his disciples who had come to condole with him: "Just as we say to a man when his ox or ass has died, 'May the Omnipotent make up for your loss!' so, too, we should say to a man on the death of his slave: 'May the Omnipotent make up for your loss!'" In other words, "condolences" offered to a master when his slave died were improper and unnecessary. Inferrentially, they were to be reserved only for the death of a "human being."

The ownership of Jewish slaves by Jews rapidly died out during the Maccabean Age and early Rabbinic period. Those times were characterized by a religious puritanism and revivalism under whose searching scrutiny passed all religious and social institutions. But following the complete fragmentation of the Jewish people by the imperial Roman juggernaut, there took place in Judea and in the various countries of Jewish settlement a deterioration in the traditional social morality. While it is true that Jews no longer were taken into bondage by other Jews, some of the less scrupulous found a loophole in the Torah legislation which, inconsistent with its usual humane outlook, permitted the ownership of slaves, provided that they were non-Jews.

In the Byzantine and medieval periods, there were wealthy Jews who, like their Christian and Islamic neighbors, kept slaves or traded in them as a commodity of commerce. In Christian countries they owned and traded in Mohammedan and pagan slaves, and in Mohammedan countries they owned and trafficked in Christian slaves. Neither Church nor Mosque, neither Christian prince nor Mohammedan ruler, saw anything wrong in the time-revered practice of slave-trading. It is actually a historic fact that many of the Church lands in Europe were tilled by slaves, and that Christian as well as Jewish slave traders supplied them when they were required. It was only in the thirteenth century that the Church finally forbade trade by Christians in *Christian* slaves; but it continued to permit the buying and selling of slaves of other religious affiliations.

Of course, medieval Christian society, until the rise of the feudal system, accepted the institution of slavery in a matter-of-fact-way; it had inherited a taste for it as well as the habit directly from Imperial Rome which had been the arch slaveocracy of the ancient world. If the Eastern Church of Byzantium and Gregory the Great (who was pope from 590–604) decreed that Jews could not own slaves, it was not because they opposed slavery but rather feared that the slaves, whether pagan or Mohammedan, might, in living together with Jews, ultimately succumb to the "Jewish superstitions." This fear arose because, during the early centuries of Christianity, there was a clear tendency on the part of many slaves owned by Jews to become converts to Judaism. The inducements for conversion, both practical and moral, were considerable.

It was quite natural for this to be so. The widely held and often aired view in the Byzantine world was that Jewish masters treated their slaves with greater humanity and leniency than did owners of other faiths. Some early Christian writers even criticized them for "spoiling" their slaves with excessive kindness. An old Rabbinic legal opinion declared:

"Mercy is the mark of piety, and no man may load his slave with a grievous yoke. No Gentile slave may be oppressed; he must receive a portion from every delicacy that his master eats; he must not be degraded, neither by word nor act; he must not be bullied nor commanded with scorn, but he must be talked to gently and he must be heard with courtesy."

It was, indeed, true that slave children were raised by Jewish masters together with their own, ofter receiving their religious education in the same schools. On reaching their majority, not a few of them were given their freedom and were often accepted, if they knocked for admission, into the Jewish fold.

Although Jews could no longer own any slaves in Christian countries, nevertheless, there was no opposition to their trafficking in non-Christian slaves. Charlemagne granted Jewish slave-traders that privilege in the eighth century. The role of the Jewish slave-traders in Europe in medieval and also in later times has often—out of animus, no doubt—been exaggerated, like that, for instance, of the Jewish moneylenders. Like the latter, there were quite a few, but in proportion to the general Jewish population, they constituted but an insignificant fraction. The great majority of Jews, conditioned by their history, their beliefs, and practices, had an aversion for slavery.

While there were a small number of Jewish slave-traders active in the United States before the Civil War—and a great many more Jews who were pro-slavery—they hardly represented the sentiment and stand of the majority of American Jewry. Prominent in the Abolition cause were individual Jews such as Ernestine Rose, Michael Heilprin, and Rabbi David Einhorn. Perhaps a true reflection of this antislavery sentiment is found in the annual report for 1853 of the American and Foreign Anti-Slavery Society. It reads in part:

> Some of the Jews who reside in slave states have refused to have any right of property in man, or even to have any slaves about them. They do not believe anything analogous to slavery, as it exists in this country, ever prevailed among the ancient Israelites. But they profess to believe that "the belief of Abraham, enlarged by Moses, and now acknowledged by the Jews, is one of purity and morality, and one which represents the strongest possible support for civil society, especially a government based upon principles of equality and liberty of person."

See also BROTHERHOOD; CHARITY; ESSENES; ETHICAL VALUES, JEWISH; FELLOWSHIP IN ISRAEL; JUBILEE; LIFE, SANCTIFICATION OF; LOANS, FREE; MAN, DIGNITY OF; MOSES; PASSOVER; PEACE, JEWISH CONCEPT OF; PROPHETS, THE (*under* BIBLE, THE); TORAH, THE (*under* BIBLE, THE); THERAPEUTAE; UNITY OF ISRAEL; WORKER, THE.

SOCIAL JUSTICE

The Jewish dedication to the ideal of justice, historically considered, has been all-enveloping and passionate. It has formed part of the interior structure of the religious-cultural heritage of the Jews. The fact is that it is difficult to separate the ideal of justice analytically from all other ethical values created in Jewish life with which it is intertwined. Those are ideals which seem to balance and to blend into one another in an integrated harmony between idea, sentiment, and practice.

It was that way virtually from the beginning: Moses had set the course. He had taught the children of Israel, fleeing from slavery in Egypt and still writhing from the whiplash of the taskmaster: "Let justice pierce the mountain!" But his continuators—the Prophets—went even farther. They strove to pierce the minds and hearts of mankind with the moral imperative of "Justice!"

> Seek justice, relieve the oppressed,
> Judge the fatherless, plead for the widow.
>
> ISAIAH 1:17

In all of its practical applications, the Mosaic-Prophetic ideal of justice for the elimination of social inequities and for the moral guidance of the individual's conduct found classic definition during the first century in the maxim of the Talmudic Sage and grandson of Hillel, Simeon ben Gamaliel. He taught: "The world [society] rests on three foundations: on justice, on truth, and on peace." By indoctrinating the young of every generation with these ethical values, and by attempting to translate the idealistic theory into concrete practice, the teachers of Israel succeeded in awakening the personal and social conscience—the real motivating and molding force in the civilization of the Jewish people.

Because of this, the great modern French social idealist, Jean Jaurès, was able to observe: "And we would have lost much if there had not extended into the French conscience the seriousness of those great Jews who did not conceive of justice as merely a harmony of beauty (Greek), but who demanded it passionately with all the fire of their spirit, who appealed to a just God against all the powers of brutality, who called for the age when all men would be reconciled in justice and when the God whom they invoked would, according to the psalmist or prophet, 'wipe away the tears from all faces.'"

See also BROTHERHOOD; CHARITY; ESSENES; ETHICAL VALUES, JEWISH; FELLOWSHIP IN ISRAEL; JUBILEE; LABOR, DIGNITY OF; LIFE, SANCTIFICATION OF; LOANS, FREE; MAN, DIGNITY OF; MOSES; PASSOVER; PEACE, JEWISH CONCEPT OF; PHARISEES; PROPHETS, THE (*under* BIBLE, THE); SLAVERY AND THE SLAVE; THERAPEUTAE; TORAH, THE (*under* BIBLE, THE); UNITY OF ISRAEL; WORKER, THE.

SOFER (Hebrews s., meaning "scribe"; pl. SOFERIM)

Ever since the return of the Exiles from their Captivity in Babylonia, the sofer functioned as a professional copyist of the Torah. And with the increase in the sacred literature of the Jews in subsequent centuries, he found additional work in reproducing other texts, such as the Talmud, the commentaries, prayer books, and devotional and scholarly writings of various sorts. He also made copies of the Haggadah for the Passover Seder (home-service); of the Megillah (Scroll of the Book of Esther) for Purim; amulets to protect one against misfortune; ketubot (marriage contracts) for marriage ceremonies, and the Scriptural texts on parchment that are enclosed in tefillin (phylacteries) and mezuzot (*see* MEZUZAH).

It is quite an impressive achievement that, although the sofer first appeared on the Jewish scene during the fifth century B.C.E., when Ezra the Scribe and the Men of the Great Assembly (who compiled and made canonical the various writings that comprise the Bible) functioned, so sacrosanct were those works considered—especially the Five Books of Moses—that for some twenty-three hundred years, the rules and regulations governing the production (i.e. copying) of a Torah Scroll (Sefer Torah) and other sacred texts have been observed in almost every respect. Even after the introduction of printing, when Hebrew religious books in large quantities came off the presses, the ancient tradition continued: The Scroll of the Law (Sefer Torah) still had to be copied by hand by the professional sofer, and to this day it is so done.

In each generation there appeared copyists of the Torah

A sofer (Torah-copyist) at his painstaking work. Russia, early 20th century.

who faithfully reproduced the sacred texts of the Five Books of Moses (the Chumash or Pentateuch) *without making a single error!* Once textual errors were discovered, then the parchment page on which they appeared—or, occasionally, the entire Sefer Torah that had taken so many months of grueling and patience-taxing work to prepare—was condemned and hidden in a genizah (a repository for faulty Scriptural texts). The early Scribes and the Rabbinic Sages were dedicated to the protection of the definitive Hebrew Torah text for the generations still unborn, and thus they would not allow any change in it whatsoever, whether through the indifference, ignorance, or carelessness of the scribe, or through deliberate alteration or interpolation. For this they built up an elaborate technical system (*see* MASORAH). Amazingly enough, this physical "fence" around the Torah did work extremely well. It would explain the fixed and almost unaltered character of the Torah text.

This errorless copying of the Torah was a real *tour de force!* It was made possible largely because of the unusual requirements set by Rabbinical standards for the calling of the sofer. He had to be not only learned in the Law but also had to demonstrate satisfactory resources of character and powers of concentration. A dedicated, deeply religious individual, he plied his calligraphic-copyist skill with the utmost scrupulousness.

He was expected to prepare his Torah Scrolls with all possible legibility and beauty for the greater glory of God. With this as a goal, he readily submitted himself to an extraordinary self-discipline. Before sitting down to work, he had to make himself ritually clean in body, mind, and soul. He had to put on his prayer shawl and phylacteries as if he were engaging in religious worship, and these he kept on until his daily quota of work was finished. There are several old Torah Scrolls extant on which the sofer left his humble mark—not out of vanity but as a prayer asking God's forgiveness if, unwittingly, he had allowed an error to creep into the sacred text.

More than eighteen hundred years ago, the famed Judean teacher of ethics, the Scribe Ishmael, cautioned a young copyist: "My son, be careful in your work for it is the work of Heaven, lest you err either in leaving out or in adding one iota, and thereby cause the destruction of the whole world." Two centuries later, the Talmud relates, Rabbi Chisdai came upon his vain Rabbinical colleague, Chananeel, as he was transcribing a Torah Scroll, but he was doing it entirely from memory. Chisdai taunted him: "Indeed! So you are able to write the entire Torah from memory! But haven't our Sages forbidden the writing of even one letter without consulting a model copy?"

There can be no question about it: Whatever else the sofer was, he was often enough also an artist—an artist-calligrapher whose sense of beauty was cultivated in him by the painstaking craft in which he was constantly engaged. The natural drive to artistic beauty among Jews—a creative urge common to all peoples, but dammed up and sent underground by the stern Second Commandment from the fear of the religious teachers that such artistic expression might somehow lead the way back to the idolatrous worship of "graven images," found one of its vicarious outlets in the Hebrew calligraphic art of the sofer. For the kind of graphic beauty he engaged in he found enthusiastic Rabbinic sanction; more—even encouragement. An ancient religious teacher interpreted in this manner the following Scriptural verse: "This is my God, and I will beautify Him." (Exodus 15:2.) Its real meaning, said the rabbi, was: "Serve Him in a beautiful manner . . . Prepare a beautiful Scroll of the Law. Have it written in good ink with a fine quill by a sofer who is expert."

It is interesting to note in this connection that, when Jews felt the impact of an alien superior culture upon their own, the art of the sofer began to blossom. A case in point is that of the famous calligraphic work produced by the sofer in the Hellenistic metropolis of Alexandria more than two thousand years ago, where a quarter of a million Jews had been exposed for centuries to the highly developed Greek forms of architecture, painting, and sculpture. There the *sofer* even tried his hand at illuminating the text of the Torah with miniatures and decorative designs. Unfortunately, no examples of these are extant today; however, it is assumed that they probably were Hellenistic in style and technique. Nonetheless, although the Jewish religious climate in Alexandria was far more enlightened than in Judea and Babylonia, the city's rabbis declared such illustrated Seforim Torah to be a profanation of the Name (of God) and a violation of tradition and such art to be merely a work of vanity, having the unfortunate effect of distracting readers from the spiritual truths of the Torah. As a result, they summarily put a ban on the practice of illuminating manuscripts.

See also ART, CEREMONIAL; SCRIBES; TORAH SCROLL.

(Left) The sofer's three-piece tool for stitching together the parchment leaves of a Sefer Torah (Torah Scroll). (Right) The Sofer's seal. Germany, c. 1800.

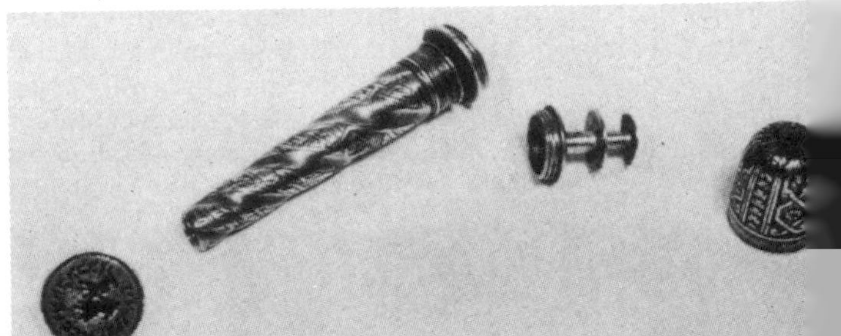

SOME ARCHITECTS OF JEWISH CIVILIZATION
Following Moses, the Prophets, Ezra the Scribe, and the unidentified Men of the Great Assembly (see TALMUD, THE), there were, in the course of the centuries, numerous rabbinic teachers, scholars, thinkers, writers and poets who, each in his own special way, made significant contributions to what may be described as "the Jewish way of life" with its distinctive patterns of attitudes, ethical values, thinking and feeling. Almost one hundred of the most important among these eminent men are to be found in the biographic thumbnail sketches which follow. References, citations, and names of others will appear in the Index of Persons.

ABA BEN JOSEPH. *See* RABBA BEN JOSEPH *(below)*.

ABBA ARIKA. *See* RAB *(below)*.

ABBAYA (Babylonia, *c.* 280–339 C.E.)
Gaon (Rector) of the Yeshibah (Talmudic Academy) of Pumbeditha. In the numerous disputations he had with his friend Rabba which were known as "The Debates between Abbaya and Rabba," he helped perfect the dialectical method of examining the legal traditions of the Babylonian Talmud.

ABRAHAM BAR CHIYYA (ABRAHAM SAVASORDA; Spain, *d. c.* 1136)
A foremost mathematician and astronomer of the Middle Ages. Greatly affected the development of scientific studies among Jews with his own original works in Hebrew (eight of which are still extant) and with his famous Hebrew encyclopedia, *The Foundation of Understanding.*

ABTALION (Judea, first century B.C.E.)
Pharisee leader and Vice-President of the Sanhedrin in Jerusalem. Although he was of Gentile descent, he was one of the most beloved Rabbinic teachers of the age and a great expositor of Scripture. Together with his colleague Shemaiah, he conducted a yeshibah in Jerusalem where Hillel, greatest of all the Rabbinic Sages, acquired his Torah-learning.

ACHAD HA-AM (meaning, in Hebrew, "one of the people"; pen-name of ASHER GINZBERG; *b.* Russia, 1856–*d.* Palestine, 1927)
Expositor of cultural Zionism in his Hebrew writings, this foremost philosopher of Jewish nationalism played a vital role in the propagation of the idea of a Universal Israel deriving its spiritual sustenance in the Diaspora from a Jewish nation and civilization flourishing in the Land of Israel.

AKIBA BEN JOSEPH (Judea, *c.* 50–135 C.E.)
Probably the foremost and most influential creator of the Talmud. In his yeshibah at B'nai Brak were raised a galaxy of eminent Rabbinic thinkers and teachers, including Meir, Simeon bar Yochai, Yoseh ben Chalafta, and Judah ben Ilai. A great legist and systematizer, Akiba, above all other Rabbinic scholars, was most responsible for the codification of the Mishnah laws, although Judah ha-Nasi (*see below*) was their final codifier (*c.* 200 C.E.). Akiba's method of interpretation of Biblical and Oral Laws became the classic tool of Talmudic learning for all the generations. The moving spirit in the Bar Kochba revolt against Rome, Akiba died a martyr's death under torture.

ALBO, JOSEPH (Spain, 1380–1444)
Noted theologian and author of *Ikkarim* ("Principles"), on the fundamentals of the Jewish religion. He reduced the dogmas of faith to three: the Existence of God, Revelation, and Reward and Punishment.

ALFASI, ISAAC BEN JACOB (*b.* North Africa, 1013–*d.* Spain, 1103)
The principal Talmudic authority of his generation, he served as a judge and as teacher of numerous scholars. His work on Rabbinic laws–Halachot (s. Halachah)–drew this encomium from Maimonides (*see below*): "The Halachot of our great teacher, Rabbi Isaac of blessed memory, have superseded all their predecessors' . . . his decisions are unassailable." Alfasi's work was referred to as "The Little Talmud" and received enormous attention from various commentators and critics besides Maimonides.

AMRAM GAON (AMRAM BEN SHESHNA; Babylonia, *d. c.* 875)
Rector (Gaon) of the Sura Academy in Babylonia until his death. He possessed, like so many of the Geonim (*which see*) of Babylonia, encyclopedic learning. He rendered numerous decisions covering all aspects of Jewish jurisprudence. His most important work was his prayer book, Siddur Rab Amram, the first complete liturgy for synagogue and home, which served as the basis for all subsequent Jewish prayer-services and rites–Sefaradic, Ashkenazic, Polish, and Oriental.

ANTIGONOS OF SOKO (Judea, third century B.C.E.)
Believed to have been the first in the line of Pharisees (Rabbinic Sages), his Greek name shows the far-reaching influence of Hellenism even in that early time. A disciple of Simon the Just, the last of the Men of the Great Assembly, his only recorded teachings are his maxims cited in Pirke Abot, the Mishnah treatise on ethics.

ARI, THE (ISAAC BEN SOLOMON LURIA also known as ARI HA-KODESH [THE HOLY ARI]: Palestine, 1534–72)
He was the founder of a system of "Practical Cabala" (as opposed to merely "Theoretical" Cabala). A visionary and moralist who practiced mortifications of the flesh, he found the celestial mysteries readily opened for him, and he imparted them to a closed circle of Cabalists. His metaphysical notions, abstruse and mystical, of the soul and its transmigrations, were eagerly adopted by the many seekers of "the hidden wisdom," including Christian scholars and divines. The Ari introduced a symbolic and mystical significance for every religious rite and ceremony. Through eighteenth-century Chasidism, he left a deep and enduring impact on Jewish life and religious thought and feeling.

ASHER BEN YECHIEL (*b.* Germany, 1250–*d.* Spain, 1328)
A Talmudic scholar of vast learning and incisiveness, he was in implacable opposition to philosophy and to all the secular knowledge which absorbed scholarship during the Arabic-Jewish Golden Age in North Africa, Spain, and the Provence. He even led the onslaught of the fundamentalists against Maimonides' (*see below*) rationalistic liberal teachings. Yet his influence on Talmudic studies was unsurpassed in the age in which he lived. His work Halachot (on the Laws) soon eclipsed the Halachot of the celebrated Isaac Alfasi (*see above*).

ASHI, CHAI BAR (Babylonia, 352–427 C.E.)
Gaon (Rector) of the Yeshibah of Sura for almost half a century, he succeeded in restoring the waning religious authority of that institution to its original supremacy. Ashi was one of the principal compilers and editors of the Babylonian Talmud (*see* TALMUD, THE).

BAAL SHEM TOB, ISRAEL BEN ELIEZER (called also THE BESHT; *b.* The Ukraine, *c.* 1700–*d.* 1760)
A visionary and social idealist in terms of religious-ethical values, the Baal Shem founded the cabalistically derived sect of Chasidim. He preached the omnipresence of God in all creation and denigrated formal worship and Talmudic study, extolling instead love, humility, ecstacy, joy, and the service of the pure heart to God and one's fellow men.

BAR KAPPARA (ELEAZAR BEN ELEAZAR HA-KAPPAR; Judea, third century C.E.)

Headed the yeshibah at Caesarea, and was the teacher of Joshua ben Levi (*see below*). Bar Kappara was greatly admired by his contemporaries for his scientific learning, his Hellenistic culture, his Hebrew verses, and his down-to-earth approach to religious problems. But because he possessed a satirical bent of mind, he also made enemies easily, including the Patriarch, Judah ha-Nasi (*see below*).

BEN AZZAI, SIMEON (second century C.E.)

This Mishnah Tanna (Sage) was almost a legendary figure because of his love for learning and his diligence to acquire it. His authority in matters of the Law was world wide and unquestioned both in Judea and Babylonia. Ben Azzai remains most famous for his exaltation of the human personality: "In the day that God created man, in His own likeness did He make him."

BEN SIRACH (SIRA). *See* JESUS BEN SIRACH (*below*).

BIALIK, CHAIM NACHMAN (*b.* Russia, 1873; settled in Palestine, 1924–*d.* Austria, 1934)

Bialik was the greatest poet nurtured by modern Hebrew literature. He gave the language new and sonorous tonalities. In the main he was a poet of idealistic pessimism, irresistibly drawn to tragic themes about Jewish destiny and martyrdom. Contemporary Jewish culture, whether in Hebrew, Yiddish, or any of a variety of other languages adopted by the Jews of the world, unmistakably reveals the great impact of his poetic genius. Some of his most famous long poems, several of which are to be found in anthologies of world poetry, are *Ha-Matmid* ("The Talmud Student"), *Be'ir ha-Harega* ("In the City of Slaughter"), *Metei Midbar* ("The Dead of the Wilderness"), and *Megillat ha-Esh* ("The Scroll of Fire"). However, juxtaposed to his tragic Muse are his lyrics that extol the joys of childhood, the raptures that reside in Nature and the redemptive powers of love and peace. A number of his songs have been set to music and have achieved the popularity of Jewish folk songs in Israel and throughout the world.

BRATZLAVER, NACHMAN. *See* NACHMAN OF BRATZLAV (*below*).

BUBER, MARTIN (*b.* Austria, 1878–settled in Israel)

Theologian and leader of the Neo-Chasidism which experienced an upsurge in many countries in the years following the Nazi period. Essentially mystical and intellectual, Buber's ideas sound deep undertones of philosophical existentialism. His adherents are found not only among liberal cultivated Jews but among their Protestant counterparts as well. Since 1938 he has taught philosophy at the Hebrew University, in Jerusalem.

CARO, JOSEPH (*b.* Spain, 1488–*d.* Palestine, 1575)

His famous rabinic code, the Shulchan Aruch, the work considered universally authoritative by Orthodox Jews, has maintained its prestige to the present day.

CHAI BAR ASHI. *See* ASHI, CHAI BAR (*above*).

CHIYYA BAR ABBA (also called CHIYYA THE ELDER; Babylonia, third century C.E.)

A Babylonian scholar, he settled in Judea and taught in Tiberias. He was eminent as a compiler of the Toseftah, the supplement to the Mishnah code of the Oral Traditions (*see* MISHNAH, *under* TALMUD, THE). He was an ardent champion of universal elementary education.

CHOFETZ CHAIM (meaning, in Hebrew, "he who desires life"; pseudonym of RABBI ISRAEL MEIR HA-COHEN; Poland, *c.* 1837–1933)

A foremost Orthodox authority on Jewish law and ritual. Beloved by the folk for his devotion to it in times of trial and for his saintly character.

CRESCAS, CHASDAI BEN ABRAHAM (Spain, 1340–1410)

A philosopher of striking originality–he deeply influenced Spinoza more than two centuries later–who nevertheless strove to keep philosophy and the Jewish religion separate. He sharply attacked the application by Maimonides and Gersonides (*see both, below*) of Aristotelianism to Judaism, declaring such a reconciliation to be artificial.

DE LEON, MOSES BEN SHEM TOB (Spain, *c.* 1250–1305)

Author of the Zohar–the "scripture" of the Cabalists–a religious-ethical work which, next to the Bible and the Talmud, wielded the greatest authority on the thinking and the folkways of the Jewish people.

DUBNER MAGGID ("Preacher of Dubno"–RABBI JACOB BEN WOLF KRANTZ; Lithuania, 1740–1804)

The most famous preacher in Yiddish in Eastern Europe. His homespun wisdom, love of people, and gaiety of spirit led him to the invention and also adaptation of hundreds of diverting parables which he employed to illustrate his moralizing sermons. He has sometimes been called "The Jewish Aesop."

EGER, RABBI AKIBA (Germany, 1761–1837)

A casuist in his Talmudic dialectics, he was accepted by his generation of Orthodox Jews as its supreme authority on Jewish law. His devotion to humanitarian ends endeared him universally to the folk except to the adherents of secular education and to Reform or Liberal Judaism, which he opposed vigorously.

ELEAZAR BEN AZARIAH (Judea, first century C.E.)

Eminent priest, teacher of the Mishnah, and a descendant of Ezra the Scribe. He taught at the academy in Yabneh with enormous success: His humane and liberal views found many disciples. It is written in the Mishnah: "With the death of Rabbi Eleazar ben Azariah was removed the 'crown' of the Sages."

ELEAZAR BEN ELEAZAR HA-KAPPAR. *See* BAR KAPPARA (*above*).

ELEAZAR BEN JUDAH OF WORMS (Franco-German Rhineland; *c.* 1176–1238)

Talmudist, astronomer, Cabalist, liturgical poet, and teacher of ethics, his works exercised great influence on the lives of the Ashkenazim (*which see*) during the medieval period.

ELIEZER BEN HYRCANUS (Judea, second century C.E.)

Wealthy fundamentalist interpreter of the Torah, defending the "eye for an eye" Scriptural law against the humane teachings of Ishmael (*see below*) who called instead for financial compensation to the injured.

ELIJAH BEN SOLOMON OF VILNA. *See* VILNER GAON (*below*).

GERSHOM, RABBENU ("Our Teacher Gershom"–GERSHOM BEN JUDAH; Germany, 960–1040)

Because he established yeshibot (s. yeshibah) in various towns of the Franco-German Rhineland, he was revered as "The Light of the Exile." To European Jewry, his religious authority was supreme, and his decision declaring polygamy a sin resulted in its virtual uprooting among the Jews in Oriental countries.

GERSONIDES (LEVI BEN GERSON; France, 1288–1344)

Among Christian Schoolmen he was famed under the names of Magister Leo Hebraeus and Leon de Bagnols. Physician and Aristotelian, he dedicated his labors to works on philosophy and the natural sciences, but he also produced religious writings in which he advanced his views on the nature of the soul, and prophecy. In his commentaries on the Bible and the Talmud, he pursued further the bold rationalistic course initiated by Maimonides (*see below*). Most influential among his religious writings was Milchamot Adonai (The Wars of the Lord).

GINZBERG, ASHER. *See* ACHAD HA-AM (*above*).

GRAETZ, HEINRICH (Germany, 1817–91)

Foremost among the historians of Jewish life and culture since the final Dispersion in 70 C.E. His monumental *History of the Jews,* completed in 1876, still remains unsurpassed in its kaleidoscopic documentation and comprehensiveness.

HAI GAON (Babylonia, *d.* 1038)

Last of the illustrious line of Geonim (*which see*), those Rabbinic intellectuals who, as heads of the yeshibot (s. yeshibah) of Babylonia, were the continuators of the Talmudic Sages in their development of Jewish knowledge and law. Hai Gaon himself was a champion of secular learning.

HALEVI, JUDAH (YEHUDAH) (*b.* Spain, 1085–*d.* Palestine, *c.* 1140)

A great figure in the galaxy of Hebrew poets of the Arabic-Jewish Golden Age in Spain, Judah Halevi was in later centuries acknowledged as the Jewish national poet because of his profound love for Zion and the poignancy with which he expressed this sentiment in verse. It has been estimated that some 300 of his liturgical poems are still in use among Jews–this in addition to some 800 of his secular poems. Aside from his poetry, Halevi achieved great renown for his apologetic dialogue, *Kuzari,* in which he presented a defense of the Jewish religion.

HESS, MOSES (*b.* Germany, 1812–*d.* France, 1875)

At first a social and political radical and an associate of Karl Marx and Friedrich Engels, Hess parted company from them when he became a Jewish nationalist. In 1862, he issued his famous Zionist work, *Rome and Jerusalem,* in which he attacked the position of many Jews–"Where I prosper, that is my fatherland!"–and he called for an upsurge of national aspiration for a Jewish "Jerusalem."

HILLEL (also called HILLEL HA-ZAKEN [HILLEL THE ELDER]; *b.* Babylonia, *c.* 30 B.C.E.–d. Judea, *c.* 20 C.E.)

The greatest of the Pharisee teachers, his ethics served as the bedrock of Rabbinic Judaism. His pursuit of chachmah (wisdom) was directed toward righteousness, and his own practice of it carried tremendous weight among the Jewish folk, who ever sought to emulate Hillel in ways of brotherly love, peace, humility, and benevolence. It has often been observed that Jesus of Nazareth, in his teachings and conduct, used the saintly Hillel as his model. Hillel founded a school of Rabbinic (Pharisaic) thought which, in its gentleness and open-mindedness, was in constant conflict with the rigorous, fundamentalist view of the rival School of Shammai. The debates between these two Pharisee groups formed the foundation of the literature of the Talmud.

HIRSCH, SAMSON RAPHAEL (Germany, 1808–88)

Chief theoretical exponent of Modern or Neo-Orthodoxy. He advanced his ideas in popular book form as *The Nineteen Letters of Ben Uziel.*

IBN ADRET, SOLOMON BEN ABRAHAM (Spain, 1235–1310)

One of the most influential among Jewish religious teachers of the Middle Ages. An ardent champion of the rationalistic spirit and of Maimonides (*see below*), he energetically opposed the incursion into Jewish studies of the mystical Cabala. His intellectual impact was great and continuous.

IBN DAUD, ABRAHAM (Spain, 1110–80)

The first eminent Jewish Aristotelian, he was also a historian and astronomer and laid the rationalistic groundwork for Maimonides' (*see below*) attempt to reconcile the Jewish religion with Greek philosophy.

IBN EZRA, ABRAHAM (Spain, 1092–1167)

A scholar of genius and a great liturgical poet of the synagogue, his many creative gifts were directed to astronomy, mathematics, and grammar. Next to Rashi's (*see below*) commentary on the Scriptures, Abraham ibn Ezra's has been most admired and considered the most authoritative. Ibn Ezra was the first to introduce into his interpretations the critical, historical, and philological methods. His name became a byword in the Jewish household for generations throughout the world.

IBN EZRA, MOSES (Spain, 1070–1138)

Neo-Platonist, mystical follower of Solomon ibn Gabirol (*see below*), his philosophy and his verse, both religious and secular, were imbued with Persian Sufi existentialism. Moses ibn Ezra did not find his peer in lyricism among the great Hebrew poets of the Middle Ages. Besides his critical history of Hebrew poetry, he also produced a philosophical treatise: *Bed of Spices.*

IBN GABIROL, SOLOMON (Spain, 1021–58)

The first Jewish Neo-Platonist philosopher in Spain, he achieved the highest eminence as both thinker and poet. His liturgical verses in Hebrew are still recited and sung in many of the world's synagogues, and his meditations and searchings of soul have not been surpassed in eloquence and transparency of sentiment by any poet. His philosophical work, *The Fountain of Life* (*Mekor Chayyim*), greatly influenced the Christian Schoolmen, and his book on morals, *Improvement of the Qualities of the Soul,* left deep imprints on the thinking of Jewish folk.

IBN PAKUDA, BACHYA BEN JOSEPH (Spain, *c.* 1050–*c.* 1100)

Ethics was Bahya's philosophical preoccupation. A thinker-scholar of vast erudition in all the branches of Greek and Arab learning, he was also thoroughly informed in rabbinic studies. His celebrated work, *Chobat ha-Lebabot* ("The Duties of the Heart"), has proven the most popular and enduring on Jewish ethics.

ISHMAEL BEN ELISHA (Judea, second century C.E.)

One of the great architects of rationalistic methodology for interpreting Scripture, he was commonly referred to in Rabbinic literature simply as "Rabbi Ishmael." His Thirteen Rules (for exposition and analysis) were universally followed by the Talmudic Sages. It is believed that he, like his colleague Rabbi Akiba, died a martyr's death for opposing Roman tyranny.

IRAEL MEIR HA-COHEN, RABBI. *See* CHOFETZ CHAIM (*above*).

ISSERLES, MOSES BEN ISRAEL (Poland, *c.* 1520–72)

Author of Mappah, a commentary and notes to Joseph

Caro's ritual code, the Shulchan Aruch (*which see*). It was by means of Isserles' commentary that the Shulchan Aruch was made acceptable to the Ashkenazim, the Jews of Central and Eastern Europe. Isserles was also a staunch defender of the rationalist views on religious matters expressed by Maimonides (*see below*) and stood opposed to the Cabala (*see also*).

JACOB BEN ASHER (*b.* Germany, 1269–*d.* Spain, 1340)

Author of the religious code Arbah Turim, Jacob ben Asher was a religious jurist of progressive ideas; he retained in his code only those rabbinic laws which had practical application to the life of his own day. His code was authoritative among the Jews for two centuries, but it was finally displaced by Joseph Caro's code, the Shulchan Aruch (Set Table).

JESUS BEN SIRACH (BEN SIRA; early second century B.C.E.)

Author of the famed Wisdom Book in the Apocrypha called Ecclesiasticus in Latin and Chachmat ben Sirach in Hebrew. This work, although it was not admitted into the Bible canon, enjoyed great popularity, first among the Jews and, subsequently, among Christians. Its aphorisms and maxims, similar to those contained in the books of Ecclesiastes and Proverbs, entered into the thinking and locutions of the Jewish people.

JOSHUA BEN CHANANIAH (Judea, second century C.E.)

Referred to in the Mishnah only as "Rabbi Joshua." Celebrated as a teacher (taught in the yeshibah at Yabneh) and as an intimate friend and disciple of Yochanan ben Zakkai (*see below*). Joshua ben Chananiah was a bold and liberal-minded religious thinker who was constantly in dispute with his ultra-conservative colleague Eliezer ben Hyrcanus (*see above*).

JOSHUA BEN GAMALA (Judea, first century B.C.E.)

Established, shortly before Judea fell (in 70 C.E.), the first comprehensive elementary universal school system in Judea—probably the first one in history. The Talmud eulogizes him thus: "Remember for good the man named Joshua ben Gamala, because were it not for him, the Torah would have been forgotten by Israel."

JOSHUA BEN LEVI(Judea, third century C.E.)

Headed the Yeshibah of Lydda. Gentle and meek, his forbearance and benevolent attitude toward his opponents made him a ready subject for folk-legendarizing. His devotion to the community and its welfare was frequently demonstrated in action.

JUDAH BEN ILAI (Judea, second century C.E.)

Called simply "Rabbi Judah" in the Mishnah, his opinions are cited more than 600 times. His great facility and eloquence in expressing himself earned for him the sobriquet Rosh ha-Meddaberim—"the First Among Speakers."

JUDAH CHASID (meaning, in Hebrew, "Judah the Pious"; Germany, *d.* 1217)

Foremost mystic and moralist among the Ashkenazim during the Middle Ages, he earned an enormous reputation and popularity for wonder-working among the plain folk of Central and Eastern Europe. To him is ascribed the composition of the seven "Songs of Unity" and the "Song of Glory," which are given great prominence in the synagogue liturgy. His moralistic work, Sefer Chasidim (Book of the Pious), became virtually a household book.

JUDAH HA-NASI (Judea, *c.* 135 C.E.–*c.* 220 C.E.)

The Patriarch of Judea, usually referred to in the Talmud simply as "Rabbi" or "Rabbenu"—"Our Teacher"—or "Rabbenu Ha-Kodesh"—"Our holy Rabbi." He earned an exalted position in Rabbinic Judaism for having codified the Mishnah (about 220 C.E.). Celebrated also as a teacher of the Oral Traditions, he raised many distinguished Rabbinic thinkers and teachers.

JUDAH (YEHUDAH) HALEVI. *See* HALEVI, JUDAH (*above*).

KAPLAN, MORDECAI (*b.* Lithuania, 1881–U.S.A.)

Professor at the Jewish Theological Seminary in New York and founder of the Reconstructionist movement in modern Judaism. Through the Society for the Advancement of Judaism, which he organized, he has exercised considerable influence in both the Conservative and Reform wings of Judaism. His principle emphases: that the Jews, whatever their religious views, are united by a common awareness of *peoplehood,* and that Judaism is not just a religion but a civilization.

KOHLER, KAUFMANN (*b.* Germany, 1843–*d.* U.S.A., 1926)

Leader, theologian, and scholar of Reform Judaism in America. His principal work, *Jewish Theology* (1910), was the first systematic examination of the principles of Judaism from the point of view of the Higher Biblical Criticism (*see* BIBLE, THE), the scientific postulates of history, and the evolutionary process of ideas. As teacher and (later) President of the Hebrew Union College in Cincinnati, he raised several generations of Liberal rabbis and scholars.

KRANTZ, RABBI JACOB BEN WOLF. *See* DUBNER MAGGID.

LEVI BEN GERSON. *See* GERSONIDES.

LEVI YITZCHOK OF BERDITCHEV, RABBI (Poland, 1740–1809)

A humble and great-hearted soul, beloved by the Chasidic folk, he was affectionately called "the Advocate [before God] of his People." Yiddish folklore abounds with charming anecdotes and exempla of his saintly and forbearing life and character.

LIPKIN, ISRAEL, OF SALANT. *See* SALANTER, ISRAEL (*below*).

LURIA, ISAAC BEN SOLOMON. *See* ARI, THE (*above*).

MAIMONIDES (MOSES BEN MAIMON, "THE RAMBAM"; *b.* Spain, 1135–*d.* Egypt, 1204)

The greatest philosopher that the Jewish people produced until the time of Spinoza (seventeenth century). Maimonides was chiefly concerned with finding the right method for reconciling the tenets of the Jewish religion with the philosophy of Aristotle. His principal religious-philosophical writings are *A Guide to the Perplexed* and the celebrated commentary, Mishneh Torah. Both works are still vastly popular and read by intellectual Jews of every conceivable outlook.

MAR SAMUEL (SAMUEL YARCHINA'AH [meaning "Samuel the Astronomer"]; Babylonia, *c.* 165–*c.* 257 C.E.)

As Gaon (Rector) of the yeshibah at Nehardea, he turned it into a worthy rival of the academy at Sura that was headed by the great Rab (*see below*). Together these two Rabbinic institutions established the religious and intellectual independence of Babylonian Jewry from the authority of Judea, bringing about the creation of the Babylonian Talmud (*see* TALMUD, THE). To that work, the intellectually enlightened and socially dedicated Mar Samuel made a large contribution.

MEIR, RABBI (called also BAAL HA-NES; Judea, second century C.E.)

A disciple of the great Tanna (Sage) Akiba (*see above*),

Meir continued his master's work of collecting and systematizing the Oral Traditions—a labor that was ended only with the codification of the Mishnah (*c.* 220 C.E.) by Meir's successor, Judah ha-Nasi (*see above*). A great and popular teacher, Meir pursued the democratic traditions of Torah-learning by bringing them down to the level of folk comprehension.

MEIR, RABBI, OF ROTHENBURG (Germany, *c.* 1215–93)

Liturgist and Talmudic scholar whose religious authority was established over all the Ashkenazic communities. His devotion to his people led him to a voluntary martyrdom: imprisoned by the Emperor Rudolph, he refused to be ransomed in order not to establish a pattern for the blackmail of other Jews.

MENDELE MOCHER SEFORIM (pen name of Solomon Jacob Abramowitsch, Russia, 1836–1917)

Mendele's unique and also incredible achievement was that he was the progenitor of two bodies of related Jewish literatures: one in Hebrew and the other in Yiddish. His masterly writings served as the seminal stream that gave life, form, and substance to the modern development of both literatures. A leading champion of the Enlightenment—the Haskalah—for the Jewish masses, he chose satire as the literary tool for indoctrinating them with liberal Western ideas and knowledge. Folksy and realistic at the same time, and steeped in the traditional lore and values of his people, his impact on the life and thought of Yiddish-speaking East European Jewry cannot be overestimated. His disciples, foremost among them Sholem Aleichem and Peretz, further explored his microcosm of the ghetto for projecting Jewish life, character and problems in sober realistic terms. His best-known Yiddish works are *Di Klatche* ("The Old Plug," 1873), *Fishke der Krumer* ("Fishke the Lame," 1869), and *Dos Vinshfingerl* ("The Wishing Ring," 1882–92).

MENDELSSOHN, MOSES (Germany, 1729–86)

To the Germans, his importance was as a philosopher; to his fellow Jews, he was important mainly as the initiator of the Jewish Enlightenment (Haskalah). A controversial figure whose sincerity and brilliance were conceded by adherent and opponent alike, his ideas and program for the Europeanization of the Jewish people ultimately led to the emergence of Reform Judaism early in the nineteenth century.

MÖLNN, JACOB BEN JOSEPH HALEVI, OF MAYENCE (Germany, 1365–1427)

The foremost religious authority of his time among the Ashkenazim of Central and Eastern Europe. Tradition holds that he composed some of the best hymn-tunes in the Ashkenazic Minhag (Rite).

MOSES BEN JACOB OF COUCY, RABBI (France, thirteenth century)

Author of the famous religious code Semag, which treats of the 613 Scriptural mitzvot (*see* MITZVAH).

MOSES BEN MAIMON. *See* MAIMONIDES (*above*).

MOSES BEN NACHMAN. *See* NACHMANIDES (*below*).

NACHMAN OF BRATZLAV (NACHMAN BRATZLAVER; The Ukraine, 1771–1811)

Mystic poet and reformer. He was the great-grandson of Israel Baal Shem-Tob (*see above*), the founder of Chasidism. Nachman strove to purify the thought and conduct of his fellow sectaries from their gross preoccupation with miracles, superstitions, and tzaddik worship. He attracted to his idealistic beliefs the best elements among the Chasidim.

NACHMANIDES (MOSES BEN NACHMAN; *b.* Spain, 1194–*d.* Palestine, *c.* 1270)

A leading writer of commentary on the Scriptures, a foremost Talmudic expounder of Rabbinic law, as well as a liturgical poet of great expressiveness, Nachmanides was forced by the stark realities of persecution to step forward in 1263 as the champion of the Jews in a circus-like public disputation against the slanderous accusations made by the apostate Jew, Pablo Christiani. The final outcome: Nachmanides was sentenced by Pope Clement IV to perpetual banishment.

PERETZ, YITZCHOK (ISAAC) LEIBUSH (Poland, 1851–1915)

Peretz was the most poetic and philosophic of the triad of great writers in modern Yiddish literature that also included Mendele Mocher Seforim and Sholem Aleichem. Without question, he was the most influential of them in leaving his stamp on the literary styles and tastes of several generations of Yiddish writers and readers. Undoubtedly, he was the most modern and cultured of the three. His works reveal astonishingly diverse ingredients—Biblical, Cabalistic, and Chasidic—and these are overlaid with a patina of religious skepticism, socialism, Zionism, and romanticism. From a synthesis of all these materials, however, he created many remarkable short stories, sketches, and plays which, surprisingly, he molded into a unity because he marked them with his own unique individuality. Some of his best-known prose writings, Chasidic and folkloristic, are *A Gilgul fun a Nigun,* ("The Reincarnation of a Melody"), *Drei Matones* ("Three Gifts"), *Oib Nisht Noch Hecher* ("If Not Still Higher!"), *Bontshe Shveig* ("Bontshe the Silent"), and *Sholom Bayyis* ("Domestic Peace").

PHILO JUDAEUS (PHILO OF ALEXANDRIA; Egypt, *c.* 20 B.C.E.–40 C.E.)

A Platonist and an idealistic mystic, Philo was the Chief Rabbi of the great Jewish community in Alexandria. Because he interwove the allegoric-ethical strands of his Jewish faith with Greek philosophy and poetry, his rabbinical and homiletical writings were, consequently, stamped with the character of Hellenistic culture, which was both poetical and mystical.

PINSKER, LEO (*b.* Poland, 1821–*d.* Russia, 1891)

A champion of the Jewish Enlightenment and the Russification of the Yiddish-speaking ghetto masses, Pinsker experienced a shattering disenchantment in his former beliefs upon the outbreak in 1881 of government-sponsored pogroms that were quickly followed by the crushing anti-Semitic May Laws. It was then that Pinsker wrote his rousing *Auto-Emancipation,* in which he advocated a return to Palestine and agricultural colonization by his fellow Jews, calling on them to rely only on themselves for their emancipation.

RAB (ABBA ARIKA; Babylonia, *d.* 247 C.E.)

Most famous of all the Rabbinic Sages of Babylonia and founder of the great yeshibah at Sura. Students from all parts of the Jewish Diaspora flocked to Rab's classes, and Sura became the seat of religious authority for all Jewry. Rab's decisions and opinions as well as his many disputations with Mar Samuel (*see above*), the talented Gaon (Rector) of the rival Yeshibah of Nehardea, virtually overflow the massive texts of the Babylonian Talmud.

RABBA BAR NACHMANI (often called simply RABBA; Babylonia, *d.* 330 C.E.)

Great Rabbinic teacher at the Yeshibah of Pumbeditha. Thousands of Talmudic scholars and students came to listen to him expound the Law (Halachah).

RABBA BEN JOSEPH (ABBA BEN JOSEPH; Babylonia 280–352 C.E.)

In his famous debates with his friend and colleague Abbaya (*see above*), he helped develop the dialectical method in the examination of legal traditions. He established his yeshibah in Machuza, where he found numerous students. He was responsible with his decisions for the introduction of new rules in ceremonial law. A popular interpreter, he gave public lectures, especially on the primary importance of Torah study.

RABBENU GERSHOM. *See* GERSHOM, RABBENU (*above*).

RABBENU TAM. *See* TAM, RABBENU (*below*).

RAMBAM, THE. *See* MAIMONIDES (*above*).

RASHI (SOLOMON BEN ISAAC OF TROYES; Franco-German Rhineland, 1040–1105)

Known as "the Prince of Commentators" because of the vast popularity of his commentaries on the Scriptures and Rabbinic law. His interpretations are characterized by clarity, succinctness, and a scrupulous attention to the literal meaning of the words in the texts. Rashi remained for centuries the foremost religious guide for the Yiddish-speaking Ashkenazim of Europe.

RESH LAKISH. *See* SIMEON BEN LAKISH (*below*).

SAADIA GAON (SAADIA BEN JOSEPH; *b.* Egypt, 882–*d.* Palestine, 942)

The most versatile of all Jewish savants in the Arab Diaspora, Saadia presided over the great Yeshibah of Sura, in Babylonia. His encyclopedic erudition and his vast culture would have distinguished him in the intellectual milieu of any age. Saadia composed works on every conceivable subject with which the culture of his Arab-Jewish society was concerned: Biblical exegesis, the Hebrew language, liturgy, grammar, law, philosophy, rabbinics, mathematics, astronomy—even the theory of music. His outstanding religious work was The Book of Faith and Doctrines (Sefer Emunat ve-De-ot).

SALANTER, ISRAEL (ISRAEL LIPKIN OF SALANT; *b.* Lithuania, 1800–*d.* Germany, 1883)

One of the most beloved of Orthodox religious leaders and teachers of modern times. He was a simple man, great-hearted and out-reaching to the plain folk. Practical-minded as well, he agitated for the teaching of trades to the ghetto youth to save it from an otherwise hopeless destiny.

SAMUEL, MAR. *See* MAR SAMUEL, (*above*).

SAVASORDA, ABRAHAM. *See* ABRAHAM BAR CHIYYA (*above*).

SCHECHTER, SOLOMON (*b.* Romania, 1847–*d.* U.S.A., 1915)

The principal expounder of Conservative Judaism in the English-speaking world, Dr. Schechter helped mold the religious thinking of thousands of rabbis and religious teachers during his long-held presidency of the Jewish Theological Seminary of America in New York. His writings on Jewish subjects were always scholarly, liberal, and urbane.

SHAMMAI (Judea, first century B.C.E.)

A contemporary and chief religious opponent among the Pharisee Sages of the "gentle" Hillel, Shammai was, essentially, a literal-minded rigorist and an uncompromising fundamentalist. The disputes and discussions on belief, law, rite, and conduct carried on between his adherents—the School of Shammai (Bet Shammai)—and their opponents of the School of Hillel (Bet Hillel) extended over many centuries and fill many pages of the Talmud.

SHERIRA GAON (SHERIRA BEN CHANINA; Babylonia, tenth century C.E.)

Gaon (Rector) of the Yeshibah of Pumbeditha. He wrote numerous rabbinical decisions preserved in Responsa (*see* RABBINICAL DECISIONS) to many questions of law raised by Jewish communities throughout the world.

SHNEOR ZALMAN (Lithuania, 1744–1813)

Foremost systematizer and exponent of Chasidism, he was called "The Rav" (The Master). In his classic work *Tanya* (1796), he laid down the guidelines for Chasidic belief and practice which were quite generally adopted by the adherents of the sect, and adapted for them the prayer service originated by Isaac Luria (*see above*), the Cabalist master of sixteenth-century Safed, Palestine. This service he termed Nussach Sefarad (the Sefaradic order of prayer).

SHOLEM ALEICHEM (pen name of Sholem Rabinowitz, *b.* Russia, 1859–*d.* U.S.A., 1916)

The best beloved and the most widely read Yiddish writer has been Sholem Aleichem, whose humorous-satirical works are unique in world literature. His uncanny understanding of the minds and souls of the plain ghetto folk, his sympathy for their character peculiarities and dilemmas—and his marvelous ear for recording their speech—made him the most persuasive and illuminating articulator of East European Jewish life in the several decades prior to World War I. Translations of his writings are to be found in more than seventy languages. Among his most esteemed works are *Tevye der Milchiger* ("Tevye the Dairyman," 1895–1916), *Menachem Mendel of Yehunetz* (1892), *Maisses far Idishe Kinder* ("Stories for Jewish Children"), and *Varmbeder* ("Spas").

SIMEON BAR YOCHAI (Judea, second century C.E.)

A foremost teacher of the Mishnah and a mystic, he is referred to 325 times in the Oral Laws as "Rabbi Simeon." A disciple of Akiba (*see above*), he was, like his master, outspoken against Roman rule and condemned to death for his beliefs. Jewish folklore is enlivened by legendary accounts of his thirteen-year sojourn in a cave in hiding from the Romans, and of the wonders he performed. The authorship of the Zohar (the "scripture" of the Cabalists) was ascribed to him by Cabalist tradition. Annually, on the eighteenth of Iyar, thousands of devout Jews in modern Israel make a pilgrimage to his supposed tomb at Merom, in Galilee.

SIMEON BEN AZZAI. *See* BEN AZZAI (*above*).

SIMEON BEN GAMALIEL, RABBAN (Judea, second century C.E.)

A celebrated Tanna (Sage) of the Mishnah, he was one of the great teachers of Jewish ethics. He was, like his father and grandfather before him, the titular Patriarch and President of the Great Sanhedrin (*see* SANHEDRIN). A direct descendant of Hillel the Elder (*see above*), Rabban Simeon emulated him in his benevolent outlook toward people and lenient interpretation of the Law. A man of broad culture, he had studied Greek philosophy, the natural sciences, and medicine, and this learning had widened and deepened his religious thinking.

SIMEON BEN LAKISH (also known as RESH LAKISH; Judea, second century C.E.)

Taught at the academy of Tiberias, which was presided over by his brother-in-law, Yochanan bar Nappacha (*see below*), the celebrated Rabbinic master. Early in his career, Resh Lakish was forced through dire need to earn his livelihood as a "strong man" and gladiator in a Roman circus. His didactic aphorisms and sayings, as recorded in the Talmud, were widely circulated among the folk in later centuries.

SIMEON BEN SHETACH (Judea, first century B.C.E.)

President of the Sanhedrin (105 B.C.E.–70 B.C.E.). A Pharisee teacher, he initiated the first elementary school system ever to exist (*see* TALMUD TORAH) in Jerusalem and other principal towns of Judea.

SOLOMON BEN ISAAC OF TROYES, RABBI. *See* RASHI (*above*).

SPINOZA, BARUCH (Holland, 1632–77)

Spinoza was the most eminent of the thinkers who sprang from the Jewish people, and he became one of the giants in world philosophy. A consistent idealist in his own way of life and a teacher of ethics which he tried to develop systematically in his principal work, *Ethics,* his thinking was profoundly influenced by the scientific rationalism of the French philosopher, René Descartes, and by the heroic example in martyrdom of the free-thinking priest, Giordano Bruno. While preparing himself for the rabbinate in the Amsterdam Yeshibah, his "heretical" views on such central teachings as immortality, free will, prophecy and miracles, subjected him to harassment, obloquy, and, finally, excommunication from the Jewish fold. Forced into exile from Amsterdam, he wrote, years later and with obvious autobiographic intent, in *Tractatus Theologico-Politicus* ("Treatise on Theology and Politics"): "What greater misfortune for a state can be conceived than that honorable men should be sent like criminals into exile because they hold diverse opinions which they cannot disguise."

Besides compiling a Hebrew grammar, Spinoza undertook in the *Tractatus* a bold and new critical analysis of the Bible and of Jewish doctrines; he proclaimed therein the intellectual independence from the authority of religion of philosophy and of the search for truth.

STEINSCHNEIDER, MORITZ (*b.* Austria, 1816–*d.* Germany, 1907).

The most scientific of all research scholars in the field of Judaica, Steinschneider made monumental contributions to Jewish bibliography. His *Catalogue of Jewish Books in the Bodleian Library* (at Oxford; 1852–60) was the first production to establish his reputation as a researcher. There followed *The Hebrew Translations During the Middle Ages and the Jews as Interpreters, Jewish Literature,* and *The Arabic Literature of the Jews.*

TAM, RABBENU (JACOB BEN MEIR TAM; France, 1100–71)

The grandson of Rashi (*see above*), he was an independent Talmudic thinker who challenged and disagreed with many of his grandfather's interpretations of Scripture and the Talmud. These questions, added to his rabbinic decisions (Responsa), he turned into a book: the famous and widely read Sefer ha-Yashar (The Book of the Just)—a work that initiated the rabbinic form of commentary called *Tosafot* (Additional Notes) on the Talmud.

TARPHON (Judea, first and second centuries C.E.)

Distinguished Tanna (Sage) of the Mishnah and a fellow teacher of Akiba at the yeshibot in Yabneh, Lydda, and B'nai Brak. Before the Romans destroyed the Temple in Jerusalem, in 70 C.E., Tarphon had performed priestly services there.

TCHERNICHOVSKY, SAUL (*b.* Russia, 1875–*d.* Israel, 1943)

Next to Chaim Nachman Bialik, Tchernichovsky ranks as the most formidable modern Hebrew poet. A hedonist with an amoral classic Greek outlook, he celebrated the sensuous joys of existence, of laughter, and of Nature renewing itself eternally. He wanted his Hebrew verses to help correct the one-sided traditional Jewish emphasis on intellectuality and the religious life permeated by what he considered a morbid puritanism. Nonetheless, as a Jew living in times that were disastrously tragic for his people, he could hardly avoid collisions with reality. Out of this painful awareness during the Nazi period in 1937 stemmed his *Baruch of Mayence* and the *Martyrs of Dortmund,* works written in the elegiac style of the Hebrew kinah. But his reputation as a great poet is more likely to rest on those poems written in the "pagan" mood: *A Sheaf of Sonnets, The Book of Idylls,* and *New Poems,* all three produced in the early nineteen twenties.

VILNER GAON (ELIJAH BEN SOLOMON OF VILNA; Lithuania, 1720–97)

The possessor of a remarkable photographic memory, he achieved almost legendary fame as a writer on Biblical and Talmudic literature. As an ascetic, he was led naturally to oppose the surface hedonism and lack of emotional discipline of the Chasidim, whom he excommunicated in a rage of zeal.

YARCHINA'AH, SAMUEL. *See* MAR SAMUEL (*above*).

YOCHANAN BAR NAPPACHA (Judea, *d.* 279 C.E.)

Usually referred to in the Talmud simply as "Rabbi Yochanan." He headed the famous Yeshibah of Tiberias for many years. Gentle and amiable to all men, Yochanan enjoyed an almost saintly reputation. He raised a generation of such eminent scholars as Eleazar ben Pedat, Chiyya bar Abba, Ammi, Abbahu, and Assi. He laid down certain fundamental rules for analyzing Rabbinical opinions and decisions in matters of law and observance—his emphasis was always on the liberal interpretation (he even believed that secular and non-Jewish studies and decorative and non-figurative mural painting [*see* ART AMONG THE JEWS] should be allowed). It should be borne in mind that Yochanan's name and citations from his opinions appear in the Talmud more frequently than those of any other Rabbinic Sage. Some scholars attribute to him the compilation—or at least the planning—of the Jerusalem Talmud or Gemara.

YOCHANAN BEN ZAKKAI (Judea, first century C.E.)

Pharisee disciple of and successor to the great Hillel (*see above*), he established the yeshibah at Yabneh, following the Destruction of the Temple and the Jewish state in 70 C.E. by the Romans. He was revered by the Jewish people as a symbol of their strong determination to preserve their religion, group identity, and culture. His moralistic sayings became widely disseminated among the folk.

YOSEH BEN CHALAFTA (Judea, second century C.E.)

A Tanna (Sage) of the Mishnah, he was a foremost disciple of Akiba (*see above*). He is believed to have been the author of the Hebrew chronicle Seder Olam Rabbah, which fixed the chronology of the Bible.

ZUNZ, LEOPOLD (Germany, 1794–1886)

Established the "Science of Judaism" in Germany in the early 1820's. Subsequently, he produced important pioneer studies on the liturgy of the synagogue, and on Jewish religious literature and cultural history.

SOUL, THE

When the religious Jews say "soul" or its equivalent, "spirit," what exactly do they have in mind? This word has been defined often enough, either in the ecstatic vein of the poets of the synagogue, so that, it shimmers with mystic imagery, or in the obscure manner of the rabbinic philosophers of the Middle Ages, so that it remains incomprehensible to the modern reader.

We first meet with the word "soul" in the Biblical Book of Genesis, which tells how God formed Adam, the first man. He made him of dust, and he "breathed into his nostrils the breath of life; and man became a living soul." Just as poetical is the aphorism in Proverbs: "The spirit of man is the lamp of the Lord."

The mystical "scripture" of the Cabalists, the Zohar, preferred a more intimate descriptive to emphasize the divine origin of the soul: "The soul is the daughter of God." This same mysticism and vagueness are found in all the Hebrew names for "soul." Their number is surprising, clearly demonstrating the great difficulty Jews found in their many efforts to define the concept. The three most commonly used Hebrew names for "soul" are *neshamah, ruach,* and *nefesh.*

In the traditional Jewish view, the soul is considered to have a separate existence of its own. But the Bible fails to make clear what its substance or essence actually is, and whether it is material or "spiritual." However, both in and out of the body, the soul is considered dependent upon the will of God. This belief of dependence on the Deity is in striking opposition to the well-known notion of Plato that the soul is entirely free and independent "because it is the only thing in the world that moves without being itself moved by anything else." Also, unlike the traditional Jewish conception, that of the Athenian philosopher did not limit possession of a soul exclusively to human beings. For Plato believed that all things in the universe, whether animate or inanimate, organic or inorganic, also had souls!

The Sages of the Talmud, certainly less sophisticated than Plato, argued from a different premise. The Torah, they said, states that God, at the time when he fashioned man, made him in his own image, breathing into Adam's inert body the breath of his own Ineffable Soul. From *this* exalted origin man derived his "holy" individuality and human dignity. Unlike all other things in creation, the Sages said, man's possession of a soul brought him into a unique relationship with God. It was the kinship of a son to his father. "God the Father" became an endearing Jewish figure of speech, and one which was adopted into Christian usage by Jesus and the Apostles.

The ancient Rabbis asked: If you strip the husk of flesh from man's being, what remains? Only the soul, they answered.

There frequently runs through Jewish religious teachings the declaration that man is the child of God; therefore, he is a co-partner with him in the divine plan of Creation. This distinction imposes on him the sacred obligation to work for the increase of godliness, truth, and justice in the world. Could the grave then be regarded logically as the end of human existence? According to the Rabbis, it was merely a stopping-off station on the long road to Eternity. They likened Olam ha-Zeh–"This World"–to a wayside inn and compared mortal man to a footsore traveler who halts in life for only a little while, to rest and take refreshment before he continues on his distant journey to Olam ha-Bah–"the World-to-Come." The higher and nobler man's stage of moral development, the closer he gets to his final goal–to redemption and the bliss of Gan Eden (Paradise).

The Rabbis of the Talmud were skilled weavers in the art of poetic allegory. They chose this particular literary form, in addition to the parable and the fable, because it proved a useful aid in making their teachings more intelligible to the simple-minded folk. And so they allegorized about the soul of man, likening it to the Shechinah (God's Ineffable Presence), stating that even as the Shechinah pervades the entire universe, so does the soul pervade the body. Just as the Creator–the First Cause–will outlast the material universe because he stands outside and above it, so too will the soul outlast its fragile tenement of flesh. As there is only one God in all the universe, so too is the soul the only inhabitant of the body. Even as God sees all, and yet is not seen himself, so too does the soul see, yet remains invisible. Just as God "rests not, neither does he sleep," so too the soul of man never is at rest, never slumbers. And finally, even as God remains unchangeably pure and ineffable "from everlasting to everlasting," so too can the spirit of man, fired by the truth and way of the Torah, aspire with confidence to become ever purer and more perfect.

Despite these and other ingenious Rabbinic explanations, the reality of such an intangible essence as the soul remained elusive, especially to the ordinary folk. What *really,* they kept on asking, was the soul? To satisfy this urgent need to understand, an infinite variety of childish speculations, fantasies, and superstitions sprang up and took firm root among the backward elements of the Jewish people. Rationalist religious teachers were deeply disturbed by these views and tried to counter them with a frank admission of their own bafflement and ignorance before the heavenly mysteries.

The twelfth-century philosopher-rabbi, Maimonides, went on to warn his fellow-Jews. "Just as a blind man is unable to form any idea about colors or a deaf one to hear sounds . . . so the body cannot comprehend the delights of the soul . . . For we live in a material world, and the only kind of pleasure we can understand is the material. But the joys of the spirit are everlasting and ceaseless. There is no resemblance of any kind between the enjoyments of the soul and those of the body."

See also IMMORTALITY; RESURRECTION; WORLD-TO-COME.

SOVIET UNION, JEWS IN. *See* HEBREW LITERATURE, MODERN; PERSECUTION IN "MODERN" DRESS; POGROMS IN SLAVIC LANDS; YIDDISH LITERATURE, MODERN; ZIONISM.

STANDARDS OF MARITAL BEHAVIOR. *See* MARRIAGE AND SEX.

"STAR OF DAVID." *See* MAGEN DAVID.

"STILL, SMALL VOICE, THE." *See* BIBLE, THE.

SUCCAH. *See* SUCCOT.

SUCCOT (Hebrew pl., meaning "booths" [s. SUCCAH]; hence [the] "Feast of Booths"; also known as [the] "Feast of Tabernacles")

What had begun in an unrecorded remote period purely as a harvest festival at the time of the full moon, in the process of religious development became fused with new but spiritualized elements in the festival of Succot. Originally, its celebration was marked by primitive rites that had magical ends in view. These were consummated by revels, with feasting and choric dancing to the liquid flutings of the double-pipe (chalil). In this respect, the Jewish rites were probably not at all distinguishable from those observed by Israel's nature-worshiping neighbors at their festivals. Yet, whatever the later and more meaningful changes, the specifically agricultural character of Succot as a harvest festival has been preserved, although in the puritanical climate of latter-day Jewish life, the pagan revels were outlawed.

According to the Bible, it was God, speaking to Moses, who had instructed the people at Mount Sinai: "And thou shalt observe . . . the feast of ingathering at the year's end."

(Exodus 34:22.) For this reason, in early times Succot was frankly a celebration marking the harvest of the crops and named, appropriately, the "Feast of Ingathering."

The festival began four days after Yom Kippur on the fifteenth day of the seventh month of Tishri. It lasted seven days, during which time the Jews were required to live in pastoral booths. And the Scriptural reason for this unusual departure from the normal way of living was "that your generations may know that I [God] made the children of Israel to dwell in booths, when I brought them out of the land of Egypt." (Leviticus 23:43.)

Once again the tireless reminder was made to the Jews that their ancestors had been slaves in Egypt. The wonderment arises why this lingering recollection of an historic experience long past and unflattering to the self-esteem of a proud people, should have been hammered so unrelentingly into the consciousness of the Jews. Quite clearly, Israel's religious teachers considered it necessary to stamp on the people's memory its national degradation and suffering in Egypt so as to be able to emphasize the more the "miracles" that God had wrought in its behalf.

The purpose of the Biblical commandment instructing all Jews to dwell in a succah or booth for seven days was to bring by vicarious experience the reality of the most epochal events–the Egyptian Bondage, the Liberation which followed, and the covenant that Israel had entered into with God at Mount Sinai–in the history of the Jews to all generations. The Alexandrian philosopher-rabbi, Philo, who flourished early in the first century, saw great ethical significance in the fact that the succah was to be dwelt in by *all* in Israel, whether great or humble, rich or poor. He considered it to be an educational instrument of democratic leveling, for it taught, he wrote, "equality–the first principle and beginning of justice."

How ancient the festival of Succot is may be judged from the chronicle of Nehemiah which he wrote during the middle of the fifth century B.C.E. In it, he stated that Ezra and the Scribes reinstituted its celebration which, according to him, had not been observed since the days of Joshua, the successor of Moses. The returning exiles from Babylonia "made themselves booths [succot], every one upon the roof of his house, and in their courts, and in the courts of the house of God [i.e., the Temple], and in the broad place of the [Temple] Water Gate, and in the broad place of the Gate of Ephraim." (Nehemiah 8:16.)

No sooner had Yom Kippur departed than the construction of the succah began. Everyone was obligated by Rabbinic law to take part in the work as a meritorious act of piety or mitzvah. Precise instructions were laid down by the Rabbis for the building of the festival booth. It was to be no less than four feet long and four feet wide and not higher than thirty feet. Every effort was made, within the limits of the material means and the level of taste of each family, to make the succah beautiful. To give it verisimilitude, the roof of each succah was made of green boughs, and the interior was festooned with all kinds of fruits, flowers, and greenery. The roof foliage was required to be so laid that through the apertures the stars could be seen, as a reminder to the worshipers that the Guardian of Israel was always watching for the safety of his people against the evil designs of its enemies.

In modern urban living, of course, there are few Jews except the very Orthodox who are prepared to go to the trouble of erecting a succah in their backyard. Consequently, each synagogue, to keep the verdant memory of the harvest festival vivid, erects its own communal succah.

As in all ancient religions, which, without exception, were male-oriented, the requirement for dwelling in the succah during the festival–or, at least, eating and studying the Torah in it–was limited to the privileged menfolk. Boys over five were included in this religious fellowship in order to accustom them to the proper observances.

In its traditional agricultural features, the practice of dwelling in the succah and the symbolic use of "the Four Species" (*see* FOUR SPECIES, THE) revealed striking similarities to the Dionysian festivals. The Greek historian of the first century, Plutarch, who was a keen and painstaking observer of the manners and customs of the various peoples of his time, noted about the celebration of Succot: "I know that their God is our Bacchus [Dionysos]." He probably derived this quite understandable impression from his observation of the succah, which was covered with vines and vine leaves, and was festooned, among other things, with clusters of grapes. This impression was further strengthened by noting that wine was being drunk in the succah during the rite of Sanctification (Kiddush) and that there was much convivial singing and dancing, just as there was among the Greeks during their harvest festivals. Furthermore, the Jewish worshipers in their rites employed the lulab, the palm branch decorated with willow branches and myrtles, which greatly resembled the Dionysian festal thyrsus-rods (in Greek: *thyrsos*) that were entwined with grape leaves and surmounted by pine cones.

The seventh day of Succot is known as Hoshanah Rabbah (i.e., the Great Hosanna). The Sages of the Mishnah called it "the Day of the Willow Branch," for it was then, with willow branches in their hands, that the priests in the Temple moved in stately procession seven times around the altar. During the Second Commonwealth, the rite became associated with the Messianic promise of redemption, and as such it was observed by the followers of Jesus when he came to Jerusalem, according to the Gospel of John.

Hoshanah Rabbah is regarded as a day of great sanctity. There is an ancient tradition that on this day, the final fate of the Jews in the year to come is sealed in the heavenly court of records. In the synagogue that morning, after the seven circuits (hakafot, *which see*) are made with the lulabim, each worshiper vigorously beats his willow branches against the bema (the raised platform in the synagogue) until they are leafless, while the entire congregation intones the hymn, "A Voice Brings Glad Tidings." This hymn peals forth triumphantly the promise of the Messiah's coming and the establishment of God's righteous Kingdom *on earth*.

The folk-imagination invested this day of Hoshanah Rabbah with all kinds of mystical significance on which the Cabalists of the Middle Ages continued to embroider. The

"Rejoicing in the Law" on Simchat Torah in an East European Chasidic Synagogue.

Scattering cakes to children in celebration of Simchat Torah. (From Leusden's Philologus Hebreo Mixtus, *Utrecht, Holland, 1657.)*

Procession with the Scrolls of the law on Simchat Torah, New York, 1892.

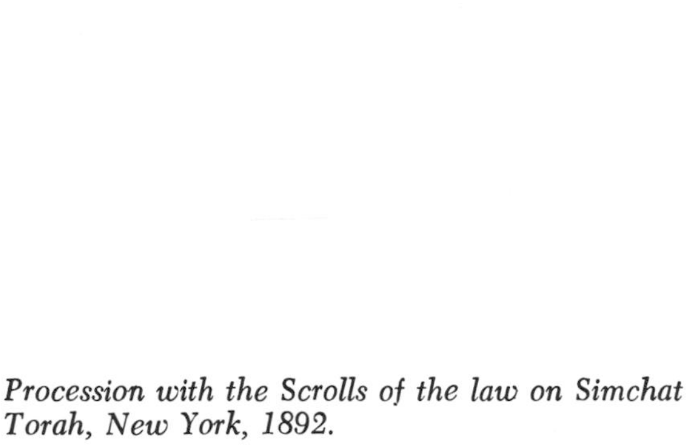

The pious Jews of every generation considered the bestowing of the Torah on Mount Sinai through Moses as the most epochal event in their more than 3,000 years' history. (Pen and ink drawing by Abraham Walkowitz, Paris, 1903.)

number seven was full of untold creative possibilities for them. Seven were the days of the Creation, seven were the illustrious men of Israel in Cabalistic count: the Patriarchs Abraham, Isaac and Jacob; Moses and Aaron, and Phineas, and David the Psalmist. Seven also were the days of the Festival of Succot.

The question occurs: Why the rite of beating willow branches? One Rabbinic rationalization attempts to allegorize it away. It holds that just as the willow tree after it loses its leaves gets them back again in the springtime, so is the repentant individual able to renew his soul even after he has fallen into evil, provided he renews for himself his faith in God. But ethical allegorizing aside, anthropologists regard the beating of willow branches as a fertility rite, of which the willow has served as a symbol in a number of religions. In ancient Greece, this rite was performed to "beat in" fertility.

Although it is an independent festival and has no connection with Succot, Shemini Atzeret (meaning "Solemn Convocation") is joined to it as an eighth day in one continuing celebration, and together these festivals make up "the Season of Our Rejoicing." What Shemini Atzeret originally stood for remains obscure. Undoubtedly, it had a primitive agricultural character. This is indicated by a special prayer-rite (Geshem) that is performed on this day in the synagogue; it is a supplication for seasonal rain.

There are also indications that Simchat Torah (meaning "Rejoicing Over the Torah"), which is observed on the day following Shemini Atzeret, originated as late as the ninth or tenth century C.E. in Babylonia. This celebrates the triumphant completion of the uninterrupted reading in the synagogue from the Torah, a task which can be accomplished either in an annual or triennial cycle. In honor of this achievement, all the children, who are not yet Bar Mitzvah or confirmed, are gathered around the bema (the reader's desk) in the center of the synagogue. A large tallit (prayer shawl) is spread over them like a shielding canopy, and a respected worshiper is called upon to read to them from the Torah. The ceremony is concluded when the rabbi blesses them by recalling the blessing that the Patriarch Jacob in Egypt pronounced over his grandsons, Ephraim and Manasseh (Genesis 48:20).

Traditionally, Simchat Torah is celebrated by the Orthodox with processions in the interior of the synagogue. Each male worshiper (including all the little boys) is afforded an opportunity to circumambulate the synagogue interior with the Torah Scroll (Sefer Torah) clasped in his arms. The most memorable part of the ceremony is the reading of the very last passage in the Pentateuch. The member of the congregation thus honored receives for this occasion the honorific title of *Chatan Torah*—"The Bridegroom of the Torah." When he has concluded reading, all cry out with verve, *"Chazak, chazak! Venit chazak!"* ("Be strong and fortified [in defense of the Torah!"]) Immediately after, another worshiper is called to the reading desk. He is named *Chatan Bereshit*—"The Bridegroom of Genesis"—for it is his privilege to resume the never-ending devotion of public Torah-reading by once again beginning with the first verse of the Bible: "In the beginning God created the heaven and the earth."

See also "FOUR SPECIES," THE; HAKAFOT.

SYNAGOGUE, THE (in Hebrew: BET HA-KNESSET, meaning "House of Assembly")

The word "synagogue" is derived from the Greek *synagoge* and means "assembly" or "congregation." No mention of the synagogue is made in the Jewish Scriptures, but it appears with great frequency in the New Testament, which was written originally in Greek. In the Greek version of the Apocrypha, there are references made to the *Proseuche,* the "House of Prayer." This word also was employed in the Greek-Jewish writings of Josephus and Philo and in the Latin satires of Juvenal to denote a synagogue. But in Judea and Babylonia, where the large Jewish populations best retained the traditional patterns and folkways, the term for "synagogue" ever remained *Bet ha-Knesset.*

Building and decorating a succah in a backyard of Tel Aviv, Israel, 1959. (Israel Office of Information.)

Procession on Succot with etrog and lulab in the Portuguese synagogue of Amsterdam. (Copper engraving by Bernard Picart, Paris, 1724.)

It is of great associative cultural interest that, as far back as Hellenistic Egypt in the pre-Christian years, the Jews there often equated the word *schola* (school) with "synagogue." Philo, the first-century rabbi-Platonist of Alexandria, eulogized in his *Life of Moses* the Jewish houses of prayer in that Hellenistic metropolis, where were taught "temperance, courage, prudence, justice, piety, holiness, and in short—of all virtues by which things human and divine are well-ordered." The intellectual-religious activity carried on in the schola, commented Philo, transformed the Jews into a community of "philosophers," namely, *talmidai chachamim*—"disciples of the wise"—which was the Hebrew equivalent. This may not have been an exaggeration at all, for the very same descriptive term was applied to Jews by Clearchus, the Greek pupil of Aristotle, when he quoted his master about a Jewish savant he had once talked with.

By the time of the Middle Ages, the word "school" had generally taken the place of "House of Assembly" or "House of Prayer" in Jewish usage. The Church Latin term for synagogue was *scuola Judaeorum* ("the Jewish School"); in Italian it was *scuola;* in Spanish, *escuela;* in Provençal, *escolo;* in French, *école;* in German, *schul;* and in Yiddish, *shul* or *sheel.* All these names are eloquent and unchanging reminders through the many centuries that the Jewish House of Prayer, which usually stood adjacent to the House of Study (Bet ha-Midrash) and often combined the functions of both at the same time, was in all countries also the intellectual center where Torah-learning was pursued in unbroken continuity and with a motivated dedication possibly never equaled in the history of religion.

When the institution of the synagogue was first initiated in Babylonia in the sixth century B.C.E., at the start of the Captivity, it signalized a far-reaching transformation, both externally and internally, of the Jewish religion. It cannot be said that this had come entirely unexpectedly. The historic and social processes of storm and stress, of growth and change, had been going on for a long time in Jewish life. Even during the eighth century B.C.E., the prophet Amos and his younger more gifted contemporary, Isaiah ben Amoz, had been inflaming thinking men's minds into earnest questioning about the authenticity and the validity of their religious values. They indicted the priesthood and the Temple sacrificial worship for their empty formalism, their soullessness, and their unconcern with moral and human values.

Savage was the jibe of Isaiah:

> To what purpose is the multitude of your sacrifices unto
> Me?
> Saith the Lord;
> I am full of the burnt-offerings of rams,
> And the fat of fed beasts.
>
> ISAIAH 1:11

All this formalism, primitive in character, changed when the many thousands of captive Jews had been driven by Nebuchadnezzar into Exile in Babylonia in 586 B.C.E. It was in adversity in a foreign land that the synagogue came into being, evolving primarily from practical considerations. The exiles, far from the Temple which lay in ruins in Jerusalem, desperately wished to maintain the continuity of their religious life in Babylonia. But since they could no longer offer sacrifices in their own sanctuary nor were permitted to build a new one in Captivity, only prayer was left to serve their religious needs: "so will we render for bullocks the offering of our own lips." In this manner, the institution of congregational prayer was first established.

There exists a poignant tradition concerning what some presume to have been the first synagogue. It is told in the Talmud that when the Jews of Jerusalem were being carried off into captivity, they snatched up on the way some of the stones from the Temple ruins and took them along into their Exile. These they worked lovingly into the masonry of the synagogue of Shaf ve-Yatib that they erected in the town of Nehardea. Because of those sacred stones this synagogue came to be known as the "House of the Shechinah" (the House of God's Presence).

The exiles, who had been colonized by their conquerors in scattered communities throughout the Euphrates-Tigris river country of Babylonia, would congregate on the Sabbath and the festivals for collective prayer and for public discussion of communal problems. On those occasions, they

Church of Santa Maria de la Blanca, Toledo, Spain. This famous edifice was originally a synagogue but was confiscated by the Church.

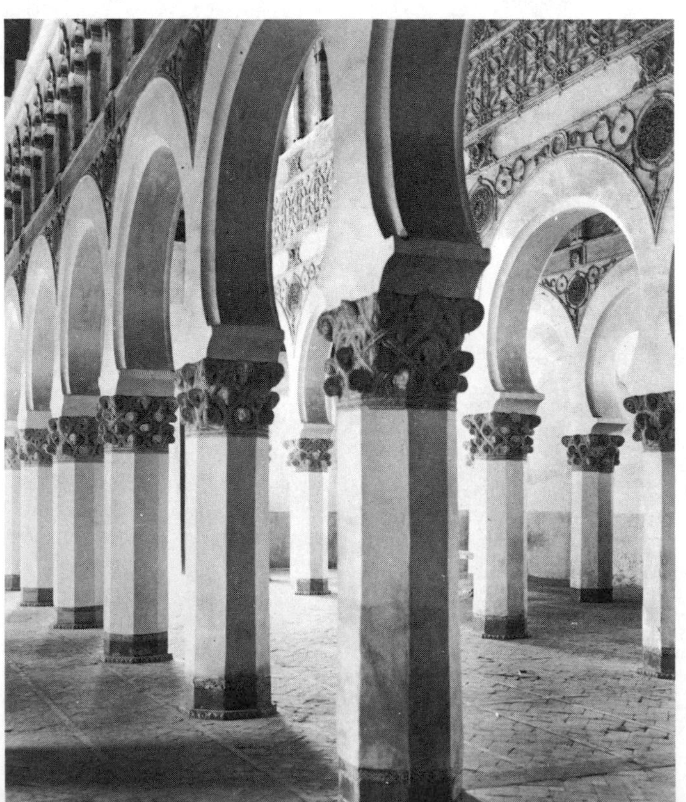

One of the most famous churches in Spain, El Transito, in Toledo, was originally a synagogue. It was converted into a Christian house of worship after it was seized by the ecclesiastical authorities, but the Hebrew inscriptions on the walls were left intact.

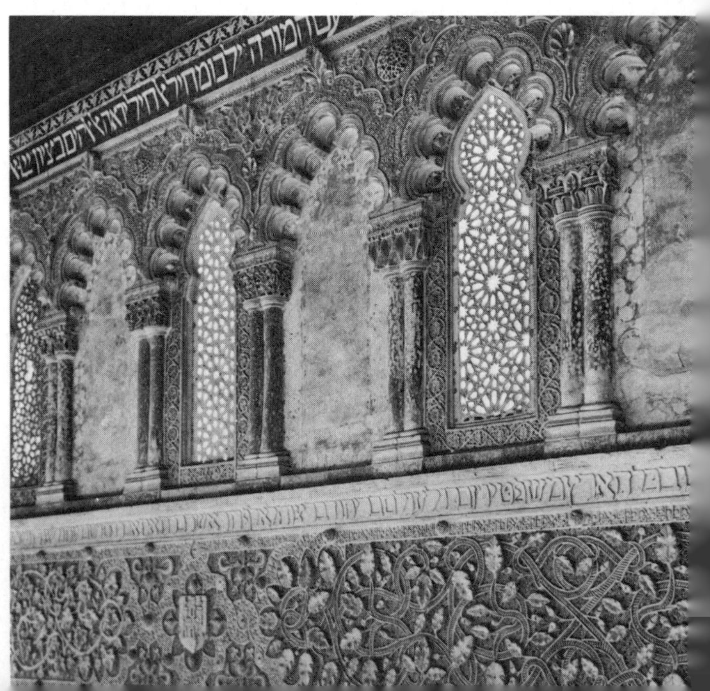

intoned prayers and sang the Hebrew psalms in unison, undoubtedly feeling drawn and held together by the warmth and fervor which their common beliefs and rites generated in them.

The institution of prayer had taken such a firm hold among the Jews in Babylonia in less than a century, that after the return of a large number of exiles to the Land of Israel and following Ezra's democratic innovation of obligatory Torah-study by the people, the popularity of animal sacrifices in the Second Temple in Jerusalem began to decline. Often, the offering of more agreeable incense was substituted for it upon the altar. From this time, a more spiritualized and rational conception of divine worship, implicit with ethical meaning, began to evolve.

Although the Temple still continued to sway powerfully the emotions and the loyalty of all Jews, its influence became largely a sentimental one, symbolic of the extraordinary attachment the Jews felt for their religion and Eretz Yisrael (the Land of Israel). Attendance at the Temple for the pious was made urgent only on the three "pilgrim festivals" of each year–Passover, Shabuot, and Succot. For the remainder of the time, however, the synagogue served as the religious and community center of the Jews. In Jerusalem itself, states the Talmud, when the Second Temple still was standing, there were busily functioning 394 synagogues.

While religious worship at the Temple in Jerusalem was carried out on a spectacular and ceremonious scale, appealing to sight and sound mainly, it was really in the humble synagogue that the Jewish folk achieved their most intimate and fulfilling religious experiences. "The Holy One–blessed be He!" declared the Talmud, "proceeds from synagogue to synagogue and from House of Study to House of Study, that he might give His blessings to Israel." Philo noted with great satisfaction: "Though the worshipers bring nothing else, in bringing themselves they offer the best sacrifices, the full and truly perfect oblation of noble living, as they honor with hymns and thanksgivings their Benefactor and Saviour–God."

One of the profoundest religious changes effected by the synagogue almost immediately upon its establishment twenty-five centuries ago was to bring communion with God directly and easily to the individual worshiper. Whereas before its development he had been able to worship the Deity only through the mediation of the priests and by means of whatever animal sacrifice he could afford to bring to the Temple altar, now, in the House of Prayer, the worshiper could commune with his God simply and unrestrainedly without the taint of crassly materialistic rites. It was, rejoiced the Rabbinic Sages, either with a prayer on his lips or with a wordless prayer in his heart that the suppliant was able in the synagogue to address himself to his "God of compassion."

It stands to reason that, under the powerful impact of this "liberation" from religious primitivism, the priestly caste began to wither away in the Jewish religion being supplanted before the Second Temple's Destruction, by a large class of Rabbinical teachers. Now the bulk of the Jews, by praying together and studying the same sacred lore, found they were being tied together by common interests and fraternal bonds of an indestructible kind. The religion of Israel, through the instrumentality of the synagogue, was thus becoming both spiritualized and the common heritage of everybody. Thereafter, wherever Jews lived in a community where a minyan (a quorum of ten male worshipers) could be assembled for prayer, it was obligatory upon them to build a synagogue, no

Remains of the Hellenistic synagogue at K'far Nachum (the Capernaum of the Gospels), 2nd century B.C.E., *where Jesus is said to have preached. (Israel Government Tourist Office.)*

Ruins of the Hellenistic synagogue at K'far Bir'am, in Northern Galilee, Israel, 2nd century B.C.E. *(Israel Government Tourist Office.)*

Greek inscription on a column excavated on the site of the Caesaria synagogue: "The gift of Theodorus, the son of Olympus, for the salvation of his daughter Matrona." Jewish use of Greek language and Greek names indicates extensive Hellenization during the first centuries of the Common Era. (American Friends of the Hebrew University.)

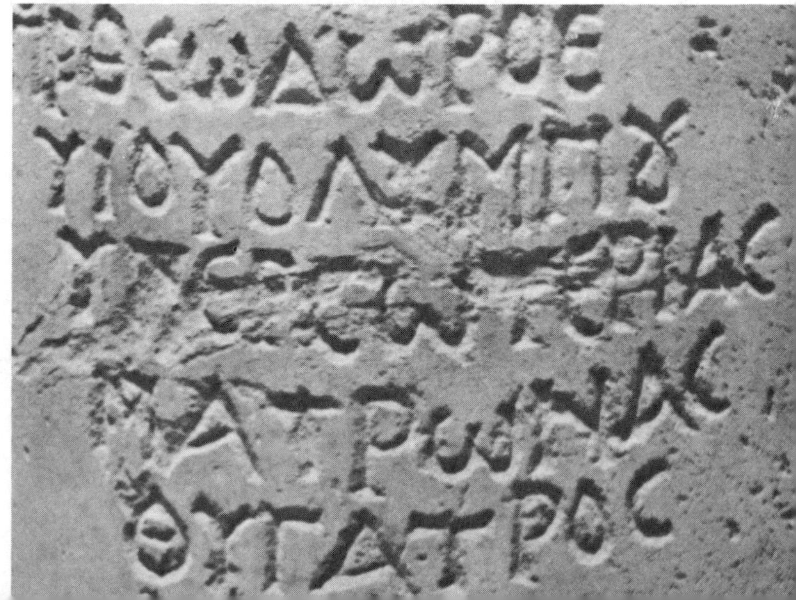

matter how poor they were or how humble the edifice they could afford. And the entire collective life centered around it.

After the burning of the Temple in Jerusalem by the Romans in 70 C.E., the synagogue took on increasingly greater importance among Jewry, which was now more dispersed than at any time before. Its religious, intellectual, and communal activities were many, being given a variety of emphases in different places. Yet the basic pattern remained everywhere about the same. The synagogue's institutional functions virtually took in the entire spectrum of interests in Jewish life. It was often, simultaneously, a House of Prayer and a House of Study. It was a communal House of Assembly as well as a House of Judgment where Rabbinical law prevailed. Not least in its social uses was its employment as a House of Charity, for it was in the synagogue that all activities of benevolence and mutual aid were carried on in Jewish group-existence: Clothing was distributed "to the naked," food was served "to the hungry," hospitality was accorded to Jewish travelers, and words of encouragement and solace were said to the downhearted, the lonely, and the afflicted. These works of "loving-kindness"–of *gemilut chasadim,* as they were eloquently referred to in Hebrew speech–underscored the high level of social responsibility and humanity that existed among Jews. This concrete identification, by works as well as by faith, of the individual with his fellow Jews led to the coining in the Talmud of one of the most significant of all folk sayings: *"Kol Yisrael chaverim."* ("All in Israel are comrades.")

It was the synagogue that held the Jews firmly together. From it–a phenomenon of cultural history–they were able to draw much of the courage and the moral will that were necessary for their continued endurance in a world that was ceaselessly threatening, persecuting, uprooting, and destroying them. The destruction of one, or even of a hundred, synagogues no longer meant the end of everything as it had for many Jews when the sanctuary on Mount Zion was destroyed by Titus. It was now taken for granted that synagogues could always be replaced by other synagogues. The people, accepting the ethical teachings of Rabbinic Judaism, already conceived of God as being infinite and omnipresent in creation. They had the certainty–and that was the crux of the matter–that wherever Jews worshiped sincerely and dealt justly and kindly with one another, there was their true "sanctuary."

In the course of only several centuries, synagogues sprang up in all the Jewish communities of Babylonia, and in every city, town, and village of Judea. In Egypt and Cyreneica, in Persia and the Crimea, in Yemen and Arabia, in Rome and Greece, in Syria and Asia Minor, and in many other countries where there were Jewish settlements, the daily life of the individual and the community became centered in the synagogue and house of study.

It is true that the idealized image of the Temple in Jerusalem always filled the inner eye of the Jew in Dispersion. Yet the perpetual mourning that the people had entered into "until the coming of the Messiah" in memory of the sanctuary that had been destroyed, discouraged the *duplication* of any physical feature of the Temple, including its architecture and its ritual vessels and ceremonial objects. It was forbidden to build a synagogue in the exact dimensions of the Temple. Although it is true that the pattern of synagogue architecture followed the same general plan as that of the Temple, having an ulam (vestibule), an echal (prayer hall), and an Aron ha-Kodesh (Holy Ark), the Rabbinic Sages nevertheless forbade the vestibule to be modeled after the Temple porch, the interior hall after the Temple court, the table for "shewbread" after the Temple table, and the menorah after the Temple menorah. With regard to the menorah–the seven-branched candelabrum–the Rabbis did permit the making of menorot, but stipulated that they could have only five, six, or eight branches.

Jews have often been perplexed by the question which comes naturally to mind of whether there actually has ever existed a style of synagogue architecture that could be labeled "traditionally Jewish." The only objective answer possible is that there has not. True, there have been "traditions" in synagogue design that conformed to the many individual alien cultures into whose framework a fragmentized Jewish life in Dispersion had been set. But each tradition, in the time-span of its operative force, from origin to decline, had but a limited range of several centuries. In any case, there has never been any substantial proof of an original "Jewish" style of architecture comparable to that of the ancient Egyptians, Greeks, or Romans. Because Jews were not free agents, they did not and were not able to excel in any of the fine arts and architecture until their civil emancipation, which only began in the nineteenth century.

No matter how segregated they were kept from the Christian population in whose midst they lived, the Jews were always exposed to–and to a certain degree were also receptive to–Gentile cultural influences. From this historic factor it logically followed that the architecture of the synagogue, and also its interior decoration and furniture, should reflect contemporary styles and even the regional tastes of the milieu in which the Jews lived. In Hellenistic times, for example, Jewish houses of worship contained the familiar features of Greek and Roman architecture of the day. In medieval southern Spain, under the rule of the Moorish caliphs and in conformity with prevailing Islamic architecture, the synagogues were built along Moorish lines, and resembled mosques. In other parts of western and southern Europe, during different centuries, the synagogues were designed according to contemporary architectural styles–whether Byzantine, Romanesque, Gothic, Renaissance, Baroque, etc. In Poland, for example, when fortress churches were being built in response to dangerous historic events from the fourteenth to the seventeenth centuries, fortress synagogues were also raised by the Jews; when wooden churches went up, Jews responded by building wooden synagogues but gave them an original architectural variation–a pagoda-like shape. In the United States today, where "modernist" architecture is currently in vogue, some sophisticated Jewish congregations have been erecting "functional" houses of worship. Outstanding examples of such synagogues are those designed by Frank Lloyd Wright, Eric Mendelssohn, and Percival Goodman.

Synagogue in Düsseldorf, Germany, built in 1904.

The old synagogue on the Heidereutegasse in Berlin. (Engraving, early 18th century.)

The Great Synagogue on Duke Street in Aldgate, London, built late in the 17th century, reconstructed in 1790, and rebuilt after World War II, when it was virtually destroyed by German bombers.

The Altneuschul *in the Prague ghetto. (Etching, early 19th century.)*

That the Jews' general cultural environment was reflected in early synagogues can be seen in those that have been turned up by archaeologists in this century in such widely scattered places as ancient Carthage, Greece, Syria, Rome, and Judea—specifically the synagogues at Beth-Alpha, Kfar Birim, Kfar Nachum (the Capernaum of the Gospels, where Jesus was said to have preached), Priene, Miletus, Hammat-Lif, Aegina, and Dura-Europos. They all show the characteristic features of Hellenistic architecture and decoration, that at Dura-Europos even boasting a fascinating series of twenty-foot-high frescoes depicting Biblical heroes and incidents. The only identifiable Jewish elements in most of these synagogues are their Hebrew inscriptions or the pictorial representations in mosaic of religious symbols—the menorah, the lulab, the shofar, and the laver.

The Great Synagogue in Alexandria, built during the second century B.C.E. but destroyed in the reign of Trajan, was esteemed as a great architectural triumph. The Talmudic Sages, who often succumbed to hyperbole, reported about its beauty: "He who has not seen the synagogue at Alexandria, has not seen the glory of Israel!" According to contemporary reports, it looked very much like a Greek or Roman Temple. It had a huge basilica with double-colonnaded courts. Upon the columns were hung ornamented golden shields, sculptured bronze wreaths, and marble tablets bearing in-

The synagogue in Cavaillon, France.

Synagogue of the German (Ashkenazic) Jews in Amsterdam. (Engraving by P. Fouquet, 18th century.)

Plaque in Hebrew and Spanish commemorating the dedication in Barcelona of the Rebbi Moshe Ben Maimon (Maimonides) Synagogue, on Rosh Hashanah, 1954. This was the first Jewish house of prayer allowed to be erected in Spain since the expulsion of the Jews in 1492. (Courtesy of David Ventura, president of the Comunidad Israelita de Barcelona.)

The synagogue in Florence, Italy, 19th century.

The unobtrusive Rebbi Moshe Ben Maimon (Maimonides) Synagogue in Barcelona—the first Jewish house of worship to be erected in Spain (in 1954) since the expulsion of the Jews in 1492.

scriptions in honor of the various Roman emperors of the age. So vast was the sanctuary that, in order to get the congregation to give the responses—"Amen!" or "Hallelujah!"—the precentor (baal tefillah) was obliged to signal from the bema in the center by waving a pennant or prayer shawl (tallit). What this synagogue's "Jewish" features were is impossible to say. Oddly, the Egyptian caste-system was followed in the seating of the worshipers. They were arranged in special sections, according to social rank, from nobles to slaves. The majority, being artisans, sat separately with their fellow guild-members: goldsmiths, silversmiths, coppersmiths, physicians, butchers, tailors, carpenters, masons, etc.

More than a thousand years later, synagogue design in Cordova and Toledo faithfully reflected the best traditions of Moorish architecture. Unquestionably, the two most beautiful synagogues in existence are those found in Toledo, Spain. If they still stand today it is due only to the "happy" accident of their having been forcibly "converted" into churches following the Expulsion from Spain in 1492. The Church of Santa María la Blanca has rows of fabulous octagonal-shaped columns, exquisite pine-apple-motifed capitals, and Moorish arches that combine to give a near-magical illusion of vastness. The other church is that El Tránsito, which had been built in 1357 by Samuel Abulafia, Jewish treasurer to King

Great Synagogue on the Tabakgasse in Budapest, Hungary. Early 19th century.

Synagogue in Trondheim, Sweden. (YIVO.)

Wooden synagogue in Jeziary, Poland. 17th or 18 century. (YIVO.)

Synagogue in Zolkiew, Poland. (Drawing by Alexander Kokulav. Early 19th century. Bezalel Museum, Jerusalem.)

"Fortress" synagogue in Tarnopol, Galicia, 17th century. One of many such contemporary Jewish houses of worship that served as defensive strongholds in times of danger. (YIVO.)

Great Synagogue in Kazimierz, suburb of Cracow. Built at end of 14th century.

Synagogue (mesjid) of the black Falasha Jews in Abyssinia. Architecturally, the structure is similar to other Falasha houses. (Photograph by Professor Wolf Leslau.)

"Rashi Synagogue" at Worms which was consecrated in 1034 C.E. *but was destroyed by the Nazis.*

Rabbi Yitzchok Nachman's synagogue in Lvov (Lemberg). Designed in Renaissance style by the architect Paolo of Rome in 1581.

Synagogue of K'ai-fêng, China (no longer in existence), which has the architectural design of a Taoist temple. (Copied by Père J. Brucker, S.J., from drawings prepared by Père Jean Domenge, S.J., in 1722.)

Temple Shaaray Zedek, Detroit, Michigan, designed by Percival Goodman, a noted architectural modernist. As in the case of the Israel Goldstein Synagogue at the Hebrew University, it illustrates the historic-cultural fact that synagogue architecture, from the time it was Greco-Roman in style, inevitably expressed the changing values and spirit of each age. (Courtesy of Percival Goodman.)

The Israel Goldstein Synagogue, during the period of construction, on the campus of the Hebrew University in Jerusalem. (Photo by Leni Sonnenfeld. American Friends of the Hebrew University.)

Pedro of Castile. Part Moorish and part Gothic in style, it has several naves which are separated by arches and columns. The walls represent a miracle of classic Islamic design. They are covered with delicate arabesques and Scriptural verses wrought with Hebrew characters in the same jewel-like manner that Arabic verses from the Koran were carved into the stones of contemporary mosques.

By another ironic twist of Jewish "destiny," the best extant example of Romanesque architecture in the synagogues of Italy is that of the Church of Santa Anna, in Trani. On one of its walls, a melancholy reminder of violent events that led to the changeover of the structure from one religion to another, is the Hebrew inscription carved in 1247 into the stone in honor of its Jewish architect: "A man of understanding, an honored member of our body [i.e., congregation]."

Until 1938, the finest Romanesque-style synagogue in Europe outside of Italy was to be found at Worms, the cultural Jewish center of the Franco-German Rhineland during the Middle Ages. There in the eleventh century the great Rashi used to worship and teach. But together with hundreds of other synagogues in Germany and Poland, this one too was blown up by the Nazis in their calculated campaign to obliterate all Jews and everything Jewish.

See also ARK CURTAIN; ARK OF THE LAW; ART, CEREMONIAL; BAAL TEFILLAH; BEMA; BET HA-MIDRASH; CHAZZAN; GABBAI; HYMNS OF THE SYNAGOGUE; KADDISH; KOL NIDRE; LAMP, PERPETUAL; LAVER; LION OF JUDAH; MAGGID; MINYAN; PRAYER AND WORSHIP; PRIESTS; PULPIT; RABBI; SERMON; SHAMMES; SHEMONEH ESREH; SIDDUR; SIDRAH; TEMPLE, THE; TORAH ORNAMENTS; TORAH-READING; TORAH SCROLL.

SYNAGOGUE, HYMNS OF THE. *See* HYMNS OF THE SYNAGOGUE.

TA'AMIM. *See* MUSICAL ACCENTS.

TA'ANIT BECHORIM. *See* FASTING AND FAST DAYS.

TA'ANIT CHALOM. *See* FASTING AND FAST DAYS.

TA'ANIT ESTHER. *See* FASTING AND FAST DAYS.

TACHRICHIM. *See* BURIAL CLOTHES.

TAHARAH. *See* BURIAL RITES AND CUSTOMS.

TALLIT (Hebrew, meaning "prayer shawl")

The Biblical commandment (in Numbers 15:37-41) instructing the individual to wear fringes on the four corners of his outer garments to serve as a visible "reminder" of his duty to observe faithfully all the 613 commandments of the Torah, was made obligatory for all Jewish males. After the breakup of Jewish national life in Judea and the fact of the Dispersion throughout the world with its accompanying persecution, the wearing of the fringed cloak or tallit which had been previously part of the ordinary and mandatory national costume of the male Jew in public, was limited by Rabbinic regulation; it became mandatory to wear it only in the synagogue or at home at the time of the recitation of the morning prayers, and on several special occasions (such as the all-day prayer services in the synagogue on Yom Kippur). It stands to reason that the wearing of the tallit had served as an identifying part of the Jew's attire, for just as the Scottish clansman who follows tradition disports prominently the distinctive tartan of his clan, so did the Jew of Judean times constantly wear the tallit for the whole world to see, although from more compelling and complex motives. Since it had been established by religious law and sanctified by tradition, wearing it became, naturally, an act of national-religious self-assertion and pride.

When the tallit became a prayer shawl, Rabbinic law did not make the wearing of it mandatory for a man until he married. However, in modern times it is usually customary for boys to begin wearing it at morning prayer or on their Bar Mitzvah. Reform congregations have dispensed with the tallit altogether, except for the rabbi or cantor.

The tallit is usually made of linen, wool, or silk, with its fringes of the same material. But since Jewish tradition has undergone many modifications in keeping with the changing times and views of various religious groups, the tallit too has experienced some drastic changes. The traditional tallit, with variations imposed in certain periods, different regions, and cultural settings, is worn today only by the Ultra-Orthodox and the sectarian Chasidim. It is elaborate, made of wool or linen, reaches down to the ankles, and envelopes in its substantial folds the entire body of the worshiper, like the cloak it originally was in Judea. However, in consonance with these utilitarian times, the Orthodox and Conservative Jews generally wear it in abbreviated form; the ordinary tallit looks today more like a scarf than a robe, and lacks the beauty and the drama of the tallit of old, with its flowing folds, beauty of hand-woven craftsmanship, and the majestic dignity lent to it by the atarah (the broad band of silver or gold embroidery or passementerie that ran along its upper edge, framing the neck and the chest).

Perhaps most impressive, esthetically, lending the charm and authenticity of its ancient Oriental folk-origin, are the solid bands of black or blue which decorate it across its width. The tradition of the black bands, of great antiquity, has a poignant motivation. It is intended as a visible sign of the perpetual mourning for the Destruction—*zecher lechurban:* "in memory of the Destruction"—of the Temple that the Jews entered into nineteen hundred years ago and that many of them still observe with a remembering loyalty perhaps unmatched in the annals of mankind.

See also TZITZIT; TALLIT KATAN.

Worshiper in silk tallit (modified modern style) at prayer in the Great Synagogue, London.

TALLIT KATAN (Hebrew, meaning "small tallit"; sometimes called ARBAH KANFOT ["four corners"])

The origin of the tallit katan is uncertain, and so is the historic period of its appearance. The first mention of it is found in the code of religious laws and regulations compiled about 1350 by Jacob ben Asher, the rabbinical authority of his day in Germany and Spain. There is the highly convincing speculation that at some particular point in the remote history of the Jewish people, during a period of intense religious persecution, the tallit could no longer be worn with impunity as the national-religious identifying cloak, which it was in Judean times. But since the Scriptural injunction (in Numbers 15:37-41) to the Jewish male that he wear tzitzit (ritual fringes) all the time to recall to him that his duty of perpetually fulfilling the precepts of the Torah was not to be violated, the tallit-cloak then became for the Jew a concealed symbol, so to speak, of his faith and identity. It went "underground"; it actually became an undergarment. It was worn like an undershirt next to the skin—not for warmth or for the intimate touch of holiness. (In Yiddish the name of the tallit katan is *leibtzudekl,* meaning "small body-covering.")

The tallit katan is a four-cornered woolen scarf, rectangular in shape. It is approximately three feet long and about one foot wide. Since it is worn as a garment falling over chest and neck in equal length, there is a rectangular

Traditional tallit-band (atarah), sewed as a border around the neck of the prayer-shawl, and made of point d'Espagne—*of silver thread and lamé. (Bezalel Museum, Jerusalem.)*

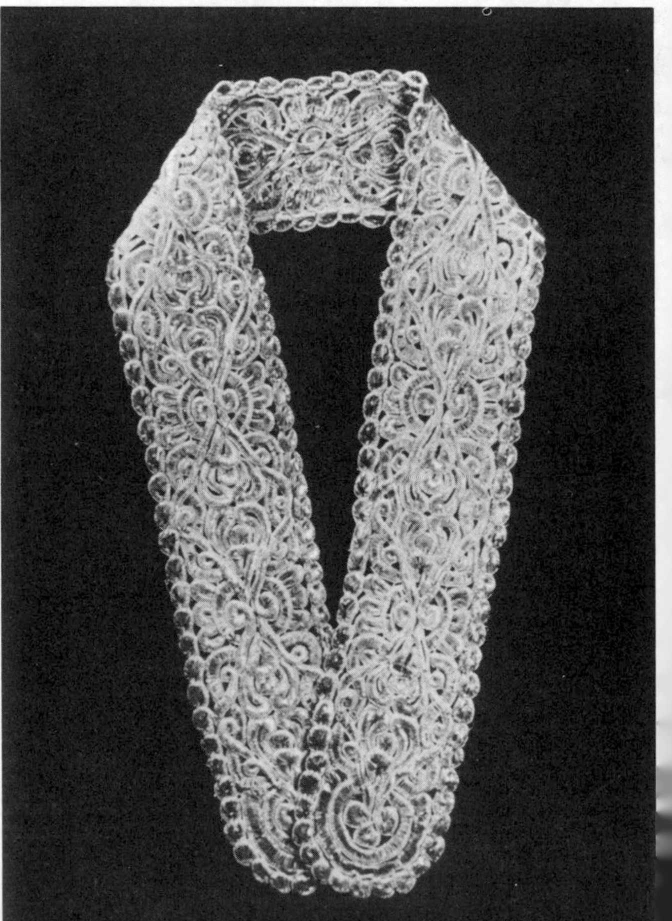

Traditional tallit worn by the Ultra-Orthodox. (Painting by Sheva Ausubel.)

cutout in the middle for the head to go through. Each of the "four corners"—arbah kanfot—is perforated by a small hole from which is suspended the tzitzit or fringe.

In East European Jewish communities in the past (and today among the Ultra-Orthodox) the religious obligation of wearing the tallit katan is imposed on little boys as soon as they are able to dress themselves. Upon rising in the morning, it is the first garment they put on after washing; at night, on going to bed, it is the last they take off.

See also TALLIT; TZITZIT.

TALMID CHACHAM (Hebrew, meaning "disciple of the wise")

The beau ideal of the Jewish people, ever since the religious-intellectual era was initiated by Ezra and the Scribes in the fifth century B.C.E., was neither king nor aristocrat, neither warrior, priest, nor rich man, but the Torah scholar—the talmid chacham. He, the humble man of learning and probity (in the Jewish scale of values, learning and a high moral character in its possessor were paired as complementary and indivisible), was honored as the "finer finest" among all men. The title of homage (i.e., talmid chacham) given to him, does not appear to have been bestowed by any special authority of learned men; it was in some intangible manner reached spontaneously by a recognition among his colleagues of his intellectual attainments and character endowments. The Rabbinic Sages whose collective teachings constitute the "Sea of the Talmud," have always been referred to in Jewish usage as *Talmidai Chachamim*—"Disciples of the Wise."

In the long, troubled history of the Jews, some of the most highly prized ego-social values of the worldly—material riches, political power, and social prestige—were deprecated as mere snares and delusions. In the end, averred the Jewish moralists, these goals turned out to be only misleading wills-o'-the-wisp, hollow shams, a coming in and a going out with the turnings of the capricious wheel of fortune. In the lands of Eastern Europe, the hard-bitten Yiddish-speaking Jews, so many of whom legal and economic discrimination had forced to become petty hucksters and shopkeepers, gave utterance to this disillusionment in one of the most beloved of all their folk-sayings, *"Toireh is di besteh schoireh"* ("Torah is the best merchandise"). This spiritual "merchandise" was, in fact, the principal commodity in the collective "commerce" of the Jewish people throughout the many centuries everywhere in the world since Talmudic times and until the modern era. Its effigy is overwhelmingly stamped on the religious and moralistic literature produced in so many languages—in Hebrew, Aramaic, Greek, Arabic, Spanish, Yiddish, Fersi-Tat (Judeo-Persian) and whatnot.

What is a chacham—a wise man—according to the Jewish tradition? The medieval Cabalists defined him as one who had the discernment to see what lay beneath the surface of things, who could distinguish between the shallow illusion of appearance and the profound truth of reality. The Cabalistic work, the Zohar, the source of "hidden wisdom" for the Jewish mystics, defined its view of the chacham in a catechism:

> What does the fool see?
> The outer garment of a person
>
> What does the wise man see?
> The inner garment—the spirit.

Did the chacham always apprehend the inner truth of everything? Not at all! The Jewish conception of the wise man was of one who blunderingly *sought* wisdom and not one who triumphantly *found* it. That is precisely the inner logic in the title *talmid chacham*: He was a "disciple of the wise," not "a wise man"—he was a perpetual student, an inquirer after truth, not a finished master preening himself smugly and facilely with the eternal verities. In Jewish religious annals, the roles of teacher and pupil, of master and disciple, often are found reversed. The Rabbinic luminary, Chanina, is quoted in the Talmud as saying: "Much have I learned from my teachers, even more from my colleagues, but most of all from my students."

The famous Lithuanian scholar, Rabbi Elijah of Vilna, reverently known to Yiddish folk as Der Vilner Gaon—*"The Genius of Vilna." Late 18th century.*

Portrait in tapestry of Rabbi Akiba Eger, the noted Talmudic scholar. Russia, early 19th century.

The portraiture of the talmid chacham in the folk mind was drawn with romaniticized ardor ever since he emerged upon the scene of Jewish community life. "He should be like the Ark of the Covenant, which was overlaid with pure gold outside and inside," says the Talmud. The teachers (the Tannaim) of the Mishnah distinguished the following character traits as the preconditions for becoming a disciple of the wise: "The way of the wise is to be modest, humble, alert and intelligent . . . to endure patiently unjust treatment . . . to make himself beloved of men . . . to be gracious in his relations with all, including those under him . . . to avoid wrongdoing . . . to judge each man according to his actions." An element of asceticism and renunciation of the world seems to have crept into this credo as well: The talmid chacham was forewarned not to take any delight in the pleasures of the world, for in those vanities, because of the very nature of his dedication, he had no portion. Stoic and austere is the Mishnah's final eulogism: "Wrapped in his mantle, he sits at the feet of the wise."

During the Middle Ages and long after, the practice was introduced in the various ghettos of Europe of exempting the talmid chacham from all payment of communal taxes. For he, totally absorbed in his Torah studies, was condemned by necessity to remain as poor as a synagogue mouse. Nonetheless, his high place in Jewish popular esteem, in spite of his poverty, remained secure.

Still living on the tongues of the Jewish folk is the ancient adage from Pirke Abot (the Sayings of the Fathers) concerning the seeker after wisdom: "In whom wisdom is—in him is everything. In whom it is not—what has he? He who has acquired it—what does he lack?"

See also CHACHMAH; ETHICAL VALUES, JEWISH; SAGES, RABBINIC; TALMUD, THE; THORAH STUDY; YESHIVAH BACHUR.

TALMIDAI CHACHAMIM. *See* SAGES, RABBINIC.

TALMUD, THE (Hebrew, derived either from LAMAD, meaning "to study" or from LIMAD, "to instruct")

The Talmud is the literary reservoir of Rabbinic Judaism that was created during the Hellenistic Age in Jewish history. It is not just one book—as is commonly taken for granted—but a *collection of many books.* The plain folk, with abounding pride, have called it "The Sea of the Talmud" (in Hebrew: *Yam ha-Talmud*). It is, in fact, a virtual library of treatises which dwell on the Rabbinic laws and regulations, traditions, customs, rites and ceremonies, and civil and criminal laws. In addition, the Talmud contains opinions, discussions and debates, and moralistic aphorisms and biographic exempla of the Rabbinic Sages. These are presented to the devout in order to inspire emulation in wisdom and ethical conduct. Not least, the Talmud attempts to pilot the Jewish masses through all the dangerous shoals of faith and living by means of popular preachments which bring into play all the arts and pedagogic devices of a highly developed folklore.

The Talmud, it needs to be emphasized, was the religious-cultural creation not just of one time but of centuries of collective striving. Its materials originated with the religious revivalism and moralistic self-searching that accompanied the Maccabean upsurge in Jewish life (second century B.C.E.), and they ended with the closing of the Babylonian Talmud (*see below*) in 500 C.E. It took literally thousands of the best minds and noblest spirits of the Jewish people over

Rock tomb of a Talmudic teacher in a catacomb at Bet Shearim. Inscriptions (on top in Hebrew and over door in Greek) read: "This is the tomb of Rabbi Isaac ben Magim." In the catacomb containing this tomb, the majority of inscriptions are in Greek—the lingua franca of the then Hellenistic world. Judea, 2nd(?) century.

a time-span of possibly seven centuries to attempt the construction of a rational synthesis of belief and observance with moral conduct and law. The Protestant Biblical scholar of the nineteenth century, Franz Delitzsch, once defined the vast scope of the Talmud "as an immense public assembly in which thousands, even tens of thousands, of voices of at least five centuries are heard to rise and comingle."

The literature of the Talmud was a logical development, elaboration, and deepening of the teachings of the Torah and of the social idealism of the Prophets. The Talmud was once aptly described in perspective "as the enlarged and illustrated Bible of Israel."

To the great majority of the informed, the Talmud stands as the authoritative code of Jewish religious beliefs, practices, and observances, even if, for many Jews, these no longer have any relevance to modern Jewish life and needs. Considered purely as a religious-legal system, the Talmud has proved to be dynamic. In a world of constant flux, it had been fashioned by its Rabbinical architects as an instrument for the adaptation of the Jewish religion to the ever changing circumstances of life. Almost two thousand years before Justice Oliver Wendell Holmes of the United States Supreme Court wrote: "The life of the law has not been logic; it has been experience," the Sages of the Talmud were already tranquilly proceeding on that progressive premise of jurisprudence in which law was made to serve as an expression of the life of man and not merely of abstract theory. "Ask me a point of law," taught the Talmudic Sage Rami bar Chami, "and though I will answer you according to reason, yet you will also find its parallel in tradition [i.e., in time-tested experience]."

THE MISHNAH

(from the Hebrew word-root SHANAH, meaning "to repeat"; i.e., the repetition of a tradition)

The creation of the Talmud caused a significant development to take place in the Jewish religion. Each of the three major divisions of this monumental work—the Mishnah (the code of Oral Laws), the Gemara (the commentary and elaboration of the Mishnah text), and the Midrash (the sermonic exposition and popular interpretation of the Bible—became a repository of the collective Jewish striving for a more harmonious and comprehensive philosophy of religious belief, observance, and conduct. Yet the main objective of the Talmudic Sages (those early architects of Rabbinic Judaism) was to draw for the Jewish people a clear design for a *total way of life.* That is why one of the most illustrious of them, Simeon ben Gamaliel, taught: "Not [Torah] learning but *doing* is the chief thing."

It is, of course, axiomatic that nothing in the human condition ever remains immobile. The only constant possible is change. Often, change results in growth, although sometimes it leads only to diversion or even to decay. The process of change has a special applicability to religious beliefs, intellectual ideas, laws, and morals. The history of the development of Rabbinic Judaism presents an excellent illustration of this cultural law.

As is well known, the Five Books of Moses—the Pentateuch—contain the written Law of Torah, which is called in Hebrew *Torah sheh-bi-Ketab* (literally: "Torah That Is Written"). But in the several centuries following the canonical compilation of the Scriptures by Ezra and the Scribes in 444 B.C.E. it was found necessary by the Scribes (Soferim; *see* SCRIBES) to supplement the written Torah with a second body of sacred jurisprudence. This code was called in Hebrew *Torah sheh be-al-Peh*—"the Oral Torah." It consisted, in the main, of such laws, regulations, decisions, opinions, and ethical teachings as had been transmitted *orally* by a relatively large number of religious authorities, each of whom usually combined in himself the varied functions of thinker, teacher, jurist, and moralist. It was a continuous chain of tradition which they handed down, each master to his disciples. But one thing is certain: Those traditions must have originated at a much earlier period, for it is reasonable to conjecture that much time had to elapse before a tradition could become definitive, accepted by the people, and then fixed and revered.

No doubt there were a number of valid reasons for the creation of new laws to supplement or to modify the already existing Scriptural laws. But surely none was more imperious than the demands of the social and material conditions in Jewish life during the Second Temple period. Changes were already at work in the economy of Judea and in the social stratifications of the people in Macabbean times. They became even more apparent following the great increase and diversification in the country's agriculture, trade, and commerce under the exploitation of the ruthlessly efficient Romans, who intended to extract for themselves every possible material profit from the Jews.

As a result, the Biblical laws no longer were found adequate for meeting new contingencies. The lack had to be corrected somehow, but it could not be done arbitrarily, for Scripture was held to be inviolable and its truths eternal. Therefore, the elaborative Oral Laws incorporated in the Mishnah code were constructed, without exception, upon the authority of either suggestions or bare statements in the Pentateuch which permitted expansion.

It needs to be kept in mind that the Mishnah represented principally the thought and teachings of the Rabbinic Sages, most of whom were undoubtedly Pharisees (*which see*). In the historic context of their age, these men were the religious-social liberals of Judea. They were not afraid of challenging the status quo, or of rejecting old, sacrosanct shibboleths. Most important of all, in the face of the fierce opposition and censure of their opponents, they had no hesitation in extending the Biblical laws to make them conform more realistically and effectively to the demands of life.

The path of the Rabbinic Sages was bestrewn more with thorns than with roses. For pitted against them were the ruling powers—the Sadducean sectaries—those fundamentalists who ruled under and collaborated with Rome in oppressing the Jewish people (*see* SADDUCEES). This class was obdurately opposed to any change in the religious laws and practices. The first-century Jewish historian of Judea, Josephus, who was a contemporary witness of those events, noted: "The Pharisees [ie., the Mishnah Sages] have made many ordinances among the people according to the tradition of their fathers, whereof there is nothing written in the Laws of Moses; for which cause they are rejected by the sect of Sadducees."

From an entirely independent source—from Philo, the rabbi-Platonist of Alexandria (*c.* 20 B.C.E.–40 C.E.)—one learns that even in Hellenistic Egypt, which was quite remote from Judean Rabbinic influences and controversies, there were current among the Jews "myriads of unwritten customs and usages." Philo made this statement almost two centuries before the final editing of the Mishnah code by Judah ha-Nasi (about the year 220 C.E.).

It was actually in great measure due to the Biblical tradition that an oral law got to be considered equally as valid as a written law. Ostensibly, in the value-scheme of Jewish religious culture, tradition was highly revered—so much that one Talmudic authority flatly declared: "Torah which is not based on tradition is not Torah." In the days of the Wandering in the Wilderness, following the departure of Israel from Egypt, Moses had appointed a council of Seventy Elders over which he presided. He created this administrative judicial body in order that it might assist him "to sit within the gates" to judge the people.

Adhering to this hallowed precedent of Mosaic times, the institution of the Men of the Great Assembly (also known as "the Men of the Great Synagogue" or "the Great Sanhedrin") was established during Second Temple days. It consisted of seventy Scribes (Soferim) and priest-scholars who were presided over by the high priest. This supreme religious-legislative-judicial body decreed many additional laws and regulations. It initiated new customs, prescribed a multitude of ritual observances and ceremonies, and established the essential pattern of the liturgy for the synagogue. However—and this is the most extraordinary aspect of its activities—it legislated and issued legal opinions orally! To write down any of the laws and regulations, the Men of the Great Assembly had decreed, was forbidden. In making this rule, they were motivated not by any superstitious notion or by caprice, but from practical considerations. For putting the Oral Laws in writing, the Men of the Great Assembly feared, might result in confusion and only lead to contradiction with the laws and commandments already found in the written Torah.

Yet memory itself is but a fragile reed; it cannot be relied upon entirely. So it is presumed—no doubt with good reason—that the Tannaim (the Rabbinic teachers of the Mishnah) in order the better to remember the unwritten laws so as not to err while, at the same time, they honored the prohibition against writing them down for public instruction, made secret and abbreviated notations of them for their personal reference. Unquestionably, a desperate need was felt by the Tannaim for memorizing the Oral Laws correctly. The Rabbinic Sage Meir, one of the prime movers in their eventual compilation as a written work, found it necessary to issue this dread admonition to the Torah scholars: "When a scholar forgets one word of his Mishnah, it is judged against him [by Heaven] as if he had forfeited his life."

In reality, the Talmudic scholars of the Middle Ages were not altogether in agreement that Judah ha-Nasi had, all by himself, committed the laws of the Mishnah to writing. Although such formidable authorities as the great scholars Abraham ibn Daud and Maimonides accepted the tradition that he actually had, a no less weighty Talmudic luminary than Rashi, seconded by several of his continuators, the French Tosafists (*see* TOSAFISTS), sharply dissented from their view. Rashi went even further in his disagreement. Basing his conclusion on internal evidence in the Talmud, he stated that not only the Mishnah itself but also its commentary, the Gemara, had not been written down at the time they originated but had been transmitted *orally* until the sixth century.

Nothwithstanding the prohibition against writing down the Oral Laws, in due time the fear of the Rabbinic Sages was only too well realized. Their scruple was frustrated by the very zeal of the many collectors and, most of all, the multitude of the traditions, laws, regulations, customs, opinions, and decisions that the Fathers of the Oral Tradition had issued in the course of several centuries. Hillel, the Pharisee Scribe and teacher of Jerusalem (*d.* 10 C.E.), who was accorded by the grateful Jewish folk the distinction of resembling Mosheh Rabbenu ("Our Teacher Moses") in wisdom, humility, patience, and "loving-kindness," was the first Rabbinic Sage to attempt to make some order out of the chaos of the oral teachings. But what happened to his code remains unknown.

A crisis was finally reached in the decades that followed the Destruction of the Second Temple in 70 C.E. With Israel dismembered and scattered and with its religious and psychological center lying in ruins, a great urgency was felt by the Sages for critically examining and compiling the unwritten laws. The difficulty of doing so, however, was compounded by the fact that, with equal zeal, different codes of Oral Traditions were being taught in the Rabbinic schools of Judea. One set of laws often contradicted the others so that there was contention and confusion.

This state of affairs eventually forced the chief religious authority of the generation, the founder of the Rabbinic academy at Yabneh, Yochanan ben Zakkai, to issue this warning to his fellow Tannaim: "He who writes down the [Oral] Laws is to be compared to one who sets fire to the Torah." At the same time he admonished the devout: "He who studies these codes will have no reward [in the World-to-Come]."

Despite Yochanan's resolute ban and following his death, when the plight of the Jewish people had become increasingly desperate because of the Hadrianic persecutions, it was decided that an authoritative codification of the Oral Laws could no longer be put off. Because of the overwhelming number of these laws, there was danger that any faulty repetition, memory failure, or unresolved contradictions among them might result in their corruption or their being entirely forgotten.

The great Akiba ben Joseph, probably the most intellectually gifted of all the Tannaim, undertook the pioneer task of collecting, sifting, critically selecting, and, finally, ordering into a rational code the vast multitude of the Oral Traditions. He thus laid the complicated editorial groundwork for the Mishnah, a work which he was not fated to complete. When he died a martyr's death at the hands of the Romans in 135 C.E. (*see* KIDDUSH HA-SHEM), his brilliant disciple Meir took up the labor of codification but was unable to bring it to a satisfactory conclusion. It was left to the Patriarch of Judea, Judah ha-Nasi, to complete the work on the Mishnah and to have it declared canonically closed about the year 200 C.E.

It was quite in keeping with the ingenuous tradition of post-Biblical practice that the prestige of a special attribution of authorship was accorded many of the Oral Traditions, a distinction, however, which they did not at all merit. As had been the case with the Book of Job, whose composition had been ascribed to the inspiration of Moses in order to facilitate its acceptance into the Biblical canon by the Men of the Great Assembly, so the intention of the Rabbinical teachers quite plainly was to make the more important among the Oral Laws unchallengeably authoritative by ascribing their origin to divine revelations that had been received by Moses on Mount Sinai but which he had not written down. "From Moses on Mount Sinai" was the awe-inspiring tag attached to many an Oral Tradition in the Mishnah. The very opening declaration in the first chapter of the Mishnah treatise which deals with piety and ethics, Pirke Abot (also known as Ethics of the Fathers or Chapters of the Fathers), advances this premise of unbroken continuity in the transmission of the Oral Laws and Traditions. It actually begins with the theophany on Mount Sinai:

> Moses received the [Oral] Law on Sinai, and handed it down to Joshua; and Joshua to the Elders; the Elders to the Prophets; and the Prophets handed it down to the Men of the Great Assembly.

Continuing the illustrious genealogy of this transmission to Simon the Just (*c.* 200 B.C.E.), "one of the last survivors of the Great Assembly," Pirke Abot reports that it was faith fully carried by word of mouth to later Rabbinic teachers from one generation to another until the time of Judah ha-Nasi.

In time, this cavalier attribution of certain traditions to Moses fell into scholarly disrepute. The noted Talmudist of medieval Germany and Spain, Asher ben Yechiel (1250–1328), sought to interpret this belief as being merely a linguistic euphemism. He conjectured that in claiming the Oral Traditions had derived from Moses, the Rabbinic Sages simply meant that "these Laws are as clear and as lucid *as if* they had been made known to Moses on Mount Sinai."

The religious teacher who first laid down the ground plan for the Mishnah was Hillel the Elder, the President of the Sanhedrin in Jerusalem. He arranged all the Oral Laws into six divisions—whether from purely arbitrary reasons or because he had inherited the pattern from a sacrosanct older Rabbinic tradition is not known. However, in this rigid ordering he was faithfully followed by the Sages Akiba ben Joseph and Meir in their own Mishnah compilations that they made more than one hundred years after his passing. Neither did the ultimate editor of the Oral Laws, Judah ha-Nasi (a devout descendant of Hillel), depart from the pattern.

The six divisions of the Mishnah are called *sedarim* (s. *seder*), meaning "orders." Altogether, they comprise a total of sixty-three *massechtot* (s. *massechtah*)—"treatises" or "tractates." In turn, each treatise is divided into *perakim* (s. *perek*)—"chapters"—and each chapter is further subdivided into paragraphs. In all, there are 523 chapters. By this arrangement, students of the Talmud have been enabled to correctly identify the laws of the Mishnah, noting treatise, chapter, and paragraph.

The contents of the Mishnah—popularly called Shas (the Hebrew acronymn for Shishah Sedarim—"the Six Orders") —are not always consistent with their division titles. They embrace a wide variety of subject matter, often unrelated, which Judah fitted into the mold of the Six Orders the best way he was able, for Hillel's pattern, which had been followed faithfully by both Akiba and Meir, Judah considered to be sacrosanct, and not to be altered or extended.

THE FIRST ORDER: SEEDS (ZERA'IM)

This deals with agricultural laws and with other matters pertaining to seeds and the produce of field and orchard, and to the ritual observances affecting them.

THE SECOND ORDER: FESTIVALS (MO'ED)

This covers the laws of the Sabbath, the Festivals, and the Fast days.

THE THIRD ORDER: WOMEN (NASHIM)

This details the laws concerning betrothal, marriage, and divorce.

THE FOURTH ORDER: DAMAGES (NEZIKIN)

This treats of civil and criminal laws.

THE FIFTH ORDER: SACRED THINGS (KODASHIM)

This deals with sacrifices, offerings, and the Temple service in Jerusalem.

THE SIXTH ORDER: PURIFICATION (TOHAROT)

This covers things "clean" and "unclean," and personal hygiene.

There is no question but that the most memorable, the most influential, and also the most revered, of all the Rabbinic Sages was Hillel the Elder. It is assumed, both by tradition and by modern scholarship, that he was the actual initiator of the movement by the many Tannaim of the Mishnah to gather and to critically examine all the Unwritten Laws, to memorize them with the utmost fidelity, and then to impart this knowledge, not in writing, but *orally* to their disciples. The latter, in their turn, were to transmit these Oral Laws and Traditions to their own disciples in a chain of dedicated continuity.

Hillel was possibly the first to formulate the Seven Basic Modes or Rules (Middot) of inferential reasoning, known as "Rabbinic logic," for the interpretation of the Scriptural laws. But one word of caution: By no means should this system of reasoning be compared with the logical method of Socrates or Aristotle. There was little in common between them, either in approach or methodology. Whenever Hillel thought that the Biblical law was inadequate for meeting certain requirements or situations in the contemporary life of the Jews, he attempted, with the aid of the reasoning tool of his Seven Modes, to extract new connotations out of the old laws. Because of the zeal he displayed in trying to make the Jewish religion an ever living and applicable force in the life of his people, he was called reverently "the Reviver of the Torah."

More than a century after Hillel, the Tanna Ishmael formulated his Thirteen Rules. These were both a modification and an extension of Hillel's. Almost at the same time, the Tanna Eliezer, son of Yoseh the Galilean, came forward with his own Thirty-three Modes. The method, employed by all these three Mishnah Sages, and one growing both in complexity and finesse with the centuries, is so technically involved, representing a type of reasoning so unfamiliar to the modern reader, that none but a disciplined Talmudist would be able to understand and apply it as, indeed, untold numbers have through many centuries.

Definitely, the Mishnah is not a legal code in the accepted modern sense. It is not a code in which every sentence, every clause, every word, and even every comma of a stated law has strict validity. The Mishnah was intended to be not a dogmatic but a flexible instrument of extra-Biblical jurisprudence. Its laws stemmed from Rabbinical opinions that on many matters were often divergent but not binding. Where there was no disagreement about a particular law among the authorities, it was stated simply and with finality. But where there was dissent among the Sages, the opinion of any one of them was weighed with equal detachment against the opinions of the others. One of the juridical rules laid down in the Mishnah, occasioned by reference to the most illustrious Rabbinic savant of his generation, Akiba ben Joseph ran thus: "Akiba's opinion is always authoritative when it is in conflict with a single scholar, but not when he is opposed by more than one scholar."

An attachment to truth and reason very often was given precedence over mere reverence for authority, no matter how illustrious. This attitude, not at all uniquely Jewish, is reminiscent of the classic saying: "I love Plato, but I love truth more." Taking this into consideration, much of the time it is not only inexact but also quite meaningless to say: "The Talmud states . . ." when in reality it frequently is only the opinion of one particular Rabbi presented there.

Recognizing the ever "unfinished" and "growing" character of the Scriptural and Rabbinic laws, as the centuries passed there took place a further modification and renewal of them by a steady stream of interpretive code-commentaries. Among the exegetical writings which exerted a powerful influence on the later development of Jewish law were the Responsa (Questions and Answers) of the Geonim (the learned Rectors of the Babylonian Rabbinical Academies during the Byzantine and premedieval period); the monumental commentary on the Mishnah code, the Mishneh Torah, by Maimonides (1135–1204); the Arbah Turim ("the Four

Towers") by Jacob ben Asher (*d.* 1340); and not least, the universally consulted (by the Orthodox) Shulchan Aruch ("the Set Table") by Joseph Caro (1488–1575) of Safed.

The Schools of Hillel and Shammai. The era of the Tannaim (Aramaic pl., meaning "Teachers," specifically, the Teachers of the Oral Law; s. Tanna) lasted approximately from about 10 C.E. to 220 C.E. It began, so it is believed, with the heated religious-legal debates between the rival Rabbinic schools of Hillel and Shammai in Jerusalem toward the end of the first century B.C.E.

It is, of course, customary to think of the Greek and Roman philosophers as men who possessed vast knowledge and who commanded an incisive logic in their groping for understanding and certainty. The Mishnah Sages, so different from the Gentile philosophers, who were secular minded, laid their emphasis on religious and ethical truths rather than on intellectual ends, and counted among them an unusually large number of distinguished minds. Their achievements are to be judged more by their humane outlook on life and by the religious-ethical goals that they set for the Jewish laws than by their actual intellectual contributions.

During the first two centuries of the Common Era, an unbroken line of eminent religious and ethical thinkers—almost legendary personalities—flourished in Judea. Besides Hillel and Shammai, there were also Rabban Gamaliel I (the Pharisee Rabbi whom Paul of Tarsus claimed as his teacher), his son, Simeon ben Gamaliel, Yochanan ben Zakkai, Eleazar ben Azariah, Joshua ben Chananiah, Akiba ben Joseph, Meir, Simeon bar Yochai, and Ishmael. All these revered teachers, in consonance with the Jewish tradition of modesty, called themselves *Talmidai Chachamim* ("Disciples of the Wise"). But later worshipful Rabbis, including Judah ha-Nasi, chose to drop the word *Talmidai* ("Disciples") and called them just *Chachamim* ("Sages").

It is quite certain that the matrix for the religious-ethical goals of these Chachamim—and not only their method of Talmudic reasoning and discussion—was either created in part or else brought to a higher state of refinement by the genius of one savant—Hillel the Elder, who taught almost one hundred years before the Temple was destroyed and Israel underwent its final Dispersion in 70 C.E.

Hillel's philosophy of life and of religious belief and practice, which his numerous gifted disciples further developed, was hammered out in controversy with the rival Rabbinic school of Shammai. The dedication to seeking truth—moral and religious truth—became for the Rabbinic Sages as much of a passionate quest as it had been for Socrates and Plato several centuries before them. Like the Greek philosophers, they too forged their ideas and moral values in the smithy of free discussion and sharpened them in the thrust and parry of controversy with their opponents. In the final analysis, the continuing debates over the religious laws and traditions between Hillel and Shammai (and, after they had died, between their disputatious disciples for centuries after) supplied the materials that make up the Talmud. There were times, though, when these fraternal wranglings were more fierce than exalted in spirit. They often reached a point of crisis. This moved one Rabbinic Sage to remark ruefully: "The one Torah has now become two Torahs!"

In mentality and character, and each in his own way, Hillel and Shammai personified the different teachings and ethical values of their rival Pharisee schools. It is not difficult to understand why Shammai's aggressive intellectual temper and passionate nature made of him an unyielding dogmatist. He grew impatient with other men's opinions when they ran counter to his own. For all that, judged by

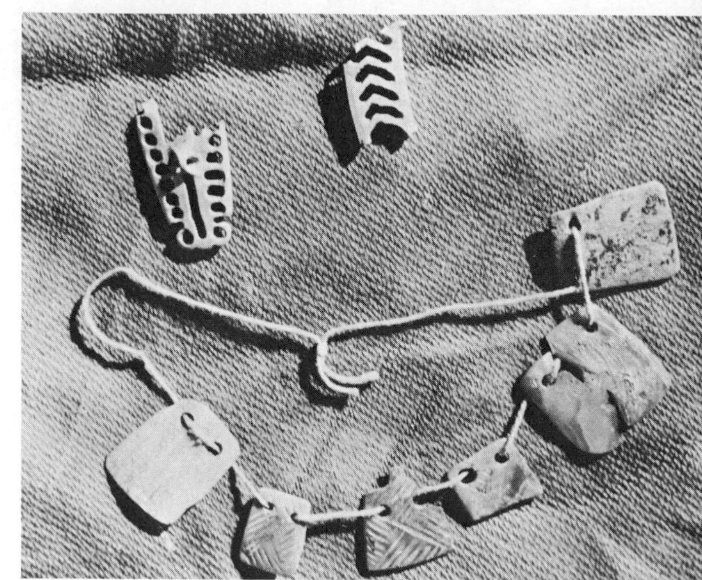

Necklace of stone and wooden ornaments found in a Judean Desert Cave in a goatskin bag that held letters by Bar Kochba, the Messianic rebel leader of 132–35 C.E. *(American Friends of the Hebrew University.)*

Woman's beadwork bag found in a Judean Desert cave. Judea, early 2nd century. (American Friends of the Hebrew University.)

Stone Sarcophagi in catacomb rock niches near Meron, Israel, presumed to be the burial place of the Rabbinic Sage Hillel the Elder and several of his disciples. Judea, 1st century. This is one of the few physical reminders extant relating to the Talmudic yeshibot and the Rabbinic Sages who taught there.

the testimony even of the Talmud, which was strongly biased against him, he was a sincere man of unimpeachable integrity and great strength of character. He acted according to his own lights, however mistaken Hillel might have thought them to be. The Hillelites, who by an inscrutable turn of history had the last word and also the best of the argument over the School of Shammai in that the compiling and editing of the Talmud fell into their hands, did not in any way try to improve the dour image that existed of him and of his zealous followers.

The Mishnah itself records that the patterns of neither liberal interpretation nor unswerving fundamentalism in matters of law were clearly defined by either of the two Sages or their respective schools. In fact, sometimes their roles were reversed. The Hebrew text prefaces a number of disputes between the two with this odd formula: "These are the *lenient* views of the School of Shammai and the *restrictive* views of the School of Hillel."

Quite a different type of man from Shammai was Hillel, as he is pictured by his own characteristic teachings and personal behavior in a portrait which is rounded out by the hero-worshiping testimony of Rabbinic tradition. Lovingly–the memory of him remains undimmed and untarnished by the passage of two thousand years–the Jewish folk have treasured his ethical and wise sayings and the examples in virtue he set with his own conduct. These breathe an indefinable gentleness and benevolence, forming, as it were, an outreaching embrace for all of mankind. One of the most cherished of his teaching maxims and one repeated tirelessly by all the generations of Jews since, has been: "Be of the disciples of Aaron; love peace and pursue peace; love your fellow men and draw them closer to the Torah."

More than once, as has been commented upon by knowledgeable Christians as well as by Jews, the ethical teachings, the social attitudes, and the personality traits of Hillel have shown an arresting resemblance to those of Jesus as they are presented in the Gospels. Furthermore, they often express the very same ideas and values, even employ similar metaphors or, on occasion, the very words used in the Gospels.

This, of course, is by no means just coincidental, nor is it to be wondered at, since both Hillel and Jesus emerged from the identical religious and social climate that had produced the Pharisee and Essene movements with their closely resembling idealistic beliefs and perfectionist practices. For historical accuracy, it should be noted, however, that it was *not* Jesus who had influenced the thinking of Hillel but quite the reverse; it was Hillel who had influenced Jesus. Hillel, it should be remembered, preceded Jesus in point of time by one generation, having died in Jerusalem in 10 C.E., when, presumably, the boy Jesus was only a few years old. Hillel was, in fact, the president of the Sanhedrin long before Jesus is assumed to have been born. The Mishnah reveals him to have been the most potent religious-ethical teacher of contemporary Jewry.

This simple matter of chronology and of Jewish cultural history should be considered of fundamental significance by Christians. It can help them understand why so many of the social ideals and moral values of Jesus, no less than those of other Jews of his time, should have been stamped with the teachings of Hillel and of the other Rabbinic Sages.

Perhaps it was because of the polarity of their approaches to the problems of life and religion that both Hillel and Shammai were impelled to found separate schools of Tannaim for the critical examination of the Oral Laws and Traditions. Considering the fact that it was the School of Hillel that was responsible for the actual compilation and writing of the Talmud, the degree of objectivity it demonstrated appears quite remarkable. The Mishnah, codified by Judah ha-Nasi, set the Talmudic pattern for presenting side by side both the majority and the dissenting opinions on any given matter of law under consideration. Nonetheless, being only human, the Mishnah Fathers of the School of Hillel, ardently supported by their Rabbinical successors, the Amoraim (s. Amora)–"Expounders" who in later centuries created the Gemara, the monumental commentary on the laws of the Mishnah–sometimes could not resist the temptation of indulging in bias. This is clearly shown in the Talmudic maxim: "Let a man be always humble and patient like Hillel and not passionate [i.e., fanatical] like Shammai."

Tomb at Meron, Israel, of the celebrated Rabbinic Sage and mystic of the 2nd century, Simeon bar Yochai.

Leaving all caution to the wind, the pro-Hillel Amoraim even laid down this guiding rule of legal procedure for all future generations: "Where the School of Shammai is opposed to the School of Hillel, the opinion of the School of Shammai is considered as if it were not cited in the Mishnah."

For more than two centuries, the rival Rabbinic schools of Hillel and Shammai contended with each other in public discussions over religious doctrine, legal principles, moral ideas, ritual practices, and social ethics. The Talmud records 316 such debates. By all indications, these debates were not always conducted with decorum and amiability; they were, often, acrimonious. In fact, on a number of occasions they even grew lamentably violent.

In most of these disputations, the School of Hillel emerged victorious. So the Talmud asks rhetorically: "What was the merit of the School of Hillel that it should have been considered the correct one?" And the answer given is that its disciples were gentle and forbearing; while they defended their own decisions, they also presented in the Mishnah text the opposing views of their rivals, and, moreover, out of traditional rabbinical courtesy, presented the views of the School of Shammai deferentially before their own.

What did the later Sages of the Talmud conclude from all this intellectual chivalry? "This teaches us that he [Hillel] who is humble, God will exalt; and he [Shammai] who exalts himself, God will abase." Also, "He [Hillel], who runs away from being great, greatness will pursue him, and he [Shammai] who pursues greatness, greatness will run away from him."

Those who entertain the notion–patently a fallacious and unflattering one–that Rabbinic Law is monolithic, rigid, and authoritarian, will find the free opposition between the two dominant religious schools of the Mishnah conclusive proof of the contrary. In large areas of belief and practice, the Jewish religion may justly be counted among the most undogmatic of the religions of mankind, reacting ever sensitively and humanely to the changing demands of life.

Pirke Abot. (Hebrew, meaning "Sayings" [literally, "Chapters"] of the Fathers often referred to simply as ABOT ["The Fathers"] called by East European Jews simply PEREK ["Chapter"]).

Pirke Abot is one of the sixty-three treatises that comprise the Mishnah. Nevertheless, it is not an integral part of that code of the Oral Laws. In reality, it is only a compilation of the popular teachings of the Rabbinic Sages, the great majority of which are based on the themes of righteous conduct, the wisdom of living, and the pursuit of true piety.

This type of instruction, modeled upon Proverbs and Ecclesiastes in the Bible, takes the folkloric forms of uninvolved sayings, aphorisms, and quintessential definitions of the principles and goals of the Jewish religion and its ethos. Some of these *sententiae,* shimmering with poetic imagery and feeling, are truly lovely. Others, throbbing with humanity or worldly wise or morally profound, are gentle and devout. They breathe a soaring spirituality found only too rarely in the scriptural writings of the other religions of mankind. All of these maxims were designed for the illumination, for the guidance in living, and for the moral improvement of the folk.

The teachings are characteristically brief; they are simply and pithily expressed, attesting to the fact that they were intended to be memorized by the devout. But keeping them in mind was only the beginning, since religious principle without practice was considered less than useless by the Rabbinic Sages. For example, the Babylonian Talmudic teacher, Rabba ben Joseph (*c.* 280–352 C.E.), stated: "He whose aim is to become pious must fulfill the words of the [Mishnah] Fathers."

Each of the five chapters in Pirke Abot (a sixth–the so-called Addition of Rabbi Meir–was added after the Mishnah had been closed, because the five chapters supplied insufficient reading material for all the Sabbaths between Passover and Shabuot) is prefaced by a proclamation. It peals forth like the principal theme in a symphony: "All in Israel have a portion in the World-to-Come! As it is said, And thy people shall be all righteous. They shall inherit the land forever, the branch of my planting, the work of my hands, that I may be exalted."

Taken by itself alone, this declaration represents one of the central postulates of Jewish religious belief. It affirms as unchallengeable truth that all human beings are considered by God to be equal, that they are fundamentally good and perfectable, and that, in the fullness of time, extending his compassion and love to his children, God their Father will redeem them all.

Committed to the folk memory of Israel are many wise and pious teachings. A few among the most treasured are the following:

Yoseh, the son of Yochanan of Jerusalem, said: "Let your house be opened wide, let the poor be members of your household."

Shemaiah said: "Love work, hate power, and do not try to be on intimate terms with those who rule."

He [Hillel the Elder] used to say: [1] "If I am not for myself, who will be for me? And if I am only for myself, what am I? And if not now–when?" [2] "The more flesh, the more worms; the more possessions, the more anxiety."

Shammai said: "Say little and do much, and receive all men with a cheerful face."

Simeon [ben Gamaliel] said: [1] "Not (Torah) learning but doing is the chief thing." [2] "By three things is the world preserved: by truth, by justice and by peace."

Eliezer said: "Let the honor of your fellow man be as dear to you as your own."

Joshua said: "The Evil Eye, the Evil Inclination, and hatred of his fellow men can drive a man out of the world."

Buried in one tomb marked by Hebrew and Aramaic inscriptions are two daughters of the preeminent Rabbinic Sages, the Patriarchs Simeon ben Gamaliel and Judah ha-Nasi. Catacombs of Bet Shearim, Judea, 2nd century.

Akiba said: "Everything is given on pledge, and a net is spread for all the living. The shop is open, the dealer gives credit, the ledger lies open, the hand writes, and whosoever wishes to borrow may come in and borrow. But the collectors regularly make their daily round, and exact payment from man, whether he likes it or not, and they have that on which they can rely for their demand. And their judgment is the judgment of truth."

It was noted by Amram, the Gaon (Rector) of the celebrated Talmudic academy (yeshibah) at Sura in Babylonia (in 856 C.E.), that it was during his time the custom among the Torah scholars and students at the yeshibah to read a chapter from Abot on the afternoon of the Sabbath. This practice must have originated a long time before. More significantly, it has continued as a revered tradition for the devout ever since then. The reflective reading from Abot takes place in the traditional synagogue on the Sabbath afternoons between Passover and Shabuot. In the home, too, on that day of spiritual self-replenishing, fathers discuss these Rabbinic sayings and maxims with their children in order to help them draw the correct lessons from them.

The pedagogic acumen of the Rabbinic teachers was indeed great, for by inserting the Pirke Abot into the very text of the siddur (prayer book) among the Sabbath prayers–a privilege not even accorded to any of the more exalted Biblical writings–the dedicated teachers of a later age sought to keep the Jewish folk constantly preoccupied with the problems of ethical conduct, in that way quickening the religiosity of the heart and the hand.

The Sayings of the Fathers harks right back to the starting point of the Oral Law–the Torah she-be-al-Peh. It begins with Moses on Mount Sinai; then it telescopes the line of its transmission from Moses to the Prophets, and from them to the Men of the Great Assembly. The golden chain of continuity is finally linked up with Hillel and Shammai, and chiefly with their great disciples, one of whom, Hillel's descendant Judah ha-Nasi, closed the canon of the Mishnah *c.* 200 C.E.

Modern critics of the Talmud–and they have been numerous–have often dwelt on the fact that the Mishnah was excessively freighted with laws and prohibitions—often trivial—on purely ritualistic and ceremonial matters. It has been charged by some that, by erecting a regulatory "fence" around the Law in order to preserve it, Rabbinic Judaism succeeded only in imposing through its massive design for formalism in worship and observance, an onerous burden on the devout. To many an enlightened Jew of today, much of this adverse criticism seems to be justified. But if one only takes the trouble to dig a little beneath the surface of the Mishnah text, one is sure to find that this allegation is not fundamenally valid.

Actually, the Mishnah tirelessly underscores the fact that what is most relevant in the practice of the Jewish religion is an inner piety, a purity of intention, and, above all, a consistency in living righteously and in fraternity with one's fellow men. For proof of this one need go no further than the simple teachings of Abot, a work which is really a distillation of all the thinking in the Talmud that is noble, humane, and just–and therefore, timeless.

TOSEFTA

(Hebrew, meaning "additions" or "supplements")

While formerly the Tosefta was regarded merely as an independent collection of commentaries on the Mishnah or Oral Law, more recent scholarship has tended to consider it as a collateral work. The authors were the second-century (C.E.) Judean Rabbinic Sages, the Tannaim–principally Akiba ben Joseph, Simeon ben Gamaliel, and Judah ha-Nasi–but the editing of the work has been attributed to the third-century Tanna, Chiyyah bar Abba.

The Tosefta is arranged in the same systematic manner as the Mishnah. It is divided into six divisions or *sedarim* (s. *seder,* meaning "order"). These divisions in turn are divided into fifty-nine treatises. Whereas the Mishnah stated the Oral Traditions in brief aphoristic form, these treatises of the *Tosefta* contain greater elaborations of them. The intention was to make them more comprehensive, and also more comprehensible.

GEMARA

(Aramaic, meaning "Completion")

While the word Talmud, as it is customarily used, is an over-all term which includes in its compass all the ancient Rabbinic writings that are gathered under its main divisions–Mishnah, Gemara, and Midrash–properly speaking, it refers to the Gemara alone. This dual application of the name has often resulted in confusion in the minds of the uninitiated.

For the greater part, the Gemara is the Rabbinic commentary on the Mishnah code. The text of the latter left itself open to further free discussion of its laws, opinions, and traditions by the simple act of juxtaposing many of the majority opinions of the Tannaim with the rejected dissenting views of equally illustrious Rabbinic colleagues. The very absence of unanimity in these decisions posed a challenge–in fact, almost an invitation–to the later Rabbinic teachers, the Amoraim or Expounders, following the codification of the Oral Laws (about 200 C.E.), to explore those disagreements: either to reconcile them or to agree upon more satisfactory decisions.

This critical re-examination led naturally to further elaborations and to new applications of the Mishnah laws. The great variety of Rabbinic discussions and opinions that are recorded in the Gemara demonstrate the fluidity and tireless probing for greater understanding by the Talmudic mentality. Yet, strictly speaking, Jewish law never remained frozen for long. Perfectionist and progressive in its philosophy, it was constantly being exposed to revision under the impact of the changing circumstances of Jewish life.

The critical review of the obscurities and contradictions in the Mishnah text was carried out by the Amoraim. They were the Rabbinic successors to the Tannaim who were the collectors and teachers of the Oral Laws. In this massive intellectual activity participated hundreds of scholars over a time-span of several centuries.

With the meticulous, and sometimes hairsplitting, zeal of seasoned legal casuists, they examined the text of the Mishnah, law by law and sentence by sentence. They tried to trace every opinion and tradition to its most authoritative source. In group discussion, they sought to reconcile every inconsistency and contradiction that they discovered. Very often, they accomplished their aim of reaching greater clarity and consistency. Also, not infrequently–as so commonly happens in all matters of legal interpretation–they only succeeded in complicating the issue more.

By and large, however, the Amoraim were remarkably open-minded thinkers. They sought the ever elusive truth wherever they thought they would be able to find it, but it was always with the devout proviso that it be well founded on the Scriptural teachings. It was a rare instance, indeed, when they succumbed to the temptation of confirming a law arbitrarily. In their approach, most of them merely imitated the enlightened example that had been set by the Tannaim. Most of the time they followed the same pattern of intellectual tolerance in their discussions. The editors of the Gemara, whenever possible, presented the dissenting opinions of the rejected minority side by side with those of the accepted majority in a method comparable to that used by the United States Supreme Court in issuing decisions.

In addition to their exhaustive discussions of the laws of the Mishnah, the Amoraim also explored a formidable and variegated body of knowledge and opinion that had little to do directly with the Mishnah text. From this reservoir, too, they wished to draw proper guidelines for the devout.

The Talmud abounds in discussion and comment on a a wide array of subjects on every conceivable situation, relationship, and value imaginable in the life, religion, and culture of the Jews during the Rabbinic Age. It dwells with earnestness and poetic feeling on the problems of faith, repentance, sin, and piety; on prayer and Torah-study; on medicine and hygiene; on mathematics and astronomy; on marriage and divorce; on ethics—especially on the just and benevolent treatment of the poor, the worker, the needy, the weak, the Gentile stranger, and the slave. It provides the scrupulous person with a chart of guidance for righteous conduct along every step of his way and for the regulation of just relationships in society, whether between parents and children, husband and wife, borrower and lender, loser and finder, judge and accused, a man and his community, Israel and the nations, and, not least, upright intercourse between Jews and Gentiles. In no other body of the religious literature of mankind can there be found such an abundance of commentary on the moral imperative for world peace and on the arts of peace, on brotherhood, and the practices of humanity.

With the single exception of the Bible, which supersedes it in authority, the Talmud in all its divisions remains the exhaustive storehouse of knowledge and illumination about Judaism, Jewish life, laws, mores, and culture.

For the uninitiated, it is necessary to underscore the fact that there is not just one Gemara or Talmud but two, each one being a commentary and interpretation in. the Aramaic language of the same Hebrew text of the Mishnah. Yet each, because of geographic cultural reasons, is significantly different from the other. It is the concensus that the more impressively intellectual and at the same time the more influential of the two interpretive works was created by the collective efforts of several hundred Amoraim who taught for three centuries in the Talmudic academies of Babylonia: in Sura, Pumneditha, Nehardea, and Machuza. This Gemara is identified as the Babylonian Talmud–Talmud Babli–and it was completed about 500 C.E. The other Gemara–the Palestinian Gemara, known as the Jerusalem Talmud or Talmud Yerushalmi—was developed perhaps by an equally great number of scholars in the Judean Rabbinical schools of Caesarea, Bene Berak, Siknin, and Lydda, but mostly in the academy of Tiberias. The latter collegium of Rabbis considered itself to be the rightful successor to the Sanhedrin, which the Romans had ordered abolished. The Jerusalem Gemara was completed, it is believed, about the end of the fourth century C.E.

Of the two, the Babylonian Gemara is by far the more voluminous. Although it comments upon only thirty-seven of the sixty-three treatises of the Mishnah, it is, in fact, seven or eight times the length of the Palestinian Talmud, which covers thirty-nine Mishnah tractates. Various hypotheses have been suggested to explain this incompleteness, but the most persuasive have been that the "missing" treatises were either never committed to writing or, during the many dreadful and turbulent times which followed the Talmudic Age, were lost or destroyed.

Why, of the two Talmuds, the Babylonian should have enjoyed a greater prestige and have had a greater impact on Jewish life and thought may be explained by the historic fact that it had been produced in the superior intellectual climate of Zoroastrian Babylonia. There the material conditions and the advanced state of the communal life of the Jews (who numbered from one to two millions) under the relatively mild rule of many of the Sassanid dynasts of Persia, were more favorable for their religious and cultural development. (It was not accidental that both Ezra and Hillel were Babylonian Jews.) At the same time, it is not to be ignored that, while the Rabbinical teachers in each of the two countries were producing their own Talmud, the Jews in the homeland were lying crushed and bleeding, first under the iron heel of Rome and later, after Constantine had made Christianity the state religion of the Empire, under that of the Roman Church as well. It is almost miraculous that the Tannaim of Palestine were able to create the Jerusalem Talmud under such circumstances.

Notwithstanding that the religious-cultural interaction between the Jewish communities of Judea and Babylonia was fraternal and thoroughgoing, it is, nonetheless, disconcerting to discover a certain rivalry in their relationship. Upon close examination, this group self-preening smacks of provincialism, the regional "better-than-thou" characteristic that is present in all national cultures. One Amora is quoted in the Babylonian Talmud as crowing (with an oddly un-Sage-like arrogance): "The scholars in Babylonia are the blossoms and flowers on the tree of the Torah." Another example of their rampant provincialism can be seen in the attitude of the Judean scholar Zeira (fourth century C.E.). He, upon his return home from a sojourn in Babylonia (notes the Jerusalem Talmud), fasted one hundred days so that he might forget all the "false" Talmudic teachings he might unconsciously have absorbed from the scholars in Babylonia!

That there were two different levels of religious culture in the two Jewries may be inferred from their own definitions of an am ha-aretz (ignoramus). In Judea, the Jew who could not recite the brief, one-sentence Shema (the affirmation of God's Unity) was considered an am ha-aretz. But in Babylonia, where the cultural standards were higher, that Jew was considered an am ha-aretz who, even though he was knowledgeable in Bible and Talmud, yet failed to grasp their spiritual-ethical meanings. This extreme intellectual preoccupation with religion, designed to draw the devout closer to a knowledge and love of God, was trenchantly expressed in a private prayer by Mar Samuel, the celebrated Gaon of the Babylonian Academy of Nehardea in the third century C.E.: "Make us intelligent that we may know Your way!"

The Talmud–and this reference is to the Mishnah, the Gemara, and the Midrash–consists of two general classifications of materials. One is called Halachah. It denotes "walking," and is a poetic allusion to walking along the well-defined path of righteousness that had been laid out for the devout in the Torah. In actuality, Halachah, comprises all the laws and regulations in the Mishnah and in both Gemaras, together with all the opinion and discussions relevant to them.

Intimately meshed with and complementary to the laws and regulations that are set forth in the Halachah are those materials which collectively are termed Agada. While the literal meaning of the word is "narrative," nonetheless the Agada includes many forms of the literary imagination and of the storyteller's art. It constitutes an immense and colorful tapestry of folklore, woven of allegories, nature myths, legends, parables, fables, moralistic anecdotes about the Rabbinic Sages, aphorisms, folk-sayings, and even jokes and witticisms.

Apart from their pedagogic intent of making plain and persuasive to the pious every nuance of meaning in Jewish beliefs, laws, ethics, and ritual observances, the Agada comprises the most significant body of the folk culture of the Jews. Its poetic, discursive manner of examining the texts of the Mishnah and supplying them with interior insights is quite unique in the religious literature of mankind. It, so to speak, puts living flesh and warm blood upon the dry bones of the Law. It was this Midrashic method of textual illumination which was taken over first by Christianity and later by Islam.

This is the way the affinitive relationship between Halachah and Agada is described in the Talmud: "Bread–that is Halachah; wine–that is Agada. By bread alone we cannot live."

The view, during the Middle Ages, widely held that the Agada contained hidden meanings which could be interpreted only allegorically, found its most illustrious exponent in Maimonides. Although himself an Aristotelian philosopher and an avowed rationalist, he, nevertheless, averred that the parables, allegories, myths, and fables in the Agada held concealed in them those "divine truths" to the search of which all philosophers in the past, both Jewish and Gentile, had dedicated their lives. If those truths, said he, were imbedded in esoteric statements, it was because of a deliberate design on the part of their creators, the Rabbinic Sages, to sharpen and deepen the understanding of Torah scholars. His counsel was: "Seek rather the inner meaning, and if you cannot find the kernel, leave the shell alone, and confess: 'I do not understand this.'"

Maimonides classified Talmudic scholars and interpreters in three categories. The first, he said, consisted of unimaginative literalists. They followed the text mechanically, word for word. A second category of scholars, who were skeptics or mockers, also chose to give the text a literal reading. Their purpose was to expose to ridicule the absurd and irrational elements in the Talmud. There was still another class of Talmudists, noted Maimonides. Numerically they were "so small that we can scarcely term them a class." These were fully cognizant that behind the façade of Talmudic allegory were to be found profound and elusive truths.

MIDRASH

(from the Hebrew verb DARASH, meaning "to expound," "to interpret," or "to deduce"; specifically, "to expound the precepts and ethical values of the Scriptures"; actually, a voluminous Talmudic literature known plurally as MIDRASHIM but considered collectively under the singular MIDRASH)

As has already been seen, the literary output of the Rabbinic teachers in the Talmudic Age seemed inexhaustible. Apparently, they never regarded any matter involving religious belief, law, and observance as being entirely settled or completed. Simultaneously and parallel with the creation of the Mishnah and the Gemara, the compilation of still another vital source of Talmudic exegesis and illumination was being carried on with great zeal. This activity did not terminate until more than one thousand years later, in 1040 C.E., when the Geonic period had come abruptly to an end. The literature was that of the Midrash.

The Midrash was a free-wheeling and imaginative interpretation of the Biblical writings, but in particular of the Five Books of Moses. It abounded in most of the literary forms known to Jews in those centuries–in wise aphorisms, moral maxims, folk proverbs, poetic metaphors, diverting analogies, legends, fables, parables, allegories, and anecdotes. In the propagation of the faith, both teacher and preacher had complementary functions to perform: the first to *persuade* and the other to *inspire* the simple folk to a love of God, to a dedication to the commandments of the Torah and the Jewish way of righteousness. The consolation that they held out as a reward to the devout was a reassurance of ultimate redemption and of the restoration of Israel's greatness in the days of the Messiah.

Actually, the Midrashim had originated as popular lectures or homilies which were delivered either in the synagogue, in the House of Study (Bet ha-Midrash), or the Talmudic academy. This was a revered custom believed to have been initiated by the Scribes of Judea or, by Antigonos of Soko in the third century B.C.E. These inspirational expositions, or sermons, were delivered on the Sabbath, on holy days–both festival and fast days–and upon the periodic appearance of the New Moon.

The Midrashic or discursive form of freely developing a popular lecture on the springboard of a Scriptural verse or passage is already apparent in some of the pre-Christian Jewish writings in the Apocrypha and the Pseudepigrapha, and in the Greek writings of Philo, the rabbinical Platonist of first-century Alexandria. The interesting fact is that Philo's numerous allegoric sermons, such as those on Moses, the Sabbath, and the precepts of Scripture, however handsomely attired in classical garb and garlanded with citations from the Greek poets and philosophers, unmistakably bear the stamp of the Rabbinic Midrash as developed in the yeshibot of Judea toward the close of the Second Temple period. No doubt from Philo and from other Jewish Hellenists whose writings were preserved by early Church Fathers like Eusebius and Clement of Alexandria, the Midrashic method of illuminating Scripture found its way directly into didactic Christian writings.

To be sure, as had been the case with all other Jewish religious writings, the Midrash, too, unswervingly adopted the Torah as the starting point and as the end, as the source and as the fount of the Jewish religion and of its own literary inspiration. While the Jewish folk faithfully observed the injunction of the Tannaim to "Search out the truths they [i.e., the Midrashim] hold," yet they were cautioned against regarding acceptance and practice of them as obligatory.

The aim of the Midrash was to illuminate the truths of the Torah less by means of rationalization and more by homely and affecting illustration. This explains why so many legends, allegories, and anecdotes in the Midrash are built around the character traits and deeds of beloved heroes from Scriptures—the Patriarchs, Moses and Aaron, several of the Prophets, David and Solomon, etc.

As in the instance of the Gemara, also the Midrash is divided into two kinds of literary materials. There are the legal or Halachic Midrashim and, to complement them, the sermonic or Agadic Midrashim. The second category is by far the more preponderant and memorable. In the Agada, the exposition of the Scriptural laws is interspersed with many diverting, moralistic, and teaching forms of folklore.

Three important works of earlier expositional Midrash which, ostensibly, were the creations of some of the Tannaim or Rabbinic Sages, are the Mechiltah (Measure), an interpretation of the Book of Exodus only partly extant; Sifrah (the Book), a commentary on Leviticus; and Sifreh (the Books), namely, Numbers and Deuteronomy. These writings were composed not in Babylonia but in Judea, and not in the vernacular Aramaic but in the new Mishnah Hebrew.

Two Rabbinic thinkers—heads of rival academies in Judea early in the second century C.E.—the Tanna Ishmael ben Elisha, who had created the Thirteen Principles of Talmudic reasoning, and his colleague, Akiba ben Joseph, left the indelible imprint of their intellects upon the above-mentioned works. Akiba, of course, was the master of Midrashic exposition and analysis. He proved himself ingenious, logical, and thorough in his attempt to systematize all legal materials and to reconcile contemporary needs with the precept of the Torah.

The Midrashim, composed in the vernacular Aramaic by the Amoraim, the Rabbinic successors to the Tannaim, and apparently edited after the Babylonian Gemara was completed (c. 500 C.E.), followed the method of organization and presentation introduced by the latter in their Biblical exegesis. The Midrashim, too, were running commentaries to the texts of particular Biblical books. An outstanding work of this character was the Midrash Rabbah (The Great Midrash). Besides containing expositions of the texts of the Five Books of Moses (treated weekly portion [sidrah] by weekly portion), it also included Midrashim on the Five Scrolls (Megillot): The Song of Songs, Ruth, Lamentations, Ecclesiastes, and Esther. There are similar exegetical Midrashim on the Psalms, Job, etc. In proper order, these Scrolls are read in the synagogue throughout the year.

While the expository Midrashim found an immense audience—the erudition of the average Jew in Torah and Mishnah was quite astonishing under the traditional Jewish culture-pattern—there yet remained an even greater number of Jews who were unable to follow the intricacies of the Halachic (legal) discourse and dialectics. For their enlightenment, the popular "preaching" Agadic Midrashim were created. These were devout and inspirational sermon-lectures couched in expressive and emotional terms. They appealed to the simple understanding of the folk, gave them spiritual insights into the Torah, stimulated their imaginations, and taught them moral and ethical values by indirection through illustrative myths, sagas, parables, and wise sayings. Many of these, unostentatious and addressed to he heart more than to the intellect, possess a haunting beauty and nobility. In later centuries, they entirely captivated such knoweldgeable Gentiles as the English poet Coleridge and the Russian writer Tolstoy. To Jewish parents, they were always considered to be among the most important silent educators of their children in piety and right conduct.

In passing, it may be culturally significant to note that it was the custom of the great second-century Mishnah Father and fable-writer Meir to lecture in diverting fashion to the women—who were, unhappily, unlettered in those days—on matters of Torah and ethics every Friday evening in the synagogue. That probably marked the beginning of the Oneg Shabbat ("Sabbath Joy") tradition.

One of the pre-eminent sources of these homiletical Midrashim is the Pesichtah. This work is often referred to as Pesichtah d'Rab Kahana because it opens with a statement by Abba bar Kahana, the Gaon of the Rabbinical Academy of Pumbeditha, Babylonia, in the ninth century. It is an anthology of 33 sermons or discourses intended for special Sabbaths, festivals, and other holy days. Other important sources are Pesichtah Rabbathi, which adheres to the general design of the earlier Pesichtah; Vayikra Rabbah, which contains 38 discourses on Leviticus; Tanchumah, a large compilation of Midrashim presumably written by Tanchumah, the fourth-century Judean Amora of that name and which is constructed upon virtually all the weekly portions (*sidrot*) of the Pentateuch; Shemot Rabbah, homilies on the Book of Exodus; Ba-Midbar Rabbah, on Numbers; and Debarim Rabbah, on Deuteronomy.

Summarizing the objectives of the Midrash, the noted pioneer of Jewish Studies, Leopold Zunz, wrote in 1832: "It is intended both to bring heaven down to the community and to lift man up to heaven. Its aim is both to exalt God and to console Israel. Therefore, the discourses contain not only myths, sagas, and moral maxims, and colloquies on retributory justice, and legends from Jewish history which treat of Israel's national greatness and unity in the past and of its prospects in the future, they contain comforting reflections calculated to give new courage to the people in Exile."

Jewish Critics and Opponents of the Talmud. This truism can always stand repeating: Judaism never was a closed system of religion. Furthermore, it was never burdened, like other faiths, with a superfluity of dogmas. Its highway of moral perfection was broad and its spiritual vistas were limitless: They took in the totality of human experience. It was only in times of insupportable strain and stress that the unprogressive elements—the legalistic, the pietistic, and the obscurantist—sought to confine Jewish belief and observance in a strait jacket of conformity. That is why—considering the enormous time-span that was traversed in the creation of the Talmud—its vast literature faithfully reflects all the different approaches, values, trends, and levels of religious culture during the Rabbinic Age. This diversity prompted the noted scholar, Solomon Schechter (1847–1915), to observe that it was entirely possible to select materials from "that wonderful mine of religious ideas"—a choice to be governed by the criteria of a special bias—and yet be able to produce thereby some sort of cohesive philosophy of Judaism. He thought that "it would be just as easy to draw up a manual for the most orthodox as to extract a *vade mecum* [a companion] for the most skeptical. . . ."

The Rabbinic views and discussions which are recorded in the Talmud range across the entire spectrum of Jewish religious experience. The great rabbinical exegete-poet-humanist of Toledo, Abraham ibn Ezra (1093–1167), was thus able to write in detached evaluation of the allegories, parables, and legends in the Gemara and Midrash: "Some of them are fine silks, but others are heavy sackcloth." Being painfully aware of the latter, Maimonides complained bitterly that there were certain scholars who, motivated by a cynical disregard for the truth, were trying to bring the great literaure of the Talmud into disrepute by one-sidedly concentrating their critical attention not on the "fine silks" but only on the "heavy sackcloth." By the process of arbitrary selection, he charged, they endeavored to cull from its numerous tractates every item of absurd reasoning, every superstition and hair-splitting exercise in logical futility. *This*—so *they* said—was the Talmud; therefore it was unworthy of the intelligent man's interest.

However, as is well known to the informed, the childlish notions, the trivia, and incongruities which mar the Talmud may also be found in the religious and philosophical writings of the Greeks and the Romans, of the Church Fathers and the medieval Christian Schoolmen.

The Talmud—if the intention is to weigh it in the balance scales of culture—should be considered as a giant literary storehouse that is stocked with a great number of different intellectual elements which, when taken together, constitute the Jewish religious civilization of the Rabbinic age. Generally, it is of a very high order—wise, gentle, humane, ethical, and enlightened. It always sounds the overtones of a love for people and a spiritual exaltation that is rarely met with in other than Jewish religious writings. Notwithstanding this, it also contains a large assortment of pointless naïvetés, taboos, superstitions, demonic lore, myths, legalistic interpretations, numerological calculations, and absurd argumentation. The sublime and the ridiculous, the profound and the superficial are often found in it in an uncomfortable and hard-to-reconcile proximity, unless one keeps in mind that these polarities represent different cultural levels among the Jews of antiquity.

There is no question but that many of the creators of the Talmud were distressed by the shallowness and the hair-splitting compulsion of some of their Rabbinic colleagues. When one Babylonian Rabbi found himself hopelessly tangled in a debate with one such casuist, he asked ironically: "Aren't you from Pumbeditha, where they draw an elephant through the eye of a needle?"

To the great majority of the Rabbinic creators of the Talmud, knowledge was never an end in itself; it was only one of the possible means for ascertaining truth—both religious and moral. These Sages had scorn for those of their colleagues who frittered away their time and energies in sterile debate, in "thumb-twisting" and legalistic interpretation of things that did not matter at all.

It possibly may come as a surprise to some that, apart from their passionate commitment to the religious and moral improvement of the individual Jew and, in extension, of Jewish society, not a few of the Talmudic thinkers revealed a strong partiality for the natural sciences. This intellectual orientation did not come suddenly; it had been growing steadily, stimulated, no doubt, by the scientific spirit of inquiry among the Egyptian, Chaldean, and Persian astronomers and physicians, and among the Greek and Roman mathematicians and physicists. They were, therefore, able to say with the Judean teacher, Eleazer bar Kappara (*c.* 200 C.E.): "He who knows how to compute the course of the sun and the revolution of the planets yet neglects to do so, of him Scripture says: 'But they regard not the work of the Lord, neither have they considered the operation of his hands.' [Isaiah 5:12.]"

Learned Jews of the Talmudic period and of later times were absorbed simultaneously in studies of religion and astronomy. This drew the following surprised observation from Theophrastus, Aristotle's pupil, in the fourth century B.C.E.: "They spend their time conversing on divine matters and observing the stars at night."

Medical investigations, too, were pursued by the Rabbinic Sages. In the fourth century of the Common Era, the most knowledgeable among the Jews' opponents, Jerome, was provoked with the Rabbis because, he said, they were frittering away their time and intellectual talents on such a vain worldly goal.

At the very time that the Mishnah was being compiled, an extraordinary baraita (addition to the Mishnah) was composed in Judea (about the year 150 C.E.) by Nehemiah, the disciple of Akiba. This work was a geometry in Hebrew, written in the same literary style as the Mishnah itself, and bore the title *Mishnah ha-Middot* (*middot* are "modes" or "rules"). The *Mishnah ha-Middot* deals principally with terms, definitions, and rules of plane and solid geometry. Since it was intended to be used as a practical reference by the land-measurers and rope-stretchers of Judea, it dispensed with the conventional proofs and demonstrations. Discussed in it by Nehemiah were the triangle, quadangle, arc, circle, rectangle, prism, cylinder, pyramid, cone, and sphere. The mathematician Hermann Schapira noted in 1880 that Nehemiah's work was the model and source for the celebrated first Arabic geometry by Mohammed ibn Musa al-Khowarizmi, almost seven hundred years later!

The late mathematician Solomon Gandz gives information on two other Rabbinic mathematicians, Eliezer Chisma and Yochanan ben Gudgaga, who were older contemporaries of Nehemiah. They, too, had been disciples in the school of Akiba and are described in the Talmud as having been great mathematicians. Their claim to fame, apparently, rested on their supposed ability to compute all the drops of water that are in the ocean. On the face of it, this claim seems fanciful, but if it is considered in the naïve context of scientific researches in antiquity, it does not appear at all surprising. It should be recalled that none other than the incomparable Archimedes (*c.* 225 B.C.E.) had himself undertaken, in a work named *The Sand Reckoner,* to count all the grains of sand necessary to fill the empty space of the universe!

For long periods in Jewish history, there was no general acceptance of Rabbinic authority. The first formidable opposition came from the sectarian Sadducees who during the period of Roman domination constituted the priestly ruling-class of Judea. Like the Samaritans, they were firmly opposed to any authority extraneous to that of the Torah (Pentateuch). Some of their ideological skirmishes with the Pharisee Sages (the creators of Rabbinic literature) are feelingly recounted in the Talmud (*see* SADDUCEES).

A second upsurge of revolt against the authority of the Talmud took place in 760 C.E. In that year, the intellectually brilliant Babylonian scholar, Anan ben David, initiated his anti-Rabbinic movement, Karaism (*see* KARAITES). Its central principle was that only the laws of the Torah and the teachings of the Prophets had any validity in the religion of Israel. The Karaites considered the Talmud a work full of falsehoods, heresies, and illogic. So numerous and embattled did they become, that the Rabbinic authorities were forced to initiate a counterattack against them. Leading in this polemical war was Saadia Gaon (892–942), the supreme Talmudic authority of the age. This internal strife often led to acrimony and violence, although it greatly diminished in intensity as Karaism declined. Yet Karaism remained a divisive force in Jewish life for almost twelve centuries, with both "Rabbanites" (Talmudists) and Karaites denying to each other the right to call themselves Jews.

See also BET HA-MIDRASH; CHACHMAH; COMMENTARIES, RABBINIC; DISPUTATIONS, RELIGIOUS; GEONIM; KARAITES; LAW, JEWISH; PHARISEES; SADDUCEES; SAGES. RABBINIC; SAHEDRIN; TORAH STUDY. STUDY; YESHIBAH; YESHIVAH BACHUR.

TALMUD, CHRISTIAN DETRACTORS AND DEFENDERS OF THE

Opposition of a different character was evinced toward the Talmud in Christian Europe during the Middle Ages and the Renaissance. It stemmed perhaps as much from primitive hatred and ignorance as from religious bigotry. This hostility was inflamed by the malice and self-seeking of meshumadim, renegades from Judaism (s. meshumad) who turned informers (pl. masorim, s. masor) against their former brethren. No name of opprobrium in the dictionary of Jewish scorn ever aroused as much revulsion as did that of *masor;* the betrayer's role of the renegade had a nightmarish aspect for the Jews of the European ghettos in medieval and later times.

One such apostate-informer in the thirteenth century was Nicholas Donin, a former Jew of La Rochelle, France, who had entered the Dominican Order. He prepared a complaint against the Jews generally and against their Talmud specifically and presented it formally to Pope Gregory IX in Rome in a brief of thirty-five particulars. Among the most curious of his allegations were these: that the materials in the Talmud were inflammatory, inciting Jews with hatred for Christians; that it cursed Jesus and uttered other vile blasphemies; that it gave religious-legal sanction to Jews to deceive, to rob, and even to murder Christians; that its authority among Jews even superseded that of Scripture, which, being also revered as revealed truth from God by Christians, could be considered by them as nothing short of outrageous blasphemy.

Persuaded by Donin that his accusations were well founded, the Pope sent transcripts of them to the kings of France, England, Portugal, Castile, Aragon, and all of the Italian principalities. At the same time, he ordered the bishops in those countries to confiscate all copies of the Talmud. In his rescript of June 9, 1242, to the archbishops of France, he wrote: "Wherefore, since this [Talmud] is said to be the chief cause that holds the Jews obstinate in their perfidy [i.e., resistance to conversion], we herewith order you by apostolic letters, that on the first Saturday of the Lent to come, in the morning, while the Jews are gathered in the synagogue, you shall . . . seize all the books of the Jews who live in your districts, and have those books carefully guarded in the possession of the Dominican and Franciscan friars . . ."

On the designated Sabbath (March 3, 1240) all copies of the Talmud were brought by the Jews of Paris to their synagogues and surrendered, under pain of death, to the Dominicans. "St." Louis IX, the French king, then ordered that a public disputation be held and four rabbis be made to confront Donin to answer his charges. Among the four rabbinical defenders of the Talmud were Yechiel of Paris and Moses of Coucy. It was a glittering assembly. Both royal court and Church turned out in the full panoply of their power. Present were the queen, the courtiers, the archbishops and bishops of the realm, and the most noted theologians. The Church referred to this trial of strength as "a Tournament for God and the Faith." It was in every essential a kind of knightly joust, except that what was missing were the chivalry and the strict rules of fair play that customarily governed combat on the "field of honor."

Vainly, Rabbi Yechiel strove to expose Donin's accusations against the Talmud as sheer inventions and misrepresentations. To the apostate's charge that the Talmud contained shameless insults against Jesus, the Virgin Mary, Christianity, and the Church, Yechiel countered with the observation that St. Jerome and other illustrious Church Fathers who had been great scholars and knowledgeable in the Talmud had never found it necessary to point out any hostile or abusive statement in it about any of these. Therefore, he asked, did it not seem remarkable that such a discovery had to wait eight or nine centuries before an uninformed renegade from his faith, clearly motivated by malice, came along to slander it?

For two days this strange tournament was fought. All the while the Jews of Paris remained locked in their synagogues, praying for divine succor for their champions. Quite obviously, the disputation was being held not for the sake of truth or reason or justice, but as propaganda for the Christian faith against the "perfidious" Jews.

The tribunal, composed of leading prelates, found the accused "prisoner"—the Talmud—guilty of all the crimes and blasphemies Donin had itemized against it in his complaint. Concerning this finding, Bishop Odo, the papal legate to France, observed later, in 1248: "We found that these books were full of innumerable errors, abuses, blasphemies, and wickedness such as arouse shame in those who speak of them and horrify the hearer to such an extent that these books cannot be tolerated in the name of God without injury to the Christian faith. . . ."

In June of 1242, twenty-four cartloads of the Talmud and other Hebrew works (it should be kept in mind that these books were not printed but were manuscript productions by copyists) were publicly burned by the Dominicans. That occasion may have set the historic precedent for the book-burning orgy by the Nazis in 1932 in Berlin.

What the effect of the symbolic incineration of the Talmud may have had on Christians is not known, but the terrible trauma it caused the Jewish psyche is well established. Elegies on the tragic event in Paris were composed by two contemporary Hebrew poets—by the German rabbi-scholar, Meir of Rothenburg, and by the liturgist Abraham Bedaresi of the Provence. Meir's lament is still recited in many Orthodox synagogues on Tishah b'Ab (the Ninth of Ab), the fast day which commemorates the Destruction of the Temple in Jerusalem. The poet gave tongue to the grief of all Jews who felt bereaved because their Talmud had been destroyed.

> I am desolate and sore bereft,
> Lo! I am a forsaken one:
> Like a sole beacon on a mountain left,
> A tower alone.

The fires that consumed the persecuted Talmud in melodramatic settings of priestly piety and mob fury burned brightly more than once in the centuries which followed. Tragically unforgettable to the Jews were the book-burnings that took place in Italy in the year 1553, at the height of the Counter Reformation. These were carried out in compliance with the papal bull issued by Julius III. The then contemporary Jewish historian, Joseph ha-Cohen, chronicled in his martyrological work, *The Vale of Tears,* how some Jewish apostates hurried to Pope Julius and complained to him: "There is a certain Talmud widely spread among the Jews and its laws are diverse from those of all peoples. It calumniates your Messiah and it ill befits the Pope to suffer it." The Pope raged: "Get hold of it and let it be burned!" And it was done as he said. Bonfires for the Talmud were lit in the principal city squares of Rome, Venice, Ferrara, Mantua, Bologna, and Ravenna. The chronicler concludes: "And the children of Israel bewailed the burning which the enemies of God had kindled."

Of course, the enemies of the Jews, however overwhelming their hatred and their powers of coercion and suppression, could not possibly destroy every single copy of the Talmud that was in existence. Yet the disputations with the Jews over that work were held to be of the greatest value to the Church. It was believed that by exposing to public scorn the wickedness of the Jews, as it was allegedly mirrored in their religious books, the faith of the Christians would be strengthened. Therefore, the Church ordered the disputations to go on. The one held in Tortosa, Spain, in 1413, resulted in the issuance of a bull by Martin V forbidding Jews to study the Talmud.

The popes who came after Gregory IX and the various Church councils that were convoked by them periodically also authorized the holding of frequent and special inquisitions. These were conducted by Doctors of Theology of the Church, ably assisted by the Jewish apostates in the roles of "experts." They instituted a strict censorship of all Hebrew books and of the Talmud especially, even after the edicts for its suppression were abrogated.

Not infrequently, the apostate-informers, who the Church wishfully presumed were well versed in the Hebrew language and knowledgeable in Jewish religious literature, were appointed to be official censors. These apostate-censors engaged in willful distortions of word-meanings. Armed with Church license and driven sometimes by a thirst for revenge on their erstwhile people, who recoiled from them for having denied their Jewish group-identity and deserted the faith of their fathers, they literally mutilated the Talmudic texts. For example, whenever the word "heathen" was used in an uncomplimentary context in the Talmud, they insisted that it was merely a cunning device for saying "Christian," and they expunged it. (Their favorite method of expunction was a heavy inkblot.) In the same way, whenever the Talmud made satirical mention of Rome, meaning the Imperial Rome of the Caesars that had oppressed the Jewish people for so long, the censors likewise insisted that what the Sages of the Talmud actually had in mind was the Holy Roman Church, so they zealously blotted out all references to Rome!

The verdict was always the same: "Guilty!"—guilty of blaspheming Jesus and the Christian religion, and guilty of being inimical to Christians and to the Church. These secret trials, together with the public disputations between Jewish apostates and rabbis, soon gave the Talmud an aura of horror, deceit, and sorcery that helped to create in the minds of the Christian masses a repugnant image of the Jew.

During the first decade of the sixteenth century, at the very beginning of the Protestant Reformation, there took place an intellectual duel between Johann Reuchlin, the Christian humanist, and Johannes Pfefferkorn (1469–1524) an apostate-informer who, although, by trade, a butcher and possessed but a smattering of Jewish learning, nevertheless, engaged in furious and "erudite" diatribes against the Jews. His principal stock in trade was the same which had served Nicholas Donin so well almost three centuries before. He averred that the principal deterrent keeping Jews from embracing Christianity was the nefarious Talmud, and to prove this, virtually repeated all of the slanders and distortions that had led to the burning of the Talmud in Paris in 1242.

Impressed by his accusations, the Emperor Maximilian issued in 1510 an edict directing a commission of five theologians and scholars to examine all Jewish writings and to order the destruction of all those that attacked or reflected adversely on the Christian faith. Among the five inquisitors was Reuchlin. An independent thinker well versed in Jewish studies, he wrote of his conclusions the following year: "I examined them [the books of the Talmud], and I wrote and responded to the command of the King to the effect that I did not know nor had I heard of such things [Pfefferkorn's charges] in the Talmudic writings."

Reuchlin was well aware of what lay behind the attack on the Talmud. Deep rumblings were already being heard within the Church itself—dissatisfactions with the Inquisition and the general state of religious affairs. There was an increasing clamor for internal reforms. This matter soon resolved itself in an unofficial lining up of two quite sharply defined groupings. In one camp stood the liberal reformers, who counted in their number some of the most progressive prelates, theologians, and scholars of the day, including Erasmus. In the opposing camp were the fundamentalist powers of the Church, who girded themselves for the defense of the status quo. The situation was astonishingly similar to that which revolved around the Dreyfus Affair almost five centuries later and over which the republicans and royalists of France fought a fateful political battle (*see* DREYFUS CASE, THE). However, in the earlier just as fiercely fought skirmish over the Talmud, Reuchlin emerged as the victor.

In order to vindicate his stand, Pfefferkorn, backed by the Dominicans, even resorted to an attack on the personal integrity and the religious loyalties of Reuchlin. He conducted a campaign of vilification against him, charging that Reuchlin had been bought off by "Jewish gold." He even manipulated an official summons to Reuchlin to stand trial for heresy before the inquisitors of the Holy Office.

Hardly a man to remain silent or on the defensive, Reuchlin proceeded to the counterattack. He stated flatly that it was their ignorance of the Talmud and their malice at having been exposed which had prompted Pfefferkorn and the Dominicans to concoct the slander against him. He wrote that "it was through my advice that their plan had come to naught," so that they, out of chagrin, had therefore complained to the Church authorities that "I was a heretic, not believing in our religion and denying its very principles."

The most advanced elements among the churchmen and intellectuals in Europe closed ranks behind Reuchlin. They realized that there was a well-organized plot afoot to punish and ruin him. They recognized also that to a great extent, his stand in defense of the Talmud was in reality one on a larger issue: It was actually concerned with his right, as a Christian and a thinker, to freedom of thought and expression—a right they desperately wished to acquire for themselves. Cardinal Edigio da Viterbo, the humanist who had engaged for many years in Hebrew studies under the instruction of the Jewish grammarian, Elijah Levita, assured Reuchlin: "In fighting for your cause we are defending not you but the Law, not the Talmud, but the Church."

Without actually intending it, or even dreaming that it could ever lead to that, Reuchlin's defense of the Talmud against the bigots in the Catholic world proved to be one of the most significant engagements of the Reformation. For this, there was no lesser authority than Martin Luther. He wrote in 1518 to Reuchlin: "Without your knowing it, you have served as an instrument of Divine Providence." Luther, however, neglected to mention the part the Talmud had played in this extraordinary drama of history.

See also TALMUD, THE; DISPUTATIONS, RELIGIOUS.

TALMUD TORAH (Hebrew, meaning "study of the Torah")

In the year 64 C.E. a revolution of a religious-cultural nature was initiated in Judea by the High Priest, Joshua ben Gamala. "Were it not for him," the Talmudic chronicler gratefully records, "the Torah would have been forgotten in Israel." What he had started was something that perhaps had never been tried before and was not to be repeated by any nation for some eighteen centuries, until the first free, universal, and obligatory public school systems were established in the United States (in Philadelphia and New York City), early in the nineteenth century.

Notes the Talmud, it was only six years before the Jewish state was trampled underfoot in 70 C.E. by the Roman legions that "Joshua ben Gamala came and instituted [a law] that teachers should be appointed in every province and in every town, and that all children above the age of six or seven were to be placed in their charge." In these schools, the attendance of children from six to thirteen was obligatory; the instruction was free. Girls, in keeping with the discriminatory practice prevailing everywhere at the time, were excluded from this instruction, but they were often taught privately, for the yearning for education was a kindling force and reached out, in different ways, to all strata of the people.

Primary schools were established in cities, towns, villages—even hamlets. The public response to the institution of the Talmud Torah (which in the beginning was also called *Bet Sefer*, meaning, in Hebrew, "House of the Book," was one of religious and patriotic enthusiasm. The confident declaration by the Jewish educators in the Talmud was: "So long as the voices of the children of Jacob are heard studying Torah in the schools, the hand of Esau will not be able to prevail against them."

It is also chronicled in the Talmud how in the beginning —presumably this referred to the period before Simeon ben Shetah had established the first schools in Jerusalem about

Talmud Torah class in Polish town. Pre-Nazi period. YIVO

80 B.C.E.—children received their religious instruction from their fathers. Since, at that juncture many fathers did not know very much themselves, the instruction was usually merely rudimentary and unsystematic.

But the general dedication by the Jews to what was considered to be perhaps their most sacred task—the acquisition of Torah-learning—stimulated the development of a remarkable philosophy of Jewish education. Many were the Rabbinic sayings (like the following) seized upon by the plain folk which ever after colored their thinking and feeling concerning the religious instruction of the young: "The very breath of the children at school preserves the world." "He who fails to instruct his child in the Torah robs him of his inheritance." Joshua ben Levi, the famed Rabbinic teacher of the third century, gave this matter supreme emphasis: "He who teaches Torah to his sons and grandsons is as if he himself had received it at Mount Sinai."

Impressive as practical illustration of Joshua's philosophy of education is presented in the Talmud by the following anecdote. One day, a Rabbinic colleague, Chiyya bar Abba, saw Joshua leading his little grandson to the Talmud Torah, seemingly in a great hurry. "Why are you in such a hurry?" asked Chiyya jokingly. Joshua flung back at him: "Why should I not be in a hurry? Do you think it is a small matter to have the privilege of standing at Mount Sinai?"

The interest in universal elementary education waned or rose with the shifting circumstances of Jewish life after the Jewish state in Judea came to an end. Dedicated men under the leadership of Yochanan ben Zakkai arose to perpetuate the practice of learning in every Jewish community of all the countries of the Dispersion. The Talmud Torah then became as indispensable for the preservation of the Jewish religion among the children as the synagogue and the House of Study (Bet ha-Midrash) were for their elders. Often all of these three institutions were housed under one roof or in adjoining buildings.

The ancient Rabbinic educators, who were the architects of the elementary Talmud Torah system, fully appreciated the need for beginning the instruction of the child as early as possible. "A child is ready to learn the aleph-bet [Hebrew alphabet] at three," it is stated in the Midrash. Why so early? "Bend the branch of a vine when it is still young and pliant. When it has grown hard and old, you will no longer be able to bend it."

Constant repetition by children of lessons they had learned was considered absolutely necessary in order that the effect of both the words and meaning of the Bible (which served as their text) might be made indelible in their memory and in their thinking. According to the Rabbis of the Talmud, this practice was predicated on what they considered to be a sound pedagogic theory: "If he [the student] learns Torah and does not go over it again and again, he is like a man who sows without reaping." This will explain why, in Jewish religious practice down the ages, the study of the Torah by the pious never faltered, never came to an end. This ceaseless repetition had at least one good result: The average good scholar was able to recite his religious texts almost word for word—a virtuosity of no mean order.

Another unusual learning method traditional for some two thousand years—and one still observed by the Orthodox—was that of having the children recite their texts out loud. This followed the epigrammatic axiom of the Rabbinic teachers: "*Open your mouth* and learn the Torah." They believed that reading the text "with the eyes" and simultaneously sounding it "with the lips," would make the recollection of it doubly strong.

At some unspecified time during the Middle Ages, among the Ashkenazim of Germany, Austria, Bohemia, and the Polish provinces, a different type of educational institution than the one hitherto known became popular. This was the privately run cheder. Nevertheless, the term Talmud Torah continued in general use, but it referred only to the *communal free elementary schools* which were established for the benefit of those children whose parents were too poor to pay for their tuition.

The chazzan's hagbahah (elevation) of the opened Torah Scroll following the reading of the week's sidrah or portion of the Pentateuch on the Sabbath. (Engraving by Bernard Picart, Amsterdam, 1725.)

But among the Spanish, Provençal, and Italian Sefaradim, who enjoyed an unusually high standard of culture, the traditional Talmud Torah continued to flourish, although with important modifications in its curriculum. For instance, a revealing account (published in 1680) of the latter-day Talmud Torah established by the refugee Sefaradim of Spanish-Portuguese stock who had settled in Amsterdam, describes these modifications. That school, which occupied a building near the synagogue, had six graded classes conducted by six teachers. In the first grade, the smallest boys were taught the aleph-bet and learned by rote a few of the fundamental Hebrew prayers and certain of the blessings. The Hebrew texts of the Five Books of Moses (the Chumash or Pentateuch), together with the traditional musical accents or mode for cantillating them, were taught in the second class. The translation of the Hebrew Bible text into Spanish, together with the marginal commentary-explanation of it by Rashi (the eleventh-century French exegete), was taught in the third class. The Prophetic Writings and miscellaneous books in the Bible, as well as the musical notation marks for guidance in the cantillation, were taught in the fourth grade. In the fifth began the study of the less difficult treatises of the Gemara of the Talmud, and here the principles of Hebrew grammar and the laws pertaining to the holy days, as catalogued in the standard manual of rites and ceremonies, the Shulchan Aruch, were also learned.

The most advanced class was taught by the rabbi himself. For boys of twelve or thirteen, their studies seem to have been astonishingly like graduate courses given in a university today. They studied, analyzed, and discussed various complex treatises of the Talmud together with their rabbinic commentaries, and turned for authoritative guidance to such involved religious-legal codes as those compiled by Maimonides, the medieval philosopher-rabbi, and the fourteenth-century savant, Jacob ben Asher.

The Talmud Torah schedule in this particular institution in Amsterdam (as it was elsewhere and at all times in the world) was arduous. It was especially trying for the small boys of three and four. They attended classes from six to ten hours daily, six days a week, all year round.

Whatever its shortcomings, because of its complete preoccupation with religious studies, the traditional Jewish primary school, whether Talmud Torah or Cheder, represented the first step in a learning discipline that conditioned for intellectuality generation after generation of Jews.

See also BIBLE, THE; CHEDER; MELAMED; MUSICAL ACCENTS; RABBI; TORAH; TORAH STUDY.

TANACH. *See* BIBLE, THE.

TANNA, TANNAIM. *See* SAGES, RABBINIC; TALMUD, THE.

TASHLICH (Hebrew, meaning "casting off")

It remains unknown when the tashlich-rite became customary among the Jews. The first mention of it in Jewish writings was by Rabbi Jacob ben Moses Halevi Mölln of Mayence (1355–1427).

Upon the conclusion of the afternoon service in the synagogue on the first day of Rosh Hashanah, pious Jews in all countries of the world wend their way to the banks of rivers, lakes, or running streams in which live fish are found. There they recite, in addition to other prayers, this verse (7:19) from the Prophet Micah: "And thou wilt cast all their sins into the depths of the sea." Fulfilling the Scriptural expression in a literal way, the devout proceed to "cast all their sins" into the water. They perform this odd rite, called *tashlich* in Hebrew, in the manner introduced by the medieval Cabalists–by shaking out their pockets of whatever stray odds and ends might be concealed there. Some merely shake the hem of their outer garment three times.

To say that the tashlich custom was of Jewish origin would be entirely incorrect. Anthropologists have met with it–or variations of it–in a number of primitive cultures. In parts of India, the villagers fill a pot with all their collected sins and float it down the river. In Siam, it is said, the accumulated sins and afflictions of every member in a community are symbolically loaded into a boat and sent drifting out to sea. This "good riddance" rite was even practiced by Christians in medieval times. The Florentine poet, Petrarch, noted some time before the middle of the fourteenth century that on June 24 of each year–a day marking the Eve of St. John–the Christians of Cologne marched in religious procession to the banks of the Rhine, where they pronounced "certain words" and cast herbs into the river. This they did, wrote the poet, in order that the waters migh wash away all their bad luck for the year ahead.

The reason for casting sins into the water is unclear; it originally must have had some association with nature-worship. Unable to furnish a reason for it on rational grounds, the latter-day rabbis tried to read into it religious significance by allegoric means. A sixteenth-century Polish rabbi explained it this way: Just as water is in perpetual motion and never remains quite the same, so too it can be with the sinner if he repents and promises not to remain the same as before–that is, his sins will drift away from him and leave him in a state of purity.

Why it was necessary for the tashlich rite to be performed over water that contained fish, a rabbinic moralist of the Middle Ages explained this way: Said he, just as a fish is caught with a net, so is a sinner caught in the net of his sins from which he cannot disentangle himself; instead, he has to submit to the mercy of divine judgment.

The performance of the tashlich rite by Jews both mystified and amused their Christian neighbors. In thinking about it, Rabbi Abraham ben Shabattai Horovitz (seventeenth century) of Cracow grew bitter. He said that the rite of emptying their pockets into the water, as performed by the literal-

The Tashlich rite at a body of water where there are live fish. (Woodcut. Germany, 1508.)

Small-town (shtetl) Jewish women at the waterside, reciting the Tashlich prayer. Poland, pre-Nazi period.

minded, was sheer mummery or worse, ". . . for it really is a desecration of the great Name of God before the nations that know of the custom. When they see Jews going to the river, they laugh and say: 'The Jews are going to shake their sins into the water.' "

Many a time, this childish but perfectly innocent rite symbolizing repentance was only too thoroughly misrepresented by the enemies of the Jews. They accused them of throwing "poison" into the rivers, lakes, and streams in order "to wipe out" the Christians. Many a bloody tragedy–the most terrifying ones were the massacres which followed the Black Death in 1348–49 (*see* MASSACRES)–affecting entire Jewish communities, resulted from these calumnies about tashlich.

See also REPENTANCE; ROSH HASHANAH; SIN AND SINNER.

TEACHERS AND THINKERS. *See* ARABIC-JEWISH "GOLDEN AGE"; BIBLE, THE; CHEDER; GEONIM; MELAMED; RABBI; SAGES, RABBINIC; SOME ARCHITECTS OF JEWISH CIVILIZATION; TALMID CHACHAM; TALMUD, THE; YESHIBAH.

TEFILLIN (Hebrew, meaning "phylacteries" or "frontlets"; from TEFILLAH, meaning "prayer")

Tefillin–or phylacteries, as they are generally known in English–constitute, like the Sabbath, circumcision, the dietary laws and tzitzit (the ritual fringes), a prominent symbol of the Jewish religion. Their central importance in Jewish religious observance may be gauged by the following parable in the Talmud: The Rabbinic Sage Eliezer related that when the Israelites came before God and complained to him: "We are eager to occupy ourselves night and day with the study of the Torah, but, alas! we cannot find the leisure time for it," God replied to them: "Perform the commandment concerning tefillin and I will consider that as if you had been studying the Torah night and day."

There was even an ancient Jewish saying: "God, too, wears tefillin."

The obligation for every male Jew to wear tefillin was stated in the commandment: "And it shall be for a sign unto thee upon they hand, and for a memorial between thine eyes, that the law of the Lord may be in thy mouth." (Exodus 13:9.)

The observing male Jew, for countless generations, in performing the daily rite of putting on tefillin every time he recited his morning prayers, was helped to remain permanently conscious of his religious duties and his Jewish group-identity. The tefillin were for him a symbol of his personal dedication to his God and to the Torah. In the optimistic words of the twelfth-cenury rabbi-philosopher Maimonides: "The sanctity of tefillin is very great. As long as they are on the head and on the arm of a man, he is modest and God-fearing and will not be distracted by merrymaking or idle talk. He will have no evil thoughts, but will devote all his thinking to truth and righteousness."

Tefillin are two individual boxes or cubes whose dimensions usually are two or three inches square. Inside each are deposited strips of parchment on which are inscribed four Biblical passages in Hebrew: Exodus 13:1-10 and 11:16, and Deuteronomy 6:4-7 and 11:13-21. The tefillin themselves are made of black leather; one is designed for the head, the other for the left hand. They are held in place by means of leather loops, knots, and long straps. Their physical form no doubt follows a very ancient tradition. The spiritual symbolism they carry must have been acquired at a more advanced level of religious thinking. The tefillin (the word is singular as well as plural) worn on the head is strapped around the forehead so that, suggestively, it may rest next to the brain; the one on the left arm rests in a position closest to the heart. This arrangement for the wearing of the "frontlets" the Talmudic teachers interpreted to signify that the Jew, when he worshiped God, did so with all his heart and with all his thoughts.

The wearing of tefillin is obligatory for all Orthodox male Jews from the time they become Bar Mitzvah, at thirteen. They put them on before commencing the recitation of the morning prayers each day except on the Sabbath and festivals. The latter exceptions are made, according to the Rabbis, because, by themselves, the holy days also consti-

Orthodox member of an Israeli settlement at his morning's devotions while standing guard during the Arab invasion in 1948. The tefillin (phylacteries) he wears are arranged in the exact pattern followed by every Jewish worshiper since Rashi established it during the Middle Ages.

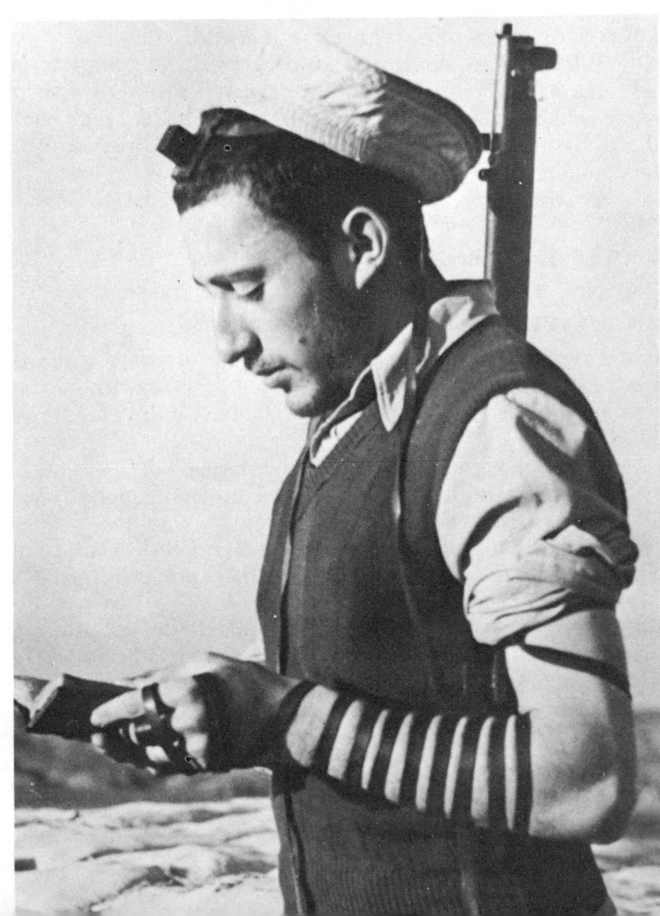

tute "signs" or "symbols" of the Jewish religious identity; consequently, the wearing of tefillin on them is considered superfluous.

Talmudic laws, which are based on Oral Tradition as well as on later practices and rabbinic views, with regard to tefillin are very numerous indeed. The sixteenth-century ritual code, the Shulchan Aruch, lists 160 laws that relate to every aspect of the physical make-up of tefillin, the ritual procedures, and the order of putting them on and taking them off; they provide for all the exigencies that might possibly govern, under any conditions, the wearing of tefillin.

The first specification is that they be "fit." What this means is that a "competent and God-fearing scribe [sofer]" write the four Biblical execerpts which are encased in the cubes. (The *sofer* who prepares the parchment text has to submit to a calligraphic as well as religious discipline that is as rigorous as that prescribed for copying a Torah Scroll [*see* TORAH SCROLL].) In addition, the tefillin and the straps which hold them in place can be made only from the skin of an animal considered ritually "clean." The sewing on each tefillin is limited to twelve stitches and must be done with thread made of the dried veins of a "clean" animal. The edges of the case are not to be scuffed, nor can the outside layer of leather show any sign of peeling or separation.

There are rigid rules for the worshiper to follow in putting on and taking off the tefillin. Tradition requires that he do so while standing, as a mark of reverence. The tefillin of the hand comes first. This is put in place on the inner side of the left arm just above the elbow, and it is held in position by a noose from the long strap hanging down its side. After its knots are tightened, the worshiper coils the tefillin strap several times around the forearm. He then proceeds to put on the tefillin of the head. This is placed in the upper middle of the forehead and the strap holding it is then looped around the head and knotted; the two ends of the strap are left hanging down and brought forward over the shoulder. When that is accomplished, the worshiper winds the hand strap three times around his middle finger (to represent the Hebrew letter *shin,* which begins the Cabalistic word Shaddai—one of the names for the Almighty). It is the custom for the worshiper to kiss the tefillin with the utmost reverence before putting them on and upon returning them to the tefillin bag in which they are stored.

The exact period when the wearing of tefillin originated is not known, although the Jewish historian Josephus, writing in the first century, referred to the rite as one that was already ancient in his time. Yet the conclusion is inescapable that, like other spiritually interpreted values in the Jewish religion, the wearing of tefillin must have had a more primitive meaning in earlier times. The thought obtrudes that the tefillin originally was an amulet—a charm worn for the protection of the wearer against the designs of his enemies and against hostile demons. More than a hint of this lies in the etymology of its name: "phylacteries." This word was derived from the Greek word *phylakterion,* meaning "fortress" or "protection." The first mention of this name for tefillin is found in the original Greek text of the Letter of Aristeas, written in Alexandria some time during the third century B.C.E. by the Greek Jew Aristeas. The word entered into general usage in Europe by means of the Greek version of the Gospel according to Matthew (23:5).

The survival of the original functional use of tefillin as a protective amulet may also be inferred from the Scriptural passage, "And all the peoples of the earth shall see that the name of the Lord is upon thee; and they shall be afraid of thee." This reference is to the Hebrew letter *shin,* which is shown on the outside of the tefillin of the hand, as described

Silver tefillin cases owned by a wealthy Polish Jew during the 18th century. The usual cases are made of leather. (Courtesy of Joseph B. Horwitz Judaica Collection, Cleveland.)

above. The Rabbinic Sages declared that when a Jew wears the tefillin of the head, it is a sign that the Shechinah (God's Radiance) rests upon him and gives him its protection against all harm. Therefore, they prohibited the total covering of the tefillin with the folds of the prayer shawl (tallit) in order that the potent *shin* might not be obscured.

There are also some grounds to associate the wearing of the tefillin of the head—considered the most sacred of the two phylacteries—with the wearing of the tallit. Like the tallit, it may have been worn as part of the identifying Jewish national costume. The probable reason for ultimately discarding its use as well as that of the tallit except during prayer is indicated in a statement by the Church Father of the fourth century, Jerome. He wrote that Jews were afraid to show themselves on the streets of his city because of the hostile attention they drew upon themselves (presumably with their identifying costume). Whether all male Jews in his time wore the head-tefillin is not clear. However, it is certain that the Mishnah Sages, some eighteen centuries ago, set an example in this respect. The Talmud records that the famed teachers, Akiba, Abbahu, and Rabba, wore tefillin all day long. From the Middle Ages on, many of the dedicated pious followed their example.

It is interesting to note that Maimonides viewed the tefillin as a super-amulet. He wrote: "But he who is accustomed to wear tefillin will live long, as it is written: 'When the Lord is upon them, they will live.' "

See also PRAYER AND WORSHIP.

TEITSCH-CHUMASH

The Teitsch-Chumash is the late-sixteenth-century paraphrase in Yiddish of the Five Books of Moses (the Pentateuch). It also includes the Haftarot (s. Haftarah), the weekly selections from the Prophets which are read together with the weekly sidrot (s. sidrah or sedrah), the portions from the Pentateuch, and the five lesser Biblical writings which are commonly referred to as Megillot (s. Megillah) or Scrolls. These are the books of Esther, Ruth, and Lamentations, The Song of Songs, and Ecclesiastes.

The etymology of Teitsch-Chumash is interesting from a philological point of view. Chumash, of course, is the Hebrew name for the Pentateuch. The word *Teitsch,* like *Teutsch,* is an older Yiddish word for *Deutsch* (i.e., "German"). Literally translated, the title *Teitsch-Chumash* means "German Pentateuch," for Yiddish, being part of the Germanic language group, was in former centuries referred to as *Teitsch,* "German") by the Jews who spoke it. In a broader sense, however, the word *Teitsch* in general Yiddish usage came to mean "translation"—specifically, "translation into Yiddish"—of the sacred Hebrew texts.

Although Teitsch-Chumash is its popular name, its original title was *Tze-enah u-Re'enah,* which in Hebrew means "Go Forth and See!" This phrase is taken from The Song of Songs (3:11): "Go forth and see, O ye daughters of

Zion!" But because Jewish women were generally ignorant of Hebrew, the title became garbled on their tongues and emerged as *Tzeneh-Reneh*, by which name it was known ever after. However, most women preferred to call it Teitsch-Chumash.

The adapter and compiler of this celebrated work, Isaac Yanover, never dreamed it would become such a revered household religious book among Yiddish-speaking women in Central and Eastern Europe, one deserving to be placed side by side with the Hebrew Bible and the daily prayer book (the siddur). But from the very first, after its publication in Prague, it enjoyed a phenomenal success. It was even given a Latin translation by a Christian scholar in 1660. It went through far more editions than any other work in Yiddish, and is still in wide use among Orthodox Yiddish-speaking women everywhere.

The Teitsch-Chumash appeared during a period of cultural backwardness for the Jews of Germany and Eastern Europe. It therefore came to fill a great void in the devotional and cultural life of Jewish women, who were not only denied a general Jewish education and an accompanying knowledge of Hebrew (in which all religious literature was written) but, in sharp contrast to their menfolk, were also limited in the exercise of the religious experience, both in the synagogue and at home. It was the ever unsatisfied hunger of the Jewish woman for even a smattering of knowledge about her peoples' religious culture that helped create the wide market for devotional works written in Yiddish, of which the Teitsch-Chumash, without question, was the shining example. The Jewish woman clung to it, receiving from it the same spiritual sustenance as did the Christian woman from The Book of Hours and The Lives of the Saints. Customarily, she read from it on the Sabbath day, when she had the opportunity to escape "beside the still waters" from the turmoil and harassments of her daily existence.

Simplifying the Hebrew Biblical text in an easy, intimate style, and being, at the same time, highly charged with emotion and a moralizing fervor, this Yiddish paraphrase of the Pentateuch often brought to the reader healing balm.

Mother reading the Teitsch-Chumash, the Yiddish paraphrase of the Pentateuch, on Sabbath afternoon. (Painting by Sheva Ausubel.)

There evolved a curious traditional vocal style for reading from the Teitsch-Chumash that required enormous concentration. This was a chanting in a devotional singsong, mostly in a minor key.

The Teitsch-Chumash, in a very literal sense, was one of the great educators of the Jewish folk during several centuries. Assessed against the requirements of its time, it was of inestimable religious, cultural, and social value. Its simple and often naïve text was full of ethical and moral reflections. Its compiler furnished copious examples from the Bible, the Talmud, and medieval religious sources to illustrate the virtues of kindness, charity, compassion, and just-dealing. In addition to its devotional and moralistic materials, the work also contained a great number of parables, allegories, legends, and folk sayings that often were poetic and inspirational and, sometimes, wise. Without any attempt at artfulness, the Teitsch-Chumash popularized Jewish history and lore with the astuteness of first-clas pedagogy. And every mother was certain to transmit the knowledge and illumination she derived from it to her children.

See also FAMILY, THE; FAMILY RELATIONS, TRADITIONAL PATTERNS OF; WOMAN, THE TREATMENT OF.

TEMPLE, THE (in Hebrew: BET HA-MIKDASH, or, simply: BAYIT, meaning "The House"—a term used also by the Canaanites)

The religious worship of all peoples, from the most primitive to the most advanced, invariably was formalized and followed fixed patterns. It is a cultural paradox that at no time in its three thousand years of history was the Jewish religion so thoroughly institutionalized as when the Temple in Jerusalem existed as the sole national sanctuary of Israel. The instinctive urge in all mankind seems to be for dramatizing its most cherished beliefs and group-values in formal emotional and symbolic terms. It led to the invention by the ancient Jews of impressive rites and ceremonies for the Temple on Mount Moriah. These were made dazzling with color, solemn with pageantry, and stirring with choric music.

The synagogues, although existing independent of the national sanctuary ever since the Babylonian Exile, after 70 C.E., when they supplanted the destroyed Temple in religious worship, seemed scarcely touched by the overpowering materialistic ecclesiasticism with which the Temple services had been imbued. Except during the relatively brief existence of the Sanhedrin (q.v.) in latter-day Judea, they never were required to submit to any central religious authority comparable to that wielded by the priestly hierarchy in the Temple in Jerusalem.

In their groping for a truer spirituality, the synagogues were able to avoid the barbarous sacrificial cult with its gory hecatombs of animal peace-offerings and sin-offerings that had been central in Temple worship. Sacrifice, it must be remembered, was not a ritual practice peculiar to the Jews alone; it was general not only in the regions of the Fertile Crescent but in most parts of the world as well. In its accepted sense, the sacrificial rite in all ancient religions was performed for the propitiation of a deity or to achieve a reconciliation with him. But according to the nineteenth-century English Biblical scholar and scientist, W. Robertson Smith, it had an additional function. It constituted "an act of social fellowship between the deity and his worshipers." *Together*, in significant communion, the god—through his surrogate, the priest—and the worshiper ate of the flesh and blood of the animal-sacrifice, and also of the "the first-fruits": vegetables, grains, wine, and oil. By eating with him the suppliant became "a kinsman" or "friend" of the god whose protection and benevolent regard he thus expected to obtain.

The details given by the Biblical chronicler of the dedication rites of the Temple of Solomon that took place in Jerusalem during the Feast of Tabernacles (Succot) about 955 B.C.E. seem staggering indeed to modern sensibilities. They attest to the overwhelming importance given to the sacrificial rites in the Temple worship. On that memorable occasion there were slaughtered upon the altar as peace-offerings "unto the Lord" a hecatomb of "two and twenty thousand oxen, and a hundred and twenty thousand sheep. So the king and all the children of Israel dedicated the house of the Lord." (I Kings 8:63.) For seven days, the king, the priests, and the people feasted and—as Robertson Smith probably would have said—"ate with the god" in fellowship.

A most revealing incident, as illustrative of the changing concept of worship in the Jewish religion, is recounted in the Talmud. Shortly after the Destruction of the Second Temple by the Romans, as the Rabbinic Sage, Yochanan ben Zakkai, was walking past the sacred ruins in company with Joshua ben Chananiah, the latter broke into lamentation over the loss of the sanctuary and the end to the hallowed cult of sacrifice. "Do not grieve, my son!" Yochanan comforted his disciple. "We still have left to us means for the atonement of sin in the performance of acts of loving-kindness. Is it not written: I desire mercy, and not sacrifice [Hosea 6:6]?"

Whatever criticism can be and actually has been leveled at the primitivism and antisocial character of this priest-domination of the Temple religion of the ancient Jews, one positive good accrued from it. Merely by virtue of the fact that it existed as the sole and central sanctuary, it acted as a powerful *national unifier* of Jewish life. In a significant way, it served as the emotional binder and religious-cultural integrator of the people during the post-Exilic period. It brought closer to realization the dream of Moses, the Prophets, and Ezra the Scribe for a clearer conception of ethical monotheism among the majority of Jews who stubbornly remained monolatrous, worshiping YHVH (the ineffable secret name of God, not to be pronounced) as the chief god in a pantheon of lesser deities. This may, in part, be inferred from the fact that in the religions of even the most advanced contemporary peoples—Egyptian, Babylonian, Phoenician, Greek, and Roman—the proliferation of numerous local sanctuaries dedicated to different "patron"-deities merely compounded the theological confusion. In that manner, they helped perpetuate primitive nature-worship—the central element in polytheism.

Always, and especially during the post-Exilic period, the Temple in Jerusalem called forth the most passionate devotion from the devout. It represented to them, in a complex psychological way that had evolved out of their unique historic experiences and ethnic culture, the supreme physical symbol of the Jewish religion. It is enough to refer to an incident that occurred in the final anguished hours during the siege of Jerusalem in 70 C.E., after the Roman soldiers, under Titus, had put the Temple to the torch. Many of the last-ditch defenders, when they saw their beloved sanctuary ablaze, cried out in anguish and leaped into the flames. They preferred to be incinerated with their Temple rather than to survive in Judea's national desolation without it.

The farther removed in point of time the Temple became to succeeding generations of Jews after they had been scattered throughout the world, the more glamorous grew its memory. The reason is easy to explain. The drabness and poverty of Jewish life everywhere in the world, the hazards and misfortunes the Jews always had to face, made them look back nostalgically to the time when the Temple still

Shekel, showing (left) representation of the Temple laver and minted in 66 C.E., at the outbreak of the revolt against Rome culminating in the Destruction of the Temple and the Jewish state four years later.

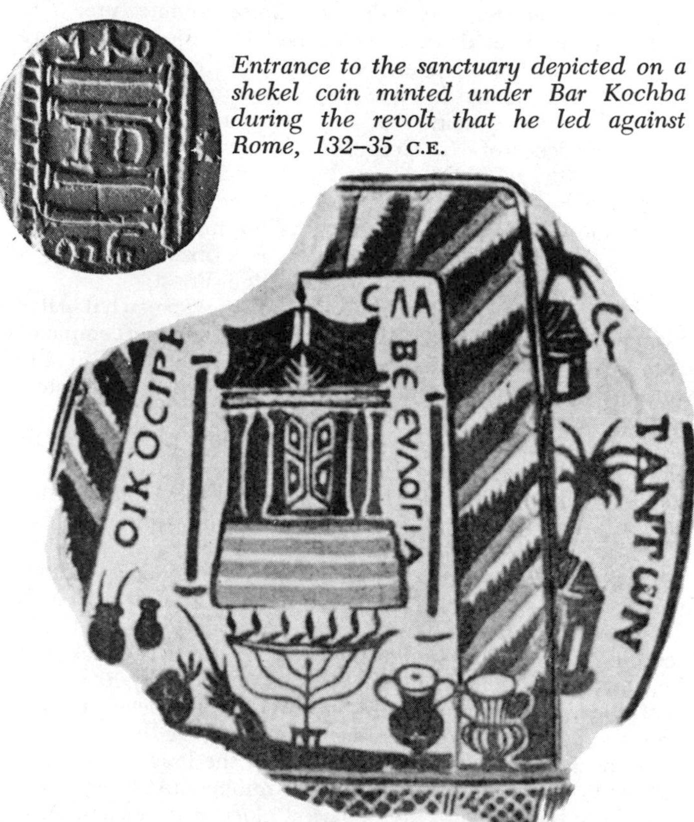

Entrance to the sanctuary depicted on a shekel coin minted under Bar Kochba during the revolt that he led against Rome, 132–35 C.E.

Depiction of the entrance to the Holy of Holies within the Temple sanctuary. Note its similarity to the Aron ha-Kodesh (Ark of the Law) in the modern synagogue. Gold glass fragment of the period before 70 C.E., found in a Jewish catacomb (rock cave cemetery) in Rome. (Vatican Museum, Rome.)

Inscription in Greek on a stone forbidding non-Jews, on the pain of death, to enter the inner courts of the Temple reconstructed by Herod, 1st century C.E. (Museum in Istanbul, Turkey.)

stood in Jerusalem, in the Golden Age of the Jewish people. It was not merely a sentiment of piety or of national pride which held Jews in rapt wonder over what they claimed were the incomparable beauties of their sanctuary on Mount Zion. It was the traditional view that the world had never seen a structure as perfect nor as beautiful.

The Alexandrian rabbinical savant of the first century, Philo, who had journeyed to Jerusalem several times for the "pilgrim festivals" (*see* HOLY DAYS) more than half a century before the Destruction, waxed ecstatic about the architectural wonders of the Temple. His opinion must not be taken lightly, considering the conditioning of his esthetic taste in Hellenistic Alexandria to Greek architecture. The sanctuary he beheld was, of course, the one which King Herod had embellished and to which he had given a new façade, Greco-Roman in style only a generation before, in 20 B.C.E. The outer precincts of the enclosure were framed by double porticoes of 162 Corinthian columns of white marble overlaid with gold. Colonnaded, too, were the open inner courts where, wrote Philo, "stood the Temple itself, beautiful beyond all possible description, as one may tell even from what is seen in the outer court; the innermost sanctuary is invisible to everyone except to the High Priest."

His enthusiasm is supported by the somewhat later testimony of the Talmud: "Whoever did not see the Temple of Herod missed seeing the most beautiful building in the world. It was constructed entirely of polished granite interspersed with marble of a dark tint, with beveled edges set in plaster. Herod even proposed to fill up the edges with gold. But the Sages advised him not to do so because the granite and the marble blended with the white plaster so as to give the Temple the appearance of waves upon the water."

The literature of the Jews in all historic periods, whether before or subsequent to the Destruction, is also rich with allusions to the fabled beauties of the Temple and of the Temple service. The medieval poetry of the synagogue and the devotional reflections of later days turn lyrical with wistfulness and tender with delicate piety whenever they refer to them. This undimming memory with the haunting power of a dream contains the ache and the longing of a disinherited and humiliated people straining to reach back vicariously for solace to the departed glory of its ancient past.

Considered objectively, the Temple which Solomon had built was neither as large nor as imposing as, for instance, some of the famed sanctuaries of the Egyptians, the Babylonians, and the Greeks. If we accept the estimate of some scholars that the Biblical cubit was the equivalent of 21.85 inches, then the Temple in Jerusalem must have been a relatively small building. Its dimensions, as noted in the Bible, were in round figures: 120 feet long, 40 feet wide, and 60 feet high. Since it took seven years for a virtual army of artisans and laborers to complete it, one cannot help but assume that its distinction did not lie so much in its elaborateness and magnificence as in its exquisite architectural design and workmanship.

The Temple structure was three stories high. Like the Canaanite temples, its interior was divided into a vestibule (ulam), an outer sanctuary (hechal), and an inner sanctuary or "Holy of Holies" (debir). Following the pattern of all heathen temples, it provided, along the walls and colonnades of the inner and outer courts, administrative, service, and utility chambers for the use of the priests and Levites; here were stored the Temple treasures, the ceremonial vestments, lighting materials for the two menorot (s. menorah), the musical instruments for the Temple service, and the sacrificial knives. Here also were pens for housing the animals to be

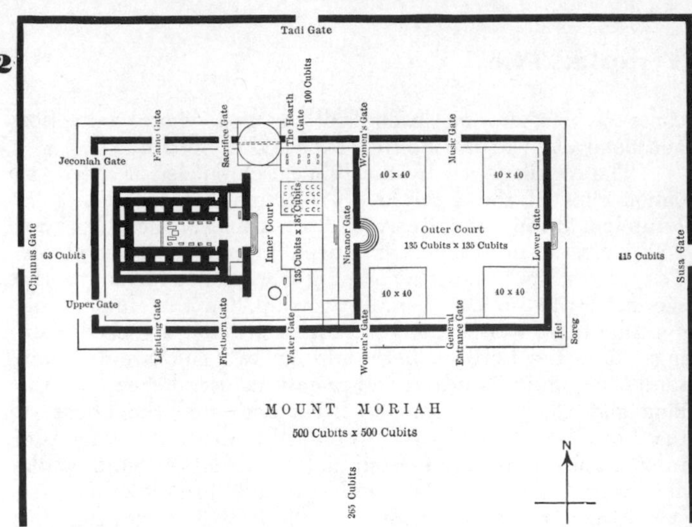

The ground-plan of the Temple as described in the Talmud. The ancient Egyptian cubit measured 20.64 inches; the Hebrew cubit is presumed to have been somewhat larger. (Drawn by Rabbi J. D. Eisenstein of New York, about 1900.)

sacrificed, areas for cutting up carcasses and taking off hides, a bakery where the shrewbread was baked daily, a ritual bath for the purification of the priests, and a woodshed.

The Temple was built of hewn stone, but its interior walls and ceilings were paneled with cedar and overlaid with gold. The floors and the folding doors were made of fir; the doorposts were of olive wood. The entire interior was ornamented with carved figures of cherubim, palm trees, and flowers and buds, all of which were also overlaid with gold.

The sanctity of every part of the Temple and of all its terraces, stairways, gates, and courts was well established. Yet there was one spot which was deemed unutterably holy and inviolable. This was the inner sanctuary—the Holy of Holies where the Ark holding the Tables of Moses reposed. Only the high priest was allowed, by priestly law, to enter into this inner sanctuary, and then only on Yom Kippur, the Day of Atonement. Anyone else daring to penetrate its sacred precincts merited death. Death too was the penalty for any non-Jew found in any part of the Temple area, not only in the Holy of Holies. This attitude was so traditional and this law so rigidly observed that almost a thousand years after the construction of the First Temple by Solomon, King Herod had a stone block put up before the entrance to the Temple area. It bore the following menacing warning in Greek: "No alien [non-Jew] may enter within the balustrade and the enclosure around the sanctuary. Whoever is caught will have only himself to blame for his death."

The Holy of Holies was built on a raised platform within the interior of the Temple. It was separated from the outer sanctuary, the hechal, by an enormous veil or curtain and by a chain of gold. It was, therefore, more like a sanctuary within a sanctuary, and was built in the form of a perfect cube, each of its dimensions being exactly 20 cubits or about 40 feet. Its ornamentation and the materials employed were identical with the rest of the building. Perhaps its most striking decorative objects were two great carved figures of cherubim, modeled after the winged angels created by the Babylonians, and probably having, like their Babylonian models, a human face, the body of an animal, and two spreading wings that, in a later period, became associated pictorially with the Western artists' conception of angels. The two cherubim were carved out of cedarwood and were overlaid with gold. Their wings met in the center of the Holy of Holies in a protecting arch, like the hands of the high priest raised in benediction. From tip to tip they measured about twenty feet. It was the popular belief that

Sculptured relief on the Arch of Titus in Rome, executed only a few years after the Destruction of Jerusalem, depicting the laurel-wreathed Roman conquerors of the Jews carrying off as their booty the sacred Temple vessels made of gold: the menorah, the trumpets, and the table of shewbread.

underneath these wings, in the Ark of the Covenant where the stone tablets of Moses were enshrined, dwelt the Shechinah—the Divine Radiance of God's Presence.

The leading artist-sculptor of these cherubim, who had also designed and wrought the altars and all the holy vessels and ritual objects for the Temple, was a half-Jew from Tyre by the name of Hiram. The king of Tyre had loaned him to Solomon for the construction of the sanctuary. He presumably had an all-around mastery of the architectural and decorative arts, judging by the Temple vessels and ceremonial objects depicted on sculptured relief on the Arch of Titus in Rome. The Biblical chronicler noted that he could "work in gold and in silver, in brass, in iron, in stone, and in timber." He was also a master-weaver and dyer, and showed great skill "in purple, in blue, and in fine linen, and in crimson."

Devout mourners grieving over the Destruction of the Temple at the "Wailing Wall" in Jerusalem, 1867.

At the entrance to the Temple interior, near the large altar of brass on which the animal sacrifices were brought, stood two pillars of bronze that the ingenious Hiram had made. These were called, for reasons strange and unknown, "Jachin" and "Boaz." They were about thirty feet high and were crowned by ten-foot capitals that were embellished with a design of carved lilies. Some archaeologists conjecture that the pillars were hollowed inside, and that their basins served as giant braziers where the burnt-offerings were consumed. The inference made is that the primitive matzebah—the large, uncut stone "set up" in early times in high places for receiving offerings of oil and the blood of animals—in the more developed First Temple period made way for the more efficient and attractive bronze columns of Jachin and Boaz.

Hiram was also responsible for the huge laver called the "molten sea," for the ten small mobile lavers on wheels, the shovels, the basins and the menorot (the seven-branched candlesticks). Besides the menorah that Bezalel had made for the Tabernacle centuries before, Hiram designed ten others for the Temple. Five of them flanked each side of the sanctuary. For the care of these menorot there were tongs and basins, firepans and snuffers, all made of gold.

The elaborate Temple service required a large variety of other ritual objects and vessels. There was, for instance, an altar of gold that was reserved exclusively for offerings of incense, and a golden table, ten handbreadths long and five wide, on which were laid the twelve loaves of shewbread baked of fine flour. These were left exposed on the table "in the presence" of the Lord for a whole week; then they were eaten ritually by the priests as holy bread.

The "molten sea" was an enormous laver designed for the frequent ablutions of the priests, who were required to wash their hands and feet before they entered into the sanctuary. The laver had a diameter of some twenty feet, and its huge basin rested on the backs of twelve cast-iron oxen. Its rim was circled by a bas-relief of lily buds and open flowers. The ten lavers on wheels were made of bronze; they were ornamented in relief with figures of cherubim, lions, and palm trees.

It can hardly come as a surprise that the Temple of Solomon, which had been designed, constructed, and decorated by architects, sculptors, goldsmiths, and other skilled craftsmen imported from Phoenician Tyre, should have revealed features of design and workmanship of ritual and ceremonial objects that were customary in Phoenician temples. The Greek historian Herodotus described two pillars that he had seen standing in front of the temple at Tyre. From his description they seemed very similar in both form and cult-function to those of Jachin and Boaz.

In any case, the architecture of the Semitic Near East, unlike the Egyptian, Greek, or Roman, never had an original face of its own. It was eclectic, borrowing selectively from various nations and cultures. The Israelite "molten sea," for example, was but a replica of the Apsu, the laver that the Babylonian priests used in their temple rites, except that the Babylonian original was chiseled out of stone and elaborately figured with sculptured relief. Then, too, the Temple in Jerusalem, like all other Near Eastern sanctuaries (which invariably followed the Babylonian model in more than one way), was built "on a high place"—on Mount Moriah.

Very likely, also, the manner of bringing sacrifices in Israel was similar to that of its neighbors. The practice in Jerusalem of using massed choirs of Levite singers and instrumentalists for their spectacular and emotional effects was an established feature of the religious service in Egypt, Babylonia, Canaan, Greece, and other countries.

This, of course, does not at all mean that there was nothing original either in the Temple itself or in the rites performed there. The genius of Israel impressed its own stamp of individuality upon its cultural borrowings from other peoples. Probably nothing in all religious literature can equal in lyrical eloquence the soul-searching Hebrew psalmody which was so important liturgically in the Temple service.

The Temple which Solomon had built, in its one-thousand-year history, went through several transformations, but those were but minor reconstructions of an external character, since there existed a sacrosanct tradition that the original design was under no circumstance to be altered in any essentials. In 586 B.C.E., about four centuries after Solomon had dedicated his sanctuary on Mount Moriah, it was destroyed by Nebuchadnezzar, the king of Babylonia. He despoiled it of its hallowed treasures—the ritual vessels and all ceremonial objects—and carried them off, together with the flower of the people, into captivity. But when the Jewish prince Sheshbazzar was allowed by King Cyrus to lead back to the Land of Israel in 538 B.C.E. the first contingent of exiles in order to initiate the restoration of the Jewish Commonwealth, he was given all the Temple vessels and appurtenances that had been taken away by Nebuchadnezzar.

The rebuilding of the ruined Temple did not begin until the reign of Darius. The work was begun in 519 B.C.E. and it was finished in three years. But this time the most sacred of all the Temple treasures—the Ark of the Covenant—no longer rested in the Holy of Holies. It, together with the Urim and Thummim—the divining objects worn in his sacerdotal breastplate by the high priest—had mysteriously disappeared. The single reference to their loss is found in the Talmud, which was written centuries later.

The Temple was rebuilt for a second time in 20-19 B.C.E. by Herod, king of Judea. Whatever changes in the structure he made were also not fundamental. The general ground-plan and the interior arrangement of the Temple of Solomon were closely adhered to, but the building was made a little higher and it was embellished by a Greco-Roman façade to conform with the prevailing Hellenistic taste of the times.

In passing, it should be noted that of the Temple edifice, nothing that might be considered authentic is left standing today except the site itself. The outer western wall of the Haram area, popularly known as "the Wailing Wall"—in Hebrew, *Kotel Ma'aravi*—and consisting of enormous blocks

The "Wailing Wall" in the Destroyed Temple area in Jerusalem. (Painting by J. L. Gérome, Paris, 19th century.)

It is believed that in this enclosure under the "Dome of the Rock" behind the metal grill on the Mosque of Omar, erected more than one thousand years ago by the Arabs on the site of the Temple in Jerusalem, there once stood the Holy of Holies. (United Nations photo.)

of hewn stone, is the only remaining physical reminder of the Temple of Herod. There, for uncounted generations, their faces pressed against its rude surfaces, pious pilgrims from all parts of the world would stand weeping, reciting dirges from the Book of Lamentations in mourning for the desolation of Zion and the vanished sanctuary. This custom has lapsed, due to the division of Jerusalem by the United Nations; today the Wailing Wall is in Jordan territory.

In every way possible, following the burning of the Temple and the sacking of Jerusalem, Jews everywhere gave themselves ceaseless reminders that without Zion they were like children bereaved of their mother. Whenever a house or synagogue was erected, it became the custom to leave a square yard unfinished on one of the walls. On it were inscribed in Hebrew the words of the Psalmist: "In Memory of the Destruction" (*Zecher l'Churban*). Not only on the Ninth of Ab (Tishah b'Ab) but also on every other day in the year were the devout to recall the national catastrophe. Too great merriment and singing, even on festivals and at weddings, were frowned upon. Instrumental music was banned from the synagogue and was not to be resumed until the coming of the Messiah. The Jews had freely chosen to go into perpetual mourning for the vanished glories of Zion.

Why were the Temple and Jerusalem destroyed? was the question which the unconsolable mourners in Israel were perpetually raising. And this they were also perpetually answering with the theologic refrain: "On account of our sins . . ."

The Rabbinic Sages, humane fathers of the people as well as down-to-earth rationalists, were greatly troubled by this obsessive grief. Joshua ben Chananiah therefore cautioned: "Not to mourn at all is impossible, because the fatal decree [i.e., the Destruction] has already been enacted. To mourn too much is likewise impossible; it is beyond human endurance."

See also ARK CURTAIN; ARK OF THE COVENANT; ARK OF THE LAW; ART, CEREMONIAL; ART AMONG THE JEWS; HIGH PRIEST; LAVER; LEVITES; MENORAH; MUSIC, ANCIENT JEWISH; MUSIC IN THE TEMPLE; MUSICAL INSTRUMENTS OF THE BIBLE; PRAYER AND WORSHIP; PRIESTLY BLESSING; PRIESTS; SYNAGOGUE, THE; TISHAH B'AB; YOM KIPPUR.

TEN COMMANDMENTS (in Hebrew: ASERET HA-DIBROT, literally meaning "The Ten Words"; English equivalent is "Decalogue," from the Greek *Dekalogos*)

The most widely known—and, indeed, the best remembered—part of the Bible is that which contains the Ten Commandments. There always has been a persistent belief, among both religious Jews and Christians, that the Ten Commandments symbolize—in fact, constitute—the quintessence of the Jewish religion. However, to any serious student of the Bible, of post-Biblical literature, and of the Talmud, such a notion appears not only erroneous but also unfortunate. Without a doubt, the reason for the popularity of this view has been the projection of the supernatural into the Biblical account, which, in its epic canvas, delineates the awesome drama at Mount Sinai, when the stone tablets of the covenant were inscribed with the "Ten Words" by the hand of Moses writing "with the finger of God" for the guidance and salvation of Israel forever.

The plain fact is that the Ten Commandments, despite the fact that historically they represented at the time the greatest advance in the moral thinking of mankind, were only rudimentary concepts. They had originated in a primitive tribalistic society that was set in a seminomadic pastoral economy. For a truer index of the Jewish religious, ethical, and social values, one has to turn to more sophisticated times, to the far more advanced teachings of the canonical Prophets and, in particular, to the ethics of later Rabbinic Judaism that are expounded in the literature of the Talmud.

Remarkably, the Bible contains two separate versions of the Ten Commandments—one in Exodus 20:1-14, the other in Deuteronomy 5:6-18 (*see* BIBLE, THE). Both texts differ, not only in language (although only slightly) but also in the contents of the Fourth Commandment, which treats of Sabbath observance. This curious discrepancy has given rise to much learned speculation in the light of the traditionalist belief that every word was revealed and written "with the finger of God." Many Biblical scholars, whether correctly or wrongly, have concluded that the two versions must have been collated by Ezra and the Scribes into the Bible canon from two different Scriptural writings. The following version in Exodus, believed to be of earlier composition, is generally favored, by Christians as well as Jews, over that in Deuteronomy:

I. I am the Lord thy God, who brought thee out of the land of Egypt, out of the house of bondage.

II. Thou shalt have no other gods before Me. Thou shalt not make unto thee a graven image, nor any manner of likeness, of any thing that is in heaven above, or that is in the earth beneath, or that is in the water under the earth; thou shalt not bow down unto them, nor serve them; for I the Lord thy God am a jealous God, visiting the iniquity of the fathers upon the children unto the third and fourth generation of them that hate Me; and showing mercy unto the thousandth generation of them that love Me and keep My commandments.

III. Thou shalt not take the name of the Lord thy God in vain; for the Lord will not hold him guiltless that taketh His name in vain.

IV. Remember the sabbath day, to keep it holy. Six days shalt thou labour, and do all thy work; but the seventh day is a sabbath unto the Lord thy God, in it thou shalt not do any manner of work, thou, nor thy son, nor thy daughter, nor thy man-servant, nor thy maid-servant, nor thy cattle, nor the stranger that is within thy gates; for in six days the Lord made heaven and earth, the sea, and all that is in them, and rested on the seventh day; wherefore the Lord blessed the Sabbath day, and hallowed it.

V. Honour thy father and thy mother, that thy days may be long upon the land which the Lord thy God giveth thee.

VI. Thou shalt not murder.

VII. Thou shalt not commit adultery.

VIII. Thou shalt not steal.

IX. Thou shalt not bear false witness against thy neighbor.

X. Thou shalt not covet thy neighbour's house; thou shalt not covet thy neighbour's wife, nor his man-servant, nor his maid-servant, nor his ox, nor his ass, nor any thing that is thy neighbour's.

Observed in their proper historical setting, the Ten Commandments clearly appear to have embodied the earliest religious legal-code adopted by the Israelites. Their ascription to Moses by the Biblical chronicle is fully persuasive, although some modern scholars would like to think that they were created in the later epoch of the Judges of

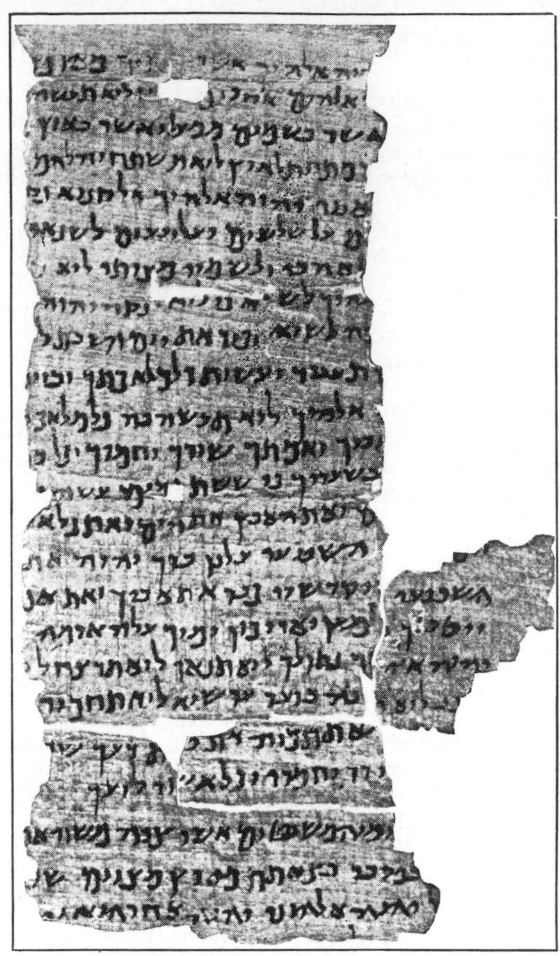

Hebrew manuscript fragment of the Decalogue, possibly the 2nd century C.E.

Bronze clock with a Hebrew time-face. On its base, flanked by two lions, are symbolic "Tables of the Law" in Hebrew. 19th century. (Courtesy of Joseph B. Horwitz Judaica Collection, Cleveland.)

The Tables of the Law, flanked by Moses and Aaron, on a Torah Breastplate. Note the Hebrew Tetragrammaton in the center that is the equivalent of YHVH; below the tables are two hands, upraised and with the fingers separated, in the position used for the priestly benediction. France, late Renaissance period.

Israel, from the twelfth to the eleventh centuries B.C.E. Whatever conclusion concerning the date of their origin one may reach, the oversimplified notion must be avoided that any moral idea or a legal system—whatever its character—springs full blown into being all at once, or is the indentifiable work of one period or of one person—even of one as supremely great as was Moses, the founder both of the Jewish religion and of the Jewish people. Cultural history has made it conclusive that, even though the formulation of an idea or of an entire system of ideas may be first noted at a given point in history, its origins and process of development must be sought for in the dimmer, diffused regions of earlier times. The probable fact is that the Israelitish legal code that is represented by the Ten Commandments must have come as the climax to centuries, perhaps even of millennia, of evolutionary growth, of painful and irresolute gropings for a better ordering of individual conduct and social relationships in the chaos, destructiveness, and immorality that disfigured so much of life in ancient society.

Despite the belief of those who "know" for a certainty that the Ten Commandments were divinely revealed by God *in person* to Moses and Israel at Mount Sinai, or that of others, more prosaic minded, who regard them merely as a legal code that had been drawn up by Moses (or even by later religious lawgivers), the student of comparative religion has no choice but to observe objectively the impact of certain non-Jewish influences upon them. Germinal ideas for several of the Commandments are clearly to be found in legal codes antedating the Jewish: in the sacred writings of the Egyptians, the Babylonians, and other culturally advanced peoples living within the Fertile Crescent. Two obvious Babylonian sources were the Code of Hammurabi (about 1700 B.C.E.) and the magical writing called Shurpû (1500-1100 B.C.E.)

But even more arresting and significant than those is a passage found in Chapter 125 of the Egyptian Book of the Dead, a work of supplications, the oldest version of which seemingly was composed by Egyptian poet-priests about 1500 B.C.E. Although its ideas are not stated in the summary and imperious manner of the Biblical Commandments but instead as a ritualistic plea by the soul of the deceased to Osiris, the Egyptian God of the Dead, nevertheless, what is made plain is the remarkable affinity it bears to five of the Ten Commandments. The soul of the deceased Egyptian is made to say in his self-defense:

I have not slighted God.
I have not slain.
I have not commanded to slay.
I have not committed fornication or impurity.
I have not stolen.
I have not spoken falsehood.

And since this text, presumably, was already in general ritualistic use in Egypt in Moses' time (early in the thirteenth century B.C.E.), it would not be farfetched to assume that he had been considerably impressed by it when he drew up the Ten Commandments.

But this much should be added: Whatever the discernible influences, the stamp of original genius that Moses placed upon it raised his code in the design of its synthesis—however primitive its ring in modern ears—to an ethical plane that was far in advance of all others in his age. It sounded, metaphorically speaking, like a trumpet blast wakening men's souls to the potentialities of their innate human nobility.

See also LAW, JEWISH; MITZVOT.

TEN PLAGUES, THE. *See* PASSOVER.

TENTH OF TEBET, FAST OF THE. *See* FASTING AND FAST DAYS.

TEREFAH (TREFAH) (Hebrew, meaning "forbidden")

Although certain animals were declared by the ritual laws to be "unclean" and therefore, *terefah*—"forbidden" to Jews—there were, in addition, prohibitions against the eating of certain parts of a "clean" animal. Classed as terefah were the blood and the fat from oxen, sheep, and goats. Nor could the hindquarters of "clean" animals be eaten. This latter prohibition was directed at the "sinew of the hip," i.e., the gluteal muscle in the thigh. Just as the heart, the brain, and other vital organs were treated as sacred by the ancient Greeks and, consequently, were taboo for eating, so was the "sinew of the hip"—that which makes movement possible—prohibited to the Israelites. A curious explanation is given for this in Genesis 32:25: "Therefore, the children of Israel eat not the sinew of the thigh-vein [namely, the sciatic nerve] which is upon the hollow of the thigh, unto this day; because he [i.e., the Angel of the Lord with whom the Patriarch Jacob wrestled] touched the hollow of his [Jacob's] thigh.

In later centuries, the word *terefah* took on a much wider compass and reached out in every dietary direction. Ritually rejected foods, governed by the minutiae of rabbinic opinions and decisions, increased vastly in number. The medieval philosopher-rabbi, Maimonides, one of the most enlightened thinkers of his age, was so alarmed by the deadening mutiplicity of the dietary laws and regulations, —particularly by the distractions and hardships they imposed upon the people—that he decided it was necessary to draw the line somewhere, even though arbitrarily. Therefore, he issued this rabbinical decision: "Seventy [indications] of terefah are the limit, and must not be increased or diminished, even though it should be found by scientific investigation that some of the injuries are not dangerous to the life of the animal, or that some unenumerated conditions are dangerous to its life. Only those indications of terefah may be followed which have been accepted by the [Talmudic] Rabbis and handed down by tradition."

In a culturally less enlightened period in Jewish life, some five centuries later, Maimonides' opinion was all but forgotten. This was due not only to the backwardness of a confining ghetto existence, but in part also to the great authority wielded by the rabbinic code, the Shulchan Aruch. That manual, compiled by Joseph Caro in the fifteenth century, succeeded in compressing a considerable part of the Jewish religious experience into a vast and sterile ritualism. Not infrequently, the extreme preoccupation of the daily religious routine in the ghetto with the trivia connected with the dietary laws, called forth sharp rebukes from earnest rabbinic writers. Like Maimonides, they too were apalled by the excessive emphasis placed on rite and ceremony to the detriment of such primary religious values as belief, problems of conscience, and ethical practice.

See also ANIMALS, "CLEAN" AND "UNCLEAN"; DIETARY LAWS; MEAT, SALTING OF; MEAT AND MILK; SHECHITAH; SHOCHET.

TESHUBAH. *See* REPENTANCE.

TETRAGRAMMATON. *See* GOD, NAMES OF; SHEM HA-MEFORASH.

THEATRE, OPPOSITION TO THE

Until relatively modern times, Jewish religious opposition to the theatre and to public entertainment was forthright and consistent. Although this attitude was already apparent even in Biblical days, it first crystallized during the degenerate period of the Roman theatre in the Augustan age (about the time of the end of the Judean state). That was a time when not only Roman rule but also Roman cultural influences, both good and bad, were infiltrating into Jewish life throughout the far-flung Roman Empire, in Judea and elsewhere. The prayer book in many a Jewish synagogue today still carries the polemical words of thanksgiving uttered by a Talmudic Sage of the first century: "I give thanks to You, O Lord my God and God of my fathers, that you have placed my portion among those who sit in the House of Study and in the House of Prayer, and that you did not cast my lot among those who frequent theatres and circuses. For I labor, and they labor; I wait and they wait: I to inherit the World-to-Come; they, the pit of destruction."

Ancient Greek drama, like the drama of all other peoples, had evolved as an integral part of the rites of religion. Some of its primitive and (from the moral point of view of Judaism and Christianity) often objectionable features had been carried over into more enlightened times in the Greco-Roman world, and these continued to enjoy public favor, although on a different cultural level, side by side with the noble Greek dramas of Aeschylus, Sophocles, and Euripides, as well as those of lesser Greek and Latin playwrights.

Theatrical tastes became more degenerate during the decline of Roman civilization, when comedies of a licentious character and lewd exhibitions by dancers and mimes became all the rage, even among the assimilated upper-class Jews in Jerusalem. In the circuses and arenas, audiences were diverted by games in which there took place mortal combats between men and wild beasts, and also between men and men. In their bestiality and cruelty, these pastimes violated every concept of humanity and morality that were part of the traditions that stemmed from the Judaism of the Prophets and the Sages.

The early Church Father, Tertullian, like the Rabbis who were his contemporaries, was revolted by "the obscenity of the theatre and the abominations of the arena." The enthusiasm for this type of entertainment among many Jews alarmed their religious leaders. It alerted them to the ever present danger of apostasy inherent in a process of cultural assimilation that was of a negative and antisocial character. Nor were the gifted Roman satirists slow to recognize the absurdities devolving from the social pretensions of a certain class of rich and fashionable Jews who, wishing to appear "more Roman than the Romans," prided themselves on being patrons of the theatre and the circus. The gibes in Latin they wrote of them still carry an acid bite.

How far this interest, interdicted by the Rabbis, went among Jews may be gauged by the fact that there were Jewish professional actors and actresses employed in the Roman theatre. Several achieved considerable repute; one of them, Alityros, was mentioned by the first-century historian, Josephus, as being "an actor, and a Jew, well-favored by Nero."

A Rabbinical anathema was drawn up to be hurled at those Jews who had joined "the scorners" among the Gentiles in their ribaldry: "Cursed be they who visit the theatre and the circus, and despise our laws!" When, in 28 B.C.E., King Herod built an amphitheatre on the edge of Jerusalem where indecent comedies and lewd pantomimes were performed and obsecene verses were sung in Greek to the accompaniment of lute and lyre, the indignation of those who were uncompromisingly devoted to Jewish moral traditions and practices knew no bounds. A multitude of them descended on the amphitheatre one night while King Herod was away—whether to stop the performance or to assassinate the king, as was charged, is not quite clear. Suffice it to say that one of the "invaders" was rent limb from limb by the audience.

However, not all types of theatrical entertainment were banned by the Rabbis. The fact remains that during the second century B.C.E., there were several serious Jewish verse-dramatists writing in Alexandria; it is believed that their works, composed in Greek, were given public performance in that enlightened Hellenized metropolis. The fragments that have survived of three such dramas, on themes drawn from the Bible, reveal an elevated religious tone. One of these, *The Exodus from Egypt*, by Ezekelios, was written in hexameter and its dramaturgy modeled upon that of Euripides. The other two fragments that are extant were written in trimeter, and are on the subject of God's Unity and the Temptation of Adam and Eve.

A general antipathy to the theatre was sedulously cultivated by Jewish religious teachers down through the many generations following. It was not until the sixteenth century, during the cultural thaw experienced by Italian Jewry of the late Renaissance, that Jews began to evince a renewed interest in it, although Leone da Modena, the rabbi-humanist of Venice, noted that there was strong opposition in the Italian-Jewish community of his day toward the theatre because of the "frivolous and indecent remarks" with which audiences were regaled. It was not until the early nineteenth century, in the wake of the Haskalah (the Jewish Enlightenment movement) in Germany, Austria, Italy, France, and England, that many Jews became enthusiastic devotees of the theatre. A marked number soon played an increasingly active and distinguished part creatively in all the branches of stage art, their contributions often helping to give new directions to them.

See also PURIM PLAY.

THEOCRACY (from the Greek *theokratia*, meaning a "state ruled by God")

It was the Jewish historian Josephus, a Hellenist of the first century writing in Greek, who first used the word "theocracy" to describe the character of ancient Jewish society and its political state. In his polemic, *Contra Apion*, he wrote: "Our legislator [i.e., Moses] . . . ordained our government to be what by a strained expression may be termed a theocracy, by ascribing the authority and the power to God."

From its very inception, ancient Israel constituted a priestly and Levitical society—"a kingdom of priests and a holy nation," as described in Exodus 19:6. God was the omnipotent ruler. The supreme authority—secular as well as religious—rested in the Torah, which served as a complete guide to the daily living of the Jew from birth to death. Every aspect of existence, economic, cultural, social, and personal, even when not centered directly in religion, was regulated or supervised by the Torah. From this remarkable situation stemmed the homogeneous character of Jewish life and culture in former times, which was penetrated almost totally by its religious-ethical values.

See also BIBLE, THE; CHOSEN PEOPLE, THE; LAW, JEWISH; MONOTHEISM; SANHEDRIN; SCRIBES.

THERAPEUTAE (from the Greek, meaning "physicians" or "healers"; inferrentially—"healers of themselves")

The Therapeutae formed a Jewish monastic order of monks and nuns which had already, long before the birth of Jesus, been established on the crest of a hill overlooking Lake Mareotis, to the south of Alexandria, in Egypt. It must have been in existence for a very long time, since Philo, the Platonist philosopher-rabbi of Alexandria (b. 20 B.C.E.), noted: "They have also writings of men of old, the founders of their way of thinking." With the single exception of Philo, who visited them and with penetrating insight described their mode of life and thought, no other reference to them is found in ancient writings. The third-century Church Father, Eusebius, erroneously considered them to be an early Christian monastic order. For that matter, it is difficult even today for many informed persons to grasp fully the fact that Christian monasticism had Jewish origins.

From all accounts, life in Hellenistic Alexandria was dissolute, cruel, and cynical; its veneer of Greek culture and intellectual sophistication was able to conceal neither its inherent bestiality and corruption nor the hopelessness underneath. The Greco-Roman world-empire was disintegrating rapidly everywhere, in part because of the evils of the slave-system, which were rotting the very foundations of ancient society.

Despairing of the world, many cultivated Alexandrian Jews resolved to become "healers of their own souls" in the same "escapist" way taken by their various counterparts, the Judean Essenes, the New Covenanters of Damascus, and the Morning Bathers (Baptists) at the River Jordan. Theirs was an idealistic pessimism that nohow could be assuaged. Refusing to compromise with the world as they found it, they escaped into a complete renunciation of it, into a utopian dream-world that was cast in ecstatic terms. They, noted Philo, "dedicated themselves to knowledge and the contemplation of the verities of nature, following the truly sacred instructions of the Prophet Moses." Thus the monastery of the Therapeutae on Lake Mareotis in Egypt and the Essenic brotherhood at Qumran on the Dead Sea in Judea were almost identical products of the same social and moral impasse of the times, although so different in their cultural settings.

According to Philo, each "healer of himself" occupied a small cell, a *monasterium*, "and closeted in this . . . [he is] initiated into the mysteries of the sanctified life." The initiate prayed, meditated deeply, and practiced austerities—ordeals of fasting and self-mortification. The daily regimen was physically severe and, except for the Sabbath and holy days, without letup. Like the Buddhist monks of India, the

Jewish monks and nuns too observed a vegetarian diet and were abstemious in their eating and drinking. When the Christian Church, centuries later, formed monastic orders, its monks and nuns merely followed in the footsteps of the Therapeutae; they took vows of chastity and renounced all sensory pleasure.

Notwithstanding that the Therapeutae stood on a far higher level culturally than the Essenes (they belonged principally to the educated Egyptian upper-classes, whereas the Judean Essenes came mostly from the ranks of the uneducated proletarians and the landless), they too devoted much time to Torah-study, searching for its "inner meaning," in this they followed the Greek Septuagint version of the Bible, since they had little or no knowledge of Hebrew.

During congregational worship, the Therapeutae chanted Psalms and sang canticles of adoration especially composed for the liturgy of their sect. On the festival of Shabuot, for example, the Therapeutae assembled in the refectory for the feast. They formed themselves into two choirs—one of men and the other of women—then, standing in the middle of the room, "they sang hymns to God composed of many measures and set to many melodies." Sometimes, the two choirs joined their voices together; at other times they sang antiphonally to each other, "hands and feet keeping time in accompaniment, and rapt with enthusiasm," They then marched in procession and wheeled and counterwheeled through the convolutions "of a choric dance." It must have been singing and dancing in the Greek Dionysian manner, for Rabbi Philo, himself a Greek of Greeks in the matter of his cultural conditioning, remarked that the singers, "having drunk as in the Bacchic rites of the strong wine of God's love," emulated the choir that had sung inspiredly at the Red Sea—the men led by Moses and the women by Miriam —"in honor of the wonders wrought there."

In the days of the Therapeutae, the lines of demarcation between races, peoples, cultures, religions, and ideas had become blurred. As a world metropolis, Alexandria was at that time the reservoir of syncretism into which flowed all civilizational streams. In this fusion, the ideology of the Therepeutae was not only a product of Jewish religious culture in particular—that is, of the social and ethical values of the Judean Essenes—but of other religions as well. No one can doubt that some of the mystical ingredients that went into its making and into its institutional form and practices, were drawn from diverse contemporary sources. For, concurrently with the Jewish Therapeutae in Egypt, there existed the mystery-cult of the Persians, the Chaldean worship of angels, demons, and the stars, the world-rejecting but wisdom-bent Gnostic anchorites, and—not least—mystical Greek-Platonist philosophers such as Philo Judaeus was.

The story of the Therapeutae, as related by Philo in his *On the Contemplative Life,* is one of the most remarkable chapters in the history of utopian questing. But perhaps its chief significance lies in the pattern it helped establish for the monastic ideals and institutions of early Christianity. Those of the Roman Catholic Church have endured with an undiminished vigor to this day.

See also ASCETICS; CHRISTIANITY, JEWISH ORIGINS OF; DEAD SEA SCROLLS; ESSENES; MONASTICISM, JEWISH; PHARISEES.

TISHAH B'AB (Hebrew, meaning the "Ninth of Ab")

In a formal sense, Tishah B'Ab is observed as a fast day. It is a day for remembering and, therefore, for mourning over the Destruction of the Temple in Jerusalem—the first time by the Babylonians, in 586 B.C.E., and the second time by the Romans, in the 70 C.E. But somehow, in the imaginative thinking of the folk, which has been macerated by the memories of many national disasters, the Ninth of Ab also became a grim symbol—a kind of reservoir into which were poured all the misfortunes of the Jews in their history. Therefore the Mishnah (the code of Oral Laws) added to the commemoration of the Destruction of the two Temples the tragic events that followed the Bar Kochba revolt in 135: the death of Bar Kochba and the butchery by the Romans of his followers three years later, climaxed by the "plowing up" of Jerusalem by order of the vindictive Roman emperor Hadrian.

During the Middle Ages, still other historic misfortunes were added to the ever growing list: the death of the Ten Martyrs (among whom were the Rabbinic Sages Akiba, Ishmael, and Chanina ben Teradion) at the time of Hadrian's persecution (*see* KIDDUSH HA-SHEM); the expulsion of the Jews from England in 1290 and from Spain in 1492; and the massacres carried out during the Crusades and by the maniacal master-butcher Rindfleisch (an early German prototype of Adolf Hitler) in 1298.

This Rabbinic saying, and variants of it, became proverbial: "He who does not mourn over the Destruction of Zion will not live to see her joy." But merely formal grief had no meaning; it was frowned upon as a spurious kind of commemoration. Long remembered, therefore, by Jews was the inquiry that was made of the Prophet Zechariah in 516 B.C.E., only seventy years after the Destruction of the First Temple. He was asked: "Should I weep [on Tishah B'Ab]?" The Prophet's reply was withering: When his questioner fasted and mourned on Tishah B'Ab, did he do so for God's sake or for his own benefit? Rather than making a display of that kind of grief (i.e., fasting and lamenting), counseled Zechariah, true piety required that one should act justly, "show mercy, and compassion by every man to his brother; and oppress not the widow nor the fatherless, the stranger nor the poor."

Tishah B'Ab has all the characteristics of shivah (the mourning period for the dead). Prohibited on Tishah B'Ab are bathing, eating, drinking, laughter, conversation, and beautifying oneself. As the "mourners" enter the synagogue they take off their shoes; they seat themselves on low stools, on overturned benches, or on the floor. No greetings are exchanged. The parochet (the decorative curtain over the Ark) is removed before the holiday as unseemly for the sober occasion; frequently, a drape of black cloth is substituted for it. The only light in the synagogue comes from the Ner Tamid (Eternal Lamp), which, hanging before the Ark, casts its gloomy flicker on the congregation, and the one dim light at the reading desk for the use of the precentor. The recitation, in a subdued minor, is from the Biblical Book of Lamentations. Its stirring dirges, implausibly attributed to the authorship of the Prophet Jeremiah, no doubt must have been composed by eyewitnesses of the Destruction of the First Temple on the Ninth of Ab, in 586 B.C.E.

In addition, kinnot (liturgical elegies; s. kinnah) of medieval composition are recited. These poems, outpourings of the millennial grief of the Jews, while sounding harsh, self-tormenting tonalities, are compensated for by a noble, Job-like melancholy. One of the most affecting of these dirges is that about the Prophet Jeremiah, who makes an impassioned plea to the three Patriarchs, the four Matriarchs, to Moses and Aaron, and to other eminences that they intercede with God on behalf of desolated Zion and afflicted Israel.

It is customary on Tishah B'Ab for those Jews who follow tradition and believe in Zechut Abot—"the Merit of the Fathers"—to pray beside the graves of their ancestors and those of illustrious rabbis. They repeat the Prophet Jeremiah's plea for the hastening of Israel's restoration and the rebuilding of Zion in the days of the Messiah. When

Chanting the Book of Lamentations on Tishah B'Ab in a Polish synagogue. The Orthodox worshipers sit on the floor or on low stools, and in stockinged feet, as during shivah (the seven-days' mourning period observed on the death of a member of one's immediate family). (Painting by Horovitz, 1870.)

that happy event occurs (the Talmudic Sages comfort the people) then Tishah B'Ab will be transformed from a day of mourning into a day of rejoicing.

Reform or Liberal Jews do not observe the Ninth of Ab; they consider its commemoration anachronistic for the modern age. And since the establishment of the State of Israel and the creation there of a dynamic Jewish society, there are many other Jews who have ceased observing Tishah B' Ab.

See also TEMPLE, THE.

TOMBSTONES (in Hebrew: MATZEBOT; S. MATZEBAH)

From all indications, the ordinary Jew of the masses during the Biblical age remained as anonymous in death as he had been in life. The plain folk, unlike the patricians, the notables, and the rich, were laid in common and unmarked graves. In reality, the burial ground of the people was treated with open contempt by its rulers, as a number of instances recorded in the Bible clearly demonstrate. When Jehoiakim, king of Judah (ruled 608-598 B.C.E.) had slain the "Prophet of the Lord," Uriah ben Shemaiah, he "cast the dead body into the graves of the children of the people." (Jeremiah 26:23).

No one really knows when stone matzebot began to mark the graves of ordinary Jews and when inscriptions carved upon them gave the names of the deceased and noted the dates of their passing. Whatever Biblical records exist refer exclusively to the illustrious and the rich. The first such mention is in Genesis 35:30: "And Jacob set up a pillar [matzebah] upon her [Rachel's] grave; the same is the pillar of Rachel's grave unto this day." But the character of the pillar mentioned bears but a remote relationship to the tombstone of today. Sacred stones and trees (asherahs) were often to be found at the site of ancient Jewish tombs. Some anthropologists believe they had primarily a ritualistic purpose and represented practices closely associated with primitive religion. These stones—rude altars, so to speak—were anointed with oil and worshiped; the blood of animal sacrifices was burned upon them in order to appease the invisible powers and thereby gain their protection. There is another school of thought which considers the ancient matzebah as being merely a warning marker declaring the burial spot to be sacred or taboo (prohibited) to all passers-by.

During the Maccabean period, when Judea fell, in part, under the cultural hegemony of Hellenism, the Jewish ruling class followed the contemporary Grecian style of building ornate family mausoleums for the dead. According to I Maccabees 13:27-9, Simon Maccabeus put up an imposing monument for his father and brothers at Modin, presumably at their burial place. It consisted of seven pyramids bearing bas-reliefs of ships and weapons of war, sculpted in polished marble. Such ostentation had been unheard of previously in Jewish mortuary customs. It prompted the comment in the Talmud: "The Jewish tombs are more beautiful than royal palaces." But from the second-century Patriarch of Judea, Simeon ben Gamaliel, came the satiric thrust that, quite understandably, the affluent dead should feel offended because the splendid monuments that adorned their graves seemed blatantly to proclaim that it was only because of them that memory of the deceased would be preserved.

After the final Dispersion, it became the Jewish custom to raise tombstones that seemed, in hardly any physical detail, to depart from their Greek and Roman models. They, too, were inscribed in Greek with the conventional eulogy of the dead. Only one distinctive feature set them apart: The Jewish epitaph ended with the three fraternal words *Shalom al Yisrael* (Peace to Israel) and the tombstone was adorned with characteristic religious symbols—menorah, shofar, lulab, laver, or palm branch. Sometimes the Greek or Latin epitaph was carried also in a Hebrew translation.

It is axiomatic that Jewish gravestones have varied in each region, being much affected by the conventional tastes and fashions of the local Gentile environment. There have been, of course, what might be called "Jewish tombstone traditions," accumulated by Jews coming from various climes and periods and transplanted in whatever places they migrated. Thus the Greco-Roman custom of interment in a stone sarcophagus, with the lid bearing the identifying epitaph—a form of burial which the wealthy Jews of Hellenistic times adopted—was carried over by them into the early Middle Ages in Europe. In the ancient Jewish graveyard of Sarajevo, Yugoslavia, may still be seen such Hellenistic-style tombs.

The custom of providing individual graves and of raising headstones became general among the Jews during the early Middle Ages. The Jews of Central and Eastern Europe—the Ashkenazim—made it traditional to set the headstone in an upright position; the Jews of Spain, Portugal, and the Balkans—the Sefaradim—laid the tombstone flat over the grave. This latter fact was noted by Henry Wadsworth Longfellow in his poem about the Jewish cemetery of Newport, Rhode Island, which had been laid out by Spanish and Portuguese Jewish settlers in 1677.

> And these sepulchral stones, so old and brown,
> That pave with level flags their burial-place,
> Seem like the tablets of the Law, thrown down
> And broken by Moses at the mountain's base.

Perhaps the most interesting of all Jewish burial grounds in Europe is the Prague cemetery. Its oldest stones, dating from medieval times, are simple slabs of sandstone, Gothic in design, and with the epitaphs cut in quaint Hebrew lettering.

During the Renaissance, the style of the tombstone underwent a transformation; it was cut in portal form, had a pointed gable, and was ornamented with animal symbols and tribal signs chiseled in the stone. Also, if the deceased was a male and of priestly descent (a Cohen), on his tombstone were depicted carved hands, upraised, and with fingers outspread in the familiar priestly benediction; if he was of Levite stock (a Levi) his stone bore upon it the representation of a jug or laver.

The Baroque period, which smothered Christian art and architecture in Europe in an excess of ornamentation, also left its gaudy impress on the tombstones of the Jews of Prague. Instead of the unadorned upright stele of previous centuries, the matzebah became a florid sarcophagus—an ohel; i.e., a "tent." It had four walls and was hollow within. However, this was only a formal memorial, because the body itself reposed beneath the sod. In such an ohel the almost legendary Rabbi Judah Löw ben Bezalel (1520-1609), the purported creator of the clay Golem (*which see*), lies interred. Like all tombstones of that period, his is flamboyant in ornamentation and in the Biblical Hebrew inscription.

Most imaginative was the way the name of the deceased was often treated; it was graphically illustrated on the tombstone according to its literal meaning. If the Hebrew name of the departed was Yehudah, a lion of Judah was carved on the stone; if Dov, a bear; if Zeb, a wolf; if Zevi, a stag. If a woman's name was Chavah (Eve), her tombstone was adorned with a scene from the Garden of Eden. The surname of Hahn was represented by the carving of a cock; that of Meisl, by a mouse.

The Jewish stonecutter—the folk-artist of the cemetery—also found much inspiration for his creative imagination in the callings and professions of the deceased. A tailor was

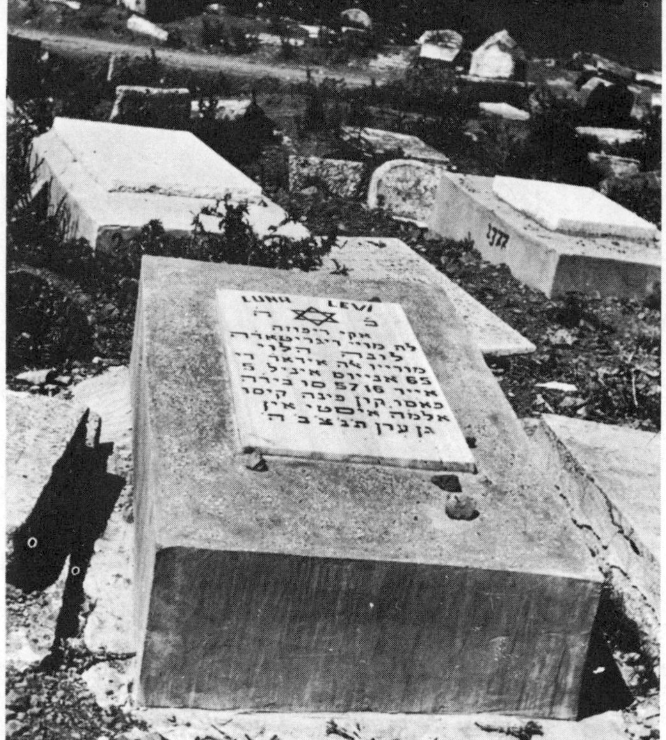

Epitaph in Ladino (Judeo-Spanish) written with Hebrew characters, in Istanbul, Turkey. Sefaradic tombstones are laid horizontally on the graves.

represented on his tombstone by a pair of scissors; a doctor, by medical pincers; an apothecary, by mortar and pestle; a goldsmith, by a crown and two chains; a musician, by a violin; a printer, by a book; and a dealer in etrogim (the citrons used ceremonially during Succot, the Feast of Tabernacles), by an etrog.

Aside from information giving the name of the deceased, the date of his death, his father's name, and, in the instance of a wife, the name of her husband, the verbally overloaded gravestone also carried, more often than not, elegies and eulogies for the departed. These were composed in Biblical Hebrew and were characteristically flowery and fulsome. The eulogy for Elijah (Elias) Levita, the famous Hebrew grammarian and Yiddish troubadour of Venice during the Renaissance, is an excellent example: "The stone cries out from the wall, and mourns . . . for our rabbi who has departed and ascended into heaven. Elijah [Note—Here Elijah Levita is flatteringly coupled with the Prophet Elijah. See II Kings 2:11.] is gone to the Lord in a whirlwind—he who shed light on the darkness of grammar and turned it into light. He ascended at the end of Shebat in the year [counting from the Creation] 5309 [namely, 1548 C.E.] and his soul is bound up in the bond of Eternal Life."

Even more pathos and extravagant metaphor is lavished on the tombstone of a Prague Jew who was buried in 1586: "With bitterness and grief I cry: 'Ariel—he has gone to God!'

Jewish cemetery in Hartford, Conn.

The "Americanized" tombstone of Reform Judaism.

Inscription in Greek and Latin on a stone tablet found in Rome, reading: "Here lies Tubias Barzaharona and his son Parecorius." Two menorot and the word shalom *in Hebrew identify the deceased as Jews. 1st century* C.E.

. . . Weep and lament, mourn and shed bitter tears. . . . He hastened to perform deeds of piety like a stag to the water-brook . . ."

Today's tombstones over Jewish graves are quite simple and matter of fact. Except perhaps for the symbol of either a menorah or a Star of David (Magen David) and a few characteristic Hebrew words inscribed upon them, many are no more traditionally Jewish than were those of Hellenistic times whose epitaphs were carved in Greek. Cemeteries of Conservative and Reform Jews display tombstones that, in shape and design, seem to be little different from those that may be found in Protestant graveyards. However, the stones over the Orthodox and Ultra-Orthodox graves, while to the beholder they may seem scornful of external beauty, nonetheless, strive to maintain some of the characteristics of the past, if not in the design of the stone, at least in the epitaph.

Tombstone in Jewish cemetery in Lublin, Poland.

Yet most Jewish tombstones—whatever the manner of the religious adherence of the deceased—follow tradition in a few details. On top are carved the Hebrew equivalents of the letters *P* and *N*. These stand for *Poh Nikbar*—"Here lies *buried*—" At the bottom are inscribed the Hebrew equivalents of the consonants *T N Z B H* (pronounced in Hebrew *Tenatzayboh*). These constitute the initial letters of the Hebrew supplication recited at the funeral service: "May his soul be bound up in the bond of Eternal Life."

It has become the custom that around the time of the first anniversary following the death, for the family and friends of the *niftar* (the departed) to gather at the graveside for the unveiling and dedication of his tombstone. Since the Talmudic age, it has been a Jewish folk-belief that it is good for one's soul to pay a visit to the graveside of a beloved person. It teaches humility and recalls to mind the emptiness of some of the values of the world and the need of devoting oneself to ideal goals and to doing good.

See also BURIAL CLOTHES; BURIAL RITES AND CUSTOMS; CEMETERIES; DEATH; IMMORTALITY; MAGEN DAVID; MENORAH; MERIT OF THE FATHERS; RESURRECTION; SHIVAH; YAHRZEIT; YIZKOR.

TORAH. *See* BIBLE, THE.

TORAH-LEARNING. *See* BET HA-MIDRASH; BIBLE, THE; CHACHMAH; CHEDER; GEONIM; TALMID CHACHAM; TALMUD, THE; TALMUD TORAH; TORAH STUDY; YESHIBAH; YESHIVAH BACHUR.

TORAH ORNAMENTS (in Hebrew: KELEH KODESH, meaning "holy vessels")

"The Tree of Life" (in Hebrew: ETZ CHAYYIM). Jewish tradition always aimed to embody abstract ideas and ideal values in terms of physical symbols. It is, therefore, not surprising to find that each of the two wooden rollers around which the parchment Torah Scroll is wound is called a "Tree of Life." The name, of course, is a poetic reference to the Torah, in accordance with the ancient Hebrew saying that runs: "The Torah is the Tree of Life to those who cleave to it."

The Wrapper (in Hebrew: MAPPAH). To tie the rolled-up Scroll of the Torah securely from top to bottom, a wrapper is provided. This consists of a band, usually made of white linen, colored silk, or velvet. It is generally four to six inches wide, and from about 75 to 150 inches long. While, in the poverty-stricken East European communities it was kept plain and unadorned, it received very marked decorative attention in Germany. There, with time, it took on more the character of folk art than of a religious article.

The German Jews, somehow and at an undetermined period, began to associate this wrapper symbolically with the male child. Among them the wrapper was, therefore, made of four strips from the swaddling clothes that an infant had worn during the rite of circumcision. When the baby finally reached the age of one year, his parents would bring him to the synagogue for the first time for the Sabbath service. There, in a brief but affectionate ceremony, the child was prompted to offer "his" wrapper to the rabbi, and the ceremony concluded with his touching or kissing the Torah. But the child's offering would not be used for tying any Torah Scroll until the Sabbath of his Bar Mitzvah, when he was thirteen. The ceremony usually concluded with the pious wish that when the boy reached manhood, he would fulfill his happy destiny in *"Torah, chuppah, . . . ma'asim tobim;"* that is, in "Torah study, marriage, and good deeds."

The Jews in Central Europe for several centuries decorated those Torah wrappers made from the swaddling clothes of an infant with all kinds of floral designs, which were either embroidered or painted from stencils. In them were also interspersed Biblical quotations in Hebrew and various representations of lions, stags, birds, etc. Often they carried illustrations in folk-art style of various religious ceremonies and of the particular sign of the zodiac under which the child (whose offering the wrappers were) had been born. In addition, the wrappers were inscribed with the name of the boy, the date of his birth, and with the names of his parents.

The Mantle. After the Torah Scroll has been securely tied with the wrapper, it is completely encased, for protection as well as beauty, in a fitted mantle or sheath which is only a little larger than the rolled-up Scroll itself. This mantle, which has an opening at the bottom, is pulled over the two Trees of Life until it rests on top of the discs which prevent the Scroll from slipping off the Trees. (The Torah mantle in use among the Sefaradim is different in that it has its opening on the side.)

The height of a mantle can be anywhere from 30 to 35 inches and the width from 30 to 35 inches. In Ashkenazic congregations, the mantle is customarily made of velvet, but sometimes it is of plush, and occasionally of silk. The most popular color is a bright red, but green, blue, purple, and white are also common. (However, the latter is used only for the High Holy Days.) The Sefaradic preference is for fine, patterned brocade, which makes embroidery and appliqué unnecessary.

The models for the modern Torah mantles have been mainly those produced during the Baroque period, in the seventeenth century. Those were embroidered or appliquéd with a profusion of floral garlands, scrollwork, Biblical illustrations, and religious symbols. Prominent among the latter were the double Tablets of the Commandments, supported on either side by a lion rampant, and, supreme over all, suspended in majesty, the Crown of the Torah—the symbol of the omnipotence of the Bible in Jewish life. Some seventeenth- and eighteenth-century embroiderers even managed to crowd into the limited space of the mantle representations of the two sacrificial pillars of Jachin and Boaz and the ceremonial vessels and furnishings used in the ancient Temple service, as described in the Bible.

Today, the Torah mantle is made far more simple, even if less beautiful and less elaborate in its design; certainly, it is less skillfully worked. The principal motif generally is the Crown of the Torah, flanked on each side by a rampant lion, and over it, embroidered in gold or silver thread and encircled by a wreath of flowers or leaves, the Hebrew words *Keter Malkut* (Crown of Royalty).

It is worthy of note that, ever since the Baroque period, the embellishments and ornamentation of the Torah mantle have been almost identical with those appearing in the Ark curtain (the parochet).

The Case. Among many Oriental congregations and some Sefaradic ones as well, the fitted Torah mantle that is customary among the Ashkenazim is not used. Instead, these Jews wrap the entire Scroll in a strip of fine silk and deposit it in a cylindrical case. This case is made either of carved wood or of ornamental metal, in sections that are held together by hinges. Some of these metal cases are hand hammered and embossed tastefully with silver. They show all manner of the arabesque ornamentation and scrollwork so popular among the Arabs of the Near and Middle East.

The Crown (in Hebrew: KETER MALKUT; that is, "Crown of Royalty"). The desire to "dress up" and to "beautify" the Scroll of the Torah in all its physical elements in order to make its public appearance in the course of the prayer service in the synagogue more impressive, resulted in the creation of

Torah-wrapper of pink silk with the name of the woman donor who embroidered it and the date on which it was presented to the synagogue. Mantua, Italy, 1766. (Courtesy of Joseph B. Horwitz Judaica Collection, Cleveland.)

four specific ornaments for it. These are the Crown of the Torah, the breastplate (tzit), the headpieces (rimmonim), and the pointer (yad) used while reading from the Torah.

Why the Crown? It is written in the Talmud: "Among all the crowns in the world, the Crown of the Torah is the most royal." The Torah Crown is unqestionably of very great antiquity in Jewish ceremonial art, although no one knows when it was first introduced. It can be made of silver alone, or of silver that has been gilded, or of a combination of silver and gold. Sometimes it is set with semiprecious colored stones. The style of workmanship, as it has come down to us from Baroque times, is usually cast, "cut out," or repoussé. When it is in its ceremonial place, the Crown of the Torah rests on top of the Trees of Life.

The greatest ornamentation of all was lavished upon the Crown. It was designed with all imaginable kinds of architectural conceits and novelties: with graceful columns, pilasters, arches, and tiny bells. The silversmith found here free play for his artistic inventiveness and skill. Since there never was any form fixed by tradition, as was the case with other Jewish ceremonial objects, on the basis of hundreds of extant Crowns made during the past several centuries, one can see that the artist-craftsmen introduced a great variety of forms and subject matter into their designs. They made representations of lions, horned stags, fanciful griffins, and eagles and other birds; also, winged cherubs, the Tablets of the Commandments, flower and leaf wreaths, and the ritual vessels and other ceremonial objects described in the Bible as having been used in the Temple service.

The Breastplate (TZIT). The silver breastplate which is hung from the Sefer Torah commemorates the breastplate (choshen) of Biblical times. According to the Bible, that was studded with twelve precious colored stones, one for each tribe of Israel, and the high priest wore it during the Temple service in Jerusalem. The period of its origin remains unknown, but it is significant that the tzit is not used at all by the Sefaradic Jews; that indicates it had a rather late origin in Central or Eastern Europe. The earliest breastplate extant today is one that had been publicly dedicated in the Ashkenazic synagogue at Amsterdam in 1612.

Like the Crown of the Torah, the breastplate is made of silver, but occasionally there is gilding on some of its parts for the purpose of contrast. The earliest examples extant, which became the models for subsequent production, stem from the showy Baroque period. It is an interesting cultural phenomenon that, because Jews lived sequestered in their walled-in ghettos, they clung longer and more tenaciously to outmoded costumes and design-patterns than their Christian neighbors. There simply exists no basis for speculating how the Torah breastplate of more remote times might have looked.

Not all breastplates are alike. Most often they are rectangular or oblong in shape. When they are square, they are designed with an arched top. Whatever the variations in their shape and size, the average dimensions are 10 to 12 inches high by 8 to 9 inches wide.

The breastplates are excessively rich in detail, and those produced in more recent times show even less taste and technical skill than their older models. They confuse and satiate the eye with their rococo ornamentation of grapevines, floral wreaths, tendrils, the pillars of Jachin and Boaz, the Crown of the Torah, and the almost ever present little bells. Often enough, insufficient surface space is provided by several small cartouches on the breastplate for illustrations of Biblical scenes containing portrayals of illustrious personages, or of the ever recurring Tables of the Ten Commandments as they were being handed down to Moses at Mount Sinai, or of Aaron, magnificent in his high-priestly robes and regalia, swinging a censer, or of a man blowing a shofar, of a Seder service, of Jews eating in a succah, of a menorah, etc.

To be sure, there is also a practical besides an ornamental or a symbolic purpose for the breastplate. In its center there is a rectangular opening behind which, manipulated by hand, are movable indicators upon which appear, to suit the particular occasion, the words Shabbat (Sabbath) and the names of the holy days (such as Rosh Hashanah, Yom Kippur, etc.).

The Headpieces (in Hebrew: pl. RIMMONIM, meaning "pomegranates," s. RIMMON). Of all ornaments fashioned for the Sefer Torah, the Headpieces are the oldest known. Just as the pomegranate is stuffed full of seeds, so do the rimmonim symbolize the wishful blessing for great fertility and population increase of Israel.

Like the pomegranate, the shape of the rimmon is round. In time, because of the great number of embellishments lavished on it, it became more elongated. In European countries, it took on an architectural—almost a monumental—character. Without a doubt, finding inspiration in the structural forms of feudal times, there developed a preference for rimmonim in the shape of towers. (Some had the form of belltowers, unmistakably suggesting the influence of church architecture.)

The rimmonim were either cast, embossed, or done in repoussé; only rarely were they gilded over or chased.

Silver Torah Breastplate (19th century) with two rampant lions supporting the Crown of the Torah over the Tables of the Ten Commandments. The Hebrew word Shabbat *(at bottom) indicates the special use of the Breastplate on the Sabbath. (Courtesy of Joseph B. Horwitz Judaica Collection, Cleveland.)*

The Pointer (in Hebrew: YAD, meaning, "hand"). The pointer was required in order to obviate the need of touching the sacred text of the Sefer Torah with the bare hand—considered an impiety—at the time of the public reading of the Scriptural portion in the synagogue. But it had still another purpose: to underscore separately each revered word of the text for fear of accidentally missing a single one. Those pointers extant today do not date back later than the seventeenth century.

The yad is a slender ornamental silver shaft which is attached to a silver chain. It is suspended from one of the two wooden Trees of Life. Traditionally, it is made in the shape of a hand, of which the pointed index finger serves as a marker. From 8 to 10 inches long, it has been made in a variety of technical combinations: It has been cast, hammered, filigreed, and chased. Sometimes it is set with semi-precious stones and is embellished with a crown or another motif, but most of the time it is plain and bare of any decoration.

In poor, Ultra-Orthodox congregations, a pointer made of bone instead of silver is not infrequently used.

See also ART, CEREMONIAL; TORAH SCROLL.

TORAH-READING (in Hebrew: KERIAT TORAH, KERIAT HA-TORAH)

The continuous reading from the Sefer Torah (the parchment scroll of the Pentateuch which rests in the Ark) during the congregational service on the Sabbath, the festivals, the fast days, and Rosh Chodesh (the Festival of the New Moon), was far more than merely a ceremonial requirement. Its principal object was instructional: that the worshipers "may hear and that they may learn."

At first, the directive fulfilling the ancient commandment in the Book of Deuteronomy ascribed to Moses—"Thou shalt read this law before all Israel in their hearing"—was meant for one single occasion: the Feast of Tabernacles (Succot), and that only during the Sabbatical or seventh "year of release."

In the year 444 B.C.E., Ezra the Scribe read from the Torah on each of the eight days of Succot before all the returned Babylonian exiles assembled in the Temple Court in Jerusalem. Five centuries later, the Jewish historian Josephus explained (in *Against Apion*), for the benefit of his educated Roman readers: "The Lawgiver [Moses] showed the Law [Torah] to be the best and most necessary means of instruction by enjoining the people to assemble not once or twice or frequently, but every week, while abstaining from all other work, in order to hear the Law and learn it in a thorough manner—a thing which all other lawgivers seem to have neglected."

This neglect in other ancient religions of the systematic study of scriptural writings by their adherents was, in most instances, due to the almost total monopoly held by the priests over the religious doctrines, ceremonies, and practices. But through the various developmental stages of the Jewish religion—Mosaic, Prophetic, and Rabbinic—there passed a continuous and growing chain of democratic tradition in which the religions experience became increasingly more personal, more general, and finally, entirely independent of mediation, whether by prophet, priest, or rabbi. Therefore, each Jew, as far as his intellectual capacities and his circumstances permitted, was expected to learn for himself the fundamental laws that were to govern his religious life.

From earliest childhood it was incessantly iterated and reiterated to the Jew that he could earn his "portion of bliss" in the World-to-Come only by his own efforts in piety and by his performance of good deeds for the benefit of his fellow men. For that reason, whenever he was honored by being "called up" to read before the entire congregation from the sidrah (the weekly portion of the Torah; pl. sidrot), he followed the instructions laid down by tradition for reciting the Scriptural text with the utmost concentration. He was expected to cantillate the Hebrew words with reverence, sincere emotion and sweetness of voice, and remain fully aware of their meaning. Religious experience was thereby brought down to the grass-roots of Jewish life.

Case for a Sefer Torah (Scroll of the Law). This type of case is in general use among Jews of the Orient. (Courtesy Joseph B. Horwitz Judaica Collection, Cleveland.)

This unflagging periodic participation in Scriptural illumination in Jewish millennial history by the plain folk and not only by the scholars and communal big-wigs, made the impact of the social and ethical teachings of the Pentateuch and the Prophetic Writings constant, indelible, and timeless. Their influence was further intensified by the additional requirement that both the weekly sidrah and its haftarah (the applicable selection from the Prophets) were to be recited by all Jews at home on the Sabbath. The reading of Scripture was thus prized as a fundamental exercise in the self-dedication of the religious to their God and the Torah as "a nation of priests."

The reading aloud from the Torah flowed on like a never ending stream in the community life of the Jew in every land. In a symbolic act of self-renewal, he began his Torah-reading all over again when he had finally come to the end, on Simchat Torah. It has been traditional for many centuries that when the concluding words from the Five Books of Moses have been read, the worshipers, as with one voice, cry out the ancient formula: *"Chazak, chazak, venit chazak!"* ("Be strong, be strong, and let us gather new strength!") What all this meant to the Jew of the ages was described in mystic terms by Simeon bar Yochai, the Mishnah Sage (Tanna) of second-century Judea: "When the

Scroll of the Torah is taken out [of the Ark] in the presence of the congregation to read therein, the heavenly Gates of Mercy open and divine love awakens."

The successful penetration of the conscious as well as the unconscious self of the Jew by the ceaseless, purposeful reading induced the Church and later the Mosque to institute this same practice of reading from scriptures in public worship. Yet more than once, under the lash of their Greek and Roman oppressors, the Jews were forbidden to read congregationally from the Torah. For instance, in the year 533, in response to the urgent complaint of the bishops of the Byzantine Church, the Emperor Justinian issued such a ban. To the bishops, zealous for the missionary triumph of Christianity in half-pagan Europe, the reading from the Torah by Jews seemed very much like overt competition with the reading from the Gospels held during the services of the Church. In addition, they took it as a challenge to the truths of the Christian faith and feared it might lead to Judaizing.

In the early centuries after the institution of the practice of Torah-reading in Judea, it took three years to complete the cycle of the Five Books of Moses, but in time, a more effective arrangement of the sidrot was made by the Babylonian rabbis which reduced the triennial period to one year. This remained almost the general practice ever since.

It was the quaint but realistically motivated custom during late Second Temple days and in the Rabbinic period which followed that the Hebrew reading from the Torah and from the Haftarah be promptly translated into the vernacular Aramaic or Greek for the benefit of those congregants who knew no Hebrew. In Hellenistic Egypt, the Torah-reading was apparently done directly from the Greek translation, for the Jews there knew little or no Hebrew. In later and culturally less liberal periods, this practice was dropped entirely. But in the Reform congregations of our day, the reading by the rabbi or cantor from the Hebrew Scroll is usually followed by a translation of the portion into English.

The traditional way of reading—or, more precisely, of cantillating—from the Torah has been by means of a system of musical accents which are called in Hebrew *neginot*. The text is half-sung, half-intoned, so it somewhat resembles the modern operatic recitativo or the speech-song. The neginot reveal a definite parental kinship to the earliest liturgical modes and Gregorian plain song which were employed in the musical service of the Church.

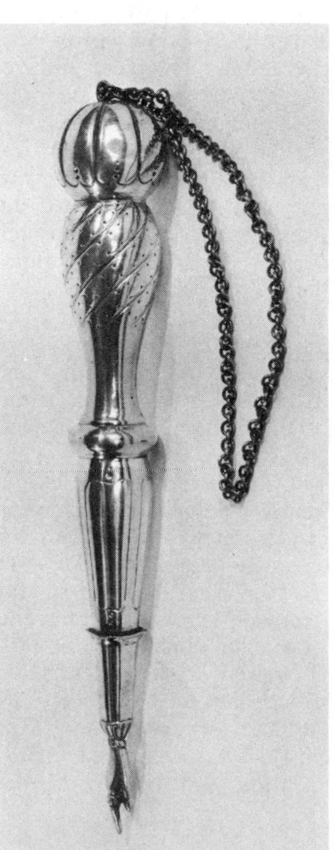

Yad (pointer), hand wrought of silver, used in underscoring the Hebrew text when reading from the Torah Scroll on the Sabbath in the synagogue. (Courtesy of Joseph B. Horwitz Judaica Collection, Cleveland.)

Among the Jews, a thorough knowledge of the accents, was required for proper cantillation of the sacred Hebrew text. There were, naturally, different identifiable modes or melodic patterns for intoning the Pentateuch, the Prophetic Writings, the Psalms, The Song of Songs, Lamentations, Job, and Esther, but even these were different in various parts of the world. A working knowledge of the modes for Scriptural reading was made an obligatory part of the curriculum in the traditional Talmud Torah and cheder. In addition, in former times, no Bar Mitzvah boy could be considered properly educated who was not able to cantillate fluently the various Scriptural books according to their distinctive musical modes.

There were wide variations also in the religious-cultural levels of Jewish communities in various places at different times, especially during periods of harsh persecution. As has been noted elsewhere in this work (*see* MUSICAL ACCENTS), reading publicly from the Sefer Torah and employing the proper traditional cantillations, proved difficult because neither accent marks nor vowel points were permitted on the sacred parchment text of the Sefer Torah. Instead, these markings had to be learned by children from non-ritualistic texts of the Pentateuch that carried the neginot. In less knowlegeable times, when the opportunity for mas-

Torah Crown, intricately designed in silver, surmounted by two Tables of the Law flanked by lions rampant. Note the animal and flower motifs, and the bells. (Courtesy of Joseph B. Horwitz Judaica Collection, Cleveland.)

tering the accents was lacking, it was found expedient to appoint for public Torah-reading one who was expert in the cantillations. This functionary was either the professional chazzan (cantor) or some learned man, and he acted in an honorific capacity as the baal koreh (master of reading). In that way, those who could not read the Hebrew text properly or did not know the cantillations were not shamed for their lack of knowledge when they were "called up" to the Torah. During the actual reading, they stood silently by, merely following the sidrah with reverent eyes. But they did recite the usual benedictions before and after the reading. In Reform congregations today, it is the cantor alone who does the Scriptural reading, and he does it minus the traditional cantillation.

The drama of one congregant's being summoned by name to the bema (the reader's platform), there to read aloud while all the worshipers act as a responsive choir, adds dignity and a deep emotionalism to the reading. "This nation is a nation only by reason of its Torah," wrote Saadia Gaon (Babylonia, tenth century), the intellectual-religious authority of that age.

The ceremonial in which the reading from the Torah is traditionally set is elaborate and was fixed by rabbinic regulations, although these have varied in different regions. During the sixteenth century, the Cabalist Joseph Caro of Safed established in his authoritative ritual code, the Shulchan Aruch, the procedure that has since been followed in the Western world. The ceremony begins with the opening wide of the doors of the Ark of the Law by the worshiper to whom has fallen this honor. This is followed by the recitation of solemn prayers and doxologies or "praisings" while the Sefer Torah still rests in the Ark. Another worshiper, also signally honored, advances to the open Ark and takes out the Scroll of the Torah. He deposits it in the extended arms of the cantor or the "master of reading." Either of these officiating worthies, wrapped in his tallit (prayer shawl) and raising high the Scrolls above the heads of the congregation, intones the Shema: "Hear, O Israel—the Lord our God the Lord is One!" The worshipers fervently repeat the words responsively. Then the reader, echoed by the congregation, proclaims the omnipotence and holiness of the Creator. In traditional congregations, with his chanting of "Magnify the Lord with me," the Sefer Torah is carried around the synagogue in procession, with all those it passes by falling in line, while the congregation, as with one voice, chants: "Thine, O Lord, is the greatness, and the power, and the glory, and the victory, and the majesty."

The Sefer Torah is borne to the bema and prepared for reading. Successively, it is divested of its silver ornaments, and its velvet, brocade, or silken mantle. Then the binder underneath is unwound, and the Sefer Torah is placed upon the reading desk, where it is unrolled to the portion of the week. The first worshiper is summoned to do the reading of the opening Scriptural passage. (This honor is termed an ALI'AH.) Tradition requires him to be either a descendant of a priest (cohen) or of a Levite of Temple times. For more than two thousand years, the ceremonial regulations surrounding the Torah-reading, although varying in minor ways from place to place, have been elaborate, precise, and stylized in the form of their execution. The one who takes out the Sefer Torah must carry it in his right arm only. In the traditional congregation, all those whom it passes by must pay it homage by escorting it in procession to the bema. Each one "called up" to read must not descend the steps of the bema until the reader who follows him has recited the opening benediction. Neither may anyone touch the Scroll with his bare hand but only with a fold of his prayer shawl. And before he begins, the reader is required to take hold of the two handles ("Trees of Life") of the Sefer Torah, and closing his eyes for greater mental concentration, recite this blessing with congregational response: "Blessed art Thou, O Lord, Giver of the Torah!" At this point, removing his hand from the left handle, he begins to read the Scriptural passage assigned to him—one consisting of at least three verses. On concluding, he again grasps the left handle of the Scroll and then, with both hands, rolls it up, reciting the blessing which exalts God, ". . . Who has given us the Law of Truth, and has planted everlasting life in our midst."

The most dramatic moment in the ceremony is reached when the Scriptural readings are ended. Then the cantor or baal koreh (master of reading) raises aloft (hagbahah) the partly unrolled Sefer Torah, revealing at least three columns of text above the heads of the worshipers. First he turns the Scroll to the right of him, then to the left, then to the front, and then behind him. The Shulchan Aruch states: "It is the duty of everyone to look upon the writing and to recite, 'And this is the Torah which Moses set before the Children of Israel . . . It is the Tree of Life to them that grasp it . . . its ways are the ways of delight, and all its paths are peace . . .'"

The ceremony of returning the Sefer Torah to the Ark is virtually the reverse of that which takes place when it is taken out. It begins with the rolling up (gelilah) of the Scroll, which is first tied with its band, then covered with its embroidered mantle, and finally adorned with its silver ornaments. As it is carried back to repose in the Ark, everyone whom it passes by rises and escorts it reverently.

So great was the Rabbinic emphasis laid on the public reading from the Scriptures that the observance of all other laws and ritual regulations were permitted to lag in its favor. Heavily burdened with the accretion of the ceremonial laws of the centuries as Torah-reading may be, the motivating purpose behind it transcended them all collectively. For the law, urgently stated, is that in the congregation where there is no Torah Scroll, the worshipers are duty bound to read aloud from any kind of Bible text that is available—even from a printed copy. The Talmudic teachers held that far more important than the observance of all rites and ceremonies was this consecrated task: "that the law of reading from the Torah be not forgotten" in Israel.

See also BIBLE, THE; CHRISTIANITY, JEWISH ORIGINS OF; HAFTARAH; MUSICAL ACCENTS; SERMON; SIDRAH; TORAH SCROLL;

TORAH SCROLL (in Hebrew: SEFER TORAH; pl. SIFREI TORAH)

The institution by Ezra the Scribe in the middle of the fifth century B.C.E. of the custom of reading aloud from the Torah (the Five Books of Moses or Pentateuch) during public worship as a form of popular instruction in the Jewish religion, became a paramount and lasting feature of the synagogue service on the Sabbath and on Holy Days. Time-honored custom also decreed that there could be no public reading from Scripture except from the specially prepared parchment Scroll. And the supreme reverence in which the Torah was held by the religious Jew not only did not allow any tampering with the Hebrew text of the Torah Scroll but did not permit any change in the manner and technique of its production, or even in its traditional form.

The scroll form was conventional for books made in ancient Judea. There is a rare drawing extant of a synagogue ark, constructed in Greco-Roman style, with round holes running through it horizontally. This would indicate that

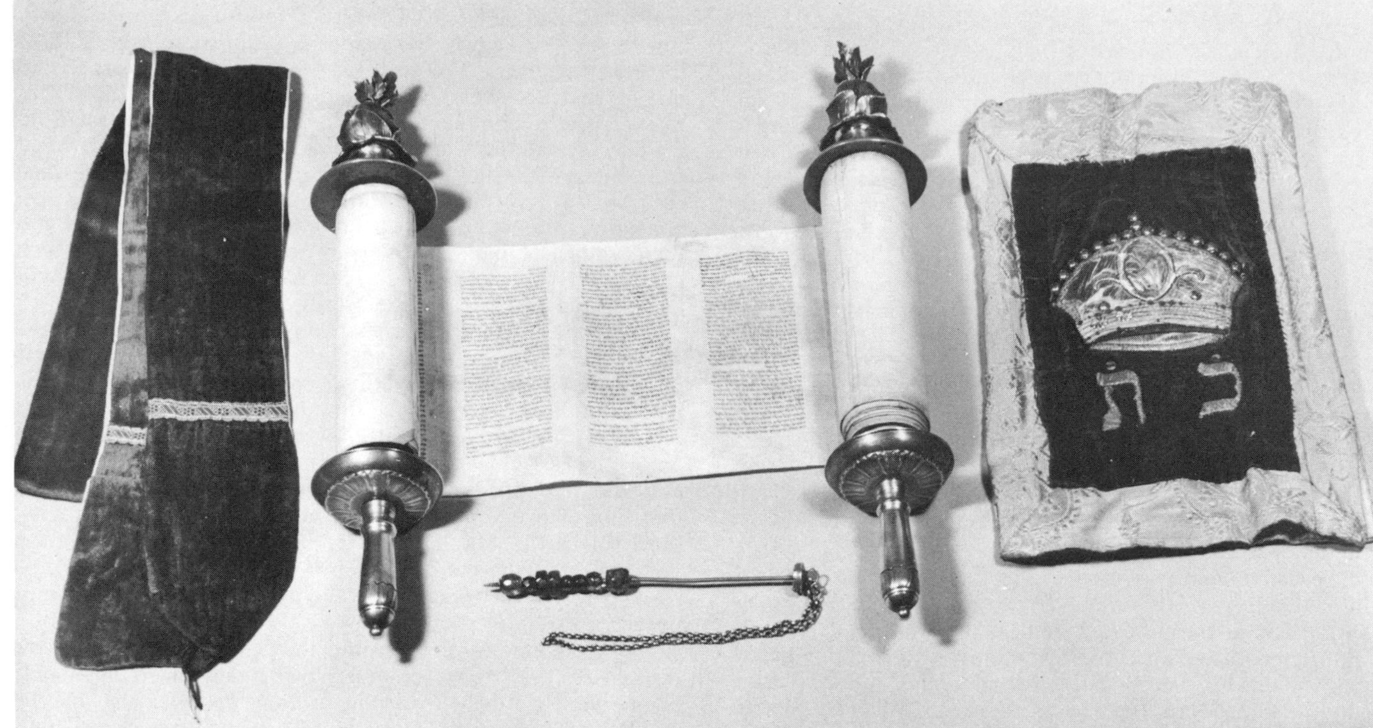

Torah Scroll (center), Torah Mantle (right), Torah Wrapper (left), silver pointer or Yad (bottom). The rollers of the Scroll are surmounted by silver finials. Late 18th century. (The Jewish Museum.)

Scrolls of the Torah or other scroll writings were probably stored in such a receptacle in ancient times. Later, in an unknown period, the practice was to build the inside of the Ark in the form of a closet or chest in which the Torah Scrolls were deposited, leaning slightly in an upright position.

It is without question true that the Torah Scroll, in both form and Hebrew calligraphic style, has remained the least changing of all Jewish religious articles. It therefore would be safe to say that the Torah Scroll, as we know it today, is pretty much like the one that was in use two thousand years ago.

The writing of a Sefer Torah was considered no routine task but a sacred rite, for it contained what every pious Jew believes to be the inspired commandments and the eternal truths revealed by God to Israel. For that reason, without being allowed any deviation, the Torah scribe (sofer), from whose painstaking hands the Scroll came, was required to follow tradition and all the Rabbinic regulations in every detail of its production. The sofer had to be dedicated. He was expected to be a man of deep piety, no mere copyist employed for a fee. To emphasize that his calligraphic work in transcribing the sacred Hebrew text was but another form of religious worship, he had to wear a prayer shawl (tallit) and phylacteries (tefillin) when he sat at his task.

In the days of the Second Temple and down to the early Middle Ages, the writing was done on leather that had to be prepared from the hides of ritually clean animals. The Dead Sea Scrolls, which were discovered in 1948 in the Palestinian Cave of Qumran, were all written on leather. But some centuries after that, parchment made from the skin of ritually clean animals was substituted. (The sheets of parchment, equal in size, were sewed together with dried tendons.) As a preliminary to his copying the new Scroll from a correct model, the sofer proceeded to divide the empty parchment pages into squares, ruling his lines carefully with a stylus. For his work, he used only the best and most enduring black ink and the finest of goose quills. He had to be eternally watchful to prevent a single error from creeping into his Scroll. While any ordinary mistake could be erased, if, how-

Embroidered velvet cloth on which the Torah Scroll is rested during public reading in the synagogue at Sabbath and festival services. The Hebrew inscription reads: "Offered from the heart by Elvira Fano. She worked willingly with her hands to serve in holiness to beautify the dwelling of the Lord, in the year 5615 [1854]." Milan, Italy. (Courtesy of Joseph B. Horwitz Judaica Collection, Cleveland.)

ever, he misspelled God's name—this was deemed a grave sin under any circumstance—he had to destroy quickly the entire page! He was allowed no leeway in anything. Rabbinical regulation minutely prescribed for him book divisions, paragraph order, and spaces between letters, words, lines, and sentences.

The sofer wrote in square Hebrew letters, and he was not allowed to insert the customary punctuation marks and vowel points for vocalization used in reading aloud. (These have been permitted only in ordinary Torah Scrolls and in printed books of the Chumash (the Pentateuch). Yet tradition required him to decorate certain letters with rudimentary drawings of full crowns (in Hebrew: pl. KETARIM, s. KETER) over them, and still other letters with lesser marks of royal distinction, i.e., coronets (in Hebrew: pl. TAGGIM, s. TAG). Since the parchment pages were continuously stiched together and wound around two rollers (the "Trees of Life"), naturally, only one side of the page—the facing side—could be written on. At the upper and lower ends of the rollers were flat wooden disks designed to keep the parchment roll from slipping off. The rollers were topped by vertical rods or handles. Usually, both disks and handles were decorated, carved, or inlaid, and were inscribed with appropriate Scriptural passages.

The art of the sofer, perhaps due to more indifferent, less dedicated, and more commercial-minded times, no doubt has declined, but Torah Scrolls are still made as they were always made.

Silver Rimmonim (finials) for the rollers on which are wound the Sefer Torah. (Courtesy of Joseph B. Horwitz Judaica Collection, Cleveland.)

Embroidered gold-brocaded Torah mantle from the Pinkas Synagogue in Prague, 1710.

A Sefer Torah dressed in its brocaded mantle and adorned with silver Rimmonim (finials) and Yad (pointer) is held during services in the Great Synagogue, London.

Most synagogues today have more than one Sefer Torah; some of the larger ones have a great many. But poor congregations can afford only one, for a Torah Scroll is expensive; it is customarily donated to the synagogue by a member as a meritorious act of piety. Its formal dedication is considered to be a very important occasion and it is celebrated by the congregation with a great deal of ceremony and a procession, sometimes through the streets adjacent to the synagogue.

It stands to reason that, because of the supreme reverence in which the Sefer Torah is held, the practice and need to "beautify" it in every manner possible arose. No single religious or ceremonial object has called forth so much adoration from the Jews nor is there another on which has been lavished so much beautiful and, sometimes, overrich decoration and ornamentation: in silver and gold, in brocades, silks, and velvets.

See also SOFER; TORAH ORNAMENTS; TORAH-READING.

TORAH STUDY

The study of the Torah assumed the character of a national-religious dedication in the fateful year of 444 B.C.E. That occurred when Ezra the Scribe and the Elders, after having compiled and edited the Five Books of Moses (the Pentateuch), assembled within the Temple courts of Jerusalem the Jews who had but recently returned from the Babylonian Captivity, to promulgate and to teach them the Scriptural commandments and the laws.

The study of the Torah of Moses (Torat Mosheh) which, from that day on, was made obligatory and ceaseless, as the highest form of religious worship, ultimately became the passionate preoccupation of the entire Jewish people. It reached its flood tide five centuries after Ezra, during the Talmudic age, when Jerusalem and the Temple were no more.

In its scheme of ideal values, the Torah was prized by the ancient Jews as the sum of all possible good. They reverenced it as the repository of that which had been divinely revealed and remained true and morally perfect for all time. In their awed estimation, it stood for the absolute and universal harmony; the world existed only because of its transcendent spiritual power. Folk myth presented it as having existed *before* existence—as having been created by God two thousand years *before* Creation—and that he had kept it tenderly cradled in his bosom all that time, until he imparted it to Moses during the Revelation at Mount Sinai.

To the Jews, the Torah served, in a daring unitary conception of religion without parallel in history, as both the means and the end for the total life of man in this world and also in the World-to-Come. To devote oneself, at whatever personal sacifice, to a perpetual study of Torah was prized more as a privilege than as a duty. "Grant us our portion in Your Torah," was the impassioned prayer of Judah ben Timah, a Tanna (Sage) of the Mishnah.

An awesome moral significance was assigned to the self-consecration of Israel for the study and the transmission of the teachings of the Torah to all the generations yet unborn. It was a sort of general priestly service in which each individual Jew, inasmuch as he considered that he belonged to "a nation of priests," was expected to play his indispensable sacerdotal part. In the golden chain of the Oral Tradition (*see* MISHNAH, *under* TALMUD), forged in Judea while the Second Temple was still standing, was this link of pious exhortation by the Rabbinic Sage known as "son of Bahgbahg": "Study it [the Torah], and study it over and over again, for everything is contained in it. Reflect upon it, and grow old and gray over it, and do not stir from it!" (Pirke Abot 5:25.)

The character of Torah-study among the Jews was unique in that it was postulated upon democratic and egalitarian principles. The significance with which the activity was endowed was as social in character as it was religious and intellectual. The general attitude was that the truth of God was not a spiritual commodity especially reserved for an elite of superior individuals; on the contrary, it belonged to each person, for each, no matter what his position might be in the world, was valued as being equal to every other person merely by virtue of the natural law which distinguished him as a human being created "in the image of God."

This cardinal religious principle about the common "ownership" of God and about every Jew's inalienable and equal share in the Torah was illustrated by the celebrated rabbinic authority, Rashi of Troyes (1040-1105) in a retelling of the following Talmudic legend: Moses had given the Torah to the Priests and the Elders. When the ordinary folk —"the Israelites—saw this, they protested indignantly: "Didn't we, too, stand before God at Mount Sinai? Surely, the Torah was also given to us! Why then do you now appoint the sons of your own tribe [Levi] the priests and the Elders, to be the lords and masters over it. One fine day they will be sure to say to us: 'The Torah was not given to you but to us!' " When Moses heard this general outcry, he rejoiced and said: "Today, at last, O Israel, you have become a people!"

But this conception of Torah went far beyond any narrow sectarian Jewish lines. Its mission was considered by the ancient Jews as being directed to all mankind for its greater benefit and happiness. For that reason the Talmud made the solemn declaration: "It is not the Torah of the priests, nor is it the Torah of the Levites, nor even the Torah of the Israelites; *It is the Torah of man!* Its gates are open to receive any righteous nation which keeps the truth and also all individuals who are good and upright in their hearts."

Many people are somewhat nebulous about the meaning of "Torah," therefore, the distinction should be made between the limited term *"the Torah"*—which merely has reference to the Pentateuch (the Five Books of Moses)—and the generic but broad term "Torah" without the article "the." The latter conception also embraces, besides the Pentateuch (which retains its position of sovereign centrality in the Jewish religion), the other twenty-two Scriptural writings that are included in the Hebrew Bible. To these must be added, in a somewhat lower order of sanctity, the vast literature of the Talmud—the Rabbinic code of the Oral Tradition which consists of the Mishnah and the Tosefta, and the Gemara and the Midrash, which comment upon, elaborate, and illuminate the Torah still further.

In later centuries, the concept of "Torah," remaining ever elastic (since it was not fixed by any arbitrary definition or rabbinic ruling), was widened by popular acceptance to include the medieval classic commentaries on the Bible and the Talmud by their foremost interpreters—Rashi, Abraham ibn Ezra, and Maimonides—and also the authoritative ritual and ceremonial codes, the Arbah Turim and the Shulchan Aruch. To these the medieval Cabalists and their eighteenth-century continuators, the Chasidim, added their own esoteric writings: the Sefer Yetzirah and the Zohar.

In all religions, the discipline that rules worship and conduct is armored with a series of incentives and deterrents, of rewards and punishments. There were always, of course, a large number of small-minded literalists among the pious Jews—indeed, they are also found in every other religion—

Reading the sidrah (weekly portion) of the Pentateuch from the Sefer Torah in the Great Synagogue of London. Note the use by the reader of the Yad (pointer) on the Torah text.

who, by formally fulfilling their religious duties to the letter of the law, expected to be recompensed by a generous God for their pains—*quid pro quo*—with ego-social and material benefits in this life and with the same rewards as the saints (tzaddikim) in the World-to-Come.

However, a far less calculating piety was fostered as a tradition through the centuries by the rabbinic moralists. They placed the major emphasis on distinterestedness in worship, ritual observance, and upright personal conduct. In the instance of the religious obligation to study Torah, the Talmudic Sages counseled that it should be pursued *for its own sake alone*. "One should not say, 'I will study Torah so that they will call me a scholar,' or 'I will study our traditions so that they will make me an Elder and will give me a seat in the Higher Academy' . . . Rather, one should say, 'I will study out of love.' "

Such a motivation for study was eulogized in Jewish life as Torah Lishmah—Torah for its own sake. But some Talmudic teachers, always realistically on guard against the temptation of mere wishful thinking, placed great reliance on the power of gradual habituation and in making haste slowly in educational conditioning. The sophisticated Babylonian teacher of the third century, Chunah, gave this astute directive: "Study the Torah even if at first it is not for its own sake, for in time it will become for its own sake."

Yet "Torah for its own sake" was studied far more often than is generally realized in our own skeptical and utilitarian times. As an intellectual activity, it was no mere trifle or simple side-interest for the devout of former centuries. Rather, it constituted a towering and undiminishing preoccupation. The individual who engaged in it *con amore*, derived a sense of exalted purpose from it. It endowed him with a moral dignity and an emotional importance of mission. For he, like all other Jews, had been indoctrinated with the certainty that the existence of all mankind—in fact, of the whole natural world—depended, in part, on his dedicated Torah-study.

The moral grandeur that the Torah scholar could acquire by his activity was glowingly described in the Talmud: "He who labors in the Torah 'for its own sake' merits many things . . . he is called 'friend,' 'beloved,' 'a lover of God,' 'a lover of mankind.' It clothes him in humility and in fear of God, and prepares him to become righteous, pious, and upright. Moreover, it keeps him far from sin and brings him over to the side of virtue. It gives him sovereignty, dominion (over himself), and discerning judgment. The secrets of the Torah are revealed to him; he becomes a never failing fountain. He thus grows modest and long-suffering, and forgives insults—in that way rising above all mundane things."

Among the Rabbinic Sages in ancient Judea, the great majority earned their daily bread literally by the sweat of their brows (*see* LABOR, DIGNITY OF) as "hewers of wood and drawers of water." Nonetheless, they devoted themselves to Torah study every moment of their free time—as the Talmudic saying goes, "by day and by night." They set the pace, the intensity, and the all-consuming urgency for all later students and scholars of sacred lore.

In every generation, the quest for God, for truth, and for righteous conduct was felt by Jews as a burning need and a moral compulsion. There was so little time in this life! This was always the plaint of these dedicated Torah-scholars. Therefore, they exhorted, one must rouse oneself by the exercise of the free will from the dream-state of the soul and from a vacuuous existence and turn instead to that which is of everlasting value and which, in the end, brings redemption.

In the Babylonian Talmud, it is related of the third-century Rabbinic teacher Chisda how he studied Torah night and day until he was utterly exhausted. When his daughters pleaded with him that he go to bed, he replied: "How can I sleep? Soon the day will come when I shall have to lie down and sleep forever. Now, while I still have time, I want to devote myself to Torah study."

The point was made over and over again by these religious savants that there was so much to learn, yet so little time to learn it in and so pitiably little to show for one's efforts! There was the ring of pathos and frustation in the lament by the great Yochanan ben Zakkai, who flourished during the first century: "If all the heavens were made of parchment, if all the trees in the forest were made into quills, and if all human beings were scribes, it still would be insufficient for me to write down all that I have learned from my teachers. And yet, all the knowledge I have been able to carry away from them is no more than the water a dog is able to lap up from the sea!"

Considering all these natural handicaps and limitations, what could be a just measure for Torah study? The inevitable answer was: hardly any! Not merely a minimum in effort but the very maximum possible—that is what was expected of the Torah-scholar. The medieval rabbinic philosopher, Maimonides, observed austerely about this duty: "Every Jew has the obligation to study the Torah, whether he be rich or poor, in good health or physically afflicted, and whether very young or so old that his strength fail him. And should one be so poor that he is supported by charity, or if

Sefaradic Jews reclining in Oriental fashion on divans in their stockinged feet, engaged in Torah study.

married and the father of a large family, he is still bound to set aside a definite time for the study of the Torah both during the day and during the night, as it is written: 'Thou shalt meditate [in the Torah] day and night.' "

In regard to general studies that individuals normally undertake, there is usually a time limit set for their completion. But that was not at all the case for the Jewish Torah-scholar. An approximation of the following catechism is often found in rabbinical devotional writings:

> "How long has a man the obligation to study Torah?"
> "Til the day he dies."
> "Why so?"
> "For as soon as a man ceases to study he forgets."

Did the student-scholar ever grow tired of his perpetual exercise in the Torah? Did he, by any chance, find the frequent repetition of it boring or monotonous?

The answer to these questions, quite naturally, depended upon the outlook of the learner. If he happened to belong to the company of dedicated Torah scholars, he studied Torah Lishmah—Torah for its own sake. In that event he would be bound to testify that every time he repeated the text, he experiencd the freshness and the thrill of a new revelation; each time he restudied any particular passage, he would seek there new and unsuspected beauties of thought and wisdom.

Since there could be no end to learning, a regimen of daily study was prescribed by the Talmudic Sages: "Just as water falls drop by drop until it swells into a stream, so it is with Torah. If a man studies two laws today, two laws tomorrow, and so on—his learning soon becomes a living stream."

Different, of course, was the attitude of the skeptical-minded and the sophisticated toward this perpetual study—toward bearing unprotestingly "the yoke of the Torah" day in and day out. It was wittily expressed by the rabbinic poet-scholar of the Provençe, Kalonymos ben Kalonymos. In his satire *Eben Bohan* ("The Touchstone"), written in 1325, he spoofed with characteristic Jewish irony about Torah study:

> . . . Which makes the Jew a luckless creature,
> For he must shun all jest and play,
> And must o'er folios night and day,
> Mosaic and Rabbinic lore,
> And books which he may think a bore.
> The Bible is not half enough:
> Glosses there are and other stuff
> In which he erudite must be . . .
> In things particularly small
> Of no significance at all.

My Father at Torah Study.
(Painting by Sheva Ausubel.)

According to the Rabbinic Sages, there were three ascending categories of Torah-learning. The first was factual (da'at) knowledge; higher still was binah (understanding) which resulted from a proper use of knowledge; the highest of all was chachmah (wisdom)—the culmination and the end-goal of all knowledge and understanding.

Modern in its educational philosophy was the traditional methodology that was developed during the Talmudic Age for acquiring Torah-learning. It was not to be a lone, individualistic quest but a collective group-effect. The Babylonian religious teacher of the third century, Chisda, gave it as his opinion that "one teacher is best for the study of Torah. But to discuss it with several teachers is better, for their different opinions will improve your understanding." The Talmud therefore counseled: "Form groups for the purpose of study, for Torah can be acquired only in a group."

Pupil and teacher—both were interchangeable roles in the intellectual ethics of Rabbinic Judaism—follow the ancient tradition that there is no one from whom it is not possible to learn something of value. The Sages taught: "If you learn from any person just one maxim, or even a single word, you owe him the respect that is due to a teacher."

Torah-Teaching. Since Torah study was such a highly

prized pursuit, it logically followed that the Torah scholar-teacher, serving as the pivotal center for the entire learning process, should be greatly revered by the plain folk. The general enthusiasm for Torah-learning after the destruction of the Second Temple resulted in a lively teaching activity in Judea as well as in the Jewish settlements of the Diaspora. As democratic champions of the people, the Rabbinic Sages were not only dedicated learners but also inspired *sharers* of learning. The gateway to knowledge was left wide open to all those who cared to enter. Said the Mishnah tanna of the second century, Yoseh ben Chalafta: "There is nothing more futile than to acquire knowledge and not to impart it to others." The moralists of the Talmud likened him who had acquired Torah knowledge but did not teach it to others who were less fortunate or less intelligent than himself to a myrtle that blooms solitarily in the desert: Who can derive any benefit from it there?

The avocation (until the Middle Ages it was no vocation) of Torah-teacher was looked upon as the ultimate function of the learning quest. By sharing his knowledge with others it neither died in him nor was it diminished in any way for himself. The ancient Rabbis taught: "The light of one candle can kindle many candles, yet its own light remains undiminished."

As an illustration of the supreme religious importance assigned by tradition to the role of the Torah-teacher the following incident is recounted in the Midrash.

> Once the two Rabbinic luminaries of the second century, Assi and Ami, went about the towns of Judea establishing schools. When they came to a certain city, they said to its inhabitants, "Go and fetch the guardians of your city!"
>
> So the people went and brought before the Rabbis the captain of the watch and the judge.
>
> "Do you mean to tell us that these men are your guardians?" demanded Assi and Ami. "Why, they are your oppressors!"
>
> The inhabitants of the city were bewildered. "Who then, in your opinion, are the guardians of our city?"
>
> The Rabbis replied: "Your true guardians are the teachers of Scripture and the Mishnah. They are the ones who meditate upon the Torah night and day and seek to teach its eternal truths to you and your sons."

The Rabbinic teaching method was unpretentious. There was a general recognition by the Sages that pedantry and involved argumentation were bad pedagogy. That is why, when the Rabbinic Sage of the second century, Akiba ben Joseph, and the illustrious Patriarch Judah ha-Nasi, who compiled the Mishnah (*c.* 200 C.E.) discovered that, when they were lecturing "profoundly," their students either became inattentive or just dozed off, they promptly stepped down from their intellectual pedestals. From that time on they talked so simply that everyone understood and paid attention to what they were saying.

This democratic tradition of the teachers' not talking over the heads of their students drew students and teachers closer. As the students' comprehension increased, so too did their gratitude and respect. It is written in the Talmud: "A teacher takes the place of a father when he instructs the youth. For that reason the students should revere him just as they do their own father."

Scholars analyzing a knotty problem in the Torah text. (Painting by Bender, late 19th century.)

The absorbed Torah scholar. (Painting by L. Pilichowski, Paris, late 19th century.)

It was the custom, when the Orthodox Jewish child was one year old, for the father to take him to the synagogue for the first time. There he was allowed to touch the Sefer Torah—"his destiny" until the day he died. (Painting by Moritz Oppenheim, Germany, early 19th century.)

Analysis and discussion of religious texts. (Woodcut, Germany, 1483.)

Swaying During Torah Study. Many people, Jews as well as Gentiles, have wondered at the strange custom among Orthodox Jews of swaying their bodies when they pray or when they are at their Torah studies. A famed fourteenth-century rabbinic codifier of religious laws, Jacob ben Asher, the compiler of the Arbah Turim, explained it this way: that at Mount Sinai the Jews "received the Torah with awe, trembling and quaking. This accounts for the swaying of the body during the study of the Torah."

Certainly, a more poetic interpretation is given in a purported colloquy between two Rabbinic Sages, as recorded in the medieval Cabalistic work, the Zohar:

Discussion of sacred texts in the Bet ha-Midrash (House of Study). (Painting by Alfred Wolmark, London, 1905.)

> RABBI YOSEH: Why is it that among all the nations the Jews alone have a custom to sway their bodies?
>
> RABBI ABBA: This illustrates the excellence of their [i.e., the Jews'] souls. "The spirit of man is the lamp of the Lord [Proverbs 20:27]" refers to them. The light of that lamp flickers and wavers in unison with the light of the Torah.

A more realistic if not poetic explanation was advanced by Judah (Yehudah) Halevi (1085-1140), the great poet-philosopher of Spain. It was to the effect that, since manuscript copies of religious works (this was long before the invention of printing) were always costly and, therefore, rare, it was but natural that a number of poor Torah-scholars would crowd around a single book at their studies. Each one in turn, standing wedged in uncomfortably sideways, and trying to snatch a quick glance at the text, could do so only by swaying his body forward and backward. The constant repetition of this motion throughout their lives caused the scholars to develop (to inject a modern psychological term) a compulsive habit of swaying while at their studies. In time, this curious habit was adopted as a religious custom (minhag) and continued even when books had become plentiful, after the introduction of printing.

See also BET HA-MIDRASH; BIBLE, THE; CHACHMAH; COMMENTARIES, RABBINICAL; MASORAH; RABBI; SAGES, RABBINIC; SHULCHAN ARUCH; TALMID CHACHAM; TEITSCH-CHUMASH; TORAH-READING; YESHIBAH; YESHIVAH BACHUR.

TOSAFISTS

The Tosafists were medieval rabbinical commentators in Lorraine and the German Rhineland who had critically examined the text of the Babylonian Talmud. Most of their writing activity was carried on during the twelfth and the thirteenth centuries. They were called Tosafists because they had appended to the commentary of the Talmud by their master Rashi (Solomon ben Isaac of Troyes, 1040–1105) their own "additions" (in Hebrew: *tosafot*).

It is a curious fact that among these independent investigators were three grandsons of Rashi—Isaac, Samuel, and Jacob ben Meir, the last of whom is better known among Jews as Rabbenu ("Our Teacher.") Tam. While they revered their master and grandfather greatly, they also criticized him freely, for they were dissatisfied with those of his conclusions which seemed to them to have been drawn from illogical premises. Within the limits of the objectives they had set for themselves, their commentaries were not continuous and unified; they merely concentrated on reconciling or explaining particular contradictions.

So highly thought of were these writings that it has become standard to flank each page of text of the Babylonian Talmud with the Rashi commentary and the supplementary tosafot of his disciples.

See also COMMENTARIES, RABBINICAL; TOSEFTA, TOSAFOT (*under* TALMUD, THE).

TOSEFTA, TOSAFOT. *See* TALMUD, THE.

TREFAH. *See* TEREFAH.

"TROUBLERS OF ISRAEL." *See* THE PROPHETS (*under* BIBLE, THE).

TRUTH, JEWISH CONCEPT OF

Although the kind of truth that the Greek and Roman philosophers sought was based on the demonstrable proofs of logic, the idea of truth handed down by Jewish tradition in the teachings of the Rabbinic Sages was manifestly of a moral nature. It was implicit with social and ethical values.

At first this truth sought merely pragmatic ends. "Ye

shall not lie to one another," admonished the Levitical moralist of ancient days. This referred only to the practices of thievery and false dealing. Then the concept of truth began to take on spiritual and affirmative goals. "Truth is the seal of God," piously stated the Talmud, which also taught that it is the divine imprimatur on the life of man and is its justification: "Speak ye every man the truth with his neighbor; execute the judgment of truth and peace in your gates," taught the Tannaim (Sages) of the Mishnah.

One of these teachers of ethics, Joshua ben Chananiah, who flourished early in the second century C.E., told how once, as he was trying to take a short cut through a field, a little girl called after him: "Why do you walk here? . . . Can't you see this is a cultivated field?" Embarrassed, the Tanna tried to justify himself: "Just look . . . there's a path here, and it's well worn too!" "That it is," retorted the child with exasperation, "but it's a path that has been made by people just as selfish as you are!"

Merciless self-criticism and a striving for moral truth became just as much of a dedication for "the teacher of righteousness" among Jews as the undeviating goal of logical truth had been for the Athenian philosopher Socrates. "Teach your tongue to say, 'I do not know,' lest you invent a falsehood and be caught in your own trap," cautioned an ancient bit of Jewish folk-wisdom. This was in line with the existing realization that not all human shoulders were strong enough to support the truth equally. Mused an anonymous realist among the Rabbinic Sages: "Truth is a heavy burden; therefore, only a few wish to carry it." But since there were always among Jews courageous truth-seekers with strong spirits and inquiring minds, the burden of the search for truth was never dropped. And this referred to the pursuit of intellectual truth as well as to moral truth, especially at times of cultural fusion, when Jewish humanists also seriously examined the postulates of the Gentile philosophers.

In the Hellenistic-Jewish intellectual world of the second century, many people could not help but wonder why it was that a pious traditionalist like Rabbi Meir should have "stooped" to study wisdom from the brilliant heretic, Elisha ben Abuyah, who finally, to the chagrin of all Jews, embraced the truths of Greek philosophy in preference to the truths of the Torah. But those who understood the character of Meir warmly defended his conduct. They said: "Rabbi Meir found in the heretic Elisha ben Abuyah a pomegranate. He threw away the hard shell but he ate the nourishing fruit inside."

The trend to synthesize intellectual with religious-moral truth grew even stronger during the Middle Ages. To reconcile faith with reason became as ardent a goal of the medieval rabbi-philosophers as it was of the Christian Schoolmen. The most eminent of these religious thinkers, the Aristotelian Maimonides (Spain, twelfth century), who applied the logical method of the Greek philosopher to prove the validity of Jewish moral and religious teachings, stated the matter concerning truth with superb bluntness: "A truth, once it is established by proof, neither gains additional force from its acceptance by all scholars, nor loses any force if all reject it."

TSHUVEH. *See* REPENTANCE.

TU BI'SHEBAT. *See* CHAMISHAH ASAR BI'SHEBAT.

TWELVE TRIBES. *See* ANIMALS, "CLEAN" AND "UNCLEAN."

TZADDIK, TZADDIKIM. *See* CHASIDIM; KIDDUSH HA-SHEM; LAMED-VAV TZADDIKIM; RABBI.

TZADOK, TZADOKIM. *See* SADDUCEES.

TZEDAKAH. *See* CHARITY; LOANS, FREE.

TZITZIT (Hebrew, meaning "[ritual] fringes"; in Yiddish: TZITZIS)

The Jewish religion provides a number of visible "reminders" —symbols constantly recalling to its masculine adherents their identity as Jews and their obligation to fulfill the 613 precepts of the Torah in their daily lives. One of these "reminders" is the tzitzit, or fringes affixed to the four corners of the tallit (the prayer shawl whose wearing is made mandatory for the morning service in the synagogue) and the tallit katan (little tallit). This latter is a garment worn daily by Orthodox males underneath their outer clothing. The Talmud justified the fringes as a recaller of the commandments on pedagogic grounds: "Seeing leads to remembering, and remembering leads to doing."

The wearing of fringes on both tallit and tallit katan had Biblical sanction. "And the Lord spoke unto Moses, saying: 'Speak unto the children of Israel, and bid them that they make them throughout the generations fringes in the corners of their garments and that they put with the fringe of each corner a thread of blue. And it shall be unto you for a fringe, that ye may look upon it, and remember all the commandments of the Lord, and do them.' " (Numbers 15:37-39.)

Why the "thread of blue"? Rabbi Meir, the poetic Sage of the second century, said: "The thread of blue in the tzitzit resembles the hue of the sea, the sea mirrors the azure of the sky, and the sky reflects the radiance from the throne of God's glory, concerning which it is written: 'Under His feet . . . a sapphire stone.' " But by the fifth century, the thread of blue had become a thread of anxiety for the pious. The dye for it was hard to come by as it was extracted from a rare species of snail called *chalzun* in Aramaic—one which, in time, had become practically unobtainable. So, reluctantly, the Rabbis abrogated the Scriptural requirement for it.

East European cheder boy wearing the obligatory tallit katan (small tallit) with tzitzit (fringes). Called also arbah kanfot *(four corners) it is worn by the Orthodox male as an undergarment during all his waking hours. (Painting by Regina Mundlak, Paris, 1912.)*

Tzitzit

There are precise and sacrosanct procedures concerning the preparation of the four fringes. Each is made up of four long woolen threads. These, drawn through a small hole in each corner of the tallit or tallit katan, are first tied together in a double knot, thus making eight half-threads. One of the threads, considerably longer than its mates, is employed as the binder for the others. First it is wound seven times around them and secured by a double knot, then it is given, consecutively, eight, eleven, and thirteen windings, and each respective winding is marked off by a double knot. In this way, the fringe has four sections, each one indicated by a double-knot.

It was not accidental that the symbolism of numbers entered into the making of the tzitzit. The Talmudic Cabalists left their mystical imprint upon it in this manner: The total number of windings in a fringe was thirty-nine, and this was the numerical value of the Hebrew letters in the two last words of the Shema: *Adonai Echod* ("the Lord is One").

There can be no question but that the tzitzit were regarded as the external identifying mark of the Jew, and, as such, were recognized by both Jew and Gentile in antiquity. After the Temple was destroyed (in 70 C.E.), they became a symbol also of the collectivity of Israel.

In the prayer caller Ahabah Rabah (With Abounding Love), which precedes the recitation of the Shema, the worshiper is required by tradition to gather up all the four tzitzit on his tallit and to petition God: "O bring us in peace [to Zion] from the four corners of the earth!" Thus the four fringes become poetic symbols of the four corners of the earth—the entire desolate range of the Jewish Dispersion—and not only of God's universal omnipotence.

TZOM GEDALIAH. *See* FASTING AND FAST DAYS.

UGANDA PROPOSAL, THE. *See* THEODOR HERZL (*under* ZIONISM).

UNITED STATES, JEWS IN. *See* JUDAISM IN THE MODERN AGE; PERSECUTION IN "MODERN" DRESS; SYNAGOGUE, THE.

UNITY OF ISRAEL

This is a fundamental tradition which was forged by the character of the Jewish religion and the necessities of history. Jews had to preserve their group solidarity or else disappear from the face of the earth. Upon religious grounds, the unity of Israel was commended as being in imitation of God, for just as God was one so were his people to be one entity. The Talmud warned: "The Messiah will not come to redeem Israel until all Jews stand united in a single fellowship."

But the main catalysts working for Jewish unity were persecution and suffering. The rabbis of ancient times were realists; they stressed the need for Jewish unity and mutual aid as the only ways to cope with a dangerous and hostile world, observing: "Single reeds can be broken, but many reeds bound together in one bundle—who can break them?"

See also FELLOWSHIP IN ISRAEL; MUTUAL AID (*under* CHARITY).

UREN KOIDESH. *See* ARK OF THE COVENANT; ARK OF THE LAW.

USURERS, USURY. *See* MONEYLENDERS; SHYLOCK MYTH, THE.

VIDDUI. *See* CONFESSION.

VISITING THE SICK. *See* SICK, VISITING THE.

VOWEL POINTS. *See* VOWEL-SOUNDS, HEBREW.

VOWEL-SOUNDS, HEBREW

It is a linguistic oddity that most Semitic languages, including Hebrew, suffer from an inadequate vowel system. While it is true that there are five vowel letters in the Hebrew alphabet—*aleph, vav, yod, ayin,* and *hay*—no phonics were indicated for them; there were perhaps just oral traditions, lost to us today, that served as hints for articulation. For reading aloud, special punctuation marks—as was the case in Babylonian, Syriac, and Arabic—were introduced at some unknown point of time in Jewish antiquity. But because there existed no uniformity in vocalization for the vowels, latter-day Rabbinical grammarians and punctuators devoted themselves to the difficult task of disentangling and rediscovering the "pure" line in the tradition of vowel vocalization.

Communication from the Jewish community in Tiberias, Palestine, to the Jewish community of Modena, Italy, asking for financial assistance. (Dr. Abraham Schwadron Collection, Israel.)

It must not be forgotten that, to the believing Jews, Hebrew was not just a language; it was claimed to have had a divine origin; it was the "sacred tongue"—*lashon ha-kodesh*—of Israel in which the repository of all revealed truth—the Torah—had been written down by Moses at the dictation of God. The urgent preoccupation of Rabbinic scholars with the Hebrew vowel-sounds was, therefore, not just a matter of technical research by grammarians; it was looked upon reverently as an essential part of Torah study and knowledge. Moreover, it also had a ritualistic aspect to it: It was necessary to find the "correct" vocalization (*see* MUSICAL ACCENTS) for the weekly portion of the Torah when it was cantillated aloud in the synagogue on the Sabbath and on holy days, a rite that constituted the spiritual climax in the entire prayer service.

The Hebrew vocalization system in use today dates back to the ninth century. It is referred to as the "Tiberian" system because it had been perfected and given authoritative form by the Yeshibah (rabbinical academy) of Tiberias in Palestine, under the guidance of the famous grammarian Aaron ben Asher. In this vocalization system, the vowel sounds are indicated by means of dots and dashes called *nekudot* (meaning "points"; s. *nekudah*). These points are placed above, below, alongside, or inside the letters. There are seven such vowel symbols: *kamatz, patach, cholam, chirik, segol, tzereh,* and *shuruk.*

At a later time, other Hebrew punctuators improved on the Tiberian system. They added new vocalization symbols. These, being placed either above or below the letter, indicated either the thinness or "fullness" of the vowel sound.

For example: the so-called "strong" or "long" vowel required the symbol *above*; the weak or short one *below*.

An unbreakable tradition was established by the Rabbinic Sages during the first centuries of the Common Era: that the Sefer Torah (the parchment Scroll containing the Five Books of Moses, out of which the weekly portion or sidrah is publicly read in the synagogue) must not carry *any* punctuation marks. The same also holds true for the Megillah (the Hebrew parchment scroll of the Book of Esther, which is read aloud on the festival of Purim in the synagogue). All other types of Torah Scrolls and all other religious writings are permitted to be marked with the vowel points.

In modern Hebrew—and also in Yiddish, which employs the Hebrew alphabet—the vocalization points are generally not used, being considered archaic and superfluous.

See also HEBREW LANGUAGE, A HISTORY OF THE; MASORAH; TORAH-READING; TORAH SCROLL.

WAILING WALL, THE. *See* TEMPLE, THE.

WANDERING JEW, THE

Just as the service of love required a special symbolism in Christian practice, so did the service of hatred call for its own. For hating the Jew, the sinister figure of "the Wandering Jew" was invented. How old this legend is—for, unmistakably, it is pure legend—no one can say. The first literary treatment of the story is found in *Flores Historiarum* ("The Flowers of History"), written in 1228 by the English monk Roger of Wendover. This account was given wider dissemination several years later by Roger's successor, Matthew Paris, in his well-know *Chronica Majora*.

The gist of this legend is that, as Jesus was dragging his cross along the Via Dolorosa to the place of his crucifixion, he was stoned, beaten, and jeered at by the Jerusalem mob. Exhausted, he tried to rest and, as the medieval English ballad piteously describes it, sought:

> To ease his burthened soule
> Upon a stone . . .

But the tale has it that the most vindictive among his tormentors, a shoemaker by the name of Joseph Cartaphilus (obviously a fictional character, since there is no mention of him anywhere in the New Testament), heartlessly would not let him pause, crying:

> ". . . Awaye, thou king of Jews,
> Thou shalt not rest thee here;
> Pass on; thy execution place
> Thou shalt not rest thee here;

At which, as he picked up his cross again, Jesus replied:

> ". . . I sure will rest, but thou shalt walk
> And have no journey stayed."

The version given of this by Matthew Paris was the more familiar: "Tarry till I come!"

As has so often happened with purely mythic materials, the story of Joseph Cartaphilus was stupefyingly repeated and reaffirmed as "gospel truth" by a long chain of Christian clerics, theologians, and preachers. And it was further disseminated in every literary and popular medium for centuries by chroniclers, poets, dramatists, and storytellers. It became universally accepted as undisputed "history."

The sinister image of the Wandering Jew, with long gray beard and malevolent eye and with staff in hand, would be conjured up by parents as a bogeyman with which to frighten misbehaving children. In 1826, the poet Heinrich Heine wrote to a friend: "Ah! How deeply rooted is the myth of the Wandering Jew! In the hush of the wooded valley, the Christian mother tells her children this frightening fairy tale. The little ones move fearfully closer to the hearth . . ."

The legend was seemingly based on the astonishing passage in the Gospel of Matthew (16:28) in which Jesus is purported to have said to the mob that jeered him along the way to his execution: "Verily I say unto you, there be some standing here which shall not taste of death till they see the Son of man coming in his kingdom." It is parenthetically to be observed that, even if the disciple of Jesus was the source for this alleged remark, it does seem incredible and inconsistent that such a vindictive curse could possibly have been uttered—whatever the provocation—by the same teacher of ethics whose evangel of redemption breathes only love and forgiveness for all mankind! But, nonetheless, since the kernel for the Wandering Jew story was to be found in an authoritative scriptural source, the legend, easily concocted, was soon enough comfortably transformed into a true historic "fact."

Repeatedly, during the Middle Ages and later, there were reports, "substantiated" by some of the highest Christian ecclesiastical authorities, that the Wandering Jew had been seen in this or that place in Europe. From 1547, when allegedly he had made his appearance in Hamburg, Germany, until 1790, when he was "spotted" on the streets in Newcastle, England, he was said to have made eighteen appearances. It is amusing to note that in 1868 (the last time he was "seen"), the Wandering Jew was paying a visit to an Irish Mormon by the name of O'Grady in the United States!

The perhaps ingenuous-sounding question arises: If the Wandering Jew lived more than nineteen centuries ago, how could he have been "seen" at such late dates? The legend itself, of course, carries the explanation. The curse Jesus supposedly laid on Joseph Cartaphilus was that he not die but be doomed to drag out his wretched existence through the ages, as a wanderer on the face of the earth, despised, persecuted, and shunned as a pariah until the Second Coming of Jesus. Why was it found so necessary to perpetuate this legend? The answer is obvious. It was to justify the "righteous" hatred for the Jews by Christians and to give a moral validity to their persecution. This was not only a doctrinal teaching of the Church as laid down in its canon law and reaffirmed repeatedly by many Councils, popes, bishops, preachers, and theologians, but it was made also the state policy of almost every ruler in Christendom.

The "Wandering Jew" legend, based on a falsification of Christ's life and teachings, actually became a cornerstone of anti-Semitism. Since Joseph Cartaphilus was metamorphosed into *every* Jew by the fanatical and the unthinking, many Christians excused their anti-Semitism in their own consciences by telling themselves they were only engaging in the "imitation of Christ" by working for the fulfillment of "his" curse on the "Christ-killers" in everyday life. Therefore, they concluded, to hate Jews and to persecute them were acts of Christian virtue.

See also CHRISTIANITY, JEWISH ORIGINS OF; CHURCH AND PERSECUTION; MASSACRES; PERSECUTION IN "MODERN" DRESS; POGROMS IN SLAVIC LANDS.

WARSAW GHETTO, BATTLE OF THE. *See* NAZIS, THE.

WEDDING CUSTOMS

Notwithstanding the strong religious coloration of Jewish family life, in Rabbinic law marriage was considered to be essentially a civil institution. In consequence, Jewish wedding-customs, often patterning themselves on those prevailing among Gentiles, have varied greatly throughout the world. They give a clear demonstration of the astonishing extent of the diffusion of folkways among peoples and religions.

In former times—but not so long ago at that—the Jewish wedding was preceded within an interval of from one month to a year by the ceremony of betrothal or engagement, called in Hebrew *erusin* or, more popularly, *tena'im* (which literally means "conditions"). These so-called conditions concerned the premarital arrangements that had been entered into by the parents of the bride and groom and fixed the nadan (dowry) and also the penalties for any breach of the agreement's conditions. The tena'im gave both parties to the contract sufficient time for calm reconsideration before they plunged into the finality of marriage.

The betrothal naturally involved a considerable expense for all concerned. For one thing, in earlier times it required, in part or in whole, the payment of the traditional mohar (the price of betrothal). This was actually a disguised and later form of the primitive practice of "wife-purchase." Then there was the additional expense incurred by the groom's father for giving the kenasmahl or "Penalty Feast" (*kenas* in Hebrew means "penalty"; *mahl* is the German for "meal"), the traditional betrothal-meal eaten by the Ashkenazim since the Middle Ages. Custom and etiquette also made mandatory the exchange of gifts between the engaged couple. It became almost obligatory for the groom to present his bride with a siddur (prayer book), a sash, a veil, fine hair-combs, and a gold engagement ring but, unlike the ostentatious practice of our day, one that was without any gem. In her turn, the bride gave to her groom a Passover Haggadah and a tallit (prayer shawl) which he was to wear in the synagogue for the first time the morning after the wedding. In more recent centuries, the bride's gift to the groom was usually a gold or silver watch and chain.

By the eleventh century, because of the general impoverishment and persecution suffered by European Jewry, it had become expedient to merge the betrothal and the wedding ceremonies and to perform them in sequence on the same day. Even so, the lavish scale of rejoicing for seven days that had been customary everywhere among Jews since the Biblical age, prompted latter-day religious authorities to place realistic, even arbitrary, limits upon wedding festivities. In 1637, for example, a communal law was enacted for the Jews of Lithuania that required the local rabbi and the elders of each town to fix the number of the wedding guests that were to be invited, allowing "for every individual according to his financial capabilities." Moreover, in order to curb the needless expense attendant on feeding the ever present wedding-crashers, the regulation specified: "No one is allowed to come to a wedding-feast unless he has been invited by the shammes [beadle]!"

Medieval marriage ceremony. To the right, a klezmer (Jewish folk musician) plays a wedding tune on the lute. Next to him stands the rabbi with the wine goblet for the recitation of the benediction. (From the Second Haggadah, Germanischer Nat. Museum, Nuremberg.)

Since every marriage worked for the biological perpetuation of the Jewish people, for many centuries it was celebrated with enthusiasm by the entire community both as a religious and as a patriotic duty. Therefore, an unusual importance was lent to the wedding procession that wound its merry way through the streets. A well-remembered Talmudic tradition had it that in the First Temple, which King Solomon had erected, there was a special Gate of the Bridegroom. There Jerusalemites would gather to watch the wedding processions enter and depart. When the groom appeared, they directed to him the customary blessing for progeny: "May God, Whose throne is set in this house, rejoice your heart with sons and daughters!"

The "sharing" in the happiness of bride and groom was valued as an act of singular merit—a mitzvah. The greatest honor was to be bestowed upon the couple on their wedding day. To this end, some of the Sages were in the habit of adjourning their classes at the yeshibah (rabbinical academy) and, accompanied by their students, following behind the wedding party in procession.

There was, understandably, a great diversity in the character of wedding processions. Jews adopted some of the local Gentile folkways in different regions and culture periods. Thus, under Hellenistic political-cultural hegemony, Jewish weddings, both in Judea itself and throughout the countries of the Diaspora, were celebrated in the Greek style. Bride and groom, temporarily invested with the symbolism of royalty, wore reed or floral crowns, and were garlanded with myrtle leaves and roses. After the Destruction of the Second Temple, in 70 C.E., the Rabbis frowned upon

Groom, wearing the compulsory Judenhut *or "Jew's hat" places the ring on the bride's finger. In lieu of a veil, the bride wears a blindfold. (From a machzor [festival prayer-book] of Germany, early 15th century.)*

the wearing of the myrtle garland; they considered it a violation of the duty to remember and mourn for the devastated sanctuary.

In Augustan Rome it was customary for the Jewish girl companions of the bride to escort the bride and groom in procession while holding lighted torches in imitation of the Roman *faces nuptiales*. Centuries later, it was noted by Rabbi Nathan ben Yechiel of Rome (1035-1106) that sending up fireworks was a festive feature of Jewish wedding processions in Arab countries in his time.

The Rabbinic law required of bride and groom that they fast on their wedding day. This was to be in atonement for all their sins in the past so that they might start their married life "with a clean slate." During the Minchah (Afternoon) service on his wedding day, the groom, and frequently also the bride, would recite before the worshipers in the synagogue the Confession of Sins (Viddui) from the Yom Kippur liturgy.

Like the ancient Romans, who contracted no marriages during the Month of May because they considered that time unpropitious, the Jews also forebore from celebrating weddings during approximately the same period, between the festivals of Passover and Shabuot. Following the example of the German-Christians in whose midst they lived, the Jews of Germany, beginning with the Middle Ages, arranged for weddings only at the time of the full moon. In similar fashion but in a reverse direction, adopting the custom from the ancient Greeks, the medieval Spanish Jews (who were the inheritors of Hellenistic-Arab folkways) held weddings only at the time of the new moon.

Among German as well as among East European Jews, Orthodox weddings took place most of the time on Friday. There were two principal reasons for preferring this day; one was conscious and the other obscure and indirect. Because Friday was followed by the Sabbath—the day of rest for the Jews—the entire community had ample opportunity for publicly rejoicing with bride and groom. Incongruously (for they had not the slightest inkling of its origin), the medieval Jews of Germany followed the custom of Christian-Germans who got married on Friday, the auspicious name-day of Freya, their pre-Christian Teutonic goddess of marriage-vows and procreation. The Germanic acculturation of the Jews living in the Rhineland towns was far greater than is generally realized.

During the fifteenth century, the ceremonial procedures and protocol for Jewish weddings had been fully charted among the Ashkenazim in Central and Eastern Europe and they were generally scrupulously observed in the latter region until the close of the nineteenth century. Traditional Chasidic and Ultra-Orthodox circles still faithfully adhere to them, but the encroachments of assimilation and modernism are rapidly causing their disappearance, in the United States and Canada, especially.

The pattern for the Jewish wedding among the Yiddish-speaking Jews of Central and Eastern Europe in former days was quite uniform. At dawn on the Friday of the wedding, the groom was escorted in festive procession from the home of his parents to the courtyard of the synagogue by his kinfolk, the rabbi and other communal dignitaries, and his friends and fellow townsmen. At the head marched the klezmorim (the ghetto folk-musicians) playing the gay tunes especially associated with Jewish weddings. In earlier times, lighted torches were carried by the wedding guests, in part for the celebration itself, and in part to illuminate the half-dark of daybreak.

Taking ceremonious leave of the groom and his family before the synagogue, the procession then turned around and hurried to the home of the bride. She too was escorted in the same gay manner as the groom to the synagogue courtyard. When bride and groom met, they clasped hands in a symbolic joining, at which all present showered them with wheat kernels or grains of barley. Three times the celebrants called out to the bridal pair in the words of the Scriptural formula: "Be fruitful and multiply!" This fertility-wishing custom expressed by symbolism is diffused among all peoples, no matter how advanced they may think themselves to be. In the United States, for example, a Gentile bride and groom are usually showered with rice. Among Jews, the custom, now discarded (except among the Ultra-Orthodox), of setting up the chuppah (wedding canopy) under the open sky in the synagogue courtyard also carried a fertility symbolism. It was meant to recall the promise that God had made to Abraham: "Thus shall thy children be, like the stars of Heaven." Also when the veil was placed upon the bride, her woman companions fervently chanted the Scriptural wish:

> "Our sister, be thou the mother of thousands of myriads;
> God make thee as Sarah, Rebekah, Rachel, and Leah!"

Centuries ago, a hen and a rooster were carried before the bride and groom in the procession as a fertility symbol. Upon the conclusion of the nuptial rite, these were flying over the chuppah with a cluck and a cackle. And since a prime symbol of reproduction (because of its roe) is the fish, the Sefaradic bride in the Near East and the Balkans was required by an ancient custom to go through the solo convolutions of the Fish Dance before the assembled wedding guests. Fish-conscious, too, for the same reason, were Russian and Polish Jews. Thus in a culinary rite of sympathetic magic—of achieving like results with like means!—the bridal couple would dine on fish the day after the wedding. Another fertility folkway was that of jumping over a bowl containg live fish.

Some quaint ways were followed in East European regions with regard to the bride. They reflected unmistakably

Bearing lighted braided candles, the father of the groom and another kinsman lead the groom ceremoniously to the chuppah (bridal canopy). Note the shtreimel (the traditional fur-trimmed hat worn by the Chasidim on Sabbath and festive occasions). Modern, New York City. (YIVO.)

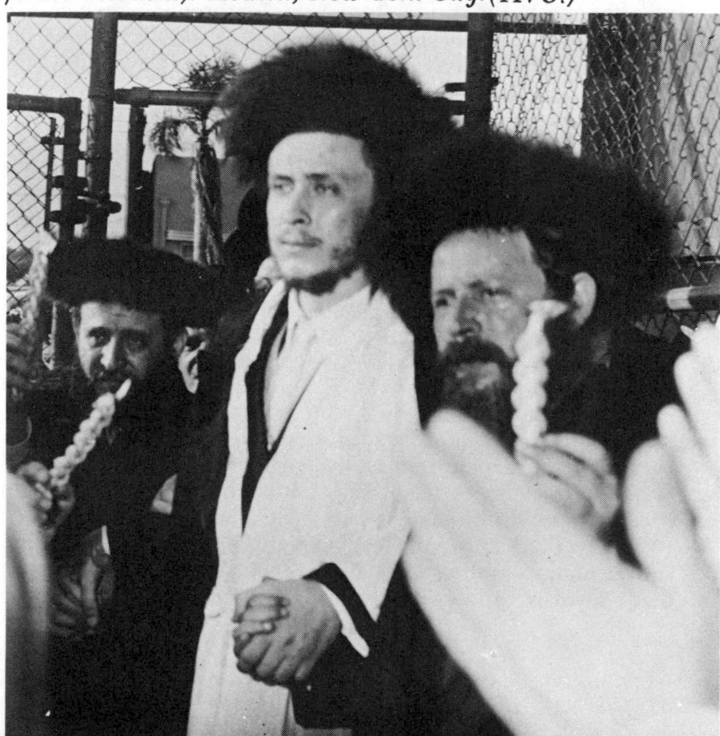

Polish, Ukrainian, Russian, Romanian, and Lithuanian peasant customs. There was, for instance, the widespread ceremony called in Yiddish *bazetzen di kaleh*—"seating the bride." This was performed half in make-believe play and half in deadly earnest; it had the charming quality of innocence present in all symbolic dramatizations of folk custom. In a manner of speaking, it represented the bride's sorrowful "enthronement" by her girl companions, wishing her sad farewell now that she was leaving their carefree maiden ranks forever. While they clustered around her, they held lighted candles in their hands. The klezmorim played dirgeful music throughout the invariably poignant ceremony of cropping off the bride's tresses—a bitter ordeal for every young girl. For these promptly substituted the sheitel (*which see*), the wig of medieval provenance that Jewish custom had made obligatory for the married woman in Germany and in the Slavic regions.

This melancholy interlude concluded, it now became the turn of the badchan that traditional and indispensable folk-bard of the ghetto and the improvisator who entertained at weddings to sing for the bride. His performance was called *bazingen di kaleh*—"singing to the bride." The bard broke into a lament keyed in a wailing minor; it was part song and part declamation. Extemporizing as he went along, he poured out a torrent of Yiddish words in a torrent of rhyming doggerel. He reminded the kaleh that now her unclouded girlhood had come to an end at last; thenceforth, she would have to wrestle with the serious anxieties and responsibilities of married life.

Already weakened by her long fast that day and unstrung by the many excitements of the wedding preparations and of her imminent marriage, the combination of the dismal tune and the melancholy reminders of the badchan made the bride break into sobs and her womenfolk weep along with her in sympathy.

At this juncture, custom considered it high time to dissipate the tragic mood that had been so deliberately induced in the bride. The klezmorim knew their cue well; they struck up gay Jewish folk dance tunes. The badchan, in the classic manner of the medieval shpielmann (*see* MERRYMAKERS, TRADITIONAL JEWISH), whose lineal descendant he was culturally, cut a few comic capers and flung out personally directed quips and jests with a dazzling rhyming virtuosity amidst the general hilarity. Everyone now went to great pains to drive away the bride's gloom. (It should be of more than casual interest that at Ukrainian peasant weddings, until a time not too remote, preceding the nuptial ceremony by the village priest, the bride, too, was "enthroned" by her girl companions. To the accompaniment of fiddlers, they too sang to her in doleful chorus and, with words and tune of a similar tearful character to that wailed by the badchan, they made her sob, also.)

Another Jewish folk custom of undetermined origin—and one still observed by the Ultra-Orthodox of East European descent—was called *badecken di kaleh*—"covering (i.e., veiling) the bride." In celebration of this, the groom, preceded by the overworked but tireless klezmorim playing wedding tunes, was escorted in procession to the bride. The two mothers of the bridal couple (they are called in Yiddish and only in connection with their special role as "in-laws" *machutènèstehs*, s. *machutènèsteh;* the two fathers are similarly *machutonim*, s. *mechuten*) hold a dish between them filled with raisins and nuts and covered with a large silk napkin. The officiating rabbi and the groom each lift a corner of the napkin and cover with it the bride's head and face. At this the two mothers, joined by all those who are present, pelt bride and groom with the raisins and nuts. (Whatever other rationalized explanation may be given for this custom, to anthropologists it is well known as a practice that in many diverse cultures is considered an effective protection against evil spirits.) Everybody present cries *"Mazel tov!"* ("Good luck"). The Sefaradim of Spanish-Portugese descent say *simmon tov* ("A good omen"). Members of the family and the wedding guests now dance a turn each with the bride. The traditional dances at Jewish weddings have been the *Mazel-tov Tanz*, the *Kosher Tanz*, and the *Machutonim Tanz*.

A religious ceremony customary among the Jews of Central and Eastern Europe—one that, with some variations, is still being followed by the Orthodox today—is performed by the rabbi while the bride and groom are standing under the chuppah. In ancient times, the chuppah, made of colorful woven fabric and enclosed on all sides, had served as the nuptial chamber for bride and groom. But in the evolutionary refining process of Jewish life, the chuppah was transformed into a canopy (similar to the baldachin, the ceremonial contraption under which great dignitaries sat in state during the Middle Ages). It was supported at each of its four corners by an ornamental pole. The material of its "roof" was made of silk, satin, or velvet, and embroidered upon it were the Hebrew rubrics: "The Voice of the Groom —The Voice of the Bride"; "The Sound of Joy—The Sound of Gladness."

The special role of the *unterfihrer* (Yiddish for "escorts") comes to attention here. Selected for this honor were two married couples; one served as escort for the bride, the other for the groom. To the sound of a stirring tune by the klezmorim band, the groom, flanked by his father and mother and unterfihrer, was conducted with ceremony to the chuppah. Immediately after, and with similar pomp, the bride was led to the chuppah by her father and mother and unterfihrer. She took her place at the right side of the groom in fulfillment of the verse of the ancient singer of Zion: "At thy right hand doth stand the queen in gold of Ophir." (Psalms 45:10.) For in Jewish tradition it is as a royal personage going to her coronation that the young bride appears on her wedding day.

Heavily veiled, the bride is led to the chuppah (marriage canopy), flanked by her mother and another relative holding lighted braided candles. Modern, New York City. (YIVO.)

The rabbi thereupon commenced to intone the prefatory prayer service, which includes the recitation of a Psalm of Thanksgiving (Psalm 100). Then, raising a goblet of wine, he pronounced the blessings in the rite of betrothal. The bride and groom each sipped from it.

It is still customary at traditionally conducted ceremonies that, as the rabbi chants the introductory prayer of betrothal, the bride, her parents, the unterfihrer, and other close kin, holding lighted candles in their hands, make seven circuits around the groom. (To draw the mystic circle in a human ring seven times was an old protective practice of the ancient Cabalists for thwarting the malicious designs of any demons who are reputedly jealous of the happiness of bride and groom.)

As the groom slips the wedding ring on the foregfinger of the bride's right hand, he recites the ancient formula of marriage: "Behold, thou art consecrated unto me by this ring, according to the law of Moses and of Israel. (*Harrey aht mekudeshet lee betabaat zu kedat Mosheh ve'Yisrael*)" The first written trace of this formula is found in the apocryphal Book of Tobit, which dates back to the second century B.C.E. There (in Chapter 7, Verse 13) Raguel "called his daughter Sarah, and he took her by the hand and gave her to Tobit to be his wife, and said: "Here, take her, according to the Law of Moses . . .'"

It was made mandatory during the Maccabean period that the rabbi read aloud to the bride the terms of the ketubah, the marriage contract which the early Rabbinic Sages of Judea had instituted in order to afford the woman, who occupied an inferior position in the male-dominated society, some financial and legal protection were she, in time, to be-

Embroidered chuppah (canopy or baldachin) under which the marriage ceremony is performed. Germany, 1733.

The marshalik or badchan (the traditional merrymaker at Jewish weddings) diverts the guests with Yiddish quips and ribbing in doggerel rhyme to the accompaniment of the klezmorin (the folk musicians of the ghetto). Galicia, late 19th century. (YIVO.)

Marriage ceremony under the chuppah (canopy) outside the synagogue. Galicia, 19th century.

come widowed or divorced. (The reading of the ketubah is still done today.) In addition to the bride and groom, two responsible men then witnessed the document by affixing their signatures to it.

With this delicate matter out of the way, the rabbi raises a second glass of wine and recites the Seven (Nuptial) Blessings (Shebah Berachot). Among these is found a striking eulogy addressed to God for making possible the happiness of marital life: "You did create joy and gladness, bridegroom and bride, mirth and exaltation, pleasure and delight, love, comradeship, peace and fellowship . . . Blessed are you, O Lord, who makes the groom to rejoice with the bride!"

The rabbi passes the wine to the bridal couple to drink. The groom breaks the glass underfoot amidst the general rejoicing to the cries of "*Mazel tov!*" or "*Simmon tov!*"

The breaking of the wineglass—seemingly a ritualistic act—has greatly puzzled students of Jewish folkways. With the discreet reservation that there is a possibility that this custom could have had a primitive origin, it is to be assumed that, at a later date, it must have acquired a more spiritual symbolism. This is to be surmised from the frequent reminders in Jewish religious writings that, even at the dizzy height of his happiness, the human being was to recall that joy is ephemeral, like a passing dream. And, therefore, in conformity with the instruction of the Psalmist, the Sages of the Talmud cautioned that man should always "rejoice with trembling" (Psalms 2:11). Perhaps that is the reason why, in some places, it became customary at weddings to pick up the shattered pieces of the wineglass (or the earthenware goblet that was used in its stead) and carefully preserve them against the day of burial of one or the other of the bridal pair. Then the pieces would serve as the shards laid over the dead eyes, there to remain until the day of the Resurrection.

Many are the proofs in Rabbinic literature of this sober assumption. The Talmud records that, when the Babylonian Sage Ashi (fourth century) observed the unbridled hilarity at his son's wedding, he was filled with consternation: "And he brought a very fine glass and broke it, and they became sad." A similar reaction had Chamnuna, the third-century Rabbinic teacher. Once, when he was asked to sing at a boisterous wedding-feast, he complied with an elegiac hymn:

"Woe to us for we must die!
Woe to us for we must die!"

And the wedding guests, startled but sobered, had no choice but to respond with the pious chorus:

"Blessed be the Truth!
Blessed be the Torah!
Our shield and our buckler."

It must have been following the Destruction of the Temple that the breaking of the wedding glass or earthenware goblet by the groom took on an additional depressing symbolism. The Rabbinic Sages had decreed that, on all occasions of rejoicing, the Jew must never allow himself to forget the desolation of Zion—his "chiefest grief"—and the breaking of the glass served as such a reminder.

On the morning following the wedding day, it being the Sabbath, the religious and community ties of the groom were made most manifest. For then when the groom entered the synagogue, to which he was escorted by his male companions, he was conducted with ceremony by the elders to a seat of honor next to the Aron ha-Kodesh (Ark of the Law). This was to be the first occasion on which he was permitted to put on the tallit which his bride had given him after their betrothal, for it could be worn by married men only. Wrapped in its flowing folds, the groom ascended the three steps to the bema (the platform) to read aloud from

A marriage ceremony in the synagogue courtyard. In the foreground, following an ancient superstition, children scramble for nuts thrown to them by women in white, to drive away evil demons from the bridal pair. (Painting by Stryowski, Galicia, 19th century.)

the weekly portion of the Torah. Thereupon, the entire congregation, as acknowledgment that it had a fraternal share in his joy, burst into song. One of the most tender of these Hebrew medieval wedding odes had for its opening line:

> Rejoice, O Bridegroom, in the wife of your youth, your comrade!

Jewish weddings of modern times have accommodated themselves to the drastically changed circumstances of Jewish life and to the prevailing tastes and customs in Western culture. There is no longer any fixed ceremony. The fragmentization of Western Jewry into different religious divisions—Ultra-Orthodox, Modern Orthodox, Chasidic, Neo-Chasidic, Conservative, and Reform—has led each to evolve its own wedding pattern. In the United States and Canada, for example, there has taken place a strange but inevitable acculturation of traditional Christian customs. These have affected the character of the various Jewish wedding-ceremonies as well as the manner in which they are celebrated. Furthermore, there have appeared in them entirely new accretions. These seem to have had no link with the past but have grown out of the special material and cultural conditions of Jewish middle-class life in America.

Jewish communal wedding rings. In European countries, in former times, rings like these, which were owned by the congregation, were used at all Jewish weddings during the ceremony. (Courtesy of Joseph B. Horwitz Judaica Collection, Cleveland.)

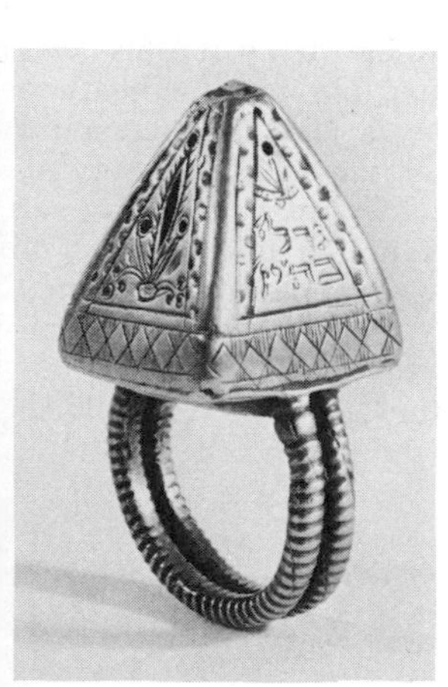

Merely to indicate a few of the accommodations and changes that have taken place in recent decades: The bridal shower and the double-ring ceremony, characteristics of marriage practices among Christians, have been widely adopted by Jews. Equally striking is the assimilation into the Jewish nuptial rite of the almost identical question put by the Christian minister to the bride and groom:

> Rabbi [to the Groom]: Do you of your own free will and consent, take ——— to be your wife; and do you promise to love, honor and cherish her throughout life? If so, answer *yes*.

Reform Judaism and, to a far less extent, Conservative Judaism, have dispensed with the traditional chuppah altogether. In its place, in many instances, has been substituted a white floral arrangement. Gone, too, from any but the weddings of the Orthodox, are the unterfihrer of old, they having been displaced by the bridesmaids and the best man. Dispensed with, as well, have been the seven days of festivity (required by custom in the olden days), the seven magical circuits made around the groom under the chuppah, and the recitation of the Seven (Nuptial) Benedictions.

Except among the Orthodox, the bride and groom no longer fast before the ceremony, and the ketubah, the contract containing the terms of the marriage settlement, is neither written nor read anymore except among the traditionalists. Only at Orthodox weddings can one still hear the old folk-tunes played by klezmorim, but these are considerably "jazzed-up" and denatured to flatter current popular tastes. But even at these weddings, incongruous elements have crept in, such as the solo-singing of "O Promise Me" and "I Love You Truly." In place of the spirited and melodious folk-tunes that used to accompany bride and groom to the chuppah in former times, one can now hear only the wedding marches of Mendelssohn and Wagner, made conventional and indispensable by general usage.

Yet this much can be said about contemporary Jewish weddings. Although the recent changes and borowings have been many and astonishingly transforming, some things, nevertheless, have remained unaltered and seemingly indestructible. These are the traditional Jewish familial attachment, the emotional warmth and the expansive conviviality of plain folk—all values and customs carried over from the social-cultural heritage of Jewish life in past centuries. They have made, and still are making, of the Jewish chasseneh (wedding), in most instances, a glowing experience for bride and groom, and a thing of joy for everybody else present.

See also FAMILY, THE; FAMILY RELATIONS, TRADITIONAL PATTERNS OF; KETUBAH; KLEZMER; MARRIAGE; MARRIAGE AND SEX; MERRYMAKERS, TRADITIONAL JEWISH; MONOGAMY; SHEITEL; WOMAN, THE TREATMENT OF.

WIG. *See* SHEITEL.

WISDOM. *See* CHACHMAH.

WISDOM BOOKS, THE. *See* BIBLE, THE.

WIVES AND HUSBANDS. *See* FAMILY RELATIONS, TRADITIONAL PATTERNS OF.

WOMAN, THE TREATMENT OF

It is no exaggeration to say that, for most of the time, Jewish women fared better at the hands of their menfolk than did the women of other peoples. This was especially true during those fervent centuries of Hellenistic times, when the Talmud was being created. It marked, among Jews, the highest development of individual and social morality, of which the fundamental theme was that all life, having been created by God, was sacred. Joined to it was this corollary: that the conduct of the individual, as well as of all society, must be governed by truth, justice, and love for one's fellow men. And the just treatment of the woman was included.

George Foot Moore, the Christian historian of the religious civilization of the ancient Jews, considered that the legal status of the woman in Biblical times "compared to its advantage with that of contemporary civilization." Furthermore, said he, "the social and the religious position of women in Judaism . . . is itself a moral achievement, and fundamental in the morals of the Jewish family."

Certainly, it is not possible to pretend that the position of the Jewish woman remained permanently fixed by Biblical and Rabbinic law, or even by custom. Nonetheless, for much of the time and in the greatest number of far-flung places where Jews lived, they succeeded in maintaining their traditional attitude of respect, gentleness, and humanity for the woman. This regard, incidentally (not that it is not widely present among other peoples), has remained a characteristic of Jewish family life. In the fourth century, the Church Father, Jerome, even chided the Jews for "pampering" their wives and allowing them too much freedom.

Truth to tell, the attitude of her menfolk toward the Jewish woman was at no time uniformly enlightened in every community—nor, in fact, even in the same community. As in every other society, there went on a continuing struggle in Jewish society between the "fundamentalists" and the "modernists," between the upholders of the *status quo ante* and those who believed in change. For that reason, the position of the woman fluctuated widely in terms of her social, legal, and religious rights. The moral values and the social outlook upon which they were based, naturally rose and fell with the historic tides.

It cannot be stressed enough that, for an incredibly long time-span, the Jews existed as a global people, living dispersed everywhere. For that very reason, the respect and regard the woman was able to awaken for herself in the Jewish masculine breast varied noticeably in different countries and during different culture-periods. It is not to be overlooked that, even during its most rigorously segregated ghetto-existence, the Jewish community everywhere was exposed to all the influences, whether for good or for ill, that stemmed from the non-Jewish world outside. In consequence, the esteem, or perhaps the lack of it, for womankind that prevailed among other peoples, also had a certain impact on the traditional Jewish attitude itself.

Comparing the position of the Jewish woman of Biblical times with that of her sex among the Philistines, Phoenicians, Babylonians, and Egyptians, we find that the non-Jewish woman, by and large, was condemned by law, religion, and social custom to an ignominious—often degraded—role in the home as well as in society. Recognition of her *as a human being* was an exceptional occurrence. Most often, together with the ass, the ox, and the camel, she was treated by her husband as a possession or as an economic asset, and sometimes with even less consideration than he usually gave his animals. She was a bearer of burdens and of children, and always of sorrows. Almost in the literal sense, she was bought and sold like any slave or chattel. Though marriage by purchase or capture was common in the early tribal days of Israel, it was finally forbidden by Mosaic law.

Even among the latter-day Greeks and Romans, who were fully justified in boasting the most advanced material and intellectual cultures in antiquity, the woman was quite generally despised, although, it must be added, she was treated by the men of her society with less grossness and with far greater gentleness than were the women of other peoples. The great respect, for instance, that Roman tradition accorded Cornelia, the noble-minded mother of the Gracchi, was quite exceptional. No less a person than Aristotle, the supreme Greek philosophic genius, uttered the disdainful attitude of the Hellenic world for womankind when he observed: "Man has the courage to command, woman has the courage to serve." And serve the Grecian woman certainly did; she was *a servant!* It has sometimes been pointed out that the grandeur of Greek civilization was made possible by the toil of millions of slaves—and, one might add, of the additional millions of Grecian wives and daughters as well.

Indignation has frequently been sounded at the gratuitous "insult" to womankind found among the early morning blessings in the Hebrew liturgy. Pious Jews have been reciting it daily in their prayers ever since the second century C.E. After first expressing his gratitude to the Creator (that he had "not made me a heathen" and "not made me a bondman"), the worshiper goes on to exult: "Blessed art thou, O Lord our God, King of the Universe, who hast not made me a woman!" It is to be inferred that many a contemporary of Rabbi Meir, the author of the blessings, must have raised a disapproving eyebrow at its inclusion in the prayer service, for we come across Rabbi Meir's own defense of it in the Talmud. Several later religious authorities tried to elaborate and improve on Meir's uneasy explanation. Continuing confusion and criticism must have called it forth. Undoubtedly, it was found necessary to reconcile the controversial blessing with the fundamental Jewish view of the woman as laid down in the Book of Genesis (5:1-2): "In the day that God created man, in the likeness of God made He him; male and female created He them and blessed them." Thus Jewish tradition states categorically that not only man but also woman was fashioned by God in his own divine image, and that he had placed upon her, as well as upon man, the seal of his blessing.

The intent of the "blessing," explained the Rabbis, was not to express disdain for the woman, nor for the heathen and the slave with whom her name is joined. How could any Jew be advised to feel scorn for the heathen? For he, like the Jew, was a child of God. Certainly the Jews, of all peoples, could not be permitted to fall into the sin of contempt for the unfortunate slave, for never were they allowed to forget that once, in Egypt, they too had eaten of the bread of affliction in the House of Bondage. And as for the Jewish woman—was it possible that any Jew would wish to derogate her who was likened to the prophetess Deborah, who was called *em b'Yisrael*—"mother in Israel?" Perhaps a more satisfactory answer could be found elsewhere, in the preachment of an ethical teacher in the Midrash: "I call heaven and earth to witness that, whether it be Jew or heathen, man or woman, freedman or slave—only according to their actions does the Divine Presence [Shechinah] rest upon them."

With regard, specifically, to the daily prayer concerning women (mentioned above), the religious teachers asserted that this was merely intended to express man's gratitude to God for having made him a man so that he might enjoy the privilege from which the Jewish woman, like the heathen and the slave, was exempted—of fulfilling the numerous positive precepts of the Torah. The woman's deprivation of this privilege was based upon the Rabbinic assumption that the man and the woman had different, though complementary, roles to play in life. The man was to be the provider and the active preserver of the Torah and the religious values; the woman was to be the preserver of the home and the teacher of her children in righteous living. By excusing the woman from the arduous and time-consuming performance of the positive precepts of the Torah, argued the Rabbis, she would be free to give her undivided attention to the equally necessary and sacred tasks of the home.

However persuasive these arguments might be, it still is not possible to overlook the fact that the Jewish woman was linked, in an excluding and negative sense, with the heathen and the slave. The effect of this exclusion, whatever the reasons, was to assign to her an inferior role in religious life as well as in society. She could not be a member of a minyan (the quorum of ten required for public worship), nor was she allowed to read from the Sefer Torah (Scroll of the Torah) before the congregation. Neither was she permitted to lead the prayer service, nor perform any public congregational function.

Similar religious discriminations, it should be pointed out, also prevailed—and still do prevail—in the Catholic Church, where, for example, the woman is excluded from all priestly functions, even being deemed undesirable for assisting at the altar. It could hardly be held irrelevant to note that the Church Fathers held even more disconcerting views about the woman than did their Rabbinic contemporaries. Their conception of her was based on the Biblical myth of creation. It was that of Eve, the seductive daughter of the earth who, by means of her innate cunning and lack of scruple, enticed Adam into eating of the forbidden fruit of knowledge, thereby bringing about his fall from virtue. This was considered, in Christian as well as Jewish tradition, a catastrophic event for the whole human race, for the expulsion from the Garden of Eden meant that man's enjoyment of all innocent bliss and a perfect state of grace had come to an end forevermore. Although this primitive view colored some areas of Jewish Rabbinic thinking—in particular, those of the pre-Christian Apocalyptic writers and the medieval and later Cabalists—among the Jews, it never was given the primary importance that it held in Christian doctrine. The Church Fathers elevated Adam's Fall into a cosmic tragedy, and upon it, they built the fundamental dogma of Original Sin, with all its attendant implications of woman's intrinsic moral unworthiness. This attitude is especially made vivid in the denunciation of woman by Tertullian, a near-contemporary of Rabbi Meir. In his treatise, "On Ornaments of Woman," he cries out: "O woman! You should always wear mourning or rags, in order to show your penitence, weeping and atoning for the crime of having corrupted mankind! You are the one who first tasted of the forbidden fruit, and transgressed the law of God. You seduced man whom the Devil himself dared not approach. Because of you, O woman, our Saviour Jesus had to die!"

It is worthy of repetition to note that the laws and opinions regulating Jewish life and conduct and found recorded in Bible and Talmud were not created all at once. They were the accretions of many centuries, so that new and more enlightened ideas stood side by side with primitive and backward ones. It is one of the less attractive features of all laws and codes that even those that fall into disuse are often kept on the statute books. This is even truer of religious laws because of the odor of sanctity attached to them. Often we stumble in the sacred literature of the Jews upon laws, regulations, and opinions about woman that are primitive and harsh, and, therefore, impossible to reconcile with the traditional Jewish evaluation of her, which is enlightened and which accords her *full equality with man as a human being.* Rather, it is the sum total of all the progressive laws and opinions about her, by far more numerous and fundamental than the negative and benighted ones, that constitutes the traditional and, therefore, dominant valuation of the Jewish woman. Furthermore, very often where the law erred, the humanizing force of folk custom entered as a corrective.

See also CHALITZAH; DIVORCE; FAMILY, THE; FAMILY RELATIONS, TRADITIONAL PATTERNS OF; MARRIAGE; MARRIAGE AND SEX.

WORKER, THE

Jewish law, both Biblical and Rabbinic, went to extraordinary pains to protect the worker, standing alone and quite helpless in ancient society, from exploitation and mistreatment. "The worker's rights take priority over all other rights," ruled the Sages of the Talmud. This was as much as laying down the principle that human rights took precedence over property rights. For that reason, the Jewish law ringed numerous safeguards around the worker's human personality, aside from any considerations about his toil, wages, and other conditions of labor. Many are the references in Jewish religious literature extolling the spiritual and social importance of work and of the worker. Jesus ben Sirach taught in his Wisdom Book, Ecclesiasticus:

> But they will maintain the fabric of the world,
> And in the handiwork of their craft is their prayer.

Why this grave and hitherto unprecedented concern with workers? A cardinal doctrine in the Jewish religion represented God to be just and merciful—i.e., humane—toward man. And since man was duty bound to emulate the Deity in all of his attributes of righteousness, Jewish law required that the worker—the humblest in the scale of social importance and, therefore, the most exposed to oppression—receive full protection from his masters.

The Rabbinic teachers of social ethics pleaded in the Talmud: "The poor man ascends the highest scaffoldings, climbs the tallest trees. For what does he expose himself to such dangers, if not for the purpose of earning his living? Be careful, therefore, not to oppress him in his wages, for it means his very life."

In ancient Jewish society, the worker was almost exclusively a day-laborer, although there were occasions when workers were hired for longer periods, but the law of the Mishnah (the code of the Oral Traditions; *see* MISHNAH, *under* TALMUD, THE) opposed any work-agreement between master and servant for more than three years. This prohibition was initiated in order that the suspicion might not arise that such an agreement was a form of voluntary slavery—an arrangement repugnant to the libertarian sensibilities of Jews.

During Biblical and post-Biblical times, the law was adamant in its insistence that the wages of the worker be paid promptly and in full at the conclusion of each work day. The Rabbinic law even guaranteed it to him. Leviticus 19:13 had stated the terms originally in precise language:

". . . the wages of a hired servant [i.e., a worker] shall not abide with thee all night until the morning." For an employer to postpone payment was to violate the commandment: "Thou shalt not oppress thy neighbor, nor rob him." And the concept of "neighbor" went beyond the narrow confines of nation or creed: The law forbade oppression of any worker ". . . whether he be of thy brethren [the Jews], or of the strangers [non-Jews] that are in thy land within thy gates." The reason for this solicitude regarding the payment of wages was expressed in Deuteronomy 24:15: ". . . for he is poor, and setteth his heart upon it."

It is remarkable that in the absolute monarchy of ancient times the Jewish worker should have been accorded the right of disposing of his own labor as he saw fit. Outside of the arbitrary power his rulers exercised to press him into forced labor gangs—or his own poverty, which often forced him to become an indentured servant to his creditor—he was free to leave his job at any time. Moreover, if he found that the conditions under which he had been hired were not being honored, he had the privilege of going out on what amounted, in ancient times, to a strike. In Hebrew, such cessation of labor or laying down of work tools was called *regiah,* meaning "rest."

Interesting are the unusual scruples shown by devout employers in abiding by the Scriptural commandment to pay the worker his *daily* hire. The Rabbinic Sage Rab Chamnunah would say to his field-laborers at the end of the work day: "Here are your souls! Take them back!" And thus saying, he would pay them their daily wage. But once, for reasons unknown, one of his workers did not wish to take away the money with him. Chamnunah began to scold him: "If it is not permitted you to deposit your body with me, how much more serious is your offense to leave your soul with me!" For without his wages to sustain himself and his family, the worker was, so to speak, deprived of his soul.

The Rabbinic law required that the worker be paid for the days he was not permitted to work—the Sabbath, festivals, and fast days. He toiled between sunrise and sunset—probably twelve hours daily. But of this time, two hours were allotted to him, in tacit recognition of his humanity, for religious worship and for meals. Agricultural toilers—and the vast majority of workers were such—were given the right to satisfy their hunger from the produce in field and garden. It was the established custom for the worker to eat at his master's table—itself an indication of social equality.

During the Talmudic era, the morality and dignity of labor had been elevated by the Rabbinic Sages in both their teachings and through the examples they themselves set by working at some manual trade for a livelihood. Consequently, the honest worker had acquired by that time a certain social status and respectability—at least among the sincerely pious.

But the same law that gave the worker protection also demanded of him a reciprocal attitude of responsibility toward his work and his employer: He was to serve his master faithfully, and he was to perform his tasks conscientiously. Maimonides, the twelfth-century rabbi-philosopher, recapitulated the ancient Rabbinic principle concerning the obligations of the worker: "Even as the employer is required not to oppress the worker, so is the worker expected not to take advantage of his employer. He must not be idle but work well and diligently. He should remember the words of our Father Jacob to his wives, Rachel and Leah: 'And ye know that with all my power I have served your father" (Genesis 31:6).

See also ESSENES; ETHICAL VALUES, JEWISH; FELLOWSHIP IN ISRAEL; JUBILEE; LABOR, DIGNITY OF; LIFE, SANCTIFICATION OF; MAN, DIGNITY OF; LOANS, FREE; PASSOVER; PROPHETS, THE (*under* BIBLE, THE); SLAVERY AND THE SLAVE; TALMUD, THE; THERAPEUTAE; UNITY OF ISRAEL.

WORLD-TO-COME (in Hebrew: OLAM HA-BAH)

Believing Jews have always been eternity minded. They have gone tirelessly in search of absolutes. To the skeptics and the free-thinkers of the second century B.C.E., the "Judgment Day" post-Biblical poet Baruch, posed this question: Had the Creator not made a Hereafter to follow man's mortal end, then of what use would it have been to give him a beginning in the first place?

For those who could not reconcile themselves to death as the end of existence, the World-to-Come carried with it the assurance of satisfying all the lacks and frustrations experienced in life. They saw Heaven and Earth interdependent, as one single unity. That is what led the Sages to declare solemnly that God would not enter into the "Heavenly Jerusalem" before the "Earthly Jerusalem" (another designation for the Kingdom of God; *see* MESSIAH, THE) would be established by means of man's striving for righteousness. They made it abundantly clear to the people that a ready-made Gan Eden (Paradise) was an illusion; Paradise could become Paradise only to the extent that people could will it into being by conducting themselves uprightly during their lifetime. Therefore, those who thought Gan Eden was created by God as a reward for the good in the Hereafter were in error. The Almighty did not make Paradise; *people did!* The Jerusalem of Heaven was built like the Earthly Jerusalem, but instead of rising stone upon stone, like the latter, it was being constructed deed upon deed upon deed of loving-kindness, justice, and truth among men.

This idealistic notion of a man-made Paradise was imaginatively spun into an allegory by Kalonymos ben Kalonymos, the Provençal poet of the synagogue in the thirteenth century. He compares the world to a vast sea. Upon it he sees sailing a tiny bark called *Man.* Fragile as it might appear, the vessel is perfect in form and most beautiful to look upon. What mysterious hand steers it along its uncharted course across the stormy sea of life to its destination—to the opposite shore? It is the guiding power of the Divine Spirit which directs it ahead, answers Kalonymos, overawed. What cargo does the vessel carry? It is the good and evil deeds which every man must bear with him to the shores of Eternity. And as each unloads his cargo, the Ruler of the Universe sits in majesty on his Throne of Judgment surrounded by the hosts of Heaven. He examines "the merchandise" and has it weighed in the scrupulous scales of his justice.

When he reaches the end of his allegory, the poet points up its moral with this exhortation: "Now, O son of man! Everything will depend on the kind of cargo you bring with you. It will decide whether you will be admitted to that place which glows with the light of eternity (Gan Eden), or whether you will be condemned to the regions where darkness reigns supreme (Gehinnom).

What have been the traditional Jewish conceptions of Gan Eden (the Garden of Eden or Paradise) and its opposite, Gehinnom (called "Gehenna" in New Testament Greek and "Hell" in English)? All religions, not only the Jewish, felt the necessity of believing in a Hereafter that was tangible, even though unseen, and whose reality could be made persuasive to the simple-minded. Because the majority of mankind always found it difficult to grasp abstract ideas, the rewards and punishments promised for the World-to-Come had to be made comprehensible and concrete to them by the use of the symbols of common knowledge and experience. Thus, Gan Eden and Gehinnom were conveniently spelled out in physical terms: They were pictured as well-ordered places, institutionalized like the various departments of living on earth. They, their geography, and their administration, were described in great detail with the precision of an architectural plan.

Actually, there have been a variety of notions concerning Gan Eden and Gehinnom, and the character of each has depended upon the degree of sophistication and culture possessed by the various teachers of religion who described them. Broadly speaking, there have been two kinds of conceptions, one hardly compatible with the other. One type has been utterly primitive, shaped by childish myth and superstition; the other has been poetic in tone and ethical in its content.

We know today how one culture borrows from another and fuses it with its own. Thus, the myth-conception of the Jewish Hereafter was, to a great extent, "syncretized" or fused with borrowings from several other ancient religions, principally from the Egyptian, Greek, and Persian. For instance, the influences of the Egyptian Osiris-cult of the dead with its notions of the Hereafter infiltrated deeply into the Judaism of the Second Temple period. Its impact must have come mainly by way of the great Jewish community of Alexandria, established by the Macedonian world-conqueror (after whom it was named) during the fourth century B.C.E. Curiously, many of the primitive-sounding notions about Gan Eden and Gehinnom strongly resemble those of their Egyptian counterparts so vividly described in the Book of the Dead, a scriptural work composed by the priest-poets of the Osiris-cult fifteen centuries before the Talmudic era began!

Despite their epochal advances in the field of personal and social ethics, the Jews could not escape altogether the influence of the cultural impacts of the surrounding world. And these, unhappily, were not always of a progressive character. The Jews could not rid themselves entirely of the nature-worshiping beliefs and practices held by neighboring peoples and present in their own tribal past. In the same way that the early Israelites conceived God to be formed in their own human image possessing all the character traits of a man, they also visualized these traits in unabashed materialistic images. It certainly is true that the most knowledgeable and clear-thinking among Jewish religious teachers, beginning with the great Prophets, sought to interpret the Biblical text and to explain the mysteries of Heaven and of the nether world in a poetic-allegoric manner. Their aim was to chart a moral course through the Torah for the guidance of men's conduct and to satisfy their spiritual needs. They were fully aware that, if they followed some of their less progressive rabbinic colleagues in the literalness of their Torah interpretations, they would soon find themselves tangled up in a maze of inconsistencies, foolishness, and superstition.

Perhaps even the enlightened Sages themselves were partly responsible for the primitive notions concerning Gehinnom and Gan Eden which flourished among the folk. Like all teachers of religion, they too were fond of symbolism. They employed the poetic metaphor and the allegoric method for the purpose of making their instruction as plain as possible to the unsophisticated. This sometimes led to confusion and misunderstanding on the part of the literal-minded. To cite but one example: The Mishnah Fathers had taught: "This world is merely a vestibule that leads to the banqueting hall of Heaven." The simple-minded must have asked: "What does one do in a banqueting hall?" Eat and drink, of course! And, since God was a most generous host and lacking in nothing, the plain folk conjured up a gourmandizing and incessant feasting as the reward of the righteous in the brilliantly illuminated "banqueting hall of Heaven" while they reclined like kings on luxurious couches . . . The *pieces de résistance* of the menu would be "leviathan" preserved in brine, and "wild ox" (*shor ha-bor*), both washed down with generous gulps of "wine preserved in the grape since the six days of Creation."

See also GAN EDEN; GEHINNOM; IMMORTALITY; REWARD AND PUNISHMENT; SIN AND SINNERS; SOUL, THE.

WORSHIP. *See* PRAYER AND WORSHIP.

WRITINGS, THE HOLY. *See* BIBLE, THE.

YAHRZEIT (from the German, meaning "anniversary"; in Yiddish: YOHRTZEIT)

References to this observance first appeared in the writings of the famous Talmudist of fifteenth-century Germany, Rabbi Jacob ben Moses Halevi Mölln (Maharil) of Mayence. However, the memorial observance of the death of one's parents and of beloved teachers was already general in the days of the Mishnah Sages, some fifteen hundred years before. It is noteworthy that in Geonic times, before the Middle Ages, it was established as a tradition to observe the yahrzeit of Moses on the seventh day of the month of Adar.

In the Talmudic period, custom required that the mourner spend the anniversary day in fasting and that he visit the grave of the deceased and recite prayers before it. During the Middle Ages, the custom was established of burning a memorial lamp for twenty-four hours. Since all people borrow one from the other certain folkways and adapt them to their needs, it is not too farfetched to deduce that this custom was derived from the Catholic practice of burning votive lamps.

The yahrzeit today is observed by attendance at religious services, and the climax is reached with the recitation of the Kaddish (q.v.) in unison with all the mourners present. In addition, tradition requires that the male mourner be called to read from the Torah in the synagogue at Sabbath prayer, or on Monday or Thursday, during the Morning Service. Among the Sefaradim (Jews of the Spanish rite), a deeper tone of prayer and homage for the soul of the departed is sounded. It takes the form of worship by means of Torah study. Friends and kin come to the home of the mourner for this purpose.

Yahrzeit (memorial) prayers recited by a worshiper in the synagogue on the anniversary of a beloved relative's death. Note the lighted memorial lamp contained in the glass (foreground). (Painting by I. Kaufmann, 19th century.)

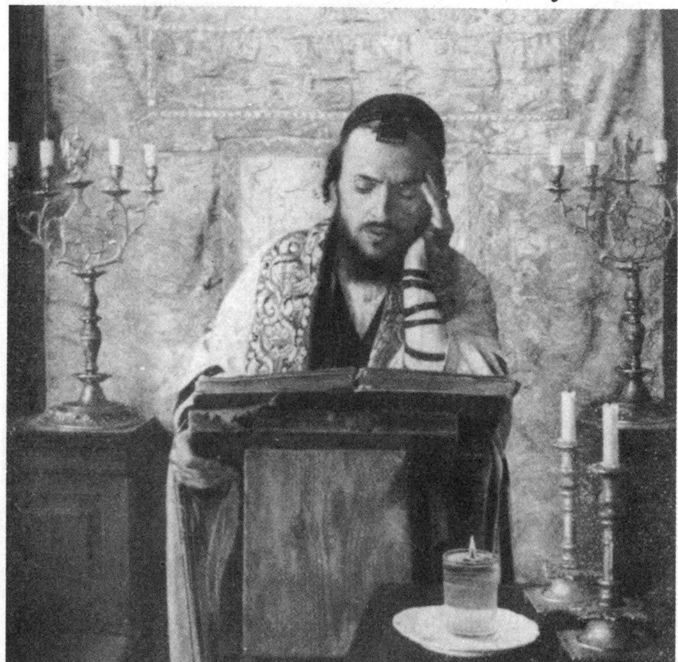

There were quaint folkways current in certain countries at various times in connection with yahrzeit. In the East European ghettos of the eighteenth and nineteenth centuries, the mourner would pass around his snuffbox to the worshipers at the end of the prayer service so that not only did he and they pray together but they sneezed together as well—as a sign of "good luck." The sectarian Chasidim, one of whose principal doctrines was worship through joy, banished all mourning on the yahrzeit of their wonder-working rabbis or tzaddikim (s. tzaddik). Instead, on that day they sang hymns of joy and, dancing in the mystic circle, offered thanks to God for having illumined their lives by sending such "saints" to lead them. The Chasidic yahrzeit ceremony ended with all participants partaking of honey cake and wine.

YAMIM NORAIM. *See* SELICHOT.

YARMULKAH. *See* HEAD COVERING.

YELLOW BADGE

Ever since antiquity, the color yellow has somehow denoted "shame." Yellow was the identifying color of the prostitute; in many countries she was required to wear yellow.

The memory of man often seems to go back far beyond recorded history. Thus, the Alexandrian writer Artapanus, in his *History of the Jews,* noted that (supposedly in the days of the Jewish Bondage) the king of Upper Egypt, Chenephres, "ordered that the Jews should wear garments which would distinguish them from the Egyptians, and thereby expose them to maltreatment." Whether the wearing of yellow was ordered as part of their distinguishing dress is not indicated. But certain it is that in 640 C.E., after the Caliph Omar, Mohammed's successor, had finished the conquest of the Jewish world for Islam, Jews were ordered to insert a yellow strip of cloth into their outer garments. In 1301 they were also required to wear yellow turbans. This latter identification was required not of Jews alone but of all "infidels," including Christians, living in Mohammedan countries. The object, of course, was to isolate the "unbeliever," to brand him as an enemy, to keep him exposed to the public eye as a pariah, and thereby discourage Mohammedans from religious, social, and cultural contact with him. Such branding was, incidentally, considered a most powerful persuader for conversion to the "true faith." In addition, it also made it conveniently easy to badger, rob, and persecute the pariah while "keeping an eye" on him.

Apparently, Pope Innocent III and the Fourth Lateran Council found this Mohammedan practice very attractive, for they decreed in 1215 that, thenceforth, all Jews were to display prominently on their breasts the Yellow Badge of Shame. In England, Henry III forced the badge on the Jews in 1218. Here it consisted of a white cloth patch, oblong in shape and two by four finger-breadths wide. The Badge of Shame in England at least had a measure of dignity about it: Its mark was of the two stone tablets of the Ten Commandments.

Louis IX of France (who was made a saint by the Church after his death), before he started out at the head of a new Crusade to the Holy Land, in 1248, ordered the Jews of his country not only to wear a badge—a yellow wheel (*rouelle*)—on the breast but also a badge on the back. This was "so that those who were thus marked might be recognized from every side." With some variations, the wearing of the yellow badge in the shape of a wheel was enforced in Poland, Hungary, Germany, and in other countries of Europe, but it took several centuries to accomplish this thoroughly.

Jews wearing the circular yellow badge. (Illustration in Bible Historiale *by Pierre Comestor, France, 14th century.)*

Yellow badge compulsory on outer garment of Jews. Rhineland, end of 16th century.

Yet there were some places where the rulers and princes of the Church were filled with an even greater ardor to put the mark of Cain (as "Christ-killers") on the Jews. In Mayence, for example, in addition to the yellow badge, the Jews were ordered in 1229 by the Diocesan Council to wear the *Judenhut* or Jew's hat; Poland followed suit in 1264, and Vienna in 1267. This hat (in Latin: *cornutum pileum*) was shaped like a sugar cone—quite like the traditional "dunce cap"—and was designed to make the Jew appear ridiculous and an object of scorn.

Curiously, the lawmakers of Christian Europe during the Middle Ages, unlike many people today, who believe you can tell who is a Jew just by looking at him, came very close to the view of the modern anthropolgists: that there is no certain means of identifying Jews by their appearance alone. Pope Innocent III and the various Church Councils were fearful that many Jews might be mistaken for Christians and, without anyone being the wiser for it, succeed in having "carnal commerce" with the faithful. To prevent this, the Provincial Council of Ravenna in 1311, "thinking that many scandals have arisen from their [the Jews] too free comingling with Christians, decreed that they should wear a wheel of yellow cloth on their outer garments, and their women a like wheel on their heads, so that they may be distinguished from Christians."

It took the French Revolution of 1789 to grant Jews their simple rights as human beings. The Republic abolished the Badge of Shame, which it considered to be not the shame of the Jews but of Europe. The example of France quickly led to its abolition everywhere in Germany, Austria, Italy, and other countries. (In England, the badge had ceased to exist upon the Jews' readmission to that country in the seventeenth century by the Lord Protector, Oliver Cromwell.)

One would have thought that the conscience-stricken world had seen at last the end of the Badge of Shame. But Adolf Hitler and Nazi Germany resurrected it on September 19, 1941. All Jews in Germany and the rest of Nazi-occupied Europe who were over six years old were then

Varieties of the Judenhut (Jew's hat) compulsory for Jews during the Middle Ages by decree of the Lateran Council in 1215. (From H. Weiss's Kostumkunde.)

Jews in the synagogue of Trent, depicted wearing the Judenhut *(Jew's hat) and allegedly plotting to "slaughter" a Christian child for "ritual" purposes. (From* History of the Murdered Christian Child in Trent, *Germany, 1475.)*

forced by law to wear it. This time the yellow badge, which could also be worn as an armlet, had a new design—a *Magen David,* or—"Star of David—and in its center the word *Jude*—"Jew."

See also CHRISTIANITY, JEWISH ORIGINS OF; CHURCH AND PERSECUTION; FEUDAL SOCIETY, POSITION OF THE JEWS IN; GHETTO; "HOST DESECRATION" CALUMNIES; MASSACRES; RITUAL MURDER SLANDERS; WANDERING JEW.

YESHIBAH (YESHIVAH) (Hebrew, meaning "Talmudic [rabbinical] college"; first used in the Talmud to mean an assembly or synod of Torah scholars deliberating under the presidency of a chief scholar; YESHIBAH [pl. YESHIBOT] is ancient Sefaradic form; YESHIVAH [pl. YESHIVOT] is Ashkenazic variant)

NOTE: For the sake of uniformity and to avoid confusiòn, the forms *yeshibah, yeshibot* are used throughout this article, even when referring to Ashkenazic institutions.

Very little is known today about the early yeshibah, the Talmudic college where the higher religious learning was pursued during the final period of the Second Commonwealth. What is known however, is that the Soferim (Scribes) and the Zekenim (Elders) taught publicly in Jerusalem and other Judean towns, and that each "raised" many disciples. The most concrete information is derived from numerous references in the Talmud to the incessant, and frequently sharp, disputations held in Jerusalem, just as the Common Era was dawning, between the two rival Rabbinic schools of Hillel the Elder and Shammai. (*See* PHARISEES; RABBINIC SAGES; TALMUD, THE; ZEALOTS.)

By that time, a new dialectical method for interpreting the Torah according to a distinctive system of logic—but one which, nevertheless, differed from that of the Greeks—had been perfected by the Tannaim (Mishnah Sages; s. Tanna). These religious scholars, legists, and moralists had been painstakingly examining and collecting the ethical teachings and traditions preserved as the Oral Laws. These were finally compiled, after several centuries, into the Mishnah Code, which forms the very core of the literature of the Talmud.

When the Second Temple was destroyed by Titus in the year 70 C.E., the humble but ubiquitous synagogue had taken its place wherever Jews lived in community. Torah study and prayer finally supplanted worship by sacrifice. Although Torah study had been diligently maintained among the Jews since the middle of the fifth century B.C.E., when Ezra had made it an absolute obligation for every male Jew, it was only with the Destruction of the national sanctuary on Mount Zion that new and overwhelming emphasis was laid upon it in the religious life of the people.

Faced with the ruin of the Jewish political state and a dispersed and decimated nation, Yochanan ben Zakkai, the foremost disciple of Hillel and his successor as leader of the Pharisees, transformed the little Yeshibah of Yabneh into the supreme religious-intellectual center of Jewry. The collegium of Rabbinic Sages that formed around Yochanan at Yabneh at the end of the first century realistically came to the realization that the new conditions (which had arisen as a result of the national disaster) in Jewish life and religious practice required prompt reinterpretation and adjustment. Thus the Yeshibah of Yabneh not only served as an educational institution for Torah learning, but, quite understandably, since the vacuum had to be filled, also took over the functions of the now defunct Great Sanhedrin (*see* ANHEDRIN) as the supreme religious authority of Jewry.

But the Yeshibah of Yabneh had a relatively short life. It closed in 135 with the crushing of Bar Kochba's revolt against Roman rule. However, other Rabbinic academies took its place in Galilee, first in Usha then in Sepphoris, where the Mishnah was codified about 200 C.E. by Judah ha-Nasi—"the Prince." In the centuries which followed, similar institutions were established in Caesarea, Lydda, and Tiberias. It was in the Yeshibah of Tiberias that, for seven or eight centuries, the central authority in Jewish religious life in Palestine and the Holy Roman Empire was vested. There the Jerusalem Talmud (as distinct from the Babylonian Talmud) was compiled and edited during the fifth century.

Because the Jews had become virtually a global people following the final Dispersion in the year 70, the Jewish communities which were established in various countries were forced to become more or less autonomous in their religious-cultural life. Yet their psychologic-emotional center was still their homeland, Judea. When the Mishnah canon of the Oral Traditions was closed, Rabbinic yeshibot on the pattern of those already established in Tiberias and other towns of Judea made their appearance in the Babylonian Jewish communities. They were first established in Nehardea and Machuza, and then in Sura and Pumbeditha. The latter two became the most authoritative in the Oriental Jewish world. The Yeshibah of Sura, it is surmised, was founded by the brilliant Rabbinic scholar Rab (Abba Arika) early in the third century. When the Yeshibah of Nehardea was ordered closed by the Persian authorities in 259, the Yeshibah of Pumbeditha was established in its place. This school was world famous for its religious-legal scholars and skilled casuists who—so their more serious rivals, the Sages of Sura—gibed, were, masters of the fine art of "making an elephant jump through the eye of a needle."

It was more in the yeshibot of Babylonia—a country where the Jews enjoyed a higher cultural development than

Students in a modern yeshibah absorbed in their Talmudic texts. Pre-Nazi-period. (Joint Distribution Committee.)

in Judea—that the character and method of Torah and Talmudic study and interpretation were perfected; they served as the model to the rest of Jewry the world over for many centuries. By almost general agreement, the yeshibah at Sura was revered as the principal Talmudic center of Babylonia. From it for hundreds of years issued forth the authoritative voice of Rabbinic Judaism to all the Jews of the world, and there the vast Babylonian Talmud was compiled and closed, *c.* 500 C.E.

It was customary for the head of the yeshibah (in Hebrew: *rosh yeshibah*) to deliver his daily lecture before the assembly of the entire student body and all the members of the faculty. This discourse usually took from two to three hours. In some academies there were two lectures delivered daily, one in the morning and the other in the afternoon.

The method of instruction employed might seem odd indeed to the modern reader. The lecturer was assisted by a Rabbinic "interpreter" and expounder called a *meturgeman.* He was a disciple of the Rabbinic Sage and was thoroughly familiar with his manner of thinking, his views, attitudes, and conclusions. After the lecture, still other Rabbinic "interpreters" would attack the problems it raised in informal discussion with small groups of students. Frequently, the interpreters would go back to the lecturer for clarification where bafflement or logical contradiction appeared.

The ancient yeshibot in Judea, and even more so those in Babylonia (especially in Sura and Pumbeditha), were far more than just institutions of higher religious education. This was in contradistinction to the medieval and modern yeshibot which had exclusively an educational character and were intended for the training of rabbis and religious scholars. The collegium of Rabbinical scholars who constituted the faculty of the ancient yeshibot received by general consent a tacit recognition of their right to perform the authoritative functions of a quasi-Sanhedrin in the adjudication and regulation of Jewish religious, moral, cultural, and social relations. Some, of course, wielded greater authority than others. One Babylonian Sage, when he regarded the positive achievements of the yeshibot at Sura and Pumbeditha, exulted: "God created these two academies in order that his promise—that the word of God should never depart from the lips of Israel—might be fulfilled."

With the eleventh century, the supreme authority of the Babylonian yeshibot went into a sharp decline, chiefly because of the persecution and religious suppression that the Jews in Persia were suffering. The result was that a mass exodus from that country took place by Jews in search of a more secure refuge in other lands. They settled mainly in North Africa, Spain, and the Provence, and thereafter the authority of the yeshibot in those places was in the ascendancy.

The fact that yeshibah instruction for students varied very little for eight or nine centuries in the East is a revelation of the enduring power of custom and culture patterns among the Jews. When Petachiah of Regensburg, the famous Jewish globetrotter of the twelfth century, visited the yeshibah in Baghdad, he noted without surprise that that institution had some two thousand students and five hundred advanced graduate scholars on its academic rolls. He pictured the rector of the yeshibah as a very magnificent personage second only in rank to the Rosh ha-Golah (Head of the Captivity; i.e., the secular head of Babylonian Jewry). The rector, observed Petachiach, "occupies a large house hung with tapestries. He is dressed in a gold-trimmed garment and sits on a raised dais, while the students sit [squat] on the floor . . . He discourses with the aid of an interpreter or explainer [i.e., the meturgeman] who answers all questions asked by the students and, if he does not know the answers, inquires of the Rosh Yeshibah. Sometimes there are several interpreters, each expounding in a different part of the yeshibah on the treatise."

Petachiach went on to make this interesting (from a historical-cultural point of view) comment: "The manner of study is with an intonation." For cantillating the Talmudic texts according to a traditional modal melody had at that time already become (and still remains) the standard manner for Talmudic study; it was (and is) also employed during the vernacular exposition and interpretation which followed.

The yeshibot of the East during the Byzantine period and the early Middle Ages followed closely the older Babylonian models. While these institutions during each culture period continued to modify the old forms of instruction and even created a few new ones, they preserved the dialectical method of analysis and logical probing which were the chief characteristics of the early Talmudic intellectualism.

Celebrated institutions of Torah-learning flourished for centuries in Cairo, Egypt, and in Kairouan, Tunisia. Their Jewish studies were set in the speculative-scientific framework of Arab-Jewish culture that, genealogically, was derived from the earlier Hellenism. With the conquest of Southern Spain by the Moors and the transplantation there of the religion of Islam and Arab culture, the North African Jewish immigrants who followed them, founded on the new soil the same kind of yeshibot they had cultivated in Egypt, Tunisia, Libya, and Morocco.

Intellectually these schools were of a high order. In some ways they were even superior to the early Christian universities of Europe; in particular, their outlook was more enlightened, their scholarly interests were more broadly humanistic. The instruction followed in the yeshibot was keyed to a critical-rational analysis of the Scriptural and Talmudic texts and to the study of the natural sciences. The philosophic method of the Greeks as filtered through Arab-Jewish Hellenism was customarily employed and there was much stimulation resulting from the free intellectual exchanges between the Rabbinic teachers and their students. Even after Moorish rule had been supplanted by Christian, the Jews in Spain succeeded in founding a number of great centers of learning in Cordova, Lucena, Málaga, Granada, Toledo, Saragossa, Valencia, Majorca, Seville, Gerona, Tortosa, and Barcelona.

All along it had been traditional for every yeshibah to be built around the instruction of some Talmudic master of great erudition. Such, for example, was Asher ben Yechiel (1250–1328) who established his school in Toledo; Moses ben Nachman, known also as Nachmanides (1194–*c.* 1270), who headed the school at Gerona; and Solomon ibn Adret (1235–1310), the traditionalist opponent of Maimonides (Moses ben Maimon; 1135–1204), who presided over the celebrated yeshibah in Barcelona.

In that same general period there was evidenced a similar preoccupation with Talmudic studies combined with secular subjects in the yeshibot of the Jewish communities of Southern Italy and the Provence. So great, in fact, was the renown of the Italian yeshibot in Bari and Otranto that it led to the coining of a grandiloquent paraphrase in Hebrew of the familiar Biblical verse: "From Bari shall go forth the Law, and the word of the Lord from Otranto!"

Certainly far less humanistic and secular-minded than the Islamic-oriented yeshibot of Spain, Italy, the Provence, and North Africa, were the Talmudic schools of the Central European Ashkenazim. The initiator of the yeshibot among them in Northern France and in Germany, from whence they proliferated into Bohemia, Moravia, Poland, Lithuania, and the Ukraine, was Rabbenu ("Our Teacher") Gershom ben Judah. That foremost rabbinic authority of the age had opened his yeshibah about the year 1000 at Mayence, in the Rhineland. The system of Talmudic learning that he inaugurated there marked the breaking away of rabbinic studies from their old philosophic-secularistic moorings.

The yeshibot in Northern France and the Provence had for centuries drawn a great many Torah students and scholars from every section of Europe. Notable especially were the schools in Champagne, Lunel, Montpellier, Marseilles, Dampière, and Paris. The wandering Spanish scholar, Rabbi Benjamin of Tudela (*d.* 1173), noted on a visit to France: "Rabbi Abraham is the principal of the yeshibah of Narbonne, from where the study of the Torah spreads into all countries . . . at Beaucaire there is a great yeshibah under Abraham ibn Daud, an eminent scholar of Torah and Talmud who attracts students from distant countries. At Marseilles, in the upper city near the fortress, is a great yeshibah which boasts of very learned scholars . . . the descendants of Rashi run yeshibot at Troyes and at Ramerupt. Paris contains many learned men whose equals are not to be found anywhere on earth." One of these "learned men," Jacob of Orléans, crossed over to England and established a yeshibah in London during the middle of the twelfth century.

Talmudic learning during the Middle Ages in Europe became a consuming passion for many. It led young hopefuls, ardent for knowledge and eager to worship God by means of Torah study, to leave home and family and, penniless, wander forth to distant, improverished, but illustrious centers of learning. An arresting example of this kind of dedication was that evidenced by the youthful Rashi (Solomon ben Isaac, *d.* 1105) of Troyes, whose name has remained for eight centuries virtually a household word in every devout Jewish home. He parted from his young wife to become a wandering student. Living under the most trying hardships, he journeyed from one yeshibah in Lorraine to another, studying Torah, but all the time "lacking bread and clothing and with a millstone around his neck."

Although yeshibot everywhere were very much alike, yet there were some striking regional divergences in their philosophy of education, in their curricula, and in their teaching and learning methods. The schools in Spain and North Africa followed a more systematic and intellectually broader course of study than those in Germany and Poland. They gave greater attention to secular learning, including sciences such as mathematics, astronomy, medicine, philosophy, grammar, and even musical theory, nothwithstanding that Talmudic studies comprised their major interest.

The yeshibot of the Franco-German region followed a different pattern, being more traditional and parochial. They were far less involved with the natural sciences and the philological examination of the Pentateuch. The fact of the matter is that they rejected the philosophical method in use in the Sefaradic institutions. They denounced it as alien to the Jewish religion, charging that it was introducing into questions of faith and practice a disruptive intellectual skepticism.

In the yeshibot of France and Germany, Rabbinic studies were carried on in depth. Usually they were limited to the study of the Bible, the literature of the Talmud, the principal commentaries, ritual codes, moralistic writings, and religious-legal opinions by individual rabbinic authorities designated by modern scholarship as *Responsa*. Nevertheless, unlike the nineteenth-century Polish and Lithuanian schools, they were not entirely divorced from non-Jewish culture. For instance, the writings of Rashi reveal some familiarity with mathematics and grammar, and one medieval German rabbi, to illustrate a Talmudic commentary, even introduced into it a number of Euclidean propositions!

It goes without saying that not everyone who wished to study there was admitted into a yeshibah. The applicant, usually seventeen or eighteen years old, first had to demonstrate the extent of his Torah-learning and his intellectual competence to the rabbinic luminary who headed the yeshibah. In order to qualify, he was expected to have a thorough grasp of the Bible, a working knowledge of Hebrew and Aramaic, an ability to use Rashi's Scriptural commentary, and, lastly, a familiarity with some of the texts of the Talmud. It must be pointed out that in former times it was held as the norm of achievement for a gifted Jewish boy in the ghetto to begin the study of the Mishnah (the Hebrew Code of Oral Law) at the age of ten. And if after seven years of further study he wished to prepare himself to be a rabbi or a serious scholar, then he was required to spend still another seven years of grinding study, from early morning till late at night, at the yeshibah.

At the time of the Renaissance there was a great outcropping of yeshibot in Germany, Moravia, Bohemia, and Silesia. Important institutions sprang up in Regensburg, Frankfurt, Breslau, Fürth, Pressburg, Nikolsburg, and Prague. Yet, strange as it may appear, the really significant yeshibot emerged at the start of the sixteenth century in the culturally most backward Jewish communities of Europe—in Poland, Lithuania, the Ukraine, and White Russia.

The most influential of all the yeshibot in the world at the time of the Renaissance was the one in Cracow, made famous by the redoubtable Talmudist and educator, Moses Isserles (1520–72). A man of considerable secular culture and strong character, he defied the religious fundamentalism of Polish Jewry in his time. He introduced into the curriculum of his yeshibah not only the study of astronomy, history, and mathematics, but also the highly controversial Aristotelian philosophic method of Maimonides (the foremost Jewish thinker of the Middle Ages), for whom he had unbounded admiration.

The intellectual-religious authority of the Polish Talmudic institutions gradually asserted itself over world Jewry following the expulsion of the Jews from Spain in 1492. Even under conditions of wildest upheaval, the harried and driven Jews of Europe managed, by a supreme effort of will and dedication to Torah-learning, to maintain many of their Talmudic institutions. But their efforts were severely circumscribed by external forces. In the yeshibot of Northern Italy—at Padua, Venice, Ferrara, Mantua, Modena, and Livorno—the harsh papal interdictions during the sixteenth and seventeenth centuries against the study of the Talmud discouraged their development. A number of private yeshibot, oriented to the mysticism of Cabala and supported by the contributions of the pious from abroad, also maintained themselves in Jerusalem and Safed. But any objective assessment would show that these rabbinic institutions never became important centers of learning. They were distinguished more for their piety and their very existence in the Holy Land, where they stood as comforting symbols to the "exiles" of Israel's ultimate restoration.

The yeshibot suffered a serious setback in Germany during the Thirty Years' War, and in Poland and the Ukraine following the terrible massacres and the devastation of Jewish life during the Cossack uprising of 1648. But they revived again during the eighteenth century, and in Lithuania most of all. There Elijah ben Solomon, the famed Vilner Gaon, himself a very gifted and erudite scholar, gave impetus with his personal example and enormous authority to the new Talmudic learning in Vilna. That city, on account of this intellectual revival, won the soubriquet of "the Jerusalem of Lithuania."

It is deserving of special comment that the Polish, Lithuanian, and Russian yeshibot during the nineteenth century, despite their desperate poverty and shabby exteriors, were shining models of democratic folk-institutions. Their teachers and students, both dedicated to Torah-learning, took fire from each other in free and stimulating discussion; they constituted but one fellowship in their common though rather one-sided quest. A mastery of the Torah and rabbinic literature and a demonstration of genuine intellectual abilities merited for their possessors the highest honors and social distinction. Such a value-standard was merely in line with the ancient Jewish tradition of reverence for both learning and the learned.

Without any intellectual frills or pretensions, all these schools functioned forthrightly as the intellectual citadels of Orthodoxy and traditional Judaism. Yet their learning discipline was not only thoroughgoing but severe. The best known of the yeshibot were in Volozhin, Mir, Slobodka, Lida, Kovno, Slonim, Minsk, Lomżah, and Radun. The Yeshibah of Volozhin, which had been established in 1803 by Rabbi Chaim ben Solomon, a protégé of the Vilner Gaon, enjoyed an unusual reputation among Jews. Before being entered on its rolls, applicants had to demonstrate clearly that they possessed exceptional scholarly capabilities.

A serious crisis arose eventually for all the yeshibot in the Russian empire. In 1887, just to cite one instance, Count Pahlen, the czarist governor of Vilna, issued orders for their modernization. They were told to introduce into their curricula courses in the Russian language, literature, and history—subjects not only foreign but considered anathema to the devout, who, in a cultural sense, were still living in "dark ages" of their own creation. At first the yeshibot complied with the "reform," but, on reconsideration, the heads of the thirteen leading rabbinic institutions concurred that "profane" studies would only "poison the minds of the students and would turn them away from the study of the Talmud." This uncompromising position led to the summary closing of the yeshibot in 1892 by order of the Russian government, but after several years they were allowed to reopen.

Despite the rapid decline in the twentieth century of ghetto isolation and cultural particularism, some of the traditional yeshibot in Eastern Europe managed to maintain themselves against this tide of change and assimilation. Yet all their efforts to perpetuate Torah-learning among the Orthodox youth came to naught. During their "liquidation of the Jewish problem" in World War II, the German Nazis put an end not only to the yeshibot but also to their teachers and students.

With the mass immigration of Jews from the countries of Eastern Europe to the United States and Canada, beginning with the early 1880's, several yeshibot, following the traditional pattern of the schools in Poland and Lithuania, were founded in New York City. The most effective and enduring among these has been the Yeshiva Rabbi Isaac Elchanan. This institution, still functioning as a school for advanced Jewish studies and for the training of Orthodox rabbis, served as the academic nucleus around which was built the nationally prominent Yeshiva University.

It should be noted in passing though that there are quite a number of Orthodox day (parochial) schools in the United States which call themselves *yeshibot,* but they do not rank academically with the traditional yeshibah that is devoted to higher Talmudic studies. Quite a few of them are religious institutions on a secondary and, in a few instances, on an elementary school level. Some of them, breaking with venerable fundamentalist tradition which has regarded Torah-learning as being exclusively a male preserve, have been equally hospitable to girls.

See also CHACHMAH; CHEDER; GEONIM; RABBI; SAGES, RABBINIC; TALMID CHACHAM; TALMUD, THE; TORAH STUDY; YESHIVAH BACHUR.

YESHIVAH BACHUR (Hebrew s., a student in an Ashkenazic yeshivah [yeshibah] or academy for higher Talmudic learning; pl. YESHIVAH BACHURIM)

The national-religious dedication of the Jews throughout their history to the perpetual study of the Torah and to its related bodies of sacred literature, spurred the establishment of yeshivot (academies for higher rabbinic learning). In these schools, the most gifted and also the most pious youths of each generation spent years of their lives in devoted Torah study; as the Hebrew description of it runs, they abandoned themselves to it "by day and by night." During the Middle Ages, the usual course of study in the European yeshivot lasted seven years. But there also were students in whom the hunger for religious knowledge and illumination remained unassuaged, and they continued as "perpetual" students (in Hebrew: MATMIDIM; s. MATMID), studying until the day they died.

Due entirely to the straitened and perilous circumstances of Jewish life in many lands, following the final Dispersion (after the end of Judea as a Jewish state), there emerged—with wide variations, of course—a recognizable type of student: the *yeshivah bachur.* He might be described as being, both by his conditioning and moral conviction, exceedingly gentle. He had a burning passion for knowledge and understanding of the sacred mysteries in the fires of which he was ready, even eager, to burn up his youth and all its normal interests and pleasures.

The general poverty of the Jews led, of course, to a life of privation and much anxiety for the dedicated yeshivah bachur. Almost two thousand years ago, when the matrix of the first yeshivah bachur (although he was not called by that name at that time) was already being fashioned in Jewish society, the Mishnah Sages held out to the bachur this design for the "career" he was freely choosing to follow: "Eat a morsel of bread with salt, drink water by measure, sleep upon the ground, and lead a life of tribulation while you toil in the Torah."

Naturally, not all yeshivah bachurim were filled with the same pure passion, intellectual gift, and endurance for Torah-learning. To many of them, the raptures of illumination or even the incentive-promise of a share of bliss in the World-to-Come was not sufficient compensation for the torments and hardships they had to endure. The Rabbinic teachers of antiquity, who possessed a fine skill for weaving analogies, allegories, and parables with which to illustrate vividly religious ideas and ethical values, inserted into the Talmud a witty analogy in respect to yeshivah bachurim: "There are four qualities among those [students] that sit before the Sages. Some are like a sponge, others variously like a funnel, a strainer, and a sieve." Why like a sponge? A student who eagerly "sucks up" learning may be compared to a sponge. Why like a funnel? The student who cannot retain knowledge is like a funnel which lets in matter at one end and lets it out at the other. Why like a strainer? That student is like a strainer who allows the wine of wisdom to runout but, nevertheless, keeps the worthless sediment. Why like a sieve? That highly selective student who shakes out the worthless chaff but retains the precious grain is like a sieve.

The models serving for the medieval and later yeshivot of Europe, the Near East, and North Africa always were those that had been created by Babylonian Jewry in Sura and Pumbeditha during the third century. In those academies of almost legendary fame was initiated an astonishing intellectual discipline in Rabbinic studies which required, on the part of their bachurim, arduous and intensive study. And this regimen, with modifications, continued in the yeshivot of Eastern Europe until relatively recent times.

During the Middle Ages, before, and in some cases even after, the onset of a religiously sanctioned hatred and organized violence against the Jews, traditional yeshivot flourished in the cities of Europe: in Barcelona, Cordova, Toledo, and Lucena in Spain; in Bari, Otranto, Padua, Pavia, Salerno, and Cremona in Italy; and in Narbonne, Troyes, Dampière, Champagne, Beaucaire, Arles, Montpellier, Avignon, and Paris in France. The support of the students in those institutions was considered the sacred responsibility of the Jewish communities in whose midst they were pursuing their studies. Rabbi Benjamin of Tudela, the compulsive traveler of the twelfth century, made it one of the principal objectives of his wanderings to visit these institutions. At the French yeshivah in Lunel, he found that "the foreign students . . . are supplied with food and clothing at community expense." To the yeshivah in Beaucaire, which was presided over by Abraham ibn Daud, one of the most illustrious philosopher-rabbis of the Middle Ages, students flocked from distant countries not only because of the intellectual eminence of its principal but also because he "provides for them from his private means, which are guite considerable."

When the ghastly massacres of the Jews that began in the wake of the Crusades and climaxed after the Black Death in 1348–49 in a seemingly endless series of bloody horrors, expulsions, and flights, Jewish community existence was virtually torn up by the roots. There no longer was any opportunity for the pauperized mass of Jews, except for the fortunate small class of the well to do, to acquire a higher religious education. The wandering yeshivah bachur now made his appearance in Jewish life. Consumed by a burning desire for greater religious and intellectual knowledge, and in his tatterdemalion state appearing no different than other beggars and vagrants, he trudged his solitary way from one center of rabbinic learning to another. Often it led him to yeshivot in foreign countries. Without means, and with the inability of the ruined Jewish communities of Europe to sustain the yeshivah bachurim for any length of time, even in the most meager way, their Torah studies were desultory; they were constantly being interrupted by the urgent need for physical survival to wander on hopefully to greener pastures. Many of these students, according to contemporary accounts, fell sick on the road. They wandered lonely, footsore and hungry along the sorrowful way of their own pious choosing. Not a few of them perished from starvation or exposure or at the hands of robbers and fanatical Christians.

Yeshivah bachur in pre-Nazi Poland. (R. Vishniak. Joint Distribution Committee.)

In Germany and Bohemia, during the Renaissance, the material conditions for the yeshivah bachurim were greatly improved. The students at the yeshivot in Fürth, Frankfurt-am-Main, Altona, Nikolsburg, Prague, Metz, and also in centers of neighboring regions—in Pressburg and Cracow—were lodged in special dormitories: "bachurim houses." They were supported by special Jewish communal taxes and by the contributions of the philanthropic.

After the middle of the sixteenth century, the new yeshivot established in Poland gradually began to overshadow in intellectual importance those of Germany and Bohemia. And this pre-eminence they continued to maintain uninterruptedly for almost four centuries until World War I.

The material conditions of the Polish yeshivot, after the Cossack massacres under Chmielnicki in 1648 (*see* POGROMS IN SLAVIC LANDS), reflected the general economic plight of Polish Jewry. A new and, in some ways, just as woeful, existence opened up for the Polish yeshivah bachur as it previously had for the wandering bachur of the fourteenth century. He became, more often then not, an object of charity. The humiliations he was not infrequently subjected to in order to be able to pursue his studies, and his sensitivity of pride in accepting his crust of bread from strangers, became proverbial in the Slavic ghetto. Practically all the time he stood but one step away from starvation. He had no place he could call his own; instead, the dreary and often unheated schoolhouse served as his home. He spent his waking hours at the long study-tables in the yeshivah classrooms; at night he would stretch out his undernourished body on the benches for uneasy sleep.

While it is undeniable that some communities which maintained yeshivot went to great lengths in order to provide the students with food and lodging, even of the most modest kind, the bachurim in other places had no choice but to accept the crumbs of private charity. They ate at the tables of the charitable pious. This practice was dubbed in expressive Yiddish *essen teg*—i.e., "eating days." (Actually, the truth was the reverse—the days were "eating" the students, devouring their self-respect.) The bachurim usually would make the rounds of the Jewish community, eating at the table of one or another household in a kind of rotation system, in periods of one or more days. Mendele Mocher Seforim, famed as "the grandfather of modern Yiddish literature," described out of first-hand experience as a hungry yeshivah bachur in nineteenth-century Russia, the gall-and-wormwood taste left in the student's mouth after dining "with the family" at the tables of his "benefactors."

To make a beginning for ending this very distressing situation, Rabbi Chaim, a Lithuanian disciple of Elijah of Vilna (the Vilner Gaon) founded in 1803 the Volozhin Yeshivah. At least, during the time they remained at this institution, its students were spared the humiliation of accepting private charity and were protected against the anxieties of an uncertain daily existence.

Orthodox Jews today maintain yeshivot in many countries. Some of these institutions are of the traditional kind; they prepare their students for the rabbinate or for teaching in religious schools. There are others, in the United States and Canada in particular, which also call themselves yeshivot, but these are little more than Jewish parochial day-schools and are, therefore, not to be confused with the yeshivot which are adult rabbinical seminaries. With reference to these latter institutions, the changed economic and social conditions of the Jews in the modern world no longer make the privations of former times necessary for the majority of their bachurim or students.

See also TORAH STUDY; YESHIBAH.

YETZER HA-RAH. *See* YETZER TOB AND YETZER HA-RAH.

YETZER TOB AND YETZER HA-RAH (Hebrew, meaning, respectively, the "Good Inclination" and the "Evil Inclination")

In post-Exilic Judaism, as well as in Zoroastrian religious belief, good and evil were paired off in a unity of contrasting opposition. That the Jews derived this dualistic notion from the Persians is pretty certain. For many centuries, following the Captivity in Babylonia, which had started in 586 B.C.E., Jews had lived in large permanent settlements among the Babylonians and Persians, comprising a population of more than one million even in the pre-Christian era. It stands to reason that they assimilated much of the alien culture in which they lived, including certain religious beliefs, for there was free and enlightened intercourse between the Persian "wise men" or magi and the Jewish "teachers of wisdom"—the Rabbinic Sages.

Yet there was a fundamental difference between the dualism found in the Parsee religion and that which was later developed independently by the Jews. In the religion of Zoroaster there were two deities, symbolic of good and evil. One was Ormuzd (the god of Light), the other was Ahriman (the god of Darkness). They were engaged with each other in an unceasing war for supremacy in the world. True, one can find an oppositional kinship between those Persian gods and the "Good Inclination-Bad Inclination" concept of the Jews, for the latter pair too were dramatized as implacable rivals locked in unending battle with each other. But that is where the similarity ends, for Rabbinic teachings endowed this conflict with a naturalistic—in fact, with almost a psychological—character, declaring "Good" and "Evil" to be, not as the Parsees would have them, supernatural forces operating *outside* of human beings, but, on the contrary, natural inclinations *inside* of human beings, struggling without cease for supremacy over the mind and soul within the "kingdom of the heart." Furthermore, stated the Sages, those antagonists within man were not absolute but conditional powers, subject to the moral controls of the mind and the decisions of the will.

From a historical perspective, the Jewish conception of the Yetzer Tob and the Yetzer ha-Rah signalized a turning-point in the ethical thinking of mankind. It was a repudiation of fatalism: Man was free to think, to choose, and to act; he did not have to go jiggling through life like a puppet manipulated by the caprice of the gods. Within its religious context, this represented a restatement of the old Biblical belief in the perfectability of man.

Despite the fact that Rabbinic discussion in the Talmud about Good and Evil is extensive, the Yetzer Tob—the "Good Inclination"—receives but the most cursory attention. It is, of course, honored and given appropriate commendation (couched in the most pious terms) as being the true support of the individual who wishes to live righteously. If its admonitions are heeded, the Sages declare, it is able to deliver the harassed soul from the silken coils of the enemy within—none other than that tireless tempter, the Inclination to Evil. And what are the admonitions of the Yetzer Tob? That man can save himself from the punishing consequences of doing evil through the intervention of good works, devoted study of Torah, and by his performance of the Mitzvot (the 613 Scriptural commandments).

The Jewish concept of the eternal struggle within man of the Yetzer Tob and Yetzer ha-Rah finds a striking analogue in the central Zoroastrian doctrine of the unending conflict between Ormuzd (Ahura Mazda), the god of light and wisdom, and Ahriman, the dragon-deity of darkness and evil.

But it is the Yetzer ha-Rah—"the Inclination to Evil"—that is given the special attention of the Rabbis. And possibly that emphasis is justified from a pedagogic point of view. In Jewish folk-thinking, the Yetzer ha-Rah, personalized for dramatic purposes, is pictured as a subtle tempter—Satan himself! He is eloquent with persuasiveness; he is a master of cunning and adroit with stratagems wherewith to entangle the unheeding foolish soul in the net of promised pleasures and gain. "The Yetzer ha-Rah is a seducer in this world and an accuser in the World-to-Come," warned the ancient moralists.

How did man ever come by his Evil Inclination? It was asked. It is "the leaven in the dough"—the agent of corruption in man—was the mournful answer. But this explanation did not satisfy the deeply reflective, challenging "Jobs" among the pious. Surely, they argued, since God foresaw everything, why did he have to create the evil seducer to torment man with his temptations and lead him to his spiritual destruction? In an extraordinary passage in the Talmud, God is described as sternly rebuking Cain for the murder of his brother, Abel. At this, the fratricide becomes incensed. Why was God blaming him? Hadn't He, the Creator, planted the Yetzer ha-Rah in his heart? Then in all fairness it was God's own fault that he, Cain, had murdered Abel!

The question arose how to reconcile the moral inconsistency represented by the Evil Inclination with the belief in the reality of God's justice and love for mankind. The Zealots, undeviating and perfectionist in their faith, chose to see in the Yetzer ha-Rah a negative force which was working for the positive good. In short, they accepted the presence of evil in mankind as a moral necessity! Asked Rabbi ben Nachman rhetorically in the third century: "Is then the Evil Inclination good," He replied to his own challenge somewhat quizzically: "Were it not for the promptings of the Yetzer ha-Rah, no man would be led to build a house nor marry a woman nor beget children nor engage in trade . . ."

Even more concerned with the problem of combating it effectively than with reconciling the existence of the Yetzer ha-Rah were the Tannaim, the religious thinkers cited in the Mishnah. They had God saying to man, as it were: "If I created the Evil Inclination to tempt you into error, I also created the Torah [i.e., truth] to keep you from error."

It was taught in the Academy of Rabbi Ishmael in Jerusalem during the second century: "When the Evil Inclination comes to seduce you—drag him to the House of Study! If he is made of stone, your study of Torah will wear him down like the steady drip of water! If he is made of iron, your study of Torah will melt him like flame!"

See also ASCETICS, JEWISH; FREE WILL; GOLDEN MEAN, THE RABBINIC; PASSIONS, MASTERY OVER; REWARD AND PUNISHMENT; SATAN; SIN AND SINNER.

YIBBUM. *See* CHALITZAH.

YIDDISH LANGUAGE, THE

The first glimmer of factual light turned on the subject of the vernacular language of the Jews who settled in the French-German Rhineland dates back to the eleventh century. A number of German words written in Hebrew characters are suddenly met with in the Responsa (rabbinical decisions and opinions) by Solomon ben Isaac of Troyes (1040–1105), better known as Rashi. He himself referred to the German of the Jews as *Loshon Ashkenaz*. A little later, other such words and expressions cropped up in the Responsa on rabbinic law by Eliezer ben Nathan of Mayence (second half of the twelfth century).

The question this raises is: How did German words first happen to enter into Hebrew religious writings at this particular juncture? Presumably, the eleventh and twelfth centuries (if not earlier) marked the beginning in a concrete, ascertainable way of the Judeo-German language which is popularly called Yiddish (from the German word *Jüdisch*, i.e., "Jewish").

It is a wry truth that, according to the facts of recorded history, the Jews spent only about a fourth of their national existence in Palestine. The rest of the time they lived in other countries as small ethnic groups set apart from the rest of the population by Christian and Mohammedan state law and religious separatism, creating in their semi-isolation their own distinctive Jewish religious culture. Wherever they lived, they learned to speak the vernacular of the inhabitants of the land. However, since ancient times it was customary for them to use the characters of the Hebrew alphabet when writing in any other language. They did this with Persian, Greek, Latin, Arabic, Spanish, Italian, French, and also with German. It was from German that Yiddish sprang.

Had Jews lived in France for a much longer period of time and in as relaitvely large numbers in settled communities and ghettos as they did in Germany, the probabilities are that they would have evolved a different kind of Yiddish language; it would have had a French rather than a German base. Four hundred years ago, the Jewish humanist and Hebrew grammarian, Elijah Levita, stated: "We German Jews are of French stock. When we were

Facsimile page from Yiddish manuscript version of the Book of Psalms, end of 15th century. (Prussian State Library, Berlin.).

Facsimile page from the printed Yiddish version of Yosippon, *Zurich, 1546. (Sulzberger Collection, Jewish Theological Seminary of America.)*

expelled from France . . . we were dispersed throughout Germany, but on our tongue have lingered many words from their language."

During the twelfth and thirteenth centuries, Jewish poets in France translated a number of Hebrew liturgical verses into French, but they transcribed the French words with Hebrew characters. There are also extant from the same medieval period several rhymed prescriptions and cures composed by Jewish doctors in French but also written with Hebrew characters. This is a clear indication that, while the French Jews were familiar with the Hebrew language, they employed it only for religious worship and study; the language they *spoke* was French.

On Yiddish tongues still linger French words and expressions of medieval origin. To cite just a few examples: The Yiddish word *alker* (alcove) came from the French *alcôve; impet* (impetuousness) from *impétuosité; goider* from *goître; benshen* (grace) from *bénédiction; davenen* (to pray) from *diviniser; sarver* (server of food) from *serviteur; kapoteh* (long coat of medieval origin still worn by some Ultra-Orthodox Jews) from *capote*.

It is a retributive historical irony that "Aryan" scholars of medieval German have found Yiddish to be one of the most fruitful sources for their studies. This is because eight or nine centuries ago, Yiddish, although it was written phonetically with Hebrew characters, represented mostly Middle High German. The Jews who spoke it followed the Swabian and Bavarian dialects. Being already literate in Hebrew, they felt no need of learning the Latin alphabet, which they self-defensively rejected as being "the monkish script." In cheder (the traditional religious elementary school), every Jewish boy acquired at very least a reading and writing competence in Hebrew, which was the obligatory language for the practice of the Jewish religion, for prayer, for reading from the Torah, etc.

There were a number of reasons why Yiddish, in its development as a language, increasingly deviated from its Germanic source. For one thing, Hebrew continued as the *lashon ha-kodesh*, the sacred language. It pervaded the entire fabric of Jewish life, which was uniquely centered in religion and in an unceasing study of the Scriptures. Therefore, it was natural that Hebrew words, terms, and expressions should be constantly on the tongues of Jews, no matter where they lived or what vernacular they spoke.

The mere technical procedure of transliterating German words with Hebrew letters and some dissimilar phonetics automatically resulted in "dialect" changes in the language. The subsequent migrations, flights, and expulsions of the Jews from country to country encouraged their assimilation of words and expressions from different languages, although the base of Yiddish always remained German. Still in active currency—but only in Yiddish—are such Old and Middle High German words as *einekel* (from *enekel*, meaning "grandchild"); *tzvugen* (from *zwagen*, "to comb"); *milgroim* (from *magrana*, "pomegranate"); *atsinder* (from *etzunt*, "now"); and *shvehr* (from *schweher*, "father-in-law").

By the thirteenth century, Yiddish already began to reveal linguistic variations from spoken German. These differences were further intensified when the massacre of Jews during the Crusades and the Black Death of 1348-49 sent tens of thousands of them fleeing for their lives from the Franco-German Rhineland into Central and Southern Germany—into Bavaria, Austria, and Bohemia—from where they proliferated into Northern Italy and the hitherto unfamiliar Polish provinces and Russia. Until that time, the Jews of Eastern Europe probably had only spoken one or another of the Slavonic languages or dialects. But beginning with the thirteenth century, they adopted Yiddish, the Middle High German dialect of their brothers from Germany. How that change was effected, however, is not altogether clear, although certain inferences may be safely drawn from the historic migratory movements of Jews hither and thither across the face of Europe.

In the centuries that followed, the religious and cultural integration of the German Jews with the Slavonic Jews was accomplished by means of Yiddish, which thenceforth became the "Jewish" language for most of the Jews on the Continent.

Philologists have often attempted to give a fractional breakdown of the component elements of Yiddish. Their estimates have varied but little. Perhaps an acceptable formula would be 70 per cent German, 20 per cent Hebrew and Aramaic, with the remaining 10 per cent consisting of Russian, Polish, Ukrainian, Slovakian, Romanian, and other loan-words.

See also JEWISH LANGUAGES.

YIDDISH LITERATURE, MODERN

Paradoxically, modern Yiddish literature developed directly out of the Haskalah, the Jewish Enlightenment movement which was started in Berlin during the second half of the eighteenth century by Moses Mendelssohn, "the German Plato"—and he had waged an uncompromising onslaught on Yiddish because it was "a corrupt jargon"! (*See* ENLIGHTENMENT, THE JEWISH.)

The modern period of Yiddish literature—and, amazingly enough, the same also holds true of modern Hebrew literature—began with the writings of Mendele Mocher Seforim ("Mendele the Bookseller"—the whimsical pen name of Solomon Jacob Abramovich, 1836–1917). His youthful disciple, Sholom Aleichem, affixed to him the folksy Yiddish soubriquet *Der Zaydeh*—"The Grandfather [of Jewish literature]." With this descriptive he wished to acknowledge that "Mendele" (his readers, with the intimacy of bosom friends, usually refer to him by his first name) was truly the *zaydeh*, the archprogenitor of himself and of all other modern Yiddish writers.

Although he was the first master to appear in Yiddish literature, Mendele had for forerunners a small number of Yiddish fiction writers, poets, playwrights, and journalists who, in intellectual terms and by their example, had helped pave the way for him. Like Mendele Mocher Seforim, they were also devotees of the Jewish Enlightenment and, in varying degrees, were also familiar with classical and European literature. Although far less gifted than he, they, too, can be said to have belonged to the modern era and to the progressive spirit that permeated it. Most noteworthy among these Yiddish Maskilim (adherents of the Haskalah) whose writings were frankly agitational in behalf of the Enlighten-

Mendele Mocher Seforim. Russia, end of 19th century.

ment, were Isaac Ber Levinsohn (1788–1860), Yitzchok Aksenfeld (1787–1862), Solomon Ettinger (1800–1855), Abraham Ber Gottlober (1811–99), Michel Gordon (1823–90), Isaac Meir Dick (1808–93), and Isaac Joel Linetzki (1839–1915).

At very best, these pioneer men of letters, writing in the modern vein, were merely taking tentative first steps in the direction of bringing into being a bona fide modern literature in Yiddish. Whatever the level of their literary competence, taste, or culture, at no time can their writings be said to have been distinguished. It is to their credit, however, that they made the first serious attempts, however faltering, to depict life and social relationships within the ghetto realistically, using an approach and treatment that were almost entirely absent in contemporary Hebrew Haskalah writings, which were marred by a purple, pseudo-Biblical rhetoric.

But carried away by their zeal as "Enlighteners," Mendele's forerunners seized upon satire as the principal weapon in their literary armory. Often enough they wielded it without any sublety—more like a club or a bludgeon—upon their pious adversaries, the Chasidim (*see* CHASIDIM) and their rebbehs (the "wonder-working" rabbis). They were unsparing in their ridicule of the Chasidim for their credulity and superstition and of their rebbehs—whom they accused of an unspiritual fondness for money—for their employment of a mystifying verbal jugglery to awe their adherents.

At the heart of the program of the Enlightenment lay the intention of exposing to laughter and scorn all in Jewish life that was alien and out of step with the progress of the world and all the warpings and vices in ghetto life. This satirical onslaught had many targets. In particular, the nineteenth-century Yiddish writers inveighed against the corruption of the communal big-wheels—the baalebatim who ruled the kahal (the semi-autonomous microcosm of the ghetto; *see* COMMUNITY, SELF-GOVERNING) with an iron hand, often showing themselves to be insensitive to the sufferings of the poor.

This simple fact deserves re-emphasis: Mendele Mocher Seforim was, indeed, the first of the great Yiddish moderns, but also, like these less-gifted Yiddish precursors, he was a Maskil, a champion of the Enlightenment which aimed to serve as the cultural bridge between the ghetto (then steeped in medievalism) and the modern world. His books, whether in Hebrew or in Yiddish—and he wrote in both of these Jewish languages with enormous facility and felicity—were imbued with the liberal spirit of the Haskalah, with its rationalistic approach to religion and its program for educational and social reforms. Contrary to the usual inclination of literary men to regard their writing principally as an art or a craft, he valued it chiefly as a tool for social progress. This programmatic approach, however, did not prevent him from evolving a brilliant literary craftsmanship and a communicative art.

In some respects, Mendele bore an arresting resemblance to the Dubner Maggid—the wandering "Preacher of Dubno," Rabbi Jacob Krantz (Lithuania, 1740-1804). Like him, Mendele was a consummate storyteller, a moralist passionately attached to his people and full to the brim with its folk wit, wisdom, and traditional ethical values. But in Mendele both the old and the new were intermeshed, and out of this fusion there resulted—as he himself came to recognize—"two Mendeles: one is the devout, the wise Jew of the House of Study [Bet ha-Midrash]; the other is the modern skeptic." Like the Preacher of Dubno, he considered that, in the field of popular education, there was to be found no method of instruction as effective as satire.

Mendele's employment of satire, far from being frivolous, carping, or malicious, seems to have been motivated and to have sprung from an urgent sense of social responsibility—from a desire to serve the group-welfare of his fellow Jews by doing his share in bringing them out of their backward ghetto existence and helping them to transform themselves into "enlightened Europeans." Sometime in the 1880's he wrote to Beszonov, a Christian and a member of the Russian Government Commission to Study the Jewish Question: "Since I love the Jews with all my heart, I have, therefore, chosen satire as my genre in the field of literature. I'm not at all afraid of uncovering and taking apart our innermost faults."

Mendele's satiric hand, dipped in both acid and honey—acid for exposing the mean and their meannesses, and honey for depicting the virtues of humble folk passing unrecognized under the shabby exterior of their poverty and ignorance—produced works that were in the populist, humanitarian tradition of Nikolai Gogol and Charles Dickens. The great cast of characters that pass in review before his searching analysis is in one way similar to the human kaleidoscope of feudal England in Chaucer's *Canterbury Tales* or even, in a more significant way, to *La Comédie Humaine* of Balzac, which encompassed the entire bourgeoisie of France. The life Mendele depicted was the Jewish microcosm of Russia and Poland—a world that was complete in itself. His imaginary ghetto towns of Tunayadevke and Glupsk, which he populated with motley types and assorted miseries, appeared to at least three generations of East European Jewish readers as real as if they had been actual places on the map and as vivid as if they themselves had lived there.

All the social classes and callings in the ghetto were bountifully represented by Mendele: rabbis, cantors, sextons, Talmudic scholars, Torah-Scroll copyists, boys' Scripture teachers, yeshivah students, ritual slaughterers, communal leaders, charity collectors, tax-farmers, innkeepers, merchants, brokers, agents, storekeepers, tailors, carpenters, cartmen, peddlers, misfits and luftmenschen (literally, "men of air; that is, men without trade or calling"), beggars and homeless wanderers. With a proper understanding of the nature of culture, Mendele once told the Jewish historian Simon Dubnow that, in the future, should a historian wish to depict the East European Jewish life of the nineteenth century, to grasp its real character he would have to read his (Mendele's) tales. This prediction has turned out to be altogether correct.

Mendele's absorbing concern not only with psychological characterization but with the depiction of the social evils that existed within the ghetto gave impetus to his creative urge, and lent verissimilitude, substance, and depth to his novels, novelettes, short stories, and plays. He laid bare with relentless objectivity all the griefs and dissonances resulting from the mad struggle for survival in the ghetto.

Mendele never gave up belaboring the corruption of power in Jewish community life. This he did with enormous satirical vigor in his play, *Di Takse, oder Di Bande Shtut Baal-Toives* ("The Tax-Office, or The Gang of Town Benefactors"). The play takes to task the petty tyrants who rule the ghetto in the mythical town of Glupsk, where the poor and the weak "have been beaten down and are being strangled like so many cats, and no one is permitted to raise his head." It deserves to be noted that at the time when Mendele published *Di Takse*, in 1869, he was living in Berditchev, and this work caused such anger among the Jewish communal leaders there that they forced him to leave town.

The author took a new approach to the problems of the Jewish masses in his allegory *Di Kliatche* ("The Old Plug" or "The Broken-down Mare"). The protagonist—"the old bag of bones"—of this fable in novel form is none other than the Jewish people, whom everybody liked to abuse and kick around. "The old mare," who is a non-resister to evil, endures her mistreatment meekly since she no longer has any energy or will left to protest.

At this juncture—dramatically expressed in *Di Kliatche*—Mendele began to revaluate for himself the goals of the Haskalah. Would Enlightenment and Westernization by themselves succeed in solving the problems of the Jewish masses? he asked rhetorically. And he hastened to answer himself: "Not ignorance is the cause for the pauperization [of the ghetto Jews] but rather, 'You can't dance before you've eaten!' Now please tell me, I beg you, what has eating got to do with education? By what right can we tell another human being not to eat, not to breathe freely until he first learns some new tricks [i.e., education]?" And the moral of Mendele's tale of the broken-down mare is: "First the right to live—only afterwards enlightenment."

It was, however, with *Fishke der Krumer* ("Fishke the Lame," 1869) that Mendele first realized his full creative potential. This novel is a parable about ghetto poverty and social neglect. It is a tale that deals with beggars, cripples, and other varieties of outcasts scurrying over the social anthill of the ghetto in a struggle for sheer physical survival. There is genuine pathos in the attachment between its two central characters—Fishke the Lame and Beila the Hunchback. Their bodies twisted, their surroundings sordid, their livelihood mean, they themselves, although despised and rejected by "respectability," nonetheless find a haven from life's cruelties and the consequences of their own follies in the love they have for each other.

A work of striking originality among the eighteen volumes of his published writings was *Dos Vinshfingerl* ("The Wishing Ring," 1888–92). Simple in form but epic in its compass, it recounts the life of a Russian Jew, Hershele, living from birth until maturity in the poverty-stricken ghetto town of *Kabtzansk* ("Pauper-Town"). A microcosm typical of all East European Jewish life, it delineates the entire physical and spiritual life of the community, its activities, problems, afflictions, ethical folkways, and religious values and practices.

Mendele's free employment of the Yiddish folk idiom, while blending it with the traditional Scriptural and Talmudic locutions, casuistical "thumb-twisting," and dialectical style of reasoning, gave the Yiddish language a plasticity and a brilliance it had never realized before. From an undisciplined polyglot vernacular he transformed it into a responsive instrument of literary expression. Concerning this contribution by his master, Yitzchok Leibush Peretz wrote: "He [Mendele] was the first to show love and devotion to the medium of his art—the Yiddish language—which he preserved and developed in all its purity, not Germanized, not Russified, not even Europeanized. Therefore, he is the first writer to have created a Yiddish style, his own individual style. Mendele speaks the language of his people."

The principal literary follower of Mendele was Sholom Aleichem (the pen name of Sholom Rabinowitz: Russia, 1859–U.S.A., 1916). In a reading of both writers, the thought unavoidably obtrudes itself that had Mendele never lived and written his tales, Sholom Aleichem, notwithstanding that some of his literary gifts outshown his master's, probably would have turned out a different sort of writer. There is to be found in both the same love for plain folk and a similar preoccupation with the problems of personality and Jewish destinies. Both shared a revulsion toward cruelty, a scorn for the pride of social caste (termed in Yiddish *yiches*), and a feeling of outrage against the oppression of the weak by the strong. Like Mendele, Sholom Aleichem, too, wrote with compassion for the poor, the maltreated, and the outcast. Moreover, he adopted the folksy, earthy approach of Mendele and even improved upon it, for he had a wonderful ear for speech.

Sholom Aleichem had a deep insight into his creative resources. Said he: "It was destined for me, by a wonderful inner power, to go hand in hand with my queer little characters, and to contemplate this vast tumultous life through an open laughter and disguised hidden tears."

Whereas Mendele was often bitter about life's injustices, his disciple was blessed with a gentle, merry nature. True, he, too, could be satirical, but he was never harsh. He could be devastatingly funny, but without being vinegary; indignant, but never self-righteous. The salient characteristic of his genius was that he could be angry yet laugh gaily at the same time, so that the sting was taken out of his barbs. He could also be sentimental, but most of the time escaped becoming syrupy; his good-natured ribbing always served as a corrective.

Sholom Aleichem's works might be said to constitute the Book of Life in the ghetto during the last decades of the nineteenth century. They exude a pulsating sense of reality—the reality of the accumulated experiences of the folk. The great humorist was steeped in Jewish lore, tradition, and folk wisdom. The characters he depicted were representative Jewish types, therefore universal. What other writers would have passed by, considering it commonplace, he endowed with individuality and distinction. His portrait gallery is immense. Every single individual who figures in his stories, novels, or monologues has his own peculiarities of speech and idiocyncrasies of personality. When his heroes or villains clash, as they so often do, they duel with fabulous retorts and with choice abuse requiring the aid of a glossary. Unabashedly, they engage in idle but deadly gossip, being fully informed of one another's vulnerabilities, upon which they pour salt and pepper. This is done with no apparent malice but good humoredly, with quips and with an air of innocence.

But this is only one aspect of Sholom Aleichem's genius for characterization. Just as impressive perhaps is his kindly feeling for all people, whoever they may be. If they are schlemiehls or schlimazels, or if they reveal fissures in their characters, it only awakens his compassion for them the more. His creed is simple: He believes in the essential goodness of plain folk, however misfit, ridiculous, or odd they might appear to others.

First one laughs heartily with Sholom Aleichem as he applies the scalpel of insight to his quaint characters. Then, upon reconsideration, one suddenly finds that the droll situations into which the characters are thrown are really tragic. Sholom Aleichem consciously tried to teach his hard-pressed fellow Jews that while it was not possible to take any but a realistic view of their troubles, it was necessary that they face them with the courage of laughter.

In addition to a great number of novelettes, short stories, sketches, monologues, and plays, Sholom Aleichem wrote a number of memorable novels in his inimitable, humorous, folksy style. The wide appeal of so many of his writings, going far beyond his Yiddish-reading audience, may be seen in the fact that some of his books have been translated into more than seventy languages. When the great Russian writer, Maxim Gorky, read *Mottl Paysi, the Cantor's Boy* in a Russian version, he thus described his reactions: "I both laughed and cried over it—a wonderful book! . . . The entire work is flooded with a deep, genuine and wise love for people—a sentiment that is so rare in our time."

Among the eight or nine novels Sholom Aleichem produced, two achieved an immense popularity. It can be justifiably claimed that they entered and shaped the thinking and feeling of the Jewish masses. These two novels were *Menachem Mendel of Yehupetz* (1892) and *Tevye der Milchiger* (1895-1916). Menachem Mendel is the original schlimazel—the everlasting pipedreamer. He is always in hot pursuit of the mirage of riches that has been the obsession of so many misfits. *Tevye der Milchiger* has a great deal in common with Menachem Mendel; he, too, is a little man, unlettered and unworldly, feeling helpless in an inhospitable world. He, too, does a lot of wishful thinking about better times which somehow never come. Although buffeted and battered by a life he had never made, he remains meek and smiling wistfully. He never loses his self-respect and dignity even at the lowest ebb of his fortune. It should be added that the reason why *Menachem Mendel* and *Tevye der Milchiger* were so beloved by Yiddish readers is that in them they saw their own lives reflected.

In the majority of cases, the shorter pieces of Sholom Aleichem—whether stories, sketches, or monologues—were composed with an eye to their recitation. The fact is that they have had a popularity even greater than his novels among Yiddish readers, who have repeatedly turned to them with more relish than even the most ardent enthusiast of Shakespeare lavishes upon the Bard's plays. In some respects, these pieces do not find their like in world literature. By the almost exclusive means of dialogue they faithfully reproduce not only the Yiddish speech and intonation but, with a seeming artlessness, achieve three-dimensional characterizations of ordinary Jews and their mode of thinking and feeling. It is not possible to know Sholom Aleichem adequately without having read his two volumes of *Maisses far Idishe Kinder* ("Stories for Jewish Children"), and the "Jews-at-the-Spa" and "Jews-on-the-Train" stories.

The third member in the triad of Yiddish literary classicists was Yitzchok Leibush Peretz (Poland, 1851-1915), early a devotee of the Haskalah. Writing at first in Hebrew, Peretz set himself the task of becoming a folk writer in the Yiddish language. Truth to tell, he became a Yiddish writer instead of a Hebrew or Polish one not because of any overflowing love for Yiddish but because he was convinced that for practical reasons the vernacular could serve as the most effective linguistic medium for bringing enlightenment to the backward Yiddish-speaking masses of Eastern Europe. This attitude he expressed very plainly in 1890: "We want to teach the people and write in *Jargon* [the derogatory name for Yiddish used by the followers of the Enlightenment (*see* YIDDISH LANGUAGE, THE)] because we have about three million Jews who understand only *Jargon*. However, we do not consider this *Jargon* as holy. We sympathize quite often with those who wish to exchange Jargon for a living language." But not many years passed before Peretz' attitude toward Yiddish changed from one of antipathy to nationalistic enthusiasm: "One people—Jews; one language—Yiddish. In this language we will gather our treasures, we will create our culture, and will further strengthen our spirit with it."

Peretz drew enormously for his writings from the raw materials of Jewish religious lore—from the folk legends, parables, and the ethical traditions and practices of the people. As a writer, he was introspective and moody and displayed a great fondness for symbolism and the poetic mode of expression. Many of his works are permeated by an undercurrent of poetic mysticism—the residue of the Chasidism that, ironically, he, an enlightened Maskil, had rejected long before. At the same time, following the Russian pogroms of 1881-82 and the repressive May Laws promulgated by the czarist government, he had turned both Zionist and revolutionary Socialist. His Jewish nationalism and social radicalism (he was active in the Bund, the Jewish Revolutionary Organization) equally with his Chasidic mysticism, deeply imprinted themselves on his writing.

Merely from this fact alone it is possible to deduce that, in his beliefs and attachments, Peretz was an eclectic rather than a confused thinker. He drew his intellectual sustenance from the most diverse sources. To the literary historian Israel Zinberg he once confided: "The Prophets influenced me deeply." And in the same breath he added his debt to intellectual skepticism: "For a long time I was under the spell of Heine and Boerne." But these by no means were the only influences. Seemingly contradictorily, he was at one and the same time a mystic Chasid and a confirmed rationalist, a literary realist and a romanticist. Although he was dominated by the populist sentiment of faith in the common people, he nonetheless also expressed his disenchantment with idealistic strivings. His disciple H. D. Nomberg recalled: "Peretz was saturated with an abysmal pessimism, with a revulsion for life."

Peretz acquired a virtuoso skill in almost every type of literary composition—short story, essay, causerie, verse, and drama. In only one form was he lacking: in novel writing. His special genius obviously lay in the short story, in the vignette which he could perfect, as a lapidary polishes a jewel.

Whatever were the other sources from which Peretz tapped his materials, it was on Chasidic themes that he emerged most fully as a creative artist. To these he devoted a major portion of his literary activity. A great many of the stories, conceived in the secularist spirit, were poetical refinements of Chasidic legends and ethical anecdotes. Peretz, always an enthusiastic collector of Jewish lore, had heard some of the tales from the lips of the folk; others he had discovered

Sholom Aleichem. Russia, c. 1900.

I. L. Peretz. Warsaw, c. 1900.

in the little groschen- ("penny-book") collections of tales about the wonder-working Chasidic rebbehs and Cabalists. But, invariably, he treated his materials in a modern impressionistic manner with mystical lyricism struck in a minor key. Rapture (in Hebrew: *hitlahavut*) and contemplation—the essential ingredients of the inner illumination sought by the Chasidim—Peretz made identifiable characteristics of his stories. For example: "The world is no more than a song and a dance . . . the life of man is a melody [nigun] which is either gay or sad, and when it is ended the soul takes its flight from the body."

The mysticism of Peretz did not always escape challenge; it even induced exasperation in the rationalists. His drama, *Di Goldene Keit* ("The Golden Chain"), which treats of the Chasid's quest for purity of faith and conduct in a life that is declared to be disfigured by sin and evil, has its heroine, Leah, raise the cry "Light! . . . let there be light!" But to Peretz' friend, the antimystical Sholom Aleichem, this "light" appeared as no light at all: "I gave him [Peretz] my opinion very frankly about *The Golden Chain.* I told him that I would gladly exchange ten such "golden chains" for one little story in his *Folkstimliche Geshichten* ['Folkloristic Stories']."

Peretz' Chasidic stories and sketches—Sholom Aleichem's lack of enthusiasm for them notwithstanding—rank among the most memorable of his productions. *A Gilgul fun a Nigun* ("The Reincarnation of a Melody"), *Oib Nisht Noch Hecher* ("If Not Still Higher") have become beloved classics in Yiddish literature. The same can be said for several of his folkloristic-style stories: *Yenkel Pessimist* ("Yenkel the Pessimist"), *Drei Matones* ("Three Gifts"), *Der Chelmer Melamed* ("The Hebrew Teacher of Chelm"), *Arupgeloste Oigen* ("Lowered Eyes"), and *Der Meshulach* ("The Messenger").

To a great extent, Peretz' stories and sketches on social and familial themes are didactic. In his celebrated short story, *Bontshe Shveig* ("Bontshe the Silent"), he expresses both pity and scorn for the Russian-Jewish workers (of the 1890's) for their attitude of meekness and non-resistance to oppression. In *Mendel Breines*, a tale of a Torah-scholar and a holy man, "the meek one" is his wife; her life is consumed in the menial service of her "saintly" husband who, unperturbed, accepts her self-sacrifice as his due. *Sholom Bayyis* ("Domestic Peace") extols the traditional solidarity of Jewish family life in the face of adversity.

Peretz' molding influence on the development of modern Yiddish literature was greater even that that of Mendele or Sholom Aleichem. His many distinguished disciples were greatly attached to him, calling him *Unser Rebbeh* ("Our Rabbi" or "Our Teacher"). Foremost among these were Sholem Asch, Bergelson, Pinski, Reisen, Yehoash, Lamed Shapiro, Dinesohn, Spektor, Jacob Gordin, Weissenberg, Nomberg, Yoinah Rosenfeld, Sh. Niger, Ansky, Hirschbein, Opatoshu, Leivick, etc. "Strictly speaking," observed the great Yiddish poet Yehoash, "it was Peretz, and no one else, who was the Father of Yiddish Literature. In a certain sense, all Yiddish writers are his disciples. Peretz brought faith into Yiddish literature. He had a vision of the edifice before even the foundation was laid."

There have been a great many talented Yiddish writers who traced their literary descent from the three "Founding Fathers." Patently, within the compass of this sketchy outline of modern Yiddish literature, it is not possible to mention them all, or even to discuss in but the barest detail those writers who are mentioned. Furthermore, it is not feasible to evaluate all those many gifted writers who are still living and whose literary course is still incomplete.

A contemporary of Peretz and traveling approximately in the same cultural direction was Yankev Dinesohn (Lithuania, 1856-1919). He was a social novelist whose works were marred by excessive sentimentality and melodramatic situations. His most successful tales were about boys—*Hershele* (1895) and *Yosseleh* (1903). He described with pathos their plight as orphans and rejects in an inhospitable world.

Mordchi Spektor (*b.* Russia, 1858–*d.* U.S.A., 1925), a follower and friend of Peretz', together with him upheld the Haskalah program of returning the misfit Jews of the ghetto to productive trades. In the 1880's he published *Der Yiddisher Muzhik* ("The Jewish Peasant"), a thesis novel with a back-to-the-land theme. This was a work which won for him a respected place in contemporary Yiddish letters. Spektor treated of another aspect of the same theme in his novel *Kalikes* ("Cripples"). Who were the "cripples"? The author indicated that they were the majority of the Jewish youth who were dragging out meaningless lives in the small towns of Eastern Europe, paying with privation for not having learned useful trades to provide them with sustenance and a meaning for their existence.

Jacob Gordin (*b.* Russia, 1853–*d.* U.S.A., 1909) was, if not the founder, certainly the "purifier" of the Yiddish drama. He was frankly imitative: His drama, *Der Yiddisher Kenig Lear* ("The Jewish King Lear") was modeled upon Shakespeare's play, *King Lear; Minna* was a Jewish reconstruction of Ibsen's *The Doll's House; Gott, Mensh un Teifel* ("God, Man and the Devil") took its central idea, symbolism, and demonic trappings from Goethe's *Faust; Di Shevuah* ("The Vow") was unmistakably derived from Hauptmann's *Fuhrmann Henschel.* Nevertheless, Gordin was a dramatist with delineative power. Notwithstanding his unoriginal plots, he was able to fill his stage-pieces with original Jewish characterizations; he poured into the borrowed molds of his stories specifically Jewish problems, values, and feelings. For that reason, the impact of his plays on the Yiddish theatre for more than half a century was unequaled by any other playwright.

One of the most talented Yiddish writers to emerge from the turmoil and disaster of Russian Jewish life in the 1880's was Shimon Shmul Frug (Russia, 1860–1916). At first he had written in Russian and achieved some renown as a poet in that language in the literary circles of St. Petersburg. But the pogroms of 1881 had turned him into an ardent Zionist. In his volume of verses, *Golus-lieder* ("Songs of Exile"), he articulated the grief of the Jew in his homelessness and persecution.

S. Ansky (pen name of Shloima Zanvil Rapoport, Russia, 1863–1920) was the most cosmopolitan of all the Yiddish writers; he wrote equally well in Russian, Hebrew, French, and Yiddish. He himself noted wryly: "My life was broken, split up, fragmentized. I do not belong among those who had the good fortune to grow up in their own environment so that their creativity had a normal character." Because he was a close student of and compiler of Jewish folklore, it was natural that it should have supplied him with the raw material for his fine tales, verse, and drama. Into his epic poem *Der Ashmedai,* about the legendary Jewish prince of demons, Asmodeus, he poured his enormous erudition in Jewish ethical folklore and demonology. But, unquestionably, the work by which Ansky will be longest remembered is the Chasidic drama *The Dybbuk* (1914). The play depicts the transmigration of a sinful soul from one body to another, yet at the same time serves also as a repository for old Jewish customs, mystic beliefs, and superstitious notions. Its success has been quite universal, and it has entered into the repertory of every important art-theatre in the world.

In the second half of the nineteenth century, in reaction

to the plight of unorganized workers in the garment industry, there emerged a number of "proletarian" poets such as Dovid Edelstadt (*b.* Russia, 1866–*d.* U.S.A., 1892) and Yosef Bovshover (*b.* Russia, 1873–*d.* U.S.A., 1915). Some of their verses were set to music and were widely sung by workers. One of the best known of these poets was Morris Wintchevsky (*b.* Poland, 1856–*d.* U.S.A., 1932). With reference to his collection, *Londoner Silhouetten,* he noted that he had written the poems included in it "under the stress of the terrible poverty I saw around me . . . of human abandonment and prostration . . ." Translated into English, and later into French, the work won the admiration of William Morris, the English pre-Raphaelite poet, and of Anatole France, the great French writer.

The most talented of all Yiddish poets of social protest was Morris Rosenfeld (*b.* Poland, 1862–*d.* U.S.A., 1923). By an odd combination of accidents, he achieved among non-Jews an international reputation equalled only by those of Sholom Aleichem and Sholem Asch. As a garment worker in the sweatshops of London and (later) New York (where he contracted tuberculosis), he received first-hand knowledge about toil, oppression, and struggle—the subjects of his verses. How such things happen no one can explain—undoubtedly it is a part of the mystery of the folklore process—but before long, Rosenfeld's verses were acquiring musical settings and being sung by workers in all the garment sweatshops of the world. When his *Songs from the Ghetto* appeared in 1898 in an English translation by Professor Leo Wiener of Harvard, they caused a stir in American literary circles. William Dean Howells, the novelist-critic, commented: "It is sufficient glory to speak to whomever reads them . . . his is their [i.e., the sweatshop workers'] misery uttering itself in music; his is their voice."

A poet of quite another outlook and temperament was Yehoash (pseudonym of Solomon Bloomgarten, *b.* Russia, 1870–*d.* U.S.A., 1927). He was one of the most intellectual among the Yiddish writers; his range of interest was reflected in the subject matter of his verse. This he drew from the rich storehouse of Jewish religious culture and history; from the Bible, the Talmud, the Zohar, and from the legends about the master-Cabalists and their continuators, the Chasidic rebbehs. He also chose his materials from medieval folk tales and from the wise saws and proverbs of the people. But not least was his passion for nature which he translated into a pure stream of poetic lyricism. He enriched Yiddish poetry with new forms adopted from world literature and created in the Yiddish language new tonalities and nuances which became a powerful stimulus for later poets seeking a more varied expressiveness and literary sophistication. His principal verse-collections were *Zun un Nepel* ("In Sun and Mist") and *Fun der Velt un Yener* ("Of this World and the Next"), both published in 1913. His translation of the entire Bible into Yiddish was a literary-scholarly achievement of great distinction.

One of the most ardent admirers of Peretz was David Pinski (*b.* Russia, 1872–*d.* Israel, 1959). His first short stories, published in 1894 under the influence of the Jewish Enlightenment in its agitation against pietism, were characterized by a biting satire. Turning next to the drama, which thereafter became his principal medium, he wrote his social play, *Isaac Sheftel* (1899), which carried an indictment of society's unconcern with the welfare of human beings. After the Kishinev pogrom in 1903, Pinski related how, "at the open graves of the Kishinev martyrs, when their blood hadn't yet time to dry, I conceived the idea of, and then began to write, my *Familia Zvi.*" In his comedy, *Der Oitzer* ("The Treasure," 1906), he attempted to show the corrupting power of money on an entire community. This stage piece had an instantaneous success, not only in New York, in the Yiddish theatre, but also in Berlin, where Max Reinhardt produced it in German. In 1920 it was staged again in New York, but this time in an English version. In 1908, Pinski wrote the verse-drama *Gabri un di Froyen* ("Gabri and the Women"), and in 1911, *Der Shtumer Mashiach* ("The Mute Messiah"). The latter drama was an allegory in a medieval setting about the Jewish people and its expectations of ultimate national redemption.

In no Yiddish writer of fiction was the talent for depicting superfluous and futile individuals among the Polish-Jewish intelligentsia as pronounced as in H. D. Nomberg (*b.* Poland, 1876–*d.* Argentina, 1927). A protégé of Peretz, he became a vivesectionist of the mordid psyche. All the characters in his stories strike attitudes and play dramatic roles—not on the stage but in real life. Their antics are artificial, but in the context of their own personalities, they seem almost natural. Nomberg deliberately places them in melodramatic situations only for the purpose of satirizing them. This he tried to accomplish in the short story "Fliegelman," and in the character of Bender in *Dos Shpiel in Liebe* ("Playing in Love").

A writer with a strong social bent was Leon Kobrin (*b.* Russia, 1872–*d.* U.S.A., 1946). In his novels, short stories, and plays he was the first uncompromising realist—or, better said, naturalist—in modern Yiddish literature. He presented almost clinical information about his characters. Their speech, their peculiarities, and the details of their physical surroundings he tried to reproduce, as it were, photographically. He depicted Jewish immigrant life in the New

Dovid Bergelson.

Sholem Asch.

Yehoash.

York tenements with skill and power. His novelette, *Yankel Boila* (1898), brought him immediate recognition. Years later he prepared a dramatic version of it that was staged by Stanislavsky at the Moscow Art Theatre. Among his most admired works were *Ghetto Dramen,* a collection of short stories (1903); and the novels *Immigration* (1909) and *A Litvish Shtetl* ("A Lithuanian Village," 1914).

With the exception of his contemporary, Sholem Asch, no Yiddish writer of his generation who was nurtured in the school of Peretz achieved such wide popularity among Yiddish readers as Avrohm Reisen (*b.* Russia, 1876–*d.* U.S.A., 1953). He was a voluminous producer of short stories on themes of Jewish ghetto-life. Many of his characters are nondescript individuals impelled by ego drives to drift helplessly along with the current. These are impecunious big-town but half-baked intellectuals, struggling shopkeepers, Hebrew teachers, cantors, preachers, the unskilled, the misfits, the social rejects—all portrayed in terms humorous, ironic, wistful, or compassionate. The celebrated Danish critic, Georg Brandes, discerned in Reisen a writer of individuality, and he judged his translated works to be an important addition to world literature.

However, Reisen's reputation among the Jewish masses rests mainly on his lyric poetry. There he occupies a unique position: One of his distinctions rests on his ability to articulate most spontaneously the spirit of the Jewish folk. Many of his verses have the transparency, the melodiousness, and the flavor of folk songs, but his lyrical talent responded mostly to situations and sentiments that expressed defeat and moods of despair. His best known lyric, "Mai Komash Malon?" ("What Does It Tell Us?"), set to a melancholy tune which is reminiscent of the cantillation in which Talmudic study is traditionally carried on, has achieved the universality of a favorite folk song.

Whenever the names of Mendele Mocher Seforim, Sholom Aleichem, and Peretz are mentioned, that of Sholem Asch (*b.* Poland, 1880–*d.* England, 1957), also springs to mind. In some significant ways, he was the logical—"the modern"—extension of their genius. His place in the historical development of Yiddish literature was described as early as 1910 by Dr. Chaim Zhitlovsky, the champion of Jewish culture in Yiddish thus: "Until Sholem Asch, Yiddish literature held only a parochial interest for Yiddish readers. Asch is the first Jewish artist who has outgrown the limitations of his [Jewish] sphere and who has incorporated in himself the spirit of European culture. This explains his popularity in the non-Jewish world." This comment was called forth by the fact that Asch's drama, *The God of Vengeance,* written when its author was only thirty, was accorded the respect of a theatrical classic by such outstanding directors as Stanislavsky, Reinhardt, and others.

Sholem Asch came to the attention of Yiddish readers in a forceful way when he was only twenty-four, upon the publication of the novelette *Dos Shtetl* ("The Small Town"). This work was an idealization of the departed glories of Jewish small-town life when it was steeped in its pious and ethical folkways. Its great success was due, in large measure, to the fact that it evoked a nostalgic response in thousands of Jews who had formerly been small-town dwellers but whom economic necessity had forced into the city slums, where they felt culturally rootless and alienated. It is indeed remarkable how persistently this theme and image of the shtetl crops up in the writings of Sholem Asch. The author remains in love with the stately rhythm of Jewish religious rite and ceremonial; he is constantly looking back with longing to the golden age of Jewish communal living, when it was still "whole" and harmonious in its religious integration. This is particularly in evidence in the novels *Di Yatisheh Tochter* ("The Middle-Class Daughter") and *Shloime Nogid* ("Rich Shloime"), as well as in the historical novels *Kiddush ha-Shem* ("Sanctification of the Name"), *Marranen* ("*Marranos*"), and *Di Kishefmacherin fun Kastilien* ("The Sorceress of Castile").

A new literary phase began for Asch following his first visit to the United States in 1910. His novels and short stories began to mirror the tumultuous life of the East Side ghetto and its sweatshop-slum-tenement setting. His first considerable piece of fiction of the American scene was *Uncle Moses* (1918), a novel about an "all-rightnik"—a newly rich immigrant who owned a sweatshop on the Bowery. Here once again is sounded the leit motiv of *Dos Shtetl:*

> Every old stone, every old house and corner is recalled with love and longing by the loyal children of Kuzmin as they sit sewing pants. And here and there a tear falls; a groan from an old Kuzmin-er is heard as he recalls the beauty of his birthplace.

In *Di Mutter* ("The Mother," 1923), the immigrant Jews, transplanted into the stony East Side tenements, sigh for the serenity and the meaningfulness of the life they left behind them in the "old country."

Perhaps the last of Asch's significant novels on a Jewish theme—namely, of the life that he knew so well at first hand—was the thesis-novel *Farn Mabl* ("Before the Flood"; 1933), which in its English version is called *Three Cities.* In this work he conceived of each of the "three cities"—St. Petersburg, Warsaw, and Moscow—as representing one act in the then recent life of Slavic Jewry. The action begins with the ritual-murder frame-up of Mendel Beilis (*see* "RITUAL-MURDER" SLANDERS) in 1913 and concludes on the triumph of the Russian Revolution.

The closing years of the life of Sholem Asch were embittered by controversy; he had deeply offended a large section of American Jewish opinion because he had made Jesus the hero of *The Nazarene* (1939), Saint Paul the central character of *The Apostle* (1943), and the Virgin Mary the heroine of *Mary* (1949). He had chosen to do this, Asch explained, in order to bolster Jewish self-esteem, which had been dangerously deflated because of denigration by the anti-Semites, especially by the Nazis. At the same time, said he, he wished to break down the prejudice of Christian readers by proving to them "that the ancient Jewish people gave *something* to mankind and, after all, was Christianity not derived from Judaism? Had not the Jews created it?"

At one time Yitzchok Meir Weissenberg (Poland, 1881–1937) was regarded as potentially the most gifted of Peretz' writer-fledglings. He took an objective approach to reality; his characters were recognizable flesh-and-blood creatures. His famous short story, "Dos Shtetl" (1906), was the complete opposite in conception and treatment of Sholem Asch's *Dos Shtetl.* Its prose style was natural and vigorous, its characters plain and crude. Just as Asch's treatment was romantic and sentimentally nostalgic, so was Weissenberg's delineation of the little town realistic and uninvolved. The misery of the poor was largely the subject of his stories, many of which dealt with Jewish toughs and the brutality of their ways. Weissenberg never stops to sentimentalize or commiserate with his hoodlums; he is a social realist without pathos. One of his truly great stories, "A Tatte Mit Bonim" ("Father and Sons") portrays rude, animalistic individuals who possess great physical strength but proportionately weak minds. They are instinctively decent, but what really snarls up their lives are their unbridled passions and their ignorance.

Never a writer of versatile talents, Lamed Shapiro (*b.* Russia, 1878–*d.* U.S.A., 1948) showed an obsessive preoccupation with themes about pogroms and incidents of Jewish self-defense. Three pogrom stories, written with moving power in 1906–09, were "Der Kush" ("The Kiss"), "In Der Toiter Shtut" ("In the Dead City") and "Der Tselem" ("The Cross"). Upon completing the last story he was filled with revulsion and declared: "Enough! No more pogroms! I cannot continue living with the pogrom in my heart!" And with that, although he subsequently wrote some fine short stories, his promising career, for all intents and purposes, came to an end. One might say that he shocked himself out of the creative process, so disturbed were his sensibilities by the horrors he wrote about.

Yoina Rosenfeld (*b.* Russia, 1882–*d.* U.S.A., 1944) was a subjective writer, rarely relying on invention or flights of the imagination. He drew chiefly from his own experience and observation for his stories, novels, and plays. *Konkerenten* ("Competitors") was a Yiddish stage success during the 1920's. Among his best short stories are those about abandoned or mistreated children, but he always had himself in mind, reliving in each of his child characters the sorrows and bitterness of his own boyhood.

The plays of Peretz Hirschbein (*b.* Lithuania, 1880–*d.* U.S.A., 1948) form the most impressive contribution to the Yiddish literature of the theatre. Their principal ingredient is East European Jewish folklore, projected in ingratiating terms of poetic phantasy. Often in their sophisticated primitivism and naïveté they are reminiscent of the paintings of Marc Chagall; at other times they recall the mystical symbolism of the Belgian playwright Maurice Maeterlinck, but it is a symbolism darkened by a gravity that is peculiarly Hirschbein's own. In the play *Einsameh Menshen* ("Lonely People"), he lays bare the melancholy tenor of his thoughts: "From one star to another there is no path . . . nor is there any path from the earth to heaven . . . each one lives alone in his little world." The most popular of his plays were folk idylls of great charm and sensibility: *Di Pusteh Kretchmah* (The Idle Inn), *Dem Schmit's Tochter* ("The Blacksmith's Daughter"), and *Greeneh Felder* ("Green Fields"). These three plays in the years before the Nazi conflagration were found in the repertories of the leading European stages, including the German.

In his novels and short stories, Joseph Opatoshu (*b.* Poland, *d.* 1887–*d.* U.S.A., 1954) was fated to remain divided between two literary styles and two different esthetic loyalties. On the one hand, he tried to follow the advice that Sholom Aleichem once gave him; "You know our ghetto and that hell called New York . . . your task is to portray the New York ghetto and the Jews of America." Accordingly, Opatoshu produced many short stories, novelettes, and novels about American Jews, writing in a realistic style. On the other hand, as a disciple of Peretz, he was also impelled to follow the nationalistic-mystical trend that his master had initiated. This aim he fully achieved in the historical novels *A Tug in Regensburg* ("A Day in Regensburg"), *Eliahu Bachur, Rabbi Akiva* (translated in 1954 as *The Last Revolt*), and *In Poilesheh Felder* ("In Polish Woods"). It was on the last-mentioned work (1915–19), which was translated into English, that his reputation as a novelist will have to rest. This is a historical novel in three parts, describing Jewish life and struggles in the stormy times before and during the Polish national uprising against czarist Russia in 1831.

Although he, too, in his formative years as a writer, had been a loyal follower of Peretz, David Bergelson (Russia, 1884–1952) soon separated himself from the romantic realism of his master and embarked on his independent course as a social realist. In his first novel, *Arum Vuksaal* ("Around the Railroad Station"), written in 1909, he depicted uncompromisingly the social swamp represented by the decaying ghetto-town. It swarmed with petty tradesmen, shopkeepers, shacher-machers (manipulators), drifters, and luftmenshen who circulated listlessly around their "business center"—the railroad station—in pursuit of elusive fortune. Pursuing the same social-psychological investigation of ghetto life but in a different sector, Bergelson's next novel of significance, published in 1913, was *Noch Ahlemen* ("After All"). Its characters were members of the Jewish intelligentsia—the sons and daughters of the very tradesmen who haunted the railroad station. These youths, in the characterizations that Bergelson gave them, represented the pathos of intellectual negativism, of living without fixed moral values and even without hope. When *Noch Ahlemen* was translated into German, the noted novelist-critic Alfred Döblin, enthusiastically placed it on the same eminence with Flaubert's *Madame Bovary* and the best novels of Thomas Mann.

During the years 1932–40, adopting the "Socialist realism" of the Soviet society in which he lived, Bergelson produced, among other works of fiction, the popular novel (in two parts) *Beim Dnieper* ("At the Dnieper"). Conceived in the grand manner, it presents a vast gallery of characters who are psychologically portrayed against their changed social setting in the communist society. Its success as a novel may be ascribed mostly to the fact that it also described a world that had passed and which Bergelson knew so well—the life of the Jews in Russia before the Revolution of 1917–18. Bergelson, it should not be forgotten, was one of the Yiddish writers who perished tragically in the U.S.S.R. in 1952, having been falsely accused of treasonable crimes—of which they were posthumously exonerated in 1956.

Many have been the Yiddish writers and intellectuals fortunate enough to have lived simultaneously in two cultural milieus—the traditional Jewish and the secular modern. Such a writer was Der Nistor (pseudonym of Pinchas Kahanovitch; Russia, 1884–1952). Strains of the Bible and the Midrash, of the Cabalistic writings and Chasidic legends, are heard in much that he wrote, especially in the tales *Hecher Fun der Erd* ("Higher than the Earth," 1910) and in *Der Kadmon* ("The Ancient Man"). In the same vein did he compose his volume of verses, *Gesang un Gebayt* ("Song and Prayer," 1912). Essentially a poet, Der Nistor was drawn to nature and demon tales, which he projected folkloristically. His most ambitious work in the years after the Bolshevik Revolution was his kaleidoscopic novel, *Di Mishpoche Mashber* ("The Family Mashber," 1940); the author's object here was to recreate in words the reality of the entire social microcosm of the Berditchew ghetto as it had existed during the pre-Soviet years.

In a sketchy survey such as this, it is hardly possible to become discursive about any writer no matter how significant his work might be; nor, for that matter, is it even possible to mention all the gifted ones by name. Yet brief reference must be made to several fine Yiddish poets in the Soviet Union who, together with Bergelson and Der Nistor, were executed in 1952 for alleged acts of treason later declared officially by the Soviet Government to have been without foundation. These writers were Peretz Markish (1895–1952), David Hofstein (1889–1952), Aaron Kushniroff (1891–1952), and Leib Kwitko (1893–1952).

Ultimately, the United States became the major locale for Yiddish literary production. It occurred during the period 1881–1914 when almost two million Jewish immigrants,

Peretz Hirschbein.

David Pinski.

Morris Rosenfeld in the 1890's.

Avrohm Reisen in the early 1950's

Abraham Sutzkever.

Itzik Manger.

Moisheh Leib Halpern.

Leivick. (Portrait by F. Horowitz.)

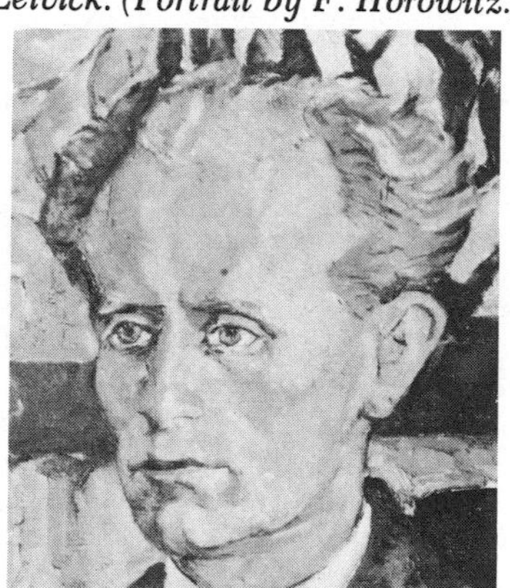

seeking a better and freer life, came to the New World from Russia, Poland, Galicia, Lithuania, and Romania. This mass immigration also brought with it a considerable number of Yiddish writers. Among these—to mention only the most important of the older writers already discussed here—were Morris Wintchevsky, Yehoash, Morris Rosenfeld, Mordchi Spektor, Yoina Rosenfeld, Jacob Gordin, Avrohm Reisen, David Pinski, Peretz Hirschbein, S. Niger, Dr. Chaim Zhitlovsky, and Leon Kobrin. Those who had arrived in the years of their maturity continued to write as they had done before. Psychologically and emotionally, because they continued to live in the past, their style as well as their themes were hardly influenced by the American environment.

But only a few years before the outbreak of World War I, the younger—and, therefore, more pliable—generation of immigrant writers made determined efforts to depict the American surroundings of which it was now a part. It is extraordinary to consider that almost all of the Yiddish writers, unlike many of the contemporary Hebrew writers, who were of middle-class derivation and therefore well educated, came from poor or working-class families. They had little or no systematic schooling, being for the most part self-taught through reading voluminously in the literatures of the world. It would seem that no group of writers who ever created in any language was economically as rootless and psychologically as maladjusted as they. Few had any trade skills; a number worked from sunrise to sundown in the garment sweatshops of New York and did their writing at night and on Sunday. Two of the leading poets earned a precarious livelihood as sign-painters, and a third was a house-painter. Still another worked in a shoe factory. Several were teachers in elementary Hebrew or Yiddish schools, and a lucky few worked in some writing or editorial capacity for the Yiddish newspapers and periodicals.

About the time that the First World War broke out, a circle of gifted writers—most of them poets—imbued with the desire to plunge into the living stream of general culture and modernity, organized themselves into a literary circle. Whimsically, they called themselves *Di Yungeh*—"The Young Ones"—in order to be distinguishable from *Di Alteh*—the "older" generation of Yiddish writers who single-mindedly depicted the life of the East European ghetto. To these "Young Ones" belonged Moisheh Nadir, Moisheh-Leib Halpern, H. Leivick, Dovid Ignatov, Isaac Raboy, Joseph Rolnick, Reuben Eisland, and Zisha Landau.

Actually, it was a very loosely joined group, for each one of its members was intensely individualistic and determined to follow his own private path as a writer. Nonetheless, in the relatively few years of its existence, it started Yiddish poetry moving along a more contemporary road. This group soon revealed the same kind of stylistic and thematic trends that marked the verse of such American poets of their day as E. A. Robinson, Amy Lowell, Vachel Lindsay, Edna St. Vincent Millay, Carl Sandburg, and Edgar Lee Masters.

H. Leivick (his full name was Leivick Halpern; *b.* Russia, 1888–*d.* U.S.A., 1962) was a poet and dramatist of arresting individuality and expressiveness; his works followed the folkloristic trend that Peretz had initiated. He was a symbolist who leaned heavily on Cabalistic mysticism. To achieve his brooding moods, he painted with dark glowing colors. "A gloomy spirit that struggles for inner clarity," is the way one Yiddish literary critic described him. His verse-drama, *Der Goilem* ("The Golem," *see* GOLEM, THE), elevated him in 1921 to the front rank of Yiddish poets. He constructed this work in eight scenes, frankly using Goethe's *Faust* as his model. The play resounds with the declamation of mystical choruses and it teems with supernatural beings that are cast in Jewish legendary lineaments. Its characters speak in musical cadences which evoke moods of unreality and terror but are, at the same time, also elevated and heroic. In 1930–32 Leivick added a second part to this drama. This he called *Di Geulah Komedia, oder, Der Goilem Cholemt* ("The Redemption Comedy, or, The Golem Dreams"). The Golem's dream is of the Messiah and, at the climax, the dream miraculously transmutes itself into reality: The shofar-blasts of the Redemption are sounded.

One of the most original among "The Young Ones" and at the same time one of the most complex of all the "originals" in Yiddish literature was Moisheh Nadir (the pen name of Yitzchok Reiss, *b.* Galicia, 1885–*d.* U.S.A., 1943). His uniqueness as a wit, satirist, poet, playwright, and critic was, however, of unequal quality in its component parts; it was marred by a certain egocentric perverseness, by an excessive fondness for saying things in a novel way.

Wit—and many times it took on a tragic note—was his forte; he himself expressed his indebtedness to those two Jewish ironists, Heinrich Heine and Peter Altenberg. From beginning to end, his writings—poems, one-act plays, causeries, chit-chat, extravaganzas, literary and theatrical critiques abounding in quips, bon mots, and a clever but compulsive play with words—occupy a very special niche in Yiddish writings. He invented new Yiddish words, expressions, and stylistic mannerisms which quickly became common. Yet Nadir was more than a verbal virtuoso; his writings often possess warmth, lyricism, and an intellectual *élan*. Among his best-known works are *In Vildeh Verterwald* ("In a Wild Word-Forest"), *Maiselach Mit a Moral* ("Little Stories with a Moral"), and *Meineh Hent Hobn Fargossen Dos Dozzigeh Blut* ("My Hands Shed This Blood").

About Moisheh-Leib Halpern (*b.* Galicia, 1886–*d.* U.S.A., 1932) one Yiddish critic once commented: "His poems are full of wild people, frightening shadows and drumbeats of despair." There was no poet quite like Halpern in Yiddish—or perhaps even in all world literature; he was a poet of extraordinary vigor and individuality. The defeatism, the masochistic self-examination, the acid sarcasm, and the rapier-like thrust of this self-hatred betray the essential tragedy of him both as man and as poet. His best verses are contained in *In New York* (1921) and *Di Goldeneh Paveh* ("The Golden Peacock," 1924).

Isaac Raboy (*b.* Poland, 1882–*d.* U.S.A., 1944) was active in a special area of fictional exploitation—the back-to-the-land movement which fired many idealistic Jewish immigrants to come from Slavic lands to the Western prairies in the United States at the turn of the twentieth century. A hard-bitten realist, Raboy depicts the struggle of the poor Jewish farmers—former city-dwellers and bookish men—with the forces of nature. He describes the monotony and loneliness of their lives, which remained as unbroken as the North Dakota plain itself, in his homesteading novels. The best of these are *Herr Goldenberg* ("Mr. Goldenberg," 1915), *Der Pas Fun Yahm* ("The Ocean Lane," 1917), *Dos Vildeh Land* ("The Wild Country," 1919), and *Der Yiddisher Cowboy* ("The Jewish Cowboy," 1943).

Besides "The Young Ones," there were other circles of youthful post-World War I writers groping for new and more significant forms of articulation. The best-known of these, and certainly the most gifted, was the group of poets calling itself *Insichisten* ("Introspectionists"). Its leaders were A. Glanz-Leyeless (*b.* Poland, 1889–U.S.A.,), Mani Leib (*b.* Russia, 1884–*d.* U.S.A., 1953), and Jacob Glatstein (*b.* Poland, 1896–U.S.A.,).

Besides verse, Glanz-Leyeless has also written literary criticisms for the Yiddish periodicals. His colleague, Mani Leib, a shoemaker by trade, developed into one of the most admired among Yiddish poets in America. His verse is characterized by delicacy, lyricism, and an emotionalism which sometimes has been criticized as being excessive and self-conscious. But perhaps the most talented member of the Introspectionists is Jacob Glatstein. His poems are distinguished by a boldness of expression, by satire, and a lusty humor. His prose works, because of their lively colorful style and wit, have also found many admirers.

A world apart in outlook from the writings of these sophisticated modernists are the novels and short stories by the brothers Israel Joshua Singer (*b.* Poland, 1893–*d.* U.S.A., 1944) and Isaac Bashevis Singer (*b.* Poland, 1904–to U.S.A., 1935). Both are realists and, at the same time, mystical in the Chasidic sense. The elder brother achieved international fame with his much translated novel, *Di Bruder Ashkenazi,* published in its English version in 1936 as *The Brothers Ashkenazi.* It recounts how German immigrants, weavers from the mills of Silesia and Saxony, settled in the town of Lodz, Poland, early in the nineteenth century and established there one of the important textile centers in Europe. The development of the town into a city, of the first few mills into an industry, is focused on the inner and outer transformation that takes place in the lives and characters of the Brothers Ashkenazi—alienated descendants of an Orthodox, community-minded leader of Lodz. Greed corrupts them and finally leads to a debacle.

In 1932, Israel Joshua Singer's play, *Yoshe Kalb* (in its English translation it was called *The Sinners*), enjoyed a great success in the New York Yiddish Art Theatre. Here, too, naturalism in characterization was fused with Cabalistic unreality on a theme about a Chasidic rebbeh who had sinned carnally and, repenting of his act, had left his home to wander like a mendicant in what the Jewish folk used to call *golus uprechten* (expiatory self-exile).

Exceptionally gifted as both novelist and short-story writer is Isaac Bashevis Singer, who has had most of his tales in Yiddish published in English translation. In the novel *Satan In Goray* (1935), he examines the problem of good and evil in a Polish Jewish community in the seventeenth century. His best-known work, *The Family Moskat* (translated into English in 1950), describes the manner of life led at a time prior to the Nazi holocaust by a wealthy Warsaw family, a kind of patriarchy presided over by Meshulam Moskat. Two other novels, *The Magician of Lublin* (1960) and *The Slave* (1962)—the latter being a historical novel about the genocidal atrocities perpetrated against the Jews of the Ukraine and Poland by the Cossacks during the uprising of 1648—have helped make Bashevis Singer a popular storyteller for discriminating English readers. But probably the fictional form that suits this writer most is the short story. This he has amply demonstrated in two collections: *Gimpel the Fool, and other stories* (1957) and *The Spinoza of Market Street* (1961). In these tales he frequently combines realism with a robust humor and a folkloristic mysticism.

Associated culturally with no particular generation of Yiddish writers, yet exercising a powerful influence upon the entire course of modern Yiddish literature as critics have been Dr. Chaim Zhitlovsky (*b.* Russia, 1865–*d.* U.S.A.,

Abraham Goldfaden, the most popular composer of musical plays in Yiddish employing the folk-idiom of the East European ghetto in the second half of the 19th century.

1943) and Shmuel Niger (pen name of Samuel Charney; *b. Russia,* 1883–*d.* U.S.A., 1955).

Dr. Zhitlovsky was a remarkable man. A leader of the revolutionary movement against czarist tyranny early in the century, he had been elected to the Russian Duma (Parliament) but was not allowed to take his seat. A philosophical writer, deeply involved in the problems of Jewish life and survival, he carried on a lifelong agitation for the adoption of *mameh-loshen*—the "mother-tongue" (i.e., Yiddish)—as the language of Jewish cultural nationalism that could unite the Jewish people in its global dispersion.

Niger was probably the foremost critic that modern Yiddish literature produced. A writer possessing a wide culture and a keen intellect, he published valuable studies on Mendele Mocher Seforim, I. L. Peretz, Leivick, and other leading writers. In this manner he and Dr. Zhitlovsky put the stamp of their thinking and judgment on virtually every trend in modern Yiddish letters.

In the various countries of Jewish settlement in the world today there still are at work quite a number of Yiddish writers, but they are writing for what may be—statistically speaking at a grass-roots level—an ever dwindling number of Yiddish readers. The most gifted of these writers are poets, of whom the best known are Abraham Sutzkever (*b.* Lithuania, 1913–Israel), Chaim Grade (*b.* Lithuania, 1910-), Binem Heller (*b.* Poland, 1908-), and Itzik Manger (*b.* Romania, 1900-France, U.S.).

Sutzkever, who drew wide attention as a prominent member of the "Young Vilna" group of Yiddish writers, remained in the city of Vilna during the Nazi occupation and fought the Germans as the leader of a partisan group. He is now a well-known and admired literary figure in Israel where, since the establishment of the Jewish state and with the position of Hebrew made secure as the primary language of the Jews there, the former overt hostility shown to the Yiddish language by the yishuv (the Israeli community) has been abandoned. Constitutionally a sensitive man and one addicted to much self-examination, Sutzkever's verse is often overburdened with a sense of tragedy which mirrors the nightmarish world in which he was forced to live during the Nazi occupation of Vilna.

At the time of the First World War, because of the destitution of his parents, Chaim Grade lived for some years in a children's home. Ultimately, he became one of the most talented poets in the "Young Vilna" group. Like his friend Sutzkever, he was scarred by his experiences during the Hitler era. Yet, although his verse has an austere bitter ring, his faith in life remains affirmative; he still believes in the virtue and need for mutual aid. In his poem "To Life I Said Yes" he declares: "My brother in peril, give me your hand!"

Different is the approach, both to life and to poetry, of Itzik Manger. His verses breathe both light and air, and he is able to evoke subtle gradations of mood and feeling. His form is polished, his poetic style is disciplined. He ranks high in the evaluation of Yiddish poets and critics alike. Frequently, his poems take on a playful, folkloristic manner and make one think of the open but self-conscious naïveté of Marc Chagall's paintings of Slavic-Jewish life and character.

Today the Yiddish language and literature (and the significant folk culture created by them) are, one might say, at the historic crossroads. The extermination of one-third of the world's Jewish population, the great majority of whom were Yiddish-speaking, has dealt grievous blows to the prospects for an active continuity of Yiddish as a living tongue and to the first-class modern literature which has been created in it. The reduction to cultural rubble of all historic Jewish centers, old institutions, and the traditional ways of life in Central and Eastern Europe has left a great void in the world Jewish community—an emptiness that is extremely hard to fill.

No one can be rash enough to turn prophet, and certainly not a prophet of gloom concerning the survival of the Jews in every country where they live provided he is still deeply rooted in the thought and speech processes and in the sentiments of millions of Jews throughout the world. Yet—to be entirely realistic—there is unmistakably in evidence a decline in the number of those for whom Yiddish is still the *mameh-loshon.* Notwithstanding some brilliant practitioners, belles-lettres in Yiddish is diminishing in quantity of production as well as in quality. The inevitable erosions caused by the language and cultural assimilation of the Jews in every country where they live provide the explanation for the ebb in the fortunes of a once great and colorful literature.

See also ENLIGHTENMENT, THE JEWISH; HEBREW LITERATURE, MODERN; YIDDISH LANGUAGE, THE.

Rudolf Schildkraut, generally acclaimed as the greatest of Yiddish actors, won international renown in the 1920's with his playing in German of the parts of Shylock in Shakespeare's Merchant of Venice, *and of Yekel (below) in Sholem Asch's* God of Vengeance (Gott fun Nekumeh) *in Max Reinhardt's repertory theatre in Berlin.*

An early production (during the 1920's) at the Jewish State Theatre in Moscow of Night in the Old Market Place *by I. L. Peretz.*

Production at the Jewish State Theatre in Moscow during the 1930's of "Two Hundred Thousand," *a stage adaptation of Sholom Aleichem's comedy,* Dos Groiseh Gevins *("The Great [Lottery] Winning").*

Bertha Kalich, star of both the Yiddish and the English stages before World War II.

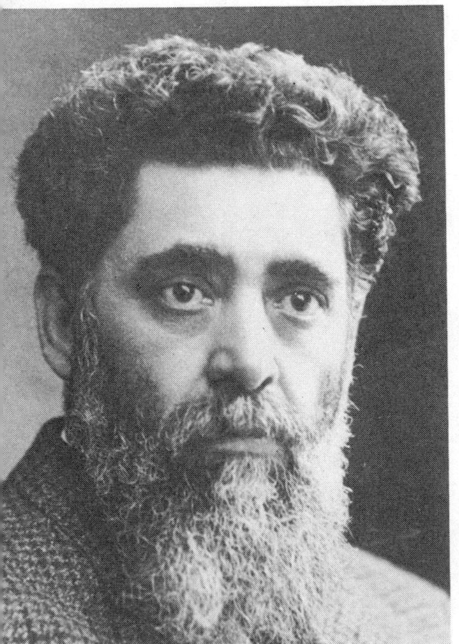

Jacob Gordin, a gifted but uneven writer of Yiddish dramas and melodramas during the late 19th century.

YIDDISH THEATRE. *See* YIDDISH LITERATURE, MODERN.

YISHUV. *See* FOLK MUSIC AND DANCE; HEBREW LANGUAGE, HISTORY OF THE; HEBREW LITERATURE, MODERN; KIBBUTZ; ZIONISM.

YIZKOR (Hebrew, meaning "May He remember")

This is the opening word of a prayer as well as the popular reference to the entire Memorial Service, called in Hebrew *Hazkarat Neshamas* (Remembering the Souls). This is observed by the Ashkenazim—those Jews who follow the German minhag (rite or custom)—in their synagogue worship. The Sefaradim—those who follow the Spanish minhag—have their own memorial prayer which they call *Hashkabah* ("Laying to Rest"). This is customarily recited during burial rites in the cemetery as well as in the synagogue while making a pledge to charity for the repose of the soul of the departed.

Yizkor undoubtedly originated during the Crusades, when many Jewish inhabitants of communities in the Rhineland were massacred by the Knights of the Cross and the fanatic mobs they led. Then, rather than face the temptation of apostasy from their faith, tens of thousands of Jews instead chose death, often in mass-suicide. In the awed estimation of the Jews of the Middle Ages, these had perished as holy martyrs, as living sacrifices for the Sanctification of God's name (*al Kiddush ha-Shem*). Accordingly, it was the custom in many Jewish communities in medieval Germany that on Yom Kippur, during the recital of the Memorial Service, the names of all the massacred—men, women, and children—be read aloud to the worshipers from the *Memorbuch* ("Memorial Book"; from the Latin *memoria*). Inasmuch as there were constantly more Jews who were being martyred, the *Memorbuch* of many a German community became appallingly long. One of the earliest of these martyr-lists was drawn up in Nuremberg. It began in 1096, with the first massacre by the Crusaders, and it eventually included the names of those who perished two-and-a-half centuries later, during the public hysteria following the Black Death.

Similar records were kept by other Rhineland communities (such as Speyer, Worms, and Mayence). However, as time passed, the recitation from the *Memorbuch* in the synagogue became a dreary and protracted exercise. The worshiper could no longer respond emotionally to the reeling off of so many names with which he had no personal association. And so, by the seventeenth century, the practice of reading from the *Memorbuch* was abandoned and the book itself become merely a local historic relic of melancholy import. Likewise, the custom that had centered around it was transformed into the Hazkarat Neshamas recited for one's beloved deceased parents. The prayer for a father (it has but a slight alteration for a mother) runs thus:

> May God remember the soul of my revered father who has gone to his repose. May his soul be bound up in the bundle of life. May his rest be glorious with fullness of joy in Thy presence, and bliss forevermore at Thy right hand.

In more modern times, the custom arose in East and Central European countries to memorialize the dead on the last days of the festivals of Passover, Succot, and Shabuot, but most particularly on Yom Kippur. In the twentieth century, whatever the degree or fervour of religious observance on the part of the individual Jew, Yizkor remains one of the most universally revered institutions of Jewish prayer. At the time of its recitation on Yom Kippur, for example, the number of worshipers in the synagogue and the emotional tension prevailing in it become markedly increased. Not a few of these worshipers are normally non-observing, but they cannot resist the appeal of filial sentiment that Yizkor holds for them.

The custom has become traditional that, upon the conclusion of the reading from the Prophets during the Yom Kippur service, the worshipers contribute to various charities in memory of the souls of their beloved who have departed.

Superstitious folkways have become intertwined with lofty meanings. For instance, a belief held by Orthodox Jews forbids all those whose parents are still living to be present during the recital of the memorial prayer—this in order to avoid the baneful influence of the Evil Eye. Those mourners who have suffered the death of a parent within the year are also required to leave the house of prayer before Yizkor is said. This regulation has a humane reason: the fear that those individuals who have been but recently bereaved might be unable to restrain their grief and thereby open up old wounds in those who are commemorating the death of parents long departed.

The rabbis of old always took the larger view that the moral instruction of the people stood above the mere pious utterance of prayers. In accordance with this, they included in the Memorial Service references of homage to the souls of the great teachers and illuminators of Israel. They wished that the living would take an object lesson in righteousness from those great men and seek to emulate them in good deeds, and in steadfastness to God, to Torah, and to the Jewish people.

Of the Geonim (the eminent rectors of the Babylonian Talmudic academies in pre-medieval times) the prayer-leader (baal tefillah) chanted in praise: "They spread the Torah in Israel, and enlightened Israel with their ordinances and books." Of the illustrious poets such as Judah (Yehudah) Halevi, Solomon ibn Gabirol, and Abraham and Moses ibn Ezra, he said: "They composed hymns of praise to the omnipresent God and strengthened the heart of Israel with their poems of piety"; of the communal leaders: "They labored on behalf of the congregations and with utmost devotion to serve the best interests of the community." And finally, uttering the fervent hope concerning those countless in every generation who had perished as martyrs, the baal tefillah prayed that "in return for their suffering, may their souls be bound up in the bundle of life with fullness of joy in thy presence, with bliss at thy right hand forevermore. Amen."

See also MERIT OF THE FATHERS.

YOBEL. *See* JUBILEE.

YOHRTZEIT. *See* YAHRZEIT.

YOM HA-DIN. *See* ROSH HASHANAH.

YOM HA-ZIKARON. *See* ROSH HASHANAH.

YOM KIPPUR (Hebrew, meaning "Day of Atonement")

Since primeval times, and on different levels of conception—all the way from the magical to the ethical—the Jews have revered the Day of Atonement as the most significant of all holy days in their religious calendar. As the centuries moved forward, their comprehension of the idea of "atonement" for sins also advanced. Ultimately, Yom Kippur became a sounding-board for all the inchoate yearnings of a people driven by an idealistic compulsion for self-improvement and social justice to examine their individual consciences. In the process, they had developed disturbing guilt feelings about their conduct, and these, in turn, led to a stark self-reappraisal and the moral cumpulsion for self-correction through repentance.

Perhaps the real significance of Yom Kippur as an instrument for a higher individual morality directed toward the good of social progress is that its observance originated at

Orthodox worshipers, each dressed in white kittel, entering the synagogue on Yom Kippur. (Painting by Moritz Oppenheim, Germany, 1873.)

the dawn of Jewish history in a primitive society. Then it was frankly an occasion for the yearly performance of the rites of "propitiation" before the Deity. It was ceremonially presented as the expression of collective contrition and atonement for transgression and misdoing by the sacrificial offering of bullocks and goats to the intonation of magical incantations and the shrill blare of music.

There are Semitic scholars who think that the very word *kippur* was a derivation of a Babylonian term meaning "to purge" or "to wipe out"; namely, to wipe out the stain of sin. Rites of such sin-cleansings performed collectively were commonplace in other ancient religions. In a direct connection with Yom Kippur were the atonement ceremonies employed by the religions of Babylonia and Canaan—ceremonies whose great impact on the rites of the Jews can hardly be exaggerated.

All ethnic peoples that were set within the constellation of Assyrian-Babylonian civilization shared, more or less, a common outlook on life and nature. Consequently, they practiced kindred magical rites. These, including that of collective atonement for sins, were predicated on the animistic belief that a separate unseen power, spirit, or "god," was indwelling in all manifestations of matter—in the sun, moon, and stars, in earth, sea, and sky, in rain, thunder, and wind, and—not least—in the corn and in other produce vital to human existence in a primitive agricultural society. Most important of all considerations for human beings—those invisible spirits or supernatural powers had to be placated with animal sacrifices, incantations, and hymns of praise so that they would refrain from doing harm to the petitioners and their flocks and crops. Instead, by the employment of these magical means it was expected the spirits would become their protectors, perhaps even their allies, in the hazardous adventure of life.

One widely diffused belief in the magic-directed religions of primitive cultures was that the sins of the individual, besides bringing him personally to grief, also infuriated the invisible powers against the entire community of which he was a member. Thus, in meting out punishment in such a strictly pastoral-agricultural society as Israel, these powers might cause the crops to fail, the water-wells to dry up, the cattle to be killed off by an epidemic, and still other calamities to occur that could disturb the balance in nature. It was, therefore, thought to be a matter of life and death for the community to appease the wrath of the gods and the spirits.

Among the many forms of primitive worship was that of atonement for sins—of abject abasement before the unseen powers. For this, it was necessary that there take place a symbolic and total cleansing of "shared guilt" within the group that would result in a wiping out each year of cul-

Rite of penitence and expiation, called malkat *(stripes), which is submitted to voluntarily by every devout Orthodox adult male on the day when Yom Kippur Eve occurs. (Engraving by Bernard Picart. Amsterdam, 1725.)*

Confession of sins in an East European Ultra-Orthodox synagogue on Yom Kippur. (Painting by L. Pilichowski, Paris, 19th century.)

pability for all misdoings. This would be a general remission of sins, and in that narrow sense, would effectuate an annual "redemption."

The sacrifice of atonement in the Biblical age was accomplished vicariously by the sacrificial offering of a "scapegoat." It should be kept in mind that, although human sacrifices were being performed in all ancient religions, they had been sternly proscribed for the Jews by Mosaic Law. The sacrifice of the scapegoat, through which there was a magical transference of collective sins from human beings to an animal, was of primitive derivation. It was performed not so much to lift the burden of sin from individuals as to drive away the residue of evil from the community in the hope of arresting the punishment of the gods upon the people. This will make it clear why on Yom Kippur, in ancient Temple days, the high priest of the Jews performed the sacrifice of the scapegoat on the altar *before* and for the benefit of the entire "Congregation of Israel."

For this ceremony, the high priest brought forward two goats as sin-offerings to God for the people. One goat, reserved by lot "for the Lord," he sacrificed on the altar. He sprinkled its blood eight times before the "mercy seat" in the inner sanctuary—the Holy of Holies—and between the staves of the Ark of the Covenant. (This was another magical rite "to make atonement for the holy place, because of the uncleanliness of the Children of Israel, and because of their trangressions . . .")

Then he solemnly confessed the people of their sins, which he placed, in magical transference, upon the head of the second goat, the "scapegoat" which was destined for the appeasement of Azazel, the evil demon who infested the wilderness. This animal was led ceremoniously up a high cliff and flung down the precipice to its death. The instant this was done, the vast multitudes who thronged the Temple area and all the surrounding hills of Jerusalem, received the concluding signal. It was the waving from one of the Temple gates of a strip of white wool, symbolizing purity. When the people saw it flutter, they shouted for joy. They took it as

Kapparah (scapegoat) rite. Galicia, late 19th century. (YIVO.)

a sign that their sins had been forgiven.

The custom of having a scapegoat sacrifice continued unbroken not merely because of its magical goals but because it was such a convenient and easy means for unburdening any feelings of sin-guilt.

After the Destruction of the Temple, in 70 C.E., when sacrifices could no longer be brought, the rite of *kapparah*—also a vicarious sacifice of atonement—was introduced among the Jews in the Diaspora. It is still being observed, but only by the most undeviating of Orthodox traditionalists. During this, the believer, holding a rooster or hen firmly by its legs, circles it over his head three times (a Cabalistic number), in the meanwhile reciting the mystical formula in which the offering of the blood of the fowl, soon to be shed by the ritual slaughterer or shochet, is to be accepted vicariously as atonement for the sins he has committed during the year gone by. Nowadays, however, there are many Orthodox Jews who, having become less enamored of this archaic ritualism, substitute for the "scapegoat rooster" the donation of a sum of money to charity.

With the final Destruction of the national sanctuary in Jerusalem, there took place the inevitable de-emphasis from collective atonement through the magical transference of all sins upon an animal scapegoat to the assumption by the individual of moral responsibility for his own actions. Then "atonement" no longer meant the automatic wiping out of wrongdoing, but a voluntary self-accounting by turning the merciless light of truth upon one's self. "Atonement" was now *repentance*—a transformation of the individual "from within," and to attain it became the objective of all the rites and prayers on Yom Kippur. The sincerity of the individual's repentance was to be tested by the alacrity with which he altered his outlook and conduct. "Every man should confess his sins and turn away from them on that day [Yom Kippur]," urged Maimonides, the philosopher-rabbi of the twelfth century.

The congregrational recitation of the litany in the Confession of Sins (Viddui) was obligatory for the searching of the soul on "the Sabbath of Sabbaths"—the poetic descriptive in the Bible for Yom Kippur. It was to be recited with inner agitation and in unison. Even if, in its outer form, it appeared to be a survival of the primitive rite of collective atonement, it was now motivated by a moral-social reason. Rabbi Isaac Luria (known as "the Ari"), a sixteenth-century master Cabalist of Safed, explained that it was "because all Israel is one body, and each Jew is a limb of that body; that is why we are *all* held responsible when one of us sins." In the social thinking of the Jewish religion, the wrong done by the individual Jew was not considered as being merely his private affair since its consequences impinged on the lives of others and, often, on the entire community.

A Christian artist's interpretation of the kapparah (scapegoat) rite on Yom Kippur. Note the kneeling figures with hands folded in prayer—a practice that is not Jewish. (Woodcut from Der Gantz Jüdisch Glaub *["The Entire Jewish Religion"] by Antonius Margaritha, Augsburg, Germany, 1530.)*

Tirelessly, with almost hypnotic effect, the long litany of the Confession recited on the Day of Atonement inventories fifty-six categories of sin. As the worshiper recites each one of these, he beats his breast over the heart with his right fist in symbolic contrition, and he repeats the formula of confession: *"Al chet . . ."* "For the sin which we have committed before Thee by . . ." And for all these enumerated wrongdoings he implores, in concert with the entire congregation: ". . . O God of Forgiveness, forgive us, pardon us, grant us remission!" Who can fail to recognize in the Hebrew *Al chet* the Latin *mea culpa*—the confession of sins recited by Roman Catholics?

Yom Kippur is observed with appropriate austerities, with continuous prayer and expressions of grief and regret. All this is done in order that the holy day be kept accordant with the moral idea of atonement. The Rabbinic Sages had concurred that indispensable to sincere atonement was "the broken heart."

The Talmud observed that, while man stands before the divine judgment on Rosh Hashanah which falls on the first day of Tishri—the first of the Ten Days of Penitence (Yamim Noraim)—the judgment of his fate is sealed on the climactic last day—Yom Kippur. Therefore, the ancient tradition, as stated in the Mishnah, was adamant: "It is forbidden on Yom Kippur to eat and to drink, to wash and to anoint onself, and to wear shoes . . ."

It was the duty of every Jew to fast on that day. Only the gravely ill were exempted. The Mishnah Sages in the second century laid down the ground rule that was to guide Jewish parents for all time. They were to accustom their children to fast by gradually increasing their hours of not eating as they grew older. Twelve-year-olds were expected to fast the entire day: from before Yom Kippur Eve to the conclusion of the holy day on the following night, after the first stars had appeared.

Beginning with the Middle Ages, the design for congregational worship in the European synagogues on the Day on Atonement was well fixed. Throughout the day, supplications were recited continuously. The menfolk wore under the tallit (prayer shawl) the kittel—the unadorned white robe that was eventually to serve as the shroud in which they would be buried. In contrast with Tishah B'Ab (the Ninth of Ab), when the Ark of the Law in the synagogue was draped in the black of mourning, on Yom Kippur the Ark was draped in spotless white. Also, the Torah Scrolls were dressed in shimmering white mantles, for white was the ancient Jewish symbol of purity and hope for God's forgiveness.

The nature of forgiveness was both carefully and sensitively defined by the Mishnah Sages. Eleazar ben Azariah declared at the end of the first century that, while a man's sins, as they affect his relations with God, can be atoned for on Yom Kippur, it is otherwise with a man's offenses against his fellow man. For these "the Day of Atonement does not atone, unless and until he has . . . redressed the wrong he has done to him."

It was the judgment of the Rabbis that "whoever offends another, even if he does it only with words, must conciliate him." The custom, therefore, arose during the Talmudic age—and it has continued to be observed by pious traditionalists to this day—that well before the Kol Nidre service commenced on the Eve of Yom Kippur, the devout would go in haste and contrition to call on those they had

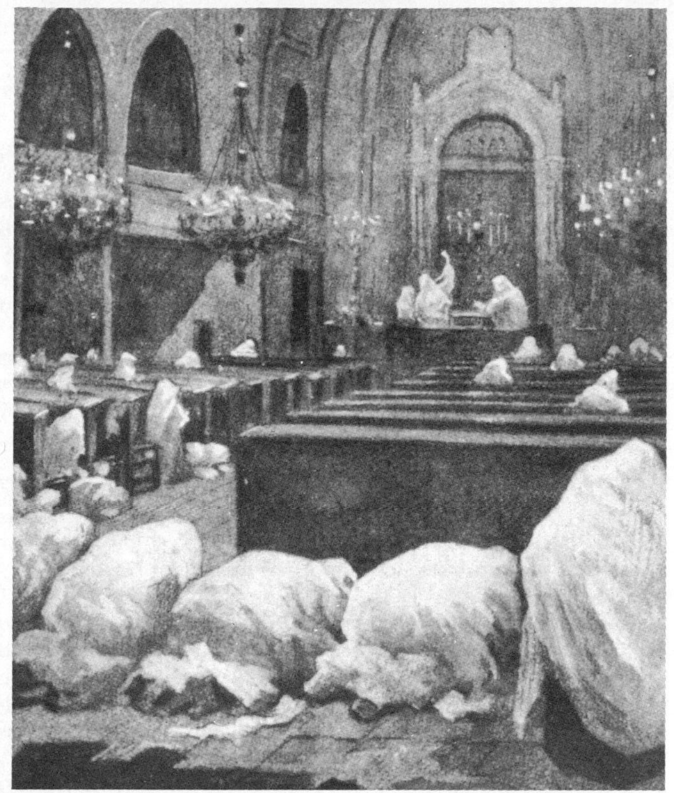

Worshipers prostrating themselves (termed in Yiddish fahlen koirim*) in a prayer of contrition on Yom Kippur. This is a survival of a very ancient custom and occurs only once a year. (Painting by an unidentified artist.)*

injured or offended, abjectly beg their forgiveness, and become reconciled with them before entering the synagogue for soul-baring worship.

A touching custom—one that recalls "the love-feast" of the sectarian Essenes of Judea—is still observed among the Yemenite Jews. At the conclusion of the evening service on the Day of Atonement in the synagogue, they embrace and kiss one another. They also bless one another with these Hebrew words: "May you receive tidings of forgiveness, pardon and atonement; may your name be inscribed in the Book of Life and of Remembrance."

See also KOL NIDRE; REPENTANCE; REWARD AND PUNISHMENT; SIN AND SINNER.

ZEALOTS (in Hebrew: pl. KANNAIM; S. KANNA)

With the exception of the rejected Samaritans (who stood outside the recognized limits of Jewish life) and of the upper-class priestly Sadducees (who were Greek assimilationists), the Jews of the Second Temple period, under the molding hands of the Pharisee teachers and scribes, were firmly anchored in traditional Judaism. Nevertheless, there was going on constantly among them a real clash of ideas, of principles, and of commitments. These ideological differences eventually led to the coalescence of separate offshoots and a breaking away from the main body of the Pharisee movement.

The schisms that took place within the Pharisee ranks present a striking illustration of the in-group incompatibilities among the various sects of Judea; they splintered and resplintered to result in still other sectarian divisions and subdivisions. At one extreme stood the gentle, life-renouncing Essenes; at the other end, the embattled patriots, terrorists, and religious authoritarians, the Zealots.

The inner fissures in Pharisaism were already discernible one generation before the appearance of Jesus, and were manifested in the constant clashes that occurred toward the beginning of the first century B.C.E. between the rival schools of the Pharisee Sages Hillel and Shammai. Hillel and his disciples and their later Rabbinic continuators were quietists by conviction. They were non-resisting pacifists and humanitarians who placed the daily practice of love and kindness in the service of one's fellow men above ritualistic observance of the religious law. It was this trend of Pharisaism, with which the Essenes has much in common, that Jesus followed several decades later.

Yom Kippur service according to the Ashkenazic (German and East European) Rite. (Engraving by Bernard Picart, Paris, 1725)

Although, like Hillel and his adherents, Shammai and his disciples also prided themselves on being dedicated guardians of the Torah and its traditions, they took a diametrically opposite approach to them and arrived at different conclusions. They were by conviction activists and literalist sticklers for the laws of the Torah. They split sophistical hairs—and sometimes their opponents' skulls as well—in passionate disagreement over the observance of the minutiae of all the commandments, laws, statutes, and regulations in Scripture. In short, they were fundamentalists who wished to institutionalize all aspects of religion into a clearly defined, codified, disciplined, authoritative, and uncompromising order.

It is, therefore, not at all surprising that it was the Rabbinical teachers of Shammai's persuasion, and not those of Hillel's, who gave direction and leadership to the Zealot wing of the Pharisee sect less than one hundred years before the destruction of Jerusalem, during the rule of Herod. In the peculiar, and also desperate, circumstances of the protracted rebellion waged by the Jews against Imperial Rome, and fitting into the pattern—although already fast dissolving—of Jewish theocratic society, the Zealots were a religious sect and, at the same time, a political organization which employed a military arm for achieving its ends. They gave vigorous leadership to the almost continuous uprisings that occurred in Judea against Roman rule.

The Zealots, avowedly, had a two fold goal: They strove, by fair means or foul, to drive the Roman oppressors and administrative leeches out of their country. At the same time, they also clung to the Messianic obsession that the military defeat of Rome was a precondition set by Heaven itself for the coming of the Redemption. One curious belief of the day, fervently accepted by the suffering Jewish masses, was that the Age of the Messiah would be preceded by "the Great War" that would put an end to all wars forever. This was envisioned, in terms mystical and eerie, as a conflict to the death between tormented Israel and the mythical armies of Gog and Magog, which together comprised a thinly veiled symbol of the Roman oppressors. The final battle, it was confidently expected, would be won by the Jews, who, although militarily inconsequential themselves, would be led by an invincible commander sent by God. This would be the Messiah ben Joseph, and he, although victorious, would nevertheless fall in the thick of the fighting. By that very symbolic token of sacrifice, he would "make straight the path" for the coming of the ultimate redeemer—the Messiah ben David!

The immense impact of the Zealots not only on the Jewish religion and historic destiny of the Jewish people but also on Christianity, has not yet been sufficiently appreciated. By concretizing the "military" phase of the Messianic expectation with a number of dramatic "redemptive" uprisings against Rome—the Gog and Magog of the legend—the Zealots stirred into action the deep emotions of the Jewish people and created in Judea a feverish climate in which the Messiah idea was able to flourish so luxuriantly.

It is self-evident that, without the fervor and the delirium of Messianic redemption, the Zealots could hardly have inspired their followers to wage such heroic and savage guerrilla warfare against the Romans, since they were but poorly armed and had no military training. They actually overwhelmed and destroyed, on one memorable occasion, twelve Roman legions in the full panoply of their might that had been sent from Antioch by the imperial legate to put down the rebellion.

The simple fact is that, in the year 6 C.E., barely one generation before Jesus began to preach in Galilee, the Jews there, maddened by hunger and oppression, had rallied in revolt around the banner of Judas the Galilean and Tzadok, a Rabbinic disciple of Shammai, the ideological opponent of Hillel the Elder. They attacked the two Roman legions that had been sent by the Legate Varus from Syria to quell the rebellion, but were defeated. A frightful butchery followed. Two thousand Zealots were nailed alive to separate crosses by the Romans, a tragic precursor of the crucifixion of Jesus by them one generation later.

The Zealot sectaries, standing far closer than the pacifist Hillelite Pharisees to the ideas and practices of the Hasideans of the Maccabean struggle in 168-165 B.C.E., took up for their battle cry the exhortation to his sons of old Mattathias, the Hasmonean priest of Modin: "Be ye zealous for the Torah, and give your lives for the covenant of your fathers!"

The Zealots well deserved their name. Their "zeal" was actually a thoroughgoing fanaticism. The very logic of their beliefs led them to a systematic employment of terror. It was directed not only against the hated Romans, but also against the equally execrated Jews who collaborated with them. Zealot guerrilla bands roved in marauding operations through the hills of Galilee. Because they used the sica, a short Roman dagger, in their work of assassination of Romans and of Jewish Romanophiles, they were called *sicarii;* namely, "sica-wielders," or, more plainly, "assassins."

Not only the biased Roman chroniclers and Josephus, the quisling Jewish historian of the time, but also the Pharisee compilers of the Talmud several centuries later—the latter because they were loyal followers of the School of Hillel—had no kind words to say for the terrorist Zealots. The Hillelites, being quietists—and that, by no means, put them in the camp with the collaborationists—were opposed on principle to acts of violence of any kind. Moreover, they bitterly opposed uprisings against Rome, for these, they were convinced, were adventuristic and most likely to turn out to be futile and catastrophic for the Jewish people. The Talmudic Sages had mostly bitter words for the Zealots, whom they called biryonim (*bandits*), a time-honored verbal salute for rebels.

It was by no means unexpected that Josephus, in wishing by casuistry to justify his own defection to the Romans in the very midst of the struggle during the Great War, should have nothing but scorn and abuse for the Zealots. He blamed them for every disaster that had befallen the Jews: "All sorts of misfortunes sprang from these men, and the nation was infected with this doctrine to an incredible degree; one violent war came upon us after another." The Zealot-inspired revolts reached a towering climax in the Great War which erupted in the year 67 and came to a tragic end three years later with the obliteration of the Jewish state and the final Dispersion of the Jewish people.

As if in refutation of his own epithets, Josephus, who was not only a very complex and unstable character but also a painstaking chronicler, went on to say that the Roman soldiers "slew the robbers [i.e., the Zealots] and their families." In response to a proclamation by King Herod offering to the rebels generous terms if they surrendered, Josephus remarked that "not one of them came willingly to him, and those that were compelled to come preferred death to captivity."

Thousands of Zealots perished in the uprisings that took place under the Roman procurators Ventidius Cumanus and Felix, who goaded the people into revolt by intolerable confiscatory taxation, by the suppression of every human right, and by an official demonstration of contempt for the Jewish religion.

Perhaps the historic incident that best illustrated the climate of terror, torture, and murder that convulsed Judea under the Romans occurred during Herod's reign. This Jewish kinglet, who was a notoriously corrupt sycophant of the Romans and a ready tool for them, had ordered a large golden eagle, the proud symbol of Imperial Rome, to be put up over the principal gate of the sacrosanct Temple on Mount Zion. This act was viewed by the people as a shocking blasphemy and a desecration of the national sanctuary. It caused an outcry of a kind that had not been heard in Judea since the defilement of the Temple by the Seleucidan conquerors in the days of the Maccabean uprising.

Now the Zealots, in devotion to their central doctrine that they recognized no ruler but God, looked upon this imperial eagle as a provocation and a challenge to their religious sensibilities. So they sent clambering to the top of the Temple gate young men who pulled down the golden eagle and broke it in pieces. All those Zealots who were involved in this daring escapade were seized and ordered by the king to be burned alive.

The effect on the people of these executions, chronicled Josephus, was shocking. "They lamented those that were put to death by Herod . . . Nor was this mourning of a private nature, but the lamentations were very great, the mourning solemn, and the weeping such as was loudly heard over all the city [Jerusalem], as being for those men who had perished for the laws of their country and for the Temple."

The Zealots promptly sounded the shofar call to battle; many thousands rallied to their standard. At first they were successful in their guerrilla attacks, but in the end, their uprising was drowned in a sea of blood by the Roman legions.

The frenzied agitation unleashed by the Zealots went on for almost a hundred years in Judea, so that sometimes it did seem that even the military might of Rome would not be able to cope with it. Nonetheless, there were many Jews in the country—those who followed Pharisee and Essenic teachings in particular—who were sincerely convinced of the futility of the armed struggle. They lamented over the terrible price that was being paid in lives. Before, and also during, the Great War which broke out in the year 67 C.E., and especially during the siege of Jerusalem, the bitter ideological conflict continued between the Zealot militants and the Pharisee pacifists who were led by the Sage Yochanan ben Zakkai. The latter were irrevocably committed to the proposition that the historic destiny of the Jews was not to be fulfilled by the naked power of the sword, but only by a steadfast dedication to the eternal verities of the Torah. Yochanan's idealistic quietism was but an echo of the triumphant proclamation by the Prophet Zechariah: "Not by power, nor by might, but by My spirit, saith the Lord of hosts." (Zechariah 4:6.)

A more sophisticated and realistic opposition to the Zealots was that advanced by Josephus, who was for a time, until he turned traitor, even a leading participant in the struggle to liberate Judea from the stranglehold of Rome. In his *Life*, he made an eloquent statement of the stand that he took against the Zealots:

> I, therefore, endeavored to put a stop to these tumultuous persons and tried to persuade them to change their minds; and I laid before their eyes against whom it was that they were going to fight, and told them that they were inferior to the Romans, not only in martial skill, but also in good fortune; and desired them not rashly, and after the most foolish manner, to bring on the dangers of the most terrible mischief upon their country, upon their families, and upon themselves . . . but I could not persuade them; for the madness of desperate men was quite too hard for me.

The determination of the Zealot leaders to continue the fight marked a decisive turning point in the history and destiny of the Jews. Rome employed the most desperate means for crushing the almost continuous rebellion. But inspired by their unshakeable belief that, in the nick of time, Heaven itself would intercede on their behalf and send the Messiah to succor them, the Zealots fought on with the strength of heroes or madmen. During the siege of Jerusalem, it was the Zealots who, by the most violent means, kept many of the wavering defenders from surrendering, despite the pleas of the Pharisee Sages against the useless carnage. It is a fact that most of them died fighting in battle, those who were captured, were savagely tortured and then slain. Some Zealots succeeded in escaping from the burning city and took refuge in the mountain fortress of Masada on the Dead Sea. When they were besieged there by the pursuing Romans, they committed suicide en masse rather than fall into the hands of their revenge-thirsty enemies.

Even the destruction of Judea as a Jewish state and the dispersion of the Jews which followed were unable to put out the fires of Zealotism. More than half a century later, during the reign of Trajan, and of his successor, Hadrian, the Rabbinic teachers Ishmael and Yoseh the Galilean went about the country preaching the duty of revolt against Rome. Despite the opposition of Akiba, the leading Rabbinic authority of the day, the insurrectionary agitation continued to mount. Under the whiplash of Hadrian's persecution, the insurrectionary movement was constantly gaining new adherents, not only among the people but also among the Pharisee pacifists. Ishmael was finally put to death for preaching treason.

When the conflagration had reached its most flaming intensity in the uprising under Simon Bar Kochba in 132–35 C.E., even the Hillelite pacifist Akiba ben Joseph was unable to resist the patriotic-Messianic frenzy. He hailed Bar Kochba as the Messiah ben Joseph in the same way that the other Zealot leaders before him, beginning with Judas the Galilean, his grandson Menachem, and Theudas (*see* MESSIAHS, WOULD-BE), were proclaimed to be God's martial instruments for ushering in the Redemption. Like Ishmael and many other Sages, Pharisee-Hillelites as well as Zealots, Akiba too ended his life as a martyr, *al-kiddush ha-Shem*, "to sancitfy the Name." In his death-agony, as the Romans tore his flesh with iron combs, he cried out the affirmation of the Shema: "Hear O Israel, the Lord our God the Lord is One!" And as his voice faltered and lingered triumphantly on the word "Echad"—"One" (so chronicles the Talmud)—he expired.

See also ESSENES; PHARISEES; SADDUCEES; SAMARITANS; THERAPEUTAE.

ZECHUT ABOT. *See* MERIT OF THE FATHERS.

ZEMIROT (Hebrew pl., meaning "Songs"; s. ZEMIRAH)

Although, in the general sense, the word *zemirot* means "songs," in popular Jewish usage it applies to the so-called table-songs. These are liturgical hymns offering thanks and praise to God at the festive family-table on the Sabbath. They are sung at the conclusion of each meal and center around the recitation of Grace, which, among Jews, occurs after eating and not before as it does among Christians. (The Chasidim also sing zemirot between courses.)

Singing zemirot is a very ancient Jewish custom; it goes back at least to the time of the Second Temple. We get an intimate glimpse of its religious goal in the account given by Philo, the first-century Hellenistic philosopher-rabbi of Alexandria, of the Jewish monastic sect in Egypt, the Therapeutae:

> After the supper they hold the sacred vigil . . . They rise up all together and, standing in the middle of the refectory, form themselves into two choirs, one of men and one of women . . . Then they sing hymns to God composed of many melodies, sometimes chanting together, sometimes taking up the harmony antiphonally, hands and feet keeping time in accompaniment . . . Lovely are the thoughts, lovely the words, and worthy of reverence the choristers, the end and aim of thoughts, words and choristers—alike in piety.

The two religious sects of latter-day Judea—the Pharisees and the Essenes—shared a philosophy of life in which God was not conceived of as being a separate value from existence. Both were considered inseparable, for God was immanent, indwelling in all creation. And so life was not departmentalized as in other religious systems, but presented as a synthesis of every one of its aspects. All that pertained to man, believed to have been created by God in His own image, was deemed holy, including the act of eating. The Talmud is replete with wise sayings concerning food, one being: "Consider your table as if it were an altar before the Lord." With the nourishment he obtained there, man sustained his life, and was thereby able to say that he loved God "with all his heart and with all his soul." Consequently, the Jew was exhorted to preoccupy himself while eating with pious reflections and to discourse on themes from the Holy Scriptures. Also, he was to thank God "with gladness" for the food that He had given him from his bounty.

Besides having words of Torah linger on his lips, the pious man could exalt his Creator in no more fitting way than with the homage of song. This especially was the favorite manner of worship among the medieval Cabalists and the Chasidim of the eighteenth and nineteenth centuries. Commented the Zohar, the "scriptures" of the Cabalists: "The gates of the Temple in Heaven may be opened only by song." And since this singing was a spontaneous freewill offering, it was, therefore, the ultimate possible in praise of the Deity. "When the heart is filled with joy it breaks into song."

The custom of singing zemirot at the Sabbath table within the emotional warmth of the family circle, experienced a revival during the eleventh and twelfth centuries. This was a time when great intellectual and cultural advances were being made by the Jews in the world of Islam, including the kingdoms of Moorish Spain. Gifted poet-rabbis composed liturgical hymns (in Hebrew: *piyyutim; s. piyyut*) in an outpouring of religious devotion. Many of these were chanted in the synagogue; still others, as zemirot, were sung in the home on the Sabbath. As in the instance of the hymns incorporated into the liturgy of the synagogue, the devotional verses of the zemirot were also set to a great conglomeration of tunes, both Jewish and non-Jewish in origin. In the latter category were melodies derived from folk music in Germany, France, the Provence, Italy, Persia, Arabia, Turkey, Greece, Spain, Portugal, Bohemia, and other countries.

During the Middle Ages, a great number of popular anthologies containing Hebrew zemirot were compiled, but they came entirely without musical notation, for that was then not in the province of Jewish knowledge. The tunes were learned by ear and were passed on to others in the same manner, like the songs of love and chivalry of the early German *Minnesinger*. The greatest difficulty of all has been to establish the correct attribution of zemirot melodies, including even those which, simply by the chemism of time, have taken on the patina of tradition. Yet one thing is certain: most of the tunes were picked up by Jewish singers in the non-Jewish world about them. Characteristically, they recast in a "Jewish" mold all varieties of Christian and Mohammedan folk music, popular songs, and even Church melodies. Not infrequently, they intertwined several motifs or musical phrases into a clever pastiche of melody. Yet, no matter how lovely the melodies sometimes were, many of the Hebrew verse-texts to which they were sung were far more eloquent and memorable.

The lively exploration by the chazzanim (cantors) in every generation of the folk songs of other peoples for melodic settings to the zemirot—in particular by the free-roaming Chasidic fancy during the nineteenth century—is indicated in a half-whimsical, half-resentful comment once made by Chopin. He wrote to a musician friend: "Poor Polish tunes! You will not in the least suspect how you will be interlarded with *Majufes.*" *Majufes* (pronounced *mah-yufes*) is the Polish-Ashkenaz way of pronouncing the Sefaradic-Hebrew "Mah Yafit," one of the most beloved of all the zemirot. The poem was composed in honor of the "Sabbath Bride"—a Cabalist mystical symbolism—by Mordecai ben Issac, a thirteenth-fourteenth century liturgical poet of Carpentras in France.

> Fair thou art, fair thou art, yea
> comely with delight,
> Joy in sorrow's darkest night.

Hundreds of musical settings were made for this zemirah alone. Like Chopin, other cultured Gentiles became fully aware of this feverish adapting and recasting activity, and they could not cease to marvel at it.

See also CHAZZAN; HYMNS OF THE SYNAGOGUE.

ZION. *See* TEMPLE, THE; ZIONISM.

ZIONISM

Although, as a national movement, Zionism dates back only to the middle of the nineteenth century, as a national concept Zion (pronounced *Tziyon* in Hebrew) is as old as the Babylonian Exile, which began in 586 B.C.E. Separation from the Land of Israel as they were being led into captivity by their conquerors rested crushingly upon the spirits of the Jewish exiles; a longing for the homeland consumed them. Turning in the direction of Judah, they then, in the words of the Psalmist, took an awesome vow:

> If I forget thee, O Jerusalem,
> Let my right hand forget her cunning.
> Let my tongue cleave to the roof of my mouth,
> If I remember thee not;
> If I set not Jerusalem
> Above my chiefest joy.
>
> PSALMS 137:5-6

In the emotionalism of this outburst may perhaps be found the key to a proper understanding of the dynamic forces that generated the Zionist movement, which was consummated politically in the establishment of the State of Israel in 1948. Nothing comparable to this passionate outcry of attachment to a land can be found in ancient writings of other peoples. To all later generations of Jews, the loss of Judea in 70 C.E. as their national and religious center only meant that, thenceforth, they were to consider themselves as *exiles* and their separation from it as *The Exile* (in Hebrew: *Galut*).

The grief-consciousness they derived from the Galut-idea never seemed to give them any respite; even after eighteen centuries they remained unresigned to it. Constantly they were turning yearning glances toward the far-off ancestral land. When they prayed, they faced in the direction of Jerusalem, and their love for the holy city and mourning for its departed glories pervaded their liturgy and their private devotions and meditations.

The hope associated with the coming of the Messiah and the Ge'ulah (Redemption)—although the prospects for its realization seemed so forlorn—was uttered every day in his life by the Jew of simple faith: "And to Jerusalem, Thy city, return in mercy . . . rebuild it soon in our days!" These thoughts, dreams, and prayers, never aging, never fading, found their most optimistic expression during the Passover Seder recitation about the Bondage and Exodus, when all participants cry out as with one voice: "Next year in Jerusalem!" (*"Le-shanah ha ba'ah bi'Yerushalauim!"*)

Subjective magic was evoked in the mind of the devout Jew whenever he conjured up the verbal images of "Zion" and "Jerusalem." ("Zion" or "Jerusalem" to Jews has always been a symbol of all Eretz Yisrael—the Land of Israel.) The Zionist leader and first President of the State of Israel, Dr. Chaim Weizmann, once expressed the thought that the persistence of the Jewish group-identity in history was the consequence of a spiritual idea that was the synthesis of "the people of Israel, the God of Israel (and) the Land of Israel." This integrated pattern of Jewish life led logically to the corollary of "the belief in a future restoration of the people to its homeland." This belief was first expressed in Babylonia, not long after the Captivity had commenced, by the Prophet Ezekiel, speaking thus in the name of God: "For I will take you from among the nations and gather you out of all countries and will bring you into your own land." (Ezekiel 36:24.)

The Jew's attachment to Zion and his certainty that the Messiah would eventually appear provided the nourishment by which his bruised psyche was sustained for almost two thousand years; it gave his people solace in its darkest hours and buoyed it up with the hope of eventual restoration to the Land of Israel. However, it was the secularist spirit of the nineteenth century, seeking social solutions for idealistic problems but in practical and not in purely religous terms, which brought the Zionist movement into existence. No doubt, the equalitarian principles existing in the "Rights of Man" thesis of the French Revolution in 1789 had stirred not only other peoples but also the Jews into an awakening of their own group-worth and dignity.

The leaders of the Jewish Enlightenment—the Haskalah—in Russia during the nineteenth century at first clung to the possibility that the Jews would attain group self-esteem and fulfillment by means of secular education. They confidently believed that if Jews could only succeed in becoming as Slavic as the Russians, the czarist government would promptly decree their civil emancipation and grant them full equality, and thus the Jewish problem, at least in the Russian Empire, would be solved once and for all. The advice of the Haskalah leaders to Jewry, therefore, was: "We must prepare ourselves for this golden future and take advantage of the opportunities offered us. We must come out of our shell, obtain a secular education, acquire Russian culture; then all else will follow." (*See* ENLIGHTENMENT, THE JEWISH.)

But what did follow was not exactly what the assimilationist idealists had expected. The harsh repressions decreed against the Jews during the reign of Nicholas I (1825–55) began to dampen the spirits of even the most ardent adherents of Enlightenment; they became a little less certain of their theorizing. The final blow to their hopes was dealt in May, 1881, when the czarist government decreed its infamous anti-Jewish laws and initiated a series of bloody pogroms throughout the Empire which left the Jews stunned and despairing. Almost overnight the hope of the Enlighteners (the Maskilim) evaporated. At this historic juncture, Zio-

Mordecai Manuel Noah.
(Portrait by John Wesley Jarvis, New York, early 19th century.)

Moses Hess.

Rabbi Zvi Hirsch Kalischer.

Zionism

nist ideas and programs, whch, even though existing, had hitherto been vague and romantically defined, began to find a fertile field among the disenchanted Jews, not only in Russia but everywhere in Europe.

During the first half of the nineteenth century, a number of utopian proposals were advanced for acquiring Palestine as a homeland for the Jews. One of the earliest of these was made in 1820 by the flamboyant editor and High Sheriff of New York, Major Mordecai Noah. When his plan for establishing a haven for persecuted Jews (on a land tract he had purchased on Grand Island, near Buffalo) collapsed, he announced, in 1824: "We will return to Zion as we went forth, bringing back the faith we carried away with us."

But Jews who belonged to the Reform branch of Judaism took the opposite stand. When the first Reform temple was established in Charleston, South Carolina, in 1841, it took for its motto: "This country is our Palestine, this city our Jerusalem, this house of God our 'Temple.'" In 1845, in Frankfort, Germany, a conference of Liberal (Reform) rabbis resolved to remove from the prayer book "the petitions for a return to the land of our forefathers and the restoration of the Jewish State." This view was entirely concurred in by Reform Jews in the United States at their rabbinical conventions held in Philadelphia in 1869 and in Pittsburgh in 1885. At the latter conference, the following plank was adopted: "We consider ourselves no longer a nation but a religious community."

The first concrete Zionist effort was begun by Zvi Hirsch Kalischer (1795–1870), an Orthodox rabbinic scholar in Germany. On the basis of Talmudic law, he averred, he had reached the conclusion that it was not at all inconsistent with a belief in the Messianic Redemption to work in a practical way for the Restoration of Israel in Palestine. In fact—he concluded with the utmost sincerity it might even hasten "the Messiah's coming." But Kalischer's pleas for a return to the soil in Eretz Yisrael fell mostly on deaf ears, for the majority of religious Jews considered his plan blasphemous. This provoked from him the outburst to his fellow Jews in the book *The Demands of Zion* (1862): "Are we worse than all the other peoples who consider their blood and possessions as nothing compared to their love for their people and country?"

As time went on, Kalischer's religious justifications for the Restoration grew less emphatic; the practical realities of colonization then came to the fore. Beginning in 1836, he had tried to interest wealthy Jews, the banker Meyer Amschel Rothschild and the British philanthropist Moses Montefiore among them, to finance his colonization projects. Only Montefiore was prevailed upon to visit Palestine in 1841. While there, he purchased an orange grove—the first one to be owned by a Jew in that country.

Perhaps the first significant result of Kalischer's agitation was that he prevailed upon Karl Netter, the Jewish philanthropist of France, to establish in 1870 through the Alliance Israelite Universelle, an agricultural school in Mikveh Israel, near Jaffa. It taught young colonists scientific methods of farming, and thus helped make possible the first modern settlements of Jewish farmers in a land still steeped in primitive tillage and feudal oppression of the Arab peasantry. It marked a historic turning point in the building of the Jewish homeland. Kalischer served as president of the "Society for the Colonization of Palestine" until his death in 1870.

There were men of action and there were also men of vigorous ideas in the Zionist movement. Probably the most distinguished among the theoretical founders of Zionism was Moses Hess (Germany, 1812–75). A philosopher, a

Leo Pinsker.

Rabbi Samuel Mohilever.

Kattowitz Conference, 1884. Rabbi Samuel Mohilever and Dr. Leo Pinsker are shown seated, fourth and fifth from left.

Hegelian, and a social revolutionary besides, he had aligned himself during his early years in collaborative political work with Karl Marx and Friedrich Engels. His published writings were on social, ethical, and political problems.

What first caused his espousal of Jewish nationalism, although he was a confirmed materialist and internationalist, is not easy to define. But there were several contributing factors which exerted, directly or indirectly, a decisive influence on his thinking. Principally, these included his personal collision with anti-Semitism and his observation of the desperate poverty of the Jewish masses and of their hopeless position as scapegoats and pariahs in a vengeful European society; the ritual-murder slander, and the riots and atrocities against the Jews in Damascus in 1840 that stemmed from it and, not least, the powerful impact on his mind made by his reading of Heinrich Graetz's monumental *History of the Jews,* which began appearing volume by volume in 1853. Thus Hess found his way back to an identification with the Jewish people after twenty years of estrangement.

It was the victorious liberation and unification movement in Italy in 1859 under the leadership of Mazzini and Garibaldi that fired Hess with the desire—and also the hope—of approximating a like liberation for the Jews. In 1862 he issued his book, *Rome and Jerusalem,* in which he expounded this intention: "If we have already lived to see the liberation of Rome from the fetters of the Middle Ages, logical reasoning requires that freedom be granted also to Jerusalem, that is to say, the Jewish people." Whatever the difficulties that would be met with in pursuit of this objective, concluded Hess confidently: "The Jews are a nation, destined to be resurrected with all other civilized nations."

Hess brooded much on his pessimistic premise that Jews would not—and indeed could not—be accepted as equals by other peoples: "We shall always remain as strangers among the nations . . ." It was his belief that even if Jews were to attain full civil emancipation and a complete cultural assimilation with their Gentile environment, they still would be regarded as second-class citizens. Therefore, Hess felt nothing but pity and contempt for those Jews who took the attitude: "Where I prosper, that is my fatherland."

In essence, the ideas Moses Hess touched upon in *Rome and Jerusalem* were seminal for the subsequent theories of Zionism. Later exponents merely elaborated upon or developed one or another of his postulates. Theodor Herzl, the principal leader of the Zionist movement, correctly acknowledged in 1901 in his Diary: "All that we are now trying to do is already to be found in this book [i.e., *Rome and Jerusalem*]." Leo Pinsker, in his famous manifesto, *Auto-Emancipation,* was but reformulating in his own forceful way the insistence of Hess that Jews, like the Italian adherents of the Risorgimento, could not rely on anyone else but themselves for their freedom. It also should not be overlooked that "the spiritual center" concept which Achad ha-Am preached many years later had a close resemblance to Moses Hess's conviction that with Palestine as its "center of activity" the Jewish people would become intellectually and spiritually great again and so would be the instrumentality for "connecting mankind and the whole world with their Creator."

An impressive figure in the history of Zionist ideology was Leo Pinsker (*b.* Poland, 1821—*d.* Russia, 1891). He was the founder of the Chibat Tziyon (Love of Zion) movement which was the immediate precursor of the World Zionist Organization under Theodor Herzl's leadership. Although he had always been an assimilationist follower of the Jewish Enlightenment, the effects on him of the pogrom that he witnessed in Odessa in 1881 were so shattering that he

Theodor Herzl. (Etching by Hermann Struck, Berlin.)

Max Nordau.

Israel Zangwill.

Zvi Hermann Schapira.

David Wolfsohn.

renounced "enlightenment" as a suitable means of solving the Jewish question. He decided instead that Jews could rely only on their own efforts for their emancipation. His pamphlet, *Auto-Emancipation* (1882), was finally adopted as the platform of the Chovevei Tziyon (Lovers of Zion) Organization, which during the first decade of its existence established more than fifty branches in a number of countries in Europe, in the United States, and in Canada.

The prime mover in this movement was Samuel Mohilever (Lithuania, 1824–98), a leading Orthodox rabbi who has been regarded as the actual founder of Mizrachi, the religious-Zionist party. A man of great energy and dedication, he threw himself into Chovevei Tziyon propaganda and organizational work, but Jewish colonization projects in Palestine remained his principle objective. The first agricultural settlements of East European Jews in Palestine were founded by a Lovers of Zion group known as Bilu (a Hebrew acronym formed by the verse in Isaiah: "O house of Jacob, come ye, and let us walk." Bilu-ite settlements included Rehovot, Rosh Pinah, Rishon-le-Zion, Zichron Ya'akov, Ekron, and Gederah.

During the period 1882–1903, about 25,000 settlers arrived in Palestine from Russia, Poland, and Romania. Life on the land was hard and frustrating. They had to contend not only with the hostility of the Turkish authorities of Palestine and with Arab attacks and depredations, but also with malaria and dysentery, and with the ungenerous soil and difficult climatic conditions. Furthermore, they found themselves at bitter odds with the old-established Ultra-Orthodox and Chasidic community of some twenty thousand pious people who had gone to the Holy Land either to die and be buried in its sacred soil, or to devote themselves to prayer and Torah study, thereby to hasten the coming of the Messiah. The new settlers, although many of them were Orthodox, with their modern rationalistic ideas and their vigor and enthusiasm for work, threatened to undermine not only the pietists, supernatural expectation of the Jewish Redemption but also their means of livelihood, for a great number of them existed on charitable contributions (chalukkah) collected from Jews throughout the world.

Theodor Herzl. The name Theodor Herzl has conjured up in

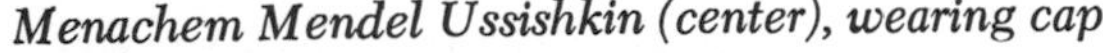
Menachem Mendel Ussishkin (center), wearing cap.

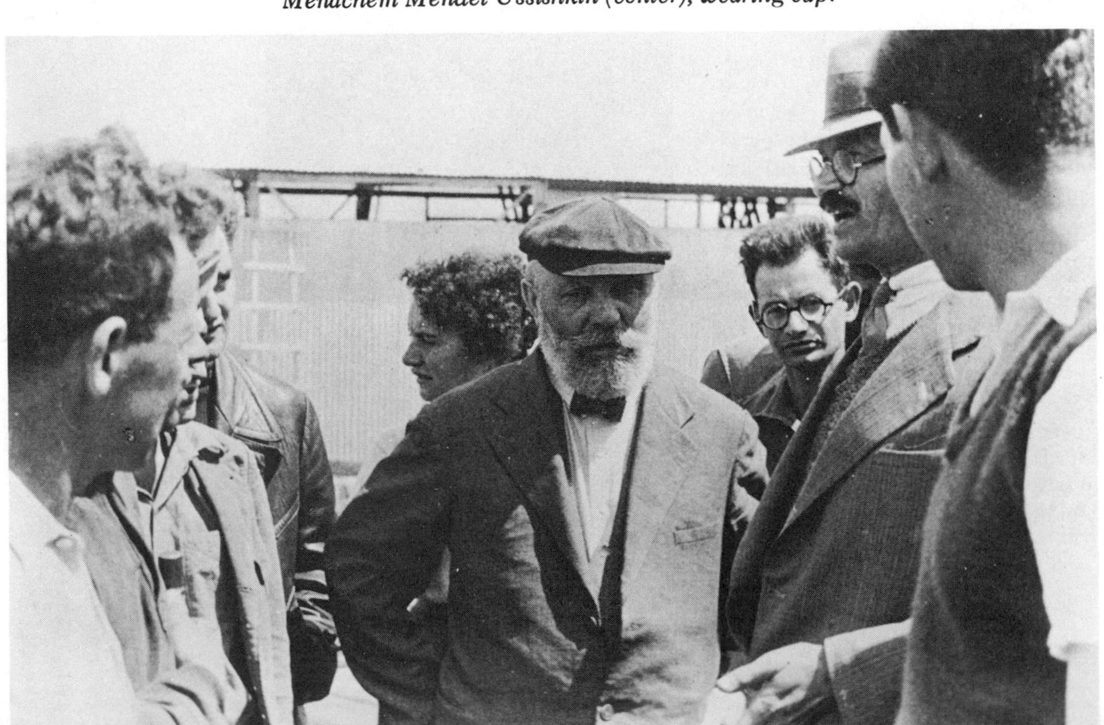

the minds of four generations of Jews the associative image of a Hebrew prophet attired in modern clothes—a patriarchal, bearded, modern-day Moses with luminous eyes, imposing in a frock coat and high silk hat. Like the liberator of the Israelites from their Bondage in Egypt, Herzl also, even though he did not quite measure up to the greatness of Moses (he himself had set up Moses as his model), applied himself to the by no means unheroic task of leading back the persecuted Jewish masses of the world to Palestine—the "Promised Land." "We want to live at last as free men on our own soil, and die quietly in our own homeland," he wrote in *The Jewish State*.

Theodor Herzl (*b.* Budapest, 1860—*d.* Vienna, 1904) was the founder of political Zionism. In January, 1895, as a journalist (with a legal background) reporting for the Viennese newspaper *Neue Freie Presse* the development of the military treason-trial of the Jewish artillery officer, Captain Alfred Dreyfus (*see* DREYFUS CASE, THE); he was present at the latter's degradation ceremony. This incident proved the turning point in Herzl's life. An assimilationist until that time and hardly aware of what Zionist activities and theories were then circulating in the world, he experienced a deep emotional crisis when he heard the French anti-Semitic mob hoot at the unfortunate Dreyfus: "Death to the Jews!"

Herzl began to give much thought to the Jewish question. He asked himself: "Why should we not help one another and leave this unhappy exile and build for ourselves a Jewish state?" In a mood blended of both inner agitation and exaltation he sat down to write his essay, *Der Judenstaat* ("The Jewish State," February 14, 1896), a pamphlet which proved of great historic significance for the Jewish people, since—at least in its broad outline—it turned out to be the blueprint for all subsequent Zionist political thinking. His central thesis was "the restoration of the Jewish State. I am absolutely convinced that I am right, though I doubt whether I shall live to see myself proved to be so."

Despite the practical application of some of his theories, Herzl was, without a doubt, a romantic idealist with a tendency to dramatize himself. "Herzl's political technique was simple to the point of naivete," the English Zionist leader, Harry Sacher, once wrote of him. His plan was to try, through personages of power such as Kaiser Wilhelm of Germany and British government ministers, to exert political influence and the requisite pressure on Sultan Abdul-Hamid II of Turkey, the then ruler of Palestine, to relinquish that country to the Jews. Of course, it could be arranged *quid pro quo* for the sultan, said Herzl: "If His Majesty the Sultan were to give us Palestine, we in turn would be able to undertake to put the finances of Turkey in proper order." This, patently, was something that could more easily be promised than fulfilled, for Herzl had an unrealistic expectation of what sacrifices Jewish men of wealth, even the Rothschilds, were ready to make for such a stupendous project.

Actually, neither Kaiser Wilhelm nor the British government showed any enthusiasm for Herzl's plan when he submitted it to them during the next few years; neither did the sultan of Turkey. Nevertheless, by dramatizing the matter publicly, he was able to arouse an intense interest, if not excitement, among the millions of Jews in Romania and Russia who, desperate in the face of ever mounting persecution, were prepared for any "miracle" to happen.

For two years following the publication of *The Jewish State* (which, incidentally, was addressed to Lord Rothschild), Herzl literally burned himself out trying to enlist support for a Jewish state in Palestine from such wealthy Jews as the London Rothschilds and Baron Maurice de Hirsch. They proved unresponsive, but it must be remembered that they were philanthropically rather than politically oriented to the Jewish question. With undisguised satirical intent Herzl wrote Baron de Hirsch in 1895: "Jewish money can be found in large amounts for a Chinese loan, for Negro railways in Africa—but for the deepest, most immediate and crying need of the Jewish people itself, is there none to be found?"

Herzl continued to seek by personal contact to influence various rulers and ministers of state in Europe on behalf

Theodor Herzl greeting Max Nordau before the First Zionist Congress in Basle, August, 1897. (Zionist Archives and Library.)

of the Jews. With them, too, he felt frustrated, receiving in each case a chilling reception. "Whom do you represent?" he would be asked politely. At long last, although reluctantly, he decided to put his faith in the support of the plain Jewish folk, most of whom were very poor. On August 29, 1897, he convoked the First Zionist Congress in Basle, Switzerland. With him at its helm stood Max Nordau (*b.* Budapest, 1849–*d.* Paris, 1923), one of the most brilliant journalists of his time.

While the Chovevei Tziyon societies had held a world congress of their movement in 1884 at Katowitz, Silesia, the conference had had little practical result. However, the First Zionist Congress in Basle took on the character, in miniature, of an unofficial world parliament of Jews. Strongly represented there was the Chovevei Tziyon movement. Herzl caustically addressed himself to its delegation when he stated in his program that no reliance could be placed on the agricultural colonization of Palestine by piecemeal methods, namely, settlement by settlement. What was required, said he, was practical colonization on a massive scale, and this could begin only as soon as there was consummated the aim of Zionism: "to create for the Jewish people a home in Palestine secured by public law." By this, he made it clear, he meant a Jewish state secured *legally* and *publicly* by international guarantees.

The enthusiasm of the majority of the delegates for the Basle Program knew no bounds. "If you only will it, then it is no fairy tale," Herzl urged. The World Zionist Organization was promptly founded and became a permanent institution. Its financial arm—the Bank (The Jewish Colonial Trust) —and its mechanism for the acquisition of land-holdings in Palestine—the Jewish National Fund (Keren Kayemeth)—were subsequently established.

Herzl noted in his diary after the First Zionist Congress: "In Basle I established a Jewish State. If I were to say that aloud today, universal laughter would be the response. Maybe in five years, certainly in fifty, everybody will recognize it." Was this intended to be a prophecy? The State of Israel was founded exactly fifty-one years later!

Whatever his rationalizations for courting only the powerful and the rich to serve his project, with the First Zionist Congress, Herzl laid down a broad democratic base for Zionist operations that made it easy for the poorest of Jews to become bona fide members of the Zionist movement. All that was required of them was adherence to the Basle Program and the annual purchase of a shekel (about twenty-five cents). Herzl thus gave Zionism a more meaningful and dignified character, diverting it from its previous rescue-and-philanthropic trend to a movement of mass political action.

Yet, despite all of this, Herzl never abandoned his conviction that the best way to acquire the Jewish State was by means of personal diplomacy. It was with an all-consuming passion that he tried to reach "important" people—the Pope, kings, statesmen, bankers, philanthropists, and the like. In his dedication to his cause, traveling from one capital to another, he not only ruined his health, but he impoverished and embittered his family. All his efforts were directed to one end (which to some of his critics seemed obsessive and quixotic): to obtain a legal charter for a Jewish state in Palestine from Sultan Abdul-Hamid of Turkey.

Twice in 1898 Herzl had audiences with Kaiser Wilhelm of Germany. He even journeyed to Saint Petersburg after the Kishinev pogrom in 1903 to urge the Imperial Russian Government, which at that time was seemingly anxious to get rid of its Jews, to bring pressure upon the Turkish government in Constantinople to give Palestine to them.

In the meantime, so great had grown the tension and despair among the Jewish masses of Russia, Poland, and Romania because of the intolerable official and unofficial persecution to which they were being subjected, that rumblings of revolt began to be heard against Herzl's personal diplomacy and his alleged autocratic manner of conducting the Zionist movement—one which, thus far, had brought no practical results. A sharp division took place in the Zionist ranks between the "Politicals," who had little interest in the colonization of Palestine and therefore supported Herzl, and the "Practicals," who numbered in their ranks such adherents as the Chovevei Tziyon enthusiasts (Chaim Weizmann [*b.* Russia, 1873–*d.* Israel, 1952] was one of them), who clamored for step-by-step colonization. What they resented most in Herzl was his bland assumption that the East European Jewish masses would be content to serve as the unquestioning foot-soldiers of the Restoration while the wealthy and highly placed Jews of Germany, England, and France would march at their head as the generals, with himself, Herzl, as the commander in chief.

His magnetic personality and great charm notwithstanding, Theodor Herzl, partly because of his un-Jewish background and perhaps partly because of an insufficient familiarity with the spirit and content of traditional Jewish life, which is sternly "democratic," engaged in unnecessary controversy with the East European Zionists. Out of this set-to, it must be admitted, he emerged only second best. An open rebellion against his leadership erupted during the Sixth Zionist Congress in Basle in August, 1903, right after the terrible Kishinev pogrom. It occurred when Herzl submitted for the consideration of the delegates an offer from Joseph Chamberlain, the British Colonial Secretary, to establish a large number of Jews—with funds from The Jewish Colonial Trust—in "a Jewish colony or settlement [in East Africa] . . ." with the "appointment of a Jewish official as the chief of the local administration . . . and permission to the colony to have a free hand in municipal legislation . . . such local autonomy being conditioned upon the right of his [Brittanic] Majesty's government to exercise general control."

This plan, referred to as "the Uganda Proposal," caused a consequent shock and furor. Delegates from Russia bitterly accused Herzl of betraying the Zionist cause, of turning it over to the use of British imperialism, of trying to divert the Zionists from establishing a homeland in their own historic Eretz Yisrael. In vain Herzl tried to defend his position: "Admittedly," he agreed, "this is not Zion, and never can be. It is only an auxiliary settlement scheme . . . It is and remains only an emergency measure [following the Kishinev pogrom] . . . and is intended to prevent the loss of dispersed parts of the [Jewish] nation."

But the indignation of the Russian and Polish delegates could not be stilled. Unappeased, they withdrew from the Conference hall in a body, being joined in their demonstration by other opposition delegates. While, on the basis of a test vote, Herzl obtained a majority, it proved to be only a Pyrrhic victory for him, for the delegations that bolted represented the great majority of shekel-paying members . . . In fact, at a special conference held later by the dissidents in Kharkov, in the Ukraine, the Russian Zionists, under the fiery leadership of Menachem Mendel Ussishkin (*b.* Russia, 1863–*d.* Palestine, 1941), repudiated "The Uganda Proposal" and demanded that greater emphasis be placed on practical colonization work in Palestine.

Although Herzl, following the imperious law of *Realpolitik*—to compromise whenever necessary—finally acceded to the demands of the dissidents for speeded-up colonization in Palestine "and not in Uganda," the excitement and strain induced in him by the acrimonious dispute had completely worn him out. He died on July 3, 1904, at the age of forty-four, of heart disease.

The great majority of Zionists found the Basle Program adequate for their expectations; at least it was a strongly organized "political" effort in a practical direction. But there was also an influencial minority consisting of the intellectual-minded, of those individuals having Jewish cultural aspirations. It was to these Zionists that the philosophical writer, Achad ha-Am ("One of the People"—the pseudonym in Hebrew of Asher Ginzberg, *b.* Russia, 1856–*d.* Palestine, 1927), addressed himself. He wished to "convert it [the national idea] into a lofty moral idea." His emphasis, consequently, was on the fashioning of a spiritual or cultural Zionism.

Achad ha-Am's contention was that the centrifugal pressures in the cultural environment of the non-Jewish world made it impossible for the "full development of the creative powers of a [minority] people according to its own specific character." What then was required for the isolated Jewish communities of the Diaspora in order to be able to fulfill their Jewish national aspirations in an overwhelmingly dominant Gentile milieu? It was required, answered the writer, "that we, too, shall be a majority in one land . . . a land in which our historic rights cannot be questioned and where in its proper historic setting our national life will develop according to our own aspirations and capabilities without being squeezed into, and confined to, limited fields of endeavor and areas of expression."

Achad ha-Am was convinced that it would not be feasible for more than a small part of world Jewry to be settled in Palestine, but he also held to the view that even a small Jewish population, developing its Jewish culture in the Hebrew language in the ancestral homeland, could become the dominant force for a Jewish national revival, both spiritual and cultural, everywhere in the lands of the Diaspora.

Following the death of Herzl, his mantle of leadership in the World Zionist Organization fell on the shoulders of his friend and well-intentioned but mediocre lieutenant, David Wolffsohn (*b.* Lithuania, 1856–*d.* Germany, 1914). Being an ardent disciple of Herzl's, Wolffsohn attempted to carry on his predecessor's policies, but he proved no match for the resourceful and determined opposition leaders of the East European "Practicals"—Ussishkin and, especially, Weizmann, who later became the first President of the independent State of Israel in 1948. They forced a collective leadership on Wolffsohn—one in which they played key roles. Thereafter, it was gibed by Weizmann's critics that he had invented "Synthetic Zionism." Supposedly, he had taken an accommodating middle-of-the-road position among all leaders of Zionist factions, thereby producing a synthesis of Herzl's political lobbying among the mighty, uniting the colonization program of the Practicals with Achad ha-Am's "cultural center" concept.

Collection box of Jewish National Fund. Germany, c. 1904.

While all this intramural wrangling was engaging the attention and energies of the Zionist leadership, the agitation among the masses for the restoration of Israel was gaining momentum. New voices were being heard, different points of view were being advanced. It was, therefore, inevitable that a large Jewish worker-element should also be drawn to Zionism, but according to its own ideological terms of reference and class interests, which were socialistic and secularistic in character, as well as nationalistic.

One need only follow the career of Aaron David Gordon (*b.* Russia, 1856–*d.* Palestine, 1922), the worker-theoretician of the "Religion of Labor" in Eretz Yisrael and the inspirer of the kvutzah-kibbutz movement (*see* HEBREW LITERATURE, MODERN; KIBBUTZ) to be able to gauge the potential dynamism of the Jewish labor trend for Palestine in the post-Herzl period. Today (in 1964), the Histadrut (the General Federation of Labor) through its political arm—the Labor Zionist Mapai Party—is the dominant force in the government of Israel, and its organizational, economic, medical, cultural, and social welfare institutions constitute a vital part of the total life of the yishuv (Israel community).

The Zionist labor movement had its inception among the Jewish workers in Russia; in 1901, under the leadership of Ber Borochov (Russia, 1881–1919), a small group of intellectual Marxists founded the Poale Zion (Zionist Workers Party). Being secularistic in their approach to the Jewish question, they could detect no contradiction in their attempt to synthesize internationalistic socialism with nationalistic Zionism. But when, in later years, the Poale Zion leaders had greatly watered down their original socialistic program, groups of militant Marxist workers coalesced around the splinter organizations Achdut Avodah (Unity of Labor), Hashomer Hatzair (The Young Watchman), and Left Poale Zion.

At the other end of the Zionist spectrum was the formidable Mizrachi (Easterners) Organization of Orthodox Jews, which had been founded in 1902 but was already foreshadowed in the activities of the rabbis Kalischer and Mohilever, several decades before. This group had a twofold aim: to agitate among Orthodox Jews for acceptance of the necessity for upbuilding the Holy Land and, at the same time, to make the influence of traditional Judaism felt in all the activities of World Zionism and the Palestinian communities. The religious Zionists, consequently, adopted the motto: "The Land of Israel for the People of Israel according to the Torah of Israel." In addition to the General Mizrachi Organization, a Religious Labor division—Hapoel Hamizrachi—came into being, as well. Together, these now constitute one organization: Mizrachi-Hapoel Hamizrachi.

The Balfour Declaration. Throughout World War I, negotiations went on in London for a Jewish homeland in Palestine. On the one side were aligned the foremost Zionist leaders—Menachem Mendel Ussishkin, Yechiel Tchlenov (the leader of the Russian Zionists), Nahum Sokolow, and Chaim Weiz-

Leaders at Sixth Zionist Congress (1903). 1) Israel Zangwill; 2) Theodor Herzl's mother; 3) Max Nordau; 4) Herzl; 5) Franz Bodenheimer; 6) Oskar Marmorek; 7) David Wolfsohn; 8) Professor Mandelstamm; 9) L. J. Greenberg; 10) Professor Otto Warburg; 11) Dr. Leopold Kahn.

Chaim Weizmann. (Israel Office of Information.)

Nahum Sokolow.

B. Borochov.

Editorial board of Achdut, *the first Zionist Labor journal in Palestine, 1912. (Seated, left to right) Joseph Chaim Brenner, the noted Hebrew writer; David Ben Gurion; and Yitzchak Ben-Zvi. The latter two achieved renown many years later as the first Prime Minister and the second President of the State of Israel, respectively.*

Joseph Trumpeldor, organizer during World War I of the Zion Mule Corps, the precursor of the Jewish Legion for Palestine. His death, resulting from his gallant defense of the Jewish settlement of Tel Chai against Arab attackers, won him acclaim as the first Jewish national hero of the Yishuv in Palestine.

mann—and with them, Dr. Moses Gaster (the Chief Rabbi of England), Lord Rothschild, and Sir Herbert Samuel; on the other side were Prime Minister David Lloyd-George and Lord Arthur James Balfour, the Foreign Minister. On November 2, 1917, Balfour sent to Rothschild the momentous letter that became known as "the Balfour Declaration." This stated that His Majesty's Government was "viewing with favour" the establishment of a Jewish National Home in Palestine.

As soon as the Declaration was issued, loud rumblings of discontent and protest started reverberating throughout the Arab nationalist and feudalist world. Arab representatives appeared before the Peace Conference at San Remo and spoke in opposition to the granting of the Palestine Mandate to Britain. It was their indignant claim that Palestine had been promised to them by Britain *as an Arab state* and not to the Jews. To the astonishment of the Zionist delegation at the Peace Conference, the Arab objectors revealed for the first time the existence of a *secret* correspondence early in 1915 between Sir Arthur Henry McMahon, British High Commissioner in Egypt, and Grand Sherif Hussein ibn-Ali of Mecca, afterward first king of the Hejaz. In it, the sherif—in consequence of a prior commitment negotiated with him by the famous British Intelligence agent, Colonel T. E. Lawrence ("Lawrence of Arabia")—undertook a diversionary revolt against the Turks, whose entry into the war on the side of Imperial Germany was regarded as imminent. In payment for this aid, the British government, on its part, promised to support at the proper time the Arab claims for an independent state to be established in a specified territory. But McMahon's "promises" to the Arabs had been adroitly couched in phraseology that was diplomatically ambiguous; there was no mention at all of Palestine in them. Yet the Arabs insisted that it was Palestine that was categorically meant and included in the oral bargain made with Hussein.

It was not long before the Zionist leaders discovered that they, too, had been "misled" in their expectations. In such verbal ambiguities was the Balfour Declaration dressed up that it was entirely possible to make different legalistic interpretations of both its general intentions and its specific promises. The British government, to whom the League of Nations had assigned its Mandate for the establishment of the Jewish homeland in Palestine in 1922, was resentful of the Jews' persistence in seeing that their own interpretation of the Declaration and of the terms of the Mandate was carried out, showed itself hostile to the Palestinian Jewish community (the yishuv) from the very start. It placed obstacles before and restrictions on every phase of settlement and construction, so that many Zionists began to question seriously the correctness of the political policy that the leadership—in particular, Dr. Weizmann—was using in placing such great reliance on the British.

Facsimile of the Balfour Declaration, November 2, 1917.

Foreign Office,
November 2nd, 1917

Dear Lord Rothschild,

I have much pleasure in conveying to you, on behalf of His Majesty's Government, the following declaration of sympathy with Jewish Zionist aspirations which has been submitted to, and approved by, the Cabinet

"His Majesty's Government view with favour the establishment in Palestine of a national home for the Jewish people, and will use their best endeavours to facilitate the achievement of this object, it being clearly understood that nothing shall be done which may prejudice the civil and religious rights of existing non-Jewish communities in Palestine, or the rights and political status enjoyed by Jews in any other country".

I should be grateful if you would bring this declaration to the knowledge of the Zionist Federation.

Yours sincerely

Arthur James Balfour

Zeeb (Vladimir) Jabotinsky in English Royal Fusileer uniform of the Jewish Legion in Palestine, 1918.

These circumstances gave rise to a serious schism in the Zionist ranks. Leading the opposition to Weizmann's policies and methods was Vladimir Jabotinsky (*b.* Russia, 1881–*d.* U.S.A., 1940), a journalist of authoritarian temperament who possessed great energy and determination. For two decades he proved himself the *enfant terrible* of the Zionist movement. He organized the Zionist Revisionist group which heaped scorn on the British intentions and indignation on the Zionist leadership. He kept on clamoring for a bona fide Jewish homeland and not for a British-ruled Jewish "colony." A maximalist in his expectations, he would not settle for less than a Jewish governing majority in *all* of Palestine, and on both sides of the Jordan River, too. He demanded not just piecemeal settlement of Palestine but a Jewish mass-immigration, to be financed by the British but to be controlled by the Jews themselves. His program required the establishment of many Jewish towns and villages not only in Judea but also in the region of Transjordan, which he claimed was Jewish by historic right.

The Balfour Declaration—the documentary arch-villain

A boatload of Jewish refugees, saved by the Allied armies from the Nazi death camps in Europe at the conclusion of World War II, are forcibly prevented from landing in Palestine by the English Army in 1947.

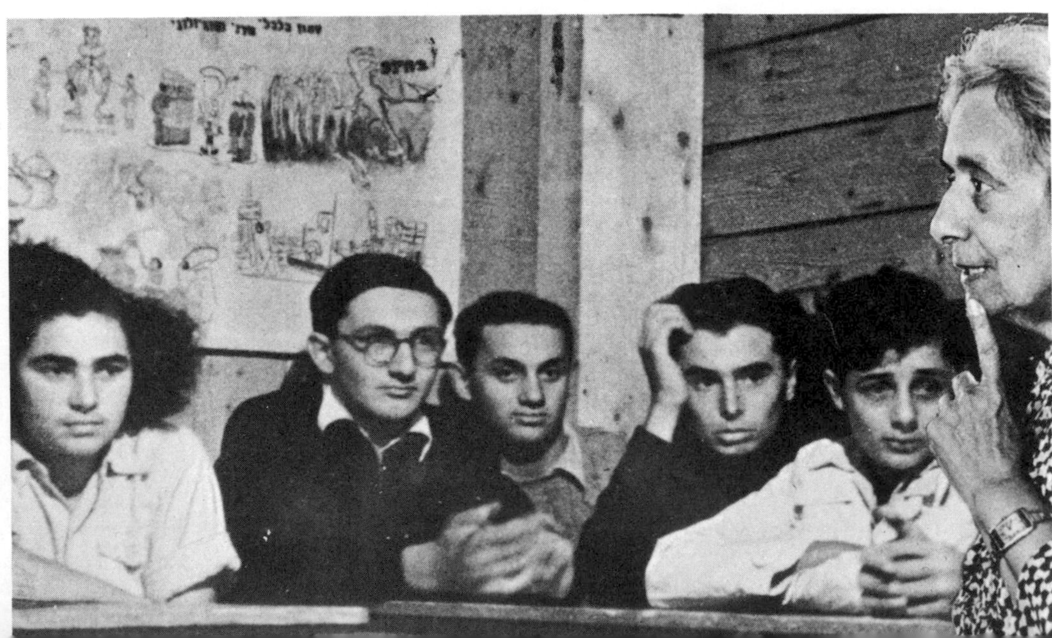

Henrietta Szold, founder and leader of Hadassah, the American Women's Zionist Organization, talking to teen-agers orphaned by the Nazis in Europe and brought to Palestine by Youth Aliyah of Hadassah. (Photo by Hadassah.)

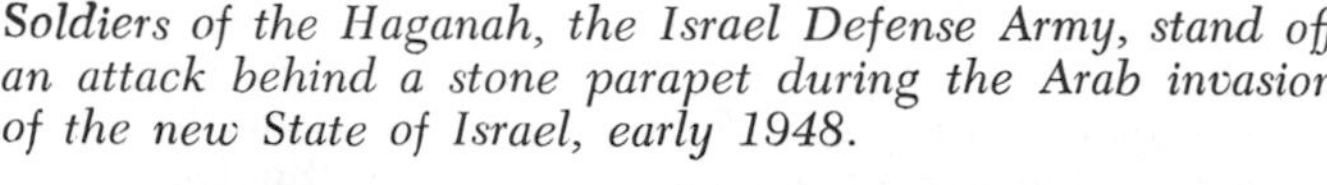
Soldiers of the Haganah, the Israel Defense Army, stand off an attack behind a stone parapet during the Arab invasion of the new State of Israel, early 1948.

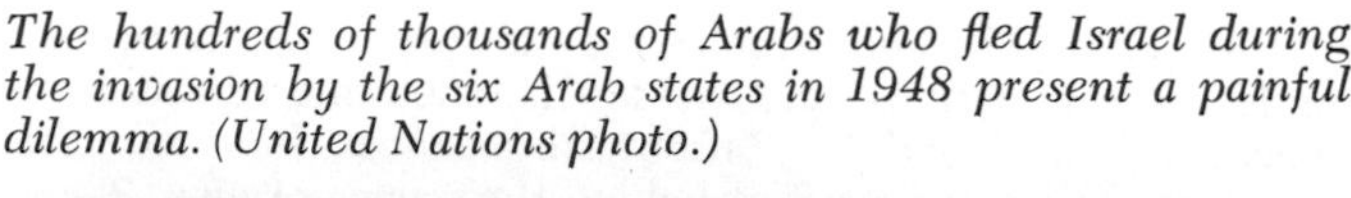
The hundreds of thousands of Arabs who fled Israel during the invasion by the six Arab states in 1948 present a painful dilemma. (United Nations photo.)

The invasion of the new State of Israel by six Arab armies in 1948 resulted in widespread destruction to Jerusalem. (Zionist Archives and Library.)

in this political crime which was causing such an uproar, endless recriminations, and worse—the shedding of much innocent Jewish blood by Arab terrorists was but one consequence—had some curious behind-the-scenes origins. These came to light seventeen years later, in 1934, after the introduction of the document, when the British Labour government set up a Palestine Royal Commission to make an inquiry into the causes for the intense Arab-Jewish hostility that had erupted in rioting and pogroms by armed Arab bands and street-mobs.

The Commission reported: "In the evidence he gave before us, Mr. Lloyd George, who was Prime Minister at that time, stated that . . . the launching of the Balfour Declaration at that time was 'due to propagandist reasons.'" These "propagandist reasons," explained by the former Prime Minister, had been decided upon by the British Cabinet because of the threat of an Allied defeat. England stood in need of all possible help. "In particular, Jewish sympathy [in appreciation for the issuance of the Balfour Declaration] would confirm the support of American Jewry . . ." In return, said Lloyd-George, concluding his testimony, Weizmann and the other Zionist leaders promised "to do their best to rally Jewish sentiment and support throughout the world to the Allied cause." (It should be added that at that juncture, England was desperately trying to get President Wilson to bring the United States into the war as an ally; therefore American Jewry could serve as a useful prod.)

In their attempt through the years that followed to pull out of their commitment to the Jews in order to mollify the clamoring Arabs, who appeared far more important to them, both economically and politically, successive British governments went to great lengths to distort, modify, and dilute Balfour's original promise for establishing a Jewish homeland. Winston Churchill made no attempt to conceal this cynical legalistic maneuver: "When it is asked what is meant by the development of a Jewish National Home in Palestine, it may be answered . . . the further development of the existing Jewish Community . . ."

To show that, at least on this subject, there was no difference of opinion between Tory and Labourite, Ramsay MacDonald, then the Prime Minister, issued in 1939 a White Paper (the Jews bitterly named it the "Black Paper") which had been drawn up by none other than Lord Passfield, that same Sidney Webb who had been the famous Socialist idealist and co-founder of Fabian socialism in England. This document gave an odd whittled down interpretation of the Balfour Declaration. Apparently the document could be interpreted in any way one chose. Drastic curbs were then placed by the authorities on further Jewish immigration. Quite obviously, the British Government seemed determined to scuttle the Balfour Declaration.

The prime importance of the running war that swirled around the Balfour Declaration year after year was that it greatly encouraged the outbreak of Arab violence against the Jews of the yishuv. The outspoken position of the British Mandatory Government—that proclaimed to the whole world that the Jews had no right whatsoever to a Jewish homeland or state in Palestine—was a carte blanche invitation to the Arabs to do everything in their power to frustrate the Jews in all their activities. The British in Palestine did little to prevent the Arab outbreaks against the Jews; nor, for that matter, did they give the latter adequate physical protection during the rioting and attacks. In consequence, the yishuv, working through the Jewish Agency's secret resistance committee, which was headed by the energetic David Ben-Gurion (*b.* Russia, 1886—Israel,), who was to become the first Prime Minister when the new State of Israel was established, decided to look after its own survival as well as it could, and it prepared for any eventuality by secretly arming its underground military force—the Haganah. The attitude taken by the Jewish Agency at the time was one in harmony with the soberly bitter reflection made in 1946 by Emanuel Neumann, the American Zionist leader, on quite another problem of Zionist tactic: "Virtue did not suffice, and weakness was no virtue."

What subsequently happened concerns far more the turbulent history of the struggle with Great Britain and the Arabs over Palestine than it does the history of Zionism. An account of the dramatic events which unfolded thickly and furiously in the final years of British rule over that unhappy region can be found in any good chronicle of the period. These events include the illegal Jewish immi-

Chaim Weizmann taking the oath as President of the Provisional Council of Israel in 1948.

The Provisional Cabinet of Israel, headed by Prime Minister David Ben Gurion, 1948.

Aerial view of Hadassah-Hebrew University Medical Center in Jerusalem. (Photo by Fred Csasznik. Courtesy of Hadassah.)

Hebrew University, Jerusalem. (Israel Office of Information.)

Weizmann Institute, Rehobot, Israel. (Israel Office of Information.)

gration, which was the Zionists answer to the large curbs imposed by the British authorities; the acts of terrorism—assassinations, bombings, kidnappings, sabotage, raids of reprisal, etc.—carried out by the underground Irgun Tzvai Leumi (National Military Organization), founded years before by Jabotinsky, and by the small but intrepid Marxist band of Fighters for the Freedom of Israel, derided by its opponents as the "Stern Gang;" the Partition of Palestine ordered by the United Nations in 1947; the reluctant departure of the British military and civilian forces, and the prompt proclamation by the yishuv of the establishment of Medinat Yisrael—the State of Israel—on May 14, 1948, an irrevocable event that was immediately followed by the simultaneous invasion of the tiny new state by the armies of six Arab nations—and their ultimate defeat.

Incredibly, Theodor Herzl's optimistic challenge to the Jewish people in 1897—"If you only will it, then it is no fairy tale!"—had found its fulfillment in 1948. But, as it always occurs in all true-life situations, the happy ending of Israel's striving to attain its Zionist goals in the ancestral land remains darkly overshadowed by the ever recurring threat of its unreconciled Arab neighbors to "drive it into the [Mediteranean] sea."

See also ERETZ YISRAEL; HEBREW LANGUAGE, HISTORY OF THE; HEBREW LITERATURE, MODERN; KIBBUTZ; MESSIAH, THE.

ZOHAR, THE. *See* CABALA.

INDEX OF PERSONS

Biographical information about many of the most important contributors to Jewish civilization appear in the text under the heading, "Some Architects of Jewish Civilization," page 421. In this index those individuals so listed are identified by the letters SAJC. Dates for many of the other entries are given here.

Italic page numbers refer to illustrations.

GENERAL INDEX

Because main entries appear in alphabetical order, they are not repeated in the index unless there are references to the topics in other entries.

The names of individuals are listed in the Index of Persons, page 541, appearing here only if a descriptive entry requires the name of a person for identification.

Italic page numbers refer to illustrations.